ENCYCLOPEDIA OF PSYCHOLOGY

ENCYCLOPEDIA OF PSYCHOLOGY

Alan E. Kazdin
Editor in Chief

VOLUME 7

AMERICAN
PSYCHOLOGICAL
ASSOCIATION

OXFORD
UNIVERSITY PRESS

2000

AMERICAN
PSYCHOLOGICAL
ASSOCIATION

Washington, D.C.

OXFORD
UNIVERSITY PRESS

Oxford   New York

Athens   Auckland   Bangkok   Bogotá   Buenos Aires   Calcutta
Cape Town   Chennai   Dar es Salaam   Delhi   Florence   Hong Kong   Istanbul
Karachi   Kuala Lumpur   Madrid   Melbourne   Mexico City   Mumbai
Nairobi   Paris   São Paulo   Singapore   Taipei   Tokyo   Toronto   Warsaw

and associated companies in
Berlin   Ibadan

Copyright © 2000 by American Psychological Association and Oxford University Press, Inc.

Published by American Psychological Association
750 First Street, NE, Washington, D.C. 20002-4242
www.apa.org
and
Oxford University Press, Inc.
198 Madison Avenue, New York, New York 10016
www.oup.com

Oxford is a registered trademark of Oxford University Press.

Library of Congress Cataloging-in-Publication Data
Encyclopedia of psychology / Alan E. Kazdin, editor in chief
p.   cm.
Includes bibliographical references and index.
1. Psychology—Encyclopedias.   I. Kazdin, Alan E.
BF31 .E52   2000   150'.3—dc21   99-055239
ISBN 1-55798-187-6 (set); ISBN 1-55798-656-8 (vol. 7)

AMERICAN PSYCHOLOGICAL ASSOCIATION STAFF

Gary R. VandenBos, Ph.D., *Publisher*
Julia Frank-McNeil, *Commissioning Editor*
Theodore J. Baroody, *Senior Development Editor*
Adrian Harris Forman, *Project Editor*

OXFORD UNIVERSITY PRESS STAFF

Karen Casey, *Publisher*
Claude Conyers, *Commissioning Editor*
Marion Osmun, *Senior Development Editor*
Matthew Giarratano, *Managing Editor*
Peri Zeenkov and Norina Frabotta, *Project Editors*
Nancy Hoagland, *Production Manager*
Jessica Ryan and Will Moore, *Production Editors*
AEIOU, Inc., *Index Editor*
AEIOU, Inc., Linda Berman, Denise McIntyre,
Space Coast Indexers, Inc., Linda Webster, *Indexers*
Suzanne Holt, *Book Design*
Joan Greenfield, *Cover Design*

3 5 7 9 8 6 4 2

Printed in the United States of America
on acid-free paper

RAPE. Most North American statutes currently define rape as the nonconsensual oral, anal, or vaginal penetration of the victim by the penis, fingers, or other parts of the body, or by objects, using force, threats of bodily harm, or by taking advantage of a victim incapable of giving consent. Penetration, however slight, completes rape; emission of semen is not required. Laws defining rape vary by state, but in contrast to older definitions, the crime of rape is no longer limited to female victims, to vaginal penetration alone, to forcible situations only, and the exclusion of spouses as possible perpetrators of rape has been dropped. Thus, rape laws criminalize assaults by intimates, as well as assaults by strangers, and they are gender neutral, suggesting that both men and women can be raped. The rape of women, however, is ten times more common than rape of men, and perpetrators are almost always men regardless of the sex of the victim. Social scientists describe multiple guises that rape takes including child rapes under the rationalization of arranged marriage, rapes by acquaintances and dates, marital rape, punitive rape to control activists for political rights, sexual torture, forced prostitution, rape of refugees, forced virginity exams, rape in war, and genocidal rape.

Prevalence

Rape is universal in that it occurs cross-culturally, though the prevalence rates differ among cultures. Rape in war is evidenced throughout the historical record and has been recorded in almost every modern armed conflict. Rape is one of the most underreported crimes in the United States and worldwide, both during peace and war. Historically, rape victims have been blamed and denigrated as damaged goods. As a result, many victims hesitate to reveal their experiences and determining prevalence rates is difficult. The United States has two federal sources of rape incidence data: the Uniform Crime Reports (UCR), which is a compilation of crimes reported to local authorities, and the National Crime Victimization Survey (NCVS), a nationwide, household-based crime victimization survey intended to determine the true amount of crime including both reported and unreported cases. The UCR reported in 1994 that 102,096 crimes reported to police qualified as rapes. The NCVS reported that 345,340 rapes (including attempts) occurred in 1994, less than one third of which were reported. However, many experts believe these are underestimates. An independent national survey estimated the number of rapes among adult women for 1992 at 683,000 compared to 313,600 from NCVS figures for the same year.

Rape risk is often given as a percent, and estimates range from 13 to 25% of women. These numbers suggest much higher chances of rape than federal estimates, partly because they represent rape *prevalence* and count women as victims if they have been raped at any point in their lifetime, as opposed to the rape *incidence* figures quoted above that count only individuals who were victimized during the preceding 12 months. Because the recovery period for rape is extensive, prevalence rates more accurately portray its true psychological toll.

Variation in prevalence rates is explained by differences in sampling and methodology—differences in the composition of samples, the questions asked, and the context in which the questions are placed. First, the method of data collection is important. If the participants are hard to reach, have language barriers, and/or do not trust the interviewer, the researcher will underdetect a sensitive issue such as rape. How the questions are asked will also affect the amount of disclosure. If the screening questions use different terms than respondents use to remember their experience, the respondent will fail to access relevant memories. Many victims do not answer affirmatively to questions that use the words "rape" or "sexual assault," either because they are not aware of the formal definitions, or because they don't want to be stigmatized as a rape victim. Commonly, women endorse affirmatively that they have had intercourse against their will because a man used force, but say no when asked if they have been raped. Finally, the context of the questioning, the timing and placement of the questions, as well as the gender and ethnicity of the person asking the questions are also important. Less than optimal methods on any of these factors can lead to underdetection of rape.

There are several findings about rape that are undisputed. The typical victim is young, with the peak risk for rape between the ages of 12 to 24 years in the United States. Worldwide, between one third and two thirds of victims are 15 years old or younger. Over 80% of rapes are committed by people victims know, and these acquaintance rapes are less likely to be reported to the police. Contrary to stereotypes, the level of violence is often equal or greater in rapes involving acquaintances, especially among partners in a steady relationship or formally married, and the fear of being seriously injured or killed may be similar.

Most studies attempting to calculate prevalence statistics across ethnicities within the United States and cross-nationally suggest that rape is a significant concern for women universally. Figures drawn from studies administered to college students in several countries show that lifetime prevalence of completed and attempted rape combined is universally above 20%. Data for the United States suggest that prevalence rates are similar for African American women and White women but that the prevalence of sexual assault is lower among recently immigrated Hispanic women. An alternate explanation for this finding, however, is that these cultures have a lower level of comfort for discussing intimate matters with a complete stranger.

Causes of Rape

Many theories have highlighted a primary cause of rape. Some focus on individual characteristics of men who commit rape, others emphasize institutional or social causation. Research suggests, however, that no single theory can explain all rapes all of the time. Current emphasis is on the development of more complex multifactor models of causation. One contributing factor to these models is based on evolution, where the goal of sexual behavior is viewed as maximizing the likelihood of passing on one's genes. In ancestral environments, men were best served by mating with as many fertile females as possible. A number of recent studies have shown that young men are more interested in partner variety, less interested in committed long-term relationships, and more willing to engage in impersonal sex than young women. This factor is limited in the explanation of rape among human beings because it cannot explain rapes lacking reproductive consequences be-

cause they involve oral or anal penetration or victims who are prepubescent or male. Furthermore, some investigators demonstrate that these results characterize only those men with backgrounds of insecure attachments to caregivers. Recent results suggest that pair bonding may be much more important to human survival than evolutionary theory recognizes.

Other causal determinants are based on physiology and neurophysiology. Most of this research involves animal studies or human correlations that don't imply causation. These studies concentrate on steroid hormones, neurotransmitters, neuronanatomical abnormalities, and brain dysfunctions, showing a correlation between biological factors and aggression. Certain psychopathology and personality traits have also been described among sexual offenders. Sexual offenders are most frequently diagnosed with antisocial personality disorder. However, the only perpetrators tested are those who are caught, and this group is a limited sample distinguished by greater poverty and lower education than rapists who remain free in the community. Even within incarcerated groups, it is frequently impossible to distinguish sex offenders from other incarcerated offenders on the basis of psychological profiles. Efforts to create typologies of rapists have led to the conclusion that there is a great deal of heterogeneity, even among the narrow range of men confined in centers for treatment of sexually dangerous persons.

Social and institutional causal factors reflect that rape is ultimately a problem of the society that spawns and perpetuates it, although it affects individuals and is perpetrated by individuals. From this perspective, rape occurs in a sociocultural context and is viewed as one manifestation of gender inequality. Gender has always been an integral organizing feature of human social structures and institutions. Social structures and institutions such as organized religion, political bodies, the military, schools, sports, peer groups, and families directly impinge on our daily lives and define the gendered sociocultural context in which we live. Understanding rape requires examination of the legal, economic, and physical power inequalities between men and women. Rape is one mechanism for maintaining these inequalities, reinforcing male dominance and female subordination in society. Some researchers report that more male-dominant societies have the highest levels of rape and that more rape is seen in preliterate societies characterized by patrilocality and an ideology of male toughness. Within the United States, rape rates in the individual states are correlated with societal-level indicators of social disorganization and inequality.

Gender inequality is represented at the level of individuals in the learned sexual scripts that guide the behavior of boys, girls, men, and women. These scripts assign different roles and behaviors to men and women and establish expectations about interactions. Heterosexual scripts are learned early. Adults and children alike are bombarded with images that equate physical and psychological domination and abuse of women with sexual pleasure through television, film, magazines, and music. Parents tend to socialize their daughters to resist sexual advances and socialize their sons to initiate sexual activity. One study found that 50% of the girls and 65% of the middle school boys sampled believed that it is acceptable for a man to force a woman to have sex if they have been dating for more than six months. Approximately 25% of the boys said that it was acceptable for a man to force sex on a woman if he had spent money on her. Men who use traditional dating scripts, where they initiate the date, pay all of the expenses, and drive the car, are more likely to be sexually aggressive than other men. Cultural norms and expectations pervade everyday life. Myths such as "women provoke rape by the way they dress" and "women say no when they mean yes" appear to prevail throughout our society. Groups who have been identified by researchers as endorsing rape stereotypes include average citizens, police officers, and judges. The prevalence of these myths helps explain why intervention efforts have often been victim-focused and have often been victim-blaming, and why the responses of health professionals, the justice system, and the family frequently increases, rather than ameliorates, the impact of rape on victims.

Cultural expectations and norms associated with alcohol use also serve to perpetuate rape. Alcohol appears to not only serve as a disinhibitor for the man, but as an excuse for his behavior after the fact. It also serves as a blaming mechanism by making the victim appear culpable for her rape. Research also suggests that alcohol may interfere with social cognitions. Men under the influence of alcohol are more likely to perceive ambiguous or neutral cues as suggestive of sexual interest and to ignore or misinterpret cues that a woman is unwilling. Alcohol may be used by young women to "medicate" the tension they experience over expressing sexuality in a double-standard environment. Although many rapes occur in the absence of alcohol, its use was reported by 75% of college student men and over 50% of the women who were involved in acquaintance rapes.

It is now accepted that multiple classes of influences, from the individual to the societal level, determine the expression of sexually aggressive behavior in men. Rather than focusing on a single set of causes, researchers understand rape as *gendered* violence, address *multiple levels of influence* from macro-social to intrapsychic and neurophysiological, and utilize a *life-span perspective* that focuses on the development of a man's violent career. People bring their past into the present in their attitudes, respond to biological drives, reflect the influences of their families and formative institutions in the sexual scripts they follow, and these features influence selection of the environments and strategies they use in pursuing intimate connection. Sexual violence is also responsive to its consequences. In a society where few men are arrested, prosecuted, or convicted of raping a female acquaintance, little constructive feedback counters the immediate reinforcement of achieving sexual aims through whatever means necessary.

Psychological Impact

Immediate responses following rape may include shock, intense fear, numbness, confusion, extreme helplessness, and/or disbelief. Many victims also experience feelings of guilt, shame, and self-blaming causal attributions that may be influenced by cultural myths about rape and unsupportive responses of their social support network. While self-blame has been found to be an adaptive means of retaining "just" world beliefs in certain trauma victims, it is not the case with rape victims who are often already blamed by their societies. Self-blame has repeatedly been found to predict poorer adjustment and greater distress in rape victims. A rape victim's cognitive beliefs and schemas about safety, power, trust, esteem, and intimacy are also often affected by this type of experience. Many experience feelings of vulnerability and loss of control that often stem from no longer believing that they are secure in the world, that the world has order and meaning, and that they are worthy persons. Some rape victims also experience a general distrust or fear of men.

The most common long-term symptoms experienced by rape victims are those of fear and anxiety. Fear is often triggered by stimuli associated with the attack itself, or situations that are perceived by the victim as reminders of rape. Generalized anxiety may lead to jumpiness, sleep disruptions, and/or a lack of concentration. Some rape victims will also experience symptoms of depression. These symptoms include sleep and appetite disturbance, a loss of interest in normal activities, a decrease in the ability to concentrate, and/or feelings of alienation and loneliness. While some rape victims actually develop major depression following the rape, others will only experience some of the symptoms, and not for extended periods of time. One study found that almost one in five raped women in the community had attempted suicide. Rape victims are also more likely than nonvictims to receive several psychiatric diagnoses including alcohol or drug abuse/dependence even several years after the assault. Some victims report deterioration in their sexual functioning following an assault, which may include a fear of sex, arousal dysfunction, and/or decreased sexual interest.

Post traumatic stress disorder (PTSD), a disorder found in many trauma survivors who have been exposed to the threat of injury or death, is the predominant psychiatric diagnosis applied to victims of rape.

Characteristic symptoms of PTSD include repeated daytime intrusive memories and/or nightmares that are so discomforting as to motivate patients to go to great lengths to avoid reminders of the trauma. PTSD has been diagnosed in as many as 94% of rape victims assessed immediately after an assault. Lifetime prevalence of PTSD is about 15% among victims of rape, a similar figure to that seen among male combat veterans. Although all women are affected in some way by the experience of rape, it is difficult to predict the magnitude of impact and the type of response. Certain demographic variables and aspects of a victim's history are somewhat predictive of the severity of distress. Being married, being elderly, having a history of other negative life stressors, and having preexisting psychological distress all have been associated with greater postassault distress; income and education are not predictive. First-time victims show more distress immediately following a rape, but prior victims experience increased stress over time, show more depression, and have a longer recovery overall. Women who are raped more than once are also more likely to abuse substances and have a lifetime diagnosis of depression. Women who have been sexually assaulted by acquaintances or family members suffer as serious psychological aftereffects as women who are assaulted by strangers, but are less likely to report their victimization to police. In addition, the actual violence may be less crucial in predicting response than the perceived threat and uncontrollability of the situation, even though number of assailants, physical threat, injury requiring medical care, and medical complications are all predictive of symptoms. Finally, research suggests that victims who were fondled and caressed tend to experience more symptoms, which may be due to later confusion with subsequent displays of affection that remind them of the attack. Social support may moderate the impact of rape, but unsupportive behavior by significant others in particular predicts poorer social adjustment. Research suggests that Asian and Mexican American women, and possibly Islamic women, have more difficult recoveries than others, possibly because of cultures that link intense, irremediable shame to rape. Though there may be a general similarity in levels of symptoms, the meaning of the experience, the meaning of the symptoms, and the preferred avenues of healing differ according to the survivor's cultural milieu. There is no "correct" or "healthy" time span for victims in coping with their assaults. For some, symptom elevation subsides by the third month, but approximately one-quarter of rape victims go on to experience long-term and sometimes severe symptoms.

Physical Impact

Rape has also long-lasting effects on health. Adult victims of sexual assault seek help from physicians twice as frequently as other women, most often in the second year following victimization. Victimization was a more powerful predictor of medical utilization among women HMO patients than other variables with well-known links to disease including smoking, drinking, life stress, age, and education. Like psychological symptoms, victims of rape may experience, to varying degrees, a wide range of physical symptoms. In the immediate aftermath of rape, nongenital injuries are seen, including abrasions and bruising as well as genital injuries including vaginal tears that can range from catastrophic to microscopic. Some reports indicate that 40% of rape victims experience some degree of nongenital injury, 54% of whom seek medical treatment. However, measured by costs and individual distress, the long-term somatic consequences of rape are more alarming. Several chronic medical diagnoses are made disproportionately among women who have a history of sexual assault including gastrointestinal syndromes, chronic pain syndromes including pelvic pain, and tension headaches.

Interventions

It has been said that women can try to avoid rape, but only men can prevent it. Therefore, a discussion of rape intervention and prevention must begin with men. Currently, cognitive behavioral interventions are used in treatment centers to try to teach offenders to identify situational and emotional states in which they are likely to reoffend and skills to avoid or cope effectively with triggers. Recent meta-analyses of sex offender treatment studies, however, have concluded that their success rates are not promising and that the research on treating sex offenders appears to suffer from intractable methodological problems, precluding any definitive conclusions.

Relatively few rape victims seek specialty mental health treatment immediately after a rape, even though resolution of rape on one's own is difficult. Many women try to block the rape from their minds or distance themselves, believing that if they don't think about it, they can put it behind them. This strategy may work for some trauma survivors. For others, recovery from rape-related symptoms is more elusive and they eventually request assistance for psychosocial or physical distress. Triggers to help-seeking include relationship breakups, persistent distress, an impending trial, or withdrawal of support from family and friends. If victims choose to seek mental health treatment, they have many options ranging from different formats such as individual and group therapy with a variety of techniques used within each format. Research on individual psychotherapy has focused on behavioral and cognitive behavioral techniques for rape victims. Behavioral exposure techniques such as in vivo flooding, systematic desensitization, and prolonged exposure treatment confront the victim with the feared situation through varying degrees of exposure or imagination. These techniques show mixed empirical results. While the prolonged exposure treatment appears to be the most helpful, all of these techniques are somewhat aversive for the victim and may result in high dropout rates or reactivation of chemical abuse and suicidal attempts unless practiced by a qualified specialist. Anxiety management techniques, such as stress inoculation training, focus more on the victims' cognitions by teaching them to feel in control of the fear, rather than activating and habituating the fear. New hybrid approaches such as cognitive processing therapy and eye movement desensitization and reprocessing therapy (EMDR) combine elements of exposure and anxiety management. Studies of these treatments have suggested efficacious outcomes. However, existing treatment evaluations are brief, the studies generally deal only with uncomplicated cases, and small numbers of participants are treated by a small number of therapists. Future research also needs to document that treatments incorporating a focus on the rape event itself are more effective than more traditional approaches aimed generally at symptoms of depression, anxiety, or sexual dysfunction.

Current individual psychotherapeutic treatments may not be appropriate for many of those in need. Of those victims who do seek out this type of treatment, 20 to 30% drop out of treatment before completion. Individual therapy for rape victims has been criticized because it reduces rape from a social issue to an individual issue and encourages women to adjust to living in a rape-supportive society by focusing energy on their own recovery, rather than by taking political action that could ultimately prevent rape. Group psychotherapeutic treatment has become the intervention choice of clinicians, as it both builds a community feeling of activism and empowerment and also provides individual support by peers who are able to validate the feelings, share grief, and counteract self-blame. Group therapy is widely used both in community-based programs and within the formal mental health system. The effort directed at evaluation of group interventions is very disproportionate to the number of survivors treated by it, however.

While no one therapy has proven to be effective for every client, and no one treatment has proven to be superior for rape-related symptoms, all efficacious treatments share common features. Such features include the avoidance of victim blame, a supportive, nonstigmatizing view of rape as a criminal victimization, an environment to overcome cognitive and behavioral avoidance, provision of information about traumatic reaction, and the expectation that symptoms will improve.

Physicians, rather than mental health professionals, are the health professionals most often approached by rape victims. Because physicians are the ones on the front lines, it is most important that they be trained to screen for victimization by violence, acknowledge disclosure, and direct women to other resources if they so desire it. Although mandated by standards of care to perform these roles, studies show that few physicians initiate discussions about violence history. Currently the bulk of victim care is provided by grassroots agencies. In addition to advocating for improved community response to rape, crisis centers support groups for survivors, offer hospital and police accompaniment services to victims, court accompaniment programs, volunteer hot lines, self-defense training, and advocacy. They also often offer training for police, court, medical, and mental health professionals, educating them about victims and the normal responses to a rape, and emphasize prevention by presenting programs to young people about rape, particularly within intimate relationships. Unfortunately, these agencies rely on funding from local and state money, which has become more and more difficult to obtain and has resulted in crisis center program cutbacks and closures.

Conclusions

Over the years, the public has believed that rape was rare. We now know better. Stereotypes have also misled the public to think that most rapes involved strangers, when the majority of perpetrators are actually known by their victims. An understanding of rape requires an acknowledgment of the social context that supports rape and a scrutiny of the systemic responses to it. Although rape affects individuals, it must be fought at a societal level, primarily through community prevention and advocacy, as well as through support of group treatment research.

Bibliography

Abbey, A., Ross, L. T., & McDuffie, D. (1995). Alcohol's role in sexual assault. In R. R. Watson (Ed.), *Drug and alcohol abuse reviews: Vol. 5. Addictive behaviors in women.* Totowa, NJ: Humana Press. Useful in learning about the complex relationship between alcohol and sexual violence.

Burnam, M. A., Stein, J. A., Golding, J. M., Siegel, J. M., Sorenson, S. B., Forsythe, A. B., & Telles, C. A. (1988). Sexual assault and mental disorders in a community population. *Journal of Consulting and Clinical Psychology, 56,* 843–850. An example of the type of methodology used to demonstrate the psychological effects of rape.

Crowell, N. A., & Burgess, A. W. (Eds.). (1996). *Understanding violence against women.* Panel on Research on Violence against Women, Committee on Law and Justice, Commission on Behavioral and Social Sciences and Education, National Research Council. Washington, DC: National Academy Press. A comprehensive review and policy analysis of rape and male partner violence focusing on the science infrastructure.

Foa, E. B., Zinbarg, R., & Rothbaum, B. O. (1992). Uncontrollability and unpredictability in posttraumatic stress disorder: Experimental evidence. *Psychological Bulletin, 112,* 218–238. Reviews human and animal research that supports the role of cognitions as mediators of the trauma-psychological distress relationship.

Frazier, P. A., & Burnett, J. W. (1994). Immediate coping strategies among rape victims. *Journal of Counseling & Development, 72,* 633–639. Reflective of the growing body of studies examining cognitive strategies for coping with the distress of rape.

Furby, L., Weinrott, M. R., & Blackshaw, L. (1989). Sex offender recidivism: A review. *Psychological Bulletin, 105,* 3–30. Documents reasons for pessimism about stopping rape through offender treatment.

Golding, J. M. (1994). Sexual assault history and physical health in randomly selected Los Angeles women. *Health Psychology, 13,* 130–138. An example of the methods for demonstrating the health impact of rape.

Kilpatrick, D. G., Seymour, A. E., & Edwards, C. N. (April 23, 1992). *Rape in America: A report to the nation.* Arlington, VA: National Crime Victims Center. A national telephone survey addressing the frequency and characteristics of rape, considered the best, but conservative, estimate of prevalence.

Koss, M. P., Goodman, L., Browne, A., Fitzgerald, L. F., Keita, G. P., & Russo, N. F. (1994). *No safe haven: Male violence against women at home, at work, and in the community.* Washington, DC: American Psychological Association. Reviews research on causes, frequency, impact, treatment, and prevention of partner violence, workplace harassment, and rape.

Koss, M. P., Heise, L., & Russo, N. F. (1994). The global health burden of rape. *Psychology of Women Quarterly, 18,* 499–527. Presents information on the prevalence of rape in developing countries, provides estimates of disability globally attributed to male violence, and describes the intersections between violence and women's health.

Lefley, H. P., Scott, C. S., Llabre, M., & Hicks, D. (1993). Cultural beliefs about rape and victims' response in three ethnic groups. *American Journal of Orthopsychiatry, 63,* 623–632. Examines how White, African American, and Hispanic ethnicity impact on response to rape.

MacKinnon, C. A. (1994). Rape, genocide, and women's human rights. In A. Stiglmayer (Ed.), *Rape: The war against women in Bosnia-Herzegovina* (pp. 183–196). Lincoln: University of Nebraska Press. Reviews the status of rape in international law.

Parrott, A., & Bechhofer, L. (Eds.). (1991). *Acquaintance rape: The hidden crime.* New York: Wiley. Contains research on college students.

Resick, P. A., & Schnicke, M. K. (1993). *Cognitive processing therapy for rape victims: A treatment manual.* Newbury Park, CA: Sage. An example of treatment packages designed for rape survivors.

Mary P. Koss and Laura Boeschen

RAPID EYE MOVEMENT. *See* Dreams, *article on* Physiology; *and* Sleep.

RASCH MODEL. Georg Rasch, a Danish mathematician, created a family of psychometric models to measure persons and items on latent traits, such as abilities, behavioral dispositions, and personality (*Probabalistic Models for Some Intelligence and Attainment Tests*, Chicago, 1960). Persons and items vary in level on the trait latent trait. Both a person's standing and an item's characteristics are estimated from the pattern of responses to test items.

The term *Rasch model* is often used to refer to Rasch's logistic model for dichotomous data (see below). Georg Rasch developed this model to measure abilities from dichotomously scored items from a battery of military tests. However, Rasch also provided the groundwork for other psychometric models which are appropriate for multiple item response categories and reading speed. Further, the term *Rasch model* is also extended to a family of logistic models that includes rating scales, partial credit models and multidimensional models. Extended coverage of these models are given by Fischer and Molenaar (*Rasch Models: Foundations, Recent Developments and Applications*, New York, 1995) and by Linden and Hambleton (*Handbook of Modern Item Response Theory*, New York, 1997). Defining features of Rasch-family models include the assumptions of constant item discriminations, minimal guessing, and a logistic relationship of item responses to the latent trait. Thus, the term *Rasch model* should be distinguished from Rasch-family models, although in the literature they are often used interchangeably.

Rasch models are a subclass of item response theory models. Item response theory models predict a person's particular response on each given item (i.e., the dependent variable). An item response theory model specifies how the person's trait level and item properties (i.e., the independent variables) combine to predict the outcome. Theoretically, it is assumed that the latent trait underlies item responses; consequently, both the person's trait level and the item's characteristics are estimated as parameters in the item response theory model. The person's estimated trait level depends not only on their success on the items, but also on the properties of the items that were administered. [*See* Item Response Theory.]

The term *Rasch model*, when used to refer to a single model, is the one-parameter logistic model (1PL) in which the dependent variable is the dichotomous response (correct versus incorrect) on an item. The independent variables (person trait level and item difficulty) combine additively in the exponential form of the 1PL model; that is, the item's difficulty is subtracted from the person's ability. The more the person's trait level exceeds the item difficulty, the higher the probability of a correct response. Each total score has only one associated trait level in the Rasch IPL which means that total score is a sufficient statistic for estimating traits. However, total score is not linearly related to trait level; the exact relationship depends on the difficulty of the items.

The estimations obtained for the Rasch model are biased by neither the estimation sample nor the particular items administered. In contrast, in classical test theory both the person's score and the item's difficulty are biased. Item difficulty is estimated by the proportion of persons in the sample who pass the items; clearly, this value depends on the level of the trait in the population. A person's trait level is linearly related to total score, which depends on the difficulty of the items that were administered.

[*See also* Scale Development.]

Susan E. Embretson and Kim A. Diehl

RATIONAL EMOTIVE BEHAVIOR THERAPY (REBT). Originated by Albert Ellis in January 1955, rational emotive behavior therapy (REBT) was the first of the major cognitive behavior therapies. Having been trained in person-centered and psychoanalytic therapy, Ellis found them to be too passive and nondirective, so he went back to philosophers—especially to several ancient Asian and Greek-Roman philosophers—who held that people largely upset themselves instead of being upset directly by early and later adversities in life. Taking a constructivist position, Ellis theorized that humans are born with strong tendencies to cope with serious practical and emotional problems by significantly changing their cognitive, emotional, and behavioral reactions to their adversities. Unlike other constructivist therapies, however, REBT holds that people are also born, as well as reared, to have strong destructivist tendencies, and are especially prone to take their goals and preferences (which are largely socially learned) and to inflate them self-defeatingly into absolutistic musts and demands. They often construct three basic self-disturbing imperatives: (1) "I *absolutely must* perform well and win significant others' approval"; (2) "Other people *have to* treat me kindly and fairly"; and (3) "My life conditions *ought to* be enjoyable and free from great frustration."

Theory of REBT

REBT theory states that once people convert their important desires and goals into absolutistic demands—which they often fail to acknowledge that they are doing—they tend to create related dysfunctional, exaggerated beliefs such as "Because I am not performing well, as I *absolutely must*, I am an *inadequate person*"; "Because you're not treating me as fairly as you *certainly should*, you are a thoroughly rotten individual"; or "Because life conditions are far worse than they *absolutely ought to be*, it's *awful, I can't bear* it, and I can't enjoy myself at all."

By consciously and/or implicitly believing, in one or more unrealistic and illogical imperatives, people very likely—though not necessarily—make themselves seriously anxious, depressed, enraged, and self-pitying. These feelings, REBT holds, are usually unhealthy or dysfunctional and are often accompanied by self-defeating behaviors such as procrastination, addiction, poor relationships, violence, and phobias. But if people change their grandiose demands to flexible preferences when their goals and desires are unfulfilled, they will tend mainly to experience healthy negative feelings—such as sorrow, regret, and frustration—and they will be significantly less disturbed and will function better.

REBT also is based on the premise that when people feel disturbed and function badly, they frequently construct unrealistic "musts" about their symptoms. Thus, they strongly believe that "I must not be depressed" and depress themselves *about* their depression; and they insistently think that "I must not procrastinate! I'm no good for procrastinating" and thereby make themselves depressed *about* their procrastination.

ABCs of Human Disturbance

The ABC theory of REBT is similar to that of cognitive-behavior therapy (CBT), such as Aaron Beck's cognitive therapy, Donald Meichenbaum's cognitive-behavior therapy, and Martin Seligman's optimism-enhancing therapy. It states that A (Adversities) may contribute heavily to C (dysfunctional emotional and behavioral Consequences); but equally important in "causing" C is B (irrational Beliefs) about A. REBT theory also hypothesizes that when therapists help clients to clearly see, and actively to Dispute (D) and change their dysfunctional Beliefs (B), and particularly to replace them with preferences instead of demands, they tend to wind up with E (Effective New Philosophies) that are usually accompanied by other functional E's—notably, Effective New Feelings and Effective New Behaviors.

The ABCDE theory of disturbance and how it can be helped by Disputing (D) clients' irrational Beliefs (B) has been tested in hundreds of studies of REBT and CBT. The great majority of these studies show, first, that people with disturbances have more frequent and more strongly held dysfunctional Beliefs than less disturbed individuals, and they tend to become less seriously disturbed with REBT treatment.

REBT theory states that people easily and often adopt and construct self-defeating and socially defeating Beliefs; practice holding on to and reinforcing them for many years; and habituate themselves to dysfunctional behaviors (e.g., phobias) that are difficult to change. Therefore, in spite of often understanding how handicapping their thoughts, feelings, and behaviors are, they often have great difficulty rectifying them and maintaining their Effective New Behaviors. Some seriously disturbed individuals, moreover, may have biochemical tendencies to be dysfunctional and may be helped to function better with REBT or other forms of therapy plus suitable psychotropic medication. Most clients or patients can be taught to understand how they frequently harm themselves; they can decide to change their self-destructive thoughts, feelings, and actions; and they can actually do so—with considerable work and practice.

Treatment Methods of REBT

In REBT clients are usually quickly shown how they are needlessly contributing and adding to their disturbances, and they are provided with a number of multifaceted cognitive, emotive, and behavioral methods that they can apply to reduce their disturbances. Cognitively, they are shown how to actively and persistently dispute their dysfunctional beliefs—especially their absolutistic musts—and how to change them to realistic and logical preferences. They are taught how to consider the cost-benefit ratio of their harmful indulgences, how to use rational coping statements, positive imagery, cognitive-distraction methods, written and audiovisual self-help materials, reframing techniques, modeling, and other rethinking methods. Emotively, they are given unconditional acceptance by the therapist, and are encouraged to use forceful self-emotive statements, shame-attacking exercises, rational role playing, vigorous disputing of irrational beliefs, humorous interventions, metaphors, and other experiential procedures. Behaviorally, they are encouraged to do activity homework, *in vivo* desensitization, risk-taking experiments, reinforcement methods, skill training, stimulus control, and relapse prevention and to participate in other retraining and reconditioning experiences.

All multifaceted REBT methods are tailor-made for the individual client in accordance with his or her assessed disturbance and how he or she reacts to the initial techniques that are used. Client and therapist collaborate in discovering and continually experimenting with general and specific procedures that work best for this particular client at this special time in his or her life.

REBT and Other Forms of Cognitive-Behavior Therapy

REBT is similar to many CBTs, such as those of Beck, Meichenbaum, and Seligman, but it differs from them in several ways: (1) It stresses the primacy of the musts in neurotic disturbance as well as the core irrational Beliefs that commonly accompany these demands, especially awfulizing, I-can't-stand-it-itis, and damning oneself and others; (2) it includes a humanistic-existential outlook, and emphasizes choice and purposiveness; (3) it stresses forceful disputing of irrational Beliefs and uses more emotive-evocative methods than most other CBTs use; (4) it favors *in vivo* desensitization and activity homework assignments; and (5) unlike the constructionist CBTs of Vittorio Guidano and Michael Mahoney, it is actively directive and educational.

Clients using REBT are shown what they can do to alleviate their presenting symptoms and to *feel* better. But if they are willing to work hard at therapy, they are also encouraged to *get* better. This involves (1) symptom alleviation; (2) long-term maintenance of therapeutic gains; and (3) making a profound philosophical change that enables them to rarely upset themselves seriously about even some of the worst adversities that may occur in their lives. This kind of change means that people acquire:

Unconditional self-acceptance and other-acceptance—accepting oneself and others no matter how poorly you and they perform.

Antimusturbation—refusing to make grandiose demands that desired goals—such as success, approval, and comfort—absolutely must be fulfilled.

High frustration tolerance—refraining from defining unfortunate events and losses as terrible and awful, and from seeing them as so bad that they absolutely must not exist.

Allergy to overgeneralizing—checking all-or-nothing, black-and-white, either/or thinking and adopting instead a flexible, alternative-seeking, and/also approach to life.

REBT, of course, does not claim that if people achieve this profound philosophical change they will have a panacea for all their emotional and behavioral ills. But it will probably help.

[*See also* Psychotherapy.]

Bibliography

Ellis, A. (1994). *Reason and emotion in psychotherapy* (revised and updated). Secaucus, NJ: Birch Lane.

Ellis, A. (1996). *Better, deeper, and more enduring brief therapy.* New York: Brunner/Mazel.

Ellis, A., & Dryden, W. (1997). *The practice of rational emotive behavior therapy* (rev. ed.). New York: Springer.

Ellis, A., & Harper, R. A. (1997). *A guide to rational living* (3rd rev. ed.). North Hollywood, CA: Melvin Powers.

Guidano, V. F. (1991). *The self in process.* New York: Guilford Press.

Mahoney, M. J. (1991). *Human change process.* New York: Basic Books.

Walen, S., DiGiuseppe, R., & Dryden, W. (1992). *A practi-*

tioner's guide to rational-emotive therapy. New York: Oxford University Press.

Albert Ellis

RATIONALISM. *See* Philosphy, *article on* Philosophy of Science.

RAYNAUD'S DISEASE is a disorder of blood vessels in the fingers and sometimes the toes in which cold or emotional stress causes a complete stoppage of blood flow. At this time, the digits turn white and feel numb or extremely cold. After a few minutes they may turn blue and/or red, accompanied by mild to severe pain. A typical attack lasts about 5 to 15 minutes and may occur daily or only occasionally, depending on the weather and the severity of the patients' disease. The disorder is four times more common in women than in men and affects about 4 to 5% of the U.S. population. There are no clear racial or ethnic preferences and no definite age of onset. There is some evidence suggesting that Raynaud's disease runs in families.

The term *Raynaud's disease* denotes the primary form of the disorder, in which the symptoms cannot be attributed to another disease. When the symptoms are caused by another disease, such as rheumatoid arthritis, the term *Raynaud's phenomenon* is used. Toxic agents, such as vinyl chloride, can also cause Raynaud's phenomenon.

Blood flow in human digits is controlled by nerves that cause blood vessels to constrict in response to cold or stress and by receptors that cause the vessels to constrict or dilate in response to chemicals that circulate in the blood. Maurice Raynaud, the French physician who identified the disease in 1854, thought that the symptoms were due to nervous system overactivity. Subsequently, Thomas Lewis (1929), an English cardiologist, advanced the theory that the symptoms were due to an abnormality of the blood vessels themselves. Although scientists do not yet know the cause of Raynaud's disease, most evidence now favors the theory of Lewis.

Lewis, followed by Freedman (1989a), produced Raynaud's attacks in patients with the disease, even though their finger nerves were blocked with local anesthesia, thus showing that the nervous system is not needed to cause an attack. Other investigators directly measured the activity of finger nerves and found no differences between Raynaud's disease patients and normal volunteers. Many researchers have measured the blood levels of circulating chemicals that affect blood vessels but have generally found no differences between persons with Raynaud's disease and those without it.

More recently, Freedman (1989b) and J. D. Coffman (1990) showed that a specific class of biochemical receptors (α_2-adrenergic receptors) in the fingers produce more blood vessel constriction in Raynaud's disease patients than in normal volunteers. Freedman (1993) then went on to show that local cooling increased this effect only in Raynaud's patients and that blockage of these receptors prevented Raynaud's attacks in the laboratory.

There are no obvious psychological factors in Raynaud's disease. Stress appears to provoke about one third of the attacks, but patients in general do not appear to differ psychologically from the general population.

A variety of drug treatments have been tried for Raynaud's disease to the end of increasing finger blood flow and decreasing cold-induced blood vessel constriction. Nifedipine is currently the drug of first choice for patients with primary Raynaud's disease. Nifedipine is a calcium slow-channel blocker that reduces the entry of calcium into cells, thereby reducing blood vessel constriction. Many studies have been done using this drug, with the average effect being a reduction in the frequency of Raynaud's attacks by about 50%. A newer, slow-release form of nifedipine may increase patient compliance because it is taken only once per day.

In the 1970s Neal Miller, an eminent behavioral psychologist, demonstrated that voluntary control of many physiological functions could be learned by providing immediate and objective external feedback of the parameter under investigation. Edward Taub, a physiological psychologist, showed that finger temperature control in humans, could be learned by using a temperature sensor on a finger to control the intensity of a light bulb viewed by the participant. Since Raynaud's attacks are characterized by sharply decreased finger temperature and blood flow, it seemed logical to train these patients to increase their finger temperature in the hope of decreasing their symptoms.

Freedman then conducted a series of studies on Raynaud's disease patients in which the effects of ten 1-hour sessions of finger temperature biofeedback were compared with those of other behavioral procedures. He found that biofeedback patients learned to increase their finger temperature and reported an average decrease in symptom frequency of 66%. When half of the training sessions were conducted under mild cold stress to better simulate the natural environment, the decline in attack frequency improved to 92%. These effects were maintained at 1- and 3-year follow-up periods conducted during the coldest months of the year. A second study was then conducted to investigate the physiological mechanism of these effects. It was found that increases in blood flow during temperature biofeedback could be obtained even when the finger nerves were blocked with a local anesthetic, suggesting that a chemical in the blood produces the effect. It was also found that the blood flow increases occurred in the smallest finger blood vessels, which is probably where the attacks occur as well. The average decline in symptom frequency was 80%, maintained at 2-year follow-up.

[*See also* Arthritis; Biofeedback; Stress; *and the biography of Neal E. Miller.*]

Bibliography

Coffman, J. D. (1991). Raynaud's phenomenon. *Hypertension, 17*, 593–602. A good review paper emphasizing pharmacological treatments.

Coffman, J. D., & Cohen, A. S. (1971). Total and capillary fingertip blood flow in Raynaud's phenomenon. *New England Journal of Medicine, 285*, 259–263. The first modern study of the pathophysiology of the disease.

Coffman, J. D., & Cohen, A. S. (1990). α_2-Adrenergic and 5-HT$_2$ receptor hypersensitivity in Raynaud's phenomenon. *Journal of Vascular and Medical Biology, 2*, 100–106.

Freedman, R. R. (1995). Raynaud's disease. In A. J. Goreczny (Ed.), *Handbook of health and rehabilitation psychology* (pp. 117–131). New York: Plenum. A review paper that emphasizes behavioral treatments for Raynaud's disease.

Freedman, R. R., Ianni, P., & Wenig, P. (1983). Behavioral treatment of Raynaud's disease. *Journal of Consulting and Clinical Psychology, 151*, 539–549. A controlled study comparing four behavioral treatments with a one-year follow-up.

Freedman, R. R., Mayes, M. D., & Sabharwal, S. C. (1989a). Induction of vasospastic attacks despite digital nerve block in Raynaud's disease and phenomenon. *Circulation, 80*, 859–862. A laboratory study demonstrating that the nervous system is not needed to produce Raynaud's attacks.

Freedman, R. R., Sabharwal, S. C., Desai, N., Wenig, P., & Mayes, M. (1989b). Increased α-adrenergic responsiveness in idiopathic Raynaud's disease. *Arthritis Rheum., 33*, 61–65.

Freedman, R. R., Sabharwal, S. C., Ianni, P., Desai, N., Wenig, P., & Mayes, M. D. (1988). Nonneural beta-adrenergic vasodilating mechanism in temperature biofeedback. *Psychosomatic Medicine, 50*, 394–401. Describes the mechanism of biofeedback treatment for Raynaud's disease, with two-year follow-up data.

Freedman, R. R., Moten, M., Migaly, P., & Mayes, M. (1993). Cold-induced potentiation of α_2-adrenergic vasoconstriction in idiopathic Raynaud's disease. *Arthritis and Rheumatism, 36*, 685–689. Describes the mechanism of cold-induced blood vessel constriction in Raynaud's disease.

Lewis, T. (1929). Experiments relating to the peripheral mechanism involved in spasmodic arrest of circulation in the fingers, a variety of Raynaud's disease. *Heart, 15*, 7–101. A classic paper describing early physiological studies of Raynaud's disease.

Robert R. Freedman

REACTANCE is a motivational state defined conceptually as an impulse to restore behavioral freedoms that are perceived to have been threatened or lost. The theory of psychological reactance stipulates the conditions that give rise to reactance and the ensuing psychological and behavioral consequences. For example, a woman who believed she was free to wear slacks to her job and then was told to wear only dresses would experience psychological reactance. How much reactance she would experience and what its consequences might be are delineated by the rest of the theory.

Determinants of Reactance

In general, behavioral freedoms are beliefs about what behaviors one can perform, when, and how to perform them. Examples include the belief that one can brush one's teeth in the morning, one can eat only vegetables, one can own a car, and one can have religious beliefs. What constitutes a threat or loss is the perception or belief that the possibility of engaging in a free behavior has been reduced or eliminated.

Given the perception that a freedom has been threatened or lost, what determines the amount of reactance experienced is the importance of the freedom. What makes a freedom important to a person is its unique instrumental value for the satisfaction of important needs. For example, for most people, the importance of the freedom to have a crisp new dollar bill is determined by its purchasing power and so it is not different from the importance of having a used dollar bill. However, if one's favorite vending machine accepted only new dollar bills, then the freedom to have a new bill would be greater than the freedom to have an old one.

With the importance of freedoms held constant, the greater the number and/or proportion of freedoms threatened or eliminated, the greater should be the magnitude of reactance. If a person expected to be able to attend any of three different movies and then found that only one was showing, he would experience more reactance than if he found two were showing. If a person thought that she could attend any of three movies and found that two were not showing, she would experience more reactance than if she had expected six, only two of which turned out not to be showing. A greater proportion of her freedoms would have been eliminated in the former than in the latter case.

When a freedom is threatened or eliminated, any implication that other freedoms are also threatened will increase the magnitude of reactance. Such implications can easily occur, and furthermore, they increase not only the number and proportion of freedoms threatened, they can easily include freedoms of greater importance than the one explicitly threatened or eliminated. Thus, if a person who really liked to eat chocolate desserts were told by his physician to reduce his consumption of hot chocolate, he might infer that his consumption of desserts was also under threat and thereby experience a great deal of reactance.

Finally, it should be noted that freedoms can be threatened or eliminated by impersonal agents such as government, business, or chance events.

Consequences of Reactance

Because psychological reactance urges a person to restore any threatened or eliminated freedom, its most direct consequence is a behavioral tendency to engage in the freedom in question. A corollary is that the behavior whose freedom is in question will increase in subjective desirability in proportion to the magnitude of reactance. A child, for example, who has been told to stop eating potato chips will experience an increase in appetite for potato chips.

While the freedom can be restored by engaging in the threatened behavior, it can also be restored by engaging in a behavior that implies possession of the freedom. For example, a person who was stopped by a deputy sheriff for driving at 40 mph in a 35-mph speed zone might then drive at 65 mph in a 50-mph speed zone, thereby implying that he really did have the freedom to drive 5 mph over the speed limit.

An individual's reactance can be reduced by the action of another person or agency. If one member of a secretarial pool were told to spend less time at the water cooler, her freedom could be restored by other members' spending increased time at the water cooler. Similarly, impersonal events such as a change in law or its enforcement, changes in business practices, and so forth can reduce reactance by restoring freedoms.

Theoretical Implications

When a person can choose only one of two or more alternatives, the contemplation of giving up one or more freedoms because of the necessity to reject one or more alternatives should constitute a threat to those freedoms, just as a decision to give up one or more should eliminate those freedoms. Both the contemplation and the decision should therefore create reactance. The reactance from contemplation should increase the perceived attractiveness of any alternative to be given up, and perhaps even decrease the attractiveness of the alternative to be chosen, both effects making the decision more difficult. However, Mills and Ford (1995) have produced evidence that this convergence in the attractiveness of choice alternatives occurs only for public evaluations; private evaluations will actually tend to diverge. Nevertheless, once the decision has been made, reactance from no longer being able to reject the chosen alternative and reactance from no longer being able to have the rejected alternative should cause a feeling of regret about the choice. Such regret effects have been experimentally demonstrated, though not as a test of reactance theory.

A second arena that involves freedoms is persuasion. People frequently believe they can adopt whatever opinion or attitude they wish and behave as they please. At a minimum, people feel they are free to hold whatever attitudes they already have and behave as they have in the past. As a consequence, persuasive communications aimed at changing a person's attitude or behavior will frequently generate reactance and a consequent increased urge to resist the persuasive attempt.

A limit to reactance from social pressure has been noted by Grisla Grabitz-Gniech (1971). She made the point that social influence processes within a group can lead members to give up freedoms rather than experience reactance. Another theoretical problem of interest was the suggestion (Wortman & Brehm, 1975) that helplessness effects should normally be preceded by reactance effects; when an individual finds it impossible to solve problems, the first response will be to try harder, the second, to become helpless.

Because psychological reactance is a way to understand resistance to influence or to change, the theory has been used to try to understand a variety of problems including compliance with rules and regulations, change in laws governing consumer products, compliance with medical regimens, reactions by juries to judicial restrictions concerning admissible evidence, how people respond to censorship, and so forth. The theory has also been used to sharpen understanding of the Type A coronary-prone behavior pattern (Rhodewalt & Strube, 1985). Individual difference measures of reactance (Dowd, Milne, & Wise, 1991) have been developed to improve understanding of various practical problems including resistance in counseling and psychotherapy. The theory has received attention from researchers in Europe, Australia, South America, and Japan.

Bibliography

Brehm, J. W. (1966). *A theory of psychological reactance*. New York: Academic Press. The original statement of the theory along with some minor research not published elsewhere. This volume is now out of print except in Japanese (Seishin Shobo).

Brehm, S. S., & Brehm, J. W. (1981). *Psychological reactance: A theory of freedom and control*. New York: Academic Press. A comprehensive review of relevant evidence produced up to 1981 and a discussion of disagreements between theory and research findings and potential resolutions. A section of this volume is devoted to application of the theory to applied problems such as therapy, sales promotions, antilittering campaigns, and so forth.

Dowd, E. T., Milne, C. R., & Wise, S. L. (1991). The therapeutic reactance scale: A measure of psychological reactance. *Journal of Counseling & Development, 69*, 541–545.

Grabitz-Gniech, G. (1971). Some restrictive conditions for

the occurence of psychological reactance. *Journal of Personality and Social Psychology, 19,* 188–196.

Mills, J., & Ford, T. E. (1995). Effects of importance of a prospective choice on private and public evaluations of the alternatives. *Personality and Social Psychology Bulletin, 21,* 256–266.

Rhodewalt, F., & Strube, M. J. (1985). A self-attribution-reactance model of recovery from injury in Type A individuals. *Journal of Applied Social Psychology, 15,* 330–344.

Wicklund, R. A. (1974). *Freedom and reactance.* Hillsdale, NJ: Erlbaum. A survey of the first 10 years of reactance research along with a critical look at the theory and research issues that have been neglected. Also useful is a discussion of how reactance theory accords with other views of freedom, including those of B. F. Skinner, Ivan Steiner, and Erich Fromm.

Wortman, C. B., & Brehm, J. W. (1975). Responses to uncontrollable outcomes: An integration of reactance theory and the learned helplessness model. In L. Berkowitz (Ed.), *Advances in experimental social psychology* (Vol. 8). New York: Academic Press.

Jack W. Brehm

REACTION TIME refers to the time that elapses from the appearance of a stimulus and the onset of the response to that stimulus. Reaction time is one of the most prevalent behavioral measures in experimental cognitive psychology and is used in other domains, such as social cognition. Other terms are also frequently used that are synonymous with reaction time, such as *response time* and *response latency.* The usefulness of reaction time measures in revealing characteristics of mental processes is made possible by a number of very simple theoretical assumptions about the organization of mental processes that intervene between stimulus onset and response onset.

Studies using reaction time (RT) measures generally instruct participants to respond as quickly as possible while still maintaining a high ($>$95%) level of accuracy. Emphasis on speed is intended to ensure that RT is an estimate of the minimum processing time. This is critical because theoretical interpretations are based on the differences in RTs across a set of experimental conditions. If participants are not responding as quickly as possible, then differences may reflect both processing time and some additional time that carries little theoretical import. To increase the accuracy of the estimate of processing time, typically a number of RTs for each condition for each subject are collected. In most cases, RTs for incorrect responses are excluded from the analyses. Additional trimming of RT data is common, although there is disagreement regarding appropriate trimming criteria. It is not unusual to eliminate correct RTs that appear to be too fast for the participant to have made the responses based on the stimuli (e.g., RTs less than 200 ms). Inappropriately long RTs may also be eliminated from the analyses although a criteria for identifying such outliers is open to question. Once the RTs have been trimmed, then a measure of central tendency is calculated, such as mean or median RT. For a set of RTs within a subject and condition, the RT distribution is virtually always positively skewed. To deal with this fact, median RTs may be used. However, mean RTs are more commonly used because the sampling error of the mean is smaller than that for the median, and the mean is an unbiased estimator, unlike the median. Moreover, certain theoretical frameworks make mean RT measures the preferred estimator (e.g., additive factors logic).

Simple RT is measured in situations in which an individual must always make the same response to the onset of a single repeated stimulus. The minimum mean simple RT appears to be just under 200 ms in young adults for easily dicriminable, suprathreshold stimuli with a fast onset (e.g., lighting an LED in a darkened room). *Choice RT* is measured in situations where the task is to select one of two possible responses contingent on the identity of the stimulus. In general, choice RT is longer than simple RT. As the number of possible responses increases, RT tends to increase linearly with the log of the number of response alternatives. This relation between RT and the number of response alternatives is called Hick's Law.

Most research using RT measures is not interested in RT per se but rather in using RTs to make inferences about underlying mental operations. However, it is not possible to observe the operation of individual mental processes. Rather, the effect of experimental manipulations believed to influence a single process can only be observed in the context of the total RT. The total RT is not only reflective of the single process of interest, but also a number of other mental processes that intervene between the presentation of the stimulus and the initiation of the response. The challenge is to attribute the change in RT to the influence of the experimental manipulation on individual mental processes. This inferential step from observed RT to underlying mental process requires a number of assumptions. Fundamentally, there is the assumption that the amount of time that a process takes is some measure of what that process does (e.g., the more to accomplish, the more time required). Beyond this, a much more detailed framework is needed for linking observed RT with mental events.

Subtraction Method

In 1869, F. C. Donders proposed the subtraction method for estimating the durations of individual processing stages. The typical experiment involved three different experimental tasks. Task A required the subject to make a simple reaction such as lifting a finger off a telegraph key once a stimulus occurs. Task B had multiple possible stimuli and multiple responses. Task C had multiple stimuli but subjects only made a single response for certain stimuli. Thus, Task B required stimulus discrimination and response selection. Task C had stimulus discrimination but no response selection. Subtracting Tack C from Task B gave the time for response selection. Subtracting Task A from Task C gave the time for the discrimination process. Donders's method led to a flurry of studies examining the influences of a variety of experimental manipulations on reaction time and the hypothesized underlying mental stages of stimulus discrimination and response selection.

There are at least two limitations to Donders's method. First, the method provides time estimates for mental processes that are already known to exist. The application of this method presumes considerable knowledge already about the organization of processes. However, such extensive information is rarely available in cognitive psychology. Second, it must be possible to devise variants of the task that either add or delete processing stages while leaving all other stages unaffected. This has been called the assumption of pure insertion and deletion. If adding or removing a stage has any effect on other stages, or if it changes the quality of task, then the values obtained from the subtraction method are no longer meaningful. Skepticism about the validity of this assumption and a host of contradictory findings led to a sharp decline in the use of reaction time measures at the beginning of the 1900s. It is important to note, however, that the assumption of pure insertion and deletion appears to be possible under some circumstances and variants of the subtraction method are used in many neuro-imaging studies.

Additive Factors Logic

The restrictive assumptions of the subtraction method meant that there were often situations where the subtraction method was not appropriate. A generalization of Donders's method, called additive factors logic, was proposed by Sternberg (1969). Additive factors logic makes three basic assumptions about how mental processes were organized. First, processing is organized into discrete stages in which only the final result of each processing stage was passed on to the next stage. Second, stages are organized in series such that processing in one stage did not begin until the completion of the prior stages. Third, the duration of a processing stage is independent of the final result of that stage. This last assumption means that one can increase the duration of a processing stage but assume that the result of the influenced stage is unaffected. In other words, experimental manipulations influence the duration, not the result of processing. In contrast to Donders's subtraction method, Sternberg's method is applied in the context of more complex factorial studies that examine the influence of multiple experimental factors within a single study. The central notion was that when two factors influenced different processing stages, then the effect of the factors would be additive. However, when two factors influenced a common processing stage, then the effect of the two factors was unlikely to be additive and the factors were more likely to interact. A more specific example should make this clearer. The classic demonstration of the additive factors method was in the context of the memory scanning task. This task required individuals to remember a short (two to six items) list of items in memory and then a probe item was presented. The task was to decide as quickly as possible whether or not the probe letter was in the memory set. The results showed that the time to make the decision on the probe letter increased linearly with the number of items in the memory set such that each additional item in the memory set increased mean RT by approximately 40 ms. Thus, increasing the memory set size increased the duration of the comparison stage. Sternberg went on to demonstrate that degrading the stimulus, a manipulation assumed to influence perceptual processing, was additive with memory set size. In other words, perceptual degradation of the stimulus (e.g., adding random dots over the probe letter) slowed response time equally regardless of the number of items in the memory set. Additive factors logic leads one to conclude that these two manipulations, perceptual degradation and memory set size, influence distinct processing stages. In contrast, the types of items in the memory set (e.g., visual figures versus words) influence the comparison process. Because this is the same process that is lengthened by increasing memory set size, the factors of item type (word or visual figure) and memory set size interact. In the aggregate, the number of mutually additive factors will equal the number of processing stages in the task.

The simplicity and power of additive factors logic led to its widespread application to research in a wide variety of areas in cognitive psychology. However, as with Donders's method, the applicability of the additive factors method has been questioned on a number of grounds. First, it is clear that processing stages frequently overlap and there are many examples of parallel processing where multiple mental processes are engaged at the same time. Moreover, identifying situations in which processing is serial rather than parallel is very difficult (see Townsend, 1974). In light of this, there have been attempts to develop more general frameworks for interpreting response time data that make less restrictive assumptions. McClelland (*Psychological Review*, 1979, *86*, 287–330) examined the consequences for interpreting RT data if one were to assume that processing was still arranged as a series of stages, but processing was cascadic rather than discrete. Cascadic processing means that information can be passed continuously from one process to the next and that at each point in time, the output of each processing stage is a "best guess" based on the available information. This allows for some processing of information to occur at later stages well before processing may actually be complete at the earlier stages. Thus, processes typically overlap in time. This formulation of information processing may be more consistent than discrete serial processing with how the brain might process information. Within this more general framework, the interpretation of additive and interactive effects is more ambiguous. The use of more detailed RT models (e.g., Ashby & Townsend, 1982) is one approach for helping to resolve this ambiguity.

Speed Accuracy Tradeoffs

Complicating the interpretation of RT data is the relationship between speed of a response and the accuracy of a response. In tasks measuring RT, participants must select a response criterion that specifies the amount of information that is sufficient for a response. This response criterion is set based on the experiment instructions, and the participant's decision of what constitutes an acceptable number of errors. The situation is similar to that of a news editor deciding when a news report is ready for broadcast. The editor may decide to broadcast the report quickly, before all of the fact checking is complete, and accept the possibility of more errors, or wait for a later broadcast after the story has been thoroughly checked. In experiments, individuals may adopt a very liberal response criterion, allowing them to make faster responses but at the cost of a higher error rate or they may adopt a conservative response criterion that results in slower responses and a lower error rate. The relationship between RT and accuracy is not linear. When RT is fast and accuracy is near chance, large gains in accuracy can be achieved with relatively small increases in RT. As accuracy increases, further increases in accuracy can be accomplished only with increasingly large increments in RT. Most experiments emphasize to participants that both speed and accuracy are important and allow participants to set their own position on the speed/accuracy function. Indeed, when error rates are low (e.g., under 5%) researchers are typically not concerned with small differences in accuracy across experimental conditions. However, it is when accuracy is high that small differences in error rates across conditions should be most concerning.

To deal with the relation between speed and accuracy, alternative experimental techniques have been developed that allow for researchers to map out the entire speed/accuracy tradeoff (SAT) function rather than just measure performance at one point on this function. In studies using this method, participants are required to respond within a certain amount of time after the onset of the stimulus and measuring accuracy. Varying the amount of time allowed between stimulus onset and response allows one to map a continuous SAT function. Unfortunately, because this procedure is laborious and requires a large amount of data per participant, it is rarely used.

Despite the limitations and interpretative ambiguities, RT measures have yielded considerable insights into the organization of mental processes. While future developments may add to the repertoire of dependent measures for studying cognition, RT measures will no doubt remain one of the dominant dependent measures in experimental psychology.

Bibliography

Luce, R. D. (1986). *Response times: Their role in inferring elementary mental organization.* New York: Oxford University Press. This book is perhaps the closest to the definitive word on the use of response times in experimental psychology; covers a range of topics from simple RT to more complicated experimental tasks; discusses both the empirical results and the mathematical frameworks for interpreting these results.

Pachella, R. G. (1974). The interpretation of reaction time in information processing research. In B. Kantowitz (Ed.), *Human information processing: Tutorials in performance and cognition* (pp. 41–82). New York: Wiley. An introduction to empirical and theoretical issues that arise when using RTs and interpreting experimental results.

Sternberg, S. (1969). Memory scanning: Mental processes revealed by reaction time experiments. *American Scientist, 57,* 421–457. A very clear description of several memory scanning experiments and how the additive factors logic can be used to study cognition.

Townsend, J. T. (1974). In B. Kantowitz (Ed.), *Human information processing: Tutorials in performance and cognition* (pp. 133–185). New York: Wiley.

Townsend, J. T., & Ashby, F. G. (1983). *Stochastic modeling of elementary psychological processes.* Cambridge, UK: Cambridge University Press. A review and tutorial on the use of mathematical concepts for understanding and modeling cognitive processing.

Daniel H. Spieler

READING. How do we read? If psychologists could understand all the mental processes involved in skilled reading, we would be close to describing the workings of the entire human mind. Thus, although we will discuss three important components of silent reading—how and when the eyes move during reading, how words are identified, why the sounds of words matter during reading—we know we will omit many important topics. First, we describe some basic facts about each component and then discuss each of them in more detail.

When we read, it seems as though our eyes move smoothly across the text. However, this is an illusion; our eyes make a series of jumps (called *saccades*) that last about 20 to 35 milliseconds. Between these saccades, our eyes are relatively still for about 200 to 250 milliseconds. It is during these *fixations* that information is encoded from the text; no information is obtained during saccades because the eyes are moving so quickly. Information extraction during reading is thus a bit like seeing a slide show in which a new "slide" with a different view of the text appears every quarter of a second or so.

The second way in which our subjective impression is an illusion is that our eyes do not move forward as relentlessly as we think; 10 to 15% of the saccades move the eyes backward in the text. Although some of these "regressions" reflect major confusion requiring us to go back some distance in the text to straighten things out, the majority go back only a few letters.

We make saccades so frequently in reading because visual acuity drops off rapidly when information gets too far away from the *fovea* (center of vision). In fact, little useful information can be extracted in reading beyond about 15 characters from fixation (about 5 degrees of visual angle in normal reading conditions). We therefore make frequent eye movements to bring new words in the text into foveal vision for detailed processing.

Although the process by which words are identified is complex, it is very fast and automatic. We estimate that the time needed to identify a word may be as little as 50 milliseconds and is often less than 200 milliseconds. Moreover, skilled readers identify words that are presented in isolation almost as quickly as when the words are preceded by a relevant context because word recognition is rapid and effortless enough to need little support from the context. In contrast, beginning and unskilled readers derive considerable benefit from relevant contexts because they identify words in isolation slowly and with errors.

When we read, we usually experience an inner voice saying the words that our eyes are falling on. This suggests that we are, at least sometimes, converting print to sound. The role of this so-called sound coding in reading is controversial, but research indicates that converting print to sound is an important part of reading, even in languages like Chinese.

Eye Movements

The average saccade length in reading is 8 to 9 characters, but the range is typically 1 to 20 characters. The average fixation duration is 225 to 250 milliseconds, but the range is often 50 to 500 milliseconds.

Figure 1 shows the record of a reader's eye movements superimposed on text. Notice that most words are fixated only once. However, some words are fixated twice, and some are not fixated at all. Since a fixation lands on or near almost all words, it is clear that the major purpose of eye movements is to bring words close to the fovea.

Much of the variability associated with fixation times and saccade lengths is due to processes involved in comprehending text: The ease or difficulty of processing a fixated word strongly influences how long the reader looks at that word. This observation is most obvious from the fact that how familiar the word is, as measured by printed-word frequency, strongly influences fixation time: A low-frequency word is fixated about 50 milliseconds longer than a high-frequency word of the same length. Fixation times do not only reflect the difficulty of identifying individual words; they also reflect the various processes that combine the meanings of individual words to form a more global understanding of the text such as (1) constructing syntactic structures of individual sentences and (2) linking the meanings of individual sentences into a coherent overall mental structure.

Although comprehension processes associated with understanding words, phrases, sentences, and larger units all influence how long the eyes fixate words, the primary influence on how far the eyes move is the length of the words in the text. Short words (three or fewer characters) are often not directly fixated but processed on the fixation prior to which they are skipped. Most of the time, readers try to move their eyes to a place in the next word that will be maximally efficient for word identification processes.

This brings us to the interesting question of how much information we utilize from each eye fixation. Phenomenologically, it seems as though we can identify words from a large region around our fixation point. However, this subjective impression is false. Remember that we move our eyes only about 1.5 words on average with each saccade. If we could identify many more words than that, why would we make so many eye fixations? The reason again has to do with decreased visual acuity the farther words are from the point of fixation.

Much research has been done to determine the size of the "perceptual span" (the region of useful vision) during an eye fixation. The best technique for this purpose limits the amount of information that is available to the reader on each fixation. In this "moving window" paradigm, readers' eye movements are monitored by an accurate eye-tracking system that is interfaced with a computer, which is interfaced with a video monitor on which text is presented. Wherever the reader looks, an experimentally controlled "window" of normal text is exposed, whereas the text is "mutilated"

When we read, it seems as though our eyes move smoothly across the text.

	*		*	*		*	*		*	*		*	*	*	*

   1   2   3   4   5 6   8 7 9 10

367 223 186   211 156 89   177 215 233 172

However, this is an illusion since our eyes make a series of jumps (called saccades) that

12 11 13 14   15   16 17   18   19   20   21 22

288 58 102 312 179   189 199   236   209   247 233 145

last about 20-35 milliseconds. Between these saccades, our eyes are relatively still for

23   24   29 25   26   27   28   30 31   32   33

308 311   264 344   201   182   266 77 149   248   219

READING. Figure 1. An excerpt from a passage of text with fixation sequence and fixation durations indicated. The asterisk represents the fixation location.

in some way outside of the window (see Figure 2). The basic logic of the method is this: If the presence of a window of a certain size has no effect on reading (i.e., reading speed and comprehension are undiminished), then readers are not extracting useful information outside of that window region.

The central finding of this research is that the perceptual span is small: Information is obtained from a region extending from about 3 to 4 characters to the left of fixation to about 15 characters to the right of fixation. Note that this is the maximum area from which information is extracted. On many fixations, the area from which information is extracted is smaller. Note also that the span is asymmetric. This asymmetry is related to attentional factors and the direction in which the eyes move, since the span is asymmetric to the left of fixation for Israeli readers reading Hebrew text (which is printed from right to left). In addition, little or no information is obtained from below the currently fixated line, which also indicates that the span is limited by attentional factors and reading experience.

Word Identification

Most of what we know about word identification comes from experiments in which skilled readers process isolated words. Although psychologists still have only vague ideas about how readers recognize the letters of the alphabet, we have made some headway with questions about how processes at various levels relate to each other. First, we consider the relation of letters to words; then we discuss how encoding the sound of a word relates to encoding its meaning.

One theory of how letter identification relates to word identification is that words are identified by a serial scan of the component letters (probably from left to right). Several lines of research, however, indicate that letters are not scanned serially at even a high rate.

One of the most important employs words presented briefly enough so that there are errors in identification. In these experiments, when readers are asked to identify a preselected letter (the last letter in WORK), they are more accurate in identifying it than in identifying a letter in isolation even when guessing is controlled. This finding has been dubbed the *word superiority effect*. The word superiority effect is inconsistent with a serial scanning hypothesis, as several letters, no matter how meaningful, would take longer to process than a single letter.

A second theory is that words are unified visual patterns or "templates" and that word identification in skilled readers is a process that occurs independently of identification of the component letters. Although this theory seems unlikely—since the logic of alphabetic languages is that words are made up of component letters—proponents argue that processing the component letters slows down word identification. This theory has been instrumental in the advocacy of "whole-word" methods of teaching reading rather than "phonics." There are several findings that rule out the "word-as-template" theory. The first is that letters in "pseudowords" (pronounceable nonwords) such as MARD are identified better than letters in isolation and about as well as letters in words. The second is that text written in aLtErNaTiNg CaSe LiKe ThIs is just about as easy to read as normal text if you practice reading it. Thus, in either case, there is no striking difference between processing familiar word forms and visual patterns seen for the first time.

The bulk of the word identification research indicates that words are identified through their component letters in parallel. That is, visual information about letters in words (and nonwords) excites component letter detectors in parallel, which in turn feed excitation and inhibition into a set of word detectors (e.g.,

When we read, it seems as though our eyes move   Normal text
    *

XXen we read, it seeXXXXXXXXXXXXXXX |
    * |
        |
XXXXXXad, it seems as tXXXXXXXXXXXX | 13-letter window
    * |
        |
XXXXXXXXXXXXXms as though our XXXX |
       *

READING. Figure 2. Example of the moving window paradigm. The first line shows normal text (with fixation location indicated by the asterisk). The next three lines show successive fixations in the moving window situation with a 13-letter window.

W in the first position excites WORD, WORK, WOOD, etc., while inhibiting CORK, CORD, CARE, etc.). The word detectors also feed back excitation and inhibition to component letters (e.g., WORK excites W in the first position but inhibits B). When sufficient visual information has accrued, only the correct word and letters will be excited because all the others will be inhibited. However, when visual information is insufficient, errors of identification may occur. In fact, several versions of such a model have accounted well for a wide variety of data on word identification (including the word superiority and pseudoword superiority effects described above).

Sound Coding

In many current theories, word detectors are viewed as being part of a "lexicon" or mental dictionary from which other information, such as the pronunciation and meaning of the word, are accessed (pretty much the way you would find them in a standard dictionary). Of interest is whether the information flow is this simple in skilled reading. That is, is the meaning of a word accessed by an analysis of its visual form without any contribution from an analysis of its sound? A considerable amount of recent data appears to argue the opposite; these data suggest that access to sound coding occurs early and is important in the access of meaning.

One piece of evidence for sound coding is that, when asked to judge whether two words are related in meaning, readers falsely respond "yes" to pairs of words like BEECH and SAND 20 to 30% of the time and more than to matched orthographic control pairs such as BENCH and SAND. This finding indicates that readers access the sound of the word before accessing its meaning. Moreover, readers make considerable errors with pairs such as SUTE and CLOTHING, indicating that the sound is not merely accessed after the lexicon is accessed. Other work, using variants of the moving window technique, has shown that sound codes are accessed early in processing—even before a word is fixated and within the first 40 milliseconds of a fixation. Interestingly, this early access of sound codes appears to transcend reading with an alphabet; many of these findings have been replicated for readers of Chinese.

The finding that encoding sound is an important part of word identification is perhaps not surprising, given that we are probably programmed biologically to understand spoken language. However, in some popular views of reading, sound coding is viewed as a bad habit, restricted to beginning and poor readers. This conclusion stems partly from the belief that sound coding is necessarily conscious or is necessarily related to subvocal speech. Although conscious sound coding often occurs in reading, and although there is evidence indicating that skilled readers engage in subvocal speech (as indicated by enhanced muscular activity in the lips and throat), neither conscious sound coding nor subvocal speech is necessary. Reading can go on without either conscious voices in the head or muscular activity. Indeed, if we force ourselves to become conscious of sound coding (i.e., continually hear a voice in our heads), silent reading slows down. However, sound coding is probably going on continuously even without our being consciously aware of it or making any muscle movements.

Finally, there are data indicating that sound coding serves a useful function beyond word identification. Sound coding is an important part of short-term memory in general and plays an important role in the process of integrating text. For example, when readers repeat something over and over again while attempting to read (e.g., saying "cola, cola, cola"), reading comprehension is disrupted, especially those aspects of comprehension that crucially depend on drawing text together from different clauses and sentences.

In summary, many complex processing activities are finely orchestrated during reading. It is clear that in order to understand reading, we need to know about these basic processes and how each contributes to the whole complex of skilled reading.

[*See also* Dyslexia; *and* Neuropsychology.]

Bibliography

Balota, D. A., Flores d'Arcais, G. B., & Rayner, K. (1990). *Comprehension processes in reading.* Hillsdale, NJ: Erlbaum. This edited volume covers all aspects of comprehension processing in reading, from word identification to discourse processing.

Crowder, R. G., & Wagner, R. K. (1992). *The psychology of reading.* New York: Oxford University Press. An easy-to-read introduction to all aspects of reading.

Gernsbacher, M. A. (Ed.). (1994). *Handbook of psycholinguistics.* San Diego, CA: Academic Press. This edited volume contains a number of excellent chapters dealing with various aspects of reading.

Huey, E. B. (1908). *The psychology and pedagogy of reading.* New York: Macmillan. This pioneering book was republished by MIT Press in 1968. It still is one of the best introductions to the issues related to understanding skilled reading.

Just, M. A., & Carpenter, P. A. (1987). *The psychology of reading and language comprehension.* Boston: Allyn & Bacon. Comprehensive coverage of all aspects of reading.

Perfetti, C. A. (1985). *Reading ability.* New York: Oxford University Press. A nice overview of issues related to reading ability differences; also contains easy-to-read overviews of important issues in reading research.

Rayner, K., & Pollatsek, A. (1989). *The psychology of reading.* Englewood Cliffs, NJ: Prentice Hall. Provides comprehensive coverage of all aspects of reading. This book is currently published by Erlbaum.

Keith Rayner and Alexander Pollatsek

REASONING. *See* Thinking, *article on* Reasoning.

RECIPROCITY. *See* Prosocial Behavior.

REFERENCE GROUP. *See* Norms.

REFUGEES. In 1951, The United Nations Convention Relating to the Status of Refugees defined a refugee as a person who has left their country of origin due to a "well-founded fear of being persecuted for reasons of race, religion, nationality, membership in a particular social group or political opinion." However, many governments subsequently recognized persons to be refugees who were victims of war, violence, and other social and political disasters and who were forced to seek asylum.

The United States Immigration and Nationality Act of 1980 defined a refugee as the following:

> A refugee, for our purpose, is any person who is outside any country of such person's nationality or, in the case of a person having no nationality, is outside any country in which such person last habitually resided, and who is unable or unwilling to return to, and is unable or unwilling to avail himself or herself of the protection of that country because of persecution on account of race, religion, nationality, membership in a particular social group, or political opinion. (Immigration and Nationality Act, 1980, p. 12)

Expanding the Definition of Refugee

A United Nations High Commission on Refugees working group reconsidered the definition of a refugee under the broader category of all those people in need of service and protection. They included (1) persons covered by the 1951 Convention; (2) persons covered by the Organization of African Unity (OAU) Convention/Cartagena Declaration; (3) persons forced to leave or prevented from returning because of man-made disasters; (4) persons forced to leave or prevented from returning because of natural or ecological disasters or extreme poverty; (5) persons who apply to be treated as (1) or, when applicable (2), but are found not to be in these categories; (6) internally displaced persons; and (7) stateless persons (Siem & Appleyard, 1991).

How Many Refugees Are There?

Although figures vary according to the different agencies monitoring the international refugee situation, it is estimated that there are close to 20 million international refugees in the world today. In addition to the international refugees, it is estimated that there are 20 million internally displaced persons who are refugees within the borders of their own countries; however, unlike refugees who cross international borders, internally displaced persons are not protected by international refugee conventions even though they may face political and/or religious persecution. Thus, the number of international refugees and internally displaced persons likely exceeds 40 million people (U.S. Committee on Refugees, 1997).

According to recent figures provided by the United States Committee for Refugees (1997), the most sizable refugee groups are from the Middle East (5.841 million), Africa (3.684 million), Europe (2.479 million), and South and Central America (1.795 million). The countries producing the largest numbers of internally displaced persons are Sudan (4 million), Afghanistan (1.2 million), Angola (1.2 million), Bosnia/Hercegovina (1 million), and Liberia (1 million). These are all considered underestimates of actual figures. Because of continuing national, regional, and international tensions and low-intensity wars, it is likely that this number will increase in future years.

The Consequences of the Refugee Experience

Many refugees are victims of famine, torture, rape, brutality, and deprivation. Their future is uncertain, and their lives are often lived in quiet anguish and despair fighting poverty, pestilence, and disease. They live amidst peril and pain. For those refugees fortunate enough to reach the haven of a refugee camp, there are often new problems to be faced, including problems of living in crowded tent cities with meager food and medical resources. And far too often, the violence of the refugee camps replaces the violence they fled (Marsella, Bornemann, Ekblad, & Orley, 1994).

Because of mounting domestic problems, many countries in North America and Europe that formerly welcomed refugees are now closing their doors to further entry. And for those few refugees fortunate enough to be admitted, there are new problems to be overcome—problems of acculturation, racism, language, work, housing, health, and personal safety. For many refugees, the process of rebuilding their lives often proves to be as traumatic as the dislocation process from which they sought refuge.

In brief, refugees and dislocated persons face numerous sequential stressors that pose serious challenges to their mental health and well-being. These typically include (1) psychological trauma associated with war, political abuse, violence, persecution, and torture; (2) medical problems including possible brain damage, spinal and skeletal injuries, infections, and malnutrition; (3) dislocation and destruction of home and family life with related economic disadvantages; (4) uprooting; (5) sense of loss and bereavement; (6) migration; (7) transitional living in refugee camps and relocation centers; (8) resettlement; (9) acculturation and culture shock; and (10) possible racial and ethnic abuse, marginalization, and isolation.

Refugee Mental Health and Well-Being

Because of the many problems the refugee must face, mental health problems are now acknowledged to be among the most common, acute, and chronic sequalae of the refugee experience. The refugee experience is associated with anxiety, fear, paranoia and suspicion, grief, guilt, despair, hopelessness, withdrawal, depression, somatization, substance abuse and alcoholism, posttraumatic stress disorders, anger, and hostility. In addition to psychiatric symptoms, there are also problems related to work, family, and marital adjustment, and in acculturation and assimilation. Life within refugee camps is associated with its own set of problems including a sense of loss, uncertainty, distrust, skepticism, helplessness, vulnerability, powerlessness, overdependency, survivor guilt, violence, crime, and social disintegration. Refugees are one of the most high-risk groups in the world for mental-health problems. (Epidemiological and clinical data on mental-health problems can be found in Marsella et al., 1994.)

Research studies and clinical commentaries all point to the tragic mental-health consequences of being a refugee. Rangaraj (1988) described the life circumstances in the following poignant words: "Outwardly, they have lost everything—family, friends, culture . . . and suddenly they are nobody. Everything is done for them—they are not left to do anything for themselves; and then there is no future for them—nobody wants them. . . . Decay seems to set in and they seem to disintegrate day by day" (Rangaraj, 1988, p. 41).

Although the mental-health risks associated with being a refugee are numerous, there are a number of factors that have been demonstrated to provide protective functions in the transit and resettlement period, including (1) maintaining the extended family; (2) availability of immediate employment; (3) access to human rights groups; (4) creation of self-help groups; (5) encouragement of cultural practices and traditions; (6) accessibility to primary health care; and (7) use of indigenous healers (Jablensky, Marsella, Ekblad, 1994).

As the international refugee problem continues to grow, host nations (i.e., those nations accepting refugees for resettlement) are being faced with many challenges regarding the acceptance of refugees, including mounting economic, political, and social costs. While many refugees are eager to begin their new lives in their host country, there are also many who will need considerable medical and mental-health services because of the traumas associated with their experiences. In addition, there is a growing reluctance among many host nations to admit refugees because of racial and cultural biases, economic concerns (i.e., jobs), and internal political dynamics (e.g., the sizable number of Palestinian refugees in Jordan creates tensions for Jordan with neighboring Israel), as well as external ones (e.g., Nepal admits Tibetan refugees from neighboring China, keeping the issue of Chinese oppression before the world). Ultimately, these problems add additional burdens to the troubled refugee psyche.

Bibliography

Holtzman, W., & Bornemann, T. (Eds.). (1990). *Mental health of immigrants and refugees*. Austin, TX: Hogg Foundation/University of Texas. Discusses the mental-health problems associated with immigrants and refugees.

Jablensky, A., Marsella, A. J., Jansson, B., Levi, L., & Ekblad, S. (1993). Refugee mental health and well-being. *Journal of Refugee Studies, 5,* 172–184. Concise overview of refugee mental-health problems with discussions of mental-health risks and disorders. Includes recommendations for research and policy.

Marsella, A. J., Bornemann, T., Ekblad, S., & Orley, J. (1994). *Amidst peril and pain: The mental health and well-being of the world's refugees.* Washington, DC: American Psychological Association. Multidisciplinary book that summarizes major mental-health, legal, and policy problems associated with refugees. Includes chapters on refugees from different areas including Africa, Asia, Latin American, and the Middle East. Discusses major mental-health challenges including trauma and violence and makes suggestions for delivery of mental health services.

Mollica R., & Lavelle, J. (1988). Southeast Asian refugees. In L. Comas-Diaz & D. Griffith (Eds.), *Clinical guidelines in cross-cultural mental health* (pp. 262–302). New York: Wiley. Detailed discussion of the mental-health problems faced by Southeast Asian refugees in the United States. Discussion includes commentary on Southeast Asian cultures and the specific problems associated with the delivery of mental-health services.

Nanda, V. (Ed.). (1989). *Refugee law and policy: International and United States responses.* New York: Greenwood Press. Excellent overview of the many legal issues involved in defining refugees and the associated national policy problems. Raises questions about the need to go beyond current definitions to accommodate growing numbers of persons faced with survival problems.

Rangaraj, A. (1988). The health status of refugees in Southeast Asia. In D. Miserz (Ed.), *Refugees: The trauma of exile* (pp. 36–45). Dordrecht, Holland: Martinus Nijhoff.

Siem, H., & Appleyard, R. (1991). *Refugee movements and human migration: Some conceptual issues.* Paper presented at International Conference on Refugee Mental Health and Well-Being. Karolinska Institute, Stockholm, Sweden.

United States Committee on Refugees. (1997). *World refugee survey—1997.* Washington, DC: U.S. Committee for Refugees (USCR). A factual report published each year by the USCR. It includes summaries of all relevant statistics on refugees (i.e., number, sources, location, costs) and sections discussing the current status of the refugee situation in different parts of the world. Considered to be one of the most authoritative publications on the topic.

Anthony J. Marsella

REGIONAL PSYCHOLOGICAL ASSOCIATIONS. [*This entry is geographically divided into two articles: Regional Psychological Associations in the United States and Regional Psychological Associations in Canada.*]

In the United States

Regional associations of psychologists have existed, in one form or another, since the early years of the twentieth century, but the youngest of the associations, the New England Psychological Association (NEPA), was not founded until 1961. Only 9 years after its founding in 1892, the American Psychological Association (APA) authorized the establishment of regional branches, and several branches were soon established. In part, the regional branches were established because of the difficulties of traveling to the APA convention, which, in the early years, was held in the eastern United States.

The oldest of the regional associations is the Southern Society for Philosophy and Psychology (SSPP), founded in 1904. The Midwestern Psychological Association was founded in 1927, but it developed from the Chicago affiliate of the APA, which had been founded in 1902, and the Eastern Psychological Association (EPA), which was founded in 1938, evolved from the New York affiliate of the APA, which had been established in 1903. The Rocky Mountain Psychological Association (RMPA), founded in 1956, developed from the Rocky Mountain Branch of the APA. The other regional associations were founded without predecessor organizations. The Western Psychological Association (WPA) was founded in 1921, the Southwestern Psychological Association (SWPA) was founded in 1954, and the Southeastern Psychological Association (SEPA) was founded in 1955.

Except for a few years during World War I and World War II, each association has held an annual meeting, one of the major functions of each of the regional associations. The emphases of the annual meetings differ from one association to another, with some emphasizing traditional experimental psychology and others emphasizing professional aspects of psychology. All have had paper sessions, symposia, presidential addresses, and invited addresses. At the beginning of each of the associations, geographic restrictions on membership were established, but recently, those restrictions have been removed. Now, people from outside the region implied by the name of the organization and even people from outside the United States are members of each of the associations.

The SSPP was established to promote psychology and philosophy in the southeastern region of the United States and is the oldest of the regional associations. It has never been affiliated officially with the APA because approximately half of its members are philosophers, who are not eligible for membership in the APA. Although it could not be an affiliate of the APA, some of its early annual meetings were held jointly with the APA. In 1908, the SSPP met with the APA and the American Philosophical Association, and there were three presidential addresses, one for each of the organizations, at this meeting. For many years, the SSPP met jointly with those two organizations and with the American Association for the Advancement of Science. The founder of the SSPP was Edward Franklin Buchner, who was the first secretary-treasurer and later was the president of the SSPP (1910). The first president of the SSPP was J. Mark Baldwin, but he did not participate actively in founding the organization. Shepherd Ivory Franz (1911), John B. Watson (1914), E. K. Strong, Jr. (1918 and 1919), and Knight Dunlap (1920) were other early presidents of the SSPP. For most annual meetings, there have been philosophy sessions, psychology sessions, and joint sessions. Attendance at the annual meetings has varied from 15 at the first meeting to as many as 350. Thirty-six charter members of the Society, including Christine Ladd-Franklin, Baldwin, and Buchner, were approved at the first meeting, and the largest number of members on record is 733 in 1993.

The WPA was founded in 1921 with 14 charter members. Lewis M. Terman was elected the first president of the WPA. Shepherd Ivory Franz (1928), E. K. Strong, Jr. (1933), and Knight Dunlap (1939), each of whom earlier had been president of the SSPP, were elected to the same office in the WPA. Fifteen of the 73 presidents of the WPA have served as president of the APA. In addition to the usual scientific programs, the WPA became involved in numerous social issues and adopted resolutions supporting academic freedom (1949), opposing California's loyalty oath (1952), and opposing the involvement of the United States in Southeast Asia (1970), among other social and political positions.

The MPA evolved from the Chicago Branch of the APA, which had been founded in 1902. Probably more than any of the other regional associations, the MPA has a center, which is Chicago. By far the greatest number of annual meetings have been held in Chicago or in the Chicago area. The Chicago Branch of the APA met regularly from 1902 until 1908, but there was a lapse of meetings between 1908 and 1925. In 1926, A. R. Gilliland called a meeting of midwestern experimental psychologists, and at that meeting, "midwestern" was used for the first time in referring to the meetings. "Experimental" in his name for the group set the tone, and the emphasis at the MPA meetings has been on traditional experimental psychology. In recent years, the MPA program has had invited papers in many of the paper sessions. Those papers often involved the presentation of innovative research in each of several research domains. The MPA had its largest number of members, 4,147, in 1977, which makes it the second largest regional association.

The EPA evolved from the New York Branch of the APA, which was established in 1903. Although the EPA formally began in 1938, its annual meetings are numbered from the 1930 meeting of the reorganized New York Branch. In 1936, the New York Branch became the Eastern Branch of the APA, and then in 1938, the name was changed to the Eastern Psychological Association. The annual meetings of the EPA have tended to be larger than the meetings of the other regional associations, with the largest attendance, 4,731, occurring in 1973 at a meeting in Washington, D.C. Members could be psychologists on the eastern seaboard from Florida to Canada. From 1948 until 1952, the EPA had a committee on academic freedom, which submitted a resolution supporting Edward C. Tolman's resistance to the California loyalty oath. In 1969, the EPA passed a resolution concerned with racial prejudice. However, the principal activity of the EPA has been the annual scientific meeting, from which the organization strayed in relatively few instances. Those annual scientific meetings frequently were very large, with more than nine hundred presentations in 1977.

The SWPA held its first annual meeting in 1953. A letter inviting psychologists to join the SWPA had been sent to those in the southwestern region of the United States by Wayne Holtzman, Harry Helson, and Saul Sells, who constituted an SWPA organizing committee. The annual meetings often have involved student awards for the best papers and, more recently, for the best poster. Attendance at the annual meeting has varied from 166 in 1957 to 835 in 1975. At the meeting in December 1954, the SWPA decided to meet in the spring rather than in the winter. Organizing a meeting for the spring of 1955 was not feasible; thus, there was no meeting in 1955.

The SEPA held its first annual meeting in Atlanta, Georgia, in 1955, following an organizational meeting at the APA Convention in New York in 1954. At that organizational meeting, John B. Wolfe was selected as the president, Dorothy C. Adkins was selected as the vice-president, and M. C. Langhorne was selected as the secretary-treasurer. SEPA is best known for its continuing education program, which began in 1965. The number of workshops reached a maximum of 44 in 1981 and has declined in recent years as other groups have begun offering continuing education workshops. The SEPA also is well known for involving women in its governance in recent years. In 1972, the executive committee established a Commission on the Status of Women, which later became the Committee on the Equality of Professional Opportunity.

The RMPA has an unusual ancestry in that there was a Rocky Mountain Branch of the APA from which RMPA evolved. The Rocky Mountain Branch also was affiliated with the Colorado-Wyoming Academy of Sciences, which had been established in 1930. In 1956, the RMPA adopted its current name and became a separate society. The territory served by the RMPA overlaps that served by the WPA and the SWPA, and there were joint meetings with the WPA in 1989, 1993, and 1998. New Mexico is claimed by the RMPA and the SWPA; the RMPA and the WPA both claim Utah; and all three associations claim Arizona.

The NEPA held its first annual meeting in 1961, and thus, it is the youngest of the regional associations. M. C. Langhorne, who had been instrumental in starting the SEPA, moved from Emory University to Trinity University in 1959, but he began to plan the NEPA even before he moved to New England. The founders, other than Langhorne, cannot be determined definitively because there is no list of charter members. Although the annual programs of the NEPA have been varied, the participation of undergraduate psychology majors has been consistent almost since the founding of the organization. The NEPA is the smallest of the regional associations, both in terms of the number of members and in terms of the attendance at the annual meetings.

The regional psychological associations always have had the holding of an annual meeting as their primary function. The nature of those meetings has varied across time and across regions, but in all cases, the annual meetings have provided forums for communication among colleagues and for the introduction of both graduate and undergraduate students to the professional and scientific meetings of psychologists.

Bibliography

Pate, J. L., & Wertheimer, M. (Eds.). (1993). *No small part: A history of regional psychological associations.* Washington, DC: American Psychological Association. A collection of histories of regional psychological associations, published as part of the centennial celebration of the founding of the American Psychological Association. Most of the information in this article is taken from this book, which contains numerous references to other sources of information about the regional associations.

James L. Pate

In Canada

There are two types of provincial/territorial psychological organizations in Canada: (1) Regulatory, with a primary mandate of public protection, operating under statutory authority to regulate the admission and practice of psychologists offering services to the public; (2) Professional/societal, with a primary mission to advance and protect psychology as an applied profession. Regulatory bodies exist only at the provincial/territorial level because responsibility for the regulation of the professions is accorded to the provinces/territories under the Canadian constitution. At the national level, two organizations, the Council of Provincial Associations of Psychologists (CPAP) and the Canadian Regis-

ter of Health Service Providers in Psychology (CRHSPP), are governed as federations of provincial/territorial organizations in which the Canadian Psychological Association (CPA) also participates.

Provincial/territorial regulatory bodies of psychology and professional/societal associations in Canada evolved autonomously, with no national support from CPA during their first quarter century. Indeed, the British Columbia Psychological Association was established in 1938, one year earlier than the founding of CPA. While this generally reflects the less centralized nature of the Canadian confederal system, it is also explained by factors particular to Canadian psychology. In sharp contrast with the American Psychological Association's espousal and support for the development of applied psychology after World War II, the Canadian Psychological Association (CPA) discouraged this prospect. CPA focused its postwar mission on the advancement of Canadian psychology as a scientific and academic discipline. Hence, CPA largely distanced itself from provincially based efforts to establish psychology as a human service profession. This prevailed well into the 1970s when CPA began a trend toward greater involvement in professional issues. By that time, professional/societal bodies had been established in all provinces.

Professional psychology is formally organized and legally regulated in all 10 Canadian provinces and 1 of the 2 territories. In 2 provinces (New Brunswick and Québec), regulatory and societal functions are largely combined in the same body, although in Québec a small professional/societal body has reemerged. In eight provinces (Alberta, British Columbia, Manitoba, Newfoundland, Nova Scotia, Ontario, Prince Edward Island, and Saskatchewan), there are distinct regulatory and professional/societal bodies.

More than 12,000 psychologists are currently members in good standing with provincial/territorial regulatory bodies of psychology. Depending on the particular terminology and functions accorded by the psychology-specific legislation of each province/territory, psychologists are certified, chartered, licensed, or registered for the practice of psychology in the jurisdiction(s) in which they practice. Every provincial/territorial regulatory body administers the admission process according to defined eligibility criteria. They also investigate and discipline psychologists for infractions of ethical and practice standards. Some conduct mandatory or voluntary peer-review activities. Most offer continuing education. Those regulatory bodies that serve as professional/societal bodies as well also undertake some or all of the other activities described hereafter for professional/societal associations. In all provinces/territories except Québec, regulatory bodies function within the provisions of the Common Law legal tradition.

A major difference across provinces/territories, however, is the educational level required for entry to practice as a "psychologist." Only the doctoral degree is recognized for this purpose in four provinces (British Columbia, Manitoba, Ontario, and Saskatchewan); four provinces (New Brunswick, Newfoudland, Nova Scotia, and Prince Edward Island) specify the doctoral degree but provide authority to the regulatory body to admit on the basis of a master's degree, subject to prescribed conditions or for a limited period of time; two provinces (Alberta and Québec) and the Northwest Territories admit on the basis of a master's degree. Two provinces (Manitoba and Ontario) also recognize master's level persons in a separate level and with a different title, "psychological associate." However, only in Ontario may psychological associates practice independently within their prescribed scope of practice. The criteria for determining an acceptable curriculum, regardless of the particular degree, is determined by each regulatory body. A variable set of other requirements, including supervised pre- and/or postgraduate experience and exams, are also set by each regulatory body. A written exam, common to most Canadian and American jurisdictions, the Examination for the Professional Practice of Psychology (EPPP), is required by eight of the Canadian regulatory bodies.

The historic absence of a cohesive national strategy for the development of professional psychology in Canada contributed greatly to the varying levels of entry to the practice of psychology across provincial/territorial jurisdictions. Notwithstanding repeated attempts to resolve this problem, organized psychology has been unable to do so. A resolution may soon be at hand. In 1994, the federal, provincial, and territorial governments concluded a wide-ranging accord, the Agreement on Internal Trade, which proposes, among other elements of a more purely commercial nature, to eliminate barriers to the free mobility of regulated professionals. While this is not the first time the prospect of an externally controlled outcome has appeared, it is the most serious. It is estimated that the profession of psychology may have three to five years to resolve this matter before the respective governments will impose a solution. Whether either event will occur remains to be determined. An interim solution has been proposed whereby doctoral-entry jurisdictions would facilitate mobility among their provinces while a parallel memorandum of agreement would accomplish this among master's degree–entry jurisdictions.

The provincial/territorial societal bodies have been the vital agents in promoting the development and advancement of professional psychology in Canada. In each jurisdiction, they were the most important force in the drive to secure statutory recognition of psychology from the first such achievement (Ontario in 1960) to the most recent (Prince Edward Island in 1990). As professional/societal bodies, provincial/territorial associations engage in a wide range of advocacy and lobbying as well as provide direct benefits such as preferred rates for various commercial services. They usually organize an annual meeting and other continuing education actvities as well as offer other forms of support to the maintenance of competence. After almost 60 years, they remain in the forefront of protecting the profession and securing the viability of its future. They vary only as a function of their membership base, ranging from approximately 40 in the Prince Edward Island Psychological Association of Canada's smallest province, to more than 1,400 in the Ontario Psychological Association (OPA) of Canada's largest province. Consequently, the means at their disposal also varies, with only one (OPA) having a full-time psychologist executive director, while others have a part-time psychologist executive director, only administrative personnel, or no staff at all.

The Council of Provincial Associations of Psychologists (CPAP) brings together all provincial/territorial regulatory and societal bodies. This federation evolved from its predecessor, the Advisory Council of Provincial Associations of Psychologists (ACPAP), which was constituted as an advisory committee of CPA in 1968. It reconstituted itself as an autonomous entity in 1983, with CPA as an affiliate member. However, it only became legally incorporated in 1995. Its primary purpose is to share information and resources among provincial/territorial bodies and to facilitate national undertakings in the common interest of its members. Given its structure and limited finances, it is rarely in a position to function as an action-oriented organization. However, it is of great value in fostering a collective understanding of issues important to professional psychology. It can also serve as a vital forum for debate on issues that are ultimately decided elsewhere. Its role as a catalyst also ensures that matters based at the provincial/territorial level are considered by other national organizations, particularly CPA and the Canadian Register of Health Service Providers in Psychology. Indeed, CPAP served as the primary vehicle for the creation of the Canadian Register in 1985. More recently, CPAP has been devoting much attention to matters of mobility and the globalization of professional services generated by the implications of the North American Free Trade Agreement and the Agreement on Internal Trade.

Now spanning six decades, the history of Canadian provincial/territorial regulatory bodies and professional/societal associations of psychology is a reflection of the contribution of hundreds of individuals. A smaller number promoted the recognition of professional psychology's legitimacy and effectiveness at the national level. Among them, Mary Wright, a distinguished child psychologist with strong applied interests, served as an early president of the Ontario Psychological Association as well as of the Canadian Psychological Association. Her career has paralleled almost exactly the emergence of professional psychology as a distinct entity. Parke Davidson went from the presidency of the British Columbia Psychological Association to prominent leadership in the Canadian Psychological Association in the 1970s when a tragically early death precluded him from contributing further to establishing ACPAP as a more vital element in CPA. Ray Berry, twice president of OPA and an early registrar of Ontario's psychology regulatory body, became the first nonacademic, applied psychologist to be elected to the presidency of CPA in the mid-1970s. Barbara Wand, also an Ontario registrar, served with Pierre Ritchie, also twice president of OPA, as the founding cochairs of CPAP in the mid-1980s. Ritchie subsequently served as CPA's executive director until 1993. The emergence of provincial/territorial issues as a priority for CPA is underscored by the selection of its last three CEOs, Timothy Hogan, Pierre Ritchie, and John Service, who have all served as provincial presidents. The isolation of professional psychology in Québec from the rest of Canada has been reduced by two of its recent presidents, Michel Sabourin and Luc Granger, later serving CPA presidential terms during the late 1980s and early 1990s. Another Québec president in the 1990s, Mario Poirier, also served as a CPAP cochair. Although Ontario and Québec, with more than half of Canada's population, have produced numerous provincial leaders who have made a national contribution, other provinces have contributed as well. CPAP cochairs include Lorraine Breault (Alberta), Jay Brolund (Manitoba), John Garland (Newfoundland), Charle Hayes (Nova Scotia), John MacDonald (British Columbia), Terez Retfalvi (New Brunswick), Philip Smith (Prince Edward Island), and Carl von Bayer (Saskatchewan).

Bibliography

Adair, J. G., Paivio, A., & Ritchie, P. L.-J. (1996). Psychology in Canada. In J. T. Spence, J. M. Darley, & D. J. Foss (Eds.). *Annual review of psychology, 45* (pp. 341–370). Comprehensive review of history and current status of Canadian psychology as well as extensive references.

Berry, R. G., Davidson, P. O., & Gibson, D. (1969). Advisory Council of Provincial Associations of Psychologists. *Canadian Psychological Review, 10,* 368–375. Provides valuable historic information.

Dobson, K., & Dobson, D. (Eds.). (1993). *Professional psychology in Canada.* Toronto: Hogrefe & Huber. Standard reference on contemporary professional psychology in Canada. Includes chapters on psychological organizations (K. Craig), regulation (B. Wand), special aspects of Québec's Civil Code (L. Granger).

Ritchie, P. L.-J., & Sabourin, M. E. (1992). Sous un même toit: Canada's functional-structural approach to the unity of psychology. *International Journal of Psychology,* 27, 311–325. Critical assessment of the particular challenges and problems confronting organized psychology in Canada.

Wright, M. J. (1971). The psychological organizations of Canada. *Canadian Psychology Review, 12,* 420–431.

Pierre L.-J. Ritchie

REHABILITATION PSYCHOLOGY. Rehabilitation psychology, in the broadest definition, focuses on the relationships between physical impairment and the person from two perspectives. The first and most important perspective is that of the insider (the person who experiences the impairment): In what ways does the fact of physical variation from the norm affect the person's life and psyche? What are the immediate and long-term consequences? And, second, how do outsiders (those who are observers) respond to another's physical variation from the norm? The focus of this dual domain of concern was defined by Barker, Wright, Meyerson, and Gonick as "variations in physique that affect the psychological situation of a person by influencing the effectiveness of his body as a tool for actions or by serving as a stimulus to himself or others" (1953, p. 1). Thus, to Barker, an early and strong influence on rehabilitation psychology, physique is both a tool and a stimulus. Disability within rehabilitation psychology is always defined as a relational phenomenon: It is a product of the individual interacting with the environment and varies both with environmental signals and with the response of the individual.

Traditionally, rehabilitation psychology's domain has been boundaried by physical impairment, which may arise from any cause (e.g., illness, trauma, birth defect, stress of daily life). The effects of such impairment (the negative effects are termed "disability" at the level of the person and "handicap" at the societal level) are the results of the interaction between the person with the impairment and the demands of the social and physical environment within which the person lives. Rehabilitation psychology defines the effects of impairment as both negative and positive, as well as neutral, depending on the construction placed on impairment by a specific person within a specific situation and by the "situation" interacting with a specific person. Such effects will be seen in all rings of the "concentric circles" within which the person dwells: within his or her intrapsychic functioning, in activities carried out in day-to-day life, in role functioning, in the person's social environment, and in the larger community. All of these arenas affect the individual with a disability, and, thus, have become the areas of interest within rehabilitation psychology.

Rehabilitation psychologists, both as clinicians and

researchers, have pursued a wide range of questions centering on the interaction of person and impairment, placed always within a specific social/physical environment: How does the insider react to sudden onset of impairment? What signals between the person and environment are critical in the individual's development and to his or her reaction to disability? What environmental elements affect the individual's functioning and well-being? How does the individual with a disability optimize his or her role functioning? What are the images of individuals with disabilities in the media, and what are the effects of such images on beliefs about disability? What attitudes do people with disabilities have about disability? How do attitudes of employers affect their hiring of or behavior toward employees with disabilities? What are the stages of adjusting to onset of impairment?

As pointed out by Beatrice Wright, a pioneering rehabilitation psychologist whose seminal and influential work was done at the University of Kansas: The general areas of interest and the specific issues that rehabilitation psychologists define within their purview have broad relevance for psychology (and human beings) in general. In terms of our understanding and assessment of the human condition, the "special" case of the person with a disability can reveal much of relevance about the "general" case, in that all individuals, over the life span, must confront challenges and losses, physical and nonphysical, internally or externally derived. And, in fact, rehabilitation psychology has both borrowed from and contributed to many fields of psychology: clinical, counseling, community, environmental, neuropsychology, developmental, health, and social.

Psychological studies of people with disabilities are of long standing. In fact, Barker et al., in their 1953 survey of the social psychology of disability, cite Galton's (1883) study of the behavioral differences of 13 pairs of adult same-sexed twins, in which one of each pair had a disability. Thereafter, however, studies of persons with disabilities were seldom carried out until the late 1940s, largely as a result then of the expansion of medical rehabilitation and clinical psychology's growing involvement in the provision of rehabilitation services.

Rehabilitation psychology (which has also been called somatopsychology) began to emerge as a field of study and clinical practice at that point. It was based on the thinking and work of social and clinical psychologists who took an interest in the situation of the person with a disability: primarily Kurt Lewin, Roger G. Barker, Beatrice A. Wright, Tamara Dembo, Gloria Leviton, Franklin Shontz, and Lee Meyerson. Much of the initial impetus sprang from Lewin's formulation, which defines behavior [B] as a function of the person [P] in the environment [E]. Given the thrust of this equation

($B = f [P, E]$), early efforts within the field became focused on adaptation to loss (of physical structure, e.g., a limb, or of function, e.g., walking). That is, interest was focused on how P differently interacts with E after loss of a characteristic attached to P. In fact, Beatrice Wright's groundbreaking text provides an in-depth exploration of the ways that people cope: "Factors within the person and factors attributable to the environment are considered in terms of how they aid psychological adjustment or, on the negative side, how they create difficulties" (1960, p. xviii).

Academic research in rehabilitation psychology has also focused on the environmental side of Lewin's equation. For example, Barker's student, Edwin Willems, and his colleagues at The Institute for Rehabilitation Research, Baylor College of Medicine, carried out a program of studies in the 1960s and 1970s to document the environmental dynamics of individuals undergoing rehabilitation. Willems, along with Sholom Vineberg, James Alexander, and Diana Rintala, among others, used behavioral observation and behavior setting methods (largely developed by Barker), to delineate how individuals with, in this case, spinal cord injuries, interact with the environment, and to document the types of signals sent by varying settings within rehabilitation facilities. A major interest was to define the types of signals from the environment that were associated with behavioral variance, including what they called behavioral "zest," or more outgoing, active behaviors.

The tradition started by Lewin, Wright, and Barker was also continued within the Rehabilitation Indicators Project at New York University Medical Center during the 1970s. As part of an effort by the Division of Rehabilitation Psychology of the American Psychological Association to contribute to accountability within rehabilitation, this project developed a series of assessment tools to document the impact of rehabilitation services on the behavioral output of people with disabilities. The goal of this effort was to locate rehabilitation outcomes in the behaviors evidenced by people with disabilities in the real world, rather than in their "passing tests" of ability within the boundaries of rehabilitation facilities. This research was associated with Leonard Diller, Wilbert Fordyce, Durand Jacobs, and Margaret Brown.

Many research contributions have emerged within rehabilitation psychology largely outside the academic traditions and concepts outlined herein. Instead, the challenge arose directly from the problems in clients' day-to-day living that confronted clinicians. For example, Diller and his colleagues (Joseph Weinberg, Yehuda Ben Yishay, Wayne Gordon, Rose Lynn Sherr, and others) created innovative techniques to help individuals with brain injury compensate for cognitive deficits. Similarly, Wilbert Fordyce at the University of Washington made significant contributions to the psychology of pain management. He adopted a behavioral approach documenting the individual's patterns of activity, to determine the patterns of behavioral output associated with pain.

In recent years, a factor shaping research in rehabilitation psychology has been the National Institute of Disability and Rehabilitation Research (NIDRR), United States Department of Education, which has been the major source of funding of psychologists within rehabilitation settings. (Recently the National Institutes of Health created the National Center on Medical Rehabilitation Research.) A large proportion of NIDRR's funds are used to support Rehabilitation Research and Training Centers. These major research and training programs are comprised of thematically interrelated projects and activities. NIDRR also supports "model systems of care" organized around specific impairments. Currently, 18 model systems exist in spinal cord injury, 15 in traumatic brain injury, and 4 in burn rehabilitation. Each model system develops a continuum of care needed to provide services to an individual from the point of injury through lifelong follow-up care. Each center in a system contributes data to a uniform data base, which is used to examine the outcomes of the program as well as for other types of research. For example, both the spinal cord injury and traumatic brain injury model systems have documented dramatic decreases in length of rehabilitation center stay that are associated with system care. Within each of these programs, greater focus is now being placed on issues of community functioning and quality of life. Although much important work continues in trying to understand the intrapsychic processes associated with disability, much more attention is being paid to the texture of day-to-day life and ways to expand opportunities.

In recent years, the consumer's voice has had greater impact on research than in the past, particularly within participatory action research (PAR). Within PAR, individuals with disabilities become full participants in diverse research roles: generating consensus on questions that need study, helping in the gathering of data, and participating in analysis of results. Thus, people with disabilities are helping to set the research agenda and are increasingly found in paid positions within research teams.

Rehabilitation psychologists have developed, both for use in research and in clinical practice, a wide variety of assessment tools to document the issues faced by individuals with specific forms of disability. Marcia J. Scherer and Laura A. Cushman (1995) discuss a variety of areas where assessment is of importance within rehabilitation psychology: coping with disability, functional assessment, neurocognitive function, behavioral assessment, pain, social support, vocational interests, neuropsychological function, personality, and awareness of deficits.

The clinical role of the rehabilitation psychologist is very broad and, on the one hand, can involve addressing the reality-based issues that the person with a disability identifies as his or her personal barriers to successful living, or, on the other, helping the individual identify environmental barriers that hinder full realization of potential. In the first instance, the psychologist might assist the person in confronting a negative self-appraisal stemming from the person's perception of activities that he or she is no longer able to perform. Or, the rehabilitation psychologist may assist the person to dissect a challenging and difficult situation into its component parts, to find ways to reorganize the "impossible" into the possible. A typical role is to help individuals with cognitive deficits to learn to compensate for their losses. The rehabilitation psychologist, functioning vis-à-vis environmental barriers, might, for example, serve as an advocate on behalf of the client with an insurance carrier to eliminate architectural barriers in the client's home. Or the psychologist might help clarify with the person his or her rights under the Americans with Disabilities Act or coach the client in challenging a community agency's role.

The rehabilitation psychologist often participates in both clinical and research endeavors as a neuropsychologist or clinical psychologist. And, in fact, as was noted above, rehabilitation psychology draws on and is related to many fields of psychology. However, the work of the rehabilitation psychologist aligns itself with unique lines of research, as well as models and conceptualizations of disability. First, the rehabilitation psychologist approaches clients with a long tradition of defining the client as an individual, with full self-determination and free choice. Thus, the psychologist within the rehabilitation tradition views the person with a disability outside the medical model. The person with the disability is the prime decision maker and is not a "patient" or a "subject." Second, the rehabilitation psychologist focuses on the assets of the person with the disability. The emphasis is on what the person does or can do rather than on what is "wrong" with the person or on what he or she cannot do. The person's assets, skills, interests, hopes, and goals form the context for working together. Another novel aspect of rehabilitation psychology is its focus on the person-environment interface. Disability, therefore, does not reside within the person, but instead in the way the environment fits or does not fit the needs and interests of the person with a physical impairment.

Currently there are no degree-granting programs in rehabilitation psychology. Predoctoral internship training programs in rehabilitation psychology exist at the Rusk Institute of Rehabilitation Medicine, New York University Medical Center, New York; the Department of Rehabilitation Medicine, the Mount Sinai Medical Center, New York; the Department of Rehabilitation Medicine, University of Washington, Seattle; and the Rehabilitation Institute of Michigan, Detroit. In 1997 the American Board of Professional Psychology approved the creation of the American Board of Rehabilitation Psychology and the granting of "Diplomate" status in rehabilitation psychology.

[*See also* Health Psychology; *and* Sport Psychology.]

Bibliography

Barker, R. G., Wright, B. A., Meyerson, L., & Gonick, M. R. (1953). *Adjustment to physical handicap and illness: A survey of the social psychology of physique and disability.* New York: Social Science Research Council. The major formulation of rehabilitation psychology, at its earliest stage of development.

Brown, M., Gordon, W. A., & Diller, L. (1984). Rehabilitation indicators. In A. Halpern & M. Fuhrer (Eds.), *Functional assessment in rehabilitation* (pp. 187–203). Baltimore: Paul H. Brookes. A conceptual summary of Rehabilitation Indicators, one approach to assessing functioning of individuals with disability, emphasizing the interaction of person and environment.

Brown, M., Gordon, W. A., & Ragnarsson, K. T. (1987). Unhandicapping the disabled: What is possible? *Archives of Physical Medicine and Rehabilitation, 68,* 206–209, 317. An example of the use of Rehabilitation Indicators to document activity of people with physical disabilities within home and community.

Dembo, T., Diller, L., Gordon, W. A., Leviton, G., & Sherr, R. L. (1973). A view of rehabilitation psychology. *American Psychologist, 28,* 719–722. An overview of rehabilitation psychology written at a mid-point in the development of the field.

Galton, F. (1883). *Inquiries into human faculty and its development.* New York: Macmillan.

Scherer, M. J., & Cushman, L. A. (1995). *Psychological assessment in medical rehabilitation.* Washington, DC: American Psychological Association.

Willems, E. P., & Halstead, L. S. (1978). An ecobehavioral approach to health status and health care. In R. G. Barker and associates (Eds.), *Habitats, environments and human behavior.* New York: Jossey-Bass. A broad view of the work of researchers at The Institute for Rehabilitation Research, which focuses on environment-person interactions as determinants of behavioral output.

Willems, E. P., & Vineberg, S. E. (1969). Direct observation of patients: The interface of environment and behavior. *Psychological Aspects of Disability, 16,* 74–88. An example of research using an ecobehavioral approach to observing activity of individuals with disabilities.

Wright, B. (1960). *Physical disability: A psychological approach.* New York: Harper & Row. A groundbreaking formulation.

Wayne A. Gordon

REID, THOMAS (1710–1796), Scottish philosopher. The recognized leader of Scottish Common Sense philosophy, Reid was educated at Marischal College, University of Aberdeen, later teaching there at King's College (1751–1764). He concluded his long academic career at the University of Glasgow where, in 1764, he occupied the chair in moral philosophy recently vacated by Adam Smith.

Reid's *Inquiry into the Human Mind* (1764) has come to be recognized as one of the most trenchant and incisive philosophical essays in the English language. Though its principal target was David Hume, the *Inquiry* also drew attention to a number of widely but uncritically accepted precepts shared by an otherwise diverse group of philosophers: Aristotle, Descartes, Locke, Berkeley, and Hume. Chief among these precepts was what Reid dubbed the "ideal" theory according to which all knowledge of the external world is mediated by the senses such that there can be only ideas of things rather than knowledge of the things themselves. On Reid's account, there is not only little to support such a theory but much to refute it. Reid noted that even the lowly caterpillar will traverse a thousand leaves until it finds one that is right for its diet. A creature whose contact with the external world is solely by way of distorting mediations can have no secure future and would stand as one of nature's mistakes. Opposing this theory, Reid advanced and defended *commonsense realism*, which is at once a pre-Darwinian version of psychological and biological adaptation and a defense of providentialist Christianity entirely compatible with Reid's Presbyterian faith.

As used (with reluctance) by Reid, the term *common sense* is not to be confused with opinion or belief or deeply held convictions. Reid defines a principle of common sense as that which one is under an obligation to take for granted in all of the ordinary encounters and transactions of daily life. Included among its principles are such logical necessities as the law of contradiction, and such psychological necessities as the awareness that the experience one is having is one's own. Such principles are grounded in the very constitution of one's being. They are from "the mint of Nature," as Reid said, and are inextricably bound up with survival and a coherent form of life.

Reid was a strenuous defender of the methods of inquiry propounded by Bacon and Newton and used by the latter with such unsurpassed success. He regarded the major errors of philosophers as the result of both a corruption of ordinary language and a tendency toward theoretical speculation undisciplined by the canons of scientific investigation. His critique of Hume's theory of causal concepts is illustrative. Hume's account leads to the conclusion that events or objects "constantly conjoin'd" in experience come to be treated as causally linked. Reid's counter is that many unfailingly conjoined experiences (e.g., day and night) are never regarded as causally related. Moreover, from the mere conjunction of events no one could derive the notion of causality unless the observer recognized some kindred power within oneself. According to Reid, it is from the recognition of oneself as having certain *active powers*—the power not only to do something but also to forbear from doing it—that one draws the inference to events occurring externally. One's direct awareness of one's own active power supports the inference that events brought about in the external world are the result of some similar antecedent power.

Modestly in his *Inquiry* but then rather more profligately in his later works, Reid set down a number of basic powers or "faculties" of the mind judged to be at the foundation of all cognitive, perceptual, and affective operations. This *faculty psychology*, which was an early version of what today are called modularity theories of mind, would be adopted by the phrenologists Franz Joseph Gall and Johann Kaspar Spurzheim in their efforts to link specific psychological functions to specific "organs" in the brain. Notwithstanding his discussion of such faculties, Reid was abidingly opposed to reductionistic modes of psychological inquiry. He criticized David Hartley's materialistic theory of mind, arguing that if thought were reducible to vibrational mechanics, one should be able to get thought from a pendulum. These and similarly wry comments were intended to impose what Reid took to be proper and sensible restraint on those who would address the complexities of mental life.

Reid's influence, both directly and by way of his celebrated student, Dugald Stewart, was broad and deep. Scottish commonsense philosophy was extremely influential at the American founding. Thomas Jefferson would declare Dugald Stewart one of the two greatest metaphysicians of the age. John Witherspoon presented commonsense philosophy to a young James Madison at Princeton, the future president taking a fifth year to study it ever more closely. Yet another native Scot and Founding Father, James Wilson, was an avowed disciple of Reid. So, too, was Victor Cousin who, in his official capacity, gave a distinctly Reidian character to precollege education in France throughout much of the nineteenth century.

Bibliography

Beanblossom, R., & Lehrer, K. (Eds.). (1983). *Thomas Reid's "Inquiry" and essays.* Indianapolis, IN: Hackett.

Freeman, E. (Ed.). (1978). *The philosophy of Thomas Reid. Monist, 61.*

Reid, T. (1967). *Works* (Vols. 1–2). (H. Bracken, Ed.). Germany: Hildesheim Georg Olms.

Daniel N. Robinson

REINFORCEMENT. *See* Operant Conditioning.

RELATIVE DEPRIVATION. *See* Deprivation.

RELAXATION TRAINING. Methods of quiescent self-inquiry leading to states of well-being are collectively referred to as relaxation, and their practice dates to 3000 BCE. Like the field of psychology that embraced it, relaxation has attained respectable scientific status in the twentieth century. More than half a century has passed since Jacobson (1929) lamented that a scientific method of relaxation did not exist. Medical treatment often included advice to relax, but instructions on how to accomplish this were limited to "take a vacation." By now a variety of relaxation techniques are well established and have earned the respect of health professionals.

Relaxation Procedures

Relaxation therapy enjoys a unique set of characteristics. No other psychological intervention can reliably produce immediate, substantive effects with most patients (Lichstein, 1988). The methods of relaxation can be categorized as either deep or brief.

Deep Methods. The three most common methods of deep relaxation are autogenic training (AT), meditation, and progressive relaxation (PR); (Lichstein, 1988). "Deep" signifies that the method may produce large physiological and experiential effects and implies that the patient must assume a static, comfortable position.

AT consists of imagining a peaceful environment and comforting bodily sensations. The standard exercises of AT are composed of six themes: limb heaviness, limb warmth, cardiac regulation, calm respiration, abdominal warmth, and cooling of the forehead. Current typical practice employs a version of AT needing several 25-minute sessions to attain mastery. The patient assumes a comfortable position and silently focuses on these sensations while imagining being in a peaceful setting.

Of the many meditation techniques, the most common type found in clinical practice is called focal meditation and consists of dwelling on a word, an image (guided imagery), or an object. Perhaps the most popular version of meditation is a generic technique called the relaxation response (Benson, 1975), defined by its four components: quiet environment, mental device, passive attitude, and comfortable position. Under these conditions, the patient silently repeats a word, a phrase, or a sound with each expiration for about 15 minutes.

Current PR practice consists of moving through

about 15 major muscle groups of the body in sequence. Each group is tensed for 5 to 10 seconds and then relaxed for 30 to 60 seconds in a 15-minute induction. PR is probably the most popular form of relaxation in clinical use.

Brief Methods. The invention of brief methods was inspired by the inability of deep methods to adequately manage frequent eruptions of stress during the day (Lichstein, 1988). The term *brief* denotes that most of these methods require less time to learn and less time to implement than the deep methods. Further, they are portable and unobtrusive and will induce only a mild to moderate level of relaxation.

Self-control relaxation is a typical example of brief relaxation. The patient first masters PR. Subsequently, the muscle tensing portion is phased out, and relaxation is invoked by recall. In addition, cue words such as "peace" are practiced during training to elicit conditioned relaxation responses when said silently. When stress threatens, the individual can recall relaxation and repeat his or her cue word without interrupting the task at hand.

AT may be abbreviated and similarly converted to a self-control format. Also, the first two standard exercises of AT, heaviness and warmth, are frequently employed as a rapid relaxation induction. The slow, soft repetition of the chant, "my arms and legs are heavy and warm," has proven to be a simple and effective method.

Paced respiration teaches patients to maintain slow breathing when anxiety threatens. Another method of breath control, deep breathing, consists of taking a deep breath, retaining the breath about 5 seconds, and exhaling slowly. Five breaths will usually produce a mild relaxation effect.

Comparative Characteristics of Relaxation Methods. The various methods of relaxation can be compared along three dimensions: structure, somatic/cognitive emphasis, and mobility. Such considerations clarify the relative strengths of the techniques and help guide clinical decisions.

The structure continuum extends from meditation to AT to PR in a low to high progression. To illustrate the utility of this dimension, individuals with a high need for structure, such as Type A individuals, may prefer the high end. A somatic/cognitive dimension produces the same sequence as above, with meditation anchoring the high cognitive and PR the high somatic end. Lastly, a mobility dimension ranks all three deep methods as low because they require sitting quietly for an extended time in a conducive environment. They may be abbreviated and transformed into high mobile methods, such as self-control relaxation. Further, a relaxed attitude (discussed below) may be cultivated by any of the static methods to foster mobility.

It is difficult to draw general conclusions about com-

parative clinical efficacy between methods. Comparative trials are not numerous, and the results are inconsistent (Lichstein, 1988).

Clinical Applications

Relaxation is used with disorders having a basis in anxiety or arousal, but the mode of application may vary (Lichstein, 1988). Relaxation therapy refers to the use of relaxation as the sole or primary intervention. However, relaxation is often enlisted as an adjunct in a subordinate role to facilitate another therapeutic technique, such as systematic desensitization. As a treatment component, relaxation has roughly equal but minority status among a set of interventions orchestrated to form a treatment package. This is most often done to address multifaceted problems wherein it is feared that neglect of any aspect would undermine therapeutic impact, as in stress management.

I have previously summarized the clinical outcome literature of relaxation applied to some two dozen distinct disorders (Lichstein, 1988). This broad applicability prompted one group of observers to call relaxation the "behavioral medicine aspirin" (Russo, Bird, & Masek, 1980). The strongest clinical results for relaxation therapy occur with anxiety, chemotherapy side effects, essential hypertension, insomnia, muscle-contraction headache, and phobias.

A general sense of the efficacy of relaxation can be gleaned from a recent meta-analysis of PR (Carlson & Hoyle, 1993). The average posttreatment effect size was $d = 0.86$, which is generally considered large.

Abiding Clinical and Research Issues

Three areas demand future attention: compliance, sustained practice, and enduring cognitive effects.

Compliance and Treatment Implementation. Typically, relaxation is taught in the therapy session, and the patient is instructed to practice daily at home. Home practice adherence is critical because the home is the primary arena of treatment exposure. Research employing empirical, unobtrusive methods of monitoring practice has shown that actual home relaxation practice may fall far short of patient reports and leave treatment exposure well below prescribed levels (Lichstein & Hoelscher, 1986).

Home practice may be viewed as but one part of treatment implementation. We have proposed a treatment implementation model as one way of understanding compliance (Lichstein, Riedel, & Grieve, 1994). Independent treatment components, termed *delivery*, *receipt*, and *enactment*, must be adequately represented to conclude that satisfactory treatment exposure occurred. The delivery component refers to the accuracy of treatment presentation (also called treatment integrity), receipt refers to the degree of the patient's mastery of treatment, and enactment refers to the extent of home practice (this component is equivalent to the usual meaning of compliance).

Faults in any component will cause the patient to deviate from the intended treatment. As examples, delivery faults may be caused by poorly trained therapists, receipt faults by impaired patients, and enactment faults by poorly motivated patients. To illustrate the implications of this model, errors in delivery or receipt will lead to compliance with the wrong treatment. Relaxation therapy, not unlike other interventions, must make strong efforts to induce high implementation and must assess the success of these efforts.

Sustained Practice. In Eastern cultures, meditation is an integral part of the practitioner's values and religious beliefs. In Western cultures, denuding relaxation of its religious and philosophical context has created discontinuity between the individual's lifestyle and values versus the relaxation task, fostering sporadic relaxation practice. Sustained relaxation practice is critical, because treatment effects accruing to relaxation therapy usually persist only as long as relaxation practice continues.

Future research has a dual task in this domain. First, the actual relationship between duration of relaxation practice and symptom return needs to be more clearly explicated. Second, methods of promoting long-term, lifestyle commitment to relaxation practice deserve serious attention.

Enduring Cognitive Effects. All schools of relaxation require the focusing of attention, and virtually every student of relaxation has difficulty doing this. Thus, mind wandering is a notorious obstacle to successful relaxation. However, another view of mind wandering, which may be called the *blessed irritant* (Lichstein, 1988), unveils a critical opportunity for nurturing a relaxed attitude. Adopting a tolerant, relaxed attitude about distracting thoughts during relaxation practice can form the basis of an enduring trait. A relaxed attitude holds the potential of pervading one's life to a greater extent than somatic effects, which begin to dissipate at the conclusion of a relaxation session. Indeed, adopting a relaxed attitude sustains somatic effects and primes the individual to calmly navigate the day's challenges (as discussed by Smith, 1990). Unfortunately, the mechanisms of cultivating such an attitude and the evaluation of its effects have received little attention. Future research would do well to remedy this neglect.

[*See also* Meditation.]

Bibliography

Benson, H. B. (1975). *The relaxation response*. New York: Morrow. This is a layperson's book that reviews relax-ation techniques and recommends a composite method of relaxation composed of features common to the variety of available methods.

Carlson, C. R., & Hoyle, R. H. (1993). Efficacy of abbreviated progressive muscle relaxation training: A quantitative review of behavioral medicine research. *Journal of Consulting and Clinical Psychology, 61*, 1059–1067.

Jacobson, E. (1929). *Progressive relaxation*. Chicago: University of Chicago Press. This text, written by the "father" of relaxation, inaugurated the modern era of relaxation and presents the classical (long) form of progressive relaxation.

Lichstein, K. L. (1988). *Clinical relaxation strategies*. New York: Wiley. This book provides a comprehensive accounting of relaxation, including theory, research, and practice.

Lichstein, K. L., & Hoelscher, T. J. (1986). A device for unobtrusive surveillance of home relaxation practice. *Behavior Modification, 10*, 219–233.

Lichstein, K. L., Riedel, B. W., & Grieve, R. (1994). Fair tests of clinical trials: A treatment implementation model. *Advances in Behaviour Research and Therapy, 16*, 1–29.

Russo, D. C., Bird, B. L., & Masek, B. J. (1980). Assessment issues in behavioral medicine. *Behavioral Assessment, 2*, 1–18.

Smith, J. C. (1990). *Cognitive-behavioral relaxation training*. New York: Springer. This is an overview of relaxation with an emphasis on cognitive mechanisms and procedures.

Kenneth L. Lichstein

RELIABILITY. The dependability of scores obtained from a psychological assessment or from a psychological test is referred to as reliability. A reliable psychological test will yield highly dependable or highly consistent results if administered to the same person or persons under similar circumstances.

Reliability Theory

The starting point for most discussions about reliability is considering what is reflected in a psychological test score. Ordinarily, a test is made up of a series of questions or items that are all intended to tap the same underlying characteristic. The score that a person obtains on the test is the sum of his or her answers to the individual items. This observed score is generally believed to be influenced by two factors: stable characteristics of the person, including the characteristic that the test is designed to measure, and irrelevant characteristics of the person or the situation.

The conceptual relationship between an observed test score and these two factors is embodied in the formula:

$$\text{Observed Score} = \text{True Score} + \text{Errors of Measurement}.$$

The concept of true score does not correspond to "truth" or to "real" scores. A true score represents a combination of all the characteristics that give consistency to a person's answers to the test items. Although it is hoped that the true score reflects the characteristic that the test was designed to measure, a test can yield consistent (i.e., reliable) scores without necessarily being valid.

Errors in measurement reflect the effects of chance factors on the test scores. Various sources of measurement error include lasting or temporary features of the person, lasting or temporary features of the test-taking situation, and unknown elements of chance. For example, errors of measurement associated with the person may occur if the person is tired, ill, distracted, or, for that matter, extraordinarily energetic while taking the test. Errors of measurement associated with the test-taking situation may result from factors such as a noisy room, poor lighting, and so on.

A theory of reliability has been based on the assumption that errors of measurement are random. If errors of measurement are indeed random, then errors could be either negative or positive and hence will average out to zero in the long run. A corollary of this is that longer tests should be more reliable than shorter tests. Further, truly random errors of measurement will not be correlated with true scores or with errors on other tests.

Moving from these assumptions, it can be shown that the variability in observed test scores is a function of the variability in the true scores plus the variability in error scores. A reliable test is thus defined as a test on which the variability due to errors of measurement is close to zero, and the variability in the observed test scores is close to the variability in the true scores.

The classic equation that links observed scores to true scores and errors of measurement can be reformulated to provide a mathematical definition for the reliability of a test:

$$\text{Reliability of a Test} = \frac{\text{True Score Variability}}{\text{Observed Score Variability}}.$$

Alternatively:

$$\text{Reliability of a Test} = \frac{\text{True Score Variability}}{\begin{array}{c}\text{True Score Variability} \\ + \text{ Errors of Measurement}\end{array}}.$$

Theoretically, true scores might be assessed by looking at a person's performance on two different but perfectly parallel tests. Any differences in observed scores would then be a function of errors of measurement. Unfortunately, parallel tests are next to impossible to develop; all measurement involves some error. In practice, we cannot measure true scores.

The Reliability Coefficient

How then is the reliability coefficient calculated? In the mid-1890s, Karl Pearson, a mathematician, developed a statistical index that reflects the relationship between two sets of variables. This statistic is called the Pearson product-moment correlation. At a simple level, a reliability coefficient is the Pearson product-moment correlation between two sets of observed scores. The size of the correlation is taken as an indication of how much variability in the test scores is due to true score variance versus error variance. For example, a Pearson product-moment correlation of 0.8 between two sets of tests scores is interpreted as meaning that 80% of the variability in the test scores is true score variability. In principle, the reliability coefficient can range from 0, indicating a perfectly unreliable test, to 1.0, indicating a perfectly reliable test.

Different versions of the correlation coefficient have subsequently been developed. The Pearson product-moment correlation is by far the most common one used when calculating a reliability coefficient. However, some psychometricians have argued that the Pearson product-moment correlation overestimates reliability because it is insensitive to differences in the average test scores obtained from the two test administrations. That is, the Pearson product-moment correlation assesses the degree to which test takers maintain their relative positions. Even if every test takers' score changed, the reliability coefficient estimated using the Pearson correlation could still be 1.0 as long as the ordering of people by the two sets of test scores did not change.

Some psychometricians advocate using more conservative types of correlation coefficients to estimate reliability, such as the intraclass correlation. The intraclass correlation is sensitive to differences in both in the slope and intercept of the test score distributions. In other words, the intraclass correlation will only yield a reliability coefficient of 1.0 if all test takers obtain identical scores on both tests. Nonetheless, if the effects of error on the two score sets are truly random, the differences between the Pearson product-moment correlation and the intraclass correlation are minimal.

Methods of Establishing Reliability

Although there are no perfectly parallel psychological tests, there are approximations to the idea of a parallel test that allow us to estimate the reliability of a set of scores obtained from a test. These are the test-retest method, the alternate-forms method, the split-half reliability method, and the internal consistency method.

Test-Retest Reliability. The test-retest approach involves administering the psychological test twice to the same people. The test-retest reliability of the test is the correlation between the two sets of scores from one test for one group of people. Because no parallel tests are involved, some theorists prefer to call test-retest reliability an index of test score stability rather than reliability per se. One possible source of error in the test-retest reliability coefficient is that people may remember their answers to some questions from the first testing session. A memory effect is likely to result in an inflated estimate of reliability using the test-retest method.

Alternate-Forms Reliability. A second method of calculating a reliability coefficient involves constructing two alternate (although not strictly parallel) forms of the test. These two tests are administered to the same group of people, usually on two separate occasions. The reliability coefficient is the correlation between the two sets of scores for one group of people who answered both alternate versions of the test.

Both the test-retest method and the alternate-forms method of estimating reliability presume that people do not change on the characteristic that the test is designed to measure. Even selecting a short interval between test administrations cannot guarantee elimination of error due to real change. Moreover, the error that comes from change in people brought about strictly by having taken the test itself is uncontrolled in the case of two separate testing sessions.

Split-Half Reliability. A third method of calculating the reliability of a test is to administer a test only once to a single group of respondents. Split-half reliability involves dividing the items from one test into two groups, calculating a score on each half test for each test respondent, and then correlating the two scores on the half tests across respondents. However, this results in a reliability coefficient for a test that is only half as long as the actual test. Based on our assumptions about random error, we know that tests with more items will tend to have higher reliabilities. To estimate the reliability of the full-length test, a correction must be applied to the split-half reliability coefficient. This correction is called the Spearman–Brown prophecy formula.

A set of test items from one test can be split into two groups in various ways, although some ways are better than others. For example, if items were divided into those that appear on the first half of the test and those that appear on the second half of the test, we could expect measurement errors due to fatigue or due to interest in the test to affect scores differentially on the two test halves. One of the better and more common methods for dividing items into groups is an odd-even split. That is, a score is calculated for each test taker on the odd-numbered items; another is calculated on the even-numbered items; and the two sets of scores are correlated.

When a test has high split-half reliability, it means that the scores people obtain on one set of items can be generalized to a second set of items intended to measure the same characteristic. The split-half reliability approach to estimating reliability gets around some problems of the test-retest and the alternate-forms estimates of reliability; nonetheless, it is still susceptible to errors that result from a split that is in any way inadequate.

Internal Consistency. Kuder and Richardson in the 1930s proposed an alternate approach for estimating test reliability based on the responses of a single group of respondents to one test. They derived various formulas to calculate the mean of all possible split-half correlations. Their approach gets around the problem that any one split-half reliability coefficient might be unduly influenced by an unlucky split of the items into two groups. Their reliability coefficient also goes beyond comparing scores on two test halves: It relates test takers' performance on each item to their performance on all the other items.

Because of its emphasis on item response coherence, this type of reliability estimate has become known as "internal consistency." High internal consistency is interpreted as evidence that all of the items on the test reflect the same underlying characteristic. All error in this approach is assumed to be error due to differences among items. The Kuder–Richardson formula 20 (K–R 20) is used to calculate the internal consistency of items that are scored dichotomously (0, 1), such as correct/incorrect or yes/no.

Shortly after Kuder and Richardson published their work, other authors applied an analysis of variance approach to estimating internal consistency. Analysis of variance is a set of statistical techniques designed to partition, or break down, the variability in scores and to assign that variability to different sources. To evaluate reliability using analysis of variance logic, test score variability is divided into variance associated with items, variance associated with persons, and total variance. The remainder variance is defined as the variance left over after variance due to items and to persons has been subtracted from the total variance. This remainder variance is treated as error variance. The variance due to persons is considered the variance of consequence. The definition of reliability can be expressed in the relationship between person variance and remainder variance, and is shown in the following version of the well-known Hoyt's formula:

$$\text{Hoyt's reliability} = \frac{\text{Person Variance}}{\text{Person Variance} + \text{Remainder Variance}}.$$

Hoyt's reliability formula is conceptually similar to the classic reliability formula that was described earlier Computationally, Hoyt's approach will yield a reliability coefficient that is identical to that produced by the K–R 20 formula for dichotomous items.

In the 1950s, Cronbach presented a more general version of the K–R 20 formula. Cronbach's alpha, or coefficient alpha as it is also called, can be computed from individual test item variances and is an estimate of the average split-half reliability coefficient for items that are scored on a continuous scale (e.g., 1 to 5). Cronbach's alpha will produce a reliability estimate that is identical to Hoyt's reliability for nondichotomous data.

Profile Reliability

Sometimes a person is given a series of tests, all related to the same underlying characteristic. For example, a person might respond to a number of subtests on an overall measure of intelligence or to different scales on a psychopathology questionnaire. How reliable are differences that may be reflected across the profile of subtest scores? Two factors are relevant. First, differences in subtest scores are usually less reliable than the subtests themselves. Second, the more highly correlated two subtests are, the less reliable are the differences between them. Consider that two highly correlated subtests approach the theoretical idea of parallel tests. Score differences reflect what the two tests do not measure in common: error variance. Cronbach has provided a formula for estimating the reliability of the difference between pairs of subtests in a profile of test scores.

Reliability of Judges

So far, reliability has been discussed in the context of psychological tests made up of self-report questions. The concept of reliability is also applicable to instances in which judges or observers assign scores to people. Consider that judges might be teachers assigning marks to essay questions or interviewers making ratings of job candidates. In the simplest case, the reliability of two judges could be calculated as the Pearson product-moment correlation between the two sets of judgments across people. If more than two judges are involved, reliability could be assessed using a version of the analysis of variance approach described above. Alternatively, Guilford developed a formula that is applied to the rank ordering of all people by all the judges. The formula estimates the reliability of a single judge. The Spearman–Brown formula would then be applied to estimate the reliability of the composite judgment.

Interpreting Reliability Coefficients

A reliability coefficient gives a general indication of how reliable a test is. So, for example, a test with a reliability of 0.80 is more reliable than a test with a reliability of 0.60. However, a reliability coefficient does not indicate how reliable actual test scores are.

Standard Error of Measurement. Standard error of measurement is a statistic that estimates the average number of points by which observed test scores and true scores differ. Of course, we cannot calculate true scores. We can use information about the reliability of

a test and the amount of variability in overall test scores for a group of people to estimate the amount of error in observed test scores. Conceptually, standard error of measurement is described as follows:

Error of Measurement in Observed Scores
= Test Variance $\times$ (1 $-$ Test Reliability).

To obtain the standard error of measurement in test score points, the actual computation uses the standard deviation of the test scores and the square root of (1 $-$ Reliability Coefficient). As an example, consider a test with a reliability coefficient of 0.84 and a standard deviation of 10. The standard error of measurement is: 10 $\times$ Square Root (1 $-$ 0.84) = 4. Standard error of measurement is interpreted like a standard deviation. An observed score on this test is assumed not to differ from a respondent's true score by more than four points approximately 67% of the time; an observed score will not differ by more than two standard errors of measurement (2 $\times$ 4 = 8 points) approximately 95% of the time; and so on.

Use of the standard error of measurement presumes that the amount of error in test scores is constant across the entire range of test scores. This may not be true. Very low or very high scores in particular may contain larger degrees of error. Rulon has a formula that permits calculation of a series of standard measurements of error for selected ranges of the test. These standard errors of measurement are compared to determine whether a single standard errors of measurement or different ones should be used when interpreting observed test scores.

Degree of Reliability. How high does a reliability coefficient have to be in order for a test to be considered reliable? Some authors have tried to propose actual numbers; most others have outlined more general considerations. Much emphasis is given to the type of decisions that will be based on the test scores (individual versus group decisions; research versus applied decisions) and to the type of test (cognitive ability/achievement versus personality tests; professionally developed versus classroom tests). The key theme is that reliability of the test must be in proportion to the importance of the decision.

Restriction of Range. One methodological consideration that has implications for understanding the size of a reliability coefficient is the amount of variability in the test scores. The purpose of a correlation is to compare the variability in one set of scores to the variability in another. When a range of scores is restricted, that is, unusually small, the correlation is decreased. Likewise, when the range of scores is extended, the correlation will be inflated. The amount of variability in test scores, and by extension the reliability coefficient, can be affected by giving the test to an inappropriate sample. To illustrate, if a test is given only to people who are preselected to be very high on the characteristic of interest, then the test scores will show a restriction of range. A reliability coefficient calculated on the test scores will be artificially low.

Conclusion

When can a test be called reliable? When test-based decisions depend heavily on the stability of the characteristic being measured, demonstration of substantial levels of test-retest reliability or alternate-forms reliability would be required. Test-retest or alternate-forms reliability are also essential for tests that tap speed of responding. Tests that involve interpretation of meaningful individual differences depend on item coherence and hence need strong internal consistency. Many test developers report more than one type of reliability coefficient for a test. Just as there is no one size of correlation that is appropriate, no one reliability coefficient is applicable to all testing situations.

[*See also* Analysis of Variance; *and* Validity.]

Bibliography

Dick, W., & Hagerty, N. (1971). *Topics in measurement: Reliability and validity.* New York: McGraw-Hill.

Friedenberg, L. (1995). *Psychological testing: Design, analysis and use.* Boston: Allyn & Bacon.

Murphy, K. R., & Davidshofer, C. O. (1997). *Psychological testing: Principles and applications* (4th ed.). Upper Saddle River, NJ: Prentice Hall.

Rust, J., & Golombuk, S. (1989). *Modern psychometrics: The science of psychological assessment.* London: Routledge.

Streiner, D. L., & Norman, G. R. (1991). *Health measurement scales: A practical guide to their development and use.* Oxford, UK: Oxford University Press.

G. Cynthia Fekken

RELIGION AND PSYCHOLOGY. [*This entry comprises two articles: a broad history of the field; and a review of the typical stances of Western psychological science toward religion. For a general discussion of the philosophy of science, see* Philosophy, *article on* Philosophy of Science.]

An Overview

The psychology of religion consists of the application of psychological theories and methods to the content of the religious traditions and to the related experiences, attitudes, and actions of individuals. This highly pluralistic field, with roots deep in the past, coalesced as a formal discipline late in the nineteenth century, a product of the reformist spirit of progressivism and the growing enthusiasm for applying the scientific attitude and methods in the human realm. Psychology of a conjectural sort had already been applied to religion by the anthropologists and others who were contributing to the emerging science of the history of religions (*Religionswissenschaften*). The new psychology that was being formalized in both Europe and the United States offered the possibility of a more systematic approach.

Two Traditions

Like psychology in general, the psychology of religion is composed of two broadly contrasting traditions. The natural-scientific or "objective" tradition rejects any direct study of experience as unscientific and uses instead the quantitative procedures of statistical-empirical psychology. The experiment is the empirical ideal for inferring causal connections, but because religion does not easily lend itself to laboratory study, most investigators in this tradition use correlational methods instead. Typically, groups of research participants are asked to complete questionnaires designed to assess their religious attitudes, behavior, and experience. Their scores on these scales are then correlated mathematically with their scores on other measures, usually of social attitudes or mental health. Religiosity scores may also be related to such factors as age, sex, educational level, and physical health status.

The human-scientific or "subjective" tradition uses methods designed to give more or less direct access to human experience. These include phenomenological description, interviews, personal document analysis, clinical and historical case studies, and other methods sensitive to the subtleties of individual experience. These methods may be used mainly to describe what a particular type of experience—deep meditation, for example—is like or to characterize the experience of some notable person. The descriptive material may also be approached hermeneutically, that is, it may be subjected to some system of interpretation.

Psychologists of religion are likewise divided in terms of their goals. Some carry out their research to promote or defend religion, or at least some form of it, as it exists today. Others aspire to purify or transform a particular religious tradition, either recovering its original spirit or reshaping it to accord with modern understandings and sensibilities. Still others seek to discredit religion, in whole or in part, either by finding its origins in natural, sometimes pathological, processes or by demonstrating that it can have serious negative consequences, both personal and social. Relatively few assume a neutral stance, pursuing their study of religion without personal investment in its outcome and the practical implications of their findings. Whole literatures have taken shape around particular combinations of methods and goals.

Beginnings in the United States

In the United States, where the field had its formal beginnings, the objective and subjective approaches were evident virtually from the start. Representing the objective perspective was the Clark school of religious psychology, which was established by Stanley Hall at Clark University in Worcester, Massachusetts, and carried forward notably by Edwin Starbuck and James Henry Leuba. Starbuck established the typical course of conversion, and of religious growth more generally, by quantifying the questionnaire replies of more than 1,400 subjects, most of whom were Protestants. Starbuck undertook his study of religion's origins not as a way of illuminating religion's nature or value, but as a means of facilitating individual growth into religious maturity.

Leuba, in contrast, sought in his writings to demonstrate that religious experience can be explained satisfactorily in terms of physiological processes. He also conducted questionnaire studies to show that scientists, especially eminent ones, tend to believe neither in a god who answers prayer nor in personal survival after death. Although he denied the existence of a supernatural realm of beings and events, Leuba nevertheless advocated the use of modified forms of religious ritual to foster inborn human ideals.

Another major contributor to the objective psychology of religion was George Albert Coe, who, then at Northwestern University, was one of the first to apply scientific methods to the study of religious experience. Deeply influenced by both Darwin and the Social Gospel movement, Coe eventually concluded that what is most crucial in religion is not exceptional experience, as some traditions emphasize, but the development of personal and social values. A founder of the Religious Education Association, Coe deeply influenced generations of liberal Protestant religious educators through his courses at Union Theological Seminary in New York City and his writings over more than 40 years, both in the psychology of religion and in the theory of religious education.

At nearly the same time that Hall, Starbuck, Leuba, and Coe were carrying out their work, William James published his classic work using the subjective approach, *The Varieties of Religious Experience* (1902). A leading psychologist and philosopher, James likewise wrote in defense of certain forms of religious faith. But rather than inferring general trends from statistical analyses of representative samples, on the model of the Clark school, or carrying out hypnotic experiments, as Coe did, James sought to make religious experience comprehensible by sympathetically presenting firsthand reports from various "religious experts." Although the *Varieties* also contains speculations regarding the causal origins of religious experience and oft-cited reflections on the qualities of its fruits, this work stands out today as a model of the descriptive, or broadly phenomenological, approach to religion. In the same tradition but emphasizing ordinary piety is a classic work by one of James's students: *The Religious Consciousness* (1920) by James Pratt.

Classic German Literature

German-speaking contributors to the psychology of religion, who have tended to be educated as philosophers or theologians rather than as psychologists, have historically preferred the descriptive approach, which seeks to illuminate religion rather than to explain or evaluate it. The best-known and most influential of these descriptive studies is Rudolf Otto's *Idea of the Holy* (1917). A philosopher and a theologian, Otto undertook to formulate the nonrational experience of "the holy," or what he called the "numinous." Experience of the "Wholly Other," Otto was to conclude, is essentially bipolar: Frighteningly awesome and overpowering, on the one hand, the numinous is alluring and fascinating, on the other.

Another influential contributor was the German philosopher, psychologist, and educator Eduard Spranger, who is widely known for his delineation of six "ideal types" of life forms, including the religious type, as well as for his existentially framed reflections on religious faith and its development. But the interpretive and historical methods used by Otto and Spranger, among others, were thought by some descriptive psychologists of religion to be too inexplicit and too dependent on uncommon intuitive gifts. Such was the view of members of the Dorpat school of religious psychology, which was founded by theologian Karl Girgensohn at Dorpat University in Dorpat (today, Tartu), Estonia. Using highly educated and well-trained observers, Girgensohn and his associates adopted the Würzburg school's laborious method of systematic experimental introspection to study cognitive and emotional responses to selected religious texts. Although first undertaken to establish the general psychological nature of religion, these studies came to focus on individual differences and the practical matters of religious education and pastoral care. The work of the Dorpat school was brought to a virtual halt by the rise of National Socialism in Germany, where much of the work was continuing under the direction of theologian Werner Gruehn, the school's leader after Girgensohn's death in 1925. The Dorpat school of theology and its Institute for Religious Psychology were dismantled after the Soviet Union annexed Estonia in 1940.

From Austria and Switzerland came yet another major trend in the German literature: the application of depth psychology to the contents of the religious traditions and the experience of exceptional religious persons. First to appear was the psychoanalytic perspective of the Austrian neuropathologist Sigmund Freud, famous for his conviction that religion is rooted in the wishes and fears of early childhood, especially those that constitute the Oedipus complex. Religion, which Freud equated with belief in a Father God and the scrupulous carrying out of fixed rituals, was declared to be a dangerous illusion that restricts the great majority of human beings to an immature phase of development.

Appearing somewhat later was the equally influential work of the Swiss psychiatrist C. G. Jung, an early associate of Freud's, who broke with him in part because of his views on religion. According to Jung's analytical psychology, the myths and symbols that constitute the religious traditions arise out of the collective unconscious, a deep-lying layer of the psyche that preserves, in the form of archetypes, the basic contours of recurring human experience. For individuals to attain maturity, Jung said, they must recognize and differentiate these powerful and conflicting factors and then integrate them into a harmonious, balanced whole. This difficult and ever-incomplete task has throughout history been facilitated primarily by the religious traditions, according to Jung. Thus, in sharp contrast to Freud, Jung argues that religion is an essential psychological function, the neglect of which may lead to neurosis in individuals and massive destructiveness in the human species.

Contributions from the French Literature

The French-language literature in the psychology of religion, although influenced from early on by both the American and the German literatures, likewise has a character of its own. The earliest and most typical studies viewed religion through the prism of psychopathology. Some investigators, such as the eminent French psychopathologists Jean-Martin Charcot, Pierre Janet, and Théodule Ribot, identified mystical and other exceptional religious states with one or another form of mental disorder. Other researchers, such as the Swiss philosopher-psychologist Ernest Murisier, looked to disordered exaggerations of religious emotion for clues to the positive functions of normal piety.

The growing literature on the psychopathology of religion soon inspired a critical response from other scholars, especially Roman Catholic ones, who cautioned against generalizing from patently inferior mystics to the great ones, whose lives are said to show exceptional harmony and productivity. Some instances of religious phenomena, such as mysticism, conversion, and possession, the Catholic scholars maintained, may result from supernatural causes rather than pathological processes. Most contributors, however, have fol-

lowed the lead of the Swiss psychologist Theodore Flournoy, who argues that psychologists of religion, in their quest for every possible causal factor, may neither affirm nor reject the existence of the transcendent realm of religious objects.

A second major trend in the French literature may be found in an eclectic Protestant tradition that combined insights from the early American investigators and the dynamic psychologies of Freud and Jung with the findings of the cognitive-developmental research inspired by the famous Swiss scholar Jean Piaget. Representatives of this eclectic literature include Piaget himself, as well as Georges Berguer, who sought to recover the profound psychological truth underlying the misleading mythic elaborations of the Christian tradition, and Pierre Bovet, who is best known for his study of the course of religious development in children and adolescents.

Further Developments

The trends described here, although arising early in the twentieth century, are in large measure still characteristic of the psychology of religion today. The ideas of James, Freud, and Jung in particular are still widely cited and critiqued. Yet there have been notable developments in some of these approaches since the revival of the field following World War II. The statistical-empirical approach, for example, has become greatly elaborated through sophisticated quasi-experimental methods and complex statistical techniques, especially factor analysis, which has been the chief instrument for exploring the dimensionality of religious faith. One conspicuous outcome is a large number of questionnaires designed to measure religiousness, the most widely used of which is the Allport-Ross Religious Orientation Scale. This instrument was designed to distinguish the intrinsic religious orientation, the harmonizing of one's whole life with religious ideals, from the extrinsic one, the pragmatic use of religion for personal and social ends.

The psychoanalytic approach has similarly undergone further development, mainly under the influence of British object-relations theory and Erik Erikson's ego psychology, which together provide a more comprehensive and constructive view of religion than Freud offered. While acknowledging that religion is peculiarly vulnerable to various types of pathological distortion, the object-relations theorists argue that, at its best, religion serves to promote individual wholeness and positive emotional relations. And whereas Freud traced religion to the child's ambivalent attitude toward the father, the object-relation theorists find religion's earliest roots in the infant's positive relation with the mother. Erikson, too, featured this connection. Religion, he said, is the societal institution that confirms the first and most basic of the ego virtues, hope, which is the outcome of loving and trust-evoking care during infancy. In Erikson's schema, religious tradition also supports the attainment of ego integrity and the virtue of wisdom, the positive fruits of the eighth and final stage of development.

Postwar Perspectives

Some new perspectives emerged with the postwar revival. Particularly notable is the biological approach. Although Flournoy, among others, had argued at the turn of the century that the physiological conditions of religious phenomena should be identified whenever possible, only recently has the growing understanding of brain mechanisms allowed informed speculation about specific organic conditions of religious experience. For example, research on epilepsy and on brain lateralization suggests that the right temporal lobe is the site of mystical experience. Similarly, endorphins—opiate-like substances that occur naturally in the brain—are thought to be the causal link between ecstatic religious practices and the altered states of consciousness that often accompany them. Other perspectives that have come to be applied to religion in the modern period include behavior and social learning theories, which address the processes by which religious behavior may be acquired through interaction with the environment, and sociobiology, which brings an evolutionary perspective to bear on religious practices by considering the genetic advantages they may confer.

Also new in the second half of the twentieth century are the interpretations of religion offered by several prominent American humanistic psychologists. Sharing a highly positive view of human potential, these humanists have been chiefly interested in religion's role in its attainment. A typical strategy is to distinguish two types of religion, one that hinders the process of self-actualization and another that promotes it. Erich Fromm, for example, contrasts authoritarian religion with its humanistic counterpart, the first entailing self-deprecating surrender to a higher power and the second a joyful striving to achieve the higher self in a context of loving relations with the world. Fromm uses this typological framework to reflect on the history of the Jewish and Christian traditions and then to propose a new humanistic religiosity, which he says is the only viable alternative to the authoritarian trends that are leading humankind to catastrophe.

The distinction that Gordon Allport drew between intrinsic and extrinsic religious orientations was similarly inspired by the disturbing realization that religion is often associated with negative social attitudes. His conviction that the more genuine, intrinsic religious orientation is likely to show the opposite pattern is grounded in his conception of the mature religious sentiment, which he describes as (1) richly and complexly differentiated; (2) independent of its origins in childhood needs; (3) consistent in its moral consequences; (4) comprehensive in its unifying function; (5) well integrated into a whole; and (6) productive of energy and value commitments in spite of faith's inevitable uncertainties. Noting that the Allport-Ross Intrinsic Subscale does not encompass all six characteristics, Batson offered his Quest Scale as a complement to it, especially to incorporate the elements of complexity and tentativeness. Although criticized on various grounds, the Intrinsic and Extrinsic scales remain widely used today, sometimes in combination with the Quest Scale, to explore the ambiguous relation of religion to a variety of social attitudes and indicators of mental health.

Yet another distinction has been drawn by Abraham Maslow, who found that mystical, or peak, experiences were fairly common among the highly self-actualized persons he was studying. Taking these egoless episodes of awe and wonder and the values and insights associated with them to constitute the core of religion, Maslow maintains that the historic religious traditions have lost their anchoring in such experiences and instead have absolutized the symbols and rituals that may once have expressed these experiences. For Maslow, there are basically two types of religion, one that fosters the core religious experience, making it available for personal growth and fulfillment, and another that suppresses such experience and splits the sacred off from the human world. Maslow proposes that humanistic psychology may serve to promote the first of these types in the form of a naturalistic faith. Both Rollo May and Viktor Frankl likewise give psychology a role in forwarding the positive side of religion, especially the experiences of awe and meaning.

The number of scholars actively engaged in the psychology of religion continues to be relatively small, but they now represent a wider geographic and linguistic range than appeared in the field's inaugural period. Particularly notable is the research that has been undertaken in recent decades in the Netherlands and the Scandinavian countries, a portion of it inspired by the work of the late Swedish psychologist of religion Hjalmar Sundén, who is best known for his applications of role theory to religion. The growing international cooperation and exchange is reflected in the symposia that have been held every three years since 1979 by the informally organized European Psychologists of Religion, as well as by the appearance in 1991 of the *International Journal for the Psychology of Religion*. Articles by European scholars are likewise becoming increasingly common in the *Journal for the Scientific Study of Religion*, which has long been the leading journal for nonsectarian social-scientific research on religion. Discussion of the difficult methodological and philosophical issues that are raised by the psychology of religion also continues internationally.

Bibliography

Batson, C. D., Schoenrade, P., & Ventis, W. L. (1993). *Religion and the individual: A social-psychological perspective.* New York: Oxford University Press. Although it treats some traditional topics, such as religious development, this work is centered on the distinction among three "dimensions" of individual religion—extrinsic, intrinsic, and quest—and their consequences for personal adjustment and concern for others.

Belzen, J. A., & Wikström, O. (Eds.). (1997). *Taking a step back: Assessments of the psychology of religion.* Uppsala: Acta Universitatis Upsaliensis. An international collection of essays on the problems and prospects of the psychology of religion.

Hood, R. W., Jr. (Ed.). (1995). *Handbook of religious experience.* Birmingham, AL: Religious Education Press. Mainly useful for the various psychological perspectives that are brought to bear on religious experience.

Hood, R. W., Jr., Spilka, B., Hunsberger, B., & Gorsuch, R. (1996). *The psychology of religion: An empirical approach* (2nd ed.). New York: Guilford Press. An exhaustive survey of the English-language empirical literature encompassing such classic topics as religious development, mysticism, and conversion, as well as contemporary research on attitudes toward death, the social psychology of religious organizations, and religion and mental adjustment.

Hyde, Kenneth E. (1990). *Religion in childhood and adolescence: A comprehensive review of the research.* Birmingham, AL: Religious Education Press. With approximately two thousand references, this is the most comprehensive work available on religious development in the first two decades of life. It also evaluates the religious influence of schools and includes nine appendices on technical issues.

James, W. (1902/1985). *The varieties of religious experience: A study in human nature.* Cambridge, MA: Harvard University Press. A volume in *The Works of William James,* this is the definitive edition of the great classic in the psychology of religion. Contains an introduction by John E. Smith and 216 pages of supplementary material.

Otto, R. (1917/1950). *The idea of the holy: An inquiry into the non-rational factor in the idea of the divine and its relation to the rational.* (J. W. Harvey, Trans.). London: Oxford University Press, 1923; 2nd ed., 1950. (First German edition 1917)

Pargament, K. I. (1997). *The psychology of religion and coping: Theory, research, practice.* New York: Guilford Press. Explores the various ways in which religious commitment may be either helpful or harmful in the complex process of coping with life crises. Much of the evidence cited in this work comes out of the author's own research group, which uses a combination of objective and subjective methods.

Pratt, J. B. (1920).*The religious consciousness: A psychological study.* New York: Macmillan. This mainly descriptive work is second only to James's *Varieties* in terms of longevity and importance in the psychology of religion. An authority on Eastern religious traditions, Pratt is famous for his extraordinary sensitivity to the subtleties of religious experience.

Wulff, D. M. (1985). Psychological approaches. In F. Whaling (Ed.), *Contemporary approaches to the study of religion: Volume 2. The social sciences* (pp. 21–88). Berlin: Mouton. Useful especially for its discussion of research methods and fundamental issues in the psychology of religion.

Wulff, D. M. (1997). *Psychology of religion: Classic and contemporary.* New York: Wiley. A comprehensive survey and critique of the psychology of religion, in the United States and abroad, from its beginnings in the nineteenth century to the present. Organized in terms of psychological perspectives, both objective and subjective, this work provides references to more than 2,000 publications.

David M. Wulff

Theories and Methods

The relationship of Western psychological science to religion has been largely unidirectional and typically has taken one of three forms. First, psychology of religion has focused on religious experience as an object of study. Second, psychological findings or theories of each of the major historic paradigms of the field have been used to revise, reinterpret, redefine, supplant, or dismiss established religious traditions, as seen in the work of such luminaries as Sigmund Freud, Carl Jung, B. F. Skinner, Carl Rogers, and Roger Sperry, and in some evolutionary psychology theorists. Third, psychologists have supplied psychological information to guide the practice of pastoral care, and have provided psychological services to and for religious individuals and communities.

Each of these forms of relationship establishes unique domains of discourse, but they share a particular perspective in which psychology regards religion—or better, religious experiences, beliefs, practices, systems, and institutions—as objects of study. The heritage of modern psychology in the Enlightenment has constrained it to identify itself narrowly in terms of a particular understanding of science with definite implications for how it should relate to religion as an object of study. But religion and psychology can and do relate in ways that transcend these unidimensional and objectified modes. These possibilities can be perceived and understood only from the vantage point of substantially broadened perspectives on both religion and psychology.

Throughout the bulk of recorded human history, the psychology of the day has been intimately intertwined with religious and philosophical systems. Comprehensive texts on the history of psychology discuss Platonic, Aristotelian, Hebraic, and Christian psychologies, each of which seamlessly connected conceptualizations of the functioning of the human self with understandings of material existence and some ultimate context for that existence. At about the time that Augustine and Pope Gregory the Great in the Christian tradition were developing still more sophisticated conceptualizations, Buddhist thinkers such as Buddhaghosa and Vasubandhu (fourth to fifth centuries CE) were developing sophisticated taxonomies for understanding psychological states and the human personality. At the cusp of the Enlightenment, American writers in the Puritan pietistic tradition, notably Jonathan Edwards and Richard Baxter, were developing theologically and philosophically sophisticated psychologies that were also grounded in careful "clinical" observation of those suffering from psychological maladies.

Most psychologists, however, give little credence to such psychologies because they lack grounding in science as it came to be understood as a result of the Enlightenment. But our understanding of both religion and psychology has been shaped by the Enlightenment. Understanding the intellectual climate of the Enlightenment aids in understanding the contemporary perspective that has amplified the differences between and obscured the common ground shared by psychology and religion.

The Enlightenment and Its Impact on Psychology

The Enlightenment can be described briefly as an intellectual movement demonstrating great confidence in human reason's capacity to discover timeless and universal truth in the form of quantifiable laws in all areas of inquiry, and hence to enhance human well-being and generate cultural progress. This search for certainty was to be grounded in foundational truths (facts) that would have no connection to values. The Scientific Revolution of the seventeenth century, it was understood, had taught the value of setting aside received tradition and using sustained, rational inquiry based on absolute certainties garnered by empirical observation to grasp absolute truths of universal scope.

Whereas natural science had begun to accomplish these goals in the study of the natural world, Enlightenment thought anticipated that similar successes were possible in all areas of concern, including ethics, political science, and psychology. The seeds of the Enlightenment germinated in the seventeenth century in the writings of Descartes, Locke, and others. The movement continued to gain force during the nineteenth and early twentieth centuries. Immanuel Kant had a profound influence on the German universities of his day, the very universities that determined the early shape of

the field of psychology. Indeed, psychology's rapid advance as a discipline paralleled almost exactly the cresting of the strength of the Enlightenment. Generally speaking, modern Western psychology exemplifies the Enlightenment mindset in its repudiation of tradition (both religious and philosophical authorities), its search for universal laws of human behavior, and its unbounded confidence in its capacity to enhance human welfare through widespread application of the products of its scientific inquiries.

The Impact of the Enlightenment on Religion

The Enlightenment had two major impacts on religion, each with important implications for psychology's relationship to religion. The first has to do with the very concept of "religion," and the second concerns the relationship of religion to science.

It is now widely understood that the concepts of "religion" and the "religions" did not exist before the Enlightenment. Given the Enlightenment prejudice in favor of the universal, it is no wonder that interest grew in the eighteenth and nineteenth centuries in the universal reality or genus ("religion") that was presumed to be behind the particularistic façade or particular species (what came to be called the "religions"). The term "religion" came to stand for a universal human capacity that was presumed to transcend particular religious institutions and traditions. Kant, in *Religion Within the Limits of Reason Alone* (New York, 1960/1793), asserted that whatever religion is, it is universally accessible to human reason, and is a universal human potential rather than the product of the independent action of a deity or a function of particular traditions.

Such a construal of religion has profound implications for relations between psychology and religion, as an analysis of a prototypical work will illustrate. *The Varieties of Religious Experience: A Study in Human Nature*, by William James (Cambridge, Mass., 1902/1985), is the most widely read work in the psychology of religion. Nicholas Lash (*Easter in Ordinary: Reflections on Human Experience and the Knowledge of God*, Notre Dame, Ind., 1988) argues that James utilized a definition of religion grounded in Enlightenment thought for the *Varieties* that determined the results of his project. He sought to study pure and universal religious experience, downplayed the cognitive element in religious experience, and presumed that this pure religious experience is necessarily mystical and occurs in solitude. Through the filter of this limiting definition, James examined the religious experience of a selective sample of accomplished males chosen for their lack of connection to religious institutions. James reported that the experience of true religion, so defined, shows remarkable uniformity, concluding, "When we survey the whole field of religion, we find a great variety in the thoughts that have prevailed there; but the feelings on the one hand and the conduct on the other are almost always the same, for Stoic, Christian and Buddhist saints are practically indistinguishable in their lives" (1902/1985, p. 397).

Much of the work relating psychology and religion in the twentieth century, at the broadest level, has resembled James's work in the *Varieties* in its search for a distinctive essence of religion or religious experience that is somehow behind or beneath more particular religions or religious experiences. Implicit in this approach is a reduction of the many appearances and expressions of religious sentiment, affiliation, and practice to an assumed universal religious consciousness that is conceptualized purely in terms of naturalistic processes and events. There is, however, no neutral vantage point from which psychological science may make judgments about what constitutes authentic religious experience, no position independent of a religious tradition or of personal religious commitments from which one can form an objective view of religious experience.

In addition to its impact on the understanding of religion itself, the Enlightenment had a substantial impact on the relationship of religion to science. While allowing religious sentiment in the subjective realm, the Enlightenment called for the rejection of religious authority and tradition, especially that of the Christian church, as a precondition for or aid to acquiring knowledge. Partially in an attempt to overthrow ecclesiastical control of higher education in England and the United States, such late-nineteenth-century propagandists as John William Draper argued that the relationship of religion and science had been, throughout history, one of bitter and intrinsic strife. This erroneous construal of the historical record nevertheless was effective as a rationale for driving traditional religion from the academy, and is commonly accepted as reality by psychologists and other scientists.

Scholars have documented, however, that in some instances, proponents of the "conflict metaphor" have fabricated conflicts where there were none, interpreted as science-religion conflict that which was really ecclesiastical conflict, and interpreted unidimensionally as science-religion conflict what was really conflict arising in a complex and multidimensional context. Conflict aside, religion actually has played a set of complex and multifaceted roles in the rise of modern science. John H. Brooke in *Science and Religion: Some Historical Perspectives* (Cambridge, England, 1991) argued that religion facilitated the development of modern science during and after the Scientific Revolution in important ways and that it should not be assumed that "when religious beliefs have functioned as primitive science, it has always been to the detriment of further inquiry" (1991, p. 29).

Proponents of an Enlightenment vision of science nonetheless sought to establish its influence in part by defining it in opposition to religious sentiment and theological discourse. This stance came to dominate and perhaps define modernity and continues today during the postmodern epoch. Once religion has been driven from a position of authority or even participation in the quest for human knowing that we call science, it can be kept isolated as an object of inquiry by construing it as fundamentally different from science or even rationality. When religion is presumed to be only about faith, values, subjectivity, significance, the nonrational, the trans-logical, feeling, or privatized and idiosyncratic meaning, religion can and will have little possible connection to science, especially when science is construed as a matter of brute facts unencumbered by human interpretation and discovered and assembled into theoretical systems by objective and depersonalized rules of inquiry. This is a flawed characterization of both science and religion. Science necessarily involves metaphysical assumptions, as most contemporary reflection in the philosophy of science shows, and religious belief and experience are often constructed on certain types of what are taken to be facts and on rationally defensible logic. That there actually is some tension between science and the religions is testimony to the fact that there is at least some degree of overlap between them. Both enterprises involve, in part and at the broadest levels, the attempt to understand everything there is.

Psychology and Religion

The literature on the relationship between psychology and religion includes significant contributions in each of the aforementioned traditional, Enlightenment-driven forms for relating science and religion. The psychology of religion, for the most part, has concerned the application of psychological theory and method to the study of religious experience. As one example, scales such as Allport and Ross's Intrinsic-Extrinsic Scale have been developed to provide a means to measure presumably universal dimensions of religious orientation. Many psychological theorists have approached religion with the aim of applying their conceptual and methodological tools to religious experience. This inevitably results in the deconstruction of religious experience into preexisting theory-driven categories derived from the metaphysical belief systems on which their particular psychological paradigm is founded. Sigmund Freud, for example, considered the origin of religious sentiment to be found in infantile helplessness and the belief in God to be anchored in Oedipal psychodynamics. Religious experience was apprehended within the conceptual limits of the paradigm and reduced to categories that were privileged within that paradigm. Efforts to understand religious experience within the perspective of psychology pose the challenge of applying models from one paradigm to another while preserving the integrity of both worldviews.

Psychology has also interfaced with religion through the infusion of psychological knowledge and theory into pastoral care, and by providing direct clinical services to religious individuals and communities. Pastoral counseling has benefited from these provisions but has typically not been an equal participant in the dialogue about the meaning of human personality and behavior. Textbooks such as the *Clinical Handbook of Pastoral Counseling*, edited by Robert J. Wicks, Richard D. Parsons, and Donald Capps (New York, 1993), illustrate the wide range of human maladies addressed within pastoral care that have integrated contributions from psychology.

A fourth type of interaction between psychology and religion is beginning to emerge, one in which religious experience, concepts, and even institutions are respected participants in the conversation about human experience. There is actually an extensive if underacknowledged literature in the history of psychology that models a true dialogue between psychology and religion. Hendrika Vande Kemp summarizes a history of integration in which this dialogue became formalized through the establishment of professional societies and journals, the appearance of degree programs and professorships, and the emergence of literature and textbooks ("Historical perspective: Religion and clinical psychology in America," pp. 71–112, in E. P. Shafranske, Ed., *Religion and the Clinical Practice of Psychology*, Washington, D.C., 1996). Further, some contributors to the psychological literature, such as Rollo May, Viktor Frankl, and James Hillman, have examined the existential dimension of psychological theory and practice. These authors, although not writing specifically on religion, nevertheless contribute to the discussion of the interface of psychology and religion and demonstrate clinically the close relations between the psychological and religious constructions of meaning. Respected clinical psychologists such as Allen Bergin are advancing this dialogue through the introduction of careful analyses of the impact of the psychotherapist's and client's values on the therapeutic process and through explicit and respectful discussion of spiritual values.

What will be required to advance this fourth type of relationship between religion and psychology, in which the religions are partners in discussions rather than objects of study? First, psychology as a discipline and profession must develop greater awareness of and respect for religious faiths and spiritual traditions. The ethical code of the American Psychological Association calls for sensitivity to and respect for religious and creedal diversity among people; however, this goal has not been fully achieved given the lack of training in diversity offered in most graduate training programs.

Respect for the religious dimension will be achieved not through learning about a reified construct of "religion/spirituality" based on psychological theory alone, but through gaining an understanding of the religious experiences, beliefs, values, morality, practices, and institutions of religious persons. The best understandings of religion are multidimensional and recognize that certain dimensions of some religions will not be present in or relevant to others.

Essential to this constructive dialogue is respect for belief in a transcendent reality, which is the central feature of religious experience, religions, and spiritual traditions. In their examinations of religious experience as a subjective phenomenon, psychologists commonly assume that the stimulus for religious experience is utterly of natural origins, whether those origins are biochemical, cognitive, psychodynamic, social psychological, or cultural in origin. But if there is a supernatural agency or realm, then it may be that God did speak to Moses out of the burning bush, or that Jesus did die on a cross only to triumph over death by rising to live again, or that Allah did speak his will to Mohammed, or that Buddha really did achieve enlightenment and determine the best path to achieving that enlightenment for all persons. If any of these claims are true, then there are likely other, nonnatural stimuli for religious experience and belief.

Second, beyond an external appreciation for religion, this analysis opens the possibility for a more cooperative dialogue between religion and psychology as a science. All science is conducted in the context of an array of metaphysical background beliefs that are often unarticulated and that are relevant to but not directly accessible to empirical testing. In areas of psychology closer to the natural sciences such metaphysical assumptions may be noncontroversial and less intrusive, but at the other extreme, personality and clinical psychology, along with aspects of other social sciences, are inescapably hermeneutical. An explicit dialogue with religion, as well as with philosophy, may sharpen the conceptual analyses and the assumptions on which they are grounded and thus improve the empirical examinations that are conducted.

This same principle applies yet more definitively in applied psychology. Don Browning in *Religious Thought and the Modern Psychologies* (Philadelphia, 1987) convincingly argues that psychotherapy systems that guide the reform of human life cannot avoid metaphysics or ethics; they necessarily go beyond the typical limits of scientific theories to answer or at least address questions of ultimate meaning and of human obligation. Even the most discrete, empirically validated anxiety intervention (or the clinician delivering the service) has some implicit answer for such questions as why the anxiety experienced is bad rather than good, what role the anxiety plays in the broader life of the client, and why the client should move in the direction offered by the therapeutic intervention. Psychologists benefit by having some knowledge of the many efforts being made by scholars in other disciplines and by religious psychologists to advance this dialogue between their disciplines and religion.

Third, understanding religion and spiritual practices provides insight into healing, coping, and change processes. Jerome Frank long ago spoke of the potency of human change processes, but he compared plodding psychological processes to the explosive potential for change associated with religious conversion and other spiritual processes. Empirical evidence is steadily accumulating that religious faith and practice is a potent change catalyst even in the realm of physical healing.

An examination of the discourse between psychology and religion leads to the conclusion that there is no neutral vantage point from which we can provide objective answers to the most important questions that face us. The Enlightenment, which produced psychology as we usually conceive of it today, is itself a tradition in much the same way that a particular historic religion is a tradition. The dialogue between psychology and religion concerns an inquiry into the inherent assumptions on which knowledge of the self and the world is formulated. The resulting literature includes both a psychology of religion in which religion is understood within the categories of psychology and a conversation between psychology and religion in which the unique approaches and traditions of each domain are given an equal voice.

Bibliography

Works on the Enlightenment and Intellectual History

MacIntyre, A. (1990). *Three rival versions of moral enquiry: Encyclopaedia, genealogy, and tradition.* Notre Dame, IN: University of Notre Dame Press.

Toulmin, S. (1990). *Cosmopolis: The hidden agenda of modernity.* Chicago: University of Chicago Press.

These are two important discussions of the impact and limitations of the Enlightenment and of our current position in intellectual history. Note that for MacIntyre, psychology is a form of moral inquiry.

Works on the Enlightenment and Religion

Harrison, P. (1990). *"Religion" and the religions in the English Enlightenment.* Cambridge: Cambridge University Press.

Smith, W. C. (1991). *The meaning and end of religion.* Minneapolis: Fortress Press. (Originally published 1962)

These are two seminal discussions of how the very concept of "religion" was a product of the Enlightenment.

Works on Religion, Science, and the Enlightenment

Lindberg, D. C. (1992). *The beginning of Western science: The European scientific tradition in philosophical, religious, and institutional context, 600 B.C. to A.D. 1450.* Chicago: University of Chicago Press.

Lindberg, D. C., & Numbers, R. L. (Eds.). (1986). *God and nature: Historical essays on the encounter between Christianity and science.* Berkeley: University of California Press.

Excellent resources for a fair understanding of the complex relationship of science and religion in historical perspective, and for understanding the development and influence of the Enlightenment.

Works on Religion and Science

Barbour, I. (1990). *Religion in an age of science: Gifford Lectures, 1989–91, Vol. 1.* New York: HarperCollins. A good summary of the impact of our contemporary understandings of science on science's relationship to religion.

Jones, S. (1994). A constructive relationship for religion with the science and profession of psychology: Perhaps the boldest model yet. *American Psychologist, 49*(3), 184–199. Contains some of the arguments advanced here in expanded form.

Marsden, G. (1997). *The outrageous idea of Christian scholarship.* New York: Oxford University Press. An informed and irenic defense of, justification for, and examination of faith informed academic scholarship in a number of disciplines from a widely respected historian. Written from a Christian perspective, Marsden's arguments are logically applicable to any religious faith perspective.

Shafranske, E. P. (Ed.). (1996). *Religion and the clinical practice of psychology.* Washington, DC: American Psychological Association. The best collection of resources for a wide-ranging discussion of religion and psychology.

Smart, N. (1993). *The world's religions: Old traditions and modern transformations.* Cambridge: Cambridge University Press. One of the many survey texts on world religions, but one that is fairer than many in respecting the uniqueness of each tradition.

Stanton L. Jones

RELIGION AND PSYCHOTHERAPY. [*This entry comprises two articles. The first article provides an overview of religious and spiritual aspects of the psychotherapeutic experience and of the function of religion in providing a belief system that assuages anxiety. The second article examines the religious and spiritual beliefs of psychologists. For a general discussion of psychotherapy, see* Psychotherapy. *See also* Christianity and Psychology; Eastern Religions and Philosophies; Islam and Psychology; Judaism and Psychology; *and* Pastoral Counseling.]

An Overview

Psychotherapy and religion actually have much in common despite historical views emphasizing their mutual antagonism. Both intend to shape personal meaning and behavior. As Perry London pointed out in *The Modes and Morals of Psychotherapy* (New York, 1964), psychotherapy cannot avoid dealing with beliefs, morals, and values. It is, in fact, infused with values. London asserted that psychotherapists serve two functions: a scientific function as manipulators of behavior and a moralistic function akin to that of a secular priesthood. Because psychotherapy essentially involves elaborating and giving meanings to human experience, it necessarily concerns beliefs, morals, and values. Psychological treatments that utilize the interpretation of human experience (such as psychoanalysis) inherently involve beliefs and can be seen to function in ways very similar to those found in religion. Psychotherapy has even been described as a "religious process" (with a short-lived journal named the *Journal of Psychotherapy as a Religious Process* in the 1950s).

Religion is fundamentally concerned with articulating meanings of human experience. Kenneth Pargament in *The Psychology of Religion and Coping: Theory, Research, Practice* (New York, 1997) defined religion as a search for significance in ways that are related to the sacred, and spirituality as a search for the sacred, so that spirituality can be viewed as the core or central function of religion. A measure of mutuality can be found in psychotherapy and religion in light of their interest in and influence on personal meaning and behavior.

Jerome Frank emphasized in *Persuasion and Healing* (Baltimore, 1973) that psychotherapy involves the process of interpersonal persuasion in which the client adopts a worldview with values and meanings that provide hope to overcome the common condition of demoralization affecting all clients. Psychotherapy therefore is seen to be very similar to other indigenous forms of healing present in certain cultures, such as spiritual healing and shamanism. Conversely, such indigenous and alternative ways of healing can be viewed as forms of psychotherapy because they provide hope to the demoralized person who is seeking help or healing.

In the last two decades, much work has been done to integrate religion or religious values and interventions more specifically with psychotherapy. Several notable books have been published in which attention has focused on the relationship between religion and psychotherapy in consideration of the value-based nature of the treatment process. There have also been books dealing more specifically with particular religions such as Christianity, Judaism, Islam, and Buddhism and their relationship to psychotherapy, or with specific schools of therapy such as psychoanalysis, behavior therapy, and cognitive therapy and their integration with religion or spirituality. In addition, research has been conducted on psychologists' religious beliefs and practices compared to those of the general population.

Religion in Clinical Practice

The actual use of religion in clinical practice or psychotherapy can be described in terms of two major models viewed as ends of a continuum: implicit and explicit integration. I have described these models in "Religion in Clinical Practice: Implicit and Explicit Integration" (in E. P. Shafranske [Ed.], *Religion and the Clinical Practice of Psychology*, Washington, D.C., 1996):

> *Implicit integration* of religion in clinical practice refers to a more covert approach that does not initiate the discussion of religious or spiritual issues and does not openly, directly, or systematically use spiritual resources like prayer and Scripture or other sacred texts. . . . *Explicit integration* . . . refers to a more overt approach that directly and systematically deals with spiritual or religious issues in therapy, and uses spiritual resources like prayer, Scripture or sacred texts, referrals to church or other religious groups or lay counselors, and other religious practices. (1996, p. 368)

Whether a therapist practices implicit or explicit integration or moves along the continuum between the two models depends first of all on the needs and interests of the client, and also on the therapist's own theoretical orientation, religious beliefs or values, personal spirituality, and clinical training. For example, explicit integration may be adopted more easily by cognitive-behavioral than psychoanalytic therapists, although the latter have also begun to deal more directly with religious issues in therapy. However, every psychologist, mindful of the Ethical Principles of Psychologists and Code of Conduct of the American Psychological Association (APA), needs to be sensitive to religion as a feature of diversity in clinical practice. The American Psychiatric Association now includes religious or spiritual problems in the *Diagnostic and Statistical Manual of Mental Disorders* (4th ed., Washington, D.C., 1994) as a V code (V 62.89). Such problems, although not defined as mental disorders, can include troubling experiences involving questioning or loss of faith, difficulties related to conversion to a new faith, or struggling with spiritual values that are not necessarily related to an organized religious institution. On the other hand, religion can, of course, also be experienced by a client in ways that may be pathological or negative. Whether religion is perceived or experienced as good or bad, positive or negative, constructive or destructive, it is nevertheless a crucial factor in the psychological functioning of many individuals.

Implicit Integration in Psychotherapy

Implicit integration does not include the use of religious or spiritual resources, nor does it place emphasis on forms of religious or spiritual discernment or counseling. Implicit integration acknowledges the value-laden nature of the psychotherapeutic process and identifies efforts to understand or construct personal meaning as constituting a form of integration. Forms of depth psychology, such as psychoanalysis, analytical psychology, existential-humanistic psychology, and transpersonal psychology, often include consideration of religious or spiritual systems of belief, representations of the sacred, values, and morality. Implicit integration includes inquiry into meaning, regardless of whether that meaning is readily identifiable with a particular religious tradition.

Explicit Integration in Psychotherapy

A crucial part of explicit integration involves the use of religious and spiritual resources in psychotherapy. P. Scott Richards and Allen E. Bergin (1997) have provided the following examples of various religious and spiritual interventions: therapist prayer, teaching spiritual concepts, reference to Scripture, spiritual self-disclosure, spiritual confrontation, spiritual assessment, religious relaxation or imagery, therapist and client prayer, blessing by a therapist, encouraging forgiveness, use of a religious community, client prayer, encouraging client confession, referral for blessing, religious journal writing, spiritual meditation, religious bibliotherapy, and Scripture memorization.

Several studies of Christian therapists in particular have shown that the most commonly used religious or spiritual interventions include prayer in different forms, teaching or quoting from Scripture, forgiveness, spiritual history, discernment, and solitude or silence. A specific example of the use of prayer is "inner healing prayer or healing of memories." Healing of memories is particularly relevant with clients who have suffered past hurts or childhood traumas that remain unresolved, and are therefore still very painful emotionally in such a way that the clients feel paralyzed or in bondage.

The following is a seven-step model described by Tan (in Shafranske, 1996, pp. 372–374) for the healing of memories or inner healing prayer:

1. Begin with prayer for God's healing and protection.
2. Conduct brief relaxation training to help the client relax as deeply as possible.
3. Guide the client in using imagery to go back to the past painful memory (which the client has previously shared openly and clearly, so there is no digging out of so-called repressed memories) and relive it.
4. After sufficient time has gone by, the therapist prays for God to provide healing grace and love to the client in whatever way is needed or appropriate. The therapist refrains from making too many specific suggestions at this time.
5. There is a period of waiting and letting go, being receptive to whatever inner healing may be experienced. The therapist will periodically ask the client,

"What's happening? What are you experiencing or feeling now?"
6. Both therapist and client then close the time of healing of memories with prayer, usually including thanksgiving.
7. The final step is reviewing the experience with the client.

A similar healing of memories intervention that makes greater use of specific religious guided imagery has also been described in a religiously oriented version of cognitive-behavioral therapy developed by Rebecca Propst.

The issue of "exorcism," or prayer for deliverance from evil spirits or demons, may come up in the context of religious psychotherapy. The therapist who practices explicit integration will need to decide whether to engage in such prayer if needed, or whether a referral of the client to a pastor or religious leader who may have more experience in dealing with situations of apparent demonization may be more appropriate or judicious.

Explicit integration of religious resources in psychotherapy also often involves teaching or quoting from Scripture or sacred texts. This should be done in a clinically sensitive way so that the therapist openly discusses with the client the meanings of specific texts, rather than stating in an authoritarian and controlling way what the client should believe about the texts. The therapist should know such texts and their interpretations well enough to engage in helpful discussions with the client. Referrals to religious groups (e.g., support groups, small groups, youth groups, 12-step groups) or religious lay counselors are other examples of the explicit use of religious resources in psychotherapy. These possible referrals should be carefully made to meet the needs of the clients. Particular attention should be paid to making an appropriate match between a religious group or lay counselor and the client.

Explicit integration often involves dealing with spiritual issues in psychotherapy. Such spiritual issues may include broad concerns like the search for meaning or direction in life, values clarification, and the fear of death. They may also include more specific issues like moral failures, sins, doubts, struggles with guilt, bitterness, an unforgiving spirit, spiritual dryness or emptiness, and even possible demonization. Again, these issues should be discussed gently and respectfully with the client. Timing or pacing is crucial. For some severely disturbed clients, it may be better to postpone dealing with difficult religious issues until the client's emotional state is more stabilized.

Explicit integration also focuses on the development of the spirituality of both therapist and client. The practice of particular spiritual disciplines by the therapist and client is often encouraged. Spiritual disciplines include practices such as meditation, prayer, fasting, study, simplicity, solitude, submission, service, confession, worship, guidance, and celebration, and more generally taking personal retreats or attending special conferences or retreats for spiritual growth.

Religion and psychotherapy, of course, involves religions other than Christianity and Judaism. Buddhism, for example, has affected some forms of psychotherapy that emphasize the need for acceptance and not necessarily the goal of change. Transcendental meditation and other meditation techniques have also been incorporated in various therapies aimed at reducing tension, anxiety, and stress. A number of alternative or newer therapies have therefore recently sprung up based on Eastern mysticism, the occult, and New Age religions or philosophies. Religion broadly defined includes all of these approaches.

Faith healing is a term often used to describe interventions for healing that call on the exercising of faith in God or a Higher Power on the part of both the therapist and the client. Prayer is often the means used, although other religious rituals (e.g., use of anointing oil or holy water) can also be included. Isaac Marks in "Behavioral Psychotherapy of Adult Neurosis" (in S. L. Garfield & A. E. Bergin, Eds., *Handbook of Psychotherapy and Behavior Change: An Empirical Analysis*, 2nd ed., New York, 1978), after reviewing a documented case of transsexualism that showed a dramatic and complete cure after only two sessions of faith healing compared to typically poor results of behavior therapy with such cases, commented that when faith healing works, it has a power far greater than that of existing psychotherapy interventions. He described the difference as that between nuclear and more conventional explosives. However dramatically the result is stated in this instance, the problem remains how to tap into the power of faith healing so that it can be used more consistently. Marks therefore challenged researchers or experimenters to study this phenomenon more thoroughly.

In addition to the obvious need for better and more research in this area of religion and psychotherapy, it is important to practice religious psychotherapy ethically. Ethical guidelines must include obtaining the informed consent of the client and not forcing the therapist's religious values or interventions on the client. Therapists should also obtain appropriate training, supervision, or consultation in the area of religion in clinical practice so that they practice in a professionally competent, clinically sensitive way and remain ethical and effective.

Three specific terms need to be defined and briefly discussed: Christian counseling, pastoral counseling, and spiritual direction. *Christian counseling* is a specific example of religious psychotherapy conducted from a Christian religious perspective. It can include both implicit and explicit integration. *Pastoral counseling* has two distinctive meanings. It can refer generally to counseling or helping people by pastors or church leaders or it can mean more specifically counseling by pastoral counselors who have received special training at the graduate level in pastoral counseling and psychotherapy that includes a definite spiritual or pastoral dimension. The American Association of Pastoral Counselors (AAPC) certifies such pastoral counselors, whereas pastors who counsel their parishioners are not usually certified pastoral counselors. Pastors often do not have advanced graduate degrees in counseling. *Spiritual direction* refers to the process of providing spiritual guidance to a person whose primary interest and focus is on growing and deepening his or her relationship with God, and not the alleviation of symptoms or problems per se. In religious psychotherapy, there is a certain degree of overlap among these three areas, although they are not synonymous.

Psychotherapeutic Ideas and Practice in Organized Religion

Psychotherapeutic ideas and practice have also impacted organized religion. Many churches and religious organizations now have counseling centers or ministries, either lay or professional. Also, 12-step programs that refer to a Higher Power more specifically (e.g., God or Jesus), as well as traditional 12-step programs for helping alcoholics, drug addicts, and others, are common in churches and other religious institutions. Many of them also have other support groups, so that they have become "therapeutic communities," with some churches preaching the gospel of "self-esteem." These developments have both positive and negative aspects. Some critics have demanded that churches and organized religion return to their foundational role as places of worship rather than being so influenced by secular psychotherapy that they ironically end up being a "secular priesthood" as well.

It may be concluded that the integration of religion and psychotherapy is an important area within applied psychology. Overall, it is a constructive and positive development in the field of psychotherapy because religion is a crucial aspect of human experience and diversity. However, more and better training, clinical experience, supervision, consultation, and empirical and qualitative research to assess the efficacy of efforts at integration, as well as theory building in this area, are required for the ultimate welfare and well-being of clients.

Bibliography

Barry, W. A., & Connolly, W. J. (1982). *The practice of spiritual direction*. San Francisco: HarperSanFrancisco. A well-known introduction to the practice of spiritual direction.

Jones, S. (1994). A constructive relationship for religion with the science and profession of psychology: Perhaps the boldest model yet. *American Psychologist, 49,* 184–199. An important article focusing on how religion can be integrated constructively with both the science and the professional practice of psychology.

Kelly, E. W. (1995). *Religion and spirituality in counseling and psychotherapy.* Alexandria, VA: American Counseling Association. A helpful introduction to the integration of religion and spirituality, broadly defined, and counseling practice.

Lovinger, R. J. (1984). *Working with religious issues in therapy.* Northvale, NJ: Jason Aronson. Deals with religious issues in psychotherapy, with a helpful discussion of countertransference issues.

Propst, R. L. (1988). *Psychotherapy in a religious framework: Spirituality in the emotional healing process.* New York: Human Sciences Press. A well-known, religiously oriented, Christian version of cognitive-behavior therapy.

Richards, P. S., & Bergin, A. E. (1997). *A spiritual strategy for counseling and psychotherapy.* Washington, DC: American Psychological Association. A comprehensive and ecumenical text on a spiritual, theistic approach to counseling and psychotherapy.

Shafranske, E. P. (Ed.). (1996). *Religion and the clinical practice of psychology.* Washington, DC: American Psychological Association. A text that has become a best-seller on religion and clinical practice or psychotherapy.

Tan, S. Y. (1994). Ethical considerations in religious psychotherapy: Potential pitfalls and unique resources. *Journal of Psychology and Theology, 22,* 389–394. An important article on practicing religious psychotherapy in an ethical, effective, and efficient way.

Worthington, E. L., Jr., Kurusu, T. A., McCullough, M. E., & Sandage, S. J. (1996). Empirical research on religion and psychotherapeutic processes and outcomes: A 10 year review and research prospectus. *Psychological Bulletin, 119,* 448–487. A key review article on a decade of empirical research in the area of religion and psychotherapy, with directions for future research.

Siang-Yang Tan

Beliefs and Training of Psychotherapists

The process and outcome of psychological treatment is influenced by many factors including objective (i.e., age, sex, ethnicity) and subjective (i.e., emotional well being, values, attitudes, and beliefs) therapist variables. The therapeutic process is shaped by both the values implicit within theoretical orientation and by the personal beliefs of the psychotherapist. It has been posited therefore that clinicians draw upon both professional and personal sources in their conduct of psychological treatment. In light of this observation, Allen E. Bergin concluded in 1991 in "Values and Religious Issues in Psychotherapy and Mental Health" (*American Psychologist, 46,* 394–403) that the notion that psychotherapy is value free or value neutral was no longer tenable. Further, the Ethical Principles of Psychologists and the Code of Conduct of the American Psychological Association (APA) (Washington, D.C., 1992) directs psychologists to take into consideration cultural, individual, and role differences, including those that are due to religion, as they affect treatment and to develop competence respective to features of diversity. These now widely held views have encouraged consideration of the role of beliefs and values within the therapeutic process, including those of a religious and spiritual nature, and have stimulated empirical inquiry into the personal and professional variables that influence clinicians' approaches to spirituality and religiosity as clinically relevant features of diversity.

Religious Preference, Affiliation, Practice, and Belief

An examination of the features of religious and spiritual belief and involvement provide a means to consider personal religiosity and to compare clinicians to the general population (to which they provide psychological treatment). Surveys of psychologists and other mental health professionals have consistently identified points of difference and similarity. Education has been found to influence the degree of salience afforded religion. Almost 9 out of 10 Americans consider religion to be important; however, those holding baccalaureate and advanced degrees are less likely to find religion to be very important. Scientists and academicians have been reported to be less religious than the general population. This is particularly the case for clinical and counseling psychologists in which less than one third report religion to be very important and more than one third report religion to be not very important. Fifty percent of psychology faculty report "none" on surveys of religious preference and are among the least religiously affiliated within the academy and among the mental health professions. Surveys of clinical and counseling psychologists find however that approximately 70% report some degree of religious affiliation. For those reporting religious preference, Judaism appears to be overrepresented, and Catholicism and Protestantism are underrepresented (in comparison to the U.S. population). Marriage and family therapists and clinical social workers appear to have higher rates of religious preference and affiliation; psychiatrists appear to be more similar to clinical psychologists.

Associated with salience and religious preference is religious involvement. Survey data suggest that approximately 40 to 45% of psychologist clinicians report regular to active participation in religion. Twenty-eight percent attended church or synagogue during the 7 days prior to the administration of a survey as compared to 42% in a national poll. Whereas almost three quarters of Americans report that their whole approach to life is based on religion, less than half of that number or about one third of clinical psychologists hold that position. The assessment of religious salience, preference, affiliation, and involvement suggests that psychologists are less committed to and involved in organized religion than the U.S. public; these differences appear to be related to the degree of affiliation and salience in institutional religiosity rather than in consideration of spiritual issues.

Turning from institutional forms of religiosity to questions of fundamental beliefs and spirituality, some fundamental differences can be identified between psychologists and most Americans. Psychologists appear to be less convinced of the existence of God, express greater doubts, and may understand the transcendent in unique ways. Survey data suggest that approximately 40% endorse ideological statements conceiving either of a personal God or transcendent aspect of human experience that some persons call God; 30 to 40% believe in a transcendent dimension; and 18 to 28% find notions of God or the transcendent to be illusory products of human imagination. Twenty-five percent agreed with the statement "I know God really exists and I have no doubts about it" in contrast to endorsement by 64% of the general population. These findings suggest differences between clinicians and the general population; however, these data do not tell the complete story.

When psychologists are asked about spirituality a different picture emerges. For example, in one study of clinical and counseling psychologists, 48% reported religion to be fairly important or very important yet when asked about spirituality 73% indicated such salience. Is this just a question of semantics? No. The differences cannot be argued away on the basis of language preference or through an assumption of equivalence between the categories of religion and spirituality. What is revealed is that many psychologists may actually be more concerned with the transcendent dimension than studies exclusively focusing on institutional expression have suggested. In this regard, they may be more similar to most Americans in their commitment to personal spirituality. Yet, this finding should not minimize the apparent differences in the form that spirituality takes. The mode of appropriation of beliefs and values may be as important as the contents of faith itself. This may be particularly relevant within the clinical setting in which beliefs and values are considered not only in terms of their impact on mental health but also in respect to personal autonomy and responsibility.

The orientation that one adopts to address questions of ultimate significance (i.e., meaning of life, personal morality) inherently involves basic attitudes and world view, including positions on epistemology (e.g., how knowledge is obtained, what can be known) and authority (e.g., upon what basis are truth statements and values asserted). Clinicians and clients may differ significantly in terms of their orientations to spiritual life

and the appropriation of faith. For example, many psychologists consider their form of religiosity to be an alternative spiritual path without reference to an organized religious body. A disparity is likely to exist within many clinical relationships concerning the role of authority and salience of an organized religious body; clients may be more likely to value the role of institutional moral teaching and authority. It must be remembered that in many instances a values congruence exists; client and clinician may share in a similar religious outlook and institutional orientation. This may be particularly the case when referrals are obtained through a member of the clergy or rabbinate. What is not known definitively are the actual impacts of faith perspective on the treatment relationship, process, and outcome. It may be that values congruence may not be equally salient across all cases. For those clients for whom religion plays a central role in shaping motivation and determining moral behavior, values congruence may be crucial in establishing a therapeutic relationship. Differences in relative importance placed on religion or spirituality by clients and clinicians may indicate a congruence or dissimilarity in fundamental orientation; however, the meaning and clinical significance of those similarities or differences remains to be empirically demonstrated.

Graduate Education and Clinical Training

Graduate education and clinical training ideally prepares clinicians to conduct treatment drawing upon respected methods of observation and evaluation as well as knowledge and expertise in psychological intervention. Survey data suggest that training respective to religious and spiritual issues in psychotherapy is minimal or absent; although the majority indicate that clinical supervision and training in this area is desirable. Over 90% of the psychologist respondents to a number of surveys reported that education and training in religious issues occurred rarely or not at all. Courses in the psychology of religion are rarely offered in graduate education, textbooks often inadequately present information regarding religious and spiritual issues, and courses aimed to develop cultural competence at times neglect the importance of religion as a clinically relevant feature of diversity. Surveys suggest however that the majority of psychologists find religious and spiritual issues to be clinically relevant and some, at times, include religious interventions within treatment. The use of such interventions appears to be based on personal religious beliefs rather than on clinical training and most often take the form of sensitivity to religious issues rather than proactive provision of explicit religious resources, such as prayer.

Comprehensive graduate education addressing the integration of religious issues within professional psychology is available though limited. There are but a few

APA-accredited doctoral programs in clinical or counseling psychology that include in their mission substantial attention to the religious or spiritual dimension. These programs offer integrative doctoral degrees that include courses in theology and spirituality, and often have a specifically religious orientation, such as Christianity.

There is some evidence that attention to religious and spiritual issues is increasing within clinical training such as the appearance of a number of texts on applied psychology and religion published by the APA and other scientific presses as well as sponsored continuing-education workshops within the field. Model curricula have been developed for medical education in psychiatry graduate education by the National Institute for Healthcare Research and for clinical training in psychology by the American Psychological Association Division 36: Psychology of Religion. There are a number of professional organizations that include consideration of religion and spirituality within psychological practice. The APA Division 36 provides a leadership role in the study of the psychology of religion, provides training resources, formally encourages scholarship and empirical research through an awards program, and offers a forum for continuing education. The Christian Association for Psychological Studies with its journal, the *Journal of Christianity and Psychology*, is an example of a guild organization dedicated to explicit integration of a given religious orientation and psychological theory and practice. Journals, such as, the *Journal for the Scientific Study of Religion*, the *International Journal for the Psychology of Religion*, the *Journal of Religion and Health*, *Counseling and Values*, the *Journal of Psychology and Christianity*, the *Journal of Psychology and Judaism*, and cross-discipline publications, such as *The Common Boundary*, contribute to the discourse on psychology and religion. Consideration of religious and spiritual issues in psychology have also been taken up in the fields of transpersonal psychology, humanistic psychology, rehabilitation psychology, social psychology, analytical psychology, and psychoanalysis. The relationship of religion and spirituality on mental and physical health requires further scientific investigation, cross-disciplinary scholarship, and attention within graduate education and clinical training in light of the value-based nature of psychological intervention, the high salience of religion for most individuals, and sensitivity to issues of diversity.

[*See also* Humanistic Psychology; *and* Transpersonal Psychology.]

Bibliography

Beutler, L. E., Machado, P. P. P., & Neufeldt, S. A. (1994). Therapist values. In A. E. Bergin & S. L. Garfield (Eds.), *The handbook of psychotherapy and behavior change* (4th ed., pp. 229–269). New York: Wiley. Provides a cogent discussion of therapist and client match which includes consideration of religious values.

Bergin, A. E., & Jensen, J. P. (1990). Religiosity of psychotherapists: A national survey. *Psychotherapy, 27(1),* 3–7. National survey of psychiatrists, psychologists, social workers, and marriage and family counselors.

Kelly, E. W. (1995). *Religion and spirituality in counseling and psychotherapy.* Alexandria, VA: American Counseling Association. A practical text discussing the religious and spiritual issues in counseling psychology.

Larsen, D. B., Lu, F. G., & Swyers, J. P. (Eds.). (1996). *Model curriculum for psychiatry residency training programs: Religion and spirituality in clinical practice.* Rockville, MD: National Institute for Healthcare Research. A comprehensive curriculum guide presenting a structured pedagogy for addressing religious and spiritual issues in assessment and treatment within psychiatry, includes class outlines and available resources.

Lovinger, R. J. (1984). *Working with religious issues in therapy.* Northvale, NJ: Jason Aronson. Practical guide to considering the religious and spiritual dimension in psychotherapy.

Richards, P. S., & Bergin, A. E. (1997). *A spiritual strategy for counseling and psychotherapy.* Washington, DC: American Psychological Association. A landmark text explicitly integrating a theistic spiritual strategy into psychology and psychotherapy.

Richards, P. S., & Bergin, A. E. (Eds.). (2000). *Handbook of psychotherapy and religious diversity: A guide for mental health professionals.* Washington, DC: American Psychological Association. An edited volume presenting a comprehensive overview of religious and spiritual issues in psychotherapy from the perspective of specific religious traditions.

Shafranske, E. P. (Ed.). (1996). *Religion and the clinical practice of psychology.* Washington, DC: American Psychological Association. Comprehensive volume addressing religion as a variable in mental health and psychological treatment. It includes theoretical, historical, and empirical overviews of the field, and examples of integration from multiple clinical orientations, and makes recommendations for treatment and training. Survey data referred to in this article were initially presented in this text.

Shafranske, E. P. (in press). Spiritual beliefs and practices of psychiatrists and other mental health professionals. *Psychiatric Annals.* This publication presents a summary of the survey data discussed in this article.

Shafranske, E. P., & Malony, H. N. (1990). Clinical psychologists' religious and spiritual orientations and their practice of psychotherapy. *Psychotherapy, 27,* 72–78. Reports the findings of a national study of clinical psychologists that includes attitudes, beliefs, and practices.

Worthington, E. L., Jr., Kurusu, T. A., McCullough, M. E., & Sanders, S. J. (1996). Empirical research on religious and psychotherapeutic processes and outcomes: A ten-year review and research prospectus. *Psychological Bulletin, 119,* 448–487. A comprehensive review of the use of religious and spiritual resources.

Edward P. Shafranske

RELIGIOUS EXPERIENCE. [*This entry comprises two articles:* Belief and Faith *and* Religious and Spiritual Practices. *The first article provides an overview of the tradition of psychological study of religious faith and belief. The second article provides a broad article on matters of religious and spiritual practice.*]

Belief and Faith

Believing is, among other things, a psychological phenomenon with cognitive, affective, and psychodynamic elements. From its inception in James and Freud to the present, belief has been a topic of interest to psychology.

William James's psychology remained closely allied with his philosophy of pragmatism, and his major writings on religion—*The Will to Believe* and the book *The Varieties of Religious Experience: A Study in Human Nature*—combine philosophical and psychological concerns. His goal in writing them was to both critique and defend religious belief on philosophical and psychological grounds. For example, while clearly recognizing that there are many unreasonable religious beliefs, in *The Will to Believe* (New York, 1912) James insists that there are many important questions that are, from the standpoint of reason and science, genuinely unanswerable. In these cases, belief is the only way to proceed. In *The Varieties of Religious Experience* (New York, 1902/1982) James frankly acknowledges that religious people often appear neurotic to the nonreligious, but he argues that the origin of a belief says nothing about its value and that religious experience often has a positive and transforming effect on those who undergo it.

This concern with the effects (or the "fruits," as he calls them) of religious experience ties James's philosophical and psychological approaches to the topic. From the pragmatists' standpoint, the value of a belief lies in its effects, and for James, the effects of religious experience are primarily in the psychological domain, in the transformation of personality.

Thus James focuses exclusively on religious experience, not on creeds, rituals, or institutions. For him private experiences form the essence of religion, and that is where the psychological investigation should begin and end. In concentrating on experience, he intentionally selects "the one-sided, exaggerated and intense" (1902/1982. p. 45) forms of religious experience rather than the more mundane ones because he feels they are more genuine and express more fully the essential components of religion.

In addition to focusing on the most intense forms of religious experience, James insists on individual differences. The very title of his masterwork underscores his concern with variety and pluralism. His basic principle is the importance of temperament in religion. He illustrates this with his distinction between the religion of the "healthy-minded" and that of the "sick soul." These are not two types of religion but rather two temperaments that shape the practice of religion: one continually positive and optimistic, the other exquisitely sensitive to life's precariousness and pain.

Despite his insistence on pluralism and the endless diversity of individual differences, in the end James seeks to bring order out of this variety by suggesting that the psychological essence of all religious convictions can be found in two sensibilities: that "there is something wrong about us as we naturally stand" and that "we are saved from the wrongness by making proper connection with the higher powers" (1902/1982, p. 508).

It is not clear that this emphasis on salvation is the core of all religion. But in *The Varieties* James clearly touches on many of the important psychological aspects of religious belief: its variety, its transforming potential, its implicit challenge to any worldview that has, in James's words "prematurely closed accounts with reality."

James's European contemporary, Sigmund Freud, called his new method "psychoanalysis," "analysis" carrying the connotation of breaking down an object of investigation into its component parts. When applied to religious material, Freud's analysis yielded two contrasting but complementary approaches.

First, in *Totem and Taboo* (London, 1912–1913), Freud gave an account of the origin of religious beliefs based on the Oedipal complex. Freud modeled the mind around three constructs. The "id" was the domain of our most infantile wishes. The baby is all id, according to Freud, totally self-centered and absorbed in its own needs. Eventually the child's self-centered demands conflict with reality because reality is never as gratifying as the child wishes. Out of the process of adapting to reality, the "ego" arises as a mediator between the wishes of the child and the demands of reality.

A crucial discovery of Freud's was that children too have sexual wishes directed toward the parent of the opposite gender. Boys not only wish to sleep with their mother, they also wish to do away with their rival, the father. A crucial reality that the child must accept is that its wish to possess its contrasexual parent is doomed. The boy renounces his desire for his mother and instead identifies with his father and the prohibition of incest that his father embodies. This identification with the law of the father becomes the nucleus of the "superego," the psychological foundation for the boy's acceptance of all of the prohibitions of culture.

Thus Freud's discussion in *Totem and Taboo* is an account of how antisocial instincts (represented by the id) become transformed into culture. The route to this transformation runs through the Oedipal complex, the result of which is the capacity to renounce infantile wishes and accept the prohibitions required by civilization. Traditionally, religion has been a major carrier of those prohibitions, and so, for Freud, civilization and religion arise together out of the same psychic process, the resolution of the Oedipal drama and the formation of the superego. Religion (and all culture), as portrayed in *Totem and Taboo*, is primarily a set of prohibitions and a system of social control.

Second, in *The Future of an Illusion* (London, 1927), Freud gave a functional analysis of the role of religion in the individual's psychic economy based on his idea of infantile narcissism. A pillar of Freud's intellectual edifice was the "reality principle"—a metaphysical theory transformed into a diagnostic category. The opposite of the reality principle was "infantile narcissism," in which the infant experiences the self as omnipotent, the center of the universe. In the course of normal development, the infant gradually learns from encounters with reality to renounce this grandiosity and accept the reality principle. Proper development involves a journey from primary process to secondary process, outgrowing the pleasure principle and embracing the reality principle. The illusory and the infantile are gradually brought under the control of the real and the rational.

If the reality principle is not sufficiently internalized, the person remains captive to a narcissistic mind set in which the reality principle is subverted by the power of fantasies about the self or another (such as God in the case of religion or the beloved in the case of romantic infatuation) possessing powers and qualities beyond what is realistic. As a continuation of a primitive mental state, these remaining infantile illusions represent the greatest danger to rationality and sanity. They involve a retreat from reality into the seductively gratifying but ultimately destructive world of illusion. Ways of knowing other than empirical science, the carrier of the reality principle, are not just logical errors or mistaken beliefs. They are psychopathologies. In Freud's view, narcissism is not only a threat to character development, it is an assault on truth.

Within this framework, Freud wrote his most sustained attack on religion, appropriately titled *The Future of an Illusion*. Illusions are defined by their appeal to narcissistic wishes. Illusions are "not necessarily false." Rather, "we call a belief an illusion when wish-fulfillment is a prominent factor" (1927, p. 31). Thus, Freud maintains that he is not discussing the truth value of religious beliefs but rather their psychological function, which is "that they are derived from human wishes" (p. 30).

Despite his methodological strictures about bracketing off the truth or falsity of religious claims, Freud is driven beyond functional analysis to dismiss religion as an "all too palpable" contradiction to reason and experience (1927, p. 54). Religion appeals to and reinforces our most infantile and narcissistic inclinations. It is culture's chief mode of denying reality. Freud's polemic against religion breaks out again and again in the midst of his discussion of religion's narcissistic roots. This is not a coincidence. The outbreak of this polemic alerts us to the possibility that Freud's own narcissistic investments are threatened by religion.

Freud's first discussion, in *Totem and Taboo*, located religion primarily in the superego. His second, in *The Future of an Illusion*, located religion primarily in the id. Religion had no place in the ego, which was the seat of rationality and the reality principle and so was reserved for natural science. In this sense, Freud's metapsychology is, among other things, an internalized representation of the nineteenth-century conflict between religion (in the form of the childish id and the tradition-bound superego) and science (in the form of the rational ego). Freud's cry "where id is, let ego be" expresses his wish that science replace religion. Religious belief, from Freud's perspective, was antithetical to rationality and an enemy to human progress.

Carl Jung was originally a member of Freud's inner circle, but eventually a permanent rupture occurred in their relationship and Jung went off on his own theoretical path. Because part of the reason for the break was Jung's apparently more open attitude toward religious material, the break between Freud and Jung institutionalized the split between psychoanalysis and religion, and the banishing of Jung from mainstream psychoanalysis also banished (until very recently) religion as a topic for psychoanalytic consideration.

Jung accepted Freud's construct of the unconscious. However, as Jung worked with patients, he noticed that themes and images in their dreams echoed themes found in art, literature, and mythology from around the world. For example, images of water were often associated with transformation, and the number 4 was often found in conjunction with themes of wholeness. Jung called these images "archetypes."

For Jung the unconscious is much more complex than for Freud. There is the "personal unconscious" that Freud discovered and that contains material from each individual's personal history. In addition, there is the "collective unconscious," which contains universal archetypes. Thus, Jung claims to have discovered the source, within the individual psyche, of all art, literature, and religion.

According to Jung, Western culture's singular reliance on linear reasoning and sensory information has left its members estranged from the greater wisdom of the collective unconscious. However, through dream analysis and religious myths and symbols, this archetypal heritage can be recovered—thus Jung's famous statement that all of his patients, in the second half of their lives, needed a religious outlook. Jung states clearly that, like James, he is referring not to creeds, institutions, or traditions, but rather to religious forms as mediators of the transforming encounter with the collective unconscious.

Jung's father was a Calvinist pastor, but in adolescence Jung found the faith of his father unconvincing. In early adulthood he subscribed wholeheartedly to Freud's faith in scientific rationalism, but his break with Freud represented a rejection of that faith too in the name of the power of the archetypal and mythical. But Jung's reappropriation of the archetypal and mythic dimensions of human experience was not a return to the beliefs of his childhood. Rather, Jung's archetypal psychology represents a recognition of the limitations of, and a movement beyond, both childish religion and rationalistic materialism into a genuinely new framework that is neither religion nor science as they are ordinarily understood.

Although both Freud and Jung conceive the origin of religious beliefs to be in the unconscious, their differences over the value of these beliefs derive from opposite images of the unconscious. For Freud the unconscious is the repository of the infantile and the neurotic, so anything arising from it will be psychologically problematic. For Jung the unconscious is the ground of a deeper wisdom, so religious beliefs have the potential to access its transforming power. Their differences over religion also reflect different definitions of health. For Freud, health is resignation to the reality principle embodied in Newtonian science. Religion, as non-rational, is therefore inevitably unhealthy. For Jung health is the integration of all levels of human experience, so religion, as the bearer of archetypal knowledge, is necessary for complete well-being.

In some ways, Jung's analytical psychology fits James's definition of religion: over-reliance on ego rationality alienates people from a deeper source of wisdom, but there is a power outside conscious control that brings health and wholeness.

The ideal of the autonomous individual is shared by Freud and Jung. More recent approaches to the dynamics of personality associated with British psychoanalysts such as W. R. D. Fairbairn, Harry Guntrip, and D. W. Winnicott begin with interpersonal experience rather than with the individual as a heuristically self-contained system of instinctual or archetypal energies. Such models have shifted the focus of psychoanalytic understanding from the isolated individual to the process of interaction. The self is created from internalized interpersonal experiences rather than from instincts and defenses or from archetypal images. It is primarily these internalized patterns of interaction, and not biological drives or universal themes, that are expressed in everyday behavior, including religious beliefs or the lack of them.

In a work foundational for this relational psychoanalysis of religion, Ana-Maria Rizzuto argued in *The Birth of the Living God* (Chicago, 1979) that each person has fashioned an internal representation of the deity out of his or her early interpersonal experiences. From internalized bits and pieces of primordial interactions—the sound of the mother's voice, the feeling of being held, the sense of security or anxiety existing in the family—children (at least in monotheistic cultures) cobble together an internal image of the divine. Later, if and when these children arrive at the entrance to a church or synagogue or mosque or temple, they do so with their "pet God already under their arm" (in Rizzuto's words).

Besides seeing belief as a relational experience, this newer psychoanalytic approach to religion uses the idea of "transitional phenomena," as articulated by the British pediatrician turned psychoanalyst D. W. Winnicott (*Playing and Reality*, New York, 1971). Watching children, Winnicott observed their tendency, at a certain developmental stage, to hold fast to certain "transitional objects" (blankets, teddy bears, and such) to facilitate their movement toward greater autonomy. Such objects exist in both the child's private world and the outer social world; they are, in Winnicott's words, "both created and found." Thus, they represent for Winnicott a domain intermediate between the world of privately constructed meanings and the impersonal, objective public sphere. This "transitional space" is, for Winnicott, the realm of play, imagination, and creativity from which culture springs. Observing a child playing with a teddy bear, Winnicott saw the precursor to the works of Shakespeare, the paintings of Rembrandt, the theories of Einstein.

Contemporary psychoanalytic writers have used Winnicott's construct to discuss religious symbols and beliefs as transitional phenomena. Winnicott is claiming an independent line of development for the symbolic realm, a claim with profound appeal for those interested in a psychological understanding of religion. Rather than deriving from the vicissitudes of instinct, the symbolic order arises out of the capacity for spontaneous creativity, first on the part of the child and later in the work of the artist, the poet, the scientist, the religious visionary, and other creators of culture. Thus, religion (and culture in general) is not something imposed on human nature in the service of instinctual control; instead, it arises naturally out of the transitional domain of human experience.

Contemporary cognitive psychologists investigate belief in terms of attributional and schematic processes. Attribution theory proposes that people make attributions about occurrences in order to make experience meaningful, to gain a feeling of control, and to maintain self-esteem. The kinds of attributions made are a function of factors such as the individual's previous attributional history, the cognitive constructs available, and the characteristics of the occurrence. For example, research suggests that people are more apt to make religious attributions when events are seen as beyond human control and/or inexplicable in terms of secular theories. James's openness to religious beliefs in response to questions deemed beyond the scope of science is an example of this attributional style.

Schema theory suggests that people process information according to preexisting cognitive frameworks, or schemas, that govern what data they pay attention to and how those data are encoded and processed. Well-established schemas improve cognitive processing efficiency. Research suggests that schema-relevant information is processed more quickly and remembered better than schema-irrelevant information. For example, an individual who believes in faith healing will quickly notice and strongly remember a patient's unexpected recovery, whereas someone without such a belief may ignore or forget about such an experience. The more salient a schema is for a person, the more that person will attend to and remember schema-relevant data and, when possible, interpret events according to that framework. As such central schemas gather more associations, they become even more salient and harder to disconfirm because they generate increasingly complex ways of interpreting experiences.

Religious beliefs fit easily into these cognitive approaches, and additional research has demonstrated the connection between religious cognitions and a variety of behaviors including coping with stress, handling life transitions, and recovering from trauma. The presence or absence of religious schemas and the attributions that follow from them can be a major predictor of how individuals manage such occurrences.

Psychology and religion are both multidimensional. The psychological investigation of religious beliefs mirrors the diversity of psychology methods, each attending to a different facet of faith: from James's descriptive phenomenology, to Freud's and Jung's probing of unconscious forces, to contemporary psychoanalytic discernment of connections between the themes of a person's belief system and the relational patterns in his or her life, to cognitive psychology's emphasis on attributions and their impact on a wide range of behaviors. Many of these investigations have had religious as well as psychological motives: James's use of religious experience to challenge the narrowness of what he called "medical materialism," Freud's wish to debunk religion in the name of science, Jung's desire to refurbish religious forms as vehicles for psychological transformation. Thus, different methods and different motivations cause these different theorists to highlight some aspects of belief and overlook others. Taken together they provide a fuller understanding of the psychological processes of belief.

Bibliography

Edinger, E. (1973). *Ego and archetype*. New York: Pelican Books. Sympathetic introduction to Jung's archetypal psychology.

Homans, P. (1979). *Jung in context*. Chicago: University of Chicago Press. Detailed analysis of the break between Jung and Freud, with special reference to its impact on Jung's psychology of religion.

Jacobs, J., & Capps, D. (Eds.). (1997). *Religion, society and psychoanalysis*. Denver: Westview Press. Covers the field with a series of critical presentations of the psychoanalytic study of religion from Freud through relational theories to the latest in French psychoanalysis.

Jones, J. (1991). *Contemporary psychoanalysis and religion*. New Haven, CT: Yale University Press. General introduction to the object-relational psychoanalysis of religion.

Spilka, B., & MacIntosh, D. (Eds.). (1997). *The psychology of religion*. Denver: Westview Press. Articles on the cognitive and social psychological approaches to religion by leading experts in the field.

James W. Jones

Religious Experiences and Practices

Scholars have not arrived at a consensus regarding the meaning of the term *religious experience*. Some definitions are all-encompassing and include a wide range of experiences associated to a greater or lesser extent with formal religion. Celebration of religious holidays, participation in rituals, virtuous living or service to others, fulfillment of religious obligations, and scriptural study are examples of religious life that may be thought of as types of religious experience.

At the other end of the spectrum, some investigators have considered religious experience to occur only when there is an episodic altered state or mystical state of consciousness in which qualitative changes in emotional intensity may occur. This altered state may or may not be associated with religious symbolism or necessarily occur within the intentional framework of a spiritual practice. The understanding of specific religious and spiritual practices is determined in part by the importance ascribed to the role of mystical states in religious experience. In contrast, many religious observances or spiritual disciplines may not lead to alterations in consciousness or emotional intensity.

William James's views have strongly influenced much contemporary psychological thinking and research concerning religious experience. He studied the mystical experiences of individuals "in their solitude." After James, much psychological research has tended to focus on mystical experience as the exemplar of authentic religious experience. This predilection has left gaps in our knowledge and appreciation of the religious and spiritual landscape. Religious traditions such as orthodox Christianity, Catholicism, Judaism, Buddhism, Hinduism, and Islam tend to embed any mystical experiences within the context of a variety of religious practices and rituals. Mystical states are accepted as aspects of spiritual life rather than as the defining features of religious experience and devotion. Within the Roman Catholic orthodox Christian faiths, for example, mystical experiences are typically seen as the outgrowth of a life of prayer and humility and acts of grace from a divine source. James Pratt, in *The Religious Consciousness: A Psychological Study* (New York, 1920), presented an early critique of a psychology of religion focusing solely on mystical experience. Understanding religious experience requires an examination of the compendium of religious and spiritual life to which mystical and nonmystical practices both contribute.

One way of categorizing religious experiences is to apply the concepts of exoteric, esoteric, and mesoteric to them. "Exoteric" refers to the outer manifestations or forms of religious experience (e.g., belief, ritual, practice) that are generally accessible within a given culture. They provide, in Clifford Geetz's words, "a general order of existence," and offer rituals which mark significant events and passages common in human experience (e.g., birth, death, adulthood) (*The Interpretation of Cultures*, New York, 1973). The "esoteric" dimension of religion is an area of inner—often hidden—knowledge and experience. This domain includes mystical and revelatory experiences. The major Western religions include the esoteric forms of Sufism (Islam), cabalistic Judaism, and esoteric Christianity. The "mesoteric" level is an intermediate level in which there is significant deepening of the experiential understanding of inner life and religious beliefs, as well as a bridging of exoteric and esoteric experiences. It includes a deepening of emotions and the beginning of contemplative awareness.

In addition to levels of religious experience, the means by which persons apprehend the spiritual have been conceptualized. In *In Search of the Miraculous*, (P. D. Ouspensky, New York, 1949) introduced the idea that different types of people have varying ways of appropriating and experiencing religion. He developed a simple typology based on the area of a person's primary adaptation to life. He postulated three prevalent types: the physical, the emotional, and the intellectual. In addition, a fourth type consists of individuals not content with the other modes of living. In Ouspensky's view, individuals in each of these types have different patterns of religious experience: The physical prefers pageantry and ritual; the emotional responds to moving tales of love and sacrifice and seeks bliss; and the intellectual focuses on conceptual clarity and concentrative meditative experiences. Only the fourth type seeks mystical or transcendent religious experiences. Although not empirically demonstrated, Ouspensky's model illustrates a perspective that encourages appreciation for many forms of religious experience.

Exoteric Religious Experience

Eighty percent of the world's population claim some religious allegiance, as reported by J. O'Brien and M. Palmer in *The State of Religion Atlas* (New York, 1993). Studies in sociology and the psychology of religion attempt to describe the constituents of this allegiance by assessing religious preference, affiliation, involvement, beliefs, and practices, as well as religious orientation. These broad categories capture the outer manifestations of faith. Studies have found that the majority of people identify with a religious tradition, adopt a set of prescribed beliefs, and participate to some degree in the tradition's spiritual practices. Research based on Gordon Allport's model of intrinsic and extrinsic religious orientation has examined the reasons behind affiliation. Such motivation may be primarily extrinsic, with religion used for the believer's ends, or may it may be intrinsic, the living out of a meaningful faith. Research on denominational religious involvement provides an account of beliefs and practices but usually does not assess esoteric or mesoteric aspects of faith or the vitality of spiritual life that may be obtained through such religious affiliation. For many, exoteric religious experience furnishes a foundation for faith that sustains throughout the course of life. Through shared beliefs, symbols, rituals, and traditions, ordinary religious experience provides in Peter Berger's words, a "sacred canopy" under which personal existence derives meaning (*The Sacred Canopy*, Garden City, New York, 1967).

Esoteric Religious Experience

Studies primarily within the psychology of religion have continued the line of investigation within the Jamesian tradition, with its emphasis on individual mystical experience of a transcendent or esoteric nature. In *Mysticism and Philosophy* (Philadelphia, 1960) W. T. Stace reported religious experience to be typified by seeing all things as one in a unifying vision, feeling a sense of timelessness and spacelessness, encountering an experience of the sacred and holy, and having a paradoxical-defying logic. Andrew Greeley asked a national sample of Americans, "Have you ever felt as though you were very close to a powerful spiritual force that seemed to lift you out of yourself?" and found that 35% reported having such an experience (*The Sociology of the Paranormal: A Reconnaissance*, Beverly Hills, Calif., 1975).

Ralph Hood, Jr. extended the Jamesian approach through a body of empirical and theoretical literature. He developed the Religious Experience Episodes Measure (REEM), the instrument most widely used to measure mystical experience. Scores on the REEM were found to be correlated with the degree to which a given faith tradition emphasized the importance of mystical experiences and also were moderately correlated with self-reported religiosity. Hood subsequently developed the Mysticism scale, in which mysticism and interpretation were identified as primary factors, with the latter further yielding factors identified as knowledge and religious. The model underlying Hood's approach included two Jamesian principles—an emphasis on mystical experience and an insistence on an experiential dimension that may or may not be interpreted either in accordance with religious traditions.

Hood concluded in his textbook, edited with Bernard Spilka and Richard L. Gorsuch, *The Psychology of Religion* (Englewood Cliffs, N.J., 1985), that mystical experiences are common and are often found in normal, healthy people. Further, he contended that these experiences need not be interpreted religiously. He found that two types of mystical experience occur, both of which involve a loss and transcendence of the self and create a sense of unity or merging. In extravertive mystical experience, there is a sense of unity with all phenomena—including the self. Introvertive mysticism is characterized by a transcendence of the phenomenal world and the phenomenal self into the realm of what is experienced as the true or timeless self. This literature embodies attempts to articulate and measure mystical experience, including the esoteric dimension of religious experience.

Psychologists, not formally associated with the psychology of religion, have also contributed to the discourse concerning mystical and esoteric religious experience. Abraham Maslow's concept of peak experiences provides one example of an attempt within Western psychology to understand religious experience. In Maslow's formulation, peak experiences are experiential episodes involving a sense of absorption in the phenomena of life that can influence a person's view of reality and approach to life. He believed that peak experiences typified only that small portion of the population he considered "self-actualized." Subsequent research has shown, however, that many people report peak experiences. Transpersonal psychology theorists such as Charles Tart and Ken Wilber have also considered transcendent or transpersonal states of consciousness and have contributed to the ongoing psychological commentary relevant to esoteric religious expression. These investigations have emphasized mystical experience as the *sine qua non* of esoteric religious experience. This focus has stimulated research but has limited the appreciation of other forms of esoteric religious experience.

There are many types of religious experience other than episodic experiences of mystical unity. Religious experiences possibly involving an altered state include visions, trance states, near-death experiences, out-of-body experiences, and possession. Other religious experiences not involving an altered state of consciousness include feelings of awe and reverence, participation in a community of believers, shamanic experiences, participation in rituals and rites, prayer and reading of Scripture either alone or in a group, dancing, and acts of repentance.

Life-changing mystical or religious experiential episodes are more central in certain religious traditions than in others. For example, in many Protestant denominations, it is incumbent on each person to take responsibility for his or her own type of religious commitment. This commitment may take the form of gradual discernment or may involve dramatic, ecstatic experience of conversion. Thus, individual esoteric experience takes a multitude of forms, originating either within or outside of specific religious traditions, and serves as a source of revelation or individual understanding—often leading to conversion or to a significant deepening of spiritual life.

Mesoteric Religious Experience

Mesoteric religious experiences reflect spiritual practices, anchored within specific traditions, that are intended to deepen faith. An entire panoply of activities within a religious context can result in nonmystical religious experiences. These experiences may begin as exoteric or outward, nonmystical forms of religiousness. With intent and through practice or grace, they may evoke powerful, life-changing esoteric experiences or the mesoteric deepening of spiritual commitments beyond ordinary observance. For example, religious rituals provide an important forum for encountering the sacred. Rituals, as discussed by Victor Turner, provide an unique liminal process in which transcendent realities can be enacted, which may bring about personal transformation (*The Ritual Process*, Chicago, 1969). Table 1 presents these practices, as well as experiences that may unwittingly produce spontaneous transformative experiences that function within the mesoteric dimension of religious experience. Underlying this discussion is the assumption that an individual's spiritual life is not a static but rather a dynamic process. James Fowler, in *Stages of Faith: The Psychology of Human Development and the Quest for Meaning* (San Francisco, 1981), presents a faith-development theory that includes structural stages and discusses the variety of modes through which faith is appropriated.

It is often necessary to take into account both the form of the practice involved and the practitioner's intent to understand the psychological meaning of a given religious experience. Forms of meditation, for example, can be found in most religious and spiritual traditions. Meditative practices range from mindfulness to concentrative meditation and include both active and passive approaches. Certain forms of meditation may require specified postures or activities. The practitioner

RELIGIOUS EXPERIENCE. Table 1. Religious and spiritual practices

---

Ascetic Practices
Fasting
Sexual abstinence
Willful submission to pain
Infliction of pain on oneself or flagellation
Voluntary poverty
Solitude
Voluntary submission to extreme environmental conditions

Contemplative Practices
Prayer, especially contemplative prayer
Silence and quiet reflection
Concentrative meditation and mindfulness
Contact with a sacred place
Visualization

Rites and Ritual Practices
Rites of passage
Chanting and drumming
Handling dangerous animals
Sleep deprivation
Trances
Ritualistic experiences of possession
Ritual mutilation

Worship
Church attendance and participation
Reading scripture
Rituals of repentance and forgiveness
Confession, supplication and thanksgiving, and purification of the emotions
Pilgrimages
Group prayer, singing, and dance

Other Spiritual Practices and Disciplines
Spiritual direction
Service to others or to a religion
Dedication to a spiritual principle
Acceptance of suffering and voluntary suffering
Intentionally carrying out meaningless tasks
Modified breathing
Drug-induced states

---

may be seated or may be engaged in a form of "moving" meditation that integrates meditation into daily activities.

Meditation may be practiced within or outside of religious or spiritual traditions. Whether such a distinction makes a difference has not been ascertained by Western psychology. Persons who engage in meditative practices do not necessarily do so for religious or spiritual purposes. One common use of meditation is relaxation; other uses include coping with stress or success in competitive athletic activities. Religious experience may be neither a goal nor a result of such meditation. Prayer also has many varieties and purposes. Contemplative prayer is different in both intent and practice from intercessory prayer. People pray to many sources of help for many types of results. Engaging in meditation or prayer is thus not necessarily connected with religious experience.

Some rituals may include combinations of practices. For example, the Native American sweat lodge ceremony includes or may include prayer, rhythmic drumming, reduced sensory stimulation (darkness), extreme environmental conditions (intense heat), chanting, concentrative meditation, repentance and forgiveness, and rededication to service.

In addition to spiritual practices, a wide range of human experiences, both ordinary and extraordinary, may contribute to spiritual development. These include sexual activity, childbirth, oxygen deprivation, depression, mania, psychotic states, traumatic stress, psychic and paranormal experiences, and epilepsy, as well as the commonplace activities of daily life, such as watching children play or enjoying a symphony. The Russian writer Fyodor Dostoevsky reported the onset of continuing mystical religious experiences after having been subject to a fake execution by the czarist government. That traumatic event triggered an epileptic seizure as well as a profound mystical experience—the first of many. Dostoevesky's unintended or spontaneous religious experience involved ongoing depression, a traumatic event, and epilepsy.

In addition to being triggered by various events, conditions, or practices, religious experiences may unfold as part of a goal-directed developmental process of the psyche. This Jungian perspective attributes many such experiences to the unfolding of a pattern leading to harmonious psychological development. Such experiences, in Jungian terms, represent accessing the energies and contents of the self, which is what Jung termed the "central archetype." "Individuation" is Jung's term for the process of becoming whole or "self-actualized." Jung viewed external events and practices as often secondary to the process of individuation in accounting for the phenomenon of religious experience.

Self-change, whether brought about by the intensity of esoteric religious experience, such as mystical experience or conversion, or gained through intentional practices of a mesoteric nature, may produce a number of effects, whether or not they occur within a religious framework. Commonly noted are changes in values, shifts in the direction of life, a greater appreciation of life and of aesthetics, reverence and thanksgiving, a feeling of love for others, renewed appreciation of nature, and a commitment to the service of self-expression.

Closing Remarks

A comprehensive study of religious experience requires investigation that goes beyond an emphasis on esoteric, mystical experience. It would examine more fully exoteric and mesoteric religious experiences, as well as the contributions of individual and cultural diversity. The issue of whether there is only one type of religious experience translated through different personalities and cultures or whether there are different kinds of religious experiences with differing meanings is still unsettled. Perhaps there is a single common core or two cores (extravertive and introvertive) of mystical experience—in addition to many other varieties of religious expression and experience.

The contemporary approach to religious experience is typified by a focus on brief experiences rather than on a continuity of religious experience. The great mystical traditions place a high value on brief episodes of religious experience, which are often important in the transformation of personality. However, of far greater value in many religions is a more gradually developing, persisting, enveloping, and often serene and joyful inner spiritual life. Such heightened spirituality occurs in part as a result of continuing devotion and practice, as might be exemplified in monastic life.

Psychological research has often decontexturalized the understanding of religious experiences, and at times, has ignored the life history, culture, and religious traditions in which such experiences might be embedded. This lack of reference to the context presumes that religious experiences are in large measure "context independent" or that context provides merely a means of formulating such experiences. Studying a wider variety of religious experiences within numerous contexts would provide more adequate knowledge concerning the role of context. To do so, psychology must step outside of the more narrow aspects of the Jamesian tradition and align with James's deeper inquisitiveness, openness, and phenomenological attitude.

This article has not touched on a fundamental question—the epistemological status of religious experience. Does the phenomenology of mystical and religious experiences represent not only a psychologically meaningful but also a valid way of perceiving realities not commonly noticed or comprehended in everyday life? Does the variety of religious experiences reflect pluralistic aspects of reality or suggest a multidimensional universe? If there is a common core of the experience of oneness to mystical experiences, does this reflect a cosmic reality, a unifying force or God? Are such experiences merely subjective illusions or do they represent veridical perceptions of the cosmos and of the meaning of life?

Current psychological thinking views religious experiences as biopsychosocial phenomena. A reductionistic tendency to limit the understanding of religious experiences to psychological, cultural, or physiological causes or to focus on empirical effects has prevailed. Psychology has not yet answered foundational questions concerning the ultimate significance of spiritual and religious experience. Perhaps answering such questions is outside the bounds of psychology as an empir-

ical discipline and is better suited to the paradigms offered by philosophy and religious studies.

[See also Cults; Meditation; Mysticism; Peak Experiences; Prosocial Behavior; and Religious Symbol, Myth, and Ritual.]

Bibliography

Batson, C. D., & Ventis, W. L. (1982). *The religious experience: A social-psychological perspective*. New York: Oxford University Press. Examines religious experience theoretically and empirically from a social psychological perspective, and includes a review of the literature on intrinsic and extrinsic religious orientation.

Beit-Hallami, B., & Argyle, M. (1997). *The psychology of religious behavior, belief, and experience*. New York: Routledge. Provides a cogent introduction to the psychology of religion.

Bucke, R. M. (1902). *Cosmic consciousness*. New York: Dutton. A classic text on mystical experience.

Eliade, M. (Ed.). (1987). *The encyclopedia of religion* (16 vols.). New York: Macmillan. Definitive reference in religion.

Goleman, D. (1977). *The varieties of the meditative experience*. New York: Dutton. A lucid and accessible discussion of the psychology and practice of meditation.

Gurdjieff, G. I. (1963). *All and everything: Beelzebub's tales to his grandson*. New York: Dutton. A challenging text introducing the esoteric mystical tradition.

Hood, R. W. (Ed.). (1995). *Handbook of religious experience*. Birmingham, AL: Religious Education Press. This edited handbook is a significant volume that presents psychological commentaries on a variety of religious traditions and includes essays in the psychology of religion from a multitude of psychological perspectives, including clinical, developmental, social, and cognitive psychologies.

Hood, R. W., Jr., Spilka, B., Hunsberger, B., & Gorsuch, R. L. (1996). *The psychology of religion: An empirical approach*. New York: Guilford Press. Scholarly presentation of the psychology of religion emphasizing the empirical approach.

James, W. (1902). *The varieties of religious experience: A study in human behavior*. New York: Longmans, Green. Classic work in the psychology of religion that influenced its theory and method of study.

Maslow, A. H. (1970). *The farther reaches of human nature*. New York: Harper & Row. Influential collection of essays concerning the fourth force in psychology, transpersonal psychology, including a discussion of peak experiences.

Ouspensky, P. D. (1949). *In search of the miraculous*. New York: Harcourt. A discussion of mystical experience and cosmology based on the spiritual teachings of G. I. Gurdjieff.

Saint John of the Cross. (1990). *Dark night of the soul* (E. Pears, Trans.). New York: Doubleday. An exemplary spiritual narrative.

Smart, N. (1997). *The religious experience* (5th ed.). Englewood Cliffs, NJ: Prentice Hall. Accessible history of religious experience examining the major world religions.

Underhill, E. (1912). *Mysticism: A study in the nature and development of man's spiritual consciousness.* New York: Dutton. A classic exposition on religious experience.

Wilber, K. (1977). *The spectrum of consciousness.* Wheaton, IL: Theosophical Publishing. Early work of this transpersonal theorist integrating Eastern and Western psychologies and examining the evolution of consciousness.

Wulff, D. (1997). *Psychology of religion: Classic and contemporary.* New York: Wiley. An authoritative text, encyclopedic in its coverage of the history, methods, and findings of the psychology of religion. Takes a comprehensive view of religious and spiritual experience.

Robert N. Sollod and Edward P. Shafranske

RELIGIOUS SYMBOL, MYTH, AND RITUAL

RELIGIOUS SYMBOL, MYTH, AND RITUAL are features of culture that give form to individual and collective experiences. Each serves to signify and to maintain social standing, morality, and convention, as well as to convey through words and actions experiences of the holy that cannot be described literally. Symbols, myths, and rituals are entwined within indigenous religious settings to establish coherence of meaning and provide a *Weltanschauung* in which individual existence is located. Further, the discourse of religious symbolism, akin to artistic expression, provides a portal for transcending the profane world of ordinary experience and offers the possibility of encountering the numinous. Religious symbolism, mythology, and ritual partake of a unique character in which words, objects, places, stories, and actions sanctify experience. Each evokes meaning and emotion and motivates those initiated within a given religious culture. Whereas signs may be universally accessible, religious signification is disclosed within the bounds of the culture of the initiated.

Religious Symbolization

A central question has concerned the origin and nature of symbols. Symbols may be seen as individually created in the moment, furnished by popular culture, or discovered within a collective, universal unconscious. Ernst Cassirer considered the capacity for symbol making to be a ubiquitous form of human mentation. Susanne K. Langer, in *Philosophy in a New Key: A Study in the Symbolism of Reason, Rite, and Art* (Cambridge, Mass., 1967), went further in asserting "the need for symbolization" and concluded that a "thinking organism must be forever furnishing symbolic versions of its experiences . . . it is not the essential act of thought that is symbolization, but an act *essential to thought*, and prior to it" (p. 41). Symbols are distinct from literal signification (or signs) in light of the building up of

meanings that occurs within formation and communication. Georg Gadamer described symbol formation as a transformation in which the original object of symbolization becomes related to the universes of meaning associated with the symbol usage. Paul Ricoeur observed that symbols are profound in their opaqueness, in which meanings are layered on one another, producing inexhaustible depth. Hans-Claude Levi-Strauss proposed that mythic narratives reveal universal tendencies in human cognition in which binary categories are related. These vantage points suggest the universal nature of symbol formation and view symbols as the artifacts of contents and processes of individual minds within cultural settings.

Religious symbolization reflects both personally created and culturally anchored systems of meaning. In contrast to signs, which represent only what is tangibly and empirically available, symbols possess the ability to clothe the ineffable in humanly accessible terms. Approaching the transcendent on the religious stage encourages processes of symbolization, which traverse private experience and public expression. As symbols unify a community of believers, their influence goes beyond the existential function of creating meaning to shape behavior and affiliation. Religious symbols are not separate from mythology and ritual but rather are housed in culturally sanctioned stories that provide an aura of factuality and authority to their explanations.

Among the psychological theorists who have addressed the subject of religious symbolism, Sigmund Freud and C. G. Jung are unique in their approaches. Freud examined the associational properties of the mind, particularly in respect to dreams, and put forward a view of symbolization that considered symbols to be personal creations that contain the imprints of multiple influences of history, both personal (ontogenetic) and archaic (phylogenetic), as well as expressions of wish fulfillment. Symbols are the results of unconscious conflict and compromise. To Freud, religious symbolism, myth, and ritual reflected deeply held unconscious ties to parental figures within Oedipal and pre-Oedipal dynamics, as well as revealing the prehistory of humanity. Contemporary psychoanalytic thinkers consider religious symbols to be dynamic representations created in the here and now that serve multiple functions and bear the impressions of countless identifications and internalizations.

Jung was equally interested in symbolism; however, unlike Freud, he emphasized individual symbolic expression within the context of an objective or collective unconscious. He believed that symbolic communication aimed at disclosure rather than guise. In *Psychological Types* (New York, 1923), Jung interpreted symbolic expression to be "the best possible formulation for a relatively *unknown* thing" (p. 602). Religious symbolization served that aim and was intimately connected with archetypes, which reflected inherited modes of psychic functioning. In this regard, religious symbols, myth, and rituals allow for the discovery of *a priori* archetypes pointing to ultimate truths.

Religious Myth

Myths are stories embedded within the vocabulary of a given culture that speak of ultimate realities, answer fundamental questions, and establish principles of social conduct. Myths provide a vernacular in which common knowledge and perception are imbued with transcendent significance. Myths, as distinct from epics, resonate with the authority of religious institutions and depict the suprahistorical presence of the divine. Religious myths are afforded status as they are recited within extraordinary settings—at sacred places and at specific times—often involving ritual action. Mircea Eliade identified as fundamental the cosmogomic myth, which not only tells of the birth of the world but, more important, provides a model in which contemporary relationships within the world are oriented. Bronislaw Malinowski argued that myths emerged out of sociological processes and functioned to provide social cohesion. The explanations that myths provide are secondary to their establishment of social order. Levi-Strauss offered an alternative view that myths, despite their apparent diversity, reflect innate structures of cognition. Myths, in this view, reveal the basic structures of human cognition grappling with larger-than-life questions.

Religious Ritual

Rituals serve an important role in the transmission of culture-bound beliefs, symbols, and myths. Whether such systems of meaning are viewed as serving primarily existential, social, or cognitive functions, rituals bring the community together to celebrate particular events within a given worldview. Through the vernacular of ritual, significant human events, such as birth, deaths, and coming of age, are contextualized. Symbolic acts are performed in rituals through the immediate viscera of the body, eliciting intense perceptions, sensations, and emotions. Such dramatic performances evoke credibility in the cultural ethos and reinforce across generations beliefs, social status, and order within the community. Eliade suggested that the purpose of rituals is to memorialize and renew "hierophanies" (self-disclosures of the holy) and "kratophanies" (revelations of overwhelming power). Rituals provide entry into the "liminal," in which common experience (profane) is brought into relation with the transcendent (sacred). Rituals are performed to influence nature; to mark important individual and communal events, including rites of passage; to provide transformation, healing, and salvation; and to honor the holy, transcendent dimension. Victor Turner opined that ritual elements provide the experience of standing outside of ordinary social structures and produce a sense of *communitas* in which a felt unity is experienced. This view allows for consideration of ritual action that exists outside of normative or majority culture.

Individual and cultural identity is fashioned out of symbols, myths, and rituals. The relevance of a given religious symbolic order depends on its ability to evoke persuasive and credible representations of reality, to make sense of the ineffable, to support social cohesion, and to instill moods and motivations on which individual identity is forged. Symbolic systems that fail in these regards cease to be alive and become artifacts for the study of past cultures.

Bibliography

Campbell, J. (1949/1972). *The hero with a thousand faces.* Princeton, NJ: Princeton University Press. The study of the hero cycle, as popularized by Joseph Campbell, is an exemplar of the ability of myth to depict and shape views of developmental epochs and models of identity within multiple cultural settings.

Eliade, M. (1959). *The sacred and the profane: The nature of religion* (W. R. Trask, Trans.). New York: Harcourt, Brace & World. Influential and highly accessible work in the study of myth, symbolism, and ritual.

Eliade, M. (Ed.). (1987). *The encyclopedia of religion.* New York: Macmillan. Authoritative multivolume encyclopedia that contains excellent essays and annotated bibliographies on religious symbolism, myth, and ritual.

Levinson, D., & Ember, M. (Eds.). (1996). *Encyclopedia of cultural anthropology.* New York: Holt. An excellent introduction to the development of anthropological approaches to the study of symbols, myths, and rituals, including a discussion of symbolic anthropology and specific essays on rites of passages and mythic forms across cultures.

Malinowski, B. (1992). *Malinowski and the work of myth.* Princeton, NJ: Princeton University Press. A reader of influential works by Malinowski selected and introduced by Ivan Strenski. Provides a useful introduction to his body of literature.

Meissner, W. W. (1984). *Psychoanalysis and religious experience.* New Haven, CT: Yale University Press. Presents Freud's approach to religion, including his analysis of religious symbolism and myth, as well as an overview of contemporary psychoanalytic approaches to religious experience. Ana-Maria Rizzuto's *The Birth of the Living God* (Chicago, 1979) provides an excellent introduction with a slant toward clinical understanding. Edward Shafranske's "Freudian Theory in Religious Experience" (in R. Hood's *Handbook of Religious Experience,* Birmingham, AL, 1995) presents a succinct discussion of Freud's ontogenetic and phylogenetic approaches to religion.

Strenski, I. (1987). *Four theories of myth in twentieth-*

century history. London: Macmillan. A scholarly comparative analysis of the works of Ernst Cassirer, Bronislaw Malinowski, Mircea Eliade, Claude Levi-Strauss, and Emil Durkheim.

Whitmont, E. C. (1969). *The symbolic quest*. New York: Putnam. A scholarly and accessible text summarizing Jung's approach to psychology, including discussions of symbolism and mythology. Popular works by James Hillman and Robert Sanford provide additional examples of analytical psychology approaches to myth.

Edward P. Shafranske

RELIGIOUS TRADITIONS. *See* Christianity and Psychology; Cults, Eastern Religions and Philosophies; Hellenistic Psychology; Islam and Psychology; *and* Judaism and Psychology.

RELIGIOUS VALUES AND MENTAL HEALTH. Do religious beliefs, values, and behaviors promote mental health or do they cause mental illness and emotional disturbance? This question, a source of controversy since the beginnings of modern psychology, can be better understood if the historical and philosophical development of psychology is considered. Psychology emerged as a discipline in the late nineteenth and early twentieth centuries, the Age of Science, when modern scientists were successfully challenging religious authority and tradition. Scientists' assumptions about the nature of reality often conflicted directly with religious and spiritual views of the world, including the foundational assumption of naturalism, which asserts that human beings and the universe can be completely understood without reference to God or transcendent influences.

To avoid religion and establish psychology and psychiatry as respected sciences, early leaders of psychology accepted naturalism and other prevailing philosophies of the day. Many of them also portrayed religion as harmful or irrelevant to mental health. For example, in the *Future of an Illusion* (New York, 1927/1961), Sigmund Freud called religion "the universal obsessional neurosis of humanity" (p. 43) and stated that "the effect of religious consolations may be likened to that of a narcotic" (p. 29). John B. Watson (*Psychology from the Standpoint of a Behaviorist*, Dover, N. H., 1924/1983) and B. F. Skinner (*Beyond Freedom and Dignity*, New York, 1971) viewed religious beliefs and behaviors as superstitions learned through reinforcement and conditioning.

Not all early leaders of psychology viewed religion negatively; some believed that mature religion can promote mental health. For example, William James suggested "healthy-minded" and "sick soul" ways of being religious, with healthy-minded religion as optimistic, extroverted, happy, and social and sick soul religion as pessimistic, anxious, melancholy, and introverted (*The Varieties of Religious Experience: A Study in Human Nature*, Cambridge, Mass., 1902/1985). Carl Jung believed that religious and spiritual beliefs give life the meaning essential for psychic wholeness. He asserted that none of his religious patients over the age of 35 was healed without regaining his or her religious outlook ("Psychotherapists or the Clergy," in *The Collected Works of C. G. Jung*, vol. 11, 2nd ed., Princeton, N.J., pp. 327–347, 1969). Gordon W. Allport, with collaborator J. M. Ross, believed that there are both healthy ("intrinsic") and unhealthy ("extrinsic") ways of being religious; intrinsic people "find their master motive in religion. . . . Having embraced a creed the individual endeavors to internalize it and follow it fully," but extrinsic people "use religion for their own ends. . . . The embraced creed is lightly held or else selectively shaped to fit more primary needs" (p. 434) (*Journal of Personality and Social Psychology*, 1967, 5, 432–443).

Despite these more positive views of religion, the powerful influence of the naturalistic assumptions and antireligious views of Freud, Watson, Skinner, and others influenced many professionals during the twentieth century to hold negative views of religion and its effects on mental health. As recently as 1980, Albert Ellis (*Journal of Consulting and Clinical Psychology*, 48, 635–639), the founder of rational-emotive behavior therapy, hypothesized that religiosity is "in many respects equivalent to irrational thinking and emotional disturbance . . . the less religious [people] are, the more emotionally healthy they will tend to be" (p. 637).

Research on Religion and Mental Health

Although many scholars had theorized about a relationship between religion and mental health, until the second half of the twentieth century little empirical research was done. Many studies on religion and mental health began to appear in the professional literature in the 1950s, 1960s, and 1970s. Along with several articles and book chapters that reviewed these studies, textbooks such as Michael Argyle and Benjamin Beit-Hallahmi's *The Social Psychology of Religion* (London, 1975), and edited volumes by H. Newton Malony (*Current Perspectives in the Psychology of Religion*, Grand Rapids, Mich., 1977) and Merton Strommen (*Research on Religious Development: A Comprehensive Handbook*, New York, 1971) contributed to an emerging literature.

The reviewers generally agreed that many studies showed no relationship between religious participation and mental health, others found it to be associated with greater mental disturbance, and still others with less disturbance. Some reviewers emphasized the negative findings, consistent with attitudes of social scientists at the time, although one reviewer criticized social scientists for their prejudice and their negative portrayal of conventional religion in the absence of empirical evidence. Most reviewers agreed that better quality research was needed to clarify inconsistent findings and to advance understanding.

In the early 1980s, two influential reviews of the research on religion and mental health, by C. Daniel Batson and W. Larry Ventis (*The Religious Experience: A Social-Psychological Perspective*, New York, 1982) and Allen E. Bergin (1983, *Professional Psychology: Research and Practice*, 14, 170–184) concluded that when all the studies are considered together, no consistent relationship between these two phenomena is discernible. Both reviews emphasized that mental health and religion are complex multidimensional phenomena; because diverse measures of religion and mental health were used in these studies, combining the results did little to promote understanding. Batson and Ventis demonstrated that when studies are categorized according to their definitions of mental health and religiousness, certain types of religiousness (e.g., intrinsic) are associated with some types of mental health (e.g., freedom from worry and guilt) but not with others (e.g., open-mindedness and flexibility).

Emphasizing this same point, Bergin called for researchers to define and measure religiousness and mental health more precisely in future studies, acknowledging that perhaps both the positive and negative correlations are correct. He argued that crude measures of religiousness, such as church membership or frequency of church attendance, may not be as useful as more precise measures, such as intrinsic and extrinsic religiousness. Bergin also pointed out that biases against religion in psychology have become embedded in empirical research, prejudicing the results of studies. He encouraged researchers to be more open to healthy forms of religion and to avoid using mental health measures that characterize religious beliefs as pathological.

Partly as a result of the Batson and Ventis and Bergin reviews, as well as a growing professional and societal interest in religious and spiritual issues, the 1980s and 1990s saw a significant increase in higher quality research in this domain. Several authors have reviewed this new body of research, making possible a number of additional conclusions. The conclusions summarized hereafter are based primarily on the works of Harold G. Koenig (*Is Religion Good for Your Health? The Effects of Religion on Physical and Mental Health*, Binghamton, N.Y., 1997), P. Scott Richards and Allen E. Bergin (*A Spiritual Strategy for Counseling and Psychotherapy*, Washington, D.C., 1997), and Edward P. Shafranske (*Religion and the Clinical Practice of Psychology*, Washington, D.C., 1996).

Current findings on religion and mental health can be grouped into three different categories: (1) psychological adjustment, (2) pathological social conduct, and (3) serious mental disorders. Much research during the past two decades has also examined the relationships between religion and (4) physical health.

Religion and Psychological Adjustment. Many studies have shown that religiously committed people tend to report greater subjective well-being and life satisfaction. This finding seems robust, as a variety of measures of well-being have been used with many different samples. Several large epidemiological studies have found negative relationships between religious participation and psychological distress.

People who engage in religious coping behaviors (e.g., praying, reading sacred writings, meditating, seeking support from religious leaders and religious community) during stressful times tend to adjust better to crises and problems. One study found that hospitalized patients who engage frequently in religious coping experience less depression than other patients. Evidence shows that people who turn to God for help in coping with stress, serious illness, and death have less anxiety, less depression, greater self-esteem and psychosocial competence, and better physical health.

Many studies have examined the relations between religion and anxiety, with inconsistent findings. There is, however, consistent evidence that intrinsically religious people report less anxiety, including less death anxiety. They also experience more freedom from worry and neurotic guilt (i.e., guilt in the absence of wrongdoing that causes depression, anxiety, or obsessions) than do less religious people. Intrinsic people do score higher on measures of healthy guilt, suggesting that they are more likely to experience guilt or remorse over actual wrongdoings and to engage in repentance and restitution.

Several studies of nonclinical population samples have shown that religious commitment is usually associated with lower levels of depression. Some evidence also suggests that church attendance is strongly predictive of less depression in elderly people. Whether religiously committed people experience lower rates of major clinical depression or bipolar disorder is unknown.

Many studies have examined the relationship between religion and self-esteem, with mixed findings, which may be due to the use of a variety of religious and self-esteem measures. Additionally, bias against religious people is evident in some self-esteem measures (e.g., admitting that one is religious reduces one's self-esteem score). More research on this topic and more care in the selection of religious and self-esteem measures may yield greater clarity. For example, evidence indicates that intrinsic religiousness is often positively associated with dimensions of self-esteem such as feelings of personal competence and control.

Pathological Social Conduct. Although various

forms of social conduct such as divorce, alcohol and drug abuse, teen pregnancy, suicide, crime, and delinquency are not direct indicators of mental health status, there is a strong relationship between mental illness and pathological social conduct. Thus, it is pertinent to comment on research regarding religion and social conduct. Studies have consistently shown that people who attend church are less likely to divorce. Some have argued that this is a result of religious prohibitions against divorce rather than to happier marriages; however, studies have also consistently shown a positive relationship between religious participation and marital satisfaction and adjustment.

Considerable evidence indicates that people with high levels of religious involvement are less likely to use or abuse alcohol, with lower rates among members of denominations that discourage or prohibit alcohol consumption. There is also extensive evidence that religiously committed people are less likely to use or abuse drugs.

Many studies have reported positive correlations between religious involvement and inhibition of premarital sexual behavior, with denominations that have clear, unambiguous prohibitions against premarital sex having lower rates of premarital sex and teenage pregnancy than others. Research has consistently shown that although religious attitudes do not distinguish delinquents from nondelinquents, religious commitment, as measured by church attendance, is negatively associated with delinquency. Finally, numerous studies have found that religiously committed people report fewer suicidal impulses and more negative attitudes toward suicide, and they commit suicide less often than nonreligious people.

The relationship between religion and moral development also involves somewhat mixed, controversial findings. Research based on Lawrence Kohlberg's theory of moral development has revealed that conservative religious people tend to have lower moral reasoning scores than liberal religious or nonreligious people. Some scholars have concluded that conservative religious ideologies promote conventional moral standards but stifle or impair internalization of more principled moral values. Others have found evidence that measures of Kohlberg's stages of moral development are biased against conservative religious people, who often use spiritual, theistic criteria that may conflict with Kohlberg's justice-based moral considerations.

Despite the moral reasoning controversy, evidence indicates that religious commitment is positively associated with moral behavior. Devoutly religious people generally adhere to more stringent moral standards, curbing personal desire or gain to promote the welfare of others and of society (e.g., not gambling, drinking, or engaging in premarital or extramarital sex). Evidence further suggests that intrinsic religious commitment is positively associated with empathy and altruism. However, it has been argued that intrinsic religious commitment is associated more with a desire to appear altruistic and helpful than with altruistic behavior. More research is needed to resolve this controversy.

Religion and Serious Mental Illness. Considerably less evidence is available on the relationship between religion and serious mental illness (e.g., major affective disorders, personality disorders, eating disorders, schizophrenia and other psychotic disorders) than on the other four categories, and the evidence that exists is ambiguous. Although psychotic patients often manifest religious delusions, the presence of religious ideation in itself does not necessarily mean that a patient is devout. Nor does it mean that religion has caused or contributed to the psychosis.

Some studies have found that seriously mentally ill patients are less religious than better functioning patients; however, causality remains unclear. Seriously mentally ill people may drop out of religious activities as well as other activities, with religious involvement doing nothing to prevent the mental illness. More studies are needed that compare mentally ill with mentally healthy groups, assessing the rates of occurrence of serious clinical disorders within random samples of specific religious denominations or within other specifically defined religious and nonreligious subgroups.

Religion and Physical Health. Considerable evidence indicates that religious commitment is positively associated with better physical health. Religious people have a lower prevalence of a wide range of illnesses, including cancer, cardiovascular disease, and hypertension. As a group, religiously committed people tend to live longer and to respond better once they have been diagnosed with an illness. Several studies have found that people's religious beliefs help them to cope better with their illnesses, including a reduced likelihood of severe depression and perceived disability. Religious commitment may also play a role in recovery from illness. Studies of religiously committed surgical patients have shown lower rates of postoperative mortality, less depression, and better ambulation status compared to patients with lower levels of religious commitment.

Conclusions

Most scholars now seem to agree that religion can be either healthy or unhealthy. Considerable research supports the conclusion that devout, intrinsic religious values and behaviors are more health promoting than a less devout, extrinsic orientation. The association of religious commitment with better mental and physical health has led some scholars to ask what aspects of religion may be health enhancing. One explanation is that spiritual practices such as praying, worshipping with members of one's religious community, reading sacred writings, meditating, confessing and forgiving, and seeking spiritual direction from religious leaders help people to cope better with stress and problems. In fact, evidence is increasing that such practices do promote emotional and physical healing. Additional explanations include the following: (1) religious beliefs provide people with a sense of life purpose and meaning, which lowers anxiety and promotes resiliency, hope, and peace; (2) religious affiliation provides a link with a community of believers, resulting in a feeling of belonging and social support; (3) religious beliefs may promote healthy behaviors (e.g., abstinence from alcohol and illegal drugs); and (4) there is a superempirical healing energy activated by devout religious involvement—in other words, God blesses those who love and obey him.

A few scholars continue to question the developing consensus that religious commitment is usually associated with better health. This is further evidence that both religion and mental health are complex, value-laden concepts and phenomena that are difficult to study objectively. The frequent use of correlational designs, self-report measures, and samples of college students perpetuates some of the ambiguity in this domain. The absence of modern, precise, theoretical guiding concepts has also slowed progress toward resolving some problems. Despite these impediments, recognition of the health benefits of mainstream religious involvement and commitment has increased significantly over the past twenty years.

[See also Coping; Moral Development; Religion and Psychotherapy; and Values.]

Bibliography

Benson, H. (1996). Timeless healing: The power and biology of belief. New York: Scribner. Reviews and discusses evidence that belief in God or a Higher Power contributes to better physical health.

Hood, R. W., Jr., Spilka, B., Hunsberger, B., & Gorsuch, R. L. (1996). The psychology of religion: An empirical approach. New York: Guilford Press. Reviews and discusses research on religion, mental health, and personality.

Levin, J. S. (Ed.). (1994). Religion and aging and health. Thousand Oaks, CA: Sage. Provides a scholarly treatment of research and theory on religion and health in elderly people.

Pargament, K. I. (1997). The psychology of religion and coping: Theory, research, practice. New York: Guilford Press. Provides an in-depth analysis of how religion can promote coping and health.

Strommen, M. (Ed.). (1971). Research on religious development: A comprehensive handbook. New York: Hawthorn Books. Reviews and analyzes research done in the 1950s and 1960s on religion and mental health.

Wulff, D. M. (1997). Psychology of religion: Classic and contemporary views (2nd ed.). New York: Wiley. Provides an in-depth theoretical and empirical analysis of major psychological perspectives on religion, including the views of Freud, Jung, James, Allport, and Erikson.

Allen E. Bergin and P. Scott Richards

REM SLEEP. See Dreams, article on Physiology; and Sleep.

REPLICATION IN RESEARCH. Replication in research refers to a study or studies conducted specifically to verify the results of an earlier study. The undetected equipment failure and the rare and possibly random human errors of procedure, observation, recording, computation, or report are known well enough to make scientists wary of the unreplicated experiment. When we add to the possibility of the random "fluke" common to all sciences, the fact of individual organismic differences and the possibility of systematic experimenter effects, the importance of replication looms larger still to the behavioral scientist. [See Expectancy Effects.]

What do scientists mean by "replication"? The research participants are usually different individuals and the experimenter changes over time, if not necessarily dramatically. Thus, scientists think of relative replications in terms of participants, experimenters, tasks, and situations. Three variables affecting the value, or utility, of any particular relative replication are: (1) when the replication is conducted; (2) how the replication is conducted; and (3) by whom the replication is conducted.

When the Replication Is Conducted

Replications conducted early in the history of a particular research question are usually more useful than replications conducted later in the history of that question. Weighting all replications equally, the first replication doubles our information about the research issue, the fifth replication adds 20% to our information level, and the fiftieth replication adds only 2% to our information level. Once the number of replications grows to be substantial, there is a need to evaluate and summarize the replications already available. [See Meta-Analysis.]

How the Replication Is Conducted

If scientists choose their replications to be as similar as possible to the study being replicated, the results may be more faithful to the original idea of replication but may have limited generalizability (also called external validity). The more imprecise the replications, the greater the benefit to the external validity of the tested

REPLICATION IN RESEARCH. Table 1. Effects on theory of the success of replication and the precision of replication

Precision of Replication	Result of Replication	
	Successful	Unsuccessful
Fairly precise	Supports the theory	Damages the theory
Fairly imprecise	Extends the theory	Limits the theory

relationship if the results support the relationship. If the results do not support the original finding, however, we cannot tell whether that lack of support stems from the instability of the original result or from the imprecision of the replications.

Table 1 summarizes the consequences for the theory that is derived from the initial study of (1) successful versus unsuccessful replications and (2) the precise versus the imprecise nature of the replications. Table 2 summarizes the consequences for the original investigator of (1) successful versus unsuccessful replications and (2) the precise versus imprecise nature of the replications. Compared to the theory tested by the replication, the investigator has much to lose if a fairly precise replication is unsuccessful, because such failure is often associated with ascriptions to the original investigator of having been careless, incompetent, and in some cases, even dishonest.

By Whom the Replication Is Conducted

So far we have assumed that the replications are independent of one another. The usual minimum requirement for independence is that the subjects of the replications be different persons. But what about the independence of the replicators? For example, a common situation is that in which research is conducted by a team of researchers. Sometimes these teams consist entirely of colleagues; often they are composed of one or more faculty members and postdoc-

toral students, and one or more predoctoral students. Experimenters within a single research group may reasonably be assumed to be more highly "intercorrelated" than any group of workers in the same area of interest who are not within the same research group. And perhaps students in a research group are more likely than a faculty member in the research group to be more "correlated" with their major professor. That is, students may elect to work in a given area with a given investigator *because* of their perceived and/or actual similarity of interest and associated characteristics.

The Meaning of Successful Replication

Traditionally, successful replication has been taken to mean that a null hypothesis that was rejected at time 1 is rejected again, and with the same direction of outcome, on the basis of a new study at time 2. The basic model of this usage can be seen in Table 3. The results of the first study are described dichotomously as $p < .05$ or $p > .05$ (or some other critical level, e.g., .01). Each of these two possible outcomes is further dichotomized as to the results of the second study as $p < .05$ or $p > .05$. Thus, cells A and D of Table 3 are ostensibly "failures" to replicate because one study was significant and the other was not. The problem with this traditional view of replication is that two studies could show identical magnitudes of the effect investigated and yet differ in significance level because of differences in sample sizes.

Newer, more useful views of replication success have two primary characteristics. First, the newer views focus on effect size (e.g., the magnitude of the relationship between the manipulated variable and some relevant outcome variable) as the more important summary statistic of a study with only a relatively minor interest in the statistical significance level. Second, the evaluation of whether replication has been successful is made in a continuous fashion. For example, two stud-

REPLICATION IN RESEARCH. Table 2. Effects on original investigator of the success of replication and the precision of replication

Precision of Replication	Result of Replication	
	Successful	Unsuccessful
Fairly precise	Supports the investigator	Impugns the investigator
Fairly imprecise	Supports the investigator	Impugns the investigator very little

REPLICATION IN RESEARCH. Table 3. Common model of successful replication: Judgment is dichotomous and based on significance testing

Second Study	First Study	
	$p>.05$*	$p<.05$
$p<.05$[a]	A Failure to replicate	B Successful replication
$p>.05$	C Failure to establish effect	D Failure to replicate

*By convention .05 but could be any other given level, e.g., .01.

[a] In the same tail (or direction) as the results of the first study.

ies are *not* said to be successful or unsuccessful replicates of each other, but rather the degree of failure to replicate is specified.

Bibliography

Nelson, N., Rosenthal, R., & Rosnow, R. L. (1986). Interpretation of significance levels and effect sizes by psychological researchers. *American Psychologist, 41,* 1299–1301. Documentation of psychologists' reliance on a dichotomous decision procedure accompanied by an untenable discontinuity of credibility in results varying in *p* levels.

Neuliep, J. W. (Ed.). (1990). Handbook of replication research in the behavioral and social sciences [Special issue]. *Journal of Social Behavior and Personality, 5* (4). Discussions of how the concept of replication is central to the scientific study of psychology.

Sidman, M. (1960). *Tactics of scientific research: Evaluating experimental data in psychology.* New York: Basic Books. A classic discussion of replication in small-*n* or single-case studies.

Robert Rosenthal

REPRESENTATIONAL TOOLS. The wide variety of external representations includes pictures, maps, hallmarks, scale models, musical scores, graphs, photographs, figures, and letters. Although they are used in different ways, they all share important features:

- They have a dual nature: They are what they are, but at the same time they represent something else. Paintings are composed of pigments or patterns of ink on paper, but at the same time these elements combine to generate a representation of a scene, a person, a mood, and so forth.
- They have an intentional function: They do not emanate from an object like smoke from a burning house but are purposefully produced.
- They are enduring: They are not ephemeral like gestures, speech, or sign language but lasting in time.
- They enable online interaction between their creation and a perception of what they stand for. When they are generated, producers can look at them at the same time as they are creating them.

In sum, external representations come to have meaning on their own, independent of the situation in which they were produced.

We use external representations to record music, speech, quantities, and different information about subjects and objects or to symbolize religious and mythical beliefs. The use of external representations has increased our physical and intellectual powers beyond those constrained by biology and physics. But apart from using them as helpful referential-communicative tools, we think and talk about them, so they are also domains of knowledge. Philosophers inquire about the particular ways in which external representations can be considered symbolic and about the differences between them. Anthropologists analyze them in order to provide accounts of life in ancient cultures.

The creation and use of external representations are specifically human: No animal has ever intentionally produced a permanent trace to record its behavior. However, since external representations have existed in every culture and children are exposed to them from birth, they serve as a major source of cognitive development. Any attempt to explain human development must take into account the development of external representation.

Using Pictures and Scale Models

Before the age of 2, children are able to recognize and name people and objects depicted in pictures and drawings despite previous shielding from pictorial materials. Curiously, they can use information provided by pictures and schematic drawings before they can use information provided by scale space models. Judy DeLoache's studies (1991) gave 2- and 2½-year-olds information about a toy hidden in a room. The information consisted of either a set of color photographs of the hiding places, a wide-angle color photograph of the room, or a line drawing of a room. Most 2½-year-olds were successful in finding the toy in the real room, whereas most 2-year-olds were not. However, when the same information was provided via a scale model, 2½-year-olds could not find the miniature toy as easily; only 3-year-olds were successful. The use of external representations occurred earlier with pictures than with scale models. It is as if the less realistic the medium, the easier it is to use. This might be due to the fact that complex three-dimensional objects are more likely to be treated as objects rather than as external representations. Of course, having the ability to use information conveyed by a picture does not imply that children understand that the meaning of the object is embedded in the product detached from the conditions of production.

Representation-in-Action

Until 4 or 5 years of age, children construct their external representations as representations-in-action undetachable from the conditions of production. When kindergartners and older children were asked to record a tune that they would have to recall later, they represented the important elements of the tune while drawing. For example, for each sound of the tune, they monitored how high or low pitched the sound was and correspondingly made a mark that was either high or low. The graphic output was more like a recording of action in the graphic space. Neither the child nor another person could use it to recover the tune. The production had yet to become an independent source of information. A similar process is found in the development of other representational means.

Early Drawing Development

Although children realize very early that anything that can be visually recognized can be drawn, it takes time until they include in their drawings features that enable recognition (Schierer, 1986). Before the age of 2, drawings arise in the context of intentional action that may be nonpictorial, like pretend play. According to Schierer, earliest drawings record movement or activity accompanied by roaring sounds or voices, but the content of the record does not last, and the original referent cannot be recognized from the drawn traces. It is a representation-in-action. Romancing develops during the second year of life: Children generate scribblelike marks on purpose for contexts in which referents were stipulated prior to, concomitantly with, or immediately after their drawing. Two types of graphic schemas, circular-wavy shapes and incisive dots or angular shapes, are typically found in these scribbles. Dots and lines are combined more frequently and earlier in age to stand for what is being drawn. An external observer can capture the announced intention, "It's a car," from the context but not from the drawn shapes. By the age of five, most children have developed a repertoire of forms. They explore these primitive elements not just to form recognizable human faces or other objects but as a type of form-play in which they experiment to find the most adequate among alternative forms and to experience different combinations. It is the formal component of the development of pictorial ability. The next step is characterized by "visually realistic drawings" in which the internal representation of the referent guides the child in deciding what to draw. If the child knows that cups include handles, they must appear in the drawing, although they were missing from the cup that served as a model for the child.

Early Notational Development

Conventional systems such as numbers and writing are also interesting objects of knowledge for toddlers and preschoolers. Although the main function of numbers is to evoke numerosities and the main function of writing is to evoke language, both differ from drawing because they make use of conventional notations (Harris, 1995). The alphabet and Hindu-Arabic figures are notations that consist of a limited number of distinct graphic elements that are used to form indefinite combinations. Children's formal exploration of numbers and writing precedes their use of these systems as referential-communicative tools.

Early Development of Numerical Notation. Long before being systematically taught at school, children recognize the shape of and learn the names and the social uses of figures for buses, elevators, or birthday cakes. This formal knowledge is not used to represent numerosities. If 3- to 4-year-olds are shown collections of objects, such as different quantities of toy bricks in various tins, and are asked "to put on paper" how many toy bricks there are in each tin, they do not draw a different number of pictures for each, even when they know the shape and name of the figures. For the same situation, older children usually produce a drawinglike pattern. They do not represent quantity as a feature detached from the enumerated objects but rather iterate graphically the objects in each collection.

The next step takes place when children produce a "global notation of quantity": The number of lines diminishes or increases with reductions or increments of the objects in the collections. Later, children succeed in making one-to-one correspondences with the objects in the collection. Correspondence may be obtained by icons, tallies, dots, crosses, and other nonnumerical signs, such as letters. Numerosity has been detached from the enumerated objects, and multiplicity is explicitly depicted. Sometimes one-to-one correspondence is obtained by using numerals. For example, for a collection of four buttons, the child produces 1 2 3 4 or repeats the same figure as many times as the objects are to be represented: 4 4 4 4. Although explicit one-to-one correspondence is still necessary, the same figures are now used to represent different objects. Earlier in development, when children produce iconic iterative marks, they not only need to make explicit the items in the collection, but they also need to individualize them in a way that differentiates one collection from another.

Finally, children produce unitary notations. Although sometimes the cardinality of the collection is represented by an incorrect numeral, children no longer convey information about the quality or item correspondence in the collection. Perhaps it is only after the iteration and multiplicity implicit in conventional figures has been understood through a process of external explicit iteration and one-to-one correspondence that children are prepared to use the conventional figures they recognized earlier on.

Early Development of Writing. Very early on, children can affirm that "letters are for reading," can distinguish letter shapes, and can name them. However, a long process ensues before children use this knowledge for representing language. When 3- to 6-year-olds were asked to write words and sentences dictated by an adult, the earliest productions appear as a linear, discontinuous pattern of wavy lines. Nevertheless, the outputs display the features of form common to almost any writing system in any language: linearity, presence of distinguishable units, regularity of blanks, and directionality. Similar "scrawls," however, are made for each word or sentence children are asked to write. The written product has not yet been detached from the process of production and from the notator; it has meaning in the context of the writing task.

By the age of 5 most children start using letter forms that may not correspond with their conventional sound value. Letters of the child's own name or other letters they have learned may be used in different combinations to form whatever word or sentence they are willing to write. Moreover, at this stage children's written outputs appear formally constrained by two principles: minimal number and lack of variety of letters. They usually write about three letters, and they do not repeat more than two adjacent letters. Children have discovered that a domain-specific representation is an essential condition of writing and that different words are represented by different combinations of letters. The constraints of number and variety that children impose on their written productions reflect the actual distribution of word length and intraword variation in real texts.

The next developmental shift occurs when children start to relate writing to spoken language. During the stage of formally constrained writing, children start to match parts of the words to parts of the written string, and the number and kind of letters they use are related to the acoustic length and composition of the words. It is assumed that at this stage the names of the letters help children to relate writing to spoken language, and it marks the turning point from early writing to the development of spelling.

Relationships Between Drawing, Writing, and Numbers

Although the three systems go through a similar developmental path, starting as representation-in-action and progressing through exploring formal aspects and only then to the referential aspects, the systems are not confused. Rather, the differentiation between drawing, numbers, and writing is precocious. When children's outputs in writing are compared with their drawings, only the writing outputs display linearity, distinguishable units, regularity of blanks, and consistent directionality. Moreover, even when some 2- to 3-year-olds may produce writing and drawings that are graphically indistinguishable, their motor intentions are clearly distinct (Brenneman, Massey, Machado, & Gelman, 1996). They rotate the paper or lift the pen much more frequently when writing than when drawing.

Studies using sorting tasks have shown that preliterate children consider a card as "good for reading" if it contains more than two and less than eight or nine letters and if adjacent letters are not identical. The same children, however, will not reject single figures or a long line of repeated figures as not "good for counting." They understand that any combination of figures is meaningful for numerical representation but that not every combination of letters is meaningful for written representation.

This precocious differentiation between systems does not preclude children from using drawings to express the number of objects in a collection or to record a message for a friend. When children use numbers or writing as referential-communicative tools, they focus on the content to be conveyed and resort to drawing because of the need of making it more explicit, but they are not confounding different systems as domains of knowledge.

Bibliography

Brennemann, K., Massey, C., Machado, S., & Gelman, R. (1996). Notating knowledge about words and objects: Pre-schoolers' plans differ for writing and drawing. *Cognitive Development, 11*, 397–419.

DeLoache, J. S., & Burns, N. (1993). Symbolic development in young children: Understanding models and pictures. In C. Pratt & A. Garton (Eds.), *Systems of representation in children: Development and use* (pp. 92–112). Chichester, England: Wiley.

Ferreiro, E. (1986). The interplay between information and assimilation in beginning literacy. In W. Teale & E. Sulzby (Eds.), *Emergent literacy: Writing and reading* (pp. 15–49). Norwood, NJ: Ablex.

Freeman, N. H., & Cox, M. V. (Eds.). (1985). *Visual order: The nature and development of pictorial representation.* Cambridge, England: Cambridge University Press.

Harris, R. (1995). *Signs of writing.* London: Routledge and Kegan Paul.

Hughes, M. (1986). *Children and number difficulties in learning mathematics.* Oxford, England: Blackwell.

Karmiloff Smith, A. (1992). *Beyond modularity.* Cambridge, MA: MIT Press.

Luria, A. R. (1978). The development of writing in the child. In M. Cole (Ed.), *The selected writings of A. R. Luria* (pp. 145–194). New York: Sharpe. (Original work published 1929)

Schier, S. (1986). *Deeper into pictures.* Cambridge, UK: Cambridge University Press.

Sinclair, A., Siegrist, F., & Sinclair, H. (1983). Young children's ideas about the written numbers systems. In D. Rogers & J. Sloboda (Eds.), *The acquisition of symbolic skills* (pp. 535–542). New York: Plenum Press.

Liliana Tolchinsky

REPRESSED MEMORY. In his famous essay on repression, Freud (1915/1957) wrote that "the essence of repression lies simply in turning something away, and keeping it at a distance, from the conscious" (p. 147). Behind this statement is a very simple theory of repressed memory, a theory that in later works Freud replaced with a more sophisticated approach. The simple theory of repressed memory, however, as applied to patients suffering from disorders such as hysterical paralysis of limbs and other disabling psychological symptoms, is as follows: The patient has suffered a trauma in the past, usually in childhood and often involving a sexual interaction with an older individual, such as a parent, sibling, or relative. Memories of this trauma are so destabilizing for the self that they are repressed, but they later return transformed into symptoms and psychological illness. This model of repressed memories led Freud, in his earliest psychoanalytic work, to conclude that "hysterics suffer mainly from reminiscences" (Breuer & Freud, 1893/1955). By this he meant that repressed memories of a traumatic childhood seduction, although no longer in awareness, continued to exert a powerful influence on a person's functioning, and by way of his or her unconscious effects, to cause neuroses. Attractive though this "simple" theory of repressed memory is, it was later fully rejected by Freud (1915/1957, 1926/1959) on the basis of subsequent clinical experience, from which he concluded that such "memories" were fantasies arising from a developmental process of identification with the same-sex parent.

Freud's latter conception of repression was more complex, and to complicate matters further, underwent considerable revision over at least a 30-year period. In his paper on repression (1915/1957) he drew a distinction between what he called primal repression and after-pressure (see Moore & Fine, 1990, for a review). Primal or primary repression refers to the repression of intense instinctual desires during infancy and early childhood at a point when the mind is not yet fully developed (see Freud, 1926/1959, for further comment on this point). After-pressure or secondary repression is related to primary repression in that its function is to keep from awareness wishes, feelings, and ideas associated with materials that have been subjected to primary repression. Freud's view was that the clinician encountered only secondary repression and that primary repression could not be lifted or directly dealt with. Nevertheless, remnants of primary repression may emerge in the patient's emotional response to the analyst, and indeed in the analyst's emotional response to the patient. A further development introduced by Freud was the idea that very often it was the emotional aspects of an experience that were repressed, whereas some perhaps attenuated representation of nonemotional aspects (ideas) remained available to conscious recollection. Alternatively, and with rather different consequences for psychological illness, ideational content could be repressed, whereas the emotion associated with the (repressed) ideas remained in awareness. Most important, it is abundantly clear in Freud's more fully developed thinking on repression that he placed much more emphasis on the repression of disturbing thoughts, feelings, fantasies, and images than on the repression of whole memories. This view of Freud's is based on his advanced conception of memories, stated in chapter 7 of *The Interpretation of Dreams* (1900), in which memories were conceived as multiattribute representations distributed over several different brain processing regions, a view that has only recently taken center stage in contemporary models of human memory (cf. Schacter, Norman, & Koutstaal, 1998).

In accessing such complex mental representations, it is important that retrieval processes are able both to activate attributes relevant to current tasks and to inhibit attributes that are irrelevant or that, if activated, might interfere with achieving current goals. To use an example from Bjork (1989), when leaving the supermarket and trying to recall where one parked one's car, it is fairly critical that memories of where one parked it on other occasions do not come to mind. These competitor memories may well be activated during the retrieval process but then inhibited ("turned away" in Freud's sense) before they enter consciousness; if this were not the case, then one would be in for a bewildering and exhausting search of the parking lot. This view of the role of inhibition in memory retrieval has recently received strong support from a range of laboratory studies (Bjork & Anderson, 1994). Indeed, the evidence from the laboratory shows that, under certain circumstances, recently acquired information can be inhibited or repressed by an explicit instruction to forget the material (Bjork, 1989). This type of inhibition is consciously initiated, but it has also been shown that, when accessing specific items of knowledge in long-term memory, closely associated items are automatically inhibited (Anderson, Bjork, & Bjork, 1994; Anderson & Spellman, 1995). Although yet to be extended to clinical materials (but see Cloitre, 1998), these lines of research demonstrate the operation of an inhibitory memory mechanism that could support the turning away from consciousness of disturbing thoughts and the creation of memories or other thoughts that would "screen" closely associated but disturbing knowledge, just as Freud (1989/1962) originally postulated. Recent evidence from corroborated cases of the recovery of memories of childhood sexual abuse also adds some weight to the notion of repressed details of past experiences that later can be recovered. In one study (Schooler, Bendiksen, & Ambadar, 1997) several patients remembered either that they had been abused or that their childhoods had been "difficult," but they retained no access to detailed information. One patient had apparently informed her ex-husband in a terse nonemotional statement that she had been abused as a child. All these patients subsequently recovered details of their experiences, often in response to highly specific cues, and the latter patient was surprised to learn that her ex-husband knew of her abuse, as she had forgotten her comments to him. Other studies have observed how, for example, serial killers, when reminded of their murders, immediately indulge in intense attempts at thought blocking (Christianson & Engelberg, 1997), attempts not dissimilar to laboratory procedures that induce self-directed forgetting and highly reminiscent of Freud's (1915/1957) comments on constantly applied repression. Finally, other clinical research (Harvey & Herman, 1994) has categorized survivors of childhood sexual abuse in terms of the types of access they show to specific aspects of their trauma. Essentially, the different groups show to varying degrees repression of specific events, event details, or emotions, much as might be expected if multiattribute complex knowledge structures were subject to selective inhibition (note that in this latter study neither the abuse nor amnesia were independently corroborated).

The suggestion, however, that whole sets of highly vivid, detailed, and accurate memories can be repressed and remain in an unaltered state for years or decades, later to be surprisingly recovered, remains highly contentious and currently fuels the acrimonious recovered memories debate. At the center of this debate is an uncritical, uninformed acceptance of Freud's abandoned "simple" model of repression (Conway, 1997; Kihlstrom, 1997) coupled to a naive view of memories as accurate and detailed records of experience (Loftus, 1993). All the data currently available, from both laboratory and clinic, demonstrate that human memory does not consist of detailed, literal records of experience. Rather, human memory retains a compressed record of abstract qualities of experiences, that is, the meaning of an event, in which only a few specific details, perhaps of personal importance at the time of the experience, survive over long retention intervals. In the recovered memories debate, the lessons Freud learned over a century ago seem to have been forgotten, namely, that a simple theory of repression is contradicted by the clinical material, as well as by more recent experimental evidence. Instead, a more sophisticated account is called for, one that recognizes the complex nature of the representation of knowledge in long-term memory, the constructive use of this knowledge, and the intertwining of beliefs, wishes, desires, experience, and emotion, both in actual knowledge representations and in dynamic instantiation of these in consciousness when the past is recollectively experienced (Tulving, 1985). Although current evidence is far from complete, laboratory studies reveal promising data that implicate the operation of inhibitory processes in human memory, this view is lent further support by corroborated case studies from the clinic. In conclusion, the inhibition, repression, or "turning away from consciousness" of ideas, feelings, wishes, and so forth, seems at least possible even if we do not yet know what the exact mechanisms are or how they are applied—once, several times, or constantly. What is not possible is the repression of whole sets of videolike memories (later to be recovered in pristine form). The reason is that these did not exist in the first place—human memory is not a literal record of experience, it is an interpretation of it.

[*See also* False Memory.]

Bibliography

Anderson, M. C., & Bjork, R. A. (1994). Mechanisms of inhibition in long-term memory: A new taxonomy. In D. Degenbach & T. Carr (Eds.), *Inhibitory processes in attention, memory, and language* (pp. 265–325). San Diego, CA: Academic Press.

Anderson, M. C., Bjork, R. A., & Bjork, E. L. (1994). Remembering can cause forgetting: Retrieval dynamics in long-term memory. *Journal of Experimental Psychology: Learning, Memory, and Cognition, 20,* 1063–1087.

Anderson, M. C., & Spellman, B. A. (1995). On the status of inhibitory mechanisms in cognition: Memory retrieval as a model case. *Psychological Review, 102,* 68–100.

Bjork, R. A. (1989). Retrieval inhibition as an adaptive mechanism in human memory. In H. L. Roediger III & F. I. M. Craik (Eds.), *Varieties of memory and consciousness: Essays in honor of Endel Tulving* (pp. 309–330). Hillsdale, NJ: Erlbaum.

Breuer, J., & Freud, S. (1955). *Studies on hysteria.* In J. Strachey (Ed. and Trans.), *The standard edition of the complete psychological works of Sigmund Freud* (Vol. 2). London: Hogarth Press. (Original work published 1893)

Christianson, S.-A., & Engelberg, E. (1997). Remembering and forgetting traumatic experiences: A matter of survival. In M. A. Conway (Ed.), *Recovered memories and false memories* (pp. 230–250). Oxford, England: Oxford University Press.

Cloitre, M. (1998). Intentional forgetting and clinical disorders. In J. M. Golding & C. M. MacLeod (Eds.), *Intentional forgetting: Interdisciplinary approaches* (pp. 395–412). Mahwah, NJ: Erlbaum.

Conway, M. A. (1997). Past and present: Recovered memories and false memories. In M. A. Conway (Ed.), *Recovered memories and false memories* (pp. 150–191). Oxford, England: Oxford University Press.

Freud, S. (1955). Screen memories. In J. Strachey (Ed. and Trans.), *The standard edition of the complete psychological works of Sigmund Freud* (Vol. 3, pp. 7a). London: Hogarth Press. (Original work published 1899)

Freud, S. (1957). Repression (C. M. Baines & J. Strachey, Trans.) In J. Strachey (Ed.), *The standard edition of the complete psychological works of Sigmund Freud* (Vol. 14). London: Hogarth Press. (Original work published 1915)

Freud, S. (1959). Inhibition, symptoms, and anxiety (Alix Strachey, Trans.). In J. Strachey (Ed.), *The standard edition of the complete psychological works of Sigmund Freud* (Vol. 20). London: Hogarth Press. (Original work published 1926)

Harvey, M. R., & Herman, J. L. (1994). Amnesia, partial

amnesia, and delayed recall among adult survivors of childhood trauma. *Consciousness and Cognition, 3*, 295–306.

Kihlstrom, J. F. (1997). Suffering from reminiscences: Exhumed memory, implicit memory, and the return of the repressed. In M. A. Conway (Ed.), *Recovered memories and false memories* (pp. 100–117). Oxford, England: Oxford University Press.

Loftus, E. F. (1993). The reality of repressed memories. *American Psychologist, 48*, 518–537.

Moore, B., & Fine, B. (Eds.) (1990). *Psychoanalytic terms and concepts.* New Haven, CT: American Psychoanalytic Association and Yale University Press.

Schacter, D. L., Norman, K. A., & Koustaal, W. (1998). The cognitive neuroscience of constructive memory. *Annual Review of Psychology, 49*, 289–318.

Schooler, J. W., Bendiksen, M., Ambadar, Z. (1997). Taking the middle line: Can we accommodate both fabricated and recovered memories of sexual abuse? In M. A. Conway (Ed.), *Recovered memories and false memories* (pp. 251–292). Oxford, England: Oxford University Press.

Tulving, E. (1985). Memory and consciousness. *Canadian Psychologist, 26*, 1–12.

Martin A. Conway

REPRESSION. Although usually associated with Freud, the concept and the term *repression (Verdrängung)* was introduced into psychology a half century before psychoanalysis by Johann Herbart (1824–1825) to designate the inhibition of ideas by other ideas. Because the capacity of consciousness is limited, ideas struggle for entry into consciousness, and once successful, inhibit other ideas that might supplant them. According to Herbart, the inhibited ideas do not cease to exist but pass into a "state of tendency" below the "threshold of consciousness" and can, with changed circumstances or in recombination, overthrow the ideas currently in consciousness and repress them in turn.

Undoubtedly influenced by Herbart, at least indirectly (Sand, 1988), Sigmund Freud reintroduced the notion of repression (along with cognates such as "suppression," "dissociation," "inhibition," and "exclusion") to designate a defensive form of mental inhibition (Breuer & Freud, 1893/1955). Ideas, memories, wishes, and so forth that would produce "unbearable" psychological distress are defensively inhibited and excluded from consciousness. (Such distresses were eventually subsumed by Freud [1926/1959] under the construct "anxiety.") As in Herbart's system, these ideas did not disappear but struggled for expression and—here Freud introduces a major innovation—often emerge not in consciousness but indirectly in, for example, dreams, parapraxes (trifling cognitive errors such as slips of the tongue), or the body language of hysterical symptoms (conversion); hence Freud's stance that "symptoms have meaning" or "hysterics suffer mainly from reminiscences" (Breuer & Freud, 1895/1955, p. 7).

Almost immediately, Freud began to realize that defensive repression could be more complicated than mere inhibition. Already in 1894 he noted the phenomenon of splitting, in which the cognitive and emotional facets of an emotional ideational complex were dissociated and only the emotional component repressed (Freud, 1894/1967). This defense has come to be known as isolation or intellectualization. In the next 15 years Freud introduced, usually in the most informal, passing fashion, a plethora of additional defensive "distortions" (omission, displacement, isolation, denial, doubt, regression, projection, reaction formation, dissociation, symbolization, undoing, rationalization) that, although not completely excluding the original idea from consciousness, altered it sufficiently to render it less anxiety provoking. Many of these motivated cognitive reconstructions anticipate, even sometimes in name, the classic schema-driven distortions experimentally documented by Bartlett (1932), such as "rationalization," "omission," "symbolization," "transference" (displacement), and "condensation."

In most of his writings Freud treated the various tactics of defense as merely different techniques of repression. Eventually, he tried to simplify (not with the greatest consistency) by reverting to his initial term *defense (Abwher)* to designate all the techniques of distortion, including repression, and by treating repression in its original simple sense of inhibition (Freud, 1926/1959). Repression, in this simple sense, was now just one, though central, mechanism among a large repertoire of defenses.

Every mainstream introductory psychology textbook gives an exposition of the mechanisms of defense, including repression; yet repression has become a controversial topic in recent years. The problem is the perceived difficulty of producing repression in the laboratory. The well-known critic David Holmes (1990) has gone as far as to suggest that the concept of repression should be discarded. On close examination, the issue may turn not on science but on semantics. Without apparently intending to, psychoanalytic thinkers subtly altered Freud's conception of repression (Erdelyi, 1990, 1993). The crucial change is the widely held view, laid down by Anna Freud in *The Ego and the Mechanisms of Defence* (1936/1946), that repression had to be an unconscious operation. In the later literature, suppression was treated as the conscious counterpart of repression, in which the individual consciously inhibits unwanted thoughts or feelings. Textual analysis shows, however, that for Sigmund Freud, repression could be conscious or unconscious and that suppression and repression are treated interchangeably.

The resolution of the semantic question is decisive:

If repression (suppression, etc.) is simply the defensive exclusion, conscious or unconscious, of distressing thoughts from consciousness, then there is no argument about its existence even among experimental critics. If, however, it must be shown that the process of exclusion is itself unconscious, then it becomes deeply problematic to demonstrate the mechanism experimentally since there may exist no viable experimental methodology for so doing. Even if, for example, a patient or laboratory participant insisted that he or she was not conscious of excluding some train of thought, it could still be argued that the inhibition may have been originally conscious but then forgotten (for this type of argument, see Holender, 1986).

Another problem in trying to establish repression in the laboratory is that stimuli that are truly unbearable (child molestation, signs of impending death) cannot be ethically deployed experimentally. There is no guarantee that milder variants (e.g., obscene words) are sufficient to trigger repression.

One strategy for resolving the stimulus-insufficiency problem of the laboratory has been to study repression as a trait. There are wide-ranging individual differences in reactivity to stimuli; what is merely emotional to one participant may be intolerable to another. The construct of repressiveness has been investigated (see, e.g., Weinberger, Schwartz, & Davidson, 1979), with the finding that "repressors" (defined as people who are simultaneously high in social desirability and low in self-reported anxiety) tend, for example, to remember fewer emotional memories from childhood and also to be predisposed to certain illnesses, such as cancer. Another important individual difference, prefigured by Freud in 1894, is participants' reaction to trauma, with some responding with repressive defenses and others, actually a majority, with hypervigilance and rumination (Freud, 1894/1967). Trauma victims often oscillate between the two or show mixed patterns (Horowitz, 1986). Failure to take into account such individual differences has led to much confusion in the literature.

An unexpected laboratory window to defensive repression may be provided by clinical neurology, according to Ramachandran (1995), who describes cases of right-hemisphere stroke patents exhibiting, with respect to their left hemiplegia, "an amplified version of Freudian defense mechanisms . . . caught *in flagrante delicto*" (p. 26). Some of these patients completely deny "ownership" of, for example, a paralyzed arm, claiming it belonged to another person. In a striking discovery by Edoardo Bisiasch and his colleagues (Ramachandran, 1995), when the left ear canal of some of these patients is irrigated with ice-cold water, the result is a remission of denial and a recovery of memory for the previously denied paralysis. The remission is short-lived, however. After a few hours following caloric stimulation, one of Ramachandran's participants "not only reverted to de-

nial, but also repressed the admission of paralysis that she had made during her stimulation!" (p. 35). This "experimental/clinical evidence" shows, according to Ramachandran, that "memory repression" is "a robust psychological process" (pp. 35–36).

Beyond the existence question, there is a growing research interest in the extent to which repression and other defenses are pathological or pathogenic. Emphasis has shifted in recent years (see, e.g., Lazarus, 1983; Schwartz, 1990) to the beneficial, health-enhancing correlates of repressive coping. Related work has accumulated suggesting that depressed patients may not be suffering from negative cognitive biases or irrational beliefs, as is often supposed, but rather that it is the "healthy" nondepressed participants who deploy positive biases that protectively distort reality (see, e.g., Taylor & Brown, 1988; but see Colvin & Block, 1994, for a critique of this view). Yet another study (Pennebaker, 1995) documents health benefits for the opposite of repression—the expression of distressing past experiences—in line with cathartic therapy, an early version of psychoanalysis (Breuer & Freud, 1895/1955; Erdelyi, 1985). The research literature may be pointing to the conclusion that there are both costs and benefits to defensive repression (Lazarus, 1983) and that the timing of observation, the severity of threat, and other specific circumstances may be factors.

Although many critical issues remain to be addressed, the concept of defensive inhibition is probably established beyond question, though the term *repression* may drop out and be replaced by others, such as the currently popular *cognitive avoidance, retrieval inhibition, memory bias,* or *dissociation*. This probably will not happen as long as Freud's influence in psychology remains active, even if controversial. There is also the possibility of a synergistic integration of modern cognitive psychology and the psychodynamic tradition (Erdelyi, 1990, 1993), with the harmonizing of the laboratory findings of Herman Ebbinghaus and F. C. Bartlett, who dealt with forgetting and distortion due to cognitive factors, with the clinical findings of Freud, who dealt with forgetting and distortion due to emotional factors.

Bibliography

Bartlett, F. C. (1932). *Remembering*. Cambridge, England: Cambridge University Press.

Breuer, J., & Freud, S. (1955). On the psychical mechanism of hysterical phenomena: Preliminary communication. In J. Strachey (Ed., and Trans.), *The standard edition of the complete psychological works of Sigmund Freud* (Vol. 2, pp. 3–17). London: Hogarth Press. (Original work published 1893)

Breuer, J., & Freud, S. (1955). Studies on hysteria. In J. Strachey (Ed. and Trans.), *The standard edition of the complete psychological works of Sigmund Freud* (Vol. 2, pp. 1–35) London: Hogarth Press. (Original work published 1895)

Colvin, C. R., & Block, J. (1994). Do positive illusions foster mental health? An examination of the Taylor and Brown formulation. *Psychological Bulletin, 116,* 3–20.

Davis, P. J., & Schwartz, G. E. (1987). Repression and the inaccessibility of affective memories. *Journal of Personality and Social Psychology, 52,* 155–163.

Erdelyi, M. H. (1985). *Psychoanalysis: Freud's cognitive psychology.* New York: Freeman.

Erdelyi, M. H. (1990). Repression, reconstruction, and defense: History and integration of the psychoanalytic and experimental frameworks. In L. L. Singer (Ed.), *Repression and dissociation: Implications for personality theory, psychopathology, and health* (pp. 1–31). Chicago: University of Chicago Press.

Erdelyi, M. H. (1993). Repression: The mechanism and the defense. In D. M. Wegner & J. W. Pennebaker (Eds.), *Handbook of mental control* (pp. 126–148). Englewood Cliffs, NJ: Prentice Hall.

Freud, A. (1946). *The ego and the mechanisms of defense* (C. Baines, Trans.). New York: International Universities Press. (Original work published 1936)

Freud, S. (1959). Inhibitions, symptoms and anxiety. In J. Strachey (Ed. and Trans.), *The standard edition of the complete psychological works of Sigmund Freud* (Vol. 20, pp. 77–174). London: Hogarth Press. (Original work published 1926)

Freud, S. (1967). The neuro-psychoses of defence. (J. Rickman, Trans.). In J. Strachey (Ed.), *The standard edition of the complete psychological works of Sigmund Freud* (Vol. 3, pp. 43–61). London: Hogarth Press. (Original work published 1894)

Herbart, J. F. (1824–1825). *Psychologie als Wissenschaft neu gegründet auf Erfahrung, Metaphysik und Mathematik* [Psychology as science, newly established on the basis of experience, metaphysics, and mathematics]. (2 vols.). Königsberg: Unzer.

Holender, D. (1986). Semantic activation without conscious identification in dichotic listening, parafoveal vision, and visual masking: A survey and appraisal. *Behavioral and Brain Sciences, 9,* 1–66.

Holmes, D. (1990). The evidence for repression: An examination of sixty years of research. In L. L. Singer (Ed.), *Repression and dissociation: Implications for personality theory, psychopathology, and health* (pp. 85–102). Chicago: University of Chicago Press.

Horowitz, M. J. (1986). *Stress response syndrome* (2nd ed.). Northvale, NJ: Aronson.

Lazarus, R. S. (1983). The costs and benefits of denial. In S. Bresnitz (Ed.), *Denial of stress* (pp. 1–30). New York: International Universities Press.

Pennebaker, J. (Ed.). (1995). *Emotion, disclosure, and health.* Washington, DC: American Psychological Association.

Ramachandran, V. S. (1995). Anosognosia in parietal lobe syndrome. *Consciousness and Cognition, 4,* 22–51.

Sand, R. (1988). Early nineteenth-century anticipation of Freudian theory. *International Review of Psycho-Analysis, 15,* 465–479.

Schwartz, G. E. (1990). The psychobiology of repression and health: A systems approach. In L. L. Singer (Ed.), *Repression and dissociation: Implications for personality theory, psychopathology, and health* (pp. 405–434). Chicago: University of Chicago Press.

Taylor, S. E., & Brown, J. D. (1988). Illusion and well-being: A social psychological perspective on mental health. *Psychological Bulletin, 103,* 193–210.

Weinberger, D. G., Schwartz, G., & Davidson, R. (1979). Low-anxious, high-anxious, and repressive coping styles: Psychometric patterns and behavioral and physiological responses to stress. *Journal of Abnormal Psychology, 88,* 369–380.

Matthew Hugh Erdelyi

REPRODUCTIVE SYSTEM. Because the reproductive system relies on hormonal communication and because those hormones also affect the nervous system and behavior, an understanding of basic reproductive anatomy, physiology, function, and dysfunction can provide insight into some behaviors. We will review the basic aspects of the reproductive system, paying special attention to the role of hormones and relying primarily on the animal research literature that provides this information. This animal literature, especially that dealing with the behavioral consequences of hormones, suggests specific hypotheses about how hormones might alter human behavior. As we shall see, hormones do not play nearly as powerful a role in affecting behavior in humans as in other mammals, but nevertheless, hormones do exert an influence even in our own species.

For our purposes, we may define a hormone as a chemical that is produced by and released from one part of the body and travels through the bloodstream to affect another part of the body. Most of the organs that secrete hormones are known as endocrine glands because, unlike exocrine glands such as tear ducts or sweat glands, which release fluids outside the body, endocrine glands release fluids inside the body. The endocrine glands of primary interest to the present topic are the pituitary, the gonads, and the adrenal glands. The subfield of psychology concerned with the effect of hormones on behavior is known as behavioral endocrinology. It is important to remember one aspect of behavioral endocrinology, namely, that the secretion of hormones is not normally under our conscious control or awareness. This means that, unlike, say, perceptual processes, introspection offers few clues about endocrinological processes. Therefore, we must rely even more heavily on well-controlled studies to reveal the behavioral effects of hormones. [*See* Endocrine Systems.]

Posterior Pituitary

Lying beneath the brain is the pea-sized pituitary gland. The pituitary was long considered a "master gland" because it releases many hormones that, among other things, control hormonal secretion from the other endocrine glands distributed throughout the body. However, as with so many other aspects of mammalian biology, it soon became apparent that this master gland is itself under the strict control of the brain, especially the hypothalamus, which sits immediately above the pituitary. For example, the posterior pituitary consists primarily of axons that extend down from their parent neurons in the hypothalamus. When these hypothalamic neurons are sufficiently excited by synaptic input from other brain regions, they produce an action potential that spreads down the axons, and on reaching the terminals, induces the release of a chemical into the bloodstream. Because these hypothalamic neurons release a chemical into the general circulation rather than into a synapse, they represent a hybrid between other neurons and endocrine cells and so are known as neuroendocrine cells. These hypothalamic neuroendocrine cells release one of two peptide hormones into the bloodstream: oxytocin and vasopressin. Vasopressin promotes water retention by increasing the concentration of urine, and so plays an important role in fluid regulation. Oxytocin promotes contractions of the uterus in childbirth; therefore, physicians sometimes administer synthetic forms of oxytocin to speed delivery. In mothers, oxytocin is also released by the tactile stimuli provided by a nursing infant, and acts on the mammary glands to promote milk ejection. This process is known as the "let-down reflex" and conditioning comes to play an important role, as repeated pairings of stimuli may elicit oxytocin release prior to suckling itself. Thus, the baby's crying may come to elicit the let-down reflex before suckling commences. Men also produce oxytocin, but its functional role in males remains unknown. Interestingly, a burst of oxytocin release accompanies ejaculation in male animals and humans and accompanies orgasm in women.

Anterior Pituitary

The anterior pituitary releases at least six different protein hormones, including (1) growth hormone, which acts throughout the body to promote growth and body maintenance, (2) prolactin, which acts on mammary tissues to prepare for lactation, and a series of tropic hormones, so called because they drive other endocrine glands to release their respective hormones; these include (3) thyroid-stimulating hormone, which drives the thyroid gland in the throat to release thyroid hormones, (4) adrenocorticotropic hormone (ACTH), which drives the adrenal glands to produce two classes of steroid hormones, including glucocorticoids such as cortisol (these hormones are released as part of the normal stress response) and two hormones important for our discussion of reproduction, the gonadotropins: (5) follicle-stimulating hormone

(FSH) and (6) luteinizing hormone (LH); both FSH and LH affect the gonads—the testes in men and the ovaries in women.

The timing and amount of tropic hormone released from the anterior pituitary are determined by the brain. Hypothalamic neurons release chemical factors into a specialized vascular system that delivers them to the anterior pituitary. These hypothalmic-releasing factors promote or inhibit the release of anterior pituitary tropic hormones. For example, a network of hypothalamic neurons produce gonadotropin-releasing hormone (GnRH), which causes the pituitary to release the gonadotropins FSH and/or LH. As the name indicates, gonadotropins affect the gonads. In men, FSH acts on the testes to allow sperm production, and LH promotes the testicular release of a class of steroid hormones known as androgens. The most prominent androgen is testosterone.

The Ovulatory Cycle. In women, FSH acts first on ovarian follicles to induce maturation of ova (eggs) and cause the follicles to secrete a class of steroid hormones known as estrogens. The most prominent estrogen is estrodiol. This phase of the ovulatory cycle is therefore characterized by high estrogen levels and is known as the follicular phase. After FSH has produced these effects, the hypothalamus releases a pulse of GnRH that causes the pituitary to release a pulse of LH, which acts on the ripened follicles to trigger ovulation—the physical release from the ovary of an egg that is ready for fertilization. If pregnancy is to ensure, the newly released egg must be fertilized within the fallopian tubes connecting the ovary and the uterus. In that case, the developing embryo will have sufficient time to divide so that it can implant successfully in the wall of the uterus. If the egg is fertilized after it has reached the uterus, the inner walls of the uterus will be sloughed before the embryo can implant. This loss of tissue and blood from the uterine wall provides the visible menstrual flow. [See Menstruation.]

Proper timing of hormone action is required for pregnancy. As the follicles surrounding the egg collapse, they form a corpus luteum that then releases another class of steroid hormones—the progestins such as progesterone. Progesterone is so named because it promotes gestation—pregnancy—by preparing the uterine lining to favor implantation of an embryo and the manufacture of a placenta. If pregnancy does not occur, the entire sequence of hormone secretion and effects, known as the ovulatory cycle (or menstrual cycle) will repeat. This process takes approximately 28 days in humans and 4 days in rats. For pregnancy to ensue, the developing embryo must release hormones (including human chorionic gonadotropin, detected in pregnancy tests) to interrupt the ovulatory cycle, maintaining the uterus in a condition to favor placental function until delivery. [See Pregnancy.]

Role of Gonadal Steroids

Gonadal steroids direct sexual differentiation in the fetus, promote the development of secondary sex characteristics in puberty, and maintain libido.

Sexual Differentiation. In fetal development, gonadal steroids direct sexual differentiation of the body. When a Y chromosome is present, the indifferent gonads develop into testes. If there is no Y chromosome, then the indifferent gonads develop into ovaries. From that stage on, sexual differentiation of the body is controlled by hormonal secretions from the testes. Testicular androgens direct the development of male internal genitalia, as well as the penis and scrotum. In the absence of androgens, female internal genitalia will develop, and a clitoris and labia will be formed.

An interesting syndrome of fetal development, called androgen insensitivity, illustrates an important aspect of steroid hormone action. Steroid hormones do not affect all cells, but only those cells that produce a specialized protein called a steroid receptor. When present, the steroid receptor molecule recognizes and binds to the steroid molecule. The steroid-receptor complex then binds to DNA in the cell's nucleus to increase the production of some proteins and decrease the production of others. There are different classes of steroid receptors that recognize and interact with different classes of steroid hormones. Sometimes a developing XY fetus inherits a defective gene for the androgen receptor, so that it cannot produce functional androgen receptors. This means that even though the gonads develop as testes and those testes produce androgen, the body tissues cannot respond to the androgen. Thus the androgen-insensitive individual develops internal testes but otherwise a wholly feminine exterior, including a clitoris, labia, and vagina. At birth the baby is recognized as a girl and raised as a girl. But when menses fail to begin, the client may see a physician and learn that she has a Y chromosome and internal testes. These individuals seem well adjusted to a feminine gender identity.

Puberty. There is little secretion of gonadal steroids during childhood, but at puberty the brain begins releasing GnRH, causing the anterior pituitary to produce gonadotropins and the gonads to produce steroid hormones. The steroid hormones slowly sculpt secondary sex characters. Breast development is controlled by the ratio of estrogen to androgen in circulation: the higher the ratio, the greater the breast development. Androgens promote muscle development, beard growth, and genital growth in males. Obviously these changes in both sexes are preparatory to reproduction. Development of axial hair in both sexes is due primarily to steroid hormones from the adrenal glands. It was long assumed that the rise in sexual interest at puberty was due to, or at least augmented by, the rise in gonadal steroids. But retrospective reports indicate that boys and girls feel their first romantic stirrings at about 10 years of age, before gonadal steroids rise. Since girls undergo puberty at an earlier age than boys, the fact that they report these feelings at the same age casts further doubt on the idea that puberty is responsible for them. Thus, it has been suggested that another hormonal event, the rise of steroid secretion from the adrenal glands, which begins at about 10 years of age in both sexes, may trigger or augment these sexual feelings (McClintock & Herdt, *Psychological Science*, 1997, 5, 1278–1283).

Androgens and Libido. In adulthood, gonadal steroids maintain secondary sex characteristics, and there is evidence that they also maintain sexual interest or libido. Men who lose their testes through accident or disease experience a dramatic decline in circulating androgens and also report a decline in libido. In double-blind, placebo-controlled studies, treatment of such men with testosterone significantly restored libido, as measured by self-reported sexual fantasies and sexual activity. Thus, as in other animals, androgens seem to facilitate male sexual behavior in humans. However, one cannot conclude from these results that individual differences in the sexual behavior of men can be attributed to individual differences in circulating androgen levels, and the animal literature offers an explanation for this. Male rats or guinea pigs differ in the vigor of their mating behavior, and these differences persist even if the animals are castrated and all given the same doses of androgen. Thus, the presurgery differences in sexual behavior must be due either to differences in androgen sensitivity or to differences in nonhormonal substrates of mating behavior. The latter alternative is supported by the finding that castrated male rodents continue to copulate at presurgery levels if they are given as little as one tenth of the normal amount of circulating androgen. Thus, it appears that a small amount of androgen plays a permissive role in male copulatory behavior. With no androgen, sexual behavior declines dramatically, but even a low dose of androgen will maintain sexual behavior; larger doses of androgen have no additional effect. Therefore, although androgen levels do decline gradually in aging men, it seems unlikely that they commonly fall low enough to explain a loss of libido in aged men. The widely used drug Viagra has no known effects on either androgen levels or libido. This drug inhibits a specific enzyme in the erectile tissue of the penis to stimulate erection directly.

Androgen levels in copulating males illustrate another important cornerstone of behavioral endocrinology, namely, that hormone and behavior have a reciprocal relationship. Changes in hormone levels can affect behavior, but behavior and experience can also change hormone levels. In several rodent species, it has been found that gonadally intact males secrete slightly more androgen after copulating with a female. Likewise, a male ring dove provided a sight of a female experiences a severalfold increase in androgen concentration within a few weeks. This finding that experience can alter hormone secretion is more the rule than the exception in behavioral endocrinology. Another example is the release of oxytocin in lactation mentioned above.

Because of the misperception that androgens are "male hormones," some readers may be surprised to learn that androgens may also be responsible for maintaining libido in women. But double-blind, placebo-controlled studies indicate that, in many women reporting reduced libido following surgically induced menopause, low doses of androgen can increase sexual fantasies and sexual behavior, whereas even moderate doses of estrogens do not (Sherwin, *Psychosomatic Medicine*, 1985, *47*, 339–351). In fact, women normally produce and secrete androgens from their ovaries, resulting in circulating levels about one tenth those seen in men. Presumably, it is the loss of this source of androgen in postmenopausal women that is responsible for some of the loss of libido. Androgen does not affect the other conditions benefited by estrogen treatment, such as the inhibition of bone loss and the reduced risk of Alzheimer's disease. Therefore, the growing use of estrogen replacement therapy in postmenopausal women is being supplemented in many cases with low doses of androgen.

Sexual Dimorphism in the Human Brain

In animal models, prominent sex differences in behavior are accompanied by prominent structural sex differences (sexual dimorphism) in the brain. For example, in canaries and zebra finches, in which males sing much more than do females, a network of brain nuclei is three to six times larger in volume in males than in females. In rats, a region of the hypothalamus known as the sexually dimorphic nucleus of the preoptic area (SDNPOA) is so called because it is three to five times larger in volume in males than in females. The size of the rat SDNPOA is determined by late fetal and early neonatal exposure to androgens. If males are deprived of androgens during that period, the SDNPOA will be small throughout adulthood. If females are exposed to androgen during the perinatal period, their SDNPOA will be large in adulthood. The same androgen manipulations that alter the SDNPOA also affect the behavior of these rats; those exposed perinatally to androgen will not display feminine behaviors in adulthood. Thus, in these animals, the same androgenic signals that masculinize body structure also masculinize brain structure and ensure male-typical behaviors in adulthood.

As there are also sex differences in human behavior, philosophers and scientists have long wrestled with the question of whether those differences are due to bio-

logical forces or social forces. The animal models above suggest more specific questions: Are human sex differences in behavior caused by sex differences in perinatal exposure to androgen? Alternatively, are the sex differences in adult human behavior the result of sex differences in experience provided by the family and society? There is no satisfactory demonstration to prove or disprove either of these possibilities, but it seems likely that both perinatal hormones and socialization play a role in human behavioral sex differences. The occasional reports of sexual dimorphism in the adult human brain are sometimes interpreted as favoring the role of hormones. However, only one sexual dimorphism in human brain structure has been examined across age groups—a presumed homolog of the rat SDNPOA. In human SDNPOA, sexual dimorphism is not visible in children younger than ten years of age or so. Thus, it is possible that this sexual dimorphism is the result of sex differences in social experience. All other sexual dimorphism in the human brain have been examined only in adults, so these, too, may be the result of differences in experience rather than sex differences in hormone influence. This same concern applies to the reports that homosexual men have a smaller nucleus within the hypothalamus than do heterosexual men. There are no data indicating whether the structural brain difference caused the differences in sexual orientation or the reverse. On the other hand, several estimates of heritability based on comparisons of relatives indicate that about half of the variance in sexual orientation of men and women is caused by variance of the genome. Furthermore, there is conclusive evidence that a gene on the X chromosome can increase the probability that an XY individual inheriting the gene will be homosexual as an adult. Whether any of these genetic influences on human sexual orientation act through hormonal mechanisms is unknown.

Bibliography

Becker, J., Breedlove, S. M., & Crews, D. (Eds.). (1993). *Behavioral endocrinology*. Cambridge, MA: MIT Press. Contains chapters written by some of the leaders in various subfields; for the undergraduate upper level or the graduate student level.

Blum, D. (1997). *Sex on the brain*. New York: Viking Penguin. A very readable review of many issues about biological influences on differences in human sexual behavior from a Pulitzer Prize–winning science reporter.

Nelson, R. J. (1999). *Introduction to behavioral endocrinology*. Sunderland, MA: Sinauer. A single-author review of the field that is comprehensive yet accessible for undergraduate readers.

Phoenix, C. H., Goy, R. W., Gerall, A. A., & Young, W. C. (1959). Organizing action of prenatally administered testosterone propionate on the tissues mediating mating behavior in the female guinea pig. *Endocrinology*, 65, 369–382. The classic paper proposing that early androgen exposure that masculinizes body structure may also masculinize the developing brain and therefore permanently masculinize behavior.

Rosenzweig, M. R., Leiman, A. L., & Breedlove, S. M. (1999). *Biological psychology* (2nd ed.). Sunderland, MA: Sinauer. A textbook of biological psychology that includes a chapter devoted to hormones and another devoted to sexual behavior.

S. Marc Breedlove

REPUBLIC OF IRELAND. As an academic discipline and as a profession, psychology in the Republic of Ireland was a late developer. The reasons for this include the effect on Ireland of gaining its independence from Great Britain in 1921. The following decades, which included the years of World War II, during which southern Ireland was technically neutral, were years of economic difficulty, cultural narrowness, and—except for the continual outflow of economic emigrants—international isolation. Only in the late 1950s, when government policy changed in the direction of opening up the country economically and culturally, did psychology emerge as a discipline and subsequently as a profession. The Republic of Ireland has shed its image as an underdeveloped nation and is now one of the most vibrant economies in the world, as well as one of the most culturally active nations, given its population of just 3.6 million. These changes have had profound implications for psychology in Ireland.

As elsewhere, psychology at the Irish university level has its roots in philosophy. University College Dublin (UCD), the largest university in the Republic, established a Chair of Logic and Psychology in 1909. The philosophical hue of this approach to psychology was distinctly scholastic, and it was to be nearly half a century before psychology emerged as an autonomous academic discipline. The 13 years from 1958 to 1971 saw the major academic developments that laid the foundation for contemporary Irish psychology.

With strong encouragement and support from the national trade union for primary school teachers, the first full-time course for training psychologists was established at UCD in 1958. This two-year program led to a postgraduate diploma in psychology, which was first conferred in 1960. UCD's first bachelor of arts graduates in psychology appeared in 1970. Trinity College Dublin (TCD), the oldest university in the Republic, made its first two academic appointments in psychology in 1962. A joint honors degree in psychology and philosophy was established in 1965, with an initial six graduates in 1968. University College Cork (UCC) founded its department of applied psychology in 1964,

and University College Galway (UCG) founded its department of psychology in 1971. The universities of Dublin, Cork, and Galway together form the main colleges of the National University of Ireland (NUI). Graduates of the four universities are recognized by the British Psychological Society.

All four universities offer courses up to and including the doctoral level and between them offer postgraduate professional training in many areas of psychology. Since 1997, UCD and TCD both offer the first taught doctorates in clinical psychology in the Republic of Ireland. In recent years, courses in psychology at the postgraduate level have been offered by some of the newer universities, such as Dublin City University. Psychologists have also been employed in other university departments in the Republic, notably in departments of education. The founding professors of the four university psychology departments in the Republic of Ireland were E. F. O'Doherty (UCD), Derek Forrest (TCD), Peter Dempsey (UCC), and Martin McHugh (UCG).

Development of Psychology in the Republic

The professional development of psychology in Ireland has been uneven. Although pressures from the field of education were significant in establishing psychology as an academic discipline, educational psychology is still understaffed, with only about 60 educational psychologists currently employed as such. Clinical psychology has fared better in terms of provisions for both training and employment, although here too there is ample room for development. There are about 200 clinical psychologists in the Republic. An area that has developed well in Ireland has been psychological services for those with severe learning difficulties. This is not unrelated to the fact that the needs of this population have been met largely by voluntary agencies. Postgraduate training for organizational psychologists has been important in opening the field of business and industry to psychologists. Postgraduate training in psychotherapy and counseling psychology has also evolved strongly in the last decade.

Of central importance for the professional development of psychology in Ireland has been the Psychological Society of Ireland (PSI). Founded in 1970 with 132 members, it has now grown to a membership in excess of 1,000. It held its first annual conference in 1970 and launched the *Irish Journal of Psychology* in 1971. This journal and the journal of the UCD Student Psychological Society, *The Thornfield Journal*, are the two oldest psychology journals in the Republic. In 1974 PSI established *The Irish Psychologist* as its membership bulletin. Since its inception, PSI has energetically represented both the needs of psychology and psychologists' evaluation of many issues of social importance to all relevant branches of government.

Applications and Research Considerations

All university departments of psychology and some colleges of education have active research programs. Most of this research is applied. This is partly because many of the tasks facing psychologists in Ireland are policy related, and any nonuniversity funding that is available for psychological research is used to address practical problems. Little money is available for pure or theoretical research. Consequently, university-based researchers with interests in nonapplied areas must approach their work with adaptibility and versatility.

Apart from university departments, the most significant research in educational and social areas has been carried out by the Educational Research Centre at St. Patrick's College and the Economic and Social Research Institute (ESRI), both located in Dublin. The Educational Research Centre has been the main center for research in education in the Republic of Ireland since its foundation in 1966. Much of its work has been psychological in nature and has included the development of standardized tests of ability and achievement, the evaluation of educational programs, and studies of school effectiveness, educational development, and disadvantage. ESRI is a national research center that over the years has done much important work in areas of applied social psychology. The Royal College of Surgeons in Ireland has established a center specializing in health psychology research. Many voluntary agencies are beginning to underwrite research in clinical areas.

Psychology is one of the most popular choices for university students, with the demand outstripping the supply. The immediate future of psychology in Ireland seems buoyant.

[*See also* Northern Ireland.]

Bibliography

Brady, T., & McLoone, J. (1992). Ireland. In V. S. Sexton & J. D. Hogan (Eds.), *International psychology: Views from around the world* (2nd ed., pp. 229–239). Lincoln: University of Nebraska Press.

Carr, A. (1995). Clinical psychology in Ireland: A national survey. *The Irish Journal of Psychology, 16*, (1), 1–20.

Curtis, R., & McHugh, M. (1986). *Time present and time past: A retrospection on the department of psychology, University College, Galway (1971–1986).* Galway: University College, Department of Psychology.

Forrest, D. (1992). *A short history of the psychology department, Trinity College, University of Dublin (1962–1992).* Dublin: Trinity College, Department of Psychology.

Kirakowski, J., & Delafield, G. (1982). The department of applied psychology in University College, Cork. *The Thornfield Journal, 10*, 38–54.

McHugh, M., & McLoone, J. (1980). The roots that clutch: The origins and growth of PSI. *The Irish Psychologist, 6*(10), 1–8.

McLoone, J. (1988). The development of services for people with mental handicap in Ireland: The contribution of psychologists. *The Irish Journal of Psychology, 9*(2), 205–209.

Ciarán Benson

RESEARCH DISSEMINATION. Universities are sometimes chided for their "publish-or-perish" mentality: either faculty members publish, or they lose their jobs. Media columnists, in particular, love to lambaste universities for this mentality, at the same time that they are blithely oblivious to the fact that those media columnists who do not publish last in their jobs even less time than do university faculty members.

What the columnists and many others do not realize is that publication, in particular, and dissemination, in general, is as much a part of research as is actually doing the empirical or library investigation that leads up to the dissemination. This article will consider the importance of dissemination in science, in general, and in psychology, in particular, as well as how dissemination takes place.

Why Scientific Dissemination Is Important

Students in introductory courses, whether in psychology or anything else, often learn as part of the first chapter of their textbook that, for findings to be scientific, these findings must have four characteristics: They must be verifiable, cumulative, (reasonably) parsimonious, and public. The first three characteristics typically seem quite reasonable to these students. But why must findings be made public in order to be a part of science? Why must they be disseminated?

There are at least three reasons. First, science could not be verifiable if its findings were not public. Other scientists would not know what it was that they needed to verify. Second, science could not be cumulative if its findings were not public. Scientists cannot build on the work of others if they have no way of knowing what this work is. Third, new, more parsimonious theories could not be derived from older, less streamlined theories if scientists did not have available to them the findings on which to build the new theories. Thus, what might seem like the least important characteristic of scientific work—its dissemination to the scientific public and eventually the public at large—actually proves to be the most important: Without dissemination, none of the other characteristics of scientific work could be fulfilled!

Sequence of Dissemination of Scientific Information

Typically, scientific findings are disseminated in the sequence stated above: first to the scientific public, and only then to the public at large. To some laypeople, and especially the media, such a progression may seem elitist (only scientists are given the initial opportunity to learn about new discoveries) and even an impediment to the flow of information. After all, why shouldn't the public learn right away about information that is relevant to them—such as potential new cures for chronic diseases—and that they even may have paid for through their contributions to the tax base? Nevertheless, there are three reasons why the chain of communication should start with scientists and only then filter down to the public.

First, initial reports of findings sometimes contain errors, and even fatal errors. In recent years, the media have sometimes reported hot new discoveries in advance of scientific publication. These discoveries then generate tremendous amounts of press coverage, only for the discoveries to prove to be nonreplicable and thus unverifiable. For example, "cold fusion" generated enormous publicity and wild hopes before it was shown to be nonreplicable. Had the scientists' work first been subjected to careful scientific scrutiny, the cold fusion fiasco might have been avoided. As events transpired, the scientists' careers were ruined, the university at which the research took place appeared to be foolish, money and resources were wasted in search of a will-o'-the-wisp, and science received a black eye.

Second, initial findings may be correct, but open to alternative interpretations. It is no coincidence, perhaps, that some highly opinionated investigators first publish their findings in popular books or magazines. Whereas publications in the form of scientific articles are almost always subjected to critical peer review, publications in the form of popular books do not typically receive scientific peer review; even if they do, the publishers are under no scientific obligation to take any of the reviews into account. Trade book publishers, because they are in their business to make money, may even welcome suspect findings that generate controversy and, hence, book sales. As a result, readers may be treated to a totally one-sided interpretation of a set of data. For example, findings of differences between groups in IQ are typically susceptible to multiple interpretations, but popular books and media articles often report only one interpretation as though it were fact.

Third, scientific findings, presented without appropriate cautions, can lead and actually have led to harm. Sometimes, the review process fails, as in the case of the drug, thalidomide, which caused serious birth defects in thousands of babies. More often, however, people read a report in the popular media, act on it, and may actually do themselves damage, as in the case of the use of fraudulent treatments for cancer, such as laetrile, which may displace the use of scientifically verified treatments. Even psychological findings, such as differences in IQ between groups, if improperly interpreted, may lead to counterproductive and even harmful educational policies.

Thus, proper dissemination of scientific findings is important, and such dissemination should begin with the scientific public through refereed outlets. What are some of the kinds of outlets available for the dissemination of theories and research results?

Outlets for Dissemination of Scientific Information

Scientific information may be disseminated initially through oral presentations, such as lectures and symposiums, and eventually through written publications.

Oral Presentations. Initially, psychologists and other scientists often disseminate their theories and data orally—through lectures or symposium presentations at scientific conferences. The idea is to present their ideas and their data, and to get feedback on them before the scientists even write up their theories and data. Questions and comments at scientific conferences may reveal weaknesses in the work that the scientists can then correct before they submit the work for publication. At the same time, scientists in the audiences of such conferences know that they are hearing work that, for the most part, has not yet been published and that may, therefore, be less solid than work that has passed through the scientific publication process.

Written Publications. Once scientists have gotten initial feedback from conference presentations, they write up their work for publication. Why bother to write it up? Why not just present the work at conferences, which, after all, exposes the work to the scientific public? There are three important reasons why conference presentations in no way substitute for published work.

First, conference presentations can almost never contain the detail that is contained in a scientific article or book. The result is that crucial elements and often flaws can be glossed over or even inadvertently hidden from the audience. In rare cases, scientists may purposely hide details that they know will weaken their arguments. The written work, however, exposes the flaws that may not be discernible in an oral presentation.

Second, conference presentations usually are not prepared with the same care as written publications. Scientists know that they do not need to be as assiduous in putting together all the details of their work, because there is no time for presentation of every little detail, nor is such detailed presentation even usually appropriate in an oral presentation. Flaws that may escape the scientists in preparing a conference presentation, therefore, may become more obvious to them in preparing a written publication.

Third, conference presentations are not archival. They are "here today, gone tomorrow." There is usually no written record of the presentation, so the presentation typically does not become part of the documented archives that are so important to the development of science as a cumulative enterprise, whereby scientists can build upon each other's work.

Fourth, scientific publication is important not only to others, but to scientists themselves. It is often only through the process of writing something up that scientists become fully aware of the range of both the strengths and weaknesses to be found in their work. Indeed, new ways to analyze or interpret data often first occur to scientists during the writing process.

Once the scientist has gotten feedback from oral presentations, he or she typically writes up the work. Before submitting the written work for publication, however, the scientist will often show it to colleagues in order to get an informal kind of peer review, again to anticipate problems that journal or book referees are likely to note.

Scientific Journal Articles. The scientist then submits the work for publication, typically first in a peer-refereed scientific journal. Articles may be submitted to only one scientific journal at a time, although books and book proposals may be multiply submitted. Scientific publication has a set of rules, and various disciplines have their own manuals describing their sets of rules. For example, most psychologists use the manual of the American Psychological Association (APA) (1994) as the basis for their writing. The purpose of such a manual is not to straitjacket authors, but to provide a uniform set of guidelines for writing so that readers can concentrate on what the author is saying rather than on his or her idiosyncratic way of saying it.

When an editor receives a submission, he or she usually first quickly checks over the article to make sure it is appropriate for the journal, and that it conforms to the APA or other guidelines. The editor also may check whether the submission meets the minimal quality standards for a submission to the journal. If the article survives the initial screening, the editor of the journal will usually send the article out to anywhere from two to four referees who work in an area relevant to that of the article. These referees will then send back reviews of the strengths and weaknesses of the article. Having received the reviews, the editor of the journal will then decide whether to accept the article, accept it but require minor revisions, reject the article but encourage a resubmission if major revisions are made, or reject the article outright and suggest that the author

either send it to another journal or do further work before resubmission elsewhere.

Psychology has the benefit of having a wide range of scientific journals, and typically there are multiple journals in a given field. Thus, if an author is turned down by one journal, he or she has the option of later submitting to another. The author is well advised to take into account referees' (also called reviewers') comments, however, because the referees for the next journal are likely to raise points that overlap with (but are nonidentical to) the points raised by the referees of the first journal.

There is often an informal "pecking order" of journals, so that scientists who are turned down by a higher prestige journal can then try a journal of somewhat lesser prestige in the hope that this journal will publish his or her work. Less prestigious journals are typically less selective and more willing to overlook flaws that more prestigious journals do not overlook. There is subjectivity in the reviewing process, however, and it happens from time to time that a more prestigious journal will accept an article that was turned down by a less prestigious one.

What, exactly, are the kinds of attributes that referees consider in reviewing scientific articles? There is no list that can encompass all of the possible attributes. But, typically, referees of empirical (data-based) articles look for attributes such as (1) whether there is any theory motivating the empirical work, and if so, whether the theory is reasonable; (2) whether the work deals with a problem of genuine scientific interest; (3) whether the review of literature adequately cites previous work in the area, and makes clear how the new work will go beyond this previous work; (4) whether the work actually does contribute substantially beyond what is already known from previous work; (5) whether the methods of research are adequate for addressing the problem posed in the introduction, and for drawing the conclusions that have been drawn; (6) whether the data analysis is adequate to the data generated; (7) whether the conclusions follow from the data; and (8) whether the article is written in a way that is clear and understandable.

Although scientific theories and data are typically first published in peer-reviewed scientific journals, other publication options are available. One of the less desirable, perhaps, is nonpeer-reviewed journals, which have much lower standards for publication than peer-reviewed ones. In some of these journals, the main criterion for acceptance is that the author(s) pay a publication fee. The problem with publishing in such journals is that other scientists know which ones they are, and often think less, not more, of the scientists who publish in these journals.

Scientific journals are not all of the same kind. Some journals, such as the _Journal of Experimental Psychology:_

General or the *Journal of Personality and Social Psychology* publish primarily data-based, empirical articles. Other journals, such as the *Psychological Review*, publish theories, but theories that are supported by past data as well as data that may have been collected by the investigator. The *Psychological Bulletin* is among those journals that publish conceptually based reviews of literature. Journals such as the *American Psychologist* publish articles—both empirical and nonempirical—that are likely to appeal to the full range of psychologists, whatever their specialty. A small number of journals, such as *Contemporary Psychology*, publish only book reviews or specialize in such reviews.

Chapters in Edited Books. After original publication of a psychologist's work, there are other opportunities to further disseminate the work through the medium of print. For example, a psychologist might be asked to contribute a chapter in an edited book, which is a compilation of chapters that review related bodies of work. A chapter in an edited book is often an excellent way for a psychologist to pull together a body of work he or she has done and to integrate it with the work of others. Space constraints are usually less than those in journals, so that the psychologist can write at greater length about the implications of ideas.

Because the review process for book chapters is usually much less rigorous than that for journals, speculations that would be inappropriate in a journal might be accepted or even welcome in an edited book. At the same time, scientific colleagues know that the review process for edited books is less rigorous, so they do not typically view an edited book chapter as having the same stature as an article in a refereed empirical journal. However, a chapter in a prestigious edited book, such as a handbook, can often become a classic in its field.

Monographs. Monograph publication is another option. When a psychologist or other scientist has more to say than could possibly be expressed either in an article or even a chapter, a monograph is a viable option. A monograph may be published as part of a series (for example, the Society for Research on Child Development has a monograph series), or more typically, it may be published as a book. In either case, the monograph allows the author the greatest freedom of all to express his or her ideas. Monographs published by scholarly publishers are peer reviewed much the way journal articles are, although authors are typically allowed more freedom to express themselves as they wish in monographs. Not all monographs are peer reviewed, however.

Monographs published by trade publishers (that is, publishers that specialize in high-volume bookstore sales) typically are not peer reviewed or are subject to only cursory peer review. The concern of the trade publisher is usually more with interest and readability for a lay audience than with scientific merits. At the same time, the trade publisher will sometimes seek to ensure, at the very least, that the author has reputable credentials in his or her field.

Electronic Media. Yet another option for the dissemination of scientific work is the electronic journal, or simply dissemination of ideas over the Internet. More and more journals are being published electronically, just as more and more articles are being disseminated over the Internet. Publishers typically view such publications as tantamount to paper publication: They will not republish something that has already been electronically disseminated.

The status of electronic publication in science is in transition. Although electronic journals can be refereed, articles distributed over the Internet may have received no review at all, and hence are not usually viewed as comparable in credibility to refereed scientific publications.

Conclusion

In sum, dissemination of scientific information is important to the scientific community and to the world at large. Dissemination is not an appurtenance to science: It is an integral part of the scientific process. Without it, science cannot develop. There are many options for dissemination of scientific results, but usually published articles in peer-reviewed journals are considered the sine qua non of scientific reporting.

An analysis of scientific dissemination undoes an important misconception in the public mind: that research interferes with, or can somehow be substituted for, teaching. Dissemination of research *is* teaching. It is the way scientists teach other scientists about their work. Eventually, the work that is first published in scientific journals makes its way to the general public, and to the textbooks and lectures through which students learn about science.

The best teachers are often researchers because these teachers can convey firsthand to their students the excitement and challenges of the research process, which is a major part of what students of science need to learn. At the same time, teaching is dissemination of scientific information, although typically it is not firsthand dissemination. Once we realize the importance of dissemination to science, we realize that the development of science and teaching about science are not separate and antagonistic entities, but rather interrelated and often indistinguishable entities that always have developed and always should develop in a symbiotic way.

[*See also* American Psychological Association; Data Analysis; *and* Ethics, *article on* Ethics in Publication.]

Bibliography

American Psychological Association. (1994). *Publications Manual of the American Psychological Association* (4th ed.). Washington, DC: Author.

Caplow, T., & McGee, R. J. (1958). *The academic marketplace.* New York: Basic Books. Very out of date, but still the classic work on how academe works and the role of research dissemination in the marketplace of academe.

Sternberg, R. J. (1993). *The psychologist's companion: A guide to scientific writing for students and researchers* (3rd ed.). New York: Cambridge University Press. A fairly comprehensive guide to preparing publications in psychology, including points of grammar, APA format, effective presentation, and achieving impact.

Sternberg, R. J., & Gordeeva, T. (1996). The anatomy of impact: What makes an article influential? *Psychological Science, 7,* 69–75. An empirical analysis of the factors that lead to an article having an impact on the field.

Thyer, B. A. (1994). *Successful publishing in scholarly journals.* Thousand Oaks, CA: Sage. A good review of the steps in getting a scientific article published, from start to finish.

Robert J. Sternberg

RESEARCH METHODS. [*This entry comprises two articles. The first article discusses the historical evolution and purpose of research in the field of psychology. The companion article provides a broad survey of the theories and methods of conducting research in the field. For a general discussion of the philosophy of science, see* Philosophy, *article on* Philosophy of Science. *See also* Hermeneutics.]

History of the Field

Psychology, like other sciences, is both product and process, both an accumulating body of knowledge and a set of evolving methods for constructing this knowledge. Psychology as product can be expressed in propositions (hypotheses) predicting relations between variables or, more exactly, predicting where units of observation (in psychology, usually people) fall on an interesting dependent variable as a function of where they fall on independent variables. Psychology as process includes, to use Hans Reichenbach's terms in *Experience and Prediction* (Chicago, 1938), discovery processes and justification processes, that is, research methods for generating hypotheses and for evaluating them.

Creative and Critical Aspects of Research

Practicing researchers recognize that hypothesis creation is at least as important as hypothesis testing; nevertheless, methodology books and courses in the past century of scientific psychology have focused almost entirely on hypothesis testing to the neglect of hypothesis creation. In part this neglect reflects researchers' despair of describing, much less teaching, the creative process, although McGuire (*Annual Review of Psychology,* 1997, *48,* 1–30) describes many teachable techniques for creative hypothesis generating. The neglect may stem also from the adaptive tendency to notice what is distinctive (peculiar, unpredictable) in observed processes. While science shares its hypothesis-generating techniques with other lines of inquiry, its distinctive feature is its interest in empirical hypothesis testing. [*See* Hypothesis Testing.] Novelist, priest, marketer, and psychologist may all similarly generate the same intriguing hypothesis about interpersonal relationships, but only the research psychologist will then design an empirical test of the hypothesis. This history of methodology will reflect past practice by focusing on its distinctive feature, hypothesis testing, to the neglect of its shared hypothesis-generating processes.

Criteria for Judging the Adequacy of Knowledge Representations

Hypotheses being diverse and even contradictory, their adequacy has been judged by a wide variety of criteria, the relative ascendency of which has varied across time and field. Some are intrinsic desiderata, characteristics of the knowledge representation per se, while other desiderata are extrinsic to the knowledge representation itself.

Intrinsic Criteria. The numerous intrinsic desiderata are varied and even mutually contrary. That a knowledge formulation be internally consistent is one desideratum that has been advocated for so long that it needs no description. However, dialecticians like Plato, Hegel, and Marx have advocated the opposite characteristic, internal contradiction, as a desideratum because contradiction between thesis and antithesis is the way reality operates and contradiction tends to suggest a higher synthesis. A third desideratum, novelty, is also a popular desideratum but so is its opposite, banality, in the sense that an explanation is acceptable only to the extent that it falls within the field's prevailing explanatory paradigm. For example, during the century of scientific psychology, explaining some memory relation in terms of a hypothetical neural mechanism might be well received, but explaining it by a parapsychological mechanism is likely to be scorned. Fortunately, the establishment explanatory paradigms, like society's politically correct positions, tend to change periodically.

Fifth and sixth intrinsic desiderata for evaluating a theory's adequacies are another pair of contraries, parsimony versus rococo extravagance. The law of parsimony (Occam's Razor, Morgan's Canon) has so long been appreciated as a desideratum of knowledge that it needs no defense here. However, an antithetical minority of theorists are attracted to a contrary, sixth desideratum, rococo extravagance; they seem to find theories like astrology, cabalism, neoplatonism, alchemy, and psychoanalysis appealing not in spite of but because of their complexity. Another contrasting pair of intrinsic criteria are elegant explicitness and aphoristic pithiness. Elegance in theories often takes the form of harmonious plainness (e.g., specifying rectilinear or at least monotonic relations). The use of such aesthetic criteria in choosing theories is probably underestimated. Aphoristic condensation, as an eighth desideratum, is illustrated by the appeal of oracular pronouncements by a Nietzsche or Blake, and the compellingness of proverbs and apt poetical verses.

Extrinsic Desiderata. Criteria extrinsic to the knowledge formulation that have been used to judge its adequacy usually concern its antecedents or consequences. A popular criterion has been the hypothesis's derivability from a revered text, such as the Bible or Koran, the Marxist-Leninist corpus, the complete works of Sigmund Freud, or the U.S. Constitution. Age adds reverence but reduces relevance, which is sometimes alleviated by allowing continuous revelation, as in the Roman Catholic Church and the Church of Jesus Christ of the Latter Day Saints. The status or track record of a hypothesis's originator is a second commonly used extrinsic criterion: a theory written off as implausible at first hearing may gain renewed attention when one hears that it was proposed by an admired researcher (e.g., a seemingly extravagant claim for the health value of vitamin C may be given a second look when one learns it was proposed by two-time Nobel Prize winner Linus Pauling). This *ex opere operantis* criterion is defensible, although some journals require blind reviews to lessen it.

A third extrinsic criterion for accepting knowledge is that, whoever its originator, it has been adopted by the general public or by elite gate keepers (e.g., a theory one rejected on first hearing may receive sympathetic reconsideration when one learns that it has been published in a prime journal or generously funded after high approval by a prestigious peer reviewer panel). An opposite, fourth, desideratum is the formulation's divergence from orthodoxy; novelty-hungry revisionists find a theory more attractive for its being counterintuitive, going against widely accepted commonsense trivialities. Perspectivists routinely exploit an obvious commonsensical hypothesis by asserting its contrary and then generating circumstances in which this counterintuitive contrary would obtain.

A fifth extrinsic criterion is accepting a theory to the extent that it supports the status quo. Marxist historical materialists contend that ideology arises from the institutional power structure, to the extent of producing false consciousness, identification with the aggressor, and the masses' belief in their own inferiority or culpability. Some theologians and evolutionary epistemologists argue that knowledge formulations deservedly gain credulity from being adapted to the existing power structure. An opposite sixth criterion also considers es-

tablishment political acceptance but with an opposite, subversive view that a proposition deserves acceptance to the extent it is disruptive to the existing order. This contrarian stance is illustrated by Paul Feyerabend in *Against Method* (1975) and by Simone Weil's self-disciplining reversal procedure described in *Gravity and Grace* (1952): "Method of investigation: as soon as we have thought something, try to see in what way the opposite is true." Some are led to this stance less for its cognitive productivity than for its antiauthoritarianism.

A seventh external criterion for accepting a knowledge proposition is that it be heuristically provocative. A theory (e.g., psychoanalysis) can be afflicted with internal inconsistencies, irrefutability, or disconfirmations and yet flourish if it is creatively stimulating. Pragmatism furnishes an eighth criterion for accepting even a worrisome knowledge formulation when it serves some useful purpose (e.g., worries evoked by the algebra of irrational numbers subsided when it proved useful for working out electrical circuits). Scientists professing to rely on the orthodox external criterion, survival of empirical jeopardy, may actually be depending more on these seventh and eighth criteria of heuristic provocativeness and pragmatic value. A ninth criterion, subjective feeling, also may be more often used (even in science) than is acknowledged. Respected thinkers have proposed that the researcher's subjective feeling about a knowledge formulation is the ultimate criterion of its validity (e.g., Plato's feeling of certainty and Descartes's feeling of clearness and distinctness). Researchers may give a second and third chance to a hypothesis that they feel somehow deserves to be true. Greenwald et al. (*Psychological Review*, 1986, 93, 216–229) discuss the wisdom of clinging to an appealing hypothesis despite its poor empirical track record. Empirical studies are needed to determine when and to what extent such subjective feelings of certainty do predict ultimate confirmation.

A tenth external criterion of validity in psychological research is survival of empirical jeopardy. One's theory and its implied hypotheses must be put to an empirical test in which a representative set of people are selected or manipulated so that they vary on the independent variable while being kept homogeneous on theory-extraneous variables, and are then measured on the dependent variable to determine if the distribution of scores on the independent and dependent variables covary as hypothesized. A hypothesis that cannot be put in such empirical jeopardy is regarded as unscientific. In the twentieth century, psychology's orthodox criterion for judging the adequacy of knowledge formulations has been survival of empirical jeopardy, supplemented by secondary criteria such as internal consistency and parsimony. In practice, however, psychological researchers do—and appropriately so— make substantial use of other criteria such as heuristic provocativeness, pragmatic utility, elegance, and subjective appeal.

Evolution of the Canonical External-Confrontation Criterion in Science

In each period of intellectual history some use has been made of most of the above-mentioned criteria for judging the adequacy of knowledge although in each era one or two were dominant, even if not interdictively so. Over the last two millennia there has been a progression through five establishment criteria, from dogmatism to perspectivism.

Dogmatism. The first half of the Common Era was dominated by dogmatism, which assumes that there is some corpus of revealed truth so outstanding that other knowledge propositions are valid only if derivable from (or at least not incompatible with) this dogmatic corpus. In ancient Fertile Crescent and Mediterranean civilizations this usually was religious scriptures (the Torah, the Gospels, the Koran) and their interpretations (e.g., systemizations by Rashi and other Talmudic scholars, by Augustine and other Fathers of the Church, and by al-Bukhari and other Koranic commentators). Dogmatism was hegemonic only in the first millennium of the Common Era, but it has persisted since in enclaves, not only among religious fundamentalists but also among nonreligious or even antireligious factions such as Marxists, Maoists, Freudians of the strict observance, and Constitutional jurists of the original-intent school.

Rationalism. Dogmatism, and the rationalism that succeeded it in hegemony, both judge the validity of propositions by their agreement with an accepted set of principles; but rationalism is the more sophisticated in that its basic principles are selected, not as in dogmatism for their origins, but more for their intrinsic compellingness in seeming either self-evident postulates (e.g., between any two points one and only one straight line can be drawn) or common observations (e.g., all life comes from life). A second advance is that rationalism, more clearly than dogmatism, specifies the rules by which the hypothesis's consistency with the axiomatic corpus is to be judged, usually the rules of deductive logic. Uses of rationalism can be identified in the distant past (e.g., in Hellenistic treatises like Euclid's five axioms and five common notions) but only with the flourishing of medieval scholasticism at the beginning of the second millennium CE did rationalism enjoy several centuries of widespread suzerainty in the Mediterranean world. An early marker of its emergence in Christian Europe (and contemporaneously in nearby Islamic and Hebrew learning centers) was Anselm's *Monologium* (1077 CE), responding to the challenge of his graduate student monks to show that the truths of the Faith can be developed by natural reason alone, without dogmatic recourse to revealed scripture. A generation later Abelard, in *Sic et Non*, took a second step by showing (with cautious subtlety) that rational philosophy not only can, but must, proceed independently of dogmatic theology because the scriptures speak ambiguously or are silent on essential issues. Researchers during the next several centuries used rationalism to build intellectual palaces (e.g., the *Summa Theologica*) as splendid as the stone cathedrals of flying buttresses and stained glass built by contemporaneous craftsmen.

Positivism. The next Establishment epistemology involved more dramatic revisionism in that it stood rationalism on its head, replacing deduction with induction by taking empirical observation rather than self-evident principles as its basis of argument and using rules of inductive logic made explicit by John Stuart Mill. The label positivism was popularized only in the nineteenth century by August Comte, but the substance was adumbrated centuries earlier by Frances Bacon and developed by John Locke, David Hume, Mill, and other eighteenth century empiricists who prepared the ground for the scientific revolution. Extreme positivists prescribe empirical observation for creative hypothesis generation as well as critical hypothesis testing when they propose that the researcher observes nature with an open mind until its regularities force themselves on the observer's tabula rasa.

Logical Empiricism. Positivism's successor, logical empiricism, stands in still more dramatic relation to its predecessors by being a Hegelian synthesis of the two preceding epistemological hegemonies, the earlier deductive rationalist thesis and its subsequent inductive positivist antithesis. Logical empiricism prescribes, in accord with rationalism, that the researcher should start with an a priori hypothesis along with a theory from which it can be derived; and should then, in the spirit of positivism, put this hypothesis into jeopardy by subjecting it to an empirical test. Logical empiricism emerged out of the Vienna Circle's Unity of Science movement in 1920s Vienna. German and Austrian refugees from National Socialism carried the approach to centers of U.S. psychology, Herbert Feigl to Minnesota, Gustav Bergmann to Iowa, and Carl Hempel to Yale and Princeton. By the mid-twentieth century it had melded with Percy Bridgman's operationalism to become the Establishment meta-methodology of American experimental psychology.

Perspectivism. Psychology's emerging epistemological hegemony may be perspectivism (contextualism), which stands in a complex relationship to logical empiricism, extending some Vienna Circle theses and departing dramatically from others. Among its most radical epistemological working premises is that all hypotheses, even mutually contrary ones, are true (from some perspective in some imaginable context) and that the purpose of empirical confrontation is not to test a fixed hypothesis but to discover the meaning of a fluid, inadequately grasped hypothesis.

To clarify perspectivism/contextualism's research methodology innovations it is useful to consider its responses to four rich theses contributed by logical empiricism, two pertaining to the conceptual confrontational and two to the empirical confrontational aspects of the research process. The two conceptual confrontational theses contributed by logical empiricism are: (1) that a researcher should start, not (as proposed in extreme positivism) by making observations from which a hypothesis can be induced, but rather with a theory-derived hypothesis that guides observation and data analysis. (2) Further, logical empiricism postulates that between conflicting hypotheses, one at most can be true. Perspectivism agrees with the first of these logical empiricism postulates and extends it in two directions by prescribing (a) that the hypothesis should be explained a priori, not just by one theory but by multiple theories, and (b) that the contrary hypothesis also should be posited and explained by multiple theories. An empirical research program should then be designed to investigate both the initial hypothesis and its contrary, and multiple theories that account for each. From logical empiricism's second contention, that some hypotheses are true and some false (and that between conflicting hypotheses at least one is necessarily false), perspectivism departs radically, holding with William Blake that "Everything possible to be believed is an image of truth." The perspectivist takes as a working assumption that any conceivable hypothesized relation, although usually wrong, is valid in some actual or at least imaginable situation (e.g., as physics' classical laws of motion are acceptable even though they would obtain only in a nonexisting frictionless vacuum). Briefly, perspectivism argues that if all propositions are wrong, so also are their contradictions, which implies that all propositions are true. (This goes for contraries a fortiori over contradictories; as Niels Bohr said, the opposite of a trivial truth is wrong; the opposite of a great truth is also true.)

Logical empiricism's second pair of basic postulates pertains to the empirical confrontation aspect of research, asserting: (3) that to have scientific standing, hypotheses and theories should be subjectable to empirical jeopardy; and (4) that the purpose of this empirical confrontation is to determine whether the obtained data do or do not confirm the fixed a priori hypothesis. Perspectivism agrees with Postulate 3 as far as it goes but prescribes further that the empirical confrontation should be planned, not in the form of a single tactical experiment, but as a strategic program of research that investigates in systematically varying contexts both the initial hypothesis and its contrary and multiple theories in which each is housed. Perspectivism disagrees with Postulate 4 by holding that the purpose of empirical confrontation is not to test the validity of a fixed a priori hypothesis, but to uncover the meanings of a wavering, ambiguous a priori hypothesis (and its contrary), its meanings being the pattern of contexts in which the hypothesis does and does not obtain for multiple demonstrable reasons. Thus the empirical confrontation is not so much a critical testing of the hypothesis as a continuation of the creative discovery process begun in the a priori conceptual confrontation. These perspectivist innovations have serious implications for how research methods are taught, used, reported in the literature, and applied in society. For example, they stress why and how one should design strategic multiexperiment programs of research rather than individual tactical experiments; and they prescribe how one can organize one's initial thought experiments and prestudies so that they become not thrashing-about apologetic preliminaries, but more informative even than the final well-done demonstration experiment.

The succession of hegemonies just described suggests that research methods have evolved with accelerations in time and sophistication. As regards time, successive supplantings come progressively swifter. The first hegemony, dogmatism, maintained its dominance for almost a millennium; the most recent, logical empiricism, dominated for only a half a century. The sophistication of the transitions between successive epistemological hegemonies has also been accelerating. The first transition, between dogmatism and rationalism, involved only a substitution, replacing a revealed body of truth with a set of logically coherent and plausible axioms; while the recent transition to logical empiricism involved a creative synthesis of its two predecessors, the deductive methods of rationalism and the inductive methods of positivism. We can expect an accelerating evolution of research methodology, with each new orthodoxy surpassing its predecessor in a progressively more sophisticated way and within a shorter time.

Bibliography

Buss, D. M., & Malamuth, N. (Eds.). (1995). *Sex, power, conflict: Evolutionary and feminist perspectives*. New York: Oxford University Press. Describes methods used in the evolutionary and feminist approaches, two growing movements in psychology.

Campbell, D. T. (1988). *Methodology and epistemology for social science: Selected papers*. Chicago: University of Chicago Press. A convenient collection of papers by the most influential methodologist of twentieth-century psychology, covering topics such as quasi-experimental design, convergent and discriminant validity, and evolutionary epistemology.

Cohen, M. R., & Nagel, E. (1934). *An introduction to logic and scientific method*. New York: Harcourt, Brace & Co. An analysis of the logical structure of scientific research methods that had considerable influence on several generations of mid-twentieth-century psychologists.

Denzin, N. N., & Lincoln, Y. (1994). *Handbook of qualitative research*. Thousand Oaks, CA: Sage. A survey of the less quantitative methods that may become popular in postmodern reactions.

Feigl, H. (1969). The Wiener Kreis in America. In D. Fleming & B. Bailyn (Eds.), *The intellectual migration: Europe and America, 1930–1960*. Cambridge, MA: Harvard University Press. An account of how logical empiricist approaches spread via migration from Vienna to North American psychology in the middle half of the twentieth century.

McGuire, W. J. (1989). A perspectivist approach to the strategic planning of programmatic scientific research. In B. Gholson, W. R. Shadish, R. A. Neimeyer, & A. C. Houts (Eds.), *Psychology of science: Contributions to metascience* (pp. 214–245). New York: Cambridge University Press. A description of post-logical-empiricist strategic and tactical methods for programmatic planning of research.

Mill, J. S. (1843). *A system of logic*. London: J. W. Parker. A provocative influential attempt, especially in its chapter 6 on methods of social science, to develop a modified, elegant inductivism that is actually of some use in social science.

Popper, K. (1968). *The logic of scientific discovery (Logik der Forschung, Vienna, 1934)* (2nd ed.). New York: Harper & Row Torchbook. An outgrowth of and corrective to logical empiricism that popularized falsifiability in place of verifiability as a criterion of the scientific status of theory.

William J. McGuire

Concepts and Practices

The nature of the phenomena studied by psychologists determines the methods appropriate for their investigation. In this respect psychology is a science like many other sciences.

Psychology is concerned with many different topics, and each of these requires its own set of methods, and these raise their own method issues. For example, the content of dreams cannot be studied directly, but only through self-reports. When should the report be made? Right after the dream occurs, or in the morning, or when the meaning of the dream sinks in? Reports at these different times are not identical. In contrast, the decision as to whether the subject is dreaming (i.e., is having rapid eye movements; REM) can be based on electronic recordings that can be read without disagreement. Note, however, that these eye movements were first discovered by direct observation.

Agreement between self-reports at different times and agreement between people examining recordings are only two of the kinds of replicability, or reliability, important to psychological science. Investigators are expected to be able to replicate their findings, and other investigators also expect to be able to generate much the same findings when repeating a study in a different city or country and at a different time. A phenomenon, a relationship between two variables, is taken as understood, or at least to be under control, when an investigator can reproduce it. That is, the investigator obtains the same findings in similar investigations using research plans that retain the basic characteristics of the original study but allow other characteristics to vary freely. All of these kinds of agreement and replication fall within the broad heading of reliability.

Only rarely are investigators doing basic research interested in the specific data obtained in one singular set of circumstances. Instead, they want to generate data that reveal relationships that apply elsewhere, that is, to other classes of observations, informally or formally identified. But such generalizability of findings and conclusions can occur only when the findings of the original study have some reasonable degree of replicability. [*See* Replication in Research.] This is one view of the classic issue of validity, the extent to which scientists are measuring what they want to measure, and are applying their conclusions to an appropriate set of phenomena.

Dimensions on Which Research Differs

Central to the discussion of research methods is the topic of research plans or types of research. In psychology one dimension is the degree to which the person being observed is aware of this condition. At one extreme, psychologists can study archival records or products. For example, Stanley Coren in *The Left-Hander Syndrome* (New York, 1992) examined the handedness of people in pictures created over centuries, materials produced for some purpose quite separate from that of the investigator. At the other extreme, there are experiments where the participant's head is held firmly in a frame while he or she is responding by pressing a yes button or a no button. Overlapping highly with that dimension is one for degree of investigator control over the components of the situation that may influence the observed behavior.

Except for the case of archival records, the participants in psychological research typically know they are participants, that they are being studied. Moreover, they usually have some idea about the investigator's purpose in gathering data. It is usually necessary to obtain their informed consent, to get their agreement to do what the investigator desires, for the purposes described to them. So the participants are consciously aware of the fact that they are subjects in a psychological experiment and that their behavior is being observed or recorded. To what extent does this fact generate behavior differing from how the participant would behave if there were no psychologist around? This effect on the behavior is a control instituted by the participant. It can be eliminated by using unobtrusive measures, as described by Eugene J. Webb and others in *Nonreactive Measures in the Social Sciences* (Boston, 1981). While this kind of procedure has considerable promise for assessing group behavior, it would be difficult to use in research requiring the measurement of specific individuals. It is also difficult to see how one could obtain the participants' informed consent and still make unobtrusive measurements of them. [*See* Informed Consent.]

Among the controls available to the investigator, there is control over the time and place of the interaction between investigator and participant. The range here is from receiving a questionnaire mailed with a request to complete it and mail it back in the enclosed envelope (with no real interaction in this case), to being shut up in a soundproof room as a paid subject.

Then there is the reason for the participant-investigator interaction. There may be no two-way interaction, the investigator simply studying the other person's records or products, or there may be freely volunteering participants or paid ones. They may be captive subjects, as in a class meeting where the professor is the investigator. According to the profession's Code of Ethics, students should not be forced or bullied into participation but should be given a chance to leave the room without penalty. [*See* Ethics, *article on* Ethics in Research.]

The reader can work out the problem of attributing appropriate feelings and reactions as generated by each of the several different conditions under which the leading characters in the drama may be brought together, and the effects of these reactions on responses to experimental stimuli, to highly personal questions, or to whatever is presented to them.

There is also the investigator's control over the task: What stimuli are presented to the participant? What is that person asked to do with the stimuli? In what form is the response to be (e.g., yes-no, a freely worded answer, an association)? Consider the contrast between "What is the correct answer to this question?" (as in an ability test) and "Here is an inkblot. What do you see in it?" (as in a projective personality measure).

In psychological research, it is impossible to control everything that might influence participants' behavior above and beyond the stimuli, the independent variables that are the center of the investigator's concerns. Systematic distortion can be reduced or controlled (in one sense) by randomization. For example, participants can be assigned to experimental and control groups by a table of random numbers. This procedure reduces the likelihood that the two groups will differ on any important variable, that is, any variable that is likely to distort the findings. In practical terms, the variables that you control are the ones you think are important to control and also any additional ones deemed important by the editor of the journal to which you submit your research report. [*See* Randomized Experiments.]

Measuring

Once the research plan has been outlined, the investigator has to face decisions about measuring the various variables. For each, there is the decision about what each datum will be. Will it be an observation or a score? For each stimulus or each item, will the datum be produced by an observer or by the participant? Or will it be produced by a judge who has examined a piece of behavior as recorded in some fashion? Which of these is most appropriate for that variable? To measure "self-respect," the participant being described is the most relevant data producer although someone studying how the participant is perceived by peers would want to ask peers to produce the datum. This simple example illustrates the desirability of selecting the method most appropriate to one's conceptual formulation of the variable. [*See* Data Collection.]

In psychology, one finds few complete definitions or specifications of the variables being studied. Much more common are partial definitions. In the past, the idea of operational definitions was quite popular: A variable is defined by the operation used to measure it. While the concept of operational definitions was to a large extent accepted, it was soon realized that every operation provided its own variable: In fact your administration of a standard test today would be quite distinct from my administration of that test 300 miles away tomorrow, and hence a separate variable name would be needed. All too often, the investigator feels that the common associations people have to the construct's label are sufficient to indicate what the construct is, or that explicit definitions are sufficient conceptualizations. (A construct is a conceptual entity devised by a scientist.) This author disagrees: Psychologists need much more fully spelled out statements about each investigator's variables. Psychologists are impeded rather than helped by the fact that so many of their concepts and the labels for them come from nonscientific or lay language. As we develop and study technical constructs created by psychologists, we will progress. The full specification of a variable is a large task.

We will omit here any consideration of the relative costs of collecting data by one method or another. The investigator should, however, consider how the measurement would be made under ideal conditions, using participants with unlimited time available for the investigator's activities. This will give one a chance to select the best measuring method available, given one's resources, and to take note of the discrepancy between the ideal and the feasible, and to consider how the discrepancy might affect the interpretations that may be made from the obtained data.

It is exceedingly difficult to capture in a single measuring operation all the major features of one's construct. Unless a construct is extremely simple, it is almost certain that one will need to use more than a single measuring operation to capture the core of the construct. And, as explained by Donald T. Campbell and Donald W. Fiske (*Psychological Bulletin*, 1959, 56, 91–105), one will find that two measuring operations will not agree closely unless they share the same general method of measurement. Two self-report instruments will correlate better with each other than either will with a peer-judgment instrument. The method that one uses contributes to the variance of the measurements, so two sets of measurements using the same method will show common method variance, variance quite unrelated to the conceptualizations of whatever the sets are intended to measure. This common variance will increase the obtained correlations between the two measures and thus inflate the estimated reliability, the agreement between the measures. These contributions from method may cause difficulties in interpreting the results of the research.

Processing the Data

Once the data have been collected and checked for accuracy of transcription, the investigator is ready to analyze them. That process will involve the use of one or more statistical procedures for simply describing them, for generating the mean and variation within the distribution for each variable. Then comes the major analysis; it will usually assess the relationship between the two major variables. Often, in multivariate analyses, a number of such relationships will be studied in one analysis. Do the data come out as the investigator had predicted? [*See* Hypothesis Testing.] More formally, is the investigator's hypothesis supported by the results? Frequently the data will be analyzed by more than one statistical procedure, each asking a different question of the data and generating new information about it. [*See* Data Analysis.]

Confounding

Even with a most carefully designed study, there are usually several extraneous variables that may confound the obtained relations. To take just one instance, consider a study in which different treatments (independent variables) are given to each of two groups, each treatment taking several months. Some possible problems are the following: *history*—in addition to the differential treatments, various external events may affect the two groups of participants differentially; *matura-*

tion—changes within participants may occur with the passage of time, independent of the treatment itself; *instrument decay*—the measuring instruments or the conditions of measurement may change over time; *mortality*—if subjects drop out between first and second measurements, systematic differences between the groups may develop that affect the second set of measurements or that interact with the treatment; finally, *interactions*—any one or more of these factors may interact with the treatment and confound the results.

This list is not exhaustive, even for the particular type of research plan considered. If the investigator has a research plan that guards against all of the above potential problems, there are other possible problems, such as response biases in subjects and experimenter expectancy regarding the way the experiment will come out. [*See* Artifact, *article on* Artifact in Assessment; *and* Expectancy Effects.] The experienced investigator is on the lookout for these possibilities, having learned from often-unhappy experiences with them. Before conducting an experiment, the thoughtful novice will ask an investigator more experienced in that area of research to critique the research plan.

The Whole Picture

To assess the dependent variable, the one being studied, an investigator obtains from each participant pieces of behavior or behaviors that have a particular attribute. A number of such samples are ordinarily obtained, especially when the aim is to assign to each participant a score or average measurement. Because so many things can affect each response or piece of behavior, the investigator can almost never depend upon any single measurement as representative of the behavior of any one participant. In measuring a construct, no one operation covers all of the core of the construct. Every operation also contains variance that is irrelevant to the hypothesis being tested, variance associated with the method of measuring and to extraneous variables.

Any one bit of behavior available to the investigator is determined by effects from a number of sources. Usually, one or two sources provide the principal determinants for the participants as a group, but these may not be the major sources for all subjects, and the same subject's set of responses may be affected by different sources at different points in the set. Most participants may respond to a given item from a personality inventory in terms of their general picture of themselves. A few, however, will respond in terms of one or two recent events that had a strong impact. This and other inappropriate response processes are stable over time for that person and that item and are related to instability of response to that item (see Ruth Kuncel and D. Fiske, "Stability of response process and response," *Educational and Psychological Measurement*, 1974, 39, 743–755).

More generally, what are these sources, these variables that may affect a piece of behavior? They include the focal stimuli, the theory-relevant independent variable by which the investigator predicts the participant's response to be mostly determined. It may be a stimulus or a test item. Then there is the orientation of the participant, the participant's understanding of how participants are expected to respond (or behave). This understanding may come from explicit instructions given by the investigator or from the participant's interpretation of the situation. Ordinarily, much is left to the participant. For example, on a test of ability, should the participant go rapidly, trying to answer as many items as possible, or should the participant go slowly, making sure to give the best answer possible to each item? Unless the instructions are very specific, some subjects will take one set and others the other set. These are two of the several "response sets" that have been identified and studied by psychologists.

Some of these variables that affect responses are a function of why the participant is in the research at all: Is the participant being paid, or being forced to be present by an autocratic professor, or is he or she just in it for the sport, to see what psychologists ask subjects to do? And what is the effect of the participant's perception of the experimenter, the person running the experiment? The perceived coldness or warmth of the experimenter can affect the participant's responses to painful stimuli. Is a physically attractive test administrator likely to distract partipants from the task at hand, or at least lead them to make more casual responses? The actual date of testing may be important: The responses of participants tested the day after the assassination of John F. Kennedy in November 1963 were found to be affected by their experiences of that horrible event.

Each psychological research study takes place within a culture, and most of them within just one. Hence, it is difficult to assess the multiple effects of the culture on the behavior observed. The culture gives meanings to the several components of the research plan: to the instructions, and especially to the words used in stimuli and in instructions, and also to the nature of the investigator-participant relationship. Ultimately, we must try to bring cultural factors into our research plans, our interpretations, and our theorizing and conceptualizations.

Problems with research methods have been pointed out by psychologists. Some of these problems have been solved; for example, randomizing the position of the correct alternative on multiple-choice tests. For others, no perfect resolutions are yet available and psychologists must set up research plans to minimize their potential effects. Although there is much methodological work still to be done, psychologists are becoming more sophisticated in methodology, and hence the published research is getting better.

Bibliography

Cook, T. D., & Campbell, D. T. (1979). *Quasi-experimentation: Design and analysis issues for field settings.* Chicago: Rand-McNally. A classic. In addition to what the subtitle indicates, the book contains a scholarly chapter on "Causal Inference and the Language of Experimentation" and one on four types of validity.

Fiske, A. (1995). The cultural dimensions of psychological research: Method effects imply cultural mediation. In P. Shrout & S. Fiske (Eds.), *Personality research, methods and theory* (pp. 271–294). Hillsdale, NJ: Erlbaum. Most of our research is restricted to people within our own culture. We should try to bring cultural factors into our research and our conceptualizing.

Fiske, D. W. (1971). *Measuring the concepts of personality.* Chicago: Aldine. An analysis of the difficulties encountered in conceptualizing and measuring concepts, especially those in the personality domain.

Sudman, S., & Bradburn, N. M. (1982). *Asking questions: A practical guide to questionnaire design.* San Francisco: Jossey-Bass. An introduction to the subtleties in the phrasing of questions to be posed in a research setting.

Donald W. Fiske

RESIDENTIAL TREATMENT PROGRAMS. Residential treatment of children and adolescents with behavioral and/or emotional problems is defined as specific mental-health treatment that entails removal of the child from residence in the home during such treatment. Each year more than 50,000 youngsters are treated in residential treatment centers and psychiatric hospitals in the United States, while more than 100,000 children and adolescents receive short-term treatment for mental-health problems in general hospital psychiatric units (Kiesler, Simpkins, & Morton, 1989). The specific diagnoses and problems of children treated in such settings range from schizophrenia to conduct disorder, and the duration of their treatment can be as brief as one night or as long as a lifetime. The settings within which these children receive treatment also vary considerably, from foster homes for a single child in a suburban neighborhood to programs for several hundred children, located within state psychiatric hospitals.

Historical Perspective

Historically, residential mental-health treatment for children is a fairly recent development (Mayer, Richman, & Balcerzak, 1977). Prior to the seventeenth century, virtually all care for children with developmental or mental-health problems was provided by families, or in the absence of family, by church-run facilities. In the 1600s, however, a system of public almshouses was established in England to serve destitute children. Many of the children served in these facilities had significant behavioral problems. Over the next 200 years, these dual systems of institutional child care (church and public) flourished in Europe and America. Social upheaval around the time of the Industrial Revolution increased the number of needy children, and many institutions grew to large size. With no clear treatment philosophies and chronic underfunding, poor living conditions and abuse within these institutions became widespread.

As public recognition of the poor conditions within these institutions grew in the late 1800s and early 1900s, a sentiment developed against large institutional programs for children and in favor of foster care or more "homelike" residential treatment. In response to this sentiment, many institutions adopted a decentralized or "cottage" model that placed children in smaller functional living units within the institution. Others discharged many children back to their parents or to foster homes, often inappropriately.

At the same time that these changes were affecting institutional child care, Freud's psychodynamic theories were gaining currency in mental health. These theories provided the first systematic rationale for mental-health treatment, and their influence soon extended into the area of child care. Psychoanalytic practitioners developed a model of residential treatment specifically for children with emotional disturbances. In this model, termed milieu therapy, all aspects of the environment are considered to be potentially therapeutic or countertherapeutic. This psychoanalytic model of residential treatment was to remain dominant until the late 1960s. Since that time, other theoretical orientations, particularly behaviorism, have become major contributors to the rationale behind residential treatment, and this modality has come to be regarded as a valuable intervention in cases of severe child mental-health problems. However, it is important to recognize that residential treatment is an extremely invasive intervention that involves disruption to virtually every aspect of a child's life. For that reason, it is important to view residential treatment as only one option in a continuum of possible interventions. Furthermore, treatment should be provided in the setting that is least disruptive of a child's natural environment while still allowing for effective intervention (Lyman & Wilson, 1992).

Alternatives to Residential Treatment

In addition to the degree to which residential treatment disrupts children's and families' lives, there are two other reasons why nonresidential alternatives should be considered prior to implementing residential treatment (Lyman & Wilson, 1992). First is the fact that treatment progress in residential settings frequently does not generalize very well back to the child's natural environment after discharge from the residential environment. This generalization deficit appears to be related to the artificiality of some residential treatment goals and interventions and the dissimilarity between circumstances found in residential treatment and "real life." The second reason that nonresidential alternatives should be considered first is the high cost (up to $1,000 per day or more) and the limited number of residential and inpatient beds available.

Usually, the first treatment modality considered in cases of child mental-health problems is outpatient therapy. Whether conducted according to the traditional once-a-week schedule or more often, such therapy is clearly less disruptive to a child's life than residential placement, and there is evidence to suggest that such treatment (particularly when behaviorally oriented) can be effective in remediating many child mental-health problems (Weisz & Weiss, 1993). However, outpatient treatment, even when conducted several times a week, does not offer sufficient therapeutic "impact" to effectively treat some serious child mental-health disorders. In addition, sometimes a child's behavior is dangerous to him/herself or others, or the family is unable to function with the child in the home. In these cases, outpatient therapy is a less viable choice than residential treatment.

In many cases, day treatment also offers a reasonable alternative to residential treatment. Children enrolled in day treatment are involved for 2 to 8 hours per day in structured therapeutic and educational activities while still returning to their homes after school or work hours. This compromise allows for considerable therapeutic impact but reduces the dangers of institutionalization and detachment from the family that sometimes accompany residential placement. Again, sometimes dangerous behaviors or lack of an intact, functional family dictate the use of residential treatment rather than day treatment. Day treatment environments often resemble regular schools, and placement in them is therefore more familiar to children and less disruptive of their lives than placement in a more clinical setting would be.

Another alternative to residential treatment that has demonstrated efficacy is the in-home comprehensive service. A good example of such an intervention is the Homebuilders model (Kinney, Madsen, Fleming, & Haapala, 1977). This consists of intensive crisis intervention, often conducted in the home, by trained family therapists. These therapists are on-call 24 hours a day and provide case management, behavior therapy, crisis intervention, parent training, and family therapy. Therapists frequently provide 10 or more hours of direct service per week to families while they are in crisis. When the family has stabilized, more traditional service modalities are substituted for the Homebuilders services. Outcome data support the Homebuilders program as an effective intervention that can prevent removal of a child into residential treatment (Bath, Richey, &

Haapala, 1992). Another example of an effective in-home comprehensive services program is Multi-Systemic Therapy (MST). MST is an individualized family- and community-based treatment approach that emphasizes the delivery of services within the youth's "natural" environment. This program has demonstrated its effectiveness in reducing recidivism and incarceration of juvenile offenders (Henggeler, Cunningham, Pickrel, Schoenwald, & Brondino, 1996).

Continuum of Residential Treatment Interventions

When nonresidential treatment options are ineffective or are judged inadvisable because of risk to the child, there is an inability to continue providing a residence within the family, or geographic isolation makes nonresidential treatment unfeasible, residential care must be considered. There are a number of residential alternatives that differ in duration of treatment, characteristics of the living environment, and disruptiveness to the child's life (Lyman & Campbell, 1996). Residential care provided for short periods of time (from 12 hours to 3 weeks) is usually termed respite care if its purpose is to provide relief and support for care givers. Shelter care is the term used if the purpose is to protect and comfort the child during family crises such as abuse, abandonment, or parental substance abuse or another incapacity. Shelter and respite care programs may offer formal therapeutic interventions, or they may simply provide temporary housing for the child.

Foster care involves placement (often for an extended length of time) of one or more children in a home with adults who have been screened and are monitored by a child placement agency and who are reimbursed by the agency for providing such care. Although removal from their own homes and placement with strangers constitutes a major disruption of children's lives, some aspects of life are only minimally affected. Children usually continue to attend "regular" school (perhaps even the same school) while in foster care, and the residential environment continues to be homelike, with surrogate parents rather than child-care staff. There are usually no more than four or five children in the home at a given time. There is seldom an intensive treatment philosophy in foster homes, although a fairly recent development, "therapeutic foster homes," involves more intensive, specialized training for foster parents and more explicit treatment procedures in homes with only one foster child. This model has been used effectively with more severely disturbed children who were previously thought to require institutionalization.

Group homes are differentiated from foster homes by the number of children placed in a home at one time (up to 10 or 12) and by the more "agencylike" characteristics of the residential environment. While foster parents usually act as individuals and live in their own homes, group homes are usually owned or rented by child care agencies and the staff are their employees. A number of group homes may be operated by a single child-care agency. Therefore, group homes tend to be less informal and homelike and more regimented than foster homes. A formal treatment program or philosophy is usually evident, and staff think of themselves as treatment professionals rather than "parents." Shift workers are sometimes used instead of houseparents. In most cases, children in group homes attend external schools, although some in-house educational programs have been developed. As is the case with foster care, duration of treatment in group homes may range from one month to a number of years.

Residential treatment centers are characterized by even stronger agency identification than group homes and by even less similarity to children's natural environment. These centers are usually more isolated from the community than group homes and often provide activities (including school) within the facility rather than through community resources. There is usually a well-defined treatment program and staff other than houseparents to implement it. Some programs utilize child care workers or nursing staff in addition to, or instead of, houseparents. Mental-health professionals are usually given treatment responsibility rather than on-line staff. Although some residential treatment centers serve over 100 children, usually, functional units house no more than 15 children together. Duration of treatment ranges from several months to a number of years.

The duration of treatment in inpatient hospital settings is usually shorter (less than a month) than in residential treatment centers, but the extreme dissimilarity of the hospital environment to a child's natural environment can cause such placements to be more disruptive of a child's adjustment and development than residential treatment. Typically, nursing and medical staff are used rather than child care workers and houseparents, and there is much more regimentation and structure to the daily routine. There is often little opportunity for children to engage in such normal activities as snacking, room cleaning, or outside play. School is frequently suspended during hospitalization or offered only to a limited extent on the ward. Parent contacts are often limited.

Programs that can be defined as institutional are characterized by the absence of normalizing experiences and a deemphasis on reentry back into the child's natural environment after treatment. Institutional programs are often physically and attitudinally isolated from the community and extremely regimented and impersonal in daily routine. Few opportunities are available for residents to leave the facility. Generally, the duration of treatment is measured in years. Schooling is almost always provided within the facility and parental contact is minimal and highly structured. Fortunately, there are no longer very many programs for mentally ill children and adolescents in existence that can be described as institutional in nature. This is because of the heightened humanitarian scrutiny and emphasis on deinstitutionalization that has affected many state hospitals and similar private programs. Many of these facilities have shed their institutional characteristics and are becoming more like residential treatment centers or inpatient hospital programs. However, a program of any size, under public or private jurisdiction, may be described as institutional if it fails to provide normalizing life experiences for children and deemphasizes the goal of reentry into the community for its residents.

Theoretical Models of Residential Treatment

The earliest theoretical perspective behind residential treatment was the psychoanalytic model. As expressed by August Aichorn (1939) and Bruno Bettelheim (1950), among others, this model emphasized the isolation of disturbed children from the "pathogenic" family environment and the primary role of formal psychoanalysis as a treatment agent. Psychoanalytic models of residential treatment deemphasized the importance of the efforts of direct-care staff, such as nurses and aides, in treating children and often gave little attention to issues of behavior management and daily routine. This model remained the standard for residential treatment programs from the 1930s until the advent of behaviorally oriented programs in the 1960s, despite the fact that little data have ever been presented supporting its effectiveness.

Residential treatment programs based on learning theory emerged as part of a more general dissatisfaction with the value of psychoanalytic treatment, which occurred in the 1950s and 1960s. This dissatisfaction stemmed from an absence of empirical demonstrations of the effectiveness of psychoanalytic treatment and its limited applicability to some client populations (namely, those who are retarded, psychotic, or nonverbal). Behaviorally oriented residential treatment programs view maladaptive behaviors as largely resulting from past learning experiences. These programs utilize the residential treatment environment to remediate inappropriate behaviors through systematic management of positive and negative consequences or control of stimulus-response pairings in accordance with laboratory-derived learning principles. The direct-care workers who manipulate the therapeutic environment in these programs are usually viewed as the primary treatment agents rather than those who conduct verbal psychotherapy. During the past 40 years, behavioral treatment programs have generated tremendous quantities of data in support of their effectiveness. They appear to be generally more effective than psychoanalytical or psychodynamic programs, particularly in treating children with conduct problems and poorer verbal abilities. The Teaching-Family Model, which derived from work done at Achievement Place, is a good example of behaviorally oriented residential treatment (Blase, Fixsen, Freeborn, & Jaeger, 1989) and is currently the model espoused by the Boy's Town network of residential facilities.

The medical inpatient model is largely found in hospital programs and emphasizes medical diagnosis and somatic treatment. This model demonstrates greater success when used to treat problems with organic causal components, those that are more acute in nature, and those that are amenable to pharmacological treatment. The staff employed in inpatient psychiatric units are usually medically trained and may favor organic etiological interpretations over behavioral ones. As pointed out earlier, inpatient psychiatric units frequently do not offer an effective environment for treatment of school or family relationship problems because of the deemphasis on educational programming and the limited contact between the child patient and his or her family. A growing role for psychiatric inpatient units is the periodic hospitalization of chronically mentally ill children and adolescents for the purpose of stabilizing behavior and providing respite for the family. In addition, as medical diagnostic procedures in the area of child mental health have become more relevant, psychiatric inpatient units have increasingly become places where children are housed while such diagnostic procedures as magnetic resonance imaging (MRI), computerized axial tomography (CT), and positron emission tomography (PET) scans, sleep electroencephalographs (EEGs), and laboratory assays are conducted.

The peer culture model stresses the importance of interpersonal factors, particularly peer influences, in the cause and treatment of child and adolescent mental-health problems. Most peer culture programs use group (clients plus staff) feedback regarding behavior and group control of privileges or rewards as the major components of the treatment program. The peer culture model has become the model of choice for adolescent substance-abuse programs and seems equally applicable to other externalizing disorders that are, at least in part, maintained by peer influence (Brendtro & Wasmund, 1989).

The wilderness therapy model attempts to offer real-life challenges in the wilderness that will foster prosocial values in children and adolescents, enhance their self-esteem, and help them develop better coping skills. Such programs can be relatively brief (1–4 weeks) or can constitute a child's home environment for years. The challenges offered can range from biking and mountain climbing to blue-water sailing (Bacon & Kimball, 1989).

Residential Program Characteristics

A number of practical considerations must be addressed by all residential treatment programs. Decisions regarding program characteristics are guided only partly by theoretical orientation and can determine the nature and therapeutic effectiveness of any residential program, regardless of theoretical basis. These characteristics include the physical facilities within which the program is housed; the type and number of staff employed to work with the children; the age, gender, and presenting problems of the children served; the involvement of the family in the child's treatment; the role of psychotherapy in the treatment process; the choice of procedures used to manage children's behavior; the steps taken to maintain children's involvement with the community while in treatment, and the reintegration of the child back into the family and community at discharge. A discussion of these factors can be found in Lyman and Campbell (1996).

Evaluating the Effectiveness of Residential Treatment

Numerous outcome studies concerning residential treatment exist in mental-health literature (see Lyman & Campbell, 1996). Generally, this literature suggests that most children placed in residential treatment improve over time, but that this improvement may not be greater than that of untreated control groups. Furthermore, improvement is not clearly related to the presence or absence of any specific elements of residential treatment. Behaviorally oriented programs report better outcome data than psychodynamically oriented programs, and psychotic and conduct disordered children show less improvement than children with other mental-health disorders. Parental involvement in treatment is correlated with better outcomes. The literature also suggests that the most dramatic treatment effects are seen at the time of discharge, with the differences between untreated controls and children served in residential care diminishing at extended follow-up assessments.

The outcome data for day treatment and in-home intervention programs are roughly comparable to those for residential treatment programs (Lyman & Campbell, 1996), suggesting that such programs should be considered as viable alternatives to residential treatment, particularly when the lower cost of such nonresidential options is considered.

Bibliography

Aichorn, A. (1935). *Wayward youth.* New York: Viking. This is an early description of psychoanalytically oriented residential treatment.

Bacon, S. B., & Kimball, R. (1989). The wilderness challenge model. In R. D. Lyman, S. Prentice-Dunn, & S. Gabel (Eds.), *Residential and inpatient treatment of children and adolescents* (pp. 115–144). New York: Plenum Press.

Bath, H. I., Richey, C. A., & Haapala, D. A. (1992). Child age and outcome correlates in intensive family preservation services. *Children and Youth Services Review, 14,* 389–406.

Bettelheim, B. (1950). *Love is not enough.* New York: Free Press.

Blase, K. A., Fixsen, D. L., Freeborn, K., & Jaeger, D. (1989). The behavioral model. In R. D. Lyman, S. Prentice-Dunn, & S. Gabel (Eds.), *Residential and inpatient treatment of children and adolescents* (pp. 43–59). New York: Plenum Press.

Brendtro, L. K., & Wasmund, W. (1989). The peer culture model. In R. D. Lyman, S. Prentice-Dunn, & S. Gabel (Eds.), *Residential and inpatient treatment of children and adolescents* (pp. 81–96). New York: Plenum Press.

Henggeler, S. W., Cunningham, P. B., Pickrel, S. G., Schoenwald, S. K., & Brondino, M. J. (1996). Multisystemic therapy: An effective violence prevention approach for serious juvenile offenders. *Journal of Adolescence, 19,* 47–61.

Kiesler, C. A., Simpkins, C., & Morton, T. (1989). The psychiatric inpatient treatment of children and youth in general hospitals. *American Journal of Community Psychology, 17,* 821–830.

Kinney, J. M., Madsen, B., Fleming, T., & Haapala, D. A. (1977). Homebuilders: Keeping families together. *Journal of Consulting and Clinical Psychology, 45,* 667–673.

Lyman, R. D., & Campbell, N. R. (1996). *Treating children and adolescents in residential and inpatient settings.* Thousand Oaks, CA: Sage. Provides an overview of methods and issues related to residential treatment for emotionally disturbed youth.

Lyman, R. D., & Wilson, D. R. (1992). Residential and inpatient treatment of emotionally disturbed children and adolescents. In C. E. Walker & M. C. Roberts (Eds.), *Handbook of clinical child psychology* (2nd ed., pp. 829–843). New York: Wiley-Interscience.

Mayer, M. F., Richman, L. H., & Balcerzak, E. A. (1977). *Group care of children: Crossroads and transitions.* New York: Child Welfare League.

Weisz, J. R., & Weiss, B. (1993). *Effects of psychotherapy with children and adolescents.* Newbury Park, CA: Sage.

Robert D. Lyman

RESILIENCE. How do the resilient few survive stressors to which the majority succumb? Werner and Smith (1992) followed 698 infants born in 1955 on Kauai; 30 years later they identified 201 adults (30%) as high risk for diverse bad life outcomes such as mental illness given four or more risk factors before age 2: perinatal stress, chronic poverty, uneducated parents, family discord, divorce, and parental alcoholism or mental illness. Of the 201, 72 adults (36%) avoided serious childhood learning or behavior problems, adolescent delinquency, pregnancy, or mental illness. As young adults they "lived well, worked well, and played well" (Werner & Smith, 1992). Moffitt (1989) followed 457 New Zealand males from childhood to adolescence and found 27 "recoveries" (5%) who were extremely antisocial as children but not as adolescents. McCord (1979) rated the adverse outcomes of 506 middle-aged men who had been high-risk adolescents before World War II (indicated by, for instance, convictions for FBI-indexed crimes; death before age 35; diagnosis of alcoholism, schizophrenia, or manic depression) and found that a few resilient men were free from all adverse outcomes.

In general terms, psychological resilience is the capacity to bounce back after adversity. A more precise definition of resilience emerges from the above findings and the work of Garmezy (1993), Rutter (1990), and Elder (1985). Resilience is defined as the ability to survive a stressor (or risk factor) and to avoid two or more adverse life outcomes to which the majority of normative survivors of this stressor succumb. Avoidance of multiple adverse endpoints increases the likelihood that resilience is a psychologically meaningful phenomenon and not a statistical fluke. Identification of exceptional stressors that lead to adverse outcomes in normative survivors confirms the severity of the stressor, quantifies the stressor's modal functional impact, and distinguishes exceptional from normative stressors (such as kindergarten entry) that usually occasion no more than temporary discomfort.

The resilience phenomenon, so defined, applies across the life span to survivors of acute and chronic stressors and risk factors: children who avoid disruptions in adult work and family roles despite mentally ill parents, early life in concentration camps, war zones, or impoverished households, observation of community violence, or endurance of sexual abuse; violent adolescent males and early maturing delinquent females who avoid adult criminality and family violence; Vietnam War veterans and rape survivors who avoid later post-traumatic stress disorder and substance abuse; the mutilated victim of a letter bomb or the paraplegic victim of a riding accident who avoids alcoholism and suicide. All these individuals are resilient survivors.

Resilient survivors are not invulnerable; they feel distressed during and after exposure to stressors, and they are permanently affected by their experiences. Excessive stress may both inoculate survivors with greater capacity to face new challenges and sensitize them with more existential doubt and dysphoria. There is disagreement about prospects for resilience, particularly among children. The popular view (see Egeland & Farber 1984), is that early trauma leaves no resilient survivors. In contrast, both Kagan (1976) and Macfarlane

(1964) dispute a "tape recorder" doctrine of irreversible early experience. Reconciliation of these perspectives results when we recognize that stressors and risk factors vary in their average impact on later functioning. Some commonly experienced stressors (such as sibling rivalry) induce only passing discomfort in most children. Those who "get over" sibling rivalry with no ill effects are survivors of a normative stressor, but the term resilient survivor hardly applies. Other stressors (such as early parental neglect) are followed in most "survivors" by lingering depressive symptoms and impaired peer relationships. Survivors who avoid the usual long-term adverse consequences are reasonably called "resilient." In Werner and Smith's (1992) study, 30% of high-risk children were resilient survivors of disadvantaged families, whereas in Moffitt's study (1989), 5% were resilient survivors of seriously antisocial childhood behavior.

How do resilient survivors avoid adverse outcomes? According to Block (1991), ego resilience (resourceful, flexible responses to novel or stressful situations as measured by the California Q-set) helps decide whether children work through and grow beyond their difficulties. Longitudinal and cross-cultural studies have found that high ego resiliency ratings predict empathy, delay of gratification, reasoning, problem solving, IQ, and Big Five personality traits (Agreeableness, Extraversion, Conscientiousness, Neuroticism, Openness to experience). High childhood ego resilience ratings are associated with future avoidance of adverse outcomes such as substance abuse, but such correlational evidence cannot forge a causal link between ego resilience and resilient survival. As Sroufe (1997) points out, it is important to avoid the temptation of circular reasoning—identifying people as resilient survivors simply because they score high on a paper-and-pencil measure of ego resilience.

Perhaps resilient survivors avoid adverse outcomes via adaptive, prosocial coping, including ego-resilient behavior. Coping (Lazarus & Folkman 1984), includes all purposeful reactions to stress. Maladaptive coping strategies, used consistently across time and situations, eventually engender adverse outcomes for self and others. Problem-avoidant, risky, impulsive, ill-tempered, aggressive reactions to stress (Robins & Caspi, 1998) fail to resolve controllable problems or to moderate the emotional distress attendant on uncontrollable problems while encouraging a self-absorbed, substance-abusing lifestyle to relieve negative affect. Adolescents' use of harder drugs may represent a desperate attempt to escape a hopeless personal situation by changing inner experience (Block, 1991). Maladaptive coping strategies promise instant self-gratification but diminish social support and impair functioning in family, school, work, and community roles. Persistent reliance on maladaptive coping strategies may foster the stability of antisocial behavior over time and the comorbidity of depression and aggression. Murphy and Moriarty's longitudinal study (1976) found that effective coping with everyday stress involves a balance of autonomy and sufficient dependence to seek help from others and the poststressor capacity to relax, gather strength, and attend to role responsibilities. Adaptive coping is quintessentially prosocial, according to Blechman, Prinz, and Dumas (1995). Through private contemplation and public deliberation, the individual selects and implements a feasible response with optimum consequences for self and others.

Early research and theory on coping suggested that problem-focused coping (focusing on solving problems) and self-attributions for success (taking credit for success) are always adaptive, whereas emotion-focused coping (focusing on feeling better) and self-attributions for failure (taking blame for failure) are always maladaptive. Lately (Compas, Hinden, & Gerhardt, 1995), research evidence suggests that the nature of an adaptive coping response varies with age, personal resources, social context, and stressor. Young children and people of all ages faced with uncontrollable challenges seem to fare best when avoiding, ignoring, minimizing, or reframing. Adolescents, adults, and even school-aged children faced with controllable challenges fare best when they responsibly consider, alone and with others, the long-term consequences of personal action for self and others, devise a solution for managing the challenge and attendant negative affect, and flexibly follow through with determination, self-confidence, optimism, and social support. The survivor of a severe burn told Holaday, "To do well takes a lot of determination, courage, and struggling, but it's your choice" (Holaday & McPhereson, 1997, p. 348). Although it involves risks taken on others' behalf, prosocial coping lends meaning to life in the worst of times and promotes the common good. Prosocial coping certainly minimizes adverse outcomes in the face of normative and exceptional stressors, although the extent of its contribution to resilient survival is unknown.

Resilient survival of excessive stress is attributed by Block (1991), Garmezy (1993), and Werner and Smith (1992) to a triad of protective factors: (1) personal characteristics (e.g., coping strategy, intelligence, physiological reactivity, temperament); (2) nuclear family characteristics (e.g., cohesiveness and structure, warm, skilled parenting), and (3) extrafamilial characteristics (e.g., community organization, mentoring, supportive school environment). Excessive stressors such as homelessness do not appear to have uniformly adverse effects; instead, protective factors moderate or buffer their impact. Resilient survivors describe life-changing turning points when protection levels dramatically increase due to a caring mentor, supportive spouse, or religious conversion. Psychologists once believed in clear distinctions between risk factors (child abuse) and protective factors (warm, skilled parenting). More recent research suggests that a construct such as parenting is best thought of as a bipolar risk-protection continuum ranging perhaps from very cold, rejecting, insensitive caretaking quality at the far left pole to very warm, accepting, and skilled caretaking quality at the far right pole. Every child's experience with caretakers falls somewhere along this continuum and has both direct effects on risk for bad life outcomes, such as substance abuse and mental illness, and indirect effects, such as buffering or potentiating the impact of other risk-protection factors. Summing across caretaking experiences from infancy through adolescence, consistently cold caretaking increases risk, whereas consistently warm caretaking experience reduces risk. Across gender and ethnic groups, risk-protective factors appear to be interdependent (thus a temperamentally difficult child is unlikely to engage a mentor's concern) and cumulative in their effect. However, scaling of indicators may differ between gender and ethnic groups (e.g., very tight parental supervision may be required to buffer the impact of a disorganized neighborhood on African American males). As children grow older, their personal characteristics, especially their coping styles, increasingly act as direct determinants of future adverse outcomes and as mediators of the indirect effects of past and present familial and extrafamilial risk-protection factors.

How do youth who begin life at high risk make the transition into resilience? Longitudinal research, for example, that of Brooks-Gunn (1988), Loeber (1982), Moffitt (1989), Patterson (1993), Peterson (1995), Stattin (1995), and Magnusson (1992) suggests that most young people traverse one of four developmental pathways from birth through adulthood. Competent youth (with persisting low levels of risk) and early-onset disadvantaged youth (with persisting high levels of risk) encounter predictably favorable or adverse adult outcomes, respectively. Resilient youth (with a risk level that drops from high to low by adolescence) and late-onset disadvantaged youth (with a risk level that rises from low to high by adolescence) encounter what seem at first glance incongruently favorable or adverse adult outcomes. Thus the all-around competent youngster and the early-onset delinquent share a common stability of risk-protection levels, whereas the resilient survivor of childhood abuse and the formerly well-adjusted girl who declines during adolescence into lifelong depression may share a common instability of risk-protection levels. The adult lives of resilient youth who recover during adolescence from serious childhood conduct problems and of adolescent-onset delinquents seem different and unpredictable unless changes in risk-protection levels (e.g., dramatic increments or decrements in quality of schooling, parental supervision, or association with deviant peers) are considered. As Sroufe (1997) has noted, the capacity for resilience evolves over the life span within the total context of developmental influences.

Bibliography

Blechman, E. A., Prinz, R. J., & Dumas, J. E. (1995). Coping, competence, and aggression prevention: I. Developmental model. *Applied and Preventive Psychology, 4,* 211–232.

Block, J. (1991, December). *Remarks on resilience and ego-resilience.* Paper presented at National Institute of Mental Health Conference on Fostering Resilience, Washington, DC.

Brooks-Gunn, J. (1988). Antecedents and consequences of variations in girls' maturational timing. *Journal of Adolescent Health Care, 9,* 365–373.

Compas, B. E., Hinden, B. R., & Gerhardt, C. A. (1995). Adolescent development: Pathways and processes of risk and resilience. *Annual Review of Psychology, 46,* 265–293. This excellent resource provides citations for many studies cited in the text.

Egeland, B., & Faber, E. (1984). Infant mother attachment: Factors related to its development and changes over time. *Child Development, 55,* 703–711.

Elder, G. H., Jr. (1985). Perspectives on the life course. In G. H. Elder, Jr. (Ed.), *Life course dynamics: Trajectories and transitions, 1968–1980* (pp. 23–44). Ithaca, NY: Cornell University Press.

Garmezy, N. (1993). Children in poverty: Resilience despite risk. *Psychiatry, 56,* 127–136. Garmezy introduced the term *resilience* and inspired several decades of research on stress and coping.

Gregory, L. (1995). *The "turnaround" process: Factors influencing the school success of urban youth.* New York: Academic Press.

Holaday, M., & McPhereson, R. W. (1997). Resilience and severe burns. *Journal of Counseling and Development, 75,* 346–356.

Kagan, J. (1976). Emergent themes in human development. *American Scientist, 64,* 186–196.

Lazarus, R. S., & Folkman, S. (1984). *Stress, appraisal, and coping.* New York: Springer-Verlag.

Loeber, R. (1982). The stability of antisocial behavior: A review. *Child Development, 53,* 1431–1446.

Luthar, S. (1991). Vulnerability and resilience: A study of high-risk adolescents. *Child Development, 62,* 600–616.

Magnusson, D. (1992). Individual development: A longitudinal perspective. *European Journal of Personality, 6,* 119–138.

McCord, J. (1979). Some child-rearing antecedents of criminal behavior in adult men. *Journal of Personality and Social Psychology, 37,* 1477–1486.

Mcfarlane, J. W. (1964). Perspectives on personal consistency and change from the guidance study. *Vita Humana, 7,* 115–126.

Moffitt, T. E. (1989). Accommodating self-report methods to a low-delinquency culture: A longitudinal study from New Zealand. In M. W. Klein (Ed.), *Cross-national research in self-reported crime and delinquency* (pp. 43–66). Norwell, MA: Kluwer Academic.

Murphy, L. B., & Moriarty, A. E. (1976). *Vulnerability, coping, and growth from infancy to adolescence.* New Haven, CT: Yale University Press.

Patterson, G. R. (1993). Orderly change in a stable world: The antisocial trait as a chimera. *Journal of Consulting Clinical Psychology, 61,* 911–919.

Peterson, G. (1995). The need for common principles in prevention programs for children, adolescents, and families. *Journal of Adolescent Research, 10,* 470–485.

Robins, R. W., & Caspi, A. (1998, February). *Resilient, over-controlled, and undercontrolled adolescents: Three replicable personality types.* Paper presented at the meeting of The Society for Research on Adolescence, San Diego, CA.

Rutter, M. (1990). Psychosocial resilience and protective mechanisms. In J. E. Rolf, A. S. Masten, D. Cicchetti, K. H. Neuchterlein, & S. Weintraub (Eds.), *Risk and protective factors in the development of psychopathology* (pp. 181–214). Cambridge, England: Cambridge University Press. This is one of many important empirical and theoretical contributions by Rutter to the study of resilience.

Shedler, J., & Block, J. (1990). Adolescent drug use and psychological health: A longitudinal inquiry. *American Psychologist, 45,* 612–630. The study is worth reading both for its methods and its controversial but meaningful findings.

Sroufe, L. A. (1997). Psychopathology as an outcome of development. *Development and Psychopathology, 9,* 251–268. This is an interesting contribution from a leading developmental psychologist that shows the relationship between psychopathology and resilience.

Stattin, H. (1995). The adolescent is a whole person. *Journal of Adolescence, 18,* 381–386.

Werner, E. E., & Smith, R. (1992). *Overcoming the odds: High risk children from birth to adulthood.* Ithaca, NY: Cornell University Press. This is the classic longitudinal study of resilience.

Elaine A. Blechman

RETIREMENT. As a behavior, retirement is the transition out of the labor force or the adult role of work. Retirement is also a destination—a stage of life occupied by former workers. Retirement refers, as well, to economic and societal practices that facilitate work exits and support a postemployment period of life.

The principal criteria for defining an individual as retired include reduced participation in the labor force, receipt of pension income from public or private sources, and an individual's self-identification as retired. These criteria overlap considerably, although not always exactly, so that the designation of the retired status can shift, depending on the context (Ekerdt & DeViney, 1990). In most cases, a significant reduction in employment and pension acceptance serve to define older persons as retired.

The rate of labor force participation offers one way to describe the extent of retirement in a population. By this measure, the adult population of the United States is shifting from one that largely works to one that is mainly retired within a compressed period of the life span. In the United States in 1997, 88% of males were labor force participants (full- or part-time) at ages 50 to 54 but only 28% by ages 65 to 69, and 73% of females were labor force participants at ages 50 to 54 but only 18% by ages 65 to 69 (U.S. Department of Labor, 1998). Labor force participation rates at these ages have been declining for decades, indicating what other estimates confirm has been a trend toward earlier retirement (Gendell & Siegel, 1996), a trend that seems to have leveled off in the 1990s. Retirement prior to the benchmark age of 65 is now the norm. Yet there are those who work into their 70s and 80s. Men who do so are characteristically in good health, have higher educational attainment, and express a strong distaste for retirement.

Recent studies of retirement behavior have raised awareness of the potential complexity of the retirement transition. The idealized, crisp event of retirement, identifiable and permanent, is only one pathway. There are also sequences of exit and reentry, patterns of part-time or intermittent work, and indeterminate states of partial retirement (Henretta, 1997). For economic and psychological reasons, disability rather than retirement might be a preferable identity for older persons separated from work. This multiformity of career endings requires a concept of retirement behavior as a latent set of transitions on the way to final withdrawal from the labor force.

Explaining Retirement

The broad turnover of aging cohorts of workers into cohorts of retirees is common to Western nations, and it occurs far in advance of the ages typical of death and disability. The modern ubiquity of a retirement stage can be explained at three levels. First, national governments have an interest in regulating labor markets and reducing unemployment, and individual employers have an interest in managing the stock and flow of human resources. These aims can be accomplished in part by inducing older workers to withdraw from employment. Governments and employers sponsor pension plans that partially replace lost wage income and so act as incentives to retire. Historically retirement under compulsory age rules had also been a device for prompting job exits, but this mechanism has been largely eliminated by law in the United States. Societal and firm-level policies that favor retirement are now embodied primarily in the pension incentives of the Social Security retirement program and those of individ-

ual employers. These inducements are effective; the trend toward earlier retirement has consistently paced the offer of ever more generous pensions in the period after World War II.

A second level of explanation for the labor-leisure pattern of later life can be found in beliefs about the productivity of older workers. The industrial era ushered in a dedication to progress and efficiency, and with it a bias toward younger workers. A pessimistic medical model of aging bolstered assumptions about the obsolescence of older workers (Haber & Gratton, 1994). The capacities of older workers remain an issue today. Although older workers are recognized as loyal and knowledgeable, they are also seen as less amenable to training or receptive to technological change, and prone to accidents and illness. Human factors research on age and job performance has revealed that many of these negative assumptions are unfounded, and that the productivity of older workers can be conserved with workplace interventions, training, and job redesign (Salthouse & Maurer, 1996). Absent employer accommodation, negative perceptions reduce the market value of older workers and narrow their opportunities for extended work careers.

A third explanation for retirement is older adults' desire for leisure and release from the work role. The desire for rest in later life is historically deep, but only with the modern institution of retirement (as pensioned leisure) has this goal been widely attainable. Because retirement spells both freedom and marginality, retirement motives can be mixed. The demand for leisure may arise from a developmental need for consolidation, or it may be a response to diminished work capacity or a reaction to a disagreeable work environment that drains one's self-efficacy. The nonwork time afforded by retirement can also appear as a resource for personal or social use before the end of life. Whatever the motives, workers' readiness to retire generally conforms to a contemporary conceptual map of life, socially shared, in which a retirement stage is viewed as a cultural given.

Adaptation

Because most workers expect and are expected to retire, this normative character of retirement blunts its potential as a stressful life event. Gerontological research has failed to confirm predictions that retirement is a crisis characteristically portending negative effects on well-being. This conclusion derives from research on physical and mental health, marital quality, and morale and life satisfaction (Gall, Evans, & Howard, 1997; Reitzes, Mutran, & Fernandez, 1996). Indeed, such studies tend to disclose the benefits that retirees perceive.

A minority of retirees, however, do report difficulty in adapting to retirement. About 30% of respondents in various studies say that the transition to or state of retirement is stressful (Bossé, Spiro, & Kressin, 1996), a percentage sufficient to advise vigilance toward persons who might be vulnerable to emotional problems if faced with a change in structure or daily routine. A poor experience with retirement, when it occurs, tends to coincide with rushed or unanticipated transitions or with other negative life events (e.g., illness, a drop in income). Reactions to retirement are diverse, so the search for unitary effects on well-being is not likely to be fruitful. Adaptation is perhaps better understood by paying attention to people's agency—how and why older workers have differential opportunities to arrange late-career and transition circumstances to their own advantage (Hansson, DeKoekkoek, Neece, & Patterson, 1997).

Decision Making

Issues of control and mastery are germane to the many decisions to be faced by persons approaching and entering voluntary retirement. Whereas retirement is broadly determined by pension availability—itself an expression of societal, organizational, and personnel objectives—workers often have discretion concerning the form and timing of retirement. The matrix of choices about form includes a decision not only on whether to leave the current job, but also on whether to withdraw from work altogether or continue employment in another situation, perhaps at reduced hours or in another occupational line (partial retirement at the same job is uncommon). The earlier the timing of retirement, the longer the potential span for complex or experimental pathways before advancing age forecloses employability. Pension features affect timing as well because plan incentives are often structured by the employer so that the maximum benefit is tied to a particular age or length of employment, beyond which little advantage accrues for further tenure. The retirement benefit of the current U.S. Social Security program can be elected "early," beginning at age 62 with reduced benefits, or taken at age 65 with full benefits, or delayed with increased benefits. The options are financially neutral because the total lifetime payout to a hypothetical retiree would be about the same. The choice in this case, then, can depend on other considerations.

A special kind of timing decision is required by early retirement incentive (window) programs. Designed to cut older personnel, such programs enhance existing incentives with a time-limited offer of higher benefits if one retires now. The inducement will seem a welcome opportunity to some workers but will catch others emotionally unprepared or even surprised that the firm views them as marginal.

Prospective retirees also face the task of conserving their income and assets for an uncertain span of remaining life. Whereas the Social Security retirement benefit is indexed to rise with the cost of living, many traditional pensions of the defined-benefit type are not, and so are vulnerable to inflation. Workers accepting pension income from an account-type or defined-contribution plan, such as a 401(k) plan, must specify the distribution of the money, perhaps as a lump sum to be invested, with attendant risk, or converted to installment income for a specified term. Hovering over the future, too, is the question of finances for health care, including long-term care. The present political climate of fiscal austerity does not promise further expansion of public spending for retiree health programs, so a larger share of health costs will fall to retirees themselves.

A substantial minority of workers retire because their health effectively limits further employment, but others retire strategically to conserve their health for a retirement career. Family considerations also affect the timing and form of retirement. One spouse's health, employment, and pension situation influence the planning of the other partner, so retirement intentions and behaviors may more properly be regarded as proceeding from joint or household decisions. Altogether, the intertwined decision demands of work withdrawal make reported levels of stress concerning the retirement transition conceivable and anxiety about retirement's consequences clinically relevant.

Preparation for a New Stage of Life

Retirement, as a major normative life event that is also the threshold of a new stage of life, presents the opportunity to review matters in addition to employment and finances. Health habits are one such lifestyle issue, and so is residence. Few retirees move across state lines, but stocktaking on the locale and size of the dwelling is common. This, in turn, is bound up with commitments to adult children and grandchildren and perhaps to surviving parents. In reviewing their living arrangements, men and women may have different considerations, with women being aware of a longer life expectancy, a greater likelihood of living alone, and a stronger investment in the social convoy of family and friends. Leisure commitments are also reviewed, including the issue of volunteering. Aside from general social norms about the importance of activity and engagement, the retirement role is quite open-ended.

Information on retirement planning is widely available, and in every medium (Cooper, 1994). Participation in formal preretirement programs with comprehensive extrafinancial content is uncommon, although such programs are offered in the community and by employers with more extensive benefit programs. The goal of retirement planning specialists is to have workers develop reasonable expectations about their future. Research evaluation of planning programs has been difficult because the self-selection of workers for such pro-) grams obscures the relationship between planning and later experience.

Retirement, finally, can both challenge and clarify a worker's identity. The social ambiguity of the position— one is both free and marginal—creates new bases on which to construct the self. This task turns, in part, on the extent to which work has offered affiliation, power, and competence, and whether other continuing family, social, and religious involvements can provide a footing for encountering the world (Atchley, 1989). The rising awareness of time left to live can also compel attention to one's accomplishments and what might yet be brought to fruition (Karp, 1989).

[*See also* Elder Care.]

Bibliography

Atchley, R. C. (1989). A continuity theory of normal aging. *Gerontologist, 29*, 183–190.

Bossé, R., Spiro, A., & Kressin, N. R. (1996). The psychology of retirement. In R. T. Woods (Ed.), *Handbook of the clinical psychology of ageing* (pp. 141–157). Chichester, UK: Wiley.

Cooper, J. W. (1994). Getting ready to retire: Preretirement planning programs. In A. Monk (Ed.), *The Columbia retirement handbook* (pp. 59–80). New York: Columbia University Press.

Ekerdt, D. J., & DeViney, S. (1990). On defining persons as retired. *Journal of Aging Studies, 4*, 211–229.

Gall, T. L, Evans, D. R., & Howard, J. (1997). The retirement adjustment process: Changes in the well-being of male retirees across time. *Journal of Gerontology: Psychological Sciences, 52B*, P110–P117.

Gendell, M., & Siegel, J. S. (1996). Trends in retirement age in the United States, 1955–1993, by sex and race. *Journal of Gerontology: Social Sciences, 51B*, S132–S139.

Haber, C., & Gratton, B. (1994). *Old age and the search for security: An American social history.* Bloomington: Indiana University Press.

Hansson, R. O., DeKoekkoek, P. D., Neece, W. M., & Patterson, D. W. (1997). Successful aging at work: Annual review, 1992–1996: The older worker and transitions to retirement. *Journal of Vocational Behavior, 51*, 202–233.

Henretta, J. C. (1997). Changing perspectives on retirement. *Journal of Gerontology: Social Sciences, 52*, S1–S3.

Karp, D. A. (1989). The social construction of retirement among professionals 50–60 years old. *Gerontologist, 36*, 750–760.

Reitzes, D. C., Mutran, E. J., & Fernandez, M. E. (1996). Does retirement hurt well-being? Factors influencing self-esteem and depression among retirees and workers. *Gerontologist, 36*, 649–656.

Salthouse, T. A., & Maurer, T. J. (1996). Aging, job performance, and career development. In J. E. Birren, K. W. Schaie, R. A. Abeles, M. Gatz, & T. A. Salthouse (Eds.), *Handbook of the psychology of aging* (4th ed., pp. 353–364). San Diego: Academic Press.

U.S. Department of Labor, Bureau of Labor Statistics. (1998, January). *Employment and Earnings, 45*(1), 164.

David J. Ekerdt

RETRIEVAL PROCESSES can be defined as those processes that are involved in gaining access to memory. In contrast with encoding and storage, which refer respectively to the formation and retention of memory, retrieval refers to the utilization of memory (Melton, 1963).

The experimental logic for studying retrieval processes requires holding encoding and storage conditions constant and introducing the critical manipulation in the memory test. Manipulations introduced then are likely to affect retrieval, rather than encoding and storage, even though retrieval is inevitably conditional on those prior stages.

Such manipulations involve retrieval cues, discrete parts of the information used to gain access to memories. Presented in experiments or manipulated indirectly by comparing different retrieval conditions, retrieval cues can be varied and their effects evaluated. Retrieval cues are also part of a natural environment in which events, circumstances, and thoughts bring memories to mind.

The distinction between the "availability" of information stored in memory and its "accessibility" was first delineated by Endel Tulving and Zena Pearlstone (1966). They had people study lists of words that fell into a number of different categories, such as names of weapons, occupations, or vehicles. Everyone studied the same words under the same conditions. In a later test, one group of people had to recall the words unaided in what is called a *free recall test* (in which the only cue given is "words from the studied list"). Another group had to recall the words too, but they were reminded about the categories. The category names were presented in the test as additional retrieval cues. People given these cues were able to recall many more studied words than people given the free recall test, particularly when there were longer study lists and more categories. Since everyone was treated identically before retrieval, this difference reflects retrieval problems in free recall—problems in gaining access to memory in the absence of effective retrieval cues.

What makes retrieval cues effective? A classic series of experiments by Endel Tulving, engagingly reviewed in his *Elements of Episodic Memory* (New York, 1983), led to one general answer to this question: the "encoding specificity principle" (Tulving & Thomson, 1973). According to this principle, retrieval cues will increase access to memory only if the information provided by the cues was specifically encoded when that memory was formed. For example, the cue "girl's name" may increase the likelihood of recalling ROSE as a studied word, but only if ROSE was specifically encoded then as the name of a girl. If it was encoded as the name of a flower, then not only will the cue "girl's name" not increase the likelihood of recalling ROSE, but it may actually make its recall less likely.

Stated more broadly, the encoding specificity principle asserts that access to memory is more likely when encoding and retrieval conditions match than when there is a mismatch between them. Much evidence supports this principle, including evidence of "state-dependent retrieval," in which what varies is people's physiological state. For example, it is well known that recall of memories formed under the influence of alcohol is more likely if retrieval is attempted when one is again under the influence of alcohol than when one is sober, and vice versa. Similar state-dependent retrieval effects occur with other drugs, such as marijuana. Eric Eich (1980) pointed out that these effects are "cue dependent" in the sense that they are more likely to occur with free recall tests than with cued recall or recognition. Presumably, the retrieval cues presented in those tests largely override the effects of the more subtle internal cues that are affected by the drug state. There is also some evidence that inducing differences in people's emotional mood or differences in their physical environment between the study and test impairs recall, much as in state-dependent retrieval. Some of these effects, though, have proved harder to replicate.

A similar idea to that of encoding specificity is that of "transfer appropriate processing" (Morris, Bransford, & Franks, 1977). Transfer appropriate processing also focuses on the extent to which there is a match or a mismatch between encoding and retrieval. However, it is concerned with the general kind of processing involved at each stage rather than with specific retrieval cues. For example, if words are studied more in terms of their visual appearance than in terms of their meaning and if a recognition test requires memory for the way the words appeared, people will do better than if they had paid less attention to the visual appearance of the words in the study phase and concentrated more on meaning. Transfer from study to test will be better if encoding and retrieval require similar kinds of processing and will be poorer if they do not.

Morris et al. (1977) contrasted transfer appropriate processing with "level of processing," an approach that initially had emphasized the superiority of encoding in terms of meaning without much regard to retrieval conditions (Craik & Tulving, 1975). Transfer appropriate processing has since been used to interpret differences between performance on explicit memory tests, which direct people to remember, and performance on implicit memory tests, which do not but instead assess memory indirectly by seeing how it affects people's performance on other cognitive tasks (Roediger, 1990).

The level of processing approach suggested that deeper, more meaningful encoding leads to greater "distinctiveness" in memory than shallower, less meaningful encoding. Indeed, if people are asked to memorize a list of items in which there is one isolated distinctive item—the name Ebbinghaus (author of a classic monograph on memory), say, in the middle of a list of nonsense syllables (materials he developed for his experiments)—then people will almost certainly remember the occurrence of that item. This effect has been named the *von Restorff effect*, after its discoverer (von Restorff, 1933).

Distinctive items benefit from being associated with retrieval cues that may be unique to them. The cue "famous psychologist" relates to one item in the preceding example, whereas the cue "nonsense syllables" relates to every other item in such a list. Similarly, the cue "famous psychologist" would be much less effective for recalling Ebbinghaus from a list of famous psychologists. The more items attached to a retrieval cue, the less likely it is that any particular one of them can be recalled, given that cue. Michael Watkins (1979) described this as the "cue overload principle." Between them, the encoding specificity principle and the cue overload principle suggest why much apparent forgetting is cue dependent.

"Flashbulb memories" are characterized by vivid autobiographical recollections of momentous events to which people had strong emotional reactions and regarded as having great personal significance (Brown & Kulik, 1977). Events that have been claimed to give rise to flashbulb memories include the assassination of President John F. Kennedy, the explosion of the Challenger space shuttle, and the death of Princess Diana. Although some have argued that flashbulb memories are quite different from other kinds of memory, others disagree. Although vivid, such memories are not always accurate, and they benefit to an unusual extent from repeated retelling. It may be that flashbulb memories are little more than extreme examples of distinctiveness in memory.

Although presenting retrieval cues often increases the likelihood of retrieval, presenting cues can also have "inhibitive effects." Presenting part of a set of items to be recalled as cues for recalling the other items from the set makes their recall less likely. For example, Norman Slamecka (1968) had people study a list of the most common associates of the word *butterfly* and then presented some of these associates as retrieval cues to help them recall the other associates. Those people were less likely to recall the other associates than people not given such cues. Robert Bjork (1989) drew attention to the wider importance of the concept of retrieval inhibition and to its relative neglect in memory theory. Retrieval inhibition is not well understood generally, although the negative effects of part set cuing have been related to the cue overload principle (Watkins, 1979).

Another important and even more neglected concept, although necessary for understanding retrieval processes, is "retrieval mode" (Tulving, 1983). Retrieval mode refers to what people intend to do in a given situation. It differs, for example, if people intend only to use abstract knowledge they have about the world or if they intend to retrieve personal experiences remembered as such. There is evidence for this distinction both from behavioral studies and from recent physiological studies using functional neuroimaging techniques, but little is known about how retrieval mode influences other retrieval processes.

Memory is never absolute; it is always relative to any given set of retrieval conditions. Retrieval processes are not only conditional on encoding and storage but are also influenced greatly by retrieval environment and retrieval cues. Some aspects of retrieval, such as the encoding specificity and cue overload principles, are reasonably well understood. Other aspects of retrieval, including retrieval inhibition and the relation between retrieval processes and retrieval mode, remain—at least for the time being—more mysterious.

[See also Forgetting.]

Bibliography

Bjork, R. A. (1989). Retrieval inhibition as an adaptive mechanism in human memory. In H. L. Roediger & F. I. M. Craik (Eds.), *Varieties of memory and consciousness: Essays in honour of Endel Tulving* (pp. 309–330). Hillsdale, NJ: Erlbaum.

Brown, R., & Kulik, J. (1977). Flashbulb memories. *Cognition, 5*, 73–99. The first article to describe flashbulb memories as such.

Craik, F. I. M., & Tulving, E. (1975). Depth of processing and the retention of words in episodic memory. *Journal of Experimental Psychology: General, 104*, 268–294. Substantial article describing initial tests of the level of processing approach.

Eich, J. E. (1980). The cue-dependent nature of state-dependent retrieval. *Memory & Cognition, 8*, 157–173. General review of earlier studies of state-dependent retrieval.

Melton, A. W. (1963). Implications of short-term memory for a general theory of memory. *Journal of Verbal Learning and Verbal Behavior, 2*, 1–21. Interesting theoretical article historically, including an influential definition of retrieval.

Morris, C. D., Bransford, J. D., & Franks, J. J. (1977). Levels of processing versus transfer appropriate processing. *Journal of Verbal Learning and Verbal Behavior, 16*, 519–533.

Roediger, H. L. (1990). Implicit memory: Retention without remembering. *American Psychologist, 45*, 1043–1056. Comprehensive review of implicit compared with explicit memory performance and of transfer appropriate processing versus memory systems theories.

Slamecka, N. J. (1968). An examination of trace storage in free recall. *Journal of Experimental Psychology, 76*, 504–513.

Tulving, E. (1983). *Elements of episodic memory*. New York: Oxford University Press.

Tulving, E., & Pearlstone, Z. (1966). Availability versus accessibility of information in memory for words. *Journal of Verbal Learning and Verbal Behavior, 5*, 381–391.

Tulving, E., & Thomson, D. M. (1973). Encoding specificity and retrieval processes in episodic memory. *Psychological Review, 80*, 352–372.

von Restorff, H. (1933). Uber die Wirkung von Bereichsbildungen in Spurenfeld. *Psychologische Forshung, 18*, 299–342.

Watkins, M. J. (1979). Engrams as cuegrams and forgetting as cue overload: A cuing approach to the structure of memory. In C. R. Puff (Ed.), *Memory organization and structure* (pp. 347–372). New York: Academic Press.

John M. Gardiner

RETROACTIVE INHIBITION. *See* Forgetting.

REVERSAL THEORY. Reversal theory is a general theory of motivation, emotion, and personality that also provides an integrative framework for understanding a wide variety of psychological phenomena. Such phenomena include stress, aesthetic experience, humor, crime and violence, family relationships, dangerous sport, creativity, addiction, gambling, military combat, religious ritual, and many more. Reversal theory also promotes insight into a range of clinical problems including, for example, agoraphobia, depression, juvenile delinquency, and sexual dysfunction.

The starting point is the recognition that subjective experience has structure, and hence the general approach adopted has been referred to as "structural phenomenology." More specifically, there is a set of discrete ways of experiencing the world, each providing an internal context that imparts its own meaning and flavor to the particular contents of experience. Everyone has available the same basic set and in the normal way of things, will move between them fairly frequently in the course of everyday life.

Each of these ways of experiencing the world, known as a "metamotivational state," has three related characteristics: (1) it derives from a basic psychological desire; (2) it is associated with its own range of emotions; and (3) it construes the world in its own distinctive way.

Reversal theory postulates that these metamotivational states go in pairs of opposites so that only one from each pair is active at a given moment (but one or the other will always be active). Switches between members of a pair can occur under a variety of conditions, both situational and internal, identified in the theory. The name of the theory derives from the central role that such "reversals" play in its explanations.

Here is an example of a pair of such states. The telic state (from the ancient Greek *telos* meaning "goal") is based on the desire for the achievement of important goals. The basic emotional range runs from relaxation to anxiety. The way of seeing the world is a serious-minded one in which one experiences oneself as engaged in an activity that has significance beyond itself. The opposite, paratelic state (from the ancient Greek *para*, meaning "alongside"), is based on the desire for immediate enjoyment and fun. The emotional range runs from boredom to excitement. The orientation here is a playful one in which one sees one's ongoing activity as being indulged in for its own sake. In the course of everyday life, one reverses from one way of experiencing one's actions to the other.

Something of the dynamics of these two states and the transitions between them is brought out in Figure 1, which depicts the relationship between the emotional dimensions associated with each. From this, it can be seen that reversal from one state to the other, represented by a jump from a position on one curve to a position on the other at a point immediately above or below, can produce dramatic emotional change, particularly at the extremes of the arousal dimension. For example, high anxiety can convert to high excitement in a parachutist when his parachute opens. This general picture of the experience of arousal is preferable in a number of respects to that of optimal arousal theory (with its inverted U-curve), including the way in which reversal theory accounts for the fact that very high and very low levels of arousal can be experienced as intensely pleasurable.

Three other parallel pairs of states are postulated in the theory, the idea being that experience at any given time will be informed by a combination of states—one state from each pair—although typically one of these states will be more salient than the others. These state pairs are labelled the negativistic and conformist states (which are opposite ways of experiencing rules and constraints), the mastery and sympathy states (which are opposite ways of experiencing transactions with other people and things), and the autic and alloic states (which are opposite ways of experiencing relationships with other people and things). In combination, these

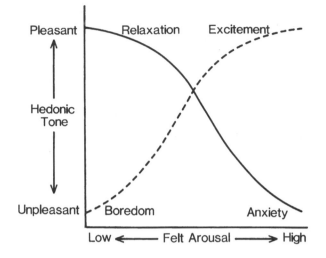

REVERSAL THEORY. Figure 1. The relationship between arousal and hedonic tone according to reversal theory. The two hypothetical curves represent opposite metamotivational states.

states give rise to emotional dimensions that can be represented by pairs of curves such as those shown in Figure 1. Between them, these states and their relationship provide a comprehensive model of the structure of emotional life. (There are also some other concepts, including state-dominance, tension, parapathic emotion, and cognitive synergy.)

Even from this short account it is apparent that reversal theory differs from other theories in significant ways. For example, all previous major theories of motivation may be seen as essentially homeostatic (i.e., unistable), whereas reversal theory is based on the more sophisticated notion of multistability. Again, the idea of static traits in personality theory is opposed in reversal theory by that of dynamic patterns of change, with intraindividual differences becoming the focus of attention. Reversal theory also emphasizes the inherent inconsistency of human nature, and some of its emotionally complex and paradoxical qualities.

The basic ideas of the theory were put forward in the mid-1970s by Kenneth Smith and Michael Apter, an English psychiatrist and psychologist, respectively. They were then developed into a full-scale theory by Apter, who gave the first detailed account (1982). Early proponents, using the theory for counseling purposes, were Stephen Murgatroyd and David Fontana, working in Wales.

Researchers and practitioners in a number of countries have taken up these ideas and between them have generated numerous papers and books. Supporting evidence comes from various sources: psychometric, experimental, psychophysiological, and clinical. Some particularly notable continuing lines of research are those of Sven Svebak and his colleagues in Norway on the psychophysiological concomitants of different metamotivational states; Kathleen O'Connell, Mary Cook, and Mary Gerkovich in Kansas City on smoking addiction and cessation; and John Kerr and his colleagues in Holland and Japan on sports performance.

Reversal theory has been used in a number of areas of applied psychology, including sports coaching, business management, and health practices.

Bibliography

Apter, M. J. (1989). *Reversal theory: Motivation, emotion and personality.* London: Routledge. Reviews the whole theory, and some of its supporting evidence, in a relatively accessible way. A good place to start.

Apter, M. J. (1992). *The dangerous edge: The psychology of excitement.* New York: Free Press. Explores in detail the reversals, healthy and unhealthy, which occur between anxiety and excitement. Written for the nonspecialist.

Apter, M. J., & Svebak, S. (1992). Reversal theory as a biological approach to individual differences. In A. Gale & M. W. Eysenck (Eds.), *Handbook of individual differences: Biological perspectives* (pp. 323–353). New York: Wiley.

Kerr, J. H. (1994). *Understanding soccer hooliganism.* Buckingham, UK: Open University Press. Applies the theory as a whole to a troubling social problem.

Kerr, J. H. (1997). *Researching subjective experience in sport: Reversal theory.* Chichester, UK: Wiley.

Kerr, J. H., Murgatroyd, S., & Apter, M. J. (Eds.). (1993). *Advances in reversal theory.* Amsterdam: Swets & Zeitlinger. A collection of 26 papers on various aspects of reversal theory.

Martin, R. A., Kuiper, N. A., Olinger, L. J., & Dobbin, J. (1987). Is stress always bad? Telic versus paratelic dominance as a stress moderating variable. *Journal of Personality and Social Psychology, 53,* 970–982.

Murgatroyd, S., & Apter, M. J. (1986). A structural-phenomenological approach to eclectic psychotherapy. In J. Norcross (Ed.), *Casebook of eclectic psychotherapy* (pp. 260–280). New York: Brunner/Mazel. Shows how reversal theory can be used in therapeutic practice.

O'Connell, K. A., Cook, M. R., Gerkovich, M. M., Potocky, M., & Swan, G. E. (1990). Reversal theory and smoking: A state-based approach to ex-smokers' highly tempting situations. *Journal of Consulting and Clinical Psychology, 58,* 489–494.

Svebak, S., & Apter, M. J. (Eds.). (1997). *Stress and health: A reversal theory perspective.* Washington, DC: Taylor & Francis.

Michael J. Apter

RÉVÈSZ, GEZA (1878–1955), Hungarian experimental psychologist. Révèsz was born in Sokiok, Hungary. He began studying law in Budapest but changed to psychology, which he studied at the University of Göttingen and then with Carl Stumpf (a musician as well as experimental psychologist of sound perception) in Berlin. He received his doctorate at Göttingen in 1905. He returned to Hungary in 1906 and was promoted through the ranks to full professor of psychology at Budapest University by 1918. After the revolution in Hungary in 1921, he emigrated and settled in Amsterdam, where he was put in charge of the psychological laboratory. From 1932, he was professor of psychology at the University of Amsterdam; he died in that city in 1955.

Révèsz experimentally investigated sight, touch, hearing, language communication, and the relationships between them. His early work concerned hearing disturbances such as amusia (inability to comprehend or produce musical sounds) and parakusia (inability to perceive individual musical notes). From 1914, he began to study musical ability, profiling the Hungarian child prodigy Ervin Nyiregyházy and devising tests for measuring musical aptitude based on the perception of rhythm, analysis of chords, and the capacity to reproduce tunes. Stumpf had initiated such testing, and Révèsz's work of 1916 through 1920 continued in this tradition; however, standardized tests were introduced by Carl Seashore in the United States in 1919, paralleling standardized intelligence tests there.

Another enduring contribution of Révèsz to music psychology is the dual component theory of pitch. Against Helmholtz, who assumed direct correspondence between frequency and pitch, in 1913 Révèsz argued that both sound quality—a phenomenological quality produced by the mind—as well as frequency were involved in pitch perception. The terms *pitch chroma* for the former, referring to the position of the tone in the octave, and *pitch height* for the latter, referring to the overall pitch level, have become standard in the literature and have received experimental confirmation.

As with pitch, in the realm of touch Révèsz and his collaborator David Katz reacted against previous attempts to reduce tactile sensations to basic qualities such as pressure, heat, and cold. Révèsz could also draw on his work on the art of the blind, in which he distinguished clearly between *haptic* and *optic* aesthetic experience and representational capability. This distinction is still being disputed.

Révèsz also studied the origins of music and of language. In cross-cultural comparisons, he emphasized tonal relationships over rhythm, another view that has been disputed. As for the origins of language, Révèsz criticized previous philosophical, biological, and anthropological theories and formulated a functional "contact" theory developing from cry to call to word.

Révèsz's views on music psychology and art of the blind continue to be debated and developed. His interests in communication were shared by students such as Hubert J. C. Duijker, who succeeded him as director of the Psychology Laboratory at Amsterdam University; Duijker campaigned against disciplinary barriers in psychology. Another student, Adriaan de Groot, worked on cognition and educational psychology, which he applied in reforming schools in the Netherlands.

[*Many of the people mentioned in this article are the subjects of independent biographical entries.*]

Bibliography

Works by Révèsz

Révèsz, G. (1970). *The psychology of a musical prodigy (Ervin Nyiregyházy)*. New York: Harcourt, Brace (reprinted from the 1925 edition). (Original work published 1916)

Révèsz, G. (1950). *Psychology and art of the blind* (H. A. Wolff, Trans.). London: Longmans & Green. Contains exposition of the psychology of space perception and comparison of sight and touch; analyzes and contributes to discourse on spatial esthetics and formalism in art. Argues that truly esthetic experience and creativity in the visual arts are not possible for persons born blind. For counterarguments, see Kennedy (1993).

Révèsz, G. (1954). *Introduction to the psychology of music* (C. I. C. de Coureg, Trans.). Norman: University of Oklahoma Press. Exposition of Révèsz's views and contributions to all aspects of music psychology.

Révèsz, G. (1956). *The origins and prehistory of language* (J. Butler, Trans.). Westport, CT: Greenwood Press. (Original work published 1946)

Works about Révèsz

Boring, E. G. (1942). *Sensation and perception in the history of experimental psychology*. New York: Appleton-Century. Boring's historiography is dated, but he gives valuable references to the work of Révèsz and his contemporaries in sound perception (pp. 379–380 and 396) and touch (pp. 512–522).

Deutsch, D. (Ed.). (1982). *Psychology of music*. New York: Academic Press. Deutsch (p. 272) has continued work on the dual component theory of pitch; references to Révèsz *passim* evaluate his contributions in music psychology in relation to more recent work.

Duijker, H. C. (1955). In memoriam: Geza Révèsz. *Acta Psychologica, 11*, 357–359. Concise account of life and work.

Haber, H. de la M. (1980). Révèsz, Geza. In S. Sadie (Ed.), *The New Grove dictionary of music and musicians* (Vol. 15, pp. 775–776). London: Macmillan. Biographical sketch and bibliography of works on music psychology.

Kennedy, J. M. (1993). *Drawing and the blind*. New Haven, CT: Yale University Press. Argues against Révèsz that representational skills and aesthetic experience of congenitally blind persons are very rich; notably the blind can represent distance graphically by perspectivelike convergence.

Barbara Whitney Keyser

REWARD STRUCTURES. *See* Interdependence, *article on* Interdependence Structures.

RIBOT, THÉODULE ARMAND (1839–1916), French philosopher and psychologist. Ribot, the founder of French scientific psychology and a prolific writer, was born in Guingamp, in northern France. His education was interrupted at the age of 17 by the need to find work. In 1862, he entered the École Normale Supérieure, graduating in 1865. He was professor of philosophy at the Vesoul Lycée from 1865 to 1868, and at the Laval Lycée from 1868 to 1872. During this last period he wrote his first book, *Contemporary English Psychology* (1870), in which he ridiculed classic philosophical psychology and defended scientific psychology, discussing the works of many English associationists little known in France. [*See* Associationism.]

In 1872, Ribot moved to Paris, wrote his Ph.D. dissertation, and attended courses at medical and clinical institutions. He successfully defended two theses at the Sorbonne in 1873, a Latin thesis on the British associationist David Hartley and a French thesis on *Psychological Heredity*. In order to survey recent movements in England and Germany, in 1875 with Alfred Espinas he translated into French Herbert Spencer's *Principles of Psychology* and in 1879 wrote *German Psychology of Today* in which he summarized the works of Fechner, Wundt, and others for a French audience. In 1876 he founded the *Revue Philosophique de la France et de l'Étranger*, devoted to new trends in philosophy and psychology. Ignoring the polemics to which his early works had given rise, he wrote monographs on diseases of memory (1881), will (1883), and personality (1885). These provide the most distinctive feature of Ribot's work in psychology: his pathological and evolutionary methods, his conviction that every mental phenomenon should be approached from the twofold point of view of its evolution and its morbid dissolution. These methods led him, for example, to propose a law of regression in the domain of memory (now named Ribot's law). According to this law, the destruction of memory is progressive. It is a regression from the newest to oldest memories, from the most voluntary to the most automatic memories.

In 1885, Ribot was placed in charge of the first course in experimental psychology at the Sorbonne. In 1888, a chair of experimental and comparative psychology was created for him at the Collège de France. He trained many students in the new psychology (e.g., Pierre Janet and Georges Dumas) and encouraged the founding at the Sorbonne of the first French laboratory of experimental psychology directed by Henry Beaunis (1889) and then by Alfred Binet (1894). He was the author of numerous other books, largely in the field of affect. Many of these have been translated into English and other languages: for example, *The Psychology of Feelings* (1986), *The Logic of Feelings* (1905), *Problems of Affective Psychology* (1910). His writings indicate that he realized, more adequately than his predecessors, the significance of affective and emotional phenomena in all of the activities of life. He retired from teaching in 1901, and continued to edit his *Revue* until his death.

Bibliography

Dugas, L. (1924). *Le philosophe Théodule Ribot* [The philosopher Théodule Ribot]. Paris: Payot.

Gunn, J. A. (1924). Ribot and his contribution to psychology. *The Monist, 34*, 1–14.

Lamarque, G. (1928). *Th. Ribot*. Paris: Michaud.

Serge Nicolas

RICHTER, CURT PAUL (1894–1988), American psychobiologist. Curt Richter may have produced more "classic" papers in psychobiology and introduced more phenomena and more techniques for studying them than any other psychologist of the twentieth century. He was the quintessential example of someone with a "nose for phenomena," a scientist who is a superb observer and experimentalist, who operates with many types of explanation (physiological, evolutionary-adaptive, psychological mechanisms), and who constantly invents new and better ways of measuring things (activity wheels, drinking "Richter" tubes, new ways to measure nest building, salivation, autonomic activity).

Curt Richter was a doctoral student of the behaviorist, John Watson, at the Johns Hopkins University, where he spent his entire academic life. His official entry into psychology, the publication of his thesis in 1922, illustrates his special genius. This work was the epitome of an antibehaviorist enterprise: a demonstration of endogenous control over behavior. An analysis of activity rhythms in rats, it was a foundation study on biological clocks in mammals. The most critical new finding was the continuation of the diurnal running cycle after the animal was placed under conditions of constant illumination, suggesting the endogenous control of the cycle. In order to do these studies of activity rhythms over periods of months, Richter invented the running wheel, a device that remains central even today to rhythm research. The work on activity rhythms gave birth to a major line of research in psychology, and became one of the themes of Richter's lifetime contribution. Further work by Richter elucidated the 4- to 5-day estrous cycle activity rhythm in female rats, demonstrated its control by ovarian hormones and the involvement of hormones and the hypothalamus in biological clocks. Studies of rhythms in humans and rats led to his "shock phase hypothesis," which holds that trauma may synchronize normally independent biological rhythms, and lead to pathological results.

Another major contribution is the work on behavioral homeostasis; indeed, Richter is the "father" of behavioral homeostasis. Following on Claude Bernard's description of the regulation of the *milieu interne*, and Walter Cannon's concept of homeostasis, Richter established the important role of behavior in regulation of body functions. He referred to this as "total self-regulatory function." This was demonstrated in many, many ways, with respect to activity rhythms, nesting, and most famously, dietary self-selection. Richter uncovered one of the paradigmatic examples of innately programmed behavior, sodium appetite in rats. Rats experiencing a sodium deficiency for the first time show an immediate preference for sources of sodium. This was studied extensively, and the approach was extended to adaptive adjustments in rat food selection in response to a variety of perturbations, including endocrine disturbances and a wide range of nutritional deficiencies. Richter established behavioral homeostasis as a fact about mammalian behavior much in the way Darwin established the theory of evolution, with a massive set of examples. His focus on innate recognition for essential nutrients, as with sodium, turned out to be an error; most specific hungers are learned. But even here, in studies of bait shyness in rats, he laid the groundwork for the current central importance of learned poison avoidance in food selection and animal learning.

The contributions of Curt Richter extend far beyond the areas of biological clocks and behavioral homeostasis (see citations below). He did important work on bait shyness, alcohol preferences, nutrition, the effects of hormones (especially thyroxin and insulin) on behavior, the neurological organization of motor systems and the autonomic nervous system, the nature of domestication, and hopelessness and voodoo death.

Curt Richter is a personification of an important type of scientist. He had a framed quote from the French physiologist, Magendie, in his office: "I compare myself to a scavenger: with my hook in my hand and my pack on my back I go about the domain of science picking what I can find." The importance and range of pickings were extraordinary: All the effects Richter reported were big, never requiring statistical validation; often accompanied by methodological innovations, covering over 20 species.

Curt Richter was a great starter. His lifetime situation at the Johns Hopkins medical school limited sharply the number of graduate students he had; but fortunately, the striking phenomena he demonstrated and began to analyze became focal in the hands of others in many areas of psychology. He provided the inspiration for the work of many biological psychologists, especially in the areas of hunger, thirst, food selection, and sodium appetite. He was a great basic scientist, but one with a serious and continued interest in pathology, and in solving both scientific and practical problems. All of this makes Richter the "compleat psychobiologist," a genius at finding, measuring, and mining many of the most substantial phenomena in mammalian behavior.

Bibliography

Blass, E. M. (Ed.). (1976). *The psychobiology of Curt Richter.* Baltimore: York Press.

Richter, C. P. (1922). A behavioristic study of the activity of the rat. *Comparative Psychology Monographs, 1,* 1–55.

Richter, C. P. (1942–1943). Total self-regulatory functions in animals and human beings. *Harvey Lecture Series, 38,* 63–103.

Richter, C. P. (1949). Domestication of the Norway rat and its implications for the problem of stress. *Life Stress and Bodily Diseases: Proceedings of the Association for Research in Nervous and Mental Disease, 29,* 19–46.

Richter, C. P. (1953). Free research versus design research. *Science, 118,* 91–93.

Richter, C. P. (1956). Salt appetite of mammals: Its dependence on instinct and metabolism. In: *L'Instinct dans le comportement des animaux et de l'homme* [The role of instinct in animal and human behavior] (pp. 577–632). Paris.

Richter, C. P. (1957). Phenomenon of sudden death in animals and man. *Psychosomatic Medicine, 19,* 191–198.

Richter, C. P. (1965). *Biological clocks in medicine and psychiatry.* Springfield, IL: Charles C. Thomas.

Richter, C. P. (1985). It's a long way to Tipperary, the land of my genes. In D. A. Dewsbury (Ed.), *Leaders in the study of animal behavior* (pp. 356–386). Lewisburg, PA: Bucknell University Press.

Richter, C. P., & Bartemeier, L. H. (1926). Decerebrate rigidity of the sloth. *Brain, 49,* 207–225.

Rozin, P. (1976). Curt Richter: The compleat psychobiologist. In E. M. Blass (Ed.), *The psychobiology of Curt Richter* (pp. xv–xxviii). Baltimore: York Press.

Paul Rozin

RIGHT TO REFUSE TREATMENT. The right to refuse treatment has been one of the most controversial issues in mental health law over the past almost 30 years. The question of whether and when people hospitalized as a result of mental illness or released to the community after hospitalization or those involved in the criminal court or correctional process may refuse mental health treatment is a complex legal, clinical, ethical, and social problem (Winick, 1997). Because the differing mental health treatment techniques produce effects that vary widely, a single, all-encompassing legal approach to the issue would be inappropriate. Instead, it is useful to conceptualize a rough continuum of intrusiveness along which the various mental health treatment techniques can be ranked based upon the nature and duration of their effects and the ability of patients to resist them (Winick, 1997).

Comparing the therapies on these bases leads to the conclusion that psychotherapy and the other verbal therapy techniques should be ranked as the least intrusive on the treatment continuum. Next in order of intrusiveness are the behavioral techniques, and after that, the psychotropic drugs. Electro-convulsive therapy would seem more intrusive than medication, and the highly experimental techniques of electronic stimulation of the brain and psychosurgery would rank as the most intrusive.

Legal limitations on involuntary treatment stem from a number of sources—statutory, administrative, international law, and judicially crafted tort and constitutional law. Although most states now have statutory and administrative limitations on enforced treatment, the limits imposed by the U.S. Constitution and its state counterparts are the most significant inasmuch as they drive other legal restrictions.

Constitutional limitations on involuntary treatment have been derived from the First Amendment's protection against intrusion into mental processes and substantive due process protection for bodily integrity, mental privacy, and individual autonomy (*Riggins v. Nevada,* 1993; *Washington v. Harper,* 1990; *Rennie v. Klein,* 1983; *Rogers v. Okin,* 1980). In addition, in more limited circumstances, the Eighth Amendment's ban on cruel and unusual punishments and the First Amendment's protection of the free exercise of religion may impose limits on involuntary treatment. In addition, equal protection principles may be invoked to question the discrepancy existing between non-mentally ill patients, for whom informed consent is a prerequisite to treatment and those suffering from mental illness, who often are treated without informed consent and over objection.

First Amendment and substantive due process protections would seem applicable to the most intrusive treatment techniques such as psychosurgery, electronic stimulation of the brain, electro-convulsive therapy, and the psychotropic drugs, but not to the less intrusive interventions such as the verbal and behavioral techniques. The level of constitutional scrutiny appropriate for the more intrusive interventions has not been clearly resolved by the Supreme Court. In *Washington v. Harper* (1990), the Court applied a reduced form of constitutional scrutiny to uphold the involuntary administration of anti-psychotic medication in a prison hospital for an inmate who was dangerous to other prisoners and staff when not taking medication. However, in *Riggins v. Nevada* (1993), the Court, in invalidating the forced medication of a criminal defendant during his trial, seemed to suggest a form of strict scrutiny, requiring a finding that involuntary medication would need to be medically appropriate and the least intrusive means of accomplishing one or more compelling governmental interests. The degree of scrutiny that the Court has applied to the constitutional claims of incarcerated prisoners has always been somewhat reduced, suggesting that the more relaxed approach of *Harper* may be limited to involuntary treatment in the prison. But whether traditional strict scrutiny, usually applied when fundamental constitutional rights are infringed, will be applied to forced treatment in the hospital and community remains unresolved.

Even if the constitutional rights invaded by unwanted treatment are deemed fundamental and strict scrutiny is applied, in some circumstances involuntary treatment will be constitutionally permissible. Governmental interests that will be deemed sufficiently compelling to outweigh the individual's assertion of a right to refuse treatment will include the police power interest in the protection of others from harm (*Washington v. Harper*, 1990), the *parens patriae* interest in protecting the well-being of individuals whose mental illness renders them incompetent to make treatment decisions for themselves, and the state's interest in restoring criminal defendants found incompetent to stand trial to competence so that they may be tried (*Riggins v. Nevada*, 1992). State statutes or administrative rules of the state's mental health department may authorize involuntary treatment in these circumstances for people who have been civilly committed or have accepted voluntary hospitalization, and for criminal defendants committed to forensic facilities as incompetent to stand trial or following an acquittal by reason of insanity (*Brakel, Parry & Wiener*, 1985; *Blackburn*, 1990; Winick, 1997). An increasing number of states also now authorize involuntary treatment on *parens patrie* grounds pursuant to statutes allowing outpatient commitment or conditional release from hospitalization.

Even when these or other compelling interests are present, strict scrutiny will require that involuntary treatment be medically appropriate and the least intrusive means of accomplishing the state's interests (*Riggins v. Nevada*, 1992). For purposes of applying this least intrusive alternative test, the burden of demonstrating the lack of success or futility of less intrusive treatments will be placed on the state and the proposed continuum of intrusiveness discussed earlier will be helpful. *Harper* makes clear that this least intrusive alternative standard will not be applied in the prison context, but *Riggins* suggests that it will be applied to involuntary treatment administered outside the prison. When the treatment at issue is less intrusive, such as verbal or behavioral therapy, courts will apply a more relaxed form of constitutional scrutiny, insisting only that such treatment bear a reasonable relationship to a legitimate (as opposed to a compelling) state interest.

Even in circumstances in which involuntary treatment is constitutionally permissible, the protections of procedural due process will often require notice and some kind of hearing before treatment may be imposed. Although some courts have required a formal adversarial judicial hearing (*Rivers v. Katz*, 1986), most have accepted the constitutionality of permitting informal and non-adversarial administrative hearings (*Washington v. Harper*, 1990; *Rennie v. Klein*, 1983; *Rogers v. Okin*, 1980). If a decision is made at the hearing to authorize involuntary treatment, the decision may need to be reviewed on a periodic basis if involuntary treatment is sought to be continued.

Of course, not all patients and offenders will seek to refuse treatment. Even when individuals have a right to refuse treatment, they may consent to it and thereby waive their right to refuse as long as the requirements of the informed consent doctrine (disclosure of treatment information, competency, and voluntariness) are satisfied (Winick, 1997). Indeed, when these requirements are satisfied, individuals may enter into advance directive instruments expressing their wishes concerning the acceptance or rejection of treatment at a future time when they may become incompetent (Winick, 1996). Although advance directive instruments are not yet in widespread use for this purpose, several states have authorized their use for mental health treatment and they seem likely to emerge as an important way of dealing with the right to refuse treatment question in the future.

In addition to legal restrictions on involuntary treatment, clinicians should be aware of ethical issues presented by forced treatment. The professional ethics of the various clinical disciplines strongly favor voluntary treatment. Moreover, psychological theory would predict that voluntary treatment is more efficacious than coerced therapy (Winick 1997, ch. 17). As a result, principles of beneficience and non-maleficience, which are at the core of professional ethics, would strongly favor voluntary approaches in the treatment area and the use of less intrusive approaches before more intrusive ones are attempted.

[*See also* Mental Health Law.]

Bibliography

Appelbaum, Paul S. (1988). The right to refuse treatment with antipsychotic medications: retrospect and prospect. *American Journal of Psychiatry and Law*, 145, 413–419.

Blackburn, L. (1990). The "therapeutic orgy" and the "right to rot" collide: the right to refuse antipsychotic drugs under state law, *Houston Law Review*, 27, 447.

Brakel, S. J., Perry, J., & Weiner, B. (1985). *The mentally disabled and the law* (3rd ed.) Chicago: American Bar Foundation.

Perlin, M. L. (1994a). *Law and mental disability*. Charlottesville, VA: Michie. A leading treatise on mental disability law.

Rennie v. Klein, 462 F. Supp. 1311 (D.N.J. 1978), modified and remanded, 653 F.2d 836 (3d Cir. 1981) (en banc), vacated and remanded, 458 U.S. 1119 (1983).

Riggins v. Nevada, 504 U.S. 127 (1992).

Rivers v. Katz, 495 N.E.2d 337 (N.Y. 1986).

Rogers v. Okin, 634 F.2d 650 (1st Cir. 1980) (en banc), vacated & remanded sub nom. *Mills v. Rogers*, 457 U.S. 291 (1982).

Washington v. Harper, 494 U.S. 210 (1990).

Winick, B. J. (1997). *The right to refuse mental health treatment*. Washington, DC: American Psychological Association.

Bruce J. Winick and David B. Wexler

RIGIDITY is a highly interesting psychological construct because it refers to two aspects of individual differences—personality and ability—that are usually regarded as separate. Verbal definitions in psychology are usually not useful, and concepts are better defined in terms of their measurement. Thus defined, rigidity is the low end of the bipolar ability factor of flexible thinking, extensively studied by Guilford and his colleagues (Guilford, 1967). In this portrayal, rigid thinkers, have conventional and fixed approaches to problem-solving that render them uncreative and convergent rather than divergent.

Rigidity, however is also conceived as a personality trait. It is an aspect of the authoritarian personality, studied by Adorno and his colleagues (Adorno, Frenkel-Brunswick, Lennson, & Sandford, 1950). Rigidity is also part of the clinical syndrome of obsessionality. Rokeach delineated dogmatism (1960), which is highly similar, and McCrae, has emphasized the importance of openness to experience (1996), which is essentially low rigidity. The construct of rigidity, albeit under different names, is important in many different approaches to understanding personality.

What are the characteristics of the rigid personality? The authoritarian personality holds rigid, unchangeable, conventional views concerning the organization of society: that it is best divided into clear hierarchies, that leaders are to be obeyed, that old wisdom is best, and that modern liberal permissiveness is the road to ruin. Authoritarians prosper in the hierarchy of the armed forces or occupations with clear-cut roles. The obsessional personality, on the other hand, has rigid ideas about more personal aspects of life. Obsessive individuals are noted for attention to hygiene, attention to detail, and a love of order and routine. They can maintain their views to the point of obstinacy. There are obvious similarities to the authoritarian personality. According to Rokeach, dogmatism can most clearly be seen in religious beliefs. The dogmatism, the rigidly held values, of those who believe strongly is well articulated in many current religious fundamentalisms throughout the world. It is also to be found among what might be called secular religions, Maoism, and the old Communism of Eastern Europe, for example. Such dogmatism is found at both poles of the political spectrum. McCrae (1996) has claimed, based entirely on empirical, atheoretical attempts to measure personality by questionnaire, that openness is one of the five pervasive personality factors (the others being extraversion, anxiety, agreeableness, and conscientiousness). He admits that his concept is allied to authoritarianism and dogmatism, and he further characterizes it as related to intolerance of ambiguity and ethnocentrism, the latter being an important aspect of authoritarianism. This work paints a vivid picture of the rigid personality as conservative, conventional, dogmatic, rule bound, ethnocentric, and obsessive. Three questions arise from this analysis of rigidity. How different are these accounts? Is it possible to reconcile them? What is the relationship between rigid thinking and personality?

The first two questions are clearly related. There are two approaches to this question, empirical and speculative. The centrality of rigidity to these differing accounts of personality suggests a solution to the first question. It is possible to see these different descriptions as different aspects of a broad personality factor that might be called rigidity. Thus the authoritarian personality refers to political aspects of rigidity, but dogmatism reflects the belief systems and attitudes consequent on rigid personality. Obsessionality refers to rigidity as it affects the conduct of everyday life, and extreme rigidity can become clinically relevant, although the precise relationship between obsessional traits and obsessive-compulsive disorder is still not clear.

The openness to experience that McCrae finds so pervasive a personality factor emphasizes the relationship of this personality trait to ability. The open-minded individual is seen as flexible and unconventional. McCrae, indeed, regards the philosopher Rousseau as an exemplar of a person high on open-mindedness—the opposite of the rigid person (1996). Kline has attempted to put this theory to the empirical test (1993). In a study of all the scales thought to be the best measures of dogmatism, obsessionality, authoritarian personality, and conservatism, all were essentially shown to measure the same factor. Rigidity is a broad personality factor related to inflexible and conventional thinking.

Bibliography

Adorno, T. W., Frenkel-Brunswick, E., Levinson, D. J., & Sandford, R. N. (1950). *The authoritarian personality*. New York: Harper & Row.

Guilford, J. P. (1967). *The nature of human intelligence*. New York: McGraw-Hill.

Kline, P. (1993). *Personality: The psychometric view*. London: Routledge.

McCrae, M. M. (1996). Social consequences of experimental openness. *Psychological Bulletin, 120*, 323–337.

Rokeach, M. (1960). *The open and closed mind*. New York: Basic Books.

Paul Kline

RISK ASSESSMENT OF VIOLENCE. *See* Violence Risk Assessment.

RITUAL. *See* Religious Symbol, Myth, and Ritual.

RIVERS, WILLIAM HALSE RIVERS (1864–1922), M.D., F.R.S., English neurologist, experimental psychologist, psychiatrist, and social anthropologist. Rivers was active during a period when the disciplines he professed were becoming fully identified. His work contributed to their development, especially in Britain.

Rivers's earliest publications, from 1888 to 1893, were in neuropathology, under the influence of John Hughlings Jackson and Michael Foster. In 1892 he spent four months at Jena attending lectures in psychiatry and physiology. In 1893 he worked with Emil Kräpelin at Heidelberg, measuring the effects of fatigue. Later that year he accepted an invitation from Foster to teach a course in the physiology of the senses at Cambridge University. At this time, he was in charge of the psychology laboratory at University College, London, and was also given space for a laboratory at Cambridge. As a result, Rivers supervised the first two psychology laboratories in Britain.

In 1898 Rivers joined the Cambridge Anthropological Expedition to the Torres Straits to supervise the measurement of Melanesians' sensory perceptions. He found it necessary to ascertain the relationships of the subjects. This led to his devising the "genealogical method" of tracing kinship that has been a basic tool of fieldwork since then.

Between 1903 and 1907 Rivers collaborated with Henry Head in a study of the peripheral sensory function, work that led to many similar studies by others. In 1908 he directed work on a project entitled "The Influence of Alcohol and other Drugs on Fatigue," which introduced the double-blind technique. In addition to the Torres Straits reports, Rivers produced *The Todas* (1906), on a tribe of southwest India, regarded as an ethnographic classic, as well as *The History of Melanesian Society* (1914) and *Kinship and Social Organization* (1914).

In 1908, along with his friend Bertrand Russell, he was elected a fellow of the Royal Society.

From 1915 to 1919 Rivers served as a military psychiatrist, treating posttraumatic stress disorder, then known by what Rivers deplored as "the unfortunate and misleading term 'shell-shock'." He was also, at war's end, involved in some of the earliest work on aviation psychology.

The titles of some of his postwar works indicate his later interests: *History and Ethnology* (1922), "The Symbolism of Rebirth" (1922), and the posthumously published *Conflict and Dream* (1923), *Psychology and Politics*, (1923), and *Medicine, Science, and Religion* (1924).

After World War I, Rivers was elected president of several organizations: in 1919, the FolkLore Society; in 1920, the medical section of the British Psychoanalytical Society; and in 1992, the Royal Anthropological Institute. Also in 1922, after some hesitation, he agreed to stand as a Labour candidate for Parliament in the general election that fall. However, he died suddenly, as a result of strangulated hernia, on 4 June 1922.

Bibliography

Langham, I. (1981). *The building of British social anthropology*. Dordrecht: Reidel.

Slobodin, R. (1997). *W. H. R. Rivers* (Rev. ed.). New York: Columbia University Press. Stroud (Glos.). UK: Sutton. (Original work published 1978)

Richard Slobodin

ROBOTICS. From the term "robot" is often said to have originated as the title of the play *Rossum's Universal Robots* by the Czech playwright Emil Capek, though linguistically the term is derived from the Serbian and Russian words for work. In engineering circles, a robot is a programmable device that can perform a variety of tasks. Most commonly, robot refers to a machine that does mechanical tasks. Typically, there is a several degree-of-freedom mechanical arm and a hand or end-effector capable of gripping or otherwise applying mechanical forces to environmental objects. One or more arms-hands may be mounted on a fixed or mobile base. A robot has a computer inside and typically has artificial sensors: interoceptors for kinesthetics and proprioception as well as exteroceptors for vision, audition, and tactile sensing. Instead of being a device to do mechanical work, robot can also mean an automatic device that physically goes to some place and gets information, like a lunar roving vehicle or spacecraft orbiting Jupiter. In this case the robot has actuators to provide mobility to the sensors (rather than sensors to provide feedback to the actuators). In popular parlance, a robot is a machine having a computer, sensors, and actuators, which behaves in a humanlike way.

Industrial Robots and Telerobots

Robots may be categorized as industrial robots or telerobots. Industrial robots are commonly used for manufacturing to perform repetitive materials processing and for manipulation tasks on assembly lines. Once programmed and set into operation, they are monitored by humans only intermittently because their operation is expected to be predictable. Examples of materials processing are paint spraying and arc welding. Examples of manipulation are moving of parts from one assembly line to another, placement of parts into jigs for stamping, drilling, or other machine operations, placing of computer chips onto circuit boards, and assembly of component parts to make up subassemblies.

Telerobots are used in a wide variety of tasks that are not repetitive and predictable, and, therefore, must be supervised by a human operator, often from a distance (hence the prefix "tele"). Telerobots have been used to perform various lifting and loading tasks in factories and warehouses, earth moving and construction tasks, and operations in hazardous environments such as space, undersea, and radioactive or chemically toxic environments. They can be programmed to perform tasks automatically for relatively short periods of time, making use of their own visual, auditory, or haptic sensors and stored computer programs between interactions with a human supervisor. Alternatively, they can embody minimal internal computation and be controlled continuously by a human through a joystick, or be controlled in master-slave fashion, where a human positions a master arm in multiple degrees-of-freedom and the slave follows exactly. The latter is more often referred to as a teleoperator. The manipulator arm on the Space Shuttle is a teleoperator. Telerobots and teleoperators are gradually coming into use for mining, cutting, and clearing trees, washing windows and cleaning floors of industrial buildings, executing dangerous police, fire, and military operations, and performing surgical procedures inside the body from outside (sometimes called "noninvasive surgery").

Human Supervisory Functions

Humans may be said to function in relation to robots in five ways : (1) planning what the robot is to do; (2) programming or teaching the robot; (3) monitoring the automatic execution of the program and diagnosing any abnormality or deviation from the intended behavior; (4) intervening to modify the robot's program, stop the robot's action, or take over control manually; and (5) aggregate and integrate results and learn from experience. Functions (1) and (2) are necessary for both industrial robots and telerobots. For the industrial robot, the programming function is done only once for many cycles of the robot's material processing or moving of parts. By contrast, for the telerobot some form of reprogramming will occur for each task, and more often than not there will be reprogramming during the course of a given task. Monitoring (function 3), intervention (function 4), and learning (function 5) are more salient human functions for telerobots than for industrial robots because, in using the former, each task to a greater or lesser degree is a new task.

Robots can be programmed using either an analogic or symbolic means of communication. Analogic communication is where the human programmer signals the desired movement of the robot by position, direction, or force applied to controls by corresponding hand movements. Joystick and mouse (cursor) controls are examples. Symbolic communication is by concatenation of alphanumeric symbols or icons signalled by button or key presses. Special programming languages have been developed for various types of robot applications.

The above five functions together comprise what is commonly called human supervisory control. This term is quite analogous to what we mean by supervision of an organization of people, but in this context, the subordinate intelligent entities are robots instead of people.

With the addition of miniature sensors and computer chips to a wide variety of technical systems, the concept of a robot (as a machine or system having its own sensors, computer, and actuators and capable of being programmed to do various tasks) can be generalized to modern aircraft, ships, trains, and highway vehicles, nuclear and chemical plants, certain hospital systems, automatic money teller and vending machines, and "smart" appliances in the home or office.

Thus, the nature of the human operation of robots and automatic machines is changing from that of being a direct manual controller to that of being a supervisory controller. In some new applications one human can supervise many robots. In a modern chemical or nuclear plant, there may be a large number of programmable automatic systems under the supervisory control of a single human operator. The new relation of human to (generalized) robot can be characterized by the prefixes super (above), tele (remote), and meta (many).

Degrees of Automation

The layperson thinks of robotics and/or automation as being mutually exclusive of human sensing and control. For example, in the factory either a human or a robot performs a task; in space it is either an astronaut or automation. This is an incorrect perception. In fact, one may think of graduated degrees of both acquisition of information and taking action, as suggested by the following scales.

Degrees of Automation of Information Acquisition

1. The computer offers no assistance: the human must get all information.
2. The computer suggests many sources of information, and
3. narrows the sources to a few,
4. guides the human to particular information,
5. responds to a question posed in restricted syntax, or
6. responds to a question posed without restricted syntax, and
7. passes the information on to the control automation if human approves, or
8. passes information on to the control automation after limited time for veto,
9. collects data from whatever sources, passes it to the action automation, and informs the human after the fact.
10. The computer collects information as it sees fit, passes it to the action automation, and bypasses the human.

Degrees of Automation of Control Action

1. The computer offers no assistance: the human must take all actions.
2. The computer offers a complete set of action alternatives, and
3. narrows the selection down to a few, or
4. suggests one alternative, and
5. executes that suggestion if the human approves, or
6. allows the human a restricted time to veto before automatic execution, or
7. executes automatically, then necessarily informs the human, or
8. informs the human only if asked, or
9. informs the human only if it, the computer, decides to.
10. The computer decides everything and acts autonomously, ignoring the human.

Social Implications

Robots pose a number of social problems and implications, especially in the manufacturing context. The following factors are causes of alienation.

1. People worry that robots can do some tasks much better than they themselves can with respect to speed and precision. Surely people should not try to compete in this arena.
2. Supervisory control tends to make people remote from the ultimate operations they are supposed to be overseeing—remote in space, desynchronized in time, and interacting with a computer instead of the end product or service itself.
3. People lose the perceptual-motor skills that in many cases gave them their identity. They become "deskilled," and, if ever called upon to use their previous well-honed skills, they have difficulty.
4. Increasingly people who use robots in their work, whether intentionally or not, do not have access to the knowledge to understand what is going on inside the robot's computer.
5. Partly as a result of the last factor, the robot/computer becomes mysterious, and the untutored user comes to attribute to the computer more capability, wisdom, or blame than is appropriate.
6. Because robotic and automated systems are growing more complex, and people are being "elevated" to roles of supervising larger and larger aggregates of hardware and software, the stakes naturally become higher. Where a human error before might have gone unnoticed and been easily corrected, now such an error can precipitate a disaster.
7. The last factor in alienation is similar to the first but is all-encompassing, namely, the fear that a "race" of machines is becoming more powerful than that of the human race. This was the theme of a Pulitzer prize–winning book (Wiener, 1964).

These seven factors, and the fears they engender, whether justified or not, must be reckoned with. Robots must be made to be not only "human friendly" but also "human trustable." Users must become computer- and automation-literate at whatever level of sophistication they can deal with.

Bibliography

Conway, L., Volz. R., & Walker, M. (1987). Teleautonomous systems: Methods and architectures for intermingling autonomous and telerobotic technology. In *Proceedings 1987 IEEE International Conference on Robotics and Automation*, 1121–1130.

Nof, S. Y. (Ed.). (1985). *Handbook of industrial robotics*. New York: Wiley.

Sayers, C. P., & Paul, R. P. (1994). An operator interface for teleprogramming employing synthetic fixtures. *Presence: Teleoperators and Virtual Environments*, 3(4), 308–320.

Sheridan, T. B. (1992). *Telerobotics, automation and human supervisory control*. Cambridge, MA: MIT Press.

Sheridan, T. B. (1997). Supervisory control. In G. Salvendy (Ed.), *Handbook of human factors* (2nd ed.). New York: Wiley.

Tachi, S., & Yasuda, K. (1994). Evaluation experiments of a teleexistence manipulation system. *Presence: Teleoperators and Virtual Environments*, 3(1), 35–44.

Vertut, J., & Coiffet, P. (1986a). *Robot technology: Vol. 3A. Teleoperation and robotics: Evolution and development*. New York: Prentice Hall.

Vertut, J., & Coiffet, P. (1986b). *Robot technology: Vol. 3B.*

Teleoperation and robotics: Applications and technology, New York: Prentice Hall.

Wiener, N. (1964). *God and golem, inc.* Cambridge, MA: MIT Press.

Thomas B. Sheridan

ROCKY MOUNTAIN PSYCHOLOGICAL ASSOCIATION. *See* Regional Psychological Associations.

ROGERS, CARL RANSOM (1902–1987), American psychologist. Rogers's conditions of therapeutic change became practice guidelines for a generation of therapists. They were deceptively simple: Try to comprehend fully the meaning and the feeling of the help seeker's communications; be emotionally "fully present," without reservations or judgments, in that relationship; and make evident your understanding through your verbal and nonverbal responsiveness. Fulfilling those conditions, you will have created circumstances that potentiate positive therapeutic change.

Rogers was born into a devoutly religious Protestant family in Oak Park, Illinois. He majored in agriculture at the University of Wisconsin but then explored a liberal religious outlook at Union Theological Seminary in New York. Shifting to psychology at Teacher's College at Columbia University, he was attracted to the ideas of Leta Hollingworth, John Dewey, and William Kilpatrick. He received a doctorate in 1931 and became staff psychologist at a community guidance clinic in Rochester, New York. While there he became intrigued with the therapy ideas of Jesse Taft, Frederick Allen, and Otto Rank. In 1940, he moved to Ohio State University, where he developed his conception of therapeutic interactions that facilitated self-understanding, described in his *Counseling and Psychotherapy* (1942). It was during his tenure at the University of Chicago from 1944 to 1957 that he most fully articulated the unique theory and the research methods that characterized the client-centered approach. In 1957, he moved back to the University of Wisconsin, this time to apply his methods to a hospitalized population. After several years of equivocal results, he moved to California, where from 1964 on he applied derivations of his therapeutic methods in groups and institutions for purposes of personal growth, organizational change, and amelioration of intergroup conflict.

Client-Centered Therapy

In Rogers's view, the sense of self is the critical referent for self-evaluation. For the ameliorative and remedial purposes of psychotherapy, self-perception and self-experiencing—not the evaluations or advice of outsiders, no matter how expert—are the important channels for self-understanding and therapeutic behavior change. The contingencies for approval laid down by others—parents, teachers, other authority figures—inevitably play a significant role in self-esteem. Psychological dysfuncton is often a result of having distorted or suppressed inner needs in an effort to satisfy the perceived standards of such dependency figures. From Rogers's perspective, continuing awareness of authentic inner desires is essential to healthy development and "self-actualization." This client-centered therapy endeavors to enable the client to reestablish that awareness. The client-centered therapist responds to the help-seeker with an accepting attitude that encourages self-chosen exploration at the individual's own pace. Client-centered therapists reflect emotional as well as cognitive comprehension of their clients' communications. This facilitates progressive self-discovery, enabling resumption of the individual's inherent tendencies toward personal growth. Successful therapy eventuates in greater self-reliance, in behavior that more authentically reflects the individual's inner impulses. Client-centered therapy was eagerly taken up by mental health professionals—chiefly by psychologists who were becoming increasingly active as psychotherapists—as an alternative to psychoanalysis and behaviorism. Many therapists were repelled by the apparent authoritarianism of the former and many others by the apparent "soullessness" of the latter. By contrast, they were drawn to Rogers's "humanistic" therapy. He was actually honored in mid-career by Columbia University, his alma mater, for having created a "democratic" psychotherapy.

Rogers has been acknowledged as *the* pioneer who opened psychotherapy to research inquiry and systematic analysis. His demonstration that therapy relationships could be recorded and analyzed was a first step in therapy research. He also maintained that there could be evaluation of process and outcomes. He used Stephenson's "Q" methodology to track transitions in clients' self-feelings at different points in the treatment process. It seemed to fit the phenomenological characteristics of client-centered theory. In addition, reports by others of client progress were gathered. Rogers and Dymond published their findings about the effectiveness of client-centered therapy in *Psychotherapy and Personality Change* (Chicago, 1954).

Challenge and Controversy

Rogers's theory and research were not received with universal enthusiasm in mental health circles. Those of different orientations were sources of skeptical criticism. Psychoanalytically oriented therapists were particularly critical of his stated therapeutic goals of complete awareness and self-direction. Some ridiculed his "fully functioning" person as "a recipe for psychopaths." Others caricatured and mimicked "standard" client-centered therapist responses that superficially seemed no more than repetitions of clients' statements. Rogers himself came to regret the "stylization" of client-centered therapist responses. A more incisive criticism was that his therapy was palliative, effective perhaps for intropunitive persons but without benefit for seriously dysfunctional individuals. It was partly in response to this challenge that he left the University of Chicago and took up a joint appointment in psychiatry and psychology at the University of Wisconsin in 1957. He would apply his therapy at a state psychiatric institution, the Mendota State Hospital.

The hospitalized population represented a difficult challenge indeed. Publications by Rogers, Gendlin, Kiesler, and Truax (1967) and by Rogers and Stevens (1967), describe their work with the hospitalized patients. Their publications include moving evocations of therapy process but also document difficulties encountered in applying Rogers's methods in that setting. Even getting the individuals to their therapy appointments was often a problem. The overall therapeutic results were equivocal. It is significant that Rogers and his colleagues made no follow-up efforts to apply his methods to extremely dysfunctional populations. From that point, he shifted away from his previous preoccupation with individual therapy and made no further revisions to his formulated position. The following years were marked by his efforts to change aspects of society through the small-group experience. His vision was nothing less than the integration of personal growth experiences—a variant of personal therapy experience within a group context—with improvement of interpersonal relations, educational renewal, democratizing intraorganizational interactions, and resolving intergroup conflict.

The Shift to Groups as Applied Social Therapy

In initial association with the Western Behavioral Sciences Institute and later at the Center for the Study of the Person in LaJolla, California, Rogers employed small-group methods to achieve the social goals he envisioned. He had become widely known and popular for his "encounter groups"—almost as much as for his conception of therapy—in Western Europe, Japan, even Russia. His way of encouraging openess and emotional expressiveness was effective, indeed, much like his demonstrated effectiveness in his role as individual therapist. Not all his attempts at "therapylike" change, however, were positively received. In fact, some of his efforts to achieve institutional change in traditionally hierachical and authoritarian systems reportedly resulted in serious functional problems for those agencies and their workers. Other efforts by Rogers to facilitate change in

seemingly intractable conflict situations or alter relationships among workers in organizations were also criticized as unrealistic. He had, of course, always emphasized humanistic values in his conceptualization of psychotherapy. His articulation of them earned him an honorable status among the world's psychologists. Application of his principles of dyadic therapy to complex multiperson, intraorganization, and interethnic conflicts, however, reflected, in the view of his critics, a tendency to oversimplification. It must be acknowledged, nevertheless, that he was not alone among contemporary psychologists in perceiving links between pathology and aggression, or between psychotherapy and peace making. Professional publications even prior to World War II provide ample evidence of lively discussion among psychologists and other mental health specialists about preventing and resolving conflict. In *A Way of Being* (Boston, 1980), written late in his career, Rogers sought to integrate the various aspects of his career, the "scientific" inquiry and theoretical formulation of his middle years with the later emotional intensity of his experiences in personal growth/encounter groups and the still later conflict resolution groups. In his later years, he increasingly relied on his personal reactions and the testimonials of gratified participants. He did not study the interaction processes in these groups as he had studied individual therapy process and outcome. To some psychologists, Rogers's status as theoretician and scientist may have been diminished by this.

His Legacy

In the 1950s and 1960s, Rogers was undoubtedly professional psychology's "intellectual hero" because of his efforts to legitimize its psychotherapeutic function and because of his pioneering studies of therapy processes and outcomes. He will be remembered for paving the way to scientifically based psychotherapy evaluation. His opposition to any mental health profession's "proprietary rights" to psychological healing was also important in the struggle by psychologists to achieve professional parity. His demonstration of the accessibility of psychotherapy processes and outcomes to systematic inquiry played a significant role in that struggle. His larger vision of employing psychotherapy to effect "desirable changes" in education, organizational democracy, and intergroup conflict resolution, however, remained elusive. He dreamed that self-directed learners could improve educational institutions, just as self-directing clients could resolve their own psychological problems; that business organizations could function as democratically interactive systems; that "emotionally open" interactions could resolve even seemingly intransigent intergroup conflicts. In this connection, it is significant that current programs of interracial "diversity training" groups on a number of college campuses have, perhaps erroneously, been attributed to his legacy. Never an "organization man," Rogers criticized hegemonic or exclusivistic definitions of practice. In his vision of therapy, there was room for multiple routes for help-giving. Therapy, itself, could be for "self-realization" as well as for remediation and for changing organizations and institutions.

[*Many of the people mentioned in this article are the subjects of independent biographical entries.*]

Bibliography

Works by Rogers

Rogers, C. R. (1942). *Counseling and psychotherapy.* Boston: Houghton Mifflin.

Rogers, C. R. (1951). *Client-centered therapy: Its major practice implications and theory.* Boston: Houghton Mifflin.

Rogers, C. R. (1959). A theory of therapy, personality and interpersonal relationships, as developed in the client-centered framework. In S. Koch (Ed.), *Psychology: A study of a science* (Vol. 3, pp. 184–256). New York: McGraw-Hill.

Rogers, C. R., Gendlin, E. T., Kiesler, D. J., & Truax, C. (1967). *The therapeutic relationship and its impact: A study of psychotherapy with schizophrenics.* Madison, WI: University of Wisconsin Press.

Rogers, C. R., & Stevens, B. (1967). *Person to person.* Moab, UT: Real People Press.

Works about Rogers

Gendlin, E. T. (1988). Carl Rogers (1902–1987). *American Psychologist, 43,* 127–128.

Rogers, C. R. (1974). In retrospect: Forty-six years. *American Psychologist, 29,* 115–123.

Martin Lakin

ROLE THEORY. A role is a comprehensive pattern for behavior and attitude that is linked to an identity, is socially identified more or less clearly as an entity, and is subject to being played recognizably by different individuals. *Basic* roles, like those attached to gender and age identities, are the most inclusive, affecting what is expected of an individual in a wide variety of situations. *Position* or *status* roles, like family and occupational roles, are linked to statuses in particular settings, though they vary in how much they carry over into other situations (a banker who gambles on his day off may be suspect). *Functional group* roles, such as "devil's advocate," "mediator," and "counselor," emerge informally as individuals acquire situational identities during sustained interaction in a group setting. *Value* roles, like hero, saint, and villain, develop around very positively or negatively valued activity.

The term *role theory* refers to a loose collection of generalizations about (1) the organization of roles in society and groups, (2) the processes of interaction between incumbents of different roles, and (3) the way individuals learn and manage the diverse complement of roles that they play under various circumstances. Underlying assumptions are that social interaction at all levels from the dyad to entire societies tends to be organized into clusters of behaviors that are thought to belong together, that individuals orient their social behavior in terms of roles they play and roles they attribute to others, that judgments of adequate or inadequate role performance constitute a major basis for assessing the worth of individuals, and that meanings are ascribed to actions according to the roles they are presumed to manifest. The stability of a system of roles and of the relationship between actors and their roles depends on three variables: *functionality*—the degree to which the role constitutes an effective strategy for dealing with relevant situations; *representationality*—the image evoked by the role; and *tenability*—the extent to which the cost/benefit ratio for the role incumbent is acceptable.

The concept of role came into general use in the behavioral sciences during the 1920s and 1930s by analogy to the theater, where the same actor might play very different parts in different plays, and different actors could play the same part quite similarly. In the most important early formulations, G. H. Mead stressed a reciprocity of role-taking and role-playing, anthropologist R. Linton (1936) identified roles as components of culture, with every social status having its accompanying role, and T. Newcomb (1950) made role a central concept in his formulation of the field of social psychology.

Approaches to role theory are most broadly classified as either *structural* or *interactional*. Structuralists, following Linton, see roles as sets of behavioral prescriptions attached to positions in organizations and statuses in society. Roles are, therefore, best described as catalogues of specific expected behaviors, complemented by sets of privileges. R. Merton (1957) introduced a more dynamic version of structural theory in which the incumbent of any position is said to play somewhat different roles in response to the varied expectations of different significant others. For example, a teacher must simultaneously take into account the somewhat different expectations of parents, administrators, students, and fellow teachers. These several roles linked to any given position are called a *role-set*. Interactional approaches, drawing upon G. H. Mead, shift the emphasis from conformity to *role-making* (Turner, 1962). By imaginatively taking the role of the other, the role incumbent improvises a suitable course of action that combines elements of creativity with conformity. People perceive and act *as if* role contents were definite and consensual, while often accepting quite unexpected behavior as a suitable or understandable manifestation of a role.

Role theory is applied in many fields of psychology. Research has revealed that roles are typically *learned* by stages, beginning with a quite formal idea of the role, moving toward a fuller but still rigid understanding as the role is practiced, and eventually progressing toward the security to develop a personalized version of the role. Roles are typically learned in pairs or sets. For example, while learning the child's role, the child must also learn much of the parent role in order to play the child role effectively. This kind of learning is facilitated by children's play in which they play at being mother, father, nurse, and other familiar identities. In the course of the many role transitions during a lifetime, learning new roles requires the often more difficult task of unlearning old roles.

At the heart of *interpersonal, group, and intergroup processes* is the *allocation* of roles, which involves negotiation between assignment to a role by others and adoption or acceptance of a role by the actor. A process of *altercasting* has been identified in which an actor attempts to entice or force others to play those roles that enable the focal person to play a preferred role. Crucial in the acceptance of a system of roles as the basis for interaction are the assigning and weighting of rights and duties.

The *self-conception*, as an organizing component of *personality*, is often described in terms of roles. Research has shown that a self-conception reflecting an organization of one's roles into a hierarchy can be predictive of behavior in choice situations (Stryker, 1987).

Perhaps the most extensive application of role theory has been to the psychology of *adjustment*. A key concept is *role strain* (Goode, 1960), a state of tension and discomfort resulting from inability to perform a role that is high in one's role hierarchy, or anxiety about being able to perform it. Role strain may result from a poor fit between the individual's dispositions, talents, or resources and the demands of a role. Role strain also results from *role conflict*. With *intrarole* conflict, the incumbent must reconcile incompatible requirements or expectations built into a role, as in the case of a parent who is expected to work hard to make a good living for the family while devoting "quality time" to the family. With *interrole* conflict, the incumbent must deal with contradictory expectations associated with different roles. Role strain has also been linked to *role overload*, common in modern society when people assume more duties than they can conscientiously perform. This linkage, however, has been challenged by S. Sieber (1974), who advanced a principle of *role accumulation*, arguing that the privileges of multiple roles often accumulate more substantially than the duties, to the incumbent's benefit. In the context of *gender roles*, and contrary to the role–overload role strain hypothesis, a preponderance of research has suggested that women who perform both homemaker and breadwinner roles feel more fulfilled than those who play only the homemaker or the occupational role.

Also important to the psychology of adjustment is identification by T. Parsons (1951) of a *sick role*, a temporary role in which the incumbent is given the *rights* of exemption from social responsibility and of being cared for, conditional upon performing the role *duties* of wanting to get well, seeking medical advice, and cooperating with medical experts, though the specific nature of the rights and duties has been shown to vary by culture and subculture. This formulation has been generalized to other *exemptive roles* such as the bereaved role and, in some cultures, a drunken role.

Bibliography

Biddle, B. J. (1979). *Role theory: Expectations, identities, and behaviors*. New York: Academic Press. A comprehensive statement with special attention to when behavior does and does not conform to expectations.

Clausen, J. A. (1986). *The life course: A sociological perspective*. Englewood Cliffs, NJ: Prentice Hall. The life course is analyzed as a series of role transitions.

Goode, W. J. (1960). A theory of role strain. *American Sociological Review, 25,* 483–496.

Linton, R. (1936). *The study of man*. New York: Appleton-Century.

Merton, R. (1957). The role set. *British Journal of Sociology 8,* 106–120.

Newcomb, T. (1950). *Social psychology*. New York: Dryden.

Parsons, T. (1951). *The social system*. Glencoe, IL: Free Press.

Sieber, S. (1974). Toward a theory of role accumulation. *American Sociological Review, 39,* 567–578.

Strauss, A. L. (1978). *Negotiations: Varieties, contexts, processes, and social order*. San Francisco: Jossey-Bass. Expands on interactionist role theory in a series of essays.

Stryker, S. (1987). Identity theory. In K. Yardley, & T. Honess (Eds.), *Self and identity: Psychosocial perspectives* (pp. 89–103). Chichester, UK: Wiley.

Turner, R. H. (1962). Role-taking: Process versus conformity. In A. Rose (Ed.), *Human behavior* (pp. 20–40). Boston: Houghton Mifflin.

Turner, R. H. (1990). Role change. *Annual Review of Sociology, 16,* 87–110. Reviews research on processes of role change.

Zurcher, L. A. (1983). *Social roles: Conformity, conflict, and creativity*. Beverly Hills: Sage. Presents several ethnographic studies of role behavior from an interactionist perspective.

Ralph H. Turner

ROMANES, GEORGE JOHN (1848–1894), Canadian/British comparative psychologist, evolutionist, and physiologist. Romanes was born in Kingston, Ontario of Scottish parents. His father, a minister and professor at Queens University (Kingston), received a large inheritance and moved the family to London before Romanes was a year old. When he died at age 46 of a cerebral hemorrhage, Romanes had achieved recognition and status in physiology and evolutionary theory. He had also written well-respected works on mental evolution and had a place in history as the first comparative psychologist. However, soon after his death, his work in animal behavior was denounced, and a tarnished reputation became his legacy in psychology. Romanes was wrongfully criticized, and the restoration of his reputation has been well underway for many years. For example, it was written that Romanes's *Mental Evolution in Animals* "is now being recognized as one of the most important books in the history of psychology" (Murray, *A History of Western Psychology*, Englewood Cliffs, NJ, 1988, p. 262).

Romanes studied theology, mathematics, and medicine at Cambridge before he settled upon physiology and evolutionary biology and earned the A.M. degree. His letter to the editor, "Permanent Variation of Colour in Fish," published in *Nature* (1873) gained Romanes notice from Charles Darwin, and they became and remained close friends until Darwin's death in 1882. Throughout his career, Romanes devoted most of his research to physiology and evolutionary biology, with 1874 to 1887 being the period of his greatest activity on the subject of mental evolution. His anatomical and physiological research on jelly fish helped establish the existence of noncontinuous nervous systems and contributed to the concept of the synapse. For this work, he received honors from the Royal Society of London and was made a Fellow. Romanes's contributions in evolutionary biology are summarized in John Burdon-Sanderson's obituary of Romanes (*Proceedings of the Royal Society of London*, 1895, 57, vii–xiv).

Romanes is best known in psychology for *Animal Intelligence* (London, 1882), *Mental Evolution in Animals* (London, 1883), and *Mental Evolution in Man* (London, 1887). Darwin assisted Romanes by giving him 40 years of collected notes on animal intelligence and the original manuscript of the "Instinct" chapter that was abbreviated in *The Origin of Species* (London, 1859). The unpublished portions of "Instinct" were included as an appendix to *Mental Evolution in Animals*.

Animal Intelligence provided foundational data for the *Mental Evolution* books. Because other data were almost nonexistent, Romanes collected anecdotes which he quoted verbatim. However, quoting verbatim often meant that behavioral descriptions useful to him were confounded with anthropomorphic interpretations that he did not accept. Yet, he was attacked for such interpretations, even when he had presented conservative, reasonable, alternative interpretations. Some of Romanes's interpretations were anthromorphic and excessive by emerging standards in the 1890s, although by today's standards, even some of those interpretations now appear acceptable. As indicated in the following quotation, Romanes was concerned about how his use of anecdotes might be perceived.

> [*Animal Intelligence*] may well seem but a small improvement upon the works of the anecdote-mongers. But if it is remembered that my object in these pages is the mapping out of animal psychology for the purposes of a subsequent synthesis, I may fairly lay claim to receive credit for sound scientific intentions, even where the only methods at my disposal may incidentally seem to minister to a mere love of anecdote. (p. vii)

Romanes's critics included influential American psychologists such as E. L. Thorndike and Margaret Washburn, and attacks on Romanes were usually linked with what some called "Morgan's canon of parsimony." By 1929, E. G. Boring observed, "The anecdotal method of Romanes . . . has become a term of opprobrium in animal psychology" (*History of Experimental Psychology*, New York, 1929, p. 464; iterated in the 1950 edition). Boring cited Morgan's canon and books as examples of reaction against Romanes's use of anecdotes and anthropomorphism. Opinions such as Boring's became the consensus view. It was overlooked or disregarded that Romanes was a competent experimentalist, and as Gray (1963) observed, "His objectivity was sufficient that, had he lived, he could have coped with even the iconoclastic Thorndike" (p. 225).

C. Lloyd Morgan is best remembered for his "principle" (Morgan's canon), a conservative guideline for interpreting animal behavior (*Introduction to Comparative Psychology*, London, 1894, p. 53). However, on the next page Morgan denied that simplicity [parsimony] was a necessary criterion. The canon was not antianthropomorphic. Elsewhere Morgan said, "human psychology is the only key to animal psychology" (Dixon quoting Morgan in *Nature*, 1892, 46, p. 392). The canon was not antianecdotal, because it did not address method, and Morgan himself used anecdotes. Later, Morgan did say that Romanes's data were "perhaps too largely anecdotal" (*Dictionary of National Biography*, New York, 1897).

Because Morgan's canon is so wrongly associated with Romanes's reputation, it would be fitting if Morgan's eulogy to Romanes could become equally well remembered:

> [B]y his patient collection of data, by his careful discussion of these data in the light of principles clearly formulated; by his wide and forcible advocacy of his views, and above all by his own observations and experiments, Mr. Romanes left a mark in this field of investigation and interpretation which is not likely to be effaced. (p. xiii in Burdon-Sanderson cited above)

Their friendship was such that Romanes, near death, asked Morgan to oversee his unfinished work, which Morgan did. It was ironic that within 5 years after Romanes's death, his "mark" would be "effaced" in the name of Morgan (Burden-Sanderson, 1895, *Proceedings of the Royal Society of London*, 57, p. xiii).

Researchers such as Wesley Mills (*Psychological Review*, 1899, 6, 262–276) defended Romanes, and scholars showed over the years that Morgan's canon was being misunderstood. However, such voices were overwhelmed by those who misrepresented Morgan's canon and used it against Romanes. There has been renewed interest since the 1980s in correcting the record on Morgan's canon and its misuse against Romanes, and it appears that Romanes's good name has been restored. It is expected that Romanes will again be respected for his careful and insightful views about mental evolution.

Bibliography

Other Works by Romanes

Romanes, E. (1902). *The life and letters of George John Romanes* (5th ed.). London: Longmans, Green. Contains biographical information by Romanes's wife, Ethel, but mostly letters (many to and from Darwin). Later editions added a few letters.

Romanes, G. J. (1885). *Jelly-fish, star-fish, and sea urchins.* London: K. Paul, Trench. A compilation of approximately ten years of Romanes's research in physiology.

Romanes, G. J. (1893). *An examination of Weismannism.* London: K. Paul, Trench. Romanes claimed some priority but expressed significant disagreement with the views of Weismann (the forerunner of the modern understanding of genetics).

Romanes, G. J. (1892–1897). *Darwin and after Darwin* (Vols. 1–3). London: K. Paul, Trench. These three volumes represent Romanes's considerable contributions to Darwin's theory of evolution, many of which were based on original research. Publication of the posthumous volumes was supervised by Morgan.

Romanes's Critics

Thorndike, E. L. (1898). Animal intelligence: An experimental study of the associative processes in animals. *Psychological Review: Series of Monograph Supplements*, 22, 1–109.

Washburn, M. F. (1908). *The animal mind.* New York: Macmillan.

Works on Romanes, Morgan, and the Misuse of Morgan's Canon

Costall, A. (1993). How Lloyd Morgan's canon backfired. *Journal of the History of the Behavioral Sciences, 29;* 113–122.

Gray, P. H. (1963). The Morgan-Romanes controversy: A contradiction in the history of comparative psychology. *Proceedings of the Montana Academy of Sciences, 23,* 225–230. Excellent examination of the relationship between Romanes and Morgan.

Thomas, R. K. (1998). Lloyd Morgan's canon. In G. Greenberg & M. Haraway (Eds). *Comparative psychology: A handbook* (pp. 156–163). New York: Garland. Examines Morgan's canon in relation to Ockham's razor, parsimony, and Romanes.

Wozniak, R. H. (1993). Conwy Lloyd Morgan, mental evolution, and the *Introduction to comparative psychology.* In C. L. Morgan, *Introduction to comparative psychology.* London: Routledge/Thoemmes. (Original work by Morgan published 1894.) This introduction to the 1993 reprinting of Morgan's classic text examines the misuse of Morgan's canon, including its misuse against Romanes.

Roger K. Thomas

RORSCHACH, HERMANN (1884–1922), Swiss psychiatrist. Rorschach spent his childhood and youth in Schaffhausen, a picturesque 700-year-old town on the Rhine, where his father was an art teacher. He was a good but not exceptional student in all of his subjects. Much has been made of his being given the nickname of "Klex" (inkblot in German) when he was initiated into the Scaphusia, a student association. Ellenberger (1954), in a definitive biography of Rorschach, provides several possible—and provocative—explanations.

When Rorschach was completing his Kantonsschule education he wavered between art and science for his life work and wrote to the famous German naturalist, Ernst Haeckel, regarding his dilemma. Haeckel, not surprisingly, advised science and Rorschach decided on medicine, but art remained a significant resource.

Following the Swiss custom of studying at several universities, Rorschach spent his first semester in Neuchatel, the next four in Zurich, then one each in Berlin and Bern before returning to Zurich for his last three terms. Every medical student was required to take at least two semesters of clinical and theoretical psychiatry. When Rorschach chose Zurich, he had the advantage of study at the Burgholzli, the world-renowned psychiatric clinic and hospital, directed by Eugen Bleuler. Here he was exposed to Bleuler's new conceptualization of schizophrenia, Freud's psychoanalytic theory, and Jung's work with word association. From the beginning of his medical studies, Rorschach had considered psychiatry. His choice was now determined.

In Zurich, Rorschach became involved with the Russian colony, and fell in love with Olga Stempelin, a fellow student who was from Russia. They married in 1910 and decided to go to Russia to live upon completion of their education. In the meantime, Rorschach obtained a residency at Munsterlingen, and while there completed his dissertation "On Reflex Hallucination and Kindred Manifestations." He received the doctor of medicine degree from the University of Zurich in 1912. While he was at Munsterlingen, working on his dissertation and trying out the new techniques of psychoanalysis on his patients, Rorschach rekindled his friendship with Konrad Gehring, a schoolmate from his Kantonschule days in Schaffhausen. Gehring was teaching in a nearby school and using inkblots to entertain his pupils. Rorschach tried inkblots with his patients, and they set up several experiments comparing the two populations.

In 1913, with his medical degree and 4 years of asylum practice, Rorschach was ready to go to Russia. He obtained a lucrative position in the fashionable Sanitarium Krukovo near Moscow. After 7 months, however, missing the opportunity to do research, he returned to Switzerland, with his wife planning to follow as soon as he was settled.

By the time he found a position at the Waldau Mental Hospital, World War I had started, impeding their reunion. He remained at Waldau for 15 months and while there he devoted his free time to the study of Swiss religious sects, which he now saw as his life work. When his wife rejoined him, he moved to a position as associate director of the Krombach Mental Hospital at Herisau, where he continued his research on the Swiss sects. He became active in the formation of a new Swiss Psychoanalytic Society and was elected vice president.

Suddenly in 1918, Rorschach's research took an unexpected turn when he began working on his own inkblot test, his *Psychodiagnostik*. The publication of a doctoral dissertation by Szymon Hens under Bleuler's direction, using inkblots as a test, may have reminded him of his early work with his friend Gehring. In some three years, Rorschach developed his standard set of inkblots, his concept of the factors of the experiment, the determinants of the responses to the apperceptions of the blots, the criteria for scoring them and arriving at a psychogram, the concept of the experience types, and his comparisons of patients of various diagnoses and of various populations. He was moving toward a comprehensive theory of personality functioning and developing the technique to describe it. His *Psychodiagnostik* was published in June 1921 as a report of a work in progress. In February, he sent a supplementary paper, *The Application of the Form Interpretation Test*, to the Psychoanalytic Society. Six weeks later Rorschach suddenly died of peritonitis. He was just 37 years old, and his final paper had to be published posthumously by Dr. Emil Oberholzer.

With Rorschach unable to develop his theories and methodology, the acceptance of the technique was slow and and limited to his colleagues and their students. After World War II, however, clinical psychology developed rapidly as a field of study and a profession, especially in the United States. In the 1950s, the emphasis was on psychodiagnosis and the Rorschach became the test of choice. During the 1960s and 1970s, psychology became increasingly involved with intervention, and the Rorschach was used as a predictor and evaluator of therapy.

Without Rorschach's direction, variations had proliferated. In the United States alone, there were at least five schools of Rorschach, with slight differences in scoring and interpretation, but vociferous disagreement: Beck (1937, 1944, 1945, 1952); Hertz (1936, 1939); Klopfer (1937, 1942); Piotrowski (1937, 1957); and Rapaport-Schafer (1946, 1954). Exner (1969) made an extensive and intensive comparison and ultimately developed what he termed the comprehensive system (1972).

[*Many of the people mentioned in this article are the subjects of independent biographical entries.*]

Bibliography

Beck, S. J. (1937). Introduction to the Rorschach method: A manual of personality study. *American Orthopsychiatric Association Monograph, 1.*

Beck, S. J. (1944). *Rorschach's Test I: Basic processes.* New York: Grune and Stratton.

Beck, S. J. (1945). *Rorschach's Test II: A variety of personality picturess.* New York: Grune and Stratton.

Beck, S. J. (1952). *Rorschach's Test III: Advances in interpretation.* New York: Grune and Stratton.

Ellenberger, H. (1954). Hermann Rorschach, M. D. 1884–1922. *Bulletin of the Menninger Clinic, 18,* 171–222. Ellenberger was able to interview and access colleagues and family members such as Dr. Olga Rorschach and provides rich information.

Exner, J. E. (1969). *The Rorschach systems.* New York: Grune and Stratton.

Exner, J. E. and Exner, D. E. (1972). How clinicians use the Rorschach. *Journal of Personality Assessment, 36,* 403–408.

Exner, J. E. (1974). *The Rorschach: A comprehensive system* (Vol. 1). New York: Wiley.

Exner, J. E. (1993). *The Rorschach: A comprehensive system: Vol. 1. Basic foundations.* (3rd ed.). New York: Wiley.

Hertz, M. R. (1936). *Frequency tables to be used in scoring the Rorschach ink-blot test.* Cleveland: Brush Foundation, Western Reserve University.

Hertz, M. R. (1939). On the standardization of the Rorschach method. *Rorschach Research Exchange, 3,* 120–133.

Klopfer, B. (1937). The present status of the theoretical development of the Rorschach method. *Rorschach Research Exchange, 1,* 142–147

Klopfer, B., & Kelley, D. (1942). *The Rorschach technique.* Yonkers, New York: World Book.

Piotrowski, Z. (1937). The M, FM, and m responses as indicators of changes in personality. *Rorschach Research Exchange, 1,* 148–156.

Piotrowski, Z. (1957). *Perceptanalysis.* New York: Macmillan.

Rapaport, D., Gill, M., & Schafer, R. (1946). *Diagnostic psychological testing, Vols. 1 and 2.* Chicago: Yearbook.

Rorschach, H. (1913). *Ueber Reflexhalluzinationen und verwandte Erscheinungen* [On reflex hallucination and kindred manifestations]. *Zeitschrift. gesellschaft fur Neurologie und Psychiatrie. 13*: 357–400. Dissertation for his medical degree.

Rorschach, H. (1942). *Psychodiagnostik* [A diagnostic test based on perception] (P. Lemkau and B. Kroninberg, Trans.; W. Morgenthaler, Ed.). New York: Grune and Stratton. (Original work published in 1921)

Schafer, R. (1954). *Psychoanalytic interpretation in Rorschach testing.* New York: Grune and Stratton.

Elizabeth B. Wolf

RORSCHACH TEST. Sometimes referred to as the Rorschach Inkblot Method, the Rorschach Test (Rorschach, 1921/1942) utilizes ten standardized inkblot cards (five black and gray, three color, and two that combine black, gray, and color) as a medium for generating information about an individual's personality. The information derived from the Rorschach is based on the assumption that the individual's perceptions, representations, and associations are selected and organized in terms of his or her internal needs, emotions, thought processes, relational patterns, and behavior. By observing the way an individual creates, organizes, and interprets his or her perceptions, psychologists gain insight into that individual's psychological functioning. The Rorschach involves the presentation of ambiguous stimuli, designed to evoke highly individualized meaning and organization, allowing the development of responses rich with unique and personal aspects of the individual. This approach to assessment avoids some of the constraints imposed by self-report measures that have a circumscribed set of responses and recognizes that not all personality characteristics are under conscious control or available to introspection.

Extensive scoring systems have been developed that provide data on the structure, content, and themes that emerge from people's responses to the inkblots (Exner, 1993; Stricker & Healy, 1990). These scoring systems can be applied in both quantitative and qualitative terms and interpreted from many different theoretical perspectives. The Rorschach also provides clinicians with ideographic information (information that is unique to that person's experience of self, others, and the world around him or her) that provides clues to important therapeutic material (Meloy, Acklin, Gacono, Murray, & Peterson, 1997). Like semistructured interviews, assessment utilizing the Rorschach is carried out within an interpersonal context, in which a clinician can evaluate the patient-clinician interaction as a source of diagnostic information. How a person negotiates the communication of idiosyncratic ideas and associations may contribute valuable information concerning diagnosis and subsequent treatment. In addition to the formal test scores, a wealth of information may be obtained through an analysis of idiosyncratic and defensive reactions of the individual to this situation.

The Rorschach Inkblot Test was first released as a monograph by Hermann Rorschach, a Swiss psychiatrist, in 1921. Utilizing what he termed a Form Interpretation Test, Rorschach investigated aspects of perception that he believed would be useful in the diagnosis of schizophrenia. Unfortunately, Rorschach died in 1922, at the age of 37, less than a year after the publication of his monograph. His untimely death did not allow him to fully develop this diagnostic method and would pose in some respects both a significant opportunity and a problem for those who would become interested in developing, expanding, and using the Rorschach Inkblot Test.

The Rorschach Inkblot Test was introduced to the United States in the late 1920s, and by the late 1950s five different scoring systems had been developed. Although each of the scoring systems shared many of the scores, criteria, and concepts found in Rorschach's original work, each also differed substantially on many issues of scoring and interpretation. This state of affairs persisted until the early 1970s, when John Exner introduced a comprehensive system for the scoring and interpretation of the Rorschach. This system reflected an empirically based integration of scores and interpretive formulations across the works of each of the previous five systems. For the past 20 years, Exner's comprehensive system has been and continues to be the standard scoring system taught and utilized in graduate training programs and internships approved by the American Psychological Association.

Conceptually based research with the Rorschach has consistently demonstrated its validity for a variety of clinical purposes (e.g., Hiller, Rosenthal, Bornstein, Berry, & Brunell-Neuleib, 1999; Viglione, 1999). Specifically, important contributions of the Rorschach to psychotherapy include identifying treatment targets (Meloy et al., 1997), indicies of termination, and engagement in, continuation of, and predicting success in psychotherapy (Alpher, Henry, & Strupp, 1990; Hilsenroth, Handler, Toman, & Padawer, 1995; Meyer & Handler, 1997). In addition, the Rorschach can be useful in selecting appropriate treatment modalities, monitoring change and improvement over time on indices of adjustment among both adolescents and adults receiving psychotherapy (e.g., Blatt & Ford, 1994; Tuber, 1983; Weiner & Exner, 1991). Properly used by informed clinicians, it functions with substantial reliability, validity, and clinical utility in answering important questions related to personality processes.

Repeated surveys of psychological test use over the past 40 years have shown a substantial, consistent, and sustained use of the Rorschach in academic training, research, and clinical settings. Surveys consistently indicate that more than 80% of graduate programs teach the Rorschach and that students regard this training as important in developing other clinical skills and understanding their patients better and very useful in their practicum and in internship training (Hilsenroth & Handler, 1995; Piotrowski & Zalewski, 1993). In regard to research applications, the Rorschach is the second most frequently researched personality assessment instrument. This rate of annual research has been stable over a 20-year period with a mean of more than 95 studies published a year. This consistently high rate of empirical investigation led the authors of a recent review to state: "Whether viewed from the perspective of research attention or practical usage, the Rorschach inkblot technique continues to be among the most popular personality assessment methods and predictions about the technique's demise would appear both unwarranted and unrealistic" (Butcher & Rouse, 1996, p. 91).

This high level of research interest is matched in applied clinical practice. In reviews of mental health facilities and private practitioners engaged in providing services, the Rorschach was found to be among the most utilized measures, at 80% or higher. Also, 90% of clinical practitioners working in the field expressed a belief that clinical psychology graduate students should be competent in Rorschach assessment.

The administration and scoring procedures for the Rorschach are standardized (Exner, 1993). The examiner and participant are seated side by side, the participant is then handed the cards one at a time and asked, "What might this be?" In the first phase (the free association phase) the examiner records all verbal material verbatim and avoids injecting any influence or direction into the situation. After responses are given to all ten cards, the second phase (the inquiry) begins, in which the examiner attempts to gain additional information and understanding from the participant to score the responses accurately. Usually this entails querying where the participant saw what he or she saw (location), the qualities of the inkblot he or she identified in the response, the various aspects of the inkblot that stimulated the response (e.g. color, movement, texture, shading, achromatic color, etc.), and what the content of the response is (e.g., human, animal, landscape, anatomy, food, fire, etc.). The inquiry phase is not used to generate new responses but simply to clarify what was perceived during the free association phase, although people often elaborate in ways that provide more insight into what they think and perceive.

Although the Rorschach has been criticized by some as an invalid or useless measure (Peterson, 1995; Wood, Nezworski, & Stejskal, 1996), this criticism appears to be incongruent with a great deal of contemporary data demonstrating its psychometric soundness and practical utility. Clinicians trained in the administration and coding of the different variables have demonstrated high levels of interrater agreement in scoring its variables (Exner, 1993; Meyer, 1997; Stricker & Healy, 1990). Extensive normative data with detailed descriptive statistics are provided for variables in Exner's comprehensive system on a sample of 700 nonpatient adults, on 1,390 children and adolescents separated by age (from 5 through 16), and on a variety of patient populations (Exner, 1993). The size and diversity of these normative and patient samples provide more standardized information than is available for most psychological assessment measures and establishes the Rorschach as adequately normed for the U.S. population (Exner, 1993). Meta-analytic studies (that is, a review of empirical results across a number of individual studies) have concluded that when used properly the Rorschach demonstrates adequate validity by usual psychometric standards comparable to self-report measures of psychopathology such as the MMPI-2 (e.g., Atkinson, Quarrington, Alp, & Cyr, 1986; Hiller et al., 1999). In addition, these reviews demonstrate that studies using theory-driven hypotheses obtain substantially higher validity coefficients for Rorschach variables than research undertaken without a theoretical or empirical rationale.

[See also Projective Techniques; Testing; and the biography of Rorschach.]

Bibliography

Alpher, V., Henry, W., & Strupp, H. (1990). Dynamic factors in patient assessment and prediction of change in short-term dynamic psychotherapy. *Psychotherapy, 27,* 350–361.

Atkinson, L., Quarrington, B., Alp, I., & Cyr, J. (1986). Rorschach validity: An empirical approach to the literature. *Journal of Clinical Psychology, 42,* 360–362.

Blatt, S., & Ford, R. (1994). *Therapeutic change: An object relations perspective.* New York: Plenum Press.

Butcher, J., & Rouse, S. (1996). Personality: Individual differences and clinical assessment. *Annual Review of Psychology, 47,* 87–111.

Exner, J. (1993). *The Rorschach: A comprehensive system: Vol. 1. Basic foundations* (3rd ed.). New York: Wiley.

Hiller, J., Rosenthal, R., Bornstein, R., Berry, D., & Brunell-Neuleib, S. (1999). A comparative meta-analysis of Rorschach and MMPI validity. *Psychological Assessment, 11,* 278–296.

Hilsenroth, M., & Handler, L. (1995). A survey of graduate students' experiences, interests, and attitudes about learning the Rorschach. *Journal of Personality Assessment, 64,* 243–257.

Hilsenroth, M., Handler, L., Toman, K., & Padawer, J. (1995). Rorschach and MMPI-2 indices of early psychotherapy termination. *Journal of Consulting and Clinical Psychology, 63,* 956–965.

Meloy, J., Acklin, M., Gacono, C., Murray, J., & Peterson, C. (Eds.). (1997). *Contemporary Rorschach interpretation.* Mahwah, NJ: Erlbaum.

Meyer, G. (1997). Assessing reliability: Critical corrections for a critical examination of the Rorschach Comprehensive System. *Psychological Assessment, 9,* 480–489.

Meyer, G., & Handler, L. (1997). The ability of the Rorschach to predict subsequent outcome: A meta-analysis of the Rorschach Prognostic Rating Scale. *Journal of Personality Assessment, 69,* 1–38.

Peterson, D. (1995). The reflective educator. *American Psychologist, 50,* 975–983.

Piotrowski, C., & Zalewski, C. (1993). Training in psychodiagnostic testing in APA-approved PsyD and PhD clinical psychology programs. *Journal of Personality Assessment, 61,* 394–405.

Rorschach, H. (1942) *Psychodiagnostics: A diagnostic test based on perception.* New York: Grune & Stratton. (Original work published 1921)

Stricker, G., & Healey, B. (1990). Projective assessment of object relations: A review of the empirical literature. *Psychological Assessment, 2,* 219–230.

Tuber, S. (1983). Children's Rorschach scores as predictors of later adjustment. *Journal of Consulting and Clinical Psychology, 51,* 379–385.

Viglione, D. (1999). A review of recent research addressing the utility of the Rorschach. *Psychological Assessment, 11,* 251–265.

Weiner, I., & Exner, J. (1991). Rorschach changes in long-term and short-term psychotherapy. *Journal of Personality Assessment, 56,* 453–465.

Wood, J., Nezworski, M., & Stejskal, W. (1996). The comprehensive system for the Rorschach: A critical examination. *Psychological Science, 7,* 3–10.

Mark J. Hilsenroth

ROUSSEAU, JEAN-JACQUES (1712–1778), Swiss French philosopher. Rousseau was the son of Isaac Rousseau, a modest watchmaker, and Susannah Bernard, an affluent minister's daughter. Tragedy struck early; Rousseau's mother died 9 days after giving birth. At the age of 16, he emigrated to Turin, Italy, where he rejected his Calvinistic upbringing and became a Roman Catholic. In 1733, he moved to Chambéry, France, where he lived with and became the lover of the Baronne Louise de Warens. Having received no formal education, it was under her patronage that Rousseau was exposed to a rich intellectual life. In 1742, he moved to Paris, hoping to succeed by composing and teaching music. Although he devoted himself to music for over a decade, his acquaintance with young Parisian intellectuals like Diderot led him to shift his focus and energy to social and political issues. In 1754, in response to a question posed by the Academy of Dijon on social inequality, Rousseau published *Discourse on the Origin and Foundations of Inequality Amongst Men.*

In 1754, Rousseau returned to Geneva and reverted to Protestantism but shortly moved back to Paris. He published *Social Contract* and *Émile* in 1762, both of which were banned in France and Switzerland for their views on natural religion and led to his persecution for the remainder of his life. He renounced his Swiss citizenship and fled France for England under the patronage of the Scottish philosopher and historian David Hume, but after a paranoid episode in which Rousseau felt that Hume and other British intellectuals were mocking him, he returned to France incognito and spent the remainder of his life justifying his controversial views in autobiographical works.

Rousseau is especially known for his political philosophy, best exemplified in his *Discourse on the Origin and Foundations of Inequality Amongst Men* (1755) and *Social Contract* (1762). In the *Discourse,* he holds that human beings are inherently good but that society corrupts them and leads them to vice. All persons were at one point equal, when they lived alone, but inequality arose when they began to form societies and compete with each other. While the *Discourse* describes how men have lost their freedom and equality, the *Social Contract* is an exposition of how individuals can recover some of it. Individuals must modify their behavior and give up their rights in accord with a general will (*volonté générale*). This general will abolishes individual liberty but in its place provides civil and property rights, which are enforced by the collective community. Although this general will can conflict at times with personal interests, it tends to promote public, common, or national interests, thus leading to a generalized freedom.

Rousseau's most important contribution to psychology is as the first great theorist of adolescence. In *Émile* (1762), he describes the upbringing of a son of nobility by a tutor with unlimited authority over him. Here he explains how development is a natural process and children should be allowed to follow their inclinations as they develop. Each child passes through successive phases and assimilates skills and knowledge appropriate to the needs of his age. As vice is introduced by external agencies (that is, society), it is the tutor's duty to protect the child and make sure he discovers and comprehends things on his own, not because he was told anything or pressured by adults.

Rousseau described adolescence as a time of heightened emotional instability and conflict, of recapitulation of earlier stages of life through which the child passes, and of the development of self-conscious thought and logical reasoning (accompanied by biological changes). G. Stanley Hall later developed his theory of individual development by combining these characteristics with Darwin's ideas about the evolution of species. Rousseau's notion that children are born good and that it is society (experience) that corrupts them (creates differences among individuals) convinced many to accept responsibility for the welfare of children. Rousseau's ideas influenced not only Hall but also other important figures of the twentieth century such as the psychoanalysts Freud and Erikson, the Swiss psychologist Piaget, and the educational psychologist Dewey.

[*Many of the people mentioned in this article are the subjects of independent biographical entries.*]

Bibliography

Cranston, M. W. (1983). *The early life and work of Jean-Jacques Rousseau, 1712–1754.* New York: Norton.

Cranston, M. W. (1991). *The noble savage: Jean-Jacques Rousseau, 1754–1762.* Chicago: University of Chicago Press.

Dent, N. J. H. (1989). *Rousseau: An introduction to his psychological, social, and political theory.* New York: Blackwell.

Grimsley, R. (1973). *The philosophy of Rousseau.* New York: Oxford University Press.

Leigh, R. A. (Ed.). (1982). *Rousseau after two hundred years: Proceedings of the Cambridge Bicentennial Colloquium.* New York: Cambridge University Press.

Shklar, J. N. (1985). *Men and citizens: A study of Rousseau's social theory.* Cambridge, UK: Cambridge University Press.

Ingrid G. Farreras

ROYCE, JOSIAH (1855–1916), American idealist philosopher. Born in California, he graduated from the University of California, Berkeley, in 1875, studied in Germany at Leipzig and Göttingen, and received his doctorate from Johns Hopkins University in 1878. Royce's unique blend of religious concerns and rationalist metaphysics and his appeal to experience and practice make him the best American representative of absolute idealism.

From 1878 to 1882 he taught English at Berkeley, continuing research on the self as knower. John Stuart Mill's social criticism and empirical methodology shaped Royce's early skeptical approach to a theory of knowledge, and Immanuel Kant's three *Critiques* led him to reconsider the role of the self and community. He began teaching philosophy at Harvard University in 1882, where he remained until his death. His colleagues included William James, Hugo Münsterberg,

George Herbert Palmer, and George Santayana (whose dissertation he supervised). These philosophers established classical American philosophy and shaped the early development of psychology when the methodologies of the two disciplines were not sharply different.

In 1883 Royce's epistemological inquiries led to a pivotal religious insight that emphasized community, individual meaning, and an Absolute Knower. In *The Religious Aspect of Philosophy* (1885), he argued that the existence of error assumes knowledge that, in turn, enables the establishment of truths in logic, ethics, and religion. Influenced by Kant's kingdom of ends, Royce focused on a universal community of moral agents in which individual moral choices, even negative ones, reaffirm the community. The idea of community guided Royce's work in history, fiction, and social psychology and his *The Spirit of Modern Philosophy* (1892).

In the two volumes of *The World and the Individual* (1899–1901), Royce develops his mature view of the relation between thought and reality in contrast to realism, mysticism, and critical rationalism. Defining an idea as a purpose seeking its object, Royce blends pragmatism with his idealistic and religious views. He develops a voluntaristic idealism in which ideas aim at the expression of the absolute will. His investigations in logic are important, particularly his concerns with the one and the many. His account of a self-representative system (a recursive function) forms a rejection of F. H. Bradley's argument that an actual infinity is self-contradictory. Royce's account of triadic relations is influenced by the American logician Charles Sanders Peirce, who gave a series of lectures at Harvard in 1898 entitled "Reasoning and the Logic of Things."

The Philosophy of Loyalty (1908/1995) develops Royce's fundamental moral principle. Recognizing the dangerous elements in blind loyalty, Royce proposes a knowledgeable, freely chosen loyalty that promotes community and individual development. This book remains one of his best known. In 1913 Royce published *The Problem of Christianity*, his last major work. Using his metaphysical analysis, he reinterprets classical religious ideas through contemporary experience and language. C. I. Lewis continued Royce's logical and epistemological concerns, and W. E. Hocking developed his metaphysical approach. Although both philosophical and psychological investigations turned from Royce's metaphysical speculations toward logical and empirical approaches, his concerns about community, the development of individuals, and the insights of religion continue to be central to American thought.

Bibliography

Works by Royce

Clendenning, J. (Ed.). (1970). *The letters of Josiah Royce.* Chicago: University of Chicago Press.

Royce, J. (1887). *The feud of Oakfield Creek: A novel of California life.* Boston: Houghton Mifflin.

Royce, J. (1899–1901). *The world and the individual* (Vols. 1–2). New York: Macmillan.

Royce, J. (1913). *The problem of Christianity: Lectures delivered at the Lowell Institute in Boston and at Manchester College, Oxford* (Vols. 1–2). New York: Macmillan.

Royce, J. (1916). *The hope of the great community.* New York: Macmillan.

Royce, J. (1995). *The philosophy of loyalty: With a new introduction by John J. McDermott.* Nashville, TN: Vanderbilt University Press. (Original work published 1908)

Works about Royce

Clendenning, J. (1998). *The life and thought of Josiah Royce.* (Rev. ed.). Nashville, TN: Vanderbilt University Press.

Kuklick, B. (1972). *Josiah Royce: An intellectual biography.* Indianapolis, IN: Bobbs-Merrill.

Oppenheim, F. M. (1967). *Bibliography of the published works of Josiah Royce.* St. Louis, MO: St. Louis University.

Oppenheim, F. M. (1993). *Royce's mature ethics.* Notre Dame, IN: University of Notre Dame Press.

Herman J. Saatkamp, Jr.

RUBIN, EDGAR (1886–1951), Danish psychologist. Best known for his perceptual research concerning figure/ground relationship and his classic illustrations of figure and ground reversing such as the vase/profile and the claw/three fingers, Rubin's scientific phenomenological approach both provided support for and clarified limitations in the Gestalt psychology description of consciousness.

Born in Copenhagen, Rubin studied philosophy and psychology at the University of Copenhagen under Harald Hoffding and Alfred Lehmann from 1904 to 1911. He was the student of Georg Elias Müller in the Institute of Psychology at Göttingen from 1911 to 1914, receiving the degree of doctor of philosophy in 1915. His dissertation, "Visually Perceived Figures: Studies in Psychological Analysis," reported his research concerning the figure/ground phenomenon. Originally published in Danish, Rubin's main work was largely ignored until 1921 when it was published in German, and the Gestalt psychologists recognized the significance of Rubin's description of the figure/ground relationship for their account of cognition.

Rubin observed that part of a stimulus array may appear to stand out (the figure) and part of it may appear to recede (the ground) as in the case of a house viewed against a landscape. Sometimes, as Rubin illustrated, in an ambiguous stimulus, figure and ground can appear to reverse. Rubin argued that this phenomenon is independent of retinal change and is determined by central factors.

Rubin also researched tactual and auditory perception, gustatory sensations during reception of food, temporal perception, and the sensation of temperature. In 1912, his earliest published work concerned the phenomenon of paradoxical warmth in which cool stimuli just below the temperature of the skin can produce a sensation of warmth.

He was consistently concerned with questions about the nature of scientific description. In rejecting classical associationism, he departed from the Danish research tradition emphasizing description by analysis and rejected Hoffding's concept of synthesis. He also objected to what he perceived as uncritical acceptance of the concept of wholeness by Gestalt psychologists. He proposed "aspective" psychology, which emphasizes the precise description of everyday phenomena.

Rubin became an instructor at the University of Copenhagen in 1916, later served as a lecturer in philosophy, and in 1920 was appointed to succeed Lehmann as professor of experimental psychology and director of the psychological laboratory. Except for two years in Sweden as visiting professor at the University of Lund, he directed the psychological laboratory at the University of Copenhagen until his death 31 years later. There were no psychological dissertations published during Rubin's tenure at the psychological laboratory. He served as president of the Danish Association for Philosophy and Psychology and president of the Tenth International Congress for Psychology in 1932. His death in 1951 followed an illness reportedly partly caused by deprivations that he encountered in his removal to Sweden during the German occupation of Denmark during World War II.

In his rejection of atomism and insistence upon scientific description, Rubin made significant contributions to the Gestalt movement and to the development of scientific phenomenology.

Bibliography

Katz, D. (1951). Edgar Rubin: 1886–1951. *Psychological Review, 58* (6), 387–388. This obituary includes information concerning Rubin's life and contributions and a picture of Rubin.

Moustgaard, I. (1975). Phenomenological descriptions after the manner of Edgar Rubin. *Journal of Phenomenological Psychology, 6* (1), 31–61. This paper includes an account of Rubin's influence on contemporary Danish psychology.

Rubin, E. (1915). *Visually perceived figures: Studies in psychological analysis.* Rubin's doctoral dissertation was first published in Danish in 1915, *Synsoplevede Figurer,* and then in German in 1921, *Visuell wahrgenommene Figuren: Studien in psychologischer Analyse.* The German translation influenced the Gestalt psychologists.

Linda R. Jeffrey

RUMORS. The definition of rumor is an unverified proposition for belief that bears topical relevance for persons actively involved in its dissemination. A critical element of rumor is that there is a lack of certainty as to the validity of its message. A story in widespread circulation that has been officially verified as false may nevertheless be considered a rumor, so long as there is a suspension of disbelief in the story's content. As an idea proposed as an explanation pertaining to matters of current or local interest, a rumor can be considered as a kind of hypothesis that reflects people's assumptions or suspicions about how the world works. A distinction can often be made between rumors that invoke hoped-for consequences (also called "wish rumors") and rumors that invoke feared or disappointing consequences (called "dread rumors").

Rumors circulate in a wide range of contexts, including social communities (e.g., the story that a local school is about to be closed), organizational settings (e.g., the assertion that there will be layoffs in the workplace), the marketplace (e.g., rumors that a company's products contain harmful ingredients), and the mass media (e.g., reports of an impending breakthrough in peace negotiations). Embellished by allegations or attributions based on circumstantial evidence, rumors thrive under conditions of social crisis, conflict, and personal trauma, and their content is apt to mirror the fears and anxieties invoked by such situations. As implied above, rumors also may be positive in nature, expressing people's hopes and desires (e.g., ruminations that a star athlete will be traded to the home team).

Rumor can be distinguished from gossip and news by considering whether the content deals with people, is significant, and is supported by evidence. Unlike gossip, which refers to relatively fleeting small talk about persons and social events, the content of both rumor and news tends to be significant and may or may not deal with people. However, news is presumed unquestionably to be based on verifiable facts whereas rumor is not, a point that led Tamotsu Shibutani to describe rumor as "improvised news." In *Improvised News: A Sociological Study of Rumor* (Indianapolis, 1966), Tamotsu Shibutani argued that rumors emerge as informal interpretations of events when information is unavailable through formal channels. Urban legends, a modern form of traditional legends, are well-developed stories that typically have surprise endings that reflect contemporary fears. Because of their unverified nature, Jean-Noël Kapferer (1987/1990) suggests that urban legends belong in the general family of rumors, albeit possessing a special narrative structure. In essence, the distinctions between these various forms often blur, and whether or not a message can be considered rumor generally depends on the context in which the message appears.

An early view of the functional nature of rumor was the psychoanalytic idea that rumors operate as a defense mechanism by serving as projections of individual needs and fantasies. Contemporary researchers, however, are more apt to regard rumor as a collective (i.e., social) phenomenon, whose dynamics can best be explained as involving a combination of psychological and situational variables. This position was first given impetus by Gordon W. Allport and Leo Postman (*The Psychology of Rumor*, New York, 1947). Based on classroom demonstration studies modeled after the popular "telephone game," they observed how certain details were characteristically eliminated (called "leveling") or selectively perceived (called "sharpening") in the communication as it was passed from one person to another in a serial transmission chain. Other researchers have argued that the observed alterations in content may have been more a function of the procedure used than an indication of how rumors operate in natural settings. In normal conversations, redundancies and clarifications are common, and, as a result, rumors often remain remarkably consistent or are elaborated as they are transmitted.

More significantly, Allport and Postman theorized that rumors are set in motion and spread when there is ambiguity regarding the true facts and when the theme of the story has some importance to speaker and listener—their "basic law of rumor." Although this principle remained the authoritative psychological explanation of rumor for many years, the lesser known work of Indian psychologist Jamuna Prasad may have been equally enlightening (*British Journal of Psychology*, 1935, *26*, 1–15). On the basis of an analysis of rumors that appeared following a devastating earthquake, Prasad concluded that, in addition to ambiguous, unfamiliar, and unverifiable aspects, rumors are generated and transmitted when conditions are emotionally disturbing or fear arousing for group members. Presumably, the anxiety induced by emotionally unstable situations provides a motivating force for rumormongering.

Several elements of these early views have been empirically validated in recent years. A program of research by Rosnow and others (*American Psychologist*, 1991, *46*, 484–496) suggests that rumors are sustained by an optimal combination of personal anxiety (an affective state characterized by apprehension about ongoing or forthcoming events), general uncertainty (free-floating doubt or ambiguity pertaining to unstable situations), and outcome-relevant involvement (i.e., importance or relevance of a situation). Credulity, or belief in the rumor, is usually a triggering mechanism for transmission. That is, unless the person perceives the rumor as bearing some degree of truth, he or she is unlikely to pass it along to others. In situations of extreme anxiety, the rumormonger's critical judgment may be blunted so that credulity plays a less active role. It appears that rumors arise out of popular imagination to restore a sense of stability when events turn unpredictable and are psychologically threatening. They are likely to endure until underlying anxieties are alleviated, provided that the communications are credible and not easily verifiable.

Because of the potentially negative effects of certain rumors in personal, economic, and political realms, researchers have begun to investigate strategies for controlling their spread. For example, Oliviane Brodin (*Decisions Marketing*, 1995, *4*, 15–26) has developed a rumor control strategy emphasizing preventive measures for reducing risk factors. Nicholas DiFonzo, Prashant Bordia, and Rosnow (*Organizational Dynamics*, 1994, *23*, 4–62) have developed theoretically based guidelines for coping with potentially harmful rumors targeted against companies. As the capabilities of social communication networks are further advanced by modern technology, rumors will continue to proliferate as a social phenomenon, evidence of which has already become apparent on the Internet.

Bibliography

Bordia, P., & Rosnow, R. L. (1998). Rumor rest stops on the information highway: Transmission patterns in a computer-mediated rumor chain. *Human Communication Research*, *25*, 163–179. Examines implications of computer-mediated communication for rumor theory and reports a content analysis of rumor discussed in a chat group on the Internet.

Goodman, R. F., & Ben-Ze'ev, A. (Eds.). (1994). *Good gossip*. Lawrence, KS: University Press of Kansas. Collection of essays and research reports balancing the pejorative connotation of gossip against its social functions.

Kapferer, J.-N. (1990). *Rumors: Uses, interpretations, and images*. New Brunswick, NJ: Transaction Books. Revised English translation of the first edition of the author's *Rumeurs: Le plus vieux média du monde*, which examines many aspects of rumor from different perspectives. (Original work published 1987)

Knopf, T. A. (1975). *Rumors, race and riots*. New Brunswick, NJ: Transaction Books, 1975. Examines the role of rumors in racial disorders, critiques the major models of rumor, and puts forward policy recommendations.

Koenig, F. (1985). *Rumor in the marketplace: The social psychology of commercial hearsay*. Dover, MA: Auburn House. Analyzes the origin of marketplace rumors and the strategies used by American commercial enterprises to control them.

Morin, E. (1971). *Rumor in Orléans*. New York: Pantheon. Sociological study of a false rumor asserting that Jewish merchants in Orléans, France, had abducted young women and shipped them to foreign centers of prostitution.

Rosnow, R. L. (1980). Psychology of rumor reconsidered. *Psychological Bulletin*, *87*, 578–591. Review of Allport and Postman's theory of rumor and a proposal for an updated conceptualization emphasizing the role of anxiety and uncertainty.

Rosnow, R. L., & Fine, G. A. (1976). *Rumor and gossip: The social psychology of hearsay*. New York: Elsevier. Examines the psychological and sociological underpinnings of rumor and gossip and provides guidelines for rumor control centers.

Zivney, T. L., Bertin, W. J., & Torabzadeh, K. M. (1996). Overreaction to takeover speculation. *Quarterly Review of Economics and Finance*, *36*, 89–115. Examination of 871 takeover rumors published in two columns of the *Wall Street Journal* and the financial consequences of trading on these rumors.

Ralph L. Rosnow and Allan J. Kimmel

RURAL COMMUNITIES. Psychologists and other scholars of human development and behavior long have sought to identify unique characteristics of rural people. Inevitably these efforts to capture the nature of the rural mind or personality failed to find substantial or particularly meaningful differences between rural people and those who were raised or lived in urban settings. The differences appeared to lie in the environments in which they lived and worked.

Rural communities came to the attention of the profession of psychology largely in the community mental health center (CMHC) movement in the early 1960s. President John F. Kennedy initiated legislation to blanket the nation with mental health centers that were required to provide five essential services in defined "catchment areas." The catchment area concept resulted in the inclusion of rural areas along with urban settings for the governance and delivery of mental health care.

Since the development of CMHCs, a variety of rural initiatives have addressed the physical and mental health of rural people and communities. Special problems and opportunities, training, administration, and program development have received attention from practitioners and scholars in community mental health and community psychology. More generally, social and behavioral scientists have sought to move beyond the perspective of professional social, health, and mental health services to understand rural life and people more broadly. For example, the National Institute of Mental Health recently has expressed its concern for rural communities by instituting significant research initiatives that focus on epidemiology, service systems, contextual characteristics, and public policy.

The purpose of this article is to discuss the rural community from the perspective of psychology, both as a profession and as a discipline. The article is divided into three general areas. First is the nature and development of the rural community, with a focus on the role of psychology. Second are the social structures that are relevant to psychology. Third are directions and recommendations for additional research among rural communities and people.

Nature and Development of the Rural Community

Most laypersons and scholars have ideas about what are the characteristics of rural environments. These ideas, however, are highly stereotypical and usually based on people's various experiences. It is important, then, that social scientists and psychologists who study rurality and rural people initially address issues of definition.

Definitions of Rural. What does the term *rural* mean? A wide range of meanings have been posited in the conceptual and empirical literature. They range from specific definitions based on the demographic data representing precise constructs to soft, subjective impressions. The validity of these definitions, then, depends on the purpose for which they are intended. Researchers and policy makers must make precise delineations of populations and typically find the Metropolitan Statistical Areas (MSA) definition of "rural" useful. The consequences of this definition are concrete and meaningful in that inclusion may affect resources or eligibility for benefits. Persons wishing to characterize rural places or experiences or to capture the flavor of the rural experience likely will find the subjective definitions more useful. The consequences of inclusion or exclusion are not so dramatic.

Precise, demographically based definitions of rural communities typically are calculated with representative populations of counties. The MSA is defined by the U.S. Office of Management and Budget (OMB) as a county or group of contiguous counties having at least one city of 50,000 people or more or having an urbanized area of 50,000 people or more and a total population of at least 100,000. Nonmetropolitan areas are defined as all other counties. These definitions attempt to assess the relative size and economic patterns of communities and the relationships between population centers as a means of classification.

Subjective definitions typically involve comparisons between small rural areas and large urban settings. Frequently they are parodies of one another. Thomas Ford, in his thorough book on rural sociology, writes, "One does not have to be a particularly astute observer to detect that contemporary life in New York City and Los Angeles is still quite different from that in Bug Tussle, Oklahoma, or Gravel Switch, Kentucky" (1977, p. 3). This type of definition is important for characterizing rural communities and focusing on the relatively small number of persons who live there.

The controversy over definitions of "rural"— whether precise specifications are more accurate than global characterizations—undergirds the perception of variability of rural communities in the United States. The differences between communities that are considered rural by any criterion appear to be rooted in particular regions of the country. What is considered rural in New England is quite different from the definition in the Deep South or the Great Plains.

Thomas Ricketts and N. Johnson-Webb (1997) recall Maria Hewitt's (1989) distinction among the topologies based on four clusters of characteristics of places to provide a unifying perspective. The clusters include population size and density, proximity to and relationships with urban areas, degree of urbanization, and principal economic activity. The characteristics represent those that affect either public policy in health care financing and services or the structure and organization of health care delivery in rural places.

Development of Rural Communities. The historical development of rural communities is as diverse as the combination of factors that make them rural. It is likely that economic and geographical factors influence the development of most communities, but there is great variability among these factors. For example, the development of rural communities is heavily influenced by their agricultural potential and by the nature and expectations of the people who live and work there. This vital link between expectations and environment is revealed in O. E. Rolvaag's account (1929) of Norwegian settlers moving across southern Minnesota into South Dakota, in which four families searched for the proper environment in which to survive and even thrive. The topography of the land, fertility of the soil, presence of water, and length of the seasons were critically important to the development of agriculture and, eventually, to the survival of the people who inhabited the communities. Later, according to Frederick Luebke (1988), transportation systems heavily influenced community development, as in the Great Plains' development with the coming of the railroads from the East and West to haul grain to markets.

The variability that characterizes the definitions of rural areas also is demonstrated in the dynamics, population configurations, and ethnic composition of these communities. While there certainly are consistencies among communities in the United States, there are no data suggesting strong commonalities across the various regions.

Psychology in Rural Settings. Psychology and psychologists have played a role in rural communities in recent years. The primary focus of psychology has been in the development of community mental health centers. At the national level, psychologists were one of the four core groups of professionals that federally funded community mental health centers (CMHCs) were required to employ. The main focus of psychological work was clinical, but psychologists quickly moved into other roles as well, including administrator, program evaluator, and educator. Other initiatives, such as Head Start and community action programs, utilized psychologists in a broad range of roles that frequently were specific to particular communities. Some of the functions carried out by psychologists focused on clinical service and patient care. Others broadened the perspective of psychologists and required them to work on problems of the larger community, particularly in the design and evaluation of prevention programs. The concept of the rural psychologist as a generalist developed from the experience of functioning in several broad roles within public health, mental health, social service, criminal justice, and community action programs.

In recent years, psychologists in rural communities have become involved in behavioral health and primary care settings. Collaboration between psychologists and traditional primary health-care providers has become a common model of service delivery in rural communities. As psychologists become more experienced and valued in primary care settings, models of collaboration develop between persons with expertise in behavioral health and those in physical health that benefit the consumers of health services.

Rural Social Structures Relevant to Psychology

Viable communities have social structures that are relevant to research and practice in psychology. Those structures in rural communities frequently include community mental health centers, churches and other religious organizations, and the agricultural extension service.

Community Mental Health Centers. The first institution to attend systematically to the mental health needs of rural people and communities, CMHCs were originally charged with the responsibility of providing five essential services to a specified catchment area: inpatient care, outpatient care, partial hospitalization, consultation and education, and 24-hour emergency services. Each center, governed by a local board, was to employ a competent staff that included at least a psychiatrist, psychologist, mental health nurse, and social worker, among other professionals, and to develop and implement plans to provide these services to its area. Evaluation of the service programs was mandated. These centers developed in virtually every state in the United States throughout the 1960s and 1970s until 1980, when President Jimmy Carter's Mental

Health Systems Act died because of lack of appropriations after Ronald Reagan became president.

Although these centers have continued to develop, they take different shapes in various states, but they still typically are responsible for service areas that include rural environments. Because the bulk of the responsibility for mental health service delivery has been transferred to state governments, the population served by community centers has shifted from the general population to the seriously mentally ill. It appears that the shifts in funding bases and service populations have reduced the responsiveness of CMHCs to community needs. The impact of this apparent shift on rural environments is unknown.

Religious Institutions. A second significant social structure relevant for psychology and psychologists in rural environments is religious institutions. However, although religious institutions remain important components of rural society, Everett Rogers (1988) points out that they are resistant to social change. This resistance sometimes hampers the acceptance of psychologists and other mental health professionals by the communities. When I was developing a community mental health center in rural southern Mississippi in the early 1970s, the pastor of a large local Southern Baptist church frequently urged his parishioners to avoid "godless psychiatrists and psychologists" and to take their troubles to God. Subsequent conversations with this man revealed his belief that the mental health professionals interfered with the relationship between God and people and that mental health problems were, in fact, spiritual in nature.

This pastor was protecting the role that the clergy had possessed for centuries before mental health professionals burst on the scene. For many years, clergy have been involved with physicians in the care of troubled people and have borne the responsibility of counseling individuals and families in the context of faith. Frequently, problems that we now interpret as mental health matters were thought of as spiritual concerns and were considered the proper domain of clergy and the church.

Given the prominence of the church in rural America, there is little doubt of the importance of religion in the sustenance of communities and in the psychological care of their residents. There appears, however, to be a less collaborative spirit between churches and mental health professionals in rural communities. The growing number of mental health professionals entering the market results in a tendency to interpret problems as psychological instead of spiritual. In the broader American society, the patterns of physical health and mental health financing, the increase in the range of disorders that are considered to be mental health problems, and the large number of providers maintain any gap that exists between religious institutions and mental health professionals. In rural communities, where there are likely to be fewer providers, cooperation and collaboration between religious institutions and mental health providers could benefit consumers of physical health and mental health care services.

County Extension Services. County extension agents, typically persons trained in agricultural techniques, have been placed in virtually every rural county in the United States. These agents, working through the agricultural extension service located in state land grant universities, represent an effort to modernize agricultural practices. Many state extension services also provide leadership in youth development and home economics. These workers assist rural families in a growing range of areas. Financial management, homemaking, parenting, and other practical activities also are offered to families through the services of extension agencies.

Everett Rogers observes that the agricultural extension services in the United States have been "highly effective" and successful in bringing agricultural technologies to farmers. In his review of the agricultural extension service, Rogers identifies the reasons for its success. These reasons include, but are not limited to, realistic budgets, technical competence, and a high degree of client contact. The extension agencies also have assumed an increasing role in assisting the nonfarm population, which is a growing component of the rural population.

In the early 1990s a new national extension initiative began. Entitled "Decisions for Health," it recognized the need to improve health-related education and resources in rural America. Numerous attempts have been made to adapt the agricultural extension model to technology transfer in other disciplines. In the field of mental and behavioral health, for example, the University of Florida's College of Health Professionals and the Institute of Food and Agricultural Sciences proposed to create the National Rural Behavioral Health Center. According to Sam Sears, Garret Evans, and Nathan Perry (1998), the center has three objectives: (1) to develop and evaluate community-based and behavioral health promotion programs that can be offered through cooperative extension services across the country; (2) to demonstrate and deliver innovative behavioral health programs designed specifically for rural communities; and (3) to train extension service employees from across the country to deliver behavioral health programs developed, demonstrated, and evaluated by the center.

In the Florida program's review of available extension services, success was noted. However, it is necessary to stress the importance of continued efforts to integrate the work of rural health service providers.

The unique challenges of the rural environment and rural psychology should be taken into account and addressed. Cooperative extension services have a long history of collaborating with community agencies to provide valuable educational programs in rural areas. To ensure that the goal of improving access to quality care for rural Americans is met, coordinated and cooperative arrangements will be helpful.

Psychological Research in Rural Communities

Psychological research in rural environments has focused on epidemiology, differences between rural and urban environments, health and mental health service systems, and the human resources required to provide care for rural people. In the last few years, much more quantitative, empirical research has occurred, resulting in the development of considerable new knowledge about rural people, their needs, and the services that must be provided to sustain them. Of equal importance, however, is the qualitative work of several scholars, including Emily Martinez-Brawley and Janet Fitchen. This work paints a more complete portrait of rural America by giving people's interpretation of their experiences of living and working away from population centers, enmeshed in families, and surviving without many of the amenities to which much of the American population has become accustomed. It is important that both quantitative and qualitative approaches be taken to research in rural America.

It is important to note that no single, consistent theoretical perspective characterizes research in rural health, mental health, or social development. This is probably because of the wide variety of disciplines that engage in rural research. Without a consistent theoretical perspective, however, our ability to gain useful knowledge is severely limited.

A potentially important theoretical approach from which to study rural people and communities, focusing on fostering the "competent community," is the behavioral-ecological perspective. A. M. Jeger and R. S. Slotnick use the competent community as a base and write, "Community enhancement for purposes of promoting the competent community is accomplished by providing environmental resources and opportunities whereby more people will be able to engage in a broader array of behaviors, or to choose from a greater number of alternatives—thereby increasing their freedom. Thus we have the beginnings of a notion of 'environmental repertoire' parallel to the individualistic notion of a behavioral repertoire" (1982, p. 34). The relationship between the psychological sense of community and the competent community is interactive; one strengthens the other. This theoretical approach can underlie the study of individuals, families and other groups, and the larger environment to develop greater knowledge that will benefit scholars, policy makers, and providers of physical health, mental health, and social services.

Both current and future psychological research involving rural communities and people must consider the enormous changes taking place in rural society and small communities. The impact of these structural changes on individuals and families is largely unknown. For example, like other parts of the country, rural America is aging rapidly. Dwindling public resources in many rural counties raise serious questions about how elderly persons will fare. There is also increasing evidence of the spread of adolescent gangs from urban settings to rural communities, presenting new challenges for law enforcement. The presence of street drugs in rural communities also presents further challenges for public providers of health and mental health care, as well as educational systems. In many rural areas, such as the Mississippi Delta, the public education system is deteriorating and teacher recruitment and retention are becoming almost impossible. The pervasive poverty characteristic of many rural areas in the country infects young and old, threatening the workforce with economic devastation.

In many ways, rural communities are excellent areas for meaningful psychological research. The development of individuals and communities can be studied in a relatively constant context. The impact of prevention and intervention programs in physical health, mental health, and social disorders can be investigated. The interaction of indigenous helpers and professional providers can be studied to understand collaborative relationships and their relative effectiveness. Clearly, rural environments offer a substantial opportunity for greater understanding of human behavior within specific contexts.

Bibliography

Childs, A. W., & Melton, G. B. (Eds.). (1983). *Rural psychology*. New York: Plenum Press.

Fitchen, J. M. (1981). *Poverty in rural America: A case study*. Boulder, CO: Westview Press.

Fitchen, J. M. (1991). *Endangered spaces, enduring places: Change, identity, and survival in rural America*. Boulder, CO: Westview Press.

Flax, J., Wagenfeld, M. O., Ivens, R., & Weiss, R. (1979). *Mental health and rural America: An overview and annotated bibliography* (DHEW Pub. No. (ADM) 78–753). Washington, DC: U.S. Government Printing Office.

Ford, T. (1977). *Rural U.S.A.* Ames, IA.

Groves, E. (1922). *The rural mind and social welfare*. Chicago: University of Chicago Press.

Harrington, M. (1962). *The other America: Poverty in the United States*. Baltimore: Penguin Books.

Hewitt, M. (1989). Defining "rural" areas: Impact on health care policy and research. Health Program Office of Technology Assessment, Congress of the United States, Washington, DC, 20510-8025.

Hollister, W. G., Edgerton, J. W., & Hunter, R. H. (1985). *Alternative services in community mental health: Programs and processes*. Chapel Hill: University of North Carolina Press.

Jeger, A. M., & Slotnick, R. S. (1982). *Community mental health and behavioral ecology*. New York:

Keller, P. A., & Murray, J. D. (1982). *Handbook of rural community mental health*. New York: Human Sciences Press.

Luebke, F. (1988). Time, place, and culture in Nebraska history. *Nebraska History*, 69(4), 150–168.

Martinez-Brawley, E. (1990). *Perspectives on the small community: Humanistic views for practitioners*. Silver Springs, MD: National Association of Social Work Press.

Ricketts, T. C., & Johnson-Webb, K. D. (1997). *What is "rural" and how to measure "rurality": A focus on health care delivery and health policy*. North Carolina Rural Health Research and Policy Analysis Center, Chapel Hill, NC. Technical Issues Paper prepared for the Federal Office of Rural Health Policy, Health Resources and Services Administration, Washington.

Rogers, E. M. (1988). The intellectual foundation and history of the Agricultural Extension Model. *Knowledge: Creation, diffusion, utilization*, 9(4), 492–510.

Rolvaag, O. E. (1929). *Giants in the earth*. New York: Harper & Brothers.

Sears, S., Evans, G., & Perry, N. (1998). *Professional Psychology*, 29, 504–507.

Wagenfeld, M., Murray, J. D., Mohatt, D. F., & DeBruyn, J. C. (1993). *Mental health and rural America: 1980–1993: An overview and annotated bibliography*. Washington, DC: U.S. Department of Health and Human Services.

David S. Hargrove

RUSH, BENJAMIN (1746–1813), American physician, humanitarian reformer, educator, and nationalist. Benjamin Rush, a visible force in American life, served as a member of the Continental Congress and signer of the Declaration of Independence. He worked briefly as surgeon general in the Continental army and as treasurer of the U.S. Mint from 1797 to 1813. Rush had a multifaceted and influential career in public service, but is remembered primarily for contributions to medical education and for pioneering work on psychiatric and psychological problems.

Rush, born in Byberry, Pennsylvania, on 4 January 1746, was the fourth of the seven children of John Rush and Susanna Hall Harvey Rush. Though his father died when Benjamin was 6, his resourceful mother liquidated the family assets, purchased a grocery business, and attended to rearing and educating her children. At 15 Rush graduated from the College of New Jersey (now Princeton University). Following a lengthy medical apprenticeship with a practicing physician, Rush entered medical school at the University of Edinburgh and completed an M.D. degree in 1768. He was elected professor of chemistry at the College of Philadelphia in 1769.

Rush lectured and wrote extensively on psychological and psychiatric topics. He is commonly regarded as the founder of American psychiatry, and his *Medical Inquiries and Observations on the Diseases of the Mind* (1812) is the first American psychiatric textbook. Rush coined the term *phrenology*, literally science of the mind, and stressed the importance of psychological topics such as emotion, memory, dreams, and perception in medical education. Rush's treatments for mental illness included unfortunate practices of bleeding, purging, and some forms of shock such as cold showers, but he also practiced enlightened treatments such as proper diet, warm baths, exercise, meaningful employment, and music therapy. He was one of the first to suggest "time out" as opposed to corporal punishment for inappropriate behaviors.

Because of his deeply held religious views Rush has sometimes been regarded as a dualist, but his persistent efforts to ground psychology in physiology suggest a pragmatic materialism. He was strongly influenced by the physiological psychology of David Hartley and the empirical philosophy of John Locke. Rush believed in mental faculties, which for him meant "capacities," but he had serious doubts about the faculty psychology of Franz Joseph Gall, who attempted to demonstrate a correspondence between cranial characteristics and mental strengths and weaknesses.

In addition to his work as a teacher and physician, Rush was an activist in numerous reform movements. He was a strong advocate for public education for both sexes, though he shared many eighteenth-century misconceptions about women's abilities. Rush was deeply dedicated to the medical and emotional needs of the poor, often treating them without payment. He was militantly opposed to slavery, public punishment, capital punishment, and the abuse of drugs such as tobacco and alcohol. Rush is not remembered for any major innovation in psychology, but like his French contemporary Philippe Pinel, he was a prominent reformer instrumental in shaping more informed and humane social attitudes toward the mentally ill.

Bibliography

Carlson, E. T., Wollock, J. L., & Noel, P. S. (Eds.). (1981). *Benjamin Rush's lectures on the mind.* Philadelphia: American Philosophical Society. A collection of edited and annotated lectures delivered to medical students by Benjamin Rush. The editors provide highly informed and helpful introductions.

Corner, G. W. (Ed.). (1948). *The autobiography of Benjamin Rush: His "Travels through life" together with his "Commonplace book" for 1789–1813.* Princeton, NJ: Princeton University Press. A lightly edited version of Rush's autobiography preceded by an introduction. The autobiography is followed by Rush's diarylike *Commonplace Book*, consisting of brief thoughts and reflections on people, and topics such as religion, death, health, and morals.

Fox, C. G., Miller, G. L., & Miller, J. C. (Eds.). (1996). *Benjamin Rush, M.D.: A bibliographic guide.* Westport, CT: Greenwood Press. A complete guide to Rush's publications along with an extensive collection of secondary sources.

Wayne Viney

RUSSIA AND THE FORMER SOVIET REPUBLICS.

The 200-year story of psychology in Russia and the former Soviet republics is a complex and fascinating one. It began under the czars and continued through the Soviet period, and on to the present day.

Psychology and the Russian Empire

Peter the Great's reign (1689–1725) brought enormous social changes throughout Russia. Bringing the Russian Orthodox Church directly under his control, creating a conscript army and navy, he went on to conquer enormous areas of territory along the Baltic Sea in the north and the Black Sea in the south. His wholesale administrative changes at both the central and local government levels and his founding of modern industries in Russia brought the country to the point where under Catherine the Great's equally despotic rule it became the leading force in Europe. It was during the eighteenth century that Russia also began its two-century long expansion into the territories of the Ottoman Empire. It was this period of expansion, change, and political power, albeit under a repressive domestic regime in the Russian Empire, that gave birth to some notable scientific, literary, and educational work. The presiding genius of the Russian Enlightenment was Mikhail Vasilyevich Lomonosov (1711–1765), whom the Russian poet Pushkin later described as the original champion of the Enlightenment in Russia: "He founded the first university, he was our university." His approach to reality was imbued with the spirit of intellectual inquiry and had more in common with modern scientific views than it did with the Russia of the eighteenth century. In addition to his view of human psychological forces as having a physical origin, he anticipated modern theories on the nature of heat and the kinetic theory of gases and did innovative work in chemistry, physics, geography, and geology. He wrote a Russian grammar, the first of its kind, and his innovative poetry changed the face of Russian poetry. In terms of psychology, he focused on the here-and-now of human lives, searching for the causes of social unrest. The journalist and publisher Nikolai Ivanovich Novikov (1744–1818) published innumerable works on the widespread social injustice of the period, activities which were eventually to lead to his imprisonment. This work derived from his belief that human beings were the central figures in the world, and his publications were intended to educate the public about ongoing issues, because he saw better education as the only solution to the nation's domestic social and economic problems.

In Ukraine, Belorus, and Lithuania from the sixteenth to the eighteenth centuries, philosophy and psychology were taught at the Brothers' Schools, educational institutions for middle- and upper-class students. Gregory Savvich Skovoroda (1722–1792), was a contemporary of Lomonosov. Though born in Ukraine, he was described as the first Russian philosopher. His views were similar to those of contemporary Christian existentialists, and they were very influential at the time, particularly his view of the "two natures" of human beings: the visible, which was created by God, and the invisible, which was God. Skovoroda divided the world into three parts: the macrocosm, the microcosm, and the symbolic (Bible), but his was primarily a person-centered doctrine. He believed that people struggle against negative forces (evil) within them, but that to do this successfully they must find the work that is truly theirs to do and live in harmony with nature. He saw the individual's self-knowledge as being essential for the improvement of the society as a whole. He wrote: "What is the heart if not the soul?" and understood empirical man as the "dream" of the true or spiritual man.

During the second half of the nineteenth century, the natural sciences, including psychology, developed rapidly in the Russian Empire. Some popular psychological theories were influenced by the natural materialist approach (A. Veselovsky, 1838–1906; A. Potebnia, a minor figure, 1835–1891; K. Kavelin, 1818–1885). I. M. Sechenov (1829–1905), who was the author, amongst other works, of *Reflexes of the Brain* (1863), sought to discover whether voluntary movements are actually reflex actions or whether there is a discrepancy between stimulus and evoked response. He developed a view of psychological processes that involved signal self-regulation and feedback. His work in studying psychology objectively as a science led to Ivan Pavlov's work on behavior and also eventually to the American behaviorist movement. At various times he worked with Helmholz, Brücke, and Claude Benard. His was a materialist view in which all human psychology was influenced by the environment. Sechenov is most often remembered today for his discovery of central inhibition.

K. Ushinski (1824–1870) saw the human emotional world as impelling the individual to action. His work, which lay somewhat outside the mainstream, understood emotions to be the basis of any action. Experimental psychology was championed by P. Urkevich (1826–1874). He saw psychological phenomena as having a material existence which made them readily comprehensible to the person who was experiencing them.

The first experimental psychology laboratories in Russia were established by N. Langue (1858–1921) in Odessa, Ukraine; A. Tokarski at Moscow University; P. Kovalevski (1849–1923) at Kharkiv, Ukraine; V. M. Bekhterev (1857–1927) at Kazan University, Tatarstan, and later St. Petersburg; and A. Lazurski (1874–1917). The Moscow Institute of Experimental Psychology was founded by Chelpanov (1862–1936), author of *Introduction to Experimental Psychology*, which was based on the courses he taught at the Institute. The Moscow Institute became the center for experimental psychology in Russia attracting such well-known Soviet psychologists as K. Kornilov, N. Rybnikov, B. Severnyiu, V. Ekzempliarsky, A. A. Smirnov (who studied the individual's relations to groups and also aspects of memory), and N. I. Zhinkin (who wrote on speech, including the psychophysics of speech sounds and the mechanisms of speech).

It was in Russia that behaviorism was first developed, and as noted above, I. M. Sechenov did major work which in turn led to the work of Pavlov, Bekhterev, A. Ukhtomsky, and the American behaviorist school. Thus, the dyad, soul-body, brain-consciousness became the triad organism-behavior-consciousness (psyche). Behaviorism was interdisciplinary in its origins pointing to the integral nature of mind-body. Ivan Pavlov (1849–1936) at the head of a large scientific team, focused for the most part on the conditioned reflex. The ways in which the organism acquires new behavioral forms and reconstructs established ones was the main focus of Pavlov's experiments.

V. M. Bekhterev, who wrote *The Foundations of the Science of Brain Functions*, developed objective psychology as the psychology of behavior, but also included consciousness as a legitimate psychological topic. One of Bekhterev's central ideas was that the organism's manifestations of its separate existence acquire features of mechanical causality and biological direction which involve the whole organism. The organism seeks to defend and affirm its existence in the course of struggling with changing environmental conditions.

A. Ukhtomsky (1875–1942) believed that it was possible to interpret the organism's behavior by means of the unity of its physiological and psychological manifestations, an idea that was to be important for both psychology and physiology. K. Kornilov (1879–1957) tried to overcome the confrontation between the psychology of consciousness (the subjective method) and the successive manifestations of behaviorism (the objective method).

Marxist ideology affected the development of psychology in the late nineteenth and early twentieth centuries, but the full impact did not take place until the Bolshevik Revolution. However, G. Chelpanov and G. Shpet (1879–1937), who was a follower of the German philosopher Edmund Husserl, formulated a new psychology that differed from both Marxist psychology and behavioral science.

The Development of Soviet Psychology

This was a period of major upheavals in the Soviet Union that affected every aspect of life.

The Development of Communist/Soviet Psychology (Social, Labor, Sports, and Military Psychology): 1917–1945. S. L. Rubinshtein (1889–1960) was a methodologist whose new methodological alternatives were based on an extensive analysis of the innate logic of psychology. It was Rubinshtein who elaborated the fundamental principles of Soviet psychology. He defined the principles of the unity of consciousness and physiology as well as of personality and development. Implementation of these principles were instrumental in enabling Rubinshtein's followers to create a new dialectical and materialistic understanding of psychology as detailed in a variety of works, such as *Fundamentals of General Psychology* (1940, 1946), *Being and Consciousness* (1957), *On Thinking and Methods of Studying it* (1958), *Principles of Psychological Development* (1959), and *Problems of General Psychology* (1973). During this period research took place in changes from somatization to psychological responses to events, visual and olfactory responses. Set theory was developed in Georgia, bringing an original approach to personality processes both conscious and unconscious. Habit formation was studied as were memory and thought processes. The concept of ability and its development were studied and became the basis for theories regarding the formation of individual psychological peculiarities. There was increased interest in Anton Semyonovich Makarenko's (1888–1939) approach to personality development on collectives. He had previously organized a home for orphans of the 1917 revolution, and his theories emphasized the importance of the collective in educating young people, along with physical labor and firm discipline.

Industrial psychology and psychometrics received a major research effort in the Soviet Union in the 1920s and 1930s. The focus was primarily on streamlining both technical school and professional education; developing methods to ensure that production lines operated at maximum efficiency; and working to prevent job-related injuries. Psychological principles were applied to the specialized problems arising in both the

army and air force. Psychometric laboratories were created in many Soviet cities. The journal *Soviet Psychometrics* was published between 1928 and 1934. In 1931 the seventh International Psychometrics Conference took place in Moscow. Sports psychology also received attention.

Within the Soviet military interest in the sociopsychological aspects of military life, along with the use of psychology in warfare began to develop between 1918 and 1920. The management of soldiers and their psychological state before and after battle, the psychological state of officers and men during battle, the overcoming of fear during combat, and group psychology all received attention.

During World War II, psychologists studied anti-aircraft camouflage, field reconnaissance, and the rehabilitation of soldiers suffering from battle fatigue or, as it is now known, posttraumatic stress disorder. Methods for counteracting snow blindness, increasing observational efficiency at air defense posts; speeding up adaptation to darkness; increasing visual and auditory sensitivity; accurate visual measurement of distance; training in quickly distinguishing moving objects, and methods of camouflaging sound were all studied.

Western educational practices became popular in Russia in the early twentieth century. This was the time when V. M. Bekhterev established the Educational Institute. Following the 1917 revolution, the educational movement expanded rapidly, and a New Marxist child psychology was developed in both sociogenetic (A. Zalkind, 1888–1936) and biogenetic (P. Blonsky, 1884–1941) directions. The task of Soviet education during this period was seen as developing a new person for the new society. While Soviet education blossomed during the 1920s and 1930s, in the early 1930s criticism arose regarding approaches to developing a creative personality along with the amount of individual attention given to each child. This was the period when the totalitarian regime needed *screw-bolts*, to use Stalin's term; people were to be small parts of the massive collective machine. In 1936, the Central Committee of the Communist Party passed a resolution berating the Soviet educational system for its alleged errors. By 1943, the political climate had changed sufficiently for the Academy of Educational Sciences to be established.

During the 1920s and 1930s, there were many psychosociological investigations of groups and collectives. V. M. Bekhterev, Z. Zaluzny, and B. Beliaev, all of whom were reflexologists, undertook extensive classification of collectives. Bekhterev determined the influence of education and sexual differences on group activity. The great Soviet educator, A. Makarenko (1888–1939) developed a classification system for groups: (1) primary group—family, class, Young Pioneer detachment; (2) secondary or broader group—school, work enterprise, military unit. He distinguished between the group's internal, local, and more distant goals involving the greater society.

Lev Vygotsky (1896–1934) was the most significant figure in the development of Soviet psychology. His work at the Institute of Psychology in Moscow from 1924 to 1934 involved the expansion of his ideas on cognitive development. Arguing that language was the central symbolic tool in society, Vygotsky emphasized social, cultural, and historical factors in cognition. His seminal work on psycholinguistics, *Thought and Language*, was published in 1934. Some of the most distinguished Soviet psychologists of the period worked with Vygotsky, including A. N. Leontiev, A. R. Luria (who studied the ways in which damage to specific parts of the brain affects behavior, mental retardation, and memory processes), A. N. Zaporozhets, D. Elkonin (who specialized in the psychology of the preschool child), L. I. Bozovich, and L. S. Slavina.

A. N. Leontiev (1903–1979) developed a thesis that physical activity lies at the basis of all psychological functions. Initially following Vygotsky, he later embraced Basov's ideas of the morphology of activity and proposed an organization of activity and transformational schema at various levels: evolution in the non-human world; in human society and history; and in the individual's own development. Leontiev emphasized that activity has a special integrity, its components being motives, purposes, and actions. The structural schema, activity–action–operation–psychophysiological functions, proposed by Leontiev in connection with the structure of the motivational sphere, was the basis for many investigations of perception, thought processes, memory, and attention; consciousness analysis was made up of meaning, sense, and sensate substance.

The Development of Experimental Psychology, Psychopathology, and Neuropsychology from 1917 to 1945

In the 1930s, extensive study of psychopathology involved research on the disintegration of the highest psychological functions and the effect of this disintegration on the developmental stages. Some of the researchers involved in this work were F. Bassin, R. Boskis, B. V. Zeigarnik, and A. R. Luria, who in addition to his other work was a pioneer in the study of neuropsychology for which he developed a phenomenological base. N. Ladigina-Cots, G. Roginsky, and N. Voitonis developed comparative psychology during the 1930s.

Soviet Psychology During the Cold War

Like earlier rulers from tsarist times onwards, Stalin intervened directly in psychology by ordering what came to be called "Pavlov's Session," a joint meeting of the Medical Sciences of the U.S.S.R. and the Academy of Sciences of the U.S.S.R. in 1950. This meeting made Pavlov's theories official dogma, that is, psychology was only to be based on physiology. However, despite this intervention psychology continued to develop in the Soviet Union.

In the 1950s and 1960s the main centers for the development of psychology were the Moscow Institute of Psychology (Academy of Pedagogical Sciences; directed by A. A. Smirnov); the department of psychology at Moscow University (A. N. Leontiev, chair); the department of psychology at Leningrad University (B. G. Ananiev, chair); the Institute of Psychology, Ukrainian Soviet Republic, at Kiev (G. Kostuk, director); and in Georgia, the D. Uznadze Institute of Psychology in Tbilisi, of which A. Prangishvili was director. *The Questions of Psychology* began publication in 1955 and the *Psychology Bulletin* was published by Moscow University. In 1971, the Moscow Institute of Psychology (now called the Institute of Psychology of the Russian Academy of Sciences) was founded with B. Lomov as director. *The Psychological Magazine* began publication in 1980.

The Development of Communist/Soviet Psychology (Industrial, Sports, and Military Psychology). As noted earlier, S. Rubinshtein developed the principle of unity of consciousness and activity which became a central theme in theoretical and experimental investigations. Rubinshtein's followers worked to demonstrate the unique nature of the human psyche and to overcome "idealism" and "naturalism" in understanding the psyche. The work of Rubinshtein, B. Ananiev, and others led to the development of a systems approach by B. Lomov, A. Krylov, and V. Rubahin. A division was made between psyche and personality. A. Brushlinsky analyzed thinking processes from a philosophical-psychological viewpoint in terms of the processes leading to prognostication. L. Ancyferova developed a theory of thinking processes as reflecting an analytic-synthetic activity, using a systems approach to reveal the regularities of psychic development in phylogenesis, the sociohistorical process in ontogenesis.

The 1960s and 1970s saw the development of a Marxist-Leninist view of social relations; the correlation between individual and social consciousness; and an understanding of personality as the totality of social relations. The processes of human communication and interactions were studied along with the psychological characteristics of social groups and personality psychology. The main task during the Soviet period was to promote control over social processes. E. S. Kuzmin, who experimented with social psychology, prepared an extensive analysis which systematized the main theoretical and practical results of social-psychological research. Social psychologists studied personality characteristics, the basic criteria for defining the stages of the socialization of the personality, a model of the mechanisms of personal disposition, and the mechanisms of the formation of social opinion. They also studied the psychology of small groups, the social influence of various leaders, the psychology of communication, personal influence in communication, psychological issues in marriage and the family, preparing people for leadership roles, elimination of social deprivation, and the reeducation of those with deviant behavior.

The end of World War II brought further development of military psychology and further analysis of psychological issues relating to combat. In the context of combat, such topics were analyzed as courage, initiative on the part of individuals in complex situations; the stages of fear, fearlessness, and panic. B. Teplov studied the psychological processes of leadership, and further studies included the processes of topographic map reading, the psychological selection of pilots, psychological pressures resulting from operating military equipment and deciphering aerial photographs.

New directions took place in industrial psychology, including engineering, aviation, aerospace, ergonomics, and management. B. Lomov (1927–1977) was the major force in this area of man-machine interactions which continued to be a central field of study.

Child Development and Educational Psychology

Work deriving from Vygotsky, Luria, and Leontiev continued. In the 1950s V. Ya. Galperin's theory of stages in the development of mental acts was described, work that was sometimes compared to that of Harry Harlow. A new system of education was developed by L. Zankov and his coworkers to raise the developmental level of elementary school children. New principles of student learning processes were developed by Elkoinin which led to the creation of experimental educational programs for Soviet schools. Elkonin also researched the theory of children's games and many other aspects of child development. Other researchers studied memory-age issues, speech and mental ability, character development, and gifted students. In educational psychology, grammar, speech development, teaching foreign languages, mathematics, and the development of imagination, were some of the topics studied. Vygotsky's view that education in itself furthers development continued to be a major motivating theme in educational psychology.

B. Ananiev (1907–1972) developed K. Ushinsky's ideas about the creation of educational anthropology as a science and suggested the idea of two types of relations between development and environment (i.e., family dynamics): homogeneous and heterogeneous. According to Ananiev, development of the human psyche is determined by the individual's social experience which acts upon the learning processes. Work, cognition, and communication were held to influence all stages of personality development.

In the 1970s considerable success was achieved in researching learning processes in preschool children, education, and psychological development. The influence of children's activities on development of sensory processes, the development of erratic behavior, speech development, prelogical thinking in preschoolers, and diagnostic methods regarding mental development in preschool children. Elkonin and Amonashvili's research on the psychological processes of 6-year-olds is of particular interest.

The Development of Experimental Psychology, Neuropsychology, Pathopsychology, and Psychophysiology. New approaches to studying thought processes were developed, much of the research emanating from Moscow University under the leadership of O. Tihomirov. The motives behind cognitive activity and their structural influence on the processes involved in solving mental tasks, and the mechanisms behind the creation of goals were also studied. A historical approach, led by A. R. Luria and P. Tulviste was founded on Vygotsky's cultural-historical concept. A cognitive approach was popular at the Kiev Institute of Psychology with investigations guided by J. Bruner's strategic approach. A new interdisciplinary scientific discipline, cognitology, was developed by B. Velychkovsky in the early 1980s.

V. Pushkin analyzed basic cybernetics concepts in relation to the psychology of thought processes. He also considered the self-regulatory process of acquiring knowledge and developed a model of dynamic systems control and analytic thought geometry. Much work was done on operational thinking, and in the early 1970s V. Pushkin successfully collaborated with experts in cybernetics on thought processes and automata.

O. Tihomirov and his colleagues studied artificial intelligence in relation to the psychology of thinking processes, emotion, motivation, and goals in relation to human cognitive activity. A. Brushlinsky studied the theoretical basis for artificial intelligence. V. Bondarovskaya applied psychological processes to computer issues. New approaches to understanding the mechanisms of creativity were proposed by Ia. Ponomarev and D. Bogiavlenskaya (who developed a diagnostic method for assessing creativity).

In psycholinguistics, A. Sokolov studied the psychological and physiological processes of mental activity.

In the 1960s and 1970s, A. R. Luria and his colleagues studied cortical functions, frontal lobe activity and the regulation of psychical processes, the neuropsychological structure of problem solving, and language and consciousness, among other topics. B. Zeigharnik (1900–1988) and her colleagues studied problems associated with cognitive activity in the pathology of mental diseases. She was the first researcher in Soviet psychology to study the pathology of personality, collaborating with A. R. Luria, G. Suhareva, and A. Shmanian on a number of papers relating to psychopathology.

E. Sokolov took an interdisciplinary approach to psychical processes and the mechanics of neurons combining psychology, neurophysiology, and cybernetics. Information on cell functioning was obtained by means of animal experimentation. The man-neuron model was used, in particular analysis of macroreactions by means of the poly effector registration method. This enabled researchers to see behind the separate reactions to those functional systems of which the reactions are components. Computers were widely used in psychophysiological experiments.

The Development of Russian Psychology After the End of the Cold War

In 1987 a meeting of the Soviet Psychological Society declared that there were revolutionary changes in Soviet life, that new ideas were on the horizon, and that old psychological stereotypes were withering away. It was emphasized that the level of psychological research and productivity in clinical psychology must be raised. One of the most important events was the rapid publication of psychological writing that had been censored under the previous regime. Joint projects with other countries and the opening of new psychological institutes took place. Works by distinguished Russian philosophers and psychologists from earlier eras that had long been out of print again became available.

There was renewed interest in ethnopsychology (V. Petrenko) and political psychology (L. Gozman). L. Gumilev's works were published. The theory and experimental methods of psychosemantics were developed. V. Petrenko and his colleagues studied the categories of social and individual consciousness, language and consciousness.

There was increased interest in partner and family relationships, the development of children's creativity, children's mental development, and children's neuroses. Institutions were established for training clinical psychologists; for example, the Training Institute in St. Petersburg and the Institute of Group and Family Psychotherapy in Moscow. V. Lepsky studied reflexive mechanisms of consciousness and behavioral manipulation; the realization of cognitive and communication goals as a result of using the Internet (A. Voiskunsky). Most important of all, new psychology journals were established: *Archetype, Family Psychology and Family Therapy, The Practical Psychologist's Magazine, The Psychologist in the Kindergarten.*

The Development of Psychology in the Countries of the Former Soviet Union

For the most part, the countries which made up the former Soviet Union were first annexed by Peter the Great in the early eighteenth century. There was ongoing activity in psychology in most of these countries, which obviously fluctuated in intensity in the course of two world wars and ongoing political repression.

Ukraine. From the beginning of the twentieth century, a number of established figures in science worked in Ukraine as both researchers and university professors. These scientists included some who have already been mentioned here: A. Potebnia, N. Lange, G. Rossolimo, S. Ananjin, G. Chelpanov, and I. Sykorski did research and also taught. In the Soviet period, A. Makarenko, G. Kostuk, A. Zaluzni, A. Raevski, and D. Nikolenko did significant work. The Kharkiv (Kharkov in Russian) Psychological Institute was founded, and A. N. Leontiev, A. R. Luria, P. Galperin, A. Zaporozethz, and L. Bozovitz, worked there during the 1930s. The Labor Institute was established in 1921 in Kharkov, providing a base for the work of F. Dunaevski, U. Syrkin, P. Rubinshtein, and Z. Chukmarev). The Institute of Psychology of the Ukrainian Education Ministry was founded in 1945.

G. Kostuk's (1899–1982) work is well known, both in the development of a theory and methodology of psychological science along with child development psychology (the correlation between child rearing and education). He is noted for works on the psychology of thought (1951) and essays on the history of psychology in Ukraine (1959). Many of Kostuk's students and colleagues still work at the Kiev Institute of Psychology, which is now a part of the Ukrainian Academy of Pedagogical Sciences.

Psychological Associations in Ukraine. These organizations include the Psychological Society of Ukraine, Ukrainian Association of Professional Psychologists, Kiev Association of Practical Psychologists and Psychotherapists, and Ukrainian Association of Political Psychology.

The Main Areas of Study by Ukrainian Psychologists. Among the many areas studied are preschool education and child development issues; self-esteem in the school-age child; the development of moral views by school-age children and the psychological sequelae; labor-technology educational development; the development of technical skills; the psychology of technological ideas; cybernetics and factory workers, designers, and computer programmers; strategic thinking. The psychological issues around pilot selection is an important area, as it is regarding the selection of drivers and teachers (E. Milerian). V. Moliako has developed a creative training system. The theoretical and practical problems of the younger generation's professional orientation has been the subject of research by B. Fedorishin.

Psychologists in Ukraine are engaged in ongoing work on problems of educational psychology; learning in school-age children. E. Mashbitz and A. Dovgiallo have studied the problems inherent in the computerization of education. Other topics include the development of thinking in mentally retarded children; providing better educational opportunities for special needs children; psycholinguistics; using technology to diagnose mental development in preschool children; and the methodological problems of psychology.

Kiev State University psychologists have studied the history of psychology; psychological aspects of computer-aided design; social psychological problems; psychodiagnostics; and the psychology of the intellect (V. Trofimov, L. Burlachuk, M. Holodnaia).

The department of psychology at Kharkiv University was headed for many years by P. Zinchenko (1903–1969), who was the author of works on the psychological aspects of memory, including involuntary memorizing. Kharkiv University psychologists are studying engineering psychology and memory problems. D. Elkonin and V. Davydov have a large experimental research program under way on the development of theoretical thinking in younger schoolchildren.

Psychologists at Poltava Pedagogical University are studying personality psychology, psychodiagnostics, and political psychology.

Georgia. Psychology has been studied in Georgia since the early years of the twentieth century. D. Uznadze (1886–1950) was the prime mover in establishing psychology in Georgia. In 1927, he founded the Georgian Society of Psychologists (the first of its kind in the then Soviet Union). In the late 1920s he introduced set theory and began constructing a general psychological theory based on it. The core of this theory is the dual nature of mental constructs and physical behavior, which working together provide a psychological preparation for a forthcoming activity. The set precedes the mental-physical activity and determines its general direction and the specific and unique nature of its realization. This experimental work was parallel to that of Fechner, Charpentier, and Piaget, who referred to Uznadze's effect. Such important set characteristics as excitability, diffused, static, or dynamic character, stability, and unconsciousness received attention. In 1941, Uznadze focused on problems of perception and thought processes in children.

In 1943, the psychology department of the Georgian Academy of Science became the Institute of Psychology. Set theory continued to be prominent as a research topic, and such aspects of it as sensation, perception, the psychology of the imagination, memory, attention, thought processes, language and speech, emotions, and

habit formation were studied. Differential psychology developed, and I. Bzalava, K. Mdivani, and M. Sakvarelidze used set theory in studying psychopathology. The social set concept was researched and social psychological phenomena were studied, including role conflicts, interpersonal relationships, and conformity.

Beginning in the 1970s, educational psychology developed, particularly as it related to 6-year-olds, elementary school education, the developmental stages of learning, and the typology of learning. In addition, labor and engineering psychology, comparative psychology, sport's psychology, and the psychology of creativity were prominent research topics.

In 1978, the international symposium on problems relating to unconsciousness took place in Tbilisi (*The Unconscious: Nature, Functions, Methods, Research*, Tbilisi, 1978, Vols. 1–3).

Armenia. The Erevan State University and the Institute of Russian and Foreign Languages both have psychology departments. Among the major research areas are the history of psychology, personality, ethnic psychology (O. Tutundjian); theoretical ideas and the subconscious; the mechanisms of intuition (A. Nalchadjian); child development (G. Ovsepian); the development of sensory function (E. Alexandrian); speech problems and their effects on child development; personality formation (M. Mazmanian, and O. Tutundjian).

Research in workforce psychology has been carried out by O. Tutudjian and D. Oganesian, including machine operation. Other areas include sport's psychology, social psychology, child psychology, and problems with personal frustration and defense mechanisms (A. Nalchadjian and G. Mkrtchian). Adaptation among retired people, psychopathology and medical psychology, and rehabilitation work (after the Armenian earthquake) were the subject of researches by L. Aganesian and A. Megrabian.

Kirghistan. Psychology was launched in Kirghistan in the 1950s. By 1968, a branch of the Psychological Society of the U.S.S.R. had opened (now the Psychological Society of Kirghistan). Research on comprehension, the senses, and communication was undertaken. The senses are considered to be the basic language function. Prominence is given to the development of social sense as a means to effective living (A. Brudni). Brudni demonstrated three independent areas of understanding in addition to the traditional studying of work, education, and games, and added to the latter three areas, child care, considering it to be essential to personality development. Other topics studied include a systems approach to thought processes; communication problems; the influence of contemporary movies on young people's values; aspects of the psychology of teaching; early forms of critical thinking. A method of analyzing texts was developed by A. Brudni (*Psychology of Hermeneutics*, Moscow, 1998).

Other Former Soviet Republics. Belorus and Moldava both have psychology departments in their universities. In Kazakhstan psychologists are studying communication problems and speech development among multilingual school-age children. In Tajikistant there are about 100 psychologists working at the university and teacher training institutes. There are a total of 5 psychology departments in all. Child rearing methods and education in a multilingual milieu are being studied. In Uzbekistan there are 3 universities and 16 teacher training institutes, an Institute of Pedagogical Sciences, a Physical Training Institute, a Culture Institute, and pedalogical colleges. There are more than 180 members of the Uzbek Psychological Society. Developmental psychology, psychodiagnostics, and psychology as it relates to Eastern thought are some of the subjects being researched. In Turkmenistan psychologists work at teacher training universities and study child and educational psychology.

Bibliography

Abulhanova-Slavskaia, L. A., & Brushlinskiy, A. V. (1989). *Philosophically psychological concepts of S. L. Rubinshtein.* Moscow: Nauka. [in Russian]

Ananiev, B. G. (1980). *Selected psychological works* (Vols. 1–2). Moscow: Pedagogica. [in Russian]

Davydov. V. (Ed.). (1981). *Scientific art of L. S. Vygotsky and modern psychology.* Abstracts of reports from the All-State Conference, Moscow, 23–25 June 1981, Moscow, USSR: Academy of Pedagogical Sciences. [in Russian]

Elkonin, D. B. (1978). *The psychology of the game.* Moscow-Pedagogica. [in Russian]

Galperin, P. Ia. (1976). *Introduction to psychology.* Moscow: Moscow University. [in Russian]

Gipenreiter, U. B. (1996). *Introduction to general psychology.* Moscow: CheRo. [in Russian]

Graham, L. R. (1987). *Science, philosophy, and human behavior in the Soviet Union.* New York: Columbia University Press.

Leontiev, A. N. (1983). *Selected psychological works* (Vols. 1–2). Moscow: Pedagogica. [in Russian]

Lomov, B. F. (1984). *Methodological and theoretical problems of psychology.* Moscow: Nauka. [in Russian]

Luria, A. P. *The stages of the covered way.* Moscow: Moscow University. [in Russian]

Nebylitsyn, V. D. (1976). *Psychophysiological investigations of individual differences.* Moscow: Nauka. [in Russian]

Romenets, V. A. (1995). *The history of psychology from the fifteenth to the beginning of the twentieth century.* Kiev, Ukraine: Vyshcha Shkola. [in Ukrainian]

Rubinshtein, S. L. (1946). *The basics of general psychology.* Moscow: Uchpedgiz. [in Russian]

Sokolov, M. (Ed.). (1961). *From the history of Russian psychology.* Moscow: Russian Academy of Pedagogical Sciences. [in Russian]

Yaroshevskiy, M. G. (1976). *The history of psychology* (2nd ed.). Moscow: Mysl'. [in Russian]

Yaroshevskiy, M. G. (1997). *The history of psychology: From ancient times to the middle of the twentieth century* (2nd ed.). Moscow Academia. [in Russian]

Valentyna Bondarovska

SAD. *See* Seasonal Affective Disorder.

SADISM. *See* Sexual Sadism.

SADNESS. The emotion of sadness may be the most prevalent negative emotion, and it is the key emotion in depression. Sadness is also the central emotion in grief and mourning. Many occasions of sadness, however, bear no relation to depression or to intense grief. Even a small loss or minor setback can trigger a little sadness and cause people to slow down and reflect on what is happening to them.

Causes

Separation from family and friends causes sadness in people of all cultures. The extreme case of separation that occurs when a loved one or close friend dies leads to the protracted sadness in grief and mourning. Causes of sadness also include the loss of a pet or any prized possession. Even what might appear to others as a trivial loss might trigger at least low intensity sadness. Disappointment and failure also cause sadness. These may be more salient causes when one sees oneself as the root of the disappointment or failure. An example is failure to reach a goal. Blaming oneself for uncontrollable failures or losses may exacerbate sadness into the more emotionally complex condition of depression.

Individuals differ in their proneness to sadness. Just as some people are consistently more jovial than others, some are more likely to experience a sad mood. Thresholds for sadness and other emotions play a role in the development of temperament and personality. Research has shown that the genes account for about half the variability in traits of personality. Genes also play a role in the development of depression.

The Feeling of Sadness

Although people have little trouble recognizing when they are sad, almost everyone finds it difficult to describe. Sad people say they are blue, downhearted, discouraged, or in a low mood. They may report feeling tired and listless and show decreased interest in things around them. The subjective state of sadness causes a slowing of the processes of the mind and body. One's face and body droop and thus contribute literally and symbolically to feeling low. The apparent decrease in energy may have a biological basis. Decreased sympathetic nervous system activity and changes in levels of neurotransmitters, like serotonin, may lower energy. However, research has not clarified the distinction between fatigue resulting from physical work and the feeling of tiredness that accompanies sadness and, more particularly, depression. Sadness creates some tension but not nearly as much as anger or fear.

The Expression of Sadness

The facial expression of sadness is innate and universal. Components of the expression appear in the first weeks of life. There are two main components. The first consists of oblique brows. The inner corners of the brows move up and slightly inward. This pattern looks a little like a wide inverted "V." The drawing of the mouth corners downward is the second component of the facial expression of sadness. In these movement patterns, slightly squinted eyes and a puckered (sometimes quivering) chin also signal sadness. By age two or three, the individual can exercise voluntary control over the voluntary facial muscles of the sadness expression. Even in early childhood, one can voluntarily display facial signals of sadness.

A body of contemporary research supports an idea

proposed by Charles Darwin and William James: An individual can use the expression of sadness to exercise a degree of control over the feeling of sadness. Thus, voluntarily assuming or suppressing the expression of sadness may increase or decrease the feeling of the emotion.

Functions of Sadness

Like other negative emotions, sadness has characteristics that have positive or adaptive value. One positive aspect of sadness, its power to strengthen social bonds, suggests that its history and evolution parallel that of the human species. We are social by nature, and we improve our adaptiveness by strengthening social bonds with family and friends. Indeed, the work of Jane Goodall shows that nonhuman primates (e.g., chimpanzees) react strongly to the death of their young. They behave as though they are experiencing a state of sadness or grief.

The role of sadness in empathy and altruism also suggests that it may be basic to social life. If we experience no sadness for the plight of another, we may experience no empathy. If we experience no vicarious sadness or empathy, we may be less inclined to help. Research has shown that children who feel sad at the misfortune of other children are more inclined to share with them.

The Development and Socialization of Sadness

Once the infant can experience the feeling of sadness, the quality of the conscious experience of sadness may remain constant over the life span. Increased cognitive ability and experience, however, will greatly expand the repertoire of events that cause sadness. These same factors contribute to an increase in the variety of responses that we make in coping with sadness. Developmental changes in experiences of sadness begin with the formation of bonds between the emotions and cognitive systems. These connections result in a sadness system or network that links the feeling of sadness with relevant thoughts and actions. Sadness motivates different thoughts and actions across situations and individuals. The adaptiveness of these thoughts and actions depends, in part, on our memories of past sad events and what we have learned through socialization.

Tomkins's theory of the socialization of sadness offers insights into the development of emotion dynamics, coping behavior, and traits of personality. For example, he noted that repeated physical punishment aimed at controlling a child's crying may result in the child's forming a connection between sadness and fear. The resulting sadness-fear bond would mean that any event (for example, a personal loss) that triggered sadness and crying might also cause fear and jeopardize the development of physical courage. Tomkins also suggested that parents' responding to a child's crying with indifference or rejection might lead to a connection between sadness and shame. This would mean that any disappointment or loss could cause sadness coupled with shame. Sadness and shame together would make coping with sadness more difficult and withdrawal more likely.

Coping with Sadness

One way to cope with sadness is to take advantage of the slowing effect it has on thinking and action. Thinking through things more slowly may provide new insights into the causes of sadness and how to address them. It is important to combine activity with thought and to avoid excessive rumination. Continuing to ponder unchangeable outcomes may only increase one's sadness. Ordinarily, sadness diminishes with the passage of time, but both time and sadness will pass more quickly in response to constructive activity. Such activities may include plans to treat yourself and a friend or loved one. Talking to a trusted friend can also help.

Thinking about happy times can decrease sadness. Recalling pleasant events of the past and anticipating good times in the future have a salubrious effect. It may prove effective to list past and future happy events and concentrate on the most salient one.

A change in environment can also relieve sadness. Sadness, like depression, decreases interest in things outside the self. After a reasonable amount of reflection on the self, a walk or ride through the neighborhood or to a park will offer a variety of interest-eliciting stimuli. Activating the emotion of interest will counteract sadness.

Research has shown that exercise has positive effects on mood. Even a brief walk may alleviate sadness. For most people, moderate to vigorous exercise increases both positive mood and energy. Exercise physiologists and psychologists agree on the therapeutic value of exercise, but they do not know precisely what mediates the beneficial effects. One possibility is that the physical activity increases energy and relieves tension. Another is that the exercise directs thoughts into different channels and away from the negative events that caused the sadness. Also, moderate to vigorous exercise for about one half-hour increases certain proteins (endorphins) and other neurotransmitters that occur naturally in the brain. The increase in these neurotransmitters may enhance positive mood.

Bibliography

Barnett, M. A., Howard, J. A., Melton, E. M., & Dino, G. A. (1982). Effect of inducing sadness about self or other on helping behavior in high and low empathic children. *Child Development, 53,* 920–923.

Bowlby, J. (1980). *Attachment and loss.* New York: Basic Books.

Darwin, C. (1965). *The expression of the emotions in man and animals.* Chicago: University of Chicago Press. (Original work published 1872)

Finman, R., & Berkowitz, I. (1989). Some factors influencing the effect of depressed mood on anger and overt hostility toward another. *Journal of Research in Personality, 23,* 70–84.

Garber, J., Braafladt, N., & Weiss, B. (1995). Affect regulation in depressed and nondepressed children and young adolescents. *Development and Psychopathology, 7,* 93–115.

Goodall, J. (1988). *In the shadow of man.* Boston: Houghton Mifflin.

Izard, C. E. (1994). Innate and universal facial expressions: Evidence from developmental and cross-cultural research. *Psychological Bulletin, 115,* 288–299.

Nolen-Hoeksema, S., Parker, L. E., & Larson, J. (1994). Ruminative coping with depressed mood following loss. *Journal of Personality and Social Psychology, 67,* 92–104.

Thayer, R. E., Newman, J. R., & McClain, T. M. (1994). Self-regulation of mood: Strategies for changing a bad mood, raising energy, and reducing tension. *Journal of Personality and Social Psychology, 67,* 910–925.

Tomkins, S. S. (1963). *Affect, imagery, consciousness. Vol. 2: The negative affects.* New York: Springer.

Carroll Izard

SALES PSYCHOLOGY. *See* Consumer Psychology; *and* Media Effects.

SAMPLING denotes the science and art, the theory and practice, of selecting a sample of *n* from a population of *N* elements, in order to make statistical inferences from statistics based on the sample to the population values (parameters) of the frame population. The parameters most commonly estimated are population totals or population means, which often are proportions. But sample statistics are also used for more complex and multivariate parameters, such as regression coefficients and tests of significance. Methods similar to those used in the sampling of human populations are also applied to animals, plants, and mineral populations.

Modern methods of sampling have been developed mostly since 1945 and have been utilized more in some human behavioral and social sciences than in others; more in sociology, political science, and social psychology than in clinical psychology and anthropology; more for large, national samples than for small clinical studies. The methods of survey sampling should yield sample designs that are suited to the complex distributions of real populations; and the need for complex sample designs gives rise to the discipline. It is simple enough to sample from a pot of soup or from an urn of lottery balls. And a sample from a good, up-to-date list of students of a single school or members of the American Psychological Association (APA) needs no specialist. But good samples of adults or farmers of the United States (or Brazil, China, etc.) need complex designs. Five criteria for good designs are: (a) Probability sampling: known, positive probabilities P_i of selection for all N elements in the frame population. (b) Measurability: probability samples designed to permit computing from the sample data, valid and useful estimates of sampling errors. (c) Useful goals and representativeness: to rule out trivial populations that may be easy to sample but difficult to use as bases for meaningful inferences. (d) Feasibility and practicality: planned freedom from obstacles to achieving sampling procedures as designed and intended. For example, "Select a random sample" is not a feasible instruction to interviewers, because the human mind is poorly designed for this task. (e) Efficiency and economy: achieving the greatest accuracy for allowed cost; or (equally) achieving the survey's goals with minimal costs.

Probability Sampling

Probability sampling requires more than a definition, model, and desire; it often depends on difficult practical procedures. Specifically, the logical and practical requirements imply this chain: statistical inference → probability sampling → objective, mechanical selection → lists, frames. We need mechanical selection procedures because nature does not hand us randomized mixtures, and because the minds of humans—whether clerks, psychologists, or statisticians—are poor randomizing devices. Mechanical procedures in practice mean selections (by a trained person) from a table of random numbers (or equivalent); and those selections denote the numbers of the listing units with which the population elements can be readily and uniquely identified in the selection frame.

A perfect list (designated as L–E) should be complete, up-to-date (current), available, and should facilitate location; and it must have listing units (L) with one-to-one correspondence with the elements (E). It should contain unique numbers, but the numbering may be nonconsecutive (like social security numbers) or alphabetical. The list of students of a school can be adequate for selecting from that population. However, no available lists of all persons or households in the United States, nor in most countries, exist, and it would be much too expensive to construct one against continual changes. (Good lists exist in some northern European and a few other countries.) Therefore, the methods of sampling frame and area sampling were created. Mobile humans (and other populations) can be identified with dwellings that are located at addresses, segments, blocks, tracts, and counties. With proper identifications, definitions, and procedures we can select multistage area probability samples, beginning with counties and going down in stages to dwellings, and then to persons, families, television sets, and anything that can be associated with dwellings.

Frame Problems

The available lists and frames are always imperfect, and the most common and useful art of a sampler is to detect, assess, and correct the imperfections. If the imperfections can be assessed to be negligible, they may be measured, declared, and neglected; but many lists suffer from serious imperfections of too many specific kinds to be listed. But they can be classed into four fundamental types, which are denoted with departures from the one-to-one correspondence (L–E) with distinct elements: (a) blanks and foreign elements (L–O)—the elements may have moved or died, or were nonmembers of the survey population, (b) missing elements (O–E), also known as incomplete frames and noncoverage—these entail most serious and difficult consequences, and volumes have been written about missing units; (c) duplicate (L–E–L) (multiple) listings—this also relates to the subject of dual (or multiple) frames for selection; and (d) clusters of elements (E–L–E) under single listings—small clusters are common and not troublesome. All four of these types can occur not only with elements, but are also common with larger sampling units of clusters of elements. Failure to correct these deficiencies, or using wrong methods, are the most common and needless sources of sampling biases.

There are many kinds of nonprobability samples, too many to define and describe, and they lack theories and textbooks, although they are common in practice. Typical or representative people (often taxi drivers, bankers, etc.) are commonly presented by journalists. Judgmental choice may be used to select a representative or typical school or village. Quota sampling is used widely for political opinion polls and market research; and there are great varieties of procedures and skills. Ad hoc and convenience samples are exemplified by patients of a clinic or clinician. Volunteer subjects who answer a notice or advertisement have been used. These may be the worst.

The methods of survey sampling deal with three principal kinds of complexities of real populations: stratification, clustering and multistage sampling, and weighting.

Element Sampling

A good (not perfect) list of students of a school is ordinarily available; no such lists exist for all students in the United States, much less for all adults. Generally, representativeness for large populations tends to con-flict with simplicity of selection. It is possible to select n random numbers to identify an unrestricted random sample with replacement. But it is better to select n different random numbers to identify n elements for a simple random sample (SRS) of n without replacement. This is a basic standard model in survey sampling with which other selection methods are compared. However, it is often more convenient to compute and use a sampling fraction $f = 1/F = n/N$ for selecting the sample. Then a simple robust procedure is selecting a systematic sample with F as the selection interval: after a random start from 1 to F, the interval F is laid off repeatedly until the end of the list.

Most lists contain some inner ordering of classification; for example, a school's students may be listed by classes and a university's students by disciplines or departments. Thus, a systematic sample will not be simply random but stratified (layered) by the classes on the list. Hence, a systematic sampling serves as an easy method for selecting a proportionate stratified random element sample. Furthermore, instead of merely accepting the naturally available ordering, the sampler can sort the listings with meaningful and available variables into optimal strata: the greatest possible heterogeneity between strata results in the greatest homogeneity within strata.

Cluster Sampling

An equal probability selection of complete clusters serves as a simple introduction. Suppose that the list of A fourth-grade classes of a state is available and we decide to select a systematic sample of 100 classes with the sampling inverval $F = A/100$. The sampling rate (fraction, probability) is $f = 100/A$ for every class; and thus for every fourth-grade student, if we take the complete classes. The number of students will vary somewhat around an average of $B = 30$ per class, so the number (n) of students is 3,000 only approximately. In practical cluster sampling it is more robust and simple to fix the rates and allow sample sizes to vary with the clusters. Furthermore, taking complete clusters is convenient when their sizes may be neither too large nor too variable.

Subsampling, Multistage Sampling

Often the available clusters are too large and smaller complete clusters are unavailable and cannot be created easily. But they can be created with subsampling; for example, those hundred classes can be made to yield an average of $b = 3$ from the $B = 30$ students, with the sampling equation $f = (100/A)(1/10) = 10/A$. One hundred clusters will be created, each about $b = 3$ in size. That would be a sample of only $n = (3)(100) = 300$; but a sample of $n = (3)(1,000)$ students can be created with $f = (1,000/A)(1/10) = 100/A$ if resources can support a sample of 1,000 classes. All population elements have the same selection probability, and the sample clusters are about equal (b = 3), when class sizes are roughly equal.

Multistage sampling must often be extended to more stages. For example, a national sample of school children in the United States may involve counties × school districts × schools × classes × children. A sample of adults of the United States often involves counties × areas × tracts × blocks × segments × dwellings × persons. Most of these involve designs with probabilities proportional to size (PPS) to select counties and blocks with greatly variable sizes. Dwellings and schools served here as our frames for identifying persons, but other frames also have been used for special populations such as hospitals, firms, and institutions.

Unequal Probabilities and Weighting

Instead of equal probabilities f, sample elements may receive unequal probabilities P_i of selection for one or more of these reasons: (a) higher selection rates for small but important domains (states, districts, ethnic groups); (b) higher rates for optimal allocations to domains with lower unit costs or higher unit variances; (c) frame problems as discussed above, and/or (d) unequal nonresponse rates. These inequalities of selection should be compensated with inverse weighting of the sample cases.

Telephone Surveys

Since about 1975 telephone sampling has become popular in the United States, Europe, and much of the developed world, as household ownership of telephones passed the 90% mark in many countries. Telephone instead of face-to-face interviewing was used even earlier for reinterviews, and the two methods combined, powerfully reduce the costs. Computer-assisted telephone interviewing (CATI) further facilitates these methods. Unique identification of persons with household telephone numbers also has the four types of frame problems noted earlier and needs similar care. For samples that need more than the 90+% telephone coverage of households, dual frames have been used to include the nonowners with area dwelling sampling.

Telephone sampling has greatly facilitated the sampling of national household populations, allowing surveys by firms and institutions without the technical resources needed for good doorstep interviewing. This success is a direct cause of its abuse by hosts of careless entrepreneurs, and especially by marketeers who cloak selling under the guise of surveys. This helped to create widespread refusals to participate. Also, three mistakes are often made through carelessness or ignorance: (a) failure to identify households and persons with the telephone numbers; (b) accepting the person who answers as representative; (c) failure to make recalls on nonresponses. I believe that in the 1990s most telephone surveys have lower or much lower than 80% responses, whereas the best doorstep surveys have over 80%.

Biases, Variable Errors, and Nonresponses

The total errors of surveys are often separated conveniently into variable errors and biases. Sampling errors are mostly variable, and they depend (inversely) on the numbers of diverse sampling units. The nonsampling survey errors, on the other hand, are mostly constant (systematic) biases that are not decreased with sample sizes. These are the errors of measurement (observation), called response errors in interview surveys. Nonresponse errors (missing units) result from missing cases due to refusals or not-at-homes. The size and nature of nonresponses vary tremendously and volumes are written about them. Noncoverage denotes parts of the desired population that the sampling frame fails to cover and it is difficult even to estimate its size. Item nonresponse refers to missing answers from otherwise mostly complete interviews (responses), and useful answers can be supplied with modern imputation methods from other respondents and other correlated items. Biases and variable errors are generally combined in the mean-square errors (MSE): $\text{MSE}(\bar{y}) = \text{Bias}^2(\bar{y}) + \text{Var}(\bar{y})$. But we must be warned that their total sizes and relative sizes vary greatly even in the same sample, and the bias terms especially vary greatly between variables in the same survey sample.

Sampling Errors

Unlike descriptive statistics (like $\bar{y}$, s_y, and r_{xy}), sampling errors depend strongly on the design, and the complex formulas of variances for the great variety of complex sample designs occupy a central part of sampling courses. The classical variances, like $var(\bar{y}) = s^2_y/n$, can vastly underestimate the true variability of complex clustered samples. The ratios of underestimation have been readily measured with the design effects $deft^2 = var(\bar{y})/(s^2_y/n)$ in many thousands of computations of actual $var(\bar{y})$, and also of $var(b)$ for other statistics b. Though most of those ratios lie between one and two, many are up to eight or more.

Mean-square errors also offer the framework to frequent broad questions of strategy for choosing between alternative methods and objectives. Should we aim for a large representative national sample even if it means cheaper and worse measurements, and perhaps even nonprobability sampling; hence large potential biases, even if small sampling errors? Or is it better to accept a high-quality study, based on and with statistical inference restricted to a small localized population? Or perhaps good samples restricted to a few sites? The small samples may have smaller biases, but the larger samples will have smaller sampling errors. These may be most important for the subclasses and their comparisons. Although we cannot assign exact values for the biases and sampling errors, the mean-square errors provide the only framework for their strategic comparisons.

Omitted Sampling Methods

Finally, several methods of sampling were omitted in order to concentrate only on methods of frequent use in population sampling. Capture-recapture methods are central for sampling fish and wildlife but rare and marginal for humans, used only rarely for nomads and the homeless. Quality-control methods are central for testing nuts and bolts, electric bulbs, and so on. They also have been used for editing survey schedules. Both methods have a large body of literature but not in books on survey sampling. However, those books do cover several methods that are important and used occasionally in sampling.

Designs for periodic surveys are natural extensions with special techniques, and they have widespread and increasing uses and a vast literature. National panels of persons and families over many years yield rich data on individual changes. Multipopulation and multinational surveys are becoming more common and better designed for their special needs and opportunities. Recently a multinational sample of psychiatric epidemiology has been started! Multiphase sampling denotes samples in two (or more) phases: First, a large sample collects inexpensive but inaccurate screening information; that information is used for designing a subsample for the second, expensive, accurate phase. Multiple (or deep) stratification or controlled selection are the names given for probability selection of small numbers of units, with many stratifying controls for better representativeness. This complex method is used for selecting a small number of clinics, or counties, when costs prohibit a wider spread.

[See also Back-Translation; and Survey Methodology.]

Bibliography

Cochran, W. G. (1977). *Sampling techniques* (3rd ed.). New York: Wiley. A classical textbook for courses in sampling theory, with derivations of all variance formulas, requiring only algebra using the summation Σ.

Groves, R. M., et al. (Eds.). (1988). *Telephone survey methodology*. New York: Wiley. Compendium of 32 chapters by over 40 experts on all aspects of global developments.

Kish, L. (1965). *Survey sampling*. New York: Wiley. Reference book on the practical aspects of actual surveys, oriented chiefly to human populations and the social sciences.

Kish, L. (1987). *Statistical design for research*. New York: Wiley. Theoretical and methodological (not mathematical) aspects linking the designs of survey samples, randomized experiments, and controlled observations.

Moser, C. A., & Kalton, G. (1971). *Survey methods in social investigations* (2nd ed.). London: Heinemann. Introduction to all aspects of survey methods and related social investigations.

Rosenthal, R., & Rosnow, R. L. (1975). *The volunteer subject*. New York: Wiley. The characteristics of volunteers for research participation, the resulting artifacts, and procedures for estimating and reducing bias.

Leslie Kish

SANFORD, EDMUND CLARK (1859–1924), American experimental psychologist. Sanford was born in Oakland, California, the son of Edmund P. and Jennie E. (Clark) Sanford. He earned a bachelor's degree at the University of California in Berkeley (1883), taught for a year at Oahu College in Honolulu, then enrolled at Johns Hopkins University in Baltimore, where he earned a doctorate in experimental psychology in 1887. He taught there at the university for a year as instructor (1888). His dissertation topic was on perception, an investigation of the relative legibility of small letters (*American Journal of Psychology*, 1888, *1*, 402–435). During his time at Johns Hopkins, he came under the mentorship of G. Stanley Hall, professor of psychology and one of the discipline's founders. Sanford remained close to Hall for the rest of his career.

When Hall was named first president of Clark University in Worcester, Massachusetts, Sanford was his initial faculty recruit. Sanford then became affiliated with Clark for the rest of his life. He directed the laboratory and was instructor (1889–1892) and assistant professor (1892–1900) of psychology, then professor (1900–1909) of experimental and comparative psychology. In 1909, he was named president of Clark College, the undergraduate counterpart of Clark University (separate schools, same building). In 1920, upon Hall's retirement and the merging of Clark University and College, Sanford returned to the faculty. He died in 1924, just as he was planning to retire to California.

Sanford is noted as a teacher, writer, and inventor of scientific equipment. He also contributed to the professionalization of psychology in America through his coeditorship of the *American Journal of Psychology* and his active involvement during the formative years of the American Psychological Association. He was elected the eleventh president of the association in 1902. Sanford's major contribution to teaching was his laboratory manual for the experimental psychology course, the first to be published in English. It was produced in installments in the *American Journal of Psychology* between 1891 and 1896, then published in book form. It was called *A Course in Experimental Psychology 1: Sensation and Perception* (Boston, 1898). Sanford planned to write a second volume covering higher mental processes, but the book was never written. Sanford's first volume was designed to acquaint the student with basic laboratory procedures in the experimental study of sensory and perceptual processes, and it helped to standardize the training of research psychologists, until replaced in the early twentieth century by the more elaborate manuals of Edward B. Titchener.

One section of the manual concerned apparatus and illustrated Sanford's other main contribution—his creativity as a designer of research instruments. His best-known invention was the Sanford Vernier Chronoscope, used for reaction time studies. Sanford also deserves credit for pioneering one of experimental psychology's most famous procedures—maze learning in rats. To investigate the rat's "home-finding" tendencies, Sanford suggested building a rat-sized replica of England's famous hedge maze at Hampton Court. The idea resulted in a series of investigations on the topic by Sanford's student Willard Small in 1900 and established a procedure that continues to be widely used.

[*Many of the people mentioned in this article are the subjects of independent biographical entries.*]

Bibliography

Goodwin, C. J. (1987). In Hall's shadow: Edmund Clark Sanford (1859–1924). *Journal of the History of the Behavioral Sciences, 23*, 153–168. A description of Sanford's career and contributions, including an analysis of the relationship with his mentor, G. Stanley Hall, and his closest colleague, E. B. Titchener of Cornell.

Sanford, E. C. (1893). Some practical suggestions on the equipment of a psychological laboratory. *American Journal of Psychology, 5*, 429–438. Provides insight into the nature of experimental psychology in the 1890s by describing what was needed for a state of the art laboratory as well as one on a bare-bones budget.

Sanford, E. C. (1903). Psychology and physics. *Psychological Review, 10*, 105–119. Sanford's presidential address to the American Psychological Association, in which he cautioned against psychology modeling itself too closely on physics.

Wilson, L. N. (Ed.). (1925). *Edmund Clark Sanford: In memoriam.* Worcester, MA: Clark University Press. Includes obituaries by Titchener, William Burnham of Clark, and Mary Calkins of Wellesley, a brief biography by Sanford's sister, testimonials from colleagues and former students, and a complete bibliography of Sanford's work.

C. James Goodwin

SANTAYANA, GEORGE (1863–1952), American naturalist philosopher. Born in Spain, he came to Boston in 1872, where he learned English in Miss Welshman's kindergarten. He was a student at the Boston Latin School and Harvard University, from which he received his doctorate in 1889. His naturalism was coupled with a deep respect for art, religion, and philosophical history, making him a major representative of American naturalistic philosophy. In addition, he was a principal member of the literati of his day, and his autobiography, *Persons and Places* (Holzberger & Saatkamp, 1986–1994), and his one novel, *The Last Puritan* (Holzberger & Saatkamp, 1986–1994), were Book-of-the-Month Club best sellers and led to his appearance on the cover of *Time* magazine (3 February 1936).

A permanent resident of Spain only from 1863 to 1872, he retained his Spanish citizenship throughout his life and frequently returned to visit family, to write, and to vacation. In his autobiography, *Persons and Places*, he describes his life as having three parts: (1) "Background," which covers the years 1863 to 1886, including his childhood in Spain through his Harvard undergraduate years; (2) "On Both Sides of the Atlantic," which encompasses his Harvard graduate and professorate days and his trans-Atlantic penchant for European travel during the years 1886 through 1912; and (3) "All on One Side," covering the years 1912 to 1952 when, as a retired professor, he traveled through Europe, eventually establishing Rome as his center of activity.

Santayana's philosophical roots lie in classical Greek and Roman naturalism, Spinoza's ethics, Royce's idealism, and James's pragmatism. His first book, *The Sense of Beauty* (Holzberger & Saatkamp, 1986–1994), foreshadowed his naturalism and also highlighted his criticism of pragmatism as being too dependent on literary psychology, an approach that relied on human experience and consciousness rather than the underlying natural causes discoverable through the empirical sciences. He defined beauty as pleasure objectified, emphasizing its natural base in animal desire. Later Santayana criticized this account of beauty as being too subjective (*Scepticism and Animal Faith*, 1923) and, perhaps, too influenced by James's radical empiricism. For the mature Santayana, relying on experience alone was neither good philosophy nor psychology because it overlooked the imaginative role of the human intellect, the plasticity of physical and social circumstances, and the determining natural causes.

The five books of *The Life of Reason: Or, The Phases of Human Progress* (1905–1906) established him as a principal force in the philosophy of the twentieth century. Surveying religions, societies, arts, and the sciences of the Western world, Santayana addressed the issue of establishing human practices that were consistent with reason. From this work came the often-quoted warning to those who do not remember (and understand) the past: They are condemned to repeat it (*Reason in Common Sense*).

Santayana's mature philosophy did not appear until more than two decades later, when he published *Scepticism and Animal Faith* (1923) and the four books of *Realms of Being* (1942). Here Santayana's naturalism, coupled with his account of art's lyrical voice, came to full development. Challenging American and English philosophy and psychology, Santayana focused on animal action and displaced privileged mentalistic accounts with his pragmatic naturalism. His antifoundationalism and emphasis on aesthetics and his view of philosophy as literature anticipated many developments in philosophy and literary criticism that occurred in the latter half of the twentieth century. His thoroughgoing naturalism served as a criticism of Dewey's more humanistic approach and of James's mentalistic, experiential philosophy.

Presenting a remarkable synthesis of European and American thought, Santayana's Hispanic heritage and his clear sense of being an outsider in America captured the apprehensions and divisions facing the United States at the turn of the millennium. Yet his delight in life, his focus on celebration and aesthetics, and his clear appreciation of the natural causes of animal action set him apart from most philosophers and highlight his contributions to understanding and delighting in human behavior, particularly in societies that value scientific explanations of human action.

Bibliography

Works by Santayana

Santayana, G. (1905–1906). *The life of reason: Or, the phases of human progress* (Vols. 1–5). New York: Scribner.

Santayana, G. (1942). *Realms of being*. New York: Scribners. (Original work published)

Santayana, G. (1946). *The idea of Christ in the Gospels or God in man*. New York: Scribners.

Holzberger, W. G., & Saatkamp, H. J. (Eds.). (1986–1994). *The works of George Santayana* (Vols. 1–4). Cambridge, MA: MIT Press.

Holzberger, W. G. & Saatkamp Jr., H. J. (Eds.) (1990). *Interpretations of poetry and religion*. Vol. 3 of *The works of George Santayana*. Cambridge, MA: MIT Press.

Holzberger, W. G. & Saatkamp Jr., H. J. (Eds.) (1994). *The last puritan: A memoir in the form of a novel*. Vol. 4 of *The works of George Santayana*. Cambridge, MA: MIT Press.

Holzberger, W. G. & Saatkamp Jr., H. J. (Eds.) (1986). *Persons and places: Fragments of autobiography*. Vol. 1 of *The works of George Santayana*. Cambridge, MA: MIT Press.

Holzberger, W. G. & Saatkamp Jr., H. J. (Eds.) (1988). *The sense of beauty: Being the outlines of aesthetic theory*. Vol. 2 of *The works of George Santayana*. Cambridge, MA: MIT Press.

Works about Santayana

Arnett, W. E. (1955). *Santayana and the sense of beauty*. Bloomington: Indiana University Press.

Ashmore, J. (1966). *Santayana, art and aesthetics*. Cleveland, OH: Press of Case Western Reserve University.

Cory, D. (1955). *The letters of George Santayana*. New York: Scribners.

Hughson, L. (1977). *Thresholds of reality: George Santayana and modernist poetics*. Port Washington, NY: Kennikat Press.

Jones, J., & Saatkamp, H. J., Jr., (1982). *George Santayana: A bibliographical checklist, 1880–1980*. Bowling Green: Philosophy Documentation Center.

Kerr-Lawson, A., & Saatkamp, H. J., Jr., (Eds.). 1983–1997). *Overheard in Seville: Bulletin of the Santayana Society* (Nos. 1–15). College Station, TX: University of Texas, Department of Philosophy, Santayana Edition.

Lachs. J. (Ed.). (1967). *Animal faith and spiritual life: Previously unpublished and uncollected writings by George Santayana with critical essays on his thought*. New York: Appleton-Century-Crofts.

Levinson, H. S. (1992). *Santayana, pragmatism, and the spiritual life*. Chapel Hill: University of North Carolina Press.

McCormick, J. (1987). *George Santayana: A biography*. New York: Knopf.

Schilpp, P. A. (Ed.). (1940). *Library of living philosophers: Vol. 2. The philosophy of George Santayana*. Evanston, IL: Northwestern University Press.

Sprigge, T. L. S. (1995). *Santayana: An examination of his philosophy* (2nd ed.). London: Routledge.

Herman J. Saatkamp, Jr.

SAVANT SYNDROME is a rare but spectacular condition in which persons with severe mental handicap, usually from mental retardation or autistic disorder, have astonishing islands of ability or brilliance that stand in stark, markedly incongruous, jarring contrast to overall mental handicap. While the incidence of savant syndrome is about evenly divided (50%) between the two developmental (congenital) disabilities of mental retardation and autistic disorder, in occasional instances, such savant abilities unexpectedly emerge in a previously normal child or adult following brain injury or disease (acquired). Those individuals whose special ability or genius is remarkable, but only in contrast to the overall handicap, are called talented savants. Those persons with a much rarer form of the condition, in whom the ability or brilliance is not only spectacular in contrast to overall mental handicap but would be spectacular even if seen in a normal person, are called prodigious savants. There are fewer than 100 prodigious savants in the entire world literature on this topic in the past century, and there are probably fewer than 25 prodigious savants living worldwide at present. Savant syndrome occurs approximately four times more frequently in males than females.

Such islands of genius residing in an otherwise severely mentally handicapped person was a condition first named idiot savant by John Langdon Down, who is better known for having named Down syndrome, a common form of mental retardation. In an 1887 lecture before the Medical Society of London, Down shared his 30-year experience as the superintendent of Earlswood Asylum during which he was struck by the extraordinary paradox of superiority and deficiency occurring in the same patient. Contrasting that superiority and deficiency, he aptly combined the term *idiot* (at that time an accepted scientific term for IQ below 25) with the word *savant* from the French word *savoir*, meaning "to know" or "man of learning." While originally perhaps creatively descriptive, the term *idiot savant* has been generally discarded now because of its colloquial, pejorative connotation and has been replaced by savant syndrome or simply savant. Nevertheless, *idiot savant* still appears even today as the reference term in much of the world scientific literature on this topic. Actually, idiot savant was a misnomer since almost all of the reported cases have occurred in persons with IQs above 40, not below 25, as Down originally presumed.

An early but remarkably astute description of this disorder appeared in a 1914 textbook, *Mental Deficiency*, by Alfred F. Tredgold, a London physician. The chapter on the idiot savant is trailblazing and still endures as a classic, even in later editions of what is still a standard text in the British Commonwealth and America. He meticulously and colorfully describes over 25 cases of such extraordinary abilities including art, language, music, memory, mathematics, and heightened sensory acuity. He concludes the chapter with an elaborate description of a famous early savant, the genius of Earlswood Asylum, whom other early investigators also had described in detail. Both Down and Tredgold commented on the intriguingly narrow range of special abilities in savants, given the wide range of human abilities overall, and on the rarity of savant syndrome in females. Both those observations remain accurate today.

Savant skills occur within a narrow but constant range of human mental capacity, generally in five areas: calendar calculating; mathematical ability, including lightning calculating; art (drawing, painting, or sculpting); music (usually the piano with perfect pitch); and mechanical ability or dexterity. In some instances unusual language acquisition or multilingual abilities (polyglot savants) have been reported, but they are rare. Other skills, also less frequently reported, include map memorizing; exquisite sensory discrimination such as enhanced sense of touch or smell; and spatial skills (unusually perceptive visual measurement ability, sense of direction, or appreciation of time without knowledge of a clock face).

The most common savant skill is musical ability. A regularly occurring triad of musical genius, blindness (particularly from premature birth and retrolental fibroplasia), and autism among prodigious savants is particularly striking. Equally striking and intriguing is the fact that calendar-calculating ability, a very infrequent and obscure skill in normal persons, coexists commonly in savants alongside the principal savant talent. These persons are able to name the day of the week when given a date past or future, with no sense of how they do it. Calendar calculating is probably the most exhaustively studied savant skill since it is the most easily quantified (range of years), can be objectively measured (accuracy and response time), and does occur in some normal persons who can articulate methodology or formulas. Yet after all this intense study, savant methodology still remains largely unexplained since neither elaborate memorization alone nor deliberate use of common algorithms can account for this extraordinary savant prodigiousness with the calendar.

In some cases of savant syndrome a single special skill exists; in others several skills exist simultaneously. The skills tend to be right hemisphere in type—nonsymbolic, artistic, concrete, directly perceived—in contrast to the left hemisphere type, which tend to be more sequential, logical, and symbolic, including language specialization.

Whatever the special skills, they are always linked with phenomenal memory within the skill area itself, and in many instances huge stores of unrelated trivia (license plates, zip codes, telephone numbers, dates, sports) coexist as well. Such savant memory, however, is of a special type—very narrow but exceedingly deep within those narrow confines. Such memory has been accurately described as memory without reckoning, a type of remembering generally referred to as habit or procedural memory. It relies on a more primitive circuitry (corticolimbic) than does higher level (corticostriatal) cognitive or associative memory used more commonly and regularly in normal persons.

Approximately 10% of persons with autistic disorder have some savant abilities; that percentage is much higher than in other developmental disabilities such as mental retardation where in an institutionalized population that figure may be only 1:2,000. Since mental retardation is much more common than autistic disorder, however, approximately 50% of persons with savant syndrome have mental retardation stemming from congenital or acquired causes, and 50% have autistic disorder. Thus not all persons with autistic disorder are savants, and not all savants have autistic disorder.

Theories to explain savant syndrome include eidetic imagery, inherited skills, concrete thinking with inability to think abstractly, compensation and reinforcement, and left brain injury with right brain compensation. These theories are summarized, and the syndrome reviewed more broadly in detail, including historical details and cases reports over this past century, in *Extraordinary People* (New York, 1989) and in a 1988 review article, "The Idiot Savant: A Review of the Syndrome" (*American Journal of Psychiatry*, 145, 563–572), both by Darold A. Treffert. To the extent that imaging studies have been carried out on savants, they do show left hemisphere damage and suggest that one plausible explanation in many savants is left brain damage from prenatal, perinatal, or postnatal central nervous system (CNS) damage with migratory, right brain compensation, coupled with corresponding damage to higher level, cognitive (corticostriatal) memory circuitry with compensatory take-over of lower level habit (cortical-limbic) memory. This could account for the linking of predominantly right brain skills with habit memory so characteristic of savant syndrome.

In addition to idiosyncratic brain circuitry, intense concentration, practice, and repetition are characteristic, and crucial, to production of savant syndrome. Such mindless repetition—unconscious reckoning—can produce in some savants sufficient coding so that access to some noncognitive structure or algorithms can be automatically attained giving the savant access, unconsciously, to what are called the rules of music or rules of mathematics. Such unconscious algorithms allow them to carry out automatically complex musical or mathematical tasks or calendar calculating, for example, with no sense or explanation available to them of how it is they are able to do those things. In the prodigious savant, however, some inherited factors may be operative as well, since it is doubtful that practice alone could account for the detailed access to vast rules of music, art, or mathematics that is innate in these persons. Once established, intense concentration, practice, compensatory drives, and reinforcement by family, teachers, and others play a major role in developing and polishing the savant skills and memory linked so characteristically, uniformly, and dramatically in this syndrome.

One of the prenatal CNS injury mechanisms that may explain the disproportionate number of males in savant syndrome is the neurotoxic effect of circulating testosterone on the left hemisphere in the male fetus based on observations reported by Norman Geschwind and Albert Galaburda, Harvard neurologists, in *Cerebral Lateralization* (Cambridge, Mass., 1987). Since the left brain completes its development later than the right brain, it is at risk for CNS damage for a longer period of time to the circulating testosterone (which can be neurotoxic) in male fetuses; left CNS damage, with right brain compensation, may account for the high male: female ratio not only in savant syndrome, but also in autism, stuttering, hyperactivity, and learning disabilities as well.

The Academy Award–winning 1988 film *Rainman*, in which Dustin Hoffman depicted a high-functioning autistic savant, made *savant* a household word. It is important to point out, however, that what is seen in that movie are savant skills (lightning calculating, memorization etc.) grafted onto autistic disorder (narrowed emotions, obsessive sameness, rituals, etc.) in a person who functions at a high level for autism. Not all autistic persons function at such a high level, and not all autistic persons have savant skills.

In dealing with savant skills, a debate has long raged over whether to train the talent or eliminate the defect. For many years it was feared that helping the savant achieve a higher level of functioning with treatment—eliminating the defect—would result in a loss of special skills in that there would be a trade-off of right brain special skills for left brain language acquisition, for example. While some cases have reported such a dreaded trade-off and loss of special skills with normalization, that generally has turned out not to be the case. Quite to the contrary: Focusing on training the talent, instead of eliminating the defect, has been the most useful approach toward increasing socialization, language, and independence in savants. In such approaches the special skills of the savant, rather than being seen as odd, frivolous, trivial, or distracting, become a useful treatment tool as conduit toward normalization in these special persons. Some schools have begun to include persons with savant syndrome into classes for the gifted and talented as a method of further enhancing this normalization.

Two related conditions merit special mention. In 1944, an Austrian psychiatrist, Hans Asperger, described a condition in which persons with rather severe psychiatric impairments showed some exceptional skill or talent disproportionate to overall intellectual ability and linked with extraordinary capacity for memorization. There is debate whether Asperger's disorder is separate from autistic disorder or whether it is only a variant of autism with most persons operating at the high end of the spectrum in terms of overall function, and that question remains unsettled. Whatever the outcome of that debate, many persons with savant syndrome do carry a diagnosis of Asperger's disorder.

The link between Williams syndrome and savant syndrome is likewise interesting and frequent. In 1961, British cardiologist J. C. P. Williams described a genetic disorder in children characterized by mental retardation, distinctive elfin-like facial features, aortic stenosis, elevated calcium levels, and autistic-like behaviors. Unique to these otherwise very intellectually impaired persons, however, is a rich, expansive, grammatically complex vocabulary with striking conversation and richly expansive story-telling skills. Equally striking, in contrast to usual autistic withdrawal, are extremely outgoing personality traits and highly expressive social interests and behaviors. In addition, remarkable musical abilities are often seen in Williams syndrome. This combination of a distinctive pixie-like appearance with what has been called a cocktail personality, including expansive and expressive speech and precocious musical skills, provides a very intriguing and unique mix of ability and disability. The unusual circumstance of impaired general intellect but spared and even precocious language abilities challenges theories about the usual linkage of language and cognition. Adding research interest in this condition is the fact that a specific genetic defect on chromosome 7 has been identified as the etiologic mechanism for this disorder. That genetic defect makes elastin production deficient in Williams syndrome, and many investigators think that the same elastin gene deletion accounts for the cardiovascular as well as neurodevelopmental brain abnormalities.

Over a century has passed since John Langdon Down first recorded his observations about savants. Since that time reports have been largely anecdotal, with no uniform nomenclature, standardized testing, or control sample comparisons. However, studies are now being done that do use more uniform terminology, standardized testing, and similar laboratory techniques, including brain imaging; comparing and contrasting savant populations to nonsavant developmentally disabled persons; and normal controls, including some nondisabled persons with savant-like skills or precociousness. Robyn Young, an Australian psychologist, reported the largest single group of talented and prodigious savants (51) studied to date with standardized testing and family histories. Four common tendencies were seen in that population: autistic disorder or autistic-like behaviors; preoccupation and persistence with areas of interest; idiosyncratic, divergent cognitive abilities but always with well-developed memory; and presence of savant-type skills and higher intelligence among family members. Bernard Rimland, a San Diego, California, psychologist who through his Autism Research Institute has over 20,000 autistic persons in his case registry, has reported on the incidence of savant skills in autism. Beate Hermelin and Neil O'Connor, British researchers, have carried out studies on savant calendar calculating, drawing, and musical skills comparing and contrasting savant and nonsavant developmentally disabled populations, and, more recently, comparing and contrasting skills and abilities in savants with prodigious and talented normal persons, to explore the similarities and differences between savant syndrome in handicapped persons and precocity and unusual ability in normal persons.

Many questions remain unanswered. Why are savant skills generally confined to five characteristic areas, given the wide range of abilities in the human repertoire? Why is the obscure skill of calendar calculating so common among savants, given its infrequent appearance in normal persons? How do they do it? Do these extraordinary abilities in some areas, despite general low levels of intellectual functioning, challenge the concept of general intelligence (IQ)? Are we a series of separate intelligences rather than having an overall general intelligence? What does the appearance of savant skills in previously normal persons after CNS insult say about hidden potential in all of us?

The savant syndrome has, to this point, largely been viewed, sometimes frivolously, as a curiosity astonishing but unexplained. But until we can understand and account for the savant syndrome, we cannot fully understand ourselves, for no model of brain function, particularly memory, will be complete until it can incorporate and explain this intriguing and paradoxical juxtaposition of overall severe disability with islands of extraordinary superiority.

Interested persons can obtain additional updated information on savant syndrome at http://www.wismed.com/foundation/savant.htm.

Bibliography

Attwood, T. *Asperger's syndrome.* London: Jessica Kingsley. An excellent resource on Asperger's for both professionals and parents.

Blakeslee, S. (1994, August 2). Odd disorder of brain may offer new clues to basis of language. *New York Times.* A report of a 1994 research symposium on Williams syndrome outlining implications of this disorder for the field of cognitive neuroscience.

Frith, U. (1991). *Autism and Asperger syndrome.* Cambridge, UK: Cambridge University Press. A comprehensive review of Autism and Asperger's disorders compared and contrasted, including savant skills.

Lenhoff, H., Wang, P., Greenberg, F., & Bellugi, N. (1997, December). Williams syndrome and the brain. *Scientific American, 277* (6) pp. 42–47. A useful description of current knowledge regarding Williams syndrome.

Miller, L. (1989). *Musical savants: Exceptional skills in the mentally retarded.* Hillsdale, NJ: Erlbaum. A detailed, systematic investigation of a childhood musical savant plus a comprehensive review of all such studies to date. Provides an extensive bibliography on musical savants.

Nettelbeck, T., & Young, R. (1996). Intelligence and savant syndrome: Is the whole greater than the sum of the fragments? *Intelligence, 22,* 49–68. A very thorough debate as to whether savant syndrome is consistent with the theory of a general intelligence factor, or the theory of multiple intelligences each supported by a specialized neural system. This article also summarizes standardized test findings and family histories in Young's 51 savant cases, the largest single sample to date. Additionally the interface between talent, creativity, and intelligence is explored and an extensive, contemporary bibliography is provided (62 citations).

Rimland, B., & Fine, D. (1988). Special talents of autistic savants. In L. Obler & D. Fein (Eds.), *The exceptional brain* (pp. 474–492). New York: Guilford Press. A documentation of the nature and extent of savant skills in autistic persons.

Treffert, D. (1988). An unlikely virtuoso: Leslie Lemke and the story of savant syndrome. *Sciences, January/February*, 28–35. An overview article on savant syndrome summarizing concisely information on history, case reports, research findings, and implications for understanding brain function contained in two following references.

Treffert, D. (1988). The idiot savant: A review of the syndrome. *American Journal of Psychiatry, 145*, 563–572. A readily available summary review article on the history of savant syndrome, early and subsequent savants, clinical characteristics, etiology theories, research findings, with an extensive bibliography on savant syndrome both in autism and other developmental disabilities, congenital and acquired.

Treffert, D. (1989). *Extraordinary people: Understanding the "idiot savant."* New York: Harper & Row. The most comprehensive sourcebook available of history, case examples, theories, research findings, and future directions of research on Savant syndrome. Several prodigious savants are profiled in depth. 155 references. This book also appeared in a paperback edition (*Extraordinary people: Understanding Savant syndrome*, Ballantine, 1989), in which the film *Rainman* and its portrayal of an autistic savant are discussed along with several new savant examples.

Williams, J., Barratt-Boyes, B., & Lowe, J. (1961). Supravalvular aortic stenosis. *Circulation, 24*, 1311–1318. Williams's original description of this disorder.

Darold A. Treffert

SCALE DEVELOPMENT. A psychological scale is analogous to a scale for measuring weight; psychological scales measure a property of a person or a group of persons. Psychologists usually distinguish between tests, which seek to measure cognitive abilities or knowledge by measuring maximum performance, and scales of personality or attitude or other attributes, which assess characteristic behavior or preferences. This article focuses on personality and attitude scales, but many of the same measurement principles apply equally to tests. The term *item* is used in psychology to refer to an individual stimulus, such as a statement or question, to which a respondent indicates an answer. These responses are scored according to rules contained in scoring keys. Aggregations of individual item scores are referred to as scale scores.

External Method of Scale Construction

There are three broad methods for scale development, the external method, the construct method, and the factor analytic method. The external approach to scale construction begins by identifying some outcome that one wishes to predict or, possibly, to assess the traits associated with a particular outcome. For example, one might wish to determine whether or not a given respondent possesses career interests similar to those of petroleum engineers, or whether or not a certain psychiatric patient can be classified with a diagnosis of paranoid personality. To develop scales to aid in identifying such qualities using the external method, one would assemble an item pool relevant to the domain of vocational interests or of psychopathology. One would then identify a representative criterion group of petroleum engineers or of patients diagnosed as having paranoid personality. One would also identify parallel groups from the general population matched with the criterion groups on such attributes as age, sex, and education. Sets of questionnaire items would then be administered to both critical and comparison groups. Vocational interest items that showed distinctly different response patterns between petroleum engineers and the general population would be retained for further analysis. Similarly, psychopathological items to which persons diagnosed as having paranoid personality answered differently from a general population group would be retained. After initial item selection, it is customary to cross-validate the selected items on new critical and comparison groups to minimize the inclusion of items due to chance. At this point the scales are ready for norming and validation.

The external strategy of scale development has several advantages. The method guarantees a certain level of validity. The external method also is believed to permit the development of a scale with only modest knowledge of the psychological attributes of the group constituting the criterion. An added advantage is that the method is relatively easy to explain and to defend to the lay public should the need arise.

There are also several disadvantages of the external method. (1) It is often difficult to identify groups that are truly representative of the target group—one's sample of petroleum engineers might be limited to those returning questionnaires rather than to the entire population—or one might identify only persons coming to the attention of mental health professionals rather than all persons diagnosable as having paranoid personality. (2) Scales constructed using the external method are usually heterogeneous in terms of the traits they measure. When they are used operationally, it is difficult to know why a person received a certain score. Thus, a person might have obtained a certain score on the paranoid personality scale because that person was disputatious and argumentative, but not suspicious, or because the person was suspicious, but not argumentative. (3) Scales constructed using the external method are susceptible to irrelevant differences between critical and comparison groups. Even if groups are matched on salient demographic characteristics such as age and sex, other differences can contribute irrelevant systematic bias in the selection of items. For example, persons chosen from a list of members of a petroleum engineering society might contain a substantial number of persons who are actually working at different jobs, such as the job of manager. (4) The generalizability of scales constructed at a particular time with a particular critical group can be limited. External scales require frequent updating. (5) The selection of an appropriate item pool is of paramount importance. This consideration challenges the traditional view that one can proceed in ignorance of the traits to be assessed. (6) The external approach is susceptible to response styles, sources of systematic method variance such as a tendency to respond "dislike" to a wide variety of vocational interest items. These response styles may or may not contribute to empirical validity, but they always interfere with drawing inferences about the traits underlying scale scores. Some early defenders of the external method (Meehl, 1945) argued that the item content of externally constructed scales is of little importance; the measure of a good scale is its ability to distinguish groups, not the interpretability of responses to particular items or of the traits underlying scale scores. But others (Jackson, 1971; Loevinger, 1957) have observed that external scales that make such assumptions can contribute little to a cumulative psychological science.

Construct Method of Scale Construction

Unlike the external method, the construct method requires hypotheses about the traits or dispositions underlying a scale. It customarily requires a number of steps, which can be summarized in a series of questions (Jackson, 1970). (1) What precisely is to be measured? Can a cogent definition be formulated? Are there facets implied by the definition? For example, a scale for general risk taking might contain facets for monetary, physical, social, and ethical risk taking. (2) In what medium will items be created? Usually simple verbal statements are employed, but possible other materials include pictorial items, simple adjectives, or responses to situations presented verbally, by video, or by computer. (3) What situations are likely to elicit the trait in question? Can the situations be formulated in a facet-by-situation template to guide item construction? For example, the measurement of ethical risk taking would embody situations in which the respondent is confronted with the possibility of gain in exchange for compromising ethical principles, where there is a possibility that transgressions will be discovered and punished. (4) What response format will be employed? Vocational interest scales typically call for preferences, personality scales seek information about characteristic behavior, and attitude scales typically call for agree-disagree responses. Judgments about other people or institutions can take these or other forms. A number of studies have indicated that respondents prefer a variable response format with a number of points to simple dichotomous scales of the true-false or agree-disagree

variety. Indeed, scales constructed with variable response options are generally more reliable and thus provide more information per item. The prevalence of binary true-false or agree-disagree formats is explained by their ease of hand scoring. A special format is the forced-choice method. This method involves the pairing of two or more statements that are almost identical in desirability; the respondent is asked to choose the one that is most characteristic of him or her. This method is useful under at least two circumstances: when faking is expected, as in a job selection situation, and to avoid response biases. To suppress faking, two equally attractive choices are presented, only one of which has been shown to relate to a criterion such as job performance. To avoid response biases such as a tendency to respond "like" to vocational interest items, activities are paired with equally popular alternatives. The respondent chooses only one, which is scored as the preferred activity. (5) What measurement model is to be employed? Although a variety of underlying measurement models and item types are possible (Green, 1954), the great majority of scales employ the method of summated ratings, in which item responses are summed to yield a scale score, based on the assumption of a single underlying factor to which all items are related.

Factor Analytic Method of Scale Construction

The factor analytic method begins with a pool of heterogeneous items relevant to the domain of interest and identifies clusters of items that are answered similarly by persons who possess the relevant traits. Thus, a questionnaire assessing personality disorders might contain items reflecting traits relevant to the functioning of persons with personality disorder. Factor analysis might be used to sort items into separate constituent traits like suspiciousness and argumentativeness. There are many other quantitative methods for clustering items, but factor analytic methods are most widely used.

A scale developed using factor analysis begins with assembling the item pool and administering it to a heterogeneous sample of people in which variation is expected in the broad characteristics to be assessed. Relationships are determined by computing product-moment correlation coefficients between responses to every item and every other item. Factor analysis of these correlations yields latent variables, that is, new broader trait dimensions that are believed to be fundamental dimensions of the domain, whether of personality, vocational interests, or psychopathology. This venture can be undertaken in an exploratory fashion when one is uncertain about the nature and number of factors that exist or in a confirmatory mode when one wishes to evaluate hypotheses about the nature of the underlying traits by specifying in advance a certain pattern of factors and evaluating the degree to which this pattern occurs empirically. There is a body of knowledge regarding the use of statistical models of factor analysis for evaluating hypotheses in confirmatory factor analysis.

The effective use of factor analysis for scale development is strongly dependent on the quality of the item pool used initially. Both the quality of the items and their comprehensiveness are critical. Obviously, one cannot expect to find essential factors if relevant items have been omitted, and poorly conceived or written items can yield uninterpretable results. Factor analysis can also yield factors that are real but not traceable to the traits of interest. For example, personality questionnaires yield a general factor of desirability responding and attitude scales yield a general factor of agreement-disagreement with items, particularly when items are ambiguous or when the attitudes are not important to respondents. It is difficult to distinguish factors due to item content from those due to respondents' styles of responding.

Development and Analysis of the Item Pool

The development of an item pool is an art that depends on the adequacy of definitions of the domain and its underlying traits, sensitivity to sources of irrelevant variance such as irrelevant content or extreme desirability, and the psychological judgment of the item writers. Lest this sound like too daunting a task, several studies (e.g., Ashton & Goldberg, 1973) have demonstrated that even when no item selection is imposed, university students without specialized training given adequate trait definitions can equal or exceed the validities obtained using external methods.

Research (Holden, Fekken, & Jackson, 1985) has identified item characteristics associated with the validity of verbal personality scales. Some of these include short rather than long items, absence of negations, reference to characteristic behavior rather than calling for agreement with general sentiments, and reference to broad trait attributions rather than to specific behaviors. After a substantial item pool is developed, ideally containing at least five times the number of items ultimately desired, items should be subjected to statistical analysis. The classical psychometric approach often used in combination with the construct method is to correlate each item with its own scale and select those items with the highest correlation. Refinements include identifying items that not only correlate highly with their own scale but that also correlate minimally with irrelevant scales or with scales reflecting generalized response styles, such as desirability responding. Thus, an item designed for a risk-taking scale should not correlate higher with an impulsivity scale if both scales are to be included in the battery. Items chosen in this way usually produce reliable scales that are not excessively correlated with other scales. A battery of scales so constructed tends to be more valid than less reliable, more highly intercorrelated scales. A similar approach may be undertaken using factor analysis.

Norming and Validation

Scale scores have little intrinsic meaning unless one can compare them to a reference group. Norming is undertaken by administering the scale to a reference group and computing scale statistics. These statistics permit the comparison of individual scores with those from the norming group. The normative sample should be chosen to be relevant to the manner in which the scale will be used. Norming studies are usually designed systematically to take account of demographic characteristics impacting the trait. Ideally, norms are gathered using stratified random sampling of a specified population in which such characteristics as age, sex, and socioeconomic status define sampling blocks. In practice, participant refusal constrains random sampling. Accordingly, many norming samples are drawn so as to duplicate the characteristics of the intended population without strictly random sampling. In such cases, it is important that selection methods do not create biases in estimates of central tendency and variability.

Scales can be validated, that is, shown to correlate with real-world behavior, in an almost infinite variety of ways. For example, an anxiety scale might be validated by comparing high and low scorers in eye blink rate while experiencing experimentally induced stress. A scale for shallow affect has been validated by demonstrating that persons low in affect favor the death penalty for prisoners. A critical hurdle for personality measures is the demonstration of convergent and discriminant validity (Campbell & Fiske, 1959). This embodies the requirement that a trait measure should correlate more highly with an indicant of the same trait measured by a different method than it does with measures of irrelevant traits. For example, a scale measuring anxiety should yield higher relationships with clinical ratings of anxiety than with clinical ratings of suspiciousness. This requirement was formulated in recognition of the fact that psychological scales reflect trait-method composites. The goal of measurement is thus to maximize the saturation of relevant trait variance in scales while minimizing variance traceable to irrelevant traits and to the particular method of measurement.

Computer Assessment

It is almost always possible to administer a paper-and-pencil scale by computer, and most people prefer computer administration. There is now a body of research indicating that responses to questionnaire items are generally unaffected by computer administration, provided that the format has not been changed. For example, people can be expected to report having headaches about as often on paper as by computer. But even apparently unimportant format changes can create problems. For example, paper-and-pencil adjective checklists requiring respondents to check only those adjectives that were descriptive of them yielded very different scores when computer administration required respondents to answer "true" or "false" to every adjective. But such changes are typically unintended consequences of computer adaptation of tests rather than representing intrinsic differences between computer and paper-and-pencil administration.

The promise of computer-aided scale administration goes well beyond the essentially trivial adaptation of existing paper-and-pencil tests. Two promising directions are the gathering of response time data and the use of computer adaptive assessment. Response latency measures have been shown to add incremental validity to scale scores in the assessment of psychopathology (Holden & Fekken, 1993) and are a promising means of detecting faking (people require more time to fake).

Computer adaptive testing can be employed in one of two ways: for locating, with fewer items, the respondent's exact location on the underlying trait and for identifying from a set of many trait dimensions those that best characterize the respondent. In the first instance, computer administration would diagnose the respondent's score on a trait such as anxiety by taking account of previous responses to successively presented items that are closer to that individual's exact location on the underlying dimension of anxiety. An example of the second application of computer adaptive testing is the use of a vocational interest measure with a large number of interest dimensions in which the algorithm identifies the few characteristics most descriptive of the respondent's high-interest areas. The questions could be adapted in such a way as to identify in the first instance clusters of high interest and, within each cluster, more refined measures of interest while eliminating dimensions of low interest. Most existing vocational interest measures cannot, for example, distinguish reliably between interests in different medical specialties because there are so many other interest areas to cover. But if a person is found to have high interests in the general medical area, a computer adaptive strategy would give less attention to scales in which the respondent initially indicated low interest and more attention to those of high interest such as different medical specialties. The time usually devoted to areas of less interest could then be devoted more effectively to a finer-grained analysis of differential interests in a narrower cluster. Computer adaptive testing offers the promise of powerful new assessment strategies, but it also challenges assessment specialists to develop new theoretical foundations to guide the enterprise and more extensive item pools to capitalize on its promise.

Bibliography

Ashton, S. G., & Goldberg, L. R. (1973). In response to Jackson's challenge: The comparative validity of personality scales constructed by the external (empirical) strategy and scales developed intuitively by experts, novices, and laymen. *Journal of Research in Personality, 7,* 1–20.

Campbell, D. T., & Fiske, D. W. (1959). Convergent and discriminant validation by the multitrait-multimethod matrix. *Psychological Bulletin, 56,* 81–105.

Green, B. F., Jr. (1954). Attitude measurement. In G. Lindsey (Ed.), *Handbook of social psychology* (Vol. 1, pp. 335–369). Cambridge, MA: Addison-Wesley.

Holden, R. R., & Fekken, G. C. (1993). Can personality test item response latencies have construct validity? Issues of reliability and covergent and discriminant validity. *Personality and Individual Differences, 15,* 243–248.

Holden, R. R., Fekken, G. C., & Jackson, D. N. (1985). Structured personality test item characteristics and validity. *Journal of Research in Personality, 19,* 386–394.

Jackson, D. N. (1970). A sequential system for personality scale development. In C. D. Spielberg (Ed.), *Current topics in clinical and community psychology* (Vol. 2, pp. 61–96). New York: Academic Press.

Jackson, D. N. (1971). The dynamics of structured personality tests: 1971. *Psychological Review, 78,* 229–248.

Loevinger, J. (1957). Objective tests as instruments of psychological theory. *Psychological Reports, 3,* 635–694.

Meehl, P. (1945). The dynamics of "structured" personality tests. *Journal of Clinical Psychology, 1,* 296–303.

Douglas N. Jackson

SCANDINAVIA. *See* Finland; Norway; *and* Sweden.

SCENE PERCEPTION is the visual perception of an environment as viewed by an observer at a given time. It includes not only the perception of individual objects, but also such things as their relative locations and expectations about what other kinds of objects might be encountered.

Given that scene perception is so effortless for most observers, it might be thought of as something easy to understand. However, the amount of effort required by a process often bears little relation to its underlying complexity. A closer look shows that scene perception is a highly complex activity and that any account of it must deal with several difficult issues: What exactly is

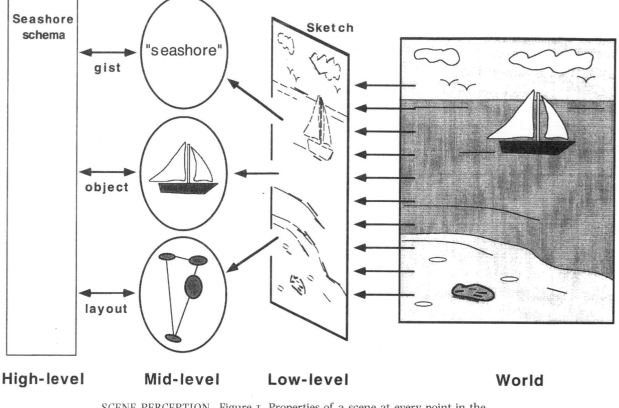

High-level   **Mid-level**   **Low-level**   **World**

SCENE PERCEPTION. Figure 1. Properties of a scene at every point in the visual field.

a scene? What aspects of it do we represent? What are the processes involved? Finding the answers to these questions has proven to be extraordinarily difficult.

However, answers are being found, and a general understanding of scene perception is beginning to emerge. Interestingly, this emerging picture shows that much of our subjective experience as observers is highly misleading, at least in regards to the way that things are carried out. In particular, the impression of a stable picturelike representation somewhere in our heads turns out to be largely an illusion.

To see how this comes about, imagine a seashore where there is a sailboat, some rocks, clouds, and perhaps a few other objects (see Figure 1). How do we perceive this scene? Intuitively, it seems that the set of objects in the environment would give rise to a corresponding set of representations in the observer. Thus, there would be detailed representations of the sailboat, clouds, and so forth, with each representation describing the identity, location, and "meaning" of the item it refers to. In this view, the goal of scene perception is to form a literal re-presentation of the world, with all of its visible structure represented concurrently and in great detail everywhere. This representation then serves as the basis for all subsequent visual processing.

As it turns out, however, memory for visual detail is generally quite short-lived (around 100 milliseconds (ms), Irwin, 1996). And since successive eye fixations are usually separated by at least 150 to 200 ms, it follows that their contents cannot be integrated into a complete, detailed representation. Conversely, it has also been found that a complete, detailed representation is not necessary—the meaning of a scene (e.g., whether or not it is a seashore) can be determined within 100 to 120 ms (Biederman, 1981; Potter, 1976), a time that allows recognition of only a few objects. Evidently, a small set of object and scene properties is enough to provide us with an impression of a scene that is complete and detailed everywhere.

This realization causes a shift in perspective: scene representations are no longer structures built up from eye movements and attentional shifts, but rather are rapidly formed structures that can guide such activities. More generally, the goal of scene perception appears to be the establishment of an immediate context for various aspects of visual processing, as well as for visuomotor operations such as reaching or locomotion.

How might this be done? Scene perception is a special case of visual perception, and so likely involves the same processing levels as vision generally. [*See* Vision and Sight.] The first of these is low-level processing, which uses the incoming light to recover simple properties of the environment visible to the observer, such as the color of the sky or the texture of the clouds. The second is mid-level processing, concerned with more complex tasks, such as separating the sailboat from its background and representing it as a distinct object with its own size, shape, and colors. Finally, there is high-level processing, concerned with issues of meaning. For example, high-level processes might identify a mid-level object as a sailboat and a scene as a seashore, and so allow us to expect such things as seagulls, whitecaps, and fishing boats.

The exact nature of the processes involved in scene perception is largely unknown. However, at least some understanding—summarized in the following sections—has been obtained of the kinds of operations carried out at each level, and their interactions with each other.

Low-Level Processing

Scene perception begins with the creation of a detailed maplike representation, or sketch, obtained from the pattern of light that falls on the retina (Marr, 1982). This sketch describes the properties of the scene at every point in the visual field (see Figure 1). These can be simple image-based features (color, size, etc.) or more complex scene-based properties (three-dimensional slant, surface curvature, etc.) obtained by "quick and dirty" interpretation processes. Thus, when looking at the seashore, the sketch will indicate "white" at regions corresponding to the sails and the surrounding clouds, and "blue" at regions corresponding to the sky. It will also describe the distribution of other properties as well, for example, indicating a degree of surface curvature at regions corresponding to the sail and the clouds, and no curvature at regions corresponding to the sky.

In the absence of attention, these low-level representations are volatile, their contents being overwritten by subsequent stimuli or else fading away a few hundred milliseconds after light stops entering the eyes (Rensink, 2000). Thus, at any particular fixation the sketch effectively exists only as long as the eyes do not move. As such, although the sketch is detailed, it is not stable—it must be constantly regenerated, with a new sketch formed with each new fixation.

Mid-Level Processing

The volatile, ever-changing representations of low-level vision cannot support the stable perception we have of a scene. Instead, this must be accomplished by a different set of representations that owe their stability to some form of short-term memory. Because such memory is costly, only a few aspects of scene structure can be given stable representation. These appear to include object structure, scene layout, and scene gist (see Fig-

ure 1). The extent to which these aspects are determined independently of each other is unknown.

Object Structure. Although visual detail is generally volatile, information about a small number of objects can be held across an eye movement or temporal interruption (Irwin, 1996; Rensink, 2000). This is likely done by attentional mechanisms that can store several attributes of an object—such as its shape, location, or the arrangement of its parts—in visual short-term memory (Irwin, 1996). Thus, if attention is given to the sailboat at the seashore, its representation would contain information such as the shape of its hull and sails, and perhaps the relative location of the sails with respect to each other and the hull. This representation will remain stable (in short-term memory) as long as attention is directed to the sailboat.

The capacity of short-term memory is severely limited, so little accumulation of object structure is possible (Irwin, 1996). And, although facilitation of processing can occur between related objects viewed in succession, this is restricted to the past few objects viewed (Henderson, 1992). Consequently, only a few object representations are in play at any time, with a limited amount of information in each. This strongly suggests that object representation is dynamic: Although all the objects in a scene cannot be represented simultaneously, eye movements and attentional shifts are coordinated such that a stable representation of any selected object can be formed whenever needed (Rensink, 2000).

Scene Layout. Just as there appears to be a stable representation of the arrangement of parts within an object, so there appears to be a stable representation of the arrangement, or layout, of objects within a scene. The layout of the seashore, for example, might be described by the relative position of the sailboat, rocks, clouds, and shoreline with respect to each other. Such information is vital if the limited information obtained from individual eye fixations is to be integrated into a structure capable of directing subsequent eye movements and attentional shifts.

Layout is sometimes thought to be represented by a schematic map, which describes the locations of various objects in the scene without a detailed description of their structure or identity (Hochberg, 1978). Such a minimal description is sufficient for the guidance of many actions, such as reaching or obstacle avoidance. And the lack of detailed description allows the map to be constructed quickly and with minimal memory. However, little is known about the particular aspects of layout that are represented or how a layout representation might be formed.

Scene Gist. The most abstract aspect of a scene is its meaning, or gist. In the case of the above example, the gist would simply be "seashore." Similarly, a scene with several boats and a dock might be perceived as "harbor." Other examples of gist would be "farmyard," "shopping center," or "city." Gist is a highly invariant quantity, remaining constant over many different eye positions and viewpoints, as well as over many changes in the composition and layout of objects in an environment. As such, it can potentially provide a stable context for other processes, such as object recognition.

Experiments based on naming and categorization show that gist can be determined within 100 to 120 ms of presentation (Potter, 1976). Only a few objects can be perceived within this time, suggesting that the perception of gist may be based on the perception of two or three key objects. For example, if an object were recognized as a sailboat, it would suggest that the scene is a seashore, harbor, or open sea; if a beach were also recognized, it would reduce the set of candidates to "seashore." Another possibility is that gist can be determined without perceiving objects at all (Henderson, 1992). This position is supported by the finding that different gists can be determined simultaneously at different spatial scales, without any need for attention (Oliva & Schyns, 1997). This suggests that gist may be invoked by low-level features diagnostic of scene category, such as the distributions of line orientations or colors in the image.

High-Level Processing

The considerable invariance of object structure, scene layout, and scene gist over different viewing positions implies that they often remain constant over relatively long stretches of time. This allows the long-term learning of their occurrence in various scenes. The result of this is a scene schema, an interlinked collection of representations in long-term memory that describes such things as the kinds of objects that occur together and how they might be positioned relative to each other. The information in a schema can constrain the kinds of objects expected, and perhaps also indicate their importance for the task at hand (Friedman, 1979).

In contrast to the simple structures that invoke it, the contents of a schema can be relatively sophisticated. For instance, schemas are believed to include an inventory of objects likely to be present in the scene. In the case of a seashore schema, this inventory could include rocks, clouds, a beach, boats, and possibly a few other objects. Various aspects of layout information may also be stored, such as the relative locations of the inventory objects (Mandler & Ritchey, 1977).

Interaction of Systems

Although details are far from clear, it appears that a relatively simple set of interactions may underlie most of scene perception (see Figure 1). When viewing a scene, the low-level processes provide a constantly regenerating sketch of the properties visible to the viewer. A subset of these properties could determine scene gist and layout, which then invoke a scene schema. Subsequent processes could attempt to verify the schema and supply it with the information needed to carry out any required actions (Friedman, 1979). When an unexpected object is encountered, more sophisticated (attentional) processes could reevaluate the object, reevaluate the gist, or learn a new association between the two. Meanwhile, the layout could be used as a direct check on the current interpretation, as well as provide spatial guidance of attention to appropriate items.

Such an account of scene perception creates an apparent paradox: If detailed representations are short-lived and stable representations contain little detail, how can our impression of a scene be both detailed and stable? The solution to this lies in the "just in time" nature of object representation, in which a stable representation of an object can be formed whenever needed through the coordinated use of attentional shifts and eye movements. Provided that only a few objects need to be represented at any one time, such a dynamic representation has all the power of a static one while requiring much less in the way of processing resources (Rensink, 2000).

[*See also* Visual Illusions.]

Bibliography

Biederman, I. (1981). On the semantics of a glance at a scene. In M. Kubovy & J. R. Pomerantz (Eds.), *Perceptual organization* (pp. 213–253). Hillsdale, NJ: Erlbaum.

Fisher, D. F., Monty, R. A., & Senders, J. W. (1981). *Eye movements: Cognition and visual perception.* Hillsdale, NJ: Erlbaum.

Friedman, A. (1979). Framing pictures: The role of knowledge in automatized encoding and memory for gist. *Journal of Experimental Psychology: General, 108,* 318–355.

Henderson, J. M. (1992). Object identification in context: The visual processing of natural scenes. *Canadian Journal of Psychology, 46,* 319–341.

Hochberg, J. E. (1978). *Perception* (2nd ed., pp. 158–211). Englewood Cliffs, NJ: Prentice Hall.

Irwin, D. E. (1996). Integrating information across saccadic eye movements. *Current Directions in Psychological Science, 5,* 94–100.

Mandler, J., & Ritchey, G. H. (1977). Long-term memory for pictures. *Journal of Experimental Psychology: Human Learning and Memory, 3,* 386–396.

Marr, D. (1982). *Vision.* San Francisco: Freeman.

Monty, R. A., & Senders, J. W. (1976). *Eye movements and psychological processes.* Hillsdale, NJ: Erlbaum.

Oliva, A., & Schyns, P. G. (1997). Coarse blobs or fine edges? Evidence that information diagnosticity changes the perception of complex visual stimuli. *Cognitive Psychology, 34,* 72–107.

Potter, M. C. (1976). Short-term conceptual memory for pictures. *Journal of Experimental Psychology: Human Learning and Memory, 2,* 509–522.

Rensink, R. A. (2000). The dynamic representation of scenes. *Visual Cognition*, 7, 17–42.

Rayner, K. (1992). *Eye movements and visual cognition: Scene perception and reading.* New York: Springer.

Simons, D. J. (Ed.). (2000). [Special issue on change blindness and visual memory.] *Visual Cognition*, 7.

Ronald A. Rensink

SCHACHTER, STANLEY (1922–1997), American social psychologist. In the aftermath of World War II, a remarkable collection of young scholars migrated to the Massachusetts Institute of Technology (MIT) to work with one of the leading founders of modern social psychology, Kurt Lewin. This group—which included Kurt Back, Leon Festinger, Harold Kelley, Stanley Schachter, and John Thibaut, among others—became the major intellectual force that shaped and guided social psychology during the last half of the century. It is difficult to envision what social psychology would be like today without the legacy of Lewin's "first generation" of American social psychologists. Beyond question, Schachter was one of the most influential and creative scholars in this pioneering group.

Schachter was born in New York City. He entered Yale University just before World War II, eventually receiving a bachelor's degree in 1942 and a master's degree in 1944. Schachter served in the armed forces from 1944 to 1946, during which time he published his first research. Most of this work focused on the visual problems and perceptual distortions experienced by air force pilots, especially during night flights. A keen interest in how basic research could be used to solve applied problems permeated nearly all of the research that Schachter conducted over the next 50 years of his career.

In 1946, Schachter entered the doctoral program at MIT to work with Lewin. Unfortunately, Lewin died shortly after Schachter arrived in Cambridge. One of Lewin's senior students—Leon Festinger—took over as Schachter's supervisor, launching a rich collaborative professional relationship as well as a lifelong friendship. When Festinger moved to the University of Michigan in 1948, Schachter followed, completing his graduate education at Michigan in 1949. Schachter's dissertation, which examined how individuals who express deviant opinions in small groups are treated by majority group members who disagree with them (Schachter, 1951), became a widely cited, classic article in social psychology. To the end of his career, Schachter's dissertation remained one of the articles of which he was proudest.

In 1949, Schachter took a job at the Laboratory for Research in Social Relations at the University of Minnesota, eventually becoming a full professor. Some of his most important research was conducted at Minnesota. In the 1950s, Schachter authored or coauthored five books, four of which had considerable impact on the nascent field of social psychology. These books included *Social Pressures in Informal Groups* (New York, 1950), which was based largely on Schachter's dissertation research; *Theory and Experiment in Social Communication* (Ann Arbor, Mich., 1950); *When Prophecy Fails* (Minneapolis, Minn., 1956), which showed how cognitive dissonance theory could explain behavior following disconfirmed expectancies; and *The Psychology of Affiliation* (Stanford, Calif. 1959), which explored links between fear and affiliation. During this fertile period, Schachter also published several articles, including some classic studies on rumor transmission (Back, et al., 1950) and the topics of group cohesion and persuasion.

In 1961, Schachter joined the department of psychology at Columbia University, where he remained until the end of his career. Immediately after arriving at Columbia, he published his ingenious and controversial studies on the cognitive, social, and physiological determinants of emotional experience (Schachter & Singer, 1962). Although some of the conclusions of this research have been challenged, Schachter demonstrated that attributions people make about the sources of their physiological arousal are malleable and showed how social cues in the environment can be used to infer emotional states. This research was groundbreaking because it focused on how biological (physiological) processes and cognitive (attribution) processes jointly influence social perception and behavior. Many of Schachter's closest friends felt that he probably underestimated the significant role this line of research played in instigating the wave of attribution theory and research that swept across social psychology in the late 1960s and early 1970s.

During the mid-1960s, Schachter's research interests began to turn to more applied problems. He conducted work on topics such as the relation between birth order and educational attainment (Schachter, 1963), the origins of criminal behavior (Schachter & Latané, 1964), the perception of pain (Nisbett & Schachter, 1966), and perhaps most notably the causes of obesity (Schachter, 1968). Schachter's research on obesity demonstrated that the eating patterns of obese people tend to be governed by the apparent time of day (external cues) rather than by their own hunger sensations (internal cues). Most of his work in the 1960s was influenced by his fascination with how attribution processes affect social perception, self-perception, and social behavior. By the mid-1970s, Schachter's applied interests shifted to smoking, especially nicotine regulation in heavy smokers (Schachter, 1977) and the effects of urinary pH on smoking behavior (Silverstein, Kozlowski, & Schachter, 1977). He knew that nicotine was addictive and how it produced withdrawal symptoms more than 15 years before the tobacco industry admitted these associations publicly.

In 1983, Schachter was elected to the National Academy of Science. In 1984, he received the Distinguished Scientist Award from the Society of Experimental Social Psychology. During the mid-1980s and early 1990s, Schachter focused on trends in the stock market (Hood, Andreassen, & Schachter, 1985). Near the end of his career, he published some of his most creative work on how speech dysfluencies reveal the structure of knowledge (Schachter, Christenfield, Ravina, & Bilous, 1991).

Perhaps the greatest legacy that Schachter left to social psychology was a line of students who have had distinguished careers of their own. These include Bibb Latané, Richard Nisbett, Patricia Pliner, Judith Rodin, Lee Ross, Jerome Singer, Stewart Valins, and Ladd Wheeler, to name just a few. These "second generation" scholars—the academic grandchildren of Lewin—have themselves affected and, in some cases, radically altered the course of contemporary social psychology during the last two decades.

Like many in Lewin's "first generation," Schachter designed experiments that told a good, ego-involving story, and they were framed around important research questions rather than specific research methods or narrow, faddish topics. This predilection drew him away from mainstream social psychology in the late 1960s, when he began to address fundamental questions about the nature of obesity and smoking. When he died in the summer of 1997, an obituary in *Time Magazine* claimed that Schachter was a scholar who specialized in studying and documenting obvious patterns of behavior. In reality, his creative and powerful approaches to studying social behavior shed such clear light on various social phenomena that they became obvious only in the wake of his pioneering research.

[*Many of the people mentioned in this article are the subjects of independent biographical entries.*]

Bibliography

Back, K., Festinger, L., Hymovitch, W., Kelley, H., Schachter, S., & Thibaut, J. (1950). The methodology of studying rumor transmission. *Human Relations, 3,* 307–312.

Hood, D. C., Andreassen, P., & Schachter, S. (1985). Random and non-random walks on the new stock exchange. *Journal of Economic Behavior and Organization, 6,* 331–338.

Nisbett, R. E., & Schachter, S. (1966). Cognitive manipulation of pain. *Journal of Experimental Social Psychology, 2,* 227–236.

Schachter, S. (1951). Deviation, rejection and communication. *Journal of Abnormal and Social Psychology, 46,* 190–207.

Schachter, S. (1963). Birth order, eminence, and higher education. *American Sociological Review, 28,* 757–768.

Schachter, S. (1968). Obesity and eating. *Science, 161,* 751–756.

Schachter, S. (1977). Nicotine regulation in heavy and light smokers. *Journal of Experimental Psychology: General, 106,* 5–12.

Schachter, S., Christenfield, N. J. S., Ravina, B., & Bilous, F. R. (1991). Speech disfluency and the structure of knowledge. *Journal of Personality and Social Psychology, 60,* 362–367.

Schachter, S., & Latané, B. (1964). Crime, cognition and the autonomic nervous system. In D. Levine (Ed.). *Nebraska symposium on motivation* (pp. 221–273). Lincoln: University of Nebraska Press.

Schachter, S., & Singer, J. (1962). Cognitive, social, and physiological determinants of emotional state. *Psychological Review, 69,* 379–399.

Silverstein, B., Kozlowski, L. T., & Schachter, S. (1977). Social life, cigarette smoking, and urinary pH. *Journal of Experimental Psychology: General, 106,* 20–23.

Jeffry A. Simpson

SCHEDULES OF REINFORCEMENT are prescriptions for arranging reinforcing consequences with respect to operant behavior. Technically, reinforcement schedules can be described without reference to the behavior they generate. In one type of scheduling arrangement, for example, a response only after some fixed period of time has elapsed is reinforced, that is, a fixed-interval schedule (see below). Although such a formal description may be useful for classification purposes, a complete account of schedules must also include descriptions of schedule performance. As it is normally used, the term *schedules of reinforcement* refers broadly to the interaction between reinforcement schedule contingencies and the performance engendered by them.

Interest in reinforcement schedules can be traced to the work in the mid-1930s of B. F. Skinner, who found that intermittent scheduling of reinforcement could organize and sustain behavior over extended periods of time. [*See the biography of Skinner.*] Since then, reinforcement schedules have been used in a variety of different ways by behavioral scientists. The utility of schedules lies mainly in their ability to produce orderly and predictable patterns of behavior over time and across a variety of different circumstances. With reinforcement schedules, a performance can be "customized" to the needs of a particular question, making schedules valuable methodological tools for investigating a wide range of environmental and biological variables. At the same time, schedules have served as important topics of investigation in their own right, for the light they shed on basic behavioral processes.

Schedules are normally studied under laboratory

conditions where performance can be directly measured and variables carefully controlled. The most common measure of schedule performance is its rate of occurrence (responses per unit time), although other measures (for example, latency, time between responses, time between reinforcers) are frequently used as well. Especially useful in the analysis of schedule patterns is a device known as a cumulative recorder, which generates a graph of the cumulated response frequency over time and in relation to schedule contingencies.

Reinforcement can be made available upon completion of a specified number of responses (ratio schedule) or upon the first response after some period of time has elapsed (interval schedule). The requirements for reinforcement may remain the same from one reinforcer to the next (fixed schedule) or may vary around some average value (variable schedule). These combinations of scheduling arrangements yield four basic schedule types: fixed ratio (FR), variable ratio (VR), fixed interval (FI), and variable interval (VI).

Each basic schedule type produces its own distinctive performance—a kind of behavioral signature—that remains roughly invariant across different responses, reinforcers, and species. Fixed schedules (FR and FI) are typified by a two-state ("break-run") pattern, in which a pause ("break") just after reinforcement gives way to a period of high-rate responding ("run") until reinforcement, whereupon the pattern repeats. The transition from the break to the run is somewhat more gradual under FI than under FR schedules. Fixed ratio responding is typified by an all-or-none pattern, occurring at virtually a constant rate once it begins, whereas FI responding shows a positively accelerated slope throughout the interval (sometimes called a scallop from its appearance on a cumulative record). On both FR and FI schedules, the length of the break following reinforcement (or postreinforcement pause) varies systematically with the requirements for reinforcement: the more responses or time required, the longer the pause. Such pausing is greatly attenuated, if not eliminated entirely, on variable schedules (VR and VI), which tend to produce constant, steady rates of responding between reinforcers.

The schedule one uses depends on the particular experimental question and the type of patterning desired. The two-state patterning created under FR and FI schedules has been useful in assessing the selective effects of an independent variable on different aspects of performance. The uniform response patterning created by VR and VI schedules makes them ideal baselines against which to assess the effects of other variables (for example, drugs, deprivation, lesions, to name just a few).

These basic schedules can be combined in an almost unlimited number of ways. The most common schedule combinations are those in which two or more schedules are arranged in serial (sequential schedules) or in parallel (concurrent schedules). In one type of sequential schedule, two or more independent schedules alternate within a session, each providing its own reinforcement. When individual schedule components are signaled by distinct exteroceptive stimuli (multiple schedule), component rates and patterns are characteristic of each schedule in isolation. When individual component stimuli are unsignaled (mixed schedule), behavior is less differentiated across different schedule components.

In a second type of sequential schedule, schedule components are presented successively with reinforcement provided upon completion of all schedule components in the sequence. When the component stimuli are signaled (chained schedule) and the number of components are few, component rates and patterns resemble those maintained by each schedule when presented singly. With three or more component schedules (sometimes called extended chained schedules), rates in early components (or links) of the chain deteriorate. When the component stimuli are unsignaled (tandem schedule), rates across components are more uniform and performance decrements in early links are greatly attenuated. In a variation of an extended chained schedule, known as a higher-order schedule, completion of each schedule component is treated as a unitary response that is itself reinforced according to another schedule.

In a concurrent schedule, two or more independent schedules are in effect at the same time. The schedules are normally associated with spatially distinct operanda such that responses cannot occur on more than one schedule at a time. The patterns of behavior generated by concurrent schedules are a complex function of many interacting variables, but in general the relative allocation of behavior is proportional to the relative allocation of reinforcement provided by the schedules.

As with basic schedules, schedule combinations have been used in a variety of ways. Multiple schedules provide a valuable technique for within-session comparisons of different independent variables. Although behavior in one component is sometimes affected by the schedule in another component (contrast, induction), such interactions are outweighed by the considerable methodological benefits of multiple schedules. Chained schedules have been used extensively in the study of sequential organization and in conditioned (secondary) reinforcement. Mixed and tandem schedules serve as useful controls for the effects of added stimuli in multiple and chained schedules, respectively. Higher order schedules have been useful in the analysis and synthesis of behavioral units. Concurrent schedules have been used extensively in the study of choice behavior.

This brief overview has emphasized the practical benefits of schedules. Indeed, the ease with which schedules can be used to generate virtually any behavioral pattern makes them extremely valuable as methodological tools. But schedules are more than mere assays for investigating other variables; schedules also modulate the effects of those variables on behavior. In addition, schedules create units that serve as building blocks out of which complex behavior emerges and are thus of scientific interest in their own right. For all of these reasons, schedules have played and continue to play a central role in the psychology of learning and behavior.

[*See also* Operant Conditioning.]

Bibliography

Ferster, C. B., & Skinner, B. F. (1957). *Schedules of reinforcement*. New York: Appleton-Century-Crofts. Considered the encyclopedia of schedules, this book is significant not only for its exhaustive coverage of the subject matter—over 900 figures (mostly cumulative records) summarizing over 70,000 experimental hours—but for providing a framework for studying and interpreting schedule effects.

Lattal, K. A. (1991). Scheduling positive reinforcers. In I. H. Iversen & K. A. Lattal (Eds.), *Experimental analysis of behavior* (pp. 87–134). Amsterdam: Elsevier. An overview of the most commonly used schedules and their characteristic effects, with a particular emphasis on practical and methodological considerations.

Skinner, B. F. (1938). *The behavior of organisms*. New York: Appleton-Century-Crofts. The first systematic exploration of intermittent scheduling of reinforcement, including some of the basic schedules still in use today.

Thompson, T., & Grabowski, J. G. (1972). *Reinforcement schedules and multioperant analysis*. New York: Appleton-Century-Crofts. Provides systematic coverage of schedules in a programmed text format, with material divided into small, incrementally arranged units. Useful for students with little or no background in behavior principles.

Zeiler, M. (1977). Schedules of reinforcement: The controlling variables. In W. K. Honig & J. E. R. Staddon (Eds.), *Handbook of operant behavior* (pp. 201–232). Englewood Cliffs, NJ: Prentice Hall. A comprehensive empirical review and theoretical analysis of reinforcement schedules. Particularly helpful is the discussion of schedule effects in relation to specific controlling variables, and of the role schedules play in the creation and integration of behavioral units.

Timothy D. Hackenberg

SCHEMA. A cognitive structure that represents knowledge about a concept or type of stimulus, including its attributes and the relations among those attributes, is called a schema. Schemas represent general broad knowledge abstracted across many particular instances. Schemas are viewed as everyday subjective theories about how the world operates. They include people's informal theories about objects (washing machines), personality traits (extroversion), self (as independent), social roles (librarian), social groups (African Americans), and event scripts (eating in a restaurant). The term *schema* is sometimes also used to describe a content-free rule for making inferences, as in causal schemas (people's informal theories about how to infer causality). A schema may include nonverbal knowledge, as in an infant's sensorimotor schemas.

Schema theories assume that schemas generalize over instances, resulting in a mental abstraction stored in memory. Unlike prototypes, which also are assumed to generalize over instances, schemas may (1) omit irrelevant or unimportant features, whereas a prototype represents all the features of the generic instance, and (2) specify links among the concept's attributes, whereas a prototype may specify a list of features but not internally organize the list. Exemplar theories, in contrast to both schemas and prototypes, posit multiple mental representations of specific stimuli or experiences, derived from either direct or secondhand experience.

History

Over the history of the schema concept in cognitive, social, and developmental psychology, it has provided a configural contrast to elemental views of mental representation. In each case it emphasizes a Gestalt whole with emergent properties beyond simple combinations of the isolated parts. Schema theory emerged in Frederick Bartlett's *Remembering* (Cambridge, Mass., 1932), which described memory for figures, pictures, and stories. Offered in explicit opposition to then-dominant views that memory was a collection of isolated elements, the theory described how people organize stories and experiences into patterns that facilitate understanding and behavior. Similarly, Solomon Asch (*Journal of Abnormal and Social Psychology*, 1946, 41, 1230–1240) proposed that people's impressions of others form an organized, coherent Gestalt in which each element relates to the whole. Relatedly, Jerome Bruner (in H. Gruber, G. Terrell, & M. Wertheimer, Eds., *Contemporary Approaches to Cognition*, Cambridge, Mass., 1957) described how perceivers use organized prior knowledge to "go beyond the information given" in their inferences. And Fritz Heider (*The Psychology of Interpersonal Relations*, New York, 1958) posited balanced configurations of social relationships (e.g., agreeing friends) that form good psychological units out of the constituent pieces (two people, an attitude object) and their relationships (liking). Jean Piaget, for example in *The Origins of Intelligence in Children* (1952), described how children engage "the coordination of the new with the old, which foretells the process of judgment" (p. 43). All these approaches emphasize assimilation to the patterned configuration, generalized from experience, in contrast to the accumulation of isolated elements or completely fresh reactions to each encounter with a stimulus.

Schema theories moved into experimental psychology along with the cognitive revolution of the 1960s and 1970s. Cognitive psychologists noted the role of schemas (expectations, generalizations, and inferences) in memory for text: Coherent frameworks guide memory for relevant material; the quantity and accuracy of people's memory increases when they have an appropriate organizing theme for a text; and people recognize material faster when they apply a schema. In the late 1970s, social and personality psychologists identified recognition speed and confidence for schema-consistent social material, particularly as applied to self-schemas, personality concepts, and social events. The schema concept met with some resistance, mainly directed to its perceived redundancy with older concepts, such as cognitive psychology's associative memory models (a more elemental approach) and social psychology's attitude concept (a less cognitive structural approach).

Current Findings

Some of the first novel findings from a schematic approach concerned schemas as unitary representations. That is, some evidence suggests that activating a portion of the schema tends to activate the whole unit at once, in an all-or-none fashion. This unitary feature of schemas makes them both efficient to use and difficult to unpack and undo. Thus remembering one attribute of the concept retrieves the whole concept, but falsifying one attribute may require relearning the entire concept, with considerable interference.

Schemas may be cued by labels or by categorization based on salient features. People, for example, can be categorized according to gender, race, and age within milliseconds. Schema-based encoding then eliminates redundant information, fills in missing details, rearranges minor disorder, and disambiguates confusions in the first moments of perception, especially in well-learned schemas. People interpret ambiguous or missing information to fit familiar schemas. Inconsistent information elicits attention and requires longer processing time than consistent information, and it either may be resolved in favor of confirming a well-developed schema, may cause the schema to be abandoned as inappropriate, or may be combined with the schema as a tagged exception or deviation. Schema-irrelevant information is virtually ignored.

Subsequent recognition generally favors schema-consistent memory, especially if uncorrected for guessing. Guessing generally follows the schema. Free recall depends on the strength of the schematic expectation: Strong, well-established schemas show a congruency advantage in free recall. Weaker, experimentally induced schemas show an incongruency advantage when the inconsistency is evaluative as well as descriptive, when they concern an individual human target (for whom consistency is otherwise expected), when they involve an explicit impression-formation goal, and when the task is located within a single, uninterrupted experimental session. The schematic congruency advantage seems more characteristic of demanding, complex, realistic settings and people who are not especially motivated.

Schema use in judgment can be uncorrelated with recall for the original data, as the schema becomes functionally independent of its origins. Schema use does depend on the perceiver's goals and the information at hand. Given adequate fit, judgments often are schematic, especially if rapid and motivated mainly by avoiding indecision and ambiguity. Given questionable fit, judgments tend to compromise between schema and conflicting data, especially if they are slower and motivated mainly by accuracy. Alternatively, given major contradictions, judgments may be aschematic if no appropriate schema is clearly applicable.

Schema Development and Change

People learn schemas from direct experience or from other people's abstract communications, though these secondhand schemas tend to incorporate less variability than the self-generated kind. People rapidly generalize, sometimes as early as encountering two instances, and schemas become more abstract, complex, organized, compact, and resilient with increased experience. Pressures toward schema maintenance include the reinterpretation of ambiguous or mixed information to fit the schema, polarization induced by mere thought, and the cost of constructing a new schema. Schemas do change in response to clear disconfirmation, encounters with alternative schemas, and scrutiny of the unique individual instance.

Conclusion

Schemas have been criticized as absurdly constructionist, theoretically imprecise, operationally not falsifiable, or repackaged earlier vintages. In addition, newer models that incorporate both abstractions and mental representations of instances aim to eliminate the need for a separate concept representing the generic case. Undaunted, psychological researchers in a single recent year continued applying the schema concept to study a variety of topics such as text processing, self-concept, personality disorders, visual perception, body image, managerial and political decision making, math instruction, clinical diagnosis, sexuality, marketing, verbal causality, criminal justice, leadership, health behavior, intended actions, story construction, stereotypes, causal explanations, geometry tests, pragmatic reasoning, gender roles, reading comprehension, close relationships, and propensity to sue. The schema concept unarguably has had considerable heuristic value.

Bibliography

Anderson, R. C., & Pichert, J. W. (1978). Recall of previously unrecallable information following a shift in perspective. *Journal of Verbal Learning and Verbal Behavior*, *17*, 1–12. An early demonstration of schema use in text comprehension.

Bransford, J. D., & Franks, J. J. (1971). The abstraction of linguistic ideas. *Cognitive Psychology*, *2*, 331–350. An early demonstration of schema use in text comprehension.

Brewer, W. F., & Nakamura, G. V. (1984). The nature and functions of schemas. In R. S. Wyer & T. K. Srull (Eds.), *Handbook of social cognition* (Vol. 1, pp. 119–160). Hillsdale, NJ: Erlbaum. A review that includes both social and cognitive applications of the schema concept.

Fiske, S. T., & Linville, P. W. (1980). What does the schema concept buy us? *Personality and Social Psychology Bulletin*, *6*, 543–557. A reply to social psychological critics of the schema concept.

Fiske, S. T., & Taylor, S. E. (1991). *Social cognition*. New York: McGraw-Hill. Chapter 4, "Social Categories and Schemas," and Chapter 5, "Conditions of Schema Use," review historical and contemporaneous research and theory, mostly concerning schemas in social settings.

Mandler, J. (1979). Categorical and schematic organization in memory. In C. R. Puff (Ed.), *Memory organization and structure* (pp. 259–299). New York: Academic Press. An early review of the schema concept in cognitive psychology.

Markus, H., & Zajonc, R. B. (1985). The cognitive perspective in social psychology. In G. Lindzey & E. Aronson (Eds.), *The handbook of social psychology* (3rd ed., Vol. 1, pp. 137–230). New York: Random House. Describes the schema concept in the context of cognitive social psychology.

Owens, J., Bower, G. H., & Black, J. B. (1979). The "soap-opera" effect in story recall. *Memory and Cognition*, *7*, 185–191. An early demonstration of schema use in text comprehension.

Schank, R. C., & Abelson, R. P. (1977). *Scripts, plans, goals, and understanding: An inquiry into human knowledge structures*. Hillsdale, NJ: Erlbaum. An influential discussion of scripts in text processing.

Smith, E. (1998). Mental representation and memory. In D. T. Gilbert, S. T. Fiske, & G. Lindzey (Eds.), *The handbook of social psychology* (4th ed., Vol. 1, pp. 391–445). New York: McGraw-Hill. A comparative discussion of mechanisms posited for mental representation, including associative networks, schemas, exemplars, and distributed representations.

Smith, E. E., Adams, N., & Schorr, D. (1978). Fact retrieval and the paradox of interference. *Cognitive Psychology*, *10*, 438–464. An early demonstration of schema use in text comprehension.

Smith, E. E., & Medin, D. L. (1981). *Categories and concepts*. Cambridge, MA: Harvard University Press. Compares classic and modern views of categorization.

Susan T. Fiske

SCHIZOID PERSONALITY DISORDER. *See* Schizophrenia.

SCHIZOPHRENIA. Most individuals encountering a person with schizophrenia will recognize that person as quite strange and very different, at least during the acute phase. Such patients appear "out of touch" with reality, in that they behave in highly atypical ways. They verbalize ideas and beliefs that seem bizarre; they exhibit strange and dramatic behaviors; and they manifest unexpected emotion. It is common to feel confused, uncomfortable, and perhaps frightened when interacting with a person with schizophrenia, because they seem to be living in and responding to a world that operates on principles quite different from those of most other people.

Characteristics and Symptoms

The concept of schizophrenia as most typically used was introduced by Eugen Bleuler in the early 1900s. Emil Kraepelin also provided an early definition. [*See the biographies of Bleuler and Kraepelin.*] The essential features of schizophrenia, as defined by Bleuler, involved a cognitive disorder, that is, a thought disorder whereby the individual does not make the same logical conclusions as others in his or her society or social group; an affective disorder, that is, the apparent absence of affect or the manifestation of socially defined inappropriate affect; and social autism, that is, the creation of interpersonal distance from others by either the patient withdrawing or the patient threatening others or manifesting bizarre behavior that causes others to withdraw from the patient. Bleuler viewed hallucinations and delusions as secondary symptoms that were not necessarily present with all patients and were not essential for making the diagnosis of schizophrenia. Hallucinations are generally referred to as disturbances of perception, with the patient claiming to hear or see something that others do not hear or see. Delusions are strongly held personal beliefs which are inconsistent with known facts but which the patient continues to believe despite the contradictory evidence. [*See* Delusions; *and* Hallucinations.]

The current, most widely used criteria for diagnosing schizophrenia are in the *Diagnostic and Statistical Manual of Mental Disorders* (*DSM–IV*; American Psychiatric Association, 1994). For a diagnosis of schizophrenia, *DSM–IV* requires, during the significant portion of a one-month period, the presence of at least two of the following symptoms: grossly disorganized or catatonic behavior, disorganized speech, delusions, hallucinations, and negative symptoms (such as affective flattening, apathy, inattention). However, when the delusions are extremely bizarre or hallucinations involve hearing voices, only the presence of one such symptom is needed for a diagnosis. Occupational or social dysfunction must be present such that there is a marked decrease from a previous achievement level attained in work, interpersonal relations, or self-care prior to the onset of the severe symptoms. And, there must be continuous signs of disturbance for at least 6 months. *DMS-IV* no longer requires the "onset before the age of 45" as was required in *DSM–III-R*. [*See* Diagnostic and Statistical Manual of Mental Disorders.]

In addition, *DSM–IV* requires that, before making the diagnosis of schizophrenia, several other diagnoses must be considered and ruled out. Particularly, it is necessary to exclude schizoaffective disorder or mood disorders with psychotic features, as well as excluding cases where the psychotic reaction is due to substances (such as an abused drug or a side effect of a prescribed drug) or to a general medical condition. *DSM–IV* also provides an opportunity to classify the course of the schizophrenic symptoms, including episodic, continuous, single episode, and several other patterns. The subtypes available for classification under *DSM–IV* are paranoid, disorganized, catatonic, undifferentiated, and residual.

Much research, particularly since 1950, has been conducted to try to classify the symptoms of schizophrenia into meaningful patterns for purposes of making reliable and valid diagnoses—which would hopefully be associated with the most appropriate and effective treatments. While considerable progress has been made in such diagnostic efforts, the reliability and predictive validity of subtyping remain unscientific, and the usefulness of refined subtyping of schizophrenia for selecting treatment and predictive outcome remains unfulfilled.

A promising line of research that has emerged in the last 20 years has divided schizophrenic symptoms into two clusters, referred to as "positive symptoms" and "negative symptoms" (Crow, 1980; Andreasen, 1982). The first term, "positive symptoms," refers to symptoms that tend to be present in individuals with schizophrenia but not in other individuals. These so-called positive symptoms of schizophrenia include marked thought disorder (manifested by incoherence or illogicality), bizarre or disorganized behavior, delusions, and/or hallucinations. "Negative symptoms" refer to mental functions that are normally present in healthy individuals but which are found to be lacking or deteriorating in individuals with schizophrenia. These so-called negative symptoms include affective flattening, asociality, apathy, attentional impairment, and poverty of speech and content of speech. More recently, Andreasen et al. (Arndt, Andreasen, Flaum, Miller, et al., 1995) have presented empirical data suggestive of a three-dimensional model of schizophrenia. Working from a principal component analysis of the major features of schizophrenic symptoms suggested a negative symptom dimension, a disorganization dimension, and a psychotic processes dimension. Positive symptoms tend to attract clinical attention and to be treatment responsive, while negative symptoms are less spectacular but more insidious and disabling—and less responsive to treatment.

Epidemiology

Individuals with schizophrenia are found in every culture, every geographic region of the world, and at all historical periods of time. Incidence of schizophrenia refers to the number of new cases of schizophrenia detected in a given period, and it is most typically stated in terms of an annual incidence rate. The annual incidence rate in industrialized countries, according to a World Health Organization study, is between 16 and 28 cases per 1,000 individuals (or between 1 and 3%), a finding that is consistent over a number of years using different diagnostic procedures across varying conditions. The prevalence rate of schizophrenia refers to the number of individuals diagnosable with schizophrenia at a given moment or period in time; prevalence rates are most typically stated in terms of either annual prevalence or lifetime prevalence. Annual prevalence rates in industrialized countries are typically estimated to be in the range of 0.2 to 7.4 per 1,000 individuals; lifetime prevalence is estimated between 0.9 and 8.3 per 1,000 individuals (although the U.S. Epidemiological Catchment Area project did find rates as high as 19 per 1,000, but this might be related to the poor reliability of the diagnostic instrument used). Incidence and prevalence appear to be somewhat higher in industrialized countries than in nonindustrialized countries. Such a difference could either be related to greater stress in industrialized countries or to better health care services and improved detection of cases.

Schizophrenia is generally seen as a disorder with onset in early adulthood. Onset of schizophrenic symptoms most typically occurs between the ages of 18 and 30 years. Rates of schizophrenia in children and in adolescents is generally low (1 in 10,000 or less), and when it occurs in these age groups it is typically quite severe. Males are somewhat more likely to meet diagnostic criteria for schizophrenia slightly earlier in age than females. The most frequent age range for onset of schizophrenic symptoms for males is 18 to 25 years, whereas for females it is 26 to 45 years. There is no consistent explanation for these differences in age of onset of severe schizophrenic symptomatology. In general, age of onset is before age 45 in 75% of the cases of schizophrenia, and age of onset is before 60 years in 90% of cases.

However, successively older cohorts will also show a decreasing proportion of individuals with schizophrenia. This occurs for several reasons. First, some of them die. Between the ages of 40 and 64, individuals diagnosed with schizophrenia die at a higher annual rate than their counterparts in the general population. In the Netherlands, research has found such individuals dying at a rate double that of the general population; in the United States, data suggest a rate between 2.5 and 2.9 times greater than the general population. The higher mortality rates among individuals with schizophrenia do not imply higher suicide rates for this group. Although suicide is the leading single cause of death among individuals with schizophrenia in the 40 to 64 age range, the suicide rate for this group is actually lower (at 6.36) than the suicide rate for the overall population (7.39) and for individuals suffering from depression (10.08). The life span of patients with schizophrenia is, on average, about 10 years shorter than general population averages (Brown, 1997).

Second, some individuals with schizophrenia get better. Contrary to a model of a chronic and continually declining condition, a good proportion of individuals with schizophrenia "get better" as they age, if a truly long-term perspective is taken. Such a long-term perspective, however, translates into more than 20 years. However, this information about the eventual long-term functioning of individuals with schizophrenia is relatively new, and it gives cause for renewed optimism about schizophrenia. Bleuler (1978), Gross and Huber (1973), and Ciompi (1980) report findings based on 20-year follow-ups. The general findings are (1) 20 to 25% of young individuals with schizophrenia get better with treatment in the first 6 months to 2 years; and (2) another 35 to 40% experience a significant reduction in symptoms—and this improved functioning allows them to live relatively normal lives outside of hospitals with only minor or mild continuing symptoms, with longer-term treatment. Thus, 60 to 65% of individuals with schizophrenia will, basically, recover and live reasonably normal lives, but only after many years of serious dysfunction and disability.

Similar findings have been reported in the United States (Harding, Brooks, Ashikaga, Strauss, et al., 1987a, 1987b). As part of a pioneering rehabilitation program in the mid-1950s that involved a planned deinstitutionalization program with initial community support after discharge, the 269 most chronic patients, hospitalized an average of 16 years, were followed. At follow-up, over 60% of the sample were over age 60. The most striking finding was that only 3% of the sample was hospitalized, while, depending on definition and criteria, between 17 and 34% were "cured" and functioning in the community in a superior manner. The majority of patients were manifesting modest symptoms but were living in the community, supporting themselves, and engaging in normal interpersonal and social interactions.

Treatment

There is no single uniformly recommended treatment of choice for schizophrenia. The symptoms of schizophrenia are many and varied, and different patterns of patient response have been noted with any and all forms of interventions.

Antipsychotic drugs (or neuroleptics) are generally viewed as having an important role in managing schizophrenia, reducing acute psychotic episodes and reducing the frequency of relapse and rehospitalization. Modern psychopharmacological treatment of schizophrenia began in the early 1950s with chlorpromazine (Thorazine). Other phenothiazine derivatives were later developed by different drug pharmacies as antipsychotic agents. More recently, in the 1990s, newer "atypical" antipsychotic drugs were introduced, starting with clozapine (Clozaril). Such antipsychotic drugs reduce the positive symptoms of schizophrenia, such as hallucinations and delusions.

However, antipsychotic drugs do not "cure" schizophrenia. Moreover, reductions in hallucinations and delusions do not necessarily translate into the ability to effectively function outside of a hospital, care for oneself, work, and interact socially. And, antipsychotic drugs have significant negative side effects. These effects include extrapyramidal reactions, increased motoric agitation, muscle spasms (with abnormal posturing of head and neck), and Parkinsonism-like symptoms. Long-term use of antipsychotic drugs causes permanent neurological damage, referred to as "tardive dyskinesia"; 25 to 40% of patients managed with such drugs.

Individuals with schizophrenia need psychosocial treatment, not just antipsychotic drugs. Such patients typically become dysfunctional during periods of critical psychological, social, and educational development. Because of this, they generally have not benefited fully from their educational experiences, did not fully experience all of the normal social and interpersonal events of adolescence and early adulthood, and have often not developed work and career skills. Psychotherapy, social skills training, and vocational counseling and job training may be critically necessary for long-term functioning outside of a hospital or other protective environment.

Psychotherapy, provided by a well-trained and experienced psychotherapist, can be critical to long-term functioning of individuals with schizophrenia (Karon &

VandenBos, 1981). Such psychotherapy consists of regularly scheduled talks between the patient and the psychologist, in which current and/or past problems, thoughts, feelings, behaviors, and relationships are reviewed and explored. Working together, the patient and psychotherapist consider the patient's earlier experiences, how the patient coped with them, what assumptions and expectations that patient (rightly or wrongly) formed from them, and how these assumptions and expectations interact with real world events currently happening in the patient's life—leading to successful coping or unsuccessful symptoms and dysfunction. The patient learns, through insight, psychoeducational information, and examination of interpersonal behavioral patterns, how to function in a more appropriate, effective, and personally satisfying way. Family education, family psychotherapy, and self-help groups can also assist in such psychological development and behavior change.

Schizophrenia is a severe and disabling psychological disorder, which usually involves a long period of extreme distress and dysfunction. However, there is hope for individuals with schizophrenia and their families. Antipsychotic drugs can lessen the terrifying psychotic symptoms, and psychotherapy can shorten the period of dysfunction and improve the chances that the patient will return to the highest possible level of functioning.

Bibliography

American Psychiatric Association. (1994). *Diagnostic and statistical manual of mental disorders* (4th ed.). Washington, DC: Author.

Andreasen, N. C. (1982). Negative symptoms in schizophrenia: Definition and reliability. *Archives of General Psychiatry, 39,* 784–788.

Arndt, S., Andreasen, N. C., Flaum, M., Miller, D., & Nopoulos, P. (1995). A longitudinal study of symptom dimensions in schizophrenia: Prediction and patterns of change. *Archives of General Psychiatry, 52,* 352–360.

Bleuler, M. (1978). *The schizophrenic disorders: Long-term patient and family studies.* New Haven: Yale University Press.

Brown, S. (1997). Excess mortality of schizophrenics: A meta-analysis. *British Journal of Psychiatry, 171,* 502–508.

Ciompi, L. (1980). Catamnesic long-term study on the course of life and aging of schizophrenics. *Schizophrenia Bulletin, 6,* 606–617.

Crow, T. J. (1980). Molecular pathology of schizophrenia: More than one disease process? *British Medical Journal, 280*(6207), 66–68.

Gross, G., & Huber, G. (1973). Prognosis of schizophrenia. *Psychiatria Clinica, 6,* 1–16.

Harding, C. M., Brooks, G. W., Ashikaga, T., Strauss, J. S., & Breier, A. (1987a). The Vermont longitudinal study of persons with severe mental illness: I. Methodology, study sample, and overall status 32 years later. *American Journal of Psychiatry, 144,* 718–726.

Harding, C. M., Brooks, G. W., Ashikaga, T., Strauss, J. S., & Breier, A. (1987b). The Vermont longitudinal study of persons with severe mental illness: II. Long-term outcome of subjects who retrospectively met DSM–III criteria for schizophrenia. *American Journal of Psychiatry, 144,* 727–735.

Karon, B. P., & VandenBos, G. R. (1981). *Psychotherapy of schizophrenia: The treatment of choice.* New York: Aronson.

Kraepelin, E. (1971). *Dementia praecox and paraphrenia* (R. M. Barclay, Trans.; G. M. Robertson, Ed.). Huntington, NY: Krieger. (Original work published 1909–1913, original translation of selected portions published 1919)

Gary R. VandenBos

SCHLOSBERG, HAROLD (1904–1964), experimental psychologist. Schlosberg studied at Princeton University, receiving his doctorate in 1928. That year he became a member of the faculty of the department of psychology at Brown University, where he taught until his death. In 1954, he became chair of the department of psychology.

Schlosberg took an enormous interest in the design of the Walter S. Hunter Laboratory of Psychology, a building that was envisioned as being perfect for the needs of a psychology department. With research laboratories devoted to sensation, perception, learning, and what was then called physiological psychology (and now called behavioral neuroscience), the building was built in 1958.

Schlosberg guided the department into a planned expansion that made it possible for the department to provide a broad range of courses to undergraduates, but which provided a depth of research experience for graduate students in experimental psychology. He emphasized to graduate students the importance of doing research beginning in the first year of study and continuing throughout the graduate program. He enjoyed all aspects of the research process, including the construction of apparatus. Moreover, he regularly taught an introductory course in psychology with a laboratory that provided students with experience in the experimental study of reaction time, perception, learning, and memory. Schlosberg also supported undergraduate laboratory courses in perception, learning, and physiological psychology and instituted an undergraduate research thesis as the central part of an honors program, one of the many traditions that can be recognized in current programs.

Schlosberg's research interests were almost as broad as the field of experimental psychology, including learning, psychophysics, perception, and emotion. In experimental studies, he found principles of conditioning that applied to humans and other animals, and he made important contributions to the emerging consensus that the role of reinforcement contingent upon a response (as described by Edward L. Thorndike) was different from the role of reinforcement contingent upon a stimulus (as described by Ivan P. Pavlov). His studies of the recognition of emotion extended the procedures of psychophysical scaling to stimuli that could not be readily described on physical dimensions. His experiments on perception explored the important effects of backward masking. In addition, he did research on motivated behavior, such as hoarding of rats, the effect of effort on choice, and on skill learning.

The breadth of Scholsberg's interests was demonstrated in the revised version of Robert S. Woodworth's *Experimental Psychology* (New York, 1954). Schlosberg's breadth of scholarship and interests was not characteristic of most psychologists in the latter half of the twentieth century, although it may now be returning with the increasing emphasis on interdisciplinary research and collaboration.

[*Many of the people mentioned in this article are the subjects of independent biographical entries.*]

Bibliography

Schlosberg, H. (1928). A study of the conditioned patellar reflex. *Journal of Experimental Psychology, 11,* 468–494.

Schlosberg, H. (1937). The relationship between success and the laws of conditioning. *Psychological Review, 44,* 379–394.

Schlosberg, H. (1954). Three dimensions of emotion. *Psychological Review, 61,* 81–88.

Schlosberg, H. (1965). Time relations in serial visual perception. *Canadian Psychologist, 6a,* 1961–1972.

Russell M. Church

SCHOOL-BASED COLLABORATION AND TEAMING. In workplaces across settings, including business, mental health, and education, collaboration and teaming are seen as positive contributions to effective practice (Arcaro, 1995; Maeroff, 1993; Platt, 1994). Recent work on school culture and school restructuring has confirmed that schools, just as other workplaces, benefit from collaboration (Fullan & Hargreaves, 1991; Little, 1990; Rosenholtz, 1989) and well-implemented teams (see, for example, Maeroff, 1993). Although collaboration and teams are currently in vogue, school cultures have not historically been highly collaborative workplaces in the United States (Fullan & Hargreaves, 1991; Little, 1990). As a result, implementation of meaningful collaboration opportunities and well-functioning teams in schools, especially ones without norms supportive of collaboration, requires considerable investment in terms of facilitation and training (Arcaro, 1995).

The Rationale for Collaboration and Teaming

The growth of collaborative practice in schools has been fueled by a variety of factors, including "the acceleration of professional specialization and fragmentation . . . increases in size and complexity of service organizations, and broadened conceptions of the interrelated nature of human problems and the need for comprehensive professional approaches" (Billups, 1987, p. 146). Collaboration is thought also to facilitate meaningful opportunities for learning for diverse student populations and to increase the possibility of solving problems that more traditional school cultures fail to address adequately (Thousand & Villa, 1992). The concept of collaboration has been applied to nearly all areas of schooling, including participatory forms of organization, such as site-based management in administration; mentoring, peer coaching and team teaching among classroom teachers; inclusive programming in special education; professional development schools as bridges between schools and colleges of education; and emphasis on partnerships with families (Pugach & Johnson, 1995). The emerging concept in the school restructuring movement is that effective schools serve as learning organizations, dependent upon developing a sense of community as well as the habits and skills of collaboration in both students and staff.

Some empirical work supports collaboration as an effective strategy in schools. Rosenholtz's (1989) widely cited study, *In Teachers' Workplace,* concluded that "when collaborative norms undergird . . . groups, they bring new ideas, fresh ways of looking at things, and a stock of collective knowledge that is more fruitful than any one person's working alone" (p. 41). She demonstrated the ways in which isolation in schools is dysfunctional and how collaboration may facilitate problem solving at the classroom level, providing increased opportunity for teachers to improve their technical expertise and create improved learning opportunities for their students. Weinstein, Madison, and Kuklinski (1995) found that collaborative meetings among teachers enabled them to engage in the critical work of integrating new research-based ideas into their normal patterns of work. In a project designed to raise expectations for high school students at risk, the collaborative structure facilitated conditions described as stimulating and supportive; they not only "focused systematic inquiry, provided resources . . . , built linkages among people and between roles, empowered individuals, and reinforced positive change" (p. 153) but also enabled the teachers to move from a focus on obstacles to change to opportunities and strategies to overcome the obstacles.

Teaming as a structure for collaborative problem solving has also been on the increase. Many reasons exist for team development in schools. First, teams are mandated by law or district policy for specific functions, such as the multidisciplinary team (MDT) required in special education law and regulation. The MDT was included in the special education law, Public Law 94-142, in the 1970s and has continued to be integral to the special education process in America. Basically, the law mandated a team that would use multiple criteria and sources to make decisions about the classification and placement of students with disabling conditions. An additional reason for the use of teams in the special education process was the belief that group decision making would be a safeguard against individual bias and errors in judgment with respect to the disproportionate classification of minority group members as handicapped (Maher & Yoshida, 1985).

The team concept within special education was based on research drawn from the behavioral science literature on group decision making, but little direct evidence existed that it would facilitate good decision making in the special education process (Maher & Yoshida, 1985). Group problem solving is best in situations requiring unusual solutions, whereas the special education teams largely decide on eligibility and placement: "With these choice constraints, it is not surprising that MDT's demonstrate similar outcomes as groups in business of no greater effectiveness than individuals when decisions are made routinely and in quantity" (Maher & Yoshida, 1985, p. 17). Implementation of the MDT has been considered problematic from the beginning, with many problems identified in the research (Rosenfield & Gravois, 1999).

A second major reason for the use of teams in schools is that they are considered a structure that can better address a problem, issue, or situation than can an individual working alone (Platt, 1994; Rosenfield & Gravois, in press). There are many references in the literature on teams stating that more heads are better than just one or two, and that this benefit is enhanced when the group includes individuals with diverse training and professional expertise. With increasing professional specialization and demands upon schools, the need grew for structures enabling professionals and other involved individuals to work collaboratively, not only to assist students with special needs but also to cope with macroissues such as prevention and intervention at the systems or society levels (Rosenfield & Gravois, 1999). A variety of team models operating as problem-solving support structures have proliferated in the last 20 years, although the research base for these models has not kept pace with their growth in number (Rosenfield & Gravois, 1999).

Effective Models of Collaboration and Teaming

Collaboration is a process that can be implemented in many forms. Little (1990) has defined strong and weak kinds of collaboration in schools, some of them leading to little positive impact; episodic witnessing of other teachers' classrooms and telling stories about experiences, ready availability of mutual aid or helping, and routine sharing of materials and methods are viewed as weak forms, whereas joint work (including, for example, team teaching, planning, and action research) yield more positive outcomes. Fullan and Hargreaves (1991) distinguish between the existence of collaboration and a culture of collaboration that permeates the school. They also developed a continuum of weak to strong types of collaboration: (1) balkanzation, that is, "a culture made up of separate and sometimes competing groups, jockeying for position and supremacy" (p. 52); (2) comfortable collaboration, which "restricts the extent to which teachers can inquire into and advise one another about their practice" (p. 55), leaving intact major elements of prevailing privacy norms; (3) contrived collegiality, usually administratively imposed and "characterized by a set of formal, specific, bureaucratic procedures to increase the attention being given to joint teacher planning, consultation and other forms of working together" (p. 58), which can either facilitate or impede collaboration; and (4) interactive professionalism, in which school staff develop norms of continuous improvement; reflection in, on, and about practice, and greater professional mastery, efficacy, and satisfaction.

Translating a culture of interactive professionalism into an effective team structure requires a number of key ingredients: (1) team members must understand and agree on the function and mission of the team; (2) there must be a clear assignment and acceptance of roles and responsibilities by team members; (3) there must be an explicit and public commitment from administrators supporting the team's mission; (4) team members must establish and maintain communication processes for member-to-member exchange, as well as processes to cope with intrateam conflict when it arises; (5) meetings must be perceived as events that accomplish results; and (6) team members must develop and routinely use common problem-solving strategies in which problems are identified and analyzed, interventions are generated in response to the problems identified, and data are used to evaluate progress toward goals (Arcaro, 1995; Rosenfield & Gravois, 1999).

Barriers to Collaboration and Teaming

Much has been written about how school culture acts as a barrier to collaboration and teaming (e.g., Rosenholtz, 1989). According to Rosenholtz, although "uncertainty is endemic to teaching, even under the best of circumstances, norms of self-reliance in isolated schools leave teachers even more uncertain about a technical culture and instructional practice" (1989, p. 69). As a result, the more difficult problems become unsolvable. Modifying the cultural norms in schools is, in fact, what the practices of collaborating and teaming are designed to do.

Two major barriers that affect collaboration and teaming, along with the norms of self-reliance and privacy that permeate schools, are time and diversity. Perhaps the biggest perceived obstacle to developing collaborative norms in schools is time, particularly for teachers (Fullan & Hargreaves, 1991; Rosenholtz, 1989). Hargreaves (1990) contrasts the distinction between the polychronic time perspective of teachers, which emphasizes personal relationships and "flexible management of simultaneous demands in the densely packed world of the classroom" (p. 319) in comparison to the more linear, monochronic time perspective of administrators and agents of change, with their sets of objectives to be achieved. A deeper understanding of how time is perceived by teachers is emerging and may contribute to addressing this concern.

Although schools have found many creative ways to generate time for these activities, it is rare for school systems to accept how much time may be required for the work of collaboration and teaming and for the training needed to ensure effective teams (Rosenfield & Gravois, 1999). Teachers view time spent with other adults as less important than time spent with students. Rarely do school boards allocate the resources that would enable substantial time for teachers outside the classroom. Moreover, changes in school schedules to allow for more collaboration, such as extending or shortening the school day, affect families as well as staff. Psychologists in schools also complain about finding time for consultation and collaboration, even in those schools that have engaged in some restructuring to ensure such activities. It is important to study how schools can effectively generate useful and meaningful time for collaboration.

The second barrier grows out of one of the strengths of collaboration and teaming—bringing together diverse individuals generates a potential source of conflict. Rosenfield and Gravois (1999) summarized research findings indicating that

> a lack of interdisciplinary collaboration and trust, territoriality, mixed participation by differing professional roles . . . , and differing conceptualizions of another's role and function are a few of the difficulties found in actual team practices. (p. 1032)

Jackson and Ruderman (1995) suggest that work team diversity should be broadly defined, to include

the following areas: "demographic diversity (e.g., based on gender, ethnicity, age), psychological diversity (e.g., based on values, beliefs, knowledge), and organizational diversity (e.g., based on tenure, occupation, hierarchical level)" (p. 3). Like other workplace sites, educational settings are subject to the entire diversity domain, and diversity affects both the cohesion and productivity of groups. As schools seek to diversify the racial composition of their faculty, for example, ethnic differences can lead to lack of cohesion among group members. Hargreaves (1990) comments that elementary school classroom culture is predominately female, with a "high sensitivity to unpredictabilities and particularities of context, to the importance of interpersonal relationships, and to the successful completion of the tasks in hand" (p. 311), factors that may be less hospitable to the planning and reflection of the collaborative process. Different roles bring different perspectives. Psychologists who work in schools often focus on individual needs, whereas teachers are more concerned with groups and curricula. Principals and teachers often differ both in their focus and their gender. Finding ways to capture the positive aspects of diversity while dealing with the inevitable differences that diversity brings to the group process contributes to a productive team.

Implications for Psychologists Working with Schools

Collaboration and teaming are structural changes; by themselves they are only weakly related to changes that have a more powerful effect, such as teaching practices. However, they provide the context for the more substantial restructuring in schools that is widely considered essential to school reform and improved outcomes for students.

The increasing focus on collaboration and teaming provides a challenge to behavioral scientists to develop better theories for understanding behavior within organizations (Jackson & Ruderman, 1995). Research on effective implementation and outcomes of collaboration and teaming are still emerging (Rosenfield & Gravois, 1999). Psychology has much to contribute to making collaboration and teaming more effective processes, through understanding of interpersonal and group dynamics, problem solving and communication processes, and research and evaluation design.

Bibliography

Arcaro, J. S. (1995). *Teams in education: Creating an integrated approach.* Delray Beach, FL: St. Lucie Press.
Billups, J. O. (1987). Interpersonal team process. *Theory into Practice, 26,* 146–152.

Fullan, M. G., & Hargreaves, A. (1991). *What's worth fighting for? Working together for your school.* Andover, MA: Regional Laboratory for Educational Improvement of Northeast and Islands.

Hargreaves, A. (1990). Teachers' work and the politics of time and space. *Qualitative Studies in Education, 3,* 303–320.

Jackson, S. E., & Ruderman, M. N. (1995). Introduction: Perspectives for understanding diverse work teams. In S. E. Jackson & M. N. Ruderman (Eds.), *Diversity in work teams: Research paradigms for a changing workplace* (pp. 1–13). Washington, DC: American Psychological Association.

Little, J. W. (1990). The persistence of privacy: Autonomy and initiative in teachers' professional relations. *Teachers College Record, 91,* 509–536.

Maeroff, G. I. (1993). *Team building for school change.* New York: Teachers College Press.

Maher, C., & Yoshida, R. (1985). Multidisciplinary teams in schools. In T. Kratochwill (Ed.), *Advances in school psychology* (Vol. 4, pp. 13–44). Hillsdale, NJ: Erlbaum.

Platt, L. J. (1994). Why bother with teams? An overview. In Commission on Interprofessional Education and Practice (Eds.), *Interprofessional care and collaborative practice* (pp. 3–10). Pacific Grove, CA: Brooks/Cole.

Pugach, M. C., & Johnson, L. J. (1995). *Collaborative practitioners, collaborative schools.* Denver: Love.

Rosenfield, S., & Gravois, T. A. (1999). Working with teams in the school. In C. Reynolds & T. Gutkin (Eds.), *Handbook of school psychology* (3rd ed., pp. 1025–1040). New York: Wiley.

Rosenholtz, S. J. (1989). *In teachers' workplace: The social organization of schools.* New York: Longman.

Thousand, J. S., & Villa, R. A. (1992). Collaborative teams: A powerful tool in school restructuring. In R. A. Villa, J. S. Thousand, W. Stainback, & S. Stainback (Eds.), *Restructuring for caring and effective education: An administrative guide to creating heterogeneous schools* (pp. 73–108). Baltimore, MD: Brookes.

Weinstein, R. S., Madison, S. M., & Kuklinski, M. R. (1995). Raising expectations in schooling: Obstacles and opportunities for change. *American Educational Research Journal, 32* (1), 121–159.

Sylvia Rosenfield

SCHOOL CONSULTATION. Consultation services in schools and related settings have received increased support over recent years because of their documented efficiency and efficacy. Psychologists working in schools are recognizing the desirability of such services to address the needs of an increasingly complex population of students. Consultation is defined as an indirect problem-solving and decision-making model that involves the cooperative efforts of a consultant (specialist) and consultees (teachers, parents, caregivers) to clarify primary needs and issues and to develop, implement, and evaluate appropriate strategies for intervention.

Theoretical and Guiding Frameworks

There are three general models of consultation (behavioral, mental health, and organizational development) that vary along a number of dimensions, including theoretical framework, goals, procedures, and empirical support. Behavioral consultation and its variants are most prevalent in school-related practice.

In a traditional sense, behavioral consultation has relied solely on applied behavioral theory as the framework for services (including definition and analysis of problems, development of interventions, and evaluation of outcomes). Behavioral theory continues to provide the primary structural backdrop for this model; however, in recent years researchers have identified the need to expand the conceptual and procedural bases of behavioral consultation to understand, explain, and address complex referral concerns. Currently, many emphasize a broadened framework for consultation practice, incorporating the conceptual advances of ecological systems theory with the empirically validated structured template provided by behavioral models.

In a seminal article, Urie Bronfenbrenner (1977) emphasized the importance of ecological considerations in child development by recognizing that a child is part of a number of interrelated systems, each with reciprocal and bidirectional influence on the others. The "microsystem" and the "mesosystem" are the subsystems that are most readily addressed in consultation. The microsystem is defined as the immediate setting or system within which an individual functions at any one point in time, such as a classroom, neighborhood, or home setting. Attention at this level addresses problems as they occur in an isolated setting or environment. The mesosystem is concerned with relationships among immediate systems in an individual's environment, such as interrelations among the home and school settings. Attention at this level allows for the identification and resolution of broader issues as they are manifested across systems and as they are influenced by intersystemic variables.

In traditional consultation approaches, the focus may be a client's "target problem" as manifested within and across settings. Considering an ecological-behavioral orientation, however, consultation also can allow for the identification and management of systemic or contextual variables that relate to referral issues. For example, variance in opinions, values, or beliefs among parents, teachers, administrators, or other caregivers may affect programs or practices related to a child's academic or behavioral difficulties and influence the child's academic or social development. In a strict behavioral orientation, one may focus on the academic or behavioral difficulty inherent in the child. In a broadened "ecobehavioral" model, however, a consultant may focus on congruence among caregivers and the "match" within and across environments as important contributors to a child's functioning. An appropriate intervention may therefore address client-focused issues and also seek to increase concordance among home, school, and other systems.

An additional consideration of ecological-behavioral approaches to consultation emphasizes the need to recognize the shared influence of these systems and strive toward systems integration in the identification, analysis, and resolution or management of problems. This highlights the importance of home-school-community partnerships and models of consultation that are structured toward comprehensive and coordinated services. Conjoint behavioral consultation, described by Sheridan, Kratochwill, and Bergan (1996), is a model that promotes integrated services across home, school, and community in both theory and practice.

Consultation Procedures

In both behavioral consultation and conjoint behavioral consultation, services are implemented through structured interactions among consultants and consultees. The role of the consultant is to guide the consultation process. An effective consultant structures consultation practices through the use of both process expertise (knowledge of the goals and procedures of behavioral consultation) and content expertise (experience with the presenting problem and appropriate interventions). Specifically, consultants use a structured interview format to guide participants through the identification of issues or concerns that are the target of consultation, the collection of information about presenting difficulties, the development of an appropriate intervention plan, and the evaluation of outcomes in relation to consultation goals. In most cases the consultant in a school setting is a psychologist, counselor, or special educator.

A consultee is an individual responsible for delivering the intervention or program to resolve a presenting issue. The consultee primarily contributes content expertise by sharing relevant information and unique knowledge about the client and presenting problem, by collecting data concerning the problem, and by implementing the plan. Consultees are usually educators, parents, or paraprofessionals. In behavioral consultation, as it was initially described, a single teacher or parent was considered the consultee. The development of conjoint behavioral consultation broadened the scope of the process by including multiple consultees in consultation and by expanding the breadth and scope of consultation interventions.

The client role must also be considered in consultation. In school consultation, the client is typically a student or group of students for whom consultation services are provided. Clients are generally responsible for participating in the treatment program with the expectation for positive change, and their level of participation within the consultation process can vary depending on various case characteristics.

As articulated in seminal works by John Bergan and Thomas Kratochwill (Bergan & Kratochwill, 1990, Kratochwill & Bergan, 1990), behavioral consultation is conducted through four problem-solving stages. Together, the consultant and consultees engage in problem identification, problem analysis, treatment (plan) implementation, and treatment (plan) evaluation. These stages are operationalized through the use of three structured interviews. In the Problem Identification Interview (PII) consultants and consultees define a target behavior, identify important environmental conditions that influence the problem, describe the scope and strength of the problem, agree on a goal for behavior change, and establish a procedure for collection of baseline data. The PII is the most important of the stages because the success of future stages hinges on the development of a specific and precise definition of the target behavior. This is often challenging because clients may present with a number of difficulties. It is the consultant's responsibility to assist the consultee in determining the most important and valid issue to be addressed in consultation.

Following a baseline data collection period, the Problem Analysis Interview (PAI) is conducted. The objectives of the PAI can be further delineated into two phases: problem analysis and plan design. The objectives of the analysis phase are to evaluate the baseline data, determine if the target issue warrants intervention, and conduct a thorough functional analysis. A careful analysis of the conditions surrounding a problem leads to the development of an appropriate intervention plan that will elicit behavior change in the client and be deemed acceptable to the consultee. The third stage of consultation involves implementation of the treatment plan and ongoing data collection by the consultee. Although there is no formal interview conducted at this stage, the consultant is typically involved in monitoring implementation of the plan and providing training to the consultee as necessary. It is important that throughout this stage the consultant maintain close contact with the consultee and monitor any unintended side effects or behavioral contrasts.

Finally, the Treatment Evaluation Interview (TEI) is conducted to evaluate the effectiveness of the intervention by inspecting behavioral data, to discuss strategies regarding the continuation, modification, or termination of the treatment plan, and to discuss procedures for promoting maintenance and generalization of treatment gains.

Goals in Consultation

Primary goals in behavioral consultation models encompass both outcome and process variables. Generally speaking, consultation goals center around engendering change in the client and preventing future problems through the development of consultees' skills and competencies. Whereas the former has been supported repeatedly in consultation research, the effectiveness of consultation as a preventive model is unclear.

Along with the general outcome goals are specific consultation objectives that increase the likelihood that an intervention will result in positive behavior change. Such objectives include obtaining comprehensive and functional data, establishing consistent treatment plans across settings to enhance maintenance and generalization, and providing consultees with skills to engage independently in future problem solving.

Although more difficult to operationalize and measure, it is believed that process goals contribute uniquely to the efficacy of behavioral consultation and therefore also are important to consider. Some important process goals include establishing intersystemic partnerships, increasing commitments to consultation goals, recognizing the need to conceptualize problems as occurring across and not only within systems, promoting shared ownership for problem definition and solution, and increasing the diversity of available expertise and resources.

Consultation Research

Reviews of the empirical literature have supported consultation as an effective model of service delivery. In a review of consultation outcome literature, Sheridan, Welch, and Orme (1996) reported that 76% of the studies reviewed demonstrated at least some positive outcomes. When the outcomes were analyzed by model, behavioral consultation outcomes appeared most favorable. Nearly all (95%) of the studies using behaviorally based models reported positive outcomes. Furthermore, methodological standards were more rigorous in behavioral consultation studies than in those studies using other models. The largest percentage of negative findings was in studies that did not specify a model of consultation. Thus it appears that a clearly articulated model is important for increasing positive outcomes.

Along with examining outcomes, some researchers have examined the process of consultation in order to determine which factors in the consultation process lead to positive outcomes. Early research by John Bergan and his colleagues (Anderson, Kratochwill, & Bergan, 1986; Bergan & Tombari, 1975, 1976) demonstrated that among the most important process variables in consultation are accurate problem identification and the use of behavioral (rather than medical or psychodynamic) problem interpretations.

Another important process variable identified in the consultation research literature is the manner in which the consultant communicates. Consultees appear to prefer "common sense" language to psychological jargon (Witt, Moe, Gutkin, & Andrews, 1984). Moreover, eliciting input from consultees is beneficial, because teachers are more likely to identify resources and methods for implementing interventions if the consultant asks them, rather than tells them, how they can identify and use resources (Bergan & Neumann, 1980).

Collaboration between the consultant and consultee(s) has historically been assumed to increase the effectiveness of consultation; however, this assumption has been widely contested. William Erchul (1987) found that consultants who are directive in consultation interviews are more effective than consultants who are not directive. Some have interpreted this finding to mean that collaboration is not effective in consultation; however, collaboration and control are not necessarily mutually exclusive. In a paper presented at the annual conference of the American Psychological Association Terry Gutkin (1997) suggested that collaboration and control represent a false dichotomy and that there are at least two dimensions to consider in the consultation process: collaboration/coercion and directive/nondirective. Within this framework, a consultant can be collaborative and directive (as well as any of the other three possible combinations). A collaborative/directive framework implies a relationship in which the consultant and consultee(s) each has a valuable role in the consultation process, but one in which their roles are different. As alluded to earlier, an important role for the consultant is leadership of the consultation interview, eliciting and organizing valuable input from consultees.

An exciting research direction in consultation is the movement by various researchers toward an ecobehavioral, cross-systems model of consultation. Specifically, researchers are beginning to examine the effectiveness of involving consultees from various systems in a child's life. Along these lines, the investigation of team-based consultation guided by a consultant who brings together individuals representing various systems and mobilizes them toward providing integrated and comprehensive services is needed. This type of consultation may be viewed within a developmental consultation framework in which multisystems consultation is used as a format to address long-term issues in the child's life, rather than the more time-limited consultation generally used in schools to bring specific problems to swift resolution.

Future research must continue to increase in methodological rigor. Specifically, consultation researchers should (1) specify the consultation model and procedures used, (2) increase the use of various forms of experimental designs, (3) use direct, objective, multiple measures, (4) attend to outcomes beyond the client level, and (5) pay greater attention to integrity issues. Finally, process issues in consultation (such as collaboration/control) continue to be an engaging and important research direction. Research in this area must clearly define the constructs under investigation (such as collaboration) and use process analyses that investigate complex interactions between participants.

Bibliography

Anderson, T. K., Kratochwill, T. R., & Bergan, J. R. (1986). Training teachers in behavioral consultation and therapy: An analysis of verbal behaviors. *Journal of School Psychology, 24*, 229–241.

Bergan, J. R., & Kratochwill, T. R. (1990). *Behavioral consultation and therapy*. New York: Plenum. A comprehensive source that presents detailed descriptions of historical and contemporary issues and procedures surrounding behavioral consultation as a model of indirect services.

Bergan, J. R., & Neumann, A. (1980). The identification of resources and constraints influencing plan design in consultation. *Journal of School Psychology, 18*, 317–323.

Bergan, J. R., & Tombari, M. L. (1975). The analysis of verbal interactions occurring during consultation. *Journal of School Psychology, 13*, 209–226.

Bergan, J. R., & Tombari, M. L. (1976). Consultant skill and efficiency and the implementation and outcomes of consultation. *Journal of School Psychology, 14*, 3–14.

Bronfenbrenner, U. (1977). Toward an experimental ecology of human development. *American Psychologist, 32*, 513–529.

Erchul, W. P. (1987). A relational communication analysis of control in school consultation. *Professional School Psychology, 2*, 113–124.

Erchul, W. P. (1993). Selected interpersonal perspectives in consultation research. *School Psychology Quarterly, 8*, 38–49. Describes several studies that investigated relational communication patterns in school-based consultation and interprets findings in terms of the importance of teamwork and cooperation in effective consultation relationships.

Erchul, W. P., & Martens, B. K. (1997). *School consultation: Conceptual and empirical bases of practice*. New York: Plenum. Describes an integrated theoretical model for school-based consultation that incorporates behavioral, mental health, and social psychological tenets.

Gresham, F. M., & Noell, G. (1992). Documenting the effectiveness of consultation outcomes. In J. E. Zins, T. R. Kratochwill, & S. N. Elliott (Eds.), *Handbook of consultation services for children: Applications in educational and clinical settings* (pp. 249–273). San Francisco: Jossey-Bass. Presents alternative approaches to documenting outcomes in consultation and offers various methods as important in furthering the consultation knowledge base.

Gutkin, T. B. (1993). Conducting consultation research. In J. E. Zins, T. R. Kratochwill, & S. N. Elliott (Eds.), *Handbook of consultation services for children: Applications in educational and clinical settings* (pp. 227–248). San Francisco: Jossey-Bass. Provides a critique of previous consultation research and offers suggestions for researchers interested in conducting research in important aspects of consultation practice.

Gutkin, T. B. (1997, August). *Collaborative versus directive/expert school-based consultation: Reviewing and resolving a false dichotomy*. Paper presented at the annual convention of the American Psychological Association, Chicago.

Kratochwill, T. R., & Bergan, J. R. (1990). *Behavioral consultation in applied settings: An individual guide*. New York: Plenum. A practitioner-oriented guidebook describing the general stages and procedures of behavioral consultation, with interview guides, checklists, and chapter quizzes.

Kratochwill, T. R., Elliott, S. N., & Busse, R. (1995). Behavior consultation: A five-year evaluation of consultant and client outcomes. *School Psychology Quarterly, 10*, 87–117. Describes a 5-year study aimed at training school psychology students in behavioral consultation and provides extensive data (including small-*N* and meta-analyses) documenting effects on consultant-trainees and clients.

Sheridan, S. M., Kratochwill, T. R., & Bergan, J. R. (1996). *Conjoint behavioral consultation: A procedural manual*. New York: Plenum. A guidebook that presents practical issues surrounding the extension of behavioral consultation to incorporate multiple systems in a client's life, including modified interview forms, discussion questions, and case examples.

Sheridan, S. M., Welch, M., & Orme, S. (1996). Is consultation effective? A review of outcome research. *Remedial and Special Education, 17*, 341–354. Reviews the school-based consultation outcome research across behavioral, mental health, and organizational models, critiques methods and designs used in past investigations, and suggests future directions for research.

Witt, J. C., Moe, G., Gutkin, T. B., & Andrews, L. (1984). The effect of saying the same thing in different ways: The problem of language and jargon in school-based consultation. *Journal of School Psychology, 22*, 361–367.

Zins, J. E., Kratochwill, T. R., & Elliott, S. N. (1993). *The handbook of consultation services for children: Applications in educational and clinical settings*. San Francisco: Jossey-Bass. A comprehensive edited source that includes sections pertaining to consultation theory, practice, and research.

Susan M. Sheridan, Jaqui R. Richard, and Tracine Y. Smoot

SCHOOL DROPOUT. Approximately 15% of students in American high schools drop out each year (U.S. Department of Education, 1995). It is perhaps as misleading to talk about a typical drop-out rate, however, as it is to talk about a typical school. Although there are numerous reasons for the disparity in drop-out rates between high schools, the most profound variable is socioeconomic status. It is widely known that the percentage of students who graduate from high school is highly determined by the socioeconomic level of the school (see, for example, Rossi, 1994). In many affluent, suburban school districts, the drop-out rate is 1% or less; in some urban districts the rate is 70% or higher. Fine (1991) commented: "Dropping out of high school is, in some schools, a nearly anomalous event. In other schools, it is a shared tradition" (p. 21).

Despite the difference in prevalence, dropping out of school has negative consequences, regardless of the economic level of the student. For example, data from the most recent census show that 65% of African Americans without a high school diploma live in poverty, while less than 25% of graduates fall into this category (U.S. Department of Education, 1995). Moreover, attainment of a high school education is barely sufficient to enable students to function in a society that is becoming increasingly complex and technologically sophisticated. Clearly, students who fail to attain even a minimal level of education have little hope of achieving economic success.

The nation's economic prosperity is inextricably linked to the quality of education. Whether the nation embraces the ideological concept of equality of educational opportunity, there is usually an assertion that the powerful forces of international competition, advanced technological skills, and domestic social agendas demand that all students attain a quality education. Even if a nation is able to achieve the highest possible quality in all of its educational endeavors, this means nothing for those who are unable or unwilling to participate fully. Perhaps for these reasons, a 90% graduation rate was targeted in the Goals 2000: Educate America Act (U.S. Government, 1995).

A national goal to increase the graduation rates, or any effort to reduce the drop-out rates, generates at least three explicit challenges: (1) the need to define and clarify the concept of dropout; (2) the need to differentiate the salient characteristics of dropouts for predictive purposes; and (3) the need for reliable data to develop preventive measures and intervention services.

Defining Dropout

Graduation and drop-out rates are among the criteria used to measure the effectiveness of schools. Despite the importance of drop-out data, a common definition of dropout or an acceptable methodological procedure to ensure accurate and reliable data is enmeshed in conceptual ambiguity and ideological positions motivated by institutional interests (Clements, 1991; Hahn, Danzberger, & Lefkowitz, 1987; Hammack, 1986).

There is near consensus that approximately 25% of American students leave school before graduation (Clements, 1991, 1996). Nevertheless, there is a perception that drop-out rates are ill-conceived, ideologically based, and often misleading (Fine, 1991). School districts have established their own methodology to determine drop-out rates. Hahn, Danzberger, and Lefkowitz (1987) correctly note that the problem of inconsistency in calculating drop-out rates partially lies in the fact that "in many localities, no central, state, or city-wide authority rigorously scrutinizes the drop-out count or methodologies for compiling school leavers" (p. 9).

One of the most widely regarded strategies for the statistical analysis of drop-out rates is advanced by the National Center for Educational Statistics (NCES), which computes drop-out rates in three ways: (1) event rates, (2) status rates, and (3) cohort rates (McMillen, Kaufman, & Whitener, 1993). Given the various ways in which drop-out rates are defined and the different methodological procedures utilized in their calculation, the three ways popularized by NCES bring much-needed conceptual clarity to the issue and merit further elaboration.

Event rates are calculated from the annual data on the proportion of students who drop out without completing high school. It is this annual comparative analysis that is likely to drive policy decisions about school improvement.

Status rates are the cumulative rates measuring the proportion of individuals in the population who have not completed high school regardless of when they drop out. If the effectiveness of the educational system is partially measured by the proportion of students graduating from high school, and if education is indeed a moral and economic imperative, the magnitude of the drop-out problem must be ascertained. Thus, the status rate is a central variable to be factored into school improvement plans regardless of their conceptual framework.

Cohort rates measure the drop-out rate of a single group of students relative to their age and grade peers within a specified time.

Regardless of the strategy used to calculate a drop-out rate, there is substantial evidence that the rate is significantly influenced by socioeconomic status, racial/ethnic factors, and school experiences (Alexander, Entwisle, & Horsey, 1997). Despite the persistence of several factors that contribute to students leaving school before graduation, an overall reduction in drop-out rates has occurred over the past decade (McMillen, Kaufman, & Whitener, 1993). National emphasis on the personal and economic costs of dropping out of school is the impetus to research efforts to identify the differentiating characteristics of dropouts (Barrington & Hendricks, 1989); the family lifestyles and values related to the developmental pathway to school failure (Garnier, Stein, & Jacobs, 1997); the background of poverty that underlies poor school performance (Ensminger & Slusarcick, 1992); and the preventive measures to support school graduation.

Demographic Characteristics of Dropouts

Extensive literature focuses on the prediction of dropping out of school as a basis for early remediation. In general, this literature has investigated demographic and psychologically based variables (e.g., self-esteem) to derive a model for predicting who is most likely to leave school prior to graduation. The major finding from this research is relatively easy to state: students who are poor are far more likely to drop out of school than students from privileged backgrounds (Fine, 1991; Rossi, 1994). Beyond this, however, differences within cohorts have been also noted. Specifically, several variables have been related to dropping out of school in one or more studies:

- Gender: Males are more likely to drop out of school than females (Alexander, Entwisle, & Horsey, 1997; Hodgkinson, 1985).
- Race: African Americans are more likely to drop out compared to Caucasians; and Latinos drop out more frequently than do African Americans. Asian Americans are least likely of all ethnic and racial groups to drop out. (Alexander, Entwisle, & Horsey, 1997; Fine, 1991).
- Grade retention: Students who have been retained in one or more grades are more likely to drop out (Barrington & Hendricks, 1898; Garnier, Stein, & Jacobs, 1997).
- Academic performance: Students who show a clear pattern of academic problems by the third grade and/or who perform poorly on standardized tests are more likely to drop out (Cairns, Cairns, & Neckerman, 1989; Schneider, Svetvilas, & Baker, 1994).
- Mobility: Students whose families move more than twice during their school years, and especially when these moves occur after the seventh grade, are more likely to drop out (Ensminger & Slusarcick, 1992; Rumsberger, 1990).

Drop-Out Prevention Efforts

The literature on school dropouts has traditionally placed the focus of causality within one or more of three broad categories: the individual, the school, and the family or community. Consequently, efforts at dropout prevention have focused on these areas.

Programs Focused on the Individual

For conceptual clarity, drop-out prevention programs that focus on the individual can be divided into two broad categories: those that attempt to improve some characteristic of the individual student that consequently enhances his or her chances of graduating from high school and those that attempt to decrease the impact of negative influences. Some of the major programmatic efforts from both of these categories are:

1. Academic improvement programs. One of the most direct links to dropping out of school is poor academic performance. Consequently, many school districts have implemented a variety of remediation programs involving tutoring, individualized instruction, and competency-based instruction to keep at-risk students at a level where continued school attendance is a reasonable alternative (Hahn, Danzberger, & Lefkowitz, 1987).
2. Motivational improvement programs. These programs typically attempt to increase traits such as achievement motivation and self-esteem, which have been shown to characterize students who persevere in school (Zimmerman & Arunkumar, 1995).
3. Scholarship and tuition-guarantee programs. These programs promise support for higher education if the student graduates from high school. The programs are based on the assumption that students will stay in school if they perceive a possibility for further education beyond high school (U.S. General Accounting Office, 1993).
4. Mentoring programs. Based on the assumption that students who drop out of school lack appropriate role models and sufficient support, these programs provide students with mentors who act in these capacities. Mentors may be successful adults who are similar to the student (for example, in gender and race) or academically successful peers (Grannis, 1994).
5. Programs that attempt to decrease grade retention. It has been recognized for some time that one of the strongest predictors of dropping out of high school is retention at an earlier grade. Consequently, programs have been established to help students compensate for their failure to keep pace with their age cohorts (Smith & Shepard, 1988).
6. Pregnancy and drug-prevention programs. Students who become pregnant or who are addicted to drugs are far more likely to drop out of school. Programs to avoid these problems, or to overcome their impact, often have the effect of decreasing school dropout rates (Hahn, Danzberger, & Lefkowitz, 1987).

School-Wide Efforts to Address Dropouts

A growing body of research locates the causes of dropping out within the school rather than the student. This research focuses on the school as a system that supports or does not support students remaining and on the degree to which the schools themselves work to hold on to these students or inadvertently drive them out (Fine, 1991; Renihan & Renihan, 1995; Wehlage & Rutter, 1986).

Calls for reform focus on how responsive schools are to students' needs. Often, efforts to improve a school's ability to retain students focus on changing the climate of the school. Effective schools provide at-risk students with a community of support (Wehlage et al., 1989). Several authors conceptualize successful schools as those that create a caring community and emphasize the student's position as an important member of the community (Cuban, 1989). Some call for a redefinition of the teaching role to place greater emphasis on the caring relationship between teacher an student (Wehlage et al., 1989). The school is seen as a site where responsiveness and pastoral care are used to provide meaningful experiences for students who are at risk of dropping out (Renihan & Renihan, 1995).

Programs That Focus on the Family and Community

A wide variety of programs attempt to influence the support that students receive from their families or communities. It is widely recognized that family support can be a vital element in keeping a student in school. Programs have been developed in which parents are actively recruited to work with the school to provide the necessary support for at-risk students. Programs have also been implemented using school-business partnerships where students work part-time while maintaining their status as full-time students. Other programs involve the active support of various community organizations (churches, social organizations, and other religious groups), which provide services and support to students to keep them in school.

Bibliography

Alexander, K. L., Entwisle, D. R., & Horsey, C. S. (1997). From first grade forward: Early foundations of high school drop-out. *Sociology of Education, 70,* 87–107.

Barrington, B. L., & Hendricks, B. (1989). Differentiating characteristics of high school graduates, drop-outs, and nongraduates. *Journal of Educational Research, 82(6),* 309–319.

Cairns, B. C., Cairns, B. D., & Neckerman, H. J. (1989). Early school drop-out: Configuration and determinants. *Child Development, 60,* 1437–1452.

Clements, B. S. (1991). What is a drop-out? Pilot program collects meaningful data for improving schools. *Equity and Excellence, 25(1),* 5–8.

Cuban, L. (1989) The "at risk" label and the problem of urban school reform. *Phi Delta Kappan, 70,* 780–801.

Encyclopedia of American Education. (1996).

Ensminger, M., & Slusarcick, A. (1992). Paths to high school graduation or drop-out: A longitudinal study of a first-grade cohort. *Sociology of Education, 65,* 95–113.

Fine, M. (1991). *Framing drop-outs: Notes on the politics of an urban public high school.* Albany, NY: State University of New York Press.

Garnier, H. E., Stein, J. A., & Jacobs, J. K. (1997). The process of dropping out of school: A 19-year perspective. *American Educational Research Journal, 34(2),* 395–419.

Grannis, J. C. (1994). The drop-out prevention initiative in New York City. In R. J. Rossi (Ed.), *Schools and students at risk.* New York: Teachers College Press.

Hahn, A., Danzberger, T. S., & Lefkowitz, A. (1987). *Drop-outs in America: Enough is known for action.* Washington, DC: Institute for Educational Leadership.

Hammack, F. (1986). Large school systems' drop-out reports: An analysis of definitions, procedures and findings. In G. Natriello (Ed.), *School drop-outs, patterns and policies.* New York: Teachers College Press.

Hodgkinson, H. (1985). *All one system: Demographics of education, kindergarten through graduate school.* Washington, DC: Institute for Educational Leadership.

McMillen, M., Kaufman, P., & Whitener, S. (1993). *Drop-out rates in the United States: 1993.* Washington, DC: U.S. Department of Education, National Center for Educational Statistics.

Renihan, F. I., & Renihan, P. J. (1995). Responsive high schools: Structuring success for the at-risk student. *High School Journal, 79(1),* 1–13.

Rossi, R. J. (1994). *Schools and students at risk.* New York: Teachers College Press.

Rumsberger, R. W. (1983). Dropping out of high school: The influence of race, sex and family background. *American Educational Research Journal, 20,* 199–220.

Schneider, S. J., Svetvilas, N., & Baker, A. M. (1994). *Tomorrow's drop-outs in today's schools.* Paper presented at the annual meeting of the American Educational Research Association, New Orleans.

Smith, M., & Shepard, L. (1988). Flunking grades: A recapitulation. In L. Shepard & M. Smith (Eds.), *Flunking grades: Research and policies on retention.* Philadelphia: Falmer.

U.S. Department of Education. (1995). *Digest of Education Statistics.* Washington, DC: National Center for Education Statistics.

U.S. General Accounting Office. (1993). *Promising practice: Private programs guaranteeing student aid for higher education.* Washington, DC.

Wehlage et al. (1989). *Reducing the risk: Schools as communities of support.* London; New York: Falmer Press.

Wehlage, J. H., & Rutter, R. A. (1986). Dropping out of school: How much do schools contribute to the problem? *Teachers College Record, 87(3),* 374–392.

Zimmerman, M. A., & Arunkumar, R. (1995). Resiliency research: Implications for schools and policy. *Society for Research in Child Development, 8,* 1–17.

*Trevor E. Sewell, Joseph P. DuCette,
and Erin McNamara Horvat*

SCHOOL EFFECTIVENESS AND IMPROVEMENT

are both relatively recent disciplines within educational, psychological, and social research. Effectiveness research is concerned with factors that promote student intellectual and social growth and in general, has been a research-oriented discipline lacking strong links with practice. The improvement enterprise, by contrast, has been more concerned with improving practice than researching factors associated with improvement. Both disciplines have been developed, to some extent, by individuals outside educational research communities in countries such as the United States and the United Kingdom. In the case of school effectiveness in Britain, for example, major contributions came from sociomedical research, the child guidance community, child psychiatry and epidemiology. Marginal affiliation of effectiveness researchers within educational research communities is no longer important, given the existence of the discipline's separate professional association, The International Congress for School Effectiveness and Improvement (ICSEI); a journal, *School Effectiveness and School Improvement*; and associated proceedings.

The increase in the quantity of research on school effectiveness and improvement, the quality of research designs and methodology, and the impact of research in determining national policies on education is a marked contrast to the research paradigms of more than 30 years ago. In the 1960s there was a prevalent belief that "schools made no difference," born of the research by Coleman and colleagues (1966) that showed that family and individual factors are the best predictors of student achievement. Psychological research in the 1960s and 1970s, with its emphasis on the primacy of early development and on a psychological paradigm of inquiry, contributed to this view by concentrating on individual and family factors.

Effectiveness

Effectiveness research into the school's impact on student development has grown enormously (see review in Scheerens & Bosker, 1997). In the United States, early contributions came from practice and research backgrounds and have recently been supported by cohort studies that examine school and classroom impact on development (Teddlie & Stringfield, 1993). Current research is sensitive to possible variation in "what works" by different contexts, such as school socioeconomic background, school governance, school location in urban and rural settings, and school-age phase. In the United Kingdom, advances have occurred through rigorous research methodologies for studying school effects, the development of multilevel methods of analysis, a literature on the school-level determinants of student progress, and the use of measures of both social and academic gains. In the Netherlands, the strong research traditions in learning and instruction have meant that effective instruction has developed as a focus of interest, together with theories that link together student inputs, processes, and outcomes conceptually (Scheerens & Creemers, 1990).

Improvement

In school improvement, one perceives a different discipline historically in its conceptual and methodological paradigm (Reynolds et al., 1996). School improvement developed reactively out of the failure of innovations in education in the 1960s and 1970s to take root in schools and affect outcomes (Reynolds, 1988). Whereas these innovations were organizationally based, developed outside the school, evaluated qualitatively, and concerned with changing the formal organization and curricular contents of schooling, the new paradigm loosely associated with authorities such as Fullan (1991) and Hopkins, Ainscow, and West (1994) emphasized the importance of change in school culture, the necessity of ownership of the school improvement strategy by the school itself, and the importance of collegiality and laterality within schools to enhance implementation of school improvement efforts.

School effectiveness and school improvement researchers spawned a considerable literature, but because of their adherence to different sets of beliefs concerning disciplinary goals and methodologies, they found it hard to work jointly to improve education. Although school effectiveness knowledge can be viewed as the "content" and school improvement knowledge as the "vehicle" of school change, in reality few programs were attempted that merged knowledge. Only in the last few years have elements of a merged paradigm become apparent (Reynolds et al., 1996). The elements are:

- A commitment to utilizing all bodies of knowledge from all disciplinary locations, whether they be school effectiveness, school improvement, teacher effectiveness, or program evaluation.
- A commitment to "pull all relevant levers" when intervening in schools, especially the lever of the classroom, which explains considerably more variance in pupil outcomes than the school or district levels.
- A commitment to use mixed methods to establish relationships between school and classroom factors and student outcomes and qualitative data to explain them.

Methodology

The methodology that has been common in school effectiveness research involves collection of data on three sets of factors, inputs (the students arriving at schools and their personal, intellectual, and familial characteristics), outputs (the cognitive and affective outcomes produced at the end of the schooling process), and processes (the educational factors at district, school, and classroom levels that can affect outcomes). Early analyses were relatively simple, involving multivariate techniques such as multiple regression to predict school means from the intake characteristics (using a number of schools to establish the relationship) and then utilizing school process data to account for schools' variation in their "added value" based on a comparison of actual student achievement with predicted achievement. Since the mid-1980s, there has been a gain in popularity of multilevel methods that permit the apportionment of variance to multiple levels of the educational process (child, teacher and classroom, school, district, region, nation, etc.) and that permit the evaluation of "slants on slopes," the varying nature of the relationship between individual children and their teachers, or the variation between teachers and departments in their students' gain within the same school. Such methods are now axiomatic within school effectiveness research, but it is interesting to note that conventional multivariate analysis (factor analysis, path analysis, and multiple regression) gives estimates of explained variance similar to these more advanced methods.

School improvement research has rarely used quantitative analyses but has recently seen projects utilizing multilevel analyses to judge the variation in student gains from different "off-the-shelf" and school-generated improvement programs and the factors responsible for schools' differentials in their improvement trajectories over time.

The Contribution of Psychology

Psychology and psychologists have played a considerable role in the evolution of school effectiveness as a discipline and a lesser but still important role in school improvement. School effectiveness has been particularly influenced by the model of J. B. Carroll (1963), which offers a relevant set of factors at the student and classroom level. This model was originally developed to predict the success of training in foreign languages and defines student achievement, or the degree of learning, as a function of the time spent divided by the time needed by a student. Time needed is influenced by factors at the student level (aptitude, task-specific skills) and ability to understand instruction (general intelligence), and at the classroom level, namely the quality of instruction. Time spent is influenced by student factors (perseverance over time) and by the time allowed for learning by the teacher. Research on mastery learning, time spent and student achievement, and opportunity to learn, operationalized as the curriculum content a teacher covers, have all been influential outgrowths of this paradigm.

Social psychology has also had an impact on school effectiveness in the area of internal locus of control, which was entered into the school effectiveness literature by Coleman et al. (1966), Brookover et al. (1979), and Teddlie and Stringfield (1993), who used student "sense of futility" scales and scales measuring students' and teachers' internal and external locus of control in the school. The evolution of the concepts of teacher and student expectations started in experimental studies in psychology in the 1960s and was applied in the form of the self-fulfilling prophecy in the classic *Pyg-malion in the Classroom* study (Rosenthal & Jacobsen, 1968), which in turn heavily influenced the research designs of Brookover and colleagues (1979), Hallinger and Murphy (1986), and Teddlie and Stringfield (1993), in which the source of expectations is analyzed from home, school, and the socioeconomic status of catchment areas. A further influence of social psychology has been in the area of student self-concept or self-esteem, in which it has been used as an intervening variable between expectations and achievement, an outcome variable, and a predictor variable related to achievement.

Organizational psychology also has had an influence on school effectiveness research, particularly in the area of organizational climate. The widespread use of measures such as the Organizational Climate Description Questionnaire (OCDQ), Pupil Control Ideology (PCI), and Organizational Health Inventory (OHI) is also an area in which psychology has had an impact within effectiveness research.

The final area of psychological impact has been that of teacher effectiveness. Developing as a separate field, significant relationships have been reported between teacher behaviors and student achievement (Brophy & Good, 1986), progressing from correlational studies to quasi-experiments in which the alteration of classroom processes produced achievement gains. By the mid-1980s, a substantial literature had developed covering issues such as pacing and quantity of instruction, opportunity to learn, classroom management, use of praise, questioning, and the social psychological climate of the classroom. Many of the originally psychologically developed classroom observation systems have been used in effectiveness research (see summary in Schaffer, Nesselrodt, & Stringfield, 1994).

Conclusions

It is likely that psychological perspectives and research will have an enhanced role in the future of effectiveness and improvement research and practice. Whereas, historically, there has been little interaction between psychology and improvement research, enhanced interest in ineffective schools is leading to borrowing perspectives from abnormal psychology, social relations, psychiatry, and human relations to conceptualize the factors worthy of study prior to the development of context-specific improvement initiatives. Researchers are also increasingly aware of the need for new, more contemporary outcomes of schooling to be measured, particularly the learning-to-learn skills that are necessary for successful learning processes. Many argue that these skills contribute to outcomes, although it is not clear how large their contribution actually is (Palincsar & McPhail, 1993).

Finally, new perspectives on the process of learning itself have reconceptualized learning as an active process in which students construct knowledge and skills by working with the content, which differs from a passive role of the student as a learner to be instructed. Whereas older models of instruction aim at direct transfer, new models consider learning as knowledge construction, in which the student plays the active part. Ideas about active learning change the role of the teacher in that the student is responsible for learning. The teacher is seen as a manager and orchestrator of the learning process, and not a person who delivers the instruction. This implies that teachers teach students how to learn (Weinstein & Mayer, 1986).

Contemporary views on learning have resulted in new models for instruction, or at least in adaptations of the direct instruction model. The new models put greater emphasis on the students as active, responsible learners in cooperation with their teachers and with other students. Examples of the new instructional models are reciprocal teaching (Brown & Palincsar, 1989), modeling (Schoenfeld, 1985), procedural facilitation (Scardamalia & Bereiter, 1985), and cognitive apprenticeship (Collins, Brown, & Newman, 1989). Further interaction between psychology and school effectiveness is likely to be functional for both disciplines.

Bibliography

Brookover, W. B., Beady, C., Flood, P., Schweitzer, J., & Wisenbaker, J. (1979). *Schools, social systems and student achievement: Schools can make a difference.* New York: Praeger.

Brophy, J., & Good, T. L. (1986). Teacher behavior and student achievement. In M. C. Wittrock (Ed.), *Handbook of research on teaching* (3rd ed., pp. 328–375). New York: Macmillan.

Brown, A. L., & Palincsar, A. S. (1989). Guided, cooperative learning and individual knowledge acquisition. In L. B. Resnick (Ed.), *Knowing, learning and instruction* (pp. 393–453). Hillsdale: Erlbaum.

Carroll, J. B. (1963). A model of school learning. *Teachers College Record, 64*(8), 723–733.

Coleman, J. S., Campbell, E., Hobson, C., McPartland, J., Mood, A., Weinfeld, R., & York, R. (1966). *Equality of educational opportunity.* Washington, DC: U.S. Government Printing Office.

Collins, A., Brown, J. S., & Newman, S. E. (1989) Cognitive apprenticeship: Teaching the crafts of reading, writing, and mathematics. In L. B. Resnick (Ed.), *Knowing, learning and instruction* (pp. 453–495). Hillsdale: Erlbaum.

Fullan, M. (1991). *The new meaning of educational change.* London: Cassell.

Hallinger, P., & Murphy, J. (1986). The social context of effective schools. *American Journal of Education, 94,* 328–355.

Hopkins, D., Ainscow, M., & West, M. (1994). *School improvement in an era of change.* London: Cassell.

Palincsar, A. S., & McPhail, J. C. (1993) A critique of the

metaphor of distillation in "Toward a knowledge base for school learning." *Review of Educational Research, 63*(3), 327–334.

Reynolds, D. (1988). British school improvement research: The contribution of qualitative studies. *International Journal of Qualitative Studies in Education, 1*(2), 143–154.

Reynolds, D., Creemers, B. P. M., Hopkins, D., Stoll, L., & Bollen, R. (1996). *Making good schools.* London: Routledge.

Rosenthal, R. & Jacobsen, L. (1968). *Pygmalion in the classroom.* New York: Holt, Rinehart, & Winston.

Scardamalia, M., & Bereiter, C. (1985). Development of dialectical processes in composition. In D. R. Olson, N. Torrance, & A. Hildyard (Eds.), *Literacy, language and learning* (pp. 307–329). Cambridge, England: Cambridge University Press.

Schaffer, E. C., Nesselrodt, P. S., & Stringfield, S. (1994). The contributions of classroom observations to school effectiveness research. In D. Reynolds, B. P. M. Creemers, P. S. Nesselrodt, E. C. Schaffer, S. Stringfield, & C. Teddlie (Eds.), *Advances in school effectiveness research and practice* (pp. 133–152) London: Pergamon.

Scheerens, J., & Bosker, R. (1997). *The foundations of school effectiveness.* Oxford, England: Pergamon Press.

Scheerens, J., & Creemers, B. P. M. (1990). Conceptualizing school effectiveness. In B. P. M. Creemers & J. Scheerens (Eds.), *Developments in school effectiveness research* [Special issue]. *International Journal of Educational Research, 13*(7), 691–706.

Schoenfeld, A. H. (1985). *Mathematical problem solving.* New York: Academic Press.

Teddlie, C. & Stringfield, S. (1993). *Schools make a difference: Lessons learned from a 10-year study of school effects.* New York: Teachers College Press.

Weinstein, C. E., & Mayer, R. E. (1986). The teaching of learning strategies. In M. C. Wittrock (Ed.), *Handbook of research on teaching* (pp. 315–328). New York: Macmillan.

David Reynolds, Bert Creemers, and Gerry Reezigt

SCHOOL PHOBIA. *See* School Refusal; *and* Specific Phobia.

SCHOOL PSYCHOLOGY. [*This entry provides a broad history of the field from its inception to the present.*]

A specialty of professional psychology, school psychology is "the application of psychological knowledge and skills within educational settings to directly or indirectly enhance the development and learning of children" (Thomas, 1996, p. 345). Though most practitioners work in public school settings, they increasingly deliver services in other settings, including private schools, clinics, correctional institutions, private practice, and colleges and universities. Broadly considered, a school psychologist is a professional psychological practitioner whose general purpose is to bring a psychological perspective to bear on the problems of educators and the clients educators serve. This perspective is derived from a broad base of training in educational and psychological foundations as well as specialty preparation, resulting in the provision of comprehensive psychological services of a direct and indirect nature. (Fagan & Wise, 1994, p. 3)

A detailed definition has also been approved by the International School Psychology Association (Oakland & Cunningham, 1997).

There are an estimated 25,000 persons in the field of school psychology in the United States and perhaps 87,000 worldwide (Oakland & Cunningham, 1992) employed under various titles, most often "school psychologist" or "educational psychologist." Preparation programs are offered in approximately 230 U.S. institutions of higher education, awarding master's, specialist, and doctoral level degrees. Approximately two thirds have specialist-level preparation (60 graduate semester hours), and about 25% hold doctoral degrees. Most school psychologists are employed by public school systems, work on a 9- or 10-month contract, and are paid competitive salaries for nondoctoral psychological practitioners. Salaries vary as a function of school system location, practitioner education, and years of experience. In the mid-1990s, the average salary for all practitioners was estimated at $43,000.

Practitioners, trainers, and students are organized in state associations of school psychologists, commonly affiliated with the National Association of School Psychologists (NASP), whose membership numbers around 21,000. The field is also served by the Division of School Psychology of the American Psychological Association (APA), whose membership is approximately 2,500. The principal journals of the field in the United States include *Journal of School Psychology* (begun in 1963), *Psychology in the Schools* (1964), *School Psychology Review* (1972), and *School Psychology Quarterly* (1986). On the international level, the primary publication is *School Psychology International* (begun in 1979), and several countries publish journals primarily for school psychologists (e.g., *Canadian Journal of School Psychology* or Switzerland's *Psychology and Education*). Professional literature is also provided through state, national, and international newsletters, an array of journals in related fields (e.g., *Journal of Psychoeducational Assessment*), and books specific to the field. Nonprint media information and electronic "literature" are also currently available.

Practitioners are credentialed through state education agencies, typically at the nondoctoral level for school-based practice, and by state boards of examiners in psychology, typically at the doctoral level, for private, independent, and nonschool practice (often as health service providers). Practice is regulated by these agencies as well as by the codes of ethics of the major professional associations (APA and NASP).

School psychologists distribute their services across the areas of assessment, consultation, interventions, administrative assignments, continuing education and professional growth, in-service teaching and staff development, research, and program evaluation. Assessment, consultation, and intervention activities account for more than 90% of practitioner time. Assessment services for children with suspected disabilities have broadened in the past 20 years to incorporate alternatives to standardized assessment and to include more consultation and interventions with both exceptional and regular schoolchildren.

History

School psychology emerged in the late nineteenth and early twentieth centuries from the interplay of people and events associated with child study, clinical psychology, compulsory schooling, and special education. The origin of the term "school psychologist" in the United States appears to be from a 1911 translation of an article by William Stern from the German-language psychology literature. Of particular note are the contributions of Lightner Witmer and Granville Stanley Hall, bellwethers of clinical psychology and child study, respectively (Fagan, 1992). Hall's emphasis on the normal child and his association with child development and educational psychology and Witmer's emphasis on the abnormal and exceptional child and his association with clinical psychology and with the founding of the first psychological clinic in the United States set in motion practice and research arenas that are discernible to the present day (Fagan, 1996; McReynolds, 1987). Though most psychological practice specialties have early connections to clinical and applied psychology, school psychology has been connected to development in professional education as well. For example, calls for reform and accountability in public schooling have influenced the documentation of services and their impact in school psychology. Changes in the delivery of services have also been affected by the managed health care movement of the latter twentieth century.

Though they had origins in Witmer's first psychological clinic, school psychological services developed in public school districts, first in Chicago (1899), then in most urban and large city districts by 1913 (Wallin, 1914). Suburban and rural services developed later and were spurred by state and federal legislation for the handicapped and the general evolution of the field of special education. Practitioner growth was slow for several decades, with perhaps only 200 by 1920 and 1,000 by 1950. By 1970 there were 5,000 people in the field and more than 20,000 by 1990 (Fagan, 1995). Services emerged in the major cities of the eastern United States and spread rapidly to the Great Lakes area and the far west. Practitioner distribution corresponds closely to the distribution of the school population nationwide. One measure of the delivery of school psychological services has been the ratio of school psychologists to the number of schoolchildren served. The nationwide ratio is approximately 1:2,000, though the range is considerably broad. The NASP recommends a ratio of 1:1,000. For many years the ratio was much worse; as recently as 1974, the ratio was estimated at 1:4,800.

Both men and women have figured prominently in the history of school psychology and its leadership (French, 1988). Arnold Gesell is reputed to be the first person to hold employment with the title "school psychologist." The first book specifically about school psychology was written by Gertrude Hildreth (Hildreth, 1930). Other noteworthy contributors include Harry Baker, Jack Bardon, Calvin Catterall, Norma Cutts, Ethel Cornell, Frances Mullen, Grace Munson, Harriet O'Shea, and Helen Thompson Woolley (see Fagan & Warden, 1996). The field has always been well represented by both males and females; perhaps never less than 30% have been women, and currently at least 70% of the field's members are women.

Training programs emerged in the late 1920s, the first at New York University. Other early programs were at Pennsylvania State University, the University of Michigan, and the University of Illinois. Program growth was rapid in the 1960s and 1970s, following strong job demand for practitioners, growth in special educational services, and guidelines for accreditation and credentialing. The number of school psychology program institutions has remained around 200 to 220 for the past decade, despite growth in the number of accredited doctoral programs.

Credentialing of practitioners dates to the use of a licensing examination for school psychologists in the New York City schools in the mid-1920s. New York and Pennsylvania were the first states to have certification through their state departments of education in the mid-1930s. Certification grew steadily in the 1940s, and its growth paralleled that of independent practice licensure for psychologists during the period 1946–1976. By the late 1970s all states offered credentials from both state departments of education and state psychology boards.

The field struggled for identity for several decades. With the post–World War II baby boom and associated growth in school enrollments, demand for school psychologists grew rapidly. Subsequently, there emerged rapid growth of credentialing of practitioners, the development of training programs, and regulation of the field in terms of accreditation, legislation, and credentialing requirements. The field was greatly affected by a series of federal laws and litigations related to the education of children with disabilities. These developments ushered in an era of closer scrutiny of services, regulations and practice guidelines, and accountability. By the late 1970s, the field had established a strong and clear identity.

Overall, the history of the field has been divided into two general periods of development, the "hybrid" years and the "thoroughbred" years. The former reflects the period roughly from 1890 to 1969, when the field was emerging from a mixture of various fields of study and practice and the primary role of the practitioner was the assessment of referred children for possible special education placement. In contrast, the thoroughbred years, from 1970 to the present, are characterized by a general purification of the field's identity by establishing its own symbols of professionalization. In this period, practitioners more consistently have come from accredited school psychology programs staffed by school psychologist faculty and have obtained employment as school psychologists with credentials specific to the field of school psychology. Unlike the earlier period, practitioners in the thoroughbred years have their own state and national associations and a literature specifically about and for school psychologists.

Throughout its history, school psychology has straddled the arenas of psychology and education, attempting to carve for itself a unique practice and research arena, though continuing to be influenced by the forces of both fields. The success of these struggles is witnessed in the overall identity of the field and the much increased publication and research activity in the past thirty years. The field's primary areas of research are in psychoeducational assessment of children with disabilities, consultation, and interventions for both academic and personal-social behavior.

Training Requirements

The APA advocates the doctoral level as the appropriate entry level for the independent practice of school psychology, whereas the NASP advocates the specialist degree level. Programs specifically in school psychology are accredited at the doctoral level by both APA and NASP, the latter through an agreement with the National Council for Accreditation of Teacher Education (NCATE), and at the specialist level solely by NASP and NCATE. At the state level, programs are often formally approved by the state's education agency. Training guidelines are available from both APA and NASP and include comprehensive preparation in educational and psychological foundations, specialty preparation, and field experiences, including a minimum of one school year or more of internship. Doctoral level internships are expected to consist of approximately 1,500 clock hours, whereas nondoctoral internships are expected to consist of at least 1,200.

School psychology training programs are administered in departments of psychology in colleges of arts and sciences and in various departments in colleges of education. In many respects, training has evolved in connection with trends in the training for clinical, counseling, and educational psychology. Until the 1930s there were few discernible differences in the preparation of professional psychologists. With the increasing differentiation of psychology and the evolution of practice specialties, school psychology, like other areas, developed its own training identity by the late 1960s. However, there are important distinctions between psychological practitioners based on preparation, clients, service settings, and services rendered. Like industrial psychology, school psychology has many setting-specific determinants of training, credentialing, and practice. Nevertheless, school psychology shares several aspects of practice with clinical and counseling psychology and with educational psychology, a research field not generally considered a practice specialty of psychology.

Professional Organizations

The largest organization for school psychologists in the world is the National Association of School Psychologists, founded in 1969. The NASP governance consists of officers and delegates from each of the 50 states, the District of Columbia, and Puerto Rico. The Division of School Psychology of the APA was founded during the reorganization of the APA in 1945. It is not governed by geographic representation but rather by officers and vice presidents for particular areas (e.g., education, training, and scientific affairs; social and ethical responsibility and ethnic minority affairs (see Fagan, 1993). The International School Psychology association, though its membership is less than 1,000, represents the interests of the field from a global perspective.

Although many school psychologists belong to other groups (e.g., Council for Exceptional Children), most maintain an affiliation with only one national organization, most often the NASP. School psychologists have joined their respective state associations at a high rate; perhaps 80% or more hold state membership. All state and national associations conduct one or more annual conventions.

Future Directions

Conferences on the future of school psychology were held in the early 1980s (e.g., the Spring Hill and Olympia conferences). Along with the publication in 1984 of a *Blueprint for Training and Practice* (National School Psychology Inservice Training Network, 1984) and its

revision (Ysseldyke et al., 1997), these conferences have helped to keep the field abreast of changes and to plan for the future. School psychologists will continue to train and practice primarily at the nondoctoral level, though a gradually increasing percentage will hold the doctoral degree. Since most will continue to be based in public schools, employment opportunities and salaries will be linked to developments in public education. However, the increasing interest in persons with school psychology training and experience and the growth in the number of doctoral recipients will help to expand the employment opportunities in nonschool settings. The roles and functions of practitioners will remain similar so long as schools are responsible for the education and general health care of exceptional and at-risk student populations. Subspecialty training by some practitioners will continue to expand services in specific areas, such as services for preschool children, postsecondary school services, and neuropsychology.

With the pending retirements of practitioners and trainers who entered the field in the 1960s and 1970s, strong academic and field employment demand should continue. Employment opportunities will remain favorable in large urban districts and in rural and remote settings and for practitioners of minority backgrounds or who are bilingual. Increasing opportunities will be available for school psychologists whose additional training qualifies them for positions in school administration.

[*See also* Academic Assessment–Intervention Link; Academic Assessment of Performance; Academic Intervention; Buros Mental Measurements Yearbook; Classrooms; Developmental Psychology; Educational Psychology; Educational Testing Service; Elementary Education; Preschool Education; Psychometrics; Secondary Education; *and* Teachers.]

Bibliography

Cutts, N. E. (Ed.). (1955). *School psychologists at mid-century*. Washington, DC: American Psychological Association.

Fagan, T. K. (1986). The historical origins and growth of programs to prepare school psychologists in the United States. *Journal of School Psychology 24*(1), 9–22.

Fagan, T. K. (1990). Research on the history of school psychology: Recent developments, significance, resources, and future directions. In T. R. Kratochwill (Ed.), *Advances in school psychology* (Vol. 7, pp. 151–182). Hillsdale, NJ: Erlbaum.

Fagan, T. K. (1992). Compulsory schooling, child study, clinical psychology, and special education: Origins of school psychology. *American Psychologist, 47*, 236–243.

Fagan, T. K. (1993). Separate but equal: School psychology's search for organizational identity. *Journal of School Psychology, 31*, 3–90.

Fagan, T. K. (1995). Trends in the history of school psychology in the United States. In A. Thomas & J. Grimes (Eds.), *Best practices in school psychology—III* (pp. 59–67). Washington, DC: National Association of School Psychologists.

Fagan, T. K. (1996). Witmer's contributions to school psychological services. *American Psychologist, 51,* 241–243.

Fagan, T. K., & Warden, P. G. (Eds.). (1996). *Historical encyclopedia of school psychology.* Westport, CT: Greenwood.

Fagan, T. K., & Wise, P. S. (1994). *School psychology: Past, present, and future.* White Plains, NY: Longman.

French, J. L. (1988). Grandmothers I wish I knew: Contributions of women to the history of school psychology. *Professional School Psychology, 3,* 51–68.

Hildreth, G. H. (1930). *Psychological service for school problems.* Yonkers-on-Hudson, NY: World Book.

McReynolds, P. (1987). Lightner Witmer: Little known founder of clinical psychology. *American Psychologist, 42,* 849–858.

National School Psychology Inservice Training Network. (1984). *School psychology: A blueprint for training and practice.* Minneapolis, MN: Author.

Oakland, T. D., & Cunningham, J. L. (1992). A survey of school psychology in developed and developing countries. *School Psychology International, 13,* 99–129.

Oakland, T., & Cunningham, J. (1997). International School Psychology Association definition of school psychology. *School Psychology International, 18,* 195–200.

Thomas, A. (1996). School psychology. In T. K. Fagan & P. G. Warden (Eds.), *Historical encyclopedia of school psychology* (pp. 345–347). Westport, CT: Greenwood.

Wallin, J. E. W. (1914). *The mental health of the school child.* New Haven, CT: Yale University Press.

Witmer, L. (1907). Clinical psychology. *Psychological Clinic, 1,* 1–9.

Ysseldyke, J., Dawson, P., Lehr, C., Reschly, D., Reynolds, M., & Telzrow, C. (1997). *School psychology: A blueprint for training and practice—II.* Bethesda, MD: National Association of School Psychologists.

Thomas K. Fagan

SCHOOL READINESS. A serious human development problem, especially in poor areas, is school failure and dropout. It leads to high rates of repetition of first-year classes and low rates of remaining to the final year of the basic educational cycle (UNESCO, 1991; UNICEF, 1991). Especially in less developed countries, in which universal schooling has not yet been achieved, this problem entails severe economic and human costs. Thus the World Bank (1988) estimated that the average cost for each student who completes primary school in sub-Saharan Africa is 50% higher due to repetition and dropout.

One of the many factors involved is poor preparation of the child for school. It is a multifaceted factor involving both the child and his or her environment.

"School readiness" is currently defined in terms of the child's activity level, social competence and psychological preparedness, and cognitive abilities, including preliteracy and prenumeracy skills. It is also reflected in the positive orientation and support of the child's family (Myers, 1992). Each one of these concepts needs explanation.

Activity level of the child refers to health and nutritional status, which affects both the child's school attendance rates and concentration level in class. For example, an early report (Berg, 1981) showed that in some Latin American countries children may miss up to one third of the school year due to illness and poor health. Nutritional levels also are of crucial significance. Children with protein-energy malnutrition or vitamin and mineral deficiencies are found to be less active and attentive and more apathetic than their adequately nourished peers. In the case of iron deficiency, iron supplementation increases school performance (Myers, 1992; Pollitt & Metallinos-Katsaras, 1990).

Social competence and psychological preparedness affect adaptation to and coping with various school requirements, and basic cognitive abilities enable the child to handle the school material adequately. Research in developmental psychology consistently points to the crucial importance of early years for the overall development of the child, ranging from language to social competence and maturity, from cognitive abilities to life skills development. What happens in preschool years directly affects what happens in school.

Family support has to do with a positive orientation to the child's "student role," which would be reflected in such behaviors as allowing the child time to go to school and do homework, helping the child with schoolwork, interest in the school, and especially in the context of poverty, forgoing the child's economic and material contributions to the family for the sake of his or her school advancement. An early attendance to the child's overall development, particularly in providing the child with a "literate home environment," contributes greatly to the child's preparation for school.

The crucial role of environmental factors in human development has at times been undermined by the dominant organismic/maturational models. Current advances in biological and genetic research also tend to weaken the perceived relative importance of context. The old nature/nurture controversy tends to linger on. This has negative scientific and policy outcomes, with less attention being paid to discovering the adverse environmental conditions of development and to ameliorating them. Yet, as noted by Bronfenbrenner and Ceci (1993), "Humans have genetic potentials . . . that are appreciably greater than those that are presently realized, and . . . progress toward such realization can be achieved through the provision of environments in which proximal processes can be enhanced, but which are always within the limits of human genetic potential" (p. 315).

School readiness can be conceptualized as a developmental problem based on the assumption of some standard of adequacy that can be established and measured. Despite the rich research tradition and accumulated knowledge in developmental psychology, there is a dearth of standards of adequacy that can be used to assess general school readiness. Culturally valid age-specific psychological developmental norms, based on cross-cultural research, need to be established to parallel pediatric growth norms. Such norms are required if developmental arrears are to be corrected, especially in contexts of poverty, in which the early development of children suffers (e.g., Kagitcibasi, 1996; Kaur & Saraswathi, 1992; Landers, 1992; Savasir, Sezgin & Erol, 1992).

School readiness is one area in which environmental intervention can go a long way. Early enrichment programs go back several decades, and a great deal of research has been conducted to assess their effectiveness (for reviews, see Kagitcibasi, 1996, 1997; Meisels & Shonhoff, 1990; Myers, 1992; Seitz, 1990; Yoshikawa, 1994; Young, 1997). There is much diversity in goals, approaches, targets, timing, and setting of early support programs; for example, in terms of whether they are child- or parent-centered, whether they are home- or center-based, whether they involve only educational intervention or extend to health-nutrition support, whether they start at infancy or later, and so on. Though there is debate about what produces optimal results, it is generally agreed that programs that involve the parents and family as well as the child and those that have multiple goals lead to more sustainable positive gains.

Early intervention programs for school readiness go back to the era of President Lyndon Johnson in the United States. In Europe, early childhood care and education have a longer past and a history of providing wider coverage of children (Kamerman, 1991). In the rest of the world, early education is a more recent phenomenon, reaching a relatively smaller proportion of children. However, great strides have been made even in the less developed countries to increase coverage, though quality of care is a moot question (Myers, 1992).

A final point of consideration is that, just as children should be ready for school, schools should also be ready for children (Myers, 1992). This is particularly important in less developed countries in which large classes, inadequately trained teachers, lack of educational materials, irrelevant and "foreign" curricula, and general inaccessibility of schools (in terms of distances to be traveled and costs incurred) decrease the performance of even "prepared" children. Preparation of children

and schools have an interactive synergistic relationship. Developmentally prepared children increase the quality of schools, and better quality schools promote children's overall development. For this benign cycle to occur, educational policies should be informed by sound research and should, in turn, induce greater investment in education.

Bibliography

Berg, A. (1981). *Malnourished people: A policy review*. Washington DC: World Bank.

Brofenbrenner, U., & Ceci, S. J. (1993). Heredity, environment and the question "how?" A first approximation. In R. Plomin & G. E. McClearn (Eds.), *Children, families and government: Perspectives on American social policy* (pp. 393–414). New York: Cambridge University Press.

Kagitcibasi, C. (1996). *Family and human development across cultures*. Mahwah, NJ: Erlbaum.

Kagitcibasi, C. (1997). Parent education and child development. In M. E. Young (Ed.), *Early child development* (pp. 243–272). New York: Elsevier.

Kamerman, S. B. (1991). Child care policies and programs: An international overview. *Journal of Social Issues, 47*, 179–196.

Kaur, B., & Saraswathi, T. S. (1992). New directions in human development and and family studies: Research, policy and program interfaces. *International Journal of Psychology, 27*, 333–349.

Landers, C. (1992). *Measuring the development of young children: A comparative view of screening and assessment techniques*. New York: UN/C: Consultative Group on Early Childhood Care and Development.

Meisels, S. J., & Shonhoff, J. P. (Eds.). (1990). *Handbook of early childhood intervention*. Cambridge, U.K.: Cambridge University Press.

Myers, R. (1992). *The 12 who survive*. London: Routledge.

Pollitt, R., & Metallinos-Katsaras, E. (1990). Iron deficiency and behavior. Constructs, methods and validity of the findings. In R. J. Wurtman and J. J. Wurtman (Eds.), *Nutrition and the brain: Vol. 8. Behavioral effects of metals and their biochemical mechanisms* (pp. 101–146). New York: Raven.

Savasir, I., Sezgin, N., & Erol, N. (1992). 0–6 Yas Cocuklari icin gelisim tarama envanteri gelistirilmesi. [Devising a developmental screening inventory for 0–6-year-old children]. *Turk Psikiyatri Dergisi, 3*, 33–38.

Seitz, V. (1990). Intervention programs for impoverished children: A comparison of educational and family support models. *Annals of Child Development, 7*, 73–103.

UNESCO (1991). *The world education report*. Paris: Author.

UNICEF (1991). *The state of the world's children*. New York: Author.

World Bank (1988). *Education in sub-Saharan Africa, policies for adjustment, revitalization, expansion*. Washington, DC: Author.

Yoshikawa, H. (1994). Prevention as cumulative protection: Effects of early family support and education on chronic delinquency and its risks. *Psychological Bulletin*, 115, 28–54.

Young, M. E. (Ed.). (1997). *Early child development: Investing in our children's future*. New York: Elsevier.

Cigdem Kagitcibasi

SCHOOL REFUSAL (also known as school phobia and school avoidance) is a heterogeneous problem that involves extreme reluctance to attend school for a variety of reasons. Although there is a lack of consensus on the definition, etiology, and treatment of school refusal (Kearney, Eisen, & Silverman, 1995; Paige, 1997), the following criteria for school refusal are recommended (Berg, Nichols, & Pritchard, 1969; King, Ollendick, & Tonge, 1995):

1. Severe difficulty attending school that often results in prolonged absence
2. Severe emotional upset when faced with the prospect of going to school, including excessive fearfulness, temper outbursts, or complaints of feeling ill (e.g., stomachache or headache)
3. Staying at home with the parent's knowledge when the student should be at school
4. Absence of antisocial characteristics (e.g., lying, stealing, and destructiveness).

The latter two criteria differentiate school refusal from truancy. Truants tend to miss school without parental knowledge. Also, school refusal is more often associated with anxiety, whereas school truancy is more often associated with conduct disorders. Prolonged absence has been operationalized as being absent from school at least 40% of the time for at least a 4-week period or as being more than one standard deviation above the child's school's average attendance rates (Granell de Aldaz, Vivas, Gelfand, & Feldman, 1984; King et al., 1995).

There is no single clinical presentation of school refusal. School refusal can be acute and short-lived or in other cases chronic and prolonged. There are, however, three main groups of school refusers: (1) those who present with long histories of separation anxiety, depression, and at times oppositional and conduct problems; (2) those who display a circumscribed fear of one or more aspects of the school itself (e.g., of public speaking), and (3) those who display a combination of separation anxiety or depression and specific fears or phobias (King et al., 1995).

Reports of the prevalence of school refusal vary depending on definitions and criteria used. Nevertheless, rates are consistently low worldwide. For example, using Berg et al.'s (1969) criteria elaborated above, a rate of 0.4% was reported in the United States (Ollendick &

Mayer, 1984); and in a Venezuelan study (Granell de Aldaz et al., 1984), the rate of identification ranged from 0.4 to 5.4%, depending on the stringency of the criteria. Despite its low prevalence, school refusal consistently has been represented in 1 to 6% of clinic referrals, and its clinical significance is reflected in the attention given to this topic in the professional literature (Kearney & Beasley, 1994; Ollendick & Mayer, 1984).

Demographic studies reflect disagreement concerning the age of onset of school refusal, but it appears that the disorder can occur at any age and often occurs during school entry (ages 5 to 6 years) and major school transitions (ages 11 to 12 years) (King et al., 1995). However, the characterization of school refusal in youth may depend on age; that is, younger students tend to express separation anxiety with family members, and older students tend to have more school-specific fears or phobias (Last, Francis, Hersen, Kazdin, & Strauss, 1987). Studies regarding gender and socioeconomic status differences in prevalence rates are inconclusive (King et al., 1995).

Causes of school refusal are complex. Contributing variables can include constitutional vulnerability (for example, having a "difficult" temperament), learning history, parental psychopathology, family dysfunction, stressful events at school and/or home (such as a change of schools or illness of the student or parent), miscommunication between professionals concerning plans for intervention, and other school-related problems (King et al., 1995; Paige, 1997). Several theoretical explanations for school refusal have been advanced, most prominent of which are learning and psychodynamic theories. Psychodynamic theory postulates that a dysfunctional parent-child (typically mother-child) relationship is at the root of the problem. This relationship is characterized by repressed anxiety and mutual dependency and hostility. From a traditional learning theory perspective, school refusal is a learned behavior that results in school avoidance. More specifically, preschool children can experience separation anxiety from parents who are strong reinforcers and are seen as a refuge when the child is in a frightening situation. Also, parents can reinforce the child's behavior by being overly concerned about his or her safety (Paige, 1997). From the more recently developed cognitive-behavioral learning perspective, contributions of cognitions (negative self-talk) to school refusal is one of the more promising and largely unexplored areas of study (King et al., 1995).

Because of the complexity and heterogeneity of school refusal symptoms, assessment should include multiple methods (e.g., behavioral observation and rating scales) and sources (e.g., parent and teacher reports and self-monitoring). Also, collaborative team interventions should involve the student, family, school, and other service providers. Examples of treatment modalities are psychotherapy, hypnosis, family counseling, parent and social skills training, and behavioral treatments (including systematic desensitization and contingency management, which involves applying consequences for appropriate and inappropriate behaviors) (Paige, 1993). Although drug therapy should be considered in the multidimensional treatment of school refusal (particularly when depression and/or separation anxiety are involved), it must be used with caution because of the possibility of drug side effects (King et al., 1995).

School refusal can have a significant impact on the child, family, and school. The prognosis for school refusal is affected by many variables, but major prognostic indicators include age of onset, intellectual functioning, severity of the disorder, and time before treatment is initiated. In particular, a successful outcome for school refusers is more likely when there is early identification of the problem and initiation of a comprehensive treatment program (Paige, 1997). Without proper treatment, school refusers may be at risk for continued psychological disturbance in adulthood, including depression, anxiety, agoraphobia, antisocial and criminal behavior, alcoholism, and marital and work-related difficulties (Kearney et al., 1995; King et al., 1995; Paige, 1993).

Bibliography

Berg, I., Nichols, K., & Pritchard, C. (1969). School phobia: Its classification and relationship to dependency. *Journal of Child Psychology and Psychiatry, 10,* 123–141. Originally delineated school refusal criteria currently in common use.

Granell de Aldaz, E., Vivas, E., Gelfand, D. M., & Feldman, L. (1984). Estimating the prevalence of school refusal and school-related fears: A Venezuelan sample. *Journal of Nervous and Mental Disease, 172,* 722–729.

Kearney, C. A., & Beasley, J. F. (1994). The clinical treatment of school refusal behavior: A survey of referral and practice characteristics. *Psychology in the Schools, 31,* 128–132. Describes the results of a survey of 63 clinicians in the United States concerning client characteristics and treatment success.

Kearney, C. A., Eisen, A. R., & Silverman, W. K. (1995). The legend and myth of school phobia. *School Psychology Quarterly, 10,* 65–85.

King, N. J., Ollendick, T. H., & Tonge, B. J. (1995). *School refusal: Assessment and treatment.* Boston: Allyn & Bacon. Written from a clinical behavioral perspective for professionals responsible for the management of school refusers.

Last, C. G., Francis, G., Hersen, M., Kazdin, A. E., & Strauss, C. C. (1987). Separation anxiety and school phobia: A comparison using *DSM–III* criteria. *American Journal of Psychiatry, 144,* 653–657.

Ollendick, T. H., & Mayer, J. A. (1984). School phobia. In S. M. Turner (Ed.), *Behavioral theories and treatment of anxiety* (pp. 367–411). New York: Plenum.

Paige, L. Z. (1993). *The identification and treatment of school phobia.* Silver Spring, MD: National Association of School Psychologists. Includes decision matrices and treatment guidelines and is written primarily for school psychologists.

Paige, L. Z. (1997). School phobia, school refusal, and school avoidance. In G. G. Bear, K. M. Minke, & A. Thomas (Eds.), *Children's needs II: Development, problems, and alternatives* (pp. 339–347). Washington, DC: National Association of School Psychologists.

Sylvia Z. Ramirez

SCHOOL SUSPENSION AND EXPULSION. Suspension is a procedure used by a school to punish students for what the school views as serious forms of misbehavior. Suspension consists of removing the offending student from the regularly assigned classroom for a specified period of time. Similar to time-out but of longer duration, suspension is intended to be aversive: As a consequence of the misbehavior, the student is sent to an alternative setting in which participation in regular classroom activities, assumed to be desirable to the student, is denied.

The alternative setting to which the offending student is sent is located either within the school building (in-school suspension) or elsewhere (out-of-school suspension; with the student's home or an alternative education program being the most common out-of-school settings). Removing a student from school for more than 10 days is generally considered expulsion, not suspension (Hartwig & Ruesch, 1994), although this distinction is an arbitrary one that is not always made. School district policies and/or state laws generally dictate the behaviors for which a student can be suspended or expelled, the number of days the suspension or expulsion lasts, and the student's due process rights.

Approximately 1 million students receive out-of-school suspension and 1.4 million receive in-school suspension (Jones & Jones, 1998). Physical aggression is the most common behavior leading to suspension and expulsion. Other behaviors for which students are often suspended are talking back to school staff, using obscene language, smoking, use of alcohol, lack of cooperation, classroom disruption, extortion, excessive tardiness, skipping class, and forging parent signatures (Costenbader & Markson, 1998; Morgan-D'Atrio, Northup, LaFleur, & Spera, 1996).

Expulsion is typically applied to the most serious rule violations, such as violent behavior, possession of weapons or drugs, and other criminal acts. As a result of a "zero tolerance" attitude toward such behavior in the schools, federal laws have recently emerged mandating the use of expulsion. The federal Gun-Free Schools Act of 1993 requires expulsion whenever any student knowingly possesses a weapon. Other federal laws (Individuals with Disabilities Act Amendments of 1997; Rehabilitation Act of 1973), however, restrict the use of suspension and expulsion for children with disabilities.

Removal from the classroom is intended not only to punish the offending student, but also to deter students from engaging in the same behavior and to protect the right of all students and teachers to a safe and orderly learning environment. For most students, suspension and expulsion serve as effective sanctions or deterrents of inappropriate behavior. The punishment's severity communicates to students the school's expectations about appropriate behavior and its intolerance of inappropriate behavior, with an intent to foster internalization of the school's and society's values.

Whereas many of the limitations of suspension and expulsion are the same as those that apply to punishment procedures in general, others are more specific to removing students from the educational environment. Punishment fails to address factors underlying the student's problem behavior, does not teach replacement behaviors such as prosocial alternatives, has questionable long-term effects, may harm the student-teacher relationship, and is likely to foster resentment, retaliation, and/or emotions that are counterproductive to learning (Hyman, 1997; Martens & Meller, 1990). Suspension and expulsion may actually have paradoxical effects, resulting in negative reinforcement of the very behaviors being disciplined (Tobin, Sugai, & Colvin, 1996)—that is, suspension and expulsion allow students to escape from situations they find aversive, including frustrating academic tasks, peer rejection, and an atmosphere they frequently perceive as noncaring and of little relevance to their career goals. Unless instruction is provided while the student is removed from the classroom, suspension and expulsion are likely to delay achievement, which, in turn, increases the risk of academic failure and dropping out of school. Additionally, out-of-school suspension and expulsion may increase student exposure to negative peer models and crime, especially when the student is released to a home or community in which behavior goes unsupervised and unmonitored (Walker et al., 1996). Students themselves perceive suspension as of little or no value in reducing behavior problems (Costenbader & Markson, 1998).

Given the above shortcomings, few researchers endorse suspension and expulsion as primary methods for dealing with discipline problems, recommending instead that they be employed only after a variety of

other strategies fail. Such strategies include proactive classroom management strategies for preventing misbehavior, instructive strategies for teaching behaviors that should replace those that led to the suspension, and milder punishment-oriented strategies such as time-out, withdrawing privileges, and parent conferences (Bear, 1998a). Preventive strategies include frequent monitoring through eye contact and physical proximity, use of humor, cuing of appropriate behavior, praising the student and peers, asking rhetorical questions, and garnering the support of parents. Instructive strategies, used to promote self-discipline, include teaching social problem-solving and social decision-making skills, moral reasoning, and the self-regulation of emotions and behavior. Research shows that it is the combination of preventive and instructive strategies, rather than corrective strategies per se, that best differentiate teachers who are effective or ineffective as classroom managers (Brophy, 1996; Gettinger, 1988).

Most educators and researchers agree that suspension and expulsion should not be used alone but should be combined with intervention strategies that target factors that contribute to or explain the student's behavior. Because suspended students comprise a heterogeneous group, it is important that schools target a wide range of factors, both proximal and distal, for intervention. These would include individual student factors (e.g., behavioral, cognitive, and emotional deficits and excesses), classroom and school factors (e.g., instructional strategies, the curriculum, school atmosphere), peer factors (e.g., peer acceptance or rejection, role models), and home and community factors (parenting, family stressors, availability of weapons and drugs, exposure to violence). An assessment of such factors, conducted either formally by a school psychologist or informally by administrators, teachers, or other school staff, should be conducted to determine which, if any, of these factors should be addressed and to what extent (Batsche & Knoff, 1995; Bear, 1998b).

Assessment linked to broad-based and sustained interventions that are delivered at school, home, and community is particularly necessary for responding to students with histories of chronic antisocial behavior. For such students, the interventions shown to be most effective are social problem solving and social decision making, parent management training or family therapy, and a variety of classroom and schoolwide interventions for promoting the expectation and norm of prosocial behavior (Bear, 1998b; Quinn, Osher, Hoffman, & Hanley, 1998).

Bibliography

Batsche, G. M., & Knoff, H. M. (1995). Linking assessment to intervention. In A. Thomas & J. Grimes (Eds.), *Best practices in school psychology* (Vol. 3, pp. 577–578). Bethesda, MD: National Association of School Psychologists.

Bear, G. G. (1998a). School discipline in the United States: Prevention, correction, and long-term social development. *School Psychology Review, 27,* 14–32.

Bear, G. G. (1998b). *Interim alternative educational settings: Related research and program considerations.* Alexandria, VA: National Association of State Directors of Special Education.

Brophy, J. E. (1996). *Teaching problem students.* New York: Guilford Press.

Costenbader, V., & Markson, S. (1998). School suspension: A study with secondary school students. *Journal of School Psychology, 36,* 59–82.

Gettinger, M. (1988). Methods of proactive classroom management. *School Psychology Review, 17,* 227–242.

Hartwig, E. P., & Ruesch, G. M. (1994). *Disciplining students with disabilities: A synthesis of critical and emerging issues.* Alexandria, VA: National Association of State Directors of Special Education.

Hyman, I. A. (1997). *School discipline and school violence: A teacher variance approach.* Boston: Allyn & Bacon.

Jones, V. G., & Jones. L. S. (1998). *Comprehensive classroom management: Creating communities and solving problems.* Boston: Allyn & Bacon.

Martens, B. K., & Meller, P. J. (1990). The application of behavioral principles to educational settings. In T. B. Gutkin & C. R. Reynolds (Eds.), *Handbook of school psychology* (pp. 612–634). New York: Wiley.

Morgan-D'Atrio, C., Northup, J., LaFleur, L., & Spera, S. (1996). Toward prescriptive alternatives to suspensions: A preliminary evaluation. *Behavior Disorders, 21,* 190–200.

Quinn, M. M., Osher, D., Hoffman, C., & Hanley, T. (1998). *Safe, drug-free, and effective schools for all students: What works!* Washington, DC: Center for Effective Collaboration and Practice.

Tobin, T., Sugai, G., & Colvin, G. (1996). Patterns in middle school discipline records. *Journal of Emotional and Behavioral Disorders, 4,* 82–94.

Walker, H. M., Horner, R. H., Sugai, G., Bullis, M., Sprague, J. R., Bricker, D., & Kaufman, M. (1996). Integrated approaches to preventing antisocial behavior patterns among school-age children and youth. *Journal of Emotional and Behavioral Disorders, 4,* 194–209.

George G. Bear

SCHOOL TRANSITIONS. Transitions in life can mark opportunities for transformation in self-definition and interpersonal relationships. One common differentiating feature of transitions is whether they are normative or nonnormative. Normative transitions are scheduled or anticipated transitions such as marriage or the transition into junior high school; nonnormative transitions are unscheduled and unanticipated changes such as the sudden death of a parent or the transfer into a new school in the middle of an academic year.

In this article, we review the literature on the academic and behavioral outcomes that have been associated with both nonnormative and normative school transitions. We examine the individual and ecological factors that place students at risk for or protect them from maladaptive outcomes as well as the processes that mediate these outcomes during the transition from one school to another. Finally, we review some prevention programs designed to facilitate smoother and less problematic school transitions.

Nonnormative school transitions are commonplace in the United States because of the high rate of residential mobility. As a result, many school-aged children and adolescents experience one or more off-time school transfers. The rates of unscheduled transfers are highest among elementary school children, and younger children experience greater negative effects than older children. By third grade, over 40% of elementary school children attend two or more schools and 17% attend three or more schools (labeled frequent movers). Frequent movers constitute 25% of inner-city and 30% of low-income children. In many urban school classrooms, annual turnover rates of 50% are not unusual. Psychologists and education specialists believe that nonnormative school transfers represent risky transitions because of the separation and loss associated with friends and familiar places, changes in the curriculum and teacher expectations, and the inappropriate placement of students because of delays in the transfer of school records, which is a common occurrence.

Although a number of studies examine the impact of school transfers on academic achievement, this research often fails to differentiate between transfers that occur at the commencement of an academic year and those that occur during the course of an academic year. Nevertheless, the general consensus is that students who make frequent school transfers are more likely to do poorly in school. Children who transfer from one school to another are more likely to receive lower grades, perform below grade level in math and reading, and be held back a grade.

The pattern of research findings comes into even clearer focus when the studies are differentiated according to the socioeconomic status of the sample. Highly mobile students are more likely to come from low-income, single-parent, minimally educated, or unemployed households; often, these students did not perform well academically prior to the unscheduled school transfer. In sum, the negative effects of school transfer seem to exacerbate poor academic performance for the students doing most poorly prior to the school transfer.

There are few studies on the impact of unscheduled school transfers on psychosocial outcomes. When self-esteem is the outcome of interest, generally no difference is found between mobile and nonmobile students. On the other hand, some studies find that transfer students exhibit more behavior problems.

As suggested above, the negative effects of school mobility are most evident for low-income students. When middle-class children or children from military families are the focus of the study, school transfers become less problematic; in some instances, students even benefit from the transfer. Why do such differences exist? We need to look at the reason for the school transfer and the similarity between the old and new schools. Middle-class families are more likely to move for a job promotion (upward mobility) or an expanding family. In addition, children from military families often transfer into a new school that is remarkably similar in its structure and curriculum to that of the old one. In contrast, low-income families are more likely to move due to unemployment, loss of housing, and/or marital disruption (downward mobility); each school may be very different from the previous one. Residential moves may be seen as beneficial to middle-class families, but may create added stressors for low-income families.

At a different level of analysis, the deleterious effects of school mobility for low-income children may be due to the inefficiency of school record transfer systems. Placement of transfer students is difficult because it generally takes 2 to 6 weeks for school records to arrive at the new school. With records unavailable, schools with high rates of mobile populations often do not have the time to assess and place students in age-appropriate classes. When school records do arrive at the new school, they are often incompatible with the current school's records because the form and quality of records differ across states and districts. In addition, teachers receive little or no notice of the withdrawal or enrollment of students and find it distracting to have students move in and out of their classrooms throughout the school year. Some teachers adversely prejudge students who transfer into their classrooms in the middle of the school year.

Prevention of the risks associated with school mobility is possible. A common prevention program assigns newly arriving transfer students a buddy who tutors students of the same gender and grade. In one study of students transferring into urban, parochial elementary schools, gains in achievement were found when a buddy system was used. Improving the school record transfer system also could be used to overcome the problems often experienced by highly mobile student populations. Several states are piloting a new record transfer system: Exchange of Permanent Records Electronically for Students and Schools (ExPRESS). The ExPRESS system electronically sends student records to the new school. This new system is time-efficient and cost-effective; it reduces the cost of mailing records,

eliminates the need and cost of retesting and immunizing new students, and leads to more appropriate age- and ability-class placements.

Normative school transitions affect everyone, in contrast to nonnormative school transitions that affect only selected students. These transitions occur when students make the scheduled transition into elementary, middle/junior high, or senior high school. Each school transition presents children with different demands and challenges that yield different effects. With each transition, children face increased environmental demands, disruptions in their existing patterns of social relationships with peers and adults (social regularities), and different norms and expectations.

Entry into elementary school is viewed as a critical period for development. Children leave the smaller and more flexible setting of preschool or home that emphasizes play, a setting where they received considerable adult attention, for a larger, more rigidly scheduled, and rule-bound setting that focuses upon achievement and where teachers spend less time with each child. Academic expectations and testing become important for the first time, and grouping according to ability often begins. Though research is scant, the elementary school transition appears to be most deleterious for economically at-risk children for whom discontinuity between home and school is greatest. Even less research is available on how to manage entry into elementary school, but some of the practical literature suggests that the transition will be most effectively managed when activities and events are designed to overcome the discontinuities that disrupt children's learning and development.

When children move into junior high school, they encounter an altogether new system of rules and routines. Students change subject matter, teachers, and peer groups approximately every 45 minutes. As youngest children in this new environment, they suddenly find themselves low in social status. Teachers, too, face a challenging situation of large classrooms for short periods of time with less opportunity to get to know the children. Order and control of these large groups of ever-changing "strangers" tends to take precedence over other pedagogical objectives. This inhibits teachers' abilities to foster student autonomy and reduces their pedagogical flexibility. As such, small working groups, common in elementary school classrooms, are rare in junior high school classrooms. Ability tracking is more fully implemented; movement from a low track to a higher track is rare.

In addition to the ecological changes that occur as students make this normative school transition, they experience biological, cognitive, and interpersonal changes. Girls begin puberty, and early developing girls are often pressured to begin dating. Early adolescents strive for independence, struggling between wanting the security of the family and wanting to be independent. Students want more control in what goes on in the classroom and school, but junior high school teachers withdraw many of the privileges given to students in elementary school, focus more on discipline, and trust their students less than elementary school teachers. This occurs when the need for increased trust and independence is becoming foremost in the adolescent's mind. Youths also become more performance oriented and are aware of what others, including teachers and classmates, think of them. Moreover, the evolving peer culture, with both the pressure and need to fit in, place adolescents at increased risk for drug use and delinquency.

This normative transition from elementary to junior high school has been a focal point of research and policy debate during the past two decades. Studies uniformly find poor academic adjustment after the transition. Precipitous declines in self-esteem are consistent among studies of urban and large suburban school districts, but infrequent in studies of suburban middle-class communities or small cities. Some studies suggest that girls, particularly when they experience the early onset of puberty, are at greater risk than boys for declines in self-esteem.

Several scholars theorize that declines in self-esteem and academic achievement result from the developmental mismatch that occurs when the new structure and social ecology of the junior high school collides with the adolescent's evolving biological, cognitive, and interpersonal needs and motivations. A process of disengagement from school ensues and is characterized by increased academic demands and hassles, less involvement in extracurricular activities, and less perceived support from school personnel.

Students once again face a major disruption in their lives during the transition to senior high school. Again, the physical setting changes, teachers change, and classmates and social status change. Academic tracking is fully implemented. The pressure to perform well academically is even greater since it is clearly linked to future educational and career prospects. Concurrent with these changes in the school ecology, disruptive behavior, substance abuse, and school dropout peak. Thus, it is often assumed that the transition is directly related to these negative outcomes. Ample evidence does suggest that this transition results in declines in academic performance and engagement. However, declines in self-esteem and rises in social deviance have not been linked directly to the transition to high school.

To prevent academic and socioemotional difficulties, educators and interventionists often develop programs to inoculate children before or shortly after they make a risky normative school transition. The goal is to strengthen their competencies and resources and to enable them to resolve future dilemmas and conflicts. For example, all youth in a grade or classroom may be provided with a series of lectures and exercises in decision-making and social problem-solving. Although many of these programs have considerable utility, they rely primarily on changes made by the children themselves. Little attention is paid to the disruption in the school ecology they experience after a transition.

Recently, we have seen the implementation of policies aimed at restructuring the organization of secondary schools, with an emphasis on creating smaller educational units. This ecological approach of changing the school environment to better fit with students' needs is in stark contrast to more common prevention programs aimed at changing the students to fit within the schools' structure. These more innovative school reform efforts have been referred to as schools-within-schools, house systems, and academies. Implicit in the efforts aimed at school restructuring is to increase students' and staffs' engagement, empowerment, and sense of ownership. Not only do these programs alter the physical and social context of education, but they also change the day-to-day social regularities among all the school's inhabitants. Such reforms have been implemented primarily at the transition to senior high school; research, however, suggests that effects of such innovative strategies would be greatest at the time of the transition to junior high schools, in accordance with the developmental mismatch hypothesis.

The School Transitional Environment Project (STEP) is an excellent example of a program focused upon reducing the flux in the transition to senior high school. Youth making the transition to an inner-city high school were randomly assigned to either a small learning environment in one section of the school or the normal school curriculum. STEP students moved through all their primary classes (e.g., English, math) as a single unit, and one adult was assigned to each child as a counselor. Thus, STEP students and teachers experience dramatically different social regularities. The long-term findings were impressive: 76% percent of the STEP youth versus only 57% of the control youth remained in school by the twelfth grade.

For educators, policy makers, and the public at large, academic failure and school dropout are dramatic and poignant events. As the rates of these negative outcomes peak shortly after entry into high school, the high school transition has received the greatest attention. However, we believe that the path to school disengagement begins at the time of the transition to junior high school, and more prevention efforts need to be made to reduce the flux and turbulence associated with this earlier transition. In that vein, it is encouraging that recent efforts aimed at restructuring the physical and social environment of the junior high school are beginning to be implemented on an experimental basis.

Bibliography

Alexander, K. L., Entwisle, D. R., & Dauber, S. L. (1996). Children in motion: School transfers and elementary school performance. *The Journal of Educational Research, 90*, 3–12.

Eccles, J. S., Midgley, C., Wigfield, A., Buchanan, C. M., Reuman, D. A., Flanagan, C., & MacIver, D. (1993). Development during adolescence: The impact of stage-environment fit on young adolescents' experiences in schools and families. *American Psychologist, 48*, 90–101.

Entwisle, D. R., & Alexander, K. L. (1993). Entry into school: The beginning school transition and educational stratification in the United States. *Annual Review of Sociology, 19*, 401–423.

Government Accounting Office. (1994). *Elementary school children: Many change schools frequently, harming their education.* Gaithersburg, MD: Author.

Lipsitz, J, Jackson, A. W., & Austin, L. M. (1997, March). What works in middle-grades school reform. *Phi Delta Kappan*, 517–556.

Love, J. M., Logue, M. E., Trudeau, J. V., & Thayer, K. (1992). *Transitions to kindergarten in American schools: Final report of the National Transition Study.* Washington, DC: U.S. Department of Education.

Ruble, D. N., & Seidman, E. (1996). Social transitions: Windows into social psychological processes. In E. T. Higgins & A. W. Kruglanski (Eds), *Social psychology: Handbook of basic principles* (pp. 830–856). New York: Guilford Press.

Seidman, E., & French, S. E. (1997). Normative school transitions among urban adolescents: When, where, and how to intervene. In H. J. Walberg, O. Reyes, & R. P. Weissberg (Eds.), *Children and youth: Interdisciplinary perspectives* (pp. 166–189). Thousand Oaks, CA: Sage.

Simmons, R. G., & Blyth, D. A. (1987). *Moving into adolescence: The impact of pubertal change and school context.* Hawthorne, NY: Aldine.

Stief, E. A. (1994). *Transitions to school.* Washington, DC: National Governors' Association.

Edward Seidman and Sabine E. French

SCHOPENHAUER, ARTHUR (1788–1860), German philosopher. Schopenhauer's impact on the development of psychology is best measured by his influence on the first generation of depth psychologists, including Sigmund Freud, Carl Jung, and Otto Rank. Anticipating Freud's notion of the id and his treatment of sexuality, Schopenhauer viewed the "will" as a blind, driving force, expressing itself most directly through the sexual drive. Indeed, Freud credited Schopenhauer with anticipating his own discovery of the omnipresence of the sexual drive as the prime motive for human action. Moreover, Freud explicitly acknowledged that Schopenhauer's will was equivalent to the mental instincts of psychoanalysis and the unconscious. As a young scholar, Schopenhauer identified repression as a potential cause of mental illness. When Rank presented the relevant passage to Freud, the latter denied that he had been previously exposed to Schopenhauer's ideas on this topic. Other Freudian topics apparently prefigured by Schopenhauer include parapraxes, primary process thought, dream processes, and a technique of free association for the recovery of lost memories.

Despite the numerous similarities between Freud and Schopenhauer's thought, Freud insisted that he only read Schopenhauer late in life, namely, after 1915. Scholars continue to debate the reliability of Freud's disclaimer, pointing out that at the very least Freud was exposed to Schopenhauer's ideas indirectly, through his participation in a reading society in his youth and by his reading of secondary literature, especially the writings of the philosopher Eduard von Hartmann. Freud's exposure to Schopenhauer was probably also facilitated through contact with academic and professional mentors interested in Schopenhauer's ideas. More critical commentators have also pointed out that some of Freud's writings prior to 1915 contained detailed references to Schopenhauer and his work.

In contrast with Freud's explicit denial of Schopenhauer's direct intellectual patrimony, both Jung and Rank celebrated Schopenhauer's early influence on their intellectual development. Whereas Jung traced his own view of the unconscious in part to the writings of Schopenhauer and his intellectual descendent Hartmann, Rank viewed Schopenhauer as the direct philosophical forerunner of psychoanalysis. Indeed, Rank traced the historical development of the idea of libido from the Greek philosophers to Schopenhauer. In like manner, Jung viewed his own treatment of individuation as an advancement of Schopenhauer's ideas and Schopenhauer's notion of the "idea" as fundamentally equivalent to his own notion of the archetype. Jung also found in Schopenhauer support for his own understanding of synchronicity, even though Jung implicitly rejected Schopenhauer's appeal to a determining first cause as an adequate explanation.

By assigning primacy to the functioning of an unconscious will over the conscious mind, Schopenhauer laid the foundation for subsequent explorations of the first generation of depth psychologists. Rarely read today by either American philosophers or psychologists, Schopenhauer's legacy as a proto-depth psychologist remains largely unappreciated. Whereas for some psychologists Schopenhauer's philosophical method and his anti-intellectualist leanings limit his relevance to the science of psychology, for others his work continues to serve as a brilliant, psychologically astute testimony to both the power and the limits of human consciousness.

[*Many of the people mentioned in this article are the subjects of independent biographical entries.*]

Bibliography

Ellenberger, H. F. (1970). *The discovery of the unconscious: The history and evolution of dynamic psychiatry.* New York: Basic Books. An excellent, comprehensive treatment of the intellectual currents that influenced the development of the idea of the unconscious, including contributions made by Schopenhauer and his followers.

Gupta, R. K. (1975). Freud and Schopenhauer. *Journal of the History of Ideas, 36,* 721–728.

Janaway, C. (1994). *Schopenhauer.* Oxford: Oxford University Press. A recently published, readable biography of Schopenhauer by a first-rate scholar.

Jarrett, J. L. (1981). Schopenhauer and Jung. *Spring: An annual of archetypal psychology and Jungian thought.* Dallas, TX: Spring.

Schopenhauer, A. (1958). *The world as will and representation.* (2 vols.). (E. F. J. Payne, Trans.). New York: Dover. (Original work published 1819.) This work contains most of Schopenhauer's ideas considered anticipatory of later depth psychological thought.

Michael C. Luebbert

SCHUMANN, FRIEDRICH (1862–1940), German experimental psychologist. Schumann was representative of the natural science orientation of many early student/propagators of experimental psychology. His experiments and his skillful construction of apparatus were important components of the new discipline, although the experiments seem less important now. Sponsored early by Georg E. Müller, he became the one person who most reliably carried out the organizational tasks that left his mentor free to develop extensive works in memory, cognition, and color theory. He also sponsored Max Wertheimer and Wolfgang Köhler's entries into the faculties of Prussian universities.

Schumann was born in Hildesheim, a small city just south of Hannover. His father was a *Gymnasium* teacher. Schumann went to study physics at Göttingen University in 1881. He completed his dissertation with Eduard Riecke in 1887. He also qualified in philosophy. For the written exam, Müller required him to write a critique of the memory research in Hermann Ebbinghaus's *Über das Gedächtnis* (On Memory). The excellence of his criticism led to collaboration with Müller on the first major study of memory after Ebbinghaus, a study that utilized the first memory drum and provided the standards for serial anticipation methods. While the collaboration was in progress, Schumann became the first person sponsored by Müller for a *Habilitation*, the step required to begin teaching as a *Privatdozent*. Schumann's work, drawing on his ability to construct precisely crafted apparatus, measured the thresholds of short time intervals and sharply criticized the work of Wundt's students, Georg Dietze and Ernst Meumann. Shortly after, in 1894, Schumann became Carl Stumpf's assistant at the newly created *Institut für experimentelle Psychologie* in Berlin.

Although Schumann and Stumpf did not get along, Schumann produced important work on motion perception, visual illusions, and part-whole relationships (which are sometimes seen as precursors to Gestalt psychology). During this time, he made the acquaintance of Robert Sommer, the Giessen Professor of Psychiatry who was to sponsor the formation of the *Deutsche Gesellschaft für experimentelle Psychologie* (DGeP) in 1903. During the years 1899–1903, Schumann helped plan the new organization and after its formation became *Schriftführer*, or general dues collector and report organizer, for the publication of the biennial meetings from 1904 to 1914.

In 1905, Schumann was chosen to succeed Meumann as professor of psychology in Zurich and in 1909, on Ebbinghaus's death, he became the publisher of the psychological component of the *Zeitschrift für Psychologie und Physiologie der Sinnesorgane.* In 1909, Karl Marbe, professor in Frankfurt, replaced Oswald Külpe as professor in Würzburg, and in 1910, Schumann was selected for Marbe's chair of the *Handelsakademie* (which became the Frankfurt university in 1914)—a position that included its own precision machinist.

Much of Schumann's intellectual work was not published in the *Zeitschrift* but in six volumes concerned with intellectual processes, *Beiträge zur Analyse der Gesichtswahrnehmungen* (Contributions to the Analysis of Visual Perception). At Frankfurt, he continued his research; his most obvious contribution to psychology was the sponsorship of the *Habilitation* works of Wolfgang Köhler and Max Wertheimer, thus, earning him the title of godfather of Gestalt psychology. After World War I, increasingly debilitated by stomach problems, he successively laid down his DGeP roles, as well as his other professorial duties. In 1927, he was succeeded by Max Wertheimer. He died in Frankfurt am Main.

[*Many of the people mentioned in this article are the subjects of independent biographical entries.*]

Bibliography

Esper, E. A. (1966). Max Meyer: The making of a scientific isolate. *Journal of the History of the Behavioral Sciences,*

2, 341–366. Includes an account of Schumann's difficulties with Stumpf, which is not entirely easy to interpret.

Kroh, O. (1935). Georg Elias Müller. Ein Nachruf [Georg Elias Müller. A eulogy]. *Zeitschrift für Psychologie, 135* (3), 150–190. The primary source for describing the beginnings of memory research, in which Kroh reports the results of his conversations with Müller and Schumann.

Metzger, W. (1940). Friedrich Schumann. Ein Nachruf [A eulogy]. *Zeitschrift für Psychologie, 148,* 1–18. Appears to be the only obituary, outside of newspapers, for Schumann. Metzger admits that he did not know Schumann well and got much of the information from Kroh.

Müller, G. E., & Schumann, F. (1894). Experimentelle Beiträge zur Untersuchungen des Gedächtnisses [Experimental contributions on the investigation of memory]. *Zeitschrift fur Psychologie und Physiologie der Sinnesorgane, 6,* 81–190, and *6,* 257–339. The major memory work of Müller and Schumann. In it, Schumann's roles as a subject and experimenter in the 13 experiments are clearly detailed. Schumann, however, did not list it in his *curriculum vitae,* which suggests that he did not see himself as having a large intellectual role in the choice and interpretation of the experiments.

Schumann, F. (1932). *Curriculum vitae.* In C. Murchison (Ed.), *Psychological Register* (Vol. 3, p. 872). Worcester, MA: Clark University Press. Prepared by Schumann himself, the best source of material by Schumann and his associates, since many of his publications, privately printed, do not appear in the *Cumulative Psychological Abstracts.*

Universität Göttingen. (1962). *Catalogus Professorum Gottingensium* [Catalogue of the professors in Göttingen], collected by W. Ebel. Göttingen, Germany: Vandenhoek & Ruprecht. The authoritative source for Schumann's dates.

Edward J. Haupt

SCIENTIST-PRACTITIONER MODEL. The training model for clinical psychology that was adopted as the official model by the American Psychological Association (APA) in 1949 is referred to as the scientist/practioner model. It also has been referred to as the Boulder model after the site of the first national conference on training in clinical psychology where the recommendations for the adoption of the model by the APA were made.

Although clinical psychology in the United States had existed for over 50 years, its growth, like that of the parent field of psychology, had been slow, and there were only a small number of clinical psychologists in the early 1940s. However, the Second World War with its attendant tragic consequences had a significant impact on clinical psychology. The large number of psychiatric casualties and the relatively small number of psychiatrists available to care for them led to an increased demand for mental health workers from other related fields. In the U.S. army this resulted in the commissioning of clinical psychologists as second lieutenants in the fall of 1944. When the war was over, the burden of caring for the large number of psychiatric casualties in the military services fell largely to the Veterans Administration (VA). To meet this need, the VA created new positions for clinical psychologists patterned after those developed in the army. Also, because of the need for additional trained personnel, both the VA and the Public Health Service asked the APA to provide the names of universities that had satisfactory training programs.

Prior to this time, there were no truly organized clinical psychology training programs as we know them today. The request for training universities, however, influenced the APA to consider the matter of training standards for university programs in clinical psychology. The APA appointed a committee on clinical psychology training chaired by David Shakow in the spring of 1947. The committee's report, usually referred to as the Shakow report, was published in the *American Psychologist* in December 1947 (Vol. 2, pp. 539–558). The report emphasized the goals and principles of a desirable program rather than attempting to provide detailed specifics; "If we recognize that clinical psychology is both a science and an art calling for scientific rigor tempered by personal and social sensitivity, we can specify these goals fairly clearly" (p. 540). These views reflected emphases that were later incorporated in the report of the Boulder Conference and came to be known as the scientist/practitioner model.

Basic Features of the Model

The Boulder Conference was a 2-week meeting, held in 1949, to consider the necessary and desirable training components for university programs in clinical psychology and to make the necessary recommendations for university training as well as a procedure for accreditation. The 72 participants mainly represented the university programs currently given accredited status. A variety of topics were discussed and a number of recommendations made. The title of clinical psychologist, for example, was to be reserved for individuals who had received a doctoral degree in psychology from a recognized university. Following the recommendations of the Shakow Committee, the conference participants recommended an integrated graduate program that emphasized six major areas of study: (1) general psychology; (2) psychodynamics of behavior; (3) diagnostic methods; (4) research methods; (5) related disciplines; and (6) therapy. The program was also to be a 4-year program and include 1-year internship during the third year. Three areas, diagnosis, therapy, and research, were designated as the major functions of the clinical psychologist. The unique role of the clinical psychologist in research was once again emphasized. "Probably of greatest significance was the firm decision to establish as a major goal the training of the clinical psychologist as *both* a scientist and as a practitioner at the Ph.D. level" (Garfield, 1983, p. 12). Here was the essence of what became known as the scientist/practitioner model, and it was a reasonable conclusion. After all, the field of psychology was to a great extent an academic and research-oriented field, and if university departments of psychology were to train clinical psychologists to a high level of skill, the Ph.D. degree would appear to be the logical degree. Training for the Ph.D. degree also meant an emphasis on research training. This also signified a potentially unique skill of the psychologist among those trained for clinical work.

At the same time, there was a realization of the need for training in the clinical applied areas of diagnosis and therapy, which were now to be added or superimposed on the traditional academic and research areas of psychology. Securing competent and experienced teachers and supervisors in these areas was also viewed as an important task for the training universities.

It was clear that the scientist/practitioner model was viewed by the participants at the Boulder Conference as a truly unique one. The preface to the official report said:

> The development of the profession of clinical psychology constituted something of an educational experiment in that clinical psychologists are being trained both as scientists and as practitioners. Most professions base their practices on one or more sciences and train their future members in a separate professional school. In contrast, clinical psychologists are trained concurrently in both the theoretical (scientific) and applied (clinical) aspects of psychology. The training occurs not in professional schools but in the graduate schools of our colleges and universities. (Raimy, 1950, p. v)

Despite this lofty objective, there were some questions and doubts about its feasibility. Can these very different interests, values, and even personal qualities be combined within the same individual? Nevertheless, the scientist/practitioner model was favorably received and approved as the model of training for clinical psychologists in the United States. Although there were conflicts later between individuals and groups representing the two different value orientations, the Boulder Model remained the dominant model for a period of about 25 years. For example, at the Conference on the Professional Preparation of the Clinical Psychologist held in Chicago in 1965, several other models were considered, including a primarily professional model and one called the psychologist-psychotherapist. Nevertheless, the scientist/practitioner model was again approved overwhelmingly:

> Having given careful consideration to a variety of alternatives to the Scientist-Professional model, and having agreed to be open to evidence of the effectiveness of alternate programs, the conferees nonetheless decidedly reaffirmed their belief that the Scientist-Professional model offered the best hope for the continued development of clinical psychology. (Hoch, Ross, & Winder, 1966, p. 74).

Other Training Models

Despite the apparent support for the scientist/practitioner model, some primarily professional models appeared within a few years. A Psy.D. program of training was introduced in 1968 at the University of Illinois. It was a 4-year program in which the formal research training was omitted and practical clinical training substituted. The basis for the new program was that most clinical psychologists were not interested in research, that the university programs overemphasized training in research, and that practical clinical training tended to be slighted. The Psy.D. degree was required in order to clearly identify the clinical psychologist. This new program was offered alongside the regular Ph.D. program.

Needless to say, the Psy.D. program at Illinois was a radical departure from the accepted scientist/practitioner program. However, within a short time professional psychologists in California, with the support of their state psychological association, developed plans for a professional school of psychology completely independent of any university (Pottharst, 1970). It was the first free-standing autonomous professional school of psychology. Although the program of the California school offered a Ph.D. degree, it was clearly not identical with the traditional scientist/practitioner model of training. The faculty were mainly practitioners, most were part-time instructors, and the emphasis was on professional training. Much larger classes were admitted, and generally most students completed the program in 4 years, as contrasted with an average of 5 to 6 years in most university programs.

Since the early 1970s, the professional schools have grown significantly; many offer both Ph.D. and Psy.D. degrees, and a few universities also offer Psy.D. degrees although the University of Illinois program was discontinued some years ago. The free-standing professional schools graduate a large number of clinical psychologists, at least half of the total annual output. With such different emphasis and values, there have been conflicts and debates from time to time on the efficacy of the training models. In 1990, for example, the National Conference on Scientist-Practitioner Education and Training for the Professional Practice of Psychology was held in Gainesville, Florida. The "conference was designed with the overall goal of producing a policy document that would describe the current and anticipated future characteristics of the scientist-practitioner model" (p. 1) and was sponsored by 20 organizations. Basic to all of the discussion was the view that

> The scientist-practitioner model of education in psychology is an integrative approach to science and practice wherein each must continually inform the other . . . Scientist-practitioner psychologists embody a research orientation in their practice and a practice relevance in their research. Thus, a scientist-practitioner is not defined by a job title or a role, but rather by an integrated approach to both science and practice. (Proceedings, National Conference on Scientist-Practitioner Education and Training for the Professional Practice of Psychology, p. 7)

This is the heart of the model, and it is still vibrant 50 years after its inception.

[*See also* Practitioner Model; *and* Training.]

Bibliography

American Psychological Association, Committee on Training in Clinical Psychology. (1947). Recommended graduate training program in clinical psychology. *American Psychologist, 2,* 539–558. This committee was chaired by David Shakow, who played a leading role in the formulation of the scientist/practitioner model.

Belar, C. & Perry, N. W. (Eds.). (1990). *Proceedings of the National Conference on Scientist-Practitioner Education and Training for the Professional Practice of Psychology* (January 16–20, Gainesville, FL). (Available from Professional Resource Press, P.O. Box 15560, Sarasota, FL 34277–1560.)

Garfield, S. L. (1983). *Clinical psychology: The study of personality and behavior* (2nd ed.). New York: Aldine. This book provides a brief history of clinical psychology and the various training models.

Hoch, E. L., Ross, A. O., & Winder, C. L. (Eds.). (1966). *Professional preparation of clinical psychologists.* Washington, DC.: American Psychological Association. This is the official report of the Chicago Conference, which reaffirmed the scientist/practitioner model.

Peterson, D. R. (1969). Attitudes concerning the doctor of psychology program. *Professional Psychology, 1,* 44–97.

Pottharst, K. E. (1970). To review vitality and provide a challenge in training—The California School of Professional Training. *Professional Psychology, 1,* 123–130.

Raimy, V. (Ed.). (1950). *Training in clinical psychology.* New York: Prentice Hall. The official report of the Boulder Conference and its recommendations for training.

Sol L. Garfield

SCL-90-R is a 90-item self-report symptom inventory developed by Leonard Derogatis (1975, 1994) to measure the psychological symptoms and distress of community, medical, and psychiatric respondents. The Symptom Checklist-90-R (SCL-90-R) represents symptomatic distress in terms of nine primary symptom dimensions and three global indices. The symptom dimensions are labeled Somatization (SOM), Obsessive-Compulsive (OBS), Interpersonal Sensitivity (INT), Depression (DEP), Anxiety (ANX), Hostility (HOS), Phobic Anxiety (PHOB), Paranoid Ideation (PAR), and Psychoticism (PSY). The global measures are termed the Global Severity Index (GSI), the Positive Symptom Distress Index (PSDI), and the Positive Symptom Total (PST).

The SCL-90-R represents a direct outgrowth of the Hopkins Symptom Checklist (HSCL) developed by Derogatis and his colleagues (1974), which maintains considerable continuity with previous inventories, such as the Cornell Medical Index by Wider (1948) and, to some degree, with the original self-report symptom inventory, the Personal Data Sheet by Woodworth (1918). The SCL-90-R was developed in response to limitations in the HSCL, primarily its limited scope of psychopathology, and because the HSCL was not designed for clinical applications.

The SCL-90-R is one component in an integrated series of psychological instruments, which includes the Brief Symptom Inventory (BSI), a 53-item brief version of the scale, and two matched clinician rating scales, the Derogatis Psychiatric Rating Scale and the SCL-90 Analogue Scale (1993). Gender-keyed norms are available for the SCL-90-R and the BSI for community adults, community adolescents, psychiatric outpatients, and psychiatric inpatients. The SCL-90-R and the BSI are designed for use with adults and adolescents over the age of 13 years and are written at a sixth-grade reading level.

In terms of psychometric properties, the internal consistency reliabilities for the scales of the SCL-90-R range from 0.77 to 0.90; comparable coefficients for the BSI range from 0.71 to 0.85. Test-retest reliability for the SCL-90-R with a one-week interval ranged between 0.80 and 0.90, and the analogous coefficients for the BSI ranged from 0.68 to 0.91 over a 2-week interval. Acceptable interrater reliability has been demonstrated for the matching clinical rating scales.

The dimensional structures of both the SCL-90-R (Derogatis & Cleary, 1977) and the BSI® (Derogatis, 1993) have been confirmed in empirical studies with large samples, and convergent-discriminant validation for the SCL-90-R has been demonstrated relative to the Minnesota Multiphasic Personality Inventory (Derogatis, Rickels, & Rock, 1975), the Middlesex Hospital Questionnaire (Boleloucky & Horvath, 1974), the CES-D and the Hamilton Rating Scale for Depression (Weissman, Scholomskas, Pottenger, Prusoff, & Locke, 1977), and the General Hospital Questionnaire (GHQ-28) (Koeter,

1992). In a comprehensive series of validation studies, Peveler and Fairburn (1990) demonstrated aspects of convergent-discriminative, predictive, and construct validity for the SCL-90-R using the Present State Examination, a detailed, structured clinical interview, as an external criterion standard. Concerning predictive or criterion-oriented validity, there are currently over 1,000 published studies with the SCL-90-R and more than 700 involving the BSI, which demonstrate the high sensitivity of these inventories to an extremely broad range of clinical effects. Recent reviews of the applications of these scales as outcomes measures in psychiatric, medical, and community populations, as well as specifically with psychotherapeutic, psychopharmacologic, and psychosocial interventions, have been provided by Derogatis and Lazarus (1994) and by Derogatis and Derogatis (1996).

The SCL-90-R and the BSI are currently available in 26 languages, including Spanish, French, German, Russian, Italian, Portuguese, Dutch, Swiss, Japanese, Chinese, Korean, Vietnamese, Hebrew, and Arabic. The tests are distributed by National Computer Systems (NCS) of Minnetonka, Minnesota.

Bibliography

Boleloucky, Z., & Horvath, M. (1974). The SCL-90-R® rating scale: First experience with the Czech version. *Activitas Nervosa Superior, 16,* 115–116.

Derogatis, L. R. (1975). *The SCL-90-R®.* Baltimore: Clinical Psychometric Research.

Derogatis, L. R. (1993). *The Brief Symptom Inventory (BSI®: Administration, scoring and procedures manual* (3rd ed.). Minneapolis: National Computer Systems.

Derogatis, L. R. (1994). *SCL-90-R®: Administration, scoring and procedures manual* (3rd ed.). Minneapolis: National Computer Systems.

Derogatis, L. R., & Cleary, P. (1977). Confirmation of the dimensional structure of the SCL-90-R®: A study in construct validation. *Journal of Clinical Psychology, 33,* 981–989.

Derogatis, L. R., & Derogatis, M. F. (1996). The SCL-90-R® and the BSI®. In B. Spilker (Ed.), *Quality of life and pharmacoeconomics in clinical trials* (2nd ed., pp. 323–335). Philadelphia: Lippincott-Raven.

Derogatis, L. R., & Lazarus, L. (1994). The SCL-90-R®, Brief Symptom Inventory, and matching clinical rating scales. In M. Maruish (Ed.), *The use of psychological testing for treatment planning and outcomes assessment* (pp. 217–248). New York: Erlbaum.

Derogatis, L. R., Lipman, R. S., Rickels, K., Uhlenhuth, E. H., & Covi, L. (1974). The Hopkins Symptom Checklist (HSCL): A self-report symptom inventory. *Behavioral Science, 19,* 1–15.

Derogatis, L. R., Rickels, K., & Rock, A. (1976). The SCL-90-R® and the MMPI: A step in the validation of a new self-report scale. *British Journal of Psychiatry, 128,* 280–289.

Koeter, M. W. (1992). Validity of the GHQ and SCL-90-R® Anxiety and Depression scales. *Journal of Affective Disorders, 24,* 271–279.

Peveler, R. C., & Fairburn, C. G. (1990). Measurement of neurotic symptoms by self-report questionnaire. *Psychological Medicine, 20,* 873–879.

Weissman, M., Scholomskas, D., Pottenger, M., Prusoff, B. A., & Locke, B. Z. (1977). Assessing depressive symptoms in five psychiatric populations: A validation study. *American Journal of Epidemiology, 106,* 203–214.

Wider, A. (1948). *The Cornell medical index.* San Antonio, TX: Psychological Corp.

Woodworth, R. S. (1918) *The personal data sheet.* Chicago: Stoelting.

Leonard R. Derogatis

SCOTLAND. Scottish psychology has two roots, which it shares with psychology in general, in the protopsychological thought of the eighteenth century. One of these consists of the works of Scottish Associationists (thinkers concerned with the relationships among sensations, ideas of sensations, and ideas themselves); the other consists of the works of the writers of the Scottish enlightenment, either opposed to, or little concerned with, the Associationist speculations. Richards (1992) shows that only a few of the major texts on the history of psychology devote about equal attention to the two roots; most favor Scottish Associationism. This disparity accords well with the tradition of seeking the origins of psychology in philosophy rather than in other emergent disciplines into which, by the eighteenth century, philosophy was clearly dividing itself. Such an approach casts an unreal light on the work of a majority of the present-day psychologists, to whom philosophical problems of the mind-body relationship, for example, are of relatively little interest but who are concerned either with investigations involving empirically definable concepts or with the application of psychology to concrete problems.

The Scottish contribution to the Associationist debate is weighty, and within it Hume's (1711–1776) contribution is dominant. His sceptical arguments have influenced the development of psychology in two ways: (1) by causing reexamination of the notion of certainty as applied to empirical findings (see Gregory, 1987) and (2) by provoking the vehement reaction of Thomas Reid (1710–1796) and the Common Sense school, who were concerned about the moral implications of Humean scepticism. Reid was a professor of philosophy in Aberdeen and in Glasgow. His first major work was *An Inquiry into the Human Mind on the Principles of Common Sense* (1762); after its publication he repeatedly attacked the "metaphysical lunacy" of scepticism. Two books summarize his life's work: *Essays on the Intellectual Powers of Man* (1785) and *Essays on the Active Powers of Man* (1788).

Dugald Stewart (1753–1827), professor at the University of Edinburgh, did much to consolidate and clarify Reid's seminal notions by publishing *Elements of the Philosophy of the Human Mind* (1954–1958; vol. 1 in 1792, vol. 2 in 1814) and by contributing two very timely articles to the *Encyclopedia Britannica*. His junior colleague Thomas Brown (1778–1820), author of *Lectures on the Philosophy of the Human Mind* (1820), was the third member of the Scottish Common-Sense school.

Other savants of the Scottish Enlightenment achieved international standing by exploring the three main preoccupations of the time: the structure of human society, language, and the awareness of actions. The first of these issues inevitably involves a continuum extending from selfishness to amicable disposition. Adam Ferguson (1723–1816), professor at Edinburgh, in his *Essay on the History of Civil Society* (1767 [1980]) favored the latter bound as the cement of society. The human, he thought, was a "progressive animal." Adam Smith (1723–1790), the founder of economics and professor at Glasgow, agreed with this view in his *Theory of Moral Sentiments* (1759 [1976]) but seemed less ardent in *The Inquiry into the Causes of the Wealth of Nations* (1776 [1992]), the treatise that brought him fame. Smith also speculated about the origin of language. He shared this interest with Lord Monboddo (1714–1799), who, in his six-volume *Of the Origin and Progress of Language* (1773–1792 [1967]), put forward the view that "language was not natural to man" and that a "political state is necessary for its invention."

Contemporaneously with these studies, Robert Whytt (1714–1766), professor of medicine in Edinburgh, investigated involuntary responses by observing reflexes of frogs whose spinal cords had been cut. The findings were reported in his *Essay on the Vital and Involuntary Motions of Animals* (1751).

Alexander Bain (1818–1907), the son of an Aberdeen weaver and early in his life a weaver himself, gathered these disparate strands and wove them together so that psychology became a distinct discipline based on systematic observations—in short, a science. He did that by writing two books and by launching the first psychological journal in English. The books, *The Senses and the Intellect* (1855 [1894]) and *The Emotions and the Will* (1859 [1899]), advocated that findings of various disciplines as well as the psychologist's interpretation should be used in the search for psychological theories and thus explicitly recognized the importance of all empirical data. The journal, *Mind*, was launched in 1876. Bain then held the Chair of Logic and Rhetoric at the University of Aberdeen, and this had yet another effect:

In 1896, the University of Aberdeen appointed a lecturer in psychology. The person appointed to this first lectureship in psychology in Scotland (and in Great Britain) was George Frederick Stout (1986–1944), the editor of *Mind*, the author of *Analytic Psychology* (1896), and soon to be the author of a *Manual of Psychology* (1899). Lectureships in psychology at other Scottish universities followed. There were, at that time, four universities in Scotland: St. Andrews (1411; 1927; 1963), Glasgow (1451; 1907; 1947), Aberdeen (1495; 1896; 1947), and Edinburgh (1583; 1906; 1931), and each of them, albeit with differing alacrity, made such an appointment (dates in parentheses are those of the foundation of the university, appointment of the first lecturer in psychology, and creation of a chair in psychology). The time lapses between the appointments of first lecturers and the creation of the chairs show that the discipline was not enthusiastically embraced by the universities. The newly established departments were small, and their laboratories were used mainly for demonstrations to students whose main subject of study was not psychology but education—future teachers, educational psychologists, and administrators. Under these circumstances Scottish domination of psychological theorizing on a grand scale began to wane, and teaching and investigation of issues of immediate concern became the chief pursuits of the Scottish departments. Investigations of thinking and of sensory integration were carried out in Glasgow by H. J. Watt (1879–1925), who had recently returned from Germany. Interest in pupil evaluation led to development of an extensive body of psychological tests at Moray House in Edinburgh under the guidance if G. H. Thompson. These tests were used widely both in the United Kingdom and overseas. In order to assess the scores and to gain understanding of the structure of abilities that these revealed, Thompson used factor analysis, both greatly extending and elucidating the technique (Thompson, 1939). Other applied issues were also tackled. The department of psychology in Edinburgh engaged in systematic testing of printers' apprentices mainly by means of a battery of psychomotor tests, thus opening the entry to the realm of occupational psychology, and ran a clinic for children and juveniles, thus making first steps in child guidance.

Clinical instruction was not at that time offered by the universities, and potential clinicians obtained their training by working as apprentices with an established clinician. Such training was provided at the Crichton Royal Hospital in Dumfries, where John Raven (the designer of Raven's matrices) provided guidance.

After World War II, Scottish universities experienced two phases of rapid expansion, one in the 1960s, and another in the 1990s, both of which led to an increase in the number of students of psychology. The effect of the second phase was to increase the number of institutions in which psychology was taught, often as a part of broad degree programs. The first phase has led to the establishment of the universities of Dundee, Strathclyde (in Glasgow), and Stirling and facilitated the introduction of new syllabi; thus, for example, at Strathclyde, where G. Jahoda became the first incumbent of the chair of psychology, cross-cultural psychology, a subject not previously offered in Scotland, was introduced. Another notable effect of the first phase was the reinvigoration of psychology at St. Andrews, by the creation of a chair and appointment of M. Jeeves as its first incumbent in (1969). The department, which had then only a single lecturer, is now thought to be the prime research department in the country, especially noted for its studies of neuropsychology, perception, and primatology.

Practice of Psychology

The first degree, which is normally obtained after 4 years of training, is not thought to be sufficient qualification for the practice of psychology as a profession; further formal training is thought desirable.

In clinical psychology such training extends over a period of 2 to 3 years. It is offered at the universities of Edinburgh and Glasgow. Since the National Health Service controls most of the establishments in which clinical psychologists are employed, it practically dictates the nature of the training needed. Similarly, in the field of educational psychology, the local educational authorities are practically the only employers, and they decide on the appropriateness of training. In occupational psychology a large number of employers offer a greater variety of opportunities. Most psychology graduates do not remain within academic psychology but enter a variety of callings in which psychological training is thought to be useful.

Scottish psychologists can become members of both British psychological societies, the Experimental Psychology Society and the British Psychological Society; the former is concerned only with the science of psychology, and the latter, whose concerns are more extensive, has a Scottish branch. The Royal Society of Edinburgh elects psychologists to its membership.

[See also England.]

Bibliography

Bain, A. (1894). The senses and the intellect (4th ed.). London: Longmans Green.

Bain, A. (1899). The emotions and the will (4th ed.). London: Longmans Green.

Brown, T. (1820). Lectures on the philosophy of the human mind. Edinburgh: Tait.

Ferguson, A. (1980). Essay on the history of civil society (1st ed., reprinted with introduction by L. Schneider). New Brunswick: Transaction Books.

Gregory, R. L. (1987). Oxford companion to mind. Oxford: Oxford University Press. A reference text that elucidates many of the issues touched on in this brief entry.

Monboddo, Lord (James Burnett). (1967). Of the origin and progress of language. Menston (Yorks): Scolar Press.

Reid, T. (1969). The essay on intellectual powers. Cambridge, MA: MIT Press.

Reid, T. (1977). The essay on active power. New York: Garland.

Richards, G. (1992). Mental machinery: Part 1. London: Athlone Press. Presents the origins and consequences of psychological ideas and examines Scottish contributions made between 1600 and 1850.

Smith, A. (1976). Theory of moral sentiments (R. R. Raphael & A. L. Macfie, Eds.). Oxford: Clarendon Press. This edition includes Smith's essay on language.

Smith, A. (1992). The inquiry into the causes of the wealth of nations (F. R. Glahe, Ed.). New York: Rowman and Littlefield.

Stewart, D. (1954–1958). Collected works of Dugald Stewart (W. Hamilton, Ed.). Edinburgh: Constable. The Elements are contained in Vols. 2–4 of the set.

Stout, G. F. (1896). Analytic psychology. New York: Sonnenschein.

Stout, G. F. (1899). The manual of psychology. London Tutorial Press.

Thompson, G. H. (1939). The factorial analysis of human ability. London: University of London Press. (A revised and extended edition was published in 1946.)

Whytt, R. (1751). An essay on vital and other involuntary motions of animals. Edinburgh: Balfour & Neill.

Jan B. Derẹgowski

SCOTT, WALTER DILL (1869–1955), American psychologist. Scott was born near Cooksville, Illinois. He graduated from Northwestern University in 1895 and pursued graduate study in the Leipzig, Germany, laboratory of Wilhelm Wundt in 1900, writing a dissertation on the psychology of impulses.

Scott returned to Northwestern in 1900 as a lecturer in psychology and pedagogy. There he pursued an interest in applied psychology that began with a 1901 lecture on the psychology of advertising. The head of one of Chicago's largest advertising agencies, John Mahin, was in attendance at that lecture. Mahin was intrigued by Scott's remarks and asked if he would write a series of articles on the psychology of advertising.

Mahin's Magazine began monthly publication in 1902 and Scott contributed an article in each of the first 12 issues. He covered a variety of subjects including habit, laws of association, suggestion, perception, argumentation, and mental imagery. Only one of the articles was based on any research by Scott, a study on the legibility of typefaces of timetables for the Burlington Railroad. Those dozen articles were republished in 1903 as Scott's first book, The Theory of Advertising (Boston, Mass.). In the next 8 years, he published four more books in applied psychology, on advertising, public speaking, human efficiency, and influencing individuals in business. He was arguably the first American psychologist to be identified as a business psychologist.

Scott's most important work as a psychologist came during World War I. His work in employee selection before the war—work completed when he was director of Carnegie Institute of Technology's Bureau of Salesmanship Research—prepared him well for assuming a similar role for the military. As head of the Committee on the Classification of Personnel in the Army (CCPA), Scott modified his "Rating Scale for Selecting Salesmen" for use in selecting army captains. Of all the mental testing efforts by psychologists during the war, this program proved to be the most successful. Scott opposed the emphasis on intelligence testing and instead focused on functional measures of behavior (such as decision making and accuracy) that proved to be better predictors of job performance. For his work, Scott was awarded the prestigious Distinguished Service Medal of the United States in 1919, the only psychologist to be so decorated. This work and subsequent studies were the basis for his most influential book, *Personnel Management* (Chicago, 1923).

In 1919, Scott and several members of the CCPA founded a psychological consulting firm called the Scott Company. Scott served as president and chief fundraiser for the company. The company did well principally due to Scott's contacts, but when Scott left in 1920 to become president of Northwestern University, business began to fall off, and the company closed in 1923. Scott spent the final 19 years of his professional life as one of the most successful administrators in Northwestern's history. His legacy to contemporary psychology was his work in business psychology, particularly personnel selection and management, and he is recognized as one of the earliest pioneers in what is today called industrial-organizational psychology.

Bibliography

Jacobson, J. Z. (1951). *Scott of Northwestern: The life story of a pioneer in psychology and education.* Chicago: Mariano. There are no full-length biographical treatments of Scott other than this one, which provides little information about his work.

Scott, W. D. (1911). *Increasing human efficiency in business.* New York: Macmillan.

Scott, W. D. (1911). *Influencing men in business.* New York: Ronald.

Von Mayrhauser, R. T. (1989). Making intelligence functional: Walter Dill Scott and applied psychological testing in World War I. *Journal of the History of the Behavioral Sciences, 25,* 60–72.

Ludy T. Benjamin, Jr.

SCRIPT. *See* Schema.

SCRIPTURE, EDWARD WHEELER (1864–1945), American psychologist, phoneticist, and speech therapist. After graduating from the College of the City of New York (1884), Scripture studied in Europe. His 1891 doctoral dissertation at the University of Leipzig (directed by Wilhelm Wundt) addressed the associative course of thought and won him a one-year position at Clark University. In 1892, he moved to Yale University, where he soon began issuing volumes of *Studies from the Yale Psychological Laboratory.*

Scripture's teaching at Yale emphasized extreme experimental precision. His research addressed such phenomena as the localization of sound, the size-weight illusion, and the effect of rhythm on movement. Although his stress on instruments made his experiments seem "more [like] telegraphy than psychology" to one well-known student (Carl E. Seashore), many of his colleagues soon began using the apparatus he designed.

At Yale, Scripture wrote two popular books, *Thinking, Feeling, Doing* (1895) and *The New Psychology* (1897), both of which harshly criticized many of his contemporaries for the "endless speculation and flimsy guesswork" of their "armchair psychology." Such comments angered many colleagues; William James called him "shallow, and a complete barbarian." But others found the ample plagiarism in *Thinking, Feeling, Doing* from a recent translation of one of Wundt's books by Edward B. Titchener and James E. Creighton even more despicable. Scripture gradually refocused his research on "the psychology of expression, especially by speech." His *Elements of Experimental Phonetics* (1902) introduced soon-to-be-standard methods and apparatus for experiments on speech. But the following year he was fired from Yale.

A grant from the Carnegie Institution of Washington allowed Scripture to continue his research in Europe, and his *Researches in Experimental Phonetics: The Study of Speech Curves* (1906) further defined that speciality's emphasis on the physiology of speech production. In that year he earned a doctor of medicine degree at Munich and soon returned to New York. There he became associate in psychiatry at Columbia University's College of Physicians and Surgeons and established a private practice in speech therapy. His *Stuttering and Lisping* (1912; revised as *Stuttering, Lisping and Correction of Speech of the Deaf*, 1923) approached stuttering as a "typical psychoneurosis" to be treated both through modified psychoanalytic techniques and exercises designed to correct faulty speech patterns.

In the mid-1910s, Scripture moved to London, where he continued his therapeutic and research work. In 1924, he also became professor of experimental phonetics at the University of Vienna. He retired from his Austrian position in the mid-1930s and returned to England, where he continued his work until his death.

Few late-nineteenth-century American psychologists could be called modest, and they readily tolerated their colleagues' arrogance when it accompanied actual achievement. But most disliked Scripture and agreed with Hugo Münsterberg when he called Scripture an experimentalist but not a psychologist. Few mourned his departure from Yale in 1903, and 20 years later, even as his London colleagues agreed that stuttering required a mix of treatments, they responded similarly when he moved to Vienna. His personality thus severely limited his influence, even in a field in which his legacy has lasted.

Bibliography

Berry, M. F. (1965). Historical vignettes of leadership in speech and hearing: I. Speech pathology: Edward Wheeler Scripture (1864–1945) [and] May Kirk Scripture (1865–1943). *ASHA 7*, 8–9.

Eldridge, M. (1968). *A history of the treatment of speech disorders.* London: Livingstone.

Hardcastle, W. J. (1981). Experimental studies of lingual coarticulation. In R. E. Asher & E. J. A. Henderson (Eds.), *Towards a history of phonetics* (pp. 50–56). Edinburgh: Edinburgh University Press.

Scripture, E. W. (1936). Autobiography. In C. Murchison (Ed.), *History of psychology in autobiography* (Vol. 3, pp. 231–261). Worcester, MA: Clark University Press.

Sokal, M. M. (1980). The psychological career of Edward Wheeler Scripture. In J. Brozek & L. J. Pongratz (Eds.), *Historiography of modern psychology: Aims, resources, and approaches* (pp. 255–278). Toronto, Ontario, Canada: Hogrefe.

Michael M. Sokal

SEARS, PAULINE S. (1908–1993), American psychologist. Pauline Kirkpatrick Snedden completed her undergraduate degree in psychology at Stanford University (1930), her master's degree in child guidance at Teachers College, Columbia University (1931), and her doctoral degree in psychology at Yale University (1939). At Stanford, she met Robert Sears, and they became interested in psychology through Professors Paul Farnsworth and Louis Terman. Snedden and Sears were married in 1932, forming a personal and professional union of 57 years and producing research vital to child psychology and human development. [*See the biography of Robert R. Sears.*]

Pauline Sears began her professional career as a clinical instructor at Yale. In 1942, she and Robert Sears went to the Child Welfare Research Station, University of Iowa, pioneering research methodologies, including multiple assessment procedures with children, time-sampled observations in preschools, and doll play procedures for studying children's fantasies about family relationships. These procedures enabled researchers to test specific theory-based hypotheses about parental-child relationships. In 1949, Sears became a faculty member in the Harvard School of Education, pursuing her research interests in child development with a focus on psychological factors affecting school performance. She returned to Stanford in 1953, continuing as a faculty member until her retirement in 1973.

Sears is renowned for her groundbreaking work on self-esteem and motivation in children. At Yale, inspired by Kurt Lewin's views of aspiration, she produced her first major work, a classical study of the effects of school success and failure on children's aspirations. [*See the biography of Lewin.*] At Harvard, she utilized systematic observation of teaching styles to study teachers' effects on motivation and achievement in children with different initial aptitudes. She was the principal investigator of a 5-year study at Stanford on achievement motivation in elementary schools. This work culminated in the publication of *In Pursuit of Self Esteem* (Belmont, Calif., 1964), a book of case studies on achievement motivation and self-esteem coauthored with Virginia Sherman.

At the Stanford Center of Research and Development in Teaching, Sears brought rigorous research standards to important educational issues, including the effects of computer-assisted instruction, accelerated math programs for girls, and teaching strategies for effective reinforcement of culturally different children. She published pioneering work on the differential treatment of male and female students by teachers, initially raising the question of whether classrooms were biased in favor of boys.

Sears authored more than 30 articles, monographs, and chapters, published in technical/professional journals in psychology, education, and child development. A member of Sigma XI, the American Psychological Association, American Educational Research Association, and the Society for Research in Child Development, she bridged the fields of psychology and education through a lifetime of thoughtful research, applying hard research methodologies to heretofore "soft" areas such as self-esteem, motivation, and teaching style.

In 1980, Sears and her husband were awarded the American Psychological Association Gold Medal Award for their "distinguished and long continued record of scientific and scholarly accomplishments [as] psychologists who for decades have inspired both students and colleagues in the study of human development and whose efforts have furthered the applications of knowledge to the education and social betterment of children."

Bibliography

Sears, P. S. (1963). *The effect of classroom conditions on the strength of achievement motive and work output on elementary school children.* Stanford, CA: Stanford University School of Education. Report of the 5-year study on achievement motivation funded by the U.S. Department of Education and the Ford Foundation.

Sears, P. S. (Ed.). (1971). *Intellectual development.* New York: Wiley. A book of readings sponsored by the American Educational Research Association.

Carolyn L. Compton

SEARS, ROBERT R. (1908–1989), American psychologist. Born in Palo Alto, California, the son of Jesse B. Sears, a Stanford University faculty member, Robert Sears attended Stanford with aspirations of becoming a writer but graduated in 1929 with a baccalaureate degree in psychology. After graduation, and at the urging of Paul Farnsworth and Harry Harlow, he began graduate studies at Yale University to work with Clark Hull.

While at Yale, Sears began his work on the conditioned reflex and the study of the unconscious, two disparate interests that would lead him to the path of social learning theory. Sears was joined at Yale by a former Stanford classmate, Pauline (Pat) Snedden, whom he married in 1932 and with whom he collaborated on many projects. Sears received his Ph.D. in psychology in 1932 after completing a dissertation on the conditionability of decorticate goldfish.

After Yale, Sears joined the faculty at the University of Illinois, where he taught courses on personality and developed an interest in the relationship between personality and motivation. As a way of gathering clinical experience, Sears served as the clinical psychologist for the Institute for Juvenile Research traveling clinic. It was there that he began research on the objective study of defense mechanisms.

Sears left Illinois in 1936 to return to Yale as a member of the Institute of Human Relations. Under the directorship of Mark May, Sears was given the daunting task of constructing a unified behavioral science along with researchers such as John Dollard, Carl Hovland, Neal Miller, and G. P. Murdock. Their research, linking frustration and aggression, became a landmark work in the area of social behavior. Sears began work, at this time, on a monograph on experimental tests of psychoanalytic concepts. At Yale, Pauline received her Ph.D. in clinical psychology, and in 1942 the Searses left Yale for the University of Iowa, where Robert became professor of psychology and director of the Child Welfare Research Station.

At the Research Station, Sears began his career as a developmental psychologist. His work at Illinois and Yale on the empirical evidence for psychoanalytic theory had made him a leading figure in that area. However, he then turned his attention to the differences in children's personalities. His research on aggression in children led him to use dolls, classroom observations, and parental interviews to study the effect of child rearing on aggression. It is this focus on the role of parental child-rearing practices on behavior and personality and the design of objective measures to study development for which Sears is most recognized.

In 1949, after developing a research program for the study of development, Sears left Iowa to join the faculty of Harvard University and establish the Laboratory of Human Development there. He was joined by Eleanor Maccoby, Harry Levin, and Edgar Lowell, who were to be key collaborators in the future. At Harvard, Sears began research into identification processes and cross-cultural differences in dependency and aggression as continuation of the work on factors affecting the development of personality started at Iowa. In 1953, he left Harvard and returned to Stanford as the psychology department head; he remained there for the rest of his career.

At Stanford, Sears continued his program of research into the effects of socialization on development. His books, *Patterns of Child Rearing* (1957) and *Identification and Child Rearing* (1965), and his many journal articles demonstrated multiple objective techniques for measuring the relationship between child-rearing techniques, social environment, and the development of identification, morality, and aggressiveness in children. With the departure of Lewis Terman from Stanford, Sears took over the Terman longitudinal study of giftedness. He reported on the five surveys of the Terman sample collected between 1960 and 1986 in journal articles and the book *The Gifted in Later Maturity* (1995). Sears also served as the dean of the School of the Humanities and Sciences at Stanford from 1961 to 1970.

In addition to his place in developmental psychology, Sears was elected to the American Academy of Arts and Sciences, served as president of the American Psychological Association in 1951 and president of the Society for Research in Child Development (SRCD) from 1973 to 1975, and was an editor of the SRCD monograph series from 1971 to 1975. He and Pauline received the American Psychological Foundation's Gold Medal Award in 1980 for lifetime contributions to psychology. However, it was his work on objectifying the study of development and identifying the role of socialization in the development of personality that set Sears apart in the history of psychology.

Bibliography

Cronbach, L. J., Hastorf, A. H., Hilgard, E. R., & Maccoby, E. E. (1990). Robert R. Sears (1908–1989). *American Psychologist, 45,* 663–664.

Dollard, J., Doob, L. W., Miller, N. E., Mowrer, O. H., & Sears, R. R. (1939). *Frustration and aggression.* New Haven, CT: Yale University Press. Seminal work on the relationship between frustration, aggression, and behavioral responses in people.

Grusec, J. E. (1994). Social learning theory and developmental psychology: The legacies of Robert R. Sears and Albert Bandura. *Developmental Psychology, 28,* 776–786. Article emphasizing the role of Sears and Bandura in developing social cognitive explanations of development and their influence in the current field of developmental psychology.

Holahan, C. K., & Sears, R. R. (1995). *The gifted group in later maturity.* Stanford, CA: Stanford University Press. Descriptions of the most recent longitudinal studies concerning the Terman gifted group. Describes data collected on the Terman sample through later maturity describing some of the factors that influence successful aging.

Sears, R. R. (1943). *Survey of objective studies of psychoanalytic concepts,* Bulletin No. 51. New York: Social Science Research Council. Monograph reviewing the empirical evidence in psychology contributing proof of the existence of psychoanalytic concepts, such as defense mechanisms.

Sears, R. R. (1980). Robert R. Sears (autobiography). In G. Lindzey (Ed.), *A history of psychology in autobiography* (Vol. 7). San Francisco: Freeman.

Sears, R. R. Maccoby, E. E., & Levin, H. (1957). *Patterns of child rearing.* Evanston, IL: Row, Peterson. Seminal work describing research done with 379 mothers relating patterns of parenting with personality characteristics of their children.

Sears, R. R., Rau, L., & Alpert, R. (1965). *Identification and child rearing.* Stanford, CA: Stanford University Press. An intensive study of 40 families, investigating the role parents and social environment play in the development of differing types of identification, gender role, adult role, and morality.

Katherine N. Saunders

SEASHORE, CARL EMIL (1866–1949), American psychologist. Seashore was born Carl Emil Sjöstrand in Mörlunda, Sweden. In 1869, his family moved to Iowa and anglicized its name. In 1891, Seashore graduated from Gustavus Adolphus College as valedictorian and went to Yale University to study philosophy with George Trumbull Ladd. [*See biography of Ladd.*]

Although initially impressed by Ladd's scholarship, Seashore soon became disenchanted with his reliance on the authority of textbooks and gradually redirected his attention toward the new experimental psychology. His first laboratory work with Edward Wheeler Scripture depended so heavily on instruments that it seemed to Seashore more like telegraphy than a branch of philosophy. But he soon grew to appreciate both Scripture's emphasis on student initiative and the profes-

sional opportunities in American universities for psychologists with laboratory training. His 1895 Scripture-directed doctoral dissertation, *Illusions and Hallucinations in Normal Life,* addressed important perceptual questions by use of experimentation. He remained at Yale as an assistant for two years to sharpen his laboratory skills.

In 1897, Seashore became assistant professor at the State University of Iowa with charge of the psychological laboratory. By 1902, he was promoted to professor. Three years later Seashore became head of the department of philosophy and psychology and in 1908 became dean of the university's graduate college. At Iowa, Seashore developed an influential career as one of the few leading American psychologists of his generation who was neither native-born nor the scion of an upper-middle-class family. His own psychological and administrative work helped to establish the State University of Iowa's significant place in both the American psychological and educational communities of the twentieth century.

At Iowa, Seashore worked to enhance the role of the university's psychological laboratory. He developed courses that drilled undergraduates in the basics of psychology and experimental work, published the influential *Elementary Experiments in Psychology* (New York, 1908), and (for graduate students) emphasized the design and construction of instruments. For many years, he regularly reviewed new laboratory apparatus in the *Psychological Bulletin,* and before 1900 (with the help of Iowa physicist Charles Bowman) he designed and built an audiometer that electrically generated stimulus tones of standard intensities. Mass produced by the Stoelting Company, these devices were used for decades in public schools throughout America to test students' hearing.

Seashore always wanted to apply his science further, and as early as 1901 he wrote on the value of general psychological tests. He developed his most important contribution to psychology by building on his continuing interest in music and developing methods of measuring musical aptitude and talent. He broke down what he was studying into (what he took to be) its sensory and perceptual elements, which (for him) included the ability to distinguish differences in pitch, time, rhythm, loudness, and the like. In 1899, he began to publish articles in psychological journals on tests to measure such abilities and, by 1906, periodicals such as *The Musician* and *Musical Quarterly* and *Etude* asked him to describe his tests for their readers. Physicians and music schools (as well as psychological laboratories) gradually adopted many components of his tests, and in 1919, Seashore published *The Psychology of Musical Talent* and issued phonograph records with standard tones so his tests could be performed without special equipment. His 1937 book, *Psychology of Music,* brought together all of his previous studies, and in 1940 he issued (with several students) a revision of (what had come to be called) the Seashore Measures of Musical Talent.

Seashore built the department into one of the first large-scale midwestern graduate departments of psychology. As dean of the graduate college at Iowa, Seashore never hesitated applying his psychological ideas and using his position to direct university priorities toward areas in which he was interested. He took pride that his department of psychology worked closely with other university units, including the Child Welfare Research Station and Psychiatric Hospital, for which it operated a psychological clinic. He helped build strong programs in other scientific fields, and under his leadership, the graduate college developed a well-deserved national reputation. Meanwhile, his interest in individual differences led to a serious concern with gifted children, and through the 1920s he led a National Research Council project that urged school systems to section classes on the basis of (tested) ability.

Bibliography

Works by Seashore

Seashore, C. E. (1930). Autobiography. In C. Murchison (Ed.), *History of psychology in autobiography* (Vol. 1, pp. 225–297). Worcester, MA: Clark University Press.

Seashore, C. E. (1942). *Pioneering in psychology.* Iowa City: University of Iowa Series on Aims and Progress of Research.

Seashore, C. E. (1964). *Psychology and life.* Iowa City: Privately printed.

Works about Seashore

Bathurst, J. E., & Sinclair, R. D. (1928). A complete annotated bibliography of the writings of Seashore. *Psychological Monographs, 39,* 3–23.

Davis, A. B., & Merzbach, U. C. (1975). *Early auditory studies: Activities in the psychology laboratories of American universities.* Washington: Smithsonian Institution Press.

Kendler, H. H. (1989). The Iowa tradition. *American Psychologist, 44,* 1124–1132.

Stoddard, G. D. (1950). Carl Emil Seashore, 1866–1949. *American Journal of Psychology, 63,* 456–462.

Michael M. Sokal

SEASONAL AFFECTIVE DISORDER (SAD), also known as mid-winter or seasonal depression, is characterized foremost by at least two major depressive episodes occurring in 2 consecutive years, at a particular time of year, and with the absence of depressive symptoms at other times of year (American Psychiatric Association, 1994). Common symptoms include increased need for sleep, increased appetite, and carbohydrate craving (Rosenthal et al., 1984). Although described in the literature early in the twentieth century, organized clinical research programs have existed only for about 20 years.

Factors known to be associated with an increased prevalence of the disorder include young adult age, those living in high latitudes (presumably related to the decrease in the duration of daytime sunlight in the winter months), and female gender (American Psychiatric Association, 1994). Prevalence rates in countries or regions of countries at high latitudes have been estimated as high as 12% of a general population survey in Denmark (Dam, Jakobsen, & Mellerup, 1998) and 9% in Alaska (Booker & Hellekson, 1992), to relatively lower figures of 4% of a general population survey in Iceland (Magnusson & Stefansson, 1993) and 2% of a survey of psychiatric nurses in England (Eagles, Mercer, Boshier, & Jamieson, 1996). Differences between prevalence rates across studies may be attributable to differences in correction for age and gender, populations surveyed, and the selection of screening instruments.

Etiology: Theoretical Framework from Animal Studies

In many mammals and other vertebrates, the pineal hormone melatonin is secreted in response to darkness, bright light can inhibit its release, and it appears to act as an internal calendar, allowing the regulation and timing of seasonal-dependent behaviors such as breeding (as reviewed in Cassone & Natesan, 1997). This has lead researchers to speculate that in humans, the decreased length of daylight in the winter months, also known as a shorter photoperiod, which is particularly evident at higher latitudes, could result in a longer duration of melatonin release. Thus, it is thought that through direct or indirect mechanisms, the shorter photoperiod and hence longer duration of melatonin release may play causal roles in the pathogenesis of SAD (Young, Meaden, Fogg, Cherin, & Eastman, 1997; see also review by Wehr, 1997).

Phototherapy

Early results suggested that application of artificial bright light ("phototherapy"), applied in both the early morning and late evening hours, or the evening hours alone, led to the remission of symptoms (Rosenthal et al., 1984; Rosenthal et al., 1985). This antidepressant effect was hypothesized to be due to a direct antidepressant effect of light, the suppression of endogenous melatonin release or modulation of another mediating neurotransmitter, or an effect on the timing of the endogenous circadian pacemaker. However, contradictory to the melatonin inhibition hypothesis, phototherapy during the middle of the day when melatonin secretion is already partially or completely suppressed has also been shown to be effective (Terman et al., 1989; Wehr et al., 1986).

Evidence has been collected in support of the theory that SAD patients have a phase delay of their endogenous circadian pacemaker relative to their habitual waking and sleeping times, and hence their exposure to a light-dark cycle (Avery et al., 1997; Lewy, Sack, & Singer, 1985). This would suggest that morning light exposure would be indicated to phase advance the SAD patients' internal circadian rhythms back into proper alignment with their sleep/wake schedules. However, comparisons of morning versus evening phototherapy have found them to have equal antidepressant effects in SAD patients, regardless of possible circadian phase misalignment (Wirz-Justice et al., 1993), arguing against the phase delay hypothesis. Differences in patient populations and treatment protocols prohibit firm conclusions on the strength of the phase delay hypothesis.

There is also evidence that the efficacy of phototherapy in SAD may follow a dose-response relationship. Increased light intensity and/or the duration of light exposure have been shown to improve treatment response (Terman et al., 1990). In most studies, the artificial bright light is provided by a special box or bank of fluorescent tubes capable of producing light intensities in the range of 2,500 to 10,000 lux. For comparison, average indoor room light is in the range of 100 to 150 lux, and direct midday sunlight is in the range of 100,000 to 150,000 lux.

Future Directions

Future studies may further clarify several issues that remain unresolved, including the efficacy of natural sunlight as an antidepressant in SAD (as in Wirz-Justice et al., 1996), the possibility of using a less intrusive and time-consuming phototherapeutic intervention, the role of novel pharmacologic agents in treatment, and the unexplained gender difference seen in the prevalence data.

[See also Depression; and Mood Disorders.]

Bibliography

American Psychiatric Association. (1994). *Diagnostic and statistical manual of mental disorders* (4th ed). Washington, DC: Author.

Avery, D. H., Dahl, K., Savage, M. V., Brengelmann, G. L., Larsen, L. H., Kenny, M. A., Eder, D. N., Vitiello, M. V., & Prinz, P. N. (1997). Circadian temperature and cortisol rhythms during a constant routine are phase-delayed in hypersomnic winter depression. *Biological Psychiatry, 41*, 1109–1123.

Booker, J. M., & Hellekson, C. J. (1992). Prevalence of seasonal affective disorder in Alaska. *American Journal of Psychiatry, 149*, 1176–1182.

Cassone, V. M., & Natesan, A. K. (1997). Time and time again: The phylogeny of melatonin as a transducer of biological time. *Journal of Biological Rhythms, 12*(6), 489–497.

Dam, H., Jakobsen, K., & Mellerup, E. (1998). Prevalence of winter depression in Denmark. *Acta Psychiatrica Scandinavica, 97*, 1–4.

Eagles, J. M., Mercer, G., Boshier, A. J., & Jamieson, F. (1996). Seasonal affective disorder among psychiatric nurses in Aberdeen. *Journal of Affective Disorders, 37*, 129–135.

Lewy, A. J., Sack, R. L., & Singer, C. M. (1985). Treating phase-typed chronobiologic sleep and mood disorders using appropriately time bright artificial light. *Psychopharmacology Bulletin, 21*, 368–372.

Magnusson, A., & Stefansson, J. G. (1993). Prevalence of seasonal affective disorder in Iceland. *Archives of General Psychiatry, 50*, 941–946.

Rosenthal, N. E., Sack, D. A., Gillin, J. C., Lewy, A. N. J., Goodwin, F. K., Davenport, Y., Mueller, P. S., Newsome, D. A., & Wehr, T. A. (1984). Seasonal affective disorder: A description of the syndrome and preliminary findings with light therapy. *Archives of General Psychiatry, 41*, 72–80.

Rosenthal, N. E., Sack, D. A., Carpenter, C. J., Parry, B. L., Mendelson, W. B., & Wehr, T. A. (1985). Antidepressant effect of light in seasonal affective disorder. *American Journal of Psychiatry, 142*, 163–170.

Terman, M., Terman, J. S., Quitkin, F. M., McGrath, P. J., Stewart, J. W., & Rafferty, B. (1989). Light therapy for seasonal affective disorder: A review of efficacy. *Neuropsychopharmacology, 2*(1), 1–22.

Terman, J. S., Terman, M., Schlager, D., Rafferty, B., Rosofsky, M., Link, M. J., Gallin, P. F., & Quitkin, F. M. (1990). Efficacy of brief, intense light exposure for treatment of winter depression. *Psychopharmacology Bulletin, 26*(1), 3–11.

Wehr, T. A. (1997). Melatonin and seasonal rhythms. *Journal of Biological Rhythms, 12*(6), 518–527.

Wehr, T. A., Jacobsen, F. M., Sack, D. A., Arendt, J., Tamarkin, L., & Rosenthal, N. E. (1986). Phototherapy of seasonal affective disorder. *Archives of General Psychiatry, 43*, 870–875.

Wirz-Justice, A., Graw, P., Krauchi, K., Gisin, B., Jochum, A., Arendt, J., Fisch, H.-U., Buddeberg, C., & Poldinger, W. (1993). Light therapy in seasonal affective disorder is independent of time of day or circadian phase. *Archives of General Psychiatry, 50*, 929–937.

Wirz-Justice, A., Graw, P., Krauchi, K., Sarrafzadeh, A., English, J., Arendt, J., & Sand, L. (1996). "Natural" light treatment of seasonal affective disorder. *Journal of Affective Disorders, 37*, 109–120.

Young, M. A., Meaden, P. M., Fogg, L. F., Cherin, E. A., & Eastman, C. I. (1997). Which environmental variables are related to the onset of seasonal affective disorder? *Journal of Abnormal Psychology, 106*(4), 554–562.

James K. Wyatt

SECHENOV, IVAN MIKHAILOVICH (1829–1905), Russian physiologist. Sechenov attended medical school at Moscow University and became a doctor in 1856. After 3½ years in western Europe, in the major physiological laboratories of the day, he accepted his first position as assistant professor of physiology in the Medico-Surgical Academy at St. Petersburg. Subsequently, he held positions at the Universities of Odessa, St. Petersburg, and Moscow. Throughout his life, Sechenov campaigned to make psychology a part of physiology. For him, psychology was the study of the reflexes of the brain, by methods that must be strictly physiological. He died of pneumonia in November 1905.

Sechenov believed that all behavior is reflexive, whether that behavior is simple or complex, involuntary or voluntary, sane or crazy. He treated reflexes as three-part units consisting of a sensory nerve, a connecting nerve, and a motor nerve. Anticipating Charles Sherrington, he also recognized that, although they could not be seen—even through a microscope—these components must be separated by the gaps that we now call synapses. In bold extensions of the reflex concept, he emphasized the roles of excitation and inhibition in reflex action and proposed that reflexes are modifiable by association. [See the biography of Sherrington.] He made the argument for reflex interpretations of human actions by tracing the associative history of behavior to its origins in infancy.

The only capabilities of neonates are a sensitivity to stimulation and a repertoire of reflexes that are elicited en masse by appropriate stimuli. For example, the infant has a tendency to react to any brightly colored object. These reactions are associated with many different stimuli. For one important example, sometimes they occur with self-produced stimulation and sometimes without it. The resulting associations are quite different when a little boy sees a toy in his own hand from what they are when he sees the same toy in his mother's hand. The elaboration of these latter associations produces an individual's self-concept. Self-esteem is a learned emotional reaction to that concept.

Emotionality, like other behavior, is subject to the laws of association. In the course of growing up, the infant's emotions are modified by experience. Continuing the previous example, the passion initially evoked by colored objects transfers successively to colored pictures of a knight in a storybook, to the experience (or imagination) of being dressed in the bright clothing of a knight, to the conception of oneself-as-knight, and finally to the abstract attributes of knightly action—bravery, dependability, and love of truth. Thus, what began as the uncoordinated reflex reaction of the infant to brightly colored objects evolves into a sense of personal worth. This evolution is an evolution of reflexes—nothing more.

In Russia, Sechenov is regarded as the founder of the science of the "higher nervous activity," that is, psychology. His major ideas were accepted by Ivan Pav-lov—who called Sechenov's "associations" "conditional (conditioned) reflexes"—and they remain important in Russian physiology today.

[See also Russia and the Former Soviet Republics; Self-Concept and Self-Representation; Self-Esteem; Synapses; and the biography of Pavlov.]

Bibliography

Kimble, G. A. (1967). Sechenov and the anticipation of conditioning theory. In G. A. Kimble (Ed.), *Foundations of conditioning and learning* (pp. 3–21). New York: Appleton-Century-Crofts.

Kimble, G. A. (1996). Ivan Mikhailovich Sechenov: Pioneer in Russian reflexology. In G. A. Kimble, C. A. Boneau, & M. Wertheimer (Eds.), *Portraits of pioneers in psychology* (Vol. 2, pp. 33–45). Washington, DC, & Mahwah, NJ: American Psychological Association & Erlbaum.

Kostoyants, K. (1965). Addendum. In I. M. Sechenov, *Reflexes of the brain* (S. Belsky, Trans.). Cambridge, MA: MIT Press.

Sechenov, I. M. (no date). *Selected physiological and psychological works*. Moscow: Foreign Languages Publishing House.

Gregory A. Kimble

SECONDARY EDUCATION. Adolescence is commonly recognized as one of the most distinctive periods in the human life span. This era is signaled by physiological changes associated with puberty. Adolescence is also marked by major changes in self-views and alterations in relationships with parents and peers. Schools for adolescents are a common feature of contemporary educational systems. It has been argued that the idea of providing schooling specifically for adolescents had existed in ancient Greece and Rome (Brough, 1995). In the United States, particularly, the contemporary forms of schooling for adolescents are middle or junior high schools and high schools. This article focuses on the nature of public secondary schooling for adolescents and the roles psychologists play in them. Here, secondary schools refer to middle, junior high, and high schools.

History, Structure and Purposes of Secondary Schools

Prior to the nineteenth century, in the United States schooling for adolescents was available primarily to the children of the wealthy, who were sent to private seminaries and academies prior to attending college. For a few other adolescents, schooling took the form of individual apprenticeships to skilled artisans. This pattern changed with the establishment of the first public high school in Boston in 1821 (Reese, 1995). The appearance of public high schools also coincided with the advent of the idea of graded classrooms with elementary grades leading to secondary ones (Reese, 1995). During the remainder of the nineteenth century, public high schools rapidly expanded and became available to larger segments of the U.S. population. The dominant school structure was 8 years of elementary schooling followed by 4 years at the secondary level (Brough, 1995).

By the beginning of the twentieth century, this structural arrangement was being questioned. One of the major forces driving concerns for restructuring schools in the United States was the work of psychologist G. Stanley Hall on adolescence and individual differences, particularly his description of the developmental changes associated with early adolescence (Brough, 1995). In response to this work and to increasing urbanization and industrialization, junior high schools, incorporating grades seven through nine, were created. They were to be geared to early adolescents. In addition to their academic functions, junior high schools were expected to address the social and psychological concerns of early adolescents and help smooth the transition from elementary to secondary school by providing opportunities for these children to explore their talents, receive personal guidance, and develop social skills (Brough, 1995).

By the middle of the twentieth century, junior high schools were being criticized by educators who argued they had become miniature high schools and were not fulfilling their original purposes. The middle school movement, which began in the 1960s, once again focused on the psychological development of early adolescence as the major underpinning of its structure. Middle schools generally serve students in grades 6 through 8 and are supposed to be organized to support personal and social exploration and emotional development as well as academic growth. The degree to which these goals are being met is debated.

Secondary schools differ from elementary schools in a number of ways. First, high schools tend to be much larger than elementary schools with respect to both physical structure and the number of students served. Second, high schools are more complex organizations. Most often they are formally organized into subject-based departments that form the central basis of teacher identity (McLaughlin & Talbert, 1990). Third, according to Louis, Marks, and Kruse (1996) high schools differ from elementary schools in important aspects of culture and functioning. Specifically, in elementary schools teachers are expected to take on a more nurturing, surrogate parent role with their young students, whereas in high schools teacher-student relationships are more distant and formal.

In addition, at the elementary level, a primary function of the staff is the socialization of students, whereas at the secondary level, a major function involves differentiating among students and providing them with experiences related to their future social status. One way in which they carry out this function is through tracking, the placement of students into different curriculums within a school (Oakes & Guiton, 1995). These authors point out that, particularly in the public sector, the comprehensive high school is most common. This type of secondary structure attempts to accommodate wide individual differences by providing a range of curriculum experiences that "include academic courses from remedial to advanced placement levels and vocational offerings ranging from introductory avocational industrial arts classes, to business courses that teach generic skills to courses that prepare the non college bound for work" (Oakes & Guiton, 1995, p. 23). Although tracking ostensibly is a means to meet different students' needs, it often is differentiated along racial, ethnic, and class lines that result in middle-class White and Asian students being placed in higher tracks while poor, African American, and Latino students end up in lower tracks (Oakes & Guiton, 1995).

In summary, schools that are targeted specifically toward adolescents have a relatively long history. The particular forms they have taken have varied somewhat during the twentieth century partly in response to changes in the society and partly to increased knowledge about the developmental characteristics of adolescence. Despite these changes in structure, however, the purposes of secondary schooling in the United States have been relatively consistent over time.

According to Reese (1995) education is one important vehicle for maintaining social stability in societies. Newmann (1998) argues that, historically, education has had three major goals: (1) to prepare students to be participants in the economic life of the society, (2) to prepare them to be good citizens, and (3) to help them develop skills that would enable them to find personal fulfillment in life. These goals have been incorporated into secondary schooling from its beginnings. In classes and extracurricular activities, middle and high schools attempt to convey academic knowledge and socialize the personal and social attributes valued by the society. By the late nineteenth century, high schools were characterized as having the "twin goals of training minds and training morals" (Reese, 1995, p. 102).

Perhaps because of their overarching goal of perpetuating society, in general, secondary schools have tended to reinforce existing socioeconomic, racial, and ethnic stratifications. In the 1800s most high school students were White, middle-class, and native born and the curriculum reflected Anglo-Saxon Protestant history, culture, and values. Although African Americans began to build schools for their children shortly after slavery was declared illegal, they were often not admitted to public schools. Secondary schooling for African Americans was not common until well into the twentieth century, and this was often in segregated and unequal settings (Reese, 1995).

For more than two decades, secondary schools in the United States and in other countries have been challenged to serve student populations that are characterized by increasing cultural, social, physical, and economic diversity. As a result they now have to teach students who bring different demands, approaches, and needs to the institution. In addition, at the close of the twentieth century, many communities are pressuring secondary schools to prepare students for an increasingly technological and global world. For many middle and high schools, these challenges have proved to be more than they have been able to handle. As a result, secondary schools in the United States and in some other countries have come under fire for failing to educate students effectively. Specifically, the quality of secondary schooling in the United States is sharply differentiated according to the racial and socioeconomic status of the students served. These criticisms have spawned a number of school-reform movements that have raised questions about the structure and purposes of secondary schools.

Interpersonal Relationships in Adolescence

The physical and psychological changes that begin with puberty are associated with changes in the perceptions and expectations others have of the adolescent. Altered perceptions and expectations, in turn, have a significant impact on the nature of children's interactions with others. Many adolescents experience changes in their relationships with adults, particularly those who are significant in their lives, namely parents and teachers. Relationships between adolescents and these adults often become more difficult than at younger ages. Eccles et al. (1996) argue that the increased difficulty in relationships between adolescents and their parents and teachers is the result of "a mismatch between the needs of developing adolescents and their experiences at school and at home" (Eccles et al., 1996, p. 267). Eccles's research findings suggest that beginning in early adolescence, youth seek relationships with adults that are close but allow them increased opportunities for independence and autonomy. In addition, adolescents have increased concerns about their self-esteem and social status. Eccles and colleagues found that the junior high or middle schools adolescents enter tend to be organized in a manner that diminishes opportunities for students to form close relationships with teachers. Furthermore, school and classroom organization at the secondary level tends to highlight students' status and threaten self-esteem through "comparative and public evaluation" (Eccles et al., 1996, p. 274). Eccles and colleagues have studied adolescents in their families and

find that many families tend to become more controlling at this period of development, thus further limiting opportunities for autonomy and threatening self-esteem. Interestingly, parent involvement with their children's schools often decreases when children become adolescents.

While relationships between the adolescents and their parents and teachers may become more difficult during this period, peer relationships among adolescents often become more salient. It has been argued that the social support that adolescents obtain from their peers has significant impact on their personal development as well as their academic engagement in school (Newmann, 1998).

Self-Views of Adolescents

A hallmark of adolescence involves changes in self-views. Two significant areas of change during this period are in identity and motivation. Changes in these areas affect adolescents' perceptions of school, their relationships with teachers and peers, and their achievement outcomes.

As young people move into adolescence, questions regarding personal and social identity become increasingly important. It has been argued that the types of school experiences these young people have impact on these identity processes (Swanson, Spencer, & Petersen, 1998). For example, adolescents who have consistently frustrating or negative academic and social experiences in schools are likely to experience diminished feelings of self-worth, self-efficacy, competence, and commitment. This, in turn, can lead to feelings of lowered academic competence and disengagement from school. While all adolescents may experience these frustrations in school, adolescents of color, particularly males, may be especially vulnerable because they are more likely to be viewed and evaluated negatively in the school setting (Swanson, Spencer, & Petersen, 1998).

A number of researchers have documented declines in motivation when students enter middle or junior high school (Andermann & Maehr, 1994; Eccles et al., 1996). Unfortunately, these declines often continue throughout the high school years. Researchers suggest that the school policies and pegagogical practices typical of middle and high schools are major contributors to decreases in motivation. Andermann and Maehr (1994) argue that in early adolescence students begin to make a distinction between effort and ability. Furthermore, they tend to think of ability as a fixed trait. At the same time, they are moving into school structures that emphasize ability as a major facet of academic achievement through increases in testing, tracking, and singling out students to perform academically in public. Many students thus become much more vulnerable to fears of failure. To avoid failure, they become disengaged from school and are less motivated to attempt achievement (Andermann & Maehr, 1994).

Adolescents are struggling to develop a coherent sense of personal identity. Included in this identity formation are perceptions of self-worth, competence, self-determination, and autonomy. The experiences adolescents have in schools may have a profound impact on these aspects of development. School organizational structures and instructional practices may impede identity development and lead to decreased motivation among adolescents. These effects may be especially significant for minority and poor adolescents, whose status in society is often compromised inside and outside of the school setting.

Role of Psychologists

Psychologists have played major roles in secondary education for many years. These roles have been both direct and indirect. Indirectly, psychologists have had a great deal of influence on high schools through their research on adolescent development and learning. Since the pioneering work of G. Stanley Hall, psychologists have increased knowledge about adolescents' physical, cognitive, personal, and social development. The findings of this research have influenced secondary school policies and practices. Psychologists have also been indirectly involved in secondary schooling through their work in the development of standardized tests and other assessment tools. These tools often serve as the primary means of determining students' progress through school. In addition, these tools often are major determinants of the types of opportunities adolescents will have available to them upon leaving high school.

Traditionally, psychologists have also had direct involvement in schools as counselors and school psychologists. Counselors have customarily been concerned with the child's vocational aspirations. School psychologists have traditionally been concerned with identifying students who are purportedly in need of special educational and supportive services not available in the traditional classroom and consulting with school staff around the provision of these services.

With the increased concern about school effectiveness, psychologists have been urged to take on more active roles in secondary school settings. One area of concern has been the need to improve the school performance and experience of poor children (Turozzi & Uro, 1997). Interest in the education of poor children was spurred by the War on Poverty initiated by President Lyndon Johnson. The Elementary and Secondary Education Act (ESEA) was established in 1965 and focused on improving education for poor children in kindergarten through the end of high school. Although the ESEA originally focused on providing additional and compensatory academic support to poor children, a number of researchers and practitioners began to question this limited focus. By the time the ESEA was redesigned through the Improving America's Schools Act (IASA) of 1994, there was recognition that providing effective educational opportunities to poor children would require major changes in school organizational patterns, curriculum designs, instructional practices, and relationships with students and their families (Turozzi & Uro, 1997). Psychologists, particularly school psychologists, have roles in implementing these broad changes. Rather than focus solely on the psychological characteristics of the child, school psychologists are urged to work collaboratively with school staff, parents, and the community served by the school. Psychologists are encouraged to take responsibility for providing input in the areas of student assessment, curriculum development, and staff training (Turozzi & Uro, 1997).

Although school reform has improved academic achievement as its primary focus, there has been increased awareness that academic achievement is mitigated by a host of social, cultural, and psychological factors emanating from and impinging on children. Kolbe, Collins, and Cortese (1997) note that adolescence is a period when children seem to be particularly likely to establish behavior patterns that have negative consequences for them and their communities. Some of the patterns that place adolescents at risk include alcohol and drug abuse, tobacco addiction, eating disorders, uncontrolled aggression, and risky sexual behavior (Kolbe, Collins, & Cortese, 1997). Psychologists have the capacity to play important roles in the prevention of these behaviors in the school setting. Specifically, psychologists could work closely with school health-care workers as well as other school staff, adolescents, and their families to implement this effort. Furthermore, preventative work with adolescents can be addressed by research psychologists as well as practitioners (Kolbe et al., 1997).

Summary

Almost all societies provide some types of formal educational experiences for children and youth. In the United States, public secondary schooling has existed for over 150 years and private institutions for adolescents have existed even longer. Middle and high schools have as their primary goal the preparation of adolescents to be productive workers and positive citizens of their society. These goals help perpetuate the society. To meet these goals, schools have to function as one of the major socialization agents, along with parents, of youth.

For almost a century, psychologists have been integrally linked with middle and high schools. Psychological theory and research about the developmental nature of adolescence, learning, assessment, motivation, and identity formation has profoundly shaped the structure and function of secondary schools. Psychologists who are practitioners work directly with middle and high school students in the areas of assessment, counseling, and the identification and remediation of students with special needs and disabilities.

Within the past 20 years, secondary schooling has undergone dramatic changes in two areas. First, the student population has become increasingly diverse. Secondary schools that once served only the children of elite White families now must serve students who represent not only both genders but also a wide variety of cultures, religions, ethnicities, sexual orientations, and races, who come from increasingly disparate economic backgrounds and who have a range of physical abilities and disabilities. In general, secondary schools' response to this diversity has had limited effectiveness.

Second, secondary schools have been pressured to expand their conceptions of their functions. This has been a result of several factors, including (1) increased knowledge about the nature of adolescents and their vulnerability to incorporating negative behavioral patterns, (2) pressure from communities to prepare students to function in a complex technological and global world effectively, and (3) recognition that academic outcomes are strongly influenced by a variety of cultural, psychological, and social factors.

These changes have important implications for the roles that psychologists play in secondary schools. Several authors have argued that psychologists take on roles of expanded scope and leadership to help schools cope with these issues. However, these new roles will require changes in psychologists' training, research, and practice. Short and Talley (1997) suggest that to be effective in secondary schools, psychologists will have to be trained to work in a variety of settings, across disciplines, and with a number of populations.

Bibliography

Andermann, E. M., & Maehr, M. L. (1994). Motivation and schooling in the middle grades. *Review of Educational Research, 64,* 287–309. Provides a thorough review of theory and research explaining changes in adolescent motivation and its impact on achievement.

Brough, J. A. (1995). Middle level education: An historical perspective. In M. J. Wavering (Ed.), *Educating young adolescents: Life in the middle* (pp. 27–51). New York: Garland. Provides a comprehensive discussion of the psychological characteristics of early adolescence and the philosophical, organizational, curricular, and pedagogical bases of middle schools.

Eccles, J. S., Flanagan, C., Lord, S., Midgley, C., Roeser, R., & Yee, D. (1996). Schools, families and early adolescents: What are we doing wrong and what can we do instead? *Journal of Developmental and Behavioral Pediatrics, 14,* 267–276. Describes several empirical studies of adolescents in schools and families.

Kolbe, L. J., Collins, J., & Cortese, P. (1997). Building the capacity of schools to improve the health of the nation: A call for assistance from psychologists. *American Psychologist, 52,* 256–265. This issue contains a special section on psychologists' roles in schools and suggests directions for the future.

Louis, K. S., Marks, H. M., & Kruse, S. (1996). Teachers professional community in restructuring schools. *American Educational Research Journal, 33,* 757–798.

McLaughlin, M. W., & Talbert, J. E. (1990). The contexts in question: The secondary school workplace. In M. W. McLaughlin, J. E. Talbert, & N. Bascia (Eds.), *The contexts of teaching in secondary schools* (pp. 1–14). New York: Teachers College Press.

Newmann, F. M. (1998). How secondary schools contribute to academic success. In K. Borman & B. Schneider (Eds.), *The adolescent years: Social influences and educational challenges* (pp. 88–108). Ninety-seventh yearbook of the National Society for the Study of Education. Part 1. Chicago: University of Chicago Press. This yearbook includes articles focusing on understanding adolescence within the social contexts of contemporary families, schools, and work settings.

Oakes, J., & Guiton, G. (1995) Matchmaking: The dynamics of high school tracking decisions. *American Educational Research Journal, 32,* 3–33. This article provides an explanation of the rationale for and results of tracking.

Reese, W. J. (1995). *The origins of the American high school.* New Haven: Yale University Press. A comprehensive discussion of the intellectual, cultural, and social forces that shaped public secondary education in the United States.

Short, R. J., & Talley, P. C. (1997). Rethinking psychology and the schools. *American Psychologist, 52,* 234–240.

Swanson, D. P., Spencer, M. B., & Petersen, A. (1998). Identity formation in adolescence. In K. Borman & B. Schneider (Eds.), *The adolescent years: Social influences and educational challenges* (pp. 18–41). Ninety-seventh yearbook of the National Society for the Study of Education. Part 1. Chicago: University of Chicago Press.

Turozzi, G. N., & Uro, G. (1997). Education reform in the United States: National policy in support of local efforts for school improvement. *American Psychologist, 52,* 241–249.

Diane S. Pollard

SECONDARY INTERVENTION. *See* Intervention.

SEDATIVES. *See* Depressants, Sedatives, and Hypnotics.

SEGUIN, EDOUARD (1812–1880), French American physician and special educator. The major contribution of Seguin is the diagnostic teaching method he developed for children who were isolated from others due to severe sensory difficulties and/or by a combination of mental and physical problems. The system was based on techniques used with sensory disabled children and extended for use with those with mental and/or physical disabilities. Seguin's work, based on study with Jean Itard, was initiated in two hospitals in Paris and, as a result of his efforts, spread to other European countries and the United States. As part of that work, he developed in the 1860s a means of measuring cognitive development with form boards that was still being used 100 years later and was recognized as being more culturally fair than more verbally oriented measures.

Born in Clamecy, France, the son of a physician, Seguin was a person of many talents: writer, educator, physician, and reformer. Through political and economic articles he expressed humanitarian concerns, which he often backed up with individual action. In the 1830s he was an art critic in Paris, and later he studied medicine with Itard. Finding success with physiological training of selected mentally retarded patients, Itard encouraged the younger Seguin to start schools in which children with delayed development could receive much individual attention. Seguin's approach moved beyond Itard's continuous repetitions of sensory stimulation to include more abstract and higher level work. In 1846, Seguin published what became the standard textbook on mental retardation for the rest of the century.

Seguin's work was well received on the continent and in the United States. However, sensing more individual freedom in America than in France, Seguin moved to the United States in 1850. His system was incorporated in the program of the first state school for the mentally retarded in America under the direction of Samuel Gridley Howe. He continued writing in both French and English and consulted or spent short periods of time on the staff of mental institutions in Europe and in Boston and Barre, Massachusetts; Albany and Syracuse, New York; Cleveland, Ohio; and at the Pennsylvania Training School (now Elwyn Institute).

As the schools began to serve more and more children, the staffs of these institutions could not provide the social, physiological, and educational methods he developed and advocated, especially individualized training. Feuds with administrators were not uncommon.

According to Rosen (Seguin, 1875), Seguin's system, which relied heavily on observation in different conditions to develop recommendations, still provides guidance for training in special education programs today. Modern methods and curricula are derived from his work. Principles developed by Seguin were credited by Maria Montessori as guiding her system for teaching.

Many psychologists used a Seguin form board or one based on those he developed. The final Seguin board included a circle, star, triangle, and seven other wooden block forms to be placed in holes in a rectangular board from which they might have been cut. Henry Goddard's adaptation included the original 10 forms. Lightner Witmer's 11-form version included both an isosceles and an equilateral triangle, was more convenient in size than Seguin's, and was the best standardized of those used early in the twentieth century. The isosceles triangle was very difficult for preschool children to place, but the two triangles were helpful in differentiating among slowly developing adolescents and adults.

A Seguin form board was included as a subtest in the 1928, 1933, and 1947 versions of Grace Arthur's *Point Scale of Performance Tests* and others in the twentieth century. The Seguin boards could be presented by pantomime for the hard of hearing or with non-English speakers.

Boards evolved with pieces that needed to be assembled to fit into the holes. As the tasks became more difficult, the examiner could observe the child or adult thinking about solutions and trying varying approaches. Children who could get the forms in the holes quickly were clearly not retarded. According to Grace Kent (1950), the form boards might be measures of "stupidity" more than intelligence, but, by whatever generic name, psychologists liked them because, in a battery of instruments, they enabled the examiner to observe whether "trial and error" or force or thoughtful behavior might be occurring.

[*Many of the people mentioned in this article are the subjects of independent biographical entries.*]

Bibliography

Works by Seguin

Seguin, E. (1846). *Traitement moral, hygiene et education des idiots et des autres enfants arrieres ou retardes dans leur developpement* [The medical treatment, hygiene, and education of retarded people and other backward children retarded in their development]. Paris: Bailliere.

Seguin, E. (1866). *Idiocy and its treatment by the physiological method*. New York: William Wood (reprinted in 1907 by Teachers College, Columbia University).

Seguin, E. (1976). *Report on education: A facsimile reproduction* (Introduction by Marvin Rosen). Delmar, NY: Scholars' Facsimiles & Reprints. Available: http://www.eb.com:180/cgi-bin/g?DocF=micro/535/73.html (Original work published 1875)

Works about Seguin

Kanner, L. (1960). Itard, Seguin, Howe—Three pioneers in the education of retarded children. *American Journal of Mental Deficiency, 65,* 2–10.

Kent, G. H. (1950). *Mental tests in clinics for children.* Toronto: Van Nostrand.

Talbot, M. E. (1964). *Edouard Seguin: A study of an educa-*

tional approach to the treatment of mentally defective children. New York: Teachers College Press.

Joseph L. French

SELECTIVE ATTENTION. *See* Attention; *and* Attention-Deficit/Hyperactivity Disorder.

SELF-ASSESSMENT. *See* Self-Concept and Self-Representation; Self-Esteem; *and* Self-Regulation.

SELF-AWARENESS. *See* Self-Consciousness.

SELF-CATEGORIZATION. *See* Social Identity.

SELF-CONCEPT AND SELF-REPRESENTATION. Self-concepts contribute to a sense of identity over time. The conscious representation of self-concepts is dependent in part on unconscious schematizations of self. These are generalizations from prior memories and fantasies. It is helpful to reserve the term *self-concept* for the more declarative knowledge that people have, and *self-schemas* for the usually unconscious, procedurally based knowledge. Self-concepts are usually available to consciousness but some may be inhibited from representation. The latter might be unconscious, yet influence judgment, mood, and action patterns.

Each individual has a repertoire of self-schemas, which may be activated variably, to produce different states of mind. Each person can have multiple self-concepts, even contradictory ones. Regarded this way, *self-organization* is relatively complex. There may be various self-schemas that are arranged into supraordinate configurations. Different self-schemas can contain different, even antithetical traits such as shyness and vanity. With maturation throughout the life cycle, a person may connect the different traits and have a progressively more integrated self-organization. But some people remain subject to dissociations, segregations, and splitting of such meanings.

The many types of information that might be a part of self-schemas or self-concepts include body images, values, roles in regard to others, status in the world, persistent personally symbolic memories, goals, plans, intentions, and expectations of what will happen in the future. Subjective self-conceptualization may mirror the real physical, emotional, and mental features of an individual or it may reflect the product of fantasies. Because of different motivations for developing meanings about the self, there may be a variety of desired, dreaded, ideal, realistic, past, present, and future self-conceptualizations.

Self-schemas are organized packages of meanings, a patterned aggregation of elements. The connected and associated beliefs of a particular self-schema make up a usually nonconscious mental model, or cognitive map. Each person will have a repertoire of self-schemas, and within that repertoire there will be more or less active units.

Each unit has an effect upon information processing. The activated self-schemas influence current internal working models which, when depicted in consciousness, lead to specific self-concepts. Some schematized attributes lead to consciousness, to declarative knowledge, as when a woman says, "I am being a good mother." In other instances, the knowledge is schematized but unconscious or procedural: she behaves like a good mother but may not have a conscious experience that she is such.

As already mentioned, the person may have, in different states of mind, self-concepts that seem contradictory or irreconcilable. The person can learn to integrate these experiences, developing supraordinate self-schemas. These supraordinate schemas contain a nested hierarchy of subordinate schemas. Psychotherapy often aims at such a process. The work helps patients to integrate discrepancies within sets of self-concepts so the person has a continuous self-conceptualization over time. Such processes help the individual to see oneself as a complex person capable of both accepting and mastering contradictory traits.

One of the many elements in self-schemas are body images, cognitive maps of the physical self. The imagined self and the actual somatic styles of an individual are influenced by these body images. Declarative statements like "I am too fat" are influenced by their symbolic representations and also by ideal body images. Thus, the person may exhibit to others a systematic variance in how he or she walks, gestures, or expresses the self through voice or facial expressions, in different states of mind. When ideal body images are active, the movements and sensations may be flowing and graceful; when dreaded body images are active, they may be awkward and constricted.

Observers can infer another person's self-concepts by listening to his or her narratives and watching how he or she uses the body. Observers can then form inferences about what the other person's body images and self-schemas might be. The observers' reports might not be the same as the self-reports of conscious representations by the subject person.

Especially difficult for observers to infer are the intentions of self that may go with certain self-schemas. These are usually a private area of knowledge, and the use of frank expression is necessary in psychotherapy in order to get at such material. Self-concepts are often reflected in how the person describes others. That is, the person may have a self-concept or a self-schema that is part of an associational matrix that can be called a *role relationship model*.

An important concept already mentioned is that of the *supraordinate self-schema*. A supraordinate self-schema is formed from a synthesis of lower order networks of associations into larger networks. It is an organization or configuration of many smaller systems for establishing who the self is, and how and why the self will act.

People with few supraordinate schemes, or with supraordinate schemas that have many contradictory self-representations, are vulnerable to explosive shifts in state. They may dissociate conscious memory of various identity experiences. Their behaviors often surprise their associates because they shift states of mind so readily. They also use more defensive control processes to distort reality, leading to expressions of irrational, compensatory self-concepts such as a state of grandiosity, for example. The reason is that, if they do not use these defensive control processes, they may find themselves flooded with shame, or a chaotic sense of loss of identity. The defenses enable them, perhaps irrationally, to bolster self-esteem.

[*See also* Pesonality.]

Bibliography

Horowitz, M. (1987). *States of mind: Configuration analysis of individual personality* (2nd ed.). New York: Plenum.

Horowitz, M. J., Eells, T., Singer, J., & Salovey, P. (1995). Role relationship models for case formulation. *Archives of General Psychiatry, 53,* 627–632. Featured paper with eight commentaries.

Markus, H., & Wurf, E. (1987). The dynamic self-concept: A social psychological perspective. *Annual Review of Psychology 38,* 299–337.

Westen, D. (1992). The cognitive self and the psychoanalytic self: Can we put our selves together? *Psychological Inquiry, 3,* 1–13.

Mardi Horowitz

SELF-CONSCIOUSNESS is a personality trait associated with the tendency to reflect on or think about oneself. People differ in the degree to which they tend to focus on and think consciously about themselves. Some individuals reflect on themselves much of the time; others do so only rarely. People who frequently think about themselves are characterized as high in self-consciousness. Unlike lay definitions of the term, psychological use of the term self-consciousness refers only to individual differences in self-reflection and does not connote embarrassment or awkwardness.

Interest in self-consciousness grew out of research on the effects on people's behavior and emotion of focusing attention on oneself. Research on self-awareness (or self-focused attention) showed that directing attention toward oneself elicits a comparison process in which the person compares his or her behavior to a relevant personal standard (such as a goal, attitude, or value) and tries to bring his or her behavior in line with the standard. Thus, when people are self-focused, they tend to behave more consistently with their standards than when they are not self-focused. Researchers developed an interest in the trait of self-consciousness when it became apparent that people differ markedly in their propensity to self-focus.

Private and Public Self-Consciousness

Many researchers distinguish between two varieties of self-consciousness—private and public. Private self-consciousness is the degree to which people think about private, internal aspects of themselves that are not directly open to observation by other people—for example, their own thoughts, motives, and feelings. Public self-consciousness is the degree to which people think about public, external aspects of themselves that can be observed by others, such as their physical appearance, mannerisms, and overt behavior. Research shows that private and public self-consciousness should be regarded as two separate, weakly correlated personality dimensions rather than as opposite ends of a single dimension.

The utility of the private-public distinction, which can be traced to William James, is supported by research showing that private and public self-consciousness relate to behavior differently. Focusing attention on private aspects of oneself increases adherence to personally held standards, whereas attending to public aspects of oneself increases reliance on social, consensually held standards. Thus, private and public self-consciousness predict the degree to which people are influenced by privately held standards versus social norms and expectations, respectively.

Private self-consciousness is associated with a clearer view of oneself, a greater adherence to one's personal standards, and a higher sensitivity to stressful events. People who are high in private self-consciousness behave more consistently with their privately held attitudes and values than people who are low in private self-consciousness. They are also less likely to conform to erroneous group judgments and more resistant to coercion. Because their own perceptions and beliefs are particularly salient and clear, their views tend to hold sway over those of other people. Privately self-conscious people are also more accurate in reporting information about themselves and more likely to dispute inaccurate information about themselves from other sources, presumably because their heightened tendency to self-reflect enhances their self-understanding. Furthermore, compared to people who are low in private self-consciousness, the descriptions that high privately self-conscious people provide of themselves are less likely to be biased by extraneous factors, such as the response format of questionnaires on which they rate themselves, leading questions, or offhand comments made by other people. Because their self-reports are less affected by irrelevant factors, they respond more consistently to psychological scales across repeated assessments (that is, the test-retest reliability of their responses is higher). When thinking about how they would like to be in the future, people who are high in private self-consciousness rely more heavily on their personal standards than people low in self-consciousness. Private self-consciousness is also associated with stronger, more dysphoric reactions to stressful events, presumably because privately self-conscious people tend to mull over personal experiences and their implications.

People who are high in public self-consciousness tend to reflect on the public aspects of themselves and, thus, are particularly attuned to how they are perceived and evaluated by other people. As a result, public self-consciousness is correlated with the amount of attention that people devote to their appearance—for example, the importance they place on clothing and make-up, their physical attractiveness, and the nature of the impressions other people form of them. Emotionally, people who are publicly self-conscious are more socially anxious and able to be embarrassed, more worried about others' evaluations of their physiques, more prone to blushing, and more sensitive to being shunned than people who are low in public self-consciousness. Because they are concerned with making desired impressions, people with high public self-consciousness are more likely to conform to others' incorrect decisions than people with low public self-consciousness, even when those decisions involve relatively unambiguous perceptual tasks (such as counting metronome clicks). Also, when thinking about how they would like to be in the future, publicly self-conscious people rely heavily on how they think other people want them to be.

Measurement

The most widely used measure of self-consciousness is the Self-Consciousness Scale, which includes separate subscales for the measurement of private and public self-consciousness. (The Self-Consciousness Scale also includes a social anxiety subscale that is not directly relevant to the measurement of self-consciousness.) The Self-Consciousness Scale has demonstrated reliability and validity as a measure of individual differences in self-consciousness, although some evidence suggests that the private self-consciousness subscale may tap two distinct aspects of private self-consciousness—the awareness of one's internal states and the extent to which the person tends to self-reflect.

The Self-Consciousness Scale has been translated into several languages, including Chinese, French, German, Brazilian, Dutch, and Turkish. Not only have cross-cultural differences in self-consciousness been observed, but evidence suggests that private and public self-consciousness may relate differently to one another in certain other cultures than they do in American samples.

[See also Self-Concept and Self-Representation; and Self-Esteem.]

Bibliography

Buss, A. H. (1980). *Self-consciousness and social anxiety*. San Francisco: Freeman.

Carver, C. S., & Scheier, M. F. (1981). *Attention and self-regulation: A control-theory approach to human behavior*. New York: Springer-Verlag.

Fenigstein, A. (1987). On the nature of public and private self-consciousness. *Journal of Personality, 55*, 543–554.

Fenigstein, A., Scheier, M. F., & Buss, A. H. (1975). Public and private self-consciousness—Assessment and theory. *Journal of Consulting and Clinical Psychology, 43*, 522–527. Includes the most commonly used version of the Self-Consciousness Scale.

Scheier, M. F., & Carver, C. S. (1985). The Self-Consciousness Scale: A revised version for use with general populations. *Journal of Applied Social Psychology, 15*, 687–699.

Wicklund, R. A., & Gollwitzer, P. M. (1987). The fallacy of the private-public self-focus distinction. *Journal of Personality, 55*, 491–523. Raises questions about the theoretical viability of the distinction between private and public self-consciousness.

Mark R. Leary

SELF-CONTROL. *See* Self-Regulation.

SELF-DISCLOSURE refers to the process by which individuals reveal personal thoughts, feelings, and experiences to other people. It has traditionally been one of the most commonly studied features of relationship development, in part because many theorists see it not only as a hallmark of successful relationships, but also of emotional well-being. Greater self-disclosure involves breadth and depth and has both descriptive and evaluative elements, so it is not limited to specific bits of information but rather considers the personal significance of nominally private facts and feelings. Whereas early research operationalized self-disclosure primarily in terms of normatively private information, more recent conceptions ascribe the greatest intimacy to disclosures of personal emotions and self-perceptions (e.g., feelings, fears, wishes, and needs). In some accounts, verbalizing current feelings about a relationship to one's partner is thought to be particularly self-revealing.

Four perspectives have been used to study self-disclosure. The relationship stage approach was introduced by Altman and Taylor (1973), whose social-penetration theory likened self-disclosure to the peeling of an onion: Acquaintance deepens as individuals successively divulge more personal information, one layer at a time, eventually revealing their innermost selves to each other. The extensive empirical literature that derives from social-penetration theory supports their general proposition, although rates of progression vary markedly, with some relationships speeding through less disclosing levels of intimacy and others developing more gradually. Of course, these patterns describe optimum levels in a given relationship. Even in the most intimate relationships, conversation is far more frequently casual and superficial. Research also confirms the importance of mutuality—relationships appear to develop best when partners reciprocate each other's level of disclosure.

The individual differences approach to self-disclosure was inspired by the seminal writings of Jourard, who sought to identify dispositional factors responsible for self-disclosure tendencies (1968). Many such variables have been studied (such as extraversion, shyness, social anxiety, and sex-role orientation), with mixed results, leading some researchers to favor a personality-situation interaction model (i.e., that traits may enhance or diminish sensitivities to different situational or relational cues). Studies of one individual difference variable, gender, have abounded. Dindia's and Allen's meta-analysis of 205 studies established that women tend to self-disclose more intimately than men, and that women are more often the target of self-disclosure than men (1992). Some studies suggest that these differences may vary substantially from the North American findings in other, and especially non-Western, cultures.

A somewhat more functional perspective is offered by studies that concentrate on the interpersonal goals served by self-disclosure. Self-disclosure may be enacted for any of several purposes: for example, to elicit a supportive response; to foster a deepening relationship; to unburden the self; or to manipulate the other into complementary self-revelations. That self-disclosure may be

an effective strategy for accomplishing social goals seems clear. For example, self-disclosures of distress usually evoke sympathetic responses. Also, meta-analyses have shown that self-disclosure tends to elicit attraction and liking, and that liking in turn elicits self-disclosure.

Functional goal-based analyses highlight the relational nature of self-disclosure; that is, although dispositional characteristics of the discloser and target may account for meaningful differences in self-disclosure, by far the most compelling determinants depend on the unique relationship that disclosers and targets have with each other. Another way to say this is that few people disclose their innermost secrets universally, and few remain pervasively silent; most people vary self-disclosures from one partner to another, and these variations are thought to depend on relationship qualities. Nevertheless, the processes by which a particular partner's responses encourage or inhibit self-disclosure are not well understood, even though some analyses of intimacy and social support afford them a critical role.

The fourth and final approach is concerned with self-disclosure as a social skill. These investigations work from the assumption that there are reliable, cross-situation differences in people's ability to discern what an appropriate self-disclosure would be, and then to enact that disclosure. In a parallel vein, there are similar differences (sometimes called responsiveness) in people's ability to elicit self-disclosure from others. Implicit in this approach is the idea that there are norms, sometimes called rules or expectations, that define appropriate self-disclosure, and responses to disclosures by others. These norms are shaped by many factors, including social roles, situational factors, past experience, and relationship-relevant predispositions. One such rule is that self-disclosure should be personalistic—specific to particular friends—rather than globally distributed throughout one's social network. The norm of reciprocity—interaction partners' tendency to match each other on the depth and breadth of self-disclosure—has also received extensive empirical support. Another consistent finding is that too little or too much disclosure, in relation to personal preferences or situational norms, tends to hamper relationship development. In extreme cases, such divergences may be evidence of psychopathology.

Self-disclosure is customarily studied in several ways, most commonly with prescaled assessments of topics one has discussed, or is willing to discuss, with a partner; self-report and/or partner-report descriptions of communication patterns; and independent ratings or content analyses of speech or writing samples. These methods emphasize verbal self-disclosure. Most researchers acknowledge that intimacy is often communicated in other ways, particularly through nonverbal expressions of affect (e.g., facial expressions, eye contact, touch, and paralanguage), but also through behaviors from which inferences about the discloser may be drawn (e.g., not returning a suitor's telephone calls). Although such factors undoubtedly play important roles in moderating the meaning of verbal self-disclosure, this often subtle interplay has received relatively sparse empirical or theoretical attention. These processes are likely to be important as the field moves away from unifaceted models that conceive of relationship intimacy as a singular function of self-disclosure depth, and instead construes self-disclosure as one of several factors that contribute to establishing, maintaining, enhancing, and diminishing intimacy.

Bibliography

Altman, I., & Taylor, D. A. (1973). *Social penetration: The development of interpersonal relationships.* New York: Holt, Rinehart, & Winston.

Collins, N. L., & Miller, L. (1994). Self-disclosure and liking: A meta-analytic review. *Psychological Bulletin, 116,* 457–475.

Derlega, V. J., Metts, S., Petronio, S., & Margulis, S. T. (1993). *Self-disclosure.* Newbury Park, CA: Sage.

Dindia, K., & Allen, M. (1992). Sex differences in self-disclosure: A meta-analysis. *Psychological Bulletin, 112,* 106–124.

Jourard, S. (1968). *Disclosing man to himself.* New York: Van Nostrand.

Miller, L. C., & Read, S. J. (1987). Why am I telling you this? Self-disclosure in a goal-based model of personality. In V. J. Derlega and J. H. Berg (Eds.), *Self-disclosure: Theory, research, and therapy* (pp. 35–58). New York: Plenum Press.

Reis, H. T. (1998). Gender differences in intimacy and related behaviors: Context and processs. In D. J. Canary & K. Dindia (Eds.), *Sex differences and similarities in communication: Critical essays and empirical investigations of sex and gender in interaction* (pp. 203–231). Mahwah, NJ: Erlbaum.

Reis, H. T., & Patrick, B. (1996). Attachment and intimacy: Component process. In A. Kruglanski & E. T. Higgins (Eds.), *Social psychology: Handbook of basic principles* (pp. 523–563). New York: Guilford Press.

Harry T. Reis

SELF-EFFICACY. Perceived self-efficacy is people's beliefs in their capabilities to perform in ways that give them control over events that affect their lives. Efficacy beliefs form the foundation of human agency. Unless people believe that they can produce results by their actions, they have little incentive to act.

Sources of Self-Efficacy

There are four major ways of developing a strong sense of efficacy. The most effective is through mastery experiences. Successes build a belief in one's efficacy. Failures undermine it. If people have only easy successes, then they are easily discouraged by failure. Development of a resilient sense of efficacy requires experience in overcoming obstacles through perseverant effort.

The second way of creating and strengthening beliefs of personal efficacy is through social modeling. If people see others like themselves succeed by sustained effort, then they come to believe that they, too, have the capacity to do so. Observing the failures of others instills doubts about one's own ability to master similar activities. Competent models also build efficacy by conveying knowledge and skills for managing environmental demands.

Social persuasion is the third way of strengthening people's beliefs in their efficacy. If people are persuaded that they have what it takes to succeed, they then exert more effort than if they harbor self-doubts and dwell on personal deficiencies when problems arise. But effective social persuaders do more than convey faith in people's capabilities. They arrange things for others in ways that bring success and avoid placing them prematurely in situations where they are likely to fail.

People also rely on their physical and emotional states to judge their capabilities. They read their tension, anxiety, and depression as signs of personal deficiency. In activities that require strength and stamina, they interpret fatigue and pain as indicators of low physical efficacy.

Diverse Effects of Self-Efficacy

Beliefs of personal efficacy regulate human functioning through four major types of process; cognitive, motivational, emotional, and choice. Much human behavior is regulated by forethought. People of high efficacy set challenges for themselves and visualize success scenarios that provide positive guides for performance. Those who doubt their efficacy visualize failure scenarios that undermine performances by dwelling on things that can go wrong. A major function of thought is to enable people to predict events and to exercise control over them. People of high efficacy show greater cognitive resourcefulness, strategic flexibility, and effectiveness in managing their environment.

Efficacy beliefs play a central role in the self-regulation of motivation. Most human motivation is generated cognitively by goal aspirations and the material, social, and self-evaluative costs and benefits anticipated for difficult courses of action. People of high perceived efficacy set motivating goals for themselves, they expect their efforts to produce favorable results, they view obstacles as surmountable, and they figure out ways to overcome them.

People's beliefs in their coping efficacy also affect how much stress, anxiety, and depression they experience in threatening or taxing situations. Those who believe they can manage threats and adversities view them as less inimical and act in ways that reduce their aversiveness or change them for the better. People have to live with a psychic environment that is largely of their own making. Many human distresses result from failures of control over perturbing thoughts. Beliefs of coping efficacy facilitate the exercise of control over perturbing and dejecting rumination.

People are partly the products of their environments. By choosing their environments, they can have a hand in what they become. Beliefs of personal efficacy can, therefore, play a key role in shaping the courses lives take by influencing the types of activities and environments people choose. In self-development through choice processes, destinies are shaped by selection of environments known to cultivate valued potentialities and lifestyles.

People with a low sense of efficacy avoid difficult tasks that they view as threats. They have low aspirations and weak commitment to their goals. They turn inward on their self-doubts instead of thinking about how to perform successfully. When faced with difficult tasks, they dwell on obstacles, the consequences of failure, and their personal deficiencies. Failure makes them lose faith in themselves because they take it as evidence of their inherent incapability. They slacken or give up in the face of difficulty, recover slowly from setbacks, and easily fall victim to stress and depression.

People with high perceived self-efficacy, by contrast, approach difficult tasks as challenges to be mastered rather than threats to be avoided. They develop interest in what they do, set high goals, and sustain strong commitments. They concentrate on the task, not on themselves. They attribute their failures to remediable lack of knowledge or skill, or insufficient effort. They redouble their effort in the face of obstacles and soon recover their self-assurance after a setback. This outlook sustains motivation, reduces stress, and lowers vulnerability to depression.

Everyday reality is strewn with difficulties—full of impediments, adversities, setbacks, frustrations, and inequities. People must have a robust sense of personal efficacy to sustain the perseverant effort needed to succeed. In pursuits strewn with impediments, realists either forsake difficult pursuits, abort their efforts prematurely when difficulties arise, or become cynical about the prospects of effecting change. An optimistic sense of efficacy is an adaptive bias that promotes accomplishments and emotional well-being; it is not a cognitive failing.

Collective Efficacy

People do not live as isolates. They work together to secure what they cannot accomplish on their own. People's shared beliefs in their collective efficacy to produce desired outcomes is a crucial ingredient of group agency. Such beliefs influence the type of futures people seek to achieve through collective action, how well they use their resources, how much effort they put into their group endeavor, their staying power when collective efforts fail to produce quick results or meet forcible opposition, and their vulnerability to the discouragement that can beset those taking on tough problems that are not easily controllable.

Some people live in individualistically oriented cultures, others in more collectivistically oriented ones. If people are to work together successfully, the members have to perform their particular roles well. A strong sense of efficacy is, therefore, vital for successful functioning regardless of whether it is achieved individually or by people working in concert.

[See also Personality.]

Bibliography

Bandura, A. (Ed.). (1995). *Self-efficacy in changing societies.* New York: Cambridge University Press.

Bandura, A. (1997). *Self-efficacy: The exercise of control.* New York: Freeman.

Maddux, J. E. (Ed.). (1995). *Self-efficacy, adaptation, and adjustment: Theory, research and application.* New York: Plenum.

Schwarzer, R. (Ed.). (1992). *Self-efficacy: Thought control of action.* Washington, DC: Hemisphere.

Albert Bandura

SELF-ESTEEM. Evaluation is the most fundamental response we have to objects and events in the world around us. When that evaluative response concerns ourselves it is known as self-esteem. Self-esteem is a global evaluation reflecting our view of our accomplishments and capabilities, our values, our bodies, others' responses to us, and even, on occasion, our possessions. Low or negative self-esteem is often aversive and is correlated with depression. Positive self-esteem is thought to be important to psychological adjustment.

Mechanisms for Maintaining Self-Esteem

Contemporary research has uncovered so many different mechanisms that appear to affect self-esteem that they have been collectively referred to as the self zoo (Tesser, Martin, & Cornell, 1996). We can touch on only a small sample here. For example, there are a number of studies that indicate that simply giving an individual an opportunity to espouse his or her cherished values can positively affect self-esteem (e.g., Steele, 1988).

Esteem is often affected by how well or poorly a person performs, particularly in comparison to others. According to the self-evaluation maintenance model (e.g., Tesser, 1988), the impact of relative performance on self-evaluation is determined by the psychological closeness of self and other and the relevance of the performance dimension to one's self-definition. Being outperformed on a highly self-relevant dimension by a close other will threaten self-esteem via a comparison process; being outperformed on a minimally self-relevant dimension by a close other might actually increase self-esteem via "basking in reflected glory." See Tesser (1988) for a review of validating research.

According to the theory of cognitive dissonance (Aronson, 1969), doing something that is inconsistent with an important belief or value may be threatening to the self and motivates the individual to restore consistency. For example, an individual who endorses a defective product for very little reward will experience more inconsistency/threat and be under greater pressure to restore consistency than an individual who endorses the product for a huge reward. Thus, we would expect the former individual more than the latter to come to believe that the product is really effective. Numerous studies support this kind of prediction.

The mechanisms that affect self-esteem are often quite unlike one another. Merely affirming who one is, self-other performance differentials, and belief discrepancies all affect self-esteem. Because these mechanisms are so different from one another, there is a question of whether self-esteem maintenance is a unitary process or several independent mechanisms. If self-esteem were a unitary process, then engaging in one mechanism would repair damage to self-esteem due to a different mechanism. For example, affirming the self would repair a reduction in self-esteem due to behaving inconsistently. If the mechanisms were independent then the only way to repair a threat from one mechanism would be by engaging the same mechanism. A threat to self-esteem based on the discrepancy between act and belief, for example, could only be restored by changing the relevant attitude and not by simply reaffirming an important (but irrelevant) value or basking in a friend's reflected glory. Research (Steele, 1988; Tesser, Martin, & Cornell, 1996) suggests that self-esteem is, indeed, a unitary process and not a collection of independent processes. If we think of each of these mechanisms as a stream, then self-esteem is the confluence where they come together to influence one another. More work is needed to help us understand the precise process(es) by which this influence comes about.

Self-Concept and Self-Esteem

The distinction between cognitive and affective responses dovetails with the concepts of self-concept and self-esteem. Self-concept refers to what we believe about ourselves and self-esteem is related to how we feel about or evaluate ourselves. There is substantial research on the processes by which we come to know ourselves, how information about the self is processed differently from other information, and the way information about the self is structured. Strongly endorsed characteristics of the self are associated with cognitive structures called schemas (Markus, 1977). These self-schemas are easily evoked, they guide us to relevant information, and they are resistant to change.

Self-concept and self-esteem are related. Generally persons who believe they are moral, competent, good-looking, and so on will have higher self-esteem than persons who do not hold such beliefs. But there is a more subtle structural relationship between self-esteem and self-concept; the more clearly defined one's self-concept, the higher one's self-esteem (Campbell, 1990).

Some Correlates of Self-Esteem

Because self-esteem is so important to psychological functioning, we might expect it to be correlated with a variety of other variables. Indeed, it is. Self-esteem has been reported to be associated with desire for control, hope, achievement motivation, loneliness (negatively), self-determination, anxiety (negatively), positive affect, need for approval, depression (negatively), and aggression (negatively; e.g., Wylie, 1974). Historically, one could caricature the work on self-esteem as follows: Self-esteem, a good thing, is associated with the presence of other good things and the absence of bad things. The world is not that simple.

Work on aggression makes the point extremely well (Baumeister, Smart, & Boden, 1996). Although there have been a number of suggestions that violent behavior is associated with low self-esteem, Baumeister, Smart, and Boden's (1996) interdisciplinary review of the evidence is not consistent with this expectation. Rather, they find that violence becomes more likely when a person's highly favorable view of self is contradicted by another person or situation. An individual whose positive self-view is accurate is less likely to be confronted with contradictory information than an individual whose positive self-view is inflated, unstable, or unclear. Their review suggests that murder and assault, rape, and domestic violence are often associated with threats to honor and threats to feelings of male superiority. Moreover, unstable persons with high self-esteem are more aggressive than others (Kernis & Waschull, 1995).

Measuring Self-Esteem

From the perspective of measurement, it may be useful to think of self-esteem as a traitlike construct. As noted, there is work that shows situational effects on self-esteem and the importance of temporal instability in self-esteem. Nevertheless, there may be aspects of self-esteem that are cross-situationally consistent and relatively enduring, and the trait approach has proven quite useful. Most contemporary measures of self-esteem are based on self-reports using structured response alternatives.

The most widely used measure of self-esteem is a 10-item instrument devised by Morris Rosenberg (1965). The items elicit reports of the extent to which respondents endorse straightforward self-evaluative statements, such as "I feel that I am a person of worth, at least on an equal basis with others." Generally, for each statement one of the following response options is available: Strongly Agree, Agree, Disagree, Strongly Disagree. In typical Likert fashion, each item is weighted by strength of agreement/disagreement and the weights are summed over items to produce a total score. The scale is reasonably internally consistent and reliable over time.

There are two crucial issues involved in interpreting such self-report scores. First, will persons accurately report their self-esteem? Here one must be concerned with a variety of issues that psychometricians deal with perennially. Do different participants use the scale with the same calibration? What are the influences of response sets such as the tendency to agree and, particularly in the case of self-esteem, to try to appear socially desirable? The second issue is even more fundamental than the first. Do individuals even know how positively they evaluate the self? Are there aspects of self-esteem that are consequential but not available to conscious awareness? Some of the work reviewed above suggests that there are often aspects of self-esteem that are consequential for behavior but work outside of the individual's conscious awareness. Indeed, recent work on implicit memory and automaticity in stereotypes and attitudes has suggested that there may be important, implicit, or, in other words, nonconscious elements of self-esteem. The notion of implicit or unconscious self-esteem has a well-developed history in psychoanalysis (Westen, 1992).

Greenwald and Banaji (1995) define implicit self-esteem as "the introspectively unidentified (or inaccurately identified) effect of the self-attitude on evaluation of self-associated and self-dissociated objects" (p. 11). They see evidence for implicit self-esteem in a variety of well-established phenomena: The "mere ownership effect," in which objects become more positively evaluated by simply belonging to the self; the "minimal group effect," whereby regardless of how arbitrary the grouping, members of one's own group are treated more favorably then members of other groups; and the "initial letter effect" whereby individuals tend to like the letters in their own names, particularly the first letters of their names, more than other alphabet letters. No "standard measure" of implicit self-esteem has yet surfaced although researchers are exploring a variety of possibilities. Given its popularity in other areas of current work, it seems likely such a measure will involve latencies in making judgments involving the self.

The Impact of Culture

Culture appears to play a large role in determining how one construes the self. According to Markus and Kitayama (1991), Western cultures (e.g., the United States) and Eastern cultures (e.g., Japan) differ markedly in self-construal. The former is associated with an independent view of self, the latter with an interdependent view of self. For example, the kinds of tasks confronting the self for Western versus Eastern cultures may be described as follows: be unique versus belong, fit in; express self versus occupy one's proper place; realize internal attributes versus engage in appropriate action; promote own goals versus promote others' goals; be direct, "say what's on your mind" versus be indirect, "read other's mind" (Markus & Kitayama, 1991, Table 1, p. 230). In Western cultures, others are important as sources of comparison; in Eastern cultures one's relationship with others helps to define the self. In Western cultures self-esteem is associated with being able to express one's internal convictions, being a "winner" (or being associated with winners), and validating internal attributes. In Eastern cultures, one is "self-satisfied" to the extent that one can fit in and harmonize with the social context. These descriptions and a number of cross-cultural studies suggest that the difference between Eastern versus Western construals of self is substantial. Understanding this difference may help to explain other behavioral differences between these cultures.

[*See also* Self-Concept and Self-Representation.]

Bibliography

Aronson, E. (1969). The theory of cognitive dissonance: A current perspective. In L. Berkowitz (Ed.), *Advances in experimental social psychology* (Vol. 4, pp. 2–32). New York: Academic Press.

Baumeister, R. F., Smart, L., & Boden, J. M. (1996). Relation of threatened egotism to violence and aggression: The dark side of high self-esteem. *Psychological Review, 103*, 5–33.

Campbell, J. D. (1990). Self-esteem and clarity of the self-concept. *Journal of Personality and Social Psychology, 99*, 538–549.

Greenwald, A. G., & Banaji. M. (1995). Implicit social cognition: Attitudes, self-esteem, and stereotypes. *Psychological Review, 102,* 4–27.

Kernis, M. H., & Waschull, S. B. (1995). The interactive roles of stability and level of self-esteem: Research and theory. In M. P. Zanna (Ed.), *Advances in experimental social psychology* (Vol. 27, pp. 94–142). San Diego, CA: Academic Press.

Markus, H. (1977). Self-schemata and processing information about the self. *Journal of Personality and Social Psychology, 35,* 63–78.

Markus, H., & Kitayama, S. (1991). Culture and the self: Implications for cognition, emotion, and motivation. *Psychological Review, 98,* 224–253.

Rosenberg, M. (1965). *Society and the adolescent self-image.* Princeton, NJ: Princeton University Press.

Steele, C. M. (1988). The psychology of self-affirmation: Sustaining the integrity of self. In L. Berkowitz (Ed.), *Advances in experimental social psychology* (Vol. 21, pp. 261–302). New York: Academic Press.

Tesser, A. (1988). Toward a self-evaluation maintenance model of social behavior. In L. Berkowitz (Ed.), *Advances in experimental social psychology* (Vol. 21, pp. 181–227). New York: Academic Press.

Tesser, A., Martin, L., & Cornell, D. (1996). On the substitutability of self-protective mechanisms. In P. M. Gollwitzer & J. A. Bargh (Eds.), *The psychology of action: Linking motivation and cognition to behavior* (pp. 48–68). New York: Guilford Press.

Westen, D. (1992). The cognitive self and the psychoanalytic self: Can we put ourselves together? *Psychological Inquiry, 3,* 1–14.

Wylie, R. C. (1974). *The self-concept* (Rev. ed., Vol. 1) Lincoln: University of Nebraska Press.

Abraham Tesser

SELF-EVALUATION. *See* Self-Concept and Self-Representation.

SELF-FOCUSED ATTENTION. *See* Defense Mechanisms; *and* Self-Consciousness.

SELF-FULFILLING PROPHECY. In social interactions, people often use their preconceived beliefs and expectations about others to guide their behavior. Their behavior, in turn, may influence their interaction partners to act in ways that confirm the initial beliefs. This phenomenon, in which belief creates reality, is known by several names—the self-fulfilling prophecy, expectancy confirmation, and behavioral confirmation.

Research on this phenomenon comes predominantly from two domains: field studies of teacher expectations and laboratory studies of social interaction sequences. For example, Rosenthal and Jacobson (1968) demonstrated that teachers who were led to expect particular patterns of performance from their students acted in ways that created a self-fulfilling prophecy—the actual performance of the students, measured 8 months later, confirmed the teachers' initial expectations. Laboratory investigations of behavioral confirmation in social interaction typically have documented how one person (the perceiver), having adopted erroneous beliefs about another person (the target), acts in ways that lead the target to confirm these beliefs. In one experiment, Snyder, Tanke, and Berscheid (1977) examined the effects on interactions between college-aged men and women of the stereotyped belief that physically attractive people have appealing personalities. Before a telephone conversation with a female partner, each man was randomly assigned a photograph (ostensibly of his partner) of a physically attractive or a physically unattractive woman. Men who believed their partners to be attractive treated them with more warmth and friendliness than men who believed their partners to be unattractive. As a result, women thought to be attractive reciprocated these overtures and actually came to behave in a friendly and sociable manner; in contrast, women thought to be unattractive became cool and aloof during the conversations.

Self-fulfilling prophecies have been demonstrated in a wide variety of contexts and for a wide range of expectations, including beliefs about gender, race, age, and personality, as well as expectations of being liked or disliked, hypotheses about other people, self-images, imputations of stigma, and arbitrary designations of ability (see Jussim, 1986; Miller & Turnbull, 1986; Snyder, 1984, 1992). Discussions of the mechanisms of these phenomena have focused on four steps in the interaction sequence: (1) perceivers adopt beliefs about targets, (2) perceivers treat targets as if these beliefs were true, (3) targets assimilate their behavior to perceivers' overtures, and (4) perceivers interpret targets' behavior as confirming their beliefs. Much research has examined the second step of this sequence, specifically how perceivers elicit confirmation of their beliefs. Snyder and Swann (1978) suggested that self-fulfilling effects may result from confirmatory hypothesis-testing strategies. Perceivers motivated to determine whether a target fits their expectation typically ask questions that preferentially seek confirmatory evidence. Studies suggest that these confirmatory strategies also may reflect perceivers' social competence and help to create an appearance of empathy between perceivers and targets (e.g., Dardenne & Leyens, 1995; Leyens, Dardenne, & Fiske, 1998). Thus confirmatory strategies may have social value, increasing the smoothness and pleasantness of interaction, at the same time as they may initiate self-fulfilling prophecy sequences.

Researchers have also examined the psychological processes that underlie and motivate behavioral confirmation and disconfirmation. That is, they have sought to understand why perceivers act on their beliefs in ways that initiate self-fulfilling prophecies and why targets come to behave in ways that confirm or disconfirm expectations. Thus studies have examined the goals that perceivers and targets bring to their interactions and how these interaction goals influence the dynamics and outcomes of the ensuing interactions (e.g., Hilton & Darley, 1991). Other analyses have focused on the social and psychological functions served by the activities of perceivers and targets; this research has revealed that, when behavioral confirmation occurs in interactions between new acquaintances, perceivers typically have been acting to acquire knowledge about their partner, whereas targets have been seeking to facilitate the interaction (see Snyder, 1992).

Structural characteristics of interactions (such as the relative power and status of perceivers and targets) and their influence on self-fulfilling prophecies have also received attention. Copeland (1994) examined interactions in which either the perceiver or the target was randomly assigned to have power over the other's outcomes (by deciding eligibility for a prize). A self-fulfilling prophecy was demonstrated only when the perceiver had the power; when targets had the power, no such effect occurred. This suggests that power dynamics may underlie the perpetuation of social stereotypes by way of the self-fulfilling prophecy.

Still, as widespread as self-fulfilling effects appear, they are not inevitable. Evidence suggests that there may be definite functional and structural prerequisites for self-fulfilling prophecies to occur; that is, specific motivations of perceivers and targets (see Snyder, 1992), as well as the power differential inherent in their roles (e.g., Copeland, 1994), may be necessary to initiate the phenomenon of behavioral confirmation. Additionally, in some naturalistic settings, when expectations are based on especially valid or detailed information (such as a previous year's academic performance), relationships between expectations and later behavior may be due to the accuracy of the expectations to a greater extent than to the self-fulfilling aspects of the expectations (see Jussim, Eccles, & Madon, 1996). Under certain circumstances (for example, when perceivers are motivated to make targets like them; Neuberg, Judice, Virdin, & Carrillo, 1993), too, actions by perceivers and targets produce interactions culminating in the target's behaving contrary to the perceiver's expectations—behavioral disconfirmation (see Snyder, 1984, 1992). In some of these latter studies, however, perceivers clung to their initial expectations, thus demonstrating perceptual confirmation in the face of behavioral disconfirmation.

Although relatively little research has examined the longer-term consequences of self-fulfilling prophecies, several continuing effects are possible. First, targets' self-concepts may change as a result of self-perception of their confirmatory actions (e.g., Bem, 1972). Second, "evidence" of confirmation may be taken by perceivers to justify further expectation-based treatment of targets that could have life-affecting consequences.

For social scientists, then, the self-fulfilling prophecy is of special importance. It casts the reciprocal relationship between "subjective" cognition and "objective" behavior in ongoing social interaction into high relief, allowing focused research with significant theoretical and practical implications.

Bibliography

Bem, D. J. (1972). Self-perception theory. In L. Berkowitz (Ed.), *Advances in experimental social psychology* (Vol. 6, pp. 1–62). New York: Academic Press.

Copeland, J. T. (1994). Prophecies of power: Motivational implications of social power for behavioral confirmation. *Journal of Personality and Social Psychology, 67,* 264–277.

Dardenne, B., & Leyens, J. P. (1995). Confirmation bias as a social skill. *Personality and Social Psychology Bulletin, 21,* 1229–1239.

Hilton, J. L., & Darley, J. M. (1991). The effects of interaction goals on person perception. In M. P. Zanna (Ed.), *Advances in experimental social psychology* (Vol. 24, pp. 236–267). Orlando, FL: Academic Press.

Jussim, L. (1986). Self-fulfilling prophecies: A theoretical and integrative review. *Psychological Review, 93,* 429–445. Reviews research on teachers' expectations in the classroom.

Jussim, L., Eccles, J., & Madon, S. (1996). Social perception, social stereotypes, and teacher expectations: Accuracy and the quest for the powerful self-fulfilling prophecy. In M. P. Zanna (Ed.), *Advances in experimental social psychology* (Vol. 28, pp. 281–388). Orlando, FL: Academic Press.

Leyens, J. P., Dardenne, B., & Fiske, S. T. (1998). Why and under what circumstances is a hypothesis-consistent testing preferred in interviews? *British Journal of Social Psychology.*

Miller, D. T., & Turnbull, W. (1986). Expectancies and interpersonal processes. *Annual Review of Psychology, 37,* 233–256. Reviews research on perceptual confirmation and behavioral confirmation.

Neuberg, S., Judice, T. N., Virdin, L. M., & Carrillo, M. A. (1993). Perceiver self-presentation goals as moderators of expectancy influences: Ingratiation and the disconfirmation of negative expectancies. *Journal of Personality and Social Psychology, 64,* 409–420.

Rosenthal, R., & Jacobson, L. (1968). *Pygmalion in the classroom: Teacher expectation and pupils' intellectual development.* New York: Holt, Rinehart, & Winston.

Snyder, M. (1984). When belief creates reality. In L. Berkowitz (Ed.), *Advances in experimental social psychology* (Vol. 18, pp. 248–305). Orlando, FL: Academic Press.

Reviews the literature on behavioral confirmation in social interaction.

Snyder, M. (1992). Motivational foundations of behavioral confirmation. In M. P. Zanna (Ed.), *Advances in experimental social psychology* (Vol. 25, pp. 67–114). Orlando, FL: Academic Press. Details a theory of the motivations that lead perceivers and targets to confirm expectations.

Snyder, M., & Swann, W. B., Jr. (1978). Hypothesis-testing processes in social interaction. *Journal of Personality and Social Psychology, 36,* 1202–1212.

Snyder, M., Tanke, E. D., & Berscheid, E. (1977). Social perception and interpersonal behavior: On the self-fulfilling nature of social stereotypes. *Journal of Personality and Social Psychology, 35,* 656–666.

Mark Snyder and Arthur A. Stukas, Jr.

SELF-HELP THERAPY. *See* Mutual-Help and Self-Help.

SELF-MONITORING. *See* Self-Concept and Self-Representation.

SELF-PRESENTATION. *See* Impression Management; *and* Self-Concept and Self-Representation.

SELF-PSYCHOLOGY. *See* Psychoanalysis; *and the biography of Rogers.*

SELF-REGULATION. The root of the word *motivation* is "to move." The movement concerns approaching or avoiding some outcome by making something happen or not happen. Self-regulation occurs when people attempt to approach or avoid some outcome through their own actions, states, or attributes by doing or not doing something, being or not being something. There are three central issues concerning people's self-regulation that have been examined in the psychological literature—why it occurs, how it occurs, and what occurs after it succeeds or fails.

Why Does Self-Regulation Occur?

From the ancient Greeks through seventeenth- and eighteenth century British philosophers to twentieth-century psychologists, the dominant answer to this question has been that people self-regulate in order to approach pleasure and avoid pain—the hedonic principle. This basic answer to why people self-regulate appears throughout psychology, including theories of emotion in psychobiology, conditioning in animal learning, decision making in cognitive and organizational psychology, consistency in social psychology, and achievement motivation in personality psychology. In his classic book *Beyond the Pleasure Principle* (1920/1950), Freud describes how even the reality principle, which goes "beyond pleasure" in its sensitivity to environmental demands, simply modifies the pleasure principle by making avoiding pain almost equal in importance to gaining pleasure. (For a review of the hedonic principle, see Higgins, 1997).

The distinction between intrinsic and extrinsic reasons for self-regulation provides another answer to why self-regulation occurs. This distinction does not contradict the hedonic principle, but it highlights the fact that the reason a person approaches or engages in some activity also matters. People can engage in an activity as an end in itself (intrinsic motivation), as when a person plays with something to learn how it works, or people can engage in the same activity as simply a means to an end (extrinsic motivation), as when a person does an activity just to please someone else who has asked him or her to do it (see Deci & Ryan, 1985; Kruglanski, 1975). If the initial engagement in an activity is perceived as controlled by others, a person's interest in engaging again in the activity can be undermined.

How Does Self-Regulation Occur?

This is a central question for psychologists because just knowing that people approach pleasure and avoid pain is insufficient to account for the observed complexities of people's self-regulation. There are three general answers to the question of how people approach pleasure and avoid pain. One is regulatory anticipation. Freud (1920/1950) described self-regulation as a "hedonism of the future" in which behavior and other psychical activities are driven by anticipations of pleasure to be approached (wishes) and anticipations of pain to be avoided (fears). Mowrer (1960) proposed that the fundamental nature of self-regulation was to approach hoped-for end states and avoid feared end states. Atkinson's (1964) theory of achievement motivation distinguished between the approach tendencies of individuals with a "hope of success" and the avoidance tendencies of individuals with a "fear of failure." The principle of regulatory anticipation is important because it concerns the role of expectancies in self-regulation.

A second general answer to how self-regulation approaches pleasure and avoids pain is regulatory reference. Independent of whether pleasant or painful outcomes are anticipated, self-regulatory movement can have either desired or undesired end states as its reference point. Anticipating a pleasant outcome, for example, could involve either approach movement in reference to a desired end state or avoidance movement in reference to an undesired end state. Depending on the reference point, different pleasant emotions would be experienced—such as a feeling of satisfaction from successfully attaining an A in a course versus a feeling of relief at successfully avoiding less than an A in the course. The distinction between desired end states and undesired end states as reference points for approach versus avoidance movement, respectively, is found in animal-learning, clinical, and social psychological models of self-regulation. Regulatory reference as a principle of self-regulation is most developed in control-process models (Carver & Scheier, 1981). The principle of regulatory reference is important because it concerns the role of standards in self-regulation.

A third general answer to how self-regulation occurs concerns the strategic means by which outcomes are attained. Independent of whether pleasant or painful outcomes are anticipated and whether the reference point for movement is a desired end state or an undesired end state, there are different strategies that can be used to attain some outcome. To attain the desired goal, such as receiving an A in a course, people can use either approach strategies (e.g., pursue all means of advancement) or avoidance strategies (e.g., carefully avoid any mistakes). There are two types of regulatory focus that influence the strategies selected. The first type is a promotion focus that represents a desired goal as the presence of a positive outcome, such as when goals are represented as accomplishments or aspirations. The second type is a prevention focus that represents a desired goal as the absence of a negative outcome, such as when goals are represented as safety or responsibility. Individuals in a promotion focus tend to use approach strategies for goal attainment, whereas individuals in a prevention focus tend to use avoidance strategies. The principle of regulatory focus is important because it concerns the role of strategic inclinations in self-regulation. (See Higgins, 1997, for a review of the principles of regulatory anticipation, reference, and focus.)

The principles of regulatory anticipation, reference, and focus provide general answers to the question of how self-regulation occurs. There are also more specific answers. There are specific self-regulatory strategies and tactics for strengthening willpower or maintaining self-control in the face of temptations, distractions, and barriers that challenge self-regulation (Mischel, Cantor, & Feldman, 1996). There are also specific strategies for controlling what enters conscious thought. The psychological literature has described both unconscious (or preconscious) mechanisms for defending against unwanted thoughts or urges and conscious effortful strategies of mental control (Wegner & Wenzlaff, 1996). Perceptions of self-control also influence how self-regulation occurs, such as people's self-evaluations of how they are doing and their self-efficacy beliefs (Bandura, 1986). How self-regulation functions also varies across different phases of goal attainment, such as the "deliberative" mindset, when a person must decide which goal to pursue, and the "implemental" mindset, when a person must commit to a plan of action (Gollwitzer, 1990).

What Occurs When Self-Regulation Succeeds or Fails?

Self-regulation is not involved only when a person works to approach or avoid some outcome. Individuals also experience pleasant or painful states after such approach or avoidance succeeds or fails, and these states themselves become targets of self-regulation. A central issue is how people deal with the pain of self-regulatory failure. Some responses to failure, such as denial, can be dysfunctional and impair subsequent self-regulation. Severe impairment from dysfunctional responses can produce clinical symptoms. But even for nonpathological responses, there are different ways that individuals respond to self-regulatory failure. Individuals respond differently depending on how they interpret the implications of the failure, such as whether they interpret failure on a test as reflecting low intelligence that cannot be changed or as just a current state that can be improved through learning (Dweck & Leggett, 1988). Individuals also vary in whether their coping strategies involve dealing with the failure itself by attempting to change whatever made it occur (problem-focused coping) or whether they involve dealing with the pain that the failure produced by attempting to reduce the pain itself (emotion-focused coping; Lazarus, 1966).

Self-regulation is fundamental to people's lives. It not only concerns why and how people attain their goals, fulfill their needs, and cope with life problems, but it also underlies the very nature of everyday experiences of living.

Bibliography

Atkinson, J. W. (1964). *An introduction to motivation*. Princeton, NJ: Van Nostrand.

Bandura, A. (1986). *Social foundations of thought and action: A social cognitive theory*. Englewood Cliffs, NJ: Prentice Hall.

Carver, C. S., & Scheier, M. F. (1981). *Attention and self-regulation: A control-theory approach to human behavior*. New York: Springer-Verlag.

Deci, E. L., & Ryan, R. M. (1985). *Intrinsic motivation and self-determination in human behavior.* New York: Plenum Press.

Dweck, C. S., & Leggett, E. L. (1988). A social-cognitive approach to motivation and personality. *Psychological Review, 95,* 256–273.

Freud, S. (1950). *Beyond the pleasure principle.* New York: Liveright. (Original work published 1920)

Gollwitzer, P. M. (1990). Action phases and mind-sets. In E. T. Higgins & R. M. Sorrentino (Eds.), *Handbook of motivation and cognition: Foundations of social behavior* (Vol. 2, pp. 53–92). New York: Guilford Press.

Higgins, E. T. (1997). Beyond pleasure and pain. *American Psychologist, 52,* 1280–1300.

Kruglanski, A. W. (1975). The endogenous-exogenous partition in attribution theory. *Psychological Review, 82,* 387–406.

Lazarus, R. S. (1966). *Psychological stress and the coping process.* New York: McGraw-Hill.

Mischel, W., Cantor, N., & Feldman, S. (1996). Principles of self-regulation: The nature of willpower and self-control. In E. T. Higgins & A. W. Kruglanski (Eds.), *Social psychology: Handbook of basic principles* (pp. 329–360). New York: Guilford Press.

Mowrer, O. H. (1960). *Learning theory and behavior.* New York: Wiley.

Wegner, D. M., & Wenzlaff, R. M. (1996). Mental control. In E. T. Higgins & A. W. Kruglanski (Eds.), *Social psychology: Handbook of basic principles* (pp. 466–492). New York: Guilford Press.

E. Tory Higgins

SELF-REPORT can be defined as a respondent's direct appraisal of his or her standing with respect to a target construct or behavior. Such reports can be collected using a variety of strategies—from structured interviews to standardized inventories to mailed surveys. In collecting self-report data, the psychologist makes a very important assumption: that people are capable of meaningful introspection about their psychological status on the variable of interest and can be relied on to report about it in a meaningful way.

An argument for the use of self-report data can be made on intuitive grounds. Who knows more about a person's own feelings and motivations than the person him- or herself? Nevertheless, the logical counterargument also deserves careful consideration: What if self-reports are simply not veridical? We consider these possibilities as we explore the history of self-report, its use, and its validity and invalidity in various domains.

History of Self-Report

Like many important innovations in psychological science, the modern self-report questionnaire may be traced back to Francis Galton, a brilliant British scientist active in the late nineteenth century. Galton is well known for his interest in the origins of human individual differences and the so-called nature versus nurture debate (a phrase he coined). To learn more about the role of nature versus nurture in the achievement of eminence in science, Galton wrote a series of questions designed to tap scientists' own opinions regarding their professional interests and achievements. Did they believe their interest in science was due to nature or nurture? Obviously, Galton's data were subjective in nature, as he was simply asking for peoples' opinions, rather than directly disentangling the roles of nature and nurture (although he also outlined the basic logic of using twins to do precisely that). Nevertheless, Galton's work presaged the modern "opinion polls" that have become so much a part of our daily lives. The very idea of asking an identified sample of people what their opinions are on an important issue of the day may be traced to Galton's innovative ideas.

A subsequent historical development in the use of self-report data—like other key historical moments in psychological testing—can be traced to World War I. With the United States at war, those professionals in the fledging field of psychology wanted to help with the effort. Thus, Robert Woodworth, of the psychology department at Columbia University, developed the Personal Data Sheet to aid in identifying recruits who were unfit for duty. The Data Sheet asked about problematic "neurotic" symptoms (e.g., sleepwalking) and was scored simply by adding up the number of symptoms the respondent endorsed. The scale was obviously prone to dissimulation, for example, faking responses to avoid military service. Although this was a problem for the Personal Data Sheet, it highlighted an important issue to be addressed by future self-report measures. Specifically, more sophisticated self-report inventories were later developed to detect both problematic psychological symptoms and potential dissimulation simultaneously (e.g., the Minnesota Multiphasic Personality Inventory or MMPI).

Indeed, the question of the veridicality of self-report became a major stumbling block for the method as psychologists in later decades (the 1950s and 1960s) debated whether self-report inventories were simply measures of response styles rather than measures of important psychological characteristics. A response style refers to the idea that people are responding to self-report items in a manner that is independent of their intended content. Thus, instead of measuring what one intends to measure, one is instead unwittingly measuring something like acquiescence (the tendency to say "yes" or "true") or social desirability (the tendency to endorse items that describe characteristics that most people find desirable, such as kindness or popularity). For example, much effort was expended in determining if a large part of the variance in responses to the MMPI could be attributed to social desirability, rather than to actual maladjustment (Block, 1965).

Block's conclusion was that MMPI responses contained more substance (actual maladjustment) than style (social desirability).

Such debates are important for a developing science, and they continue to promote valuable intellectual interchange to this day. Nevertheless, we feel that a pragmatic view on the utility of a self-report measure is most useful for the daily work of a psychologist. Essentially, the value of a self-report instrument comes down to its construct validity; does a given self-report instrument generate data that behave as they should, given current theories about important behavioral, psychological, and social outcomes that should be linked to that instrument?

Status of Self-Report in Psychological Research

Self-report has served psychological science well. The main virtues of self-report measures are ease of administration and relatively lower cost. In a typical self-report study, respondents are given a questionnaire on which they record their responses. Alternative means of collecting psychological data, such as observer ratings or physiological measures, require additional expenditure of money and effort, such as identifying and recruiting observers or purchasing expensive equipment and training assistants in its use. Thus, if self-reports in a given domain can be trusted, they represent a more efficient means of gathering data.

When can self-reports be trusted? As noted, they can be trusted when empirical evidence has shown that they generate valid data. For example, many self-report instruments of personality traits are valid. First, respondents' descriptions of themselves on self-report personality instruments agree with descriptions offered by observers who know the respondents well. Second, self-report measures of personality are highly predictive of important and consequential outcomes, such as crime, health-risk behaviors, and mental disorders. Another domain in which self-report has been used successfully is the field of coping research. Coping styles, assessed via self-report, have been useful in predicting adjustment to a variety of life challenges.

There are problems, however, in relying too heavily on self-report, even in the study of personality and coping. When assessments are made using only one method, any relationship between scales may be due to shared method of assessment, rather than relationships between constructs. Such method variance is ubiquitous, and its influence can be understood only by assessing constructs using varied methods. Thus, even in domains where self-reports are valid, they need not represent the sole source of data. Indeed, self-reports can be profitably thought of as one prong of a multifaceted data collection strategy.

Consider research on delinquency. A common assumption is that official sources of delinquency data, such as police reports, provide the most valid data. After all, the police have no reason to misrepresent a person's criminal record; their work relies on the accuracy of such records. The problem is that because of differential detection of deviance by the police only a fraction of the total illegal behavior in a population is reflected in official statistics. Specifically, White, middle-class, and female offenders are often underrepresented in official crime statistics. Thus, delinquency researchers have turned to self-reports as a less biased source of data. Self-reports of delinquency, however, are not without shortcomings. For example, they have been criticized for including trivial items, such as questions about defiance of parents. In addition, concerns have been raised about overreporting by less delinquent youth, who may endorse behaviors such as "assault" in reference to their most recent fight with their sibling. Similarly, concerns have been raised about underreporting by more delinquent youth, whose multiple delinquent actions may lose their salience. Thus, most delinquency experts regard the complementary use of official and self-report delinquency data as the optimal data collection strategy.

Consider also research on emotion. Some theories of emotion (for example, William James's view that emotions are, in essence, physiological responses) place self-reports on the periphery. Indeed, emotion is an area in which much research is performed using non-self-report indices, such as physiological measures. Such physiological measures have certain advantages over self-report, especially when the variable of interest is changes in emotions during a brief period of time. For example, many physiological measures are better at tracking changes in emotional experience because they are continually "on-line." Thus, they can sample such experiences at a higher frequency than repeated self-reports. In addition, the act of completing a self-report measure may alter emotional experience or interfere with the manipulation of emotions. For example, during exposure to an emotion-eliciting stimulus (e.g., a videotape), the act of completing self-report inventories may distract the respondent from the stimulus. Nevertheless, a complete theory of emotion should account for self-reported experiences of emotion, as well as physiological and behavioral concomitants. The subjective experience of an emotion (for example, the feeling of sadness, such that a person would report "I am sad") is as legitimately a part of emotional experience as behavior or physiology. Hence, emotion research, like delinquency research, is an area in which multiple measures—self-reports, behavioral measures, and physiological measures—are profitably used together to triangulate on the topic of interest.

Finally, self-report measures of substance use and abuse have many of the usual advantages of self-report measures in any area: They are easy to administer and score and are relatively less expensive than other modes of assessment (e.g., toxicology screens). However, beginning clinicians are often taught that the first rule of substance abuse assessment is that substance users are notoriously inaccurate. Such a perspective is limiting because current views in the field emphasize the context-dependent nature of substance abuse assessment. That is, self-reports in and of themselves are not reliable or unreliable, valid or invalid—their status depends on many factors. For example, memory problems resulting from heavy use of alcohol (i.e., alcohol-related dementia) could diminish the accuracy of self-report even if the respondent is motivated to respond honestly. Also, variables like treatment status and the consequences of providing a self-report can impact on reliability and/or validity. Thus, no invariant rule of thumb applies to all self-reports of substance use and abuse. Attention to the context in which such self-reports are collected is essential in determining their likely value.

In summary, self-report data are used frequently, often provide valid data, and are often used to complement other types of assessment. The value and role of self-reports in the assessment of any specific construct is best evaluated on a domain-by-domain and study-by-study basis. Universal recommendations, even within a specific area, are unwise because various contextual factors can influence the validity and utility of self-reports. Thus, it is incumbent upon the users of self-report instruments to document that their particular measure behaves as it should, given current theories about the construct it measures.

Limitations

Despite the popularity of self-report as a method of psychological assessment and its strengths in many areas, it is not without its limitations. First, not all reporters can be relied on to make reliable self-report judgments. Obviously, self-report methods of assessment cannot be used to study animal behavior. With regard to human participants, limitations in verbal skills or reading comprehension may preclude the use of self-report. For example, children may not possess the reading skills or the cognitive capacity to reflect and report on their own behavior. Thus, the assessment of abnormal behavior in children typically relies on the reports of knowledgeable others (e.g., teachers, parents). In addition, any individual who is developmentally delayed or has suffered a head injury should not be assessed via self-report. In such cases, ratings from knowledgeable others should be obtained.

Second, not all constructs of interest to psychologists can be studied via self-report. For example, some aspects of psychological functioning are believed to be unconscious. By definition, elements of the unconscious (e.g., defense mechanisms) are inaccessible to conscious introspection, and therefore cannot be assessed via self-report. Accordingly, alternative methods of assessment, such as projective tests (e.g., the Rorschach or the Thematic Apperception Test), have been developed for the measurement of unconscious motives.

Third, some constructs are jointly defined by both self-reports and data from another domain. For example, mental disorders are typically assessed by asking people to report on their recent experiences and observing not only the content of the reports, but also their form. For instance, although various self-report indices of psychotic thinking have been developed and are valuable clinical and research tools, they are not the primary means of rendering a psychiatric diagnosis, such as schizophrenia. The additional information needed for a clinical diagnosis is provided by a trained interviewer, who elicits the patient's self-report but augments this by observing the patient's behavior. Thus, although an individual with paranoid delusions may endorse a self-report item such as "other people are out to get me," the clinical interviewer can augment this information by seeing how it matches with his or her behavioral observations made during the interview (such as whether the patient scans the interview room continuously or seems to mistrust the interviewer's motives). The trained interviewer brings configural knowledge, involving both self-report and behavioral observation, to bear on the diagnostic assessment.

Finally, other constructs are not typically assessed via self-report because they are better assessed by comparing an individual's behavior against the behavior of others. For example, even though intelligence tests resemble self-report tests, in that respondents read and answer a series of questions, they cannot be considered self-report. At no time are respondents asked to report their perception of where they lie on the dimension of intelligence. Instead, items on an intelligence test elicit behaviors from the respondent that, when taken together, indicate his or her position on the underlying dimension of intelligence. Other tests of this type include assessments of short-term memory and achievement tests.

Process of Self-Report

Although the process of self-report seems simple enough—individuals typically read a question and then decide among various response options—it can be broken down into separate cognitive tasks. As with any process, problems anywhere along the way can derail the entire enterprise. By identifying and examining each component of the self-report process separately, researchers can find ways to improve their self-report measures.

When presented with a self-report question, the first task is comprehension, in which the respondent evaluates the meaning of the question. Comprehension can be disrupted by the use of scientific jargon or vague terms. It can be improved by ensuring that questions or items are phrased in ways that are easily understood by the people for whom the measure is intended. For example, some investigators have found that the language in questionnaires developed using college students must be simplified when such questionnaires are given to general population samples. Comprehension can be checked by piloting a new measure on a small sample from the population of interest, and then debriefing the respondents to determine if their understanding of the questions agrees with the meaning intended by the investigator.

The second task is information retrieval, in which respondents search their memory for relevant information. Problems at this stage occur when the individual is asked to recall too much information. To improve recall, the researcher could narrow the target of the question or the time frame involved. In addition, the researcher could provide visual aids to help with memory retrieval, rather than simply asking people to "look back across their entire lives." For example, respondents could be presented with a chart, on which various developmental milestones (e.g., marriage, birth of first child) are placed. Respondents can be prompted to, for example, "think back to the year when you got married." Such a procedure reduces the cognitive load placed on respondents and improves the quality of self-report data.

The third task is the judgment and decision stage, in which the respondent evaluates the retrieved information and determines whether it is sufficient to answer the question. Problems in this stage can occur if respondents deem their information incomplete yet offer a response. This problem may be circumvented by allowing respondents to indicate that they "don't know" or "can't remember." Such responses need not invalidate an item, as investigators can work with respondents who select these options to improve information retrieval and arrive at a "best guess" estimate. In addition, careful attention to response options and instructions can improve performance at this stage. For example, it is possible to clarify whether respondents are being asked to judge how their behavior compares to others, to their typical behavior, or in absolute terms. When such standards are provided, respondents are better able to judge the sufficiency of their information retrieval.

Even if the question is understood, information retrieval is sufficient, and a meaningful judgment is rendered, the respondent still has to execute a response. A variety of factors may interfere with this last stage of the self-report process. For example, respondents may choose a response that does not reflect their true belief because they wish to foster a certain impression or they do not want to acknowledge their own socially undesirable behavior. To avoid these potential biases, researchers need to impress upon the respondents the confidentiality of their responses during the informed consent process.

Recent research suggests that the manner in which people respond to an assessment instrument may influence the results. Specifically, computers have been used to gather self-report data regarding sexual behavior and drug use in adolescents. When results from the computer-guided assessments were compared to results from the more traditional paper-and-pencil questionnaires, it was found that adolescents were more likely to report engaging in certain high-risk behaviors when recording their answers directly into a computer (Turner et al., 1998).

Bibliography

Baker, T. B., & Brandon, T. H. (1990). Validity of self-reports in basic research. *Behavioral Assessment, 12,* 33–51. Reviews the utility of self-report measures in research on addiction.

Block, J. (1965). *Challenge of response sets.* New York: Appleton-Century. Historically important book that examines and counters the claim that self-report personality instruments assess only response sets.

Butcher, J. N. (1999). Research design in objective personality assessment. In P. C. Kendall, J. N. Butcher, & G. Holmbeck (Eds.), *Handbook of research methods in clinical psychology* (2nd ed., pp. 155–182). New York: Wiley. Thorough review of issues and strategies in conducting personality assessment via self-report.

Kenrick, D. T., & Funder, D. C. (1988). Profiting from controversy: Lessons from the person-situation debate. *American Psychologist, 43,* 23–34. Reaffirms the value of self-report measures of personality by countering various claims about the unreality and irrelevance of personality traits.

McCrae, R. R., & Costa, P. T., Jr., (1990). *Personality in adulthood.* New York: Guilford Press. Reviews a successful body of research based on a self-report instrument of personality. Documents that such self-reports are reliable, valid, and converge with the reports of knowledgeable others.

Schecter, S., & Herrmann, D. (1997). The proper use of self-report questions in effective measurement of health outcomes. *Evaluation and the Health Professions, 20*(1), 28–46. Outlines the cognitive processes involved in responding to self-report questionnaires, and provides suggestions for improving self-report data.

Tomarken, A. J. (1995). A psychometric perspective on psychophysiological measures. *Psychological Assessment, 7,* 387–395. Examines how psychophysiological measures have been used to complement self-report in the study of emotion.

Turner, C. F., Ku, L., Rogers, S. M., Lindberg, L. D., Pleck, J. H., & Sonenstein, F. L. (1998). Adolescent sexual behavior, drug use, and violence: Increased reporting with computer survey technology. *Science, 280,* 867–873. Provides a demonstration that results of a self-report survey can be influenced by method of assessment. Specifically, adolescents were more likely to admit to certain high-risk behaviors when entering their responses directly into a computer than when completing a paper-and-pencil version of the same survey.

Robert F. Krueger and Kristen C. Kling

SELF-REPRESENTATION. *See* Personality; *and* Self-Concept and Self-Representation.

SELF-SCHEMA. *See* Self-Concept and Self-Representation.

SELF-VERIFICATION. *See* Self-Concept and Self-Representation.

SEMANTIC DIFFERENTIAL. Charles E. Osgood and his coworkers developed the semantic differential, which is a scaling and association method used to study the multidimensionality of meaning as a relational concept, or what they described as the meaning of "meaning." Osgood was inspired by earlier research on synesthesia, a phenomenon in which sensations belonging to one sense or mode are associated with another variable. Studies by H. S. T. Odbert and others (*Journal of General Psychology,* 1942, *26,* 153–173), including work that involved Osgood (*Journal of General Psychology,* 1942, *26,* 199–222), indicated that stimuli from several modalities may have shared meanings. Examples included the association of the color green with the mood created by Delius's *On Hearing the First Cuckoo in Spring* and the association of red with the mood created by Wagner's *Rienzi Overture.* Osgood concluded that imagery found in synesthesia is intimately connected with language metaphor, and that both represent "semantic" relations comprising more than just one spatial dimension of associated meaning.

The purpose of the semantic differential is to "differentiate" the meaning of a concept by having respondents judge it against a series of seven-point scales in which the ends of each scale are extreme opposites (also called bipolar scales). For example, subjects might be asked to judge the concept of "father" by placing a check mark where they feel the concept lies on the following scales:

```
happy  __ : __ : __ : __ : __ : __ : __  sad
hard   __ : __ : __ : __ : __ : __ : __  soft
slow   __ : __ : __ : __ : __ : __ : __  fast
```

In factor-analysis studies conducted in different cultures, Osgood and his associates found that the meaning of a variety of different concepts could be best represented by three primary dimensions, which they named evaluation, potency, and activity. In statistical terms the evaluation dimension accounts for approximately half of the extractable variance, whereas the potency and activity dimensions (together referred to as *dynamism*) each account for approximately half as much variance as the evaluation dimension. [*See* Factor Analysis.] Certain bipolar scales were found to tap into these dimensions. To tap the evaluation dimension, scales were anchored by such bipolar terms as *bad-good, unpleasant-pleasant, negative-positive, ugly-beautiful, cruel-kind, unfair-fair,* and *worthless-valuable.* Scales used to measure the potency dimension were anchored by *weak-strong, light-heavy, small-large, soft-hard,* and *thin-heavy.* For the activity dimension, any of the following could be used: *slow-fast, passive-active,* and *dull-sharp.*

If we were interested in the location of the concept on each of these three dimensions, we could average the ratings of the scales assigned to that dimension. If we were interested in seeing a profile of the concept on all the scales, we could plot a graph simply by lining up the scales and connecting the points representing the average scores. For example, in the 1968 U.S. presidential election campaign, one of Richard M. Nixon's first moves was the appointment of advertising researchers who traveled all through the United States asking people to judge the presidential candidates on a semantic differential scale, based on which it was possible to compare Nixon's profile with plotted curves for Hubert Humphrey and George Wallace. It is also feasible to construct three-dimensional graphs of semantic differential results. For example, Osgood and Zella Luria (*Journal of Abnormal and Social Psychology,* 1954, *49,* 579–591) made meaningful clinical interpretations of such graphs in a famous case of multiple personalities reported by C. H. Thigpen and H. M. Cleckley (*The Three Faces of Eve,* New York, 1957). Like other rating scales, the semantic differential is vulnerable to certain biases of self-reported data.

[*See also* Artifact, *article on* Artifact in Assessment.]

Bibliography

McGinniss, J. (1969). *The selling of the president 1968.* New York: Trident. Mentions how advertising researchers used the semantic differential to develop a campaign to close the "personality gap" between Richard M. Nixon and Hubert Humphrey in the 1968 presidential campaign.

Osgood, C. E., Suci, G. J., & Tannenbaum, P. H. (1957). *The measurement of meaning.* Urbana, IL: University of Illinois Press. A classic work that describes the development of the semantic differential and the theory of meaning propounded by Osgood and his associates.

Snider, J. G., & Osgood, C. E. (Eds.). (1969). *Semantic differential technique: A sourcebook.* Chicago: Aldine. An anthology of far-ranging semantic differential applications.

Ralph L. Rosnow

SEMANTICS. *See* Psycholinguistics, *article on* Semantics.

SENSATION SEEKING is a personality trait defined as the seeking of varied, novel, complex, and intense sensations and experiences and the willingness to take risks for the sake of such experience. The first Sensation Seeking Scale (SSS), published in 1964, was a measure of the general trait. Four subscales were subsequently developed: (1) Thrill and Adventure Seeking (through risky sports and activities), (2) Experience Seeking (through the mind and the senses), (3) Disinhibition (through social and sexual stimulation), and (4) Boredom Susceptibility (aversion to lack of change and stimulation). A total score, summing the four subscales, has been used in place of the general scale from the earlier version. A single-factor scale combining sensation seeking and impulsivity (Impulsive Sensation Seeking) has also been developed.

Behavioral Expressions

The varied behavioral expressions of sensation seeking are described in detail by Zuckerman (1979, 1994a). In sports, mountain climbers, parachutists, hang-gliders, car and motorcycle racers, scuba divers, and professional skiers score high on sensation seeking. A common expression of thrill seeking is found in everyday driving habits. High sensation seekers drive faster and more recklessly and were observed to tail-gate (follow other cars closely at high speeds) in an actual driving test.

Sensation seekers are attracted to vocations involving exciting experiences, like firefighting, emergency room work, air-traffic control, and work involving extensive traveling or variety. When confined to monotonous desk jobs they report high job dissatisfaction.

High sensation seekers have a short-term hedonistic attitude toward intimate relationships, whereas low sensation seekers tend to be more pragmatic, evaluating potential partners' long-term assets. High sensation seekers who are single tend to engage in more varied sexual activities with more partners. There is a high degree of assortative mating (mate selection based on similarity of traits) for sensation seeking, which is unusual for other personality traits. Marked discrepancies in sensation seeking are found in couples coming for marital therapy.

High sensation seekers like designs and art works that are complex and/or emotionally evocative. They like explicit sex and horror films as well as sexual and violent themes in other media. They like the most intense kinds of rock music. They tend to channel surf (switch channels frequently) or engage in other activities when watching television. They enjoy sexual and nonsense types of humor. Low sensation seekers prefer more predictable and less arousing art and media forms, such as situation comedy, quiet background music, and pastoral nature paintings.

High sensation seekers are more likely than low sensation seekers to smoke, drink heavily, and use illicit drugs. Sensation seeking in preadolescents predicts later alcohol and drug use and abuse. Among drug abusers, sensation seeking is most strongly related to the number of drugs used rather than to the preference for any one type of drug.

Children with conduct disorders and adults with antisocial and borderline personality disorders are high sensation seekers. Sensation seeking, particularly disinhibition, predicts delinquency in adolescents. People with bipolar (manic-depressive) disorders tend to be high sensation seekers even when they are not in the manic state. Pathological gamblers who are not involved in treatment programs tend to be high sensation seekers. Impulsive sensation seekers in a laboratory gambling experiment tend to persist in betting in the face of cumulative losses, a pattern that is characteristic in pathological gamblers.

Biosocial Bases

Studies of twins raised together or separately in adopted families show a high degree of heritability (about 60% genetic) for the trait. There is no evidence of an influence of shared environment on the trait. Specific environmental influences account for most of the nongenetic variance. These influences may be peers or life experiences specifically affecting only one member of the family. Judging from the high level of assortative mating and reports of peer behavior, there is a great deal of gene-environment correlation, that is, high sensation seekers select friends and peer groups who reinforce their own natural predilections, and low sensation seekers seek out quieter and more reliable friends.

Moderately intense and novel stimuli tend to elicit physiological responses indicative of attention and interest in high sensation seekers but weaker responses in low sensation seekers. Increasing intensities of stimuli evoke augmented cortical responses in high sensation seekers, whereas low sensation seekers show a reduction of cortical response at the higher intensities of stimulation, perhaps indicative of a stronger inhibitory tendency. Studies of cortical augmenter and reducer types among cats and rats show that these psychophysiological traits are related to behavioral characteristics analogous to sensation seeking in humans, for example, explorativeness, fearlessness in novel situations, willingness to drink alcohol solutions, and a deficit in ability to restrain behavior when responding for reward.

High sensation seekers have high levels of testosterone, and low sensation seekers have average levels of this hormone. Men tend to be higher sensation seekers than women on all of the SSS scales, except experience seeking, and this could be due in some part to hormonal differences. High sensation seekers have lower levels of the enzyme monoamine oxidase type B (MAO-B), which regulates monoamine neurotransmitters, particularly dopamine, in the brain. Low levels of MAO are related to various behavioral expressions of sensation seekers, such as failed inhibitions in a motor task, risky behavior in an investment game, mountain climbing, alcohol and drug use and abuse, and criminality.

Monoamine oxidase type B is highly heritable and stable, and differences between persons are reliable over time. MAO is even related to behavioral differences among infants in the first 3 days of life. I believe that low MAO-B is an indicator of high dopaminergic activity and weak serotonergic activity in the brain. Comparative studies suggest that dopamine is the basis of a generalized approach motive and serotonin is involved in the capacity to inhibit approach behavior. A third monoamine, norepinephrine, is related to arousability, and plays a role in alarm and panic. A metabolite of norepinephrine obtained from cerebrospinal fluid was negatively correlated with sensation seeking, suggesting that arousal in this system is weaker in high sensation seekers, providing another explanation of their fearlessness in risky situations.

[See also Accidents; Alcoholism; Antisocial Personality Disorder; Attention; Bipolar Disorder; Borderline Personality Disorder; Boredom; Criminality; Delinquency; Drug Abuse; Impulsivity; Marriage Therapy; Personality Trait; Sex Therapy; Smoking; and Sport Psychology.]

Bibliography

Fulker, D. W., Eysenck, S. B. G., & Zuckerman, M. (1980). A genetic and environmental analysis of sensation seeking. *Journal of Research in Personality, 14*, 261–281. A biometric-genetic twin study of sensation seeking trait analyzing genetic and environmental variance in the total score and the separate subscales.

Zuckerman, M. (1971). Dimensions of sensation seeking. *Journal of Consulting and Clinical Psychology, 36*, 45–52. Describes the original factor analytic research revealing the four subfactors in the broader sensation-seeking trait.

Zuckerman, M. (1979). *Sensation seeking: Beyond the optimal level of arousal.* Hillsdale, NJ: Erlbaum. The first book on sensation seeking summarizing theoretical background, development of questionnaire scales and empirical studies 1964–1979.

Zuckerman, M. (1984). Sensation seeking: A comparative approach to a human trait. *Behavioral and Brain Sciences, 7*, 413–471. Summary of the biological bases of sensation seeking comparing behavioral and biological correlates in humans and experimental evidence of biological bases of behavioral patterns in other species.

Zuckerman, M. (1990). The psychophysiology of sensation seeking. *Journal of Personality, 58*, 313–345. Summary of findings on sensation seeking and psychophysiological basal levels of arousal and arousability in reactions to novelty and intensity of stimulation.

Zuckerman, M. (1994a) *Behavioral expressions and biosocial bases of sensation seeking.* New York: Cambridge University Press. Summarizes new theoretical models and empirical studies between 1979 and 1994. A basic summary of field.

Zuckerman, M. (1994b). Impulsive unsocialized sensation seeking: The biological foundations of a basic dimension of personality. In J. E. Bates & T. D. Wachs (Eds.), *Temperament: Individual differences at the interface of biology and behavior* (pp. 219–255). Washington, DC: American Psychological Association. A basic discussion of the biological bases of the impulsive sensation-seeking trait, including recent comparative studies of cats and rats.

Zuckerman, M., Buchsbaum, M. S., & Murphy, D. L. (1980). Sensation seeking and its biological correlates. *Psychological Bulletin, 88*, 187–214. Summary of the psychophysiological and biochemical correlates of sensation seeking and parallels between animal and human research findings.

Zuckerman, M., Kuhlman, D. M., Joireman, J., Teta, P., & Kraft, M. (1993). A comparison of three structural models for personality: The big three, the big five, and and the alternative five. *Journal of Personality and Social Psychology, 65*, 757–768. A comparison of the supertrait of impulsive sensation seeking with traits in other major personality systems, discusses the development of a scale to measure impulsive sensation seeking and other major traits in the alternative-five.

Zuckerman, M., Kuhlman, D. M., Thornquist, M., & Kiers, H. (1991). Five (or three) robust questionnaire scale factors of personality without culture. *Personality and Individual Differences, 12*, 929–941. Describes the factor analyses that confirmed a major factor defined by impulsivity and all four SSS subscales, at one pole, and scales measuring socialization, need for cognitive structure (restraint), responsibility, and inhibition of aggression, at the other pole. The factor was labeled Impulsive Unsocialized Sensation Seeking.

Marvin Zuckerman

SENSORY STORES. Researchers have long hypothesized that each sensory modality has some way of retaining physical information in a relatively precategorical or unprocessed form beyond the physical duration of a stimulus. This mechanism is called sensory memory. The majority of research on sensory memory has focused on the visual and auditory modalities, with a small amount of energy devoted to the tactile modality and relatively little research on the olfactory (smell) or gustatory (taste) systems. There are two main reasons for this: Those unstudied modalities tend to be nonverbal, and in the chemical senses (olfactory and gustatory), it is difficult to tell when exactly the actual physical sensation is gone and memory begins. Visual sensory memory is usually referred to as iconic memory, and auditory sensory memory is usually referred to as echoic memory. These terms convey the type of information that these stores supposedly retain. For example, the information in echoic memory is like an echo, the same information removed in time.

Two main theoretical positions have been taken to describe sensory memory. The multiple-stores view sees sensory memory as a storage receptacle, a temporary buffer for briefly holding sensory information until it can be processed further. In this view, each sensory modality has its own buffer that can have different characteristics in terms of storage capacity, storage time, decay of information, and rate of transfer to short-term memory. In contrast, the proceduralist view suggests that memory is the natural consequence of the processing that was performed on a stimulus. According to this view, there are no memory stores per se, just a lingering residue of operations that were engaged in the original event. For example, the levels of processing framework (Craik & Lockhart, 1972) proposes that memory is the result of a successive series of analyses, of which the first involves an analysis of the purely sensory information. Only later can postcategorical information be extracted. Proceduralists believe that it is not that information is in separate stores necessarily, but rather that different analyses are performed on the information, which results in different memory traces.

Visual Sensory Memory

The most influential early studies of visual sensory memory were conducted by George Sperling in 1960. In his experiments, people saw a 3 × 4 matrix of letters that was displayed for only 50 milliseconds (ms). When asked to recall all of the letters (the whole report condition), they were able to report only about three or four of the letters. However, the participants in Sperling's experiment said that they saw all of the letters but that the unreported letters faded away or dissolved in the time it took them to report the first few letters. In order to test this introspection, Sperling included a partial report condition in which participants were asked to report only part of the array. After the array had been turned off, a high, medium, or low tone signaled which row of letters to report—those in the top, middle, or bottom rows, respectively. Using this technique, Sperling was able to estimate that participants had about nine letters available to them when the tone was sounded immediately after the offset of the visual array. The partial report scores dropped dramatically the longer the delay between the offset of the visual array and the tone cue. At about a one-second delay, partial report was no better than whole report.

Subsequent research focused on examining various aspects of iconic memory in more detail, particularly its duration. Haber and Standing (1970) tested the subjective duration of a 3 × 3 matrix, much like that used by Sperling. They had participants adjust an auditory click to mark the beginning and end of their experience of the stimulus array. Participants consistently overestimated the duration of the display, indicating that they "saw" it for about 100 ms after its offset. Similar estimates of the duration of the persistence of a visual stimulus were supported using a variety of experimental techniques, including masking the target with a bright flash.

Whereas Sperling had estimated the duration of visual sensory memory to be somewhere between a quarter second and a half second, the studies of visual persistence by Haber and Standing and others seemed to indicate that the duration was far shorter, only about 100 ms. These two estimates can be reconciled by assuming that there are two types of visual sensory storage. The system termed visible persistence refers to a sort of afterimage that takes place at the level of the retina. The system termed iconic memory is not truly sensory, and it is characterized by the recoding of some of the basic features of the stimulus into other forms.

The findings support the idea of two systems because visible persistence and iconic memory appear to follow different empirical laws. When using a task such as that used by Sperling, the duration of iconic memory is not related to the duration of the stimulus presentation as long as the stimulus is presented for more than 100 ms. Also, iconic memory is not very strongly affected by the luminance, or brightness, of the stimulus array. Intrusion errors in reporting letters from a partial report technique often sound like or rhyme with the correct letter. Finally, what is lost during the delay in the partial report technique seems to be the location of an item rather than what items were presented: With increasing delay between the offset of the stimulus array and the probe, there is no decrease in the accuracy of identifying a letter, but there is a decrease in assigning a location to that letter. This fits with studies of visual attention demonstrating that people can identify an item before they can locate it in space. These data also refute the idea that iconic memory is made up of a precategorical or unanalyzed representation of the original physical stimulus, as originally suggested by Sperling.

On the other hand, when techniques for determining the length of visual persistence are used, such as subjective duration, both the duration and luminance of the display affect performance in an interesting way: Brighter and briefer displays appear to persist longer than dimmer and longer displays. This is consistent with a retinal—or at least lower level—basis for this effect. This short visual sensory memory does appear to be truly a reflection of the original stimulus. The idea that there are two versions of visual sensory memory is also compatible with a proceduralist view of sensory memory, which assumes memory is composed of the lingering effects of the processes performed on the stimulus at each level of processing.

Auditory Sensory Memory

Crowder and Morton (1969) proposed a model of auditory sensory memory that they called "precategorical acoustic storage," or PAS. PAS was originally developed to account for the modality effect in serial recall. Serial recall is a technique whereby participants are asked to recall a list of items in the order in which they were presented. When the items are played out loud, performance decreases over serial positions, with one important exception: The final item is recalled almost as well as the first item—the recency effect. However, when presentation is visual there is no recency effect. The difference in recall of the final item due to presentation modality is called the modality effect. PAS explained the recency and modality effects by assuming that each item in an auditory sequence enters an echoic store and then lingers in a precategorical or unprocessed form. This store can then provide additional information that can later be used to identify and interpret the acoustic signals. Because items in this store linger much longer than those in the corresponding visual store, there is an advantage for information processed by ear as compared to that processed by eye. In PAS, each succeeding item interferes with information about the preceding item. Evidence consistent with this came from studies on the stimulus suffix effect, in which the addition of an extra, unrecalled item—the stimulus suffix—erased most of the auditory advantage. The potency of the suffix depended on the physical similarity (such as location or voice) between the suffix and the list items and was not affected by conceptual or semantic similarity. This sensitivity to physical attributes and an insensitivity to conceptual attributes is what would be expected if the store were precategorical. Later studies showed that the recency effect was not restricted to the auditory modality but that tactile and kinesthetic information resulted in large recency effects as well. Furthermore, there is some question as to whether the information is precategorical, because the potency of the suffix could be modulated by the interpretation of the suffix as speech or nonspeech.

As with iconic memory, there are competing estimates of the temporal duration of echoic memory. Efron (1970) asked participants to judge the simultaneity of the offset of an auditory stimulus with the onset of a visual stimulus. Participants were allowed to adjust the duration of the interval until the apparent offset of one stimulus coincided with the onset of the second stimulus. When the stimuli were of short duration (under 130 ms) listeners consistently overestimated the sound by about 200 ms. This was assumed to be because of the sensory persistence of the sound: Participants were still hearing the sound even after it had stopped. Other estimates of the duration of the short auditory store have fallen within 150 to 350 ms. It has been suggested that the 150 to 350 ms could be assumed to be the duration of the stimulus plus the time taken to process it. However, estimates of the duration of echoic memory from the modality and suffix paradigms have been as long as 5 to 10 seconds.

Thus, like iconic memory, there are two very different estimates of the duration of echoic memory. There seems to be good evidence for two separate auditory sensory stores—short and long. The long auditory store underlies the modality and suffix effects and lasts on the order of 2 to 10 seconds. The short auditory store seems to be a result of more peripheral processes, perhaps in the ear itself. For example, when two brief sounds are presented in rapid succession, the second sound can prevent detection and recognition of the first. These phenomena are called detection masking and backward masking. The ability of the second sound to interfere with the first decreases depending on the delay between the sounds, up to about 250 to 350 ms. The data seem to indicate that there are at least two auditory storage mechanisms similar in nature (but not in duration) to those found in the visual modality.

Tactile Sensory Memory

The research on tactile sensory memory is somewhat sparser than that of the auditory and visual equivalents. However, many researchers studying tactile sensory memory have used techniques similar to those described above in the visual and auditory sections, with similar results. The partial report advantage decreases as the delay between stimulus offset and cue onset increases. In addition, the sensation of a touch persists for a short time after stimulation is withdrawn. Tactile modality and suffix effects have also been demonstrated.

Neurophysiological Correlates of Sensory Memory

Recently, there has been a great deal of interest in using neurophysiological techniques to provide converging evidence for sensory memory. The main measure that has been associated with auditory sensory memory is called mismatch negativity, or MMN. MMN is a change in the electrical activity of the brain elicited by a discriminable change in a repetitive sound. The existence of MMN implies that each stimulus leaves a neural trace in the brain that encodes its physical characteristics (Näätänen, 1992). MMN is thought to reflect an automatic comparison process between an incoming deviant stimulus and the neuronal representation of the repeated stimulus. It has been used to measure the duration of auditory sensory memory, and estimates of its duration are similar to those found using behavioral techniques. The hypothesized two auditory stores discussed above are also supported by neurophysiological evidence. There has been little neurophysiological research exploring iconic memory, perhaps because of its very brief duration. Research on neurophysiological correlates of tactile sensory memory is also still in its infancy.

But What Is It For?

Many people have asked what is sensory memory for? For auditory sensory memory, the answer seems fairly straightforward: In order to understand complex auditory stimuli (such as speech or music), the acoustic signal needs to be integrated across durations lasting from a few hundred milliseconds to a couple of seconds. This can be accomplished only if there is some way of briefly retaining the earlier auditory sensation until later parts of the signal have been perceived. A similar argument could be made for tactile sensory memory: It would be useful to know where a stimulus had made contact with the skin after the stimulus has been removed in order to examine the skin for damage.

However, given that the visual environment remains in view continuously, the explanation for why there may exist a visual sensory store is a little more problematic. Haber (1983) facetiously suggested that iconic memory was only useful for reading in a lightning storm at night. The suggestion is that visual sensory memory may not actually serve a purpose, but rather is an artifact of how certain experiments are conducted. Others have argued that there is a real use for visual sensory memory: Contrary to phenomenological experience, which is of a continuous, stable visual scene, the eyes make a series of saccades, or jerky, ballistic movements. During the saccade, the normal visual processes are suppressed, and for the most part, no information is registered during the motion. Thus, visual sensory memory may be used to integrate across multiple fixations in order to build up a constant view of the world.

Summary

There is good evidence for sensory memory mechanisms in both the visual and auditory modalities, although each system results in a trace that varies in duration and capacity. The mechanisms can be described in terms of either separate storage systems or different processes. Less evidence is available for the other senses, although the little that has been done parallels the results observed for the visual and auditory modalities.

[See also Memory.]

Bibliography

Coltheart, M. (1983). Iconic memory. *Philosophical Transactions of the Royal Society of London, B, 302*, 283–294. A review of the literature on iconic memory.

Cowan, N. (1984). On short and long auditory stores. *Psychological Bulletin, 96*, 341–370. A review of the literature on echoic memory.

Craik, F. I. M., & Lockhart, R. S. (1972). Levels of processing: A framework for memory research. *Journal of Verbal Learning and Verbal Behavior, 11*, 671–684.

Crowder, R. G., & Morton, J. (1969). Precategorical acoustic storage (PAS). *Perception and Psychophysics, 5*, 365–373.

Efron, R. (1970). The minimum duration of a perception. *Neuropsychologia, 8*, 57–63.

Haber, R. N., & Standing, L. (1970). Direct estimates of the apparent duration of a flash. *Canadian Journal of Psychology, 24*, 216–229.

Hill, J. W., & Bliss, J. C. (1968). Modeling a tactile sensory register. *Perception and Psychophysics, 4*, 91–101. A model of tactile sensory memory.

Näätänen, R. (1992). *Attention and brain function.* Hillsdale, NJ: Erlbaum. A review of the neurophysiological correlates of echoic memory.

Sperling, G. (1960). The information available in brief visual presentations. *Psychological Monographs, 74* (Whole No. 498).

Robert G. Crowder and Aimée M. Surprenant

SENSORY SYSTEMS. Sensation can be studied at many different levels: from introspection, to quantitative experimental psychology, to the neurobiology of sensory neurons. The psychological aspects of human sensation are well known, due to more than a century of work on the quantitative measurement of sensory processing, a field known as psychophysics. Over the past several decades, neurobiological research has traced sensation from peripheral receptors to the responses of neurons in the cerebral cortex. While sensory systems have been studied on many different animal models, here we concentrate on sensory systems in mammals. This research has provided a mechanistic understanding of much of what we know about the psychology of perception.

Psychophysics of Sensory Systems

Psychophysics is concerned with the quantification of psychological experience in general, and of sensation in particular. Much of what we know of the attributes and capabilities of sensory systems has been learned over the past 150 years of psychophysical research. This rich psychophysical literature has formed the foundation of most subsequent work on the neurobiology of sensation. These two fields continue to inform each other. The interplay between psychophysics and neurobiology is perhaps the best example of mental processes being explained in terms of neural mechanisms.

The most fundamental division in psychophysics is between threshold psychophysics and suprathreshold psychophysics. Threshold psychophysics is concerned with the limits of sensation: the faintest sound or the lowest concentration of a chemical that can be sensed. Suprathreshold psychophysics deals with the quality of sensation, such as a judgment of relative loudness or the identification of a certain smell. The qualities studied in suprathreshold psychophysics can range from the simple, such as color, to the complex, such as symmetry or the perceptual grouping of disparate elements.

Studies of psychophysical thresholds have demonstrated the extreme sensitivity of sensation. In a classical study by Hecht, Schlaer, and Pirenne (1942), it was found that human observers could reliably detect a stimulus consisting of only a few photons. From this finding, they postulated that individual photoreceptors should produce measurable responses to single photons. Neurobiologists have subsequently affirmed this prediction. In the auditory system, sensitivity is perhaps even greater. Sound is perceived by detection of changes in pressure, or equivalently, by the displacement of air molecules. Displacements can be detected that are as small as 1/10,000 the wavelength of visible light.

Most of sensation, however, is concerned not with detecting the presence of a stimulus but with analyzing its features. Because of the variety of sensory experience, suprathreshold psychophysics is a much broader field than threshold psychophysics. At the simplest level, suprathreshold stimuli can be distinguished according to their magnitude. The relationship between stimulus magnitude and perception is summarized by

two laws. The laws are named for their nineteenth-century discoverers, both pioneers in psychophysical research. Fechner's law states that the perceived strength of a sensory stimulus is proportional to the logarithm of the stimulus magnitude. Weber's law states that the smallest detectable difference between two stimuli is proportional to their magnitude. For instance, two weights might be distinguishable only if they differ by at least 10% (the ratio is referred to as the Weber fraction). Because the two laws are closely related, they are often referred to as the *Weber-Fechner law*. Versions of the Weber-Fechner law have been demonstrated for all sensory systems. Further, its neural substrate has been demonstrated, both in the responses of sensory receptors themselves and in the responses of more central neurons.

Other areas of suprathreshold psychophysics are concerned not with the quantification of magnitude but with quality. At one extreme, the ability to discriminate between simple qualities, such as different colors or odors, can provide information about the properties of sensory receptors. At the other extreme, complex discriminations, such as between different views of three-dimensional objects, may provide information about how the cerebral cortex represents sensory information.

Physiology of Sensory Systems

In mammals, there are separate sensory systems for each of the five classical senses: vision, hearing, touch, taste, and smell. The neural systems—referred to as visual, auditory, somatosensory, gustatory, and olfactory—consist of *receptors*, which transduce certain stimuli into neural signals, and the neurons in the central nervous system with which they communicate.

Sensory Receptors. The receptors for the five senses are referred to as exteroceptors. Another class, proprioceptors, senses the internal configuration and motion of the body. Although the term usually refers to receptors in the musculoskeletal system, it is sometimes used for those in the vestibular system, which sense the orientation and motion of the head in space. Chemical receptors in the internal organs are called interoceptors.

All sensation begins with receptors, such as the rod and cone cells in the retina that are sensitive to light, or the cells in the taste buds that respond to chemicals. Each of these receptors responds in a stereotyped fashion to specific kinds of stimuli. The form of energy that evokes a response in a receptor or a neuron is dependent on the particular sensory modality. Within each modality, there are usually several different qualities. In somatosensation, there are different classes of receptors in the skin that respond to different sorts of stimuli. Some respond best to light touch, others to vibration or flutter, yet others to either hot or cold. In the auditory system, the receptors, known as hair cells, are all very similar, but, depending on their location in the inner ear, they respond to a different range of tones. In the eye, color vision is dependent on the three different classes of receptors that are preferentially sensitive to different ranges of wavelengths: long (red to yellow), middle (yellow to green), and short (blue). Finally, the chemical senses, taste and smell, depend on a large number of different receptors, each of which is sensitive to a range of different chemicals.

Although the sensation of different qualities is dependent on the different types of receptors, it is rarely true that particular qualities are signaled by the activation of only one type of receptor. For instance, a green light will excite the middle wavelength cones, but also, more weakly, the long wavelength cones. The sensation of green stems from neurons that respond to the difference in the activity between these two cone classes; these neurons will respond best when the middle wavelength signal is stronger than the long wavelength signal. This is a general principle. Most peripheral receptors respond to a broad range of stimuli, but finer distinctions between stimuli are made by neurons that compare the activity of different receptors.

Sensory transduction consists of the transformation of a particular form of energy into a change in the electrical potential across a receptor's cell membrane. All neurons have a resting membrane potential, the voltage difference between the interior of the neuron and the exterior. This potential can be altered either in a graded fashion or in an all-or-none fashion, with the generation of action potentials. Action potentials are generated by receptors in the periphery such as somatosensory receptors, muscle proprioceptors, and visceral receptors. An action potential travels down the axon of such a neuron, to the axon terminal, which then releases neurotransmitter. The neurotransmitter, in turn, influences the activity of subsequent neurons in the processing stream. In such a system, the strength of a sensory input is signaled by the rate at which action potentials are fired.

In other systems, sensory input changes the membrane potential of the receptors, but no action potentials are fired. Examples include the hair cells of the inner ear or the photoreceptors of the retina. In these systems, the second-order neurons are much closer to the sensory receptors. Hair cells will respond to sounds of a certain frequency (that is, a certain tone). The louder the sound, the more depolarized the hair cell and the more neurotransmitter it releases. Photoreceptors work in the opposite fashion. They respond to light, but the more light that falls on them, the less neurotransmitter they release. Both of these receptors can signal the presence of very weak stimuli, or very slight increments or decrements in stimulus intensity. By contrast, almost all other neurons in the nervous system

fire action potentials. Sensory neurons that respond with a graded signal transmit this information to subsequent neurons that encode the same information in the rate or timing of action potentials. The output neurons in the eye and the middle ear, for instance, fire action potentials that transmit information to the brain.

The Physiology of Sensory Neurons. Sensory information is transmitted to the brain along a number of different pathways. Some of the sensory information that reaches the brain, however, is not available to conscious perception. For instance, the receptors in the carotid artery that sense the oxygen concentration in the blood do not lead to what can be called a perception of low or high oxygen. Even some pathways of visual information are unavailable to perception, such as the pathways that guide involuntary eye movements (even though the same information may reach consciousness through other pathways). Here, we concentrate on the sensory pathways that reach conscious perception.

The cerebral cortex is involved with most, if not all, conscious perception of sensory input. Except for olfaction, all the classical senses reach the cerebral cortex by way of the thalamus. The neurons that reach the thalamus are not peripheral receptors; they are neurons that are several levels of processing away from the receptors. In the somatosensory system, for instance, the sensory neurons connect with neurons in the spinal cord that project to the thalamus. The pathway from sensory receptors to thalamus is different in each system, but one feature is common: by the time sensory information reaches the thalamus it has gone through significant neural processing. In the auditory system, the second-order neurons (those that receive input from the hair cells) provide input to several nuclei in the brain stem. While the hair cells themselves can only signal the intensity, timing, and frequency of a sound, the neurons in these brain stem nuclei encode much more complex attributes, such as the relative amplitude or timing of the sounds presented to the two ears. In the visual system, the output neurons of the retina (the ganglion cells) connect directly with the thalamus, but considerable neural processing goes on between photoreceptors and these ganglion cells.

The most common way to describe the responses of a sensory neuron is by characterizing what is known as its receptive field. In vision and the somatosensory system, the concept of receptive field has a simple interpretation: it is the area on the skin or on the retina that can be stimulated to evoke a neural response. The receptive field can be described in terms of the receptors that evoke a response, but also in a more abstract sense, by the stimulus that evokes a response. Thus, an auditory neuron has a receptive field that can be described either by the range of tones to which it responds or by the receptors that cause this response.

Neurons respond to their inputs with either by excitation or inhibition. Loosely speaking, therefore, the receptive field of a neuron is created by adding together some incoming information and subtracting other information. Much of the early processing of sensory information, up to the stage of the thalamus, is involved in detecting change, or contrast. The most prevalent form of contrast detection is achieved by a mechanism called lateral inhibition, first described in the 1930s in the visual system of invertebrates. A sensory neuron that exhibits lateral inhibition is one that is excited by a given receptor but inhibited by neighboring receptors. In vision, lateral inhibition is seen in neurons that respond to light at one position but are inhibited by light at surrounding positions. In the auditory system, lateral inhibition is seen in neurons that respond to a narrow range of tones but are inhibited by lower or higher tones. These neurons are excited indirectly by certain hair cells but inhibited indirectly by the neighboring hair cells.

While the thalamic input to the cerebral cortex represents a highly processed version of the sensory input, the cortex performs considerably more complex transformations. These transformations are performed in stages, in different cortical areas. Primary sensory areas receive input from the thalamus. Higher order sensory areas receive input from other cortical areas. Although this implies a strong hierarchy, there are both feedback and feedforward connections between areas. Primary cortical areas perform certain limited operations on their inputs. For instance, in somatosensory, visual, and auditory cortex, there are neurons that are sensitive to the direction of motion. These neurons respond preferentially to stroking the skin in a specific direction, to a visual object moving in a specific direction, or to an upward rather than downward sequence of tones. The transformations performed by higher-order cortical areas, best studied in the visual system, are less well understood. At the highest levels, areas have been found that might encode the motion and rotation of extended visual objects, or others that respond best to familiar figures, such as faces.

[See also Hearing; Smell; Taste; Touch; and Vision and Sight.]

Bibliography

Barlow, H., & Mollon, J. (Eds.). (1982). The senses. Cambridge, UK: Cambridge University Press. An overview of the psychophysics and neurobiology of each sensory system.

Boring, E. G. (1950). A history of experimental psychology (2nd ed.). Englewood Cliffs, NJ: Prentice Hall. A fascinating treatment of early research in psychophysics.

Gescheider, G. A. (1997). Psychophysics: The fundamentals. Mahwah, NJ: Erlbaum.

Hubel, D. H. (1988). Eye, brain, and vision. New York: Freeman.

McIlwain, J. T. (1996). An introduction to the biology of vision. Cambridge, UK: Cambridge University Press.

Purves, D., Augustine, G., Fitzpatrick, D., Katz, L., La-Mantia, A., & McNamara, J. (Eds.). (1997). Neuroscience. Sunderland, MA: Sinauer.

Shepherd, G. M. (1994). Neurobiology (3rd ed.). New York: Oxford University Press.

Zigmond, M., Bloom, F., Landis, S., Roberts, J., & Squire, L. (Eds.). (1998). Fundamental neuroscience. San Diego, CA: Academic Press.

R. Clay Reid

SEX DIFFERENCES. See Gender Roles; Gender, Sex, and Culture, article on Sex Differences and Gender Differences; and Gender Socialization.

SEX DISCRIMINATION. See Discrimination.

SEXISM is gender-based prejudice or discrimination. It encompasses restrictive beliefs, negative attitudes, and unfair or discriminatory judgments and treatment. Sexism can occur at multiple levels: individual, organizational, institutional, and cultural. Psychological research on sexism has been conducted at the individual level, for instance, by documenting individual differences in sexist beliefs or attitudes and demonstrating discriminatory treatment or the stereotyping of specific people. Most psychological research has been concerned with sexism against women. This is because of women's lower status and power at a cultural level, which then manifests itself in institutional and organizational practices as well as policies and individual beliefs, attitudes, and actions. In contrast, the definition given here includes prejudice and discrimination against men as well as women. The two prejudices can be linked, for instance, restricting men to occupational roles or prescribing how they should behave in heterosexual relationships has repercussions for women. Finally, when gender is specified in our definition or sexism, we are referring to the gender label that one gives to oneself or the label that is assigned to a person by another. In contrast, heterosexism refers to beliefs, attitudes, and behaviors about sexual orientation. However, heterosexism and sexism are intimately related. Prejudice against lesbians can prevent women from speaking out against sexism. Furthermore, just as a career woman may violate traditional gender roles for occupations, being a lesbian or a gay male violates traditional gender roles for sexual behavior. Thus, heterosexism can lead to sexism by silencing efforts to obtain gender equality or by pressuring women and men to conform to traditional gender roles in terms of sexual behaviors. Similar relationships likely exist for beliefs, attitudes, and behaviors based upon other gender-related group membership, especially those that violate traditional gender norms (e.g., feminists and heavy women). Thus, although there are likely overlaps between sexism and heterosexism, the definition of sexism presented here does not specifically address prejudice or discrimination directed at a person because of their sexual orientation.

Sexist Beliefs or Attitudes

Examination of the ways that sexist beliefs are measured reveals insights into different characterizations of sexist beliefs. These scales also help identify individuals who presumably would be more likely to behave in a discriminatory manner.

Traditional Sex-Role or Gender-Role Beliefs. Early measures of sexist beliefs and attitudes focused on the endorsement of traditional gender roles for women. The first such measure was developed by Kirkpatrick (1936). Since then, there have been many variations in measures of gender-role related beliefs. One popular measure has been Spence and Helmreich's Attitudes Toward Women Scale (AWS, 1972). Contrary to its name, it is not actually a measure of attitudes toward women, defined as general evaluations of women (Eagly & Mladinic, 1984). The Attitude Toward Women Scale actually measures prescriptive beliefs about women's roles and preference for the differential treatment of women and men (Swim & Campbell, 2000). The long history of its use has allowed assessment of changes in beliefs over time and across different samples. As one might expect, gender differences on the AWS typically emerge with men being more likely than women to endorse traditional gender roles. Other group differences have also been documented, including regional differences with those in the South more likely than those in the rest of the United States to endorse traditional gender roles, and age or cohort differences, with older individuals being more likely to endorse traditional gender roles than younger individuals.

The tendency to endorse traditional gender roles has waned over the years (Twenge, 1997). While some authors have claimed that there has been a backlash in terms of people returning to more sexist beliefs, particularly in the 1980s, the temporal pattern indicates this is not the case. Neither women nor men became more conservative in the 1980s with respect to endorsement of gender roles. Rather, women's tendency to become more liberal earlier on resulted in the largest gender differences in beliefs emerging in the 1980s.

Although the AWS focused on beliefs about women's roles, sexist beliefs can also include beliefs about men. Egalitarian attitudes on the Sex Role Egalitarian Scale (King & King, 1997), reflect openness to both women and men violating gender roles. Moreover, attitudes about men's roles are independent of attitudes about women's roles, such that a person can have relatively liberal attitudes about women's roles but still hold more conservative attitudes about men's roles (Thompson, Pleck, & Ferrera, 1992). One can also focus on specific unfavorable beliefs about characteristics associated with men. For instance, although scales measuring beliefs about proper behavior for men have often been used to assess men's attitudes about their own gender, Iazzo (1983) developed a scale to assess women's attitudes about men and includes measurement of unfavorable beliefs about men, such as their perceived lack of commitment to marriage and family.

Modern Sexism. Endorsement of traditional gender roles has been considered an overt form of sexist beliefs or attitudes. But it is possible that there are also more covert and subtle sexist beliefs and attitudes. Covert sexism refers to the tendency to hide sexist beliefs or attitudes and reveal them only when it is believed that one will not suffer publicly for them. Covert sexism also includes gender-based discrimination perpetrated in a clandestine manner. Subtle sexism refers to unequal treatment that may not be noticed, because it is part of normal everyday behavior either because it is subtle or perceived to be of low importance. The recognition that sexism includes covert and subtle sexism as well as overt sexist beliefs led to theories about modern sexism (Benokraitus & Feagin, 1995; Swim & Cohen, 1997). Scales measuring modern sexist beliefs examine endorsement of the following ideas: Discrimination against women is no longer a problem; women complain too much about discrimination; and women have received too much special treatment and attention by the government and the news media. Endorsement of these statements may reflect hidden prejudicial beliefs or less sensitivity to the presence of subtle sexism (Swim & Cohen, 1997).

Ambivalent Sexism. Attitudes about women are not uniformly negative. Glick and Fiske (1996) argue that attitudes about women can be considered ambivalent because they contain both benevolent and hostile elements. For instance, paternalistic beliefs reflect care and concern for women even while treating women as children. Thus, benevolent forms of sexist beliefs may coexist with more hostile or dominative forms. When they co-occur ambivalence is said to characterize beliefs about women and possibly men as well (Glick & Fiske, 1999).

Related Gender Attitudes. Other measures, such as Burt's Rape Myth Acceptance scale (1980) and Pryor's Likelihood to Sexually Harass scale (1987) were not specifically designed to measure sexism. However, endorsement of such beliefs arguably supports the oppression of women. As such, they can be considered methods of identifying sexist individuals. Another set of scales assessing attitudes and beliefs about women are those that measure commitment to feminism and obtaining gender equality. Being egalitarian or nonsexist on scales such as the Attitude Toward Women scale is consistent with being a feminist. However, having egalitarian or nonsexist beliefs does not necessarily reflect feminist identification. Scales that assess this latter orientation include Bargard and Hyde's (1991) measure of feminist identification. People who are more feminist identified are likely to hold nontraditional gender-role beliefs for both women and men and less modern and ambivalent sexist beliefs. It is possible that the same individuals hold more unfavorable beliefs about characteristics associated with men (Iazzo, 1983).

Gender Stereotypes. Endorsement of gender stereotypes has often been used as an indicator of sexist beliefs. This was based on the assumption that gender stereotypes were negative and consisted of inappropriate generalizations. Although some early assessments of gender stereotypes suggested that beliefs about women were more negative than beliefs about men (Broverman, Vogel, Broverman, Clarkson, & Rosenkrantz, 1972), more recent analyses indicate that this early finding was a result of a methodological artifact (Widiger & Settle, 1987). Furthermore, the content of stereotypes about women have been found not to be more negative than those beliefs about men, nor are they necessarily inaccurate (Eagly & Mladinic, 1994; Swim, 1994). It is more likely that negative beliefs are embedded in subtypes about women and men, such as views about feminists. It is more accurate to say that stereotypes about women reflect beliefs about their predominant communal or expressive qualities, while stereotypes about men reflect beliefs in their agentic or instrumental qualities. Both sets of stereotypes are likely based on observation of women and men in different roles (Eagly, 1987). In addition to differential traits associated with men and women gender stereotypes include expectations about sex-based roles, physical appearance, abilities, occupations, and sexual orientation.

Despite the evidence that gender stereotypes are not necessarily negative and inaccurate, they still can be a basis for sexism. For instance, misapplication of the stereotypes to individuals can be prejudicial or discriminatory. Furthermore, stereotypes can be prejudicial and discriminatory if they are considered prescriptive rather than descriptive, and they are used as justifications for the status quo.

Discrimination

Examination of the way people judge, perceive, and treat individual women and men reveals the type and prevalence of experiences that can lead to or maintain status differences between women and men.

Judgments and Perceptions. One of the first studies to demonstrate that people evaluate women and men differently was a study by Goldberg (1968). He demonstrated that women evaluated a female author of an essay with a masculine topic less favorably than a male author of the same essay. A similar paradigm was used to study attributions for women's and men's work. For instance, Deaux and Emswiller (1974) demonstrated that people were more likely to attribute more effort and less ability to women's performance on a task as compared to men's identical performance on the same task. The pattern of attributions across several studies was said to support gender stereotypes by attributing women's failures and men's successes to stable causes (such as ability and task difficulty), and women's successes and men's failures to unstable causes (such as effort and luck). However, quantitative reviews (meta-analyses) have challenged the strength of these conclusions (Swim & Campbell, 2000). The results of these meta-analyses indicate a small but significant tendency to evaluate and judge the performance of men more favorably than the performance of women, and a small tendency to attribute different causes for men's and women's successes and failures.

There are a number of different interpretations of these surprisingly small average differences. As is the case with any meta-analysis, conclusions are based upon averages across many studies, and there are many possible conditions that could moderate the size of the differences. Bias against women may occur when several particular features co-occur. For instance, a low-status woman who is perceived to be unattractive, performs a masculine task, and is evaluated by a male who endorses traditional gender roles and has little information about the woman, may be rated substantially lower then a similarly situated man. Other interpretations depend upon one's willingness to generalize research findings coming primarily from laboratory contexts (where people mostly evaluate fictitious people in contrived situations) to field settings (Campbell, 1968). The loosest assessment of the generalizability would mean that one would assume that the small differences in judging women's and men's would be replicated in field settings. Even if one assumes this, it is important to remember that small but significant differences across a group and across one person's life may be consequential. Small differences can result in a large number of unfair evaluations within a large population and within one individual's lifetime. The difference could result in large numbers of unfair evaluations that could have cumulative effects. The importance placed on size of the difference found in the meta-analyses depends on one's willingness to generalize research findings coming primarily from laboratory contexts (where people mostly evaluate fictitious people in contrived situations) to field settings (Campbell, 1968).

A more restrictive assessment of the generalizability

of the findings would mean that one is willing to generalize the direction but not the size of the effect. Thus, one would assume that women would be judged less favorably than men, but differences between the lab and field settings would preclude predicting what the size of the difference would be in the field settings. Larger differences in field settings might exist because gender is often minimally manipulated in laboratory studies by altering the name of the person being evaluated. Gender may be more salient in field settings because of the context or may be confounded with masculine and feminine attributes, such as appearance or the style of interacting, which could increase the likelihood that gender would influence evaluations (Swim & Campbell, 2000).

The most restrictive assessment of the generalizability of the findings would mean that one is willing to say that the lab studies indicate that gender can influence judgments, but one cannot predict either the direction or the size of the effect in field settings. In other words, laboratory studies may be able to assess cognitive processes but not the prevalence of gender-based judgments. It may be the case that lab studies have not optimally tested the impact of gender-related beliefs and attitudes on the judgments and perceptions of women and men. People may not be using the same criteria in evaluating performance by women and men, using instead what Beirnat and Manus call shifting standards (1994). In judging work quality, they may be comparing women to other women and men to other men, instead of comparing women and men to a similar objective standard. Differences in ratings might very well be larger if the same standard were used for judging both women and men. Furthermore, larger gender biases may be revealed were one to observe subtle nonverbal reactions to contributions by women and men instead of relying on written evaluations. Stereotypes can also impact perceptions in other ways, such as through memory distortions of what women and men have done or in the ways that people construe the meaning of identical behaviors performed by women and men (Swim & Campbell, 2000).

Finally, evaluations of particular individuals are a complex process involving many categories of judgments. For instance, the likelihood that perceptions and judgments of individuals will be influenced by category information (e.g., gender) likely involves (1) whether gender versus other information about a person is most salient, activated, and perceived to be relevant to or diagnostic of the attribute being assessed, and (2) what the judge's motivations are when making judgments about others (Swim & Campbell, 2000).

Treatment of Women and Men. In addition to differential judgments of women and men, sexism can be expressed in behavior. These include blatant or overt sexist treatment as well as covert or subtle treatment.

Thus, like different types of attitudes, behaviors can reveal blatant preferences for one gender over the other, or the preferences may be hidden or so embedded in our culture and everyday behavior that they go unnoticed. In short, sexist treatment may be regarded as a type of stressor; that is, it can come in the form of major life events as well as daily hassles. Major life events include missing particular opportunities (e.g., jobs or promotions) or acts of rape, abuse, and sexual harassment. Daily hassles include comments about one's appearance, observing sexist portrayals in the media, exposure to derogatory or demeaning labels, hearing or reading language that excludes women (e.g., use of generic words such as he or man), experiencing pressures to behave in line with traditional gender roles, and being subjected to street remarks (Swim, Cohen, & Hyers, 1998). These everyday forms of prejudice can be blatant, covert, or subtle. Furthermore, women and men can both be targets of everyday sexism, but women are more likely than men to report experiencing these events, which is consistent with women's general lower status and power in our society.

Discriminatory treatment can also occur in the form of behavioral confirmation, or self-fulfilling prophecies. For example, a person who expects that women would be more involved in raising children might be more likely to ask a mother than a father to volunteer for school activities for their child, increasing the likelihood that mothers would be more involved in child care. The extent to which this happens, however, is likely to be context dependent (Deaux & LaFrance, 1988). For instance, situations differ in the extent to which they prime gender-stereotypic beliefs. Furthermore, targets of these expectations may differ in their tendency to confirm or disconfirm other's beliefs. Gender composition of a group is a context of particular importance when determining whether people will be treated in a sexist manner. When a person is a solo member of their gender in a group (or represent about 25% or less of the group), they are more salient and more likely to be stereotyped than if they are in the majority. These effects have been found to result in more negative repercussions for women than men (Cohen & Swim, 1997).

Summary

There are a wide variety of types of beliefs and behaviors that can be considered measures of sexism. These include endorsement of traditional gender-role beliefs and gender stereotypes, lack of sensitivity or commitment to obtaining equality, and benevolent and hostile beliefs and acts toward women. Sexist beliefs about men may also exist; however, this area has not been studied to the same extent as sexist beliefs about women. There is also a wide variety of ways that discrimination can occur: in the form of biased judgments and perceptions, major life events, and everyday forms of blatant, covert, and subtle sexism.

[*See also* Discrimination; *and* Prejudice.]

Bibliography

Bargard, A. & Hyde, J. S. (1991). Women's studies: A study of feminist identity development in women. *Psychology of Women Quarterly, 15,* 181–201.

Benokraitis, N. V. & Feagin, J. R. (1995). *Modern sexism* (2nd ed.). Englewood Cliffs, NJ: Prentice Hall.

Biernat, M., & Manus, M. (1994). Shifting standards and stereotype-based judgments. *Journal of Personality and Social Psychology, 66,* 5–20.

Broverman, I. K., Vogel, S. R., Broverman, D. M., Clarkson, F. E., & Rosenkrantz, P. S. (1972). Sex-role stereotypes: A current appraisal. *Journal of Social Issues, 28,* 59–78.

Burt, M. (1980). Cultural myths and supports for rape. *Journal of Personality and Social Psychology, 38,* 217–230.

Campbell, J. P. (1986). Labs, fields, and straw results. In E. A. Locke (Ed.), *Generalizing from laboratory to field settings* (pp. 264–279). Lexington, MA: Lexington Books.

Cohen, L. L., & Swim, J. K. (1995). The differential impact of gender ratios on women and men: Tokenism, self-confidence, and expectations. *Personality and Social Psychology Bulletin, 21,* 876–884.

Deaux, K., & Emswiller, T. (1974). Explanations of successful performance on sex-linked tasks: What is skill for the male is luck for the female. *Journal of Personality and Social Psychology, 29,* 80–85.

Deaux, K., & La France, M. (in press). Gender. In D. Gilbert, S. T. Fiske, & G. Lindzey (Eds.), *Handbook of social psychology* (4th ed. pp. 788–827). New York: McGraw-Hill.

Eagly, A. H. (1987). *Sex differences in social behavior: A social-role interpretation.* Hillsdale, NJ: Erlbaum.

Eagly, A. H., & Mladinic, A. (1994). Are people prejudiced against women? Some answers from research on attitudes, gender stereotypes, and judgments of competence. In W. Stroebe & M. Hewstone (Eds.), *European review of social psychology* (Vol. 5, pp. 1–35). New York: Wiley.

Glick, P., & Fiske, S. T. (1996). The Ambivalent Sexism Inventory: Differentiating hostile and benevolent sexism. *Journal of Personality and Social Psychology, 70,* 491–512.

Glick, P., & Fiske, S. T. (1999). The Ambivalence Toward Men Inventory: Differentiating hostile and benevolent beliefs about men. *Psychology of Women Quarterly, 23,* 519–546.

Goldberg, P. (1968). Are women prejudiced against women? *Transaction, 5,* 28–30.

Iazzo, A. N. (1983). The construction and validation of attitudes toward men scale. *Psychological Record, 33,* 371–378.

King, L. A., & King, D. W. (1997). Sex-Role Egalitarianism Scale: Development, psychometric properties, and recommendations for future research. *Psychology of Women Quarterly, 21,* 71–88.

Kirkpatrick, C. (1936). The construction of a belief-pattern scale for measuring attitudes toward feminism. *Journal of Social Psychology, 7,* 421–437.

Pryor, J. B. (1987). Sexual harassment proclivities in men. *Sex Roles, 17,* 269–290.

Spence, J. T., & Helmreich, R. L. (1972) The Attitudes Toward Women Scale: An objective instrument to measure the attitudes toward the rights and roles of women in contemporary society. *JSAS: Catalog of Selected Documents in Psychology, 2,* 66–67 (Ms. No. 153).

Swim, J. K. (1994). Perceived versus meta-analytic effect sizes: An assessment of the accuracy of gender stereotypes. *Journal of Personality and Social Psychology, 66,* 21–36.

Swim, J. K. & Campbell, B. (2000). Sexism: Beliefs, attitudes, and behaviors. In R. Brown & S. Gaertner (Eds.), *The handbook of social psychology: Intergroup relations* (Vol. 4). Oxford, England: Blackwell.

Swim, J. K., & Cohen, L. L. (1997). Overt, covert, and subtle sexism: A comparison between the Attitudes Toward Women and Modern Sexism scales. *Psychology of Women Quarterly, 21,* 103–118.

Swim, J. K., Cohen, L. L., & Hyers, L. L. (1998). Experiencing everyday prejudice and discrimination. In J. K. Swim & C. Stangor (Eds.), Prejudice: The target's perspective. New York: Academic Press.

Thompson, E. H., Pleck, J. H., & Ferrera, D. L. (1992). Men and masculinities: Scales for masculinity ideology and masculinity-related constructs. *Sex Roles, 27,* 573–607.

Twenge, J. M. (1997). Attitudes toward women, 1970–1995: A meta-analysis. *Psychology of Women Quarterly, 21,* 35–52.

Widiger, T. A., & Settle, S. A. (1987). Broverman et al. revisited: An artifactual sex bias. *Journal of Personality and Social Psychology, 53,* 463–469

Janet K. Swim

SEX ROLES. *See* Gender Roles.

SEX-ROLE SOCIALIZATION. *See* Gender Socialization.

SEX SEGREGATION. Although "segregation" refers to the physical separation of groups, "sex segregation" usually denotes a sexual division of labor that concentrates the sexes in different occupations, jobs, or workplaces. Sex segregation is pervasive. In 1990, over half of women workers would have had to change occupations to eliminate occupational-level segregation. The sexes are even more segregated at the job level because workers within the same occupation are segregated into different firms and different jobs. Sex segregation, which operates in conjunction with race-ethnic segregation, engenders and legitimates unequal treatment because economic, social, and psychological rewards are distributed through people's jobs.

According to a socialization perspective, the sexes pursue different occupations because sex-role socialization instills in females and males different values, skills, and personality traits as well as a taste for activities labeled appropriate for one's sex. Neoclassical economists assume that segregation reflects the sexes' preferences, given their roles in the traditional sexual division of domestic labor, with men choosing jobs to maximize earnings and women selecting jobs that facilitate child rearing. However, the sexes' similar job values (both value high pay, autonomy, prestige, and advancement opportunities) are inconsistent with both perspectives. Also, adults' occupations are weakly associated with their youthful aspirations, and workers frequently move between more and less sex-typed occupations. These and other findings suggest that the opportunities and sanctions that adults workers encounter are more important for their jobs than their preadult socialization or adult sex roles.

Employers strongly influence the level of segregation because they assign workers to jobs. To the extent that workers choose their jobs, they select them from the few alternatives employers offer them. Customarily, employers have reserved the best jobs for men, either out of loyalty to their own sex, sex biases, or sex stereotypes. Sex stereotypes affect hiring and promotion through statistical discrimination, a process in which employers generalize stereotyped attributes of a group to all its members, and through sex-biased evaluation of workers' performance—especially in sex-atypical jobs. Some personnel practices, such as whether employers fill jobs through referrals by current workers or formal methods, affect the level of segregation because informal networks tend to be sex segregated while formal methods make jobs more widely accessible. Employers can reduce the effects of sex stereotypes and biases through formal personnel practices (e.g., widely advertising and posting all openings) and using objective criteria for evaluating job applicants and promotion candidates.

Sex segregation produces disparities in the sexes' pay, authority, and mobility opportunities. The sex composition of jobs affects various job rewards and working conditions, in part because the cultural devaluation of women leads to the undervaluation of customarily female activities. Sex segregation also affects workers' senses of self-worth and entitlement, both through the overvaluation of male activities and the undervaluation of female activities. Segregation also perpetuates sex inequality by reinforcing the idea that the sexes differ in fundamental ways that require a sexual division of labor, by reducing the likelihood of equal-status contact between the sexes, and by creating same-sex reference groups through which workers assess their rewards.

Bibliography

Baron, J. N., & Pfeffer, J. (1994). The social psychology of organizations and inequality. *Social Psychology Quarterly, 57,* 190–209. Discusses consequences of sex-typed jobs within work organizations.

England, P. (1992). *Comparable worth: Theories and evidence.* New York: Gruyter. Reviews theoretical and empirical linkages between sex segregation and sex disparity in pay.

Jacobs, J. A. (1989). *Revolving doors.* Stanford, CA: Stanford University Press. Uses longitudinal data to estimate relationship between workers' occupational aspirations and their jobs at various points in life cycle. Discusses social forces that preserve sex segregation despite considerable mobility by individual workers across more and less sex-typed jobs.

Reskin, B. F. (1993). Sex segregation in the workplace. *Annual Review of Sociology, 19,* 241–270. Reviews empirical research on extent, causes, and consequences of segregation.

Reskin, B. F., & Roos, P. A. (1990). *Jobs queues, gender queues: Explaining women's inroads into male occupations.* Philadelphia: Temple University Press. Provides theoretical framework for shifting sex composition of occupations based on case studies of 14 customarily male occupations that feminized in the 1970s and 1980s.

Barbara Reskin

SEX STEREOTYPES. *See* Stereotypes.

SEX STRATIFICATION. Social stratification refers to structured inequality in the distribution of prestige, power, property, and other valued resources. Sex stratification is the unequal distribution of such resources based on sex, although its expression is conditioned by other ascribed characteristics, such as age, color, ethnicity, and sexual orientation. Sex stratification is manifest in most societies in men's disproportionate control of economic resources and power and their greater prestige. Men's economic advantages stem from their greater likelihood of being paid for their work and—among paid workers—their higher average earnings (in 1996, U.S. men employed full-time earned 35% more than similarly employed women). These differences in opportunities for paid employment and in earnings raise men's likelihood of being wealthy and women's risk of being poor. Sex stratification in power allows men to set the degree of intimacy in interpersonal relations, enjoy greater freedom of movement, and enjoy authority over women. Differences manifest in family decision making and the sexual division of domestic and paid work. At the macro level, men monopolize political power and control major social institutions, including law, education, media, commerce, medicine, religion, science, and the arts.

Affecting and reflecting the extent of sex stratification are gender ideologies and specific institutional arrangements. Traditional gender ideology contends that women differ fundamentally from and are inferior to men, facts that warrant sex differentiation and unequal treatment. Sex differentiation is expressed in a myriad of ways, especially in a sexual division of labor that requires men's but not women's attachment to the labor force, thereby fostering women's economic dependence. The ideology of male superiority grants men more opportunities and rewards than women that in turn men's foster paternalistic control by rendering women dependent on men for protection and support. Women's emotional dependence is exacerbated by socialization that encourages them to seek happiness in heterosexual relationships. Women's legal dependence is achieved by disenfranchising women and by laws that require or allow unequal treatment. Women have reduced their legal dependence on men by winning the vote, increasing their political participation, and challenging discriminatory laws. The convergence in the sexes' labor force participation and the narrowing earnings gap have lessened women's economic dependence on men.

Families, schools, the media, and other social institutions disseminate gender ideologies that may heighten or weaken sex stratification. Sex segregated activities and the preferential valuation of male traits and activities transmit a traditional gender ideology; coeducation undermines sex differentiation and hence stratification. The mass media can reinforce or erode sex stereotypes through their depiction of the sexes. Underlying most systems of stratification is the use of force. The asymmetry between the sexes in sexual and domestic violence and in sexual harassment reflects its use in maintaining sex stratification.

Economic and demographic factors affect the extent of sex inequality (for example, war-time labor shortages reduced it). So too do the efforts of interested parties. In challenging stereotyping and discrimination by sex, feminist movements have weakened traditional gender ideology and sex stratification.

Bibliography

Amott, T. (1993). *Caught in the crisis.* New York: Monthly Review Press. Assesses the impact of the U.S. economy on sex inequality in the workforce and family.

Chafetz, J. S. (1998). *Handbook of gender sociology.* New York: Plenum. A comprehensive handbook on gender that includes many chapters related to sex stratification.

Henley, N. & Freeman, J. (1975). The sexual politics of interpersonal behavior. In J. Freeman (Ed.), *Women: A feminist perspective* (pp. 391–401). Mountain View, CA: Mayfield. An analysis of sex stratification in interpersonal relations.

Jackman, M. R. (1994). *The velvet glove: Paternalism and conflict in gender, class, and race relations.* Berkeley: University of California Press. Develops a relational approach to sex stratification drawing on classical theories, integrates sex, class, and gender stratification, and tests her approach with survey data.

Reskin, B. F. (1988). Bringing the men back in: Sex differentiation and the devaluation of women's work. *Gender & Society, 2,* 58–81. Examines the importance of sex differentiation, segregation, and devaluation in systems of sex stratification.

Spain, D. & Bianchi, S. M., (1996). *Balancing act: Motherhood, marriage, and employment among American women.* New York: Russell Sage. Uses 1990 census data to compare the sexes' educational, family, and economic positions.

Barbara Reskin

SEX THERAPY refers to a multimodal therapeutic approach designed to improve sexual functioning. Sex therapy rests on the assumption that sexual performance problems are caused by a combination of lack of knowledge, misinformation, and faulty learning. This form of treatment is offered by mental health professionals who are trained in the use of these techniques and in their underlying theoretical basis. These techniques are most appropriately applied to the treatment of sexual dysfunctions that involve persistent and recurrent difficulties in the sexual response cycle or pain during sexual intercourse (American Psychiatric Association, *Diagnostic and Statistical Manual of Mental Disorders,* 1994). Sexual dysfunctions may involve deficient sexual desire, problems achieving sexual arousal such as erectile dysfunction, difficulties reaching orgasm, or the experience of severe pain during actual or attempted intercourse.

The origin of sex therapy is largely traced to the work of William Masters and Virginia Johnson in the 1960s and 1970s. Masters, a gynecologist, and his associate, Johnson, began their research on sexuality and on sexual dysfunctions at Washington University in St. Louis. Their efforts culminated in the publications of two books, *Human Sexual Response* (Boston, 1966) and *Human Sexual Inadequacy* (Boston, 1970), both of which were highly influential and remain important contributions in the history of sex therapy. Although some treatments for sexual dysfunctions were available prior to this time, Masters and Johnson's work was truly innovative. They advocated the use of a male-female therapy team and an intensive but brief (2 weeks) intervention, and they conceptualized sexual dysfunction as a relationship problem rather than a problem that afflicted one individual. The popularity of Masters and Johnson's approach to sex therapy, however, was mostly due to the unprecedented success rates that they reported, nearly 80%.

Following these developments, the field of sex therapy underwent rapid growth. A growing number of professionals sought training in sex therapy, more books and journals were devoted to the subject, and other professionals began distinguishing themselves for their contributions to sex therapy. Helen Singer Kaplan (1974), for example, combined some insights and techniques of psychoanalysis with the more behavioral methods employed by Masters and Johnson. Kaplan argued that sexual dysfunctions may sometimes result from deep-seated emotional problems that would require a more in-depth approach to treatment.

Sex therapy has since undergone a major identity change. Medical problems have increasingly been shown to play a role in many cases of sexual dysfunction. Consequently, medical treatments have become increasingly popular. Individual cases presenting for sex therapy have grown increasingly complex. Clients presenting for sex therapy today are more likely to have long-term sexual problems, to have relationship issues, to be older, and to be in poor health (Rosen & Leiblum, 1995). The brief, problem-focused sex therapy originated by Masters and Johnson is not as well suited for such complex cases, although many of the techniques they developed remain widely used by sex therapists.

Techniques

Several different techniques are commonly used in sex therapy but they share the common goals of providing education, reducing performance anxiety, improving communication, and teaching skills to improve sexual pleasuring for both partners. Sex therapy incorporates homework assignments to be rehearsed at home, and these would ideally involve the participation of the partner.

Education. Education in the form of providing information is the most common component of sex therapy. Education may consist of offering information on normal sexual functioning, anatomy, gender differences, normal age-related changes in functioning, and the effects of diseases, medications, and drugs on sexual health. Because sexually dysfunctional couples commonly hold unrealistic beliefs, education may be helpful in debunking myths about sexual performance. Education in sex therapy is usually provided in the form of reading assignments and educational films. The use of written materials is a useful adjunct to other techniques in sex therapy (van Lankveld, 1998).

Couples Therapy. Because a number of relationship problems can lead to sexual dissatisfaction, couples therapy has become an almost standard component of sex therapy (Weeks & Hof, 1987). Relationship issues relating to trust, unresolved resentment, power struggles, poor communication, jealousy, or insecurity may precipitate, or contribute to, problems with sexual functioning. In short, sexual dysfunction may be a sign of broader relationship problems. Communication training is offered to assist couples with active listening and effective talking. Couples that do not communicate effectively are typically unable to resolve relationship problems, and they are likely to have difficulty discussing any sensitive subject, including sex. Additionally, problem-solving and negotiation skills are usually taught in couples therapy. Finally, unresolved feelings or any "unfinished business" must be addressed and worked through in order for couples to achieve emotional and sexual intimacy.

Cognitive Restructuring. Sex therapy virtually always requires the modification of clients' negative attitudes about sex. Conflicted sexual attitudes may originate from a puritanical upbringing, traumatic experiences, or a host of other repressive influences. In such cases, negative attitudes about sex are systematically challenged by the therapist. As the client successfully "tests" more positive attitudes and beliefs in sexual interactions, they are likely to become assimilated. In addition, any intrusive and distracting thoughts are addressed by teaching clients to become less concerned with their sexual performance and more focused on pleasurable sensations. This goal is greatly enhanced by the use of the sensate focus technique.

Sensate Focus. The goal of sensate focus, a technique developed by Masters and Johnson, is to teach couples to focus on the sensations that are occurring during a sexual interaction rather than on their performance. Focusing on sensations, rather than on goals, serves to reduce performance anxiety and rebuild a sense of mastery. A man with erection problems, for example, and his partner would be instructed to gradually spend time being affectionate and enjoying pleasurable feelings through nonsexual massaging. They would be instructed to initially postpone intercourse for some time while focusing on sensations, ultimately eliminating performance anxiety and fear of failure. Several steps, each of which may require several weeks, are employed. In the first step, the couple is instructed to practice nongenital touching. Genital touching occurs in the next step. Sexual intercourse is resumed in the last step but only after the couple has succeeded in reducing performance anxiety and has successfully become less performance oriented.

Squeeze Technique. This technique, also developed by Masters and Johnson, is employed with couples who are experiencing problems with premature ejaculation. If a man has recurring difficulty controlling the timing of his orgasm, and he and his partner are both dissatisfied, the squeeze technique may be beneficial for achieving more control over ejaculation. Over several practice sessions at home, the man is instructed to self-stimulate to the point at which he feels ejaculation is inevitable. He then squeezes the tip of his penis firmly for 10 seconds, thereby preventing orgasm. The procedure is to be repeated several times in each session before ejaculation. With practice, the technique helps the man gain some degree of control over the timing of ejaculation. The technique may be practiced with the assistance of a partner who would perform the squeezing on cue.

Stop-Start Technique. An alternative technique that is even more commonly used in the treatment of premature ejaculation is the stop-start method. Developed by Semans in 1956, the technique is designed to condition greater ejaculatory control by helping the male learn to identify the sensations that precede orgasm. Stimulation by the man or his partner is to be stopped at the point of impending orgasm and only resumed when the sensations have dissipated. With repeated experience stopping stimulation prior to orgasm, the male and his partner will gain some degree of control over ejaculation.

Individual Psychotherapy. Individual therapy is sometimes offered as an adjunct to sex therapy in cases where an individual has problems that may be contributing to sexual dysfunction. Alternatively, individual psychological difficulties may detract from the effectiveness of sex therapy or cause relapses. Persons who have experienced sexual trauma in the past may require individual therapy to overcome the sequelae of the trauma. Depressed individuals will usually need treatment for their mood disorder before sex therapy can be initiated. These and other psychological difficulties may have to be addressed in individual psychotherapy in order to effectively implement sex therapy techniques.

Effectiveness

More recent sex therapy outcome studies have documented more modest findings than the original success rates reported by Masters and Johnson (Boston, 1970). A number of factors may account for the discrepancy, including the complexity of cases in recent studies, diversity in applications of sex therapy, and the availability of options to traditional sex therapy. In contrast to Masters and Johnson, who viewed most sexual dysfunctions as resulting from ignorance and psychological factors, therapists today conceptualize these difficulties as stemming from the complex interplay of psychological, physical, and sociocultural factors. In addition, contemporary sex therapists encounter problems that were not even included in the original Masters and Johnson studies, such as inhibited and compulsive sexual desire disorders. Preliminary findings suggest that these disorders are relatively resistant to change and not readily amenable to standard sex therapy techniques. Couples therapy is rapidly becoming an integral component of sex therapy as relationship problems commonly play a role in sexual dysfunction. Hypoactive sexual desire, for example, is typically associated with relationship problems. Women with low sexual desire often are dissatisfied with the communication, expectations, and problem solving in their relationships (Beck, Bozman, & Qualtrough, 1991; Stuart, Hammond, & Pett, 1988). They frequently complain of a lack of romance and emotional closeness, and they perceive their partners as tending to overemphasize sex at the expense of emotional intimacy. For persons who are dissatisfied with their relationships, sex may come to be viewed as yet another obligation or duty (Stuart, Hammond, & Pett, 1988).

Medical interventions represent popular and sometimes efficient alternatives to traditional sex therapy. The past few decades have witnessed a proliferation of surgical and medical treatments. Interventions for erectile dysfunction include surgical implants, intrapenile injections, and various pump and constriction devices. Oral medications to improve erectile function are among the most popular and promising of all medical interventions. The medication Viagra (sildenafil) for erectile dysfunction, for example, became the fastest selling prescription drug in history shortly after it was introduced in 1998. Unfortunately, most of these interventions have some drawbacks, including unpleasant side effects, unknown risks from long-term use, and costs. Moreover, medical interventions do not rectify the relationship and psychological problems that may be causing or contributing to the sexual dysfunction. Some research (e.g., Hawton, Catalan, & Fagg, 1992) has shown that couples' communication skills are the single most important predictor of treatment success for erectile disorder.

Another challenge in evaluating the effectiveness of sex therapy results from the fact that success at the conclusion of therapy does not guarantee long-term gains. Relapse rates in one third of treated clients are not uncommon. Therefore, an accurate evaluation of the efficacy of sex therapy requires both short-term and long-term follow-up.

Treatment outcome studies suggest that sex therapy is beneficial for nearly two thirds of persons with sexual dysfunction. The degree of improvement is variable, ranging from modest improvements in sexual functioning to complete symptom removal. For most clients, these improvements will be lasting, although one third or more will experience a relapse within months following therapy. Some studies suggest that couples counseling and cognitive restructuring are often effective components, but there remain many questions about the active ingredients in effective sex therapy.

Future Directions

There is an ongoing need for research on the effectiveness of sex therapy. In addition to identifying the effective components and matching the most effective techniques with the appropriate disorders, we need to learn how to efficaciously combine sex therapy with medical interventions. Sex therapy should ultimately evolve into a multidisciplinary approach to solving sexual problems that have multifactorial origins. Additionally, interventions designed to prevent relapses need to be developed and systematically evaluated.

Finally, there is a critical need for research on the etiology of sexual dysfunctions. The contribution of physical, psychological, and sociocultural factors in the development of sexual problems needs to be clarified so that interventions can be tailored to identified risk factors. Historically, most studies on the causes of sexual dysfunctions have investigated male problems at the expense of female sexual disorders. Further, there is little information on the applicability of sex therapy to such problems as inhibited sexual desire or to the problems associated with sexual trauma and abuse. Advances in sex therapy are contingent on accurate formulations of the etiology of sexual dysfunction.

Bibliography

American Psychiatric Association. (1994). *Diagnostic and statistical manual of mental disorders* (4th ed.). Washington, DC: Author.

Beck, J. G., Bozman, A., & Qualtrough, T. (1991). The experience of sexual desire: Psychological correlates in a college sample. *Journal of Sex Research, 28,* 443–456.

Hawton, K., Catalan, J., & Fagg, J. (1992). Sex therapy for erectile dysfunction: Characteristics of couples, treatment outcome and prognostic factors. *Archives of Sexual Behavior, 21,* 161–172.

Kaplan, H. S. (1974). *The new sex therapy.* New York: Brunner/Mazel.

Leiblum, S. R., & Rosen, R. C. (1989). *Principles and practice of sex therapy: Update for the 1990s.* New York: Guilford Press.

Rosen, R. C., & Leiblum, S. R. (1995). Treatment of sexual disorders in the 1990s: An integrated approach. *Journal of Consulting and Clinical Psychology, 63,* 877–890.

Stuart, F., Hammond, C., & Pett, M. (1988). Inhibited sexual desire in women. *Archives of Sexual Behavior, 16,* 91–106.

Van Lankveld, J. J. D. M. (1998). Bibliotherapy in the treatment of sexual dysfunctions: A meta-analysis. *Journal of Consulting and Clinical Psychology, 66,* 702–708.

Weeks, G. R., & Hof, L. (1987). *Integrating sex and marital therapy: A clinical guide.* New York: Brunner/Mazel.

Wincze, J. P., & Carey, M. P. (1991). *Sexual dysfunction: A guide for assessment and treatment.* New York: Guilford Press.

Richard D. McAnulty

SEXUAL CONDITIONING is a form of learning in which some type of sexual stimulation serves as the reinforcer. The reinforcer may be exposure to the visual, olfactory, and/or auditory features of a potential sexual partner, or it may be copulation with the sexual partner. Sexual conditioning is of interest because the sexual behavior system provides excellent opportunities to study a number of important issues, including the adaptive significance of learning, interactions between learning and unconditioned or instinctive behavior, interactions between learning and motivation, and the contributions of learning to evolution. Studies of sexual learning may also contribute to the development of therapeutic procedures for the treatment of various forms of sexual dysfunction.

Sexual conditioning may be conducted using either instrumental or Pavlovian conditioning procedures. In instrumental sexual conditioning, the participant is required to perform a specified response to obtain access to the reinforcer. In Pavlovian sexual conditioning, the sexual reinforcer or unconditioned stimulus (US) is presented in combination with a conditioned stimulus (CS). With both conditioning methods, the magnitude of the resultant learning effect is related to how much of the sexual behavior sequence the participant is allowed to complete during his or her interactions with the sexual reinforcer. In general, exposure to a sexual partner without tactile contact does not produce as robust learning as the opportunity to engage in copulatory behavior.

Although a few empirical studies of sexual conditioning have been conducted with human participants, most of the research has involved other animal species. In initial studies of instrumental sexual conditioning, male rats were required to run the length of a straight alley to obtain access to a sexually receptive female. In other studies, male rats have been required to press a response lever to obtain access to a sexually receptive female. In analogous experiments, female rats were required to perform an instrumental response to obtain access to a sexually active male. Such procedures have been used to investigate the motivational and physiological bases of the sexual learning, but little work has been done to analyze the learning mechanisms of instrumental sexual conditioning.

Sexual conditioning has been investigated in greater detail using Pavlovian conditioning procedures with a fish species (the blue gourami, *Trichogaster trichopterus*), domesticated rats (*Rattus norvegicus*), domesticated quail *Coturnix japonica*, and to a limited extent with human males. All major Pavlovian conditioning phenomena that have been documented in more conventional conditioning situations also have been found in animal studies of sexual conditioning. These phenomena include acquisition, extinction, discrimination learning, trace conditioning, blocking, second-order conditioning, and contextual conditioning.

The conditioned response that is learned in sexual

Pavlovian conditioning depends on the type of conditioned stimulus that is used and the interval between the CS and the US during the training trials. For example, studies with male quail have shown that with an "arbitrary" CS and a short CS–US interval (1 minute), the conditioned response is approaching the conditioned stimulus (akin to "focal search" behavior). The same CS presented with a 20-minute CS–US interval results in nondirected locomotor behavior (akin to "general search" behavior) as the conditioned response.

Pavlovian conditioning procedures also have been found to activate copulatory behavior in males. Such conditioned activation of copulatory behavior can occur in two different ways, one direct and the other indirect. In the direct effect, copulatory behavior is elicited directly by a conditioned stimulus. This requires the use of a short CS–US interval and a conditioned stimulus that includes species typical features of a female US, at least initially. Direct elicitation of copulatory behavior by a sexually conditioned stimulus has not been extensively investigated. In the second learning mechanism, copulatory behavior is not elicited directly by a conditioned stimulus, but the CS facilitates copulatory behavior that occurs when a potential sexual partner is presented. Such CS-induced facilitation of copulatory behavior has been demonstrated in fish, laboratory rats, and domesticated quail. Furthermore, the CS-induced facilitation of sexual behavior can result in significant increases in sperm release and numbers of offspring produced.

Bibliography

Domjan, M. (1998). Going wild in the laboratory: Learning about species typical cues. In D. L. Medin (Ed.), *The psychology of learning and motivation* (Vol. 38, pp. 155–186). San Diego, CA: Academic Press. Describes the special role of species typical cues in the conditioning of sexual behavior.

Domjan, M., Blesbois, E., & Williams, J. (1998). The adaptive significance of sexual conditioning: Pavlovian conditioning of sperm release. *Psychological Science, 9,* 411–415. Recent study demonstrating the effects of sexual conditioning on sperm release.

Domjan, M., & Holloway, K. S. (1998). Sexual learning. In G. Greenberg & M. M. Harraway (Eds.), *Comparative psychology: A handbook* (pp. 602–613). New York: Garland. General review of research on sexual conditioning in a variety of species.

Hollis, K. L., Pharr, V. L., Dumas, M. J., Britton, G. B., & Field, J. (1997). Classical conditioning provides paternity advantage for territorial male blue gouramis (*Trichogaster trichopterus*). *Journal of Comparative Psychology, III,* 219–225. Demonstrates how sexual conditioning can dramatically increase reproductive fitness.

O'Donohue, W., & Plaud, J. J. (1994). The conditioning of human sexual arousal. *Archives of Sexual Behavior, 23,* 321–344. Provides a critical review of research on sexual conditioning in human participants.

Michael Domjan

SEXUAL DISORDERS. The *Diagnostic and Statistical Manual of Mental Disorders* (4th ed. 1994), published by the American Psychiatric Association, identifies three types of sexual disorders: (1) sexual dysfunctions, (2) paraphilias, and (3) gender identity disorders.

Sexual Dysfunctions

Healthy sexual functioning is currently understood to be comprised of three stages: (1) desire (an interest in being sexual), (2) excitement (the state of arousal that occurs as a result of sexual stimulation), and (3) orgasm (the peaking of sexual pleasure). An impairment or disturbance in one or more of these stages constitutes a sexual disorder.

Havelock Ellis (1906) was one of the first sexologists who attempted to formally define sexual functioning. He theorized that sexual functioning had two stages: tumescence (i.e., the engorgement of the genitals with blood resulting in erection in males and vaginal lubrication in females), and detumescence (i.e., the outflow of blood from the genitals following orgasm). During the 1950s and 1960s William Masters and Virginia Johnson conducted extensive laboratory observational studies of 382 women and 312 men in more than 10,000 episodes of sexual activity (Masters, Johnson, & Kolodny, 1994). Based on their research, they suggested that sexual functioning in healthy adults proceeded through four stages: excitement, plateau, orgasm, and resolution. A decade later both Harold Lief (1977) and Helen Singer Kaplan (1977) independently suggested that there was a stage preliminary to the excitement stage identified by Masters and Johnson. This preliminary stage, later defined as sexual desire, consisted of an individual's cognitive and affective readiness for, and interest in, sexual activity. Kaplan suggested that the sexual response cycle, as developed by Masters and Johnson, be reconceptualized as consisting of three phases: desire, excitement, and orgasm. Her position was that the high prevalence of desire phase disorders substantiated this need for a triphasic model of sexual response. While the current thinking is that these stages are less discrete and more overlapping, Kaplan's model has served as a useful way to conceptualize sexual functioning and, conversely, sexual disorders.

As our understanding of sexual functioning has changed, so have changes occurred in the treatment of sexual disorders, especially in the 1990s. Treatment methods developed in the 1970s by Masters and Johnson focused on anxiety and performance anxiety in particular as the primary factors in the development and maintenance of a sexual disorder. Later, however, sexual disorders came to be seen as much more complex and influenced by biological, psychological, and interpersonal factors, a view that has brought significant changes in the practice of sex therapy. Interest increased in discovering the biological factors that might underlie any given sexual disorder, as well as the sexual concomitants of disease and illness. In addition, there was a significant upsurge in the use of pharmacological interventions. This medicalization of sex therapy expanded the treatment for sexual disorders into more traditional avenues of health care, with primary care and family practice physicians, urologists, and gynecologists more frequently assessing and treating sexual disorders.

The following definitions of the various sexual disorders for each phase of the sexual response cycle and a section on sexual pain disorders are taken from the *Diagnostic and Statistical Manual of Mental Disorders* (4th ed., 1994) of the American Psychiatric Association. In addition to the assessment criteria included for each disorder, all disorders should be evaluated along two dimensions. The disorder can be primary or life-long (the problem has always existed) or secondary or acquired (the problem is of recent onset and develops after a period of normal functioning). Second, a disorder can be generalized (occurs across all sexual situations, partners, or method of stimulation) or situational (is limited to certain situations, partners, or methods of stimulation). Third, more than one disorder can exist at the same time, or one disorder (the primary disorder) can cause a second disorder (the secondary disorder).

Sexual Desire Disorders. There are two types of desire disorders: hypoactive sexual desire disorder and sexual aversion disorder. Hypoactive sexual desire disorder is defined as persistently deficient or absent sexual fantasies and desire for sexual activity. Sexual aversion disorder is defined as persistent aversion to and avoidance of all, or almost all, genital sexual contact with a sexual partner. Whereas individuals with hypoactive sexual desire are often neutral or indifferent to sexual activity, those with sexual aversion disorder exhibit disgust, fear, and often panic toward any or all types of sexual activity. Research suggests that men and women differ in psychological and interpersonal factors associated with hypoactive sexual desire (Donahey & Carroll, 1993). Desire disorders are among the most difficult of the sexual disorders to define or diagnose, primarily because of the lack of consensus regarding a definition of sexual desire or measurement approaches (Lieblum & Rosen, 1989).

Arousal Disorders. For both men and women, sexual arousal consists of a subjective sense of sexual excitement and pleasure coupled with physiological changes. An arousal disorder exists when an individual is unable to attain or maintain physiological arousal despite a subjective sense of arousal or pleasure or, despite physiological arousal, does not subjectively feel pleasure from the sexual interaction. Sexual arousal difficulties in women are referred to as female sexual arousal disorder. In men, sexual arousal difficulties are referred to as male erectile disorder.

Female sexual arousal disorder can occur as a result of a vascular, neurological, or hormonal impairment or from medications that suppress the nervous system. Clinical reports suggest that a prior history of sexual abuse can be a factor, as can psychological or interpersonal factors (e.g., depression, anxiety, stress, intimacy fears, anger, relationship distress).

Many of the same physical, psychological, and interpersonal factors that may account for female sexual arousal disorder can be etiological factors in male erectile disorder. Additional factors include Peyronie's disease; a curvature in the penis that can interfere with blood flow; cigarette smoking (may constrict blood flow); and chronic alcohol consumption (may instigate premature neuropathy). Up until the 1980s it was believed that erectile dysfunction was frequently a psychogenic problem, with anger and anxiety being regarded as the two key factors. Since then the pendulum has swung the other way, with increasing interest and emphasis in erectile physiology, extensive research into the various physical factors that often compromise erectile functioning, and the introduction and availability of pharmacological treatments.

Orgasm Disorders. Orgasm has been described as the peaking of sexual pleasure. From a physical standpoint, Masters and Johnson described it as the release of sexual tension and rhythmic contractions of the perineal muscles, anal sphincter, and pelvic reproductive organs. In men, orgasm is also accompanied by the release of semen. In women who experience orgasm, there are contractions of the wall of the outer third of the vagina.

Female orgasmic disorder refers to the persistent or recurrent delay in, or absence of, orgasm in a female despite normal sexual arousal. It is important to note that absence of orgasm during sexual intercourse, even on a regular basis, is not considered to be a sexual disorder if orgasms occur during other types of sexual stimulation (e.g., masturbation, manual, or oral stimulation). An orgasm disorder is diagnosed when, despite any type of stimulation, a woman is unable to have an orgasm or, despite being able to orgasm during masturbation, is unable to be orgasmic with a partner.

Medications, especially those affecting the vascular or central nervous system, and medical conditions often affect a woman's ability to have an orgasm. Alcohol can delay latency time of orgasm and decrease its intensity. The effects of hormonal variation on orgasm are unclear. Most studies show that hormone replacement therapy influences desire and arousal much more than orgasm.

Possible psychological and interpersonal factors include many of the factors identified for the disorders already mentioned. It is also very common for some women with inhibited orgasm disorder to report discomfort or fear of losing control, fainting, or being too vulnerable with a partner by being orgasmic.

There are two types of orgasm disorders in men. The first, male orgasmic disorder, is defined as the persistent or recurrent difficulty or inability to achieve orgasm despite the presence of adequate desire, arousal, and stimulation. It is usually restricted to an inability to reach orgasm in the vagina, with orgasm possible with other types of stimulation. It is distinct from retrograde ejaculation, in which ejaculation occurs but the fluid travels backward and into the bladder rather than forward and through the urethra. Inhibited male orgasm can occur as a side effect of some medications. Psychological and interpersonal factors may include fear of pregnancy, ambivalence about the relationship, intimacy fears, reluctance to give up control, anger toward the partner, sexual boredom, or performance anxiety. Male orgasmic disorder is not commonly diagnosed and is believed to be relatively rare in the general population.

Premature ejaculation refers to ejaculation with minimal sexual stimulation or ejaculation before, upon, or shortly after penetration and before the person wishes. For a diagnosis to be made, there has to be a consistent pattern of rapid ejaculation. Men who have trouble controlling the rapidity of ejaculation only in certain instances are not considered to have this disorder. Such a great majority of males report early ejaculation in their initial intercourse experiences that it is almost a universal male experience. As more experience is attained with intercourse, ejaculatory control is improved. Men with good ejaculatory control are able to recognize signs of sexual arousal that precede and trigger ejaculation. Consequently, they are able to use compensatory strategies to avoid reaching the point where ejaculation begins (e.g., slowing the tempo of intercourse). For men with premature ejaculation, this awareness seems to be missing. Ejaculation proceeds straight from excitement to ejaculation.

Medical problems are rarely responsible for this disorder. Current thinking suggests that the most important elements in the development of premature ejaculation may be a result of (1) early sexual experiences that conditioned rapid response, or (2) anxiety that is activated in sexual situations. Other etiological factors to consider include hypersensitivity to penile arousal, low frequency of sexual intercourse, concern with erectile functioning, and relationship conflict with the partner.

Sexual Pain Disorder. There are two types of sexual pain disorder. The first, vaginismus, is the involuntary contraction of the muscles controlling the vaginal opening, such that it interferes significantly with achieving successful penetration and intercourse. Most physical conditions (e.g., vaginal infections, endometriosis, episiotomy) are not directly responsible for vaginismus but may be associated with vaginismus indirectly through conditioning. If a woman experiences pain upon intercourse or with a pelvic examination, this may consequently lead to a self-protecting tightening of the vaginal muscles. There are some physical factors that do prevent penetration of the vagina, but these occur rarely (e.g., rigid hymen, stenosis of the vagina). Typically, vaginismus occurs due to a belief that penetration will be extremely painful. As a result of this belief, a phobic avoidance of intercourse usually occurs.

Dyspareunia, the second type of pain disorder, is defined as recurrent or persistent pain in either a male or female before, during, or after sexual intercourse. Women report this as a problem much more frequently than men. Etiological factors contributing to dyspareunia in men include urinary tract infection, sexually transmitted disease, uncircumcised penis, and Peyronie's disease. Etiological factors contributing to dyspareunia in women are much more numerous. The most common factor is vaginal dryness. It is rare for psychological factors to be the primary cause of dyspareunia; however, clinical reports suggest that guilt or anxiety regarding sexual behavior or activity, or previous sexual trauma, can affect arousal, which, in turn, affects vaginal lubrication, resulting in painful intercourse.

Paraphilias

Paraphilia refers to intense sexual fantasies or behaviors that are considered abnormal by society. As described by *DSM–IV* (1994), the essential features of a paraphilia are recurrent, intense sexually arousing fantasies, sexual urges, or behaviors generally involving (1) nonhuman objects, (2) the suffering or humiliation of oneself or one's partner, or (3) children or other nonconsenting persons, that occur over a period of at least 6 months. For some people, these types of fantasies or conditions are necessary for erotic arousal and are always included in sexual activity. These people rarely seek treatment and will do so only if their behavior has become problematic with sexual partners or society. A small number will seek treatment on their own if their fantasies or behavior cause them to feel significant shame, guilt, or depression for engaging in thoughts or behavior considered socially unacceptable. In other instances, the paraphiliac preferences occur only episodically, and the individual is able to function sexually at other times without paraphiliac fantasies or stimuli. For a diagnosis of paraphilia, *DSM–IV* also considers the extent of clinically significant distress or impairment in social, occupational, or other important areas of functioning that occurs as a result of the paraphilic behavior or fantasy. Paraphilias can range from sexual fantasies that are never acted out to behaviors in which sexual arousal is complementary (e.g., the sadist and sexual masochist), to behaviors that are considered criminal (e.g., sexual contact with children, rape, exhibitionism, and voyeurism). The *DSM–IV* classifies paraphilias into the following eight categories.

Exhibitionism. The primary feature of exhibitionism involves recurrent, intense sexually arousing fantasies, sexual urges, or behaviors involving the exposure of one's genitals to an unsuspecting stranger. There is usually no attempt for further contact with the stranger. Most exhibitionists have the desire to shock or surprise the observer. In some cases, there is the thought that the observer will become sexually aroused. Males are usually diagnosed with this disorder, although women, too, can be exhibitionists.

Fetishism. The paraphiliac focus in fetishism involves the use of nonliving objects for sexual arousal. Items commonly used are women's undergarments, shoes, boots, stockings, or other women's garments. Individuals with fetishism usually masturbate while holding, rubbing, or smelling the fetish object or may want the sexual partner to wear the object during sexual activity. For some males, the fetish object may be necessary for obtaining an erection.

Frotteurism. Frotteurism is characterized by recurrent, intense sexually arousing fantasies, sexual urges, or behaviors involving touching and rubbing against a nonconsenting person. The behavior usually occurs in crowded places (e.g., public transportation) in which the individual (almost always male) rubs his genitals against the person's thighs or buttocks or fondles her breasts or genitalia. Fantasies of an exclusive relationship with this person often accompany the behavior. To avoid detection, the individual escapes into the crowd after engaging in the behavior. Frotteurism usually begins in adolescence and declines in frequency by mid-adulthood.

Pedophilia. Pedophilia involves sexual interest and activity with a prepubescent child. To be diagnosed with pedophilia, an individual must be 16 years old and at least 5 years older than the victim. Pedophiles usually describe an attraction to children of a particular age range and often of a particular gender. However, some individuals are sexually aroused by both male and female children. Statistically, it is reported that more pedophiles are interested in girls than boys, but those who are more interested in boys are twice as likely to return to their sexual behavior after legal action or psychiatric treatment (Charlton, 1997). Some individuals with pedophilia are sexually attracted to only children, whereas others can be attracted to both adults and children.

Sexual Masochism. Sexual masochism is defined as recurrent, intense sexually arousing fantasies, sexual urges, or behaviors involving the actual act of being humiliated, beaten, bound, or otherwise made to suffer. When masochism exists in fantasy, images of rape, sexual torture, slavery, being spanked, and being forced to have sex are used for masturbation (Charlton, 1997). Sexual arousal regarding such images is said to occur early in life and remain an ongoing pattern. For some of the individuals who acted on their masochistic fantasies or urges, this behavior may remain the same over years; for others, the severity of the masochistic acts may increase over time, resulting at times in injury or even death. [*See* Sexual Masochism.]

Sexual Sadism. The paraphiliac focus involves recurrent, intense sexually arousing fantasies, sexual urges, or behaviors involving acts in which the psychological or physical suffering (including humiliation) of the victim is sexually exciting to the person. It can exist on a continuum from scenarios of dominance to murder. The sadist is more likely to be male and has engaged in this behavior since early adulthood. As with sexual masochism, for some individuals the behavior may remain the same over years; for others, the severity of the sadism increases until the person is apprehended for physically injuring or even killing his or her victims. [*See* Sexual Sadism.]

Transvestic Fetishism. The paraphilic focus involves a heterosexual male who becomes sexually aroused by cross-dressing and imagining himself as the female object of his sexual fantasy. For some individuals the motivation for cross-dressing changes over time. It can become a way to manage depression and anxiety, or it can gradually develop into increasing discomfort with one's gender role and identity, leading to gender dysphoria.

Voyeurism. Voyeurism involves the act of observing unsuspecting individuals who are naked, in the process of undressing, or engaging in sexual behavior. The act of looking is what is arousing for the individual, and usually no sexual activity with the observed person is sought. Masturbation may occur during the act of looking or later in response to what the individual has witnessed.

Gender Identity Disorder

Gender identity is the sense of being a male or female. A gender identity disorder represents a profound disturbance of the individual's sense of identity with regard to maleness or femaleness. To be diagnosed with gender identity disorder, two components must be present. These are (1) a strong and persistent desire to be, or the insistence that one is, of the other gender, and (2) evidence of persistent discomfort about one's assigned gender or a sense of inappropriateness in the gender role of that sex. Gender identity disorder is manifested differently across the life cycle. In young children, distress is manifested by unhappiness about their assigned sex. Older children often fail to develop same-sex relationships and skills, leading to rejection and a sense of isolation. In adolescents and adults, preoccupation with cross-gender desires often interferes with occupational functioning and interpersonal relationships. To varying degrees, adults with this disorder usually adopt the behavior, dress, and mannerisms of the other gender. The more discomfort the individual feels regarding his or her assigned gender, the greater the preoccupation with getting rid of primary and secondary sex characteristics (e.g., receiving hormones, obtaining surgery). Unlike transvestic fetishism, this is not for the sole purpose of deriving sexual pleasure, but rather for purposes of gender identity.

[See also Exhibitionism; Fetishism; Pedophilia; Sexual Masochism; Sexual Sadism; Transsexualism; Transvestism; and Voyeurism.]

Bibliography

American Psychiatric Association. (1994). *Diagnostic and statistical manual of mental disorders* (4th ed.). Washington, DC: Author.

Arndt, W. B., Jr. (1991). *Gender disorders and the paraphilias.* Madison, CT: International Universities Press.

Charlton, R. (1997). *Treating sexual disorders.* San Francisco: Jossey-Bass.

Donahey, K., & Carroll, R. (1993). Gender differences in factors associated with hypoactive sexual desire. *Journal of Sex & Marital Therapy, 19(1),* 25–39.

Ellis, H. (1906). *Studies in the psychology of sex* (Vols. 1–7). New York: Random House.

Kaplan, H. S. (1977). Hypoactive sexual desire. *Journal of Sex & Marital Therapy, 3,* 3–9.

Lieblum, S., & Rosen, R. (1989). *Principles and practice of sex therapy: An update for the 1990's.* New York: Guilford Press.

Lief, H. (1977). Inhibited sexual desire. *Medical Aspects of Human Sexuality, 11(7),* 94–95.

Masters, W., Johnson, V., & Kolodny, R. (1994). *Heterosexuality.* New York: HarperCollins.

Steiner, B. W. (1985). *Gender dysphoria: Development, research, and management.* New York: Plenum Press.

Karen M. Donahey

SEXUAL DYSFUNCTIONS. Difficulties in the desire, arousal, or orgasm phase of the sexual response cycle, which interfere with full sexual expression and enjoyment, are sexual dysfunctions. When it was first addressed by clinicians such as Krafft-Ebing (1902), sexual dysfunction was thought to be caused by childhood masturbation or excessive adult sexual activity. It therefore followed that treatment was focused on preventing childhood masturbation and reducing sexual activity for adults. Freud's (1962 [1905]) view of sexual dysfunction as a symptom of failure to resolve the Oedipal complex was dominant for many years, despite the ineffectiveness of psychoanalytic treatment of dysfunction.

The first challenges to Freudian views of sexual dysfunction were advanced by behavior therapists, such as Wolpe (1958). Anxiety was seen as the cause of sexual dysfunction, and systematic desensitization was used to reduce anxiety. Treatment involved having the patient visualize a hierarchy of sexual behavior items during deep muscle relaxation. The patient then engaged in the hierarchy items, again during relaxation.

Modern Sex Therapy: Masters and Johnson. Masters and Johnson's study (1966) of the physiology of sexual response led to their revolutionary therapy for sexual dysfunction (1970). They noted that dysfunctions involved effects of negative cultural and familial messages about sex, often accompanied by a general lack of knowledge about sexuality. They stressed that having a sexual failure experience frequently led to the development of an anxious, self-evaluative spectator role, which maintained the occurrence of the sexual dysfunction. Masters and Johnson (1970) also developed specific sexual techniques to overcome particular problems; their approach focused not only on reducing anxiety, but also on teaching the patients good sexual stimulation techniques.

Postmodern Sex Therapy: Theoretical Concepts and Principles. Postmodern sex therapy (LoPiccolo, 1997) adds elements of cognitive therapy and couple systemic therapy to the Masters and Johnson (1970) model. In addition, for some dysfunctions, the role of physiologic causation (illness and medication side effects) is considered. Cognitive factors such as beliefs about the meaning of sexuality, self-esteem, and gender role expectations may be addressed. Couple systemic issues are addressed, as sexual dysfunction may be both causative of, and resultant from, difficulties around issues such as power and control, conflict resolution, intimacy and trust, the need for personal space in the relationship, and general dyadic happiness.

Sexual Dysfunctions Affecting Males and Females

Both sexes may experience dysfunction at any point in the human sexual response cycle (e.g., desire, arousal, or orgasm phases). Although there are differences in the way disorder becomes manifest in certain phases of the sexual response cycle due to the underlying biological and physical differences between the sexes, both men and women experience hypoactive sexual desire, sexual aversion, and dyspareunia.

Hypoactive Sexual Desire and Sexual Aversion. Hypoactive sexual desire is a marked lack of any interest in sexual fantasies or activities that causes distress or interpersonal difficulty. Presentation of this particular complaint has become common in recent years. Although societal norms for levels of male and female sexual desire fluctuate across time and culture, true hypoactive sexual desire disorder exists independent of current social expectations of "normal" sexual desire. Sexual aversion extends beyond low desire to include negative emotional reactions to sexual situations that include revulsion, fear, or disgust.

Underlying causative factors for low sexual desire and/or sexual aversion are numerous and often intertwined. Negative messages about sexuality from parents, religion, and other significant socializing agents; past sexual trauma; past experience from other relationships; cultural context; emotional components such as fear, anxiety, and suspicion; life stress and competing demands on time and energy; and a general unwillingness, or lack, of available sexual partners can all combine to cause low sexual desire or sexual aversion.

The following treatment approach for low sexual desire and sexual aversion has been found to be fairly successful for both males and females (Schover & LoPiccolo, 1982). Nonetheless, due to the likelihood that numerous complex psychological issues underlie hypoactive sexual desire and sexual aversion, a longer program of treatment is typically required for these disorders than for the other sexual dysfunctions (LoPiccolo & Friedman, 1988). First, therapy focuses on assisting the client to become more aware of the exact nature of his or her negative emotions regarding sex and sexuality. Quite often clients state that they have worked through any negative affective associations linked with sexuality. However, such changes are often superficial, leaving residual anxiety, fear, resentment, vulnerability, anger, and so on that serve to block the normal biological sex drive that all people have. The next step of therapy involves the development of insight into the etiology of the negative affect identified in the first phase of treatment. Negative messages from the client's religion, culture, family, and current and past relationships are explored. Having identified and gained insight into his or her negative emotional associations, the client is now ready to progress to the next phase of treatment wherein cognitive techniques are applied to the irrational thoughts and emotions that inhibit sexual desire. Patients generate coping statements to combat and offset the impact of entrenched beliefs regarding sexuality, thus enabling them to change those not-so-helpful core beliefs. Finally, after the cognitive foundation work has been done, the client is ready for the final phase of treatment wherein sensate focus, skill training, and other general behavioral sex therapy procedures are introduced. Specific interventions for heightening sex drive include having the client keep a desire diary in which he or she records sexual thoughts and feelings, having the client read books and view films with good erotic content, and encouraging the client to develop his or her own sexual fantasies. All of these activities make sexual thoughts and cues more readily available to the client. Nonsexual affection, consisting of simple hugs, squeezes, and pats, as well as pleasurable shared activities such as dancing and walking together, are also encouraged to help strengthen feelings of sensual enjoyment and sexual attraction. Finally, if there are systemic issues in the couple's relationship that encroach upon the development of intimacy, they need to be addressed.

Dyspareunia. Dyspareunia is defined as "recurrent or persistent genital pain associated with sexual intercourse in either a male or a female" (American Psychiatric Association, *Diagnostic and Statistical Manual of Mental Disorders*, 1994, p. 513) that causes significant distress or interpersonal difficulty. However, dyspareunia is far more common in women than in men (Masters & Johnson, 1970).

Most cases of painful sex involve some physiological abnormality, such as unrepaired damage following childbirth or an imperforate hymen in women and prostate conditions in men. Therefore, an examination by a gynecologist or urologist who is expert in this area is essential (O'Donohue & Geer, 1993). However, to be diagnosed as dyspareunia by *DSM–IV* criteria, the condition cannot be attributed solely to the effects of a general medical condition (e.g., endometriosis, scar tissue, pelvic pathology, etc.) nor can it be due to lack of lubrication or vaginismus. It should be noted, however, that dyspareunia in women and vaginismus are closely linked given that repeated dyspareunia is likely to lead to vaginismus (discussed later in this entry).

Since psychogenic dyspareunia in women is often attributed to a lack of arousal and is commonly linked with vaginismus, the specific techniques for enhancing female orgasm and alleviating vaginismus are used to treat this disorder once all medical causative factors have been properly addressed (O'Donohue & Geer, 1993). Many patients often find relief from dyspareunia by using an artificial genital lubricant. Relaxation training (Kaplan, 1974) also is incorporated often in the treatment for dyspareunia. Dyspareunia in males is almost always related to an underlying medical condition or problem.

Male Sexual Dysfunction

Disorders of the arousal and orgasm phase of the sexual response cycle that are unique to males are as follows.

Erectile Dysfunction. Erectile dysfunction is failure of the penis to become erect, or to maintain erection, thus preventing intercourse. It is now understood that it often results from an interaction of physical and psychological causes (LoPiccolo, 1997). Physical causes include disruption of blood flow to the penis, neurological illness such as diabetes, surgical damage following prostatectomy, and medication side effects. Psychological causes include lack of adequate physical stimulation of the penis and, most important, performance anxiety and the spectator role. That is, once a man begins to have erectile failure, he enters each sexual encounter with anxiety and self-observes to see if he will again fail to get an erection. This emotional set prevents arousal, and the erection problem becomes a self-maintaining cycle.

To deal with these issues, the patient couple learns sensate focus, which involves simple kissing and caressing, without any breast or genital contact, and attempts at intercourse are not allowed. The focus is on sensuality, without any pressure to be directly sexual. In the next phase of treatment, the partner caresses the man's penis but stops caressing it should he get an erection, until he loses it. This exercise teaches them that erections occur naturally in response to stimulation, as long as the couple does not focus on performance. Next, the couple resumes intercourse; the man lies on his back, and the woman kneels above him and uses her fingers to push his nonerect penis into her vagina. This procedure, known as the stuffing technique, frees him from having to have a rigid penis to accomplish entry. The couple is instructed to achieve the woman's orgasm through manual or oral sex, again reducing pressure on the man to perform. Finally, the couple resumes full sexual activity, with no further restrictions.

These procedures work well in cases in which there is no major organic impairment of erection. Physical intervention may be needed, however, for men with major physical problems as factors in their erection problem. For these men, one approach is surgical implantation of a penile prosthesis, which produces an artificial erection. One nonsurgical approach is the use of a vacuum erection device (VED). A hollow cylinder is connected to a hand pump, which pumps the air out of the cylinder and leaves the penis in a partial vacuum. This draws blood into the penis and produces an erection. The cylinder is removed, and a rubber constriction ring is placed around the base of the penis to maintain the erection. While effective in many cases, the VED does interfere with the spontaneity of sex, as the man must take time to use it during lovemaking. Another nonsurgical treatment for men with medically based erectile failure is the injection of drugs that dilate the penile arteries. The patient self-injects a small dose directly into the penis at mid-shaft a few minutes before lovemaking, with erections resulting for most men. With appropriate dosage, the erection subsides following ejaculation. Much research has been devoted to the development of dilating drugs that can be taken orally rather than injected into the penis. One such drug, Viagra®, since FDA approval, has been prescribed widely.

Premature Ejaculation. Premature ejaculation is defined as ejaculation that occurs with minimal stimulation, before or shortly after entry of the penis, and causing distress to the patient. Simple short duration of penis intercourse is not the definitive criterion, as duration may be artificially increased by eliminating any foreplay activities or by the patient engaging in distracting thoughts or even painful activities (such as the man deliberately biting his own tongue during intercourse).

The causes of premature ejaculation remain poorly understood. While rapid ejaculation is very common for younger men and for men who have sexual activity only infrequently, true premature ejaculation is seen in men of all ages and in men who have a normal frequency of sexual activity. It is clear that organic or medical issues are not causative factors in premature ejaculation.

Despite this lack of understanding of causality, premature ejaculation is treated with almost a 100% success rate by direct behavioral retraining procedures (Masters & Johnson, 1970). In the stop-start or pause procedure, the penis is manually stimulated until the man is fairly highly aroused. The couple then pauses until his arousal subsides, and then the stimulation is resumed. This sequence is repeated several times before stimulation is carried through to ejaculation, so the man ultimately experiences much more total time of stimulation than he has ever experienced before ejaculation and learns to have a higher threshold for ejaculation. The squeeze procedure is much like the stop-start procedure, except that when stimulation is stopped, the woman firmly squeezes the penis between her thumb and forefinger, at the place were the head of the penis joins the shaft. This squeeze seems to reduce arousal further for many men. After a few weeks of this training, the necessity of pausing diminishes. The couple then progresses to putting the penis in the vagina but without any thrusting movements. Again, if the man rapidly becomes highly aroused, the penis is withdrawn and the couple waits for arousal to subside. When good tolerance for inactive containment of the penis is achieved, the training procedure is repeated during active thrusting. Generally, 2 to 3 months of practice are sufficient to enable a man to enjoy prolonged intercourse without any need for pauses or squeezes.

Male Orgasmic Disorder. This condition refers to the man who has persistent delay in reaching orgasm or is unable to reach orgasm despite receiving adequate sexual stimulation. While orgasmic disorders are quite common in women, orgasmic disorder is rare in men.

The *DSM–IV* specifies that cases that involve any

medical or medication effects and cases with coexisting erectile dysfunction, do not qualify for diagnosis of male orgasmic disorder. However, in clinical practice, the vast majority of men seen with this condition do have some physiological condition that is central to the causality. The most common conditions are neurological injury or disease and the effects of sedating medication or drugs, including alcohol.

Male orgasm disorder is treated by reducing performance anxiety and increasing the level of sexual stimulation. The couple are instructed that during sex the penis is to be caressed manually (and, if acceptable to them, orally) until the man is aroused but that stimulation is to stop whenever he feels he might be close to having an orgasm. This technique reduces goal-focused anxiety about performance and allows the man to enjoy the sexual pleasure provided by the caressing. An electric vibrator may be used to increase the intensity of stimulation. For men with neurological damage, therapy is likely to include some physiological treatment, possibly a drug that increases arousal of the sympathetic nervous system, or stimulation of the anus with a vibrator to trigger the ejaculation reflex.

Female Sexual Dysfunction

Disorders of the arousal and orgasm phase of the sexual response cycle, and sexual pain disorders, that are unique to females are as follows.

Female Arousal and Orgasmic Disorder. Female sexual arousal disorder is defined as "persistent or recurrent inability to attain, or to maintain until completion of the sexual activity, an adequate lubrication-swelling response of sexual excitement" (*DSM–IV*, 1994, p. 502). Female orgasmic disorder is the "persistent or recurrent delay in, or absence of, orgasm following a normal sexual excitement phase" (p. 506). In both disorders, the disturbance causes marked distress or interpersonal difficulty. Orgasmic disorders are specified along the following axes: generalized versus situational, lifelong versus acquired, and due to psychological factors versus due to combined factors. Although conceptualized as discrete disorders, arousal disorder is treated in conjunction with orgasm disorder, as orgasm is not possible if arousal is not attained.

Arousal and orgasm disorders in women can be due to any number of things, including family of origin learning history, systemic issues in the couple's relationship, intrapsychic or cognitive issues, operant issues in the couple's day-to-day environment, and physiological or medical issues.

One treatment for generalized, life-long inorgasmia that has been shown to be effective (Morokoff & LoPiccolo, 1986) is described in *Becoming Orgasmic* (Heiman & LoPiccolo, 1988). The program involves several steps that an individual may complete on her own as a self-help course with the aide of an accompanying book and video (LoPiccolo, 1980) or with the guidance of a trained therapist. Before beginning the more active phase of treatment, the individual is encouraged to do an in-depth examination of her beliefs about sexuality, sensuality, and being female. Discovering the origins of her fears and hopes about becoming a fully sexual woman may prove helpful to her as she progresses through the remaining steps. Next, she acquires knowledge about sexuality. Even in a culture where images of and information about sexuality are readily available, many people find they have unanswered questions about their bodies, genitals, and the female sexual response. Diagrams and reading materials are used to provide the information the client may need in order to dispel sexually related misconceptions.

The second step of the program involves the woman visually and tactilely exploring her entire body. With the aid of a mirror, she is encouraged to examine her genitals. Many women, discouraged by social mores against autoeroticism and discovery, have never seen their labia or clitoris. The purpose of this step is to help her overcome any possible discomfort she may have with her body and develop a complete sense of herself as a sexual adult.

In the third step, the woman is instructed to locate the sensitive areas on her entire body (e.g., lips, thighs, inner wrists, etc.). Quite often, women who experience difficulty achieving orgasms have very little awareness of pleasurable somatic sensations in general, and erotic ones in particular. When she is comfortable acknowledging her body as a source of pleasurable sensations, she is encouraged to expand her exploration to include more erogenous zones, such as her breasts, her genitals, and especially her clitoris. Actual stimulation of the areas is the focus of the next phase of treatment. The woman learns how to touch, caress, and massage all erotic places on her body in such a way as to be comfortable, accepting, and pleasured by her developing awareness of herself as a sexual person. She then is invited to incorporate sexual pictures, stories, and her own fantasies into her developing autoerotic practices. She is encouraged to write her own erotic fantasy as a means of creatively exploring the range of sexual material by which she will allow herself to become aroused.

The next step of the treatment program involves three phases. If the woman has not yet experienced an orgasm during the preceding phases of erotic self-pleasuring and enhanced erotic self-pleasuring, she is encouraged to experiment with using an electric vibrator to increase the intensity of stimulation. The second phase of this step involves acting out a very exaggerated orgasm to assist her with overcoming any fears that she may have about losing control or looking silly during a real orgasm. Quite often once the most feared behavioral worst case scenario is role-played, the real thing is much less intimidating; thus another block to orgasm is removed. Finally, the woman is encouraged to use orgasm triggers, such as tilting her head back, holding her breath while simultaneously tensing her diaphragm as if trying to exhale, arching her feet and pointing her toes, contracting her pelvic muscles, tensing her leg muscles, and thrusting/rocking her pelvis. Many women have found any one, or combination, of these behaviors to be helpful in triggering an orgasm.

Integrating Masters and Johnson's sensate focus procedure with the woman's individual progress is the goal of the next step. This step involves the participation of the woman's sexual partner to facilitate increased communication and sexual skill development. During this step the woman demonstrates for her partner how she prefers to be stimulated and how she can have orgasm. Many women find it easier to do this step if they have the opportunity to observe how their partner prefers to be erotically stimulated; thus partners first demonstrate self-stimulation to orgasm in order to assist the patient with disinhibition. Once the woman is comfortable self-stimulating in the presence of her partner, she teaches her partner how she likes to be touched. Her partner rests his or her hand on hers as she masturbates to orgasm. Once she is comfortable with this, she may guide her partner's hand to teach him or her how she likes to be touched. The couple is then encouraged to continue progressing until her partner is able to stimulate her to orgasm with manual, oral, or vibrator stimulation. Finally, for heterosexual couples, the woman and her partner are encouraged to explore coital positions that permit one or the other of them to continue to stimulate her clitoris during intercourse (assuming the couple has set as a goal the occurrence of her orgasm during penile/vaginal penetration).

Vaginismus. Vaginismus is defined as the "recurrent or persistent involuntary contraction of the perineal muscles surrounding the outer third of the vagina when vaginal penetration . . . is attempted" (DSM–IV, p. 513).

The exact cause of vaginismus, as with many sexual dysfunctions, is unknown. However, untreated dyspareunia is often a precursor for the development of vaginismus. Although the spastic contractions of vaginismus may develop due to painful intercourse caused by medical conditions, it is not uncommon for them to persist after the medical condition is treated and has resolved. Vaginismus is more common in younger women, women who have been sexually traumatized, and women who hold negative beliefs about sex and sexuality.

When a woman presents for treatment of vaginismus it is absolutely imperative to refer her for a gynecological examination. Once this is accomplished, psychological and behavioral treatment may proceed. It is especially important to stress to the couple that adequate stimulation (e.g., caressing, massaging) is important to ensure adequate lubrication, pleasure, and arousal instead of fear or pain. Part of the purpose of treatment is to assist the patient with unlearning the connection of pain with intercourse. Cognitive work should accompany the following behavioral protocol to address the origins of possible beliefs and fears that may contribute to vaginismus (e.g., "nice girls don't do that," "it will hurt," etc.).

The first step in treating vaginismus is to stress that it is critical that the woman progress at her own pace through the treatment protocol, because working hard to make quick progress is almost always countertherapeutic. The first step is to train the woman to become more aware of all of her somatic sensations, not just those more directly related to her presenting complaint. To that end, deep muscle relaxation and diaphragmatic breathing training is undertaken to help her relax and gain voluntary control over her major muscle groups. Kegel exercises (contracting and relaxing the vaginal muscles repeatedly) are then prescribed to help the woman learn to gain volitional control of her pubococcygeal muscle (which is part of the pelvic floor and surrounds the vagina). To assist in overcoming fear of penetration and to become acquainted with the somatic sensations associated with vaginal containment, the woman is taught to use a set of gradually larger dilators, which she inserts in her vagina at home and at her own pace. It is critical to emphasize that dilator insertion is done gently, not with vigorous thrusting motion. In addition, the woman should not progress to the next larger dilator until she is able to comfortably contain the previous smaller one. Later, when the woman can comfortably insert the largest dilator, she begins to guide her partner as he or she slowly and gently inserts the graduated dilators. Again, it is important to stress that dilator insertion is not done forcefully or with repetitive thrusting motions. If it is found that the woman is not able to comfortably contain a dilator in the presence of her partner that she was able to contain previously, the couple is encouraged not to force the larger dilator but to use a smaller one so as to not injure or traumatize her. Next, for heterosexual couples, her partner lies passively on his back while she kneels above him and gradually inserts his erect penis into her vagina at a pace that is comfortable to her. Once the woman is able to contain her partner's penis comfortably, the couple may begin to add thrusting motions and to explore various intercourse positions that are enjoyable to both of them.

Conclusions and Future Directions

Although psychology has made great strides in understanding and treating sexual dysfunctions, the etiology of many of these disorders is not yet understood completely. Obviously they are multiply determined; the explanation that they are resultant solely from experiencing childhood sexual trauma is inadequate since not all individuals who experience negative sexual events eventually develop sexual dysfunction(s). Further research into the origins of the various sexual dysfunctions may inform and refine further treatment interventions. Nonetheless, the sexual dysfunctions represent one of psychology's success stories in that the treatment protocols that have been developed to date have been proven to have relatively high success rates. Treatment approaches have expanded beyond the early practice of screening out concurrent marital problems and now include systemic interventions that address the sexual dysfunction in the context of the couple's relationship. By combining behavioral sex therapy procedures with cognitive, couple systemic, and, in some cases, medical interventions, effective treatment is available for most cases of sexual dysfunction. Clearly, further research on Viagra® and other drugs designed to treat sexual dysfunction is indicated. The effects of such drugs over time on the individual patient, as well as their role in altering the dynamic of a couple experiencing a sexual dysfunction in one or both partners, will become better known over time. A need may arise to provide information and guidelines for the appropriate referral of individuals with a sexual dysfunction to marital therapy. Although addressing the symptom of a sexual dysfunction may provide temporary relief to the patient, such treatment does not necessarily allow for the resolution of marital issues that may exacerbate and/or maintain the disorder.

Bibliography

American Psychiatric Association. (1994). *Diagnostic and statistical manual of mental disorders* (4th ed.). Washington, DC: Author.

Freud, S. (1962). *Three essays on the theory of female sexuality.* (Reprint). New York: Avon. (Original work published 1905)

Heiman, J. R., & LoPiccolo, J. (1988). *Becoming orgasmic: A personal and sexual growth program for women* (rev. and expanded ed.). New York: Simon & Schuster. Provides specifics on an empirically supported treatment program for orgasmic disorder; appropriate for professionals and clients.

Kaplan, H. S. (1974). *The new sex therapy.* New York: Brunner/Mazel.

Krafft-Ebing, R. (1902). *Psychopathia sexualis.* Brooklyn, NY: Physicians and Surgeons Books.

Lieblum, S. R., & Rosen, R. C. (Eds.). (1989). *Principles and practice of sex therapy* (2nd ed.). New York: Guilford Press.

LoPiccolo, J. (1980). *Becoming orgasmic* [Videotape]. (Available from Focus International, 14 Oregon Drive, Huntington Station, NY 11746). Designed to compliment the *Becoming orgasmic* book; provides guidance for completing the treatment program.

LoPiccolo, J. (1997). Sex therapy: A post modern model. In S. J. Lynn & J. P. Garske (Eds.), *Contemporary psychotherapies: Models and methods.* Monterey, CA: Brooks/Cole.

LoPiccolo, J., & Friedman, J. R. (1988). Broad spectrum treatment of low sexual desire: Integration of cognitive, behavioral, and systemic treatment. In S. Leiblum & R. Rosen (Eds.), *Sexual desire disorders.* New York: Guilford.

Masters, W. H., & Johnson, V. E. (1970). *Human sexual inadequacy.* Boston: Little, Brown. One of the classic texts in the field of sex therapy, it revolutionized thinking of sexual dysfunctions and described the first time-effective treatments for these disorders.

Morokoff, P. H., & LoPiccolo, J. (1986). A comparative evaluation of minimal therapist contact and 15-session treatment for female orgasmic dysfunction. *Journal of Consulting and Clinical Psychology, 54,* 294–300.

O'Donohue, W., & Geer, J. H. (Eds.). (1993). *Handbook of sexual dysfunctions: Assessment and treatment.* Boston: Allyn & Bacon. Provides thorough and technical information on the psychological and medical aspects of sexual dysfunction.

Schover, L., & LoPiccolo, J. (1982). Treatment effectiveness for dysfunctions of sexual desire. *Journal of Sex and Marital Therapy, 8,* 179–197.

Wolpe, J. (1958). *Psychotherapy by reciprocal inhibition.* Stanford, CA: Stanford University Press.

Zilbergeld, B. (1992). *The new male sexuality.* New York: Bantam Books. Provides comprehensive information on male sexuality; suitable for professionals and clients.

Joseph LoPiccolo and Lynn M. Van Male

SEXUAL HARASSMENT. As used in the psychological literature, sexual harassment refers to noxious interpersonal behaviors targeted at individuals on the basis of their sex. Although some of these behaviors meet the criteria for illegal sex discrimination, psychologists have focused on a broader spectrum, independent of the law's shifting criteria. Women have been shown to confront a variety of psychologically noxious workplace experiences; particular instances vary considerably in their nature and intensity and may or may not meet the current legal criteria for harassment. This is particularly so given that legal criteria evolve and change based on regulatory definitions, case law, appellate decisions, and the like.

Definitions

Sexual harassment can be defined from at least three different perspectives. At lower levels of inference are basic behavioral definitions, that is, the specification of which actions can be classified as harassment. A number of schemes have been proposed, with Fitzgerald, Gelfand, and Drasgow's (1996) tripartite model of gender harassment, unwanted sexual attention, and sexual coercion enjoying wide acceptance. Gender harassment refers to hostile or offensive behavior (e.g., "jokes," catcalls, and obscene pictures); unwanted sexual attention is just that, and sexual coercion refers to the use of some form of power to leverage sexual cooperation.

Psychological definitions, on the other hand, tend to emphasize cognitive construal and reactions of the target. Tracking the stress and coping literature, Fitzgerald, Swan, and Fischer (1997) define harassment psychologically as "unwanted sex-related behavior at work that is appraised by the recipient as offensive, exceeding her resources, or threatening her well-being."

At higher levels of inference are legal frameworks that articulate criteria for determining when harassment rises to the level of sex discrimination. Influential guidelines promulgated by the U.S. Equal Employment Opportunity Commission (EEOC) state that harassment occurs when cooperation is made a condition of employment, is the basis for employment decisions, or the behavior substantially interferes with work performance or creates an intimidating, hostile, or offensive working environment (EEOC, 1980). Current case law suggests that harassment must: (1) require sexual cooperation in return for some job-related consideration (quid pro quo harassment); or (2) be sufficiently severe to have created an intimidating and hostile working environment in which the situation is both objectively offensive (i.e., to a reasonable person in similar circumstances) as well as subjectively offensive to the target. Actual psychological injury is not a necessary element of the claim.

Measurement

A number of inventories exist to assess the prevalence of harassing behavior, including: (1) the U.S. Merit Systems Protection Board items (U.S. MSPB, 1981); (2) a similar set of items developed by Gutek (1985); and (3) the Sexual Experiences Questionnaire (SEQ), developed by Fitzgerald and her colleagues (Fitzgerald et al., 1996). The MSPB items provide an efficient screen for many widespread forms of harassment and, having been utilized in multiple waves of data collection, represent a rich archive of data. The SEQ, on the other hand, has the advantage of being theoretically grounded, psychometrically sophisticated, and well-validated. Efforts are currently underway to equate the two instruments.

Prevalence

It is difficult to form precise estimates of the extent of sexual harassment: Figures range from a low of 17.5% (taking only supervisor behavior into account; Dansky & Kilpatrick, 1997) to a high of 53% (Gutek, 1985) and rise even higher in organizations with a masculinized job context. Most estimates converge on a rate of 50%; not surprisingly, the most severe harassing behaviors are the least common, while less dramatic behavior is more widespread. Such estimates include experiences that may or may not meet legal criteria for sex discrimination. Consequently, statements such as "One of every two American women will experience some form of sexual harassment during her lifetime" should be understood as empirically rather than legally based. (It is conventional to refer to harassment targets as she, and perpetrators as he, while recognizing that this is not inevitably the case.)

Antecedents

Antecedents refers to those factors that have been associated with higher levels of harassment.

Target Factors. Considerable attention has been directed to identifying factors associated with higher levels of harassment, including characteristics of targets, perpetrators, and organizational context. Although the possibility of individual differences in vulnerability has been pursued, there appears to be no canonical victim. Some evidence suggests that targets are more often younger, less educated, and less powerful than their harassers, as well as being more likely single and generally (at least when Caucasian) of the same race. However, it is also true that targets can be older than their harassers, hold more formal power, and be targeted by men of other races.

Some have speculated that racial and ethnic minority women may be at higher risk because of their greater economic vulnerability and the sexual stereotypes that often attach to women of color. Evidence on this point has been mixed. Recent studies suggest that minority status appears to be associated with elevated risk, but given the association of ethnicity to other factors, the actual critical factors are unknown.

Perpetrator Factors. Although victims appear to reliably share little but their gender, this may not be true of perpetrators. Pryor offers strong evidence for the existence of a (presumably stable) personality characteristic: likelihood to sexually harass (LSH). Men scoring higher on LSH tend to subscribe to adversarial sexual beliefs, authoritarianism, lack of empathy, traditional sex role attitudes, and can be reliably identified by their behavior in a laboratory situation (Pryor, 1987). More recently, Bargh and his colleagues found a cognitive connection between sex and power among men high in LSH (1995).

Organizational Factors. Evidence also shows that contextual factors play a key role in inhibiting or facilitating sexual harassment. Gutek has shown that a skewed gender ratio, in which one sex dramatically outnumbers the other, heightens the salience of gender role characteristics and expectations, leading to the "spillover" of sex role expectations into the workplace and the greater likelihood of sexual harassment (1985).

Hulin, Fitzgerald, and Drasgow make the most explicit case for organizational conditions as antecedents to sexual harassment (1997). Like Gutek (1985), they emphasize the importance of gender context on the job (i.e., gender ratio, gender traditionality of the work, and gender of supervisor), but propose that organizational climate, that is, shared perceptions of the organization's tolerance for harassing behavior, is critical to determining the level of harassment in the workplace. Organizational tolerance includes perceived risk for reporting harassment, the likelihood of being taken seriously, and the likelihood of meaningful sanctions for offenders. A number of studies provide support for this model and organizational conditions are rapidly emerging as possibly the key factor inhibiting or facilitating sexual harassment.

Responses

By now it is well established that most instances of harassment are never reported; rather, studies show that the most common victim responses are to ignore the behavior, deflect it, or avoid the perpetrator to whatever degree possible. Although some women do confront their harassers directly, only a small proportion notify anyone in management and even fewer actually lodge formal complaints.

Research has also examined what targets actually do when faced with harassment and what factors affect the likelihood that they will report it. Responses include active problem solving (e.g., confrontation and reporting) as well as cognitions such as denial, detachment, and reframing. These latter reactions appear ubiquitous among victims, and their effectiveness for protecting them, at least on a psychological level, remains unknown.

Several studies have identified factors that influence assertive responses, such as making a formal report. Brooks and Perot (1991) found that the frequency of the behavior was a powerful predictor, as were feminist attitudes. Subsequent studies have confirmed that targets are more likely to report situations that appear intractable and, although traits such as assertiveness may play a role, the stance and climate of the organization is also a major influence. For example, at least one study suggests that victim reluctance to report is well grounded (Hesson-McInnis & Fitzgerald, 1997).

Outcomes

A number of rigorously designed studies have demonstrated the individual and organizational costs of sexual harassment. Schneider, Swan, and Fitzgerald (1997) found that women experiencing offensive sex-related behavior at work were less satisfied with their jobs, less

committed to the organization, more anxious, more depressed, and had more health problems than their co-workers. Fitzgerald and her colleagues (1997) found that this relationship held even after controlling for the impact of occupational stress, and Dansky and Kilpatrick (1995) found that victims were more likely to meet the criteria for major depression and posttraumatic stress disorder than nonvictims. Although sexual harassment is not necessarily traumatic in nature, it does represent the quotidian gender-related stressor to which many women are exposed on a relatively ongoing basis. Magley and colleagues have demonstrated that the effects of such experiences "kick in" at relatively low levels of exposure (1999).

Factors Leading to Harm

Little is known about the factors leading to negative consequences or the process by which they do so; outcomes are a function of multiple influences. The nature and extent of the behavior itself matters: whether it takes a verbal or physical form, the power of the perpetrator, as well as its severity (e.g., frequency, intensity, and duration). Individual factors include economic vulnerability, lack of social and/or organizational power, and (possibly) traditional vulnerability markers such as age, race, and ethnic minority status. Finally, contextual factors are thought to play a major role, especially organizational climate. According to a stress-and-coping perspective, effects are moderated by whether the target cognitively appraises the experience as irrelevant, benign, or threatening.

Theoretical Models

Tangri, Burt, and Johnson (1982) proposed three possible explanations for the occurrence of sexual harassment: biological, organizational power and opportunity, and sociocultural relations. They concluded, however, that only the second and third had any support from the data available at that time, a conclusion with which subsequent writers have agreed.

Gutek's (1985) sex-role spillover model suggests that harassment arises from strongly skewed gender-ratios that sexualize the workplace and stimulate the inappropriate transfer of traditional sex role expectations. According to this formulation, gender-skewed workgroups have higher levels of harassing behavior, a hypothesis strongly supported by data, at least for male-dominated workforces.

Pryor has articulated a person-environment interaction model, proposing that harassment arises when individuals with a propensity to harass find themselves in an organization tolerant of such behavior, as evidenced by a lack of policies and procedures, weak management norms, and the like (Pryor, LaVite, & Stoller, 1993). His model thus incorporates a tolerant organizational climate while also taking into account individual differences among the human actors involved. His laboratory studies offer powerful support for this formulation.

Finally, the Illinois group (Fitzgerald, Hulin, and Drasgow, 1995) proposes that harassment arises from (1) a masculinized job context and (2) a tolerant organizational climate leading to negative job-related, psychological, and health-related outcomes for those that experience it. Outcomes are hypothesized to be moderated by the target's vulnerability (economic, psychological, etc.) as well as her methods for coping with the experience. The model has received strong empirical support.

Interventions

Despite the organizational and human costs of sexual harassment, few effective interventions have been developed. Efforts that have so far appeared in the literature generally consist of attempts to convey information and change attitudes, assuming that behavior change will follow. In contrast, Grundmann, O'Donohue, and Peterson (1997) provide a sophisticated although as yet untried framework for developing interventions on a variety of levels.

Conclusion

Conceptualized legally, organizationally, or as one aspect of the larger social problem of violence against women, sexual harassment represents a serious and pervasive problem. Although considerable progress has been made at the descriptive and theoretical levels, effective interventions remain elusive. It is here that the greatest need for research remains.

Bibliography

Bargh, J. A., Raymond, P., Pryor, J. B., & Strack, F. (1995). Attractiveness of the underling: An automatic power-sex association and its consequences for sexual harassment and aggression. *Journal of Personality and Social Psychology, 68*, 768–781.

Brooks, L., & Perot, A. R. (1991). Reporting sexual harassment: Exploring a predictive model. *Psychology of Women Quarterly, 15*, 31–47.

Dansky, B., & Kilpatrick, D. (1997). Effects of sexual harassment. In W. O'Donohue (Ed.), *Sexual harassment: Theory, research, and treatment* (pp. 152–174). New York: Allyn & Bacon.

Equal Employment Opportunity Commission. (1980). *Fair employment practices, labor relations reporter.* (EEOC 1980 Guidelines on sexual harassment.) Washington, DC: Bureau of National Affairs.

Fitzgerald, L. F., Gelfand, M. J., & Drasgow, F. (1996). Measuring sexual harassment: Theoretical and technical advances. *Basic and Applied Social Psychology, 17*, 25–445.

Fitzgerald, L. F., Hulin, C. L., & Drasgow, F. (1995). The antecedents and consequences of sexual harassment in organizations: An integrated process model. In S. Sauter & G. Keita (Eds.), *Job stress 2000: Emergent issues.* Washington, DC: American Psychological Association.

Fitzgerald, L. F., Hulin, C. L., Drasgow, F., Gelfand, M., & Magley, V. (1997). Antecedents and consequences of sexual harassment in organizations: A test of an integrated model. *Journal of Applied Psychology, 82*, 578–589.

Fitzgerald, L. F., Swan, S., & Fischer, K. (1995). Why didn't she just report him? The psychological and legal context of women's responses to sexual harassment. *Journal of Social Issues, 51*, 117–183.

Grundmann, E. O., O'Donohue, W., & Peterson, S. H. (1997). The prevention of sexual harassment. In W. O'Donohue (Ed.), *Sexual harassment: Theory, research, and treatment* (pp. 175–184). Boston: Allyn & Bacon.

Gutek, B. (1985). *Sex and the workplace.* San Francisco: Jossey-Bass.

Hesson-McInnis, M. S., & Fitzgerald, L. F. (1997). Sexual harassment: A preliminary test of an integrative model. *Journal of Applied Social Psychology, 27*, 877–901.

Hulin, C. L., Fitzgerald, L. F., & Drasgow, F. (1996). Organizational influences on sexual harassment. In B. Gutek & M. Stockdale (Eds.), *Women and work* (Vol. 6). Newberry Park, CA: Sage.

Magley, V. J., Waldo, C., Drasgow, F., & Fitzgerald, L. F. (1999). The impact of sexual harassment on military personnel: Is it the same for men and women? *Military Psychology.*

Pryor, J. B. (1987). Sexual harassment proclivities in men. *Sex Roles, 17*, 269–290.

Pryor, J. B., LaVite, C. M., & Stoller, L. M. (1993). A social-psychological analysis of sexual harassment: The person/situation interaction. *Journal of Vocational Behavior, 42*, 68–83.

Schneider, K. T., Swan, S., & Fitzgerald, L. F. (1997). Job-related and psychological effects of sexual harassment in the workplace: Empirical evidence from two organizations. *Journal of Applied Psychology, 82*, 401–415.

Tangri, S. S., Burt, M. R., & Johnson, L. N. B. (1982). Sexual harassment at work: Three explanatory models. *Journal of Social Issues, 38*, 33–54.

U.S. Merit Systems Protection Board. (1981). *Sexual harassment of federal workers: Is it a problem?* Washington, DC: U.S. Government Printing Office.

Louise F. Fitzgerald

SEXUALITY. *See* Bisexuality; Heterosexuality; *and* Homosexuality.

SEXUALLY TRANSMITTED DISEASES. With the exception of human immunodeficiency virus (HIV), sexually transmitted diseases (STDs) in the United States constitute a largely hidden epidemic, in part because of a national reluctance to address sexual issues in an open manner (Institute of Medicine, 1997). Improvements in surveillance, diagnosis, and treatment—and perhaps also changes in sexual behavior occurring in response to the threat of acquired immune deficiency syndrome (AIDS)—have brought about declines in the overall national prevalence of some STDs. In 1996, the gonorrhea rate in the United States was 124 cases per 100,000 persons, and the syphilis rate was only 4.3 cases per 100,000 people, levels lower than at any time since the 1970s (U.S. Department of Health and Human Services, 1997). In contrast, however, rates of chlamydia have increased steadily from 47.8 cases per 100,000 persons in 1987 to 194.5 in 1996, and upward trends continue in the prevalence of genital herpes simplex virus infections (U.S. Department of Health and Human Services, 1997). For most of these diseases, there are dramatic differences in rates among different population segments, with women, ethnic minorities, and persons in the American South overrepresented relative to other groups. Although overshadowed in public attention by HIV/AIDS, "traditional" STDs are of substantial public health concern because their consequences can include infertility, ectopic pregnancy, reproductive cancers, pelvic inflammatory disease, and chronic pelvic pain and because lesion-causing STDs can facilitate the transmission of HIV infection.

Between 600,000 and 900,000 Americans are believed to have HIV at the present time, and at least 40,000 new infections are being contracted each year in the United States. Worldwide, HIV is an epidemic still largely out of control, with more than 25 million persons infected and approximately 10,000 persons believed to be contracting new HIV infections daily. The vast majority of HIV infections in the world occur through heterosexual transmission. In the United States, 35 to 50% of new HIV infections occur among injection drug users, 25 to 40% among gay men, and about 25% among women, who are now primarily contracting the disease due to heterosexual contact with infected partners.

STDs and HIV Primary Prevention

Primary prevention of STDs and HIV refers to strategies that help individuals avoid contracting these infections. Since all STDs and most HIV infections are contracted during sex, the primary prevention of these diseases involves encouraging behavior changes to reduce risky sexual behaviors. These changes can include abstaining from sex altogether—most often a goal in programs undertaken with young people—as well as using barrier protections and refraining from sex with partners who might have STDs or HIV.

Because of the attention given to AIDS since the early 1980s, research evaluating the effectiveness of sexual risk behavior reduction interventions has usually been approached more from the perspective of preventing HIV than STDs. Since risk for HIV is lessened by the same behavior changes that also reduce risk for many other STDs, reductions in unprotected sex in vulnerable populations should have favorable impact on risk for both HIV infection and other types of STDs.

Theories Underlying Behavioral Approaches to STD and HIV Prevention. Theoretical models that form the framework for behavior change interventions for STD and HIV prevention are the same theoretical models that have long been used to guide behavior change interventions in health areas unrelated to sex. In essence, the field has adapted behavior change principles used in interventions to promote change in nonsexual health risk behaviors (such as cigarette smoking cessation, cardiovascular risk reduction, substance use curtailment, and cancer prevention) to the issue of changing sexual behaviors that confer risk for STDs and HIV.

Social-cognitive or cognitive-behavioral theory has guided many STD/HIV prevention interventions reported in the literature. The origins of this framework can be traced to Bandura's (1977) formulation of social learning, which emphasizes the role of behavioral and cognitive skill acquisition as a determinant of success in enacting behavior change. Social-cognitive STD/HIV prevention intervention approaches usually combine risk-behavior education with structured opportunities for learning behavioral skills needed to effect behavior change; these skills often include proficiency in properly using condoms, assertively resisting partner pressures to engage in unwanted or unprotected sex, and skills for safer sex negotiation with partners who are resistant to condom use. Because social-cognitive theory emphasizes the role played by positive outcome expectancies, perceived self-efficacy, and reinforcement for enacting change, interventions based on this model often encourage individuals to identify the benefits associated with reducing risk for STDs and HIV and increase feelings of confidence for enacting behavior change.

The theory of reasoned action proposed by Fishbein and Ajzen (1975) has also been widely adapted to developing interventions for STD and HIV risk reduction. This model emphasizes the linkage between an individual's attitudes and beliefs and the strength of his or her behavior change intentions and, in turn, the linkage of these intentions to actual behavior change. Research has shown that condom use in a specific situation can be strongly predicted by asking a person how much he or she intends to use a condom in that situation. Reasoned action theory postulates that strength of intentions is influenced by positive or negative attitudes toward the action, beliefs, and expectancies held by the individual, and other cognitive processes. STD/HIV prevention interventions based on reasoned action theory tend to directly focus on promoting positive attitudes, beliefs, and intentions to adopt risk reduction behavior changes. These often involve the development of positive attitudes and beliefs concerning condom use or, especially in interventions with young people, refraining from sex at an early age.

"Stages of change" formulations as proposed by Prochaska and DiClemente (1983) have also guided some sexual risk behavior reduction interventions. Stages-of-change models postulate that people can be characterized at different levels of readiness for change. These stages range from not presently contemplating change in a health risk behavior to contemplating change, from being ready to act to acting, and from initially acting to then successfully maintaining change over a long period of time. Stages of change models emphasize that one must intervene so as to "move" the individual further along a continuum toward action and maintenance. With respect to STD/HIV prevention, this model suggests that different types of intervention may be needed at different points along the change readiness spectrum. For example, a person who is not yet contemplating condom use may not yet be "ready" for skills training in how to use condoms; at these earlier contemplative points, attitudes or belief-focused intervention may be fundamental. In contrast, persons already sensitized and ready to act to reduce STD risk—perhaps following an STD diagnosis—may not require motivation as much as they require practical assistance in learning ways to implement behavior change.

Community norm and attitude change models constitute other frameworks that have guided STD/HIV prevention programs directed toward community populations. These approaches generally seek to create new population norms and attitudes encouraging avoidance of risky behavior.

"Diffusion of innovation" theory, originally proposed by Rogers (1983), postulates that normative change in a community population can be produced when a sufficient number of key, popular "opinion leaders" within that population endorse and model a behavior change, gradually causing that change to "diffuse," be adopted by others, and eventually become an accepted new norm in the population. Applied to STD/HIV prevention, the visible endorsement of condom use by key opinion leaders can influence the normative perceptions of others toward using condoms. In addition, some community-level STD/HIV prevention interventions have made use of multifaceted community campaigns to create public interest, acceptance, and adoption of new behavior standards. "Social marketing" approaches to condom use employ targeted media campaigns to promote positive attitudes toward condoms and to increase their availability.

Brief Sexual Risk Behavior Reduction Inter-

ventions in STD Clinics. Based on the premise that persons who have just contracted STDs may be especially motivated to avoid future disease and given the known risk of persons recently diagnosed with STDs, several studies have evaluated the impact of brief, single-session sexual risk behavior reduction programs offered to patients in STD treatment settings. Solomon and DeJong (1989), for example, evaluated a videotape intervention designed to promote positive attitudes toward condoms among patients treated in an STD clinic. The video portrayed condom use as sexually appealing and socially acceptable and modeled communication skills for encouraging one's sexual partner to use condoms. Relative to members of a control group who received "standard care" STD treatment and clinic counseling, patients exposed to the videotape intervention showed evidence of improved attitudes toward condoms and more often took free condoms that were available in the clinic. Cohen, Dent, and MacKinnon (1991) evaluated a one-session intervention, also undertaken in STD clinics, that taught condom use skills and encouraged positive attitudes toward their use. Intervention participants had a lower rate of returns for treatment of subsequent STDs than did patients in a standard-care control group. Other research has shown that when such video-based STD clinic interventions are supplemented by opportunities to discuss and personally practice skill-building exercises such as condom use negotiation, patients are more likely to take free condoms (O'Donnell, Doval, Duran, & O'Donnell, 1995).

Multiple-Session Small-Group Interventions. In contrast to the brief intervention programs just discussed that have been shown primarily to improve short-term attitudes toward condom use and to increase the number of patients taking condoms in STD clinics, another set of studies has evaluated the impact of more intensive small-group interventions on persons' sexual behavior practices. Evaluations of these sexual risk reduction interventions have been undertaken with gay or bisexual men (Kelly, St. Lawrence, Hood, & Brasfield, 1989; Valdiserri et al., 1989), women at risk for HIV and STDs (DiClemente & Wingood, 1995; Kelly et al., 1994), and at-risk and predominantly ethnic minority adolescents (Jemmott, Jemmott, & Fong, 1992; Rotheram-Borus, Koopman, Haignere, & Davies, 1991; St. Lawrence, Brasfied, Jefferson, Alleyene, & Shirley, 1995).

Although small-group interventions have varied in intensity, from single-session workshops lasting several hours to a series of 12 or more group sessions, and although these programs have been tailored to address sexual-risk issues unique to each population, the programs also share many common features. All have included risk education to ensure that participants understand which sexual practices confer risk for HIV/STDs and what steps can be taken to reduce risk. All of the small-group interventions have incorporated practice exercises to strengthen participants' skills in enacting behavior change. These skills typically include correct condom use, negotiation of safer sex practices with partners, and assertiveness skills to effectively resist pressures to engage in unprotected or unwanted sex. The small-group programs also incorporated exercises to strengthen participants' positive attitudes toward condom use, enhance their intentions and readiness to avoid high-risk sexual practices, and teach them how to manage future situations or relationships that are likely to create risk. Finally, the group interventions have utilized reinforcement techniques to support participants' behavior change intentions and actions, often eliciting group member support to create peer norms favoring condom use, deferral of sex, or other risk reduction behavior changes.

The outcomes of these interventions are usually assessed by interviewing or administering risk-characteristic measures to participants both before and following intervention, and comparing their changes to those of persons in a control group. Interventions of the type described here have been shown to increase knowledge of risky behaviors and positive attitudes toward condom use, to increase participants' risk reduction behavioral skills, and to produce changes in sexual risk behavior characteristics, including reductions in frequency of unprotected intercourse, increases in condom use and other safer sex practices, and reductions in number of sexual partners. In some studies, evidence of positive benefit has been established for as long as one year following intervention participation.

Community-Level Sexual Risk Reduction Interventions. Because HIV infection and STDs are often concentrated in certain community segments, community-level and population-focused STD and HIV prevention interventions have also been undertaken. In contrast to approaches that utilize counseling or small-group techniques with individuals, community-level interventions attempt to reduce the prevalence of high-risk sexual behavior practices within larger populations, often through the use of media, social marketing, outreach, and social influence intervention methods.

One example of this approach is the AIDS Community Demonstration Projects undertaken by the Centers for Disease Control and Prevention (1996). Across several U.S. cities, population subgroups at high risk for HIV and STDs were identified. These included commercial sex workers, female partners of injection drug users, women at risk, youth in high-risk situations, and men who have sex with men. Baseline risk behavior characteristics were assessed through brief street interviews conducted with members of the identified populations. Community-level interventions were then undertaken in some of the cities. The interventions made use of sexual risk reduction behavior change messages delivered to members of the target populations in media campaigns, through street outreach, and through publicized "role model" stories that portrayed how other people in the same target population successfully made risk reduction changes. Extending beyond risk education, the campaigns attempted to strengthen risk reduction attitudes, beliefs, intentions, and behavior change readiness. Follow-up street interviews conducted with target population members in the communities revealed favorable impact of the intervention on these risk characteristics, as well as evidence of increased condom use in some population segments.

In another example of a community-level sexual risk reduction effort, Kelly and colleagues (1997) first surveyed men entering gay bars in eight small U.S. cities concerning their sexual practices. In four of the cities, an intervention was undertaken that identified persons within each bar who were most popular and well liked among gay men in the clubs. Borrowing from diffusion of innovation theory, cadres of these key and natural "opinion leaders" were recruited, taught, and engaged to systematically carry out conversations with their friends and acquaintances that endorsed the importance of safer sex practices. One year later, surveys were repeated of all men entering the four intervention and four comparison gay bars. Relative to men in the comparison cities who exhibited little sexual behavior change, men in the cities in which interventions had taken place showed reductions of more than 50% in mean frequency of unprotected high-risk sex. These findings indicate that key peers can help to shape the sexual behavior norms within their social networks.

Taken together, research on STD and HIV prevention interventions shows that psychological behavior change principles can be successfully applied to the challenge of developing sexual risk reduction interventions. Interventions based on these principles have proven effective with a range of populations vulnerable to HIV and other STDs.

Psychological Consequences of STDs and HIV

Some STDs—most notably syphilis—can directly cause severe neurological damage if undetected and untreated. The consequences of other STDs, which include infertility, ectopic pregnancy, and reproductive cancers, may create a range of psychological adjustment and coping problems related to these health and disease outcomes. As a chronic STD that can be managed but not cured, genital herpes can greatly affect the sexual relationships, self-esteem, and adjustment of persons who have contracted the disease.

By far the greatest level of attention has been directed to the psychological coping ability of persons living with HIV infection (Kelly & Murphy, 1992). When

AIDS first appeared, there were reports of alarming rates of suicide and of pervasive and severe psychological distress among persons diagnosed with HIV infection and AIDS. The combination of stigma associated with AIDS and the prospect of debilitating disease and early death undoubtedly contributed to these early patterns. Beginning in the 1980s, with the advent of antiretroviral medications to better manage HIV-related opportunistic illnesses and with at least some reduction in AIDS-related stigma, different psychological patterns were observed. Although depression, adjustment disorders, and suicide are still found among some persons living with HIV, the majority of HIV-affected persons do not show pervasive, sustained, and severe psychological distress. Especially for HIV-positive gay men with good social supports, access to medical treatment, and optimistic beliefs concerning the effectiveness of new treatments, the psychological coping patterns exhibited by an individual following HIV diagnosis tend to parallel those of the same individual prior to diagnosis. Coping issues faced by HIV-positive women—especially disadvantaged women with many other social, economic, and psychological life stressors—are often different from those confronting men and require special support (Kelly & Murphy, 1992).

Psychological interventions can benefit distressed persons with HIV and other chronic STDs, such as genital herpes. Support groups and both individual and group therapies that focus on the development of adaptive coping skills have been shown to reduce depression, anxiety, and somatic preoccupations, as well as substance use and patterns of continued unprotected sex in patients who were initially distressed. Such interventions often include attention to effective cognitive, behavioral, and social coping skills; stress management; the development of social supports; communication skills; and opportunities to express concerns and receive support from others with similar experiences.

Finally, given that STDs and HIV involve not only the person with the disease but also sexual partners and others close to the individual, mental health interventions have also been developed to meet the needs of these people. Examples of these psychological interventions include counseling for couples in which one of the two has been diagnosed with HIV or a chronic STD and also programs to meet the psychological coping needs of caregivers to AIDS patients and persons bereaved following the death of a loved one from AIDS.

[See also Acquired Immune Deficiency Syndrome.]

Bibliography

Bandura, A. (1977). Social learning theory. Englewood Cliffs, NJ: Prentice Hall.

Centers for Disease Control and Prevention (1996). Community-level prevention of human immunodeficiency virus infection among high-risk populations: The AIDS Community Demonstration Project. Morbidity and Mortality Weekly Report, 45, 1–24.

Cohen, D., Dent, C., & MacKinnon, D. (1991). Condom skills education and sexually transmitted disease reinfection. Journal of Sex Research, 28, 139–144.

DiClemente, R. J., & Wingood, G. M. (1995). A randomized controlled trial of an HIV sexual risk reduction intervention for young African American women. Journal of the American Medical Association, 274, 1271–1276.

Fishbein, M., & Ajzen, I. (1975). Belief, attitude, intention, and behavior: An introduction to theory and research. Reading, MA: Addison-Wesley.

Institute of Medicine. (1997). The hidden epidemic: Confronting sexually transmitted diseases. Washington, DC: National Academy Press.

Jemmott, J. B., Jemmott, L. S., & Fong, G. T. (1992). Reductions in HIV risk-associated sexual behaviors among Black male adolescents: Effects of an AIDS prevention intervention. American Journal of Public Health, 82, 372–377.

Kelly, J. A., & Murphy, D. A. (1992). Psychological interventions with AIDS and HIV: Prevention and treatment. Journal of Consulting and Clinical Psychology, 60, 576–585.

Kelly, J. A., Murphy, D. A., Sikkema, K. J., McAuliffe, T. L., Roffman, R. A., Solomon, L. J., Winett, R. A., Kalichman, S. C., & the Community HIV Prevention Research Collaborative (1997). Randomized, controlled community-level HIV prevention intervention for sexual risk behaviour among homosexual men in U.S. cities. Lancet, 350, 1500–1505.

Kelly, J. A., Murphy, D. A., Washington, C. D., Wilson, T. S., Koob, J. J., Davis, D. R., Ledezema, G., & Davantes, B. (1994). The effects of HIV/AIDS intervention groups for high-risk women in urban clinics. American Journal of Public Health, 84, 1918–1922.

Kelly, J. A., St. Lawrence, J. S., Hood, H. V., & Brasfield, T. L. (1989). Behavioral intervention to reduce AIDS risk activities. Journal of Consulting and Clinical Psychology, 57, 60–67.

O'Donnell, L. N., Doval, A. S., Duran, R., & O'Donnell, C. (1995). Video-based sexually transmitted disease patient education: Its impact on condom acquisition. American Journal of Public Health, 85, 817–822.

Prochaska, J. D., & DiClemente, C. C. (1983). Stages and processes of self-change of smoking: Toward an integrative model of change. Journal of Consulting and Clinical Psychology, 51, 390–395.

Rogers, E. E. (1983). Diffusion of innovations. New York: Free Press.

Rotheram-Borus, M. J., Koopman, C., Haignere, C., & Davies, M. (1991). Reducing HIV sexual risk behavior among runaway adolescents. Journal of the American Medical Association, 266, 1237–1241.

St. Lawrence, J. S., Brasfield, T. L., Jefferson, K. W., Alleyene, E., & Shirley, A. (1995). Cognitive-behavioral intervention to reduce African American adolescents' risk for HIV infection. Journal of Consulting and Clinical Psychology, 63, 221–237.

Solomon, M. Z., & DeJong, W. (1989). Preventing AIDS and

other STDs through condom promotion: A patient education intervention. *American Journal of Public Health, 79,* 453–458.

U.S. Department of Health and Human Services. (1997). *Sexually transmitted disease surveillance, 1996.* Atlanta, GA: Division of STD Prevention, Centers for Disease Control and Prevention.

Valdiserri, R. O., Lyter, D., Leviton, L., Callahan, C., Kingsley, L. A., & Rinaldo, C. (1989). AIDS prevention in homosexual and bisexual men: Results of a randomized trial evaluating two risk reduction interventions. *AIDS, 3,* 21–26.

Jeffrey A. Kelly

SEXUAL MASOCHISM involves sexual arousal associated with the actual act (not simulation) of suffering, including being humiliated, beaten, and bound. Masochism may take place individually (e.g., self-mutilation) or with a partner (e.g., restraint, blindfolding, paddling, spanking, whipping, beating, electrical shocks). One potentially lethal form of sexual masochism is hypoxyphilia (autoerotic asphyxia) in which choking (e.g., via chest compression, noose, plastic bag) is associated with sexual arousal. Pain tolerance may increase during sexual arousal, but it has been contended that masochists also carefully seek to avoid injury. Sexual masochism may involve cross-dressing, but sexual arousal is associated with being forced to cross-dress rather than the act of cross-dressing itself. There is a paucity of empirical research on masochism. Much of the literature on masochism involves case studies because adequate samples of masochists are difficult to identify and study.

Baumeister (1988b) compared masochism to other behaviors that people engage in to escape self-awareness, such as physical exercise, intoxication, meditative techniques, and being a fan or spectator. The pain involved in masochism may shift higher level self-awareness to the physical self. Thus, pain may serve as a narcotic for masochists. Masochistic fantasies, urges, or behavior become pathological when they create significant distress or impairment in a person's functioning.

Baumeister (1988a, 1988b, 1997) has conceptualized masochistic behavior as more consistent with stereotypically feminine than masculine roles. For example, masochistic behavior includes self-sacrifice, serving others, and suffering for the sake of others. In addition, male masochists may be more likely to dress and act like women than female masochists are to dress and act like men (Baumeister, 1997). Moreover, there may be gender differences in the content of male and female masochists' fantasies. Baumeister (1988a) examined the letters of sadistic and masochistic men and women

to a popular sadomasochistic magazine. Although it is likely that the magazine chose to publish the letters that would seem most appealing to their audience and thus may represent stereotypes, these letters may provide at least some evidence of role expectations of male and female masochists. Letters from male masochists were significantly more likely to involve themes of physical pain and of oral humiliation, including having the masochist kiss the partner's feet or buttocks, putting underwear in the masochist's mouth, or having the masochist consume sexual fluids other than in the context of oral sex. Letters from women were significantly more likely to involve genital intercourse. Women's masochistic behavior was viewed as an exaggeration of stereotypical feminine roles (Baumeister, 1988a).

Women's sexual submission fantasies do not necessarily reflect a wish to be raped. In these submission fantasies, women are typically in control. Women's erotic rape fantasies most commonly involve a sexually attractive man who is irresistibly sexually stimulated by the woman's sexual attractiveness. Leitenberg and Henning (1995) discussed four different explanations that have been proposed for women's sexual submission fantasies. One explanation involves sexual power in which a man cannot resist or control himself. A second involves sex guilt, in which a woman may feel blameless if she involuntarily engages in sexual behavior. A third, feminist explanation is that women's submission fantasies are symptomatic of a male dominant culture. Finally, victims of sexual abuse may become conditioned to associate submission with sexual arousal.

Masochism has also been proposed as an explanation of abused women who remain in relationships with abusers. However, views of victims as masochistic cater to the blaming of victims as having somehow provoked the abuse. Victims often remain in abusive relationships because they are dependent in many ways on the abuser, not because they are aroused by or enjoy the abuse. Leaving an abusive relationship may also create the threat of even greater abuse to the woman or her children.

Prevalence

Sexually masochistic behaviors are relatively rare. The frequency of masochistic activities in both college and male clinical samples ranges from 1 to 3%. There are no gender differences in self-reported masochistic activities in college samples, perhaps because of the restricted amount of such activity for either gender. Nevertheless, sexual masochism is the only paraphilia that is very commonly diagnosed among females, with a sex ratio of 20 males to each female.

Masochistic fantasies may be more common than actual masochistic behavior. Consistent with the lack of gender differences in masochistic behavior, recent data suggest a lack of gender differences in the occurrence of masochistic fantasies. Thirty percent of men reported fantasies of being forced to submit to sexual acts, and 35% of women did so. Few persons admitted to fantasies of being sexually degraded, including 6% of men and 9% of women. These percentages of being forced to submit to sexual acts and to being sexually degraded correspond to the percentages of men who have fantasies of forcing a partner to submit to sexual acts (29%) and who had fantasies of sexually degrading a partner (9%). Only 13% of women have fantasies of forcing a sexual partner to submit to sexual acts, and only 3% have fantasies of degrading a sexual partner. Although data have not been gathered on the percentages of men and women who fantasized about perpetrating bondage, there are significant ethnic differences in bondage fantasies. Whereas only 29% of Asian Canadian men and 26% of Asian Canadian women reported having fantasies of being tied up or bound during sexual activities, 51% of non-Asian men and 46% of non-Asian women reported such fantasies (Meston, Trapnell, & Gorzalka, 1996).

Treatment

There are no controlled outcome data on the treatment of sexual masochism. Antiandrogen treatments have been demonstrated to be effective in reducing other paraphilic behaviors, and it is probable that such treatments would also reduce the sexual motivation for masochistic behaviors. Individual approaches have focused on increasing self-esteem. Among sadomasochistic couples a proposed focus is a corrective interpersonal experience (Glickauf-Hughes, 1996). However, to the extent that sadistic and masochistic behaviors are sexually gratifying for a couple, it would appear that these behaviors would be difficult to change and that such couples would not be seen in clinical situations without some imbalance in the relationship (e.g., excessive harm as a result of sadomasochistic activities).

[See also Sexual Disorders.]

Bibliography

Baumeister, R. F. (1988a). Gender differences in masochistic scripts. *Journal of Sex Research, 25,* 478–499.

Baumeister, R. F. (1988b). Masochism as escape from self. *Journal of Sex Research, 25,* 28–59.

Baumeister, R. F. (1997). The enigmatic appeal of sexual masochism: Why people desire pain, bondage, and humiliation in sex. *Journal of Social and Clinical Psychology, 16,* 133–149.

Glickauf-Hughes, C. (1996). Sadomasochistic interactions. In F. W. Kaslow (Ed.), *Handbook of relational diagnosis and dysfunctional family patterns* (pp. 270–286). New York: Wiley.

Leitenberg, H., & Henning, K. (1995). Sexual fantasy. *Psychological Bulletin, 3,* 469–496.

Meston, C. M., Trapnell, P. D., & Gorzalka, B. B. (1996). Ethnic and gender differences in sexuality: Variations in sexual behavior between Asian and non-Asian university students. *Archives of Sexual Behavior, 25,* 33–72.

Gordon C. Nagayama Hall

SEXUAL ORIENTATION concerns an individual's erotic interest in males, females, or both. Historically, sexual orientation has been conceptualized in typological terms. Those oriented to others of their own biological sex are lesbian if female, gay if male; those oriented to the other sex are heterosexual; and, those people whose erotic focus is on both males and females are called bisexual. Same-sex and bisexual sexual orientations have been subject to intense cultural sanctions, remaining controversial in contemporary society. Although public attitudes about same-sex sexual orientation have become somewhat less negative, there is ample evidence of pervasive prejudice and victimization of lesbians, gay men, and bisexual people. For instance, in nearly half of the United States, consensual same-sex sexual activity between adults is illegal. Only a handful of states protect lesbian, gay, and bisexual people from discrimination in employment, housing, and public accommodations. And, disclosed lesbians, gay males, and bisexual women and men cannot serve in the U.S. military unless there is evidence that they will not engage in sexual activity. This strong negative bias against nonheterosexual sexual orientations has seriously interfered with efforts to understand sexual orientation and its development.

Sexual orientation is a theoretical construct composed of four components. The first component, sexual attraction, is at the core of sexual orientation. The labeling of this attraction as reflecting a particular sexual orientation—self-identification as lesbian, gay, bisexual, or heterosexual—is the second component. It is possible to experience attraction yet not attribute it to a sexual orientation. Disclosure of attraction and self-identification to others is the third component. While lesbian-, gay-, and bisexual-identified people must explicitly inform others of their orientation if they wish others to know, heterosexual people do not generally disclose their orientation to others. This process, called coming out, is usually under the conscious control of the individual. The fourth component of sexual orientation is sexual behavior. Many experience sexual attraction without engaging in sexual behavior; however, sexual behavior can lead to rethinking one's sexual orientation. These four components are not perfectly synchronized and indeed may appear inconsistent (e.g., an individual can have strong same-sex attraction but engage only in heterosexual sexual behavior).

Systematic research on the prevalence of different

sexual orientations began with the well-known interview-based studies conducted by the Kinsey Institute after World War II. Kinsey and his colleagues advanced the study of sexual orientation by proposing that sexual orientation constituted a continuum from exclusively same-sex oriented to exclusively other-sex oriented. They also found that same-sex sexual arousal was common (half of the males and about one quarter of the females reported same-sex sexual response by age 45) and that same-sex sexual experience was less frequent than arousal (37% of the males and 13% of the females reported a same-sex sexual experience to orgasm by age 45). Fewer interviewees could be labeled exclusively lesbian or gay over their entire lives; about 10% of the males and 4% of the females demonstrated consistent same-sex sexual orientations for several consecutive years past adolescence.

More recent research suggests that these figures may have overestimated same-sex sexual orientations. Based on data collected in 1988 in the United States, the United Kingdom, and France, one set of investigators found that less than 1% of all respondents acknowledged a same-sex sexual orientation. On the other hand, 21% of U.S., 16% of U.K., and 18% of French males reported same-sex attraction or behavior since age 15; for females, 18% of U.S., 19% of U.K., and 18% of French respondents reported same-sex attraction or behavior. Similar discrepancies between attraction, behavior, and self-identification were found in a random sample of 3,432 respondents interviewed in 1992. About 6% of the males and 4% of the females acknowledged being sexually attracted to others of their sex; 5% of the males and 4% of the females reported same-sex sexual contact since age 18; and 2.8% of the males and 1.4% of the females self-identified as lesbian, gay, or bisexual. Importantly, 9% of the males in the largest cities in the study self-labeled as gay, compared with 3 to 4% in suburban areas, and to 1% in rural settings; comparable figures for females were similarly skewed toward higher percentages of urban residents acknowledging same-sex sexual orientation. It thus appears crucial to assess multiple dimensions of sexual orientation. In addition, the relative acknowledgment of same-sex attraction versus self-identification as lesbian, gay, or bisexual suggests that stigma is still associated with same-sex and bisexual sexual orientations. Thus, incidence measures that rely on self-report are likely to lead to underestimation of same-sex and bisexual sexual orientations even in anonymous surveys.

Nearly all the interest in the development of sexual orientation has been directed to understanding same-sex sexual orientation rather than the processes and mechanisms by which heterosexual-identified individuals develop their sexual orientation. Indeed, development of same-sex sexual orientation was earlier often framed within a psychopathology model. The presumption was that same-sex sexual orientation was a dysfunctional developmental outcome whose etiology required explanation. Basing their views on clinical experiences with adult gay men and lesbians, psychoanalytic and psychodynamic theorists argued that same-sex sexual orientation was generally induced early in life by disordered family relationship patterns. The landmark studies of psychologist Evelyn Hooker seriously challenged the equation of same-sex sexual orientation with psychopathology. Comparing gay men drawn from nonclinical settings to similar heterosexual men, Hooker found no differences in psychological adjustment. Her studies, published in the 1960s, in combination with additional research and pressure from lesbian/gay rights activists, contributed to the removal of homosexuality from the American Psychiatric Association's list of mental disorders in 1973. The removal of homosexuality from psychiatric nosology has had a profound effect on efforts to understand the nature of sexual orientation.

Current explanations of the development of sexual orientation can be characterized as deriving from either essentialist or social constructionist perspectives. Essentialist views assume that sexual orientation is a stable individual difference variable and typically focus on sexual attraction as the defining characteristic. Social constructionist views, on the other hand, conceptualize sexual orientation as highly responsive to social and cultural circumstances and hence highly variable. In addition, social constructionist views of sexual orientation hypothesize that different cultural and social groups construct different sexual orientations at different historical periods. Research based on essential thinking endeavors to discover the basic elements and causes of sexual orientation. Social constructionist researchers view efforts at finding causes to be potentially misleading. In particular, the social constructionist perspective objects to reification of sexual orientation as a unitary "essence" not subject to social, cultural, and historical influences. In a general sense, essentialist research employs traditional, quantitative research methods, whereas social constructionist research emphasizes more exploratory, qualitative research methods.

Recent research on the biological determinants of sexual orientation has examined neuroendocrine differences between heterosexual-identified and lesbian/gay-identified adults. However, no consistent proof of hormonal variability related to sexual orientation has been found to date. Biologically based research has investigated the neuroanatomical features. Le Vay reported (1996) significant portmortem brain differences between male heterosexuals and gay males. But this study has been critiqued on a number of grounds and has not yet been replicated, nor has a comparable study of females been done.

There is some evidence for a genetic contribution to

sexual orientation. Studies have found that gay and lesbian adults report more known gay and lesbian siblings than heterosexual men and women report. Ten percent of gay males report gay brothers, compared to 1% of heterosexual males; lesbians report that 13% of their sisters are also lesbians, whereas only 2% of heterosexual women's sisters are reported to be lesbian. In addition, studies comparing monozygotic and dizygotic twins with nontwin siblings show that same-sex sexual orientation occurs more often in monozygotic twins, although this finding is more pronounced for males than for females. Other evidence of a genetic contribution to sexual orientation comes from molecular analyses that link a DNA marker on a specific region of the X-chromosome (Xq28) to male sexual orientation. This study has yet to be replicated, and a similar study of female same-sex sexual orientation did not find a genetic marker.

Much less research has been conducted on social antecedants of sexual orientation. Indeed, the degree to which early psychological experience contributes to the development of different sexual orientations is unknown. Findings from studies of gender development show that adult gay men and, to a lesser degree, lesbians report that they engaged in more gender-atypical behavior during childhood than heterosexual males and females. However, the source of this gender-atypical behavior is unknown. No carefully conducted large-scale research has investigated psychological aspects of familial and other environments during childhood and related these to adult sexual orientation.

More developmental work has been directed to the study of adolescents who define themselves as lesbian, gay, or bisexual. This research suggests that adolescents who self-identify as lesbian, gay, or bisexual are aware of same-sex attractions at about age 10, on the average, label themselves as lesbian, gay, or bisexual several years after this, and typically disclose their sexual orientation to another person for the first time at about age 16. In other words, same-sex attraction emerges in early to middle adolescence, and other components of sexual orientation occur later. There is, however, considerable variability among lesbian, gay, and bisexual youths as to the timing of these developmental milestones; lesbian and bisexual females achieve these milestones at generally later ages than gay and bisexual males. It should also be noted that same-sex sexual behavior usually follows the awareness of same-sex sexual attraction. In one study, an average of 4 years transpired between youths' awareness of same-sex attraction and same-sex sexual activity, but findings indicate that sexual orientation development accelerates during puberty. This research also shows that many high school youths are aware that they are lesbian, gay, or bisexual even though they have told no one and have not engaged in same-sex sexual activity. In addition, there are indications that lesbian, gay, and bisexual youths experience considerable stress if they remain nondisclosed, but that they experience many difficult challenges if they come out. There has been much professional interest in documenting mental health and other problems of these youths, given the recognition that stigma and victimization contribute to adjustment problems. Although no longitudinal studies have been yet conducted to follow lesbian, gay, and bisexual youths over time to assess the frequency and determine causes of problems they experience, findings suggest more suicide attempts in this population than in heterosexual identified youths. There is also evidence of verbal and physical abuse of lesbian, gay, and bisexual youths who are open about their sexual orientation.

Much remains to be learned about the development of sexual orientations during early childhood and adolescence. The earlier research work documenting that lesbian, gay, and bisexual individuals are not specifically afflicted with mental illness has evolved to efforts to understand the life challenges of lesbian, gay, and bisexual individuals. Considerable research is also examining whether same-sex committed adult relationships differ from committed heterosexual relationships (they appear to be quite similar) and exploring the development of children raised within same-sex families (they are generally similar to children raised in heterosexual families). Much has also been learned about gay and bisexual males as a result of research related to the HIV/AIDS epidemic. The increasing methodological rigor of these efforts will result in a more precise understanding of sexual orientation as it develops over the life course.

Bibliography

Bohan, J. S. (1996). *Sexual orientation: Coming to terms.* New York: Routledge.

Cabaj, R. P., & Stein, T. S. (Eds.). *Textbook of homosexuality and mental health.* Washington, DC: American Psychiatric Press.

D'Augelli, A. R., & Patterson, C. J. (Eds.). (1995). *Lesbian, gay, and bisexual identities over the lifespan: Psychological perspectives.* New York: Oxford University Press.

Garnets, L. D., & Kimmel, L. D. (Eds.). (1993). *Psychological perspectives on lesbian and gay male experiences.* New York: Columbia University Press.

Gonsiorek, J. C., & Weinrich, J. D. (Eds.). (1991). *Homosexuality: Research implications for public policy.* Newbury Park, CA: Sage.

Hamer, D., & Copeland, P. (1994). *The science of desire: The search for the gay gene and the biology of behavior.* New York: Simon & Schuster.

Herek, G. M, & Greene, B. (Eds.). (1995). *AIDS, identity, and community: The HIV epidemic and lesbians and gay men.* Thousand Oaks, CA: Sage.

LeVay, S. (1996). *Queer science: The use and abuse of research into homosexuality.* Cambridge, MA: MIT Press.

McWhirter, D. P., Sanders, S. A., & Reinisch, J. M. (Eds.). (1990). *Homosexuality/heterosexuality: Concepts of sexual orientation.* New York: Oxford University Press.

Patterson, C. J., & D'Augelli, A. R. (Eds.). (1998). *Lesbian, gay, and bisexual identities and the family: Psychological perspectives.* New York: Oxford University Press.

Rothblum, E. D., & Bond, L. A. (Eds.). (1996). *Preventing heterosexism and homophobia.* Thousand Oaks, CA: Sage.

Savin-Williams, R. C., & Cohen, K. M. (Eds.). *The lives of lesbians, gay, and bisexuals.* New York: Harcourt Brace.

Anthony R. D'Augelli

SEXUAL SADISM involves recurrent, intense sexual fantasies, sexual urges, or behaviors involving actual acts in which the psychological or physical suffering, including humiliation, of a victim is sexually arousing to a person. Sadistic fantasies or behavior include domination (e.g., forcing the victim to act like an animal), restraint, blindfolding, paddling, spanking, whipping, pinching, beating, burning, electrical shocks, cutting, stabbing, strangulation, torture, mutilation, or killing. Such fantasies and behavior appear to be a function of urges to obtain control or dominance over another person. Sadistic fantasies or behavior may occur during sexual activity with consenting (e.g., masochists) or nonconsenting partners. Sadism and masochism often exist in the same individual.

Sadistic rapists appear to substantially differ from nonsadistic rapists. Although many rapes appear to be sadistic, sexual sadism is characteristic of only a minority of rapists. Most rapists are more sexually aroused by consenting than by sadistic or other nonconsenting sexual stimuli. The murder of victims by sexual offenders is also not necessarily diagnostic of sexual sadism. Among sexual offenders who murder victims, 30 to 58% are diagnosed as sexual sadists. However, there may be a higher prevalence (86–90%) of antisocial personality disorders among sadists than among other sexual offenders.

Sadistic sexual offenders appear to be more sexually deviant than other paraphiliacs. They are more likely than nonsadistic sexual offenders to have engaged in other paraphilias (e.g., cross-dressing, voyeurism, scatological telephone calls, indecent exposure). Sadists are also more likely than other paraphiliacs to abuse alcohol. Sadists anally rape victims or force victims to perform fellatio and experience sexual dysfunction during the offense at a greater rate than other sexual offenders. There is evidence that sadists are more impulsive

and reoffend at a faster rate than other rapists; other evidence suggests that sadists who have attempted or committed homicide are more likely than nonsadists to deliberately plan their offenses.

Sadistic behavior may be associated with childhood victimization experiences. A history of being sexually victimized is common among sadists but not significantly more common than among nonsadist sexual offenders. Sadists who victimize adults may be different in this respect than nonsadistic rapists of adults who may have more limited histories of sexual abuse than other sexual offenders, such as child molesters. However, sadists are more likely than nonsadistic sexual offenders to have been physically abused during childhood. Thus, it appears that a combination of sexual and physical abuse during childhood may be associated with later sadistic behavior.

A minority of pedophiles perpetrate physical violence against the children they sexually victimize, but most may not qualify as sadistic. Only 11% of a forensic sample of 263 pedophilic men used physical force against victims, and not all of these men are necessarily sadistic (Greenberg, Bradford, & Curry, 1996). Consistent with sexual arousal patterns for most rapists of adults, mean sexual arousal patterns revealed less sexual arousal among both physically aggressive and less aggressive pedophiles in response to coercive, sadistic, and assaultive stimuli than to consenting stimuli. This pattern is also consistent with the sexual arousal patterns of child molesters in other large samples.

Classification

Clinician diagnoses of sadism are somewhat less reliable than what is generally considered acceptable for psychological tests. An interrater kappa of 0.60 has been reported for clinician ratings of sadism based on child molesters' clinical records (Knight, Carter, & Prentky, 1989). However, such clinician ratings of sadism are correlated at best only 0.30 with offenders' self-reported sadistic behavior (Knight, Prentky, & Cerce, 1994). This discrepancy between clinician ratings and offenders' self-reports is not simply a function of offender defensiveness, which was assessed to be relatively minimal. Moreover, the reliability of self-reports of sadism was good, with alphas for self-report scales involving sadism ranging from 0.82 to 0.95. The discrepancy between clinical ratings and offenders' self-reports might be attributable to the method by which the clinical ratings were obtained. The clinical ratings of sadism relied heavily on the amount of violence involved in sexual offending. However, since not all violent sexual offenders are sexually aroused by sadistic activity, offense characteristics may be analogous to a phenotype that may or may not reflect the genotype.

Penile tumescence in response to verbal depictions

of sadistic stimuli may be considered to be less subjective and may be somewhat more reliable than clinical ratings in assessing sexual sadism. The test-retest reliability of penile tumescence in response to sadistic stimuli approaches an acceptable range from a psychometric perspective. Test-retest reliabilities range from 0.69 to 0.82 among rapists and child molesters for adult sadistic stimuli. Test-retest reliability for child sadistic stimuli was 0.75 among child molesters and rapists (Hall, Proctor, & Nelson, 1988) and 0.70 among community men (Hall, Hirschman, & Oliver, 1995).

Although penile tumescence measures appear reliable, they appear not to have discriminant validity in identifying sadists. Penile tumescence to sadistic stimuli in two studies were greater among sexual offenders than among nonoffenders (Fedora et al., 1992; Seto & Kuban, 1996). However, penile tumescence measures failed to discriminate between sexual offenders who were independently diagnosed as sadistic or nonsadistic. Moreover, in both studies, mean profiles for sadistic and nonsadistic sexual offenders indicated greater arousal to consenting than to coercive stimuli, including sadistic stimuli. The ability of penile tumescence measures to discriminate between sexually deviant individuals and normals and failure to discriminate within groups of sexually deviant groups has also been reported in other studies.

Penile tumescence assessment of the paraphilias is susceptible to both false negatives and false positives. Fifty to 80% of sexual offenders and nonoffenders have been found to be able to inhibit their penile tumescence during assessments. Thus, the absence of penile response to sadistic stimuli does not necessarily rule out the possibility of sadism. Moreover, some men, particularly those who are unable to voluntarily inhibit their sexual arousal, are highly arousable to stimuli that do not necessarily correspond with their behavior. Thus, penile tumescence in response to sadistic stimuli does not necessarily reflect sadistic behavior.

Prevalence and Incidence

As with the other paraphilias, sexual sadism is much more common among men. Men were more likely than women to report sadistic fantasies in a large sample of Canadian college students (Meston, Trapnell, & Gorzalka, 1996). Whereas 9% of men reported having fantasies of degrading a sex partner, only 3% of women did so. Fantasies of forcing a partner to submit to sexual acts were reported by 29% of men but only 13% of women. Eleven percent of men and 4% of women reported fantasies of whipping or beating a sexual partner. In a study of penile tumescence in response to sadistic stimuli, 5% of a normal control sample exhibited a significant level of sexual arousal to such stimuli (Fedora et al., 1992).

Sadistic behavior may be less common than sadistic fantasies and arousal. Only 1% of college men admitted to degrading a partner during sexual activity. Sadism is a relatively uncommon paraphilia in clinical samples. In a sample of 1,025 paraphiliacs seen for an outpatient evaluation, 4% of adolescents and 2% of adults were diagnosed as sexually sadistic (Abel, Osborn, & Twigg, 1993). In an inpatient sample of 277 rapists and 239 child molesters, 10% of rapists and 6% of child molesters were classified as sadistic (Knight & Prentky, 1993). It is possible that these low rates of sadistic fantasies and behavior are a function of the social undesirability of sadism and of efforts of sadists to avoid detection.

Treatment

Controlled-outcome studies that specifically identify sexual sadists are not available. However, a meta-analysis of recent sexual offender treatment outcome studies suggests that cognitive-behavioral treatments and antiandrogen drugs are more effective in reducing recidivism among child molesters and rapists than are other treatment approaches or no treatment (Hall, 1995). It is possible that some of the child molesters and rapists in these studies were sadistic. Nevertheless, the extreme psychopathology involved in sexual sadism may make it less amenable to treatment than other paraphilias.

[See also Sexual Disorders.]

Bibliography

Abel, G. G., Osborn, C. A., & Twigg, D. A. (1993). Sexual assault throughout the life span: Adult offenders with juvenile histories. In H. E. Barbaree, W. L. Marshall, & S. M. Hudson (Eds.), *The juvenile sex offender* (pp. 104–117). New York: Guilford.

Fedora, O., Reddon, J. R., Morrison, J. W., Fedora, S. K., Pascoe, H., & Yeudall, L. T. (1992). Sadism and other paraphilias in normal controls and aggressive and non-aggressive sex offenders. *Archives of Sexual Behavior, 21,* 1–15.

Greenberg, D. M., Bradford, J. M. W., & Curry, S. (1996). Are pedophiles with aggressive tendencies more sexually violent? *Bulletin of the Academy of Psychiatry and Law, 24,* 225–235.

Hall, G. C. N. (1995). Sexual offender recidivism revisited: A meta-analysis of recent treatment studies. *Journal of Consulting and Clinical Psychology, 63,* 802–809.

Hall, G. C. N., Hirschman, R., & Oliver, L. L. (1995). Sexual arousal and arousability to pedophilic stimuli in a community sample of "normal" men. *Behavior Therapy, 26,* 681–694.

Hall, G. C. N., Proctor, W. C., & Nelson, G. M. (1988). The validity of physiological measures of pedophilic sexual arousal in a sexual offender population. *Journal of Consulting and Clinical Psychology, 56,* 118–122.

Knight, R. A., Carter, D. L., & Prentky, R. A. (1989). A system for the classification of child molesters: Reliability and application. *Journal of Interpersonal Violence, 4,* 3–23.

Knight, R. A., & Prentky, R. A. (1987). The developmental antecedents and adult adaptations of rapist subtypes. *Criminal Justice and Behavior, 14,* 403–426.

Knight, R. A., & Prentky, R. A. (1993). Exploring characteristics for classifying juvenile sex offenders. In H. E. Barbaree, W. L. Marshall, & S. M. Hudson (Eds.), *The juvenile sex offender* (pp. 45–83). New York: Guilford.

Knight, R. A., Prentky, R. A., & Cerce, D. D. (1994). The development, reliability, and validity of an inventory for the multidimensional assessment of sex and aggression. *Criminal Justice and Behavior, 21,* 72–94.

Meston, C. M., Trapnell, P. D., & Gorzalka, B. B. (1996). Ethnic and gender differences in sexuality: Variations in sexual behavior between Asian and non-Asian university students. *Archives of Sexual Behavior, 25,* 33–72.

Seto, M. C., & Kuban, M. (1996). Criterion-related validity of a phallometric test for paraphilic rape and sadism. *Behaviour Research & Therapy, 34,* 175–183.

Gordon C. Nagayama Hall

SHAKOW, DAVID (1901–1981), American psychologist. Shakow belongs to the second generation of clinical psychologists, those who began their careers in the period from about 1910 to 1940. The first generation consisted of turn-of-the-century psychologists such as Alfred Binet, Shepherd Ivory Franz, and Lightner Witmer. These early clinicians perforce entered a field that had no formal or sanctioned course of preparation. There also was little encouragement for their interest or profession from psychologists concerned that they be regarded as scientists. Thus it was usually up to the student to put together from what courses were available a suitable educational background and to fashion from on-the-job training appropriate clinical skills. The roles of clinical psychologists during this time were those of researcher, psychometrician, and teacher. Shakow was a product of this somewhat haphazard professional situation.

He entered Harvard University to study psychology in 1925. During this period he worked with Frederic Lyman Wells at the Boston Psychopathic Hospital (Wells was an early clinician who in 1906 took over the psychological laboratory at McLean Hospital) and then at Worcester State Hospital with Grace Kent in developing form boards that could be used as tests.

At Harvard, Shakow did graduate work in experimental psychology under Boring, which led to a dissertation on subliminal perception. The results of this research were inconclusive and not accepted for his doctorate. However, at Worcester State Hospital, where he worked from 1928 to 1946, Shakow continued to collaborate on research projects and advance his clinical understanding. He did research with Milton Erickson on hypnotically induced complexes, with A. J. Harris on the significance of scatter on the Stanford–Binet Intelligence Scale, with Saul Rosenzweig on the use of the tautophone as a projective method (a person heard a voice speaking unintelligibly and was required to guess what was said), and with many others on a series of studies investigating the performance of schizophrenics.

Throughout his career, Shakow had two major programs of research. First, he studied motor behaviors, such as speed of tapping, reaction time, and performance on the pursuit rotor (a person is asked to keep the end of a rod in contact with a rotating disk) among subgroups of schizophrenic patients and normals. He concluded that schizophrenics had a problem in assuming and maintaining a set, or readiness to respond, and that this resulted in decrements and great variability in their performance. Shakow thought this could also be construed as a problem in attending and found that the schizophrenics could improve their scores and become less variable with practice.

His second major research endeavor was in psychoanalysis, for which he prepared by studies in that area and by undergoing a personal analysis. After receiving his doctrate in general experimental psychology from Harvard in 1942 with a dissertation on schizophrenia, Shakow left Worcester State Hospital in 1946 to become professor of psychology at the College of Medicine of the University of Illinois in Chicago. In 1948, he received a conjoint appointment at the University of Chicago, where he tried, without too much success, to make sense of psychoanalytic sessions that had been recorded. He conducted a similar study at the National Institute of Mental Health, where he was chief of the laboratory in psychology from 1956 to 1966 and senior research scientist from 1966 until his retirement. Although this study had the benefit of a psychoanalyst who added his own thoughts to what was openly said during his sessions, the data proved refractory.

Shakow's contributions to the profession of clinical psychology, more than his research, earned him the esteem of his colleagues. In the years prior to the end of World War II, psychologists recognized that there would be a great demand for clinicians to meet the needs of returning military personnel. Shakow chaired a joint committee of the American Psychological Association and the American Association of Applied Psychology that sought to determine how psychology could best address this expected shortage of practitioners. In 1945, this committee recommended that training and education be provided through existing graduate programs in psychology, rather than by the creation of new schools or departments. Further, they recommended a four-year program: In the first year or so the student would be grounded in psychological theories, research methodology, and psychology as a science; the second and third years would provide a growing emphasis in clinical courses, practica, and internship training; and the fourth year would immerse the student in doctoral research and the dissertation. To a large extent, these recommendations were adopted.

In 1947, the American Psychological Association Committee on Training, chaired by Shakow, specified that a clinical curriculum include general or experimental psychology, statistics, psychodiagnostics, psychological tests, psychodynamics, psychotherapy, and related disciplines, such as sociology, physiology, and anthropology. This report endorsed the roles of the clinical psychologist as psychotherapist, scientist, and diagnostician. The model for the clinician was the scientist-practitioner, a model embodied by Shakow and one that he endorsed and continued to promote throughout his life. It was dominant for a generation and remains viable to the present.

[See also American Psychological Association; Clinical Psychology; Doctoral Degree; Experimental Psychology; National Institute of Mental Health; Projective Techniques; Psychoanalysis; Schizophrenia; Scientist-Practitioner Model; Stanford–Binet Intelligence Scale; and the biographies of Binet, Boring, Franz, and Witmer.]

Bibliography

Reisman, J. M. (1991). A history of clinical psychology (2nd ed.). New York: Hemisphere.

Shakow, D. (1960). The recorded interview as an objective approach to research in psychoanalysis. Psychoanalytic Quarterly, 29, 82–97.

Shakow, D. (1965). Seventeen years later: Clinical psychology in the light of the 1947 Committee on Training in Clinical Psychology report. American Psychologist, 20, 353–362.

Shakow, D. (1969). Clinical psychology as a science and as a profession: A forty-year odyssey. Chicago: Aldine.

Shakow, D. (1972). The Worcester State Hospital research on schizophrenia (1927–1946). Journal of Abnormal Psychology, 80, 67–110.

Shakow, D., & Rosenzweig, S. (1939–1940). The use of the tautophone ("verbal summator") as an auditory apperceptive test for the study of personality. Character and Personality, 8, 216–226.

John M. Reisman

SHAME. American psychologist Helen Block Lewis referred to shame as the sleeper emotion—a powerful and ubiquitous human experience that has long been overlooked in the therapist's office, the researcher's lab, and our day-to-day lives. Feelings of shame can have a profound effect on psychological adjustment and relationships with other people, but these feelings nonetheless often go undetected. People rarely speak of their shame experiences. Denial and a desire for concealment are part of the phenomenology of shame itself. We shrink from our own feelings of shame, just as we recoil from others in the midst of a shame experience. Shame is an altogether unwelcome event. To further muddy the waters, shame frequently masquerades as other emotions—hiding behind guilt, lurking behind anger, fueling depression.

Moreover, people's tendency to confuse shame with guilt helped relegate shame to a footnote in psychology's first century. In professional writings and in everyday conversation, shame and guilt are mentioned in the same breath as interchangeable emotion words, or (more often) guilt is used as a catchall term for elements of both emotions. Even the father of psychoanalysis largely neglected the distinction between shame and guilt; in his earlier work, Freud briefly discussed shame as a reaction formation against sexually exhibitionistic impulses, but in his later writings he essentially ignored the construct of shame, focusing instead on a rather cognitive conception of guilt as an outcome of ego-superego conflicts. In fact, numerous contemporary psychoanalysts have suggested that, in developing a theory that focused almost exclusively on guilt, Freud often mislabeled his patients' shame experiences as guilt.

In decades following, several post-Freudian theorists made explicit attempts to distinguish between shame and guilt. With the emergence of self psychology, shame gained an even more prominent place in clinical theory. At the same time, inspired by the groundbreaking work of Helen Block Lewis and fueled by the affect revolution, researchers began systematic empirical inquiry into the nature and implications of shame. Thus, over the past 25 years, the sleeper emotion has awakened, and we now have a much better sense of how this fundamental human emotion operates, distinct from guilt.

The Difference Between Shame and Guilt

When people make a distinction between shame and guilt, they often refer to differences in the content or structure of events eliciting these emotions. The assumption is that certain kinds of situations lead to shame whereas other kinds of situations lead to guilt. For example, there is a long-standing notion that shame is a more public emotion, arising from public exposure and disapproval, whereas guilt is a more private experience arising from self-generated pangs of conscience. As it turns out, there is little empirical support for this public-private distinction. Analyses of adults' recollections of personal shame and guilt experiences indicate that other people are no more likely to be aware of shame-inducing behaviors than guilt-inducing behaviors. When feeling shame, people may be more focused on others' evaluations, but actual public scrutiny is just as likely in the case of guilt. By the same token, shame and guilt do not fundamentally differ in terms of the types of failures or transgressions involved.

The crux of the difference between shame and guilt has to do with the focus of one's negative evaluation. When people feel guilt, they feel bad about a specific behavior. When people feel shame, they feel bad about themselves. Empirical research indicates that this differential emphasis on self ("*I* did that horrible thing.") versus behavior ("I *did* that horrible *thing*.") gives rise to very different phenomenological experiences. Whereas feelings of guilt (about a specific behavior) involve a sense of tension, remorse, and regret over the bad thing done, feelings of shame involve a painful scrutiny of the entire self—a feeling that "*I* am an unworthy, incompetent or bad person." People in the midst of a shame experience often report a sense of shrinking, of being small. They feel worthless and powerless. And they feel exposed. Although shame does not necessarily involve an actual observing audience present to witness one's shortcomings, there is often the imagery of how one's defective self would appear to others—as unworthy and reprehensible. [*See* Guilt.]

The Contrasting Motivations of Shame and Guilt: Hiding Versus Amending

Not surprisingly, phenomenological studies of shame and guilt indicate that these emotions lead to very different motivations or action tendencies in interpersonal contexts. A consistent finding is that the tension, remorse, and regret of guilt motivates corrective action—confessing, apologizing, or somehow undoing the harm that was done. In sharp contrast, shame is more likely to motivate an avoidance response. Shame is generally a more painful experience than guilt; it often involves a sense of exposure and a preoccupation with others' opinions. People feeling shame often report a desire to flee from the shame-inducing situation, to sink into the floor and disappear. And at the same time, denial of responsibility or of the behavior itself is not uncommon. Thus, shamed individuals seek to hide their misdeeds and the self from others, in an effort to escape from the pain of shame. (In fact, some developmental researchers use avoidant versus reparative patterns of behavior as early markers of shame-prone versus guilt-prone styles among toddlers.) Guilt is apt to orient people in a constructive, proactive, future-oriented direction; shame is apt to drive people to separate, distance, and defend.

Shamed into Anger: Some Further Motivational Features of Shame

Shame not only motivates avoidant behavior, but also can motivate a defensive, retaliative anger. During a shame experience, hostility is initially directed toward the self. A shamed individual feels like a bad person because of some transgression or error. As the self is painfully scrutinized and negatively evaluated, the person in the midst of a shame episode is apt to feel trapped and overwhelmed. This, in turn, can lead the person to engage in all sorts of defensive maneuvers. One way to protect the self and to regain a sense of control and agency is to redirect that hostility and blame outward—turning the tables, as it were.

Consistent with this notion, empirical studies have demonstrated a link between shame and anger, in specific situations and at the level of personality dispositions. For example, studies of both children and adults indicate that shame-prone individuals are also prone to feeling anger and hostility. Moreover, once angered, shame-prone individuals are inclined to manage their anger in an unconstructive fashion. In a recent cross-sectional developmental study of children, adolescents, college students, and adults, proneness to shame was consistently related to malevolent intentions; direct, indirect, and displaced aggression; self-directed hostility; and projected negative long-term consequences of everyday episodes of anger. (In contrast, guilt was generally associated with constructive means of handling anger.) Similar findings have been observed at the situational level. For example, in a study of real-life episodes of anger among romantically involved couples, shamed partners were significantly more angry, more likely to engage in aggressive behavior, and less likely to elicit conciliatory behavior from their partners.

More Reasons to Prefer a Nonshame-Prone Partner: Interpersonal Empathy

The link between shame and maladaptive anger raises more general questions about the interpersonal sensitivity of the shame-prone person. Are shame-prone individuals less empathic than their peers? Numerous studies of children, college students, and adults have examined the relationship among shame-proneness, guilt-proneness, and dispositional empathy. The results are quite consistent. Guilt-prone individuals are generally empathic individuals. In contrast, shame-proneness has been repeatedly associated with an impaired capacity for other-oriented empathy and a propensity for self-oriented personal distress responses. Similar findings are evident when considering feelings of shame and guilt in the moment. Individual differences aside, when people describe personal shame (versus guilt) experiences, they convey less empathy for others involved. Moreover, people induced to feel shame exhibit less empathy than their unshamed counterparts.

The inverse relationship between shame and empathy is not surprising. Feelings of shame involve a marked self-focus, drawing one's attention away from the distressed other, back on to the self. Shamed individuals are less concerned with the hurt caused to others and more concerned with negative characteristics of the self.

Taken together, a range of research studies—employing diverse samples, measures, and methods—converge at the same practical bottom line: all things being equal, it is better if your friend, partner, parent, child, or boss feels guilt rather than shame. Shame often motivates behaviors that, in one way or another, are likely to interfere with interpersonal relationships. Either path—shamed withdrawal or shamed rage—involves behaviors that are unlikely to rectify the negative effects of one's transgressions.

Shame-Proneness and Psychological Symptoms

Empirical research paints a rather foreboding picture of the interpersonal adjustment of shame-prone individuals. Does the tendency to experience shame about the entire self leave one vulnerable to psychological problems, as well? Researchers consistently report a relationship between proneness to shame and a whole host of psychological symptoms, including depression, anxiety, eating-disorder symptoms, subclinical sociopathy, and low self-esteem. The link between shame and psychological problems appears to be robust across measurement methods and across diverse age groups and populations. Moreover, the relationship between shame-proneness and depression is strong, even after controlling for attributional style. People who frequently experience feelings of shame are more apt to develop psychological symptoms, compared to their nonshame-prone peers.

The Adaptive Functions of Shame

The theory and research reviewed thus far have emphasized the dark side of shame, underscoring negative consequences of this emotion both for psychological adjustment and for interpersonal behavior. Obvious questions, then, are, "Why do we have the capacity to experience this emotion anyway?" and "What adaptive purpose might it serve?"

Some theorists have suggested that shame plays an important role in regulating experiences of excessive interest and excitement. The notion is that, especially at very early stages of development, some mechanism is needed to put the brakes on interest and excitement in social interactions, helping the young child disengage when it is appropriate to do so. Others, taking an evolutionary approach, have focused on the appeasement functions of shame and its role in diffusing aggressive behavior among conspecifics. It's also been suggested that the motivation to withdraw—so often a component of the shame experience—may be useful in interrupting potentially threatening social interactions until the shamed individual has a chance to regroup.

Finally, there is the widely held assumption that painful feelings of shame help people avoid doing wrong, decreasing the likelihood of transgression and impropriety. As it turns out, there is surprisingly little direct evidence of this inhibitory function of shame. But indirect evidence suggests that shame is not as effective as guilt in guiding us down a moral path. For example, adults' self-reported moral behaviors are substantially positively correlated with proneness to guilt but are unrelated to proneness to shame. Together with other results showing that shame is associated with impaired empathy, a tendency to deny responsibility, and destructive responses to anger, there is good reason to question the moral self-regulatory function of shame in many contexts.

Cultural Variations

Researchers have only begun to examine cultural differences in the self-conscious emotions. Recent cross-cultural research has challenged the notion that there are distinct shame and guilt cultures. People around the globe experience both shame and guilt in the course of daily life. There are suggestions, however, that the meaning and functions of these self-conscious emotions may vary with cultural context. In particular, some theorists have made the compelling argument that the experience and implications of shame and guilt may differ fundamentally depending on whether a given culture emphasizes an interdependent or independent construal of the self. These are, after all, self-conscious emotions fundamentally rooted in the self. Consistent with this notion, several recent studies suggest that, compared to cultures emphasizing an independent self, in interdependent, collectivist, or honor cultures people are more inclined to express and share their shame experiences; children understand the meaning of the term shame at an earlier age; and (perhaps most significant) the experience of shame appears to have fewer negative effects.

It's important to emphasize that the vast majority of research summarized in this article was conducted in the United States, a culture that fosters an independent construction of the self. In the coming years, cross-cultural research will no doubt reveal important areas in which culture moderates key relationships between shame and social-psychological adjustment. One might speculate that the adaptive potential of shame may be more evident in interdependent contexts.

Bibliography

Barrett, K. C., Zahn-Waxler, C., & Cole, P. M. (1993). Avoiders versus amenders: Implications for the investigation of shame and guilt during toddlerhood? *Cognition and Emotion, 7,* 481–505.

Freud, S. (1953). Three essays on the theory of sexuality. In J. Strachey (Ed. and Trans.), *The standard edition of the complete psychological works of Sigmund Freud* (Vol. 7, pp. 153–243). London: Hogarth Press. (Original work published 1905)

Gilbert, P. (1997). The evolution of social attractivenenss and its role in shame, humiliation, guilt, and therapy. *British Journal of Medical Psychology, 70,* 113–147.

Harder, D. W., Cutler, L., & Rockart, L. (1992). Assessment of shame and guilt and their relationship to psychopathology. *Journal of Personality Assessment, 59,* 584–604.

Kitayama, S., Markus, H. R., & Matsumoto, H. (1995). Culture, self, and emotion: A cultural perspective on "self-conscious" emotion. In J. P. Tangney & K. W. Fischer (Eds.), *Self-conscious emotions: Shame, guilt, embarrassment, and pride* (pp. 439–464). New York: Guilford Press.

Lewis, H. B. (1971). *Shame and guilt in neurosis.* New York: International Universities Press.

Lewis, M. (1992). *Shame: The exposed self.* New York: Free Press.

Morrison, A. P. (1989). *Shame: The underside of narcissism.* Hillsdale, NJ: Analytic Press.

Nathanson, D. L. (Ed.). (1987). *The many faces of shame.* New York: Guilford Press.

Scheff, T. J. (1987). The shame-rage spiral: A case study of an interminable quarrel. In H. B. Lewis (Ed.), *The role of shame in symptom formation* (pp. 109–149). Hillsdale, NJ: Erlbaum.

Tangney, J. P., & Fischer, K. W. (Eds.), *Self-conscious emotions: Shame, guilt, embarrassment, and pride.* New York: Guilford.

Tangney, J. P., Miller, R. S., Flicker, L., & Barlow, D. H. (1996). Are shame, guilt and embarrassment distinct emotions? *Journal of Personality and Social Psychology, 70,* 1256–1269.

Tangney, J. P., Wagner, P. E., Barlow, D. H., Marschall, D. E., & Gramzow, R. (1996). The relation of shame and guilt to constructive vs. destructive responses to anger across the lifespan. *Journal of Personality and Social Psychology, 70,* 797–809.

June Price Tangney

SHEPARD, ROGER N. (1929–   ), American experimental and cognitive psychologist. Shepard made significant theoretical, methodological, and experimental contributions that influenced the development of mathematical and cognitive psychology and that transformed the study of mental imagery and complex psychological scaling. His childhood fascination with Euclidean geometry lead him to study how individuals represent the external world by an internal psychological space that can be described with mathematical techniques, some of which he invented.

Shepard earned his doctoral degree at Yale University in 1955. After a research fellowship with George Miller at Harvard University (1956–1958), he joined the teaching staff of Bell Telephone Laboratories, rising to head of the learning processes and measurement department (1963–1966). He briefly returned to Harvard as a professor of psychology and director of the Psychological Laboratories (1966–1968), before receiving an appointment in 1968 as professor of psychology at his undergraduate alma mater, Stanford University. Shepard received the APA Distinguished Contribution to Psychology Award in 1976 and became emeritus professor at Stanford in 1994.

Early in his career, Shepard developed mathematical models to describe response and stimulus generalization. He was able to demonstrate the invariance of generalization by measuring the dissimilarity of a set of stimuli from a central stimulus in psychological dimensions, rather than in the physical dimensions of the stimuli themselves. The same law of generalization held regardless of what kind of physical stimuli were examined. Later, he turned to the study of recognition memory and, in a frequently cited study, demonstrated the near flawless capacity of humans to recognize pictures previously viewed, even after a week's time lapse. By the early 1970s, Shepard was widely acknowledged for his work in three areas: multidimensional scaling, the experimental study of imagery, and universal laws that connect the psychological and physical sciences.

Nonmetric multidimensional scaling was invented by Shepard in 1961. It is a form of psychological scaling applied to a subject's judgments of similarity and dissimilarity among a set of stimuli. The judgments are then represented by the researcher as points in a dimensional space where the distance between the points reflects the corresponding distance between the stimuli. The spatial (geometric) structure extracted from the plot of the points is held to represent the psychological structure employed by the individual in judging the stimuli. Thus, nonmetric multidimensional scaling permits a metric description of similarities based on ordinal data. The attributes of the stimuli that were used by the individual in making the judgments can often be identified by use of the procedure, thus revealing the hidden structural nature of the judgments. Multidimensional refers to the fact that, through the technique, physical stimuli may be scaled in terms of the values on the psychological dimensions employed by the subjects.

The study of imagery was dormant in psychology for many decades, until the appearance of new experimental procedures for its study in the late 1960s. One of the most important of these procedures was mental rotation, first described by Shepard in 1968. The mental rotation procedure presents a viewer with a drawing of a pair of figures (or letters). When the first figure (or letter) is rotated in the imagination, it may be made isomorphic (or if it is a mirror image of the figure, nonisomorphic) with the second member of the pair. The reaction time required for an observer to arrive at a judgment is a linear function of the number of degrees through which the first figure must be rotated to be made congruent with the second figure. In rotating the image internally, paths that correspond to an external rotation of the object are transversed. Mental rotation and related studies provided evidence that some of our representations are stored as images rather than as propositions, that images have spatial features similar to their corresponding external objects, and that imagery and perception may share similar mechanisms. Shepard argued that while the relationship between an external object and its corresponding internal image may not be isomorphic, the two can be shown to be related functionally, a fact he termed second-order isomorphism. A summary of his work may be found in *Mental Images and Their Transformation*, by Shepard and Lynn Cooper (Cambridge, Mass., 1982).

In a manner that follows from his search for psychological laws and universals, Shepard has argued that the mind contains the kind of structured representations it does—for example, three dimensions to represent color—because, among other reasons, the physical world has shaped the mind through the course of evolution; therefore, the mind takes a form in which there will necessarily be a correspondence between mental representations and regularities of the external world. General principles constrain the psychological structures one could discover, yielding the possibility of genuine universal laws or principles of mind. Since the constraints do not stem from the brain per se, but rather from the physical world that constructed the brain, it may be possible to discover mental universals with systems other than the wet tissue of the brain.

Bibliography

Distinguished scientific contribution awards: Roger N. Shepard. (1977). *American Psychologist, 32,* 62–67. A biographical sketch of Shepard's childhood and professional career with a list of his publications through 1972.

Shepard, R. N. (1967). Recognition memory for words, sentences, and pictures. *Journal of Verbal Learning and Verbal Behavior, 6,* 156–163. Classic paper on an individual's memory for previously viewed pictures.

Shepard, R. N. (1978). The mental image. *American Psychologist, 33,* 125–137. A discussion of the history and innovations in the study of mental imagery.

Shepard, R. N. (1988). George Miller's data and the development of methods for representing cognitive structures. In W. Hirst (Ed.), *The making of cognitive science:*

Essays in honor of George A. Miller. Cambridge, UK: Cambridge University Press. An illustration of mutidimensional scaling and a discussion by Shepard of his early postdoctoral research activities with George Miller.

Shepard, R. N. (1995). Mental universals: Toward a twenty-first century science of mind. In R. L. Solso & D. W. Massaro (Eds.), *The science of mind: 2001 and beyond* (pp. 50–62). New York: Oxford University Press. An excellent summary of Shepard's argument for universal mental principles, including several examples.

Terry Knapp

SHERIF, MUZAFER (1906–1988), Turkish social psychologist. One of the most influential social psychologists of the twentieth century, Sherif was born into a Moslem family in Ödemiś, Turkey. He studied at Izmir International College and Istanbul University before entering graduate work at Harvard University in 1929. There, Sherif's focus on the role of group norms in human behavior put him at odds with Gordon Allport's more individualistic approach to social psychology. As a result, he transferred to Columbia University, where he completed a doctoral dissertation under Gardner Murphy on the patterning of unstructured situations into group norms (Sherif, 1935). [*See the biography of Gordon Allport.*]

In Sherif's classic dissertation studies, subjects first judged alone and then with others the distance of illusory movement of a pinpoint of light in a dark room, the well-known autokinetic phenomenon. Judgments made alone were standardized into personally unique ranges, whereas judgments rendered aloud with other participants were standardized into group norms. In *The Psychology of Social Norms* (1936), Sherif extended his conception of group norms to internalized values, attitudes, roles, and key components of the self that, as major internal anchorages, influence cognitive outcomes.

Four central assumptions guided these and Sherif's later works:

1. *Human behavior is normative.* Human interaction over time produces social norms, which motivate and regulate much of human behavior, including the expression of biogenic needs.
2. *Reality of groups.* Although groups are emergent products, they are real, existing at their own level and not reducible to the sum of their parts, the individual members, and their characteristics. As in other part-whole relationships, the dominant influence is from the group to the member.
3. *Properties of real groups validate experimental findings.* Since groups are real, an understanding of that reality in its natural setting provides the basis for judg-

ing the validity of experimental findings. A social assembly lacking the defining properties of a group is but a "togetherness situation," the study of which has no validity for real-life groups.

4. *Frame of reference.* Perception and behavior are determined in bipolar fashion by external and internal factors, the interdependent totality of which Sherif termed "frame of reference." Internal factors predominate when they are intense, the stimulus is ambiguous, and external factors under the reverse conditions.

Sherif's 1935 and 1936 works helped spawn the "New Look" in psychology, the widespread practice of studying motivational factors through their influence on cognitive processes. They also sparked numerous studies of social influence under varying conditions of stimulus ambiguity, and stimulated the development of novel theories, including Harry Helson's theory of adaptation level (1947, 1948), which aimed at quantifying Sherif's conception of frame of reference.

In 1936, Sherif returned to Turkey, where he taught at the Gazi Institute and Ankara University. In Ankara, his opposition to the pro-Nazi attitudes and policies of Turkish officials resulted in his arrest and imprisonment for "actions inimical to the national interest" (Trotter, 1985, p. 56). His release from prison and return to the United States in 1945 were secured through diplomatic efforts initiated by his American colleagues. He never returned to Turkey, nor did he ever apply for American citizenship.

During 2 subsequent years at Princeton University, Sherif collaborated with Hadley Cantril on the compendious *Psychology of Ego-Involvements* (Sherif & Cantril, 1947), which dealt with the anchoring effects of varying sources of ego-involvement, including reference groups, and on perception and judgment. This work expanded the concept of the reference group into a broad social theory by distinguishing reference groups (those an individual identifies with) from membership groups (those the individual actually belongs to). Reference-group theory was widely adopted as a framework for explaining the effects of status, attitude formation, and judgments of in-group and out-group members.

After a brief stay at Yale University, Sherif spent the years from 1949 to 1966 at the University of Oklahoma, where he founded the Institute of Group Relations and produced 12 books and 43 articles or chapters, mostly on intra- and intergroup relations, social judgment, and attitude change. The two most influential of these were the Robbers Cave Experiment, a landmark study of group competition and cooperation (Sherif, Harvey, White, Hood, & Sherif, 1954, 1988), and the social-judgment theory of attitude change (Sherif & Hovland, 1961), which, as an important the-

ory of attitude change, generated intensive research on the determinants of responses to persuasive communication. Interest in this theory has waned appreciably only recently. In 1966, Sherif became professor of sociology at Pennsylvania State University, where he completed his career, publishing five additional books despite ill health and other setbacks.

Sherif received numerous honors in recognition of his work, including prestigious awards from the American Psychological Association and the American Sociological Association. However, a high sense of deservedness, born perhaps from a sense of marginality and insecurity compounded by a long-term struggle with manic-depression (Harvey, 1989), caused him to view such recognition as inadequate and engendered a rivalry toward other highly acclaimed social psychologists, particularly those who failed to credit his work. These feelings were strongest toward the prominent members of Kurt Lewin's group-dynamics tradition, whose status he considered undeserved, and from having been gained through research on artificially designed or "quick groups" rather than natural groups. Sherif's views on the reality of groups, the powerful effects of norms, and the limits of laboratory research continue to serve as valuable counterpoints to American psychology's experimental and individualistic emphases.

Bibliography

Harvey, O. J. (1989). Muzafer Sherif (1906–1988). *American Psychologist, 44,* 1325–1326.

Helson, H. (1947). Adaptation level as frame of reference for predictions of psychophysical data. *American Journal of Psychology, 60,* 1–29.

Helson, H. (1948). Adaptation level as a basis for a quantitative theory of frames of reference. *Psychological Review, 55,* 297–313.

Sherif, M. (1935). A study of some social factors in perception. *Archives of Psychology, 27,* 1–60.

Sherif, M. (1936). *The psychology of social norms.* New York: Harper.

Sherif, M., & Cantril, H. (1947). *The psychology of ego-involvements.* New York: Wiley.

Sherif, M., Harvey, O. J., White, B. J., Hood, W. R., & Sherif, C. W. (1954). *Intergroup conflict and cooperation: The robbers cave experiment.* Norman, OK: Multilithed.

Sherif, M., Harvey, O. J., White, B. J., Hood, W. R., & Sherif, C. W. (1988). *The robbers cave experiment: Intergroup conflict and cooperation.* Middletown, CT: Wesleyan University Press.

Sherif, M., & Hovland, C. I. (1961). *Social judgment: Assimilation and contrast effects in communication and attitude change.* New Haven, CT: Yale University Press.

Trotter, R. (1985). Profile: Muzafer Sherif: A life of conflict and goals. *Psychology Today,* 55–59.

O. J. Harvey

SHERRINGTON, CHARLES SCOTT (1857–1952), English physiologist. Charles Scott Sherrington was born into a London physician's family on 27 November 1857. In 1880 Sherrington entered Gonville and Caius College, Cambridge, receiving his degree in 1883. Two years later he qualified in medicine at St. Thomas Hospital, after which he spent a year in Rudolf Virchow's Berlin laboratory. Upon returning to England, Sherrington held appointments at St. Thomas Hospital, the University of London, the University of Liverpool, and the University of Oxford. Despite an early interest in pathology, Sherrington would turn his attention to the nervous system and behavior, primarily through the influence of Cambridge physiologist John Langley.

The Integrative Action of the Nervous System, Sherrington's seminal work, appeared in 1906. Derived from his 1904 Yale University Silliman Lectures and dedicated to David Ferrier, this landmark book produced data and concepts that altered neurophysiology. Therein he described spinal reflexes in decerebrate animals. Deducing his neurophysiological conclusions from behavioral data, he found that the reflex is not an isolated arc but an integrated action of the entire organism. Sherrington introduced terms such as *proprioceptive, nociceptive, recruitment, neuron,* and *synapse,* and concepts such as the motor unit, the final common pathway, the neuronal excitatory threshold, excitatory and inhibitory neural states, and spatial and temporal summation. These terms and concepts would become foundational in both neuroscience and psychology.

Sherrington demonstrated that stimulating muscles produced simultaneous inhibition in antagonistic muscles, and that muscular activation is important not only in movement but also in posture. He studied eye movement and established that the cortical terminations of the left and right are separate rather than merging. He also found that visceral sensations substantiate rather than initiate emotion, thus providing experimental evidence against the James-Lange theory of emotion. Topics that garnered Sherrington's attention besides the nervous system include bacteriology (especially cholera), histology, the formation of scar tissue, and cancer metabolisms. Many of Sherrington's students also became prominent researchers (e.g., Sir John C. Eccles). Not only the consummate scientist, Sherrington was also a published poet (*The Assaying of Brabantius and Other Verse,* 1925) and philosopher. He best expressed his philosophical thought in his University of Edinburgh Gifford Lectures, entitled "Man on His Nature" (1937–1938).

King George V knighted Sherrington in 1922, and in 1932 Sherrington received the Nobel Prize in medicine. He died of heart failure in Eastbourne, England, on 4 March 1952.

Bibliography

Fulton, J. F. (1952). Sir Charles Scott Sherrington. *Journal of Neurophysiology, 15,* 167–190.

Gallistel, C. R. (1980). *The organization of action: A new synthesis.* Hillsdale, NJ: Erlbaum. This helpful book places Sherrington's work in the context of other great contributions to our understanding of movement.

Sherrington, C. S. (1906). *The integrative action of the nervous system.* New York: Scribner's.

Sherrington, C. S. (1940). *Man on his nature.* Cambridge, England: Cambridge University Press.

Randall D. Wight

SHORT-TERM THERAPY. *See* Brief Therapy.

SHYNESS is the term most often used to label feelings of anxiety and inhibition in social situations. Common synonyms include timidity, bashfulness, self-consciousness, reticence, and social anxiety. The experience of shyness typically involves three components. Global feelings of emotional arousal and specific physiological complaints, such as upset stomach, pounding heart, sweating, or blushing, define the somatic anxiety component of shyness. Acute public self-consciousness, self-deprecating thoughts, and worries about being evaluated negatively by others constitute the second, cognitive component of shyness. The third component includes observable behavior such as quietness, cautiousness, awkward body language, gaze aversion, and social withdrawal. Situations differ in their power to evoke these reactions of social anxiety. Ratings of shyness-eliciting situations reveal that interactions with strangers, encounters requiring assertive behavior, and explicitly evaluative settings such as interviews provoke the strongest feelings of social anxiety.

Psychologists since William James (*The Principles of Psychology,* New York, 1890) have speculated about the function or usefulness of shyness in humans and other animals. From an evolutionary perspective on emotional development, a moderate amount of wariness regarding strangers and unfamiliar or unpredictable situations has considerable adaptive value. Social anxiety is functional when it motivates preparation and rehearsal for important interpersonal events, and shyness also helps to facilitate cooperative group living by inhibiting individual behavior that is socially unacceptable. The complete absence of susceptibility to feeling shy has been recognized as an antisocial characteristic since at least the time of the ancient Greeks.

Situational shyness as a transitory emotional state appears to be a normal aspect of human development and everyday adult life. In a cross-cultural survey Philip G. Zimbardo (*Shyness*, Reading, Mass., 1977) found that less than 10% of respondents reported that they had never felt shy. For some people, however, shyness is more than a temporary situational response; it occurs with sufficient frequency and intensity to be considered a personality trait. About 30 to 40% of adults in the United States label themselves as dispositionally shy persons. Three quarters of the shy respondents said that they did not like being so shy, and two thirds of them considered their shyness to be a personal problem. Although shyness does have some positive connotations, such as modesty or gentleness, it is generally rated as an undesirable characteristic. Viewed as a personality trait, shyness is defined as the tendency to feel tense, worried, or awkward during social interactions, especially with unfamiliar people.

Some people prefer to spend time alone rather than with others but also feel comfortable when they are in social settings. Such people are nonanxious introverts, who may be unsociable but are not shy. The opposite of shyness is social self-confidence, not extraversion. The problem for truly shy people is that their anxiety prevents them from participating in social life when they want to or need to. Longitudinal research indicates that when shyness continues into adulthood it can create significant barriers to satisfaction in love, work, recreation, and friendship. As a result, shy adults tend to be more lonely and less happy than those who are not shy.

Research in behavior genetics indicates that shyness is the personality trait in the normal range of individual differences that has the largest genetic component. According to Jerome Kagan (*Galen's Prophecy: Temperament in Human Nature*, New York, 1994) about 15 to 20% of infants typically respond to a new situation or stimulus, such as an unfamiliar toy, person, or place, by withdrawing and becoming either emotionally subdued or upset (crying, fussing, and fretting). He has suggested that this pattern of temperamental reactivity to novelty is related to a lower threshold for arousal in sites in the amygdala. Infants with this highly reactive temperament in the first year of life are more likely to be wary or fearful of strangers at the end of the second year and are also more likely to be described as shy by their kindergarten teachers than are children with an opposite, behaviorally uninhibited temperament.

Slightly more than half of shy adults report that they first became troubled by shyness between the ages of 8 and 14. According to Arnold H. Buss (*Self-Consciousness and Social Anxiety*, San Francisco, 1980), they do not appear to have the temperamental predisposition for becoming shy and inhibited. Instead, late-developing shyness is caused by the adjustment problems of social development normally encountered in the transition from childhood to adolescence. The bodily changes of puberty, the newly acquired cognitive ability to think abstractly about the self and the environment, and the new demands and opportunities resulting from changing social roles combine to make adolescents feel intensely self-conscious and socially awkward.

The developmental peak for shyness occurs around age 14, when two thirds of the girls and more than half of the boys identify themselves as shy. Late-developing shyness, however, seems to be less likely to endure than the early developing temperamental predisposition. Only 50% of survey respondents who first became shy during later childhood and early adolescence still consider themselves to be shy by age 21, whereas 75% of young adults who say they were shy in early childhood continue to identify themselves as shy persons. Extremely shy individuals have an increased risk of developing anxiety disorders such as social phobia.

Cultural differences in the prevalence of shyness may reflect the impact of socialization practices. In Israel, children tend to be praised for being self-confident and often are included in adult conversations, two factors that may account for the low level of shyness reported by Israelis. In Japan, on the other hand, the incidence of shyness is much higher than in the United States. Japanese culture values harmony and tends to encourage dependency and quiet loyalty to one's superiors. Talkative or assertive individuals risk being considered immature or insincere, and there is a high level of concern about avoiding the shame of failure. All of these values may promote shyness yet also make it a somewhat less socially undesirable personality trait. In contrast, American cultural values that emphasize competition, individual achievement, and material success appear to create an environment in which it is particularly difficult for the shy person to feel secure and worthwhile.

Bibliography

Beidel, D. C., & Turner, S. M. (1998). *Shy children, phobic adults: Nature and treatment of social phobia.* Washington, DC: American Psychological Association. Describes pharmacological, behavioral, and cognitive treatments for extreme shyness and social phobia.

Cheek, J. M., & Cheek, B. (1990). *Conquering shyness.* New York: Dell. A revised edition of this self-help book for adolescents and adults, currently out of print, is planned for 1999 by Jason Aronson Publishers.

Jones, W. H., Cheek, J. M., & Briggs, S. R. (Eds.). (1986). *Shyness: Perspectives on research and treatment.* New York: Plenum. Includes 27 chapters that provide comprehensive coverage of development, personality, social behavior, and therapy.

Leary, M. R., & Kowalski, R. M. (1995). *Social anxiety.* New

York: Guilford. Presents a social psychological approach with an emphasis on self-presentation.

Leitenberg, H. (Ed.). (1990). *Handbook of social and evaluation anxiety*. New York: Plenum.

Schmidt, L. A., & Schulkin, J. (Eds.). (1999). *Extreme fear, shyness, and social phobia: Origins, biological mechanisms, and clinical outcomes*. New York: Oxford University Press.

Jonathan M. Cheek

SIBLING RELATIONSHIPS. The sibling relationship is one of the longest lasting relationships in most people's lives, and one of the most prevalent: 80 to 85% of the children and adults in the United States have a brother or sister. Yet siblings have received little attention in psychological research and theory. Perhaps because of the legacy of psychoanalytic theory, researchers have focused on the mother-child relationship and neglected other family relationships. With one notable exception (Koch, 1960), psychologists did not begin studying the sibling relationship until the late 1970s.

Characteristics of Sibling Relationships in Childhood, Adolescence, and Adulthood

The sibling relationship begins with enormous changes in the life of a first-born child. He or she must adjust from having undivided parental attention to sharing it with an infant. Most studies have found that after the birth of a sibling, older siblings display increased anxiety and aggression toward either the new baby or their parents. Additionally, older children often regress developmentally, for example, in the areas of toilet training or sleeping (Teti, 1992). There are individual differences in how children adjust to this change, however. Two studies have shown that in families in which parents involved the older sibling in the care of the baby and discussed the baby's needs and desires, siblings had particularly close relationships later (Dunn & Kendrick, 1982; Howe & Ross, 1990). In addition, children with more difficult and less adaptable temperaments were more distressed by the birth of a younger sibling than children with easier temperaments (Thomas, Birch, Chess, & Robbins, 1961).

In early childhood, siblings spend a great deal of time together and, in fact, spend more time together than do parents with their children (Crouter & McHale, 1989). The sibling relationship is affectively rich and varies along independent dimensions of affection, hostility, and rivalry. In the early stages of the sibling relationship, when children are infants and preschoolers, the older sibling usually takes on a leadership role and teaches the younger sibling, while the younger sibling often imitates the older sibling (Dunn, 1983). Sibling relationships in middle childhood tend to be more egalitarian than those in early childhood (Buhrmester &

Furman, 1990; Vandell, Minnett, & Santrock, 1987). Perhaps as younger siblings become more cognitively sophisticated they are better able to communicate and negotiate with their older siblings, and a more egalitarian relationship develops. As siblings move into adolescence their relationships become more distant than in childhood. Levels of both affection and hostility are lower in adolescence than in childhood (Buhrmester & Furman, 1990; Stocker & Dunn, 1994). Moreover, siblings spend less time together as adolescents than they did as children.

Most of the research on sibling relationships in adulthood has focused on the elderly. However, in one recent study, sibling relationships in early adulthood, like those in childhood, varied along independent dimensions of warmth, conflict, and rivalry. Contact between siblings (e.g. phone calls and letters) but not geographic proximity was associated with more affectionate and less rivalrous relationships (Stocker, Lanthier, & Furman, 1997). In an observational study, young adult siblings who felt close to each other had more positive affect, fewer power struggles, and lower heart rate activity than siblings who rated their relationships as distant (Shortt & Gottman, 1997). Middle-aged and elderly adults report feeling close and accepting of their siblings (Bedford, 1989; Cicirelli, 1982; Gold, 1989; Seltzer, 1989). The data about conflict are more variable. For example, when self-report data are used, siblings report very low levels of conflict (Cicirelli, 1982; Gold, 1989). Among adults participating in small-group discussions, however, 45% reported feeling rivalry toward their brothers and sisters (Ross & Milgram, 1982).

Most of the information about sibling relationships at different developmental stages is based on cross-sectional data. However, the few longitudinal studies completed have found stability in individual differences in the quality of sibling relationships from early to middle childhood (Dunn, 1983; Stocker & Dunn, 1991) and from middle childhood to early adolescence (Dunn, Slomkowski, & Beardsall, 1994). Longitudinal research has not yet been completed on changes in sibling relationships from childhood or adolescence to adulthood.

Individual Differences in the Quality of Sibling Relationships

Discussed here are demographic variables, cultural influences, temperament, illness and disabilities, and step-siblings and adopted siblings.

Demographic Variables. A great deal of research has examined the effects of demographic variables such as the age-spacing between siblings or siblings' genders on the quality of sibling relationships. In general, this line of research has yielded few consistent findings, and many studies have found that these types of variables are not related to individual differences in sibling relationships (Dunn, 1992; Teti, 1992). Demographic variables are typically markers for more process oriented factors. For example, a study may show that the age-spacing between siblings is related to sibling affection. What researchers need to discover is what it is about age-spacing that is important to how siblings behave with each other.

Cultural Influences. Most of the research on cultural influences on sibling relationships has been anthropological studies of children in non-Western cultures. This work has shown that the definition of a sibling varies by culture. For example, in some South Asian cultures, siblings and cousins are not distinguished from each other (Weisner, 1993). In many non-Western cultures, older siblings, rather than parents, are the primary caretakers for their infant siblings. These types of sibling relationships are probably qualitatively different than those found in Western cultures in which older siblings are primarily companions rather than caretakers. In many nonindustrial cultures, interdependence, social obligations, and cooperation between siblings, especially in adulthood, are stressed to a much greater extent than in Western cultures (Weisner, 1993). We know virtually nothing about the influences of ethnicity and subcultures on sibling relationships within industrialized countries.

Temperament. Research on sibling relationships in childhood and adolescence has shown that children's sociability is associated with sibling warmth and emotionality is linked to conflict and rivalry in sibling relationships (Brody, Stoneman, & Burke, 1987; Stocker, Dunn, & Plomin, 1989). Moreover, the match between siblings' temperaments is related to the quality of their relationship (Munn & Dunn, 1988). There has been very little research on the influence of temperament on adolescent and adult sibling relationships.

Siblings with Illnesses and Disabilities. There is great variability in the sibling relationships of children and adults with illnesses and disabilities. For example, a school-aged child might have a younger sibling with cancer, or an adolescent could have an older sibling with autism. Early research in this area looked for deficits in the sibling relationships of children with illnesses or disabilities, but did not find general deficits. Instead, like the sibling relationships of typically developing children, variations were due to other factors such as parents' attitudes about the ill child's difficulties or the developmental level of each child (McHale & Harris, 1992). There has been almost no research on the quality of adult sibling relationships involving an individual with an illness or disability. However, this is an important area for research because the increasing longevity of adults with mental retardation and other disorders means that more siblings will assume responsibility for their care when parents die.

Step-Siblings and Adopted Siblings. Sibling re-

lationships in step-families have been found to be more conflictual than those in intact families (Hetherington, 1988). Boys have more problematic sibling relationships than girls in divorced families or than children in intact families (MacKinnon, 1989). Like most research on divorce and marital conflict, findings suggest that the quality of the spousal or ex-spousal relationship is more closely tied to variations in sibling relationships than the social address variable of marital status (Hetherington, 1988; MacKinnon, 1989). Research to date has not examined the quality of sibling relationships that develop between adopted siblings.

Association Between Sibling Relationships and Other Relationships

Discussed here are the connections between sibling relationships and parent-child relationships, parents' marital relationships, and friendships and peer relationships.

Sibling Relationships and Parent-Child Relationships. Numerous studies have documented associations between sibling relationships and parent-child relationships. Most of this research has focused on mothers and much less is known about links between father-child relationships and sibling relationships. In general, findings indicate that there are positive associations between these relationships. Thus, in families in which parent-child relationships are warm and supportive, sibling relationships are also characterized by high levels of affection. Conflictual parent-child relationships are associated with hostile and rivalrous sibling relationships (Dunn, 1992). A number of theories have been proposed to explain the processes behind these associations. Modeling and social learning theory suggest that children model behavior with their siblings that they have learned in their relationships with parents. Attachment theory proposes that based on their early relationships with their parents, children develop internal working models or schemas of relationships that then shape the types of relationships they develop with their siblings (Teti, 1992). Children's stable characteristics, such as temperamental difficulty or sociability, may also elicit similar responses from both parents and siblings, leading to similarity in the relationships (Stocker et al., 1989).

In addition to associations between each sibling's relationship with his or her parent, differences in parents' behavior toward each sibling are related to the quality of sibling relationships. For example, conflictual sibling relationships have been associated with differences in mothers' behavior toward each sibling. In contrast, siblings have more positive relationships when parents treat them similarly (Brody, Stoneman, & Burke, 1987; Bryant & Crockenberg, 1990; Hetherington, 1988; Stocker, Dunn, & Plomin, 1989; Dunn & Plomin, 1990).

Researchers have yet to pinpoint the mechanism that connects differential parental treatment to sibling conflict. Children may react to inequities in their parents' behavior by feeling jealous and in turn behaving aggressively toward their brothers and sisters. It is also possible that in families in which one sibling is particularly hostile to his or her brother or sister, parents respond by treating that sibling less favorably. A question that remains unanswered is whether differential treatment operates differently in various types of families. If the overall level of parental warmth is low, for example, differential treatment may have a greater impact on the sibling relationship, because children may be competing for limited amounts of affection and attention. Differential treatment may be less important in families that are characterized by high levels of parental warmth and affection. Children in these families may be more accepting of differences in their parents' treatment of them and their siblings.

Sibling Relationships and Parents' Marital Relationships. Although this topic has received relatively little attention, associations between the quality of parents' marital or exmarital relationships and children's sibling relationships have been documented. Sibling relationships have been found to be more conflictual in families in which parents were unhappily married than in families in which parents were satisfied with their marriages (Brody, Stoneman, McCoy, & Forehand, 1992; MacKinnon, 1989; Stocker, Ahmed, & Stall, 1997). This may be because children model conflictual behavior they have observed between their parents with their siblings. Marital conflict may also be related to the sibling relationship through disruptions in parent-child relationships. For example, hostility and conflict in the marital relationship has been shown to spill over into the parent-child relationship (Kerig, Cowan, & Cowan, 1993) and hostility in parent-child relationships is associated with more conflictual and rivalrous sibling relationships (Dunn, 1992; Teti, 1992). Additionally, parents who have unhappy marriages may be preoccupied with their marital difficulties and thus be unavailable to manage their children's sibling relationships. Finally, conflict between siblings is stressful for parents and could increase levels of hostility and antagonism between parents. Despite the positive links between marital conflict and hostile sibling relationships, some research suggests that siblings can act as supports for each other in such situations. For example, Jenkins and Smith (1990) found that in families with high levels of marital discord, children with close relationships with brothers and sisters had fewer adjustment difficulties than those with conflictual sibling relationships.

Sibling Relationships, Friendships, and Peer Relationships. The associations between sibling relationships and children's close friendships appear to be complex and may vary with children's developmental level. Preschool-aged siblings who were affectionate to their friends were found to be particularly affectionate with their infant siblings (Kramer & Gottman, 1992). Among school-aged children, in contrast, children who were competitive and controlling with their siblings were warm and affectionate with their close friends (Stocker & Dunn, 1991). Other studies have found no links between sibling relationships and friendships. In general, fewer associations between sibling relationships and peer status have been found than between sibling relationships and friendships (Stocker & Dunn, 1991). However, in one recent study, school-aged boys who had aggressive interactions with their siblings were not well accepted by their peers (MacKinnon-Lewis, Starnes, Volling, & Johnson, 1997). There is no information available about associations between sibling relationships and friendships in adulthood.

Sibling Relationships and Individual Outcome

Sociocognitive development and psychological adjustments are discussed here in connection with sibling relationships.

Sibling Relationships and Sociocognitive Development. Piaget first noted that children's social and moral understanding is influenced by their interactions with other children (Piaget, 1932). These observations have been extended by research on siblings in early childhood. For example, in their relationships with siblings, preschoolers demonstrate sociocognitive abilities much earlier than traditional cognitive development theories would predict. Two- and three-year-old children were capable of interpreting the feelings and intentions of their younger siblings. In their efforts to comfort as well as their sophisticated techniques for teasing siblings, children demonstrated quite advanced perspective taking (Dunn, 1988). Furthermore, longitudinal associations between sibling relationship quality and children's sociocognitive development have been found. For example, in one study, children's affection and cooperation toward their siblings when they were 3 years old predicted their ability to take the perspective of another 7 months later (Dunn, Brown, Slomkowski, Tesla, & Youngblade, 1995). Recent research also has found associations between the quality of the sibling relationship in young adulthood and affective-perspective taking. Young adults who rated their sibling relationships as close had higher scores on measures of emotional and cognitive empathy than did those who rated their sibling relationships as distant (Shortt & Gottman, 1997). Because these results are based on correlational analyses, it is unclear if being in an affectionate sibling relationship promotes the development of sociocognitive skills or if children who are skilled at perspective taking and other sociocognitive abilities are more capable of forming positive relationships with siblings than other children are.

Sibling Relationships and Psychological Adjustment. Research on siblings in childhood, adolescence, and adulthood has found links between the quality of sibling relationships and individuals' well-being and mental health. Children and adolescents who have conflictual and rivalrous sibling relationships have been found to have high levels of anxiety, depression, and externalizing problems, as well as poor self-esteem and school adjustment (Dunn, Slomkowski, Beardsall, & Rende, 1994; McHale & Pawetko, 1992; Stocker, 1994; Stormshak, Bellanti, Bierman, & CPPRG, 1996). In families of aggressive children, siblings model and negatively reinforce each other's aggressive behavior, leading to increases in antisocial behavior (Patterson, 1986). Moreover, conflict in the sibling relationship in early adulthood was associated with poorer overall psychological adjustment (Stocker, Lanthier, & Furman, 1997). Supportive sibling relationships, in contrast, have been linked to decreased anxiety and greater maturity in young adolescents (East & Rook, 1992). As these data are correlational, we do not know if the experience in the sibling relationship has a causal impact on individuals' psychological adjustment or if people who are psychologically healthy are better able to develop supportive relationships with their brothers and sisters than people with adjustment difficulties.

Differences Between Siblings

One of the most consistent and striking findings about siblings is that they differ from each other on most measures of personality and psychopathology as much as any two people randomly selected from the population (Dunn & Plomin, 1990). Why should brothers and sisters who grow up in the same family and share 50% of their heritable genes be so different? Researchers have discovered that even though they live in the same family, siblings experience different environments within that family. As discussed above, parents treat siblings differently and these differences have been linked to differences in siblings' outcomes (Dunn & Plomin, 1990). Behavioral geneticists have found that differences in sibling experiences (nonshared environmental measures, e.g. different levels of parental affection or attention) account for more of the variance in individuals' outcomes than similarities in their experiences (shared environmental measures, e.g., parental educational level). Siblings also have different experiences outside of the family: For example, they interact with different peers and teachers. Several theoretical explanations have been offered to explain these findings. Family systems theorists and some family sociologists have suggested that each member of the family

develops a unique role in order to ensure family harmony. Along these lines, siblings may develop different personalities and interests to avoid competing in the same arena for parental affection and attention (Schachter, 1982). Another possibility is that differences in siblings' innate characteristics, such as temperament, elicit different reactions from parents and others, thus contributing to and promoting already existing differences between siblings (Scarr & Grajek, 1982).

Conclusions and Future Directions for Research on Sibling Relationships

Psychologists have discovered a great deal about sibling relationships in the last 20 years. Most of this research has focused on preschool and school-aged, white, middle-class children. More information is needed on sibling relationships in adolescence and adulthood. It would be most helpful if this research were longitudinal, so that we could learn about stability and change in the sibling relationships across development. Much more information is needed about variations and similarities in sibling relationships in different cultural groups both within the United States and across the globe. Similarly, more information is needed about sibling relationships in single-parent families, blended families, and relationships between adopted siblings and foster siblings. Because there is a trend toward single-child families in some countries, research is needed on the consequences of not having a sibling on children's development. Finally, little is known about the impact of stressful situations on sibling relationships. We need to know more about the influence of poverty, war, and mental illness on the developing sibling relationship. Despite these gaps in the literature, in the last 20 years, researchers have come a long way in discovering the complexities of the longest lasting relationship in most peoples' lives.

[*See also* Birth Order.]

Bibliography

Bedford, V. B. (Ed.). (1989). [Special issue on adult sibling relationships]. *Journal of Family Issues, 10.* This is the most conclusive collection of articles on sibling relationships in adulthood. Articles from several different disciplines are represented.

Brody, G., Stoneman, Z., & Burke, M. (1987). Child temperaments, maternal differential behavior, and sibling relationships. *Developmental Psychology, 23,* 354–362.

Brody, G., Stoneman, Z., McCoy, J. K., & Forehand, R. (1992). Contemporaneous and longitudinal associations of sibling conflict with family relationship assessments and family discussions about sibling problems. *Child Development, 63,* 391–400.

Bryant, B. K., & Crockenberg, S. (1990). Correlates and dimensions of prosocial behavior: A study of female siblings with their mothers. *Child Development, 51,* 529–544.

Buhrmester, D., & Furman, W. (1990). Age differences in perceptions of sibling relationships in middle childhood and adolescence. *Child Development, 63,* 82–92.

Cicirelli, V. C. (1982). Sibling influence throughout the lifespan. In M. E Lamb & B. Sutton-Smith (Eds.), *Sibling relationships: Their nature and significance across the lifespan* (pp. 267–284). Hillsdale, NJ: Erlbaum.

Crouter, A., & McHale, S. (1989, April). *Childrearing in dual and single earner families: Implications for the development of school-age children.* Paper presented at the biennial meeting of the Society for Research in Child Development, Kansas City, MO.

Dunn, J. (1983). Sibling relationships in early childhood. *Child Development, 54,* 787–811. This is one of the classic conceptual and review articles on sibling relationships.

Dunn, J. (1988). *The beginnings of social understanding.* Cambridge, MA: Harvard University Press. Summarizes findings on sibling relationships and children's cognitive and moral development.

Dunn, J. (1992). Sisters and brothers: Current issues in developmental research. In F. Boer & J. Dunn (Eds.), *Children's sibling relationships: Developmental and clinical issues* (pp. 1–18). Hillsdale, NJ: Erlbaum.

Dunn, J., Brown, J., Slomkowski, C., Tesla, C., & Youngblade, L. (1995). Young children's understanding of feelings and beliefs: Individual differences and their antecedents. *Child Development.*

Dunn, J., & Kendrick, C. (1982). *Siblings: Love, envy and understanding.* Cambridge: Harvard University Press.

Dunn, J., & Plomin, R. (1990). *Separate lives: Why siblings are so different.* New York: Basic Books. This book reviews current theory and research on differences between siblings.

Dunn, J., Slomkowski, C., & Beardsall, L. (1994). Sibling relationships from the preschool period through middle childhood and adolescence. *Developmental Psychology, 30,* 315–324.

Dunn, J., Slomkowski, C, Beardsall, L., & Rende, R. (1994). Adjustment in middle childhood and early adolescence: Links with earlier and contemporary sibling relationships. *Journal of Child Psychology and Psychiatry, 35(3),* 491–504.

East, P. L., & Rook, K. S. (1992). Compensatory patterns of support among children's peer relationships: A test using school friends, nonschool friends, and siblings. *Developmental Psychology, 28,* 163–172.

Gold, D. (1989). Sibling relationships in old age: A typology. *International Journal of Aging and Human Development, 28,* 37–51.

Hetherington, E. M. (1988). Parents, children, and siblings six years after divorce. In R. A. Hinde & J. Stevenson-Hinde (Eds.), *Relationships within families: Mutual influences* (pp. 311–331). New York: Oxford University Press.

Howe, N., & Ross, H. S. (1990). Socialization, perspective-taking, and the sibling relationship. *Developmental Psychology, 26,* 160–165.

Jenkins, J. M., & Smith, M. A. (1990). Factors protecting children living in disharmonious homes: Maternal reports. *Journal of the American Academy of Child and Adolescent Psychiatry, 29,* 60–69.

Kerig, P. K., Cowan, P. A., & Cowan, C. P. (1993). Marital quality and gender differences in parent-child interaction. *Developmental Psychology, 29(6),* 931–939.

Koch, H. L. (1960). The relation of certain formal attributes of siblings to attitudes held toward each other and toward their parents. *Monographs of the Society for Research in Child Development, 25* (Serial no. 78).

Kramer, L., & Gottman, J. M. (1992). Becoming a sibling: "With a little help from my friends." *Developmental Psychology, 28,* 685–699.

MacKinnon, C. (1989). An observational investigation of sibling interactions in married and divorced families. *Developmental Psychology, 25,* 36–44.

MacKinnon-Lewis, C., Starnes, R., Volling, B., & Johnson, S. (1997). Perceptions of parenting as predictors of boys' sibling and peer relations. *Developmental Psychology, 33(6),* 1024–1031.

McHale, S. M., & Harris, V. S. (1992). Children's experiences with disabled and nondisabled siblings: Links with personal adjustment and relationship evaluations. In J. Dunn & F. Boer (Eds.), *Children's sibling relationships: Developmental and clinical issues.* (pp. 83–100). Hillsdale, NJ: Erlbaum. This article provides a literature review and results from a study on sibling relationships of disabled children.

McHale, S. M., & Pawetko, T. M. (1992). Differential treatment in two family contexts. *Child Development, 63,* 68–81.

Munn, P., & Dunn, J. (1988). Temperament and the developing relationship between siblings. *International Journal of Behavioral development, 12,* 433–451.

Patterson, G. R. (1986). Performance models for antisocial boys. *American Psychologist, 41,* 432–444.

Piaget, J. (1932). *The moral judgment of the child.* London: Routledge & Kegan Paul.

Ross, H. G., & Milgram, J. L. (1982). Important variables in adult sibling relationships: A qualitative study. In M. E. Lamb & B. Sutton-Smith (Eds.), *Sibling relationships: Their significance across the life-span* (pp. 225–249). Hillsdale, NJ: Erlbaum.

Scarr, S., & Grajek, S. (1982). Similarities and differences among siblings. In M. E. Lamb & B. Sutton-Smith (Eds.), *Sibling relationships: Their significance across the life-span* (pp. 225–249). Hillsdale, NJ: Erlbaum.

Schachter, F. (1982). Sibling deidentification and split-parent identification: A family tetrad. In M. E. Lamb & B. Sutton-Smith (Eds.), *Sibling relationships: Their significance across the life-span* (pp. 123–151). Hillsdale, NJ: Erlbaum.

Seltzer, M. M. (1989). The three r's of life cycle sibships: Rivalry, reconstruction and relationships. *American Behavioral Scientists, 33,* 107–115.

Shortt, J. W., & Gottman, J. M. (1997). Closeness in young adult sibling relationships: Affective and physiological processes. *Social Development, 6(2),* 142–164.

Stocker, C. (1994). Children's perceptions of relationships

with siblings, friends, and mothers: Compensatory processes and links with adjustment. *Journal of Child Psychology and Psychiatry, 35(8),* 1447–1459.

Stocker, C., Ahmed, K., & Stall, M. (1997). Marital satisfaction and maternal emotional expressiveness: Links with children's sibling relationships. *Social Development, 6(3),* 371–383.

Stocker, C., & Dunn, J. (1991). Sibling relationships in childhood: Links with friendships and peer relationships. *British Journal of Developmental Psychology, 8,* 227–244.

Stocker, C., & Dunn, J. (1994). Sibling relationships in childhood and adolescence. In J. C. DeFries, R. Plomin, & D. Fulker (Eds.), *Nature and nurture during middle childhood* (pp. 214–232). Cambridge, MA: Blackwell.

Stocker, C., Dunn, J., & Plomin, R. (1989). Sibling relationships: Links with child temperament, maternal behavior, and family structure. *Child Development, 60,* 715–727.

Stocker, C., Lanthier, R., & Furman, W. (1997). Sibling relationships in early adulthood. *Journal of Family Psychology, 11,* 210–221.

Stormshak, E. A., Bellanti, C. J., Bierman, K. L., & CPPRG. (1996). The quality of sibling relationships and the development of social competence and behavioral control in aggressive children. *Developmental Psychology, 32,* 79–89.

Teti, D. (1992). Sibling interaction. In V. B. Van Hasselt & M. Hersen (Eds.), *Handbook of social development: A life-span perspective* (pp. 201–228). New York: Plenum Press. This chapter provides a thorough review of research findings on sibling relationships in infancy and early childhood.

Thomas, A., Birch, H. G., Chess, S., & Robbins, A. (1961). Individuality in responses of children to similar environmental situations, *American Journal of Orthopsychiatry, 117,* 798–803.

Vandell, D. L., Minnett, A. M., & Santrock, J. W. (1987). Age differences in sibling relationships during middle childhood. *Journal of Applied Developmental Psychology, 8,* 247–257.

Weisner, T. S. (1993). Overview: Siblings similarity and difference in different cultures. In C. W. Nuckolls (Ed.), *Siblings in South Asia: Brothers and sisters in cultural context* (pp. 1–18). New York: Guilford Press. This chapter provides an overview of theoretical and conceptual issues relevant to the influence of culture on sibling relationships.

Clare M. Stocker

SIGHT. *See* Color Vision; Sensory Systems; Spatial Vision; *and* Vision and Sight.

SIGNAL DETECTION THEORY. *See* Psychophysics.

SIGNIFICANCE TESTING. *See* Data Analysis.

SIGN LANGUAGES. Sign languages are used primarily by deaf people throughout the world. These languages are articulated with the face, hands, and arms rather than with the vocal tract, and they are perceived visually rather than auditorily. Sign languages have arisen as autonomous languages and are not derived from spoken languages. They are passed down from one generation of deaf people to the next, and deaf children acquire sign language from their deaf parents in the same way that hearing children acquire spoken language. Sign languages are rich and complex linguistic systems that conform to the universal properties found in all human languages.

The Origin of Sign Languages

A sign language emerges when isolated deaf people come together to form a community, often when a school for the deaf is established. Prior to this, no sign language exists; rather, there are only isolated deaf individuals who use what is called "home sign": an idiosyncratic gestural system used within the family. As these previously isolated individuals interact with each other, a form of intercommunication arises—a "pidgin" between home sign systems. This pidgin form constitutes an intermediate stage between home sign and the emergence of a full-fledged sign language. The pidgin sign language conventionalizes sign forms across the community, but grammatical processes are quite variable and unsystematic. Young deaf children who are exposed to this pidgin filter out the noise and produce a more systematic form with more complex grammatical processes. A true sign language emerges when the first generation of deaf children acquires the sign pidgin as their first language.

The origin of American Sign Language (ASL; the language used by deaf people in the United States and parts of Canada) can be traced to the establishment of a large community of deaf people in France in 1761. These people attended the first public school for the deaf, and the sign language that arose within this community is still used today in France. In 1817, Laurent Clerc, a deaf teacher from this French school, established the first deaf public school in the United States, and he brought French Sign Language with him. The gestural systems of the American children attending this school mixed with French Sign Language to create a new form that was no longer recognizable as French Sign Language. ASL still contains a historical resemblance to French Sign Language, and it is worth noting that ASL does not resemble British Sign Language (the languages are mutually unintelligible), despite the fact that the surrounding spoken language is the same.

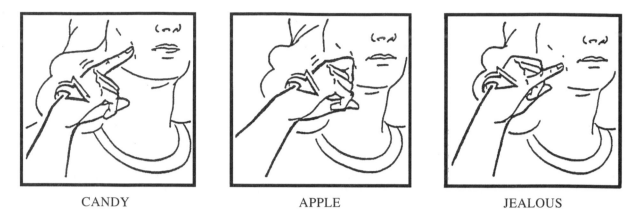

CANDY   APPLE   JEALOUS

SIGN LANGUAGES. Figure 1. Part of the phonological system of American Sign Language. The signs contrast only in hand shape. (Copyright © Ursula Bellugi, The Salk Institute.)

The Linguistic Structure of American Sign Language

American Sign Language is one of the most widely studied sign languages. The structure of ASL, like those of other signed languages, exhibits many of the same properties and follows the same universal principles as spoken languages.

Phonology. Is it possible to have a phonological system that is not based on sound? In spoken languages, words are constructed out of sounds that in and of themselves have no meaning. The words "cat" and "pat" differ only in the initial sounds, which have no inherent meanings of their own. Similarly, signs are constructed out of components that are themselves meaningless and are combined to create words. Signs are composed of four basic phonological parameters: hand shape, location, movement, and palm orientation. Figure 1 illustrates three ASL signs that differ only in hand shape. Signs are also distinguished by their location on the body or face and by their movement. Several different types of path movement occur in ASL (e.g., circling, arc, straight), and signs can contain "internal" movement, such as wiggling of the fingers or changes in hand shape. Sign languages also exhibit other phonological properties that were once thought to be found only in speech. For example, signs have a level of syllabic structure that is governed by rules similar to those that apply to syllables in spoken languages. The fact that signed languages exhibit phonological properties despite the completely different set of articulators (e.g., the hands vs. the tongue) attests to the universality and abstractness of sublexical structure in human languages.

Morphology. ASL contains the same basic form classes as spoken languages—nouns, verbs, adjectives, pronouns, and adverbs—but it has a very different system of word formation. In English and in most spoken languages, morphologically complex words are most often formed by adding prefixes or suffixes to a word stem. In ASL, these forms are created by nesting a sign stem within dynamic movement contours and planes in space. Figure 2 illustrates the base form GIVE, along with several inflected forms that can be embedded within one another and that convey slightly different meanings. ASL has many verbal inflections that convey temporal information about the action, for example, whether the action was habitual, iterative, or continual. These inflections do not occur in English, but they are found in other languages of the world. In addition, ASL contains morphological rules for deriving nouns from verbs, for creating compound words, and for numeral incorporation.

ASL does not have many prepositions and instead encodes spatial relations through morphological devices. ASL uses a system of classifiers that classify an object according to its semantic and/or visual-geometric properties. ASL classifiers are embedded in verbs of motion and location that describe the movement and position of objects and/or people in space. For example, to express "the bicycle is beside the fence," a vehicle classifier is used for *bicycle* and is positioned in space next to a visual-geometric classifier for *fence* ("long-sectioned rectangular object"). The ASL expression tends to be much more explicit than the English preposition "beside" because the ASL classifier verbs of location also indicate the orientation and proximity of the fence and bicycle with respect to each other (e.g., whether the bicycle is close to the fence, facing the fence, etc.). Although this system appears mimetic, it is not. ASL expressions of location and motion have an internal structure that comprises a closed set of clas-

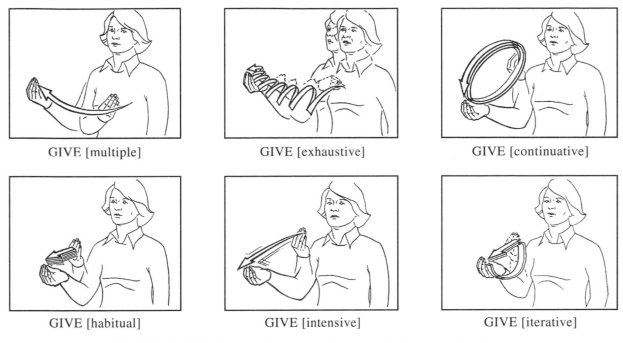

GIVE [multiple]   GIVE [exhaustive]   GIVE [continuative]

GIVE [habitual]   GIVE [intensive]   GIVE [iterative]

SIGN LANGUAGES. Figure 2. Morphological processes in American Sign Language. The aspectual meanings of the verbal inflections are given in brackets. (Copyright © Ursula Bellugi, The Salk Institute.)

sifier forms and movements that are combined in rule-governed ways.

Syntax. The canonical word order for ASL is Subject Verb Object; however, ASL word order is much more flexible than that of English. ASL morphology can mark the relationship between words, and thus ASL does not need to rely on word order to convey grammatical relations such as subject or object. Similar to Italian and unlike English, ASL allows "subjectless" sentences. For example, it is possible to sign the following (signs are notated as English glosses in uppercase): TODAY SUNDAY. MUST VISIT MY MOTHER. In English these two sentences would require subjects (subjects are underlined): "Today, *it*'s Sunday. *I* must visit my mother." The constraint on overt subjects is just one of the ways in which the syntax of ASL differs from English (but is similar to other languages). Many of the syntactic functions that are fulfilled in spoken languages by word order or case marking are expressed in ASL by spatial mechanisms. For example, when noun phrases are introduced into ASL discourse, they may be associated with a location in signing space. Once a referent has been associated with a spatial location, the signer may then refer to that referent by using a pronominal sign directed toward that location. In addition, verbs can move with respect to these loci to indicate subject and object relations. Overall, the same linguistic functions found in the world's languages are expressed within

ASL syntax and discourse, but the form these functions take is often distinctly spatial.

Facial Expressions and Sign Language

The face carries both linguistic and emotional information for ASL signers. Both hearing and deaf people use their faces in the same way to convey emotional information—these expressions (e.g., happy, sad, angry) are universal. However, ASL signers also use facial expressions to convey linguistic contrasts. Linguistic and emotional facial expressions differ in their scope and timing and in the face muscles that are used. Grammatical facial expressions have a clear onset and offset, and they are coordinated with specific parts of the signed sentence. Emotional expressions have more global and inconsistent onset and offset patterns, and they are not timed to co-occur with specific signs or parts of a signed sentence. Examples of linguistic facial expression include marking for adverbials, topics, questions, conditionals, and relative clauses.

The study of facial expressions in ASL is providing insight into the interface between biology and behavior. Emotional expressions are produced consistently and universally by children by one year of age. Emotional facial expressions also appear to be associated with specific neural substrates that are distinct from those involved in language. How does the linguistic system underlying the use of grammatical facial expressions interact with the biologically programmed use of emotional facial expressions? Current research suggests that different neural systems may subserve linguistic and emotional facial expressions—the left hemisphere appears to be involved in recognizing linguistic facial expressions, whereas the right hemisphere is important for producing emotional facial expressions. In addition, although deaf children produce emotional facial expressions very early (as do hearing children), they acquire linguistic facial expressions later and with a quite different pattern of development that reflects their (unconscious) analysis of these facial signals as part of a linguistic system.

The Impact of Sign Language Use on Visual-Spatial Cognition

The habitual use of a visual-spatial language such as ASL appears to have an impact on nonlinguistic aspects of visual-spatial cognition. The effects appear to be due to linguistic experience rather than to deafness, because hearing people who learned ASL as their first language from their deaf parents exhibit the same patterns of performance as deaf ASL signers. Sign language experience appears to enhance or alter performance within the following cognitive domains:

Motion Processing. Signers categorize motion patterns differently from nonsigners, grouping linguistically significant motions together. Signers have a heightened sensitivity to certain perceptual qualities of nonlinguistic motion. Specifically, they appear to be better able to distinguish between transitional and purposeful motion compared with nonsigners. Finally, signers exhibit a left-hemisphere dominance for detecting motion in the periphery of vision, whereas nonsigners show a right-hemisphere advantage. This finding suggests that the acquisition of a signed language can alter the brain areas responsible for motion perception.

Face Processing. ASL signers exhibit an enhanced ability to discriminate among faces that are very similar and to recognize subtle changes in specific facial features. These are skills that are strongly tied to recognizing and interpreting ASL linguistic facial expressions. Signers and nonsigners do not differ in their ability to recognize individual faces from memory or in their gestalt face processing abilities. To identify and categorize ASL facial expressions, signers do not need to recognize the person, and the gestalt aspects of the face (e.g., the shape of the face) remain unaffected by variations in linguistic facial expression. Sign language use appears to enhance only those face processing skills that must be generalized across unique individuals and that are relevant to interpreting subtle differences in local feature configurations.

Mental Imagery. ASL signers exhibit a superior ability to generate and transform mental images. Signers have faster reaction times for tasks that involve mental rotation—for example, deciding whether two objects are the same or mirror images, regardless of orientation. Signers are also faster on tasks that require them to generate an image (e.g., of a letter). Image generation may occur frequently during ASL discourse because under certain conditions signers articulate verbs as if they imagine referents as present in the space around them. Furthermore, classifier verbs of motion and location often require relatively precise representation of visual-spatial relations, and this explicit encoding may require the generation of visual mental images. Finally, mental rotation may be involved in understanding certain types of spatial descriptions when signers are face to face. When understanding the description of a spatial scene from a specific viewpoint (e.g., the entrance to a room), the addressee may have to mentally reverse the spatial arrays created by the signer such that a spatial location established on the right of the person signing (and thus on the left of the addressee) is understood as on the right in the scene being described. The habitual use of these imagery skills during language processing appears to facilitate mental imagery within nonlinguistic domains.

Neural Organization for Sign Language

Decades of research indicate that the left cerebral hemisphere is dominant for language such that linguistic abilities are more impaired by damage to the left hemisphere than to the right. The study of sign language provides special insight into the basis for this cerebral asymmetry. For example, the left hemisphere may be specialized for processing linguistic information or for more general functions on which language depends, such as rapid auditory processing or the execution of complex motor movements. Research with deaf signers who have suffered unilateral brain injury indicates that the left hemisphere is dominant for sign language, despite the modality difference. Left hemisphere damage produces sign language aphasias, but damage to the right hemisphere does not. Sign aphasias are similar to those observed with spoken language. For example, signers with left hemisphere damage may produce dysfluent signing with little grammatical morphology. Lesions to a different area within the left hemisphere produce fluent signing with many paraphasias (phonological or semantic errors that create nonsense signs). Signers with left hemisphere damage also have much poorer sign comprehension than those who suffer damage to the right hemisphere.

This pattern of linguistic deficits does not appear to be simply a function of deficits in general spatial cognitive ability. Right hemisphere–damaged signers exhibit much more severe impairments of visual-spatial abilities, such as perceiving spatial orientation, apprehending perspective within a drawing, or interpreting spatial configurations, than signers with left-hemisphere damage. Furthermore, the difference in linguistic impairment between left- and right-lesioned signers is not a function of group differences in age at time of test, age of the onset of deafness, or age of first exposure to ASL. None of these variables correlate with linguistic impairment (as measured by the ASL version of the Boston Diagnostic Aphasia Exam).

The neural organization for sign language indicates that left hemispheric specialization for language is not based on hearing or speech. Given that sign language relies primarily on spatial information rather than on rapidly changing temporal information to encode linguistic distinctions, left hemisphere dominance for language does not arise from a general competence for processing fast temporal changes. Furthermore, left hemisphere damage can spare the execution of complex motor movements that are nonlinguistic (e.g., pantomime or nonrepresentational movements) but can impair the production of sign language. Thus the disruption to sign language is not due to a general disruption of motor control. The results from signers with unilateral brain lesions suggests that the basis for the left hemispheric specialization for language lies in the nature of linguistic systems rather than in the sensory characteristics of the linguistic signal or in the motor aspects of language production.

Bibliography

Klima, E. S., & Bellugi, U. (1979). *The signs of language*. Cambridge, MA: Harvard University Press. A classic book in the field of sign language studies. Contains discussions of iconicity, historical change, memory for signs, grammatical processes in ASL, and sign poetry.

Lillo-Martin, D. (1999). Modality effects and modularity in language acquisition: The acquisition of American Sign Language. In T. K. Bhatia & W. C. Ritchie (Eds.), *Handbook of language acquisition* (pp. 531–567). San Diego, CA: Academic Press. Reviews the sign language acquisition literature from manual babbling to syntax.

The Origin of Sign Languages

Kegl, J., Senghas, A., & Coppola, M. (1999). Creation through contact: Sign language emergence and sign language change in Nicaragua. In M. DeGraff (Ed.), *Language creation and language change: Creolization, diachrony, and development*. Cambridge, MA: MIT Press. Documents the birth of Nicaraguan Sign Language.

Lane, H. (1984). *When the mind hears: A history of the deaf*. New York: Random House.

Sign Language Structure

Corina, D., & Sandler, W. (1993). On the nature of phonological structure in sign language. *Phonology, 10*, 165–207.

Valli, C., & Lucas, C. (1995). *Linguistics of American Sign Language* (2nd ed.). Washington, DC: Gallaudet University Press.

Facial Expression and Sign Language

Corina, D. (1989). Recognition of affective and noncanonical linguistic facial expressions in hearing and deaf subjects. *Brain and Cognition, 9*, 227–237. Reports left-hemisphere involvement for recognizing linguistic facial expressions.

Reilly, J., McIntire, M., & Bellugi, U. (1991). Faces: The relationship between language and affect. In V. Volterra & C. Erting (Eds.), *From gesture to language in hearing and deaf children* (pp. 128–141). New York: Springer-Verlag. Provides a microanalysis of linguistic and emotional facial expressions and describes the acquisition of linguistic expressions by deaf children.

Sign Language and Cognition

Emmorey, K. (1998). The impact of sign language use on visual-spatial cognition. In M. Marschark & D. Clark (Eds.), *Psychological perspectives on deafness* (pp. 19–52). Mahwah, NJ: Erlbaum. Reviews literature on the effects of sign language use for motion processing, face processing, and mental imagery.

Emmorey, K., Kosslyn, S. M., & Bellugi, U. (1993). Visual imagery and visual-spatial language: Enhanced imagery abilities in deaf and hearing ASL signers. *Cognition, 46*, 139–181.

Neural Organization for Sign Language

Hickok, G., Bellugi, U., & Klima, E. S. (1996). The neurobiology of signed language and its implications for the neural organization of language. *Nature, 381*, 699–702.

Poizner, H., Klima, E. S., & Bellugi, U. (1987). *What the hands reveal about the brain*. Cambridge, MA: MIT Press. Provides in-depth case studies of several deaf signers with unilateral right- or left-hemisphere lesions.

Karen Emmorey

SIMARRO, LUIS (1851–1921), Spanish neurologist and psychiatrist. Often considered to be the "founding father" of experimental psychology in Spain, Simarro studied medicine in Valencia and Madrid. After getting his doctoral degree in 1875, he joined the staff of the Free Institution of Education, at the time the most active center promoting the modernization of Spanish science and education. Simarro's lectures on the physiology of the nervous system at the Free Institution (1878) show his deep acquaintance with current research on the subject.

In 1880, Simarro went to Paris in order to further his training. He worked in histology, physiology, psychiatry, and neurology with such eminent specialists as Mathias Duval, Louis-Antoine Ranvier, Charles Richet, Valentin Magnan, and Jean-Martin Charcot. It was then that he became acquainted with Golgi's method for staining the nervous tissue, which he was to pass on to his colleague Cajal in 1887. [See the biography of *Charcot*.]

On his return in 1885, he started a private practice in neurology and psychiatry with wide social success. He continued his collaboration with the Free Institution through other organizations that were founded under the Institution's influence. Such was the case of the Pedagogical Museum, where Simarro lectured on physiological psychology and founded the earliest Spanish laboratory of a psychological significance (1893).

His psychopedagogical concerns are best shown in several papers, including "Mental Overwork in Education" (1889), where he examined the environmental conditions and the physiological mechanisms responsible for mental fatigue. His "Diseases of the Nervous System" (1898), a diagnostic guide revealing the influence of Emil Kraepelin, Charcot, and Magnan, is a good example of his neurological and neuropsychiatric interests.

In 1902, Simarro was appointed professor of experimental psychology at the University of Madrid, the first psychology chair ever created in a Spanish university. He held an associationistic, physiologically based view of psychological phenomena, which he conceived as functionally adaptive. His main contribution to psychological theory was his concept of "iteration" (1902), denoting the process of formation through repetition of organized paths in the nervous centers. Simarro considered iteration as a physiological precondition for the association of mental elements and ideas, as well as movements in instinct and habit.

Always politically and intellectually a radical, he was a member of the Féderation Internationale de la Libre Pensée. In 1909, he led an international campaign in favor of the anarchist pedagogue Francisco Ferrer, who was held responsible for the violent protest against the government policy in Africa that led to the so-called Tragic Week in Barcelona (1909). In 1913, he founded a League for the Defense of Man and the Citizen and was elected great master of Spanish Freemasonry.

Simarro published very little, but he was highly influential and had many disciples. Some of the most eminent neurologists and psychiatrists of Spanish subsequent history (Nicolas Achúcarro, Gonzalo Lafora) were trained by him. Also among his students were many of those who spread modern psychological ideas over Spain in the late nineteenth and early twentieth centuries (Domingo Barnés, Fermín Herrero, Martín Navarro, Francisco Santamaría, and Juan Vicente Viqueira, among many others). When Simarro died, he left a considerable fortune to a foundation for the advancement of scientific psychology.

Bibliography

Works by Simarro

Simarro, L. (1878). Teorías modernas sobre la fisiología del sistema nervioso. *Boletín de la Institución Libre de Enseñanza, 2,* 167–168, 176–177.

Simarro, L. (1879). Teorías modernas sobre la fisiología del sistema nervioso. *Boletín de la Institución Libre de Enseñanza, 3,* 22–23, 31–32, 37–38, 46–47, 53–54, 61–63, 79, 126–127.

Simarro, L. (1889). El exceso de trabajo mental en la enseñanza [Mental overwork in education]. *Boletín de la Institución Libre de Enseñanza, 13,* 37–39, 88–91, 369–373.

Simarro, L. (1898). Enfermedades del sistema nervioso [Diseases of the Nervous System]. In *Vademecum clínico terapéutico.* Madrid: Romo y Fussel.

Simarro, L. (1902). De la iteración. *Boletín de la Institución Libre de Enseñanza, 26,* 348–352.

Simarro, L. (Ed.). (1910). *El proceso Ferrer y la opinión europea.* Madrid: Imp. Eduardo Arias.

There is no modern edition of Simarro's works.

Works about Simarro

Bandrés, J., Llavona, R., & Campos, J. J. (1996). Luis Simarro. In M. Saiz & D. Saiz (Eds.), *Personajes para una historia de la psicología en España* (pp. 185–199). Madrid: Pirámide. A short but illuminating biographical account discussing the many facets of Simarro's professional and intellectual activity.

Campos, J. J., & Llavona, R. (Eds.). (1987). Los orígenes de la psicología científica en España: el doctor Simarro. *Investigaciones psicológicas, 4.* Monographic issue including papers on Simarro's scientific contributions by several specialists.

Carpintero, H. (1982). The introduction of scientific psychology in Spain. In W. Woodward & M. G. Ash (Eds.), *Problematic science: Psychology in nineteenth-century thought.* New York: Praeger. A short overview in English of the origins of modern psychology in Spain.

Carpintero, H. (1994). *Historia de la psicología en España.* Madrid: Eudema. The most complete overall view of Spanish psychological history.

Kaplan, T. (1971). Luis Simarro's psychological theories. *Actas del III Congreso Nacional de Historia de la Medicina, 2,* 545–555. An overview, in English, of Simarro's psychological contribution.

Lafuente, E., & Carpintero, H. (1994). *Luis Simarro y los orígenes de la psicología científica en España.* Madrid: UNED. A videotaped account of Simarro's life, work, and times, including a booklet with an annotated bibliography.

Enrique Lafuente

SIMON, HERBERT ALEXANDER (1916–) American economist, political scientist, and cognitive psychologist. Simon's ideas and theoretical proposals have profoundly impacted many fields. A founder of modern cognitive science with his seminal contributions to artificial intelligence (AI) and information-processing models of human cognition, he has received high recognition for his contributions to science in general (National Medal of Science) and to individual disciplines such as economics (the Nobel Prize), psychology, computer science, political science, public administration, and operations research.

Simon grew up in Milwaukee, Wisconsin, He completed undergraduate and doctoral degrees in political science at the University of Chicago, receiving considerable training in methods for modeling economic and social phenomena formally, including the models of classical economics that assume essentially perfect human rationality.

Before completing his doctorate, he was engaged (1936–1942) in research on methods for assessing the effectiveness of government services. From his exposure to actual decision-making processes in organizations, he concluded that the classical model of perfect rationality was unrealistic and began to build an alternative theory of bounded rationality, taking into account the limits on human knowledge and calculating capacity and the frequent incommensurability of values. He developed these ideas in his dissertation in 1942, which was expanded into his 1947 book *Administrative Behavior* (New York, 4th ed., 1997), containing the seminal ideas recognized by the Nobel Memorial Award in Economics in 1978.

After working as a political scientist at Illinois Institute of Technology in Chicago (1942–1949), Simon moved to Pittsburgh, Pennsylvania, to help organize the new Graduate School of Industrial Administration of Carnegie Institute of Technology (later Carnegie-Mellon University). During this period, Simon carried on empirical research on decision making in business firms and worked on a general framework for describing human behavior in organizations that included analysis of the effects of social interactions in groups upon decision making.

In the early 1950s, Simon became aware of the possibilities of using the then-new computers to model human decision-making and problem-solving processes symbolically (non-numerically). The team of Simon, Allen Newell, and Cliff Shaw constructed and demonstrated computer programs able to solve problems, like proving theorems in logic, that are challenging for intelligent humans. This revolutionary discovery led to the emergence of a field within computer science that designs programs exhibiting artificial intelligence.

Of more relevance to the study of human thinking, Newell, Shaw, and Simon designed AI programs that used sequences of steps to generate their solutions similar to the thoughts that human subjects verbalized when they solved the same problems. These explicit models showed that the trial-and-error character of human problem solving does not reflect irrationality but reveals the effects of incomplete knowledge of problem structure and the need to work with simplified and partial descriptions of tasks (bounded rationality). To implement these models, Newell, Shaw, and Simon in-

vented list processing languages, based on associative linkages in memory and property lists (directed associations), which remain the standard programming languages for cognitive modeling.

In their comprehensive theory of human information-tion processing, Newell and Simon in their book *Human Problem Solving* (Englewood Cliffs, N.J., 1972), showed how problem solving could be described by successive transformations of knowledge structures. Each cognitive processing step employs a combination of elementary information processes that respect the known limits of human memory capacity (for example, about seven chunks in short-term memory). The cognitive architecture, specified elementary information processes, and memory stores with fixed capacities constrain the simulation models to reproduce human thinking in the performance of tasks. These simulation models use only skills and knowledge that can be shown to be available to the human subjects whose behavior is modeled.

Newell and Simon introduced task analysis to identify the solution methods for specific problems that meet these conditions. An important product of this research was the General Problem Solver (1960), which showed how problem solving could be accomplished by selective (heuristic) search using means–ends analysis: recursively comparing the present situation with the goal situation to find differences between them and to apply operators to remove these differences. Another byproduct was the application to cognitive modeling of production system languages, whose instructions are condition–action (similar to stimulus–response) statements, which can model learning by self-modification.

Within this framework, Newell and Simon explicated and integrated many earlier theoretical ideas on the structure of thinking based on self-analysis and introspection (Otto Selz), or based on think-aloud protocols (Karl Duncker). Subsequently, Anders Ericsson and Simon in their book *Protocol Analysis: Verbal Reports as Data* (Cambridge, MA, 1993) described the cognitive processes mediating different types of verbal reports, such as introspection and thinking aloud, and showed how protocol analysis of verbal reports could be adapted to provide rigorous standards for other types of process data, such as reaction times and eye fixations.

In one of the most influential lines of his research in the 1960s and 1970s, Simon, with colleagues and students, sought to account for thinking at high levels of expertise within the cognitive framework developed and validated for traditional laboratory tasks. Bill Chase and Simon extended the pioneering studies by Adriaan De Groot and showed that the superiority of grandmasters in chess is limited to activities relevant to chess playing and reflects the chess-specific patterns and associated knowledge acquired over more than a decade of experience. These demonstrations of the critical role of acquired knowledge in attaining superior performance led to a growing body of studies of the structure of expertise in many domains, such as physics and medicine.

Simon and his colleagues also proposed successful information-processing models of phenomena that involve creative thinking, such as insight problem solving and scientific discovery. Simon also developed and refined the architecture of EPAM (elementary perceiver and memorizer) to account for a growing body of empirical phenomena that involve learning, memory, and categorization. Other research, focused on the CaMeRa program, showed how mental representations, visual and verbal, are used to reason in problem-solving situations.

Simon's life long efforts to understand the processes of decision making led him to general theories of human information processing and thinking. His numerous innovative explicit mechanisms and simulation models for cognitive phenomena and the experimental evidence testing them have become an important part of the body of contemporary psychology and have raised its level of precision.

[*Many of the people mentioned in this article are the subjects of independent biographical entries.*]

Bibliography

Simon, H. A. (1957). *Models of man: Mathematical essays on rational human behavior in a social setting.* New York: Wiley.

Simon, H. A. (1996). *The sciences of the artificial* (3rd ed.). Cambridge, MA: MIT Press.

Simon, H. A. (1979–1989). *Models of thought* (Vols. 1–2). New Haven, CT: Yale University Press.

Simon, H. A. (1996). *Models of my life.* Cambridge, MA: MIT Press.

Simon, H. A., Langley, P., Bradshaw, G., & Zytkow, J. M. (1987). *Scientific discovery: Computational explorations of the creative processes.* Cambridge, MA: MIT Press.

K. Anders Ericsson

SIMON, THÉODORE (1873–1961), French psychologist. Born in Dijon, France on 10 July 1873, Théodore Simon became interested in psychology early in his life and began reading Alfred Binet's already famous books. Enrolled at the Paris medical school, his interest in psychology grew as his clinical experience deepened. In 1899, when he became an intern at the asylum for abnormal children at Perray-Vaucluse, near Paris, he succeeded in drawing Binet's attention to his clinical work and material. Binet at that time was pursuing a study of the correlation between physical growth and intellectual development. This work, carried out in the Paris public schools, was continued at Perray-Vaucluse, and resulted in Simon's medical thesis in 1900. From 1901 to 1905, Simon worked in different hospitals (Sainte-Anne, Dury-les-Amiens) and was attending psychiatrist at Saint Yon hospital from 1905 to 1920.

It would be vain to dissociate Simon's name from that of Binet in the work they accomplished together, and to try to separate their individual contributions from their work in common. In 1904, the French Ministry of Education planned a survey of the public schools for the detection of mentally retarded children. A commitee which included Binet was appointed for this task. The association between Simon and Binet led to the psychological examination of severely retarded adult patients. During their examination of these adults, a number of tests brought responses consistent with the clinical impression of the degree of retardation. In a second step, using the same tests to examine a large group of normal Parisian children, responses were found to be consistent with the subjects' chronological ages. Thus the comparison of defective adults having various degrees of retardation with normal children of various ages provided the concept of "mental age." Norms for different ages were experimentally determined, and the scale of intelligence was constructed on the basis of this new device. Thus, together with Binet, Simon introduced into modern clinical psychology the first scale for measuring intelligence. The intelligence initial scale was published in 1905, with revised forms in 1908 and 1911, in *L'année psychologique*, the journal founded by Binet in 1895. Simon always remained critical of the immoderate use of intelligence tests and was inclined to believe that the success of the scale had prevented his fellow psychologists from comprehending the great goal of Binet: understanding human beings, their nature, and their development. Simon always remained faithful to the Binet–Simon scale, never wishing to change it out of respect for Binet's memory.

In addition to the famous Binet-Simon scale of intelligence, Simon edited the *Bulletin* of the Société Alfred Binet from 1912 to 1960. In 1920, he returned as medical director to the colony at Perray-Vaucluse, where he remained until 1930. He was then medical director of the Henri-Rousselle Hospital before his retirement in late 1936.

[*See also the biography of Binet.*]

Bibliography

Binet, A., & Simon, T. (1973). *The development of intelligence in children (The Binet–Simon Scale).* New York: Arno Press. English translations of the famous 1905, 1908, and 1911 Binet–Simon tests, and their original introductions by the authors.

Wolf, T. H. (1961). An individual who made a difference. *American Psychologist, 16,* 245–248. An interesting account of a late interview with Simon.

Serge Nicolas

SIMPLE PHOBIA. *See* Specific Phobia.

SINGLE-CASE EXPERIMENTAL DESIGN. Individual-case experimental designs (also called within-subject, individual subject, or, less accurately, $N = 1$ or single-case experimental designs) describe a set of procedures used by psychologists to evaluate the effects of independent variables on the behavior of individual organisms. Sometimes the analysis involves only one subject, as in clinical treatment of behavior disorders. More typically the effects of a given independent variable are examined in several subjects concurrently as a supplementary way of assessing reliability, with a focus on the degree to which, for each individual, the intervention or independent variable was effective. Generality of effects is assessed through systematic replications, still using similar designs. [*See* Case Study; Reliability; *and* Replication in Research.]

Background

Systematic scientific study of individual subjects can be traced back more than a century to the French physiologist Claude Bernard's *Introduction to the Study of Experimental Medicine* (New York, 1957 [first published in 1865]). The formative years of psychology, too, were characterized by intensive studies of one or a few subjects, especially those involving the psychophysical methods, which established a lineage of research in sensation and perception that continues to this day. Among the most famous research that applied single-subject methods to other psychological topics was that of the German experimental psychologist Hermann Ebbinghaus, whose early work on remembering was conducted largely on himself as a subject. [*See the biography of Ebbinghaus.*] Although early experiments in psychology sometimes employed group averages in their analyses, inferential statistical analysis was not common in this field until the 1930s. [*See* Data Analysis.] One researcher who explicitly declined to go that route was the pioneering American psychologist B. F. Skinner. [*See the biography of Skinner.*]

Beginning in the tradition of experimental physiology, Skinner conducted a series of seminal experiments during the early 1930s demonstrating systematic control over the behavior of individual subjects as functions of numerous environmental manipulations. In his *Behavior of Organisms* (New York, 1938), Skinner concluded that inferential statistics were neither necessary nor sufficient for the analysis of behavior. Rather, such analysis required reducing variability through control of the individual organism's environment so that the effects of systematically manipulated variables could be clearly discerned. This approach continued to be refined, first in laboratory settings with animals and later with humans in both laboratory and applied settings. Both the strategy and tactics of the approach were summarized in Murray Sidman's *Tactics of Scientific Research* (New York, 1960), which remains a standard reference, especially for basic researchers.

Features of Individual-Case Methods

Individual-case techniques begin with assessment of each individual's behavior under initial, constant conditions, yielding baseline data against which subsequent conditions can be assessed. Once stability of behavior has been verified, an environmental change is implemented. Quantified and portrayed as an independent variable, that change may involve a physical dimension of the situation, some static variable such as food coloring in a child's snacks, or, more typically, a dynamic feature involving consequences of behavior. Following assessment of behavior under the changed conditions, the initial, baseline conditions are reinstated while the behavior continues to be observed to determine whether the original performance will recur, thereby assuring that any observed changes were not due merely to the passage of time. This simple sequence is called an A-B-A or reversal design, where A denotes the baseline and B the treatment phase. While a typical experiment includes several subjects, each is exposed to all conditions, and any observed changes in behavior are assessed against the subject's own baseline and not against a group average. If, in applied work, the B condition proves to have beneficial effects, the sequence typically is extended to include a return to that condition (A-B-A-B design), which provides a direct replication of the effects of the independent variable.

The degree of variability in behavior during both the baseline and the intervention periods affects one's judgments of robustness of the effects. Usually the assessment is accomplished mainly by graphing the data onto a chart, with evaluation focused on whether or not the effect is obvious upon visual inspection, sometimes supplemented by quantitative analysis. A given condition is typically continued until stability criteria are met; occasionally such analyses, both visual and quantitative, are supplemented with inferential statistical analyses, but the latter are viewed as secondary to direct demonstration of experimental control.

Fundamental to the strategy of individual-subject designs is systematic replication. The simplest form is to repeat the procedure with a closely comparable subject and assess whether similar results are obtained. Such replications might also be accomplished in varied settings, such as home versus school. Another form is designated as A-B-A-C-A-D, or some variation thereof, where the letters other than *A* identify different values of the independent variable. This type of systematic replication is particularly useful because it enables the construction of functional relations between different values of an independent variable and behavior. If orderly differences are found in relation to the magnitude of the independent variable, one can be increasingly confident of the effects of each separate condition. Such orderly results also may reduce the need for repeated returns to baseline conditions, provided that occasional replications of earlier values of the independent variable prove consistent. The generality of behavioral phenomena and effects is addressed by means of systematic replications that involve subjects with differing characteristics as well as new environmental contexts.

When two or more experimental features are systematically varied along continua, the result is a strategy analogous to factorial designs in the group-design tradition, where separate groups receive unique combinations of the independent variables. [*See* Randomized Experiments.] The two strategies differ, however, in that the effects of those continua, and of particular combinations of variables that would identify a cell within a factorial design, can be evaluated for each individual in the within-subject replications. This means that in practical applications the individual-case version of this strategy allows each individual to be exposed to the most potent combination of variables.

Alternative Individual-Case Designs

The reversal design and its variants have limitations that have led to the use of some alternative individual-case techniques, each of which is applicable to a particular conceptual issue or procedural constraint. For example, practical or ethical considerations sometimes make it undesirable or unfeasible to restore the original baseline condition after an intervention. [*See* Ethics, *article on* Ethics in Research.] In such cases, multiple baseline designs may be used, whereby two or more categories of behavior are assessed concurrently. These may be different response classes of an individual subject within a single setting (e.g., a child's on-task studying, appropriate requests for help, and disruptions of other children's work). They also may be the same classes of behavior but in different settings (e.g., the same child's behavior with different adults present), or they may be similar behavior of different individuals in a single setting. Following baseline assessments, the independent variable is applied to one behavior category of one person while the other recorded behavior (of that person or of others) continues in the baseline condition. If only the behavior addressed by the independent variable shows accompanying change, the effect is presumed to be attributable to the independent variable. Further evaluation is accomplished by subsequently exposing the other recorded categories of behavior to the same intervention in sequence; if again only the targeted behavior shows systematic change, the effect is further confirmed.

Other techniques are suitable for other special conditions. For example, yoked control designs allow the equating of one dynamic variable in real time while simultaneously varying another. Thus, to assess the effect of a contingency between behavior and food delivery, the rate of food delivery can be held equal by a yoked control procedure while the contingency is either present or absent in different conditions. The probe design is another example, whereby brief presentations of an independent variable can be evaluated; this is especially useful for assessing expensive or potentially deleterious manipulations.

Strengths and Weaknesses

An obvious advantage of within-case designs is that one need not recruit large numbers of comparable subjects, which may be crucial when particular/unusual medical or behavioral characteristics are of concern. Reducing the number of subjects also has been of interest to those concerned with minimizing animal use for ethical reasons. The few subjects needed, however, typically must participate in the research for relatively long periods. Also, within-case designs tend to be time- and labor-intensive, and their requirements may conflict with practical constraints such as the subjects' school terms or their employment.

Within-case designs have practical advantages arising from the frequent, often day-to-day monitoring of data. If the closely monitored interventions prove effective they might be quickly improved upon; if they are proving ineffective, one can take corrective measures at once. These techniques also facilitate the individual tailoring of independent variables based on each participant's own baseline and circumstances.

In addition, a strong conceptual basis for favoring these designs in certain circumstances is their highlighting the importance of individual histories for the understanding of current behavior. Every subject arrives in an experiment with a history of interacting with its environment—histories that are tapped only indirectly by techniques based on brief assessments of many subjects. Individual-case designs enable direct examination of how such histories of behavior-environment interaction work, supporting a flexible, systematic but relatively informal approach to experimentation that readily translates into educational practice or clinical interventions. A substantial basic and applied literature involving the use of nonhuman as well as human subjects, both adults and children, attests to the viability and utility of this family of techniques.

Bibliography

Barlow, D. H. (1984). *Single-case experimental designs* (2nd ed.). New York: Allyn & Bacon. A basic exposition of within-case research designs as addressed to clinical and other applied problems.

Hersen, M. (1982). Single-case experimental designs. In A. S. Bellack, M. Hersen, & A. E. Kazden (Eds.), *International handbook of behavior modification and therapy* (pp. 167–203) New York: Plenum. An essay that begins by discussing variability and its implications, followed by a summary of basic research designs with some illustrative data.

Iversen, I. H., & Lattal, K. A. (1991). *Techniques in the behavioral and neural sciences: Vol. 6. Experimental analysis of behavior (Parts 1 and 2)*. Amsterdam: Elsevier. A two-volume set describing rationale and strategies as well as technical details relevant to specific domains of basic research focused on behavior of the individual organism.

Johnston, J. M., & Pennypacker, H. S. (1993a). *Strategies and tactics of behavioral research* (2nd ed.). Hillsdale, NJ: Erlbaum. A thorough discussion of the rationale of explanation that has provided the conceptual background of research focused upon the behavior of individual organisms.

Johnston, J. M., & Pennypacker, H. S. (1993b). *Readings for strategies and tactics of behavioral research* (2nd ed.). Hillsdale, NJ: Erlbaum. A thoroughly annotated collection of articles discussing and illustrating the issues that arise in the analysis and presentation of data in the use of within-case reserch designs.

Philip N. Hineline and Kennon A. Lattal

SITUATED COGNITION. The central tenet of a situated cognition perspective is that all cognitions are inextricably embedded in the contexts (situations) in which they occur. In this view, the physical, social, and cultural environments are as much a part of learning as the individual person, and context remains an integral part of what is learned. Learning is seen as being "situated" in the learning situation, both constrained and guided by the environment, and even defined by that environment. In essence, learning and knowledge—perhaps it is better to say "knowing"—cannot be separated from its context.

If one were to try to "locate" knowing, situated cognition theorists would propose that it does not exist inside the head of the knower, nor does it reside in features of the environment; rather, knowing is inherent in the interaction among the learner, the activity, the tools used, and aspects of the environment in which it develops. What is learned cannot be separated from how it is learned and used; rather, what is learned actually embodies the context in which that learning occurred. As James Greeno et al. (1993) note, just as motion is not a property of an object, knowing is not a characteristic of the individual. The motion of any moving object must always be seen in terms of a particular frame of reference: how it was set in motion, its speed, its direction, its acceleration, and the surface it is moving on or the space it is moving through. This frame of reference does not simply influence the motion of the object; rather, motion is inherent in the relationship between the object and that particular frame of reference. Similarly, context does not simply influence knowing, reasoning, and other forms of cognition; these cognitions are inherent in the relationship between the person and the situation in which the person engages in those cognitive activities.

In situated cognition it is important to remember that physical, social, and cultural environments are not just the places where learning takes place. These contexts embody personal goals, the activity or task, purposes ascribed to the activity, tools, social roles, cultural traditions, social and historical practices, as well as other people.

Because knowing is so tied to its specific learning context, we cannot talk about what someone knows without reference to the situation in which that knowing takes place. Thus, some situated learning theorists (e.g., Greeno et al., 1993), define knowing as the ability to interact with things and people in a situation, and they define learning as improvement in the ability to participate in a situated activity. This raises important questions about our understanding of such issues as transfer of learning (i.e., How can the ability to participate in one situated activity be transferred to another, differently situated activity?), effective instructional practices (i.e., How can learning be promoted?), and appropriate assessment (i.e., How can knowing and learning be measured?).

One of the problems that situated-cognition theorists have noted is that school learning often remains largely inert—not readily applied either in other situations within the same academic discipline, across disciplines, or in nonschool contexts such as work and everyday life outside the classroom. This indicates a failure to transfer. Similarly, much of the knowledge and skills that children acquire during their everyday activities outside of school fail to transfer to the classroom. A frequently cited example of this phenomenon is research reported by Nunes and her colleagues (1993). They found that young Brazilian street vendors who were able to perform mathematical calculations during business transactions on the street were unable to perform the very same math operations with the same numbers in a school context. The street vendors' failure to transfer street math to a school math context was explained by the differences in contexts. Although the numbers and operations were the same, the purposes of the activities differed, as did other contextual features such as the people involved, the materials used, and the places in which the activities took place. These contextual features were as much a part of the learning as the mathematics, and made the learning situations quite different. The difference in contexts apparently precluded transfer.

Situated Cognition and Transfer

Although there is lack of agreement among situated-learning theorists on how to address the issue of transfer, some theorists take the position that transfer is influenced by the structures of situated activity, taking note that situatedness involves not only physical context, but also social and cultural context. Thus, structures of situated activity include not only interactions of the individual with objects in the initial activity and the transfer situation, but also interactions with other people involved, the meanings that are constructed regarding the task, the importance attributed to information and to aspects of the activity, the social roles assumed by participants, and the interaction of each of these with each other.

For example, the goals of an activity, as socially defined, dictate what aspects of the situated activity are important and, therefore, what the individual pays attention to and talks about with others, which further determines meanings and significance. These social interactions can be structured in ways that encourage the individual to relate the situated activity experience to previous experiences and to other similar activities, so that the individual builds up an understanding of a domain of situations, thus promoting transfer. According to James Greeno and his colleagues, such social interactions "influence people's understanding about what constitutes a domain of situations, so that activities that occur in different situations that belong to the domain can be expected to benefit from a common set of learning experiences" (1993, p. 100). Understanding a domain of situations promotes transfer within that domain.

Effective instruction structures interactions during learning to capitalize on this notion of domains of situations; effective assessment looks at the extent to which an individual carries the learned activity from the initial learning situation to the domain transfer situations. A situated cognition perspective emphasizes instruction that focuses on everyday cognition, use of real-world tasks and activities, and apprenticeship learning (cf. "anchored instruction" as defined by the Cognition and Technology Group at Vanderbilt, 1990). Situated cognition also stresses assessment that is performance-based or in some way meets the criteria of authentic assessment.

Situated Cognition: A Challenge to Information Processing

Although situated cognition theories differ from information-processing theories, there is debate about the extent to which these two theoretical perspectives conflict or are compatible. Whereas Alonzo Vera and Herb Simon argue that the situated-cognition perspective can be incorporated into the information-processing view and is actually just a special case of information-processing (1993), William Clancy and others hotly debate this issue and contend that information-processing is one aspect of what occurs during situated cognition (1993).

In the information-processing paradigm, the model on which cognitive psychology is based, knowledge and thought are properties of the individual (they are "inside the head," so to speak) and understanding involves a process of pattern matching and identification. Sensory information from the external world is matched with information retrieved from an internal memory store (long-term memory) to identify perceptions, which are then represented in working memory (a short-term memory storage). To make further sense of this representation, it is matched with patterns obtained from an extensive search of memories held in long-term memory. Meanings and understandings are then concluded based on these pattern matches.

In contrast to this focus on the individual as information processor, the situated cognition perspective emphasizes the importance of context: the environment, the activity, social interaction, and historical and cultural practice. Understanding is not achieved through retrieval and matching, but rather involves direct information pickup—direct perception. What information is picked up is determined by the perceiver's present goals, intentions, and interaction with the current social context, and also by what is afforded by that context—its possibilities and limitations (cf. Gibson's notion of "affordances"). In this view, perception, identification of situations, and understanding are all co-determined by an interaction of person and environment. An extended critique of situated cognition and how it challenges theories of information processing can be found in a special issue of *Cognitive Science*, 17, 1993, devoted to situated cognition.

Situated Cognition and Constructionism

Although many theorists see situated cognition as very different from, and even incompatible with, constructionism, others contend that situated cognition is actually a form of constructionism. This confusion may have to do with definitions of the terms constructionism and constructivism. Piagetian notions of knowledge construction suggest that knowledge is constructed by the individual and is "in the head" of that individual. Social constructionists contend that knowledge is constructed in social interaction—it is coconstructed, and each individual's knowledge constructions are unique (to a greater or lesser extent) because they depend upon the particular characteristics of that individual and the specific context(s) in which they are constructed. If the term constructivism is reserved for discussions of Piagetian theory of development, and constructionism is used in describing socially determined constructions, as in Vygotskian theory, then situated cognition and constructionism are compatible.

Research Issues

The situated cognition perspective has important implications for how researchers study cognition. One implication of this view is that knowledge, as well as cognitive activities such as knowledge construction, task performance, and problem solving, can only be understood by studying them within the specific situations in which they emerge and evolve. And, because cognition is not only physically situated, it is also socially and culturally situated, those situations are complex. This calls for situated cognition research to be conducted in authentic real-world environments only.

Bibliography

Brown, J. S., Collins, A., & Duguid, P. (1989). Situated cognition and the culture of learning. *Educational Researcher*, Jan.–Feb., 32–42.

Clancy, W. (1993). Situated action: A neuropsychological interpretation response to Vera and Simon. *Cognitive Science, 17*, 87–95.

Cognition and Technology Group at Vanderbilt. (1990). Anchored instruction and its relationship to situated cognition. *Educational Researcher, Aug–Sept.*, 2–10.

Greeno, J., Smith, D. R., & Moore, J. L. (1993). Transfer of situated learning. In D. Detterman & R. Sternberg (Eds.), *Transfer on trial* (pp. 98–124). Norwood, NJ: Ablex.

Kirshner, D., & Whitson, A. (Eds.). (1997). *Situated cognition: Social, semiotic, and psychological perspectives.* Mahwah, NJ: Erlbaum.

Lave, J. (1988). *Cognition in practice: Mind, mathematics, and culture in everyday life.* Cambridge, England: Cambridge University Press.

Lave, J., & Wenger, E. (1990). *Situated learning: Legitimate peripheral practice.* New York: Cambridge University Press.

Nunes, T., Schliemann, A. D., & Carraher, D. W. (1993). *Street mathematics and school mathematics.* New York: Cambridge University Press.

Resnick, L. B. (1997). *Discourse, tools, and reasoning: Essays on situated cognition.* New York: Springer. A clear and comprehensive treatment of current research and

thinking in situated cognition and how it fits into various disciplines.

Vera, A., & Simon, H. (1993). Situated action: A symbolic interpretation. *Cognitive Science, 17*, 7–47.

Alison King

SITUATION AWARENESS. In everyday parlance, the term *situation awareness* (SA) means the up-to-the-minute cognizance or awareness required to move about, operate equipment, or maintain a system. The automobile driver requires situation awareness in order to safely operate a vehicle in a rapidly changing environment. The driver needs to understand the position of the vehicle in relation to the road and other traffic, the speed limit under which the vehicle is currently operating, the capabilities of the car itself and any special circumstances, such as weather conditions that may influence driver decision-making. The driver uses senses—eyes and ears and perhaps nose and touch—to take in information and process it to build a conceptual model of the situation. The process of building up situation awareness is called situation assessment.

The term *SA* has emerged as a psychological concept because it captures a characteristic of human performance that is not directly observable, but that psychologists, especially engineering psychologists or human-factors specialists, have been asked to assess or purposefully manipulate because of its importance to everyday living and working. Defining SA in a way that is susceptible to measurement, different from generalized performance capacity, and usefully distinguishable from other concepts like perception, workload, or attention has proved difficult (Pew, in press). The most widely quoted definition of situation awareness was contributed by Endsley: "Situation awareness is the perception of the elements in the environment within a volume of time and space, the comprehension of their meaning and the projection of their status in the near future" (1988, p. 97).

Communities of analysts involved with human performance, including military planners, training specialists, military and commercial aviation experts, accident investigators, and power plant engineers, to mention just a few, find the concept useful because for them it expresses an important, but separable element of successful performance.

Most definitions of SA, like the one above, focus on the awareness part and neglect the definition of a situation. Situation awareness is context-dependent. What awareness is appropriate will depend on the specific circumstances that define the situation. On the one hand, it is helpful if situations are stable enough that particular SA requirements change only infrequently, so that we can assess whether they have been satisfied.

On the other hand, contexts change more or less continuously. We must be prepared to expect SA requirements to shift with changing contexts. With these concepts in mind, a "situation" may be formally defined as: a coherent collection of environmental conditions and system states with which the participant is interacting and that can be uniquely characterized by a set of information, knowledge, and response options.

Awareness is the more standard part of the definition. Awareness is a unique human characteristic that implies the perception, information, and/or knowledge characterizing the situation. The list below shows the elements of which a system operator or crew member should be cognizant.

- Current state of the system and its environment (including all relevant variables)
- Predicted state in the "near" future
- Information and knowledge required in support of the crew's current activities
- Prioritized list of current goal(s)
- Currently active goal, subgoal, and task
- Time
- Information and knowledge needed to support anticipated "near" future contexts

In this list the elements, while generally consistent with Endsley (1988), generalize her proposal to include the awareness of current goals and tasks as well as maintain a perspective on the temporal status of goal accomplishment. Keeping track of the time course of goal/task completion is important because it plays a critical role in planning and task management. It is typically implicit in definitions of SA, but should be explicit.

It is also important to note that, while much of the SA literature focuses on spatial awareness, there are many other aspects of systems and their operations of which awareness is required. In addition to spatial awareness, which is self-explanatory, there is a need to consider activity or mission and goal awareness, which refer to the need to keep current with the phase of the activity and the currently active goals to be satisfied. System awareness is especially important in complex, highly-automated systems. Resource awareness is needed to keep track of the state of currently available resources, including physical and human resources. One needs to be aware of human resources because the current activities of other crew members impact their availability for critical tasks. This is different from crew awareness, which refers to the need for the team of crew members to share their information and interpretation of current system events. They need to be operating in a common framework of information at all times (Morgan, Herschler, Wiener, & Salas, 1993).

In a recent assessment of the important aspects of human performance that need to be represented to capture its essence, situation awareness was listed along with attention, memory, planning, decision-making, learning, and managing multiple tasks (Pew & Mavor, 1998). It is in this context, of the analysis of human information-processing characteristics, that SA is most often linked.

Bibliography

Endsley, M. R. (1988). Design and evaluation for situation awareness enhancement. In *Proceedings of the Human Factors Society Thirty-second Annual Meeting* (Vol. 1). Santa Monica, CA: Human Factors Society.

Garland, D. J., & Endlsey, M. R. (Eds.). (1995). *Proceedings of the International Conference on Experimental Analysis and Measurement of Situation Awareness*. Daytona Beach, FL: Embry-Riddle Aeronautical University Press.

Gilson, R. D., Garland, D. J., & Koonce, J. M. (Eds.). (1994). *Situational awareness in complex systems*. Daytona Beach, FL: Embry-Riddle Aeronautical University Press.

Morgan, B. B., Herschler, D. A., Weiner, E. L., & Salas, E. (1993). Implications of automation technology for aircrew coordination and performance. In W. B. Rouse (Ed.), *Human/technology interaction in complex systems* (Vol. 6, pp. 105–136). Greenwich, CT: JAI Press.

Pew, R. W. (in press). The state of situation awareness measurement: circa 1996. In D. Garland & M. R. Endsley (Eds.), *Experimental analysis and measurement of situation awareness*. Mahwah, NJ: Erlbaum.

Pew, R. W., & Mavor, A. S. (Eds.). (1998). *Modeling human and organizational behavior: Application to military simulations*. Washington, DC: National Academy Press.

Richard W. Pew

SIXTEEN PERSONALITY FACTOR QUESTIONNAIRE. The Sixteen Personality Factor Questionnaire (16PF) is one of the oldest and most widely used instruments for assessing normal-range personality characteristics with adults. Its name derives from its ability to measure 16 reasonably independent and essentially normal categories that originally emerged from a series of factor analyses of the trait universe. Test results are useful in understanding personal adjustment and in predicting a wide range of socially important behaviors, such as occupational preferences and job performance.

The primary author of the 16PF, English-born Raymond B. Cattell, began research on the test by exploring the entire universe of trait elements. Cattell adopted the position that "all aspects of human personality which are or have been of importance, interest, or utility have already become recorded in the substance of language" (*Journal of Abnormal and Social Psychology*, 1943, *38*, p. 483). As an operational definition of the universe, he took the anthology of trait terms that Allport and Odbert found in *Webster's New Unabridged International*

Dictionary. Starting with the 4,504 terms they called personal traits, he and a colleague began to reduce the list to a more manageable number that could be empirically analyzed. Cattell subsequently applied a variety of analytic methods, most especially factor analysis, to reduce this large set of characteristics to a more exact and more fundamental set of elements that he judged to be "source traits." Cattell's argument drew on analogy to the physical sciences. In the same way that water, for example, could be conceptualized as a weighted combination of more fundamental elements (hydrogen and oxygen), human characteristics such as creativity or depression could be conceptualized as weighted combinations of more fundamental source traits. Cattell pursued his search systematically. The first version of the 16PF did not appear until more than a decade after Cattell began his studies. During that period he considered a variety of methods of assessment, including ratings, self-report, and objective behavioral measures. Congruity of results across media led him to conclusions about what constituted the most fundamental personality dimensions.

The structure that Cattell discovered formed the blueprint for the test. Over time the test has undergone several major and minor revisions, most recently in 1993. Partly as a function of advances in research, some redefinition of the scales took place after 1949. Since 1956, however, the scales have largely retained their current, basic meaning.

The most recent version of the test contains 185 items, requires 35 to 50 minutes to complete, and has a fifth-grade reading level. Adaptations of the test have been developed to accommodate a variety of populations. For example, an edition in American Sign Language has been validated for use with hearing-impaired populations. One edition, Form E, was developed for use within populations whose literacy skills are severely limited. Translations of the test have been prepared in nearly 50 languages around the world, and norms exist for adult populations in nearly as many countries.

The average test-retest scale reliability coefficient is 0.80 over intervals of a few weeks and 0.70 over intervals of several months. Both gender-specific and gender-neutral norms are provided for test users.

The primary scales of the test, which are designated by alphanumeric symbols, are as follows: A-Warmth, B-Reasoning, C-Emotional Stability, E-Dominance, F-Liveliness, G-Rule-Consciousness, H-Social Boldness, I-Sensitivity, L-Vigilance, M-Abstractedness, N-Privateness, O-Apprehension, Q_1-Openness to Change, Q_2-Self-reliance, Q_3-Perfectionism, Q_4-Tension. Scoring formulas have also been developed to assess characteristics that reflect blends of the primary scales. The most important of these, called "global factors," assess features similar to those described as the Big Five in contemporary personality research (e.g., Extroversion,

Neuroticism, Conscientiousness, Agreeableness, and Openness to Experience). In addition to these global factors, the 16PF can be scored for approximately 100 scales that derive from years of research on 16PF applications in clinical, counseling, and organizational psychology.

In addition to the substantive scales just described, the 16PF provides indexes that address test-taking attitude. The current edition has three response style indicators: Impression Management, Infrequency, and Acquiescence. These scales are helpful in identifying response patterns that are statistically unusual and require alternative interpretive strategies.

Although it can easily be and usually is hand scored, the 16PF was among the earliest of personality tests to be interpreted by computer. A large number of programs exist to examine the test scores within specific contexts, such as marriage counseling, career development, and organizational performance. Both mail-in and on-site services are available for the 16PF.

As a test of normal-range adult personality, the 16PF's content overlaps with that of other instruments, such as the California Psychological Inventory and the NEO Personality Inventory, which are similarly oriented. Correlational studies show that relationships among individual scales of these inventories are often quite high. However, high correlations may convey a sense of identify that is unwarranted. The multivariate personality model that underlies the 16PF is quite distinctive and embedded within a broader framework that addresses individual differences in learning and development.

A major strength of the 16PF lies in the extensive body of research findings that have accumulated over time. Several thousand published articles and books have provided a rich database that is equaled by very few instruments. Cattell's own research has provided a detailed analysis of how the characteristics measured by the test change and develop throughout the life span. Much is also known about how test scores relate to occupational preference, job performance, academic interests, interpersonal attraction, and marital satisfaction. The 16PF was not specifically designed for use with clinical populations and is, by itself, weak in assessing major affective and cognitive disturbances. However, a significant body of clinical research suggests that the test can be usefully applied in understanding the dynamics of adjustment and personality disorders, addiction, and spousal abuse. Carefully conducted longitudinal studies have also identified physical health risk factors among the primary scales. For example, test scores have been shown to be predictive of subsequent heart attacks in symptom-free adults.

Over 50 years, the 16PF has developed into a widely used instrument for assessing adult personality. A long history of empirical research with the test by Cattell combined with roots in a well-established theory provide a rich source of interpretation for test users.

[*See also the biography of Cattell.*]

Bibliography

Allport, G. W., & Odbert, H. S. (1936). Trait-names, a psycho-lexical study. *Psychological Monographs* (Whole no. 47).

Cattell, R. B. (1943). The description of personality: Basic traits resolved into clusters. *Journal of Abnormal and Social Psychology, 38,* 476–506.

Cattell, R. B. (1973). *Personality and mood by questionnaire.* San Francisco: Jossey-Bass.

Cattell, R. B. (1979). *Personality and learning theory: Vol. 1. The structure of personality in its environment.* New York: Springer.

Cattell, R. B. (1980). *Personality and learning theory: Vol. 2. A systems theory of maturation and structured learning.* New York: Springer.

Cattell, R. B., Eber, H. W., & Tatsuoka, M. M. (1970). *Handbook for the Sixteen Personality Factor Questionnaire.* Champaign, IL: IPAT.

Krug, S. E. (1986). Solid state psychology: The role of the computer in human assessment. In R. B. Cattell & R. C. Johnson (Eds.), *Functional psychological testing: Principles and instruments* (pp. 127–141). New York: Brunner/Mazel.

Krug, S. E. (1993). *Psychware sourcebook: A reference guide to computer-based products for assessment in psychology, business, and education* (4th ed.). Champaign, IL: MetriTech.

Krug, S. E., & Johns, E. F. (1990). The 16PF. In C. E. Watkins, Jr., & V. L. Campbell (Eds.), *Testing in counseling practice* (pp. 63–90). Hillsdale, NJ: Erlbaum.

Russell, M. T., & Karol, D. L. (1994). *16PF administrator's manual.* Champaign, IL: IPAT.

Samuel E. Krug

SKINNER, BURRHUS FREDERIC (1904–1990), American psychologist. As a noted behaviorist, inventor, educational innovator, and social critic, Skinner is widely known for his seminal laboratory research on operant conditioning and for his trenchant critiques of both academic and commonsense psychology. He was born in Susquehanna, Pennsylvania, a small town that developed around an Erie Railroad repair center built in the 1850s. He attended Hamilton College (1922–1926), majoring in English. After a "dark year" spent in a fruitless attempt to start a career as a fiction writer while living at his parents' home (at that point, in Scranton, Pennsylvania), he decided that he was a psychologist and, more specifically, a behaviorist. He had had a minimal acquaintance with psychology from his undergraduate education and personal reading; he enrolled for graduate training in psychology at Harvard University in 1928.

Skinner received the doctorate in 1931 and remained at Harvard on fellowship support until 1936, when he obtained his first faculty appointment at the University of Minnesota (1936–1945). Subsequently, after serving 3 years (1945–1948) as department chair at Indiana University, he became a professor of psychology at Harvard. After his retirement in 1974, he continued to write and lecture until he died of complications of leukemia in 1990.

Skinner began his career as a laboratory investigator of animal learning and behavior, but he diverged increasingly from other American behaviorists such as Clark Hull, O. Hobart Mowrer, Kenneth Spence, and Edward C. Tolman. He formulated a distinctive kind of behaviorism (which he called radical behaviorism), developed an institutionalized enterprise of behavioral research and application now known as behavior analysis, and attained much greater public visibility than his contemporaries. In an unusually long career of 61 years, he published 19 books and 189 articles and essays and became the most widely visible psychologist of the twentieth century.

Roots of Skinner's Career

We can account for quite a few features of Skinner's distinctive psychology if we adopt—as a convenient working assumption—his thesis (Skinner, 1971, 1974, 1981) that the environment is largely responsible for individual achievements, because it is the environment inhabited by an organism that selects, shapes, and sustains its (typically successful) behavior. Four aspects of Skinner's background were important in shaping his distinctive version of behaviorism.

First, as an undergraduate Skinner was stirred by the cultural criticism of the 1920s—including the writings of H. G. Wells, Bertrand Russell, and Sinclair Lewis—and became a convert to the "scientism" that these writers espoused. Throughout his career, Skinner exhibited a thoroughly dismissive attitude toward commonsense psychology; he was distrustful of the vernacular because of its close etymological relation to prescientific theories of human nature that he viewed as mistaken and misleading. Consequently, he questioned the effectiveness of twentieth-century Western cultural practices, which typically embodied those theories (Skinner, 1971; see also Skinner, 1948, 1987).

Second, Skinner's undergraduate education laid the foundation for a lifelong interest in literary (that is conceptual) subjects, and thus he was more daring than most of his contemporaries in tackling conceptual problems in psychology. Accordingly, he wrote books on language-in-use (Skinner, 1957) and the philosophy of behaviorism (Skinner, 1974), as well as numerous articles on the confusions that arise when psychologists adopt concepts from the vernacular for scientific uses (Skinner, 1974, 1989). By comparison, the projects of his behaviorist peers were more conservatively restricted to the concerns of laboratory research.

Third, the circumstances of Skinner's training kept him at a distance from mainstream psychology. When in 1928 Skinner chose Harvard's department of philosophy and psychology for his graduate training, Harvard was an institution thoroughly unsuited to his aspiration to become a behaviorist. Walter Hunter, visiting professor from Clark University, was the only behaviorist on a faculty that favored traditional topics concerning conscious human (mostly sensory-perceptual) experience. This inhospitable setting provided Skinner with targets for sharpening his behaviorist criticisms but also drove him into the Department of Physiology in search of training in behavioral research (Skinner, 1979). There, William J. Crozier (a disciple of the physiologist Jacques Loeb) mentored Skinner in his early laboratory research, including the research for his dissertation. In addition, Crozier's scientific attitudes steered Skinner toward a descriptive metapsychology that looked with disfavor on elaborate and premature theorizing. The most important—though unintended—result, however, was that Skinner's training in physiology was accomplished at the expense of a grounding in psychology. He never acquired a thorough and professionally typical familiarity with the psychological literature. His distinctiveness was, in part, made possible by this breakdown in his socialization as a psychologist.

Fourth, during Skinner's formative years, psychologists were influenced by speculations in the philosophy of science about which scientific practices had been most responsible for the progress of the natural sciences into the early twentieth century. In particular, various versions of positivism singled out different aspects of scientific work as crucial to progress. Skinner, for his part, was affected by the writings of Francis Bacon, in the application of scientific method to human problems, and Ernst Mach, in scientific work per se (Skinner, 1976, 1979). The resulting conjunction of ideas was unusual among psychologists, and it supported attitudes and projects that placed Skinner in strong opposition to his peers. When it was fashionable to develop ambitiously complex theories of learning, Skinner (1950) questioned the practice; when the application of behavioral research to alleviate human problems was regarded as a distant hope (for example, K. W. Spence, *Behavior Theory and Conditioning*, New Haven, Conn., 1956), Skinner developed such applications; when statistical analysis was in vogue, Skinner (1956) was openly critical of such practices.

Of the world beyond academic psychology, it is safe to say that many circumstances pushed Skinner into the role of public figure. His stance as a critic of American societal arrangements (Skinner, 1971, 1987) and as a designer of behaviorist alternatives, whether fictional (Skinner, 1948) or programmatic (Skinner, 1971), departed from what at the time were characteristically professorial attitudes of ivory-tower neutrality regarding American cultural practices and genteel disavowal of efforts to attract mass media notice.

From Laboratory to Public Arena

There is a sharp contrast between Skinner's empiricist caution in employing psychological concepts when he did his laboratory research, particularly in the first half of his career, and his zealous readiness to extend laboratory-derived concepts and principles to the social world and to interpret human activity as operant behavior shaped by reinforcement contingencies in the social environment, especially in the second half of his career. What facilitated Skinner's transition from laboratory researcher to public figure was a kind of conceptual elasticity: in lieu of the intervening variables of such elaborate theories as those of Hull, Spence, and Tolman, Skinner employed flexible concepts (reinforcement delay, shaping, contingency, stimulus, and so forth) that he had carefully employed in laboratory research and then confidently extended to the human social world. (In a widely cited critique, the linguist Noam Chomsky found such extensions of laboratory-based concepts indefensible; *Language*, 1959, 35, 26–58.)

Moreover, starting as early as the "dark year" at Scranton, Skinner kept a notebook of reflections and observations. After becoming a behaviorist, he continued this practice, and his *Notebooks* (Epstein, Ed., Englewood Cliffs, N.J., 1980) provides a fascinating sample of speculations, plausible extrapolations, and illustrations of laboratory-based principles drawn from his personal experience. In addition, Skinner had the technical skill to develop apparatus and procedures to check on the validity of his musings as possible solutions to real-world problems. The second and third of Skinner's autobiographical volumes describe the personal context for such inventions or techniques as the baby-tender, teaching machine, programmed instruction, and other creations of Skinnerian applied psychology.

Radical-Behaviorist Meta-Theory

Over the course of his career, Skinner developed an environmentalist philosophy that pictured behavior as a product of environmental selection (Skinner, 1981). It is the environment that selects viable mutations in the evolution of plants and animals, and, in the life history of an organism, its operant behavior is selected, shaped, and sustained by the reinforcement contingencies that hold (or are arranged) between its behaviors and their consequences. In the case of humans, it is the environment of societal arrangements that is responsible for socially significant behavior. Skinner was sharply critical of the notion that individuals are creatively autonomous agents responsible for their own behavior. Cultures that presuppose individual autonomy and responsibility and defend individual liberties by minimizing effective social controls embrace a mistaken theory of human behavior and, according to Skinner, are likely to be less effective in promoting behavior that contributes to cultural survival (Skinner, 1971, 1987).

In his radical behaviorism, Skinner also endorsed materialism. According to him, what are typically called mental states (in the "inside story" that humans can tell about themselves and that are assumed to exist in the minds of animals) are internal conditions that are either physical stimulation (for example, of sensory receptors in the viscera) or nonpublic activities (for example, "thinking"). Thus his behaviorism encompassed and reinterpreted phenomena that appear to be nonbehavioral: emotions, feelings, thinking, planning, and so on. Skinner's proposal that the realm of subjectivity is physical and behavioral appeared to be a denial of mentality, whereas it only expressed a repudiation of dualism. On the other hand, Skinner's writings typically downplayed the importance of the inner realm in the explanation or interpretation of behavior, human and otherwise, and thus prompted resistance, rejection, and misunderstanding by a nonbehaviorist audience accustomed to accepting commonsense psychology as true.

Misunderstandings

Controversial public figures typically provoke misinterpretation, and Skinner was such a case. The fact that his proposals ran counter to conventional beliefs (as articulated in commonsense psychology) about the distinctiveness of humans, their spiritual nature, the significance of mind, and the reality of human freedom and creativity surely played a role in the reception of his ideas. Despite a variety of publications that expounded his philosophy, numerous misunderstandings persisted: (1) that he opposed all theorizing (but see his 1950 paper); (2) that he proposed an "empty organism" picture of humans (but see his 1974 book); (3) that he was unable to accommodate instinct (but see his 1981 article and his *Cumulative Record*); (4) that his proposals for social improvement were punitive, Pavlovian, coercive, and authoritarian (but see his 1948, 1971, and 1974 books); and (5) that he regarded people as machines (but see his 1974 book). Other misunderstandings are illuminated by A. Charles Catania and Steven Harnad (in their book, *The Selection of Behavior*, New York, 1988).

Skinner's Status

Skinner's accomplishments were recognized throughout his career. He was elected to the National Academy of Sciences and the Society of Experimental Psychologists, receiving the latter organization's Warren Medal in 1942. To the surprise of some, he was designated Humanist of the Year in 1972 by the American Humanist Association. He received the Distinguished Scientific Contribution Award from the American Psychological Association in 1958, and the association acknowledged his career-long achievements by giving him its Lifetime Scientific Contribution Award shortly before his death in 1990.

Skinner's wide visibility stemmed from many factors, including his substantive accomplishments as a researcher, his contributions in the public arena, and his skillful use of conceptual criticism to shock the established order. He remained an outspoken and unrepentant behaviorist to the end of his life, even as mainstream experimental psychology embraced a cognitive theoretical vocabulary and as research interests in memory and cognitive processes greatly expanded at the expense of the earlier focus on learning and behavior. Such a shift—deemed by some a revolutionary change of "paradigm"—may have the effect of permanently devaluing Skinner's significance, and indeed at present the experimental-psychology mainstream has succeeded in marginalizing Skinner by ignoring his work, although behavior analysis has remained a viable minority tradition. A wholesale eclipse of Skinner's importance, however, does not seem likely, given his success in establishing institutions in psychotherapy, in human and animal experimental psychology, and in the helping professions that employ the practices, strategies, ideas, and philosophy that he developed.

[*Many of the people mentioned in this article are the subjects of independent biographical entries.*]

Bibliography

Works by Skinner

Skinner, B. F. (1938). *Behavior of organisms.* New York: Appleton-Century-Crofts. Skinner's systematic behavior theory, heavily based on the laboratory research that he later abandoned to pursue the implications of behavior "control."

Skinner, B. F. (1948). *Walden two.* New York: Macmillan. Fictional societal engineering based on reinforcement principles discovered in the animal laboratory.

Skinner, B. F. (1950). Are theories of learning necessary? *Psychological Review, 57,* 193–216. Classic indictment of ambitious and (according to Skinner) premature efforts at theory development.

Skinner, B. F. (1956). A case history in scientific method. *American Psychologist, 11,* 221–233. A humorous but pointed critique of statistical and hypotheticodeductive methods in psychology.

Skinner, B. F. (1957). *Verbal behavior.* New York: Appleton-Century-Crofts. Skinner's major work on language.

Skinner, B. F. (1968). *The technology of teaching.* New York:

Appleton-Century-Crofts. Skinner's improvements of education.

Skinner, B. F. (1971). *Beyond freedom and dignity*. New York: Knopf. Skinner's critique of Western cultural practices that aggrandize the individual at the expense of cultural survival; accessible and thought provoking.

Skinner, B. F. (1972). *Cumulative record* (3rd ed.). New York: Appleton-Century-Crofts. A wide-ranging selection of Skinner's writings through the 1960s.

Skinner, B. F. (1974). *About behaviorism*. New York: Knopf. Radical behaviorism for the intelligent layperson.

Skinner, B. F. (1976, 1979, 1983). *Particulars of my life, The shaping of a behaviorist, A matter of consequences*. New York: Knopf. Skinner's detail-rich account of his life.

Skinner, B. F. (1981). Selection by consequences. *Science, 213*, 501–504. A concise statement of Skinner's environmentalism.

Skinner, B. F. (1987). *Upon further reflection*. Englewood Cliffs, NJ: Prentice Hall. An interesting anthology of Skinner's later writings about improving societal arrangements.

Skinner, B. F. (1989). The origins of cognitive thought. *American Psychologist, 44*, 13–18. Etymology of mentalism, aimed at exposing the prescientific character of cognitive language.

Works about Skinner

Bjork, D. W. (1993). *B. F. Skinner: A life*. New York: Basic Books. The premier biography; situates Skinner culturally as an original voice in the American tug-of-war between the quest for individual freedom and societal claims upon the individual, with Skinner's 1971 book the focal point.

Lattal, K. A. (Ed.). (1992). Reflections on B. F. Skinner and psychology [Special issue]. *American Psychologist, 47*, 1269–1533. Twenty-five articles, ranging from the technical to the philosophical, published shortly after Skinner's death.

Smith, L. D., & Woodward, W. R. (Eds.). (1996). *B. F. Skinner and behaviorism in American culture*. Bethlehem, PA: Lehigh University Press. See also Todd & Morris (1995).

Todd, J. T., & Morris, E. K. (Eds.). (1995). *Modern perspectives on B. F. Skinner and contemporary behaviorism*. Westport, CT: Greenwood. Along with Smith & Woodward (1996), a good anthology of current professional writing on Skinner's distinctiveness and importance.

Wiener, D. N. (1996). *B. F. Skinner: Benign anarchist*. Boston: Allyn & Bacon. An engaging and readable biography that attempts to draw out the person behind the public persona and reputation.

Stephen R. Coleman

SKINNER BOX. *See* Operant Conditioning.

SKIN SENSES. *See* Touch.

SLEEP. In the mid-1700s, the English essayist Samuel Johnson described sleep as a gentle tyrant before whom all behaviors bowed down each day. He noted that no researcher had yet found the efficient or final causes of this mysterious power. An explosion of interdisciplinary research, beginning in the 1950s, has done much to inform us about the dimensions of this dark kingdom and its underlying mechanisms, and to reveal its efficient causes.

In the 1930s, a method of measuring the beginning, end, and ongoing process of sleep was discovered. With the onset of sleep, the electroencephalogram (EEG) tracings of electrical activity of the brain changed and displayed a systematic pattern during sleep. Beginning in 1953, while exploring these EEG patterns, the discovery that ignited contemporary sleep research was made. During sleep, about every 100 minutes, the EEG patterns display the characteristics of waking, and this period was accompanied by rapid eye movements. When awakened during these periods, subjects reported that they were dreaming. This finding affirmed the notion that sleep was an active process, added stimulus to the search for the neurophysiological bases of sleep, incorporated the cognitive world of dreaming, and attracted a broad interdisciplinary group of researchers. [*See* Dreams.]

In the late 1960s and early 1970s, the concept of sleep as a biological rhythm began to emerge. A biological rhythm is a biological variation that occurs in a regular time sequence and is based on an endogenous (internal) timing. By the 1980s, the concept of sleep as a biological rhythm had been thoroughly incorporated. Then there was a distinct shift from basic research to applications in the areas of sleep disorders, pharmacology, and areas such as shift work, jet lag, and highway accidents. [*See* Circadian Rhythms; *and* Sleep Disorders.]

The Dimensions of Sleep

The electroencephalogram (*electro* = "electrical," *encephalon* = "brain area," *gram* = "recording") measures microvolt electrical changes from electrodes attached to the brain area. These recordings are described in terms of their frequency and amplitude. In the late 1930s, it was noted that, with the onset of sleep, EEG pattern changes were apparent. In the waking person, the brain waves show a mixed, high-frequency pattern of low amplitude and of less than 50 microvolt amplitude. Sleep is indicated by the onset of Stage 1 sleep, which has a mixed frequency of low amplitude in the 2 to 7 cycles per second (cps) range. This is followed by Stage 2, which is characterized by "sleep spindles," short bursts (0.5 seconds to 2 seconds) of regular 8 to 10 cps waves. Stages 3 and 4 (slow-wave sleep) are identified by the emergence of intermittent 2 to 4 cps waves of increased amplitude

(100–150 microvolts). Stage 4 is signaled by a record of more than 50% slow-wave sleep.

In the 1950s, while exploring the patterns of sleep, Nathaniel Kleitman, a pioneer in contemporary sleep research, and his associates made a remarkable discovery. Within the sleep process, about every 100 minutes, the EEG pattern shifted to an appearance of wakefulness, and this shift was accompanied by rapid eye movements (REMs). When awakened from sleep during this stage (Stage 1–REM) persons would report that they had been dreaming.

All night recordings of sleep revealed that there were consistent patterns of sleep across the night. Young adults would move from Stage 1, Stage 2, and Stage 3 to Stage 4 with occasional regressions to earlier stages. After about 90 to 100 minutes, a brief episode of Stage 1–REM sleep of about 5–10 minutes would occur. In the second period, sleep would return to Stage 2 mixed with Stage 3, and, occasionally, Stage 4. Again, after about 100 minutes, there would be an emergent period of a longer Stage 1–REM period. The third period would be dominantly Stage 2, with perhaps a brief period of Stage 3 followed by a longer Stage 1–REM episode. Further sleep would be, dominantly, Stage 2 with longer episodes of Stage 1–REM that may last for 30 minutes. Stage 4 sleep was almost exclusively placed in the first one third of the night, and Stage 1–REM became increasingly present in the last half of the night. Almost all introductory psychology textbooks describe these measurements in detail.

The EEG rapidly became a dominant aspect of sleep research. Sleep could be measured without interference with the process itself. The EEG could be used to index sleep in infants, the elderly, and animals, and could identify the presence of dreaming. In the early period of sleep research, the EEG became the definition of sleep, and the focus of research was turned inward toward the stages of sleep, the neurophysiological explorations of the sleep process, and the cognitive exploration of dreams.

However, it is apparent that sleep has another and broader set of dimensions. This was particularly emphasized with the observations of the sleep of nonhuman animals and across the age range of humans. It was spread across the 24 hours of the day in a variety of patterns. To describe these differences it was necessary to include the dimensions of total sleep time, the number and length of sleep episodes, and the placement of these episodes in a 24-hour period. Without attending to this complex array of sleep behavior and its interaction with other behaviors, sleep would lie in isolation, in its EEG onset and termination.

The Determinants of Sleep

As sleep research advanced, it became apparent that sleep was systematically influenced by three primary factors: a sleep need, the timing of sleep, and behavioral control.

Sleep as a Need. One of the most apparent facts about sleep is that there is a sleep need that is related to length of time awake. Simply stated, the longer the time awake, the sleepier one becomes. A good measure of this need is the speed of sleep onset when the time of sleep onset and behavioral controls are held constant. Figure 1 plots this relationship through the first 24 hours of wakefulness. The decrease in sleep latency (indicating an increased sleep need) continues until about 60 hours of wakefulness, when sleep onset is immediate. If, instead of continuing awake across the 24 hours, a full night's sleep had occurred, the sleep need would have been eliminated. If less than a full night's sleep is obtained there will be a residual sleep need.

Sleep as a Timed System. One of the most important discoveries of contemporary sleep research was that sleep is a biological rhythm. Experimental evidence of this aspect of sleep came from studies in which sleep was displaced from its usual nighttime schedule to other times within the 24-hour period. These experiments included shift work, jet lag designs, and other than 24-hour schedules, such as 2 hours awake/1 hour asleep schedules, or 12 hours awake/6 hours asleep schedules, and sleep in environments with no time cues.

These studies revealed that sleep was organized as an internally timed circadian, or 24-hour, system. Figure 1 displays this circadian effect on sleep latencies across a 24-hour period when prior wakefulness and behavioral controls are held constant. The circadian effect begins to rise shortly before the person awakes and rises across the daytime period to a high point shortly before bedtime. Then there is a rapid decline across the sleep period until the early morning rise.

Figure 1 displays the independently obtained tendencies. However, in a real-life sequence, sleep typically occurs during the nighttime phase, and these tendencies interact with each other as time passes. The tendencies, indexed as latencies, have an algebraical summed effect. If sleep occurs from, say, 11 P.M. to 7 A.M., the sleep need is reduced to the minimum point pictured at 7 A.M. The circadian effect is also low at this point but beginning to rise. This may serve as a cue for awakening. Although the sleep need is beginning to rise during the day, this effect is offset by the rising circadian tendency. Paradoxically, the circadian tendency is at its maximum point at 11 P.M., shortly before bedtime. This "forbidden zone," in which sleep onset is difficult, has now been well established. Shortly thereafter, the circadian tendency begins to diminish. This may serve as the signal for sleep onset. It should also be noted that, during the nighttime period, although the sleep need is being re-

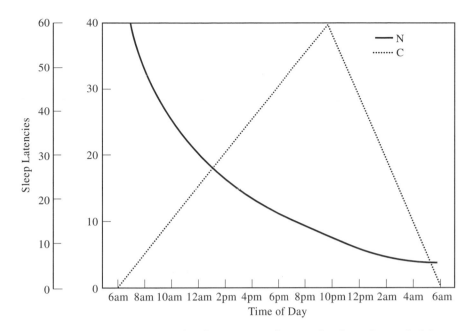

SLEEP. Figure 1. Hypothetical scales, across 24 hours, of independent wakefulness tendencies of sleep need (N) and circadian tendencies (C). These are measured by minutes to sleep onset. Note different scales for circadian tendencies (0 to 40 minutes) and need tendencies (0 to 60 minutes).

duced by sleep, at about 4 A.M. there is still a residual sleep need and a diminishing circadian tendency. It is this combination that produces the problems of shift work and jet lag.

Behavioral Control. Voluntarily or involuntarily, within limits, sleep can be delayed, shortened, or displaced in time. This inhibition of sleep has advantages and disadvantages. It permits us to extend our wakefulness, terminate our sleep, or reorganize our schedules for pleasures or demands. However, these inhibitions may, as in insomnias or noisy environments, be involuntary. Even when self-imposed, they are to varying degrees in violation of the underlying controls of sleep need and the rhythmic system. For example, as discussed above, if one continues without sleep by going on shift work or continuing to drive an automobile, one is courting the maximum combined effects of both an undiminished sleep need and a minimum circadian effect.

The Modulators of Sleep

The three primary determinants of sleep helps us understand the sleep of young healthy human adults. However, across the animal kingdom, sleep is very different from species to species, the sleep of infants and the elderly differs, and there are wide individual differences in sleep. These are all controlled by a complex neurophysiological system that may be affected by drugs. The system may also become quite disordered.

Within the perspective of the primary determinants, let us consider these modifiers.

Species. The array of sleep across the animal kingdom is remarkably varied. For predictive purposes, need and rhythmic and behavior components must be modified for each species. The sleep need varies from a few hours in 24 to many hours. A few examples: 2 to 4 hours (sheep, goats, cows, and deer); 8 hours (humans, rabbits, pigs, and monkeys); 12 hours (rats, gorillas, raccoons, and squirrels); 18 to 20 hours (armadillos, opossums, brown bats, and sloths). The rhythmic controls are also varied. Owls, bats, and rodents are nocturnal; humans and primates are diurnal. The number and length of the sleep episodes also vary widely. For example, the rat has short bursts of wakefulness and sleep in both light and dark periods. The average length of a sleep episode in the light is about 20 minutes, and about 15 minutes in the dark.

Both the timing and need levels for sleep reflect the evolutionary pressures in the development of sleep in each species relative to predator relationships and foraging requirements. For example, most grazing animals have low sleep needs, sleep in short bursts, and are generally acircadian. This reflects the 24-hour availability of forage and the need to avoid long sleep periods in order to remain in the herd.

The sleep structure of animals, as measured by the EEG, is also species specific. Almost all vertebrate species, including birds, have periodic episodes of "active" sleep resembling REM sleep. The amounts of "active" sleep vary from about 1% in birds to about 30% in cats. However, most species have only a two-phase sleep of "active" sleep and "passive" (slow-wave) sleep.

Age. Sleep is a developmental process, with sleep need, rhythmic timing, and behavioral control changing with age. This is apparent in the development of human sleep patterns. At birth, sleep need averages 16 hours and declines rapidly to about 12 hours by the age of 5. There is a further decline to about 10 hours in teens, and stabilizes at 7 to 8 hours for the young adult. From this point, the sleep need remains constant until the 60s. At this time, about one third of older persons begin to increase their amount of sleep and about 5% reduce their daily sleep. Changes in the rhythmic aspects of sleep are also evident. The newborn rapidly begins to develop a pattern of predominantly nighttime sleep; about 11 hours at night and 2 daytime naps of about an hour. By the age of 2, the nighttime sleep has become consolidated; about 25% of children are taking two naps, about 70% percent are taking a single daytime nap, and about 5% have begun to skip naps. By the age of 5, most children have begun to nap irregularly. There is a reemergence of napping in older persons in their 60s and beyond. In a detailed study of 50- to 60-year-old active persons, about 25% reported no napping and about 40% reported from one to four naps during a 2-week period. Napping increases with further aging.

Aging also is accompanied by increased awakening during the nighttime sleep period. In a sample of healthy 50- to 70-year-old persons, about 40% of men and 20% of women had 30 minutes or more of awake time after sleep onset. This tendency increases with further aging. The combined data on napping and the breakdown of the nighttime sleep is generally interpreted as evidence for the deterioration of the circadian control of the sleep process.

Individual Differences. Across species, at any age level, sleep needs, the rhythmic component, and behavioral control display individual differences. These are well documented in humans, based on estimates of sleep need from the amount of sleep obtained. At birth the range of differences, from the average of 16 hours, extends from about 20 hours to 12 hours for the 24-hour period. In young adults, from an average of 7 to 8 hours, the standard deviation of sleep hours is 1 hour. This means that about 68% of individuals need between 6½ and 8½ hours of sleep each night, about 14% will need between 5½ and 6½, or 8½ and 9½ hours, and about 2% will need less than 5½ or more than 9½ hours.

Sleep diaries of 2 weeks or move provide evidence for our behavioral control of sleep. These diaries reveal that sleep amount varies during weekdays by an average of 45 minutes from night to night, and on weekends sleep is 1 hour longer than on weekdays.

There have been few studies of individual differences in the rhythmic factors of sleep. However, strong evidence for individual differences are seen in the rates of development described above under the topic of aging.

Central Nervous System Controls. Sleep is controlled by neurophysiological mechanisms that underlie the need, rhythmic, and behavioral controls of sleep. Impositions on these mechanisms by drugs or dysfunctions of the mechanisms will modulate these determinants.

From the earliest times there has been speculation about these internal mechanisms. These speculations were fueled by the explosive development of information about the underlying physiology and neurology of organisms, which began in the mid-nineteenth century. Each new discovery often brought an assertion about its role as a sleep determinant. These included theories about vascular anemia or congestion, oxygen depletion, or neural inhibition. By the early twentieth century there were at least 18 "humoral" substances that had been implicated and dozens of neuronal "inhibitory" theories. Each new discovery modified each earlier hypothesis.

By the 1920s, the techniques for exploring the central nervous system had become highly sophisticated. Landmark findings that located the primary control mechanisms of sleep and waking in the mid-brain emerged in rapid order. In 1935, Frederick Bremer, a Belgian physiologist, reported that when the mid-brain was isolated from the cortex (cerveau isole), there was a state of continuous sleep. However, when the transection occurred at the spinal cord (encephale isole) there was a normal alternation of sleep and waking. In 1935, Giuseppi Morruzi and Thomas Magoun reported that stimulation of the reticular activating section of the mid-brain in a "sleeping" cat with a spinal transection resulted in a waking EEG. In 1952, Michel Jouvet, a French neurophysiologist, found the precise control area for REM sleep in the pontine area of the reticular activating system. In 1972, a crucial finding relative to sleep was the discovery of the role of the suprachiasmic nucleus in the control of biological rhythms. In 1977, it was demonstrated that there was a loss of the sleep/wake rhythms resulting from lesions in this area.

In addition to these lesion and stimulation studies, there have been intensive studies of the neurochemical control of sleep. These have implicated serotonin, peptides, norepinephrine, and acetycholine in the control of sleep. More recently, there has been a flurry of research examining the role of cytokine molecules, which are produced by immune cells. [*See* Brain; *and* Electrophysiology and Psychophysiology.]

We have learned that sleep and waking are related to a complex set of neuroanatomical and neurochemical relationships centered primarily within the midbrain. However, we are less certain about which are causal and which are correlative relations and precisely how this system results in sleep and waking.

Drugs. Sleep is modified by drugs, as they effect the central nervous system. Drugs or stimulants may modulate sleep latencies and, more recently, have modified the rhythmic components of sleep. They are used in the control of sleep disorders and have been found useful in controlling the effects of shift work and jet lag transitions. [*See* Depressants, Sedatives, and Hypnotics.]

Sleep Disorders. Sleep need, sleep timing, and sleep behavioral control variables are modulated by sleep disorders. Some of these effects are mediated by central nervous system dysfunctions in narcolepsy, disorders of arousal, sleep apnea, and hypersomnia. Others are the result of chronic behavioral control problems, such as sleep schedule disorders and some insomnias. Still others may be a mixture of determinants, such as drug dependency, psychiatric disorders, and some insomnias. [*See* Insomnia; *and* Sleep Disorders.]

The Consequences of Sleep Variation

The onset and termination of sleep, and the placement and continuity of sleep episodes, may be modified. These may be voluntary extensions of wakefulness, early termination of sleep, or displacement of sleep from its regularly occurring time. These may be the involuntary effects of sleep disorders or imposed environmental demands or interferences. These variations of the sleep process result in loss of sleep and affect the sleep need or modify the rhythmic occurrence of sleep.

Effects of Sleep Loss. A recent series of studies of rats extended their sleep deprivation to the point of "imminent death." Their survival time ranged from 11 to 32 days (an average of 20 days). These experiments provided evidence that sleep is necessary for survival. A provocative result of one experiment was that animals whose sleep deprivation was terminated at the point of near "imminent death" showed complete or almost complete recovery after 15 days of ad libitum sleep.

Human sleep deprivation has been experimentally extended to 20 hours (8.5 days) and a young high school student stayed awake, under observation, for 11 days. There was no evidence of any substantial physiological changes in these subjects. However, many experiments involving 2 and 3 days of sleep deprivation have now established substantial behavioral effects.

Although the effects of sleep deprivation can be detected in the first night of deprivation, clearly measurable effects begin after about 36 hours. When there is an effect of deprivation, the increasing effect appears in a wavelike fashion. For example, in a 3-night deprivation experiment, while performance continues to deteriorate across the experiment, performance on the second day will be better than on the first night, and performance on the third day will be better than on the second night. This is the combined effect of the interaction of sleep need and the circadian effect discussed above.

There are inevitable subjective changes; sleepiness increases and mood effects are apparent with increasing amounts of sleep deprivation. The subjects begin to struggle to stay awake and longer tasks are approached with reluctance. The effects vary with the task to be performed. Our basic capacities to perform are resistant to sleep deprivation. We can see or hear or perform manual tasks without impairment. When we call upon well-learned tasks or procedures they are intact. We can learn and recall simple short-term tasks. However, tasks that require self-imposed, intensive, or extensive attention will be affected. For example, with increasing sleep deprivation the addition of two-digit numbers will result in few numbers totaled without an increase in errors. With increasing sleep deprivation, if persons are required to turn off a signal that appears briefly at random intervals of between 1 and 10 seconds, most of the responses will be in the nondeprived range, but there will be an increased number of delayed reaction times. If the task requires the detection of an infrequently occurring signal across an extended time period, under conditions of sleep deprivation these signals will be missed. When this diminished attentional capacity is combined with the increased subjective tendencies, the behavioral consequences will be evident in tasks such as driving, reading, signal detection, or maintaining complex procedural rules.

The more typical condition of sleep deprivation is partial sleep deprivation, when individuals reduce their sleep on one or more nights. As noted above, on workdays in industrialized countries, sleep averages typically about 1 hour less than on nonworkdays. One or two nights of reduced sleep are not likely to have marked effects on our basic capacity to perform. However, more extended partial deprivation will result in a sleep debt that evidences itself in an increased inability to sustain attention and our unwillingness to continue to perform tasks.

Shifts in Sleep Timing. When the sleep period is displaced in time, such as in shift work or jet travel, both sleep and performance may be affected. For example, if a person begins to work on a night shift from 10 P.M. to 6 A.M., the work performance will be occurring during the trough of the wavelike period described above. In short, performance will be occurring in a "circadian slump." The effects on attention and subjective states will be those associated with sleep deprivation.

Second, as the person goes to sleep at, say, 8 A.M., the sleep stage patterning during this period will be modified, with REM sleep occurring at the onset of sleep and Stage 4 sleep being displaced. Furthermore, there will be an increase in awakening, and there will often be an early termination of sleep. If this schedule is maintained, sleep can be reorganized in its new time. The various shift work schedules are compromises that attempt to minimize these effects. [*See* Circadian Rhythms, *article on* Circadian Rhythm Disorders.]

Sleep, then, is an evolved, species-specific, need state that is organized in a circadian system. The pattern of sleep within 24 hours unfolds in a developmental sequence and displays a range of individual differences. There is a set of underlying mechanisms in the central nervous system that serves this process. Within limits, sleep, voluntarily or involuntarily, may be behaviorally controlled. Voluntarily, we can displace sleep in time or inhibit sleep by extending wakefulness. Involuntarily, sleep may become disordered. These variations will affect the underlying need or circadian components of the sleep system. The consequences in our daily lives will range from minimal to severe.

Bibliography

Carskadon, M. A. (Ed.). (1993). *Encyclopedia of sleep and dreaming.* New York: Macmillan.

Chase, M. H. (Ed.). (1972–1997). *Sleep research* (Vols. 1–25). Los Angeles: Brain Information Service/Brain Research Institute. An annual bibliography of sleep research and the abstracts of papers presented at annual meetings of the Association of Professional Sleep Societies.

Dement, W. C. (1999). *The promise of sleep.* New York: Random House. A highly readable account of the growth of contemporary sleep medicine by one of its pioneers.

Dinges, D. F., & Broughton, R. J. (Eds.). (1989). *Sleep and alertness: Chronobiological, behavioral, and medical aspects of napping.* New York: Raven Press. A comprehensive analysis of napping, including developmental, cultural, and rhythmic aspects.

Hobson, J. A. (1989). *Sleep.* New York: Scientific American Library. Excellent coverage of the brain and sleep, the evolution of sleep, and the development of sleep.

Journal of Sleep Research (published since 1992). The quarterly journal of the European Sleep Research Society, which publishes current international research papers and reviews.

Kleitman N. (1963). *Sleep and wakefulness.* Chicago: University of Chicago Press. A comprehensive review of sleep research up to and including the beginning of contemporary research by a major figure in the field. Includes over 4,000 references ranging from the early Greeks to the early 1960s on all aspects of sleep.

Lavie, P. (1993). *The enchanted world of sleep.* New Haven, CT: Yale University Press. A very readable coverage of contemporary sleep research told from a personal perspective by one of its most talented researchers. Excellent review of both basic research and sleep medicine. Particularly strong on rhythmic aspects of sleep.

Meddis, R. (1977). *The sleep instinct.* Boston: Routledge & Kegan Paul. A nontechnical exploration of sleep from an evolutionary perspective about the development and functions of sleep. Strong emphasis on animal sleep.

Monk, T. H. (1991). *Sleep, sleepiness, and performance.* New York: Wiley. Excellent coverage of the effects of sleep deprivation and shift work on performance.

Sleep (published since 1976). A monthly publication of sleep research reports and reviews published by the Association of the American Sleep Disorders Association and the Sleep Research Society.

Steriade, M., & McCarley, R. W. (1990). *Brainstem control of wakefulness and sleep.* New York: Plenum Press. An examination of the experimental data on the anatomical and cellular physiology of behavioral and physiological aspects of sleep and waking.

Wilse Bernard Webb

SLEEP APNEA is a disorder of respiration during sleep that can have a major impact on the health, as well as the cognitive, emotional, and social functioning of the individual. An apneic event is defined as a sleep-related pause in respiration lasting 10 or more seconds. If these pauses occur at a rate of 10 or more per hour of sleep, a diagnosis of sleep apnea is confirmed. In severe sleep apnea, this rate can reach 100 or more per hour. A second type of event that contributes to this diagnosis is an hypopnea. This term refers to a reduction in airflow rather than its complete cessation. It is identified when an arousal from sleep occurs due to this reduced airflow. The frequency of these two types of events in a 7-hour period of sleep yields an hourly rate of sleep-disordered breathing known as the Apnea Plus Hypopnea Index, or A+HI.

There are two main forms of sleep apnea, obstructive and central. The obstructive, which is by far the most common, is identified when a cessation and/or the reduction of airflow at the nose or mouth occurs while the effort to breath at the level of the chest and/or abdomen continues. This is called an upper airway obstruction, and the disorder is referred to as obstructive sleep apnea, or OSA. In central apnea, the chest effort also stops.

Since OSA is a problem confined to sleep, the onset is difficult to observe. There are 2 symptoms that bring this disorder to the attention of the patient: snoring and daytime sleepiness. Typically, the patient has been a benign snorer for some time before this increases in loudness signals an increase in resistance in the airway. The next step in the development of this disorder is a collapse of the airway as it closes completely, leading to an apneic pause of at least 10 seconds. Behaviorally, this obstruction terminates with a snort and a brief awakening while the patient gasps for air. More often the change from benign snoring is first noted by the bed partner whose sleep is disturbed by the irregular, noisy breathing. The patient may fail to recognize the problem until the bed partner elects to sleep separately. Marital difficulties are common in those suffering from this disorder.

The second symptom that alerts the patient to the presence of a problem is a growing difficulty in remaining awake during the day. This excessive daytime sleepiness is most apparent when the patient is sedentary—driving, watching TV, in group meetings, or reading. This tendency to fall asleep may result in a warning from an employer or a motor vehicle accident before the patient realizes the extent to which their level of alertness is affected. In one study, sleep apnea patients were found to have motor vehicle accidents at seven times the rate of subjects without apnea. The profound daytime sleepiness has two causes: the first is the frequent interruptions of sleep and the second is the drop in the level of oxygen in the blood reaching the brain. When the apneic episodes are frequent and prolonged, the patient will wake with a morning headache, become increasingly sleepy in the daytime, and may begin to show signs of cognitive impairment and mood disorder.

Nocturnal snoring and daytime sleepiness are only two of the associated signs of this problem. A gain in weight is also strongly associated. Although not all sleep apneic patients are obese, the change from being a benign snorer to one with OSA is usually heralded by weight gain. Typically, the patient has some structural features that predispose them to this condition: a short thick neck, a backward-positioned lower jaw, a low-hanging soft palate, an enlarged uvula and tonsils, and a broad-based tongue—something that compromises the degree of airway space. As daytime sleepiness increases, the patient reduces their level of physical activity and may eat high calorie foods to increase their energy level. This combination leads to further weight gain and compounds the problem.

There are other behavioral components that add to the difficulty of maintaining respiration during sleep: the consumption of alcohol in the evening hours and sleeping in the supine position. Muscle tone is naturally reduced during sleep, and the effect of alcohol is to reduce the tone in the upper airway muscles, further increasing the likelihood of their collapse. A similar logic explains the effect of sleeping on the back. The tongue looses tone in sleep, and if there is a narrow or crowded space behind the tongue and the patient sleeps on their back, it is likely that the flaccid tongue will get pulled backward during inspiration and this will episodically block the top of the airway.

Recent epidemiologic studies have established that the prevalence of this disorder is much more common than was supposed on the basis of patients applying for treatment. It is two to three times more common in men who are habitual snorers than in women. Two percent of women and 4% of men in a middle-aged workforce sample met the minimal criteria for a diagnosis. When these figures were extrapolated to the general population aged 30 to 60, those reaching an A+HI rate of equal or greater than 10 respiratory events per hour of sleep was 5% of women and 15% of men. This study and others define the risk factors for this problem to be middle age, male gender, habitual snoring, and obesity. This problem has also been associated with arterial hypertension and an increased risk of cardiovascular disease. Even when the hypertension has been medicated, those with severe OSA are hard to control. Overnight sleep studies show that the usual drop in morning blood pressure as compared to that in the evening does not always take place, and often the morning blood pressure is even higher. A study of the healthcare costs of patients with this disorder show that these are two to three times as high as the costs for matched control subjects.

The psychological and social costs have not been estimated as precisely. However, it is known that patients severely affected have cognitive difficulties, mood disorders, sexual dysfunction, difficulty coping with marital responsibility, a high accident rate, and job disability.

Treatment of this disorder has evolved from a reliance on surgery—first tracheostomy, then uvuloplatophyrngeoplasty, and more recently an outpatient procedure that trims the excess tissue of the soft palate and reduces the size of the uvula with a laser-assisted uvuloplatoplasty. Currently, mechanical assistance with continuous positive airway pressure devices (CPAPs) have become the standard in the field for severe sleep apnea. These latter devices have become very sophisticated and now include compliance meters to check the number of hours it is used. Snoring and mild sleep apnea may be treated with oral appliances fitted by a dentist to open the airway, weight loss programs, sleep position training to avoid supine sleep, or a combination of these, with education to avoid alcohol, sleeping pills, and other medications that depress the respiratory rate.

Without doubt, the most clearly successful treatment is CPAP. This involves a nasal mask attached to a compressor to force room air through the nose to keep the airway from collapsing during sleep. However, there is a problem of acceptance of this treatment by patients, and long-term compliance is an issue. The efficacy of this treatment has been tested not only for its control of snoring, respiratory pauses, and episodes of oxygen desaturation in sleep, but also for its effect in reducing daytime symptoms such as sleepiness, depression, and reversing some of the cognitive impairment in these patients. It appears that patients who use the CPAP will show increases in ability to remain awake during the day, increase their level of vigilance, reduce their diastolic blood pressure even without losing weight, and significantly reduce their scores on a test of depression. However, when there has been severe nocturnal reduction of blood oxygen saturation, not all of the cognitive difficulties show improvement. These include planning ability and manual dexterity, which are sensitive to loss of oxygen to the brain.

No other treatment approach, such as surgery, weight loss, oral appliances, sleep-position training, or improved health habits has been tested for its effectiveness on the associated waking symptoms of this disorder. In fact, only a few studies of their ability to control the disorder have been done. Most of the studies that have been done have looked only at the acute effect, and very little is known of the long-term effectiveness of any of these treatments. What is clear is that OSA is a health problem with major ramifications affecting the middle-aged workforce and its ability to function socially, economically, and psychologically, for which effective treatment that is acceptable to the patient on a long-term basis has yet to be developed.

[*See also* Sleep Disorders.]

Bibliography

Bedard, M., Monplaisir, J., Malo, J, Richer, F., & Rouleau, I. (1993). Persistent neuropsychological deficits and vigilance impairment in sleep apnea syndrome after treatment with continuous positive airway pressure (CPAP). *Journal of Clinical and Experimental Neuropsychology, 15,* 330–341.

Cartwright, R. (1984). The effect of sleep position on sleep apnea severity. *Sleep, 7,* 110–114.

Cartwright, R., & Knight, R. (1987). Silent partners: The wives of sleep apneic patients. *Sleep, 10,* 244–248.

Findley L., Unverzagt, M., & Suratt, P. (1988). Automobile accidents involving patients with obstructive sleep apnea. *American Review of Respiratory Disease, 138,* 337–340.

Guilliminault, C., Eldridge, G., Simmons, F., & Dement, W. (1977). Sleep apnea syndrome due to upper airway obstruction: A review of 25 cases. *Archives of Internal Medicine 137,* 296–300. An early description of this disorder.

Kryger, M., Roos, L., Delavie, K., Walld, R., & Horrocks, J. (1996). Utilization of health-care services in patients with severe obstructive sleep apnea. *Sleep, 19,* S111–S116.

Kribbs, N., Pack, A., Kline, L., Smith, P., Schwartz, A., Schubert, N., Redline, S., Henry, J., Getsy, J., & Dinges, D. (1993). Objective measurement of patterns of nasal CPAP use by patients with obstructive sleep apnea. *American Review of Respiratory Disease, 147,* 887–895.

Lowe, A. (1994). Dental appliances for the treatment of snoring and obstructive sleep apnea. In M. Kryger, T. Roth, & W. Dement (Eds.), *Principles and practice of sleep medicine* (2nd ed., pp. 722–735). Philadelphia: Saunders.

Millman, R., Fogel, B., McNamara, M., & Carlisle, C. (1990). Depression as a manifestation of obstructive sleep apnea: Reversal with nasal continuous positive airway pressure. *Journal of Clinical Psychiatry, 51,* 309–310.

Millman, R., Redline, S., Carlisle, C., Assaf, A., & Levinson, P. (1991). Daytime hypertension in obstructive sleep apnea: Prevalence and contributing risk factors. *Chest, 99,* 861–866.

Sullivan, C., Berthan-Jones, M., Issa, F., & Ives, L. (1981). Reversal of obstructive sleep apnea by continuous positive airway pressure applied through the nares. *Lancet, 1,* 862–865.

Walker, R., Grigg-Damberger, M., & Gopalsami, C. (1997). Uvulopalatopharyngoplasty versus laser-assisted uvulopalatoplasty for the treatment of obstructive sleep apnea. *Laryngoscope, 107,* 76–82.

Young, T., Palta, M., Dempsey, J., Skatrud, J., Weber, S., & Badr, S. (1993). The occurrence of sleep-disordered breathing among middle-aged adults. *New England Journal of Medicine, 17,* 1230–1235. The study of 602 employed men and women habitual snorers and nonsnorers to establish the prevalence of OSA and the associated risk factors.

Rosalind Cartwright

SLEEP DISORDERS. Rechtschaffen wrote, "if sleep does not serve an absolutely vital function, then it is the biggest mistake the evolutionary process has ever made" (1972). More than simple inactivity, sleep involves loss of consciousness, vulnerability to attack, and takes time away from gathering food and procreating. From the moment of sleep onset, sleep places the body at risk for a variety of syndromes, disorders, and diseases.

Some sleep disorders appear to result from the relaxation of muscles during non-rapid-eye-movement (non-REM) sleep, the inhibition of muscle activity during REM sleep, or abnormal muscle activity that results when these mechanisms fail to engage. Sleep apnea, for example, is characterized by repeated episodes of diminished or absent airflow during sleep. Even partial apneas (hypopneas) and relatively minor changes in airway resistance may have deleterious effects on sleep. The cause appears to be a susceptibility of the upper airway to collapse during sleep, based on anatomy, muscle tone, and changes in the ventilatory response to hypercarbia. Apnea often responds to mechanical treatments, the most common being nasal continuous positive air pressure (CPAP).

Although rhythms of body temperature and hormone release are robust, the circadian rhythm of sleep appears to be more fragile, and may be disrupted by internal and external factors. The tendency to fall asleep appears to be regulated by at least two processes, one associated with sleep "homeostasis" and another with circadian rhythms. Either of these processes may be affected by internal and external factors. For example, the pressures of modern society to reduce total sleep time may lead to disruption of the homeostatic process; shift work and travel may disrupt circadian rhythms. Psychiatric disorders, such as anxiety or depression, may have adverse effects on sleep either directly or through their effects on circadian rhythms. Medications, alcohol, cigarettes, and caffeine may also prompt sleep complaints. After an initial perturbation, which may be either psychological (as from the death of a spouse) or physiological (as from jet lag), sleep disturbances may be perpetuated by a variety of conditioned elements.

Many researchers are reexploring the concept of sleep states, as new disorders have been described that appear to involve the dissociation of components of sleep stages. Narcolepsy, characterized by attacks of irresistible sleepiness, may represent the intrusion of REM sleep into waking. This intrusion is also evident in the accessory symptoms of narcolepsy, such as sleep paralysis and hypnagogic hallucinations. The concept of "dissociated states" has repeatedly emerged in writings about parasomnias. Intrusion of aspects of wakefulness into non-REM sleep may cause a variety of movement disorders ranging from periodic muscle contractions to complex behaviors during episodes of sleepwalking. The active inhibition of muscle activity during REM sleep may fail in some patients, resulting in motor activity apparently stimulated by dreaming.

Sleep Apnea Syndrome

The coexistence of symptoms of obesity, drowsiness, and cardiovascular abnormalities has merited comment ranging from scientific articles to characters in popular fiction for more than 100 years. The pathogenesis of these symptoms became clear when Lugaresi and colleagues described the beneficial effects of tracheostomy in two patients with "hypersomnia with periodic breathing" (1973).

The first patient, a 65-year-old woman, snored loudly since infancy. In the 4 years prior to evaluation, she had the progressive development of "fits of sleep" during the day. She would fall asleep while standing and would awaken just in time to avoid falling. At sleep onset she began having periodic episodes of apnea lasting up to 90 seconds, and increasing in duration during REM sleep. She was treated with amphetamines, which failed to improve her sleepiness at a dose of 60 mg per day. In a follow-up sleep recording she slept 17 out of 19 hours, and severe pulmonary hypertension was re-

corded. A tracheostomy was recommended, but she refused. Two months later, when she became cyanotic and was able to stay awake for only a few minutes at a time, her family brought her to a local hospital. A tracheostomy was performed, and her excessive sleepiness resolved over a few days. A subsequent polysomnogram showed normal respiration and markedly improved pulmonary arterial pressure.

Lugaresi's second patient, a 10-year-old boy, was able to stay awake only when engaged in physical activity. He fell asleep whenever engaged in mental activity and his performance in school was "minimal." These symptoms persisted despite two tonsillectomies. He had right heart failure by electrocardiogram. His polysomnogram showed obstructive apneas lasting as long as 95 seconds; he had marked pulmonary hypertension and blood gasses that showed decreased oxygen saturation and an intense hypercapnic respiratory acidosis. All symptoms resolved quickly with tracheostomy.

It is of interest that neither of these patients fits the common perception of a typical sleep apnea sufferer: middle-aged, obese, and male. Also, few sleep apnea patients have the florid symptoms described by Lugaresi. The diagnostic manual for sleep disorders (American Sleep Disorders Association, 1997) notes that sufferers may be unaware of clinical features, such as excessive sleepiness or insomnia, which are observed by others. Loud snoring, often accompanied by choking or gagging sounds, is a consistent complaint from bed partners of sleep apnea patients. Some complain of morning headaches or dry mouth. Many are brought to the sleep center by angry spouses, as a result of threats from supervisors at work, or following accidents occurring as a result of falling asleep while driving.

The polysomnogram provides an objective measure of the frequency and duration of apneas during sleep. A random sample of 602 men and women in Wisconsin found that approximately 9% of men and 4% of women between the ages of 30 and 60 had 15 or more episodes of apnea per hour of sleep (Young et al., 1993). However, the frequency of apnea may not be the critical measure of severity. In some patients, marked oxygen desaturations or cardiac arrhythmias during apneas may prompt treatment.

At the time of this writing, tracheostomy is rarely used to treat sleep apnea. In the vast majority of patients, airway patency can be maintained by nasal continuous positive air pressure (CPAP) delivered via a mask or nasal inserts. Most patients are able to tolerate this treatment, and heated humidification or "bilevel" pressure can be used to improve patient compliance. Newer machines can sense apnea and increase pressure levels when it occurs. Daytime sleepiness and cardiovascular variables are improved when apnea is treated with CPAP. Cognitive, affective, and quality of life improvements have also been demonstrated with adequate treatment of sleep apnea. Other treatment options include pharyngeoplasty, mandibular advancement (either by surgery or oral appliance), and nasal dilation. These latter options have yet to be proven as effective as CPAP or tracheostomy, and are often recommended for patients with mild apnea or those who are unable to tolerate CPAP.

Sleep Propensity

In Western cultures, expectations regarding sleep patterns are based on the assumption that the drive for sleep is maximal at the time when sleep is initiated and continues at a high level until a sufficient amount of sleep has been obtained to allow full alertness until the next appropriate time for initiation of sleep. This requires that sleepiness resulting from sleep deprivation and circadian processes are "in phase," reaching maximal levels at the same time. Models have been developed such that measurement of the duration of prior wakefulness and body temperature rhythm permits the accurate prediction of the duration of sleep. This "two-process" system (see Borbély et al., 1989, for review) predicts fragmented sleep and decreased performance when circadian rhythms and homeostatic mechanisms do not coincide. When sleep begins at an inappropriate time, it is often described as "nonrestorative." When waking occurs during periods of usual sleep and body temperature is low, poor performance on psychomotor tests and dysphoria may result.

In some individuals, especially younger adults, the circadian component may not coincide with school or work schedules, and delayed sleep-phase insomnia may result. Older patients may have advanced sleep phase, resulting in early bedtimes and early morning awakening. These sleep disorders appear to arise from age-related changes in the period of the circadian clock. Society favors advanced sleep phase, at least until patients become residents of senior citizen's homes. Some sleep disorders may arise as a result of extrinsic factors, such as jet lag or parents setting bedtimes.

Extrinsic effects on sleep are typically short-lived, whereas the contribution of genetic factors on sleep may be profound. Twin studies have been used to estimate heritability quotients for circadian and homeostatic components of sleep. Significant results have been reported for almost all age groups. The inheritance of sleep disorders has been recognized for many years; narcolepsy, obstructive sleep apnea syndrome, and restless legs syndrome may occur in multiple members of the same family. Inherited sleep propensity may account for a "short-sleeper" or "long-sleeper" diagnosis. With regard to circadian rhythms, animal research has focused on a genetic mutation that results in an abnormally short circadian period. Transplantation of the suprachiasmatic nucleus of a mutant mouse into the brain of a normal mouse causes a normal mouse to demonstrate the mutant circadian rhythm. This suggests that, in addition to age, inherited aspects of circadian rhythms may account for delayed and advanced sleep-phase disorders.

Psychiatric Disorders and Iatrogenic Insomnia

Sleep disturbance is a complaint in as many as 75% of individuals with psychiatric disorders. Complaints of early morning awakening and fragmented sleep are suggestive of depression, which is also associated with reduced latency to REM sleep. Many researchers have postulated a circadian rhythm abnormality as a component of some forms of depression, such as seasonal affective disorder. Alterations of the sleep pattern may serve as a biological marker for depression, as they can occur prior to the onset of clinical symptoms and may persist despite resolution of the clinical symptoms (see review by Reynolds & Kupfer, 1987).

Medications, especially those used for the treatment of depression, may cause disruption of sleep. Serotonin reuptake inhibitors have been documented to cause nightmares, sleep fragmentation, and unusual polysomnographic features. Hypnotics are frequently recommended by primary care physicians as an alternative to a sleep disorders evaluation. These medications confer a risk of tolerance and withdrawal effects, and are often used on an intermittent basis that serves to perpetuate behaviors that contribute to insomnia. Many patients attempt to treat insomnia with alcohol at bedtime, which aids in sleep onset but increases sleep disruption and reduces the amount of REM sleep. Recent studies have shown that caffeine may have disruptive effects on sleep lasting as much as twelve hours.

Persistent insomnia, regardless of its cause, is frequently accompanied by expectations of poor sleep. These factors are often thought to sustain insomnia even when the precipitating factors have resolved. A variety of "sleep hygiene" issues may also contribute to sleep disturbance. At times, treatment of the behavioral component may be sufficient to eliminate complaints of insomnia. Behavioral treatments may also be a useful adjunct to pharmacological treatments.

Dissociated States

The states of waking and sleep are defined by a constellation of psychophysiological variables. At a minimum, polygraphic measurement of electroencephalographic activity, eye movements, and muscle activity are necessary to discriminate between waking, non-rapid-eye-movement (NREM) and REM sleep. Sleep has often been thought to consist of a progression from one state to another, with all of the constellation of variables that define a state changing at the same time. Experienced polysomnographers have known for many years that this is not always the case. Sawtooth waves typically occur during REM sleep, but may precede by several minutes the onset of rapid eye movements and loss of muscle tone in some individuals. Animal researchers have identified subcortical indicators of the sleep stage that may progress from one stage to another before cortical and physiologic markers show changes. Mahowald and Schenck have conceptualized a range of sleep disorders as "dissociated states," in which one or more of the variables associated with a sleep stage occur inappropriately (1991). Among the disorders that they feel can be viewed in this way are narcolepsy, sleepwalking and other non-REM parasomnias, and REM behavior disorder.

Narcolepsy. Narcolepsy is characterized by sleep attacks, which may be uncontrollable and which may occur at inappropriate times, such as when driving. Patients often report vivid and disturbing dreams, which led to speculation that the cause of narcolepsy was a conversion reaction. In attempting to study the dreams of narcoleptics, Vogel made the surprising discovery that the latency to REM sleep was abnormally short, at times with an immediate transition from waking to REM (1960). Three "accessory" symptoms often accompany sleepiness in narcolepsy. These include cataplexy, the sudden loss of muscle tone with surprise or strong emotion; sleep paralysis, an inability to move for several seconds or a few minutes at sleep onset or on awakening; and hypnagogic hallucinations, vivid images or sounds at sleep onset. Rechtschaffen and Dement, reviewing these symptoms, concluded that narcolepsy involved "precocious triggering of REM phenomena" during waking (1969). Cataplexy and sleep paralysis appear to involve the active inhibition of muscle tone that occurs during REM sleep, whereas hypnagogic hallucinations may represent an inappropriate timing of dreaming.

Narcolepsy is used by some clinicians in a broad sense to include those with hypersomnia who may have none of the accessory symptoms. Others withhold the term *narcolepsy* to refer only to patients who also have cataplexy (see Aldrich, 1996). Narcolepsy has a typical age of onset, with symptoms usually appearing between the ages of 15 and 25. There is also a genetic predisposition to narcolepsy, as well as a strong association with an HLA antigen. The diagnosis of narcolepsy remains a clinical one—the presence of the antigen is neither necessary nor sufficient to make the diagnosis. The Multiple Sleep Latency Test is the most commonly used laboratory study to confirm a diagnosis of narcolepsy. The presence of REM sleep on more than one of the naps and an average sleep latency of less than 7 minutes is strong evidence that the diagnosis is correct, but medications or withdrawal from medica-

tions can produce false positive results, and with repeated testing, examples of false negative results have been demonstrated.

A diagnosis of idiopathic hypersomnia is given to patients with clinical histories of excessive somnolence, reduced latency on the Multiple Sleep Latency Test, and the absence of other causes of hypersomnia, such as sleep apnea. These patients may develop cataplexy or other accessory symptoms, or on repeat testing may have REM sleep during the Multiple Sleep Latency Test. In practice, most of these individuals are treated in the same way as narcoleptics.

Rechtschaffen and Dement suspected that REM-suppressing stimulants would provide the best treatment of narcolepsy (1969), and this continues to be the preferred treatment. Methylphenidate, pemoline, and various forms of amphetamine have been used with good results, although objective measures of sleepiness in treated narcoleptics often fail to reach normal levels. Medication abuse is infrequent, and most patients report satisfaction with their level of treatment. Tricyclic antidepressants are often added as treatment for cataplexy.

Non-REM Parasomnias. Walking, talking, bedwetting, and night terrors during sleep are now characterized as non-REM parasomnias. The events usually occur in the first half of the night. The nature of these behaviors initially led to the conclusion that the events were caused by "acting out a dream." Broughton noted that the events arose from polygraphically determined non-REM sleep and that patients did not recall a dream when woken from the events (1968). He argued that non-REM parasomnias might be a function of abrupt arousal from delta sleep (Stages 3 and 4). Patients woken during REM sleep become lucid quickly and often recall a dream. Patients woken from non-REM sleep had behaviors similar to those of patients during sleepwalking episodes, including "mental confusion with poorly coordinated automatic behavior, distant or slurred speech, relative nonreactivity, retrograde amnesia, and a lack of dream recall." In children, the presence of these parasomnias is often regarded as a normal "developmental" phenomenon (Ferber, 1985). Getting a child out of bed and standing during delta sleep often in itself precipitates a sleepwalking episode. In nearly all cases, treatment is not considered necessary, and the events usually resolve with age.

When these events persist into adulthood they may be associated with violence, eating, or sexual behavior. Pedley and Guilleminault (1977) described patients with "episodic nocturnal wanderings," including bizarre, violent behaviors. A recent issue of the journal *Sleep* was devoted to forensic issues raised by these violent behaviors during sleep (Guilleminault, Kushida, & Leger, 1995). Adults with non-REM parasomnias may or may not have a history of events in childhood. Sleep apnea, periodic limb movement disorder, and a variety of medications may trigger the events. In some individuals, removal of the trigger is sufficient to resolve the events.

There is considerable controversy regarding the origin of non-REM parasomnias, with many researchers becoming convinced that abnormal brain electrical activity might play a role in some forms and others holding to the abnormal arousal hypothesis. The efficacy of anticonvulsant medications does not resolve this controversy, as anticonvulsants are effective in treating a number of clearly nonepileptic problems such as pain syndromes. The avoidance of medications that fragment sleep, alcohol, and sleep deprivation may be effective in reducing the frequency of events. If necessary, other medications such as tricyclic antidepressants or benzodiazepines may be used.

REM Behavior Disorder. Early animal experiments determined that the inhibition of muscle activity during REM sleep depends on the integrity of the locus coeruleus. This small nucleus in the brain stem is circumscribed in many animals, but is somewhat diffuse in humans. In cats, lesions in this area resulted in dramatic behaviors during apparent sleep, such as leaping about the cage or chasing after mice that were not there. In 1985, Schenck and colleagues described "REM behavior disorder," a parasomnia thought to arise from dysfunction of the locus coeruleus, which fails to provide tonic muscle inhibition during REM sleep (see review by Schenck & Mahowald, 1996). Episodes recorded in the sleep laboratory begin during REM sleep. They are characterized by aggressive or exploratory behaviors and do not include eating or sexual behavior. Patients report that the dreams that are enacted are more violent and confrontational than their usual dreams. The patients with REM behavior disorder who seek help in a sleep disorders center often report multiple injuries as a result of acting out their dreams. Some patients attempt to leave the bedroom through a closed window. Bed partners are occasionally injured. However, few patients complain of daytime sleepiness despite considerable disruption of nocturnal sleep.

More than half of the patients with REM behavior disorder have another neurological disorder, the most common being Parkinsonism. In some patients, the symptoms of REM behavior disorder preceded the onset of Parkinsonian symptoms. Narcolepsy may also occur in association with REM behavior disorder. There are a few reports of stress, psychiatric illness, or abrupt cessation of REM-suppressing medications precipitating the onset of REM behavior disorder.

REM behavior disorder frequently responds to treatment with clonazepam. Tricyclic antidepressants, carbamazepine, carbidopa/levadopa, and gabapentin may also be effective. The mechanism of these treatments is unknown.

Periodic Limb Movement Disorder. With the advent of polysomnography, many patients have been noted to have brief bursts of muscle activity from the limbs, which are associated with EEG signs of arousal. The bursts last ½ to 5 seconds and recur with great regularity with a period that usually falls between 20 and 40 seconds. Some patients have as many as 600 movements in a single night, resulting in marked abnormalities of sleep architecture. This pattern was initially called nocturnal myoclonus, but the movements are more prolonged than myoclonus and the activity may occur during the day. Night to night variability is high. The prevalence is estimated at 5% of young adults and as high as 44% of older adults (see Montplaisir et al., 1994, for review).

There is considerable controversy regarding the significance of these movements. They may be recorded in uncomplaining patients, such as those who undergo polysomnograms for the evaluation of impotence. Mendelson has reported that the frequency of movements during sleep does not correlate with daytime sleepiness as measured by the Multiple Sleep Latency Test (1996). However, as Picchietti and Walters have noted, it would be incorrect to assume that this lack of correlation means that periodic limb movement disorder has no clinical significance (1996). First, periodic limb movements are evident before sleep onset, and may prevent sleep onset at night and increase the latency to sleep in daytime naps. Second, other objective measures may be more sensitive to the physiological effects of periodic limb movements. Reaction time increases, lapses, and changes in "creative" thinking may result from this disorder. Many patients come to the laboratory with subjective complaints of mood disturbance, irritability, and discomfort associated with bed partners' complaints of frequent movements during sleep. Clinicians with experience in treating this disorder are also swayed by reports of improvement with treatment.

Some patients with periodic limb movement disorder by polysomnography also complain of restless legs. This syndrome produces characteristic complaints of an inability to sit or lie still, and is associated with feelings of itchiness, burning, or crawling sensations, typically in the legs. These may be temporarily relieved by voluntary movement such as stretching or walking. One patient with this disorder kept an exercise bicycle by his bed and would get up and pedal for 20 minutes when his symptoms occurred in the middle of the night. In some patients with severe symptoms, activities such as driving or playing cards, which require long periods in the same position, may be curtailed. These symptoms typically have a circadian rhythm, reaching a peak in the late evening.

The treatment of periodic limb movement disorder and restless legs syndrome is often difficult. Benzodiazepines may be helpful, but are often too sedating to use for daytime symptoms and may be associated with tolerance. Opiates have been used with good results, but many patients worry about addiction or develop gastrointestinal complaints. Carbidopa/levadopa has also been used to treat this syndrome in many patients. A few develop "augmentation," in which the nighttime symptoms are resolved but the daytime symptoms worsen. Other dopaminergic drugs may be effective without this side effect. More recently, gabapentin has been shown to relieve the symptoms and has relatively few side effects. Experienced clinicians often warn patients that treatment consists of a trial and error process and may take some time before an effective treatment regime is established. The nature of this process suggests that periodic limb movement disorder and restless legs syndrome may result from a variety of causes, and at some point it might be possible to predict which patients will respond to certain medications.

Conclusion

The function or functions of sleep remain unknown, but the field of sleep disorders medicine has grown and a variety of treatments are available to normalize sleep. Rechtschaffen argued that even though we do not know the function of sleep, we should continue to pursue treatments that improve the quality of life of people who suffer from sleep disorders.

The field of sleep disorders medicine has been criticized because there is a paucity of data conclusively demonstrating mortality and morbidity resulting from disorders such as sleep apnea (Wright et al., 1997). From outcome measures and epidemiological studies, there is considerable pressure to assess the cost-effectiveness of treating sleep disorders. However, despite the current lack of objective evidence, there are few clinicians working in this field who do not know that when sleep abnormalities are adequately treated, patients report dramatic improvements in their quality of life.

[See also Enuresis; Circadian Rhythms, *article on* Circadian Rhythm Disorders; Insomnia; Narcolepsy; Nightmares; Night Terrors; Sleep Apnea; Sleeptalking; *and* Sleepwalking.]

Bibliography

Aldrich, M. (1996). The clinical spectrum of narcolepsy and idiopathic hypersomnia. *Neurology, 46,* 393–401.

American Sleep Disorders Association. (1997). *International Classification of Sleep Disorders, Revised: Diagnostic and Coding Manual.* Rochester, MN: American Sleep Disorders Association.

Broughton, R. (1968). Sleep disorders: Disorders of arousal? *Science, 159,* 1070–1078.

Ferber, R. (1985). *Solve your child's sleep problems.* New York: Simon & Schuster.

Guilleminault, C., Kushida, C., & Leger, D. (1995). Forensic sleep medicine and nocturnal wandering. *Sleep, 18,* 721–723.

Lugaresi, E., Coccagna, G., Mantovani, M., & Brignani, F. (1973). Effects of tracheostomy in two cases of hypersomnia with periodic breathing. *Journal of Neurology, Neurosurgery, and Psychiatry, 36,* 15–26.

Mahowald, M., & Schenck, C. (1991). Status dissociatus—A perspective on states of being. *Sleep, 14,* 69–79.

Mendelson, W. (1996). Are periodic leg movements associated with clinical sleep disturbance? *Sleep, 19,* 219–223.

Montplaisir, J., Godbout, R., Pelletier, G., & Warnes, H. (1994). Restless legs syndrome and periodic limb movements during sleep. In M. H. Kryger, T. Roth, & W. C. Dement (Eds.), *Principles and practice of sleep medicine* (pp. 589–597). London: Saunders.

Pedley, T., & Guilleminault, C. (1977). Episodic nocturnal wanderings responsive to anticonvulsant drug therapy. *Annals of Neurology, 2,* 30–35.

Picchietti, D. L., & Walters, A. S. (1996). The symptomatology of periodic limb movement disorder. *Sleep, 19,* 747.

Rechtschaffen, A. (1972). The control of sleep. In W. A. Hunt (Ed.), *Human behavior and its control* (pp. 75–92). Cambridge, MA: Schenkman Press.

Rechtschaffen, A., & Dement, W. C. (1969). Narcolepsy and hypersomnia. In A. Kales (Ed.), *Sleep: Physiology and pathology* (pp. 119–130). Philadelphia: Lippincott.

Reynolds III, C. F., & Kupfer, D. (1987). Sleep research in affective illness: State of the art circa 1987. *Sleep, 10,* 199–215.

Schenck, C. H., & Mahowald, M. (1996). REM sleep parasomnias. *Neurologic Clinics, 14,* 697–720.

Vogel, G. (1960). Studies in psychophysiology of dreams: 3, The dream of narcolepsy. *Archives of General Psychiatry (Chicago), 3,* 421–428.

Wright, J., Johns, R., Watt, I., Melville, A., & Sheldon, T. (1997). Health effects of obstructive sleep apnea and the effectiveness of continuous positive airways pressure: a systematic review of the research evidence. *British Medical Journal, 314,* 851–860.

Young, T., Palta, M., Dempsey, J., Skatrud, J., Weber, S., & Badr, S. (1993). The occurrence of sleep-disordered breathing among middle-aged adults. *New England Journal of Medicine, 328,* 1230–1235.

Richard S. Rosenberg

SLEEPTALKING. Vocalization during sleep is referred to as sleeptalking or *somniloquy*. These terms are often used as synonyms for *sleep utterance*. Sleeptalking or somniloquy, however, refers to speech, whereas sleep utterance refers to any sound made during sleep, including talking, laughing, crying, humming, and groaning. The structural and physical characteristics of sleeptalking are extremely variable. Speech may range from utterances that are brief, infrequent, and devoid of emotional content and that occur entirely in the absence of external input to vocalizations that last for several minutes at a time, are affectively expressive and responsive to external stimuli, and are grammatically correct and coherent. Interestingly, even in instances in which the sleeptalker has conversed lucidly, the individual usually cannot recall the event.

Sleeptalking is reported as occurring most frequently in children and young adults (usually ending by age 25) and is thought only rarely to begin in adulthood. In a review of the literature on sleeptalking, Arkin (1981) conservatively estimated that 7 to 15% of the population report sleeptalking. The lifetime incidence percentages are, however, much higher. Here it is estimated that 31 to 75% of the population report sleeptalking at some point in their lifetime (Arkin, 1981). The notion that there is a developmental decline in sleeptalking and a low prevalence of the behavior in adults, however, should be accepted with some degree of caution. The data may be limited given that the speaker is usually unaware of the behavior and relies on the observations of parents, roommates, and bed partners when self-reporting. Also open to question are whether adult onset is rare and whether this form of sleeptalking lacks clinical correlates.

Apart from population prevalence and incidence data, there is also some evidence that the parasomnias (disorders that intrude into the sleep process and are not primarily disorders of sleep and wake states per se) in general, and sleeptalking in particular, may have a genetic component. For example, Abe and Shimakawa (1966) found an increased likelihood of sleeptalking in children of parents who have a history of sleeptalking. More specifically, if one or both parents had a history of sleeptalking or sleepwalking, 30% of the offspring also exhibited such behaviors. When the parents had no history of sleeptalking or sleepwalking, only about 5% of the children exhibited such behaviors (Abe, Amatomi, & Oda, 1984).

Sleeptalking is thought to be largely idiopathic and to have a benign course. This said, sleeptalking does tend to co-occur with other parasomnias and sleep disorders and may occur in association with diseases and drugs that affect the central nervous system. Sleeptalking reliably occurs in association with sleepwalking and night terrors, and there is evidence that sleeptalking can occur in association with narcolepsy, sleep apnea, nocturnal rocking syndromes, nocturnal seizures, and sleep paralysis. Sleeptalking may also occur in relation to central nervous system disease, trauma, or with substance use or abuse (e.g., brain damage, brain disease, brain tumors, toxic or drug induced states, drug withdrawal states, and/or mental retardation).

Finally, there is the question of whether sleeptalking occurs in association with dreaming. If dreaming is defined to mean any instance in which the individual is awakened and reports cognitive activity (images or thoughts), then the question is what proportion of sleeptalking events (utterances or speech) are accompanied by concordant cognitive activity. Over the course of several studies, Arkin (1981) found that when participants were awakened from sleeptalking episodes, they reported cognitive activity that was clearly associated with the verbalizations about 50% of the time. If, however, dreaming is defined as the mentation that occurs during REM sleep, then it would appear that sleeptalking is not tightly linked to dreaming. Although about 85% of awakenings from REM sleep (as against about 15% of NREM sleep) are associated with dream reports, the stagewise occurrence of sleeptalking is not similarly distributed. Studies by Arkin (1970c), confirming early work by Rechtshaffen (1962), suggests that sleeptalking, or at least sleep utterances, occur more frequently in NREM (77.9%) than in REM (22.1%) sleep. The NREM stagewise distribution of sleeptalking is as follows: Stage 1, 0.1%; Stage 2, 22.5%; Stage 3, 23.9%; Stage 4, 31.4% (Arkin, 1981).

Given the conservative perspective that neither dreaming nor sleeptalking occurs exclusively in REM sleep, one is left to wonder whether complexity, grammatical correctness, and concordance vary as a function of sleep stage. As to complexity, Arkin and Toth (1970) found that duration of utterance did not especially vary between sleep stages (Stage 2, 8.2 words; Stages 3–4, 10.5 words; Stage 1, 12.6 words; Stage REM, 11.3 words; Arkin, 1981). As to the grammatical correctness of sleeptalking, Arkin (1991) found that REM sleep speech, syntax, and inflection tends to be like wakefulness. In contrast, NREM sleep speech tends to be characterized by gibberish, clang associations (an association of words that sound alike), neologisms, and perseveration (Arkin, 1991). Finally, as to concordance, Arkin (1981) evaluated this fact by comparing participants' reported sleep mentation with the content of their sleep utterances. It was found that reports from REM sleep were more concordant than those from NREM sleep (REM speeches, 79.2%; Stage 2 speeches, 45.8%, Stage 3–4 speeches, 21.1%; Arkin, 1981).

Sleeptalking is, perhaps, the most paradoxical of all the behaviors that occur during sleep. This said, this parasomnia has garnered very little interest and has not been extensively studied. Further investigation of this phenomenon may be informative regarding the ontogeny of sleep, cognitive activity during sleep, and what constitutes normal variations in CNS functions during sleep.

[See also Sleep Disorders.]

Bibliography

Abe, K., & Shimakawa, M. (1966). Predisposition to sleep-talking. *Psychiatric Neurology, 152*, 306–312.

Abe, K., Amatomi, M., & Oda, N. (1984). Sleepwalking and recurrent sleeptalking in children of childhood sleepwalkers. *American Journal of Psychiatry, 141*(6), 800–801.

Arkin, A. M. (1981). *Sleep-talking: Psychology and psychophysiology*. Hillsdale, NJ: Erlbaum.

Arkin, A. M. (1991). Sleeptalking. In S. J. Ellman & J. S. Antrobus (Eds.), *The mind in sleep* (pp. 415–436). New York: Wiley.

Arkin, A. M., Toth, M. F., Baker, J., & Hastey, J. M. (1970). The degree of concordance between the content of sleeptalking and mentation recalled in wakefulness. *Journal of Nervous and Mental Disease, 151*, 375–393.

Arkin, A. M., Toth, M. F., & Esrachi, O. (1970, March). *Electrographic aspects of sleeptalking* (abstract). Paper presented at the meeting of the Association for the Psychophysiological Study of Sleep, Santa Fe. *Psychophysiology, 7*, 354.

Rechtschaffen, A., Goodenough, R. R., & Shapiro, A. (1962). Patterns of sleeptalking. *Archives of General Psychiatry, 7*, 418–426.

Michael Perlis and Henry Orff

SLEEPWALKING, also known as somnambulism, is considered one of the parasomnias, a group of sleep disorders defined as "undesirable physical phenomena that occur predominantly during sleep" (Diagnostic Classification Steering Committee, 1990). Like other parasomnias, such as sleep terrors or confusional arousals, sleepwalking rarely has a significant impact on the quality or quantity of nocturnal sleep or on subsequent daytime functioning, although this can occur in more extreme cases. More commonly, a sleepwalker will present for treatment because of embarrassment or out of concern that the sleepwalking behavior may disturb others or result in significant injury.

Clinical Features

A common misconception about sleepwalking is that the sleepwalker is acting out a rapid-eye-movement (REM) sleep dream. Because skeletal muscle paralysis is the rule in REM sleep, such an occurrence is unlikely, except in the case of a rare condition known as REM-sleep behavior disorder. Most sleepwalking episodes originate from an arousal out of the deepest stages of sleep, collectively known as delta or slow-wave sleep. Because of the depth of sleep, such an arousal may be incomplete, leading to automatic behaviors that range from sitting up in bed to panicked attempts to escape an imagined danger. Attempts to communicate with the sleepwalker may yield no response or an inappropriate response, and if the sleepwalker is awakened, disorientation and even aggressive behavior may result. When the individual eventually reaches full wakefulness, there is usually retrograde amnesia for the sleepwalking episode.

Due to the temporal distribution of slow-wave sleep, most sleepwalking episodes occur during the first third of the sleep period. Conditions that tend to accentuate slow-wave sleep, such as prior sleep deprivation, febrile illness, or certain psychoactive medications increase the likelihood that sleepwalking will occur. Also, sleepwalking is more prevalent in children than adults, possibly because slow-wave sleep tends to decline with age. Disorders that fragment sleep, such as obstructive sleep apnea, may provoke the occurrence of sleepwalking, and some experts have shown that making noise or simply standing the individual up during slow-wave sleep can produce sleepwalking.

Estimates of the prevalence of sleepwalking depend on the frequency of the events, ranging from 1% (frequent) to 15% (infrequent) of the population (Diagnostic Classification Steering Committee, 1990). The disorder appears to occur equally often in both sexes, and almost always begins before age 11 (Fisher & Wilson, 1987). The tendency to sleepwalk appears to be genetically transmitted. Children of sleepwalkers are significantly more likely to sleepwalk than the children of normal sleepers, and the concordance of sleepwalking among monozygotic twins is six times that of dizygotic twins (Bakwin, 1970). Because not all individuals with a positive family history exhibit sleepwalking behavior themselves, researchers have proposed a diathesis/stress model for the disorder (Moldofsky, Gilbert, Lue, & MacLean, 1995), but further controlled research is needed to confirm the model.

Complications

The unpredictable nature of an individual's behavior during a sleepwalking episode makes possible a variety of significant physical and psychosocial complications. Sleepwalkers have been known to walk out onto balconies or window ledges, and falls and other accidents resulting in serious injury can occur. In other cases, sleepwalkers have run through glass doors or jumped out windows in a panicked state, and locks often fail to deter the sleepwalker from leaving the house and wandering out into the street. Behavior as complex as driving an automobile or operating other machinery while sleepwalking has also been reported.

In a few rare instances, violence, including homicide, has been documented for sleepwalking individuals. Bed partners and other individuals in the home have been struck, stabbed, and strangled by sleepwalkers who, in many cases, believed at the time that they were actually protecting their spouses or families from intruders. In one extensively investigated case, a 23-year-old Canadian man, during an apparent episode of sleepwalking, got into his car, drove more than 10 miles to the home of his mother-in-law, and stabbed her to death. He was eventually acquitted of the crime, due in part to an extensive medical evaluation that revealed a strong personal and family history for parasomnias, sleep laboratory findings consistent with sleepwalking, and the presence of precipitating factors (e.g., sleep deprivation and alcohol use) just prior to the incident (Broughton et al., 1994).

The consequences of sleepwalking need not be physically harmful to be a source of distress for the afflicted individual. A sleepwalker may empty the contents of a cabinet onto the floor or urinate in a closet during the night, discovering the aftermath of the behavior the following morning. Such actions are particularly embarrassing when the sleepwalker is sharing sleeping accommodations with others. Recently there have also been reports of excessive nocturnal food consumption by sleepwalkers who may have difficulty controlling their weight because of this condition.

There remains considerable debate over whether sleepwalking is associated with emotional disturbance. If the sleepwalking originates prior to age 10, overt psychopathology is uncommon, but some researchers have reported an increased prevalence of personality disorders and other psychological problems among individuals with later-onset sleepwalking (Kales et al., 1980). There is as yet insufficient evidence to determine if emotional trauma or personality characteristics are causative factors in the manifestation of sleepwalking.

Treatment

For children, sleepwalking tends to be a self-limiting disorder that resolves spontaneously with maturation (Klackenberg, 1982). In less severe cases, patients and their families may be advised to take the necessary precautions to ensure that the household environment is safe and that the risk of injury to the sleepwalker is minimal. Advice to modify practices that may affect the occurrence of sleepwalking (e.g., sleep deprivation, an inconsistent sleep schedule, and the use of certain drugs and alcohol) may also be included in treatment.

When more aggressive treatment is indicated, medications may be used. Diazepam and other benzodiazepines have been shown to be effective for suppressing sleepwalking activity, possibly through the reduction of slow-wave sleep and/or the general sedative effects of such medication. Other research has indicated that certain tricyclic antidepressants, imipramine in particular, may be effective as well, although the mechanism of action is unclear.

The effects of psychological treatments for sleepwalking are less well documented. Hypnosis, insight-oriented therapy, and behavior therapy have all been employed to treat this disorder, but few controlled clinical studies have been published. In most cases, reassurance to the patient and the family is sufficient to quell anxiety about the condition and to allow for its successful resolution.

[*See also* Accidents; Amnesia; Antidepressants; Behavior Therapy; Hypnosis; Personality Disorders; Sleep; Sleep Apnea; Sleep Disorders; *and* Sleeptalking.]

Bibliography

Bakwin, H. (1970). Sleepwalking in twins. *Lancet, 11,* 446–447.

Broughton, R., Billings, R., Cartwright, R., Doucette, D., Edmeads, J., Dewardh, M., Ervin, F., Orchard, B., Hill, R., & Turrell, G. (1994). Homicidal somnambulism: A case report. *Sleep, 17,* 253–264. A fascinating account of the criminal trial and medical evaluation of man who allegedly killed his mother-in-law during a sleepwalking episode.

Diagnostic Classification Steering Committee. (1990). *International classification of sleep disorders: Diagnostic and coding manual.* Rochester, MN: American Sleep Disorders Association. Sleep medicine's official diagnostic and classification manual; this supersedes the previous nosology, published in 1979.

Fisher, B. E., & Wilson, A. E. (1987). Selected sleep disturbances in schoolchildren reported by parents: Prevalence, interrelationships, behavioral correlates, and parental attributions. *Perceptual and Motor Skills, 64,* 1147–1157.

Kales, A., Soldatos, C. R., Caldwell, A. B., Kales, J. D., Humphrey, F. J., II, Charney, D. S., & Schweitzer, P. K. (1980). Somnambulism: Clinical characteristics and personality patterns. *Archives of General Psychiatry, 37,* 1406–1410.

Klackenberg, G. (1982). Somnambulism in childhood—Prevalence, course, and behavioral correlations. *Acta Paediatrica Scandinavica, 71,* 495–499.

Moldofsky, H., Gilbert, R., Lue, F. A., & MacLean, A. W., (1995). Sleep-related violence. *Sleep, 18,* 731–739. Proposes a diathesis-stress model for sleepwalking and other parasomnias.

Ozbayrak, K. R., & Berlin, R. M. (1995). Sleepwalking in children and adolescents. In C. E. Schaefer (Ed.), *Clinical handbook of sleep disorders in children.* Northvale, NJ: Jason Aronson.

Mark J. Chambers

SMALL, WILLARD S. (1870–1943). American psychologist. Born in Massachusetts, Small received his doctorate in comparative psychology in 1900 at Clark University. Small's research focused on the formation of associations, which he considered the basis of animal intelligence. To assess the mental processes of white rats, he designed a model of the intricate garden maze at the Hampton Court Palace in England. Small's innovation initiated the long tradition of maze research in the study of learning and behavior.

Small believed that any experimental assessment of intelligence must be carried out in a way that did not disturb the animals' "natural proclivities." "The chief difficulty of [animal] experimentation lies in controlling the conditions of the problem without interfering with the natural instincts and proclivities of the animal" (Small, 1900, p. 133). The maze was an attempt to do both. It consisted of a labyrinth of as many thirty alleys surrounding a central food source. Seven alleys led nowhere, permitting the precise measurement of errors. With the maze, Small described the formation of associations under controlled conditions, while satisfying the animal's "propensity for winding passages," represented psychologically as a "rat-hole consciousness" (1901, p. 229).

Small's method was designed to control precisely behavior in natural context. But he distrusted the use of strictly quantitative over precisely descriptive measures. His results, emphasizing association, trial and error, and the value of success, agreed with those of Edward L. Thorndike; but Small believed that Thorndike's "graphic" method overlooked key aspects of the rat's mind. Small's method, by contrast, explicitly included the observer's subjective interpretation of the data, thereby permitting assessment of "animal intelligence in actual operation . . . rather than in . . . its general form" (1901, p. 210). Small stressed that Thorndike's method obscured the emergence of intentional action. He noted that rats were by nature indecisive. When they first enter the maze, animals have no "ideated end," no goal. But, after a long process of trial and error, they gradually begin to discriminate critical points, decrease their hesitation and indecision, and "confidently" choose correct options. "The selection of [correct] paths begins to be purposive" (p. 212).

Many of Small's test rats were female, and he was careful to note sex differences in performance: Males always solved problems more quickly and with fewer errors than females, who showed "deference" to males. Small, however, did not consider this evidence of sex differences in intelligence. Moreover, he observed greater sex differences in the behavior of wild versus albino rats and concluded that domestication had reduced differences between the sexes. Noting that civilization itself is domestication, Small inferred that culture probably diminishes sex differences in humans, too. For this reason, he thought it reasonable to promote sexual equality in the "aims, conquests, and education of the sexes" (1901, p. 212).

Clark University was founded by Granville Stanley Hall, and both Small's early research and his later career reflect Hall's developmental emphasis (Small, 1899). After leaving Clark, Small entered educational administration, and from 1923 to 1940 he was dean of the College of Education of the University of Maryland. His Clark maze research was, however, the first experimental analysis of animal learning using the maze. Small's work, therefore, laid the foundation for the tradition of maze research that dominated experimental psychology in the middle of the twentieth century.

[Many of the people mentioned in this article are the subjects of independent biographical entries.]

Bibliography

Small, W. S. (1899). Notes on the psychic development of the young white rat. *American Journal of Psychology, 11,* 80–100.

Small, W. S. (1900). An experimental study of the mental processes of the rat. *American Journal of Psychology, 11,* 133–165.

Small, W. S. (1901). Experimental study of the mental processes of the rat: II. *American Journal of Psychology, 12,* 206–239.

Cheryl A. Logan

SMELL. [*This entry surveys the behavioral, biological, and functional aspects of olfaction.*]

The sense of smell, along with its sister sense of taste, monitors the intake of environmental nutrients and airborne chemicals required for life and largely determines the flavor and palatability of foods and beverages. In addition to purveying esthetic pleasures, this system warns the organism of tainted or spoiled foods, leaking natural gas, polluted air, and smoke. Decrements in the ability to smell are relatively common in our species, particularly in the elderly, and olfactory dysfunction can serve as a marker for a number of serious diseases, including Alzheimer's disease and idiopathic Parkinson's disease. Decreased "taste" perception during deglutition largely reflects the loss of stimulation of the olfactory receptors via the retronasal route, as the gustatory system, whose taste buds are redundantly innervated by several cranial nerves (i.e., CN VII, IX, & X), is much more resilient to damage from viruses, head trauma, and other insults.

Basic Anatomy and Physiology of the Olfactory System

Since the time of the early Greeks and up through the seventeenth and eighteenth centuries, it was widely believed that odorants enter the brain via the foramina of the cribriform plate and somehow create vibrations or other activity within the fluid of the ventricles, producing the sensation of smell. This view made intuitive sense in that these same openings appeared to be the source of nasal secretions (humors) that originated within the brain. When the foramina became blocked, thereby altering the flow of the humors, such symptoms as anosmia, headaches, runny noses, high fever, and general malaise occurred. This general view persisted even when it became apparent that the reception of odorants likely occurs within the nasal mucosa, as exemplified by the following quotation from *Five Treatises* written in 1681 by the famous English anatomist and physician, Thomas Willis:

> The Sieve-like Bone in divers Animals is variously perforated for the manifold necessity and difference of smelling. A Process from the Dura Mater and manifold nervous Fibres pass through every one of its holes, and besmear the inside of the Nostrils. But as the impressions of sensible things, or sensible Species, continued as it were by the undulation or waving of the animal Spirits, ascend through the passages of these bodies stretched out from the Organ towards the Sensory; so the humidities watring the same bodies, for as much as somethimes they may be more superfluous than usual, may distil into the Nostrils through the same ways. For indeed such humors as are perpetually to be sent away from the brain, ought so copiously to be poured upon the Organs of Smelling, as we shall shew hereafter, when we shall speak particularly of the smelling Nerves; in the mean time, that there is such a way of Excretion opening into the Nostrils, some observations, taken of sick people troubled with Cephalick diseases, do further perswade.

> A virgin living in this City, was afflicted a long time with a most cruel Head-ach, and in the midst of her pain much and thin yellow Serum daily flowed out from her Nostrils; the last Winter this Excretion stopped for some time, and then the sick party growing worse in the Head, fell into cruel Convulsions, with stupidity; and within three days dyed Apoplectical. Her Head being opened, that king of yellow Latex overflowed the deeper turnings and windings of the Brain and its interior Cavity or Ventricles. . . . I could hear bring many other reasons, which might seem to perswade, that the Ventricles of the Brain, of the Cavity made by the complicature or folding up of its border, is a mere sink of the excrementitious Humor; and that the humors there congested, are purged out by the Nose and Palate.

Following the microscopic identification of the secretory glands within the nasal mucosa by C. V. Schneider and R. Lower in the mid- to late 1600s, the earlier views of olfactory transduction were abandoned in favor of activation of neural elements within the nasal cavity proper. Research performed largely in the twentieth century has led to our current perspective that odorants are detected by proteinaceous receptors located on cilia extending from the bipolar cells that collectively make up the olfactory nerve (CN I) and possibly by receptors on microvillae from the poorly understood microvillar cells (see Figure 1). Such research has also shown that some odorants produce irritation, warming, cooling, and other somatosensory sensations via trigeminal nerve (CN V) afferents distributed throughout the nasal mucosa, as well as via nerve endings within the pharynx and oral cavity (e.g., glossopharyngeal [CN IX] and vagus [CN X] afferents). However, the qualitative sensations commonly termed *odor* seem to be mediated solely by the olfactory receptor cells (CN I).

Olfactory transduction reflects a sequence of physicochemical and biological processes. First, odorants must be absorbed into the nasal mucus and must diffuse or be actively transported to the cilia of the bipolar receptor cells; second, odorants must bind or somehow interact with receptive elements on these cilia; third, action potentials must ultimately be generated within the receptor neurons as a result of such binding or interaction; and fourth, filtering, integration, and interpretation of the incoming information must occur in higher brain structures, beginning with initial relay stations in the olfactory bulb (termed glomeruli) and ending in higher order structures, including segments of the temporal and frontal lobes. Although the olfactory pathways are largely ipsilateral, bilateral connections do exist via the anterior olfactory nuclei and anterior commissure. Unlike other sensory systems, the olfactory system directly projects to primary cortex without synapsing within the thalamus. The functional significance of this arrangement is not entirely clear, but it may result in responses that are less dominated or influenced by higher order cognitive processes. Clearly, the olfactory system is closely intertwined with limbic centers involved in arousal, emotion, feeding, memory, reproduction, and hedonics, and initial responses to many odors are of an immediate and evaluative, good/bad, nature.

Small water-soluble proteins, termed *odorant binding proteins*, appear to assist the movement of hydrophobic, but generally lipid-soluble, molecules through the mucus to the receptor proteins of the olfactory cilia. Such assistance may be selective, and some of these proteins may serve to inactivate odorant molecules or filter the number of such molecules reaching the receptors. For example, some odor-induced signals appear to be rapidly abolished by detoxification or biotransformation enzymes within the mucus.

Different models of ligand/receptor interactions have been proposed, although little is known about the specific nature of the odorant/receptor interactions. Genetic diversity in vertebrate olfactory receptors appears to be the rule, as a large multigene family seems to code for odorant receptor proteins with seven transmembrane domains. The genes in this multigene family number in the hundreds, if not thousands, implying that the vast array of perceptual odor experiences de-

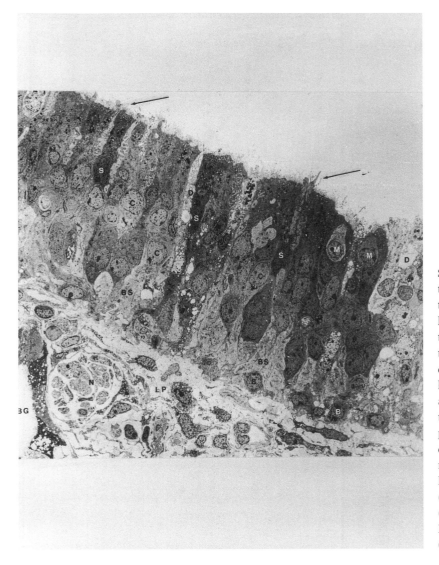

SMELL. Figure 1. Low-power electron micrograph ($\times$1000) of a longitudinal section through a biopsy of human olfactory mucosa taken from the superior nasal septum. Four cell types are indicated: ciliated bipolar olfactory receptor cells (C), microvillar cells (M), supporting cells (S), and basal cells (B). The arrows point to ciliated olfactory knobs of the bipolar receptor cells. Also depicted are degenerating cells (D), the basal segment of supporting cells (BS), the lamina propria (LP), a nerve bundle (N), and a Bowman's gland (BG). (Photograph courtesy of David T. Moran, DTM Enterprises, Boulder, Colorado.)

rives, in large part, from a wide range of ligand specificities.

It has been known for nearly half a decade, mainly from single-cell electrophysiological recordings, that individual receptor cells respond to a wide variety of odorants, leading to their characterization as "generalists." Upon closer scrutiny, however, such cells rarely respond to exactly the same sets of stimuli, allowing for the possibility of cross-neuron coding. Recent *in situ* hybridization studies in rodents provide three new pieces of information about the distribution of receptors on olfactory receptor cells and the relationship of such cells to higher order structures. First, most olfactory receptor genes appear to be expressed in only about 0.1% of the olfactory sensory neuron population, in agreement with the notion that each sensory neuron expresses only one or at most a few receptor genes. Second, neurons expressing the same gene seem to be randomly distributed within one of several (e.g., in the

mouse, four) well-defined "spatial zones" that typically span the anterior/posterior axis of the epithelium. Neurons that presumably recognize the same odors (i.e., express the same olfactory receptor genes) are more or less confined to the same zone. Third, axons of neurons that express the same odorant receptor tend to converge on a small number of glomeruli within the olfactory bulb. This suggests that each glomerulus may be dedicated to only one or a very small number of receptor types. The glomerular map may thus provide a key to the structural determinants of odorant quality that are shared by different odorants and recognized by different receptors.

As in all sensory systems, central brain structures play an important role in determining whether odors can be identified or recognized. This is amply illustrated in a recent study of olfaction in patients with multiple sclerosis (MS). In such individuals, the ability to identify odors is strongly and inversely correlated with the

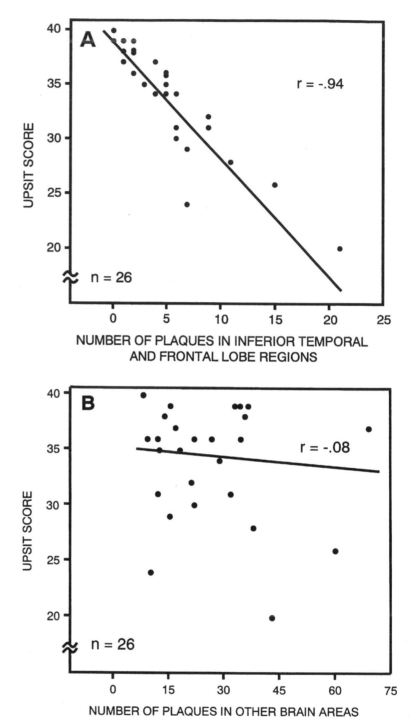

SMELL. Figure 2. Relationship between scores on the University of Pennsylvania Smell Identification Test (UPSIT) and the numbers of multiple sclerosis-related plaques in olfactory (A) and nonolfactory (B) brain regions. (From Doty et al., 1997. Copyright 1997 by The Massachusetts Medical Society.)

number of MS-related plaques within the primary and secondary olfactory cortices, as determined using high-resolution magnetic resonance imaging (MRI). Such a correlation is not present between odor identification test scores and the number of plaques in regions outside of the primary and secondary olfactory cortices, demonstrating the specificity of this phenomenon to central olfactory structures (see Figure 2).

Psychophysical Measurement of Human Olfactory Function

The last two decades have witnessed a renaissance in quantitative psychophysical assessment of olfactory function. In general, olfactory tests can be divided into threshold and suprathreshold measures. The most popular threshold tests include those employing either single ascending stimulus presentation procedures or staircase techniques. Examples of suprathreshold tests include tests of odor identification and discrimination and tests employing scaling procedures, such as category rating or magnitude estimation techniques. The most widely used olfactory test is the University of Pennsylvania Smell Identification Test (UPSIT), a 40-item standardized "scratch and sniff" test commercially available as the Smell Identification Test (Sensonics, Inc., Haddon Heights, N.J.). This standardized test is highly reliable (r = 0.94) and provides an indication of overall function (normosmia; mild, moderate or severe microsmia; anosmia), as well as a percentile rank value of the examinee's test score relative to persons of equivalent age and gender, as determined from norms based upon nearly 4,000 men and women. This test is now routinely used in thousands of clinics, laboratories, and industrial centers throughout the world and is perhaps analogous to the eye chart used for assessing visual acuity.

As in the case of psychological tests, the reliability of an olfactory test is related to its length. Reliability is higher, for example, for staircase detection thresholds that repeatedly sample the perithreshold region than for single ascending series detection thresholds that sample the perithreshold region only once. Reliability is also higher for forced-choice than for non-forced-choice tests. However, despite high reliability, the nominal validity of some olfactory tests can be questioned, and presently the degree to which nominally disparate olfactory tests measure disparate sensory processes is not clear. Principal component analyses suggest that a number of nominally distinct olfactory tests (e.g., tests of odor detection, memory, and identification) measure, to a large degree, the same component of variance in the normal population. Hence, one has to be careful about assuming that a given test result is due to pathology in the supposed trait or physiological mechanism nominally measured by the test. For example, if a test of "odor memory" is administered to a person whose olfactory neuroepithelium is damaged, the low scores may have little or nothing to do with the brain circuits associated with odor memory per se, yet the literal interpretation would be that such circuits are dysfunctional.

Adaptive Properties of the Olfactory System

Like other sensory systems, continuous exposure of the olfactory system to a stimulus results in a decline in perceptual response, that is, adaptation. Rarely, however, is adaptation to an odor complete, and psychological factors, such as a person's belief about the toxic influences of the odorant, can alter the magnitude and duration of the adaptation. Furthermore, adaptation to one odorant can result in adaptation to another (so-called cross-adaptation), although the degree of cross-adaptation need not be symmetrical. In other words, adaptation to odor A may produce a larger degree of adaptation to odor B than adaptation to odor B produces in odor A.

In general, after a few minutes of continuous exposure to an odorant, its perceived intensity decreases to 30 or 40% of its original magnitude and stays at this level for some period of time. However, differences are present among odorants, and adaptation can be very rapid and nearly complete for some stimuli (e.g., many musks). Recent studies in which participants are exposed in their own homes to an odorant for several weeks have revealed odor-specific shifts in detection threshold, as well as in perceived intensity, which last in some cases for a number of weeks after the exposure period. The physiological basis for such long-lasting adaptive effects is not known, although both central and peripheral factors may be involved. It is well established that if one side of the nose is adapted to an odorant, the other side also exhibits some degree of adaptation, presumably reflecting changes in central brain mechanisms. Such cross-nostril adaptation, however, is typically less than the adaptation observed on the side of continuous odorant exposure.

Classification of Olfactory Disorders

The nomenclature for olfactory dysfunction is straightforward. Anosmia refers to loss of the ability to smell, whereas hyposmia or microsmia refers to diminished ability to smell. Dysosmia is distorted or perverted smell perception, such as when a rose smells more like garbage than a rose (parosmia, cacosmia) or when a medicine-like smell is present in the absence of odor stimulation following head trauma (phantosmia). General or total anosmia implies inability to smell all odorants on both sides of the nose. Partial anosmia implies an inability to smell certain odorants. In some cases, partial anosmia is indicative of decreased sensitivity to a broad spectrum of odorants (general hyposmia), with the decrement exceeding the absolute threshold for only some odorants. Specific anosmia, the inability to smell one or a few odorants in the presence of an otherwise normal sense of smell, is rarely a reason for medical consultation. Hyperosmia is a rare condition of abnormally acute smell function. This can be seen, for example, in some epileptic patients prior to the onset of ictal activity.

Olfactory dysfunction can be either bilateral or unilateral (sometimes termed binasal or uninasal). Thus, if a person has anosmia on the left side of the nose but not the right, the condition is described as unilateral left anosmia. Anosmia that is present on both sides of the nose is termed bilateral anosmia, or, as noted above, total anosmia.

SMELL. Figure 3. Scores on the University of Pennsylvania Smell Identification Test (UPSIT) as a function of age in a large heterogeneous group of subjects. Numbers by data point indicate sample sizes. Filled circles indicate women ($n = 1,158$), and open squares indicate men ($n = 797$). (From Doty et al., 1984. Copyright 1984 by the American Association for the Advancement of Science.)

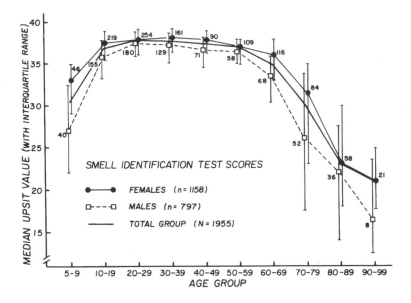

Factors Influencing the Ability to Smell

Many factors influence the ability to smell. Cigarette smoking produces a decrement in the ability to smell that can be reversed to some degree, depending upon the duration and extent of smoking and the time since cessation. Women, on average, have a better sense of smell than men, a phenomenon particularly evident after the age of 65 years. This sex difference may reflect, at least to some degree, protective influences of estrogen on the olfactory membrane. Thus it has recently been shown that ovariectomized rats receiving daily injections of 17β-estradiol have less functional olfactory loss following the administration of the olfactotoxicant 3-methyl indole than do rats that are treated with oil vehicle alone.

As alluded to earlier, age is strongly correlated with the ability to smell. Between 65 and 80 years of age, nearly half of the population experiences major loss in the ability to smell, whereas after the age of 80 this increases to approximately three fourths of the population (Figure 3). Although the decline in olfactory function may occur more for some odorants than others (depending upon such factors as the odorant's threshold and the nature of the function relating odorant concentration to perceived intensity), it is present for a wide spectrum of odorants. In general, persons who evidence comparatively low sensitivity to one odorant typically evidence low sensitivity to others, whereas those who evidence comparatively high sensitivity to an odorant typically evidence high sensitivity to others. With the possible exception of specific anosmias, such observations suggest that a "general olfactory acuity" factor exists, analogous to the general intelligence factor derived from items of intelligence tests.

The underlying mechanism of age-related losses of smell function seems to relate, at least in part, to progressive deterioration of the olfactory membrane and a subsequent secondary decrease in the number of olfactory glomeruli, with little change in the olfactory cortex. The degree to which age-related metabolic factors influence tissue susceptibility to damage is not clear, although aging is accompanied by a regression of the vessels within the olfactory neuroepithelium and by the loss of cells within its basal layers. Despite the fact that the olfactory receptor cells have the capacity to reconstitute themselves periodically, this plasticity seems to be altered by age-related processes. For example, in studies of rodent and amphibian epithelia, the ratio of dead or dying cells to the number of receptor cells increases with age, implying that receptor cells from older individuals have less mitotic activity than those from younger ones. Following chemical destruction of the olfactory receptors of mice with zinc sulfate or methylformimino-methylester, morphological repair is slower or nonexistent in older animals, unlike the case with younger ones, indicating that the neurogenic process alters with age. Interestingly, there is now evidence in humans that age-related occlusion of the foramina of the cribriform plate by bone growth can block the axonal projections from the olfactory epithelium to the olfactory bulb, providing an explanation for the olfactory loss of some elderly individuals.

In addition to being influenced by sex and age, the olfactory system can be altered by head trauma and numerous diseases. Although most of us have experienced temporary olfactory loss due to blockage from inflammation or the formation of excessive mucus from upper respiratory infections, permanent loss can also occur from such infections, a phenomenon that typi-

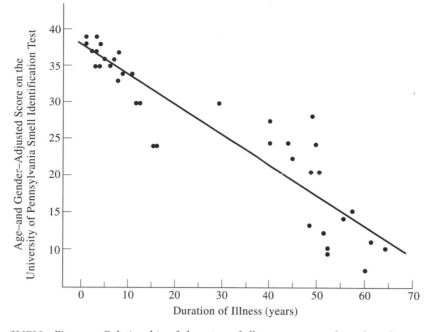

SMELL. Figure 4. Relationship of duration of illness to age- and gender-adjusted scores on the University of Pennsylvania Smell Identification Test in 38 patients with schizophrenia. (From Moberg et al., 1997. Copyright 1997 by the American Psychiatric Association.)

cally occurs after the age of 40 years. Indeed, upper respiratory infections appear to be the most common cause of permanent olfactory loss, presumably as a result of viral or bacterial damage to the olfactory neuroepithelium. Another common cause of olfactory loss is nasal inflammation due to allergies, which usually resolves following medical management but can, as in the case of upper respiratory infections, lead to permanent losses in function when chronic. Head trauma, particularly blows to the back of the head that induce coup contra coup movement of the brain and shearing of the olfactory filaments at the level of the cribriform plate, is also a common reason for permanent loss of olfactory function.

Largely as a result of the development of the UPSIT, we now know that olfactory dysfunction is among the first signs of Alzheimer's disease and idiopathic Parkinson's disease (PD) and that a number of movement disorders frequently misdiagnosed as PD are accompanied by little or no olfactory loss (e.g., progressive supranuclear palsy; essential tremor). Indeed, it is now clear that, in patients with PD, olfactory loss is more prevalent than several of the cardinal motor signs of this disorder (e.g., tremor), making olfactory testing a useful adjunct in the early diagnosis of PD. Recently, an inverse relationship was noted in schizophrenia between odor identification test scores and disease duration, implying that elements

of the olfactory system may undergo progressive deterioration in what up to this time had been viewed as neurodevelopmental disorder (see Figure 4). Indeed, odor identification test scores are the only known neuropsychological measure of disease progression in schizophrenia.

Conclusion

The sense of smell is of primary significance to humans, despite being taken for granted and, for the most part, being poorly understood. In addition to serving to protect the organism from harmful environmental agents, as well as enhancing the palatability of foods and beverages and the quality of life, this sensory system provides a unique index of brain function not tapped by most other sensory systems. Perhaps it is for this reason that olfactory dysfunction is among the first signs of a number of neurodegenerative diseases, making its measurement of considerable value in early diagnosis and pharmacological intervention.

[*See also* Sensory Systems.]

Bibliography

Breipohl, W., Mackay-Sim, A., Grandt, D., Rehn, B., & Darrelamann, C. (1986). Neurogenesis in the vertebrate main olfactory epithelium. In W. Breipohl (Ed.), *Ontog-*

eny of olfaction (pp. 21–33). Berlin, Germany: Springer-Verlag.

Buck, L., & Axel, R. (1991). A novel multigene family may encode odorant receptors: A molecular basis for odor recognition. *Cell, 65*, 175–187.

Cometto-Muñiz, J. E., & Cain, W. S. (1995). Olfactory adaptation. In R. L. Doty (Ed.), *Handbook of olfaction and gustation* (pp. 257–282). New York: Dekker.

Dahl, A. R. (1988). The effect of cytochrome P-450-dependent metabolism and other enzyme activities on olfaction. In R. L. Margolis & T. V. Getchell (Eds.), *Molecular neurobiology of the olfactory system* (pp. 51–70). New York: Plenum Press.

Dalton, P., & Wysocki, C. J. (1996). The nature and duration of adaptation following long-term odor exposure. *Perception and Psychophysics, 58*, 781–792.

Deems, D. A., Doty, R. L., Settle, R. G., Moore-Gillon, V., Shaman, P., Mester, A. F., Kimmelman, C. P., Brightman, V. J., & Snow, J. B., Jr. (1991). Smell and taste disorders: A study of 750 patients from the University of Pennsylvania Smell and Taste Center. *Archives of Otolaryngology: Head and Neck Surgery, 117*, 519–528.

Dhong, H.-J., Chung, S.-Y., & Doty, R. L. (in press). Estrogen protects against 3-methylindole-induced olfactory loss. *Brain Research, 824*, 312–315.

Doty, R. L. (1991). Olfactory dysfunction in neurodegenerative disorders. In T. V. Getchell, R. L. Doty, L. M. Bartoshuk, & J. B. Snow, Jr. (Eds.), *Smell and taste in health and disease* (pp. 735–751). New York: Raven.

Doty, R. L., Bromley, S. M., & Stern, M. B. (1995). Olfactory testing as an aid in the diagnosis of Parkinson's disease: Development of optimal discrimination criteria. *Neurodegeneration, 4*, 93–97.

Doty, R. L., Golbe, L. I., McKeown, D. A., Stern, M. B., Lehrach, C. M., & Crawford, D. (1993). Olfactory testing differentiates between progressive supranuclear palsy and idiopathic Parkinson's disease. *Neurology, 43*, 962–965.

Doty, R. L., & Kobal, G. (1995). Current trends in the measurement of olfactory function. In R. L. Doty (Ed.), *Handbook of olfaction and gustation* (pp. 191–225). New York: Dekker.

Doty, R. L., Li, C., Mannon, L. J., & Yousem, D. M. (1997). Olfactory dysfunction in multiple sclerosis. *New England Journal of Medicine, 336*, 1918–1919.

Doty, R. L., McKeown, D. A., & Lee, W. W. (1995). A study of the test-retest reliability of ten olfactory tests. *Chemical Senses, 20*, 645–656.

Doty, R. L., Shaman, P., Applebaum, S. I., Giberson, R., Sikorski, L., & Rosenberg, L. (1984). Smell identification ability: Changes with age. *Science, 226*, 1441–1443.

Doty, R. L., Smith, R., McKeown, D. A., & Raj, J. (1994). Tests of human olfactory function: Principal components analysis suggests that most measure a common source of variance. *Perception and Psychophysics, 56*, 701–707.

Frye, R. E., Schwartz, B., & Doty, R. L. (1990). Dose-related effects of cigarette smoking on olfactory function. *Journal of the American Medical Association, 263*, 1233–1236.

Hinds, J. W., & McNelly, N. A. (1981). Aging in the rat ol-

factory system: Correlation of changes in the olfactory epithelium and olfactory bulb. *Journal of Comparative Neurology, 203*, 441–454.

Kalmey, J. K., Thewissen, J. G., & Dluzen, D. E. (1998). Age-related size reduction of foramina in the cribriform plate. *Anatomical Record, 251*, 326–329.

Matulionis, D. H. (1982). Effects of the aging process on olfactory neuron plasticity. In W. Breipohl (Ed.), *Olfaction and endocrine regulation* (pp. 299–308). London: IRL Press.

Moberg, P. J., Doty, R. L., Turetsky, B. I., Arnold, S. E., Mahr, R. N., Gur, R. C., & Gur, R. E. (1997). Olfactory identification deficits in schizophrenia: Correlation with duration of illness. *American Journal of Psychiatry, 154*, 1016–1018.

Moran, D. T., Rowley, J. C., III, Jafek, B. W., & Lovell, M. A. (1982). The fine structure of the olfactory mucosa in man. *Journal of Neurocytology, 11*, 721–746.

Naessen, R. (1971). An enquiry on the morphological characteristics and possible changes with age in the olfactory region of man. *Acta Oto-Laryngologica, 71*, 49–62.

Nakashima, T., Kimmelman, C. P., & Snow, J. B., Jr. (1984). Structure of human fetal and adult olfactory neuroepithelium. *Archives of Otolaryngology, 110*, 641–646.

Pevsner, J., Reed, R. R., Feinstein, P. B., & Snyder, S. H. (1988). Molecular cloning of odorant binding protein: Member of a ligand carrier family. *Science, 241*, 336–339.

Rowley, J. C., Moran, D. T., & Jafek, B. W. (1989). Peroxidase backfills suggest the mammalian olfactory epithelium contains a second morphologically distinct class of bipolar sensory neuron: The microvillar cell. *Brain Research, 502*, 387–400.

Smith, C. G. (1942). Age incident of atrophy of olfactory nerves in man. *Journal of Comparative Neurology, 77*, 589–594.

Sullivan, S. L., Ressler, K. J., & Buck, L. B. (1995). Spatial patterning and information coding in the olfactory system. *Current Opinion in Genetics and Development, 5*, 516–523.

Richard L. Doty

SMOKING

SMOKING. Tobacco smoking is a complex behavioral activity with wide-ranging health and social implications. Smoking is based on the self-administration of nicotine—a tertiary amine synthesized by the tobacco plant as a pesticide—whose pharmacological profile includes powerful subjective, behavioral, physiological, and neuroendocrine effects.

Economics and Health

Tobacco was consumed by native populations in the Americas long before recorded history, typically chewed or brewed for religious or medicinal purposes. Reports of tobacco smoking are found in Christopher Columbus's diary of 1492, dating the introduction of tobacco to Europeans. From that time on, despite sporadic attempts by various religious and medical authorities to discourage its use, tobacco spread rapidly throughout the world. By the beginning of the sixteenth century, the tobacco trade had become sufficiently regularized that increasing tariffs and duties made it the darling of tax collectors and the sustainer of European royal treasuries; by the seventeenth century, tobacco had become a principal source of revenue for the English monarchy.

Until the mid- to late nineteenth century, tobacco was mostly consumed in pipes and in the form of snuff, with lesser amounts in cigars, smokeless tobacco plugs, and other means. The modern cigarette did not come into its own until after the American Civil War. Its popularity was made possible largely by the combined development of flue-cured tobacco, which provided a "milder" (lower pH) tobacco smoke that could be inhaled deeply into the lungs, and the Bonsack automatic cigarette-making machine, which could manufacture the equivalent of 40 times the number of cigarettes rolled by hand in a day and which brought the price of the cigarette within the reach of a mass market. In the great international conflicts of the twentieth century, cigarettes were deemed essential to war effort, and consumption in men rose dramatically in World Wars I and II. Beginning in the 1920s, one after another of the remaining tobacco taboos were broken, and even children were targeted for promotion. The continuing search for unsaturated markets also took advantage of social changes in the status of women, and cigarette advertisers began to portray women who smoked as thin, beautiful, and glamorous role models. At present, the United States tobacco industry generates around $50 billion per year, with a combined direct and indirect impact of $64.9 billion, about 2.3% of the gross national product (Huber & Pandina, 1997). In the aggregate, the industry accounts for about 1.2 million jobs and $39.1 billion in employment compensation, which goes a long way to explaining the industry's economic and political clout and serves as eloquent testimonial to society's addiction to tobacco.

Unfortunately, cigarette smoking is also associated with over 450,000 premature deaths in the United States alone each year—25% of all deaths (Bartecchi, Mackenzie, & Schrier, 1994). Chronic bronchitis and emphysema account for 70,000 deaths—57,000 of which can be attributed to cigarette smoking. Smoking has proven to be the cause not only of most cases of chronic obstructive pulmonary disease but also of 90% of bronchogenic carcinoma (106,000 deaths per year) and nearly 35% of fatal myocardial infarctions (115,000 deaths a year). Lung cancer is now the leading form of cancer in women, having surpassed breast cancer. Although fewer than 30% of Americans now smoke, the pathophysiological consequences of the habit account for nearly 60% of all direct health care costs, with expenditures estimated to be in excess of $68 billion annually (Huber & Pandina, 1997).

Prevalence and Demographics

In response to the growing evidence of adverse health effects, the prevalence of smoking in men and women has shown a steady decline in the United States (MacKenzie et al., 1994). From a peak of 44% of adults (50% of men and 33% of women) smoking in the mid-1960s, the number declined to less than 27% by the late 1980s. At present, the percentage of smokers within the population has more or less leveled off, with 24% prevalence in 1990 and 25% in 1994. Significant differences in smoking rates by race or ethnicity were no longer evident by 1995. Despite some differences in patterns of initiation, maintenance, and cessation, once social disapprobation was overcome, the history of smoking in women paralleled that of men (Pomerleau, Beman, Gritz, Marks, & Goeters, 1994)—females now appear to have reached a rough parity with their male counterparts with respect to smoking. Reports indicate that smoking rates of young people in the United States are rising once again, increasing by 45% in tenth graders (14 to 16 years of age) and by 20% in twelfth graders (16 to 18 years of age) in 1995—and the increase is more pronounced in girls (Huber & Pandina, 1997).

For youngsters who smoke, about 25% started by the age of 12, 50% by ages 13 and 14, and 90% by age 20 (Pomerleau et al., 1994). Groups of young people who are at particular risk for initiation include students in a vocational track, students with chronic educational and behavioral problems, children who are substance abusers, and children from single-parent families. "Latchkey children" are almost twice as likely to begin smoking as other children, regardless of socioeconomic status. Generally, there is an inverse relationship between smoking initiation and educational aspiration, with an initiation rate of 8% for college-bound students compared with 19% for students whose education ends with high school. Cultural constraints against tobacco use do not protect indefinitely, as indicated by the success of advertising and marketing campaigns by the tobacco industry to make cigarette smoking attractive and desirable to Hispanic women. Furthermore, it is important to realize that the overall decline in cigarette consumption in the United States over the past 30 years has prompted vigorous compensatory activity by the domestic tobacco industry to capture new international markets. The possibilities are unlimited: Countries with low prevalence of smoking represent new markets, and those with high prevalence of smoking provide opportunities for creating new brand loyalties.

An important change in the global demographics of smoking is now occurring as smoking becomes the habit of the disadvantaged, the less affluent, and the less educated. The successful creation of an antismoking climate in many societies has had the beneficial impact of discouraging many potential social or casual smokers from taking up the habit, as well as persuading discretionary smokers to quit. Unfortunately, the more successful a particular country's antismoking public health efforts, the more refractory and nicotine dependent are the remaining smokers in that nation (Fagerstrom et al., 1996).

Initiation and Maintenance

Initiation into tobacco use was once so common as to serve as a growing-up ritual. For young men in many parts of the world, this is still the norm. Having friends who smoke is a good predictor of smoking status, reflecting the contribution of peer pressure and other social factors in initiation. Smoking by parents and older siblings is also predictive, bringing attention to the contribution of genetic factors. Concordance rates for smokers are consistently higher in monozygotic than in dizogotic twins, even when the twins are brought up separately—supporting the role of genes in smoking. Overall heritability of smoking has been shown to be in excess of 50% (Pomerleau, 1995).

The nature of the behavioral traits and biological capacity for reinforcement that create susceptibility to nicotine dependence is still not well understood. Given nearly universal experimentation with tobacco, the differentiation manifested by regular smokers, occasional smokers, and nonsmokers suggests that a critical source for some of the variability is genetic. Since it is evident that smoking status is determined by self-selection rather than by random assignment, it would seem that some people are "destined" to become smokers, regardless of environmental factors. Support for these ideas come from several sources, including: (1) human laboratory experiments in which pure nicotine was used to study reactivity in nonsmokers and in regular smokers (during *ad libitum* smoking as well as in abstinence); (2) studies in which heavy and light smokers, ex-smokers, and nonsmokers were asked to recall their early experiences with smoking; and (3) investigations of first-dose reactivity in genetically pure lines of mice, suggesting that initial sensitivity to nicotine serves as an indicator of reinforcement value and potential for dependence in subsequent exposure (Pomerleau, 1995).

One fourth of the nicotine taken into the lungs during smoking reaches the brain in about 15 seconds, resulting in nearly immediate effects. Although potent peripheral actions occur, the weight of the evidence shows that the reinforcing effects of nicotine from smoking are centrally mediated. Nicotine temporarily enhances visual surveillance, reaction time, mental efficiency, rapid information processing, and memory recall. Nicotine acts on cholinergic receptors in dopamine pathways in the ventral tegmental ("brain reward") area in a manner similar to that produced by heroin, cocaine, and amphetamines, providing a plausible mechanism for explaining positive reinforcement from nicotine self-administration. In addition, nicotine has the ability to alter the bioavailability of a wide variety of other neuroregulators.

By smoking, smokers gain not only relief from annoying nicotine withdrawal symptoms—depressed mood, insomnia, irritability and anger, anxiety, difficulty concentrating and restlessness, and increased appetite—but may also obtain temporary improvements in performance or affect. In such a manner, ordinary activities, such as socializing, finishing a meal, and driving an automobile, as well as tasks that demand focused attention and vigilance, such as test taking, and various dysphoric states (e.g., anxiety and sadness) eventually become powerful cues for smoking through conditioning. The number of affective states or performance demands that can function as cues for smoking is potentially quite large, providing an explanation for the thorough interweaving of the smoking habit into the fabric of daily living. The observed behavioral and subjective effects of smoking share a remarkable concordance with the known neuroregulatory actions of nicotine. Thus, because nicotine alters the bioavailability of numerous behaviorally and physiologically active neuroregulators, it can be used by smokers to produce a variety of transient reinforcing effects—both positive and negative reinforcements (Pomerleau & Pomerleau, 1984).

Until quite recently, nicotine dependence resulting from tobacco use was not classified as drug abuse, partly because nicotine use was not associated with obvious intoxication and also because the habit was not considered disruptive of productive activity or socially undesirable. This is no longer the case. The cumulative finding of more than 2,500 scientific papers summarized in the *1988 Surgeon General's Report* of the U.S. Department of Health and Human Services reached the unequivocal conclusion that cigarettes and other forms of tobacco are addicting, that nicotine is the drug in tobacco that causes addiction, and that the pharmacological and behavioral processes that determine tobacco addiction are similar to those that determine addiction to such drugs as heroin and cocaine. Nicotine dependence implies a pattern of heavy consumption that is resistant to change, as well as nicotine tolerance and the regulation of nicotine intake within relatively narrow limits. For most smokers, withdrawal symptoms emerge a few hours to a day after abstaining from nicotine, distress peaks within two to three days, and most symptoms dissipate over a period of a few weeks to a few months.

In the past 30 years, the prevalence of smoking in adults in the United States has decreased by nearly one third, and nearly half of all people who ever smoked have quit. With such numbers of people defecting from the ranks of tobacco users, it is evident that smoking is no longer randomly distributed throughout the population. As "easy quitters" and casual smokers are eliminated from the smoker pool, the smokers who remain evince greater reliance on nicotine. Among the possible explanations for the over determination of the smoking habit in such individuals is that they are more susceptible to nicotine's reinforcing effects (Pomerleau, 1995) and/or that they utilize nicotine to help overcome preexisting psychological conditions that cause distress, suboptimal function, or both (Pomerleau, 1997).

These conditions—serving as cofactors for smoking—may well increase the likelihood of smoking because nicotine provides partial relief, further, when smokers with cofactors attempt to abstain, distress or dysfunction from the underlying condition returns or is exacerbated, persisting well beyond the usual duration of nicotine withdrawal symptoms. Comorbid conditions include depression, premenstrual syndrome, eating disorders, anxiety disorders, adult attention-deficit/hyperactivity disorder, and schizophrenia (Pomerleau, 1997). Of the various cofactors, history of depression has the most robust association, with linkage persisting even when other comorbid conditions are factored out. Patients with a history of depression fail at more than twice the rate of those without history of depression, and there is a strong genetic association between smoking and major depression, suggesting that common inherited factors of a neurobiological nature must be operative (Kendler et al., 1993).

Treatment and Prevention

Over the last three decades, the focus of smoking control has shifted from the clinic to the community, from the laboratory to the field, and from treatment to policy. With the recognition that only a minority of smokers will attend formal clinics, the emphasis has been on promoting smoking cessation through broader channels. Self-help approaches and minimal interventions have come to the fore, and the effort to help smokers quit has moved to health care settings, the workplace, and the community. The cumulative effect of these efforts, coinciding with dramatic changes in public policies and attitudes, has been remarkable (Shiffman, 1993). Between 1965 and 1987, the prevalence of smoking dropped from 40 to 29% in the United States and, although some of the decline is attributable to prevention in youth, much of it reflects smoking cessation in adults. The quit ratio—the percentage of smokers who have quit—rose from 30 to 45% during this time. Though much of this change occurred independently of formal smoking-cessation programs, highly dependent, refractory smokers—a growing proportion of the smoking population—will continue to require more intensive, individualized interventions (American Psychiatric Association, 1996); further, much conceptual innovation for managing smoking at the societal level has its origins in the clinic.

Behavioral approaches to the treatment of smoking, for example, multicomponent, stimulus control, contingency management programs, first came into prominence in the 1970s and were associated with significant improvement in abstinence rates, with some programs reporting sustained quitting in excess of 30% (Shiffman, 1993). Nicotine replacement therapies—nicotine gum (polacrilex), transdermal nicotine patch, nicotine nasal spray—constituted the next major advance, doubling the chances of quitting and increasing the effectiveness of strictly behavioral approaches. A number of nonnicotine pharmacotherapies for smoking are in various stages of development and testing (Benowitz, 1996). Taking into account the powerful contribution of cofactors for smoking such as depression and dysphoria, it is not surprising that antidepressants have emerged among the more promising of the new products. Recent evidence suggests that nonnicotine pharmacotherapies can be combined with nicotine replacement therapy to meet the special needs of nicotine-dependent smokers with cofactors.

Prevention is the capstone of tobacco control, and prevention comes down to stopping young people from starting. For example, in the United States, 90% of people who smoke began by the age of 20, and this proportion is similar in other countries. Initially, smoking education programs in schools focused mainly on the health hazards of smoking and did not have much of an effect on smoking behavior. In the 1980s, school education programs based on social learning theory focused on the personal and social skills needed to resist social pressures to smoke, but, although these programs delayed the onset of smoking, they did not prevent it. Though mass media campaigns have not been shown to be particularly cost effective in changing adolescent smoking behavior, unpaid public service announcements and media advocacy have had considerable impact on public opinion and policy makers. As a category, communitywide antismoking campaigns have varied in effectiveness, though some have evinced long-lasting effects, albeit at considerable expense (McNeill, 1997).

Among the measures for decreasing youth access, restricting tobacco sales might be effective, but typically the laws are not enforced systematically. A total ban on all forms of tobacco advertising, sponsorship, and promotion might well prevent young people from coming under the sway of the tobacco purveyors, but summing up the political will to carry out such policies has been difficult in most countries—Norway and Canada are notable exceptions in this regard. Of particular promise is the fact that there is an inverse relationship between price and cigarette consumption, suggesting that taxation could be used as a tobacco control policy by government; for example, in Canada, doubling the price of cigarettes (adjusted for inflation) reduced adult consumption by 35% and teenage consumption by 62% (McNeill, 1997). Finally, from the public health perspective of harm reduction, it is interesting to observe that cigarettes—the most harmful nicotine delivery systems available—are readily available everywhere, whereas the nicotine delivery products developed by pharmaceutical companies are highly regulated and often require a physicians's prescription—despite the absence of tobacco smoke and its attendant hazards.

Conclusion

If tobacco products were made available today for the first time, governments would be hard pressed to permit their sale. Although history has dictated some harsh lessons with respect to the personal and societal harm associated with tobacco use, tobacco companies continue to justify their products as legal, part of the culture, and of great economic importance. As Slade (1997) points out, however, slavery was once rationalized with similar arguments. Although it may not be practicable to ban tobacco products entirely, the time has come to manage these products and the industry that makes them to minimize harm to society. The movement to obtain reparations from the tobacco industry in the United States represents a crucial opportunity for changing the direction of the events of the past 400 years, for, in return for some immunity from class action suits arising from smoking-related illnesses, the tobacco industry would pay large sums of money to government agencies over several decades. These incremental resources might serve to fund prevention and treatment for smoking as well as to support research that leads to a better understanding of biobehavioral susceptibility to nicotine. This movement may engender more effective public policies for tobacco control, sparing future generations this devastating health blight.

[*See also* Addictive Personality.]

Bibliography

American Psychiatric Association. (1996). Practice guideline for the treatment of patients with nicotine dependence. *American Journal of Psychiatry, 153* (Suppl. 10), 1–31.

Bartecchi, C. E., MacKenzie, T. D., & Schrier, R. W. (1994). The human costs of tobacco use: 1. *New England Journal of Medicine, 330,* 907–912.

Benowitz, N. L. (1996). Pharmacology of nicotine: Addiction and therapeutics. *Annual Review of Pharmacology and Toxicology, 36,* 597–613.

Fagerstrom, K. O., Kunze, M., Schoberberger, R., Breslau, N., Hughes, J. R., Hurt, R. D., Puska, P., Ramstrom, L., & Zatonski, W. (1996). Nicotine dependence versus smoking prevalence: Comparisons among countries and categories of smokers. *Tobacco Control, 5,* 52–56.

Huber, G. L., & Pandina, R. J. (1997). The economics of tobacco use. In C. T. Bolliger & K. O. Fagerstrom (Eds.), *Progress in respiratory research: Vol. 28. The tobacco epidemic* (pp. 12–63), Basel, Switzerland: Karger.

Kendler, K. S., Neale, M. C., MacLean, C. J., Heath, A. C., Eaves, L. J., & Kessler, R. C. (1993). Smoking and major depression: A causal analysis. *Archives of Genetic Psychiatry, 50,* 36–43.

MacKenzie, T. D., Bartecchi, C. E., & Schrier, R. W. (1994). The human costs of tobacco use: 2. *New England Journal of Medicine, 330,* 975–980.

McNeill, A. (1997). Preventing the onset of tobacco use. In C. T. Bolliger & K. O. Fagerstrom (Eds.), *Progress in respiratory research: Vol. 28. The tobacco epidemic* (pp. 213–229). Basel, Switzerland: Karger.

Pomerleau, C. S. (1997). Co-factors for smoking and evolutionary psychobiology. *Addiction, 9,* 397–408.

Pomerleau, C. S., Berman, B. A., Gritz, E. R., Marks, J. L., & Goeters, S. (1994). Why some women smoke. In R. R. Watson (Ed.), *Drug and alcohol abuse reviews: Vol. 5. Addictive behaviors in women* (pp. 39–70). Totowa, NJ: Humana Press.

Pomerleau, O. F. (1995). Individual differences in sensitivity to nicotine: Implications for genetic research on nicotine dependence. *Behavior Genetics, 25,* 161–177.

Pomerleau, O. F., & Pomerleau, C. S. (1984). Neuroregulators and the reinforcement of smoking: Towards a biobehavioral explanation. *Neuroscience and biobehavioral Reviews, 8,* 503–513.

Shiffman, S. (1993). Smoking cessation treatment: Any progress? *Journal of Consulting and Clinical Psychology, 61,* 718–722.

Slade, J. (1997). Historical notes on tobacco. In C. T. Bolliger & K. O. Fagerstrom (Eds.), *Progress in respiratory research: Vol. 28. The tobacco epidemic* (pp. 1—11). Basel, Switzerland: Karger.

U.S. Department of Health and Human Services. (1988). *The health consequences of smoking: Nicotine addiction (1988 report of the Surgeon General).* Rockville, MD: Public Health Service, Office on Smoking and Health.

Ovide F. Pomerleau

SOCIAL COGNITION is an area of theory and research within social psychology that focuses on the cognitive mediation of social psychological phenomena. That is, social cognition attempts to understand social judgment and social behavior (including all the traditional topic areas of social psychology) by investigating the mental representations and processes by which they operate. As this definition suggests, social cognition has strong links with the study of attention, perception, memory, and related areas within cognitive psychology, and closely related approaches exist within other areas of psychology, particularly developmental and clinical.

Historical Background and Development

The historical background of social cognition begins with the clear separation between experimental psychology and social psychology that endured for most of the twentieth century. Whereas behaviorists such as J. B. Watson and B. F. Skinner urged experimental psychologists to reject mentalistic concepts and explanations, social psychologists elaborated theories involving such assumed causes of behavior as social norms, stereotypes or prejudice regarding social groups, and consonant or dissonant beliefs or attitudes. In this situation, social and experimental psychologists generally believed that their fields had little in common, and aside from a few applications of learning theory within social psychology, little theoretical interchange took place.

The face of experimental psychology changed radically in the 1960s and 1970s with the rise of the cognitive or information-processing perspective (e.g., Neisser, 1967). It became scientifically respectable to discuss mental representations and processes as causes of overt behavior. Against this background, the social cognition approach took shape in the early to middle 1970s. The pioneers of this area were individuals trained in social psychology who saw the opportunity to borrow from the new developments in cognitive psychology both theoretical and methodological tools that would help them to understand social psychological phenomena. Associative models of memory, schema theories, and response-time measurement methods were among the important ideas borrowed. Prominent early social cognition studies investigated priming and judgments about persons, social expectations and memory, and stereotyping in person perception (e.g., Hamilton, 1981).

By about 1980, social cognition was a recognized area of social psychology. A monograph entitled *Social Cognition, Inference, and Attribution* appeared in 1979 (Wyer & Carlston, 1979) and a collection of important papers in 1980 (Hastie et al., 1980). In 1980 the premier empirical journal of social psychology, *Journal of Personality and Social Psychology*, was divided into three topical sections, the first of which was named "Attitudes and Social Cognition." A new journal, *Social Cognition*, was founded in 1982. Finally, the first *Handbook of Social Cognition* was published in 1984 (Wyer & Srull, 1984).

As social cognition developed from a budding research interest shared by a few investigators to a recognized major subfield of social psychology, terminology and definitions evolved. In the early days, the term "person memory" was as commonly used as "social cognition," but the latter term now predominates. More important, definitions of the emerging area gradually converged. Many early writers defined social cognition as concerned with a particular topic area, centering on person perception and impression formation, or "how people think about people." The emphasis on person perception (including related topics such as attribution and stereotyping) is not altogether misplaced. The first social cognition researchers did focus on those topics but assumed that similar types of mental representations and processes would be involved in all types of judgments. Judgments about people were studied not because they were thought to be unique but for the same reasons that make the fruit fly *Drosophila* ubiquitous in genetics research: convenience and ready adaptability to the laboratory. However, a central aspect of the growth and development of social cognition was its application to an increasing range of topics, including persuasion, the self, personality, health, and personal relationships (see Wyer & Srull, 1994). By the mid-1980s, most researchers regarded social cognition as an approach rather than a specific topic area and adopted definitions like the one at the beginning of this article.

What differentiates the social cognition approach from the many respects in which social psychology had been cognitive all along? As the historical sketch above emphasized, social psychologists had studied mental representations (such as attitudes or stereotypes) as determinants of behavior for decades before the rise of social cognition. The difference is the new focus on direct investigation of mental structures and processes, which has both theoretical and methodological aspects. First, social cognition freely borrowed theoretical concepts (such as associative models of memory structures) from cognitive psychology. This borrowing allowed mental representations and processes to be treated as "hypothetical constructs," postulated to have a real existence and potentially observable effects independent of any theory, rather than as "intervening variables" introduced solely for theoretical convenience and not expected to be independently observable. For example, a social cognition researcher might assume that an attitude is an actual mental representation stored in the head and not just a conceptual summary of an individual's tendency to evaluate an object positively or negatively. From this orientation, we can ask the same questions about attitudes that we ask about any other mental representations, such as under what circumstances they become activated and able to affect judgments or behaviors.

Second, methodological tools (such as response time or recall measures) also permitted social cognition researchers to study cognitive structures and processes in greater depth than before. The difference is often summarized as a contrast between "outcome-oriented" versus "process-oriented" research strategies (Devine, Hamilton, & Ostrom, 1994; Wyer & Srull, 1984). In the former, if various factors were predicted to influence some judgment or behavior through a particular process, the factors would be manipulated and the appropriate dependent variable measured. If the pattern of results fit theoretical predictions, this fit would be taken as support for the theory, even though no direct evidence of the hypothesized process had been collected. With the development of measures for more directly assessing mediating representations and processes, including priming and response-time measurement techniques and the analysis of recall or recognition memory, researchers were no longer limited to measuring outcomes to test theories concerning processes. Research designs that were better suited to the assessment of mediation were developed and widely applied. Both these methodological shifts and the conceptualization of mental entities using theories continuous with those of cognitive psychology mark important differences between the social cognition approach and earlier cognitive approaches within social psychology.

Relationships to Neighboring Fields

Social cognition draws on topics and perspectives from both of its parent disciplines, social and cognitive psychology, but since its earliest days it has effectively been an area within social psychology.

Cognitive Psychology. The relationship of social cognition to cognitive psychology has been largely one way, with the former borrowing heavily from the latter but having little influence in the reverse direction. Only occasional social cognition papers appear in the mainstream cognitive psychology journals. This asymmetry may be explained in part by general theoretical and methodological preferences of the fields. Cognitive psychologists tend to favor more precise, even mathematically formulated theories and tighter experimental controls than are typically found in social cognition.

Some approaches in cognitive psychology typically involve less methodological precision. These include work on everyday memory or studies of text comprehension, areas that are conceptually continuous with important issues in social psychology (e.g., autobiographical memory and attributional inferences). In the early days of social cognition, many assumed that as cognitive psychologists moved from using single-word stimuli to sentences and other more complex materials that are similar to those studied in social psychology, their work would increasingly converge with social cognition. This promise has not been realized, however; even workers in these areas in cognitive psychology tend not to cite related work in social cognition.

Social cognition theorists have often discussed similarities and differences between social and nonsocial cognition. Ostrom (1984) outlined three general views. The "building-block" view holds that processes involved in nonsocial cognition are simpler and more fundamental and that social cognition can be understood by adding additional variables (such as affect or individual differences) to these processes. The "fundamentalist" position sees no differences between the cognitive processes involved in social and nonsocial tasks. Any apparent differences are attributed not to the social versus nonsocial distinction itself but to differences in such correlated properties as familiarity, complexity, self-relevance, and so forth. Finally, the "realist" position reverses the building-block position, positing that social rather than nonsocial processes are primary. One line of argument for this position is developmental: Infants inhabit a social environment and must learn to deal effectively with other people long before they directly manage the nonsocial world. Correspondingly, Ostrom cites evidence that young infants assume that physical objects share human attributes (such as autonomous movement) and only later distinguish nonsocial from social objects. In this perspective, factors such as affect, motivation, and individual differences that were viewed as "add-ons" in the building-block viewpoint become integral parts of developing cognitive abilities.

Because social cognition assumes that the same basic information-processing principles apply in both social and nonsocial domains, increased integration with cognitive psychology remains an important goal for the future. The unique contributions of social cognition to this integration may well involve issues such as interactions of affect, cognition, and motivation; effects of social interaction and social influence; effects of personal involvement; perceptions of complex, dynamically changing stimuli; and links between perception, cognition, and overt action.

Social Psychology. In the early days, many social psychologists identified social cognition as the study of person perception and viewed it as another content area of social psychology similar to the study of attitudes, small groups, and so forth. Over time it became clear that social cognition researchers viewed their principles as applying across the entire range of social psychology, an idea captured in the title of T. M. Ostrom's introductory chapter in the 1984 *Handbook of Social Cognition* (Wyer & Srull, 1984): "The Sovereignty of Social Cognition." Some readers interpreted this phrase as making the claim that social cognition would dominate the entire field and found the notion presumptuous or arrogant.

In the second edition of the *Handbook* (Wyer & Srull, 1994), Ostrom explained that "sovereignty" was meant to point to the integrative potential of the social cognition perspective; social cognition would embrace other topic areas rather than competing with or displacing them. As evidence of this trend, he cited chapters in the second *Handbook* describing the contributions of social cognition to major fields such as clinical psychology, the psychology of close relationships, consumer psychology, and health psychology. These chapters furnished strong evidence that the detailed study of cognitive representations and processes could advance understanding of virtually all of social psychology's traditional topic areas, as well as addressing important applied concerns.

Another potential misunderstanding about the nature of social cognition probably stems from a pervasive ambiguity in the key term "cognitive." This term can include all mental representations and processes (the sense intended in the label "social cognition" itself), but the same term is often used in contrast to motivation or affect—for example, in the recurring efforts to competitively test "cognitive" against "motivational" explanations of social psychological phenomena. If people took the term in this latter, narrower sense, they sometimes assumed that social cognition denied the importance of motivation or affect. In response, reviews of social cognition research (e.g., Sherman, Judd, & Park, 1989) took pains to point out that social cognition is not the only fruitful approach to social psychological issues and that research on affect, motivation, social interaction, and individual differences will also make major contributions. In fact, a major trend in social cognition today is the integrative thrust that Ostrom (1984) foresaw. Contributions toward the integration of cognition and motivation, affect, and group interaction have begun to appear.

Characteristic Features of the Social Cognition Approach

Social cognition holds that basic issues such as the organization of information in memory or the automatic versus controlled nature of cognitive processes have implications for all topic areas in social psychology. Correspondingly, handbooks and reviews of social cognition (e.g., Wyer & Srull, 1984; Sherman et al., 1989) have generally been organized around chapters or sections addressing such issues and showing their common features across topics. In contrast, in the *Handbook of Social Psychology* dating from the same period (Lindzey & Aronson, 1985), most chapters are devoted to topic areas (along with some that review specific theoretical perspectives or research methods). Social cognition researchers would view this traditional organization as less likely to encourage cross-topic conceptual integration.

Integrative Theoretical Models. Influential theories in social cognition have often been explicitly formulated to account for a wide range of phenomena rather than a few related findings obtained in a particular research paradigm. For example, the person memory model of Wyer and Srull (1989) aims to explain many types of judgments and patterns of memory retrieval about behaviors, people, or social groups. As another example, several models of judgmental correction describe how people attempt to correct their judgments when they suspect that they may have been unconsciously affected by extraneous factors. Again, all sorts of judgments, including attitudes, trait judgments about people, and self-related judgments, are explicitly included within the domain of these models.

Shifts in Emphasis in Research on Specific Topics. Virtually all topic areas of social psychology have been influenced to varying degrees by the social cognition perspective. Three areas will illustrate the general shifts in research emphasis attributable to the social cognition movement.

Causal attribution is the study of the way people assign causes to observed events, with particular emphasis on the attribution of traits such as "honest" or "friendly" based on people's observed behaviors. Attribution has been one of the most popular social psychological topics since the 1970s. Early models assumed that causal judgments were rational, almost scientific in nature. Later models paid more attention to biases and rested on assumptions either that human cognitive limitations force the use of heuristics and shortcuts or that various motives influence causal judgments. The great majority of this research used questionnaire methods, so only people's relatively thoughtful judgments could be investigated and only judgmental outcomes could be measured, not the processes that people used to make those judgments. With the rise of social cognition, attribution research more frequently applied priming, response time, or memory measures to investigate the processes as well as the contents of judgments (Smith, 1994). Process-oriented questions, particularly about whether various types of attributional judgments are made automatically or only in explicit and controlled fashion, have been addressed by numerous studies. Theoretical integration has also increased: Today most models of attribution are essentially general models of social judgment, dealing with such broad issues as how information is represented, how accessibility influences the retrieval of prior knowledge, and how multiple cues are combined to form a response.

In the area of stereotyping, research prior to the 1970s focused largely on the content of stereotypes (assessed by trait checklists or other questionnaires) and on how stereotypes might be changed (e.g., by intergroup contacts). Stereotypes have been conceptualized as cognitive representations since Lippman's famous "pictures in the head" definition in the 1920s, but social cognition brought the insight that the effects of any cognitive representation depend on details of its organization, accessibility, and so forth (Hamilton, 1994). Research now addresses structural issues such as whether stereotypes generally contain abstract information (e.g., traits linked to the group as a whole) versus more specific and episodic information (e.g., representations of specific group members' characteristics). Important process issues include the extent to which the application of stereotypes to group members is automatic and uncontrollable and the ways perceivers deal with stereotype-inconsistent information and defend or change their stereotypes. Finally, current work integrates affect and motivation into the cognitive analysis of the interlinked issues of stereotyping, prejudice, and intergroup relations (Mackie & Hamilton, 1993).

Finally, the study of attitudes has been at the core of social psychology since its earliest days. Attitudes are traditionally defined as the person's tendency to evaluate an object (another person, social group, physical object, or idea) favorably or unfavorably and are theoretically central as potential causes of behavior. As in other areas, the rise of social cognition led to correlated shifts in research methods and conceptualizations. Questionnaire methods (which lack the ability to assess less conscious or less thoughtful responses or to shed much light on details of cognitive processes) gave way to memory measures, thought-listing tasks, and response times (see Greenwald & Banaji, 1995). Other current research issues include the nature of attitude representations, which have been conceptualized (using models drawn from cognitive psychology) as associative structures, as well as their accessibility and other factors that affect the ease with which they can be activated and brought to mind to affect judgments and behavior. In the field of attitude change, prominent models have addressed how people process persuasive messages (either with or without extensive thought) and the resulting impact on attitudes. Finally, attitudes, like attributions, have been drawn within the framework of general models of social judgment, so that such issues as how information is organized, retrieved from memory, and combined into an overt response have been elaborated in a relatively general way.

Virtually any area of social psychology can supply more examples of the same point. Researchers studying close relationships now investigate how mental representations of the relationship partner are organized and how they influence affect and behavior in relationships. Researchers on group processes study how group membership is mentally represented as part of the self and the effects of this process on intragroup cooperation or intergroup relations. Personality theorists have often made use of social cognition concepts and methods in studying the self. In these areas and others there has been an ongoing trend toward the detailed analysis of the cognitive representations and processes responsible for social judgment and social behavior, as well as a continuing drive toward integrative theories that transcend specific topic areas. These trends mark the virtually pervasive impact of social cognition within social psychology. The further goal of increasing integration across areas of psychology (linking social with cognitive, developmental, clinical, and other areas) still remains largely for the future.

Bibliography

Devine, P. G., Hamilton, D. L., & Ostrom, T. M. (Eds.). (1994). *Social cognition: Impact on social psychology.* San Diego, CA: Academic Press. Valuable collection of chapters tracing the influence of social cognition in various topic areas within social psychology.

Fiske, S. T., & Taylor, S. E. (1991). *Social cognition* (2nd ed.). New York: McGraw-Hill. The first undergraduate-level textbook of social cognition.

Greenwald, A. G., & Banaji, M. R. (1995). Implicit social cognition: Attitudes, stereotypes, and self-esteem. *Psychological Review, 102,* 1–27.

Hamilton, D. L. (Ed.). (1981). *Cognitive processes in stereotyping and intergroup behavior.* Hillsdale, NJ: Erlbaum. A collection of early applications of the social cognition approach to stereotyping.

Hamilton, D. L., Stroessner, S. J., & Driscoll, D. M. (1994). In P. G. Devine, D. L. Hamilton, & T. M. Ostrom (Eds.), *Social cognition: Its impact on social psychology* (pp. 291–321). Orlando, FL: Academic Press.

Hastie, R., Ostrom, T. M., Ebbesen, E. B., Wyer, R. S., Hamilton, D. L., & Carlston, D. E. (Eds.). (1980). *Person memory.* Hillsdale, NJ: Erlbaum. Another influential early collection of chapters.

Lindzey, G., & Aronson, E. (Eds.). (1985). *Handbook of social psychology* (3rd ed.). New York: Random House. A traditionally oriented overview of social psychology dating from the time when social cognition was reaching maturity.

Mackie, D. M., & Hamilton, D. L. (Eds.). (1993). *Affect, cognition, and stereotyping.* San Diego: Academic Press. Recent integrative models of cognition and affect in stereotyping; compare to Hamilton, 1981.

Neisser, U. (1967). *Cognitive psychology.* New York: Appleton-Century-Crofts. A highly influential textbook marking the emergence of the cognitive perspective in experimental psychology.

Ostrom, T. M. (1984). The sovereignty of social cognition. In R. S. Wyer, Jr. & T. K. Srull (Eds.), *Handbook of social cognition* (Vol. 1, pp. 1–38). Hillsdale, NJ: Erlbaum.

Sherman, S. J., Judd, C. M., & Park, B. (1989). Social cognition. *Annual Review of Psychology, 40,* 281–326. Review of social cognition organized by broad principles and cross-cutting specific topic areas.

Smith, E. R. (1994). Attribution theory and research: Returning to Heider's conceptions. In P. G. Devine, D. L. Hamilton, & T. M. Ostrom (Eds.), *Social cognition: Its impact on social psychology* (pp. 77–108). Orlando, FL: Academic Press.

Wyer, R. S., & Carlston, D. E. (1979). *Social cognition, infer-*

ence, and attribution. Hillsdale, NJ: Erlbaum. An important early model of memory and social judgment processes.

Wyer, R. S., & Srull, T. K. (Eds.). (1984). *Handbook of social cognition.* Hillsdale, NJ: Erlbaum.

Wyer, R. S., & Srull, T. K. (1989). *Memory and cognition in its social context.* Hillsdale, NJ: Erlbaum. An influential general theory of memory and social judgment processes.

Wyer, R. S., & Srull, T. K. (Eds.). (1994). *Handbook of social cognition* (2nd ed.). Hillsdale, NJ: Erlbaum. The second edition reflects a shift from youthful enthusiasm to full maturity of social cognition.

Eliot R. Smith

SOCIAL-COGNITIVE THEORY explains human functioning in terms of triadic reciprocal causation. In this transactional view of self and society, internal personal factors in the form of cognitive, affective, and biological events, behavior, and environmental events all operate as interacting determinants that influence one another bidirectionally. Persons are characterized within this theoretical perspective in terms of a number of basic capabilities.

Symbolizing Capability

Social-cognitive theory assigns a central role to cognitive, vicarious, self-regulatory, and self-reflective processes in human development and functioning. The extraordinary capacity to represent events and their relationships in symbolic form provides humans with a powerful tool for comprehending their environment and for creating and managing environmental conditions that touch virtually every aspect of their lives.

Most environmental events exert their effects through cognitive processes rather than directly. Cognitive factors partly determine which environmental events are observed, what meaning is conferred on them, what emotional impact and motivating power they have, and how the information they convey is organized and preserved for future use. Through the medium of symbols people transform transient experiences into cognitive models that serve as guides for reasoning and action. By symbolizing their experiences, people give structure, meaning, and continuity to them.

People gain understanding and expand their knowledge by operating symbolically on the wealth of information derived from personal and vicarious experiences. They generate alternative solutions to problems, evaluate their likely outcomes, and pick suitable options without having to go through a laborious behavioral search.

The other distinctive human capabilities are founded on this advanced capacity for symbolization. However, in keeping with the interactional perspective, social-cognitive theory specifies the social origins of thought and the mechanisms through which social factors exert their influence on cognitive functioning.

Vicarious Capability

There are two basic modes of learning. People learn by experiencing the effects of their actions and through the power of social modeling. Natural endowment provides humans with few inborn skills. They must be developed over long periods and altered to fit changing conditions. If knowledge and skills had to be shaped laboriously by response consequences without the benefit of modeled guidance, a culture could never transmit its language, social practices, mores, and adaptive competencies. The tedious and hazardous trial-and-error learning can be cut short by social modeling.

Humans have evolved an advanced capacity for observational learning that enables them to expand their knowledge and competencies rapidly through the information conveyed by the rich variety of models. Virtually all behavioral, cognitive, and affective learning from direct experience can be achieved vicariously by observing people's actions and its consequences for them.

Much human learning occurs either designedly or unintentionally from the models in one's immediate environment. However, a vast amount of knowledge about people, places, and styles of thinking and behaving is gained from the extensive modeling in the symbolic environment of the mass media. Video and computer delivery systems feeding off telecommunications satellites are now rapidly diffusing new ideas, values, and styles of conduct worldwide. Because the symbolic environment occupies a major part of people's lives, the study of human development and acculturation in the electronic era must be broadened to include electronic acculturation. At the societal level, the electronic modes of influence are transforming how social systems operate and serving as a major vehicle for sociopolitical change.

Modeling is not simply a process of response mimicry, as commonly believed. Modeled judgments and actions may differ in specific content while embodying the same rule. For example, a model may deal with moral conflicts that differ widely in content by applying the same moral standard to them. Modeled activities thus convey rules for generative and innovative behavior. Higher level learning is achieved through abstract modeling. Once observers learn the underlying rules, they can generate new behaviors that go beyond what they have seen or heard.

Creativeness rarely springs entirely from individual inventiveness. Rather, modeling plays a prominent role in creativity. By refining preexisting innovations, synthesizing them into new procedures and adding novel elements, something new is created. When exposed to models of differing styles of thinking and behaving, observers vary in what they adopt and thereby create new blends of personal characteristics that differ from the individual models.

In addition to cultivating new competencies, modeling influences can strengthen or weaken behavioral restraints by showing the rewarding and punishing consequences of modeled courses of action. People are easily aroused by modeled emotional expression. They can therefore vicariously acquire attitudes and emotional proclivities toward places, persons, and things that have been associated with modeled fears, likes, and antipathies. And finally, the actions of models serve as social prompts that activate, channel, and support established styles of behavior.

Forethought Capability

Another distinctive human characteristic is the capacity for forethought. It enables people to transcend the dictates of their immediate environment. Most human behavior, being purposive, is regulated by forethought. The future-time perspective manifests itself in many different ways. People set goals for themselves, anticipate the likely consequences of prospective actions, and plan courses of action that are likely to produce desired outcomes and avoid detrimental ones. Through exercise of forethought, people motivate themselves and guide their actions anticipatorily. When projected over a long time course on matters of value, a forethoughtful perspective provides direction, coherence, and meaning to one's life.

Future events cannot be causes of current motivation and action because they have no actual existence. However, by being represented cognitively in the present, foreseeable future events are converted into current motivators and regulators of behavior.

People guide their behavior partly by its anticipated effects. Courses of action that are likely to produce positive outcomes are readily adopted and used; those that bring unrewarding or punishing outcomes are generally discarded. However, external consequences are not the only kind of outcomes that influence human behavior. People profit from the successes and mistakes of others, as well as from their own experiences. Observed outcomes exert their influence through the perception that one is likely to experience similar outcomes from similar actions and that one possesses the capabilities to achieve similar performances.

Because outcomes exert their influence through forethought, they have little or no behavioral or motivational impact until people discover how outcomes are linked to actions in their environment. This is no easy matter. In everyday life, actions usually produce mixed effects; the outcomes may occur immediately or be far removed in time; the same behavior may have different effects depending on where, when, and toward whom it is performed; and many situational factors influence behavioral outcomes. Such causal ambiguity provides a fertile ground for misjudgment.

Self-Regulatory Capability

People are not just knowers and performers guided by outcome expectations; they are also self-reactors with a capacity for self-direction. Successful development requires the substitution of self-regulation for external sanctions and demands. Once the capability for self-direction is developed, self-demands and self-sanctions serve as major guides, motivators, and deterrents. [*See* Self-Regulation.]

The self-regulation of motivation, affect, and action operates partly through internal standards and evaluative reactions to one's own behavior. The anticipated self-satisfaction gained from fulfilling valued standards and self-dissatisfaction with substandard performances serve as incentive motivators for personal accomplishments. The motivational effects do not stem from the standards themselves but from the evaluative reactions to one's own behavior.

Most theories of self-regulation are founded on a negative feedback system in which people strive to reduce disparities between their perceived performance and an adopted standard. But discrepancy reduction is only half the story. People are proactive, aspiring organisms. They motivate and guide their actions by creating discrepancies for themselves, by forming challenging goals and then mobilizing their resources, skills, and efforts to fulfill them.

In personal development and achievement strivings, internal standards become higher as knowledge and competencies are mastered. In social and moral conduct, people do not change quickly or easily what they regard as right or wrong or good or bad. After they adopt a standard of morality, their self-censure for conduct that violates their personal standards serves as the regulatory influence.

Moral standards do not function as invariant internal regulators of conduct. Self-regulatory mechanisms do not operate unless they are activated, and there are many psychosocial processes by which they can be selectively disengaged. The processes by which moral self-sanctions can be disengaged from inhumane conduct are by portraying such conduct as serving social and moral purposes, by contrasting it with worse inhumanities, by masking reprehensible activities or conferring respectable status upon them through sanitizing language, by displacing or diffusing responsibility for detrimental conduct, by disregarding or distorting the consequences of action, and by blaming and dehumanizing victims. Through selective disengagement of moral agency, people who behave righteously and compassionately in many spheres of their lives perpetrate illegalities and inhumanities in other areas.

Self-Reflective Capability

The capability to reflect upon oneself and the adequacy of one's thoughts and actions is another distinctly human attribute that figures prominently in social-cognitive theory. People are not only agents of action but self-examiners of their own functioning. Effective functioning requires reliable ways of distinguishing between accurate and faulty thinking. In verifying the adequacy of thought by self-reflective means, people generate ideas and act upon them or predict occurrences from them. They then judge the accuracy and functional value of their thinking from the results and use them to improve their thinking if necessary.

The verification process involves comparing how well one's thoughts match some indicator of reality. There are four modes of thought verification: enactive, vicarious, persuasory, and logical. Enactive verification relies on the closeness of the fit between one's thoughts and the results of the action they spawn. In the vicarious mode of thought verification, seeing the effects of other people's actions provides the check on the correctness of one's own thinking. When experiential verification is difficult or unfeasible, persuasory verification can occur, with people evaluating the soundness of their views by checking them against what others believe. In logical verification people can check for fallacies in their thinking by deducing from knowledge that is known and what necessarily follows from it.

These types of metacognitive activities help to promote veridical thought. But they can produce erroneous thinking as well if reality indicants are faulty. Forceful actions arising from erroneous beliefs can create social environments that confirm the misbeliefs. We are all familiar with unpleasant individuals who, through their aversive behavior, breed negative social climates wherever they go. Distorted media versions of reality can foster shared misconceptions of people, places, or things. Social verification can foster bizarre views if the people with whom one affiliates espouse peculiar beliefs. Deductive reasoning can lead one astray if the knowledge on which it is based is faulty or if biases intrude on reasoning processes.

Among the various types of self-referent thoughts, none is more central or pervasive than people's beliefs in their capabilities to exercise control over events that affect their lives. Beliefs of personal efficacy are the foundation of human agency. Unless people believe they can produce desired results by their actions, they have little incentive to act. It affects how they think, feel, act, and motivate themselves. Specifically, such beliefs regulate what people choose to do, how much effort they invest in what they undertake, how long they persevere in the face of obstacles and failure experiences, whether their thought patterns are self-hindering or self-enhancing, how much stress and despondency they experience in coping with taxing situations, and their resilience to adversity. A high sense of personal efficacy pays off in performance accomplishments and emotional well-being. In group endeavors, people's shared beliefs in their collective efficacy affect the type of futures they seek to achieve and how much they accomplish as a group.

The Nature of Human Nature

Human nature is a vast potentiality that can be developed by direct and vicarious experience into a variety of forms within biological limits. Most human competencies are heavily dependent on experience. This accounts for people's extraordinary adaptability and diversity. The endowed plasticity that is intrinsic to the nature of humans depends upon specialized neurophysiological mechanisms and structures that have evolved over time. These advanced neural systems, which are specialized for processing, retaining, and using coded information, provide the capacity for the very characteristics that are distinctly human—generative symbolization, symbolic communication, forethought, evaluative self-regulation, and reflective self-consciousness.

The human qualities that are cultivated and the life paths that become open to members of a society are partly determined by the cultural agencies to which their development is entrusted. Social systems that cultivate competencies, create opportunity structures, provide adequate resources, and permit leeway to develop diverse aspects of personal potentialities increase the likelihood that people will realize what they wish to become.

[*See also* Learning Theories.]

Bibliography

Bandura, A. (1986). *Social foundations of thought and action: A social cognitive theory.* Englewood Cliffs, NJ: Prentice Hall.

Bandura, A. (1991). Social cognitive theory of moral thought and action. In W. M. Kurtines & J. L. Gewirtz (Eds.), *Handbook of moral behavior and development: Theory, research and applications* (Vol. 1, pp. 71–129). Hillsdale, NJ: Erlbaum.

Bandura, A. (Ed.). (1995). *Self-efficacy in changing societies.* New York: Cambridge University Press.

Bandura, A. (1997). *Self-efficacy: The exercise of control.* New York: Freeman.

Cervone, D., & Williams, S. L. (1992). Social cognitive theory and personality. In G. V. Caprara & G. L. Van Heck (Eds.), *Modern personality psychology: Critical reviews and new directions* (pp. 200–252). New York: Wheatsheaf.

Locke, E. A., & Latham, G. P. (1990). *A theory of goal setting and task performance.* Englewood Cliffs, NJ: Prentice Hall.

Maddux, J. E. (Ed.). (1995). *Self-efficacy, adaptation, and adjustment: Theory, research and application.* New York: Plenum Press.

Rogers, E. M. (1982). *Diffusion of innovations* (3rd ed.). New York: Free Press.

Rosenthal, T. L. (1984). Cognitive social learning theory. In N. S. Endler & J. M. Hunt (Eds.), *Personality and the behavioral disorders* (2nd ed., Vol. 2, pp. 113–145). New York: Wiley.

Rosenthal, T. L., & Zimmerman, B. J. (1978). *Social learning and cognition.* New York: Academic Press.

Rotter, J. B. (1954). *Social learning and clinical psychology.* New York: Prentice Hall.

Schwarzer, R. (Ed.). (1992). *Self-efficacy: Thought control of action.* Washington, DC: Hemisphere.

Zimmerman, B. J., & Schunk, D. H. (Eds.). (1989). *Self-regulated learning and academic achievement: Theory, research, and practice.* New York: Springer-Verlag.

Albert Bandura

SOCIAL COMPARISON involves thinking about information concerning one or more other people in relation to the self. Drawing on his own earlier research on level of aspiration and on group processes, as well as research on reference groups, Leon Festinger in "A Theory of Social Comparison Processes" (*Human Relations*, 1954, *7*, pp. 117–140) proposed that humans have a drive to evaluate their opinions and abilities, and that when objective standards for self-evaluation are unavailable, they compare themselves with other people, preferably others who are similar to themselves.

Festinger's theory has been applied beyond opinions and abilities to emotions and to all kinds of personal attributes. Although Festinger devoted much of his theory to interpersonal processes (e.g., the need for similar others leads to pressures toward uniformity in groups), subsequent research has focused largely on the individual's selections of comparison targets and less on the individual's reactions to comparisons.

Who Is a Relevant Comparison Target?

The question of what constitutes a relevant comparison target has bedeviled researchers since the theory's inception. Festinger's similarity hypothesis was ambiguous as to whether similarity is defined in terms of the dimension under evaluation or in terms of other dimensions. For example, chefs may compare their cooking ability with those of others who are similar in their cooking ability, or with others who are similar in more general ways, such as the cooking school attended or gender. Goethals and Darley (1977) drew upon attribution theory to propose that the most meaningful comparisons occur with others who are similar in attributes related to the dimension under evaluation. Chefs can best evaluate their cooking ability if they compare themselves with chefs who have been cooking for about the same amount of time and who prepare the same types of cuisines.

Considerable evidence has attested to the importance of related attributes. It is perplexing, however, that the dimensions of similarity need not always be related to the dimension under evaluation to be relevant. For example, people often compare themselves with same-sex others, even if the dimension of comparison has little to do with gender. Similarly, the effects of comparisons are especially strong when they are with others who are similar, even if the dimension of similarity seems to bear no relation to the dimension of comparison (for example, comparisons with friends are more potent than comparisons with strangers).

Recent efforts to resolve such puzzles have focused on the question that the individual is seeking an answer to, such as, "What kind of person am I?" or "Can I accomplish this task?"

Goals and the Selection of Comparison Targets

A great deal of research has focused on how goals guide the selection of comparison targets. In the 1980s, researchers increasingly viewed the individual not as an unbiased self-evaluator but as a person with needs to reduce threats and to feel good about him- or herself. Wills (*Psychological Bulletin*, 1981, *90*, 245–271) proposed a theory of downward comparison, according to which people who are low in subjective well-being seek to feel better by comparing themselves with others who are less fortunate or who are inferior to themselves.

This theory sparked a shift toward field research, and considerable evidence of downward comparisons has emerged from diverse victimized samples. Recently, however, downward comparison theory has been challenged by a critique of the methods used (Wheeler & Miyake, *Journal of Personality and Social Psychology*, 1992, *62*, 760–773), by the identification of conditions under which downward comparisons are not self-enhancing, and by the recognition that upward comparisons—comparisons with others who are superior—also can be self-enhancing (Collins, *Psychological Bulletin*, 1996, *119*, 51–69).

More generally, the traditional view that self-evaluative motives lead to comparisons with similar others, self-improvement motives lead to upward comparisons, and self-enhancement motives lead to downward comparisons, is giving way to the view that multiple targets can serve one's goal, depending on the comparison context. Individuals also may use comparison strategies that do not involve target selection, such as carefully selecting one's comparison dimensions or avoiding comparisons altogether. Some researchers have even argued that people may create imaginary comparison targets. This view turns the original theory on its head; whereas

Festinger viewed the individual as seeking comparisons to establish reality, this view holds that the individual fabricates reality to serve his or her goals. However, this view is by no means universally accepted and, regardless of whether empirical evidence will support it, it is likely that the vast majority of comparisons occur with real people one contacts in everyday life.

Effects of Social Comparisons

The prevailing assumption has been that upward comparisons make people feel worse about themselves and that downward comparisons make them feel better, but recent studies suggest that both types of comparisons can be dispiriting or self-enhancing. What determines the impact of comparisons? An important variable identified by Tesser (in Suls & Miller, 1977) is whether the comparison involves a dimension that is central to one's self-definition. For example, a chef may take pride in her brother's superior musical ability but be demoralized by his superior cooking ability. Additional factors include whether one believes one will improve or worsen on the dimension of comparison. If one thinks one will improve, upward comparisons may be inspiring rather than demoralizing, and if one fears one will worsen, downward comparisons may be frightening rather than self-enhancing.

Measurement Issues

Social comparison has been operationalized in many ways, including the choice of another person's score to see, the desire to affiliate, self-reports of past comparisons, the effects of comparisons on mood and self-evaluation, and ratings of self versus others. These operationalizations have yielded results that do not always converge. Certain characteristics of comparisons may threaten the validity of some operationalizations; comparisons may be automatic, perhaps even outside of awareness, and inhibited by social desirability concerns. In addition, these operationalizations may capture different meanings of social comparison. Some disagreement exists about what social comparison is (Wood, *Personality and Social Psychology Bulletin*, 1996, *22*, 520–537).

Increasingly, researchers have used methods that are more naturalistic, less constrained, and that offer richer information to research participants than did the early methods of assessing social comparisons.

Bibliography

Goethals, G. R. (1986). Social comparison theory: Psychology from the lost and found. *Personality and Social Psychology Bulletin, 12,* 261–278. Fascinating chronicle of the inconstant history of social comparison research.

Goethals, G. R., & Darley, J. M. (1987). Social comparison theory: Self-evaluation and group life. In B. Mullen & G. R. Goethals (Eds.), *Theories of group behavior* (pp. 21–47). New York: Springer-Verlag. Reviews research on social comparison processes in groups.

Journal of Experimental Social Psychology, Supplement 1. (1966). This supplementary issue was devoted to social comparison research and includes the first empirical studies of the selection of upward and downward comparison targets. The studies primarily employed the rank-order paradigm.

Olson, J. M., Hermann, C. P., & Zanna, M. P. (Eds.). (1986). *Relative deprivation and social comparison: The Ontario Symposium.* Hillsdale, NJ: Erlbaum. Reviews research on relative deprivation, which involves how social comparison processes affect people's feelings of satisfaction and dissatisfaction with their personal outcomes.

Pettigrew, T. F. (1967). Social evaluation theory: Convergences and applications. In D. Levine (Ed.), *Nebraska Symposium on Motivation* (Vol. 15, pp. 241–311). Lincoln: University of Nebraska Press. Sets social comparison theory in the context of other conceptualizations that focus on references to social standards (e.g., adaptation level and reference groups).

Suls, J. M., & R. L. Miller (Eds.). (1977). *Social comparison processes: Theoretical and empirical perspectives.* Washington, DC: Hemisphere. Contributors review the literature from 1954 to the mid 1970s on opinion, ability, and emotion comparisons, and the role of social comparisons in group processes. Especially noteworthy are chapters by Goethals and Darley, Brickman and Bulman, Cottrell and Epley, Suls, and Gruder, and Wheeler and Zuckerman's commentary. Unfortunately, this book, which was pivotal in revitalizing social comparison research in the 1970s, is out of print, but it is widely owned by social psychologists and libraries.

Suls, J., & Wills, T. A. (Eds.). (1991). *Social comparison: Contemporary theory and research.* Hillsdale, NJ: Erlbaum. Contributors reviewed 1980s research, much of which emphasized downward comparisons under threatening conditions. The chapters by Tesser and by Major, Testa, and Bylsma concern determinants of the effects of comparison.

Tajfel, H., & Turner, J. C. (1986). The social identity theory of intergroup behavior. In W. G. Austin & S. Worchel (Eds.), *Psychology of intergroup relations.* Chicago: Nelson-Hall. Presents social identity theory, which emphasizes social comparison processes in intergroup relations.

Wood, J. V. (1989). Theory and research concerning social comparisons of personal attributes. *Psychological Bulletin, 106,* 231–248. Reviews research on comparisons involving abilities and personality characteristics and presents contemporary social comparison theorizing, which integrates insights of social comparison research with research on social cognition and the self.

Joanne V. Wood

SOCIAL COMPETENCE PROGRAMS. Any discussion of social competence programs must first place these interventions in a conceptual and historical context. Many psychologists now agree that good mental health is not simply the absence of maladjustment. That is, the absence of adjustment problems does not mean a person is well adjusted, just as the absence of a physical illness does not mean that a person is physically fit and healthy. Good mental health refers to a variety of positive skills and characteristics associated with successful functioning (Cowen, 1994; Goldfried & D'Zurilla, 1969; Jahoda, 1958). Social competence is one important component of good mental health and refers to one's effectiveness in social situations. This brings us to social competence programs that are interventions designed to promote or improve different types of social competencies.

History

Philosophers, psychologists, and educators have often stressed the importance of social competence, but have not been able to reach a consensus on its definition and major components (Anderson & Messick, 1974). Systematic attempts to enhance social competencies in young children probably began in the United States during the 1920s when visiting teachers (the historical forerunners of school social workers) promoted personal skills by working with individual children, their parents, and teachers. [See Prevention, article on Prevention for School-Aged Children.] Controlled-outcome studies that began appearing in the mid 1950s (e.g., Ojemann, Levitt, Lyle, & Whiteside, 1955) indicated positive effects for school-based social competence programs.

Although there are different conceptualizations of social competence, and interventions vary considerably in their scope and intent, many current programs can be categorized by their general focus on social skills or social-cognitive abilities. A social skill refers to "the ability to interact with others in a given social context in specific ways that are societally acceptable or valued and at the same time personally beneficial, mutually beneficial, or beneficial primarily to others" (Combs & Slaby, 1977, p. 162). The most commonly identified social skills include assertiveness, coping, communication and friendship-making skills, interpersonal problem-solving, and the ability to regulate or modulate one's cognitions, feelings and behaviors, which is alternately referred to as self-control or self-regulation.

Developmental research, initially fueled by Piaget's work on children's cognitive development (Flavell, 1963), has identified a set of important social-cognitive abilities that represent another line of research on social competence. These abilities include such things as social cognition, social sensitivity and judgment, social information processing, and role-taking skills. In general, these social-cognitive abilities refer to how well children and young adolescents can (a) evaluate social situations and determine what is expected or required; (b) accurately recognize the feelings and intentions of others; and, finally, (c) select social behaviors that are most appropriate for that given context (Crick & Dodge, 1994; Holmbeck & Kendall, 1991; Shirk, 1988).

Social competence programs have been applied preventively and therapeutically throughout the life span in a variety of settings. There are examples of social competence programs for children, adolescents, college students, and adults, and interventions have been offered in schools, businesses, nursing homes, and hospitals. Some interventions are offered to normal populations as a strategy in primary prevention. For instance, the expectation is that promoting social competencies should help young people master subsequent developmental tasks and deal more effectively with stress and interpersonal demands. If these goals are achieved, then future adjustment problems should be less likely. Social competence programs have also been used to help individuals of all ages with difficulties such as social isolation, depression, anxiety, various behavioral problems, marital dysfunction, and serious mental illness including schizophrenia. Several sources review social competence interventions (Beelmann, Pfingsten, & Losel, 1994; Benton & Schroeder, 1990; Christopher, Nangle, & Hansen, 1993; Durlak, 1997; Gresham, 1998; Hunter, 1995; L'Abate & Milan, 1985; Kavale, Mathur, Forness, Rutherford, & Quinn, 1997).

Outcomes

There is little disagreement about the potential value of social competence programs. After all, who would object to the notion of trying to help people function more effectively in social situations? Fortunately, outcome research indicates that many social competence programs have been effective, at least in the short term. Several issues have to be resolved, however. Future research needs to determine how mastery of targeted competencies generalizes to other behaviors and settings and to what extent program impact endures over time. There is also the question of whether the intervention produces changes in life adjustment that are practically significant.

What is required and appropriate for effective social functioning is likely to vary across settings, so the interpersonal environment cannot be ignored. Some interventions have successfully raised social competencies by changing the social environment rather than focusing exclusively on individuals. For example, when teachers reorganize their classroom routine, adopt new educational practices, and change their manner of interacting with students, students show not only improved academic performance, but also better social behavior, improved peer relationships, and greater commitment and motivation toward schoolwork (see Durlak, 1997). Therefore, another challenge for social competence interventions is determining how the social environment can be modified effectively so that it works in concert with social competency development. How can we influence government officials, co-workers, supervisors, teachers, peers, family members, and neighbors to promote and support social competencies in different settings?

The final set of questions to be answered regarding social competency interventions involve who, when, what, and how. That is, who should be targeted for intervention, when during the course of their development should interventions be offered, which specific social competencies should be targeted, and how can social competency be developed most efficiently and effectively? Several sources discuss future directions for social competence programs (Beelmann, Pfingsten, & Losel, 1994; Durlak, 1997; Gresham, 1998; Hunter, 1995; La Greca, 1993).

Bibliography

Anderson, S., & Messick, S. (1974). Social competency in young children. *Developmental Psychology, 10,* 282–293. Discusses some problems involved in defining social competency.

Beelmann, A., Pfingsten, J., & Losel, F. (1994). Effects of training social competence in children: A meta-analysis of recent evaluation studies. *Journal of Clinical Child Psychology, 23,* 260–271.

Benton, M. K., & Schroeder, H. E. (1990). Social skills training with schizophrenics: A meta-analytic evaluation. *Journal of Consulting and Clinical Psychology, 58,* 741–747.

Christopher, J. S., Nangle, D. W., & Hansen, D. J. (1993). Social-skills interventions with adolescents. *Behavior Modification, 17,* 314–338.

Combs, M., & Slaby, D. (1977). Social skills training in children. In A. E. Kazdin & B. B. Lahey (Eds.), *Advances in clinical child psychology* (Vol. 1, pp. 161–201). New York: Plenum Press.

Cowen, E. L. (1994). The enhancement of psychological wellness. *American Journal of Community Psychology, 22,* 149–180.

Crick, N. R., & Dodge, K. A. (1994). A review and reformulation of social information-processing mechanisms in children's social adjustment. *Psychological Bulletin, 115,* 74–101. Relates social-cognitive abilities to adjustment.

Durlak, J. A. (1997). *Successful prevention programs for children and adolescents.* New York: Plenum Press. Discusses successful social competence programs in prevention.

Flavell, J. H. (1963). *The developmental psychology of Jean Piaget.* Princeton, NJ: Van Nostrand.

Goldfried, M. R., & D'Zurilla, T. J. (1969). A behavioral-analytic model for assessing competence. In C. D. Spielberger (Ed.), *Current topics in clinical and community psychology* (Vol. 1, pp. 151–196).

Gresham, F. M. (1998). Social skills training with children: Social learning and applied behavioral analytic approaches. In T. S. Wilson & F. M. Gresham (Eds.), *Handbook of child behavior therapy* (pp. 475–497). New York: Plenum Press.

Holmbeck, G. N., & Kendall, P. C. (1991). Clinical-childhood-developmental interface: Implications for treatment. In P. R. Martin (Ed.), *Handbook of behavior therapy and psychological science: An integrative approach* (pp. 73–99). Elmsford, NY: Pergamon Press.

Hunter, R. H. (1995). Benefits of competency-based treatment programs. *American Psychologist, 50,* 509–513.

Jahoda, M. (1958). *Current concepts of positive mental health.* New York: Basic Books.

Kavale, K. A., Mathur, S. R., Forness, S. R., Rutherford, R. B., Jr., & Quinn, M. M. (1997). Effectiveness of social skills training for students with behavior disorders: A meta-analysis. *Advances in Learning and Behavior Disabilities, 11,* 1–26.

L'Abate, L., & Milan, M. A. (1985). *Handbook of social skills training and research.* New York: Wiley. Contains a discussion of social skills programs across a wide range of settings and populations.

La Greca, A. M. (1993). Social skills training with children: Where do we go from here? *Journal of Clinical Child Psychology, 22,* 288–298. Suggests ways to improve social skills interventions.

Ojemann, R. H., Levitt, E. E., Lyle, W. H., & Whiteside, M. F. (1955). The effects of a "causal" teacher-training program and certain curricular changes on grade school children. *Journal of Experimental Education, 24,* 95–114.

Shirk, S. R. (1988). *Cognitive development and child psychotherapy.* New York: Plenum Press.

Joseph A. Durlak

SOCIAL DESIRABILITY (SD) is a response set, one of several tendencies to respond on personality or attitude tests to features of the test or items that are irrelevant to item content and the purpose of the test. [*See* Artifact, *article on* Artifact in Assessment.] Response sets may be induced by the testing situation or by item characteristics that call them forth. They may also represent a disposition of the respondent, consistently expressed in test and other evaluative situations. In this case, the set is a response style. The SD response set is the tendency to choose socially desirable responses irrespective of the content of the items. Thus, "I frequently think of things too bad to talk about" is answered false because it is very undesirable to acknowledge that about oneself. Defined by Lee J. Cronbach (*Educational and Psychological Measurement,* 1946, 6, 475–494), response sets are regarded as threats to the validity of personality tests, since they prevent us from knowing what the response to item content might have been or they may confound a response style with the variable measured by the test.

When Albert Ellis (*Psychological Bulletin,* 1946, 43,

385–440) reviewed personality tests after almost 30 years of use, he found their validity sorely disappointing. For only a few was the evidence more positive than negative, and even the best were weak predictors of behavior. It was evident that the personality test respondent was no psychophysical observer reporting objectively on stimulus experience. The expectation that respondents would—or could—disclose characteristic behavior, feelings, or internal states via test questions had been revealed by validity research as untenable.

The chief threat was quickly understood to be whether respondents portray themselves honestly, and clearly many would not. There was frequent overuse of the "cannot say" option in some tests (true, false, cannot say), and faking good (and sometimes bad) could be shown by simple research designs. Strategies to identify response sets in personality tests were notably unsuccessful until Starke R. Hathaway and J. C. McKinley introduced the empirically devised Minnesota Multiphasic Personality Inventory (MMPI) and its three scales to detect bias—lying (L), defensiveness (K), and invalidating carelessness, scoring error, or frank deviance (F) (*Journal of Psychology*, 1940, *10*, 249–254. [*See* Minnesota Multiphasic Personality Inventory; *and the biography of Hathaway.*] These validity scales were a significant step, but neither wholly solved the problem nor provided a conceptual basis for understanding it.

Subsequently, Allen L. Edwards, in *The Social Desirability Variable in Personality Assessment and Research* (New York, 1957), adopted a new term and approach, the concept and measurement of SD. He proposed that personality questionnaire items may be arrayed on SD, "the most important single dimension on which to locate personality statements." Scaling test items and correlating SD scale values with probability of endorsement resulted in correlations in the range of 0.80 to 0.90 or better. The more socially desirable the item, the higher its likelihood of endorsement; the more undesirable, the lower the endorsement frequency. This was a radical shift in the understanding of personality test responding, from efforts to rid tests of respondent bias to an emphasis on test items themselves and a highly influential attribute. Whatever the test the specific items were drawn from, SD scale values strongly correlated with probability of endorsement.

Edwards drew a heterogeneous sample of MMPI items, submitted them to judges instructed to choose the socially desirable response, and selected those with unanimous judge agreement. These items became the Edwards SD Scale. Correlated with the MMPI and other personality inventories, substantial negative relationships were found: SD was inversely related to scores on measures of variables with invidious implications. The correlations with MMPI scales such as depression, psychasthenia, and schizophrenia, and derived scales like manifest anxiety were so high as to suggest that the assessment of personality by questionnaires was little more than an exercise in the measurement of SD. With the development of the SD scale, Edwards began to argue for individual differences in the tendency to give socially desirably responses. Given the extremely high correlations between the SD scale and other tests, he proposed simply administering the brief measure of SD and predicting the scores the respondent would obtain.

Here, though, was a dead end. An SD response set was indubitably established, but Edwards's approach led only to the conclusion that personality inventories were terminally infected by transparent item SD and by a prevalent disposition to respond desirably in self-characterization. Just how serious a problem this was became evident when Edwards, in *The Measurement of Personality Traits by Scales and Inventories* (New York, 1970), advanced the argument that individual differences in SD constitute a personality trait, one that most personality tests, whatever their intent, actually measure. But a personality trait with what meaning? There was little research on its behavioral correlates, and so the proposition that SD was an expression of personality remained mostly an unsubstantiated claim. However, in *The Challenge of Response Sets* (New York, 1965), Jack Block contended strongly that SD is really ego resiliency, based on the Edwards SD Scale's high loading on the first factor of the MMPI, a factor that reflects this substantive dimension. The scale seems to represent a favorable but not dissimulating bias in self-description, and it correlates positively and substantially with measures related to adjustment.

David Marlowe and I (1960, *Journal of Consulting Psychology, 24,* 349–354) argued that the chief problem was that no real thought had been given to the question of why respondents would base their responses on desirability. Because response sets were such a big nuisance, to be gotten rid of at any cost, few troubled to consider that test-taking itself might reveal personality. We devised an SD scale of items representing either highly desirable claims about oneself or common faults. Consistent endorsement of the desirable and rejection of the undesirable reveals an SD response style. Correlations of the Marlowe-Crowne (MCSD) Scale with clinical and derived scales of the MMPI were significant but moderate, in contrast to those of the Edwards SD scale. A children's version of the MCSD scale has been developed by Virginia C. Crandall, Vaughn J. Crandall, and Walter Katkovsky (*Journal of Consulting Psychology,* 1965, *29,* 27–36).

A series of experiments (Crowne & Marlowe, 1964) showed that the MCSD scale was related to conformity, compliance, and susceptibility to social influence, implicating a need for approval as the motive for the response style. Additional experiments showed seeking approval to involve inhibition of aggression, defensiveness, and self-protection.

Several other SD scales have been developed: the Balanced Inventory of Desirable Responding (BIDR); Responding Desirably on Attitudes and Opinions (RD-16); the California Psychological Inventory (CPI) Good Impression (Gi) scale; SD, a favorable impression scale; and there are other, less well studied scales. They are reviewed by Delroy L. Paulhus in *Measures of Personality and Social Psychological Attitudes*, J. P. Robinson, P. R. Shaver, and L. S. Wrightsman, Eds., San Diego, 1991; as he notes, statistical analyses of these and other SD scales reveal two factors: self-deception and impression management. The Edwards SD Scale loads highly on self-deception, the MCSD on both but more highly on impression management. The major personality inventories all employ SD scales, but since these SD measures were specifically devised and validated for each individual inventory, they generally will not find independent use. The Paulhus review also outlines methods to minimize or eliminate the influence of SD in personality and attitude measurement.

Removing SD does not always enhance the discriminant validity of personality measures. As Paulhus notes, it is usual to find that trying to eliminate SD diminishes the validity of the personality measures with which it is correlated. Investigators must understand the conceptual relation between SD and their personality measures before attempting to remove what may only appear to be an SD confound. A major conclusion to be drawn is that while we know a great deal about SD and its measurement, dimensionality, and correlations with personality and attitude scales, we still know relatively little about its motivational bases and how they may be evoked in test and other evaluative situations.

[*See also* Artifact, *article on* Artifact in Assessment.]

Bibliography

Crowne, D. P. (1979). *The experimental study of personality*. Hillsdale, NJ: Erlbaum. Chapter 6 (pp. 153–183) is a brief review of the development of the MCSD scale and studies of construct validity establishing the motive for approval and defensiveness in its interpretation. Studies of the development of approval dependence in children are presented.

Crowne, D. P., & Marlowe, D. (1964). *The approval motive: Studies in evaluative dependence*. New York: Wiley. Includes the development of the MCSD scale, a motive-based analysis of the testing situation, and the major construct validity studies of the need for approval.

Jackson, D. N., & Messick, S. J. (1958). Content and style in personality assessment. *Psychological Bulletin, 55*, 243–252. A thoughtful analysis of the stylistic properties of personality test items and of the expression personality styles that may mask item content.

Douglas P. Crowne

SOCIAL DISTANCE is the perceived distance between individuals or groups. Bogardus (1928) developed a scale to measure it that included statements such as "I would marry this person" (minimal distance) and "I would exclude this person from the country." He showed that in the 1920s American samples showed considerable distance toward people of different nationalities and races, accepting with very small distances only those who came from Canada and Northern Europe.

Triandis and Triandis (1960) developed a social distance scale by starting with 60 statements and standardizing them with the Thurstone method of successive intervals, which results in an equal-interval scale. The Thurstone method rejects ambiguous statements, and it results in scale values for each of the good statements. The statement that had the lowest scale value was given an arbitrary score of zero and the one with the highest value a score of 100. The remaining statements had intermediate scale values. For instance, American judges provided a scale value of 11.1 for "I would accept this person as an intimate friend"; Greek judges provided a scale value of 13.5 for "I would accept this person as a best friend." "I would accept this person as my family's friend" had a scale value of 40.9 for American judges and 24.0 for Greek judges, suggesting that the Greek judges saw these statements as corresponding to smaller social distance than did the American judges. Thus local standardizations of statements that are frequently made by members of each culture resulted in scales that were culturally sensitive but also provided equivalent measurement.

Sociometric methods, such as "tell me who among the members of this classroom would you like to go on a trip with" also provide measurements of social distance. Those who are overchosen (sociometric stars) experience small distances from their peers, while those who are underchosen experience large distances.

Small social distance is related to willingness to have intimate relationships with a person or member of a group. Mutual attraction also corresponds to small social distance. Judgments of liking of a person or group correspond to judgments of small social distance toward these stimuli.

Research on social distance generally shows that cultures have specific norms about the degrees of social distance that are "appropriate" for members of the culture to show in relation to various types of individuals and groups.

The specific behaviors that correspond to large distances are also culture-specific. For instance, in India, where ritual pollution is an important issue, "touching" is a much more critical behavior than it is in the United States, where behaviors such as "acceptance in my club" are more diagnostic.

The research by Triandis and Triandis (1962) found

that American samples had much social distance toward those of a different race, social class, and religion than themselves, while Greek samples had most social distance toward those of a different nationality and religion. Triandis, Davis, and Takezawa (1965) found that Germans emphasized social class, religion, and race, in that order, and nationality was emphasized minimally, while Japanese emphasized social class, race, and nationality; religion was not important.

Persons who believe that they will be rejected if they do not follow societal norms are especially likely to show large social distances to stimulus persons who are considered socially undesirable in their culture. Also, those who are authoritarian show larger distances to a wide range of stimulus persons than those who are low on this trait.

Bibliography

Bogardus, E. S. (1928). *Immigration and race attitudes.* Boston: Heath.

Triandis, H. C., & Triandis, L. M. (1960). Race, social class, religion, and nationality as determinants of social distance. *Journal of Abnormal and Social Psychology, 61,* 110–118.

Triandis, H. C., & Triandis, L. M. (1962). A cross-cultural study of social distance. *Psychological Monographs, 76* (No. 540, 1–21).

Triandis, H. C., Davis, E. E., & Takezawa, S-I. (1965). Some determinants of social distance among American, German, and Japanese students. *Journal of Personality and Social Psychology, 2,* 540–551.

Harry C. Triandis

SOCIAL EXCHANGE THEORY. *See* Interdependence, *article on* Interdependence Theory.

SOCIAL FACILITATION. In 1924, Floyd Allport offered a stimulus-response account of social psychology. Allport maintained that a response called forth by a nonsocial stimulus could be augmented by an incidental social stimulus. He called this contributory stimulus effect *social facilitation.* Allport reported experiments on the social facilitation of Harvard students' task performance by the sight and sound of other students. These early research participants multiplied numbers more quickly, generated word associations more quickly, and cancelled vowels more quickly when others were present than when they were not. Contemporary psychologists use the term *social facilitation* to designate any effect of the presence of others on an individual's task performance. [*See the biography of Floyd Henry Allport.*]

Two experimental paradigms have been used to study social facilitation. In the audience paradigm, research participants perform a task in front of spectators. In the coaction paradigm, they perform a task alongside others who are performing the same task. Although for purposes of comparison both of these paradigms feature a condition in which research participants perform the experimental task "alone," the validity of this control condition is often compromised. In many studies, individuals who are said to be performing a task "alone" are, in fact, in front of an experimenter. In such cases, the effects of others' presence may be difficult to discern.

Social facilitation had been documented by the late 1800s. Perusing records of bicycle races, Norman Triplett noted in 1898 that cyclists race more quickly when riding alongside competitors than when riding alone. To determine the generality of this effect, Triplett conducted an experiment in which schoolchildren turned fishing reels alone and in the presence of a coacting peer. Faster reel turning was observed when the peer was present. Although this 1898 study has been dubbed the first experiment in social psychology, it may not deserve that title. Triplett himself cited earlier (if less well-controlled) experiments on the effects of others' presence by the French scholar Manouvrier.

Social facilitation has been observed in many species. Cockroaches run more quickly when running beside other cockroaches; goldfish eat more food when feeding beside other goldfish; birds build nests more vigorously when other birds are nearby. As social psychologists have puzzled over the effects on humans of the presence of other people, biologically oriented psychologists have analyzed animal social facilitation.

In a way, the term *social facilitation* is misleading. If on occasion the presence of others facilitates an individual's task performance, as Triplett and Allport observed, performance is also often impaired by the presence of others, as when a spectator's presence impedes verbal memorization (Pessin, 1933). When is performance facilitated by the presence of others, and when is it impaired? Pondering this question in 1965, Robert Zajonc claimed that the impact of others' presence depends on the complexity of the performer's task. According to Zajonc, the presence of others functions to facilitate the performance of simple tasks and to impair the performance of complex tasks. Although verifying the importance of task complexity, subsequent research has shown that the social impairment of complex tasks is stronger than the social facilitation of simple tasks. Indeed, the accumulated results of 241 human "social facilitation" experiments led meta-analysts Charles Bond and Linda Titus (1983) to wonder whether the presence of others ever, in fact, facilitates performance quality.

Psychologists have constructed theories of social facilitation, with Robert Zajonc (1980) proposing the best known theory. According to Zajonc, the presence of others increases an individual's level of generalized drive. Generalized drive, as neobehaviorists Clark Hull and Kurt Spence (1956) claimed, functions to enhance an individual's dominant response tendency to the exclusion of competing tendencies. Theoretically, the impact of the presence of others on the performance of a task should depend on individuals' dominant response tendency when attempting that task. On simple tasks, the dominant tendency is to perform correctly, and the presence of others should facilitate performance. On complex tasks, the dominant tendency is to perform incorrectly, and the presence of others should impair performance.

Zajonc's theory rejuvenated the study of social facilitation. Many experiments were designed to test the theory, and most of the evidence was seen as supportive. When the presence of others occasioned mistakes in motor learning, caused errors in athletic performance, and influenced respondents' answers to word association tests, researchers invoked drive theory explanations. There was controversy, however, about the source of the socially induced drive. Zajonc attributed drive to the unpredictability of social stimuli and to the individual's need, in the presence of others, to be prepared for the unexpected. Psychologist Nickolas Cottrell (1972), by contrast, believed that drive reflected the individual's tendency to associate positive and negative outcomes with the presence of others.

All psychologists would agree that positive and negative outcomes may be associated with the presence of others. Many have wondered, however, whether the mere presence of others is sufficient to influence individual task performance, irrespective of this allied effect. In an experimental pursuit of mere presence, some memorable studies have been conducted. Rats have been fed in the presence of anesthetized rats; chickens have pecked at corn alongside dead chickens; undergraduates have traced spatial mazes in front of blindfolded mannequins. Results suggest that these merely present others can sometimes influence the individual, and many have regarded mere presence effects to be theoretically decisive. They reason, for example, that Cottrell's analysis of social facilitation is discredited because performance facilitations can be caused by others who are in no position to administer positive or negative outcomes (Zajonc, 1980). More recently, the theoretical significance of mere presence effects has been questioned. Robert S. Baron (1986) argued that if an individual learns to associate positive and negative outcomes with the presence of others, then others' mere presence might become a conditioned stimulus for those outcomes. From his perspective, mere presence effects are merely conditioned responses. No doubt there will be continuing debate about the minimal sufficient social stimulus.

Psychologists have proposed alternatives to the drive theory of social facilitation. A self-presentational analysis (Bond, 1982) attributes the social facilitation of task performance to the performer's instrumental regulation of a public image and social impairment to embarrassment following a loss of public esteem. Theoretically, performers lose esteem when they make mistakes on complex tasks. Self-awareness theories (Carver & Scheir, 1981) claim that the presence of others prompts individuals to compare their task performance to a situated standard. These self-evaluations may motivate performance facilitation or prompt withdrawal from the task, depending on the outcome of the evaluation. Expectations for task performance play a crucial role in a self-efficacy theory of social facilitation (Sanna, 1992). Attentional conflict has been emphasized in an influential distraction-conflict theory (Baron, 1986). The ability to visually monitor others' reactions is vital (Guerin, 1993). Social facilitation, a 100-year-old topic, continues to inspire psychologists.

Bibliography

Baron, R. S. (1986). Distraction-conflict theory: Progress and problems. In L. Berkowitz (Ed.), *Advances in experimental social psychology* (Vol. 19, pp. 1–40). New York: Academic Press. Emphasizes the impact of distraction on social facilitation.

Bond, C. F., Jr. (1982). Social facilitation: A self-presentational view. *Journal of Personality and Social Psychology*, *42*, 1042–1050.

Bond, C. F., Jr., & Titus, L. J. (1983). Social facilitation: A meta-analysis of 241 studies. *Psychological Bulletin*, *94*, 265–292. A comprehensive quantitative review of human social facilitation.

Carver, C. S., & Scheier, M. F. (1981). The self-attention-induced feedback loop and social facilitation. *Journal of Experimental Social Psychology*, *17*, 545–568.

Clayton, D. A. (1978). Socially facilitated behavior. *Quarterly Journal of Biology*, *53*, 373–392. Reviews research on animal coaction.

Cottrell, N. B. (1972). Social facilitation. In C. G. McClintock (Ed.), *Experimental social psychology* (pp. 185–236). New York: Holt, Rinehart, & Winston. A thorough exposition of the drive theory of social facilitation.

Dashiell, J. F. (1935). Experimental studies of the influence of social situations on the behavior of individual human adults. In Carl Murchison (Ed.), *A handbook of social psychology* (pp. 1097–1158). Worcester, MA: Clark University Press. Insightful review of the older literature. Clarifies the role of social facilitation in the history of experimental social psychology.

Guerin, B. (1993). *Social facilitation*. Paris: Cambridge University Press. Concludes from a critical literature review that the individual is most strongly influenced by others who cannot be visually monitored.

Paulus, P. B. (1983). Group influence on individual task performance. In P. B. Paulus (Ed.), *Basic group processes* (pp. 97–120). New York: Springer-Verlag. Offers a cognitive-motivational model to integrate work on social facilitation, social loafing, and crowding.

Pessin, J. (1933). The comparative effects of social and mechanical stimulation on memorizing. *American Journal of Psychology, 45,* 263–270.

Sanna, L. J. (1992). Self-efficacy theory: Implications for social facilitation and social loafing. *Journal of Personality and Social Psychology, 62,* 774–786.

Simmel, E. C., Hoppe, R. A., & Milton, G. A. (1968). *Social facilitation and imitative behavior*. Boston: Allyn & Bacon. A collection of conference papers that locate social facilitation with respect to several related phenomena: imitation, affiliation, and observational learning.

Spence, K. W. (1956). *Behavior theory and conditioning.* New Haven, CT: Yale University Press.

Zajonc, R. B. (1965). Social facilitation. *Science, 149,* 269–274. A classic reinterpretation of research.

Zajonc, R. B. (1980). Compresence. In P. B. Paulus (Ed.), *Psychology of group influence* (pp. 35–60). Hillsdale, NJ: Erlbaum. Contends that the mere presence of others arouses drive.

Charles F. Bond, Jr.

SOCIAL GERONTOLOGICAL THEORIES. Late-life development in socioemotional domains was presumed for many years to follow the same downward trajectory as cognitive development in later life. Loss was the central theme in nearly all of the theoretical conceptualizations, certainly in prominent models such as disengagement theory (Cumming & Henry, 1961). Even relatively positive models of social aging, such as activity theory (Havighurst & Albrecht, 1953), which placed reasons for decline outside of the individual, focused on societally based losses that place constraints on individuals' efforts to maintain a high quality of life.

Empirical findings from both clinical psychology and life span developmental psychology forced reconsideration of these models. During the 1980s empirical investigations showed reliably that older people were, on average, faring well—even better than their younger counterparts. Such findings fueled reconsideration of social and emotional aging. Despite losses in many domains, most older people maintain good mental health and enjoy important social relationships. Current theories of social and emotional aging address what has come to be known as the "paradox of aging," a phrase that refers to the fact that older people fare well emotionally and socially far into old age. Thus findings from epidemiological and survey studies of mental health inspired scholars to reconsider late-life phenomena as potential growth.

The theme that runs across theoretical models of socioemotional development in later life is one of selection. The model of selective optimization with compensation, developed by Baltes and Baltes (1990), views development essentially as increasingly optimized or expert performance within selected domains. Development at any age cannot occur without selection. All choices people make to pursue expertise in particular domains require the investment of resources that will not be allocated elsewhere.

Virtually every social theory of aging assumes that social relationships are selected as important domains to the very end of life, and some presume tacitly or explicitly that close interpersonal relationships increase in importance in old age. One important conceptual model aimed at understanding dependence in old age, for example, presumes that frail elders rely on others for assistance in part because of the social contact the assistance embodies. This "learned dependency" model is based on a programmatic line of research on dependency in old age that shows that older people who depend on others for assistance have more social contact than those who do not (Baltes, 1996). Thus even reductions in physical autonomy may entail gains in other areas, in this case, social relations.

Socioemotional selectivity theory (Carstensen, 1993), a motivational model of life span development, argues that the selection of goals is influenced by the perception of time. Because chronological age is confounded with mortality, systematic changes in goals unfold across adulthood as people perceive increasingly less time left in life. The theory claims that constraints on time are associated with the prioritization of emotional goals that are typically embedded within emotionally close social relationships. Although socioemotional selectivity theory makes life course predictions, the underlying mechanism—namely, boundaries on time—is presumed to operate throughout adulthood (Carstensen, Isaacowitz, & Charles, 1999).

Other models also suggest that older people are better able to function in social relationships because of developmental changes in which cognitive and emotional processes are better integrated. Among younger people, cognition and emotion oppose each other, making reasoning about socioemotional dilemmas difficult. However, older people, because they integrate emotion into cognition more successfully, are better able to reason about emotional issues. Blanchard-Fields and her colleagues have shown that whereas social problems that are low in emotional salience are solved similarly across age groups, social dilemmas high in emotional salience (e.g., conflict over an unwanted pregnancy) are solved better by older people (Blanchard-Fields, 1986). Labouvie-Vief and her colleagues propose that ego development, which is positively correlated with age, underlies the ability to integrate affective and cognitive processes (Labouvie-Vief, 1997). In the absence of ego development, however, advanced stages of development are unlikely to occur.

Models that posit a relinquishing of goals remain prominent in social theorizing about later life. Schulz and Heckhausen (1996), for example, argue that as people age and the potential to realize primary control over life goals diminishes, an increase in the use of secondary control strategies (e.g., cognitive strategies) serves to protect the motivational system. Brandtstädter and Rothermund (1994) also contend that the lowering of goal standards allows people to adjust psychologically to reduced competence in old age. Both of these models point to ways that motivation may change when instrumental competencies are reduced.

At this point in the field, social theories of late-life development make more specific predictions about socioemotional development. Ryff (1995), for example, considers personal growth within six subdomains, including positive self-regard, mastery, autonomy, positive relationships, a sense of meaning in life, and feelings of continued personal growth. It appears that aging is associated with increased emphasis in some domains, such as personal relationships, and a lessening of emphasis in others, such as mastery.

The field of social gerontology has been driven by empirical attempts to describe older populations more than by attempts to explain them (Bengtson, Burgess, & Parrott, 1997). Yet, as Bengtson and colleagues point out, even data-driven research holds vague and implicit expectations about relationships among variables. The failure to articulate the theoretical presumptions underlying the growing body of empirical findings about social relationships and social interaction in old age has been problematic in the field. Birren and Bengtson's 1988 edition of *Emergent Theories of Aging* helped to make theory building more central in the field, and the second edition that appeared only recently (Bengtson & Schaie, 1999) is expected to move the field further still.

In summary, early theorizing in social gerontology began with relatively negative expectations about social functioning in old age. Models that appeared during the last decade are more positive. While reasons for deterioration in some domains continue to be acknowledged and explicated, views of social and emotional functioning have been better specified. Although theories differ importantly in specific predictions about growth and decline as well as about the reasons for such change, most theoretical models of social aging allow for continued growth well into the later decades of life, particularly in the realm of social relations.

Bibliography

Baltes, M. M. (1996). *The many faces of dependency in old age.* New York: Cambridge University Press.

Baltes, P. B., & Baltes, M. M. (1990). Psychological perspectives on successful aging: The model of selective optimization with compensation. In P. B. Baltes & M. M. Baltes (Eds.), *Successful aging: Perspectives from the behavioral sciences* (pp. 1–34). New York: Cambridge University Press.

Bengtson, V. L., Burgess, E. O., & Parrott, T. M. (1997). Theory, explanation and a third generation of theoretical development in social gerontology. *Journal of Gerontology: Social Sciences, 52,* S72–S88.

Bengtson, V., & Schaie, W. (in press). *Emergent theories of aging* (2nd ed.). New York: Springer-Verlag.

Birren, J., & Bengtson, V. (1988). *Emergent theories of aging.* New York: Springer-Verlag.

Blanchard-Fields, F. (1997). The role of emotion in social cognition across the adult life span. *Annual Review of Gerontology and Geriatrics, 17,* 238–265.

Brandtstädter, J., & Rothermund, K. (1994). Self-percepts of control in middle and later adulthood: Buffering losses by rescaling goals. *Psychology and Aging. 9,* 265–283.

Carstensen, L. L. (1993). Motivation for social contact across the life span: A theory of socioemotional selectivity. In J. Jacobs (Ed.), *Nebraska Symposium on Motivation. Vol. 40: Developmental perspectives on motivation.* (pp. 209–254). Lincoln: University of Nebraska Press.

Carstensen, L. L., Isaacowitz, D., & Charles, S. T. (1999). Taking time seriously: A theory of socioemotional selectivity. *American Psychologist, 54,* 165–181.

Cumming, E., & Henry, W. H. (1961). *Growing old: The process of disengagement.* New York: Basic Books.

Havighurst, R. J., & Albrecht, R. (1953). *Older people.* New York: Longmans.

Labouvie-Vief, G. (1997). Cognitive-emotional integration in adulthood. *Annual Review of Gerontology and Geriatrics, 17,* 206–237.

Ryff, C. (1995). Psychological well-being in adult life. *Current Directions in Psychological Science, 4,* 99–104.

Schulz, R., & Heckhausen, J. (1996). A life-span model of successful aging. *American Psychologist. 51,* 702–714.

Laura L. Carstensen

SOCIAL IDENTITY is most often studied in social psychology and related fields. It is used primarily to refer to aspects of the self-concept that define the individual in terms of his or her social group or category memberships. It is one's self-definition or identity as, for example, American, Black, male, Catholic, a psychologist or, more generally, as "us" versus "them." The term can refer to a specific group membership or to the whole collection of a person's social categorical self-definitions. Nationality, ethnicity, religion, gender, age, class, occupation, language, sexual orientation, and mental and physical disability provide some of the most important bases of social identity, but social identities can also be based on more fleeting, ad hoc, or minimal social criteria.

The notion of social identity as social categorical self-definition derives from research on prejudice and intergroup relations. One classic line of research looks at the problems of self-esteem and maladjustment created by membership in minority groups and socially stigmatized identities. In the 1970s social identity theory employed the concept to explain intergroup discrimination and ethnocentrism. In the 1980s self-categorization theory argued that social identity provides the psychological basis of group formation and belongingness. Social identity in these related theoretical forms is a central concept in research on prejudice, intergroup relations, and group processes.

Social identity theory (H. Tajfel, & J. C. Turner, "An integrative theory of intergroup conflict," in W. G. Austin & S. Worchel, Eds., *The Social Psychology of Intergroup Relations*, Monterey, Calif., 1979) developed to make sense of experimental findings that the social categorization of people into distinct groups under the most minimal conditions is sufficient to cause discrimination favoring the in-group over the out-group (H. Tajfel, C. Flament, M. G. Billig, & R. F. Bundy, *European Journal of Social Psychology*, 1971, *I*, pp. 149–177). It proposes that people define and evaluate themselves in terms of their social group memberships and that they seek a positive social identity by trying to establish positively valued differences between their own and other groups. This core idea is elaborated in the theory to explain a broad range of intergroup behaviors as a function of a variety of real-world conditions. Intergroup attitudes are seen as arising from a complex interaction between people's need for positive social identity and the perceived structure of intergroup relationships in society. Nevertheless, ethnocentrism or ingroup bias, the tendency to judge, evaluate, and act so as to favor one's in-group over an out-group in an apparently unrealistic or unjustifiable way, is still widely seen as an important behavioral manifestation of the need for positive social identity.

Self-categorization theory (J. C. Turner, "Social categorization and the self-concept: A social cognitive theory of group behaviour," in E. J. Lawler, Ed., *Advances in Group Processes*, Vol. 2, Greenwich, Conn., 1985; J. C. Turner, M. A. Hogg, P. J. Oakes, S. D. Reicher, & M. S. Wetherell, *Rediscovering the Social Group: A Self-Categorization Theory*, Oxford, 1987) distinguishes between personal and social identity as different levels of self-categorization. Personal identity refers to self-categories that define the perceiver as a unique individual in contrast to other individuals, the self as "I" and "me." Social identity refers to social categorizations of self and others, self-categories that define the individual in terms of his or her shared similarities with members of certain social categories in contrast to other social categories, the self as "we" and "us." The theory proposes that as the level of self-categorization that is psychologically salient shifts from personal to social identity, self-perception becomes less personalized (i.e., individuated) and more depersonalized (i.e., more social categorical); people tend to see themselves less as individual persons, defined by their personal differences from others, and more as interchangeable representatives of their social group, defined by their intragroup similarities and intergroup differences. The theory argues that collective behavior and group processes depend on the social categorical perception of self and others. For example, the salience of a shared group identity tends to transform personal self-interest ("for me") into collective self-interest ("for us"), leading members to cooperate for common group goals rather than compete for individual advantage. Group behavior is seen to emerge from the capacity of people to categorize the self as a group and not merely as an individual person. The theory has stimulated research on social influence, cooperation, cohesion, crowd behavior, stereotyping, and depersonalization. Its key behavioral manifestations are depersonalization and its consequences. Salient social identity enhances people's perceived similarity to ingroup members, as they define themselves more in terms of the shared attributes of their group and less in terms of their individual differences, and in turn people act more as a group and less as unique persons; they become more cohesive, cooperative, and homogeneous.

A second popular meaning (derived from symbolic interactionism) refers to aspects of one's public self as presented to, perceived by, and reflected in the appraisals of other people (e.g., individuals, groups, society, the "generalized other"). It is the "looking-glass" self or selves, the self that is social because it is derived from or apparent in the reflected appraisals of others. Social identities in this sense are public selves projected in social interaction or internalizations of such public selves. They enact social roles and conform to norms to meet others' expectations and achieve desired outcomes, and contain the internalized reactions, expectations, and judgments of others. There is a wide variety of formulations going back to the beginning of the twentieth century, including more recently Stryker's identity theory ("Identity theory: Developments and extensions," in K. Yardley & T. Honess, Eds., *Self and Identity: Psychosocial Perspectives*, New York, 1987).

Where self-categorization theory distinguishes between personal and social identity and focuses on the social group as a basis for self-definition, the symbolic interactionist tradition contrasts the private and public self and focuses on the enactment of social roles and norms as the basis of the social self. In social interaction people both conform to and act to shape the expectations of others, creating desired impressions and projecting valued identities. The self becomes social, and hence reflexive, through seeing self as others see self and internalizing the reactions of others. In embodying social roles and norms, social identities provide a link between social structure and individual behavior. Research influenced by this tradition implies that our self-concepts are significantly shaped by others' perceived views of us and that much public behavior is more an attempt to present desired social identities to others (and ourselves) than a function of internal and relatively asocial psychological processes.

Both the self-categorical and public identity traditions tend to stress the variety and flexibility of people's identities across different social situations. They tend to see social identities as arising from the interaction of the person with the specific social situation and the person's behavior as being regulated and shaped by the specific identity that is salient. The distinction between people's relatively stable identifications with particular groups and roles and the salience of any social identity in a specific situation is an important one. A group or role may be chronically self-defining across time, but its influence on behavior is a function of its immediate prepotence in self-perception, which reflects varying motives, goals, and circumstances. Nevertheless, researchers in both traditions have explored the role of individual differences in social identity processes (e.g., in collective self-esteem, in-group identification, public versus private self-consciousness) and found it possible to take a more idiographic approach (e.g., K. Deaux, A. Reid, K. Mizrahi, & K. A. Ethier, *Journal of Personality and Social Psychology*, 1995, 68, 280–291). Social identity processes (rather than specific groups and roles) are usually assumed to be universal, but there is likely to be variation both within and between cultures in the degree to which collective or individual selves (social or personal identities) are emphasized.

[*See also* Ethnic and Racial Identity; *and* Identity.]

Bibliography

Deaux, K. (1996). Social identification. In E. T. Higgins & A. Kruglanski (Eds.), *Social psychology: Handbook of basic principles* (pp. 777–798). New York: Guilford Press. Recent summary and discussion of major themes and issues in contemporary research on social identification.

Hogg, M. A., & Abrams, D. (1988). *Social identifications: A social psychology of intergroup relations and group pro-cesses*. London: Routledge. Textbook on social psychology written from the perspective of social identity and self-categorization theories.

Mead, G. H. (1934). *Mind, self, and society*. Chicago: University of Chicago Press. Classic statement of symbolic interactionist view of the self.

Oakes, P. J., Haslam, S. A., & Turner, J. C. (1994). *Stereotyping and social reality*. Oxford: Blackwell. Presents a radically different view of the nature of stereotypes from the traditional picture of rigid, fixed images that distort and over-generalize group members' characteristics in the interests of cognitive economy and prejudice. Argues for the psychological validity of the stereotyping process on the basis of self-categorization theory.

Schlenker, B. R. (1980). *Impression management: The self-concept, social identity, and interpersonal relations*. Monterey, CA: Brooks/Cole. General summary of the impression management view of social identities as public selves projected in social interaction, written at textbook level.

Spears, R., Oakes, P. J., Ellemers, N., & Haslam, S. A. (Eds.). (1997). *The social psychology of stereotyping and group life*. Oxford: Blackwell. Recent collection of articles on different aspects of stereotyping and group behavior heavily influenced by social identity and self-categorization theories. Good overview of social identity perspective on stereotyping in contrast to a more individual-cognitive emphasis.

Stryker, S., & Statham, A. (1985). Symbolic interaction and role theory. In G. Lindzey & E. Aronson (Eds.), *The handbook of social psychology* (Vol. 1, 3rd ed., pp. 311–378). New York: Random House. Thorough, scholarly but difficult review of symbolic interactionist tradition including detailed discussions of the social self.

Tajfel, H. (1981). *Human groups and social categories*. Cambridge, UK: Cambridge University Press. Collection of the most important papers by the main originator of social identity theory.

Turner, J. C. (1982). Towards a cognitive redefinition of the social group. In H. Taijel (Ed.), *Social identity and intergroup relations* (pp. 15–40). Cambridge, UK: Cambridge University Press. First statement of self-categorization theory arguing for the distinction between personal and social identity and that group behavior is (depersonalized) action on the basis of shared social identity.

Turner. J. C. (1996). Henri Tajfel: An introduction. In W. P. Robinson (Ed.), *Social groups and identities: Developing the legacy of Henri Tajfel* (pp. 1–23). Oxford: Butterworth Heinemann. Summarizes the life and work of Henri Tajfel, tracing the intellectual, social and personal currents in his life that gradually led to the evolution of the most influential contemporary perspective on social identity.

John C. Turner

SOCIAL INFLUENCE THEORY is a body of concepts about how one person influences another. Study of social influence in social psychology has its roots in Musafer Sherif's and Solomon Asch's demonstrations that, in groups, individuals' judgments and opinions are influenced by and converge onto the judgments and opinions of others, and Kurt Lewin's concepts of what renders one person responsive to influence from another. Interest in social influence has ebbed and flowed in social psychology throughout its history. From the inception of counseling psychology as a specialty, counseling psychologists have been borrowing concepts from social influence theory to aid understanding of how counselors influence clients in counseling interviews. This effort has come to be called the social influence approach to counseling.

History of the Social Influence Approach

Francis Robinson, a counseling psychologist at the Ohio State University, introduced the idea that the counseling interview could be viewed as an expression of social psychology in his 1955 presidential address to the membership of the American Psychological Association (APA) Division of Counseling Psychology ("The dynamics of communication in counseling," *Journal of Counseling Psychology*, 1955, 2, 163–169). Harold Pepinsky, a contemporary of Robinson at Ohio State University, drew attention to the work of Musafer Sherif and Solomun Asch on conformity and convergence in notes published in 1960 (conformity and deviation, *Journal of Counseling Psychology*, 7, 144–146) and 1963 ("On the utility of bias in treatment," *Journal of Counseling Psychology*, 10, 402–405) and proposed that counseling is another group in which the behaviors of participants converge over time. He suggested that counselors introduce a psychological grammar of belief and ritual that clients come to endorse. He published this thesis in 1964 ("Convergence: A phenomenon in counseling and psychotherapy," *American Psychologist*, 19, 333–338). During this same time, Jerome Frank, who had done graduate work with Kurt Lewin, published his seminal book *Persuasion and Healing* (1961) in which he conceived of psychotherapy as a setting for social influence in which healing is generated through expectancy and belief.

In 1966, Arnold Goldstein argued ("Psychotherapy research by extrapolation from social psychology," *Journal of Counseling Psychology*, 13 (38–45), that ideas and research findings from social psychology could serve as a basis for selecting therapy variables for investigation, predicting their effects, and explaining findings. In 1968, Stanley Strong, then at the University of Minnesota, presented an integrated theory of the factors that affect the ability of counselors to influence clients that organized the results of research on attitude change around concepts drawn from dissonance theory, then the most active area of research and the most accepted theory in social psychology

("Counseling: An interpersonal influence process," *Journal of Counseling Psychology*, 15, 215–224). In collaboration with Lyle Schmidt (a close colleague of Harold Pepinsky, he had just arrived at Minnesota from Ohio State University) Strong generated a series of papers that demonstrated how these social influence factors could be evaluated in counseling-like situations. This combination of theory, method, and demonstration catalyzed the growing interest in social influence in counseling and stimulated hundreds of studies over the next 20 years. In this work, counseling psychologists have drawn on every theory or model of social influence that social psychologists have generated, including the theories of social power, cognitive dissonance, causal attribution, impression management, self-presentation, interpersonal processes, elaboration likelihood, self-efficacy, ethnomethodology, social construction, and discursive psychology.

Major Findings

The major findings in the 40 years of research on social influence factors in counseling are presented in two reviews: "Social Psychology and Counseling Psychology: The History, Products, and Promise of an Interface" (*Journal of Counseling Psychology*, 1992, 39, 139–157) and "Antecedents and Effects of Perceived Therapist Credibility: A Meta-Analysis" (*Journal of Counseling Psychology*, 1996, 43, 430–947), by Stanley Strong and colleagues at Virginia Commonwealth University and William Hoyt at Iowa State University, respectively.

Evidence of Social Influence. Pepinsky and his colleagues Michael Patton (now at the University of Missouri) and Naomi Meara (now at Notre Dame University) explored the notions of psychological grammar and convergence in a series of papers published between 1974 and 1981 (e.g., Meara, N. M., Pepinsky, H. B., Shannon, J. W., & Murray, W. A., "Semantic communication and expectations for counseling across three theoretical orientations," *Journal of Counseling Psychology*, 1981, 28, 110–118). They suggested that the various approaches to counseling and psychotherapy, which differ widely in what they propose as to the aspects of experiences that should be focused on in therapeutic conversations, how events are to be labeled, what is to be construed as the causes of problems, and how therapeutic change is to be understood, be considered treatment policies that counselors use as tools to do counseling. They studied numerous counseling cases using a computerized method of categorizing and analyzing the language usage of counselors and clients in their therapeutic conversations. They showed that the language usage of counselors and clients, including how client experiences were construed, converged in the course of counseling treatment in ways consistent with the counselors' treatment policies.

In a series of short-term counseling experiments in

the 1970s and 1980s in which treatment policy and counselor behavior were experimentally controlled, Strong and Charles Claiborn (then at the University of Nebraska) found that clients came to describe their problems and attribute causes for them in the ways their counselors proposed and that the widely different treatment policies that they studied all generated significant symptomatic improvement (e.g., Claiburn, C. D., Ward, S. R., & Strong, S. R., "Effects of convergence between counselor interpretations and client beliefs," *Journal of Counseling Psychology*, 1981, *28*, 101–109).

Stages of the Social Influence Process. In his 1968 formulation, Strong proposed that the influence process in counseling occurred in distinctive stages, an idea further developed by Strong and Claiborn in their book *Change through Interaction* (New York, 1982) and by Terrence Tracey, at the University of Illinois ("The Stages of Influence in Counseling and Psychotherapy," in F. Dorn, Ed., *The Social Influence Process in Counseling and Psychotherapy*, Springfield, Ill., 1986). The stage theory of influence proposes that counseling relationships begin with a period when there is a high level of agreeableness between counselor and client, during which time the counselor seeks to gain an understanding of the client's problem and to enhance the client's receptivity to influence. A second stage emerges as the counselor initiates efforts to influence the client in ways the counselor's treatment policy proposes will be helpful, efforts that introduce discord into the exchange. Finally, harmony reemerges as the client accepts the counselor's proposals and thus converges onto the psychological grammar of the counselor's treatment policy. To study this hypothesis, investigators have classified counselor and client utterances using rating schemes that allow an estimate of the degree of congruence (complementarity or accord) expressed by the relation of each utterance to its predecessor in the interview stream. In two well-executed studies, Tracey found that successful counseling treatments demonstrate the accord–discord–accord pattern over time while unsuccessful treatments do not, a finding corroborated in other studies.

Credibility and Change. Social influence theory proposes that clients' perceptions of their counselors as credible sources of information about their problems render clients responsive to counselors' efforts to influence them and thus are crucial to the success of counseling. In his 1968 paper, Strong proposed an array of cues that he hypothesized would affect clients' views of counselors' credibility (credibility was conceptualized in three components: expertness, trustworthiness, and attractiveness). Using meta-analysis, William Hoyt (1996) evaluated the relations among cues, credibility, and influence in terms of the effect sizes reported in the nearly 200 published studies of these relations. He

found that the relations among these variables were robust and much as Strong had proposed. Clearly, however, the most important source of counselor credibility is an entitlement that flows from counselors' socially sanctioned role as sources of help for personal and interpersonal difficulties.

Studies of outcomes of both laboratory-based short-term counseling experiments and counseling treatments in the field have shown consistently that perceptions of counselor credibility early in treatment significantly predict the degree of success of the treatment and that credibility assessments later in the process are even more strongly related to outcomes. The results of a number of studies, especially one by P. Paul Heppner and Martin Heesacker ("Perceived counselor characteristics, client expectations, and client satisfaction with counseling," *Journal of Counseling Psychology*, 1983, *30*, 31–39) suggest that clients continually reassess the credibility of their counselors during counseling and that unsatisfactory outcomes are associated with patterns of declining client judgments of their counselor's expertise and counselor reports that their clients are unresponsive to their attempts to help.

Present Status

The social influence approach to counseling was a vibrant source of ideas and empirical work for 40 years, after which the pace of work greatly slowed. Many of the propositions of the early formulations received solid empirical validation and, perhaps for this reason, lost their ability to inspire new empirical work. New conceptual work in the area went in two directions. One thrust had a distinctively cognitive cast and for the most part addressed what is influenced in counseling as opposed to the process of influence. This thrust is exemplified by two papers on the social-counseling interface listed in the bibliography: Heesacker and Carroll (1997) and Stoltenberg, McNeill, and Elliott (1995). Another strand of current conceptual work attempts to recast social influence in constructionist and discursive terms, exemplified by James Reed, Michael Patton, and Paul Gold ("Effects of turn-taking sequences in vocational test interpretation interviews," *Journal of Counseling Psychology*, 1993, *40*, 144–155) and Strong, Yoder, and Corcoran (1995).

[*See also* Social Psychology.]

Bibliography

Dorn, F. J. C. (Ed.). (1986). *The social influence process in counseling and psychotherapy*. Springfield, IL: Thomas. A collection of papers written by most of the primary contributors to the social influence approach in counseling psychology.

Goldstein, A. P., Heller, K., & Sechrest, L. B. (1966). *Psy-*

chotherapy and the psychology of behavior change. New York: Wiley. The early definitive work on the possibilities of extrapolation from social psychology to clinical/counseling psychology.

Heesacker, M., & Carroll, T. A. (1997). Identifying and solving impediments to the social and counseling psychology interface. *Counseling Psychologist, 25,* 171–180. Introduction to a group of papers that identify impediments to the interface and several current and promising areas of work.

Snyder, C. R., & Forsyth, D. R. (Eds.). (1991). *Handbook of social and clinical psychology: The health perspective.* New York: Pergamon. The definitive collection of papers on approaches to and findings on the social/counseling(clinical) interface.

Stoltenberg, C. D., McNeill, B. W., & Elliott, T. R. (1995). Selected translations of social psychology to counseling psychology. *Counseling Psychologist, 23,* 603–610. Introduction to a group of papers that present current ideas and areas of research in the social/counseling interface.

Strong, S. R. (1978). Social psychological approach to psychotherapy research. In S. Garfield and A. Bergin (Eds.), *Handbook of psychotherapy and behavior change.* New York: Wiley. A mid-stream exposition on the social influence approach that emphasized attribution theory.

Strong, S. R., Yoder, B., & Corcoran, J. L. (1995). Counseling: A social process for constructing personal powers. *Counseling Psychologist, 23,* 374–384. Presentation of an emerging conceptualization of social influence from a constructionist, ethnomethodology, and discursive perspective.

Stanley R. Strong

SOCIAL INTELLIGENCE. *See* Practical Intelligence.

SOCIALIZATION. *See* Infancy; Early Childhood; Middle Childhood; *and* Adolescence.

SOCIAL JUSTICE. The central finding of social justice research is that people ascribe importance, often a great deal of importance, to fairness in social relations. Research over the past 35 years has demonstrated that fairness judgments can affect whether a person chooses to cooperate with others, obey authority, and identify with groups, organizations, and institutions. Social justice phenomena have been shown to be important in political psychology, organizational psychology, psychology and law, and basic social psychology. Some social psychological theorists have argued that fairness is *the* key element in understanding why people behave the way they do toward others.

The psychological study of social justice can be traced to three seminal works. In the 1940s Samuel Stouffer and his colleagues conducted a study of U.S. military personnel. One of the major findings of this study was that soldiers' satisfaction with the conditions under which they served had a strong comparative component—that instances of dissatisfaction were more closely linked to *relative* deprivation rather than to the absolute or objective levels of deprivation a soldier experienced. Relative deprivation theories of subjective justice grew out of this finding, taking as their basic assumption the idea that reactions to outcomes and experiences depend on a comparison of one's own situation to that of others. The idea that fairness involves comparisons with others was taken further when, in the early 1960s, Stacy Adams proposed "equity theory," which stated that people compare not only outcomes but also contributions as they assess fairness in social relationships. Equity theory stated that when the ratio of contributions and outcomes differs from one person to another, people will feel distress and will act to reestablish equity. Thus, if Person A contributes twice as much to a business or relationship as Person B, but Person A receives a payoff only equal to that of B, inequity distress will result and *both* parties will act to try to restore equity, either by changing their contributions or their outcomes or by altering their perceptions of the contributions or outcomes. The third seminal work in social justice research appeared in the mid-1970s when John Thibaut and Laurens Walker demonstrated that the fairness of procedures, as well as the fairness of outcomes, can have potent effects on the evaluation of social experiences.

Current writing on the psychology of social justice tends to differentiate between the fairness of outcomes, termed distributive justice, and the fairness of process, termed procedural justice. Distributive justice research has shown that people tend to base their judgments of the fairness of outcome allocations on several different norms, including norms of equity (allocation according to each recipient's contributions to the overall good), norms of equality (equal allocations for all recipients), and norms of need (allocation according to each recipient's need for the outcome in question). These norms can come into conflict, of course, and a great deal of effort has gone into investigating the circumstances under which each is thought to be most appropriate. For example, it is often argued that need-based allocations are viewed as most appropriate in close communal relationships, while equity-based allocations are viewed as most appropriate in business or production-oriented relationships.

Whatever principles apply in a given setting, it is clear that violations of distributive justice can have a substantial impact on social relations. For example, the perception that someone is a "free-rider"—unfairly reaping benefit from others' efforts—can be a barrier to the resolution of social dilemma disputes. On the other hand, research has shown that equal distributions generally enjoy great popularity and wide acceptance across a variety of settings because equality appeals to a sense of fairness and is easy to apply.

Procedural justice research has also revealed some rules or procedures that are especially likely to inculcate a sense of fairness. The most widely researched of these is what has come to be called "voice." When people affected by a decision feel that they have been given an opportunity to voice their views and concerns, and to have these views considered by decision makers, they tend to feel that the process is fair even if they do not get all they want. Other factors that enhance feelings of procedural fairness include accounts and explanations from authorities about why decisions are made, evidence of the benevolence and neutrality of authorities, and politeness and respectful treatment at the hands of authorities.

Procedural justice has been shown to be at least as strong as distributive justice in shaping social attitudes or actions; indeed, in many situations procedural justice appears to exert even stronger effects than do distributive justice and other instrumental (outcome-oriented) concerns. For example, studies of legal behavior have shown that the fairness of procedures experienced in encounters with legal authorities is more important in determining who will subsequently obey laws than is either distributive justice or the extent to which people get what they want from the encounter. Similar findings have been documented in studies of the acceptance of court or alternative dispute resolution judgments, in the acceptance of work goals, and in evaluations of conflict resolution rules. In business settings, procedural justice has been shown to have strong effects on organizational commitment, extra-role helping, and acceptance of authority. In family contexts, there is evidence that children who have an opportunity to voice their views at home are less likely to run afoul of the law.

For both distributive and procedural justice, however, fairness is a matter of individual judgment, subject to social cognition processes. Evaluations of equity and fair process tend to vary depending on the interpretations of those involved, and work on "blaming the victim" has shown that people will sometimes distort their perceptions of others to try to see events as fair.

Current theory in the social psychology of justice suggests that people attach so much importance to fairness because fair treatment calms fears about exploitation and exclusion, two concerns that arise in many or most social relations. Fair treatment makes people feel they can safely cooperate with others and invest their own social identity in a relationship, group, or institution. In contrast, unfair treatment, whether manifested in terms of inequitable outcomes or unfair

process, exacerbates fears about exploitation and exclusion and pushes people to focus on self-protection and self-interest as they decide how to react to others.

Bibliography

Adams, J. S. (1965). Inequity in social exchange. In L. Berkowitz (Ed.), *Advances in experimental social psychology* (Vol. 2, pp. 267–299). New York: Academic Press.

Greenberg, J. (1996). *The quest for justice: Essays and experiments.* Thousand Oaks, CA: Sage.

Lerner, M. J. (1980). *The belief in a just world.* New York: Plenum Press.

Lind, E. A., & Tyler, T. R. (1988). *The social psychology of procedural justice.* New York: Plenum Press.

Stouffer, S. A., Suchman, E. A., DeVinney, L. C., Star, S. A., & Williams, R. A., Jr. (1949). *The American soldier: Adjustments during army life* (Vol. 1). Princeton: Princeton University Press.

Thibaut, J., & Walker, L. (1975). *Procedural justice: A psychological analysis.* Hillsdale, NJ: Erlbaum.

Tyler, T. R. (1990). *Why people obey the law: Procedural justice, legitimacy and compliance.* New Haven, CT: Yale University Press.

Tyler, T. R., Boeckmann, R. J., Smith, H. J., & Huo, Y. J. (1997). *Social justice in a diverse society.* Boulder, CO: Westview Press.

Walster, E., Berscheid, E., & Walster, G. W. (1978). *Equity: Theory and research.* Boston: Allyn & Bacon.

E. Allan Lind

SOCIAL LEARNING THEORY. *See* Learning; *and* Social-Cognitive Theory.

SOCIAL MOTIVATION. Motivation is the energizing force that steers people toward desired end states. Social motivation in particular is a driving force that derives from the real or imagined presence of others or from one's sense of the self as a social object. Social motivation can be manifest in cognition, emotion, or behavior that either propels us toward a desirable objective (a goal) or repels us from an undesirable state (a threat). Individuals differ in the extent to which they tend to be motivated to approach desirable goals versus to prevent negative consequences.

Two common themes are relevant to all theories of social motivation. First, discussions of social motivation should address, either implicitly or explicitly, physiological arousal, as arousal is intimately tied to motivation. The more motivated one is to achieve an end state, the more autonomic nervous system arousal one experiences. Motivational intensity is affected by one's needs, the potential outcomes of a behavior, and one's expectation that a behavior will satisfy the need and achieve the outcome. Higher motivational intensity is not always better, however; research has demonstrated that moderate levels of motivational intensity usually result in the best performance (Brehm & Self, 1989).

Second, theories of social motivation examine how other people can serve as the inspiration that guides thoughts and behavior. The following very different paradigms all address how the actual, imagined, or implied presence of others increases arousal, which energizes and steers subsequent thought and behavior.

Intrinsic and Extrinsic Motivation

One of the most influential ways of thinking about motivation has been in terms of the intrinsic or extrinsic source of motivation. Intrinsic motivation spurs behavior that is freely chosen and may be initiated due to curiosity, interest, a need for adventure, or a need for stimulation. Intrinsic motivation is not always social in nature, but when the source of motivation involves the real, imagined, or implied presence of others, it can be considered social motivation.

Extrinsic motivation, in contrast, has as its impetus some external reward or threat. Behavior that is extrinsically motivated is performed as a means to an external end (e.g., money or a job promotion). Other people can serve as extrinsic sources of motivation if these people are expected to dispense rewards or punishments. Extrinsic rewards need not be material or immediate, however; anticipated social approval, for example, can be a powerful source of social motivation.

An activity that once provided strong intrinsic rewards such as personal satisfaction and self-esteem can become extrinsically motivated if the activity is externally rewarded. For example, paying a child who already loves to read $2.00 for each completed book will serve to transform a once intrinsically motivated diversion into an extrinsically motivated activity.

Other People as Targets of Motivated Behavior

Perhaps the most fundamental type of social motivation is what Baumeister and Leary (1995) have identified as a need to belong, a basic need to forge and maintain social attachments. To satisfy our need for security and emotional connectedness, we try to create and maintain affiliations with others. Sometimes other people can be the targets of prosocial motivation; for example, we may act altruistically to aid a person in need or may volunteer to help our community. [See Altruism.] Other people can also be the targets of negative or aggressive behavior, however. Whether spurred by hormone levels, frustration, or other affective arousal; by environmental stressors; or by neurological factors,

we are quite capable of acting aggressively toward others. Indeed, it has been suggested that people may at times lash out aggressively to attain a desired level of stimulation or shunt off excess arousal and regain homeostasis.

Mental Representations of the Self

The presence of others, whether real or imagined, can cause us to turn attention inward to evaluate our goals or standards. For example, thinking about the standards of others may activate what has been termed an ought self, a mental representation of what important others think one should be (Higgins, 1987). If the current self is found wanting in relation to the ought self, guilt and anxiety can ensue, possibly spurring behavior to attempt to reduce the discrepancy.

Memories of our past behavior or status as well as constructions of our future behavior and status can also be sources of motivation. We formulate "possible selves" that are either based on our recollections of how we were in the past or how we would like to be (Markus & Nurius, 1986). Recalling the benefits derived from a certain course of action can spur us to reinitiate that set of behaviors. Alternatively, imagining future selves or states that we would like to attain can encourage us to set goals. When one's current status does not meet an internally set standard, negative emotion can result. If one feels efficacious at rectifying the discrepancy, however, goal setting and the development of a plan of action to reduce the discrepancy may ensue. Thus, internal representations of the self, inspired by the self or by others, aid us in energizing action sequences to attain the desired state.

Goal Setting

Goals, however they are inspired, serve a motivating function. Once we have chosen a particular goal (a process termed the deliberative phase), we focus on the course of action necessary to achieve that goal (a process termed the implementation phase) (Gollwitzer & Bargh, 1996). Research has shown that the process of forming behavioral goals and plans is in itself energizing; in fact, having goals that are specific rather than vague has been shown to result in improved performance. Being motivated in a certain direction does not invariably mean we will act to achieve that goal, however. At times, the intensity of motivation is insufficient to actualize effective behavior.

Goals need not be conscious to be impactful. When we commit to a goal, a latent internal state, which has been termed a "current concern," is established (Klinger, 1996). Current concerns are sensitive to goal-relevant cues in the environment. When a cue is encountered (e.g., a slice of chocolate cake if one is dieting), an emotional response is quickly activated. If this emotional arousal passes a certain threshold, we become conscious of the emotion, we think about the cue and goal, and we may initiate behavior that is relevant to the goal. Therefore, the motivating effects of goals need not always be available to conscious awareness to be powerful.

The Impression Management Perspective

As social animals, we are motivated to maintain a certain face in front of others; this face may contain role-appropriate behaviors (e.g., politeness in a customer service representative), a desire to be seen as honest or consistent, or a desire to behave consistently with one's self-concept. We attempt to affect the impression that others hold of us when we hold social goals (e.g., being admired) and may act in ways instrumental to attaining those goals (e.g., informing someone of a recent success). For example, when we know ahead of time that we will be presenting or justifying our views to others, we experience what has been termed accountability (Tetlock, 1983). Accountability motivates us to think about issues in a more complex fashion, as if we were preparing ourselves to contend with potential audience objections. In general, our desire to achieve and maintain power in interpersonal relationships may guide much of the way that we present ourselves to others.

Individuals differ in the extent to which their behavior is shaped by a desire to affect others' impressions of themselves, a personality difference that has been termed self-monitoring (Snyder, 1987). Whereas low self-monitors attend to their internal attitudes and dispositions when formulating their behavior, high self-monitors attend to situational pressures, thinking about what impression a certain audience would favor and behaving in a congruent fashion. Thus, self-monitoring affects the intensity of people's motivation to control others' impressions of themselves during social interactions.

Self-Motivations

In addition to setting goals that may be affected by the real, imagined, or implied presence of others, we have more general self-motivations that can be social in nature. We are motivated to have accurate information about the self—a need for self-assessment—that can guide action and thought. When so motivated, we seek diagnostic information to increase self-knowledge. However, we also have a self-enhancement motive—an ongoing drive to achieve and maintain a positive sense of self. This motive can lead us to ward off negative information about the self and to seek positive (even if inaccurate) information. A motive for self-verification causes us to seek information that confirms our existing self-concepts, whereas a motive for self-improvement leads us to attempt to better the self.

Effects of Motivation on Cognition

Motivation can affect what information enters conscious awareness. For example, the activation of a certain goal category leads us to ignore irrelevant stimuli and facilitates the processing of goal-relevant information. Motivation can also affect where we seek information—if the motivation for self-improvement is high, for example, we often prefer to seek information from people who are more (rather than less) fortunate on a particular dimension.

Motivation can also expand or constrain our mental processing. For example, motivation determines when we initiate and when we terminate thinking about an issue. When motivation is high, we will initiate cognitive activity more quickly and will persist in that activity for longer than when motivation is low. For example, being motivated to hold an accurate impression of another person when meeting that individual for the first time leads us to engage in more effortful processing, causing us to create a very individualized impression of the person. Similarly, being motivated to hold accurate attitudes can lead us to pay particular attention to the quality of the arguments in persuasive messages rather than to more superficial cues associated with those messages. When motivation is low, however, little consideration of the message arguments occurs.

Motivation can also bias our cognitive activity, affecting the way that we define situations. For example, causal explanations are often constructed so as to maintain a positive view of the self; we tend to attribute successful outcomes to internal causes (e.g., ability or intelligence) and unsuccessful outcomes to external factors (e.g., lack of time). The motivation to hold a positive view of the self can also affect the way we define and view the self; when adjectives have been associated with positive outcomes or consequences, we tend to define those traits so that they become self-descriptive. Motivation also affects the organization of information in memory and its subsequent retrieval. For example, the desire to see ourselves as consistent can lead us to misremember our past actions and attitudes as being more consistent with our present attitudes than is actually the case.

Motivation can also concretize various belief systems. For example, people tend to hold a certain view of the world that justifies their actions or their perceived place in the world. These worldviews may reinforce their notion of the self as good and thus are consistent with the self-enhancement motive. For example, there is a strong tendency to view the world as a just place, to believe that good things happen to good people and bad things happen to bad people. Terror management theory asserts that when we are threatened by something, for example, when we consider our own mortality, we may be motivated to increase our allegiance to cultural beliefs (Greenberg, Solomon, & Pysczcynski, 1997).

Cognitive processes can also be affected by stable individual differences that have motivational bases. For example, people differ in the extent to which they have a need for cognition, a need to think deeply about issues. People also may differ in their need for closure—some people are motivated to come to a decision on an issue quickly whereas others prefer to delay closure. People also differ in the extent to which they need to evaluate issues and to form and express opinions. See Kruglanski (1996) for a general discussion of motivated cognition.

Social Motivation and Performance

A large literature examines how the mere presence of other people can affect our performance on various tasks (Geen, 1991). The presence of others is a source of arousal, and this arousal can have facilitating or debilitating effects on performance, depending on the complexity of the task and our visibility in the group. When we are in a visible subgroup, arousal is high, facilitating our performance when tasks are relatively easy (social facilitation) but impairing our performance when tasks are more difficult (social inhibition). When we are undifferentiated among the crowd, a lessening of effort and performance occurs, and we exhibit what is termed social loafing (Harkins, Latané, & Williams, 1980). Finally, the type of motivation that we hold may affect performance; holding learning goals (attempting to gain mastery over a task) leads to better performance than holding performance goals (demonstrating high ability).

Researchers of social motivation have examined multiple sources, types, and effects of social motivation. All of this work shares in common the idea that the actual, imagined, or implied presence of others can energize and direct our thought and behavior and that exploring these processes is key to understanding the complexity of human nature.

Bibliography

Baumeister, R. F., & Leary, M. R. (1995). The need to belong: Desire for interpersonal attachments as a fundamental human motivation. *Psychological Review, 117,* 497–529.

Brehm, J. W., & Self, E. A. (1989). The intensity of motivation. *Annual Review of Psychology, 40,* 109–131.

Geen, R. G. (1991). Social motivation. *Annual Review of Psychology, 42,* 377–399.

Gollwitzer, P. M., & Bargh, J. A. (Eds.). (1996). *The psychology of action: Linking cognition and motivation to behavior.* New York: Guilford.

Greenberg, J., Solomon, S., & Pyszczynski, T. (1997). Terror management theory of self-esteem and cultural worldviews: Empirical assessments and conceptual refinements. In M. P. Zanna (Ed.), *Advances in experimental social psychology* (Vol. 29, pp. 61–139). San Diego: Academic Press.

Harkins, S. G., Latané, B., & Williams, K. (1980). Social loafing: Allocating effort or taking it easy? *Journal of Experimental Social Psychology, 16,* 457–465.

Higgins, E. T. (1987). Self-discrepancy: A theory relating self and affect. *Psychological Review, 94,* 319–340.

Klinger, E. (1996). Emotional influences on cognitive processing, with implications for theories of both. In P. M. Gollwitzer & J. A. Bargh (Eds.), *The psychology of action: Linking cognition and motivation to behavior* (pp. 168–189). New York: Guilford Press.

Kruglanski, A. W. (1996). Motivated social cognition: Principles of the interface. In E. T. Higgins & A. W. Kruglanski (Eds.), *Social psychology: Handbook of basic principles* (pp. 493–520). New York: Guilford.

Markus, H., & Nurius, P. (1986). Possible selves. *American Psychologist, 41,* 954–969.

Snyder, M. (1987). *Public appearances, private realities: The psychology of self-monitoring.* New York: Freeman.

Tetlock, P. E. (1983). Accountability and complexity of thought. *Journal of Personality and Social Psychology, 45,* 74–83.

Eugene Borgida and Lynne Mobilio

SOCIAL NETWORK ANALYSIS. [*This entry comprises two articles:* Definition and History *and* Concepts, Applications, and Methods.]

Definition and History

Social network analysis is an interdisciplinary behavioral science specialty. It is grounded in the observation that social actors are interdependent and that the links among them have important consequences for every individual. For example, links among actors permit the flow of material goods, information, affect, power, influence, social support, and social control. They provide individuals with opportunities and, at the same time, potential constraints on their behavior.

Social network analysis involves theorizing, model building and empirical research focused on uncovering the patterning of links among actors. It is concerned also with uncovering the antecedents and consequences of recurrent patterns. Its roots can be found in the work of a psychiatrist, J. L. Moreno (*Who Shall Survive?*, 1934), who introduced the approach called sociometry, and that of A. R. Radcliffe-Brown, a British social anthropologist, in a series of lectures in 1937 (*A Natural Science of Society*, 1945).

The development of social network analysis was fostered by the work of psychologist Alex Bavelas, who founded the Group Networks Laboratory at the Massachusetts Institute of Technology in 1948. Bavelas began with an intuitive notion—that the structural arrangement of ties linking members of a task-oriented group may have consequences for their productivity and morale. He proposed (1948) that the relevant structural feature was centrality, and specified centrality in exact formal terms.

This concern with clarification has characterized the social network approach from the very start. Its main concern has been to clarify traditional intuitive ideas by specifying them in formal terms. For example, quite early, two of Bavelas's students, R. D. Luce and A. D. Perry (1949), took the intuitive idea of social group and gave it a precise definition as a graph theoretic entity called a clique. At the same time, a French anthropologist, Claude Levi-Strauss (1949/1969), began with informal notions of kinship and specified a mathematical model designed to make their structural properties explicit. And another psychologist, Anatol Rapoport (1949), focused on natural populations in which some, but not all, individuals were directly linked by social ties. He produced a probability-based model of the process of information flow through such populations.

Through the 1950s and 1960s these were all separate and distinct research initiatives. They grew and attracted adherents but were not tied together. In the 1970s, new developments in discrete mathematics, particularly in graph theory, provided the tools for the construction of more general structural models. And at the same time, the growth of computer power and speed permitted the analysis of the kinds of complex relational data sets that network research generates. So at that time, partly as a consequence of these refinements, the earlier strands were knit together and the special field of social network analysis emerged.

Since that time, the social network analytic perspective has been productively applied to the study of occupational mobility, the impact of urbanization on individuals, the world political and economic system, community decision-making, social support, community, group problem-solving, diffusion, corporate interlocking, belief systems, social cognition, markets, sociology of science, exchange and power, consensus and social influence, and coalition formation (Wasserman & Faust, 1994, pp. 5–6). Additional applications include primate studies, computer-mediated communication, intra- and interorganizational structure, and marketing (Wasserman & Galaskiewicz, 1994). And finally, social network research has increasingly focused on the study of health and illness, particularly AIDS. (In 1995 a spe-

cial issue of the journal *Social Networks* [17:163–343] was edited by Alden Klovdahl and devoted entirely to network studies of HIV/AIDS.)

Bibliography

Bavelas, A. (1948). A mathematical model for small group structures. *Human Organization, 7*, 16–30.

Levi-Strauss, C. (1969). *The elementary structures of kinship* (Rev. ed., J. H. Bell, Trans.) [*Les structures elementaires de la parente*]. Boston: Beacon Press. (Original work published 1949)

Luce, R. D., & Perry, A. D. (1949). A method of matrix analysis of group structure. *Psychometrika, 14*, 95–116. The first formal model of group structure.

Rapoport, A. (1949). Outline of a probabilistic approach to animal sociology. I. *Bulletin of Mathematical Biophysics, 11*, 183–196. The first stochastic model of social networks.

Wasserman, S., & Faust, K. (1994). *Social network analysis: Methods and applications*. Cambridge, England: Cambridge University Press. A clear and detailed introduction to the entire field of social network analysis.

Wasserman, S., & Galaskiewicz, J. (Eds.). (1994). *Advances in social network analysis*. Thousand Oaks, CA: Sage. A review of some of the range of applications of the social networks paradigm.

Linton C. Freeman

Concepts, Applications, and Methods

Social network analysis is the study of social structure and its effects. It conceives of social structure as a social network: a set of social actors and a set of relational ties connecting pairs of these actors. The network's nodes (or network members) can be groups or organizations as well as persons. Network structure is analyzed using terms such as *density, centrality, prestige, mutuality,* and *role*. In addition, social network data sets often include information about actor attributes, such as age, gender, ethnicity, attitudes, and beliefs.

Social network analysis is an interdisciplinary enterprise that developed out of several research traditions, including (1) the birth of sociometry in the 1930s; (2) ethnographic efforts in the 1950s and 1960s to understand migrations from tribal villages to polyglot cities; (3) survey research since the 1950s to describe the nature of personal communities, social support, and social mobilization; and (4) archival analysis to understand the structure of interorganizational and international ties. Concepts such as transitivity, the strength of weak ties, and structural equivalence later arose from network research.

The basic premise of the social network paradigm is that knowledge about the structure of social relationships enriches explanations based on knowledge about the attributes of the actors alone. Network analysis reasons from whole to part, from structure to relation to individual, from behavior to tie. It goes beyond measurements taken on individuals to analyze data on patterns of relational ties and to examine how the existence and functioning of such ties are constrained by the social networks in which they are embedded. For example, one might measure the relations "communicate with," "live near," "feel hostility toward," and "go to for social support" on a group of workers. Some network analyses are longitudinal, viewing changing social structure as an outcome of underlying processes. Others link individuals to events (affiliation networks), such as a set of individuals participating in a set of community activities.

Network structure can be studied at many different levels: the dyad, triad, subgroup, or even the entire network. Although this allows different structural questions to be posed, it often requires the use of methods that go beyond the standard approach of treating each individual as an independent unit of analysis. This is especially true for studying a complete or whole network: a census of a well-defined population of social actors, in which all ties, of various types, among all the actors are measured. Such analyses might study structural balance in small groups, transitive flows of information through indirect ties, structural equivalence in organizations, or patterns of relations in a set of organizations.

Ego-Centered Networks and Social Support

The size and scope of complete networks generally preclude the study of all the ties in an unbounded population. To study such phenomena, researchers often use survey research to study a sample of personal networks (often called an ego-centered or local network). These are measured as the set of specified ties that link focal persons (or egos) at the centers of these networks to their alters. Such studies focus on egos' strong ties and on ties among egos' alters. The ego-centered approach leads to viewing community as a personal community: an individual's (or a household's) set of informal interpersonal ties. It analyzes relations such as kinship, weak ties, frequent contact, and providing emotional or instrumental aid. These relations can be characterized by their variety, content, and structure. Thus, analysts might study network member composition (such as the percentage of women providing emotional support), basic relational statistics (such as the strength of a tie), measures of relational association (strong ties with immediate kin are more supportive), and network structure (densely knit networks are more controlling). Research has shown that despite the decline of neighborhood or kinship solidarities, personal communities flourish as nonlocal, ego-centered networks.

Studies of ego-centered networks are important for understanding the provision of social support usually defined as the interpersonal resources conveyed by network members to each other. Network size, availability, density, and network member composition all affect how supportive a network can be and hence affect an individual's health and well-being.

Social Cognition

Social network studies of social cognition investigate how people perceive the ties of others and the social structures in which they are contained. Research has focused on how mental representations of networks (and their members) may be related to social context: (1) people's positions in social structures determine the specific information to which they are exposed, and hence, their perception; (2) structural position is related to characteristic patterns of social interactions; (3) structural position frames social cognitions by affecting people's perceptions of their social locales.

Organizations and Networks

Social network analysis allows a researcher to model the interdependencies of organization members. The paradigm provides concepts, theories, and methods to investigate how informal organizational structures intersect with formal bureaucratic structures in an organization's operations and workers' behavior. Hence it has informed many of the topics of organizational behavior, such as leadership, attitudes, work roles, turnover, and computer-supported cooperative work.

The study of interorganizational relations has also benefited from network analysis. It has been used for comprehending new organizational forms such as virtual organizations or knowledge-intensive network organizations, the structure of markets, the roles of organizations, and interlocking organizational ties. Much as network analysts tracked the move from bounded villages to unbounded cities, the network paradigm allows researchers to study amorphous organizational forms and to observe how organizational decision making is a function of particular social structures.

Methods

Social network analysts have developed methods and tools for the study of relational data. The techniques include graph theoretic methods developed by mathematicians (many of which involve counting various types of subnetworks); algebraic models popularized by mathematical sociologists and psychologists; statistical models (which include the Social Relations Model from social psychology, and generalizations of Markov random graphs); and software packages (such as *UCINET*). Yet social network analysis is more than a set of new methods; research into personal communities and social support continues to use standard statistical packages, and ethnographers and social historians have usefully applied qualitative methods in their network analyses.

Acknowledgments. Research for this article was supported by grants from the Social Science and Humanities Research Council of Canada to the University of Toronto and the National Science Foundation and the National Institutes of Health to the University of Illinois.

Bibliography

Berkowitz, S. D. (1982). *An introduction to structural analysis.* Toronto: Butterworth. An early, still useful account of the intellectual basis of social network analysis.

Burt, R. (1992). *Structural holes.* Chicago: University of Chicago Press. A widely read account of how people maneuver through their networks to get ahead in organizations.

Fischer, C. (1983). *To dwell among friends.* Chicago: University of Chicago Press. An influential study of ego-centered networks.

Granovetter, M. (1982). The strength of weak ties: A network theory revisited. In P. Marsden & N. Lin (Eds.), *Social structure and network analysis* (pp. 105–130). Newbury Park, CA: Sage. A review of the most influential publication in social network analysis.

Knoke, D. (1990). *Political networks.* Cambridge, UK: Cambridge University Press. This thoughtful book considers more than politics.

Monge, P., & Contractor, N. (1998). Emergence of communication networks. In F. Jablin & L. Putnam (Eds.), *Handbook of organizational communication.* Thousand Oaks, CA: Sage. This review concentrates on communication within and between organizations.

Nohria, N., & Eccles, R. (Eds.). (1992). *Networks and organizations.* Boston: Harvard Business School Press. A massive compilation of organizational and interorganizational network analysis.

Pattison, P. (1993). *Algebraic models for social networks.* Cambridge, UK: Cambridge University Press. Rewarding for those with serious algebraic training.

Scott, J. (1992). *Social network analysis.* London: Sage. A recent review.

Wasserman, S., & Faust, K. (1994). *Social network analysis.* Cambridge, UK: Cambridge University Press. A major book, paying special attention to statistical and mathematical analysis.

Wasserman, S., & Galaskiewicz, J. (Eds.). (1994). *Advances in social network analysis.* Newbury Park, CA: Sage. Solid recent compilation.

Wellman, B., & Berkowitz, S. D. (Eds.). (1997). *Social structures: A network approach* (Updated ed.). Greenwich, CT: JAI Press. Presents a theoretical overview plus original case studies, comparing network analysis with other approaches.

Barry Wellman and Stanley Wasserman

SOCIAL NEUROSCIENCE. The early American psychologist William James (*Principles of Psychology,* New York, 1980/1950) was among the first to articulate that neurophysiological processes underlie psychological phenomena. James further argued that developmental, environmental, and sociocultural factors influence the neurophysiological processes underlying psychological and social phenomena. Although these influences could be studied as neurophysiological transactions, James recognized that unnecessary diseconomies and conundrums would result if psychological phenomena were described only as neurophysiological events.

Studies of the neural processes associated with social or psychological functions were once limited primarily to animal models, postmortem examinations, and observations of patients who suffered trauma to, or disorders of, localized areas of the brain. Developments in functional brain imaging, electrophysiological recording, neurochemical techniques, neuroimmunologic measures, and ambulatory recording procedures have increasingly made it possible to investigate the role of neural structures and processes in humans. As neuroscientific approaches are applied to the study of diseases and to elementary cognitive and behavioral processes, subtler medical and psychological phenomena are succumbing to neuroscientific inquiry. This led to the U.S. Congress declaring the 1990s the decade of the brain.

The brain does not exist in isolation but rather is a fundamental, interacting component of a developing, aging individual who is a single actor in the larger theater of life. This theater is undeniably social, beginning with prenatal care, caregiver-infant attachment, and early childhood experiences and ending with feelings of loneliness or of embeddedness and with familial or societal decisions about care for the elderly. Mental disorders such as depression, anxiety, schizophrenia, and phobia are both determined by and are determinants of social processes. Disorders such as substance abuse, prejudice and stigmatization, family discord, worker dissatisfaction and productivity, and the spread of acquired immunodeficiency syndrome are quintessentially social as well as neurophysiological processes. Social neuroscience, a term coined by John Cacioppo and Gary Berntson (1992), refers to the study of the relationship between neural and social processes.

There is growing evidence that multilevel analyses spanning neural and social perspectives can foster comprehensive accounts of cognition, emotion, behavior, and health. First, inroads to the logic of social processes have come from theory and research in the neurosciences (e.g., brain organization and localization of function, genetic determinants of behavior). Research in the neurosciences, for instance, has influenced what are thought to be the processes underlying social attitudes and decisions. Mechanisms for differentiating hostile from hospitable environmental stimuli are imperative for the survival of species and for the formation and maintenance of social units. Noninvasive investigations of the physiological operations associated with evaluative processes provide an important window through which to view these processes without perturbing them. Research suggests that approach and withdrawal are behavioral manifestations that come from distinguishable motivational substrates. Ambivalence is a behavioral example of the concurrent activation of both positivity and negativity.

Second, the study of social processes has challenged existing theories in the neurosciences, resulting in refinements, extensions, or complete revolutions in neuroscientific theory and research. Classically, immune functions were considered to reflect specific and nonspecific physiological responses to pathogens or tissue damage. It is now clear that immune responses are heavily influenced by central nervous system processes that are affected by social interactions and processes. For instance, the effects of social context now appear to be powerful determinants of the expression of immune reactions. It is clear that an understanding of immunocompetence will be inadequate in the absence of considerations of psychosocial factors. Thus, major advances in the neurosciences can derive from increasing the scope of the analysis to include the contributions of social factors and processes.

Third, reciprocal benefits and more general psychological theories have been achieved by considering or pursuing jointly macrolevel and microlevel analyses of psychological phenomena. Evaluative categorizations and response dispositions—criterial attributes of attitudes, affect, and emotion—are fundamental and ubiquitous in behavior. All organisms have rudimentary biological mechanisms for approaching, acquiring, or ingesting certain classes of stimuli and withdrawing from, avoiding, or rejecting others. Knowledge of the organization and operating characteristics of these rudimentary mechanisms may therefore lay down, at least in broad strokes, the rules by which rudimentary biological and social factors alter evaluative categorizations and evaluative response dispositions. Decerebrate organisms, for example, display stereotyped orofacial ingestion-ejection reflexes to relevant gustatory stimuli. Furthermore, reflexive responses demonstrate a sensitivity to social and motivational variables. These inherent dispositions allow an organism, even at early stages of development and without previous experience, to respond adaptively to important classes of environmental stimuli. These reflexes also represent only a single level in what appears to be a continuum of evaluative mechanisms. With the involvement of additional subcortical structures, the reactions of the decorticate organism evidence greater directedness, integration, serial coherence, goal-orientation, and

contextual adaptability. Thus, evaluative mechanisms are not localized to specific neuraxial levels but evidence a hierarchy or representation throughout the central nervous system. With progressively higher organizational levels in evaluative mechanisms, there is a general expansion in the range and relational complexity of contextual controls and in the breadth and flexibility of adaptive response.

Fourth, deciphering the structure and function of the brain is fostered by sophisticated social psychological theories in which the elementary operations underlying complex social behaviors are explicated and by experimental paradigms that allow these social psychological operations to be studied in isolation using neuroscientific methods. Brain imaging studies of the neural bases of emotion have contrasted positive and negative emotions based on the assumption that these emotions are served by the same neural structures. Social psychological paradigms for eliciting positive and negative emotions have now been developed, and brain imaging studies in which positive and neutral emotions are contrasted and negative and neutral emotions are contrasted have indeed revealed the activation of some distinguishable neural structures during positive and negative emotions.

Fifth, the social environment shapes neural structures and processes, and vice versa. The handling of rat pups, for instance, alters maternal behavior toward the pups and affects the structure and reactivity of the hypothalamic pituitary adrenocortical system. These early influences on the stress-hormone system, in turn, affect these animals' reactions to stressors and their susceptibility to disease in later life. Multi-level analysis across social and neural levels made these effects apparent.

Bibliography

Anderson, N. B. (1998). Levels of analysis in health science: A framework for integrating sociobehavioral and biomedical research. *Annals of the New York Academy of Sciences, 840,* 563–576. Reviews a framework for interdisciplinary research between social, behavioral, and biomedical scientists.

Berntson, G. G., Boysen, S. T., & Cacioppo, J. T. (1993). Neurobehavioral organization and the cardinal principle of evaluative bivalence. *Annals of the New York Academy of Sciences, 702,* 75–102. Reviews evidence that with progressively higher organizational levels in evaluative mechanisms, there is a general expansion in the range and relational complexity of contextual controls and in the breadth and flexibility of adaptive response.

Blascovich, J. (in press). Using physiological indexes of psychological processes in social psychological research. In C. M. Judd & H. Reis (Eds.), *Handbook of advanced research methods in social psychology.* Hillsdale, NJ: Erlbaum.

Cacioppo, J. T., & Berntson, G. G. (1992). Social psychological contributions to the decade of the brain: The doctrine of multilevel analysis. *American Psychologist, 47,* 1019–1028. Outlines the rationale, approaches, and contributions of the field of social neuroscience.

Cacioppo, J. T., & Berntson, G. G. (1994). Relationship between attitudes and evaluative space: A critical review, with emphasis on the separability of positive and negative substrates. *Psychological Bulletin, 115,* 401–423. Reviews evidence from the neurosciences and the social sciences that the positive and negative substrates of attitudes are distinguishable.

Cacioppo, J. T., Berntson, G. G., & Crites, S. L., Jr. (1996). Social neuroscience: Principles of psychophysiological arousal and response. In E. T. Higgins & A. W. Kruglanski (Eds.), *Social psychology: Handbook of basic principles* (pp. 72–101). New York: Guilford Press.

Cacioppo, J. T., Crites, S. L., Jr., Gardner, W. L., & Berntson, G. G. (1994). Bioelectrical echoes from evaluative categorizations: I. A late positive brain potential that varies as a function of trait negativity and extremity. *Journal of Personality and Social Psychology, 67,* 115–125. Outlines paradigm for investigating evaluative categorizations and attitudes using event-related brain potentials.

Kiecolt-Glaser, J. K., Malarkey, W., Cacioppo, J. T., & Glaser, R. (1994). Stressful personal relationships: Endocrine and immune function. In R. Glaser & J. K. Kiecolt-Glaser (Eds.), *Handbook of human stress and immunity* (pp. 321–339). San Diego: Academic Press. Reviews evidence that interpersonal interactions and relationships influence endocrine and immune function.

Meaney, M. J., Bhatnagar, S., Larocque, S., McCormick, C. M., Shanks, N., Sharma, S., Smythe, J., Viau, V., Plotsky, P. M. (1996). Early environment and the development of individual differences in the hypothalamic-pituitary-adrenal stress response. In C. R. Pfeffer (Ed.), *Severe stress and mental disturbance in children* (pp. 85–127). Washington, DC: American Psychiatric Press. Reviews evidence that early social experiences affects the structure and function of the brain and a stress-hormone system, which in turn affects reactions to stressors and disease susceptibility in later life.

Uchino, B. N., Cacioppo, J. T., & Kiecolt-Glaser, J. K. (1996). The relationship between social support and health: A review with emphasis on underlying physiological processes. *Psychological Bulletin, 119,* 488–531. Outlines evidence that social support influences autonomic, endocrinological, and immunological function.

John T. Cacioppo, Gary G. Berntson,
John M. Ernst, and Tiffany A. Ito

SOCIAL NORMS. *See* Norms.

SOCIAL PHOBIA is an anxiety disorder characterized by extreme timidity and social inhibition. Those affected live in continual fear of doing something that will be embarrassing or humiliating, or that others will evaluate them in some negative way. These fears result in a pattern of social avoidance and inhibition that ranges from rather specific performance anxiety to virtually all situations involving the necessity for social discourse. When the pattern of fear and anxiety is circumscribed, as in the case of speech phobia, for example, the condition is referred to as the specific subtype. When there is a pervasive pattern of fear and anxiety, the term generalized subtype is used. In clinical settings, by far the most common type seen is the generalized type. The most common distressful situation is public speaking. Other situations that sometimes elicit distress include eating, drinking, writing, or typing in front of others, and social interactions such as parties, business meetings, or one-on-one conversations. Less common situations include using public lavatories, playing golf, or walking down the aisle at church. Often, the symptomatic picture includes many of these situations. The key element for social phobia is the fear of being judged negatively by others.

It is important to distinguish between typical public speaking anxiety and social phobia. A key concept is functional impairment. That is, in order to be considered a phobia, the fear must create significant emotional distress or prevent the individual from engaging in desired activities. For example, those with typical public speaking anxiety may feel somewhat anxious prior to giving a speech or going on a job interview. However, in these cases, once the event begins, the individual's anxiety diminishes and the activity is successfully completed. Those with social phobia, however, experience severe distress, in anticipation of or during the task, sometimes to the point of being unable to complete the task or avoiding it entirely. In addition, their initial severe anxiety does not diminish even if they are able to engage in the task. Similarly, the term shy is used to describe a pattern of social timidity similar to what is seen in social phobia. The relationship of shyness to social phobia is yet to be elucidated, but it has been speculated that many, but not all, of those labeled shy would meet diagnostic criteria for social phobia.

The most recent estimates of the prevalence of social phobia indicate that the 12-month prevalence rate for social phobia is 8% with the lifetime prevalence estimated to be approximately 12%. These figures, although higher than earlier estimates, are remarkably similar to emerging worldwide data. Epidemiological data are not available for children and adolescents but estimates suggest that perhaps 5% of all youth suffer from this disorder. These figures indicate that social phobia is the most common anxiety disorder. Indeed, its prevalence rate indicates that it is second in prevalence only to substance use disorders. The most common age of onset is middle adolescence, although children have been diagnosed as early as age 8.

When in a social situation, those with social phobia experience physical symptoms, subjective (cognitive) distress, and behavioral avoidance. The most common physical symptoms among adults include heart palpitations, blushing, trembling, and sweating, whereas children complain most often of headaches and stomachaches. Both adults and children will avoid social situations when possible. Adults, for example, will turn down job promotions or avoid going to college because of their fears. Among children, social isolation and school refusal characterize the most severe cases. Also, some children (most of whom are diagnosed as social phobic) refuse to speak in front of anyone other than immediate family (a condition known as selective mutism). With respect to subjective (cognitive) distress, adults endorse the presence of negative thoughts such as "I am really making a fool of myself" "They do not like me" or "What if I mess up?" In contrast, children, particularly preadolescent children, rarely report the presence of specific negative thoughts. Rather they just report that they "feel nervous."

Social phobia is considered a chronic disorder, particularly when the age of onset is prior to age 11. Social phobia results in significant emotional distress and social disruption such that academic achievement, occupational success, and interpersonal relationships are affected. With respect to treatment, both pharmacological and cognitive-behavioral treatments have been demonstrated to be efficacious. Among the pharmacological interventions, three different classes of medications appear to be efficacious, at least in the short term. These include monamine oxidase inhibitors (Phenelzine), serotonin reuptake inhibitors such as fluoxetine (Prozac), and high potency benzodiazepines (Clonazepam). Although these medications decrease social phobia symtomatology in the short term, there are few long-term follow-up data available. Of those data that do exist, relapse rates are high within a short period of time.

Behavior therapy and cognitive-behavior therapy are efficacious in treating social phobia. Available data show that there is little difference between these two forms of behavioral treatment. The results of meta-analysis, dismantling studies, and substantive reviews all indicate that the key ingredient in these interventions is exposure to the feared situation. Also, social-skills training appears to be an important element of treatment for both adults and children, particularly when the condition is of the generalized subtype. Available data indicate that the improvement rate is about 70% for these treatments and that the effects are durable. Most of the extant follow-up data are for 6 to 12 months but there are some follow-up data for as long as 5 years.

Over the past 15 years, social phobia has emerged from being called the neglected anxiety disorder to being recognized as one of the most prevalent psychological disorders in the general population, affecting individuals of all ages. Efficacious treatments exist and continued research will improve intervention efforts. Although studies relating to etiology are only just now emerging, it appears that there likely are different pathways to the development of social phobia, but there are some individuals who might be particularly vulnerable to the development of social phobia due to biological characteristics that are manifested at a very early age.

[See also Specific Phobia.]

Bibliography

Beidel, D. C., & Turner, S. M. (1998). *Shy children, phobic adults: Nature and treatment of social phobia*. Washington, DC: American Psychological Association. Provides a comprehensive discussion of social phobia in adults and children. Discusses developmental and etiological parameters, epidemiology, biological, and psychological risk factors, and pharmacological and behavioral treatments for children and adults.

Beidel, D. C., & Turner, S. M. (1999). Natural course of shyness and related conditions. In L. A. Schmidt & J. Schulkin (Eds.). *Extreme fear and shyness: Origins and outcomes* (pp. 203–223). New York: Oxford University Press. Compares and contrasts the syndromes characterized by maladaptive social anxiety and discusses their emotional and social consequences in the short and long terms.

Heimberg, R. G., Liebowitz, M. R., Hope, D. A., & Schneier, F. R. (Eds.). (1995). *Social phobia: Diagnosis, assessment, and treatment*. New York: Guilford Press. This volume provides comprehensive coverage of the social phobia syndrome, its assessment, and treatment.

Stein, M. B. (Ed.). (1995). *Social phobia: Clinical and research perspectives*. Washington, DC: American Psychiatric Press. The phenomenology, assessment, epidemiology, and treatment of social phobia is discussed. This volume contains several chapters that provide considerable coverage to biological aspects of social phobia.

Turner, S. M., Beidel, D. C., & Townsley, R. A. (1990). Social phobia: Relationship to shyness. *Behaviour Research and Therapy, 28,* 497–505. Discusses similarities and differences between shyness and social phobia.

Turner, S. M., Beidel, D. C., & Wolff, P. L. (1996). Is behavioral inhibition related to the anxiety disorders? *Clinical Psychology Review, 16,* 157–172. Discusses the relationship of behavioral inhibition, an early-appearing temperamental behavior pattern, to the anxiety disorders in general and social phobia in particular.

Samuel M. Turner

SOCIAL PSYCHOLOGY. [*This entry comprises two articles. The first article provides a historical survey of the methods that have been employed in this field. The second article profiles the assessments used in or unique to the field.*]

Methods of Study

Research in social psychology is generally carried out to construct and test causal theories. The emphasis on causation is implicit in the overall goals of the science: to understand phenomena by bringing them within the compass of general causal laws and to show how undesirable social conditions may be changed by altering their causal antecedents. Of course, some individual research studies, such as those aimed simply at describing existing states of affairs or at constructing and refining measurement instruments, do not directly address causal issues. Still, such studies are best regarded as part of an overall research process that focuses on building causal theory.

To evaluate the utility of different types of research in advancing causal theories, Cook and Campbell (1979) listed four criteria or forms of validity. Statistical conclusion validity depends on the use of appropriate statistical tests and adequate sample sizes, which are relatively independent of the choice of research methods. The other three forms of validity are closely related to research methods. Internal validity is the confidence with which one can conclude that the causal or independent variable in a study (here termed x) actually had a causal influence on the dependent variable in the particular study (y). Construct validity is the confidence with which one can draw a correspondence between the concrete variables in the particular study (x and y) and the abstract theoretical constructs that they are intended to operationalize (X and Y). Hence, construct validity assesses confidence with which a causal relationship can be inferred between X and Y. External validity takes two different forms depending on the type of research. When research is intended to apply in a simple and direct way to a defined setting and population (as public opinion surveys are intended to portray the opinions of the entire voting-age population of a state or country) then external validity measures the extent to which this sample-to-population generalization is viable. Such research is termed particularistic. In the more common situation of universalistic research, intended to test general causal theories, external validity amounts to a vaguer and more general question about the limits of the effects. Are they valid across different types of people, settings, or cultures?

Methods of research are defined by a number of cross-cutting factors including the research setting, the population studied, the research design, and the techniques of data collection used. Social psychology values methodological diversity, for as Cook and Campbell (1979) explained, a theoretical prediction that passes tests involving multiple methods is stronger than one that has been repeatedly tested in only a single way. Nevertheless, the field's mainstream and defining research method, used in probably three-quarters or more of published research, is the laboratory experiment.

Laboratory Studies

The laboratory as a research setting is defined by its flexibility. It is a stage upon which the researcher can produce and direct whatever sequence of events is required to implement a planned study. The high degree of researcher control that is possible in the lab means that experimental designs (which require control over the specific experiences of each participant) can readily be implemented. Logically, research settings and populations are independent issues. However, in practice, laboratory studies generally use college students as participants. This restriction to well-educated, generally attentive young adults carries potential limitations on external validity, which are due not to the laboratory setting itself but rather to the populations studied. These limitations are increasingly being remedied as social psychologists investigate more diverse populations.

Laboratory Experiments. Laboratory experiments are the bread and butter of social psychology (Aronson, Ellsworth, Carlsmith, & Gonzalez, 1990). The use of experimental design, in which the study's independent variable is manipulated to create randomly assigned groups of participants, means that internal validity is high and generally unproblematic. Criticism of lab experimentation generally involves its construct validity. Lab research offers many examples of effective, meaningful manipulations and valid measures of dependent variables, but also instances of variables that strike participants as artificial and meaningless and hence may not correspond to the intended theoretical constructs.

Laboratory experiments can be roughly divided into three types (Judd, Smith, & Kidder, 1991). Scenario or impact studies include some of the classics of social psychology. Researchers have had confederates posing as other participants report obviously incorrect judgments of the lengths of lines in order to test hypotheses about social influence on real participants' judgments. Other researchers have staged emergencies in the lab to assess the impact of various factors on participants' willingness to help others who appeared to be in danger. When scenario studies are effectively designed and implemented, the experiences become real for the subjects, leaving most questions about construct validity behind. For the study participants, for instance, their behaviors are responses to a real emergency in which they happen to find themselves. Still, the possibility of low construct validity due to the lab's artificiality exists, as participants may sit back and wonder whether the other participants' seeming consensus or the seeming emergency might not be contrived, just part of the experiment. Of course, the use of deception in research poses ethical as well as practical issues that must be carefully considered (T. D. Cook, in Judd, Smith, & Kidder, 1991, pp. 477–558).

Other laboratory experiments can be termed judgment studies, in which subjects assess usually complex stimuli (often including persons or social groups) and report their judgments, evaluations, inferences, or other reactions. Examples include most research on stereotyping and prejudice, in which information about an individual is presented, with different participants learning that the individual belongs to different social groups (e.g., he is Hispanic or Anglo in ethnicity). Their evaluations or judgments may reveal the content and operation of group stereotypes that affect their thinking about the target individual. Judgment studies also may be high or low in construct validity. When participants treat the task as realistic and meaningful it can assess their honest reactions to members of different groups. Even though most people other than corporate personnel officers may find making judgments about individuals described on paper an unusual task, we all do make judgments about others from secondhand information every day—whether they are characters in novels, individuals described in news stories, or ex-spouses described by our acquaintances. However, construct validity can also be low, for example if participants figure out that "they are looking at stereotypes of Hispanics here" and react to their perceptions of the research purpose rather than their perceptions of the target persons.

Finally, some laboratory experiments are performance studies in which some aspect of the participants' performance of a task reveals the thoughts or feelings that are under study. No explicit judgments (such as checking a box from 1 to 7 on a rating scale) may be required. Instead, subjects are asked to read some material and later to report all that they can recall of it or to respond to words presented on a screen by pressing a key as rapidly as possible to indicate whether each word is positive or negative. Within social psychology, performance studies are most common in the area of social cognition. In performance studies, the hypotheses and the predicted responses are generally less transparent than in judgment studies. For example, a suspicious participant may decide to respond in counterstereotypical ways to the Hispanic character he is asked to rate but will ordinarily have no idea what pattern of memory or response-time performance will confirm or falsify the hypothesis that he holds a stereotype of the group. Even if he knew the relevant pattern, his performance has real limits; he may not be able to remember more or process faster in order to falsely generate counterstereotypic data. Thus, in performance studies, construct validity depends more on the careful theoretically based validation of the data-collection method itself than on the participant's perceptions of the intentions of the study.

Laboratory Nonexperimental Studies. Although the control and flexibility that are characteristic of the laboratory can be used to good advantage to increase internal validity by implementing experimental designs, nonexperimental laboratory research is also common. The laboratory is used to set up specific conditions for participants to experience or to permit videotaping or other types of detailed observation. For example, two participants might be unobtrusively videotaped as they hold an informal get-acquainted conversation, and the videotape later coded in terms of their verbal and nonverbal behaviors. Or a small group may engage in a problem-solving task and their interactions coded for a study of leadership in informal groups. In cases like these, the flexibility and control of the laboratory can be used effectively to create the conditions under which specific observations can be made, even when no experimental manipulations are part of the research design.

Nonlaboratory Studies

Outside of the laboratory setting the researcher's ability to control events is much weaker. In particular, experimental designs (with their near-guarantee of high internal validity) are usually difficult to implement outside of the lab. In nonlaboratory (often called field) settings, construct validity can be either high or low. Important and meaningful independent and dependent variables can often be studied. Consider research on the effects of models or of the number of bystanders on an individual's probability of offering help to a person in need, or the effects of a person's self-concept on his or her psychological adjustment to a diagnosis of cancer. On the other hand, research outside the laboratory, embedded in the complexity of real life, always has to deal with a variety of potentially confounding variables.

Nonlaboratory research is sometimes simply assumed to be higher than laboratory research in external validity or generalizability, but this is not necessarily the case. In contrast to the connotation of the term "the field," diverse nonlaboratory settings such as a street corner, an industrial lunchroom, or a hospital emergency room differ among themselves at least as much as laboratory and nonlaboratory settings do. The types of people who typically inhabit these settings differ as well. Thus, the fact that a given study was conducted in a field setting does not in any way guarantee that its results will generalize to other nonlaboratory settings. The only true test of the external validity of a nonlaboratory finding (as of a laboratory finding) is replication.

Field Experiments. Experimental research outside the laboratory, though often difficult to implement, has many potential strengths. An example of a field experiment might be a study of bystanders offering help to a person in need, where a situation of apparent need is constructed (e.g., a person standing next to a disabled car by the side of the road) and researchers can assess the effects of various manipulations (such as a billboard advocating community responsibility located earlier along the road) on the number of offers of help. The manipulations would be added and removed according to a random schedule in order to assure that the groups of bystanders exposed to the different manipulations were equivalent. Internal validity is high because of the use of experimental design, while construct validity can also be high because the manipulations and measures derive from a meaningful and realistic setting. Finally, in particularistic research, external validity can be high when the field experiment takes place with the actual setting and population of interest (such as an experiment on the effects of different working conditions on productivity in an industrial setting). In universalistic research, it is important to keep in mind that nonlaboratory settings differ and the fact that a study was conducted outside the laboratory does not guarantee that its results are broadly generalizable.

Quasi-Experiments. Quasi-experimental designs (Cook & Campbell, 1979) can guard against some but not all of the threats to internal validity that true experiments rule out. However, they impose lower demands for strict control and may be easier to implement outside the laboratory than experimental designs. Quasi-experimentation usually involves manipulation but not random assignment. For example, an ad campaign promoting seat belt use may be implemented on television stations in one city but not in a comparable city which is used as a control, and changes in drivers' behavior measured in both cities. Except for the lower internal validity, the same considerations apply to quasi-experiments as to field experiments, just discussed.

Survey Research. Many social sciences including sociology and political science rely heavily on survey research methods, and some social psychological work fits this mold as well. For example, a researcher interested in the effects of intergroup contact on prejudice may conduct a survey to question people about the extent of their contacts with members of other races and also about their degree of prejudice. Surveys typically involve (a) an effort to collect data from a representative sample of the population of research interest (e.g., the voters in a particular state) or from the entire population (e.g., all the employees of a firm); and (b) the use of self-report data collection methods. Surveys may be conducted by personal interviews, telephone interviews, or written self-administered questionnaires; these modes of data collection each have their own strengths and weaknesses in terms of cost and data quality (Judd, Smith, & Kidder, 1991). The limitations of survey research include low internal validity stemming from the typically nonexperimental design (no manipulations are ordinarily employed, except for variations in question wording embedded within the questionnaire). Limitations in construct validity arise from the method of data collection (self-report, which may involve biases of various sorts). Thus, in the example survey study just mentioned, low internal validity means that low prejudice might cause increased intergroup contact (rather than the reverse causal sequence that is of theoretical interest), and low construct validity means that questions about prejudice may be answered dishonestly by respondents who believe that prejudice is socially unacceptable. The external validity of surveys can be high, especially for particularistic research where generalization from the sample to a specific target population is the key issue.

Naturalistic Observational Studies. Some research observes naturally occurring social behaviors, gaining high construct validity by measurement in realistic settings and populations, but losing internal validity through a lack of experimental design. For example, researchers interested in the climate of intergroup relations in an elementary school may unobtrusively observe the extent of racial segregation in seating patterns in the school lunchroom.

Analysis of Archival Data. Social psychologists have also tested research hypotheses by examining records kept in official or unofficial archives: government records, newspaper stories, library circulation records, and so on. For example, tests of the idea that heat increases aggression could involve examination of official weather records and crime statistics to determine whether there are more homicides on hot days. Archival data can offer objective and complete coverage of a population of interest, going beyond self-reports to assessments of real and important life outcomes, but can be weak in construct validity if archival measures do not correspond directly to the psychological construct of interest. For example, homicide as legally defined is not precisely equivalent to the psychological notion of aggression. In addition, archival data analyses typically involve nonexperimental designs and hence low internal validity.

Research Without Primary Data Collection

Some research in social psychology involves not the collection of new data but the further analysis and comparison of existing studies. This approach, termed *meta-*

analysis, involves the quantitative summary of multiple primary studies on a given topic. For example, many studies may have investigated (as their major goal or as a subsidiary issue) sex differences in helping behavior. A meta-analysis of all this research may be conducted to draw conclusions about (a) the overall or average difference (yielding the conclusion that across all the situations studied, men help more than women do or vice versa) and (b) the factors or conditions that influence the effect (e.g., conclusions that women help more than men in private situations but the reverse is true in public situations). The goals of meta-analysis are thus similar to those of conventional or narrative literature reviews, but quantitative techniques are used to make the conclusions more precise and objective (Mullen and Norman, in Judd, Smith, & Kidder, 1991, pp. 425–449). Results supported by meta-analytic methods can generally be considered quite strong on the counts of construct validity (to the extent that different studies use multiple different operationalizations of the constructs) and external validity (to the extent that the research samples a variety of settings and participant populations).

Computer simulation is not a substitute for data collection but a method for deducing the implications of a theory. A computer program is written embodying the assumptions of the theory, and then run to generate the theory's predictions under specified conditions. Simulation is most appropriately used with theories that are too complex for unaided intuition to clearly generate their predictions. When simulation is used, the other steps in the overall research process must be carried out as always: the theory's implications become research hypotheses to be tested by comparing them to actual data from research participants, and if the hypotheses mismatch the data then the theory must be modified or discarded.

As stated earlier, laboratory experimentation is by far the most common method in social psychology today, but other methods are also valued. The best-accepted research findings are those that can be obtained repeatedly in different settings and populations, with diverse research methods.

Bibliography

Abelson, R. P. (1995). *Statistics as principled argument.* Hillsdale, NJ: Erlbaum. Worthy companion to the classic Cook and Campbell (1979); a different approach to validity issues with a focus on experimental design and statistical analyses.

Aronson, E., Ellsworth, P. C., Carlsmith, J. M., & Gonzales, M. H. (1990). *Methods of research in social psychology* (2nd ed.). New York: McGraw-Hill. Comprehensive discussion of laboratory research methods in social psychology, including specific how-tos.

Cook, T. D., & Campbell, D. T. (1979). *Quasi-experimentation.* Chicago: Rand McNally. More than a source on quasi-experimental designs; includes discussion of philosophical approaches to the epistemology of the social sciences and the nature of validity.

Judd, C. M., Smith, E. R., & Kidder, L. H. (1991). *Research methods in social relations* (6th ed.). Fort Worth, TX: Holt, Rinehart, and Winston. Undergraduate-level textbook covering a broad range of methods for social and behavioral sciences, including laboratory methods, questionnaires and interviews, qualitative observation, and meta-analysis.

Mook, D. G. (1980). In defense of external invalidity. *American Psychologist, 38,* 379–388. A classic discussion of external validity and issues in generalizing from laboratory research.

Reis, H. T., & Judd, C. M. (Eds.). (in press). *Handbook of research methods in social psychology.* Cambridge, UK: Cambridge University Press. Authoritative collection of chapters covering major research methods at the advanced undergraduate or graduate level.

Rosenthal, R., & Rosnow, R. L. (1969). *Artifact in behavioral research.* Collection of articles on different problems that threaten construct or internal validity, mostly in the context of laboratory research.

Eliot R. Smith

Applied Social Psychology

One of the most interesting and attractive aspects of psychology in general and social psychology in particular is their potential for application and use to address social problems. Although some modern problems are not amenable to such application, many are, including prejudice and racism, crowding, human immunodeficiency virus (HIV) infection, inaccurate perception and interpretation of risk, smoking, obesity, and propaganda. Systematic application of research and theory on attitude change, persuasion, and social influence made important contributions to the war effort during World War II, and research since then has charted the ebb and flow of racism and studied its roots and products. Application of the basic research and theory of social psychology to problems of modern society enriches the literature and has proven useful in resolving or understanding many social issues.

Application of psychological research to explain or solve social issues is not a new enterprise. It is nearly as old as the field itself. A major impetus to this enterprise was action research, which refers to investigations that are generally problem-oriented and are designed to provide an answer to a particular question (as well as to advance theory in a given area). This approach was formulated by Kurt Lewin, a Gestalt-trained psychologist who also developed field theory and generated much of what became modern social psychology. Action research is eclectic problem-focused research that consists of a combination of laboratory and field studies and basic and applied research. Lewin and his colleagues used these principles imaginatively to conduct research on attitude change, groups, and social influence during World War II. Their work considered methods of changing people's attitudes toward the undesirable lifestyle changes brought about by the war effort (e.g., eating organ meats rather than more desirable cuts). Shortages and rationing made life more difficult, and these scientists applied existing theory to enhancing attitudes toward substitutes that were more readily available. Other research examined political and social organization in groups to identify determinants of satisfaction and productivity. Productivity in these groups was enhanced when organization and leadership were democratic and group members were involved in decision making. These and other studies of group dynamics contributed to the development of organizational psychology and to the organization of groups in industrial settings and were important in the development of worker goal-setting research.

There are no standard assessments or methods in applied social psychology. In general, the methods and measures used are the same as in basic research, although unobtrusive and archival measures may be more likely to be used. External validity, or the extent to which research can be applied or results generalized to larger populations, is a major concern in applied research, and this often complicates research considerably. For example, research intended to answer questions or solve problems in a particular group of people or situation (e.g., industrial workers, noisy neighborhoods) should be generalizable beyond the sample used in the study. The extent to which an experimental setting matches or corresponds to a real-world setting, the relevance of the situation or measures for the participants in the study, and the similarity of study outcomes to real-world outcomes are all important in determining the value of applied social psychological research.

These and other issues make applied research difficult and often demand that investigators make trade-offs, sacrificing experimental control for real-world relevance or sampling from reluctant, remote, or otherwise difficult to reach groups of people rather than convenient populations such as college students. However, social psychological theories appear to be very useful in addressing many social problems, and the measures and methods of the field are robust enough to permit such investigation. At the same time, hypothesis testing and derivation in applied research often benefit basic research as well. Continued development of applied social psychology research is important not only as a source of solutions to social problems but also as a critical element of the research enterprise.

One of the first social problems to be studied was prejudice. As early as the 1930s, studies documented the existence of prejudice and observed that prejudice and discrimination are not always correlated. Over the years, research has charted declines in the prevalence of prejudice but has noted that social pressures may have changed more than prejudiced attitudes and beliefs. That is, social conditions have changed and made it less socially appropriate to express prejudiced beliefs. There are many social pressures against admitting that one is prejudiced or making prejudiced remarks about a particular group of people. Increases in these normative pressures may have reduced reporting of prejudiced attitudes. Consequently, more apparently egalitarian attitudes may reflect a reporting bias rather than any real change in beliefs.

Attitudes are generally measured by self-report; they exist only as hypothetical constructs and reflect the contents of consciousness, a traditionally difficult entity to measure. This is hard enough to do under normal conditions, but when the attitudes are taboo or socially undesirable they are even more difficult to study. Psychologists have devised innovative ways of measuring these attitudes. One such method is the bogus pipeline, an experimental procedure in which participants are convinced that the experimenter can detect falsely reported attitudes. Once the participant accepts this premise, he or she is more likely to report true attitudes and beliefs, even if they are undesirable, because the experimenter can allegedly tell if the participant is lying.

It was hoped that application of knowledge from fields like social psychology would solve problems like prejudice and discrimination, but such deeply held beliefs are very difficult to change. Applied social psychology has not eliminated prejudice and racism, although we have learned a good deal about it and useful hypotheses and effective interventions have been developed. It may be the case that some prejudice is inevitable as people manage the surfeit of information available to them or adopt in-group/out-group attitudes to help support and maintain important social groups. Other areas of application that have had more dramatic effects include social psychological studies of health problems. For example, smoking is frequently a social behavior and almost certainly develops in the social contexts of adolescence and young adulthood. Smoking accounts for considerable morbidity in cancer and heart disease and is the number one cause of premature mortality in this country and many parts of the world. Applications of social learning theory, the use of well-known and well-liked models and spokespeople, and the modification of powerful peer pressures have been effective in preventing smoking. Studies have also suggested new ways of helping smokers quit. It appears to be very difficult to quit once the habit has been established, so a premium has been placed on prevention. Younger adolescents and children are target groups of interventions aimed at preventing the adoption of smoking. There has been a reversal of increasing smoking rates in some groups, attributed largely to the changes in societal attitudes toward smoking that occurred after 1980. Some of the social factors that led children to smoke or think smoking is cool have begun to disappear.

A related area of investigation in social psychology that reflects important application of work on social influence is in patient compliance or adherence to medical advice. If an illness or condition is diagnosed and the appropriate treatment is prescribed, one should expect that the patient will get better. However, if the patient does not follow the prescription, improvement is less likely. Whether it involves taking medications, attending screenings for surveillance of disease, making lifestyle changes (e.g., diet), or even coming back for a follow-up, patients are often noncompliant. Estimates range to well over 50% suggesting that most patients are noncompliant at some time in their health care. Research has identified several important social elements of the doctor-patient interaction that affect compliance, including satisfaction with the doctor and with one's health care, norms of one's primary reference groups, the style of communication adopted by the doctor, and the frequency of medical monitoring. Interventions designed to alter one or more of these social problems have been useful in improving patient adherence.

Research on smoking and medical compliance are now considered to be part of health psychology in spite of their social psychological roots. In fact, applications of social psychology were critical in the development of health psychology and other newer fields in psychology. Environmental psychology, organizational psychology, and the study of sex-role stereotypes and differences were all derived, in part, from applied social psychology research and theory. Other issues in health psychology that reflect such application have included the study of coronary-prone behavior or type A behavior, obesity and eating behavior, stress, social support, social comparison in interpreting heath communications, and prevention of HIV infection.

This last issue has been a watershed for applied psychology as a field. Acquired immunodeficiency syndrome (AIDS) and HIV disease are caused by infection with HIV, and people become infected in one of two primary ways, through unprotected sex or through intravenous drug use. Because there is no cure for the disease, no vaccine, and until recently little promise of effective treatment, the most productive defenses against the disease are preventive ones that help people avoid infection. These efforts involve important elements of persuasion, attitude change, and social influence; have led to development of important social psychological models or prevention; and have been characterized by application of theories such as the the-

ory of reasoned action. Programs to better educate high risk people or larger, less at risk populations have been supplemented by modeling, by providing skill training in negotiation with sexual partners and in adherence to safer sex procedures, and by tailored programs targeting smaller groups in the larger population.

Another important area of application for social psychology has been the law. Trials, investigations, jury behavior, and other aspects of the legal system are inherently social, and research has shown that it is possible to affect legal procedures and outcomes by understanding and manipulating these variables. For example, studies of mock and real juries have identified subgroups of people who are more or less likely to convict or find in a particular way, people who are more or less likely to vote for capital punishment, and people who are more or less likely to respond positively to particular evidence. Legal and moral development are also important in the overall operation of our legal system and are influenced by social processes and behavior. For example, the ways in which people perceive laws affect their reactions to them. Applied social psychology research has also addressed such issues as the causes of criminal behavior and the perception of justice, but most work in this area focuses on the criminal justice system.

The topics and issues of applied social psychology change as the times dictate, but many remain stable and unresolved. During times of war and privation, social influence theories and studies of group dynamics proved useful in shaping the war effort and resisting the rigors of combat or capture. During the postwar period when civil rights became a focal issue, research addressed prejudice, discrimination, and intervention to reduce these social ills. As the worldwide AIDS epidemic became news, researchers turned their attention and the power of several new theories to the task of preventing HIV infection. At the same time, research on environmental issues such as crowding, noise, and pollution, on the impact of television on social behavior, on psychology and law, on organizational development, and on a number of lasting issues or problems has continued. The result is an active, problem-focused effort to use what we have learned about human emotion, cognition, and social behavior to solve some of the social problems facing our world.

[See also Action Research.]

Bibliography

Bryant, F., Edwards, J., Tindale, R. S., Posavac, E. J., Heath, L., Henderson, E., & Suarez-Bakazar, Y. (1992). *Methodological issues in applied social psychology* (Vol. 2). New York: Plenum Press.

Davis, J. H. (1989). Psychology and law: The last 15 years. *Journal of Applied Social Psychology, 19,* 199–230.

Koch, L., & French, J. R. (1948). Overcoming resistance to change. *Human Relations, 1,* 512–532.

Lewin, K. (1997). *Resolving social conflict and field theory in social science.* Washington, DC: American Psychological Association.

Sigall, H. (1997). Ethical considerations in social psychological research: Is the bogus pipeline a special case? *Journal of Applied Social Psychology, 27*(7), 574–581.

Streufert, S. (1987). Applied social psychology. *Journal of Applied Social Psychology, 17,* 605–608.

Streufert, S. (1987). Decision making: Research and theory challenges for applied social psychology. *Journal of Applied Social Psychology, 17,* 609–621.

Wrighsman, L. (1991). *Psychology and the legal system* (2nd ed). Pacific Grove, CA: Brooks/Cole.

Andrew S. Baum

SOCIAL REPRESENTATIONS. Humans are social animals, living through interaction with each other. Individuals therefore do not think in isolation. Instead, they construct a framework of shared references that define how they think about the world around them. These shared references can be viewed as social representations, a concept first introduced in the early 1960s by the French social psychologist Serge Moscovici to form the basis for a new paradigm in his field (1961/1976).

Social representations concern the creation of shared knowledge by a community. They originate in daily life, in the course of interindividual communication, to facilitate our interpretation of reality and so guide our relation to the world around us (Moscovici, 1988). In this sense they are a social construction, socially elaborated and collectively shared.

As Denise Jodelet reminds us in *Madness and Social Representations* (1991), social representations have a twofold existence. For one, she insists that they are products of social thinking, structuring information and beliefs about phenomena considered significant for a given community (Kim & Berry, 1993). Yet, as social-psychological mechanisms that shape how we think and talk about an object, social representations are also processes of constructing reality—a point well explained by Uwe Flick (Smith, Harré, & Van Langenhove, 1995).

Any interaction, whether between two individuals or two groups of individuals, presupposes shared representations. It is only on the basis of these representations, which shape our beliefs, ideas, attitudes, and opinions, that we give meaning to things and come to understand each other. Because we elaborate them together and evoke them frequently, we let social representations become deeply embedded in our cultural fabric.

Theoretical Foundations

The roots of social representation theory can be found among certain early European social scientists who understood that the missing link to any general theory of society concerned the dynamic between the social and the individual (Farr, 1987). The French sociologist Emile Durkheim, for instance, distinguished between individual representations and collective representations. Moscovici's notion of social representations, an extension of Simmel's concept of "social ideas" and Vygotsky's notion of "higher mental functions," provides a synthesis between the two by stressing their interconnectedness. This reinterpretation avoids Durkheim's rather static juxtaposition, which implies an essentially stable society, in favor of a more dynamic vision of society in constant change and flux.

In his definition of social representations, Moscovici focuses on the social nature of thought and the ways in which people change their society. The importance of this approach is to have developed a new synthesis between the individual and the social. Here the interplay between internal mechanisms and the constantly changing social world is actualized through the interconnectedness of individuals. Individuals do not form their thoughts in isolation, but by influencing one another and therefore on the basis of collectively shared reifications of objects that make up our reality. In other words, we are interconnected through social representations that act as the bridge between the individual world and the social world.

Social representation theory has become influential beyond France in the rest of Europe, Latin America, and more recently, the Pacific Rim. As a general theory of human behavior, this approach lends itself to interdisciplinary work and innovative research. Moreover, it applies to a broad range of concrete situations and provides us with insights into key aspects of modern life. Research utilizing this approach has been conducted to study a variety of social phenomena, such as health and illness, madness, AIDS, intelligence, food, money, and race.

The Nature, Structure, and Functions of Social Representations

Social representations are above all prescriptive inasmuch as they compose a socially created metasystem that regulates, controls, and directs individual minds. That metasystem is a structure that unconsciously influences us, guides us when making up our minds about something, and forces us by means of conventions to take account of what others think about that object. Social representations are also consensual in the sense that they make relative, for comparison and juxtaposition, divergent views about an object. This requires a structuring core for the collective conceptualization of an object as one and the same. Finally, once representations are created, they are autonomous to the extent that they lead a life of their own and evolve beyond the reach of individuals.

The prescriptive, consensual, and autonomous nature of social representations enables them to shape the formation and orientation of our social life. As a source of prescription for normative beliefs, the core of a consensual world, and an autonomous force which orients the thoughts of individuals, they give our heterogenous society a structuring context to contain the divergent forces of conflict around a core of agreements.

In his analysis of the structure of social representations, Jean-Claude Abric proposes that their internal organization is built around a central core that contains an indispensable element or combination of elements giving the representation its meaning (1994). That central core is crystallized in the value system shared by the members of a group. Surrounding the central core is an organized constellation of peripheral elements that play an important role in concretizing the meaning of the representation.

The embeddedness of social representations in a given culture rests on two processes through which objects become represented in our minds, namely objectification and anchoring. These processes are fundamental for the elaboration, maintenance, and transformation of social representations, since they both assure the interdependence of individual cognitive existence and the social condition of life (Philogène, 1999). The objectification process is the crystallization of a new object into a figurative core so as to allow the projection of images. To objectify means to turn something abstract into something almost concrete, turning it from the level of idea to the level of existence in the physical world. At this point of concretization, people can talk about the object, and through communication the object acquires the kind of density of meaning that ultimately makes it a "natural fixture" in people's minds. The anchoring process categorizes a new object into our preexisting mental systems in order to render it familiar. Therefore, to anchor refers to the process by which a strange and unfamiliar object is reduced to our level of ordinary categories in order to set it in a familiar context. This ordering activity enables us to classify the object in question and give it an appropriate name for reference.

A representation always originates from a previous one, having altered mental and social configurations in the process. The dynamic nature of a social representation, meaning its capacity for continuous change, is rooted in its genesis, that is, in its link to preexisting representations. Consequently, the full understanding of a given representation necessarily requires us to start with those from which it was born. It is precisely this creative quality of transformation that makes the concept of social representation so useful to the study of important phenomena in the modern world.

Bibliography

Abric, J.-C. (1994). *Pratiques sociales et représentatons*. Paris:

Breakwell, G., & Canter, D. (Eds.). (1993). *Empirical approaches to social representations*. Oxford, England: Clarendon Press.

Doise, W., & Clemence, A., & Lorenzo-Cioldi, F. (1993). *The qualitative analysis of social representations*. Hemel Hempstead, England: Harvester/Wheatsheaf. The first textbook on quantitative methodology of social-representations research. An accessible and practical discussion of how to measure social representations and analyze them statistically.

Doise, W., & Palmonari, A. (Eds.). (1986). *L'étude des représentations sociales*. Neuchâtel, Switzerland: Delachaux & Niestlé. Combines an interdisciplinary definition of social representations with 7 empirical case studies applying that concept to important aspects of our culture.

Farr, R. (Ed.). (1987). Social representations [Special issue]. *Journal for the Theory of Social Behavior, 17*.

Farr, R., & Moscovoci, S. (Eds.). (1984). *Social representations*. Cambridge, England: Cambridge University Press. The first edited volume laying the foundation for research in social-representation theory. Includes several classic articles clarifying the concept of social representation.

Flick, U. (1995). In J. A. Smith, R. Harré, & L. Van Lengenhove (Ed.), *Rethinking psychology*. London: Sage.

Jodelet, D. (1991). *Madness and social representations*. Berkley: University of California Press.

Kim, U., & Berry, J. W. (1993). *Indigenous psychologies: Research and experience in cultural context*. Newbury Park, CA: Sage.

Moscovici, S. (1961/1976). *La psychanalyze, son image et son public*. Paris.

Moscovici, S. (1988). *European Journal of Social Psychology, 18*, 211–250.

Philogène, G. (1999). *From Black to African American: A new social representation*. Westport, CT: Greenwood.

Purkhardt, C. S. (1993). *Transforming social representations: A social psychology of common sense and science*. London: Routledge. An interesting perspective applying social representations theory to the dynamics of scientific knowledge.

Wagner, W. (Ed.). (1994). Symposium on social representations [Special issue]. *Social Science Information, 33*.

Wagner, W. (Ed.) (1996). Social representations revisited [Special issue]. *Journal for the Theory of Social Behavior, 26*.

Gina Philogène

SOCIAL SETTINGS. Individuals are profoundly affected by the social matrix in which they are embedded.

In recognition of this fact, behavioral scientists have developed ways to conceptualize and measure the underlying characteristics of social environments and their impacts. Fundamental advances have been made in the last 30 years. Integrated assessment procedures are available to identify the most important aspects of family, work, educational, and other social settings. Such methods can be used to describe social environments, to examine how such environments influence individuals' well-being and performance, to understand why some social settings are more cohesive, task oriented, and structured than others, and to help individuals select and create more satisfying and effective life contexts.

The Social Climate of Family, Work, and Educational Settings

Family, work, and educational settings can be described in terms of three underlying sets of social climate dimensions: relationship dimensions, personal growth or goal-orientation dimensions, and system-maintenance-and-change dimensions (Table 1). Relationship dimensions assess the quality of personal relationships in a setting; that is, how involved people are, how much they help one another, and how openly they express their feelings.

Personal-growth or goal-orientation dimensions tap the directions in which an environment encourages personal change and development. Because the purposes and goals differ so much from one setting to another, the nature of these dimensions differs as well. In families, personal-growth dimensions assess the emphasis on such areas as independence, achievement, intellectual and cultural interests, participation in social activities, and moral and religious values. In the workplace, these dimensions reflect the relative emphasis in such areas as autonomy, task orientation, and work demands. In classrooms, they focus mainly on task performance and competition.

System-maintenance-and-change dimensions include organization, clarity, control, and innovation. These dimensions measure how orderly and organized the setting is, how clear it is in its expectations, how much control it maintains, and how responsive it is to change.

These three sets of dimensions of family, work, and educational settings are associated with individuals' morale and self-confidence, personality and behavior, and distress and maladjustment. Aspects of these settings have been tied directly to these and related outcomes; in addition, researchers have considered the role of personal factors and individuals' coping styles in moderating the connections between social settings and individual outcomes.

Family Environment and Individuals' Well-Being. Cohesion, expressiveness, and intellectual-cultural orientation in families are closely associated with young children's cognitive and social development and with adolescents' academic motivation and success. Youth in more cohesive, expressive, well-organized, and socially oriented families are likely to have higher self-confidence and social competence. Youth in families that value independence and achievement tend to be assertive and self-sufficient, whereas those in supportive and well-organized families tend to have a more even temperament. In contrast, a strong emphasis on achievement in the context of high family structure and lack of cohesion is associated with depressed mood and suicidal ideation. Family conflict is linked to more behavior problems and impulsivity. Overall, youth development is promoted in families that encourage independence and provide modeling for instrumental and social skills, whereas it can be hampered in families that emphasize achievement in the context of conflict and accommodation to restrictive rules.

Among adults, high family support, independence, social integration, and organization are associated with better personal adjustment and well-being, more self-reliant and active coping, better adaptation to family crises and transitions, and less depression and distress. When a person experiences many life stressors, family support may have an especially protective effect on reducing depressed mood. Support may also lessen depression by enhancing problem-solving coping.

Work Climate and Employee Adaptation. Research in this area has shown how the interplay of relationship, personal-growth or goal-orientation, and system-maintenance-and-change dimensions affect the consequences of the workplace. Four aspects of work climate have been associated with employee distress and lack of mental and physical well-being: high job demands, insufficient opportunity to participate in decisionmaking, high supervisor control, and lack of clarity about the job and criteria for adequate performance. In general, distress is most likely when job demands are high and the individual has little discretion in deciding how to meet them. When employees are allowed to make decisions about their work, high job demands can be stimulating and can promote active problem solving and innovation.

The quality of personal relationships at work can moderate these associations. In general, coworker cohesion and supervisor support improve job attitudes and morale as well as employees' work motivation and commitment. But cohesion in the absence of task focus diminishes satisfaction and productivity; the combination of high support and moderate structure promotes these goals. Supportive relationships with coworkers and supervisors strengthen the positive influence of autonomy and task orientation and moderate the problematic consequences of highly demanding and constrained work settings.

SOCIAL SETTINGS. Table 1. Social climate dimensions in family, work, and educational settings

Type of Setting	Relationship Dimensions	Personal Growth Dimensions	System-Maintenance-and-Change Dimensions
Family	Cohesion Expressiveness Conflict	Independence Achievement Intellectual/cultural Recreational Moral/religious	Organization Control
Work	Involvement Coworker cohesion Supervisor support	Autonomy Task orientation Work pressure	Clarity Managerial control Innovation Physical comfort
Educational	Involvement Affiliation Teacher control	Task orientation Competition	Order and organization Rule clarity Teacher control Innovation

Learning Environments and Student Growth. Supportive relationships with teachers and classmates and an emphasis on student participation in well-organized classrooms promote student morale, continuing motivation to learn, and a sense of academic self-confidence. Students in task-oriented classes that set specific academic goals in the context of supportive relationships and clear structure are especially likely to do well on standard achievement tests. These students do as well in such areas as self-confidence and creativity as students in classes that are more engaging and flexible, but less task oriented and structured.

Competition and control in the absence of support often promote student anxiety and absenteeism. Substantial achievement gains can occur in classes that emphasize task performance and competition and are lower in warmth, but such classes are not as effective in fostering student creativity or continuing motivation to learn. Students in flexible classes that allow more individual freedom are more willing to work independently and have lower absence rates. The most effective schools are supportive as well as task-oriented; learning environments need to emphasize student performance, though not at the expense of engagement and support.

Common Characteristics of Growth-Promoting Environments. Overall, there appear to be some common consequences of conceptually similar social climate factors. Most generally, the relationship dimensions influence the individual's commitment to the environment, the personal growth or goal-orientation dimensions channel the direction of personal effort and change, and the system maintenance dimensions influence the efficacy of individual efforts and the health costs that can be involved. More specif-

ically, environmental systems tend to maintain or accentuate individual characteristics congruent with their dominant aspects.

Some emphasis on each of the three domains (relationship, growth, and maintenance) facilitates positive social and performance outcomes, but too much focus on any one domain can raise problems. Thus, too much emphasis on personal growth goals can lead to distress in family and work as well as educational settings. Highly structured and achievement-oriented families can create anxiety and erode adolescents' self-confidence. Similarly, high work demands can lessen job morale and elicit depression and physical symptoms. Difficult and competitive learning environments encourage cognitive growth, but they also can result in poor grades and higher student absenteeism and dropout rates.

The quality of interpersonal relationships in a setting can influence these associations. By promoting motivation and commitment, cohesive relationships amplify the influence of personal-growth dimensions and moderate the problematic consequences of highly demanding, performance-oriented environments. Supportive social bonds foster task performance and learning and are associated with better health and well-being. In a goal-directed environment, the combination of consideration and structure enhances morale and performance; however, support in the absence of clear goals can promote lethargy or rebellion.

In addition to their role in regulating and structuring a setting, the system maintenance factors can promote personal growth and ego control. Clarity of expectations about required tasks, adequate performance feedback, and moderate organization and structure all contribute to satisfaction and effectiveness. In the relative absence of these factors (i.e., when policies are ambiguous, feedback is sparse, and organizational rules are lax), there is a higher prevalence of morale and behavior problems. But an overemphasis on these system maintenance factors, especially when there is a lack of cohesion and autonomy, can restrict opportunities for personal development and create tension and defiance. These findings affirm the value of examining the interplay of relationship, personal growth, and system-maintenance factors in identifying the consequences of varying social climates.

Person-Environment Matching Models

As just noted, there are some important connections between characteristics of social settings and individuals' well-being, performance, and personal development. However, part of the influence of contextual factors depends on the personal orientation and preferences of the individuals who experience them. Pursuing this idea, some investigators have linked the congruence between individuals' preferences and social environment characteristics to individuals' outcomes.

The conceptual level (CL) matching model provides a developmental perspective for this area. The model posits that more mature individuals are able to organize their own environment, whereas those who are less mature need the stabilizing influence of a well-structured setting. For example, externally oriented individuals tend to adjust better in well-structured settings, whereas internally oriented individuals do better in more flexible environments. Similarly, people who want to explore and shape their environment and who exhibit a strong need for independence profit more from less structured environments. Such findings are consistent with the CL model, as is evidence that more mature students adjust and perform better in less structured learning environments and that variations in classroom environments are more strongly associated with adaptation among problem students than among nonproblem students.

These findings point to some potentially robust forms of person-environment congruence. As noted earlier, environmental systems tend to maintain or accentuate personal characteristics congruent with their dominant aspects. But when environmental demands either exceed individuals' preferences or tax their capacity to manage them, some personal dysfunction is likely to occur. Moderate emphasis on system maintenance factors helps to promote ego control among individuals who need or prefer a well-structured setting. But, a strong focus on these factors, especially among developmentally mature and internally oriented persons, restricts individual growth and can foster passivity. Expressive relationships typically promote morale, but highly independent or introverted persons who prefer fewer social bonds can feel hemmed in or overstimulated by interaction-oriented settings. Such findings show that personal factors must be considered when examining the linkages between contextual factors and adaptation.

Social Environments in Ecological Perspective

To understand social settings, it is important to consider their links to other aspects of an individual's life context. Specifically, we must place social environments in context and consider how the characteristics and influences of one type of setting, such as the workplace or school, may be altered by other factors in employees' and students' lives, such as aspects of their family settings. In this regard, the mesosystem has been defined as the interrelation between two or more microsystems, such as family and work or family and school. The exosystem is composed of settings that can affect a person even though the person does not take an active part in them, such as the influence of a mother's work setting on her daughter.

Family and Work Settings. The influence of the workplace is one important aspect of understanding family functioning in a broader social context. For example, a wife's experiences at work can affect her husband by altering the family environment. In this respect, three patterns of work-family interface have been identified. One is a pattern of positive carry-over, when personal gratification and information from work enrich the family. A more common pattern is one of negative carry-over, in which work overload and job role conflict cause stressors that create tension in the family. The third pattern occurs when individuals try to conserve their energy and privacy and become less available to family members.

Work and family settings compete for scarce personal resources. As work stressors increase, families often have fewer interpersonal resources available to buffer them. Thus, a boring, nonproductive job with little opportunity for personal control generates a pattern of withdrawal from the family. Highly demanding, conflict-laden job situations often elicit a pattern of tense family interaction. In contrast, family members of individuals who enjoy their work tend to experience their families as more involving and supportive.

High work demands are linked to interrole conflict and overload, which are associated with more physical symptoms and lack of job and life satisfaction. Family roles also contribute to interrole conflict. The association between work expectations, such as taking on extra duties and finishing job tasks by staying overtime, and perceived overload tends to be progressively stronger among single employees, those who are married, and those who have children. Thus, stressors in the workplace are especially likely to increase distress among individuals who have more family-related demands.

Parental work environments and extrafamilial social networks can influence the family climate and indirectly affect child functioning through their impact on parents and family life. For example, fathers' work stressors have been related to fathers' depression and, in turn, an increase in family arguments and children's adjustment and physical health problems. Conversely, fathers' positive work relationships have been associated with better family relationships and, in turn, fewer child adjustment problems. However, parents who are deeply involved in satisfying, but highly demanding professional careers may have less energy for family pursuits and thus contribute to their children's lack of well-being and behavior problems.

There are important connections between specific aspects of work, an individual's values and patterns of interaction in family and leisure settings, and his or her children's cognitive development and personal orientation. For example, parents train their children for the world they themselves know and believe their children will occupy. Persons who work in entrepreneurial settings value self-control, risk taking, and independent behavior and therefore socialize their children accordingly. In contrast, persons who work in bureaucratic settings value security and accommodation and teach their children to be obliging and to seek external direction.

Family and School Settings. Connections between family environments and school settings are as important as those between family and work, especially with respect to their influence on students' school-related attitudes and performance. For example, some aspects of family and learning environments can amplify each other. Thus, students who are in family and classroom settings both of which are high in support and structure tend to have the highest scholastic self-concepts. Stimulating home and learning environments that are more oriented toward learning help to predict more positive attitudes toward school and better academic achievement.

Joint family and school effects are likely to be most powerful when there is psychological continuity between the home and the school. One line of research has shown that youngsters do better in classrooms with rules guiding interpersonal interaction that are similar to those they experience in their families. Youngsters from cohesive families obtain better grades in cohesive classes and worse grades in coercive and laissez-faire classes. Youngsters from coercive families do better in coercive classes, less well in laissez-faire classes, and quite poorly in cohesive classes. Youngsters from laissez-faire families obtain better grades in laissez-faire classes and worse grades in cohesive classes.

Parents who are better educated are more likely to mirror the academic style of learning environments at home by praising and interacting with their child, modeling appropriate behavior, and promoting initiative and independence. Children of well-educated parents learn, in their homes, to master teaching and learning processes that are similar to those that occur in school. Because these family interactional processes are adaptive in the classroom, children who learn them have an advantage over children who do not. Conversely, the academic underachievement and high dropout rates of children from families of low socioeconomic status may be due, in part, to an abrupt discontinuity or mismatch between their home and school environments.

Recent Developments

The growth of a systems orientation and a focus on the connections between family, work, educational, and other social contexts is an important trend that complements the more established focus on individuals in psychology and the behavioral sciences. This systems perspective has led to three important developments.

Powerful Environments and Cross-Situational Influences. One development involves an enhanced focus on the differential strength of contextual factors and how cross-situational influences can modify them. The more intensive, committed, and socially integrated a setting is, the greater is its potential impact, especially on personal factors that are changing developmentally. Cohesive, homogeneous settings tend to influence incongruent individuals to change in the direction of the majority, whereas those in the majority maintain or further accentuate their attitudes and behavior in the relevant areas. A heterogeneous setting has more diverse influences and provides each person with a wider choice of options.

Powerful environments alter many of the individuals who elect to stay in them, but they also carry significant risks. Concentrating high-ability students in certain classrooms can promote their aspiration and achievement levels. But social comparison processes often work to the detriment of the less able students, who may feel less competent and alienated in such classes. Any setting that is powerful enough to produce constructive personal change is powerful enough to elicit concomitant distress. Such settings can create significant problems; other life contexts can buffer such problems. For example, youth who enjoy a cohesive family and supportive peers may experience less tension in highly competitive or controlling school settings.

The conceptual approach outlined here affirms the need for a fundamental shift in thinking about social programs and their effects. An educational or healthcare intervention is but one of the multiple life contexts and specific settings that influence personal growth and maturation. Other powerful current environments also shape mood and performance; the short-term influence of an intervention can be augmented or nullified by new environmental factors. Thus, family settings can alter the outcome of educational programs by inhibiting their effects (as when the family or peer group does not value achievement), by augmenting their effects (as when home and family factors bolster an achievement-oriented learning environment), or by compensating for their lack of effects (as when youth are taught skills at home that they have not learned in school).

The connections among settings influence the stability of the effects of intervention programs. Many of the hard-won gains of educational and social programs fade over time. This is precisely as expected on the basis of our knowledge about environmental impact and the diversity of settings to which people are exposed. Inherent in the belief that an intervention program can promote change is the assumption that other more recent environmental factors can modify it. Conversely, if community settings and life contexts can alter individuals, so can intervention programs. The use of a systems framework to identify convergent and divergent cross-setting effects may make it possible to formulate more integrated and powerful intervention programs that capitalize on family, work, and school influences.

Life Domains and Stress and Coping Theory. A second development involves a growing connection between the life domains perspective and the stress and coping model of health and well-being. More than three decades of research on stress and coping has provided a useful mapping of psychosocial constructs that help to understand a wide range of behavioral and health outcomes. Traditional approaches to the prediction of behavior and well-being rely heavily on demographic and person-centered variables. By focusing more attention on environmental influences, the stress and coping model represents a significant advance in identifying life context factors involved in health and illness. Life stressors and social resources consistently help to explain health outcomes and the influence of prevention and intervention programs on such outcomes.

The focus on separate life domains such as family, work, and educational settings has led to a differentiated approach to vulnerability and protective factors. An action-oriented self-concept organized according to individuals' goals and commitments in each domain serves to guide reliance on particular appraisal and coping styles in specific situations. When individuals invest themselves in a domain, they are likely to be especially vulnerable to disruptions in that domain. Life stressors that match the individuals' vulnerabilities in a highly salient domain are associated with more adverse health risks. Involvement in more domains leads to the development of a more complex self-system and provides protection against stressors in any one domain.

The merging of these two models has implicitly encouraged an approach that is transactional and oriented toward person-in-context. The main focus is on understanding the nature of people's commitments in specific life domains, such as the family, workplace, and peer groups, how life stressors can undermine individuals' fundamental, long-term commitments, and how domain-specific appraisal and coping strategies help people maintain their equilibrium. In this vein, research conducted in diverse life domains indicates that unhealthy environments undermine social ties and engender conflict, threaten safety, and constrain choice. In contrast, healthy environments provide opportunities for social integration and tend to be predictable and responsive.

A Transactional Perspective

The third development involves a more precise examination of the mutual relationships between people and the environments they select and create. People actively avoid certain environments and, on the basis of their needs and dispositions, choose to participate in others; in turn, these chosen environments are likely to influence people to change in desired ways. In addition, individuals' moods and behaviors may shape their social context, such as when a depressed individual's hopelessness and lack of interest leads to a reduction of support from family members and coworkers. People construct characteristic microenvironments that then reciprocate by fostering certain attitudes and behaviors. Thus, the processes involved in the choice and construction of social environments are closely interwoven with those involved in environmental impact.

Overall, there are at least three processes by which persons and environments can influence each other: a passive process by which people find themselves or are placed in environments that shape their behavior, an evocative process by which individuals elicit specific responses that then become part of their environment, and an active process by which individuals select and build specific environmental niches that maintain and accentuate their predominant dispositions.

One way in which people can influence their life contexts is to use information about the characteristics of social settings to change and improve them. For example, consultants and program evaluators have used change-oriented interventions to institute organizational development programs in work and educational settings, and clinicians have used such interventions to enhance effective family functioning. The procedures typically involve: (1) conducting an initial assessment and identifying specific goals for change, often by contrasting the actual with a preferred or ideal setting; (2) instituting new policies and cooperative ways to allocate and complete tasks that are intended to enhance a sense of involvement and performance; and (3) reassessing the setting and participants' affect and behavior to document change. Although these procedures are complex and difficult to implement, they typically lead to improvement in the environment and enhanced morale among participants.

More broadly, through a long-term process of shaping social values and the evolution of new communities, individuals as a group establish the characteristics of future environments. In this way, people can develop the social settings that then shape their own behavior and that of future generations.

Acknowledgments. Preparation of this manuscript was supported in part by the Department of Veterans Affairs Health Services Research and Development Service and NIAAA Grant AA06699.

Bibliography

Booth, A., & Dunn, J. F. (1996). *Family-school links: How do they affect educational outcomes?* Mahwah, NJ: Erlbaum. Analyzes how families provide a context that helps youngsters adapt to school environments.

Bronfenbrenner, U. (1989). Ecological systems theory. In R. Vasta (Ed.), *Annals of child development* (Vol. 6, pp. 187–249). Greenwood, CT: JAI Press. Develops a perspective on how to conceptualize social settings and their interrelationships.

Eckenrode, J., & Gore, S. (1990). *Stress between work and family.* New York: Plenum Press. Presents a stress and coping perspective on the linkages between work and family settings.

Fraser, B. J., & Walberg, H. J. (1991). *Educational environments: Evaluation, antecedents, and consequences.* Oxford, UK: Pergamon Press. Reviews the dimensions and effects of classroom learning environments.

Goldberger, L., & Breznitz, S. (Eds.). (1993). *Handbook of stress: Theoretical and clinical aspects* (2nd ed.). New York: Macmillan. Provides an overview of current research on stress and coping.

Golembiewski, R. T. (1990). *Ironies in organizational development.* New Brunswick, NJ: Transaction. Describes the conceptual background of and research on organizational development.

Holland, J. L. (1992). *Making vocational choices: A theory of vocational personalities and work environments* (2nd ed.). Odessa, FL: Psychological Assessment Resources. Sets out ideas about how individuals of different personality types select and create characteristic work environments.

Karasek, R., & Theorell, T. (1990). *Healthy work: Stress, productivity, and the reconstruction of working life.* New York: Basic Books. Reviews the influence of the psychosocial work environment on employee morale and productivity.

Kohn, M., & Schooler, C. (1983). *Work and personality:An inquiry into the impact of social stratification.* Norwood, NJ: Ablex. Describes the influence of the workplace on individuals' self-concepts, values, and behavior.

Moen, P., Elder, G. H., & Lüscher, K. (1995). *Examining lives in context: Perspectives on the ecology of human development.* Washington, DC: American Psychological Association. Provides an overview of how social context factors influence individuals over the life course.

Moos, R., & Moos, B. (1994). *Family Environment Scale manual* (3rd ed.). Palo Alto, CA: Consulting Psychologists Press. Describes dimensions of family environments and their determinants and effects.

Parke, R. D., & Kellam, S. G. (1994). *Exploring family relationships with other social contexts.* Hillsdale, NJ: Erlbaum. Describes processes linking families with other social contexts such as work and school.

Pierce, G., Sarason, B., & Sarason, I. (Eds.). (1996). *Handbook of social support and the family.* New York: Plenum Press. Reviews research on the role of social support on family relationships and outcomes.

Taylor, S. E., Repetti, R. L., & Seeman, T. (1997). Health psychology: What is an unhealthy environment and how does it get under the skin? *Annual Review of Psychology, 48,* 411–447. Examines the role of family, work, peer group, and community environments in contributing to acute and chronic health problems.

Walsh, W. B., Craik, K. H., & Price, R. H. (Eds.). (1992). *Person-environment psychology: Models and perspectives.* Hillsdale, NJ: Erlbaum. Provides an overview of theoretical perspectives on person-environment congruence.

Rudolf H. Moos

SOCIAL SKILLS TRAINING. Effective social skills are repertoires of learned behaviors used to achieve various goals and sources of reinforcement in an interpersonal context. Some social skills initiate, facilitate, and maintain interpersonal relationships such as friendships and harmonious family relations, which are in themselves rewarding. Other social skills promote need fulfillment and satisfaction within important relationships or social systems such as positive communication and conflict resolution skills in work teams or families. Some social skills, although employed in an interpersonal context, lead to reinforcement and goal attainment outside the relationship itself (e.g., job interview skills). Still other social skills, such as assertive refusal and limiting setting, serve to prevent others from infringing upon the individual's rights or removing or blocking reinforcement to which the person is otherwise entitled. Finally, other social skills lead to reinforcement and minimize negative social feedback because they conform to cultural or subcultural norms and expectations for social behavior. In summary, social skills are interpersonal behaviors that assist individuals in maximizing reinforcement in an interpersonal context and in minimizing social punishment and negative feedback. Social skills training addresses deficits in such behaviors.

Effective social skills are most often complex repertoires of behavior that include both verbal (e.g., appropriate self-disclosure, giving a compliment, or making appropriate requests) and nonverbal behaviors (e.g., eye contact, loudness and tone of voice, and physical gestures). Verbal and nonverbal responses are only loosely correlated such that different components may be the focus of intervention. Social skills also tend to be context or situation specific. For example, positive behaviors for job interviewing, expression of love and affection, and standing up assertively for one's rights are different social competencies. Within a type of socially skilled behavior, effective behavior may vary with the target of the behavior, goals of the behavior, and other aspects of the situation. Social skills training, therefore, focuses upon specific behaviors for specific situations and does not assume training of one type of social skills will transfer to other social skills or contexts. Additional training may be needed to develop other social competencies.

Failure to exhibit socially effective behavior may result from several factors. A common reason is that people have not had the opportunity to learn effective behaviors. They have not received instruction, modeling, or reinforcement for the relevant behavior in the past and do not exhibit the behavior in the present, because they have not learned it. Other individuals have learned the behavior, but for some reason these skills are not cued in situations in which they are relevant (e.g., effective conversational skills with peers of the same sex but not with peers of the opposite sex). Something about the physical, social, or cultural environment fails to prompt effective behavior demonstrated in other contexts. Culture may also play a role in the absence of socially effective behavior. All cultures have norms and rules concerning appropriate social behavior, and expected behaviors may conflict from culture to culture. For example, assertive, self-enhancing behavior in one culture may be considered selfish, intimidating, and offensive in another. Individuals may show social skill deficits in some contexts if their culture of origin deems that behavior inappropriate. Another source of socially ineffective behavior is neurological and physical conditions. Neurological deficits in some forms of mental retardation and schizophrenia may make it difficult for the individual to attend to and learn socially effective behavior and/or to attend to social, interpersonal cues and initiate appropriate behavior. Neurological and physical characteristics may change the individual's social cue value and prompt others to behave in ways that influence opportunities to learn and demonstrate socially effective behavior.

Social skills training encompasses behavioral interventions for developing, integrating, and transferring to real life specific social competencies in individuals who do not exhibit such behavior. Social skills training, with its focus on the acquisition of behavior, developed within behavioral models of psychotherapy, drawing on early work of individuals such as Andrew Salter, Joseph Wolpe, and Albert Bandura and extended by people such as Robert Alberti, Emmons, John Galassi, James Hollandsworth, Jeffrey Kelly, and Richard McFall. The focus on direct teaching of effective coping skills stood in marked contrast to the psychodynamic models of the day, which viewed social/interpersonal problems as a result of developmental difficulties, intrapsychic conflicts and traumas, ineffective defenses, and underlying personality structure. The focus of psychodynamic therapy, therefore, was on personality restructuring rather than on directly altering the behavioral deficits themselves found in social skills training.

Social skills training generally includes a series of sequential, overlapping steps or tasks. First, a careful assessment is undertaken to specify concretely the nature of deficits and the situations in which they occur. Although interviews are helpful, clients usually engage in role-plays, simulations, or real-life interactions so deficits may be observed and defined behaviorally.

When behavioral deficits and situation characteristics are clear, the therapist provides clear instructions and rationale for targeting given behaviors within the session. This ensures that clients understand the session's emphasis and primes appropriate behavior during training.

Verbal instructions and examples are followed by modeling of targeted skills. Clients are exposed to one or more models who demonstrate the skill components in ways that convey clearly the nature of the desired behavior. The therapist may augment this exposure by focusing attention on specific elements of effective behavior, and modeling may be repeated to ensure adequate exposure. The ways in which modeling is conducted vary widely, but three formats are common. Modeling may be done live as when the therapist engages in a role-play and models skill components such as eye contact or certain types of verbal responses. Modeling may be symbolic when presented by audio- or videotape. Effective skill components are prerecorded, and clients listen to or watch the symbolic model present the targeted skills (e.g., videotape portraying effective conversational or date initiation behaviors). Symbolic modeling allows behaviors to be defined and presented more precisely and frees the therapist to point out examples as they occur. Tapes can also be replayed for other purposes as well as allowing clients to review modeling outside the session. Covert modeling in which the client visualizes a model exhibiting correct behaviors leading to favorable outcomes may also be employed (e.g., visualization of a valued colleague maintaining eye contact while asking for a raise). Regardless of format, modeling is one of the primary components of social skills training programs.

Several factors facilitate such observational learning.

Modeling effects are improved if the model is the same gender and age as the client. Multiple models are better than single models, providing variations of the targeted skill behavior that facilitate acquisition of specific behaviors by an individual. Perceived similarity between client and model (i.e., clients perceive or are told the model is like them) increases identification with the model and acquisition of modeled behaviors. For many behaviors, a coping model (i.e., one who experiences some difficulties but copes successfully with the situation) is more effective than a mastery model (i.e., one who handles the situation flawlessly). Likability and attractiveness of the model also enhance effects because models who appear cold, distant, or unaffectionate are less effective than those who demonstrate warmth and affection. Consequences to the model also influence performance with modeled behavior leading to positive outcomes enhancing learning and performance more than modeled behavior leading to negative or minimal outcomes.

Observing effective behavior is followed by practice of that behavior to ensure clients not only know what to do but can actually do it. Effort is made to ensure that clients successfully demonstrate the behavior and that practice closely resembles troublesome situations in order to maximize transfer to the real world. Although the specific format of behavioral rehearsal varies with the targeted skills, five methods of practicing behavior are commonly employed. One is the use of structured role-plays or simulations to present troublesome situations and provide clients the opportunity to practice modeled skills. For example, the therapist role-plays an individual making unreasonable requests, and the client practices tactfully refusing the request. Variations on the theme, such as different unreasonable requests, are role-played within the session in order to consolidate skill components and increase self-confidence and the ability to handle a variety of situations. A second rehearsal format is covert rehearsal involving visualization of a problematic situation and visualizing others or one's self executing appropriate behavior. Covert rehearsal is generally repeated with the visualization of somewhat similar scenes. In other cases, clients rehearse behaviors in semistructured, extended interactions, a format particularly appropriate for social interactions of longer duration. For example, date initiation and conversational skill-training programs often model skill components and then arrange for interactions of several minutes' length during which clients employ modeled skills. Other individuals in these extended interactions are coached on general behavioral style such as being warm and not monopolizing, but otherwise engage in behavior typical of them in these situations. Another rehearsal format is unstructured practice in which clients observe effective behavior and then return immediately to the natural environment to practice the behavior. For example, socially isolated children are exposed to effective play behaviors and then return to free-play situations and are encouraged to engage in behaviors just modeled. A final form of practice involves client verbal rehearsal outside of therapy. Clients receive extensive instruction and modeling of appropriate verbal behavior. Detailed scripts or outlines of verbal responses may be developed. Clients then go over these aloud several times prior to encountering problematic situations (e.g., an oral exam or interview). Regardless of the format, practice of social skill components and, over time, rehearsals of longer, more complex patterns of skills are critical elements of social skills training.

Rehearsal is followed by reinforcement, feedback, and coaching. Therapists note and reinforce effort and successful rehearsal, provide corrective feedback and suggestions for improvement, and support and encourage clients as behavior is rehearsed again. If training takes place in a group, other clients may provide reinforcement and feedback. If rehearsal is videotaped, self-observation of the tape provides an additional source of feedback. This modeling-practice-reinforcement/feedback cycle is repeated until clients demonstrate skill across troublesome situations.

Once skills are established within training sessions, attention shifts to transfer of skills to naturalistic environments. Clients may contract practice in specific situations or simply apply skills whenever the opportunity arises. Experiences are recorded and discussed in the next session with success reinforced and problems troubleshot, adding new modeling and rehearsal as needed. When transfer is complete, emphasis shifts to maintenance and relapse prevention. Activities such as booster sessions, greater time between sessions, phone or written contact, development of written behavioral scripts or checklists, and review of videotapes are employed to keep client attention on continued application of skills over time and across situations.

Social skills training can be administered individually or in groups. Groups have the advantage of more people to provide information, modeling, and role-plays. Groups also provide a greater opportunity for naturalistic support and for a buddy system for support of external practice. Depending on the client population and skills being trained, training may vary in the continued focus on concrete behavior. Chronically mentally ill and retarded individuals often require a sustained focus on discrete behaviors and prompting those behaviors in the naturalistic environment, whereas college students may switch to general interpersonal strategies fairly quickly. Finally, social skills training may be integrated with other interventions (e.g., cognitive restructuring and self-instructional programs addressing cognitive distortions or relaxation interventions for heightened emotional and physiological arousal).

Social skill training is an effective intervention for a wide range of problems and populations. It has increased assertive refusal skills, assertive initiation behaviors, skills in giving compliments and providing positive feedback, resistance to peer pressure and drug refusal skills, conversational skills, heterosocial interactions and date initiation behavior, job interview skills, appropriate play behavior, and social problem-solving and conflict management skills. It has also lowered various social anxieties, depression, anger, and aggression. Populations have ranged from socially isolated children, aggressive and delinquent adolescents, college students and adults with a variety of social deficiencies, and chronically mentally ill and retarded individuals. In general, social skill training is an effective intervention, but not significantly more effective than other interventions addressing the same problem.

Bibliography

Alberti, R. E., & Emmons, M. L. (1970). *Your perfect right: A guide to assertive behavior.* San Luis Obispo, CA: Impact.

Deffenbacher, J. L., Thwaites, G. A., Wallace, T. L., & Oetting, E. R. (1994). Social skills and cognitive-relaxation approaches to general anger reduction. *Journal of Counseling Psychology, 41,* 386–396.

Galassi, J. P., & Bruch, M. A. (1992). Counseling with social interaction problems: Assertion and social anxiety. In S. D. Brown & R. W. Lent (Eds.), *Handbook of counseling psychology* (2nd ed., pp. 757–791). New York: Wiley.

Goldstein, A. P., & Glick, B. (1987). *Aggression replacement training: A comprehensive intervention for aggressive youth.* Champaign, IL: Research Press.

Kazdin, A. E. (1979). Imagery elaboration and self-efficacy in the covert modeling treatment of unassertive behavior. *Journal of Consulting and Clinical Psychology, 47,* 725–733.

Kelley, J. A. (1982). *Social-skills training.* New York: Springer.

McFall, R. M. (1976). Behavioral training: A skill-acquisition approach to clinical problems. In J. T. Spence, R. C. Carson, & J. W. Thibaut (Eds.), *Behavioral approaches to therapy* (pp. 227–259). Morristown, NJ: General Learning Press.

Jerry Lee Deffenbacher

SOCIAL SUPPORT. During the last 20 years, hundreds of published articles have addressed how our relationships with others influence our psychological and physical health. Although interpersonal relationships can be detrimental to well-being, most of this literature focuses on beneficial aspects of relationships, such as the supportive functions they may serve. The term *social support* refers to the process through which help is provided to others. This process is influenced by characteristics of the social environment and individual participants, transactions that occur between participants, the resources that are provided, and participants' perceptions of these transactions and their implications.

Concepts and Measures of Social Support

Attempts to measure social support have focused primarily on the structure of social relationships and the functions they serve. Structural support refers to quantitative aspects of relationships, such as the number and interconnectedness of people in a person's social network. Typical measures include whether people are married, have relationships with relatives and friends, and belong to social or religious groups; these measures are considered objective, reliable, and easy to administer (Brissette, Cohen, & Seeman, in press). The structural support concept that has received the greatest attention is social integration (SI), defined as the extent to which persons participate in multiple types of social relationships. Common measures of SI include the number of social roles that a person occupies and the extent or frequency of social activity that a person is engaged in.

The functional approach emphasizes the resources that other people provide. It has been suggested that social relationships may serve several major functions. First, they may provide emotional support, or reassurance that we are loved and cared for by others. Relationships may also provide instrumental or tangible support, such as assistance with material needs and daily tasks. Finally, we can receive informational support from others, such as the provision of guidance and feedback.

An additional distinction that has been made with respect to the functional aspects of relationships is between perceived and received support. Perceived support measures assess individual evaluations of whether support would be provided by social network members if needed (see Heitzmann & Kaplan, 1988, for a review of measures). There is substantial evidence that these perceptions are important for health, particularly in times of stress (Cohen & Wills, 1985). However, these perceptions may not be entirely accurate. For example, personality characteristics such as self-esteem can distort estimates of the support that is actually available from others. Other researchers view support as an interpersonal process that involves the exchange of resources between social network members; this is known as received support. Measures of received support typically assess how often different types of support were received over a specific period of time or in the context of a specific event (Heitzmann & Kaplan, 1988). This approach addresses the complexity of support provision and receipt and helps to explain why support exchanges may not always be effective. Both the perceived and received support concepts are viewed as important in understanding the impact of social relationships on health.

Development of the Social Support Construct

The study of social support has its origins in sociological research conducted in the early 1900s that was concerned with the impact of industrialization and urban migration on the maintenance of social ties (Brownell & Shumaker, 1984). This work focused on disruptions of social networks as causes of social and psychological disorder. However, it was not until the 1970s that research began to focus on the relationship of social support to physical health. This came at a time when scientists were proposing that in addition to biological factors, there may also be behavioral, social, and psychological factors involved in the etiology of disease. This work focused primarily on the physiological consequences of stress, although it was recognized that other psychosocial factors such as social support may ameliorate the negative consequences of stress or be directly beneficial for health.

Due to this emphasis on stress and health, one area of social support research focused on the implications of support for individuals who were exposed to stressful environmental conditions. It was proposed that social support may act as a buffer protecting individuals from the harmful effects of stressful conditions. This approach is known as the stress-buffering model of social support. Evidence consistent with this hypothesis has been found when people perceive that social support is available from members of their social network (Cohen & Wills, 1985).

One of the earliest and most influential studies in this area investigated whether "psychosocial assets," a measure of social and psychological resources during pregnancy, protect women from the negative effects of stress on pregnancy complications (Nuckolls, Cassel, & Caplan, 1972). Consistent with the stress-buffering model, women with a combination of high life stress and few psychosocial assets experienced more complications during pregnancy than women with high life stress and greater psychosocial assets. For women with low life stress, there were few complications overall and psychosocial assets were not related to pregnancy complications. Similar evidence has been found in dozens of other studies investigating the stress-buffering effects of social support on psychological outcomes (see Cohen & Wills, 1985, for a review). Thus, the perceived availability of support during times of need appears to be important for physical and psychological well-being.

Research examining different types of stressors suggests that stress-buffering effects may vary with the duration and nature of the stressor. One study found that while perceived support protected persons from the effects of residential crowding on psychological distress in the short term, it was not effective after long-term exposure to the stressor (Lepore, Evans, & Schneider, 1991). Stress-buffering may also depend on the needs elicited by a stressor. This approach is known as the matching hypothesis because the effectiveness of support is thought to depend on a match between the types of support that are needed and the resources that are available (Cohen & Wills, 1985). Cutrona and Russell examined whether specific types of functional support would be effective with certain types of stressors (1990). They found that emotional support was more beneficial in helping individuals cope with uncontrollable stressors, while informational support was more beneficial for those coping with controllable stressors. Even so, it is generally agreed that emotional support is protective across a wide range of stressful events.

Other studies test the stress-buffering model by examining the ability of social support to moderate the physical and psychological impact of illness and health-related events. Experimental studies investigating the effects of having a supportive companion ("doula") during labor found that this intervention reduced the duration of labor, the number of cesarean sections and forceps deliveries, and the receipt of medication to augment labor (e.g., Kennell, Klaus, McGrath, Robertson, & Hinkley, 1991). In a study of coronary bypass patients, married patients with greater support from spouses (measured as hospital visits) recovered more quickly from surgery than those with less hospital support and unmarried individuals after controlling for postoperative health status (Kulik & Mahler, 1989). These studies suggest that the provision of appropriate social support reduces the stress associated with health-related events. However, the evidence for the success of support interventions is inconsistent in the literature (Helgeson & Cohen, 1996).

In addition to the stress-buffering model of social support, it has been suggested that social support may exert direct positive effects on certain physical health outcomes independent of stress (Cohen & Wills, 1985). This hypothesis is known as the main-effect model of social support because it predicts a main effect of social support without a statistical interaction between stress and support. Argument for this model has been obtained when the relationships between structural measures of support (particularly SI) and health are examined (Cohen & Wills, 1985).

A number of studies have found that more socially integrated individuals report greater psychological well-being than their less integrated counterparts (Cohen & Wills, 1985). Numerous studies have documented a relationship between SI and mortality suggesting that SI also has important implications for physical health (see

House, Landis, & Umberson, 1988, for a review). A landmark study found that SI (marital status, having close friends and relatives, and group membership) predicted mortality over the following 9-year period such that those who were more integrated lived longer (see Berkman, 1995, for a review). Although the SI-mortality finding is generally interpreted as evidence for the main-effect model of support, most mortality studies do not test the stress-buffering model since they do not include measures of stress.

There is also evidence that SI is related to slower onset and quicker recovery from disease. This may help to explain why SI is associated with lower mortality. For example, SI is associated with increased survival in individuals following heart attacks (Berkman, 1995). A recent study showed a main effect of SI on susceptibility to infectious illness (Cohen, Doyle, Skoner, Rabin, & Gwaltney, 1997). Individuals reporting the fewest types of social relationships (one to three) were 4.2 times more likely to become ill when exposed to a common cold virus than those reporting the most types (six or more). Thus, the relationship between SI and mortality may be attributable to more socially integrated individuals being less susceptible to certain diseases and more likely to recover from disease when they are ill.

Although it was originally presumed that social relationships were associated with better health primarily through their ability to buffer stress, evidence for the main-effect model led researchers to explore alternate pathways linking support to health. An emphasis has been placed on behavioral patterns and biological processes involved in the etiology of various diseases (Cohen, 1988). Social support may promote positive health behavior, including abstaining from smoking, limiting alcohol consumption, maintaining a healthy diet, exercising regularly, and getting adequate sleep. Social support may also reduce disease risk through increased medical care seeking and compliance with medical regimens. In terms of biological mechanisms, social support has been related to better cardiovascular regulation, such as lower resting blood pressure levels (see Uchino, Cacioppo, & Kiecolt-Glaser, 1996, for a review). There is also evidence that social support is related to better immune function in physically healthy samples and in those with compromised immune systems, such as cancer patients (Uchino, Cacioppo, & Kiecolt-Glaser, 1996). While potential biological and behavioral mediators of the support-health relationship have been identified, few studies examine these processes based on a theoretical analysis of how the mediator might explain the relationship between a specific type of support and specific illness outcome.

Conclusions

Over the past two decades, substantial empirical evidence has accumulated showing that social relationships are beneficial for health. The stress-buffering model has been supported in studies examining the relationship between perceived support and health, and the main-effect model has been supported in studies of SI and health. Thus, both conceptual approaches are important in linking social relationships to health. However, there is still need for a broader, more integrated theory of support that specifies the psychological, behavioral, and biological mechanisms linking different support concepts to health.

[*See also* Prosocial Behavior.]

Bibliography

Berkman, L. F. (1995). The role of social relations in health promotion. *Psychosomatic Medicine, 57,* 245–254.

Brissette, I., Cohen, S., & Seeman, T. E. (in press). Measuring social integration and social networks. In S. Cohen, L. Underwood, & B. Gottlieb (Eds.), *Support measurement and interventions: A guide for health and social scientists.* New York: Oxford University Press. Discusses the conceptualization and measurement of social integration and social network characteristics in terms of their relevance to the study of support and health outcomes.

Brownell, A., & Shumaker, S. A. (1984). Social support: An introduction to a complex phenomenon. *Journal of Social Issues, 40*(4), 1–9. Presents a history of the social support construct.

Cohen, S. (1988). Psychosocial models of the role of social support in the etiology of physical disease. *Health Psychology, 7*(3), 269–297. Presents empirical evidence of the relationship of support to morbidity and mortality and discusses psychological and biologic mediators that may account for these associations.

Cohen, S., Doyle, W. J., Skoner, D. P., Rabin, B. S., & Gwaltney, J. M., Jr. (1997). Social ties and susceptibility to the common cold. *Journal of the American Medical Association, 277,* 1940–1944.

Cohen, S., & Wills, T. A. (1985). Stress, social support, and the buffering hypothesis. *Psychological Bulletin, 98*(2), 310–357. Reviews empirical studies that test the stress-buffering and main-effect models of support on mental and physical health outcomes.

Cutrona, C. E., & Russell, D. (1990). Type of social support and specific stress: Toward a theory of optimal matching. In B. R. Sarason, I. G. Sarason, & G. R. Pierce (Eds.), *Social support: An interactional view* (pp. 319–366). New York: Wiley.

Heitzmann, C. A., & Kaplan, R. M. (1988). Assessment of methods for measuring social support. *Health Psychology, 7*(1), 75–109.

Helgeson, V. S., & Cohen, S. (1996). Social support and adjustment to cancer: Reconciling descriptive, correlational, and intervention research. *Health Psychology, 15*(2), 135–148.

House, J. S., Landis, K. R., & Umberson, D. (1988). Social relationships and health. *Science, 241,* 540–545. Reviews epidemiological studies investigating the association between social integration and mortality and argues for a broader theory of support that identifies the mechanisms underlying this association.

Kennell, J., Klaus, M., McGrath, S., Robertson, S., & Hinkley, C. (1991). Continuous emotional support during labor in a U.S. hospital: A randomized controlled trial. *Journal of the American Medical Association, 265*(17), 2197–2201.

Kulik, J. A., & Mahler, H. I. M. (1989). Social support and recovery from surgery. *Health Psychology, 8*(2), 221–238.

Lepore, S., Evans, G. N. W., & Schneider, M. L. (1991). Dynamic role of social support in the link between chronic stress and psychological distress. *Journal of Personality and Social Psychology, 61*(6), 899–909.

Nuckolls, K. B., Cassel, J., & Kaplan, B. H. (1972). Psychosocial assets, life crisis, and the prognosis of pregnancy. *American Journal of Epidemiology, 95*(5), 431–441.

Uchino, B. N., Cacioppo, J. T., & Kiecolt-Glaser, J. K. (1996). The relationship between social support and physiological processes: A review with emphasis on underlying mechanisms and implications for health. *Psychological Bulletin, 119*(3), 488–531. Reviews empirical studies investigating the relationship between social support and cardiovascular, neuroendocrine, and immune function and discusses the potential mechanisms underlying these associations.

Pamela J. Feldman and Sheldon Cohen

SOCIETY FOR NEUROSCIENCE. Founded in 1970, the Society for Neuroscience is the world's largest organization of scientists and physicians dedicated to understanding the brain, spinal cord, and peripheral nervous system. Neuroscientists investigate the molecular and cellular levels of the nervous system—the neuronal systems responsible for sensory and motor function and the basis of higher order processes such as cognition and emotion. This research provides the basis for understanding the medical fields concerned with treating nervous system disorders. These medical specialties include neurology, neurosurgery, psychiatry, and opthalmology.

The society has grown from 500 charter members to more than 28,000 members. Regular members are residents of Canada, Mexico, and the United States, where more than 100 chapters organize local activities. The number of international members, particularly those from Japan and Europe, is increasing.

The purposes of the society are to (a) advance the understanding of the nervous system by bringing together scientists of various backgrounds and by encouraging research in all aspects of neuroscience, (b) promote education in the neurosciences, and (c) inform the public about results and implications of new research.

The exchange of information occurs at an annual fall meeting that includes more than 12,000 reports of new scientific findings and more than 20,000 participants. This meeting, the largest of its kind in the world, attracts many scientists from the Americas, Europe, and Asia and is the arena for the presentation of new results in neuroscience. A series of courses, workshops, and symposia held at the annual meeting promotes the education of society members.

A major mission of the society is to inform the public about the progress and benefits of neuroscience research. The society provides information about neuroscience to secondary school teachers and encourages its members to speak to young people about the brain and nervous system.

The society provides information to legislators through congressional visits held each spring and through testimony at budget hearings. In 1989, Congress designated the 1990s the "decade of the brain," an event the society strongly supported through a series of public presentations, symposia, and events planned with other scientific organizations.

The *Journal of Neuroscience*, published by the society twice a month, is the premier journal in the field and contains articles spanning the entire range of neuroscience research. Major sections are devoted to behavioral neuroscience, cellular and molecular neuroscience, and developmental neuroscience. The society also produces several publications for lay audiences. *Brain Facts* is a 52-page primer on the brain and nervous system. *Brain Briefings* is a series of 2-page newsletters explaining how basic neuroscience discoveries lead to clinical applications.

Other publications include a membership directory and the bimonthly *Neuroscience Newsletter*, which informs members of society activities and programs.

[*See also* Neuropsychology; *and* Neuroscience.]

Bibliography

Society for Neuroscience. Available Web site: http://www.sfn.org/. Information about the society and articles from the *Journal of Neuroscience*, available on the World Wide Web.

Joseph Carey

SOCIETY FOR PSYCHOTHERAPY RESEARCH. An international multidisciplinary scientific organization, the Society for Psychotherapy Research (SPR) supports development of knowledge in psychotherapy by fostering communication among investigators at its conferences and through its journal. The society welcomes researchers of all professions, levels of training, and theoretical orientations who are interested in the scientific study of psychotherapy.

The group that became the Society for Psychotherapy Research held its first meeting in September 1968 in San Francisco, in conjunction with the annual conference of the American Psychological Association (APA), aided by small grants from the APA Division of Psychotherapy and the American Academy of Psychotherapists. Initiative for organizing that group and founding the society was taken by Kenneth Howard and David Orlinsky, with the support of Lester Luborsky, Nathaniel Raskin, and Hans Strupp. The first official meeting of the society was held in June 1969 in Highland Park, Illinois.

Research conferences in the following years have been held at various locations in North America and Europe. These conferences have contributed directly to the development of the field by providing constructively critical yet supportive arenas for the presentation of new ideas and the discussion and assessment of new research findings. Annual SPR conferences have indirectly advanced the field by creating a sense of continuity and community and by maintaining a tradition of informal collegiality among researchers. The society encourages young researchers to participate in meetings by offering travel scholarships to students who present their work at the annual conferences.

Since its founding, the SPR has grown from an organization of about 100 North American members to an association of more than 1,300 members in 28 countries. There are now regional SPR chapters in Europe, South America, and North America, each of which generally holds its own conference in years when the society's international meeting is on another continent. Smaller groups within the society have also been organized through member initiatives; for example, local SPR chapters, such as one in the Chicago area that meets each month during the academic year, and specialized interest projects, such as the SPR Collaborative Research Network's program of studies on development in psychotherapists.

The SPR is governed by an executive council consisting of the president, the president-elect, the immediate past president, the general vice-president (who becomes president-elect), and vice-presidents from the four regional chapters. The following distinguished researchers have served as presidents of the society (in historical order): Kenneth Howard, David Orlinsky, Hans Strupp, Lester Luborsky, Allen Bergin, Sol Garfield, Aaron T. Beck, Morris Parloff, Irene Elkin Waskow, Edward Bordin, Mardi Horowitz, Stanley Imber, Alan Gurman, Arthur Auerbach, A. John Rush, Jim Mintz, Larry Beutler, Charles Marmar, Leslie Greenberg, Horst Kächele, Lorna Benjamin, Leonard Horowitz, David Shapiro, Clara Hill, Klaus Grawe, Paul Crits-Christoph, William Stiles, Marvin Goldfried, William Piper, Robert

Elliott, and Franz Caspar. Curtis Barrett, Chad Emerick, Michael Lambert, and Charles Marmar have also served as officers of the society. Since 1986, the SPR has been guided by an elected executive council and the following appointed executive officers (in historical order): Kenneth Howard, Paul Pilkonis, John Clarkin, and Paulo Machado.

Since 1991, the Society has published the quarterly scientific journal *Psychotherapy Research*. The founding editors were David Shapiro, Hans Strupp, and Klaus Grawe, succeeded in turn by Robert Elliott, Bernhard Strauss, and William Stiles.

[*See also* Psychotherapy.]

Bibliography

Bergin, A. E., & Garfield, S. L. (Eds.). (1994). *Handbook of psychotherapy and behavior change* (4th ed.). New York: Wiley.

Orlinsky, D. E. (1995). The greying and greening of SPR: A personal memoir on the forming of the Society for Psychotherapy Research. *Psychotherapy Research, 5,* 343–350.

Orlinsky, D. E., & Russell, R. L. (1994). Tradition and change in psychotherapy research. In R. L. Russell (Ed.), *Reassessing psychotherapy research.* New York: Guilford Press.

Strupp, H. H., & Howard, K. I. (1992). A brief history of psychotherapy research. In D. K. Freedheim (Ed.), *History of psychotherapy: A century of change.* Washington, DC: American Psychological Association.

David E. Orlinsky

SOCIETY FOR RESEARCH IN CHILD DEVELOPMENT. Concerned with the study of child development, the Society for Research in Child Development (SRCD) is an organization of over 5,000 members from various academic disciplines. Their disciplines include, but are not limited to, anatomy, anthropology, dentistry, home economics, linguistics, neuroscience, nursing, nutrition, pediatrics, physiology, psychiatry, psychology, public health, and sociology. Some members are also interested in applications of research, for example, clinical psychologists, lawyers, speech pathologists, and teachers at all levels from preschool through secondary school. In addition to being multidisciplinary, the society's membership is also international, with members from over 40 countries.

The child development movement in the United States started in the early 1920s but had its actual beginnings much earlier. Child development, in contrast to most traditional sciences, was formed by external social pressures broadly arising from desires for better health, rearing, education, and legal and occupational treatment of children. Movements related to child health, child study, and mental hygiene had grown and become prominent by the late nineteenth and early twentieth centuries. From these activities came the conception of the child as a responsibility of the society at large. The U.S. Children's Bureau was established at this time. Scientists were breaking new ground in the field, among them pioneers such as W. T. Porter, G. Stanley Hall, Edward L. Thorndike, L. E. Holt, Millicent Washburn Shinn, Lewis M. Terman, Bird T. Baldwin, and Arnold Gesell. The century of the child had begun.

Beardsley Ruml and Lawrence K. Frank conceived the idea of bringing together scientists from different disciplines to integrate research on the development of the child. Grants were given to universities to establish institutes or to expand programs already initiated. Funds for fellowships were established. By 1926, research centers for the study of children had been established at several major universities across the country, for example, the University of California at Berkeley, the University of Iowa, Yale University, the University of Toronto, Harvard University, and the University of Minnesota.

The scientific status of the field of child development received formal recognition in 1922–1923 through the appointment of a subcommittee on child development of the National Research Council during the chairmanship of Robert S. Woodworth, an eminent experimental psychologist. In 1925, this group became the Committee on Child Development with offices and staff in the National Academy of Sciences. The purpose of the committee was to integrate research activities and to stimulate research in child development, and it awarded fellowships, initiated conferences, and began publications. In 1927, 425 scientists were listed in the *Directory of Research in Child Development*. That same year the first volume of *Child Development Abstracts and Bibliography* was published, which became SRCD's first publication.

In 1933, the Committee on Child Development disbanded and passed the torch to the newly organized Society for Research in Child Development. The activities of SRCD expanded during the 1930s but diminished in the 1940s during World War II. The society experienced a great expansion in the mid-1950s that continued through the century's end.

The society's publications include three journals, *the Social Policy Report,* a newsletter, and a membership directory. The three journals are *Child Development* (published bimonthly; contains original articles on developmental research and theory); *Child Development Abstracts and Bibliography* (published three times a year; includes abstracts of research articles and book reviews); and *Monographs of the Society for Research in Child Development* (published two to four times a year; consists primarily of comprehensive reports of large-scale research projects or integrated programs of research).

The *Social Policy Report* is published quarterly; each issue focuses on a single topic affecting children, youth, or families and includes analysis of existing and pending legislation and contributions of research in the evolution of that legislative program.

The society hosts a biennial meeting with attendance of over 5,000. These internationally attended meetings include individual research reports, symposia, invited lectures, and discussion sessions, among other timely and historical programs.

Nearly 20% of SRCD's members are from outside the United States, representing more than 40 countries throughout the world. Special efforts are made by the society, through its Committee on International Relations, to increase interaction and communication between members of the society and all researchers in human development throughout the world.

Of great importance to the society is the establishment and maintenance of ethical standards for research with children. The Committee on Ethical Conduct in Child Development Research promulgates such standards.

The society fosters a commitment to research and training in diversity. The Committees on Ethnic and Racial Issues and Interdisciplinary Affairs have made great progress in improving, increasing, and disseminating research to members.

Under the guidance of the Committee on Child Development, Public Policy, and Public Information, the society helps to bring the results of research to bear on the formulation of policy affecting children and families. One way in which this is done is through the Government Fellows Program in Child Development. Beginning in 1978, the goals of this program have been to contribute to the effective use of scientific knowledge, to educate the scientific community about the development of public policy, and to establish a more effective liaison between scientists and federal offices. Fellows spend a year as aides or associates in various offices in federal agencies, working with staff in the translation of research to applied issues.

As research in human development expands, the need for coordination and integration among the disciplines grows. The society is constantly working to facilitate such coordination and integration and to assist in the dissemination of research findings. The society welcomes the increasing interest in child development research and seeks members who share this interest. Membership is open to any individual actively engaged in research in human development or any of the related basic sciences, in teaching relevant to human development, or in otherwise furthering the purposes of the society. Persons engaged in at least half-time graduate study in child development or a related field may apply as student members. The SCRD is currently located at the University of Michigan, in Ann Arbor.

[*See also* Developmental Psychology.]

Bibliography

Hartup, W., & Siegel, A. (Eds.). (1997, Fall). History of research in child development [Special issue]. *Newsletter of the Society for Research in Child Development.*

Marston, L. R. (Ed.). (1927). *Directory of research in child development* (reprint and circular series of the NRC, no. 76). Washington, DC: National Research Council.

Smuts, A. B., & Hagen, J. W. (1985). History and research in child development. *Monographs of the Society for Research in Child Development, 50,* 4–5.

John W. Hagen

SOCIETY OF EXPERIMENTAL PSYCHOLOGISTS. At a meeting at Princeton University in 1929, the Society of Experimental Psychologists (SEP) was established as a permanent formal organization of experimental psychologists. Its historical roots, however, stem from a group founded in 1904. Those roots, in turn, grew from dissatisfaction with the broadly inclusive American Psychological Association (APA), founded in 1892. Clashes in personalities and interests were inevitable in the formative years of the APA. E. B. Titchener of Cornell University disapproved of the APA's meeting format of reading papers, and felt that experimental research was insufficiently emphasized and excessive attention was given to philosophical reports.

Titchener's alternative was to invite the psychology department heads at Yale University, the University of Pennsylvania, Clark University, the University of Michigan, Princeton University, the University of Chicago, and the University of Iowa to meet in his laboratories at Cornell 4–5 April 1904 to establish an informal club of experimental psychologists, intended as a league of laboratories. At meetings they would give oral reports on ongoing research in a friendly experimental milieu, handle laboratory apparatus, and indulge in discussions and frank criticism. All invitees were interested, and five attended the first meeting: Charles H. Judd (Yale), Lightner Witmer (Pennsylvania), Edmund C. Sanford (Clark), Walter B. Pillsbury (Michigan), and Howard C. Warren (Princeton). Thereafter, the 2-day informal meetings were held annually at the participating university laboratories through 1928 (except for 1918) and were hosted by the laboratory head.

Titchener defined the content and was the dominant figure in the league of laboratories he had established. When he died unexpectedly in August 1927, the small group was left essentially leaderless. They were eager to maintain the established tradition, but felt that radical change was necessary. Freed of Titchener's dominance, the informal group—sometimes called Titchener's Experimentalists—began to restructure its organization by establishing a Committee of Five in 1928. Its members were Warren, Edwin G. Boring, Raymond Dodge, Herbert S. Langfeld, and Robert M. Yerkes. This was expanded to a Committee of Fifteen to meet as an "organizing nucleus" in 1929. The additional members were: Madison Bentley, Samuel Fernberger, Joseph Peterson, Walter S. Hunter, Edward S. Robinson, Edward A. Bott, Karl S. Lashley, Karl Dallenbach, Robert S. Woodworth, and Walter R. Miles.

Ten members of the organizing nucleus were present at the 1929 meeting in Princeton and decided: (a) to organize a Society of Experimental Psychologists to meet annually for informal discussions; (b) to limit the membership to North American experimental psychologists; (c) to place no other regional limitation upon membership; (d) to place no restriction on membership with regard to sex (women had been excluded from the informal group so the men could smoke); and (e) to place no restriction on the organism studied. Bylaws were adopted that specified procedures for selecting new members and imposed a size limitation of 50 members. To maintain the size limitation, members were to become fellows at age 65, retaining all rights and privileges except that of voting for new members. With the passage of time, both the twofold categorization of the group and its size limitation became major items of disputation at the normally brief business session at the annual meetings.

Following the election of the members of the organizing group, 11 additional new members were elected by this committee. The newly reorganized society thus had 26 members, including two women, Margaret F. Washburn, who had been Titchener's first doctoral student at Cornell, and June E. Downey.

The bylaws and unwritten traditions established a society that was unique in many ways. In describing the experimental club, Titchener had once written: "We don't want officers—in science of all things in this world!" In keeping with this sentiment, the SEP has no professional administrative staff. The officers are limited to a chairman who is host for that year's meeting, and a secretary treasurer who serves for 3 years. Four committees were later established: an executive committee to handle business between annual meetings; a trustee committee related to the incorporation of the society in 1936, the Howard Crosby Warren Medal Award Committee, to select an annual awardee, and a nominating committee to nominate new members. The society is periodically approached to join other societies with related interests. Such invitations are routinely rejected. The record indicates that the SEP did affiliate with the APA's reorganization in 1944, but not as a section and without representation. However, the record also indicates that this affiliation was later terminated.

With two exceptions, annual meetings have been held on university campuses and have been hosted by 40 different psychology departments. The earliest meetings were held on the East Coast, but beginning in 1949 the geographical center of gravity began to shift to the midwest, and in 1964, to the first annual meeting on the West Coast.

The society concerned itself with psychological matters during both World War I and World War II. The final session of the April 1917 meeting took place on the very day that the United States declared war on Germany. The group turned to a consideration of what American psychologists could do to assist the government in the war. The problem of selection of men for a great army and rejection of the "feeble-minded" was discussed and a committee was appointed to consider the possible relationships of psychology to military problems. An ultimate outcome was the avalanche of intelligence testing in the U.S. Army.

During World War II, the society appointed a delegate to the Intersociety Constitutional Convention, and another member served as its representative on the Emergency Committee of Psychologists under National Research Council auspices. There is an irony in these concerns and affiliations. Mental testing and applied psychology had been, of course, among Titchener's strongest taboos, but psychology had grown and broadened since then.

The problem of membership size and procedures for the election of new members has dominated the business session of the society's annual meetings for many decades. To first accommodate the pressures for increases beyond 50 members, the age of fellowship status was dropped from 65 to 60. Later, the bylaws were modified to eliminate the dual categories of member and fellow and treat the entire group as fellows with full society privileges. At the present time there are 197 fellows, although most meetings are attended by about 50 individuals.

Scientific reports are still the centerpiece at the 2-day annual meetings, and they are still accommodated within three sessions. A major event at each meeting is the announcement of the recipient of the Howard Crosby Warren Medal for Achievement in Experimental Psychology. The award is based on recent work, and in addition to the medal and a scroll there is a modest monetary award. There have been 59 annual awards since the first in 1936 (no awards were made in 1944 and 1946) and 6 made to two persons each for related or joint contributions. The Warren Medal was endowed by his widow, Catherine C. Warren, in 1936. It is a fitting memorial to an American experimental psychologist, who, like Titchener, was a student in Wilhelm Wundt's laboratory in Leipzig, an early host at Princeton of the small "league of laboratories" that preceded the SEP, and a member of the "organizing nucleus" that met at Princeton in 1929 to found the society.

Bibliography

Boring, E. G. (1938). The Society of Experimental Psychologists, 1904–1938. *American Journal of Psychology, 51*, 410–421.

Boring, E. G. (1967). Titchener's Experimentalists. *Journal of the History of the Behavioral Sciences, 3*, 315–325.

Goodwin, C. J. (1985). On the origin of Titchener's Experimentalists. *Journal of the History of the Behavioral Sciences, 21*, 383–389.

Leo M. Hurvich

SOCIETY OF EXPERIMENTAL SOCIAL PSYCHOLOGY. In 1965, a number of leading academic social psychologists took note of the increasing size of the American Psychological Association, especially the growth of Division 8 (Personality and Social Psychology) to 4,000 members. Distressed by the impediments that such growth brought to intellectual and personal contact at conventions, they founded the Society of Experimental Social Psychology (SESP). Professors Edwin Hollander, William McGuire, Albert Pepitone, Marvin Shaw, Ezra Stotland, Fred Strodtbeck, and W. Edgar Vinacke agreed to form an organization to include a relatively small number of research-oriented social psychologists. They decided to keep SESP small, with 50 members initially and limited growth thereafter. They believed that the society should exist to provide "enriched opportunity for social psychologists to mingle, share ideas, and communicate their findings."

The University of Chicago hosted the first SESP meeting on 2 September 1965. Thirty experimental social psychologists from psychology and sociology departments attended. Attendees judged the meeting a success, and the society has met every year since. University departments still host the annual meetings, although sessions have been moved to hotels from the living rooms of early hosts.

Along the way, the society has developed into an organization with formal traditions and practices, including the election of three new members to a 3-year term on its nine-member executive committee each year. The executive committee, in turn, elects a secretary-treasurer from its second-year class of members. The secretary-treasurer subsequently serves as chair (president) of the society during his or her last executive committee year. Standing committees include membership, program, and two awards committees.

The society's sole activity consists of its annual meeting, attended by about 40% of its members. Dues are nominal, as convention expenses are paid for by grants from host institutions, registration fees, and other income from the meetings.

Staying true to the initial intent of its founders, the society limits membership growth to 5% or less annually. Although this policy has increased membership to more than 600 to date, the size of the group has begun to stabilize as academic job growth has ceased and retirements and deaths take their toll. Applicants must be nominated by members, must be at least 5 years beyond having received their Ph.D.s, must have made important contributions to the empirical social psychological literature, and must be accepted by the membership committee. The society was incorporated as a nonprofit scientific and educational organization in 1991.

The program committee, consisting of representatives from the host institution and the past chair of the society, plans the annual program. By tradition, the society keeps programs small, includes plenary sessions, and provides for many informal, personal meeting opportunities. The awards committees choose a distinguished scientist from society ranks and a dissertation award winner annually. Each winner makes a presentation at the subsequent annual meeting. The dissertation award winner, chosen on the basis of dissertations completed the previous year, automatically becomes a society member, with the 5-year post-Ph.D. rule waived.

[*See also* Social Psychology.]

Bibliography

Hollander, E. P. (1968). The society of experimental social psychology: An historical note. *Journal of Personality and Social Psychology, 9,* 280–282.

Jim Blascovich

SOCIOBIOLOGY. *See* Ethology; *and* Evolutionary Psychology.

SOCIOHISTORICAL PROCESS. Change is a notion deeply embedded in everyday life and common sense. Everyone knows its meaning but not its definition. The Greek philosopher Aristotle (384–322 BCE) considered change as equivalent to movement, an idea still influencing the social sciences, where transformations and stagnation have been a main concern. It can be said that change is becoming. From a psychosocial and po-

litical perspective, change refers to planned or accidental processes of alteration producing power displacements, balancing or unbalancing human relations. Psychological studies of power are now considering it not as an object or a site but as a relation, thus challenging traditional theories, according to which only one pole of the relation controls it. All parties have the possibility of exerting power. Resistance, both active and passive, expresses that possibility, helping to explain how, in spite of domination, independence and freedom can prevail.

Change and Stability

Some notions are complementary. Such is the case of power and resistance, of change and stability. This leads to some questions: How is it that regardless of social movements and efforts of leaders, things do not change in proportion to their activity? Why do things often seem to maintain the same pace and direction that were intended to change? Why is there continuity? Why do certain patterns of behavior persist? How, in spite of cultural changes, does culture remain recognizable across time and space?

Social movements as privileged factors of social change seem to respond to the idea that they mobilize resources until they are paralyzed, an inert conception of the status quo, considering it as static. But society is essentially dynamic. Even to impede change, it is necessary to engage in intense activity and carry out many actions. And in performing those activities, many transformations are produced whose objective is to keep everything the same or to reduce the rate of change.

In dealing with social change, researchers have neglected everyday life, the realm where cultural practices are repeatedly carried out, steadying the rhythm of social life. Social constancy, then, is as complex a problem as social dynamics.

Iranian and British psychologists F. Moghaddam and Rom Harré provide an explanation for this puzzle in their social reducton theory. In this theory, a reducton is an elementary bit of social behavior, akin to the subatomic particle the proton. That elementary character derives from its being carried out without conscious effort using skills acquired by the person during the socialization process. Reductons respond to what is culturally defined as proper or correct behavior, that is, socially expected and produced in an almost automatic way, so changes planned at macrosocial levels do not consider or touch that basic behavior. According to this theory, cultural change occurs at macro levels, in institutions such as media and educational and religious systems. It also happens at micro levels, such as in daily social practices.

Activity occurring at one level can resist and oppose activity carried out at the other level. That resistance slows the pace of the intended change, which is why, in spite of revolutions, certain habits die hard. Social reducton theory states that the maximum speed of change at the macro level is greater than the maximum speed of change at the micro level, thus explaining why certain social changes take time.

Reductons are very similar to the notion French anthropologist Pierre Bourdieu calls *habitus* in his book *Esquisse d'une théorie de la pratique* (Geneva, 1972). It is characterized as (1) regularities associated with a socially structured environment; (2) durable; (3) structuring behavior while being also structured—somewhat like established and fixed behavior patterns; (4) practices and representations with a regulated and regular character, automatically carried out with neither conscious direction nor express mastery of the operations necessary to achieve their goals; (5) adjusted to collective regulation, without of specific direction; (6) allowing the person to face unexpected situations; (7) with implicit anticipation of the consequences of those situations, and constituting socially codified and expected responses; (8) tending to reproduce objective social structures of which they are an effect while at the same time maintaining them; (9) lacking strategic intention; and (10) facilitating social relationships since they act as links.

The holistic approach using the notion of habitus allows us to see how culturally established but unperceived behavior patterns maintain conduct chains that challenge neither their origin nor their finality nor their insertion in everyday life.

Experimental psychosocial research provides clear explanations of how people can resist persuasive information. Thus, forewarning about certain innovations or ideas may lead individuals to prepare defenses against them and become more resistant. Conversely, too much warning (e.g., repression or protest) may concentrate their attention on the denounced messages, facilitating cognitive changes partial to them (this is what the theory of conversion stresses) or inoculate them against the source of persuasion, whether that source is of the majority or the minority. As the theory of reactance proposes, if people fear that their freedom is at stake, they tend to reject any persuasive messages perceived as endangering it. Terrorism can have this effect. Currently, discursive psychology focuses on discourse as the realm where resistance and compliance take place and are expressed in actions done through discourse.

Change and Development

References to political, economic, or cultural changes can be found in the literature, the press, and daily talk. Those changes refer to transformations produced in relation to patterns of development. Development has been understood as a specific model of advancement or improvement in socioeconomic conditions. This assumption corresponds to the idea of progress or growth, whose roots can be traced to the nineteenth-century French philosopher Auguste Comte (1798–1857), who created the basis for the philosophical and scientific movement known as Positivism. Those ideas began to be challenged toward the end of the 1960s by sociological and economic theories of underdevelopment coming from Latin America. The 1970s introduced the psychological notion of development as control exerted by people over their environment in order to create the necessary conditions for self-fulfillment and a positive social identity. Emphasis shifted from economic factors to people as social actors.

The idea of progress is usually expressed by the milestones that modernity tags as signs of advancement, consisting of social changes oriented to certain goals, according to a model considered at a particular moment as the ideal and assumed to be atemporal and universal. The objectives to be reached by developing social changes have responded to the interests of the centers of power. From them radiate signals and directions to be followed in order to overcome deficits.

This process presupposes the use of psychological processes of social comparison and categorization not only at the individual level, but also at the institutional level. Thus, nations have been classified as either industrialized or developing countries. Industrialization has been considered the most advanced stage of development. Industry, gross national product and income, and energy consumption rate are the parameters that have been used to measure the degree of development. The "developing" category encompasses countries at different economic stages that have not yet reached the standards set by the industrialized countries. A complementary way to classify countries according to this developmental view places them in the First, Second, or Third World. These classifications contain several contradictions. Developed countries have pockets of poverty comparable to those present in developing or Third World nations. When the Berlin wall went down and Soviet control disappeared, industrialized countries formerly under Soviet influence revealed enormous socioeconomic deficiencies. In addition, nations with a gross national product much lower than that of industrialized nations can have a higher standard in important areas, such as the literacy rate. That is the case in Costa Rica and Denmark compared with countries such as Japan or Germany.

Modernity, Postmodernity, and the Individual

Each historical moment supposedly includes particular psychosocial expressions configuring socially predominating characteristics. Modernity has been said to influence personality processes, producing a person adjusted to its exigencies; a "modern" person has been characterized as oriented to the future; having a sense of self-efficacy, being democratic, egalitarian, and tolerant; being cognitively flexible; having high achievement motivation; being open to innovations and changes; being information seeking, risk taking, and individualistic; believing in equity and justice; having faith in science and technology; and using a global orientation.

These characteristics are exaggerated in postmodernity, the worldview emerging from the critique of modernity's contradictions. Postmodernity exposes the existence of a global culture of the excess (in goals, technology, information, and consumerism), saturating both the social realm and the self. Its effects can be seen in urban, educated, middle- and upper-class populations moving across space, being everywhere and belonging nowhere.

Modernity Challenged

The idea of modernity as a stage in social evolution is being challenged. French anthropologist Bruno Latour states in his book *Nous n'avons jamais été modernes* (Paris, 1994) that we have neither advanced nor retreated. People, he says, "have always actively elected elements pertaining to different times. . . . It is the election that makes time and not time that makes the election" (p. 99). Modernity considers as actual what moves at the pace fixed by industrialization and disqualifies as archaic, irrational, or conservative what does not adjust to that system. But in the same society, modern and traditional time can coexist, including tendencies that will shape the future. Therefore, time perception can be reversible, particular rather than general, and dependent on human relations.

Modernity has been seen as a global process that engulfs all nations as technology spreads and their markets open to free trade. But as some more or less spectacular social changes have shown, growth or progress does not follow a straight line. Within a society different ways of living coexist, and even when traditional ways are repressed, they can reemerge when social conditions change. An example is the fundamentalist movement in Islamic nations such as Algeria and Iran.

Nevertheless, if modernity is challenged, communication does have worldwide effects. The globalization, of communication, like that of technology, affects institutions and people, both in industrialized and in developing countries.

Social Change and Cultural Change

Social systems are not homogeneous, and this is especially evident when culture is considered. "Culture" refers to systems of interaction between people and the environment constructed by them. It refers to collective ways of life and thinking; to prescribed forms of behavior; and to visions of the world collectively constructed. Culture and society are the two faces of the same coin, but the marks made in one of them do not automatically appear in the other. Thus, the degree of growth of the economic or political system of a society does not determine its cultural development, and as noted, psychological processes do not change at the same speed that institutions do. The complexity and richness of a culture do not depend on industrialization or technological power and cannot be subject to comparisons, since their outcomes stem from domains that are different for each culture. Moreover, within a given society, the plurality of groups integrating it may change at a different pace. That could explain the simultaneous presence of traditionalist, modern, and deviant sectors, and of global and regional ways.

Explanations of Social Change

Innovations emerge both in society's mainstream and on its periphery within minority groups. But minorities, although producing changes, do not tend to generate innovations that stray from the deep tendencies dominant in culture, which slowly but steadily guide the course of transformations.

Nevertheless, minorities seem to be at the core of many social movements, and either as source or as transmitter, their role in social change has to be taken into account. A "minority" is a group with a defined social identity and specific goals that it pursues consistently and persistently, resisting the pressure of the majority to conform to or comply with the establishment. The minority's influence over the majority concerns innovation, that is, a movement of opinion produced in the majority, in the direction proposed by the minority, in spite of their conflict of ideas and interests.

This movement is generated by means of a psychological process called conversion, which consists of a subtle and complex set of cognitive and perceptive modifications. Conversion preserves the person's usual responses, but through thought processes concentrated in the minority's proposal, the person begins to diverge from her or his usual line of thinking, implicitly adopting the points of view of groups with ideas not only different from but opposed to his or her own.

A conception emerging from participatory action research is that there is a tension between majorities and minorities, producing a dialectical relation of mutual transformation. Opposition is conserved and a two-way conversion is produced, with both sources of social influence acting simultaneously.

Two processes, naturalization and familiarization, intervene in social influence. Naturalization is the process by which social events are considered as belonging to the natural order of the world. Familiarization is the assimilation of new knowledge to what the individual already knows, transforming it into something akin to the familiar knowledge. Both naturalization and familiarization can promote all sources of influence.

Other explanations also contribute to an understanding of social change. Relative deprivation theory states that transformation derives from the perception of inadequate and conflictive situations and from actions carried out to solve problems caused by these situations. Resources mobilization has also been identified as a way to deal with social discontent, changing the circumstances causing the unrest. This explanation has been expanded to include the relation between expectations about the results of action and the value attributed to those results. These perspectives do not compete with each other. They could be considered as part of the complex task of social construction.

Effects of Social Change

Social changes affect societies, groups, and individuals. Global transformations initiated with the first industrial revolution in the eighteenth century were responsible for specialization of labor, expansion and impersonality of markets, exploitation of natural energy sources, and an increase in urbanization. Other macro-level factors affecting behavior at the micro level are economic development, political orientation, and type of government (related to the degree of citizen participation allowed); external conflicts and internal struggles; population density; freedom or dependency; increasing complexity of public administration; and new power groups and institutions other than political parties, either stemming from the economic field, such as international organizations and enterprises, or emerging from civil society's movements. By contrast, the micro level influences public policies through the creation of ideas and the implementation of new modes of political action, some of which have a participatory character.

Political struggle between democratic and authoritarian tendencies has bestowed on religion a new political function: the conservation or imposition of the hegemony of certain ideas. Thus, religion has become a form of ideological warfare by being incorporated in the strategies intended to defeat opponents through the implementation of changes in acting and thinking. Thus, the advance of religious trends preaching submission and avoidance of protests, arguing that change should be left to God's will, has been associated with political passivity, indifference to dictatorships, and violations of human rights.

The church as an institution has also been affected. In predominantly Catholic developing countries, the religious social movement known as liberation theology initiated a process of change centered on the "forgotten poor majority," recognizing their social agency and mobilizing their consciousness in order to make them understand that their living conditions are the consequence not only of personal deficiencies but mainly of social and political circumstances. Through this movement, the poor majority came to recognize themselves as social actors able to transform their circumstances. This movement inspired the emergence of a liberation psychology with similar goals, studied from psychosocial political and community perspectives. Its objectives included the empowerment of communities and civil society and their political participation through alternative modes of political action.

Negative Social Identity

The process of industrialization in Europe during the eighteenth and nineteenth centuries was related to the colonial status imposed on many nations as providers of raw materials. Colonization and its aftermath have been associated with dependency and with a construction of social identity for the colonized that affects their national identity.

Negative social identity is characterized by a process of social comparison in which other groups are perceived as better than the person's own group—which is disqualified but not rejected or abandoned, as social identity theory predicts. The Other (*Alter*), strong and positive, opposes the We, strong and negative. This belief presupposes the phenomenon of altercentrism, in which the Other is the center of comparisons and a positive ideal around which national identity rotates.

A colonial past or a neocolonial present expressed in economic, cultural, and political dependency, has been associated with the construction of national hetero-images (those originated outside the nation) integrated by negative attributes that go along with limitations and deprivations in political, economic, labor, and educational areas. Those negative images tend to be internalized and reproduced by the people labeled by them. This process has consequences for their behavior as well as their institutions.

Complexity of Collective Identities

Although existing throughout history, international political and economic change has affected the emergence of what could be called supra-identities, in the sense that they overlap national identities, including the latter within a larger category containing other national groups sharing some common characteristics. Thus, several social identities associated with belonging to larger or smaller groups, related to national characteristics such as language, religion, territory, culture, or a common history and globalized modes of behavior, can coincide in a sort of concentric system in which each identity is activated according to circumstances (e.g., being from a particular city or region, a specific country, or a continent or a union of countries).

One example of a supra-identity is Latin Americanism, a social identity shared by nationals from Latin American countries, which is believed to be more positive than their respective national identities. Pan-Arabism and some religious identities, like Judaism or Islamism, are other examples. The European Union could be a developing supra-identity. The positive aspects of the supra-identity as a political idea could help to develop solidarity and peaceful ties between nations. The negative aspects could increase ethnocentrism.

Bibliography

Gergen, K. (1991). *The saturated self*. New York: Basic Books. A discussion of postmodernism, its effects on the self, and relatedness and interdependence in a globalized culture.

Hermann, M. G. (Ed.). *Political psychology*. San Francisco: Jossey-Bass. Provides a general overview of the psychopolitical approach to social change–related issues such as public opinion, leadership, conflict, international relations, protest movements, and terrorism.

Ibáñez, T. (1987). Pouvoir, conversion et changement social. In S. Moscovici & G. Mugny (Eds.), *Psychologie de la conversion* (pp. 219–238). Cousset, Switzerland: Del Val. Discusses social change and the roles of the majority and the minority, including a critique of the theory of conversion.

Martin-Baró, I. (1986). Retos y perspectivas de la psicología latinoamericana. In G. Pacheco & B. Jiménez Domínguez (Eds.), *Ignacio Martín-Baró (1942–1989). Psicología de la liberación en América Latina* (pp. 51–80). Guadalajara, Mexico: Universidad de Guadalajara-Instituto Tecnológico de Estudios Superiores de Occidente. Proposes a social and political psychology whose main goals are the liberation of minorities through deideologization, problematization of social conditions, and conscientization. Can be obtained from the University of Guadalajara Press.

Martín-Baró, I. (1990). Religion as an instrument of psychological warfare. *Journal of Social Issues, 46*(3) 93–107. Analyzes the use of religion as a political weapon, and the passivity and avoidance of social protest it can induce, illustrated by data gathered in El Salvador during the "low-intensity war" (1981–1991).

Moghaddam, F. M., & Crystal, D. S. (1997). Revolutions, samurai and reductons: The paradoxes of change and continuity in Iran and Japan. *Political Psychology, 18*(2), 355–384. Includes a description of social reducton theory and illustrates the paradox of social stability in spite of changes, with references to Iran and Japan.

Moghaddam, F. M., Taylor, D. M., & Wright, S. C. (1993). *Social psychology in cross-cultural perspective*. New York: Freeman. Discusses social change and its influence, specifically in relation to industrialization. The concepts of culture and development are explained in both traditional and modern terms.

Montero, M. (1994). Consciousness-raising, de-ideologization and conversion in community psychosocial work. *Journal of Community Psychology, 14*(1) 3–12. Defines the processes indicated in the title in relation to need assessment in communities, critically discussing the theory of active minorities and changes produced by their activity.

Montero, M. (1998). The dialectic between active minorities and majorities: A study of social influence in the community. *Journal of Community Psychology, 26*(3), 281–290. Outlines an explanation of the dialectic between majority and minority from a critical perspective, illustrated with examples from community psychosocial practice.

Moscovici, S. (1976). *Social influence and social change*. London: Academic Press. Outlines the minority influence theory, with definitions of main concepts.

Moscovici, S., & Mugny, G. (Eds.). (1987). *Psychologie de la conversion*. Cousset, Switzerland: Del Val. Presents illustrative work carried out in diverse European countries on majority-minority relations, as well as the cognitive process of conversion and its influence on social change.

Salazar, J. M. (1987). El latinoamericanismo como una idea política, In M. Montero (Ed.), *Psicología política latinoamericana* (pp. 203–223). Caracas: Panapo. Describes the concept of social supra-identity, presenting cross-national data from seven Latin American countries.

Serrano-García, I., & López-Sánchez, G. (1994). Una concepción diferente del poder y el cambio social. In M. Montero (Ed.), *Psicología social comunitaria. Teoría, método y experiencia* (pp. 211–238). Guadalajara, Mexico: Universidad de Guadalajara. Presents a theoretical and empirical view of power as a relation, inspired by the French psychologist M. Foucault and related to psychosocial community work. Can be obtained from the University of Guadalajara Press.

Smith, P. B., & Bond, M. H. (1994). *Social psychology across cultures: Analysis and perspectives*. Boston: Allyn & Bacon. Discusses psychosocial processes from a cross-cultural perspective, showing similarities and differences. The concepts of culture and social influence, as well as the consequences of cross-cultural contact, are described.

Maritza Montero

SOCIOLINGUISTICS. The term *sociolinguistics* was coined in the 1950s, and widespread interest in the field began to develop in the late 1960s. While linguists had focused on the structure and rules of language often to the exclusion of social context, sociolinguists sought to describe and explain the relationship between language and society. Joshua Fishman, an American sociolinguist, described the discipline as a consideration of who speaks what language variety to whom, in what context and for what function. The focus of sociolinguistic study has been on understanding the structured variability in everyday speech of ordinary people in normal social environments throughout the world, though the majority of the research has been carried out in urban industrial societies. Sociologists, linguists, anthropologists, social psychologists, and educators have all contributed to this interdisciplinary endeavor.

Sociolinguistics is an empirical science. A central paradigm for sociolinguistics has been the quantitative study of linguistic variation in the form of words and constructions according to speakers' group memberships (e.g., gender, class) and linguistic context (e.g., topic, setting, level of formality). This branch of linguistics was inspired by the pioneering work of American linguist William Labov, who analyzed tape-recorded interviews with informants chosen randomly as representative of various social classes, ages, and ethnic groups. Another classic example of this type of work was conducted by British sociolinguist Peter Trudgill in Norwich, England. These types of quantitative studies establish correlations between language use and social factors, but being correlational they cannot establish why people behave linguistically as they do. Sociolinguists aim to move from description to explanation, to develop adequate social theory to explain linguistic variation, and to provide a motivated account of the way language is used.

There has been no unifying theme or approach to the field, and priorities have shifted over time and are debated today. Areas of interest include patterns in language use in multilingual speech communities, language change, norms and rules for using conversation in different cultures, conversation analysis, attitudes toward language varieties and their social and educational consequences, and the relationship between language and thought.

Linguistic Variation and Group Membership

In any community, particular social groups are marked by distinctive linguistic repertoires. Regional groups and social class groups often use different *dialects*, or varieties of a language distinguished from other varieties in vocabulary, pronunciation, and grammatical patterns. These linguistic differences establish and maintain social identity. People's speech reflects their membership in multiple social groups (e.g., class, age, gender, neighborhood, or other social networks) and their varying degrees of identification with those groups.

Extensive research has been done on the linguistic markers of social class. In all societies there are inequalities in the distribution of wealth, privilege, and opportunity and these differences are reflected in speech variations. The highest classes are described as using the most *standard* forms. The term standard refers to a dialect that is normally used in writing, has undergone some degree of codification (in a grammar book or dictionary), is accepted for formal functions, is spoken by educated native speakers, and is taught to nonnative speakers. While standard dialect is not linguistically superior to nonstandard forms, it has been recognized as prestigious through its association with privileged, higher-status groups. Less prestigious social groups (in terms of education, wealth, social prestige) use more linguistic forms that are not part of standard speech.

Linguistic features provide clues to a person's ethnicity. For example, there are differences between the speech of Black and White Americans particularly among lower SES individuals. African American vernacular English (AAVE) is the name given to the nonstandard dialect of English spoken by lower class African American speakers. It is marked by such features as no "s" in third-person singular present-tense forms (e.g., "he go"), less incidence of the verb "to be" in the present tense (e.g., "he real nice"), and more use of the form "be" as a finite verb form (e.g., "she be nice"). Ethnic groups may use a distinctive language or different varieties of the same language.

Considerable research attention has been given to the study of gender and language. Few languages have sex exclusive features, or forms used only by members of one sex or the other. Most languages have sex preferential features, that is, men and women use the same speech forms but with different frequency. While early research focused on gender differences in pronunciation and grammar (e.g., women are found to use more standard forms than men), attention then shifted to gender differences in conversational strategies. In many studies, women's speech is found to be more facilitative, supportive, expressive, and directed toward solidarity than men's, while men's speech is found to be more oriented toward power, status, and problem solving. Women are found to exceed men in the use of politeness, men to exceed women in the use of interruptions. These gender differences are small in magnitude and situationally variable. Considerable controversy exists about how to explain these differences. Some attribute gender differences in speech to the differential socialization of men and women. Others argue that gender differences can be explained by differences in the social roles and power of men and women. The more rigid the sex role differences in society and the larger the power differences between men and women, the larger the linguistic differences.

Speech features also vary with age. Children use different vocabulary, pronunciation, and grammar from adults. To signal group membership and solidarity, adolescents use a distinctive vocabulary called slang, or vocabulary associated with very informal styles, and use a higher frequency of *vernacular* forms than other age groups. A vernacular language is an indigenous language variety of a given speech community that has not been standardized and is usually used in informal contexts.

Attention has been paid not only to differences in the way groups of people speak but also to how the use of accents and dialects associated with class, ethnicity, and gender affect the perception and evaluation of speakers. Speakers using speech features often associated with women are viewed as warmer and more caring but viewed more negatively on dimensions of power, competency, and intelligence. Speakers using nonstandard features tend to be downgraded in terms of competence, character, and career potential. Teachers show prejudice in their grading against children using nonstandard speech. Language, thus, contributes to social inequality, and prejudices based on dialect may restrict occupational and social mobility.

Linguistic Variation and Language Use

A major focus of sociolinguistic research has been understanding why people use different accents, linguistic styles, dialects, and even different languages depending on the occasion. Every person has a verbal or *linguistic repertoire*, or range of varieties, from which to choose depending on the context of their communication. This repertoire may be made up of styles or dialects in a monolingual community or different languages in a multilingual community.

To be a competent speaker, it is not sufficient to be able to produce grammatically correct sentences. To acquire *communicative competence*, a term introduced by American anthropological linguist Dell Hymes, speakers need both knowledge of underlying rules of grammar and knowledge of how to use language appropriately. They need the ability to select forms appropriate to the social norms for behavior in specific encounters. Speakers need to know how to carry on conversations, how to choose the appropriate variety and style to use in a specific situation. They must be able to use language for different functions, use language effectively and politely, use language to convey their multiple and overlapping group memberships. Norms for appropriate use of language may differ from one group to another or one language to another.

Topic. Speech varies depending upon the topic of conversation. A change in topic can require linguistic change. A person chooses a particular *register*, or variety of a language associated with a particular subject, topic, or activity. Register tells something about what one is doing, while dialect tells something about who one is. Registers are characterized primarily by vocabulary, but may also include phonological features, intonation patterns, speech forms; they are labeled jargon by nongroup members. Groups of people with common interests or jobs (e.g., law, sports, biochemistry, jazz, or cooking) tend to use distinguishable speech registers.

Style. The choice of speech can redefine the situation from formal to informal, serious to humorous, impersonal to personal. Speakers of any dialect can shift *styles* from formal to informal depending on the situation. Style refers to a variety of a language that differs in terms of formality from other varieties. Styles can differ in vocabulary, syntax, and pronunciation. Ceremonial occasions require formal speech, while conversation between intimates may be casual and informal. Speakers may shift styles depending upon the topic.

Participants. Language choice is influenced by the relationship between the speakers and the social distance between them. How intimate speakers are dictates how they talk to each other. If speakers are of unequal rank (e.g., due to age, occupation, class) their speech is more formal. Greater intimacy is signaled by the use of vernacular and familiar forms of address.

Functions of Speech. Language can be used to serve an affective function to express feelings, or to serve a referential function to convey objective information. It can serve a directive function to get someone to do something, or a phatic function to express solidarity and empathy with others. Any utterance can serve more than one function simultaneously. Research has focused on how language is used to take account of another person's feelings through use of politeness. Penelope Brown and Stephen Levinson conceptualized politeness in terms of American sociologist Erving Goffman's work on *face*. People have positive face needs, that is, needs to be respected, valued, and liked, and negative face needs, or needs not to feel imposed upon, constrained, or restricted. *Negative politeness* is oriented to reducing constraint imposed upon another and leads to deference, indirectness, and formality in language. *Positive politeness* is oriented toward positive face needs, making a person feel liked, respected, and valued. It is used to express solidarity and to minimize status differences, and it leads to compliments and informal language.

Speech style reflects the motives of speakers. People may switch from one variety of a language to another, or one language to another, to express different motives, such as solidarity, power, control, dominance. Howard Giles, a British social psychologist of language, and his associates developed *accommodation theory* to account for shifts people make in speech styles toward or away from the person they are speaking with depending on motives for social approval or distinctiveness. When members of two different groups speak together, *speech accommodation* may occur. Their speech styles may converge, becoming more similar through the use of the same pronunciation or vocabulary. This strategy is used to evoke social approval or attain efficiency in communication. Subordinates, for example, show convergence to the speech style of superiors. *Speech divergence* occurs when a speaker accentuates differences between self and others. Members of ethnic groups may emphasize divergence, using distinctive language to maintain a separate social identity.

Conversation Analysis. Sociolinguistic research has addressed the complex rules that exist for conducting conversation and how these rules differ from one society to another. Conversations are structured and rule governed and form nonrandom sequences of utterances. There are rules for how talk proceeds in turns, how one utterance relates to another, how topics are introduced, developed, and changed, and how conversations are brought to a close. Rules govern the interruption of another speaker, silence, directness, and indirectness.

Multilingual Communities. Sociolinguists have addressed the question of what social factors influence language choice in multilingual communities, why people choose one variety or another, switch from one to another, or move back and forth from one to another. They have studied *diglossia*, a term introduced by American linguist Charles Ferguson to describe a situation in which there are two varieties of a language that are sufficiently distinct, each of which is assigned a specific social function and is used for different purposes, and switching between the two varieties takes place. One is a prestigious standard or high variety that is used for formal and public occasions, the other a vernacular or low variety that is used under everyday circumstances. The term has been extended to cover situations in which there are two different languages involved, rather than two varieties of the same language, or even to societies in which two or more varieties are used under distinct circumstances.

A single speaker may move from the use of one language or one dialect to another in a process called *code switching*. The switch may occur from one situation to another or may occur with rapidity within the same conversation, which is often referred to as *code-mixing* and is common in multilingual societies. For example, people may switch codes as a signal of group membership or shared ethnicity with another person, or to express solidarity with another. Sociolinguists have sought to identify the points at which speakers switch codes and to search for the function or meaning of code switches.

Other Research Domains

There are several other important branches of sociolinguistic research.

Language Change. Sociolinguists have examined language change over time and how and why new forms develop, spread, are used alongside existing forms, and replace old forms. *Pidgin* and *creole* languages are examples of the way in which languages may get mixed up with one another and lead to the creation of a new variety out of two or more existing varieties. A pidgin language has no native speakers, but derives from a multilingual situation in which people must improvise a simple linguistic system in order to communicate. Often the situation involves a dominant group economically and socially whose language is highly codified. A pidgin is a simplification of the grammar and vocabulary of the dominant language group. A creole is a pidgin that has been expanded and has acquired a community of native speakers. Pidgin and creole languages were not viewed as interesting linguistic phenomena until recent years, but their history, structure, and functions have now become an important part of sociolinguistic study.

Sociolinguistics look at why changes spread, how they spread through a community, what determines the speed of language shift, and social factors responsible for spreading linguistic changes. There are 5,000 languages in the world, but the speed and extent of language shift in the modern world is leading to the complete disappearance of many languages. It has been common for minority language groups gradually to abandon their native languages and go over to another. Economic and political factors influence such language shifts. Immigrants shift toward the dominant language to get good jobs and gain greater status and social success. Sociolinguists have been interested in how minority languages can be maintained or how dying languages can be revitalized.

Language and Social Inequality. Sociolinguists today hold that all dialects are equally good systems linguistically; all are structured, complex, and rule governed. Linguistically, standard English is no better than any other variety of English. Yet nonstandard varieties have consistently been viewed as inferior through their association with less economically and socially successful social groups. Sociolinguists have entered the debates about the claims that linguistic deficiency is the cause of school failure among children of lower social classes. They are involved in questions regarding the treatment of dialect differences, the place of vernacular dialects in schools, and the merits of bilingual instruction versus monolingual instruction in the majority language. Many sociolinguists today contend that because language is a symbol of identity and group membership, it is psychologically wrong to tell children that their language, and thus they themselves, are inferior. This leads to alienation from school. A popular approach today is *bidialectalism*, which holds that children have the right to retain the use of a nonstandard dialect at home and with friends but should be taught standard varieties as the language of reading and writing at school. Both varieties are treated as valid, and children are helped to develop an ability in code-switching.

Language and Thought. After 50 years, debate

continues over the question of whether language affects thinking. The *Sapir–Whorf hypothesis*, or *Whorfian hypothesis*, named after American linguists Edward Sapir and his student Benjamin Lee Whorf, in its strong form claims that language shapes and constrains the way we experience, categorize, conceptualize, and understand the world. Language is said to provide a filter to reality. A weaker form of this hypothesis is that language does not determine the way speakers view the world, but it is influential in predisposing them to adopt a particular worldview. Concepts take shape only if people have the words to express them, such that linguistic differences produce cognitive differences. The Whorfian hypothesis is extremely difficult to test and after years of extensive research it remains controversial. Nonetheless, many hold that habitual thought may be conditioned to an extent by language and that thought predisposes certain types of observation, but thought is not constrained by language. While it is the case that both the physical and social environments of a society are reflected in its language, languages all have a way to say whatever a speaker might want to say. However, some concepts are easier to express in some languages.

One realm in which the question of language and thought has been examined is the question of whether thinking about men and women is shaped by the English language. Sociolinguists have studied sexism in language, the ways in which the English language conveys negative attitudes about women and reinforces inequalities through its representations of women. For example, there are more words in American English for a sexually active woman than for a sexually active man, and proportionately more of these words are pejorative. The skewed distribution of such terms reveals a pressure to represent women as a commodity for consumption. The generic use of masculine pronouns, the words *he* or *man* used as a sexually neutral term, marginalizes women. Feminists have argued that language not only reflects society but reproduces specific beliefs, and they have worked successfully for linguistic reform.

[*See also* Language; *and* Psycholinguistics.]

Bibliography

Basic Textbooks

Chambers, J. K. (1995). *Sociolinguistic theory: Linguistic variation and its social significance*. Oxford, UK: Blackwell. A critical synthesis of research from the central branch of sociolinguistics, which addresses covariation between linguistic variables and social variables. Accessible, comprehensive coverage addressing patterning, origins, and functions of variation in language. Provides extensive bibliography.

Holmes, J. (1992). *An introduction to sociolinguistics*. London: Longman. Highly accessible, nontechnical presentation of the field. Broad use of research examples from speech communities throughout the world. Emphasis on social and stylistic variation in speech. Extensive bibliography.

Hudson, R. A. (1996). *Sociolinguistics* (2nd ed.). Cambridge, UK: Cambridge University Press. A comprehensive and critical presentation of the field and of debates within it. Places an emphasis on relating findings to theory. Provides extensive bibliography.

Romaine, S. (1994). *Language in society: An introduction to sociolinguistics*. Oxford, UK: Oxford University Press. Accessible, informative overview of the field. Strong coverage of multilingualism and language change.

Trudgill, P. (1992). *Introducing language and society*. London: Penguin Books. Gives brief, clear definitions of terms and central concepts used in the field of sociolinguistics. Written in the form of a dictionary/encyclopedia.

Wardhaugh, R. (1998). *An introduction to sociolinguistics* (3rd ed.). Malden, MA: Blackwell. Comprehensive, critical coverage of the field in its complexity with entire chapters on subtopics treated briefly in other basic texts (e.g., pidgin and creole language, language and culture, ethnography of communication, solidarity and politeness, acting and conversing). Provides extensive bibliography.

More Specialized Readings

Coates, J. (1993). *Women, men and language* (2nd ed.). London: Longman. A solid introductory text providing a comprehensive review of research on language and gender and discussion of the consequences of these differences. Presents multiple theoretical explanations for the findings.

Coates, J. (Ed.). (1998). *Language and gender: A reader*. Oxford, UK: Blackwell. Comprehensive collection of papers from the early classics to recent investigations. Papers present multiple theoretical perspectives on the findings.

Giles, H., & St Clair, R. N. (Eds.). (1979). *Language and social psychology*. Baltimore, MD: University Park Press. Examines the influence of language on listeners' impressions, and speakers' use of language to convey feelings and attitudes.

Graddol, D., & Swann, J. (1989). *Gender voices*. Oxford, UK: Blackwell. Examines gender differences in voice, language use, conversational roles, and sexism in language; offers multiple theoretical perspectives on the relationship between language and gender.

Lucy, J. A. (1992). *Language diversity and thought: A reformulation of the linguistic relativity hypothesis*. Cambridge, UK: Cambridge University Press. Comprehensive historical review of Whorf's original hypothesis, empirical evidence related to it, and a theoretical reformulation of it based on this evidence.

McKay, S. L., & Hornberger, N. H. (Eds.). (1996). *Sociolinguistics and language teaching*. Cambridge, UK: Cambridge University Press. These articles provide an excellent critical review of sociolinguistic research on language use and attitudes toward language, and an examination of the pedagogical implications for second language teaching and the linguistically diverse classroom.

Milroy, L. (1987). *Observing and analysing natural language: A critical account of sociolinguistic method.* Oxford, UK: Blackwell. A critical overview of sociolinguistic methods for studying language use in naturally occurring social contexts. Discusses problems involved in sampling, interviewing, data analysis, and interpretation in relation to theoretical goals of research.

Thorne, B., Kramarae, C., & Henley, N. (Eds.). (1983). *Language, gender and society.* Rowley, MA: Newbury House. A selection of classic essays presenting a variety of approaches to the topic of language and gender. Provides an extensive annotated bibliography covering work on sex similarities and differences in language.

Elizabeth Aries

SOCIOPATH. *See* Antisocial Personality Disorder.

SOCRATES (470–399 BCE), Greek philosopher. Born and raised in Athens during the Periclean era, Socrates was the son of a stone mason and a midwife. Little is known about his early life, but by midlife he was active in Athenian civic and military affairs and, as a well-known intellectual, was caricatured as a philosopher in Aristophanes' satire *The Clouds* (423 BCE). Socrates lived according to his philosophical principles, shunning material comforts and spending his days debating the nature of human virtue and knowledge in the Athens marketplace (*agora*). Late in life he married Xanthippe and had three sons. At the age of 70, Socrates was accused of impiety and demoralizing the Athenian youth and was sentenced to death. Although encouraged to escape, Socrates accepted the verdict, drank a cup of hemlock, and died while conversing with a group of his students and friends.

Socrates was a transitional figure among a generation of itinerant lecturers known as Sophists. These philosophers shifted philosophy from the examination of the natural world to the examination of the human world. Sophists, such as the teacher of rhetoric Protagoras, argued that "man was the measure of all things" and claimed to be able to teach virtue (*arete*). Like the Sophists, Socrates investigated human conduct rather than the physical world, but he opposed the Sophists' relativism and their claim that *arete* could be taught. Socrates stated that "the unexamined life is not worth living" (Plato, *Apology*), but argued that each individual must learn to reflect more clearly on how best to live. Although teachers might help guide a student's search, they could not and should not provide answers.

Socrates was by all accounts an effective teacher, but because he left no written work, we are forced to rely on Plato's re-creation of him to learn about his philosophical views. Although scholars still struggle with the problem of disentangling Socrates' positions from Plato's, Plato's early dialogues (e.g., *Apology, Crito, Euthyphro, Protagoras, Gorgias*) are considered to provide the most reliable accounts of Socrates' doctrines. In these early dialogues, Socrates engages others in dialectical discussion of various moral issues, for example, the nature of piety (*Euthyphro*) or whether virtue can be taught (*Protagoras*). In each discussion, Socrates undermines traditional accounts by exposing inconsistencies in the arguments presented. As Gregory Vlastos (1991) points out, the "destructive" character of the Socratic method is not solely negative; the criticism clears the path for discussions that can lead us closer to the truth. Modern Socratic scholars, such as Vlastos, read Socrates as claiming that underlying the diversity of views expressed by individuals we can uncover a real and stable meaning of moral qualities pertaining to human functioning. This doctrine of essential truths distinguished Socrates' philosophy from that of the Sophists. However, his approach must also be differentiated from Plato's later theory of knowledge—in Socrates, the essential truths are not static and divorced from the real world but are to be discovered in the real situations encountered by individuals in their lives.

Socrates' impact on psychology stems from his careful exploration of the realm of private experience. In exploring this realm, he gave new meaning to the term *psyche.* In the older Homeric tradition *psyche* had denoted breath or spirit as the source of life; as with the loss of breath, one died when *psyche* departed. In the Socratic dialogues a new notion of the intellectual and moral qualities of *psyche* emerged, and the cultivation or care of *psyche* was held to be one of humans' highest goals. Socrates' innovation marked the beginning of psychology's fascination with the individual self or person.

Socrates contributed other germinal ideas about the *psyche,* including a discussion of conflict between reason and impulse in the psyche (Plato, *Gorgias*). This notion of intrapsychic conflict was developed more fully in Plato's later work (*Phaedrus, Republic*). Socrates raised the possibility that the soul was immortal, and Plato developed this doctrine as a key idea in his philosophy. In the *Meno,* a dialogue sometimes classified with the Socratic dialogues, the *psyche* is identified as the seat of innate knowledge, signaling Plato's shift in focus from the soul to the mind (*nous*) or reason and to the world of forms.

Socrates, as represented in the dialogues of his most famous student Plato, helped shape the Western intellectual tradition in several ways. The Socratic method, involving a willingness to admit ignorance and to explore issues through dialectical discussion, shaped philosophical inquiry and has been extolled by many educators as the ideal form of teaching. In rejecting the relativistic doctrines of the Sophists and shifting the meaning of *psyche*, Socrates identified the care and cultivation of the individual soul as a central problem for human inquiry. His focus on each individual's examination of values and the inner life presaged the view of Augustine and later the existential-phenomenological tradition that the unexamined life is not worth living.

Bibliography

Burnet, J. (1915–1916). The Socratic doctrine of the soul. *Proceedings of the British Academy, 7,* 235–59.

Cornford, F. M. (1932). *Before and after Socrates.* Cambridge: Cambridge University Press. This is a classic brief introduction to Socrates' work and influence.

Lovibond, S. (1991). Plato's theory of mind. In S. Everson (Ed.), *Companions to ancient thought: Vol. 2. Psychology* (pp. 35–55). Cambridge, England: Cambridge University Press.

Santas, G. (1979). *Socrates: Philosophy in Plato's early dialogues.* London: Routledge.

Taylor, A. E. (1933). *Socrates: The man and his thought.* London: Davies. This older work, along with Burnet (1915–1916), is still worth consulting.

Vlastos, G. (Ed.). (1971). *The philosophy of Socrates: A collection of critical essays.* Garden City, NY: Anchor Books.

Vlastos, G. (1991). *Socrates: Ironist and moral philosopher.* Ithaca, NY: Cornell University Press. Gregory Vlastos's work has served to stimulate much recent scholarship on Socrates.

Deborah F. Johnson

SOLOMON, RICHARD LESTER (1918–1995), learning and motivation theorist. Richard L. Solomon was born in Boston in 1918. He received his bachelor's degree (1940) and master's degree in psychology (1942) from Brown University, where his first research efforts were supervised by J. McV. Hunt and Harold Schlosberg. During the Second World War, he was a research psychologist for the government, working on new perceptual-motor systems for controlling the defensive gunfire of the B-29 bomber. When the war ended, Solomon returned to Brown, where he received his doctorate in 1947. He moved to Harvard's department of social relations that year, and 10 years later was promoted to a professorship. In 1960, he joined the faculty of the department of psychology of the University of Pennsylvania, where he remained until his retirement in 1984. Richard Solomon died in Boston on 12 October 1995.

Solomon conducted and directed research on an extraordinarily wide range of topics. His most influential research and theorizing concerned, one way or another, the acquisition of motivational and emotional states and the influence of those states on behavior. Richard Solomon also exerted a profound influence on the psychology of learning and motivation through the superb training he gave his many graduate students, among them such leading contributors as James Olds, Leon Kamin, Russell Church, Bruce Overmier, Robert Rescorla, Martin Seligman, Steven Maier, and Susan Mineka.

By the early 1950s, the explanation of avoidance learning was the primary goal of research in Solomon's laboratory. In a typical avoidance experiment, a dog in a two-compartment chamber called a shuttlebox received a visual warning signal followed 10 seconds later by an aversive foot shock, which it could escape by crossing to the other compartment. Moreover, if the dog crossed during the warning signal, but before shock began, the warning signal went off and shock did not occur. Dogs quickly learned to avoid shock and continued to avoid on trial after trial. The challenge was to understand what event was maintaining the avoidance behavior, once shocks were occurring only rarely. One answer, proposed by O. H. Mowrer but more fully elaborated by Solomon and his students, was called two-process theory. It argued that the warning signal came to evoke Pavlovian-conditioned fear as a result of its pairing with foot shock on early trials, so that once the avoidance response occurred and the warning signal was turned off, the resulting fear reduction reinforced the avoidance response. Avoidance was interpreted as escape from fear. Data compatible with two-process theory came from transfer-of-control experiments in which, for example, after avoidance training as above and separate Pavlovian fear conditioning to a tone paired with shock, presentation of the tone in the shuttlebox would evoke the avoidance response.

Interest in the role of Pavlovian-conditioned fear in avoidance behavior stimulated research on the role of Pavlovian processes within instrumental responding generally, and by the late 1960s transfer-of-control experiments designed to elucidate Pavlovian-instrumental interactions were being conducted in laboratories all over the world. A framework for classifying such interactions presented in a seminal 1967 paper by Rescorla and Solomon set the direction for this research, which has led to a much fuller understanding of the diverse ways in which Pavlovian conditioning and instrumental learning can interact, as well as of the associative structures of these two fundamental processes.

In the mid-1960s, Solomon's students discovered that after prior exposure to inescapable, unavoidable foot shocks most dogs subsequently failed to learn to escape shock in a new situation where escape was possible. Although he was less than enthusiastic about the revolutionary, cognitive account—the learned helplessness hypothesis—that his students formulated, Solomon agreed that the phenomenon had important implications and did his utmost to enable the students to make their case.

Beginning in the early 1970s, Solomon's primary theoretical focus was the opponent-process theory of acquired motivation, which, in contrast to his analysis of acquired fear, was a nonassociative account. Taking the phenomena of opiate addiction as a model, this view asserted that, with repeated presentations of a reinforcing or punishing event, the pattern of affective response to that event changes. The initial affective response diminishes, and the termination of the event comes to evoke an opposite affective response. Solomon always considered how results from the laboratory might apply to everyday life, and he extrapolated most freely in the case of opponent processess, from changes in emotional responses to aversive events in animals to changes in emotion as people become drug addicts, sport parachutists, or distance runners.

Bibliography

Brush, F. R., & Overmier, J. B. (Eds.). (1985). *Affect, conditioning, and cognition: Essays on the determinants of behavior.* Hillsdale, NJ: Erlbaum. In 1983, Solomon's students and colleagues gathered to honor him in his thirty-fifth academic year. His former graduate students and postdocs presented 22 scientific papers that were published in this volume. It includes a chapter "Perspectives on the psychology of Richard L. Solomon" by Leon J. Kamin, a list of Solomon's publications, and a list of his 32 students and their dissertation titles.

Overmier, J. B. (1996). Richard L. Solomon and learned helplessness. *Integrative Physiological and Behavioral Science, 31,* 331–337. Describes Solomon's role in the initiation of research on what has come to be called learned helplessness.

Overmier, J. B., & Seligman, M. E. P. (1967). Effects of inescapable shock upon subsequent escape and avoidance learning. *Journal of Comparative and Physiological Psychology, 63,* 23–33.

Rescorla, R. A. (1997). Richard Lester Solomon: 1918–1995. A biographical memoir by Robert A. Rescorla. *Biographical Memoirs, 71,* 301–314.

Rescorla, R. A., & Solomon, R. L. (1967). Two process learning theory: Relationships between Pavlovian conditioning and instrumental learning. *Psychological Review, 74,* 151–182.

Seligman, M. E. P., & Maier, S. F. (1967). Failure to escape traumatic shock. *Journal of Experimental Psychology, 74,* 1–9.

Solomon, R. L. (1964). Punishment. *American Psychologist, 19,* 239–254. Based on a 1963 presidential address to the Eastern Psychological Association. Solomon challenged the widely held misconception that punishment was generally ineffective and resulted in negative side effects, pointing out that research with animals had already revealed that punishment, used properly, is an effective way of controlling behavior. Solomon's eloquence had a corrective effect, and spurred further research on punishment.

Solomon, R. L., & Corbit, J. D. (1974). An opponent-process theory of motivation. I. Temporal dynamics of affect. *Psychological Review, 81,* 119–145.

Solomon, R. L., & Turner, L. H. (1962). Discriminative classical conditioning in dogs paralyzed by curare can later control discriminative avoidance responses in the normal state. *Psychological Review, 69,* 202–219.

Solomon, R. L., & Wynne, L. C. (1953). Traumatic avoidance learning: Acquisition in normal dogs. *Psychological Monographs, 67* (no. 354).

Vincent M. LoLordo

SOMATOFORM DISORDERS refer to a classification of psychiatric disorders in which the patient presents physical symptoms that cannot be adequately explained by a general medical condition. The somatic symptoms are clinically significant in causing distress or functional impairment but are without a clear organic basis. The manifestation of somatic symptoms in the absence of demonstrable organic pathology is thought to occur in response to a psychosocial stressor. In the fourth edition of the *Diagnostic and Statistical Manual of Mental Disorders* (*DSM–IV*; APA, 1994), the somatoform disorders include somatization disorder, conversion disorder, hypochondriasis, pain disorder, body dysmorphic disorder, and two residual categories (undifferentiated somatoform disorder and somatoform disorder not otherwise specified). [*See* Diagnostic and Statistical Manual of Mental Disorders; *and* Hypochondriasis.]

Somatization Disorder

Somatization disorder is a chronic psychiatric disorder characterized by a pattern of multiple and recurrent physical symptoms for which a medical explanation is not found, or when a medical condition is present, the level of complaint or impairment is in excess of what would be expected based on physical findings. For a symptom to be medically unexplained, there must be an absence of demonstrable organic pathology accounting for the symptom. Patients with somatization disorder typically have a long and complicated medical history distinguished by excessive treatment-seeking and a pattern of repeated unexplained physical symptoms. Commonly, patients with somatization disorder undergo unnecessary medical testing, treatments, and surgical procedures.

Somatization disorder has a long and rich history, with the earliest sources of recorded medical descriptions found in Egyptian papyrus fragments dating back to 1900 BCE. The term hysteria, which, like Briquet's syndrome, is a historical root of somatization disorder, comes from the Greek word *hysteria* ("from the uterus"). Both the Egyptians and the Greeks believed that the disorder originated in the uterus and they directed treatment toward this organ. In the seventeenth century, Thomas Sydenham advanced the modern description of hysteria as a psychological disorder, and in 1859, Paul Briquet developed the modern concept of hysteria as a chronic polysymptomatic disorder and provided the first known systematic description of its characteristics. In the 1960s, Samuel Guze further developed Briquet's descriptive diagnosis of medically unexplained somatic symptoms that he named Briquet's syndrome. Guze formulated a list of diagnostic criteria for the disorder that was modified by and introduced into the *DSM* in 1980 as somatization disorder. The current *DSM–IV* diagnosis of somatization disorder preserves much of these descriptions of the condition.

Diagnostic Criteria. The *DSM–IV* diagnosis identifies the disorder as being characterized by a history of multiple physical complaints occurring over several years and beginning before the age of 30. The somatic symptoms have no demonstrable pathology, and must result in medical treatment-seeking or cause significant impairment of social, occupational, or other functioning. The medically unexplained symptoms must be unfeigned, that is, are not under voluntary control, and must include complaints of pain symptoms in at least four different sites, two gastrointestinal symptoms, one sexual or reproductive symptom other than pain (e.g., irregular menses or erectile dysfunction), and one pseudoneurological symptom (e.g., lack of coordination).

Conversion Disorder

Conversion disorder is characterized by the presence of symptoms or deficits specific to motor or sensory function that suggest a neurological disorder but manifest in the absence of organic pathology. As a diagnostic term, conversion disorder first appeared in psychiatric nosology in *DSM–III*, which clearly distinguished *somatization disorder*, based on polysymptomatic complaints with symptoms related to various organs, and *conversion disorder*, which is monosymptomatic, with symptoms limited to motor or sensory functioning. Although conversion symptoms mimic neurological dysfunctions, the complaints or deficits usually do not follow known neuroanatomical pathways or physiological mechanisms. Instead, the presentation usually follows the patient's idea of how the body works. This accounts for the presence of complete organ or body part failure such as stocking or glove anesthesia (anesthesia that

presents as following a glove- or stocking-like pattern rather than following anatomical nerve distribution).

The term *conversion* did not appear in the lexicon of psychiatric disorders until Sigmund Freud used it to describe the expression of a repressed idea or trauma as a somatic symptom. However, conversion symptoms have their historical roots in clinical descriptions of hysteria that date back to ancient times. Paul Briquet, who characterized the disorder in terms of dysfunction of the nervous system, provided one of the first modern descriptions of conversion hysteria in the nineteenth century. Later Jean-Martin Charcot and Pierre Janet expanded Briquet's theory of the disorder and presented classic examples of conversion symptoms. Freud, working with Josef Breuer, hypothesized that repressed emotional trauma could be converted into a somatic symptom, often one that was symbolic of the original trauma.

Diagnostic Criteria. The *DSM–IV* describes conversion disorder as the presence of physically unfeigned symptoms or deficits related to voluntary sensory and motor functions that suggest a neurological or general medical condition, but for which no organic pathology is found. Diagnosis requires that antecedent psychological stressors be associated with the onset or exacerbation of the symptom or deficit. The disorder must cause clinically significant distress or impaired functioning, and the symptom or deficit must not be limited to pain or sexual dysfunction. Typical conversion symptoms are sensory symptoms (e.g., blindness), motor symptoms (e.g., paralysis), and convulsions (e.g., pseudoseizures).

Hypochondriasis

Hypochondriasis is the fear of having a disease or the belief that one has a disease based on a misinterpretation of physical signs or symptoms, but in the absence of any identifiable organic pathology and despite physician reassurances to the contrary. Whereas in somatization and conversion disorders the essential feature is a bodily complaint in the absence of demonstrable pathology, in hypochondriasis there is the additional feature of a mistaken conviction or unrealistic fear of having a disease. The patient's concerns may involve multiple body organs or systems simultaneously or at different times. The term hypochondriasis has appeared in medical writings since ancient times; however, only in the past two centuries has the term been used in its contemporary sense.

Diagnostic Criteria. The *DSM–IV* describes hypochondriasis as a preoccupied belief or fear that one has a serious disease. The preoccupation is based on a mistaken interpretation of bodily symptoms and persists despite physician reassurance and unsupportive physical evaluations. The fear or belief must cause clinically significant distress or functional impairment, must last for at least six months, and must not be better accounted for by another psychiatric illness.

Pain Disorder

The characteristic feature of pain disorder is a painful condition that is sufficiently severe to demand clinical attention, but that defies anatomical patterns, or is in gross excess of what can be physiologically explained.

Diagnosis. The pain must cause significant distress or impairment in functioning such as excessive preoccupation with the pain, inability to work, disruption in family life, and excessive treatment-seeking behavior. Psychological factors are involved in the onset and course of the pain. Two subtypes of pain disorder indicate the factors that are thought to contribute to its etiology and maintenance: pain disorder associated with psychological factors, and pain disorder associated with both psychological factors and a general medical condition.

Body Dysmorphic Disorder

The central feature of body dysmorphic disorder is a gross preoccupation with an imagined defect in physical appearance. Preoccupation can take up much of the day, and cause intense distress, avoidant behavior, suicidal ideation, and unnecessary plastic surgery. When patients do undergo surgery, they are often unsatisfied with the results, and commonly the scars become the new focus of attention or preoccupation. The clinical course of body dysmorphic disorder is usually a chronic one, with symptoms persisting and sometimes worsening over time. Descriptive accounts emphasize a high degree of suffering and impairment.

With the publication of *DSM–III–R*, body dysmorphic disorder entered psychiatric nosology with separate diagnostic status. The *DSM–III–R* also introduced the distinction between nondelusional body dysmorphic disorder and delusional disorder, a somatic type that is classified as a psychotic disorder. Historically known as dysmorphophobia, the syndrome has long been described in literature under the more general definition of an exaggerated or imagined subjective feeling of physical defect despite normal appearance.

Diagnostic Criteria. The *DSM–IV* diagnostic criteria for body dysmorphic disorder focuses on a preoccupation with an imagined defect or an excessive concern over a minor physical flaw. The preoccupation must cause physical distress or functional impairment. Individuals with this disorder often complain about some aspect of the face or head, although any body part may be the focus of concern.

Undifferentiated Somatoform Disorder

Undifferentiated somatoform disorder is a diagnosis used for individuals who do not meet diagnostic criteria for somatization or other somatoform disorders. The *DSM–IV* characterizes the disorder as the presence of one or more physical complaints that persist for at least six months in the absence of organic pathology. The symptoms cannot be better explained by a medical illness, the direct effects of a substance, or another mental disorder. The symptoms must cause clinically significant distress or impairment of functioning. Commonly reported symptoms include chronic fatigue, appetite loss, or gastrointestinal or genitourinary symptoms.

Somatoform Disorder Not Otherwise Specified

This diagnosis is used for somatoform symptoms that do not meet diagnostic criteria for any specific somatoform disorder. Examples include hypochondriacal or other unexplained somatic symptoms lasting for less than six months that are not better accounted for by a medical/neurological condition or another mental disorder. Little is known about course and treatment.

Prevalence of Somatoform Disorders

At least half of all patients who have a mental illness first exhibit a somatic symptom such as a backache or headache. Somatization disorder shows a lifetime prevalence rate of 0.2 to 2% in women and under 0.2% in men. Conversion disorder is a focus of treatment for 1 to 3% of patients referred to mental-health clinics. Hypochondriasis to is estimated to be prevalent in 4% to 9% of medical patients. Pain disorder is considered common, but its actual prevalence is unknown. Prevalence data are lacking on body dysmorphic disorder, but this disorder is less rare than formerly thought and appears to be equally prevalent in both sexes.

Differential Diagnosis

Sitting on the border between psychiatry and medicine, somatoform disorders are chronic psychiatric disorders that pose considerable diagnostic challenges. Before making the diagnosis of a somatoform disorder, a true medical illness must first be ruled out. This can often involve costly and unnecessary medical tests, which may lead to misdiagnosis and hazardous medical treatments such as surgery and other invasive procedures. A number of general medical illnesses with indistinct symptomatology are therefore difficult to diagnose and are sometimes misdiagnosed as somatoform disorders (e.g., multiple sclerosis and early-stage systemic lupus erythematosus). The diagnosis of somatoform disorders is further complicated by the existence of medical syndromes for which medical explanations are still lacking (e.g., chronic fatigue syndrome and Gulf War illnesses). In such cases it is important to acknowledge medical uncertainty and avoid misdiagnosis of somatoform disorders. Also, there are psychosomatic illnesses in which psychological factors such as stress are involved in the onset of physiological illness (e.g., asthma, hypertension, and irritable bowel syndrome), which must be distinguished from somatoform disorders. Furthermore, somatoform disorders have high rates of psychiatric comorbidity with other disorders such as depressive and anxiety disorders. When physiological or psychiatric disorders coexist with somatoform disorders, it is essential that these disorders also receive appropriate treatment. Somatoform disorders are different from malingering and factitious disorders, both of which are under volitional control.

Clinical Management

Somatoform disorders present considerable problems in their clinical management. Individuals with somatoform disorders manifest symptoms that suggest a physical disorder, and therefore they seek medical attention without recognizing a causal link between their physical distress and antecedent psychosocial stress. Partly because the diagnosis of somatoform disorders requires ruling out true physiological illnesses, the number of medical evaluations, tests, and invasive treatments is typically high among patients suffering from these disorders. Moreover, patients with somatoform disorders tend to reject a psychiatric approach to their complaints, generally preferring to seek a nonpsychiatric medical diagnosis. The frustrations endemic to the management of these disorders contribute to doctor–patient conflicts, the inclination of patients to doctor shop, and unnecessary exposure to a wide range of diagnostic and treatment modalities, at times with adverse consequences. Furthermore, these consequences entail excessive utilization of the health-care system, which contributes to its high costs.

The cornerstone of managing and treating these disorders is the development of a stable and trusting therapeutic relationship with the treating physician. Clinical management focuses on rehabilitation and improved functional capacity rather than on medical diagnosis and cure. Scheduling regular appointments and continuing medical evaluations while reducing the amount of testing and invasive treatments can foster good doctor-patient relationships while reassuring the patient that the possibility of serious medical illnesses is not being ignored. In the long term, such a constructive relationship can open the door to the discussion of the patient's symptoms as a physical response to psychosocial stress. Mental-health treatment can then be encouraged not as a substitute for, but as an addition to, medical care.

Etiological Factors in Somatoform Disorders

Several etiological factors have been proposed to explain the origin and expression of somatoform disorders. These include social learning theory, developmental theory, cultural differences, psychodynamic theory, and the influence of personality characteristics. In social learning and developmental theories, illness-related beliefs and behavior are communicated and learned in the family and social context. The child learns that the expression of somatic symptoms is a legitimate way to express psychological distress, elicit attention and help, or avoid conflict and responsibilities. In the case of body dysmorphic disorder, symptoms are thought to represent an extreme acceptance of accepted societal ideals of physical perfection and the paths to achieve them. Studies have also shown that somatic symptoms used to communicate psychosocial distress differ across cultures, suggesting that the prevalence and patterns of symptoms can be culturally specific. In psychodynamic theory, bodily symptoms provide an acceptable expression of unconscious emotional conflict. Furthermore, psychological distress or repressed feelings are understood to unconsciously convert to bodily symptoms such as in somatization and conversions disorders, or to displace onto a body part as in body dysmorphic disorder. Distinctive personality traits, such as introspectiveness and negative affectivity (neuroticism), have been associated with somatoform disorders, but while such traits may contribute to the development of somatoform disorders, they are considered neither necessary nor sufficient for precipitating the onset. In summary, etiological theories generally recognize the dominant role of psychosocial distress in precipitating somatic symptoms. Furthermore, somatoform disorders also appear to be closely tied to the family and cultural context, from which illness beliefs and behaviors are learned and reinforced. These theoretical perspectives about the etiology of somatoform disorders are largely based on clinical and anthropological observations, rather than empirical studies. Currently there is a need for more empirical research to understand the etiology of these disorders and explore successful treatment modalities. Somatoform disorders also present clearly the opportunity to further study the mind-body interface.

[*Many of the people mentioned in this entry are the subjects of independent biographical entries.*]

Bibliography

Abbey, S. E. (1996). Somatization and somatoform disorders. In J. R. Rundell & M. G. Wise (Eds.), *Textbook of consultation-liaison psychiatry* (pp. 368–401). Washington, DC: American Psychiatric Press.

American Psychiatric Association. (1994). *Diagnostic and statistical manual of mental disorders* (4th ed.). Washington, DC: Author.

Calabrese, L. V. (1994). Somatization disorder. Guest transcript: *Practical Reviews in Psychiatry, 18.*

Ford, C. V., & Folks, D. G. (1985). Conversion disorders: An overview. *Psychosomatics, 26,* 371–383.

Guze, S. B., & Perley, M. J. (1963). Observations on the natural history of hysteria. *American Journal of Psychiatry,* *119,* 960–965.

Katon, W. (1997). Somatization disorder, hypochondriasis, and conversion disorder. In D. L. Dunner (Ed.), *Current psychiatric therapy* (pp. 346–353). Philadelphia: W. B. Saunders.

Kellner, R. (1987). Hypochondriasis and somatization. *Journal of the American Medical Association, 258,* 2718–2722.

Kent, D. A., Tomasson, K., Coryell, W. (1995). Course and outcome of conversion and somatization disorders: A four-year follow-up. *Psychosomatics, 36,* 38–144.

Kirmayer, L. J., Robbins, J. M., & Paris, J. (1994). Somatoform disorders: Personality and the social matrix of somatic distress. *Journal of Abnormal Psychology, 103,* 125–136.

Lipowski, Z. J. (1988). Somatization: The concept and its clinical application. *American Journal of Psychiatry, 145,* 1358–1368.

Mersky, H., & Bogduk, N. (Eds.). (1994) *Classification of chronic pain* (2nd ed.). Seattle, WA: IASP Press.

Phillips, K. A. (1991). Body dysmorphic disorder: The distress of imagined ugliness. *American Journal of Psychiatry, 148,* 1138–1149.

Smith R. (1990). *Somatization disorder in the medical setting.* U.S. Department of Health and Human Services. (DHHS Publication No. ADM90-1631). Rockville, MD: U.S. Government Printing Office.

Sullivan, M. D. (1997). Diagnosis and treatment of pain disorder. In D. L. Dunner (Ed.), *Current psychiatric therapy* (pp. 354–358). Philadelphia: W. B. Saunders.

Veith, I. (1965). *Hysteria: The history of a disease.* Chicago: University of Chicago Press.

Wickramasekera, I. (1997, Fall). Secrets kept from the mind, but not the body and behavior: Somatoform disorders and primary care medicine. *Biofeedback, 20–22.*

Cheryl Koopman and Michele Gill

SOMNAMBULISM. *See* Sleepwalking.

SOPORIFICS. *See* Opiates.

SOUL. *See* Psyche and Soul.

SOUTH AFRICA. While global processes operate to create some homogeneity in psychological practices across contexts, activities take on a form and meaning in relation to the local social context within which they occur. Perhaps in more accentuated forms than other countries, South Africa has been through a series of major social and political transformations during the twentieth century. To understand psychology within South Africa requires a sensitivity to how such transformations have constructed the practices of South African psychology.

South Africa occupies the southernmost part of the African continent. It only became a national state in 1909 when, following the Boer Wars in which people of Dutch ancestry (Afrikaners) fought against British colonial rule, four separate colonies became the Union of South Africa. In 1961, South Africa broke its colonial ties and left the British Commonwealth to become a Republic. The ruling Afrikaans nationalist government, which had come to power in 1948, was then able to consolidate its racial policy of apartheid. Central to this policy was the Population Registration Act of 1950, which categorized people as African, Colored (people of mixed race descent), Indian (people from Asiatic descent), and White. Only people in the White category were able to vote for the national government. Under apartheid, legislation was produced that, on the basis of one's racial classification, controlled all aspects of life including movement, marriage, social contact, ownership of land, place of residence, education, health, and employment.

After more than 40 years of sustained resistance to the policy of apartheid, within and outside the country, the White nationalist government began to dismantle apartheid in 1990. The African Nationalist Congress and other political parties were unbanned, negotiations took place, and national elections were held in 1994. A democratic government of national unity was installed. In 1996, a new constitution with an entrenched bill of rights was enacted. Apartheid legislation was removed from the statute books. A process of transformation had begun.

In the 1996 census, it was estimated that South Africa had a population of 37,859,000 of which, in terms of the past racial categories, 76% was African, 13% White, 8% Colored, and 2.5% Indian. The country has the highest GNP and per capita income in Africa but is still marked by gross inequalities that are the legacies of apartheid.

Psychology in South Africa has been formed and continues to be formed by these transformations. A look at the development of psychology, and its current status and future, therefore, provides a particularly interesting example of the dynamic interaction between psychology, psychologists, and their social context.

Psychology as an Academic Discipline

Psychology first appeared in South Africa in the universities as a subdiscipline of philosophy. The University of Stellenbosch, an Afrikaans-medium university, started such a subdiscipline in 1917 and the University of Cape Town, an English-medium university, in 1920.

An independent department of psychology was started at Rhodes University in Grahamstown in 1926. South Africa's colonial history has meant that there has been a good interchange of ideas and expertise with Britain, the United States, and Europe. Mann, for example, mentions in *The Nature of Psychology* (1987) that Edward Titchener was involved in the design of the first psychology laboratory at the University of Cape Town, and John Dewey was given an Honorary Doctorate at the University of Witwatersrand in Johannesburg. Gordon Allport conducted research in South Africa in 1956. In the 1920s and 1930s many psychologists within South Africa traveled to obtain their degrees outside the country.

These links, which were curtailed during the years of the academic boycott, but have now been reestablished, have produced academic departments whose content, structure, and standards closely follow developments in the main centers of psychology.

All 21 universities in South Africa have psychology departments that teach the discipline as a social and human science. In many instances, these departments are among the largest in their respective universities. Psychology is taught, at an undergraduate level, as a major or minor subject in three-year bachelor's degree programs. A one-year postgraduate Honor's degree in psychology serves as a bridge to master's degree programs. A master's degree in psychology can follow an academic route, which involves the submission of a research-based thesis, or a professional route, which involves a course-work program in one of the following fields: research, counseling, and clinical, industrial, or educational psychology. The latter usually includes an additional year as an intern psychologist, which leads to registration as a psychologist. Research-based Ph.D. or doctorate degrees are offered at most universities. The structure and nature of professional degrees will have changed considerably by 2004 as the profession implements a new policy for professional practice.

The historical development of the professional practice of psychology (described in the next section) has led to the creation of separate departments of industrial/organizational psychology and educational psychology at many universities.

Under apartheid legislation, Black students were barred from attending the established universities and were obliged to register at universities created in the apartheid "homelands." Psychology departments were created at these universities but it was still exceptionally difficult for Black students to obtain professional training. These discriminatory practices had an important consequence. As argued, academic psychology has been largely modeled on concepts and theories developed in Britain, Europe, and the United States. The racial structure of tertiary education severely restricted a

dialogue between this mainstream psychology and the African experience, thereby inhibiting the emergence of an indigenous psychology. The voice of Black students and psychologists was heard, however, in the political forums against apartheid and here, outside the mainstream arenas, significant contributions to alternative theories and models did occur. Steve Biko, for example, who died in detention, while not being a psychologist, developed important ideas on Black identity in his formative work in building Black consciousness (*I Write What I Like, 1978*). Authors in the journal *Psychology and Society* consistently presented alternative progressive views.

In 1998, discussions on the restructuring of the profession in the light of the transformation of South African society are likely to have far-reaching impact on the training of psychologists (see section on Future Directions).

Psychology in the Domains of Education, Work, and Health

The development of psychology as a field of practice has been closely tied to South Africa's history. From their inception, psychology departments saw the discipline as an applied science, and research was directed toward contemporary social issues. Johann Louw sketches in *White Poverty and Psychology in South Africa: The Poor White Investigation of the Carnegie Commission* (1986) how this led to the professionalization of psychology. In the 1920s, adverse farming conditions and the development of the gold mines led to the movement of the rural population to the cities. Poverty increased dramatically and included in the poor were significant numbers of Afrikaans-speaking Whites. Given the rise of Afrikaans nationalism and a White government, this was seen to be a particular problem and caught the attention of psychologists. Louw reveals that among these was E. G. Malherbe, an educational psychologist, who, while studying in the United States, had met F. Keppel, the president of the Carnegie Corporation. In 1927, Keppel visited South Africa, and in 1928 the Carnegie Commission was established to investigate the "poor White" problem. Psychologists played an active role in this Commission as researchers conducting intelligence testing and measuring scholastic and educational achievement. Louw argues that this work opened the domains of education and work to psychologists. The National Bureau for Educational and Social Research was founded by the state in 1929. This Institute later became a central part of the Human Science Research Council, the statutory body that continues to promote research in the social sciences, along with the recently created National Research Foundation (NRF).

Johann Louw in *World War II, Industry and the Professionalization of South African Psychology* (1993a) has argued that World War II marked a second shift in the professionalization of psychology in South Africa. It drew psychologists more fully into the domain of work. Two important developments occurred. First, the war stimulated local manufacturing industry and prompted the need for the better selection of workers and work methods. The Leather Industries Research Institute based at Rhodes University played a formative role in this field, establishing the Personnel Research Section that later served as a model for the application of psychology in other industries such as mining. Second, psychologists were called on to develop assessment techniques for the selection of military personnel. The South African Air Force, took the initiative in this field and established the Aptitude Test Section (ATS) with Simon Biesheuvel as its leader. At its height it employed nearly ninety people. After the war, the ATS was reconstructed and eventually became the National Institute of Personnel Research (NIPR) with Biesheuvel as its first director. The NIPR emerged as an important psychological research institute, with an international reputation, in the domain of work and psychological testing. It published the journal *Psychologia Africana* (1962–1983), which provides an important record of the history of South African psychology. These developments established psychology as a professional practice within the domain of work and led to the professional category of Industrial Psychology.

The development of psychology in the domain of health followed a different route. Johann Louw et al. (1995) argue that in this domain, psychology was unable to establish itself as a central discipline. Despite the fact that behavior therapy, as a rival to psychoanalysis, has strong roots in South Africa—Joseph Wolpe and Arnold Lazarus, leaders in the field, developed their ideas in South Africa—psychologists were seen primarily as being responsible for conducting psychometric assessments of the mentally ill. Psychology was, therefore, seen as an auxiliary medical service. Posts in government service for clinical psychologists are largely located in psychiatric settings. Given the limited number of these posts, clinical psychologists have been obliged to establish themselves in private practice. There have been a number of consequences of this development.

First, it has led to the development of services largely being directed to the needs of White middle-class clients who can afford to pay professional fees. This has meant that the mental health needs of the majority of the population who cannot pay professional fees have been neglected. Second, it has perpetuated therapeutic models that have been largely "imported" from first-world settings and inhibited the development of services sensitive to the African context. Third, it has resulted in the profession organizing itself around professional

status issues in relation to other health professionals as opposed to serving public needs.

Professional Organization of Psychology

The first official national organization to speak for academic and professional psychology, the South African Psychological Association (SAPA), was founded in 1948. A major impetus for establishing the association was to develop a professional register of psychologists. In 1955, two government notices gave statutory recognition to psychology as an auxiliary medical service. Psychologists who wished to practice were then obliged to register with the South African Medical and Dental Council (SAMDC), which in 1998 became the Health Professions Council. From this point onward, the profession has operated at two levels: voluntary membership with professional associations, and obligatory registration, if one wishes to practice as a psychologist, with the Health Professions Council.

Professional Associations. In the 1950s, SAPA continued to organize around professional issues. It started a bulletin, *Psygram*, organized conferences, and developed a code of ethics. In 1956, Josephine Naidoo, who in terms of the Population Registration Act of 1950 was classified as an Indian, applied for membership. This precipitated a crisis with members split over the issue of membership. Johann Louw (1993b) documents this process. Recommendations to admit "non-Whites" at the Annual General Meeting in 1961 led to those opposed to a racially integrated association breaking away to form the Psychological Institute of the Republic of South Africa (PIRSA) in 1962. The split was not entirely on language lines, but PIRSA became a largely Afrikaans association and SAPA, an English organization.

Louw notes that the split had implications for the profession and the two national research institutes. The HSRC members became associated with PIRSA and those at the NIPR with SAPA. Organizing educational psychologists became an important aspect of PIRSA, while most industrial psychologists were linked with SAPA.

Between 1977 and 1983, psychologists in the professional fields of clinical, counseling, educational, and industrial psychology started their own special societies of which the South African Society for Clinical Psychologists was perhaps the largest.

In 1983, the SAPA and PIRSA agreed to reunite under a new nonracial constitution and the other specialized societies joined with them to form one organization, the Psychological Association of South Africa (PASA), with a number of specialized institutes. The need to have a united front in relation to the statutory organization of the profession was perhaps one of the major reasons for this amalgamation.

Although the new association continued as the major professional organization, it tended to be more conservative than the old SAPA. New splits in the profession developed mainly in response to the increasing polarization of political attitudes, stemming from greater state repression. In 1983, the Organization of Appropriate Social Services of South Africa (OASSSA) was started by psychologists and other professionals as a home for progressive social service workers opposed to apartheid. This association continued to provide an alternate progressive voice through its journal *Psychology and Society* and annual congresses. It provided an important base for the development of models and policy for mental health, community psychology, and therapeutic interventions for those who suffered detention and state violence. OASSSA subsequently merged with other organizations to become South African Health and Social Services Organization. Other smaller organizations to emerge in the late 1980s and early 1990s were Psychologists against Apartheid and the African Psychologist Forum.

These polarized circumstances began to change as apartheid was dismantled. In the prevailing spirit of negotiation, a Committee for the Reconstruction of Psychology was formed and in January 1994 at a national conference held in Cape Town, the Psychological Society of South Africa (PsySSA) was launched. This association successfully united the various factions. In July 1998, it had a membership of 1,200 psychologists and had successfully reestablished links with major psychological associations and put psychology on a sound professional footing. It continues to publish the *South African Journal of Psychology*, which was founded by SAPA in 1970 (and has incorporated *Psychologia Africana*). It also publishes the newsletter *Psytalk*.

Registration and Licensing. The establishment of a register in 1955 paved the way for the separation of the licensing of psychologists from the professional associations. In 1974, the Medical and Dental and Supplementary Services Act No 56 legislated for the creation of a Professional Board for Psychology under the South African Medical and Dental Council, to register and regulate the practice of psychology. In 1998, the act was revised and the SAMDC became the Health Professions Council. This process has changed the status of psychology to one of equality with eleven other types of medical and health practitioners including doctors and dentists.

To register as a psychologist with the professional board, an individual has to complete a recognized 5-year master's degree and an approved 12 months of internship. Five categories of psychologists exist. At the end of 1997, there were 4,563 psychologists on the register spread across the five categories: Clinical, 1,639; Counseling, 1,008; Educational, 909; Industrial, 763; and Research, 244.

In 1999, in line with the social transformation of South Africa, the Professional Board for Psychology and PsySSA approved a new policy for the training and registration of psychologists. This policy creates two levels of professional practice and a College for Professional Psychology (Professional Board for Psychology Psychological Society of South Africa, 1997).

Registration as a psychological counselor will be granted after the completion of a four-year B.Psych. degree and passing an examination set by the College for Professional Psychology. Registration as a psychologist will be granted after obtaining a D.Psych. degree (which will include a one-year internship) and passing an examination set by the college.

This new structure will be gradually introduced from 2000 and be fully implemented by 2004.

Future Directions

Postapartheid South Africa marks a fundamental break with the past. It presents new challenges and opportunities for psychology. Among these are the following.

Fundamental changes to the profession of psychology are occurring. Creating two levels to the profession is a response to the need to create more appropriate psychological services for South Africa. However, posts do not currently exist for psychological counselors in the public service. The success of the new policy will depend on the creation of employment opportunities. The new professional structure requires universities to restructure their degrees and training programs. This is likely to have far-reaching consequences for academic departments in terms of who they employ and the content of what is taught at undergraduate and postgraduate levels.

The future is likely to see changes in the role of psychology in the domain of health. The state has adopted a policy of primary health care, which focuses attention on service delivery at the community level. Don Foster, Melvyn Freeman, and Yogan Pillay (1997) have presented the implications of this for psychology. Psychologists will have to adopt new roles and operate within community mental health-care models. The tradition of community psychology generated in opposition to apartheid may provide a useful source of ideas for this.

The pressure for a more relevant psychology to serve the needs of the historically underserved will continue to exist. Changes in research institutes and policy have begun to occur. The Human Sciences Research Council, which incorporated the NIPR, is in the process of transformation. A more representative group of managers has been appointed and research programs to address contemporary social problems have been initiated. This includes promoting research at the historically Black universities. A new statutory organization to fund research in the social sciences, the National Research Foundation, has been created.

In the same way that psychology was constructed in its early history by its social context, so contemporary changes will continue to effect changes in the discipline and profession. The potential exists for the emergence of a contextually more sensitive psychology that could make a valuable contribution to psychology in its global setting.

[*See also* North Africa; *and* Sub-Saharan Africa.]

Bibliography

Biko, S. (1978). *I write what I like.* London: Heinemann. Central work on Black identity by the formative thinker of the Black Consciousness movement in South Africa who died while in detention.

Foster D., Freeman, M., & Pillay, Y. (Eds.). (1997). *Mental health policy issues for South Africa.* Pinelands, South Africa: Medical Association of South Africa. Collection of articles that reflect the contemporary debates and policy issues relating to mental health in a postapartheid South Africa.

Louw, J. (1986). White poverty and psychology in South Africa: The Poor White investigation of the Carnegie Commission. *Psychology in Society, 6,* 47–62.

Louw, J. (1993a). World War II, industry and the professionalization of South African psychology. In N. C. Manganyi, H. C. Marais, K. F. Mauer, & R. J. Prinsloo (Eds.), *A dissident amongst patriots: A Festschrift for Deodandus Strumpfer* (pp. 60–77). Pretoria, South Africa: Human Sciences Research Council.

Louw, J. (1993b). From separation to division: The origins of two psychological associations in South Africa. In N. C. Manganyi, H. C. Marais, K. F. Mauer, & R. J. Prinsloo (Eds.), *A dissident amongst patriots: A Festschrift for Deodandus Strumpfer* (pp. 243–259). Pretoria, South Africa: Human Sciences Research Council.

Louw, J., Orr, N., Horowitz, S., Vergunst, R., Tibbs, J., Roberts, K., Badroodien, G., Kaplan, S., Jeannot, C., & Nixon, M. (1995). The emergence of psychological themes in the South African Medical Journal, 1927–1975. *South African Journal of Psychology, 25* (2), 99–105.

Mann, J. (1987). The nature of psychology. In G. A. Tyson (Ed.), *An introduction to psychology* (pp. 3–24). Johannesburg: Westro Educational Books.

Professional Board for Psychology/Psychological Society of South Africa (PsySSA). (1997). *Draft policy on roles, licensing/registration, training and education within the professional field of psychology.* Pretoria, South Africa: Psychological Society of South Africa. A joint document produced by the statutory body and the professional association, which presents the proposed framework for professional practice that will fundamentally change the training and structure of psychology in South Africa. Psychological Society of South Africa. Available E-mail: Psyssa@cis.co.za

Andrew Gilbert

SOUTH AMERICA, SOUTH CONE ZONE OF. The geopolitical region made up of Argentina, Chile, and Uruguay called the Southern Cone (*Diccionario Enciclopédico Planeta,* 1984) has a low demographic growth rate. The approximately 52 million people inhabiting its vast territory share a great deal of sociocultural homogeneity: language, ethnicity, religious beliefs, political systems, and lifestyles in general. Its population is drawn mainly from southern European immigrants (Italians and Spaniards), although other minority groups also are present, such as central European Jews, Germans, Armenians, Arabs, and Japanese among others. The indigenous population has been reduced as a result of drastic campaigns of colonization and political institutionalization. Indigenous groups survive in small reserves, and only in a few cases, such as the Mapuche and Araucano Indians, are they more spread out and integrated into society. These countries were born during the first decades of the nineteenth century, breaking off from the Spanish colonial empire. In all of them the capital city concentrated a high percentage of the population and became a basic nucleus for national development in all aspects, including the economy, education, science, and professional work.

The History of Psychology

Psychology had already developed significantly in the beginning of the twentieth century, especially in the area of the Río de la Plata, as a result of the region's thriving economic situation and the knowledge provided by immigrants. One of the members of the board of directors of the V International Congress of Psychology held in Rome in 1905 was José Ingenieros, an Argentine doctor interested in criminology. A few years earlier, in 1898, Horacio Piñero had set up an experimental Institute of Psychology, and in 1901 he organized the first psychology course within the recently created University of Buenos Aires School of Liberal Arts (Foradori, 1954). In Chile, during approximately the same time period, Guillermo Mann organized a laboratory in experimental psychology at the University of Chile. He followed in the footsteps of his colleague Jorge Schneider, a disciple of Wundt and founder of the Institute of Pedagogy, where studies in psychology began in that country.

The history of psychology in the region can be divided into two large periods. The decades of the 1940s and 1950s are the dividing line between the two. During the first stage, psychology strictly followed the predominately French and German European model. The most influential writers were Théodule Ribot, Pierre Janet, and Wilhelm Wundt. In that period, studies in psychology were part of other disciplines: medicine, philosophy, and legal sciences. Its main areas of research were psychophysiology, psychopathology and comparative studies, and psychometry. Courses were taught within philosophy departments.

Two great changes took place during the 1940s. Because of the Second World War, significant waves of European scientists arrived, among them several psychoanalysts who set up their center of operations in Buenos Aires, founding the Asociación Psicoanalítica Argentina in 1942. Psychoanalysis had a tremendous impact, not only on the evolution of psychology, but also on life in the society as well. In its later development, in the mid-1970s, Buenos Aires came to be one of the world centers where psychoanalysis is most widely spread and practiced. Its influence extended throughout the country and in Uruguay, where the evolution of psychology was closely tied to developments in Argentina. Later on, that influence spread throughout Latin America.

The other important event was the emergence of psychology as an autonomous discipline. A university course of studies in psychology was created in Chile (1948), Argentina (1956), and Uruguay (1962).

Education

For many years, undergraduate studies reflected very similar plans in all three countries. A degree in psychology was based on programs lasting 4 to 5 years, which emphasized knowledge of theoretical-technical models over experimental studies. Students usually received solid training in theory as well as in various fields of application. The career normally included a postperiod of practices, mainly in psychodiagnosis and intervention procedures in clinical, educational, and labor psychology. An undergraduate degree allowed the bearer to practice as a professional in many fields. One exception was psychotherapy, which for many years was limited or had to be supervised by medical doctors. This changed in the 1980s, when psychologists became able to practice psychotherapy without restrictions. Up until the mid-1970s in Argentina and Uruguay, the predominance of psychoanalysis was accompanied by significant influence from Soviet psychology, which diminished abruptly in the 1980s. University studies in Chile were less hegemonic in orientation, with emphasis on the importance of studies referring to learning and social psychology (Vilanova, 1993).

At that time, Argentina had a dozen universities offering degrees in psychology, while both Chile and Uruguay had only two schools each. There was a rapid increase in the number of students of psychology in the region, especially in Argentina, which saw the number of schools authorized to offer those courses multiply, with many private universities joining them. This phenomenon was repeated in Chile, where there are now more than 30 institutions offering degrees in psychology.

Study programs have diversified in recent years with the inclusion of cognitive-behavioral and systemic models. Practical education has also been broadened, adding new specialties such as forensic psychology, neuropsychology, and community psychology, among others. Students have intensified their presence in social welfare centers where the need for psychologists is growing.

In Argentina and Uruguay, most teachers are professionals whose academic activity is only a part-time job, whereas Chile has a greater number of full-time professors, which enables more emphasis on basic research. Chile was also the first to have professors who had received training abroad.

Postgraduate studies came late on the scene in all three countries. Up until the 1990s, there were very few postgraduate university programs (Marín, Kennedy, & Boyce, 1987). This situation is rapidly changing due to new national policies promoting universities. Today, many centers of academic learning offer master's and doctorate degrees, especially in clinical, educational, forensic, organizational, and community psychology. An increasing number of those programs receive support from North American and European universities.

The Profession

Argentina has a high incidence of psychologists per inhabitant as a result of the spectacular growth in students of psychology in the last 20 years. In 1995, there were 120 psychologists for every 100,000 persons (Alonso, 1996). At that time, Argentina had some 40,000 psychologists, Chile, 4,000, and Uruguay, 2,000. These figures are approximate because of the lack of official registers.

The profile of psychologists indicates these dominant traits: young professionals, mostly women, with a solid and diversified theoretical education, good preparation for care-giving work, especially in the clinical field, and training to carry out community tasks. Their education is weaker in experimental psychology and methodology and is oriented to professional training rather than research (Klappenbach, 1994). The difficult economic conditions that plagued these countries for many years conspired against budgets for scientific development, especially in the social sciences. Research was restricted to small groups, and the little funding available was earmarked for programs of applied psychology. This situation began to change dramatically in the 1990s. The number of research projects grew, and dynamic policies aimed at generating a general structure for promoting this field were undertaken.

The role psychologists have played in relation to the difficult socioeconomic and political realities afflicting these countries is significant. First, many of them worked in social improvement programs to help popu-

SOUTH AMERICA, SOUTH CONE ZONE OF. Table 1. Regularly published journals

Country	Journal	Begun
Argentina	*Revista de Psicoanálisis*	1943
	Acta Psiquiátrica y Psicológica de América Latina	1954
	Revista Argentina de Psicología	1969
	Interdisciplinaria	1980
	Psico-Logos	1991
	Revista Argentina de Clínica Psicológica	1992
	Revista de Psicología y Psicoterapia de Grupo	1961
	Perspectivas Sistémicas	1988
Chile	*Revista Chilena de Psicología*	1979
	Terapia Psicológica	1982
	Psicología y Ciencias Humanas	1988
	Psicología	1990
	Estudios Psicológicos	1991
	Psikhé	1992
Uruguay	*Revista Uruguaya de Psicoanálisis*	1957
	Revista de Psicoterapia Psicoanalítica	1984
	Revista de la Sociedad de Psicología del Uruguay	1989

lation groups living in scarce-resource conditions. These psychologists played an active and extremely valuable role in fighting against the spread of scourges like acquired immunodeficiency syndrome (AIDS) and family and social violence. Second, they work courageously in care-giving programs for individuals and families who are victims of political repression.

Scientific and Professional Societies

Psychologists are generally grouped in each country into two types of organizations: professional and scientific (Ardila, 1986). The professional type, which are much more numerous, defend trade union interests. They are the Federación de Psicólogos (Argentina), Colegio de Psicólogos (Chile), and Coordinadora de Psicólogos (Uruguay). They defend the interests of the professionals, regulate the court of ethics, and usually organize periodic events for psychologists throughout the country to exchange ideas and experiences. The scientific type promote activities linked to scientific development and research and usually represent their countries in the International Union of Psychological Science. They are the Asociación Argentina de Ciencias del Comportamiento (Argentina) and Sociedad de Psicología del Uruguay (Uruguay). There are also other institutions that group psychologists according to different specialties, such as the Sociedad Chilena de Psicología Clínica (Chile).

The three countries have played active roles internationally in groups such as the Sociedad Interamericana de Psicología (SIP), in whose activities many scientists and professionals have participated. All three countries have also hosted congresses organized by the SIP.

Journals

Although many journals have been published in these countries, economic difficulties have forced numerous publications to be suspended or discontinued. Only a few have managed to survive for long periods (see Table 1 for journals that have been published on a regular basis in recent years).

The Situation of Psychology in the National Context

Psychology is heavily incorporated into the daily life in these countries. It is one of the most popular careers chosen by university students. Psychologists often appear in the media; their opinions are sought on various questions of interest to society, and they have begun to be included in government areas.

Above all, psychology is a service of daily consumption. Psychologists are regularly employed in different areas, like health, education, the courts, and business. This phenomenon is mainly seen in urban areas.

The income of psychologists covers a broad spectrum. A large number of psychologists are contracted by public businesses to perform tasks in hospitals, community health centers, schools, technical training centers, the courts, and penitentiaries, where their earnings are usually not very high due to budget restrictions.

Others are engaged in the private sector, working in the areas of development and training in companies, in advertising, and in opinion consultant offices. Their pay is higher than in the public sector.

The field of clinical activity has traditionally employed the greatest number of professionals, many of whom have had independent practices with middle to high incomes. The number of psychologists in this category has been diminishing, while more and more psychologists are being recruited by insurance companies who contract their services at much lower salary levels.

Bibliography

Alonso, M. (1996). La psicología en la república Argentina. *8vo. Congreso de Psicología.* San Luis, Argentina.

Ardila, R. (1986). *La psicología en América Latina. Pasado, presente y futuro.* México: Siglo XXI.

Diccionario Enciclopédico Planeta (1984). Barcelona: Editorial Planeta.

Foradori, I. A. (1954). *La psicología en América.* Argentina: Instituto Cultural Joaquín V. González.

Klappenbach, H. A., & Pavesi, P. (1994). Una historia de la psicología en Latinoamérica. *Rev. Latinoamericana de Psicología, 26,* 445–482.

Marín, G., Kennedy, S., & Boyce, B. C. (1987). *Latin American psychology: A guide to research and training.* Washington, DC: American Psychological Association.

Vilanova, A. R. (1993). La formación de psicólogos en Iberoamérica. *Acta Psiquiátrica y Psicológica de América Latina, 39,* 193–205.

Héctor Fernández-Alvarez

SOUTHEAST ASIA. This article reports the status of psychology in Brunei, Cambodia, Indonesia, Laos, Malaysia, Myanmar, Philippines, Singapore, Thailand, and Vietnam. The American Psychological Association (APA) has more than 3,000 international affiliates and members from as many as 121 countries. As of 11 June 1998, Cambodia, Laos, Myanmar, and Vietnam had no representation in the APA; Brunei had just one international affiliate; and the remaining five countries had both affiliates and members. Such representations in the APA imply that psychology may be at different stages of development in the Southeast Asian nations.

Table 1 lists statistics on their areas, populations, ethnic and religious groups, types of governments, and per capita gross domestic products (GDP). Note that the types of government range from a military regime in Myanmar to a presidential democracy in the Philippines and that the per capita GDP of Singapore is 34.7 times higher than that of Cambodia. Such diversity could have contributed to the uneven development of psychology in this region (Leung & Zhang, 1995).

The growth of psychology is linked to the scope for higher education (Richards & Gottfredson, 1978). In *The World of Learning 1998* (Europa Publications Limited, 1997), there is no entry for universities in Cambodia, and there is only a half-page description of the National University of Laos, reporting that it was founded in 1995 and has a faculty of education. Cambodia and Laos are thus eliminated from further consideration here.

Based on *PsycLIT: 1991–1998*, Table 2 lists the number of publications by the staffs of psychology departments in international and respective national journals.

Brunei

The University of Brunei, Darussalam (founded 1985) has a department of educational psychology at the Sultan Hassanal Bolkiah Institute of Education. The department offers courses for teacher trainees at the certificate, diploma, and degree levels. These courses are also open to students of other majors. There are nine on the teaching staff in the department: four have doctoral degrees (one Indonesia, one Canada, one United Kingdom, and one United States), and two of them hold chairs of educational psychology. Table 2 suggests that research is not the priority; the department has published only one paper.

Indonesia

The Dutch colonial government of Indonesia introduced applied psychology to the teacher training curriculum in the early 1940s (Nimpoeno, 1990) and opened an institute for psychotechnical services (Balai Psychotechniek) for the assessment of children's intellectual abilities and vocational choices. The Dutch army also had a unit for psychology (Munandar & Munandar, 1987). Both services continued after Indonesia's independence: The Balai Psychotechniek became part of the Ministry of Education and Culture (1951), and the Dutch army unit was turned into the Army Center of Psychology.

The Balai Psychotechniek later developed into the Institute of Psychology, with Slamet Iman Santoso, an Indonesian psychiatrist, as its head. With the assistance of Dutch and Indonesian experts, Santoso started a 3-year program for assistant psychologists in 1953. This program resulted in a 5- to 6-year graduate program in psychology. Within the Faculty of Medicine of the Universitas Indonesia at Jakarta (founded 1950), an independent department of psychology was established in 1955, and psychology emerged as a faculty in its own right in 1960 (Munandar & Munandar, 1987, p. 252).

There are now faculties of psychology at three other state universities, namely, Padjadjaran University at Bandung, Gadjah Mada University at Yogyakarta, and Airlangga University at Surabaya. In addition, 15 private universities (Jakarta: 3, Bandung: 2, Yogyakarta

SOUTHEAST ASIA. Table 1. Statistics on Southeast Asian countries[1]

Countries	Total Area (sq km)	Land Area (sq km)	Population (July 1996)	Ethnic Groups (%)	Religions (%)	Government	GDP[2] per capita ($US in 1995)
Brunei	5770	5270	299,939	Malay 64 Chinese 20 Others 16	Muslim 63 Buddhist 14 Christian 8 Others 15	Constitutional Sultanate	15,800
Cambodia	181,040	176,520	10,861,218	Khmer 90 Vietnamese 5 Chinese 1 Others 4	Buddhist 90 Others 10	King	660
Indonesia	1,919,440	1,826,440	206,611,600	Javanese 45 Sundanese 14 Madurese 7.5 Malay 7.5 Others 26	Muslim 87 Protestant 6 Catholic 3 Hindu 2 Buddhist 1 Others 1	Republic	3500
Laos	236,800	230,800	4,975,772	Lao Loum 68 Lao Theung 22 Lao Soung 9 Chinese 1	Buddhist 60 Others 40	Communist	1100
Malaysia	329,750	328,550	19,962,893	Malay 59 Chinese 32 Indian 9	Muslim 53[3] Buddhist 17 Chinese Folk 12 Hindu 7 Christian 6 Others 5	Constitutional Monarchy	9800
Myanmar	678,500	657,740	45,975,625	Burman 68 Shan 9 Karen 7 Rakhine 4 Chinese 3 Mon 2 Indian 2 Others 5	Buddhist 89 Christian 4 Muslim 4 Others 3	Military Regime	1000

Philippines	300,000	298,170	74,480,848	Christian Malay 91.5 Muslim Malay 4 Chinese 1.5 Others 3	Catholic 83 Protestant 9 Muslim 5 Buddhist and others 3	Republic	2530
Singapore	633	623	3,396,924	Chinese 76.4 Malay 14.9 Indian 6.4 Others 2.3	Buddhist 31.9[4] Taoist 22 Islam 14.9 Christian 12.9 Hindu 3.3 No religion 14.5 Others 0.5	Republic	22,900
Thailand	524,000	511,770	58,851,357	Thai 75 Chinese 14 Others 11	Buddhist 95[5] Muslim 3.8 Christian 0.5 Hindu 0.1 Others 0.6	Constitutional Monarchy	6900
Vietnam	329,356	325,360	73,976,973	Vietnamese 85–90 Chinese 3 Others 7–12	Buddhist, Taoist[6] Catholic, Islam, Protestant	Communist	1300

[1] U.S. Central Intelligence Agency (1996).
[2] GDP, gross domestic product.
[3] *The Economist* Publications Limited (1987). The data on religious groups are from 1980.
[4] Balachandrer (1996).
[5] Based on 1991 survey by the CIA.
[6] Percentage not given in the CIA report.

SOUTHEAST ASIA. Table 2. Number of international and national publications by the psychology staff of the Southeast Asian nations

Nations	Publications in journals		
	International	National	Total
Brunei	0	1	1
Indonesia	0	0	0
Malaysia	7	0	7
Myanmar	0	0	0
Philippines	8	40	48
Singapore	61	0	61
Thailand	2	0	2
Vietnam	0	0	0

Source: *PsycLIT* Search: 1991–June 1998.

and Central Java: 3, East Java: 6, and North Sumatra: 1) have faculties of psychology (Sarwono, 1996). The educational system and psychology syllabi of the different universities are similar. The language of instruction is Bahasa Indonesia.

There are three levels (strata) of academic education in psychology. At stratum one (S1), students take basic courses in psychology and write a short thesis. They earn the degree of Sarjana Psikologi (S.Psi.). The programs at stratum two (S2) and stratum three (S3) are equivalent to master's and doctoral degrees, respectively. The older state universities offer programs at all three strata. By 1993, for example, the Universitas Indonesia had awarded doctoral degrees to 35 students (Sarwono, 1996).

Graduates of a faculty of psychology become general practitioners. To practice as a psychologist, they need a professional degree at S2. This degree of magister of science in psychology (M.Si.) requires them to undertake four semesters of professional courses in clinical, educational, industrial and organizational, and social psychology, and to complete the relevant internships.

The Ikatan Sarjana Psikologi Indonesia—the only professional body of psychologists—founded in 1959 is now known as Himpunan Psikologi Indonesia (HIMPSI). Anyone with an S.Psi. degree is eligible to be a member, and by 1996 there were approximately 4,000 members (Sarwono, 1996). The *Jurnal Psikologi Indonesia*, a publication of the HIMPSI, has been published irregularly.

The *PsycLIT* search yielded no entry for the faculties of psychology of the Indonesian universities (see Table 2). There may be at least two reasons for this. One is the scarcity of staff with research skills. For example, of 120 staff members of the Universitas Indonesia, only 14.2% have master's degrees and 26.7% have doctoral degrees. Sarwono (1996) believes that language barrier is the second reason.

Malaysia

Psychology came to Malaysia as a service subject for the departments of anthropology and sociology and the schools of medicine and education. In the early 1960s, educational psychology and social psychology were taught under the faculties of education and arts of the Universiti Malaya and at the teachers' colleges (e.g., the Language Institute and the Malaysian Teachers' College in Penang and in Kuala Lumpur). When the faculty of medicine was started, a clinical psychology course became available to the medical students. Psychology continues to supplement the degrees in anthropology, education, sociology, social work, and medicine at the Universiti Malaya (founded 1962), Universiti Sains Malaysia (1969), Universiti Pertanian Malaysia (1971), and Universiti Kebangsaan Malaysia (1970).

In 1973, two psychologists—Wan Rafaei and Abdul Halim—organized a conference, "The Role and Functions of Social Sciences and Related Disciplines and Social Scientists in Malaysia." This conference provided a forum for discussing the potential contributions of psychology to nation-building and hence generated a greater support for the independence of psychology from other disciplines. The first step was the creation of a psychology division, with Mohammad Haji-Yusuf as its coordinator, in the department of anthropology and sociology of the Universiti Kebangsaan Malaysia. The first department of psychology was established in 1979. At that time, there were 9 staff members with master's degrees (6 Malaysians, 2 Peace Corps volunteers, and 1 Indonesian). There are now 15 staff members, 9 with doctoral degrees (4 United States, 3 Malaysia, 1 Australia, and 1 United Kingdom), and Haji-Yusuf holds the chair of psychology. Programs for degrees at all levels are available, and 6 candidates have already received doctoral degrees.

Another department of psychology was established in 1990 under the faculty of Islamic Revealed Knowledge and Human Sciences at the International Islamic University (founded 1983). Since 1996, there have been programs for bachelor of human sciences with honors in psychology and a master's in psychology (counseling and clinical psychology, industrial and organizational psychology). The goal of the master's program is to produce well-trained psychologists with an Islamic outlook and commitment. Of the 24 staff members in the department, 14 have doctoral degrees (7 United Kingdom, 4 United States, 2 India, 1 Germany), and 6 of them hold chairs of psychology.

Ward (1987) pointed out three challenges to the growth of psychology in Malaysia. First, psychology was viewed as a Western discipline, "at best irrelevant and at worst threatening to the Malaysian way of life" (p. 212). Second, there was "a deficit of trained professionals" (p. 211). Finally, there was no professional association of the psychologists. All three challenges appear to have been dealt with in the 1990s. First, inclusion of psychology within the faculty of Islamic Revealed Knowledge and Human Sciences at the International Islamic University is an excellent example of the realization that psychology is not opposed to Islam. Second, the threefold increase in the number of psychologists with a doctoral degree from 1987 to 1996 at the Universiti Kebangsaan Malaysia is a notable improvement in the quality of staff available. Finally, the *Persatuan Psikologi Malaysia* (PSIMA), the professional association established in 1988, has 100 members (Nair, 1997). In 1994, the PSIMA hosted the conference of the Afro-Asian Psychological Association at the Universiti Kebangsaan Malaysia. The PSIMA and the Universiti Kebangsaan Malaysia have also been publishing an academic journal, *Jurnal Psikologi Malaysia*, annually.

Table 2 shows seven international publications from Malaysia. Reasons for such a low research productivity rate could include the engagement of trained psychologists in administration and consulting. Moreover, "the majority of Malaysian psychologists are more prolific in Malay [than English] and tend to publish locally" (Ward, 1987, p. 208). This focus strengthens the linkage between psychology and the Malaysian way of life.

Myanmar

General and experimental psychology were earlier parts of the philosophy degree at the University of Yangon (founded 1920). Psychology was first offered as a degree subject in 1952. In 1955, a department of psychology was established with Hla Thwin as the chair of psychology. In 1958, the University of Mandalay (founded 1958) opened a department of philosophy and psychology with Sein Tu—a psychologist with doctoral training at Harvard—as the chair of psychology (Than, 1990).

Students earn B. A., B. A. Honors, and M. A. degrees in 3, 4, and 6 years, respectively. Both course work and a thesis are required for the B. A. Honors and M. A. degrees in psychology. Educational psychology is compulsory at the teacher training colleges and at the Institute of Education (Blowers & Turtle, 1987).

Most staff members obtained their first degree in Myanmar. Although they are free to do research on any topic of interest, emphasis is more on commissioned applied than basic research (Than, 1990). It is unsurprising, therefore, that the *PsycLIT* search had no entry for Myanmar (see Table 2).

Philippines

Teaching of psychology in the Philippines began within the department of philosophy of the University of the Philippines (founded 1908) and then moved from the College of Liberal Arts to the College of Education in 1918. A separate department of psychology was established in 1926, and it remained with the Graduate School of Education for a long time. The department of psychology was then transferred to the College of Arts and Science in 1960 (de Jesus, 1990) to give "a basic scientific orientation" in teaching psychology against the prevailing "applied educational perspective" (Enriquez, 1987, p. 274). Such scientific orientation had been introduced in teaching psychology at the University of San Carlos since 1954. Therefore, Turtle (1987, p. 7) regards 1954 as the year in which the first department of psychology was established in the Philippines.

There are now 139 colleges and universities that have undergraduate programs in psychology (Tan, 1998). At least six universities—Ateneo de Manila University, Centro Escolar University, de la Salle University, Manuel L. Quezon University, University of the Philippines, and University of Santo Thomas—offer doctoral training in psychology (Enriquez, 1987, p. 277).

At the professional level, there are nine national associations of psychology (de Jesus, 1990). However, the Psychological Association of the Philippines (PAP), established in 1962 (Tan, 1998), is the most active and influential. The PAP has 1,514 members and has published the *Philippine Journal of Psychology* in English regularly since 1968. It has also organized an annual conference. The PAP hosted the meetings of the International Council of Psychologists and the Afro-Asian Psychological Association in 1995 and 1998, respectively.

Table 2 shows 48 entries in the *PsycLIT* search. Of these, 16.7% were in international journals and 83.3% in the *Philippine Journal of Psychology*. This level of maturity may have been reached because of the provision for higher education and the fluency in English among the Filipinos to start. For example, the University of San Carlos and the University of Santo Thomas were founded in 1595 and 1611, respectively (Europa Publications Limited, 1997), and the Philippines is the third largest English-speaking country in the world (Enriquez, 1987, p. 285). The coming of Americans and the establishment of an American system of education in the Philippines may have further facilitated the growth of psychology (de Jesus, 1990, p. 311). In fact, the three successive heads of the department of psychology at the University of the Philippines, namely, Austine S. Alonzo, Isidro Pamlasigui, and Alfredo V. Lagmay, received their doctoral degrees from the United States.

One reaction to the foregoing American impact on psychology in the Philippines came in the form of a distinction between Philippine psychology and Filipino psychology, or Sikolohiyang Pilipino (Enriquez, 1987). The former refers to the Anglo-American perspective on psychology, the one widely held and practiced in the

Philippines. The latter refers to "the indigenous developments in the field of psychology from the Filipino perspective: the psychology borne out of the experience, thought, and orientation of the Filipino" (de Jesus, 1990, p. 335). In essence, the Sikolohiyang Pilipino uses the "local language" as the research tool, and "demands that the Filipino psychologist confront social problems and national issues as part of his responsibility" (Enriquez, 1987, p. 278). It is also argued that the "unsophisticated" *provinciano* (a rustic from the villages) of the Philippines is as much Filipino as the urbanized *Manileno*. Any psychological account of the Filipino should, therefore, reflect group differences.

The PAP has also submitted a *Psychology Act* to the Congress of the Philippines (Tan, 1998). If this act is passed, a practicing clinical psychologist must finish a master's degree and pass a licensure examination before conducting any therapy. Moreover, administration of the psychological tests and interpretation of the scores obtained would be done by a psychometrician.

Three constraints on the development of psychology in the Philippines deserve mention. First, not all psychology staff are adequately trained. For example, only 50% of the 26 full-time staff of the University of the Philippines have doctoral degrees (Tan, 1998). Second, several institutions do not have laboratory and computer facilities (de Jesus, 1990). Finally, most of the departments do not have ongoing research projects. Bernardo (1998) laments, therefore, that research culture is virtually absent.

Singapore

Psychology came to Singapore as a service subject for medical education. In 1914, King Edward VII Medical College started the first 3-month clinical course in psychological medicine. In the 1950s, psychology supplemented the programs for teachers' training (Long, 1987). At present, the National Institute of Education of the Nanyang Technological University (founded 1981) has a department of psychological studies under the School of Education. Of the 23 staff members of the department, 21 have doctoral degrees (10 United States, 4 Australia, 4 Canada, 2 Singapore, and 1 Germany). In 1997, the department launched a master's program in applied psychology (counseling and educational psychology).

In 1952, Beryl Wright, an Australian national and the Colombo Plan visitor, taught psychology in the Department of Social Studies at the University of Malaya (Long, 1987), as it was then known. Psychology continued to be taught by the part-time expatriate and local staffs for the next 15 years at the renamed University of Singapore. In 1977, Anthony Chang, a Singapore national and Australian-trained applied psychologist, joined the department of social work as a full-time instructor. A bachelor's degree in psychology

has been available in this department since 1986 (Elliott, 1999). In 1988, Sushilan Vasoo (a Ph.D. in social work and head of the department of social work) and Edwin Thumboo (a noted English poet and dean of the faculty of arts and social sciences at that time) persuaded the National University of Singapore (founded 1980) to rename the department the department of social work and psychology. Of the two chairs given to the faculty in 1997, one came to Ramadhar Singh of psychology. Clearly, psychology is now well recognized as an independent discipline in Singapore.

At the National University of Singapore, students earn bachelor's and honors degrees in 3 and 4 years, respectively. The honors program requires both course work and a thesis. Master's and doctoral degrees, however, are purely research based.

Although the psychology program started with only Godfrey Harrison, a British national, the university soon attracted both local and the expatriate staffs. All 16 current psychology staff members (9 local, 8 expatriates) with ranks of assistant professor to professor have doctoral degrees (8 United States, 8 United Kingdom, 1 Canada, and 1 Germany). This makes the National University of Singapore the first among the Southeast Asian institutions to have 100% of its staff members with doctoral degrees.

The *PsycLIT* search yielded 61 entries for the psychology staff of the two universities (see Table 2). These international publications illustrate the high quality of the staff and research programs.

The Singapore Psychological Society (SPsS) was founded in 1979. Its membership has grown from 40 in 1979 to 197 in 1998. A full member is required to have an honors degree plus 2 years of experience under the supervision of a full member of the SPsS. The SPsS organized the First Asian Conference of Psychology in Singapore in 1992 and has been trying to publish a journal of psychology. The *Singapore Psychologist* appeared irregularly during 1983–1992, and the *Asian Journal of Psychology* was published only twice in 1995. The SPsS and the Department of Social Work and Psychology of the National University of Singapore jointly released the inaugural issue of the *Asian Psychologist*, a twice-yearly publication, in January 1998.

Psychology is held in high esteem by the government of Singapore. There is a department of psychology at the Woodbridge Hospital and Institute of Mental Health under the Ministry of Health. The Applied Behavioral Sciences Department of the Ministry of Defense deals with industrial/organizational psychology and with the problems pertaining to the young national servicemen. The police force has a unit of psychology, and the prison department has its own psychologist. The Ministry of Education has psychologists in the Specialized Pupil Program branch.

The rapid growth of psychology in Singapore probably has four causes. First, if the "fundamental impetus for developing psychology in the [d]eveloping [w]orld is financial" (Leung & Zhang, 1995, p. 703), then Singapore's economic growth may be a factor in the development of psychology. Second, the quality of education is one of the top priorities of the government of Singapore, and the universities are provided with adequate funding for educational programs, research facilities and equipment, books and journals, and staff development. In fact, the Central Library of the National University of Singapore has the best collection of books and journals in the region (Elliott, 1999, p. 199). Third, the government practices meritocracy in recruitment and promotion of the staff. Finally, English—the language of most of the psychological literature (Gilgen & Gilgen, 1987)—is the main language of instruction in the schools and universities of Singapore.

Thailand

Psychology entered Thailand through the teacher training programs (Malakul, 1979), and the early lecturers were nonpsychologists. Mom Luang Tui Chumsai, trained at the University of Philippines and later at the University of Michigan, is regarded as the first experimental psychologist of Thailand. He wrote a textbook of psychology in 1943, set up the first laboratory of psychology, constructed the first Thai test of learning abilities, and founded the Psychological Association of Thailand in 1961 (Bhanthumnavin, 1990).

Despite the presence of such an influential experimental psychologist in Thailand, developmental psychology was the first to be offered at the master's level in 1955 at the International Institute for Child Study (now known as the Behavioral Science Research Institute) of the Srinakharinwirot University. A master's program in educational psychology, run by the College of Education of the Chulalongkorn University from 1963, was added in 1968.

Undergraduate programs in experimental psychology at the Thammasarat University and in industrial and school psychology at Chiengmai University became available in 1966. The first degree programs in social (1972), developmental (1974), and developmental–social psychology (1978) also became available at Ramkhamhaeng, Kasetsart, and Srinakharinwirot Universities, respectively. By 1990, 13 universities, institutes, or colleges had undergraduate programs in psychology; 9 of them had master's programs; and just 1 (Chulalongkorn University) had a doctoral program (Bhanthumnavin, 1990, Table 3, pp. 350–351). Emphasis in most of these programs is still on education, testing, guidance, and counseling rather than on experimental, industrial, and social psychology. The Chulalongkorn University elevated psychology to the level of a faculty in 1996 (Sirivunnabood et al., 1998).

The *PsycLIT* search had only two entries for Thailand (see Table 2), which raises the question of why research productivity is so low. Bhanthumnavin's analyses (1987, 1990) suggest four reasons. First, research has "been less the province of senior academics than that of graduate students" (p. 359), and most of the master's degree psychologists trained during 1955–1968 have had no undergraduate backgrounds in psychology. Second, most of the articles are published in the university's own journal or magazine. Third, it is still rare to find two noneducational psychologists at the same institution. That makes professional communication between colleagues in other specializations rather difficult. Finally, Thai psychologists are not interacting enough with colleagues from other countries.

The professional standing of a psychologist in Thailand is not encouraging. A person with a bachelor's degree in psychology is expected to be a practitioner, and membership in the Psychological Association of Thailand is open even to nonpsychologists. The number of research centers in psychology has also declined from 35 in 1977 to 23 in 1984 (Bhanthumnavin, 1990).

Thai psychologists have started linking psychology with the concepts of Buddhism, the religion of 95% of the people. This trend is best illustrated by the National Committee of Culture's publication, *Psychology: The Buddhist Approach* (1986) edited by the Bange Lang et al. (cited in Bhankinmu Navin, 1990, p. 343). Such a culture-linked presentation of psychology may restore the confidence of the Thai government in the potential of psychology and prevent the research centers of psychology from dwindling further. The Psychological Association of Thailand has become more active in the 1990s and has been promoting publication of more issues of the *Thai Journal of Psychology* (Sirivunnabood et al., 1998, footnote 1, p. 48).

Vietnam

Educational psychology has been one of the subjects offered at all the teacher training schools and colleges of Vietnam. The first department of psychology was established in 1955 at the Hanoi Teacher Training College (Hac, 1987). Early psychology was modeled on the French tradition, but later curricula and textbooks followed Soviet psychology. Two Soviet psychologists conducted a course on psychology and education during the academic year 1959–1960, and students were subsequently sent to the Soviet Union for more advanced study.

Hanoi Teacher Training College was the first to start an undergraduate degree program in psychology and education. The National Institute of Educational Sciences (founded 1961) has the Experimental Department of Children's Psychology and Pedagogics. In 1993, an institute of psychology was also established. Both of these institutions have been running graduate programs in psychology. Of the estimated 500 teachers of psychology in 1987, 3 had a second doctoral degree (D.Sc.), about 30 had a first doctoral degree (Ph.D.), and about 35 had a master's degree in psychology. This means that the remaining 86% of teachers had just an undergraduate degree.

Because psychology was expected to facilitate the national renovation and social progress envisaged by the Communist Party and Government of Vietnam, both child psychology and educational psychology prospered faster than other branches. Medical, sport, and social psychology have been developing since the early 1980s. The Vietnamese Association of Psychology and Pedagogical Sciences, founded in 1990, has 2,000 members. The *PsycLIT* search had no entry for Vietnam (see Table 2). Vietnamese psychologists publish their articles in the local newspapers (Hac, 1987) or in the new magazine *Psychology*, launched in 1996.

Concluding Comments

The foregoing national reviews lead to a conclusion that psychology in Southeast Asia is indeed at different stages of development. It is absent in Cambodia and Laos; it has entered Brunei as a service subject to education; and it has been progressing slowly in Myanmar and Vietnam. In the remaining five nations, psychology has been developing, but in different directions. Malaysia and Thailand have been linking psychological processes to their respective Islamic and Buddhist beliefs; Philippines has been moving toward an indigenous Filipino psychology; Indonesia has been showing an interest in cross-cultural psychology (10 members in the International Association of Cross-Cultural Psychology) along with its primary focus on applied psychology; and Singapore has been active in basic research (9 members in the American Psychological Society).

Of the four countries where psychology is absent or advancing slowly, Myanmar is on the western side and Cambodia, Laos, and Vietnam are on the eastern side of Southeast Asia. They all have nondemocratic forms of government and per capita GDP ranging between $660 and $1300 (see Table 1). These political and economic conditions may have impeded the growth of psychology, which is viewed as "something of a luxury" and not "a priority discipline" throughout Asia (Elliott, 1999, p. 198). In contrast, in all the five countries where industrialization has been rather rapid, psychology has been progressing. The growth of psychology in Southeast Asian nations can thus be attributed to industrialization of the economies (Gilgen & Gilgen, 1987; Leung & Zhang, 1995).

Bibliography

Association of the Commonwealth Universities, London. (1998). *Commonwealth universities yearbook 1997–98.* London: Author.

Balachandrer, S. B. (Ed.). (1996). *Singapore 1996: A review of 1995.* Singapore: Ministry of Information and the Arts.

Bernardo, A. B. I. (1998). Psychological research in the Philippines: Observations and prospects. *Philippine Journal of Psychology, 30,* 38–57.

Bhanthumnavin, D. (1987). Social history of psychology in Thailand. In G. Blowers & A. M. Turtle (Eds.), *Psychology moving East: The status of western psychology in Asia and Oceania* (pp. 71–88). Boulder, CO: Westview Press.

Bhanthumnavin, D. (1990). Thailand. In G. Shouksmith & E. A. Shauksmith (Eds.), *Psychology in Asia and the Pacific* (pp. 339–394). Bangkok, Thailand: UNESCO.

Blowers, G., & Turtle, A. M. (1987). Appendix: Notes on psychology in the Socialist Republic of the Union of Burma. In G. Blowers & A. M. Turtle (Eds.), *Psychology moving East: The status of western psychology in Asia and Oceania* (pp. 101–103). Boulder, CO: Westview Press.

de Jesus, M. L. V. (1990). Philippines. In G. Shouksmith & E. A. Shouksmith (Eds.), *Psychology in Asia and the Pacific* (pp. 311–338). Bangkok, Thailand: UNESCO.

Elliott, J. M. (1999). Studies in psychology: 1985–95. In B. H. Chua (Ed.), *Singapore studies* (pp. 182–203). Singapore: Singapore University Press.

Enriquez, V. G. (1987). Decolonizing the Filipino psyche: Impetus for the development of psychology in the Philippines. In G. Blowers & A. M. Turtle (Eds.), *Psychology moving East: The status of western psychology in Asia and Oceania* (pp. 265–287). Boulder, CO: Westview Press.

Europa Publications Limited. (1997). *The world of learning 1998.* Surrey, UK: Gresham Press.

Gilgen, A. R., & Gilgen, C. K. (1987). *International handbook of psychology.* New York: Greenwood Press.

Hac, P. M. (1987). Some observations on the historical development of psychology in the Socialist Republic of Vietnam. In G. Blowers & A. M. Turtle (Eds.), *Psychology moving East: The status of western psychology in Asia and Oceania* (pp. 89–99). Boulder, CO: Westview Press.

Leung, K., & Zhang, J. (1995). Systemic considerations: Factors facilitating and impeding the development of psychology in developing countries. *International Journal of Psychology, 30,* 693–706.

Long, F. Y. (1987). Psychology in Singapore: Its roots, context, and growth. In G. Blowers & A. M. Turtle (Eds.), *Psychology moving East: The status of western psychology in Asia and Oceania* (pp. 223–248). Boulder, CO: Westview Press.

Malakul, P. (1979). Psychology in Thailand. *Psychologia, 22,* 65–78.

Munandar, S. C. U., & Munandar, A. S. (1987). Psychology in Indonesia: Its past, present, and future. In G. Blowers & A. M. Turtle (Eds.), *Psychology moving East: The status of western psychology in Asia and Oceania* (pp. 249–263). Boulder, CO: Westview Press.

Nair, E. (1997). *Development and teaching of psychology in Asian countries* (Working Paper No. 54). Singapore: Department of Social Work and Psychology, National University of Singapore.

Nimpoeno, J. S. (1990). Indonesia. In G. Shouksmith &

E. A. Shouksmith (Eds.), *Psychology in Asia and the Pacific* (pp. 279–310). Bangkok, Thailand: UNESCO.

Richards, J. M., & Gottfredson, G. D. (1978). Geographic distribution of U.S. psychologists: A human ecological analysis. *American Psychologist, 33,* 1–9.

Sarwono, S. S. (1996). Psychology in Indonesia. *World Psychology, 2,* 177–196.

Sirivunnabood, P. B., Cholvanich, P., Wattakakosol, R., Panjamawat, C., & Barrett, M. E. (1998). Current state of psychology education in Thailand: Results of a key informant survey. *Asian Psychologist, 1,* 47–52.

Tan, A. L. (1998, March). *Philippine psychology: Growth and becoming.* Paper presented at the National Social Science Congress, Manila.

Than, U. K. M. (1990). History of western psychology in the Union of Myanmar. *Myanmar Review, 12,* 21–24.

The Economist Publications Limited (1987). *The world in figures* (5th ed.). London: Thetford Press.

Turtle. A. M. (1987). Introduction: A silk road for psychology. In G. Blowers & A. M. Turtle (Eds.), *Psychology moving East: The status of western psychology in Asia and Oceania* (pp. 1–21). Boulder, CO: Westview Press.

U.S. Central Intelligence Agency. (1996). *The world factbook 1996.* Washington, DC: Author.

Ward, C. (1987). The historical development and current status of psychology in Malaysia. In G. Blowers & A. M. Turtle (Eds.), *Psychology moving East: The status of western psychology in Asia and Oceania* (pp. 201–222). Boulder, CO: Westview Press.

Ramadhar Singh

SOUTHEASTERN PSYCHOLOGICAL ASSOCATION.
See Regional Psychological Associations.

SOUTHERN SOCIETY FOR PHILOSOPHY AND PSYCHOLOGY. *See* Regional Psychological Associations.

SOUTHWESTERN PSYCHOLOGICAL ASSOCATION.
See Regional Psychological Associations.

SOVIET REPUBLICS. *See* Russia and the Former Soviet Republics.

SPAIN. Current Spanish culture derives from a rich diversity of ethnic, religious, and national sources, and this diversity is found at the root of psychological think-ing: the first references to subjective aspects of the functioning of the human being are to be found in Seneca, San Isidoro de Sevilla, Averroës, and Maimonides, who represent, respectively, contributions from the Roman, Barbarian, Arab, and Jewish cultures. Pluralism can be considered one of the first historical characteristics in the construction of psychology in Spain.

The foundation of the Spanish state is frequently regarded as occurring at the unification of the two kingdoms of Castile and Aragon at the end of the fifteenth century. Thus, two Renaissance humanists, Luis Vives (1492–1538) and Juan Huarte de San Juan (c. 1529–1579), may be considered the pioneers of psychology in Spain. Luis Vives was interested in the study of passions (his 1532 work *De Anima et Viva* [Treatise of the Soul] precedes Descartes's *Traité des Passions* [Treatise of the passions]) and, mainly, in discovering people's abilities and skills in order to orient their education. Guided by this practical interest, Vives adopted a descriptive and analytical approach to the study of the mind. Thus, he moved away from the metaphysical study of the soul to initiate an empiricist and inductive perspective. This perspective would, in later centuries, come to characterize modern psychology (Foster Watson considered Vives its founder; see "The father of modern psychology," *Psychological Review,* 1915, 5, 333–353).

Juan Huarte de San Juan, a doctor profoundly influenced by Galen, also developed a concern for the diversity of human abilities. In his only known work, *Examen de Ingenios para las Ciencias* (Baeza, [Spain], 1575, [Examination of Men's Wits, 1596]), Huarte took it upon himself to identify the talents required for the adequate exercise of different professions in the arts and sciences. He recommended vocational counseling and personnel selection based on ability testing in order to ensure the best match of persons to occupations. In this way, his work can be considered of pioneering importance in differential psychology.

Absolutism, the strength of the Catholic Church and inquisitorial censure, and the economic bonanza resulting from the wealth produced by the American empire led to the virtual disconnection of Spain from the European scene. This dissociation restricted its participation in the development of modern philosophy and science (while there was a boom in arts such as literature and painting).

After the promise of the Renaissance period, there were now only anecdotal contributions—by physicians such as Gerónimo Cortés and clergymen such as Esteban Pujasol and Ignacio Rodríguez (who continued the tradition of Huarte in their interest in talents). Also worthy of mention are the critiques of Benito Feijoo and the sociocultural approach in the allegories of Baltasar Gracián.

This development of psychology in Spain reflects to

its interrelation with wider cultural processes in Europe. Periods of growth coincide with those of international opening and involvement, while stagnation corresponds to periods of Spain's isolation.

Modern Psychology

The liberal revolution marked Spain's renewed link to cultural processes in the rest of Europe and the diffusion, from the end of the nineteenth century, of Enlightenment ideas. The development of modern psychology in Spain was centered on its two most important cities; Luis Simarro (1851–1921) and Ramón Turró (1854–1926) founded, respectively, the schools of Madrid and Barcelona.

The Madrid School had its origins in the context of a reformist movement influenced by the German idealist Karl Christian Krause (1781–1832). This movement attempted to promote social change based on scientific approaches. To this end, the reformists were concerned with renewing the social sciences (especially those relating to education) on European lines. The movement was focused around the *Institución Libre de Enseñanza* (Free Institute of Education), a cultural institution under the leadership of Francisco Giner de los Ríos (1839–1915), whose influence among liberal intellectuals in Spain was considerable in the first third of the twentieth century.

Simarro, a psychiatrist and disciple of Jean Martin Charcot, was appointed in 1902 to the first chair of experimental psychology of Spain, at the faculty of sciences of the University of Madrid. In his work he attempted to integrate English associationism with German psychophysiology. However, more than his few works, the principal contribution of Simarro was the diffusion of the psychological works of his time. The Madrid School was especially concerned with psychology applied to educational counseling.

The Barcelona School emerged in a different context and worked in a different direction. In the region of Catalunya there was intensive industrialization (with large-scale immigration from other regions and considerable social tension) and a strengthening of Catalonin nationalism. These processes favored a flourishing culture and the development of social welfare policies—including the introduction of educational and psychological services for workers. In this context, Turró, a biologist, developed a positivist approach and focused his research on experimental and physiological research. Turró, greatly influenced by Pavlov, related knowledge to hunger, viewing learning as based on trophic reflexes that would satisfy needs. His vision of the organism as a "functional unit," where psychological processes are essentially linked to physiological mechanisms, was continued by Augusto Pi-Sunyer (1879–1965).

Outside of these two schools, Santiago Ramón y Cajal (1852–1934) applied his neuronal theory to an associationist explanation of psychological processes, though his work in this area did not have the repercussions of his contributions to the field of neuroanatomy, for which he was awarded the Nobel Prize for physiology in 1906.

Psychology achieved social prestige in Spain in the 1920s and 1930s on recovering its applied orientation and demonstrating its relevance for the implementation of welfare policies. These contributions were feasible thanks to individual personalities and to the support provided by the Second Republic. The Madrid and Barcelona schools continued under the leadership of Gonzalo Rodríguez Lafora (1886–1971) and Emilio Mira López (1896–1964), disciples of Simarro and Turró, respectively.

Lafora, a psychiatrist and neurologist, continued the Madrid tradition of interest in psychotherapy, especially in the psychoeducational treatment of mental retardation. Together with the existentialist philosopher José Ortega y Gasset and José Miguel Sacristán, he founded, in 1920, the *Archivos de Neurobiología* (Neurobiological Archives), the first scientific journal devoted, albeit partially, to psychology.

The endocrinologist Gregorio Marañon (1887–1969), working closely with Lafora and Ortega, developed studies on emotion. In "Contribution à L'Étude de L'Action Émotive de L'Adrenaline" (*Revue Francaise d'Endocrinologie*, 1924, 2, 301–325), he demonstrated the dual dimensionality, somatic and cognitive, of emotion. This was considered an antecedent of the cognitive theory of emotion developed several decades later by Stanley Schachter (*Emotion, Obesity and Crime*, New York, 1971). Marañon maintained that the endocrinological system plays a key role in the integration and regulation of somatic processes and temperament development.

Mira López, a consulting psychiatrist, worked in the field of psychotechnics, vocational counseling, and personnel selection, besides his involvement in psychological training at Barcelona University, where he was appointed to the first chair of psychiatry in Spain. He also founded two psychology journals in Catalunya. His wide network of contacts was reflected in the organization of international congresses on psychotechnics at Barcelona in 1921 and 1930. His contributions made him Spain's most important psychologist up to the Spanish Civil War. Lopez's book *Psychiatry in War* (New York, 1943) also conveyed his experience as head of psychiatric services in the Republican Army.

State support was reflected in the founding of a provincial network of Institutes for Applied Psychology and Psychotechnics. The institutes in Madrid (headed by José Germain) and Barcelona (headed by Mira López) were established for the study of traffic safety, vocational guidance, industrial psychology, and the development of psychotechnic tests.

In the context of a period of general cultural expansion, psychological knowledge was oriented to serve societal goals. The ideas of Piaget, Eduoard Claparède, Montessori, and Adler were disseminated among educators; the major works of Freud, Pavlov, Théodule Ribot, Carl Jung, Charlotte M. Bühler, Ernst Kretschmer, Kurt Koffka, Eduard Spranger, and many others were translated.

The recognition of international integration should have been the Eleventh International Congress of Psychology in Madrid in 1936. Figures of the caliber of Pierre Janet, Charles S. Myers, Jean M. Lahy, Herbert S. Langfeld, Claparède, and others had participated in its organization. However, the Spanish Civil War (1936–1939) led to the cancellation of the Congress, ended a period of progress, and imposed a new isolation for psychology in Spain.

Defeat in the Civil War led to the exile and dispersion of the principal psychologists of the time, who had supported the government of the Republic (for example, Mira López continued his work mainly in Brazil; Angel Garma, promoter of psychoanalysis, went to Argentina; Mercedes Rodrigo emigrated to Colombia). The dictatorship of General Franco, based on the army, the Catholic Church, and economic elites, imposed political conservatism contrary to previous social projects and suspicious of the applications of psychology. The Institutes of Applied Psychology in Madrid and Barcelona were given a new orientation and were put under the directorship of engineers. Publication of all the journals related to psychology (*Boletín de la Institución Libre de Enseñanza; Archivos de Neurobiología; Revista de Psicologia i Pedagogia*, founded by Mira López and Joaquín Xirau in 1933; and *Revista de Pedagogía*, directed by Luzuriaga) was suspended. In this context, psychology focused once again on the scholastic debate (led fundamentally by priests such as Manuel Barbado).

José Germain (1897–1986) represented continuity in these adverse conditions. A disciple of Lafora, and with an extensive psychological training (he worked with Claparède in Geneva and Frederic C. Bartlett in London), Germain was appointed professor of experimental psychology at the University of Madrid, for which he left the Institute of Applied Psychology. Several events that helped to shape current psychology in Spain were centered around him: he participated in the foundation of the *Revista de Psicología General y Aplicada* (1946), of a Department of Experimental Psychology (1948) in Madrid, of the *Sociedad Española de Psicología* (Spanish Association of Psychology, 1952), and of the *Escuela de Psicología y Psicotecnia* (School of Psychology and Psychotechnics) at the University of Madrid (1953, fol-

lowed in 1964 by the opening of a school at the University of Barcelona). He was reinstated as director of Madrid's *Institute of Applied Psychology* in 1956, and he influenced the training of a new generation of academic psychologists who would be responsible for the further development of psychology in Spain (such as Mariann Yela, Miguel Siguán, José Luís Pinillos, & Francisco Secadas).

Institutions

Psychology in Spain was experiencing a new period of vitality and expansion at the end of the twentieth century. One cornerstone of this expansion was the establishment of psychology programs in the context of an increasing student population and the modernization of higher education structures from the beginning of the 1980s. Five-year programs (*Licenciaturas*) of psychology were established at philosophy faculties in 1968 and in independent psychology faculties since 1980 (first at the Complutense University of Madrid). The number of students grew from around 3,000 in 1970 to 13,500 in 1975 and 34,000 in 1985, and it stabilized at around 59,000 in 1995–1996 (when the total figures for Spain were close to 1.5 million students in higher education). Undergraduate and graduate studies of psychology are currently offered at 23 universities.

The Law for University Reform (1983) was a landmark in institutional development, as it established participatory mechanisms in the government bodies and a civil service track of tenured career for academic staff. The number of tenured academic staff increased steadily from 22 in 1977 to 876 in 1990 and 1,295 in 1996, significantly diminishing the ratio of students per teacher. Finally, the vitality of academic training is reflected in the number of doctoral dissertations, which increased from 614 in the period 1976–1986 to 2,314 in the period 1987–1996.

Another cornerstone for the expansion of psychology was affluence and, related to it, the development of the welfare state in Spain after the mid-1970s. Opportunities for psychological intervention in individual and social settings increased correspondingly. This expansion was facilitated by the *Sociedad Española de Psicología* (Spanish Association of Psychology) and the *Colegio Oficial de Psicólogos* (the professional association of psychologists in Spain, founded in 1980). More than 25,000 psychologists are currently registered at the *Colegio*, which is legally recognized as the supervision body for professional practice. It sponsors congresses and meetings on basic and applied issues. The magazine of the *Colegio, Papeles del Psicólogo* (Psychologist's Papers, also available at http://www.cop.es), reflects this interest in current issues and has the largest circulation among psychology publications in Spain.

Journals

More than 40 general and specialized journals on psychology are published in Spain under the sponsorship of the *Colegio*, academic departments, scientific societies, and private organizations. At least two publish contributions in both English and Spanish, and many more are adapting their publication norms for international readership and coverage by English abstracting and indexing services.

Psychological Research

Psychological research in Spain received a new impulse with the consolidation of university departments and improved funding through the establishment of the National Plan for Scientific and Technological Research Funding in the 1980s (especially after the inclusion of matters related to psychology among the target priorities). These factors facilitated experimental and applied research (action-research, program design, and evaluation). As a result, the number of national and international publications increased substantially. The following review reflects major research programs (see Prieto, Fernandez-Ballesteros, & Carpintern, 1994).

Methodological research was strongly influenced by the work of Yela (1921–1994) on multivariate analysis applied to intelligence. Among the most salient issues, there are studies on statistical design and analysis; psychometrics and test development—often applying advanced computer technology, artificial intelligence, and item-response theory; decision theory; and methodology of behavior and program evaluation.

Research in psychobiology has developed in close relation to medical programs in neurosciences. There are also contributions in human psychophysiology and neuropsychology, and there is a growing interest in ethology.

Research on learning has developed since the early 1960s. Cognitive processes are studied, focusing on perception and attention, memory, information processing, and language, including studies on bilingualism. There is research on intelligence and learning potential and on individual differences in cognition.

Research on personality has been mainly influenced by Eysenck's model, Cattell's theory on personality and motivation, Witkin's theory on perception and personality, and Bandura's social learning theory. Many research teams have focused on the cognitive study of schizophrenia and depression. Child and adolescent depression are studied from behavioral and psychosocial approaches. An extensive research program on anxiety as a general trait has been under way since the 1970s at the Complutense University of Madrid. The assessment of behavior and environment has been well established as a central issue in every field of psychology in Spain.

The cognitive-behavioral approach has been the one most widely represented in academic health and clinical psychology. Nevertheless, the psychoanalytic orientation is also present in the academic context. The relevance of behavioral modification for many health problems has been emphasized, and specific programs on behaviors of stress, hypertension, pain and headache, public speaking, eating habits, agoraphobia, stuttering, visual health, substance abuse, and smoking have been developed. Biofeedback has been applied to problems such as myopia and headaches. Programs for learning adaptive behaviors in mental retardation have also been developed, as well as informational strategies to enhance coping behaviors in oncological patients. Community-oriented models are frequent in health psychology and in school and family contexts, including new concerns with the psychology of aging.

A great effort has been devoted to epistemological debate in social psychology. Research programs have been greatly influenced by Tajfel's Social Identity Theory and Moscovici's theories on group influence and social representation. Social-cognitive programs focus on emotions, social representations, regional identities, group perceptions and stereotypes, and minority influence. There are new active programs of research on personal values, perverse norms, and linguistic vitality.

Applied social research looks into issues of group processes and leadership delinquency, juries, and eyewitness accounts; gender socialization, identity, and stereotypes; political psychology; environmental psychology; and intervention in welfare services.

Work and organization research focuses mainly on personnel selection and assessment. Wide-ranging research programs have studied the effects of work socialization, of the transition from studying to work, and of the experiences of employment and unemployment on psychological well-being and work-related beliefs. These studies have also guided the design of intervention programs. Work motivation is approached from Hertzberg's bifactorial theory and from expectancy models. The psychological implications of the role-set are also studied, focusing on the effects of role ambiguity and role conflict upon work stress, and on the psychological effects of information technology and organizational processes. Finally, there are research teams on organizational climate and culture and on specific issues of power, participation, conflict, and negotiation.

Claparède, Piaget, and Jerome S. Bruner strongly influenced the work in developmental and educational psychology. Research is conducted on cognitive development, formal reasoning, and the construction of social, historical, and scientific concepts in order to improve teaching methods. Parents' cognition and child-rearing practices, the development of gender concepts, and moral development are also studied. The development of self-concept and self-esteem have been analyzed in cross-sectional and longitudinal research in the context of play, games, and sport.

Psychological principles largely influenced the recent design and evaluation of school curricula. Teacher–student interaction in class, as well as personality variables affecting student achievements are studied. Study strategies are analyzed, and they are applied in the development of learning-support software. Social psychological research supports intervention programs for enhancing school integration and achievement.

Interest in the history of psychology has helped disclose the patterns of continuity and change in the development of current psychology in Spain.

Professional Practice

The occupational structure of psychologists in Spain is similar to that of other welfare state societies. According to Díaz and Quintanilla (*Papeles del Psicólogo*, 1992, 52, 22–74), the principal fields for the professional practice of psychology in Spain are education (37% of practitioners) and clinical (28%). Another 15% of practitioners are involved in work and organizational psychology, 9% in social and community services, 6% in research, and 4% in traffic psychology.

Women are in a majority in the profession as a whole (65%), except in work and organizational psychology (where only one third are women). Until the 1990s, professional practice was affected by the youth of those working in psychology (at the beginning of the 1980s, only one in five had more than 5 years' experience); a certain lack of correspondence between the structure of curricular and occupational contents (such as in school and educational psychology fields); the weakness of practical aspects in the curriculum (scarce attention is paid to professional role-building, and some kind of practical training has been introduced only with the implementation of new curricula during the 1990s); and the limited possibilities of access to postgraduate training.

Assessment is the most frequent task in all fields of psychological intervention (except for community-based intervention). Many of the most frequently used tests (mainly from the United States) have been translated and validated in Spain and new tests have been developed and are widely applied in Latin America. A database of adapted and locally developed tests is available from the *Colegio Oficial de Psicólogos* (and from the catalogue of the main test publisher—TEA).

Educational psychology evolved from traditional private practice focused on assessment and treatment of learning and behavior problems in individual pupils to institutional models of school intervention. School psychology developed after the 1970s as a result of the establishment of services of educational counseling and vocational guidance, multiprofessional teams in special education, and local psychopedagogical teams. These services support the public education system by carrying out applied research and community-based development programs.

Clinical psychology is mainly carried out by private practitioners. In spite of strong deinstitutionalization, the contributions of psychologists to social services are constrained by the limited development of the public health network (comprising community-based mental health centers, mental health services at hospitals, rehabilitation units for chronic patients, and intermediate structures such as day-hospitals or therapeutic communities) and by the subordinate role of clinical psychology to psychiatry in most of these contexts. In the 1990s, a compulsory internship of specialization within the public health system was established.

Cognitive-behavioral analysis is the hegemonic clinical approach in Spain, as in the academic context. However, the psychoanalytic approach comes close to it in terms of frequency in clinical practice (humanist, systems, and eclectic approaches are far less frequent). Health psychology programs focus on health promotion and education, prevention and treatment of unhealthy behaviors and lifestyles, and intervention in the psychological aspects of diseases. A considerable quantity of welfare resources is devoted to prevention and treatment of substance abuse and the psychological aspects of acquired immunodeficiency syndrome (AIDS).

Practitioners in the field of work and organization have expanded their classical role profile of industrial psychologists dedicated to personnel selection and training and are now involved in organizational development, culture, climate, and other areas. This diversity of functions leads to a blurring of professional identity toward specific definitions more related to personnel management functions (for example, training consultant, expert in human relations, etc.).

The number of psychologists engaged in social services addressing the general population and specific social groups (e.g., women, children, the elderly, the disabled, substance abusers, and homeless people) increased steadily during the 1980s in public institutions and during the 1990s in nongovernmental organizations. In these services, community-based models of psychosocial intervention in multiprofessional teams are frequent.

Social and ecological models are applied in the new field of environmental psychology in Spain. Psychologists in this field work in public and private sectors (jointly with architects and other professionals). The endorsement of European regulations made compulsory the assessment of both the social and ecological aspects of environmental impact. Specific projects deal with urban, school, and prison planning, as well as with the assessment of environmental quality (with regard to aspects such as noise or residential satisfaction).

Spanish psychology has a long tradition of applications to driver assessment. This field recently extended to the study and prevention of traffic accidents, ergonomics, road education, social aspects of traffic, and so on. Among the newest fields of specific applications of psychology, there are practitioners working in the legal system (counseling in the processes of testimony and jury and judges' decisions and in prison systems), while a few are involved in sports contexts (implementing behavioral programs for motivation, training, and competition stress).

Development and Stagnation

The reconstruction after the Civil War, the modernization of society and higher education and, finally, the integration of Spain in international networks of economic and scientific production led to a new period of expansion for academic and professional psychology. New human and technological capital were generated in these processes.

The late development of the welfare state in Spain from the late 1970s facilitated the expansion of psychology to new areas of professional activity and applied research (counseling in educational and social services and design and assessment of programs). However, this expansion of services was restricted by reductions in social budgets after the late 1980s; in addition, the expansion in private practice was limited by the still scarce recognition of the role of the psychologist in society and by the low level of income per capita (in relation to other developed countries).

International Integration and Particularization

Despite its vitality, contemporary psychology in Spain has been relatively weak in terms of the production of original knowledge. Scientific development has been receptive (more than creative) and profoundly influenced by research carried out in the United States and Europe. The dependence and lack of original contribution (also related to a predominance of applied, rather than theoretical, orientation) that have historically characterized the development of modern psychology in Spain have reflected its subordinate status in the world scientific system.

In addition to the importation of paradigms of research and intervention, integration in international networks has been associated with the adoption of institutional models of academic and professional organization of the developed countries. The American model of organization has been implicitly accepted as the valid one for the development of research and professional associations, despite the differences in scientific and professional working conditions between the United States and Spain.

Within the scientific field, English has been generally accepted as the international language for the diffusion of knowledge. On the one hand, international publications have been accepted as the principal reference for psychological research, and most of original scientific work is published in journals in English, while half of the books published in Spain are translated from English. On the other hand, voices have been raised in defense of scientific publication in Spanish, and there have been efforts to develop a Hispano–Latin American scientific arena in that language.

Language has constituted a barrier in both directions of communication, which only began to be overcome in the 1990s. On the one hand, knowledge mediated by translation implies delayed and biased access to the primary sources of scientific knowledge, as well as highlighting weaknesses in the local production of the knowledge; on the other hand, publication in Spanish involves serious limitations for the diffusion and prestige of local scientific production.

European integration has reinforced previous institutional and academic links and the defense of specificity at an intermediate level. These trends have been reflected, for example, in the participation of the Spanish professional association in the European Federation of Professional Psychologists' Associations and in the preference for European theories of psychological functioning. Finally, the celebration of the 23rd International Congress of Applied Psychology and numerous satellite conferences in 1994 reflected this new international integration. The event provided the opportunity for first-hand international contacts to many local professional psychologists and for a reinforcement of the representation of psychologists from Spain in international associations.

Psychology and Culture

The political history of Spain has been characterized by alternation between periods of totalitarianism (the absolutism and the Franco regime) and democratic periods (the Republic and the post-Franco period). During the former periods, the Catholic Church and conservative and isolationist attitudes had an undeniable influence on education and culture. The periods of democracy, meanwhile, were characterized by openness, tolerance, and cultural growth.

In general terms, traditional culture has had a collectivist orientation, characterized by the centrality of interpersonal (hierarchical) relations within the framework of the family and other close groups. The self has been defined in interdependence with significant others, and individual goals have been subordinated to the goals of these in-groups. As a result, the development of emotional self-consciousness and autonomy has been constrained, and social behaviors in in-groups have been governed by social norms, duties, and obligations.

Modernization and affluence have reinforced individualist orientations and the more instrumental and egalitarian interpersonal relations in a greater diversity of in-groups. Thus, a more independent self-concept has developed, together with the search for individual distinctiveness. However, these processes are relatively recent. Furthermore, the high level of youth unemployment may strengthen conformity orientations and the security function of family and, conversely, weaken tendencies for intellectual and emotional autonomy. In consequence, collectivist inertia and individualist orientations may coexist in the person, often in a contradictory way, with varying intensity. This may reinforce a paradoxical tendency to apply certain collectivist norms to the in-groups and certain individualist norms to the remaining social groups.

Furthermore, various social and political processes have contributed to the strengthening of regional identities, alongside the development of the Spanish state and identity. Demands for different degrees of cultural and political autonomy have received significant support in the traditional nations (Catalunya, the Basque Country, Galicia) as well as in other regions. Finally, ethnic diversity is increased by a stable gypsy minority and recent immigration from developing countries. Spain has shifted from being a country of emigration to being a receptor of immigration—from north and sub-Saharan Africa, Latin America, and eastern Europe.

All of these processes have produced a society of great cultural richness. Nevertheless, cross-cultural research, training, and intervention are actually under-represented in Spain. Cross-cultural psychology is seldom included as a specific field in university curricula. Though cross-cultural research (on national identity, intergroup relations, and language vitality, for instance) is carried out, and many Spanish researchers are involved in international networks, this research is seldom defined as cross-cultural. Mainstream paradigms of research are dominant. This research usually transposes concepts and instruments from other cultures, assuming the equivalence of relevance and meaning in Spanish culture without any verification—with the main goal of applying (thus imposing) universal theories.

Researchers have yet to demonstrate an interest in reflecting the cultural idiosyncrasies of Spain and its regions and to devote much effort to the development of an indigenous psychology that should study the effects of idiosyncratic aspects of culture in the psychological functioning of individuals and groups. Questions of cultural diversity, immigration, and acculturation continue to be, fundamentally, the domain of social anthropologists.

The exceptions are found in the study of some idiosyncratic aspects of emotional functioning of national and regional social identity, of lasting peer groups (the

cuadrillas) in the Basque country, and of the phenomenon of perverse norms. Perverse norms reflect a cultural paradox by which, in a collectivist context that promotes loyalty toward in-groups, there is strong social tolerance toward the generalized (individualist) transgression of certain norms that serve general welfare. Beyond the norm infringement, this social behavior has perverse effects, such as reinforcing tendencies to corruption and cynicism. The study of perverse norms is, therefore, especially interesting from a cultural perspective.

[*See also* Portugal.]

Bibliography

Works in English

Carpintero, H. (1982). The introduction of scientific psychology in Spain (1875–1900). In W. Woodward & M. G. Ash (Eds.), *The problematic science: Psychology in nineteenth-century thought* (pp. 255–275). New York: Praeger. An analysis of the first steps of modern psychology by one of the main historians of psychological science in Spain.

Carpintero, H. (1992). Spain. In V. S. Sexton & J. D. Hogan (Eds.), *International psychology: Views from around the world* (pp. 364–372). Lincoln: University of Nebraska Press.

Carr, R. (1980). *Modern Spain, 1875–1980.* Oxford: Oxford University Press. A general history of modern Spain.

Finison, L. (1977). Psychologists and Spain: A historical note. *American Psychologist, 32,* 1080–1084.

Prieto, J. M. (1992). Studying psychology in Spain. *International Journal of Psychology, 27,* 350–363. A description of the curricula of psychology studies in Spain.

Prieto, J. M., & Avila, A. (Eds.). (1994). Applied psychology in Spain [Special issue]. *Applied Psychology, 43*(2). Contains specific monographs and reviews of the different professional fields of psychology in Spain.

Prieto, J. M., Fernández-Ballesteros, R., & Carpintero, H. (1994). Contemporary psychology in Spain. *Annual Review of Psychology, 45,* 51–78. A thorough review of research activity, with brief chapters on training, professional fields, publications, and institutions in Spain.

Yela, M. (1987). Spain. In A. Gilgen & C. Gilgen (Eds.), *International handbook of psychology.* New York: Greenwood Press. The point of view of one of the founders of current psychology in Spain.

Works in Spanish

Carpintero, H. (1994). *La historia de la psicología en España.* Madrid: Eudema. A textbook of the history of psychology in Spain since the Renaissance.

Pinillos, J. L., & Mayor, J. (Eds.). (1994). *Tratado de psicología general.* Madrid: Alhambra. A Spanish introductory encyclopedia to psychology.

Saiz, M., & Saiz. D. (Coord.) (1996). *Personajes para una historia de la psicología en España.* Madrid: Pirámide. A collection of monographs about the contributions of key persons in the history of psychology in Spain.

Héctor M. Grad

SPATIAL PERCEPTION. *See* Vision and Sight.

SPATIAL VISION concerns the basic mechanisms in the eye and brain that underlie our ability to encode and represent spatial patterns of light. The mechanisms of spatial vision are critical for all behavior that involves the processing of visual information.

In the natural environment, light from primary sources, such as the sun or a lamp, falls upon the surfaces of objects and some of this light is reflected toward the eye (see Figure 1). From this reflected light, the optics of the eye form an image on the retina, a thin sheet of neural tissue that lines the back of the eye. The retinal image can be quantified as a distribu-

tion of light across space, as illustrated in the middle panels of Figure 1. Although the quality of the human optical system is very good, the optics blur the image to some extent, even when the eye is in perfect focus.

When the amount of light falling on the surfaces changes by some factor (e.g., a factor of two) the retinal image intensities change by the same factor because each surface reflects a particular fixed percentage of the light. During the course of the day the amount of light falling on the various surfaces in the environment changes dramatically; however, because the percentage of light reflected from each surface remains constant, the ratio of the intensity from any given surface to the average intensity (i.e., the *contrast*) remains constant.

The image formed at the back of the eye is processed by a complex series of neural circuits in the retina, beginning with the photoreceptors and ending with the ganglion cells, whose axons form the optic nerve. These neural circuits perform a number of functions that are essential for spatial vision. The most important function of the retina is to encode the image with high resolution while preserving a wide field of view. This is accomplished with high receptor and ganglion cell sam-

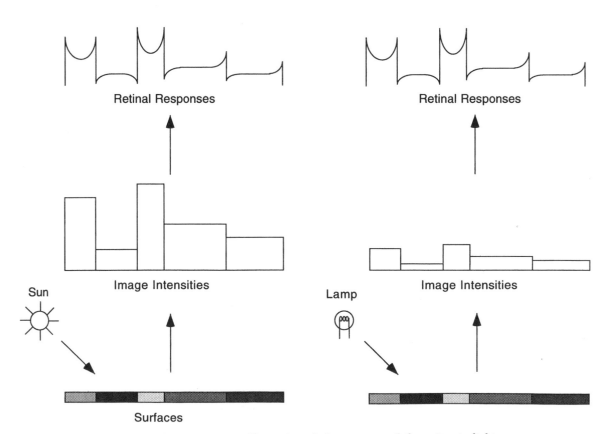

SPATIAL VISION. Figure 1. Illustration of the response of the retina to light reflected from surfaces in the environment under different levels of ambient illumination. Because of adaptation mechanisms the retina produces nearly equivalent responses to the same surfaces independent of the level of illumination.

pling density in the center of the image (in the fovea) and with decreasing sampling density away from the center. Eye movements are used to direct the fovea to regions of interest in the image. Encoding the entire retinal image at the same resolution as in the fovea would require an impossibly large optic nerve to carry the information to the brain, and an impossibly large brain (visual cortex) to process the information. Another important function of the retina is to compensate for the enormous variation in light level that occurs in the environment. Useful spatial vision requires that the retina produce reliable responses to small differences in surface reflectances at low light levels and high light levels. This is accomplished in large part with light adaptation mechanisms that adjust the neural amplification based upon the ambient light level. As indicated in Figure 1, the retina produces approximately the same response to a spatial arrangement of surface reflectances independent of the ambient light level. Another important function of the retina is to transmit, in an economical fashion, information that is critical for high level processing such as object recognition. This is accomplished with neural receptive fields, organized in a center/surround fashion, which preserve or enhance edge and contour information.

Over the past several decades, the standard behavioral method for quantifying sensitivity to spatial patterns has been to measure the minimum contrast required to detect sine wave grating patterns, at different spatial frequencies. A sine wave grating is a striped pattern in which the intensity varies sinusoidally along one axis and is constant along the other; the spatial frequency is the number of cycles per degree of visual angle (cpd) and the contrast is the modulation amplitude divided by the average intensity (one degree is equivalent, approximately, to width of an index finger viewed at arm's length). One virtue of sine wave stimuli is that all spatial patterns can be described as a sum of sine waves, and hence measurements of sensitivity to sine waves can be of value in predicting sensitivity to other patterns.

Each contour in Figure 2 plots the highest spatial frequency that can be detected at a given contrast, as a function of the distance from the center of the fovea, in degrees of visual angle. At a given contrast, only those spatial frequencies below the contour are visible. For example, at 10% contrast and 16 degrees eccentricity only spatial frequencies below 3 cpd are visible. As can be seen, the spatial resolution (the finest grating that can be seen) declines dramatically as a function of retinal eccentricity. This decline in resolution acuity matches what would be expected from the decline in sampling density of the ganglion cells. Blurring by the optics of the eye is the major factor determining the resolution acuity in the fovea, typically 40–60 cpd for 100% contrast gratings. (Under some circumstances,

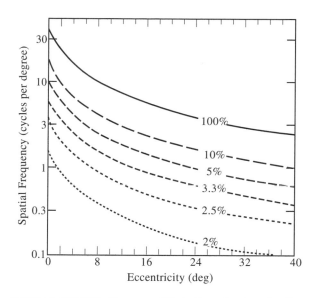

SPATIAL VISION. Figure 2. Effect of contrast and retinal eccentricity on acuity. Each contour represents the highest spatial frequency that can be detected; all frequencies below the contour are visible, at the given contrast. (Based upon the data of Robson and Graham, 1981.)

human observers are able to detect changes in relative position smaller than the diameter of a single cone. Although this result seems surprising, it can be understood by noting that, no matter how small the stimulus, more than one photoreceptor is being stimulated because of the blur produced by the optics of the eye.)

The contours in Figure 2 represent measurements made at a mean luminance similar to that of indoor lighting. Retinal light adaptation mechanisms keep the curves relatively stable across most daylight conditions; at lower light levels, sensitivity to higher spatial frequencies declines.

The contours in Figure 2 are typical of measurements where the stimuli are presented for time intervals similar to natural fixation durations (approximately 200 ms); for shorter durations the contrast thresholds increase at all spatial frequencies, for longer durations the contrast thresholds increase at lower spatial frequencies.

The vast majority of retinal ganglion cells send projections to the lateral geniculate nucleus (lgn); these projections carry most of the information relevant for spatial vision. Three different categories of ganglion cell (P, M, and K) project to separate layers in the lgn. The P cells outnumber, by eight to one, the other two categories, which are about equal in number. The P cells appear to provide most of the neural inputs supporting spatial vision; damage to the P cells severely impairs spatial vision.

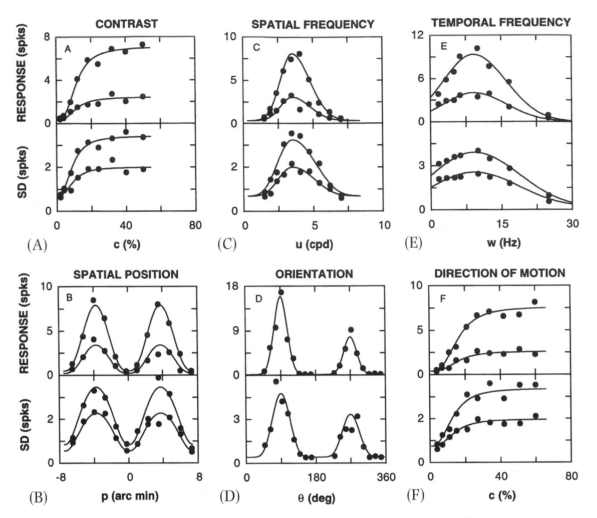

SPATIAL VISION. Figure 3. Responses of respresentative neurons, recorded within the primary visual cortex of the macaque monkey, along a number of fundamental stimulus dimensions. The upper panels plot the mean responses and the lower panels the standard deviations. Cortical neurons are quite selective along the dimensions of spatial frequency, orientation, and spatial position. (From Geisler and Albrecht, 1997. Copyright 1997 by Cambridge University Press.)

The three categories of lgn neurons relay the information from the eye to specific target zones in the primary visual cortex. Similar to neurons in the retina and lgn, cortical neurons have receptive fields that are localized in space; however, they are considerably more selective along a variety of stimulus dimensions. This selectivity is illustrated in Figure 3, which shows the responses of typical cortical neurons along the dimensions of contrast, spatial frequency (size), temporal frequency (speed), spatial position, orientation, and direction of motion. For each stimulus dimension, the upper panel shows the mean response (for stimulus durations of 200 ms), and the lower panel shows the standard deviation of the response. The plots for the mean and

standard deviation are very similar to each other because the variance of a cortical neuron's response is proportional to the mean of the response.

Consider first the dimension of spatial frequency. Figure 3 shows the response of a representative neuron as a function of spatial frequency measured at two different contrasts. This neuron responds optimally to a spatial frequency of 4 cpd and is rather narrowly tuned, in that the response falls off rapidly for both higher and lower spatial frequencies. In comparison, retinal and lgn neurons are broadly tuned. The degree of selectivity is characterized by the width of the curve at half height (the bandwidth). For this neuron the bandwidth is 1.2 octaves. Cortical neurons differ in both their optimal spatial frequency (from less than 0.5 cpd to greater than 20 cpd) and bandwidth (from less than 1 octave to more than 2 octaves). Importantly, the spatial frequency tuning of cortical cells does not change with contrast; the solid curves in the figure differ only by a scaling factor.

Consider next the dimension of orientation. Figure 3D shows the response of a representative neuron as a function of orientation. This neuron responds optimally to horizontal stimuli (90°, 270°), prefers movement in the upward direction (90°), and is rather narrowly tuned (the bandwidth is 22°). In comparison, retinal and lgn neurons are not orientation selective. Cortical neurons differ widely in their optimal orientation (0° to 360°) and in their orientation bandwidth (5° to nonoriented). Similar to spatial frequency tuning, the orientation tuning of cortical cells does not change with contrast.

Figure 3B shows the response of a cell as a function of the spatial position of a sine wave grating (of the optimal orientation and spatial frequency) measured at two different contrasts. This neuron responds optimally when the stimulus is placed in a particular spatial position and is rather narrowly tuned: The bandwidth is 4 minutes of visual angle. (The tuning function has two peaks because the stimulus was reversing in contrast over time; a big temporal modulation in response is produced when either a light bar or a dark bar of the grating is lined up with the receptive field.) Cortical neurons differ in their position bandwidth, and neurons selective to higher spatial frequencies are generally more narrowly tuned. In addition, cortical cells can be segregated into two populations based upon their position tuning: complex cells produce nearly equivalent responses no matter where the stimulus falls within the receptive field, whereas simple cells require precise positioning within the receptive field. Once again, the tuning does not change with contrast.

In comparison to the dimensions of spatial frequency, orientation, and position, cortical neurons are relatively broadly tuned along the dimension of temporal frequency (see Figure 3E). Most cortical neurons respond across nearly the entire behavioral range of temporal sensitivity.

Figures 3A and 3F show the responses of representative neurons as a function of contrast measured for the optimal and a nonoptimal spatial frequency (A), and for the optimal and nonoptimal direction of motion (F). As can be seen, the response initially increases rapidly with contrast and then saturates. Cortical cells differ widely in the contrast at which response saturation occurs. Responses measured as a function of contrast reveal two nonlinear properties that have important consequences for spatial vision. One is an accelerating nonlinearity that is easily seen when the response functions are plotted in log coordinates. This nonlinearity increases the selectivity of cortical cells along all of the stimulus dimensions; without this nonlinearity cortical neurons would be more broadly tuned. The second nonlinearity is contrast normalization, which causes the response saturation to occur at the same contrast for all stimuli, optimal and nonoptimal. Because of this nonlinearity, the tuning of cortical neurons does not change with contrast.

Psychophysical studies provide evidence for selectivity that is similar to the selectivity in the primary visual cortex. For example, prolonged viewing of a high contrast adapting grating elevates the contrast threshold for a narrow range of spatial frequencies and orientations near that of the adapting grating, over a localized region in space. Similarly, presentation of a high contrast masking grating elevates thresholds for simultaneously presented target gratings whose frequency and orientation are similar to that of the masking grating. For both of these psychophysical paradigms, the elevation in threshold across frequency and orientation is similar in shape to the neural tuning curves shown in Figures 3C and 3D. These studies have led to the development of models that are based on the concept of multiple spatial frequency- and orientation-tuned channels. Such models have been able to account for many of the basic facts concerning the detection and discrimination of simple spatial patterns, particularly when the contrast nonlinearities (see above) are incorporated.

Several explanations have been proposed for the emergence of stimulus selectivity in the visual cortex. One suggestion is that the selectivity is part of a hierarchical process, leading to individual neurons that signal the presence of specific real-world objects. Another suggestion is that the selectivity reflects a low redundancy code that is well-matched to the statistics of natural images. An alternative hypothesis is that the selectivity is a critical step in segregating objects from their context. Objects within the natural environment are generally located within a very complex context. The selectivity of visual cortical neurons permits recognition of local image properties, which allows subsequent grouping mechanisms to bind together only those local contours that define the object.

[*See also* Color Vision; *and* Vision and Sight.]

Bibliography

DeValois, R. L., & DeValois, K. K. (1990). *Spatial vision.* New York: Oxford University Press.

Geisler, W. S., & Albrecht, D. G. (1997). Visual cortex neurons in monkeys and cats: Detection, discrimination, and identification. *Visual neuroscience, 14,* 897–919.

Geisler, W. S., & Albrecht, D. G. (2000). Spatial vision: Single neurons and perception. In K. K. DeValois (Ed.), *Seeing.* New York: Academic Press.

Graham, N. (1989). *Visual pattern analyzers.* New York: Oxford University Press.

Hubel, D. H. (1988). *Eye, brain, and vision*. New York: Freeman.

Regan, D. (Ed.). (1991). *Spatial vision*. New York: Macmillan.

Robson, J. G., & Graham, N. (1981). Probability summation and regional variation in contrast sensitivity across the visual field. *Vision Research, 21,* 409–418.

Rodieck, R. W. (1998). *The first steps in seeing*. Sunderland, MA: Sinauer.

Spillman, L., & Werner, J. (1990). *Visual perception: The neurophysiological foundations*. San Diego: Academic Press, Inc.

Wandell, B. A. (1995). *Foundations of vision*. Sunderland, MA: Sinauer.

Wilson S. Geisler and Duane G. Albrecht

SPEARMAN, CHARLES EDWARD (1863–1945), British psychologist and psychometrician. Like many young men from minor aristocratic families, Charles Spearman settled upon military service on leaving school. He served for 15 years, mostly in India, mixing the normal duties and pursuits of an infantry officer with reading about philosophy (a boyhood interest) and psychology. It seems that he had little sympathy with the empiricist and associationist ideologies of contemporary British psychology but became intrigued by the more scientific approach that was gaining ground in Germany. So in 1897 the 34-four-year-old, self-taught psychologist resigned his commission and went to Leipzig to study experimental psychology in Wundt's laboratory, from which he eventually obtained a doctorate (for work on spatial perception) in 1906.

His studies were drawn out longer than expected by a recall in 1900 to serve during the South African war. But this was not wasted time for Spearman because he had the opportunity to carry out the pioneering work that laid the foundations of his "two-factor" theory of human ability and of the statistical method now known as factor analysis.

Spearman's simple and elegant theory posited an underlying function common to all intellectual activity and a second function specific to the task; these two elements, or factors, were eventually called *g* and *s*. Not only would individuals possess *g* (and *s*) to different degrees, but *g* would be called on to different extents by different tasks. To demonstrate the feasibility of this representation, Spearman adapted correlational methods pioneered by Karl Pearson, which he then applied to scores on a "hotchpotch" of mental ability tests carried out on schoolchildren.

Spearman argued that, once the influence of extraneous variables and observational errors had been eliminated as far as possible, the pattern of intercorrelations of the test scores accorded with the notion of a common element entering into any intellectual activity to a certain and quantifiable degree. This rudimentary factor analysis promised an index of general intelligence, a measure that had for so long eluded those concerned with psychological testing. However, Spearman's theory, so confidently propounded in the *American Journal of Psychology* (1904), did not gain universal approval, and, for almost three decades, he battled against critics on both sides of the Atlantic who either dismissed the idea that human intelligence could be captured in so simple a fashion or denied the existence of a common factor *g* or found grievous fault with the mathematical or statistical arguments.

After a second trip to Leipzig, Spearman became reader in experimental psychology at University College, London, in 1907, where his research again focused on developing the two-factor theory of human intellectual ability. This work reached its peak in 1927 with the publication of *The Abilities of Man*. By the early 1930s, though, younger and more mathematically sophisticated hands were busying themselves with the multiple-factor theories that gradually overshadowed Spearman's own seductively simple system.

Nowadays, Spearman's name conjures up a rank correlation measure, a formula for assessing test reliability, and perhaps a primitive version of factor analysis. But Spearman himself regarded this psychometric and statistical work as secondary to his far more ambitious mission—establishing fundamental laws of psychology that would encompass not just the processes inherent in the two-factor theory but all cognitive activity. His main contribution here, as set out in *The Nature of "Intelligence" and the Principles of Cognition* (1923), proposed an empirically grounded theory of knowledge (or epistemology) called *noëgenesis*. This synthesis of eighteenth- and nineteenth-century philosophical ideas characterized people as actively extracting relationships between events and generalizing these relationships to new situations. These notions have been rediscovered by cognitive psychologists studying analogical reasoning.

Spearman remained at University College as Grote Professor of the Philosophy of Mind and Logic (1911) and later as professor of psychology (1928) until retiring in 1931. However, retirement did not mean abandoning academic work, for he wrote numerous journal articles and several books, as well as traveling widely. Indeed, his last publication (still defending a slightly altered, though recognizable, quantity *g*) appeared after his death in 1945 (*Human Ability*, 1950). By his own considerable intellectual achievements and his ability to marshal legions of colleagues, assistants, and research students from all over the world into a coordinated program of work, Spearman succeeded in establishing the first significant center of psychological research in Britain. The distinctive badge of the "London School" was its emphasis on the rigorous application of the scientific and statistical method to the study of human abilities—principles espoused by Francis Galton several decades earlier.

Bibliography

Works by Spearman

Spearman, C. (1904a). The proof and measurement of association between two things. *American Journal of Psychology, 15,* 72–101.

Spearman, C. (1904b). "General intelligence" objectively determined and measured. *American Journal of Psychology, 15,* 202–293. This complementary pair of articles, published while Spearman was still a student, covers the theoretical, methodological, and statistical foundations of the two-factor theory.

Spearman, C. (1923). *The nature of "intelligence" and the principles of cognition.* London: Macmillan. This is a difficult but most comprehensive single exposition of the noëgenetic principles.

Spearman, C. (1927). *The abilities of man, their nature and measurement.* London: Macmillan. This is the definitive account of the two-factor theory and its ramifications.

Spearman, C. (1930a). *Creative mind.* London: Cambridge University Press. This book details the application of noëgenesis to artistic creativity.

Spearman, C. (1930b). C. Spearman. In C. Murchison (Ed.), *A history of psychology in autobiography* (Vol. 1, pp. 299–331). Worcester, MA: Clark University Press. This is primarily an intellectual autobiography.

Spearman, C. (1937). *Psychology down the ages* (Vols. 1–2). London: Macmillan. This book presents a highly partisan account of the history of psychology.

Spearman, C., & Wynn Jones, L. (1950). *Human ability.* London: Macmillan. Published posthumously, this was intended to be a revised version of *The Abilities of Man.* However, in the hands of Wynn Jones (a former student), it became a more compromised and revisionist account of the two-factor theory.

Works about Spearman

Lovie, P., & Lovie, A. D. (1996). Charles Edward Spearman, F. R. S. (1863–1945). *Notes and records of the Royal Society of London, 50,* 75–88. This contains new biographical information and some family photographs.

Thomson, G. (1946). Charles Spearman 1863–1945. *Obituary notices of Fellows of the Royal Society, 5,* 372–385. Written by Spearman's most implacable British critic, this is most useful for its complete bibliography of Spearman's published work.

P. Lovie and A. D. Lovie

SPECIAL EDUCATION. A variety of disabling conditions exist, such as mental retardation, sensory impairments (blindness and visual impairments, deafness and hearing impairments), physical disabilities (cerebral palsy, spina bifida), communication disorders, learning disabilities, behavior disorders, autism, and other health impairments. These conditions can be caused by a number of factors, including genetic inheritance, chromosomal abnormalities, insults to the central nervous system, intrauterine exposure to toxins (e.g., alcohol), trauma during birth (e.g., anoxia), postnatal injuries and diseases, and a number of risk factors (e.g., prematurity, low maternal education, and poverty). Special education is a field devoted to providing educational services to infants, children, and youth who have disabling conditions, and to giving support to their families. The purpose of special education is to assist those children and youth in becoming independent, productive, and valued members of their communities.

Historically, society's attributions about the causes of disabling conditions ranged from curses to blessings conferred by gods. As a result, the treatment of persons with disabilities ranged from infanticide or neglect to keeping them as jesters for entertainment. Until recent advances in medical practice, many infants with disabilities did not live; the lives of those who did were harsh. The first known treatment endeavors occurred with persons who were blind and deaf in the 1700s and were expanded to other disabilities in the 1800s. These attempts, however, were exceptions rather than the rule, and they were often initiated by physicians rather than educators or psychologists. Beginning in the 1800s and continuing into the middle portion of the twentieth century, persons with disabilities, particularly those with mental retardation, were sent to residential institutions. In these facilities the quality of treatment varied, but emphasis was usually on custodial care rather than education and rehabilitation. In the early 1900s, eugenics was practiced in the United States. Later, persons with disabilities were systematically exterminated by Hitler's government though policies based, in part, on the assumptions of the eugenics movement in the United States.

Through efforts of parents and other concerned individuals, special education classes and schools began to be established in the early 1900s and became progressively more common during the middle portion of the century. Concomitantly, the deinstitutionalization movement was initiated, producing a need for community services. Public education, however, was not assured for children with disabilities, particularly for those with more severe conditions. Through a series of successful court cases and the lobbying efforts of parents, parent associations, and professional societies, the U.S. Congress passed Public Law 94-142 in 1975. This law mandated a free appropriate public education for all school-age children and youth regardless of the type and severity of the student's disabilities; no school-age individual could be denied access to educational services. The law also:

1. Specified that the educational services must be provided in the least restrictive appropriate environment
2. Guaranteed parents a role in making educational decisions
3. Required that an individualized educational program (IEP) for each student with disabilities be developed by a multidisciplinary team with the participation of the student's parents (and the student if possible)
4. Required that nondiscriminatory assessment practices be used for placement and instructional planning decisions
5. Specified regular reviews of the student's progress
6. Afforded the students and parents with rights of due process. In 1986, an amendment to this law extended special education and related services to infants and preschoolers with disabilities and to their families.

In the United States, public education is currently responsible for providing special education services to preschoolers (starting at age 3) and continuing throughout the individual's educational experiences until age 21. Services for infants and toddlers are administered by an agency selected by each state. Services for infants and preschoolers are provided in a range of settings (the child's home, child care centers, early intervention programs, Head Start, or the public schools). Services for school age children and youth are provided almost exclusively by the public schools.

Psychologists contribute to special education at the research and practice levels. At the research level, many theories of human development (e.g., ecological psychology, behavioral psychology, and constructivist perspectives) have functioned as a base from which special education practices are derived. Psychologists often are responsible for developing the assessment tools that are used for making placement and programming decisions in special education. In addition, the research methods (e.g., from statistical procedures to single-case experimental designs) developed by psychologists are often employed in special education research. At the practice level, psychologists typically serve two major roles. First, psychologists assess children who are referred for special education services. That testing typically includes assessments of intelligence and adaptive behavior. Second, psychologists consult with other school personnel, particularly around students' problematic behavior. Psychologists' time in schools is often devoted more to testing than to consultation, and their consultation time is often more focused on addressing students' problematic behaviors than on instructional and curricular issues.

Research in special education has drawn on a variety of investigative models, including descriptive methods and experimental methods. Although traditional large-group research methods have been useful to special education investigators, other methods such as single-case experimental methods and ethnographic methods also have been used. These methods are employed, in many cases, because of the tremendous heterogeneity in the children being studied.

Much special education research has focused on issues that have their origins in the application of the law's provisions. The least restrictive environment provision (educating students with disabilities as much as possible with nondisabled peers) has been known in practice as mainstreaming, the general education initiative, and inclusion. This practice has been the focus of ongoing research and debate for each age level (preschoolers through adolescents) and for each level of disability severity (i.e., those with mild and severe disabilities). The practice is based on assumptions that separate is not equal, segregated classes carry stigmatizing effects, and students without disabilities can function as models of adaptive behaviors and are competent social and interactive partners for students with disabilities. In general, the research indicates that with adequate supports, preschoolers with disabilities accrue meaningful advantages from being educated with their nondisabled peers. At the older ages, the picture is more complicated. General education teachers tend to be willing to accept students with disabilities in their classes, many students with disabilities spend some time each day in classes with regular education students, the education of students without disabilities does not appear to be harmed from inclusion, and there are examples of exemplary schools that engage in such practices. For inclusion to be successful, strong leadership in the schools is needed, ongoing support and training must be available to teachers, accessible and competent assistance must exist from special educators and other specialists, support from families is needed, and barriers that arise must be addressed systematically. When these factors are absent, students with disabilities can be placed in regular education classes, but their learning may be relatively minimal. It is important to note, however, that a lack of consensus exists about including children with disabilities in regular education classes full time.

Another major area of research activity has focused on devising early intervention services for infants and young children with disabilities and their families. Since infants and preschoolers rarely attend public schools, this research has focused on how to provide services in children's homes and child care programs. A number of models and procedures have been developed for delivering early intervention services across a range of different settings in which young children spend time. A great deal of research has focused on promoting children's language and communicative behavior and their social interactions with others. This research has produced a number of useful intervention techniques and procedures for measuring children's behavior in context. A major area of research has focused on how to support families of children with disabilities. General consensus has emerged that: (1) attending to the priorities and concerns of families as they define them is central to appropriate family services; (2) establishing a supportive relationship that is not expert-client in nature is critical; (3) using informal and formal support networks is necessary; and (4) helping families access resources in their communities is desirable. Although families often seek information about their child, the child's care, and potential services, the manner in which that information is provided is central to how useful the information will be.

A major function of schools, and thus special education services, is to promote students' learning. Many students with disabilities (e.g., those with mental retardation, learning disabilities, and sensory impairments) present significant learning and instructional challenges. Instructional research in special education has focused on a number of areas:

1. Understanding how students with various disabilities learn different types of skills (academic, communication, life skills, etc.)
2. Developing instruction procedures and strategies
3. Providing instruction that produces generalized learning
4. Evaluating instructional arrangements (e.g., small group instruction, cooperative learning, peer tutoring)
5. Applying the findings from this research in actual classrooms.

In general, this research suggests that many students with disabilities learn in ways that are similar to other students, can be taught meaningful skills, require strategies that are more precise and systematic in their applications than are commonly used in general education, and can learn to apply their skills if that application is promoted.

Besides focusing on how to teach students with disabilities, a great deal of effort has been devoted to identifying the appropriate educational outcomes for those students. The academic curriculum for students without disabilities is appropriate for many students with disabilities, particularly those with learning disabilities, speech-language disorders, behavior disorders, orthopedic disorders, and sensory impairments. They may need assistance in how to learn that curriculum, but its content is similar to their nondisabled peers. For other students, the outcomes of the curriculum must be modified. For example, for students with severe mental retardation, the outcomes focus on acquiring and using various skills: communication, social, independent living (e.g., cooking and laundry), community (e.g., making purchases in the community and using public transportation), leisure, and vocational.

Some students with disabilities engage in behaviors that are not acceptable in their homes, schools, and communities. A great deal of research has been devoted to this issue. It currently suggests that the motivational and contextual factors that contribute to the occurrence of the problem behavior must be assessed through interviews, observations, and other analytic procedures. Interventions are derived from the assessment results and then implemented and adjusted as needed. These general procedures have been applied to a wide range of problematic behaviors, including severe problems such as self-injury. Much of this work has direct origins in behavioral psychology.

An area of practice that has received research attention as well as being the topic of numerous court cases deals with placement practices. In some instances, it appears that non-Caucasian students are more likely to be placed in special education. The reasons for this are varied, including lack of appropriate testing instruments and discriminatory placement practices. In general, it is recognized that bias can occur at each level of the placement process, including referral, testing practices, decision-making, and parent involvement procedures.

Another major area of research activity has focused on issues and practices related to promoting transitions from school to the world of work. This research is based on the findings that many young adults with disabilities are not employed or are underemployed and have fairly undesirable lifestyle outcomes. As a result, plans must be developed for youth who are getting ready to make the transition from public school services. Young people with disabilities often receive instruction related to securing employment, vocational skills focusing on how to do different jobs, and the social skills for functioning on the job. In general, emphasis is placed on securing competitive employment in the community as compared to having students work in programs designed only for persons with disabilities. For young adults with significant disabilities, a major area of need is ensuring that they have supportive social networks after they leave public education.

[See also Mainstreaming and Inclusion.]

Bibliography

Bailey, D. B., & Wolery, M. (1992). *Teaching infants and preschoolers with disabilities* (2nd ed.). Englewood Cliffs, NJ: Prentice Hall. Provides a comprehensive approach to issues and practices related to planning and implementing early intervention programs for infants and young children with disabilities.

Blackhurst, A. E., & Berdine, W. H. (1993). *An introduction to special education* (3rd ed.). New York: HarperCollins. An introduction to the field of special education with easy to read yet comprehensive chapters.

Dunst, C. J., Trivette, C. M., & Deal, A. G. (1994). *Supporting and strengthening families: Vol. 1 Methods, strategies, and practices.* Cambridge, MA: Brookline. Provides a comprehensive summary of the foundations and practices for working with and supporting families of children with disabilities.

Kauffman, J. M. (1996). *Characteristics of emotional and behavioral disorders of children and youth* (6th ed.). Englewood Cliffs, NJ: Prentice Hall. Provides a comprehensive discussion of the issues related to identifying, assessing, and educating students with behavior disorders.

Kirk, S. A., Gallagher, J. J., & Anastasiow, N. J. (1997). *Educating exceptional children* (8th ed.). Boston: Houghton Mifflin. A classic introduction to special education.

Koegel, L. K., Koegel, R. L., & Dunlap, G. (Eds.). (1996). *Positive behavioral support: Including people with difficult behaviors in the community.* Baltimore: Brookes. Provides a comprehensive description of many of the issues involved in addressing the problematic behavior of individuals with disabilities.

Lerner, J. W. (1996). *Learning disabilities: Theories, diagnosis, and teaching strategies* (7th ed.). Boston: Houghton Mifflin. A description of the issues related to identifying and educating children with learning disabilities.

Salvia, J., & Ysseldyke, J. E. (1998). *Assessment* (7th ed.). Boston: Houghton Mifflin. A classic and comprehensive treatment of the issues and practices related to testing and assessing students with disabilities.

Turnbull, H. R. (1993). *Free appropriate public education: The law and children with disabilities* (4th ed.). Denver: Love. Interprets the legal foundations and issues related to educating students with disabilities.

Westling, D. L., & Fox, L. (1995). *Teaching students with severe disabilities.* Englewood Cliffs, NJ: Prentice Hall. Discusses issues and practices for educating students with significant disabilities.

Mark Wolery

SPECIFIC PHOBIA. Fears of certain objects or situations are quite common and are seen in both children and adults. Many of these fears are transitory and have no significant impact on an individual's life. However, for a subgroup of individuals, these fears become a marked source of distress; this condition is called specific phobia. Specific (formerly "simple") phobias are persistent fears of certain objects or situations. To be a diagnosable phobia, the fear must be recognized by the individual as excessive or unreasonable, although this will not always be the case for children, who may not recognize this dimension. Contact with the feared object or situation almost always provokes an immediate fear response. Avoiding contact with the feared situation is common, as is significant apprehension before contact and distress on contact (American Psychiatric Association, 1994).

The current diagnostic criteria categorize specific phobias into four primary subtypes: animal (e.g., spiders, dogs), natural environment (e.g., water, heights, thunderstorms), blood, injection, and injury (e.g., needles), and situational (e.g., claustrophobia, tunnels, elevators, flying). A residual "other" subtype is also included for fears that do not fit into one of the four categories (e.g., choking, loud noises).

Specific phobias are very common, affecting approximately 10–11% of the population at some point in their lives (Kessler et al., 1994), making specific phobias one of the most common psychiatric disorders. The four subtypes are quite common. A recent work (Fredrikson, Annas, Fischer, & Wik, 1996) showed a point-prevalence rate of 13.2% for situational phobias, 7.9% for animal phobias, and 3.0% for blood, injury, and injection phobias.

There are meaningful differences between the subtypes of specific phobias that affect both symptom presentation and patterns of onset. Typically, exposure to a phobic situation or object evokes fear and activation of the sympathetic nervous system, characterized by accelerated heart rate and increased blood pressure. A notable exception to this presentation is found in blood, injury, and injection phobics, where the individual experiences a subjective feeling of disgust (Page, 1994) and fears of the consequences of confronting blood or injury, such as fainting (Rachman, 1990). In addition to differences in subjective experience, the physiological response differs from that seen in individuals with other types of specific phobias. Instead of the traditional sympathetic activation, blood, injury, and injection phobics show a biphasic response consisting of an initial increase in sympathetic arousal followed by a marked decrease in blood pressure and heart rate, sometimes resulting in fainting (Öst, 1996; Page, 1994). This differential response requires alterations to treatment.

The other meaningful difference in subtypes of specific phobias concerns the age of onset of the fears. As noted above, fears are characteristic of childhood and reflect normal developmental stages. Fears such as those of animals, strangers, and the dark represent a normal and transient developmental experience. However, for a subset of individuals these fears become chronic, with individuals generally dating the onset of their phobias to childhood. Animal phobias develop earliest, with the mean age of onset being about 7 years of age. Blood phobias are next, developing at about 9 years of age; dental phobias at 12 years; and claustrophobia much later, at about 20 years (Öst, 1987). These clear differences in age of onset suggest the heterogeneity of the diagnostic group.

Specific phobias are generally two to four times more common in women than in men (Bourdon et al., 1988;

Fredrikson et al., 1996). This difference is especially true for animal and situational fears, although men and women report more similar rates of blood, injury, and injection phobias. Interestingly, in women, some fears, such as fear of flying, appear to increase with age, whereas other fears, such as injection phobias, tend to decrease. This pattern is not seen in men (Fredrikson et al., 1996). The reasons for the gender differences are not clear. Some investigators have suggested theories of increased genetic vulnerability (Merckelbach et al., 1996), whereas others have emphasized social facilitation through increased exposure to fearful models for women (Fredrikson et al., 1996).

Various modes of onset for specific phobias have been proposed. Some individuals report aversive conditioning experiences (e.g., being bitten by a dog), whereas others endorse acquisition through vicarious processes (e.g., seeing someone else bitten by a dog). Classical conditioning has been discussed as an etiological factor in specific phobias for over 50 years, and this appears to account for the onset of phobias in some individuals. For example, traumatic dental experiences appear to be the largest cause of dental phobias (Moore, Brodsgaard, & Birn, 1991). Yet classical conditioning cannot account for a number of important findings. First, individuals can develop fears in the absence of an aversive experience. Two other related sources of information seem important in onset: modeling and negative information (Rachman, 1990), so that direct contact and aversive experiences are not necessary for phobic acquisition. Second, some objects and situations seem more potent in evoking phobic responses than others. This situation, which has been termed preparedness by Seligman (1971), refers to an innate predisposition to develop fears in relation to some stimuli because avoidance of these stimuli has evolutionary survival value (e.g., snakes, heights). This hypothesis has been criticized on both theoretical (McNally, 1995) and empirical (McNally & Foa, 1986) grounds and has not been shown to have relevance for treatment outcomes.

Recent attention has been directed to the role of cognitions in the maintenance of specific phobias. For example, Thorpe and Salkovskis (1995) reported that specific phobics are associated with a network of beliefs about the phobic object that concerns harm from the object, associated danger to the individual, and perceptions related to one's ability to control and cope with the phobic situation. At least one study has revealed enhanced treatment efficacy by adding a cognitive treatment component to more traditional exposure-based treatments for claustrophobia (Craske, Mohlman, Yi, Glover, & Valeri, 1995). Although a relatively new area of investigation, cognitive factors and biases may be shown to play a meaningful role in their maintenance.

The consensus in the literature on specific phobias is that exposure-based treatments are the treatments of choice. Exposure-based treatments include flooding either imaginally or *in vivo*, systematic desensitization, and participant modeling. Overall effectiveness rates range from 77 to 90% (Öst, 1996). Treatments for specific phobias tend to be fairly brief (a few sessions), and Öst and colleagues have developed a single-session treatment protocol that appears equally effective with various circumscribed specific phobias (Öst, 1989).

One important variant in exposure is the treatment of blood, injury, and injection phobics, whose vasovagal response requires alterations of typical exposure paradigms. An approach termed applied tension combines exposure with muscle tension to decrease the likelihood of fainting.

Although treatment success is high, individuals with specific phobias are rarely seen in clinical practice. Early estimates suggested that one in one thousand individuals with a phobia were receiving treatment (Agras, Sylvester, & Oliveau, 1969). There appear to be several reasons that phobic individuals may not seek treatment. First, the fear is circumscribed and thus may not appear to significantly impact the individual's life. A second and related factor is that the phobic individual may be able to structure life in a way that avoids contact with the feared object or situation. Finally, the fear may be a source of embarrassment for the individual, leading to a reticence to disclose it. When individuals with specific phobias do present for treatment, they are generally in significant distress and are experiencing meaningful impairment in functioning.

In sum, specific phobias are among the most common psychiatric disorders. They generally occur far more often in women than in men and have a young age of onset. Meaningful differences are apparent among the subtypes. Behavioral treatments are highly effective, although many phobics never present for treatment. Recent trends in the literature reflect an interest in the role of cognitions in the maintenance of specific phobias and the development of very brief treatment protocols.

[*See also* Homophobia; Social Phobia; *and* Xenophobia.]

Bibliography

Agras, S., Sylvester, D., & Oliveau, D. (1969). The epidemiology of common fears and phobias. *Comprehensive Psychiatry, 10,* 151–156.

American Psychiatric Association. (1994). *Diagnostic and statistical manual of mental disorders* (4th ed.). Washington, DC: Author.

Bourdon, K. H., Boyd, J. H., Rae, D. S., Burns, B. J., Thompson, J. W., & Locke, B. Z. (1988). Gender differences in phobias: Results of the ECA community survey. *Journal of Anxiety Disorders, 2,* 227–241.

Craske, M. G., Mohlman, J., Yi, J., Glover, D., & Valeri, S. (1995). Treatment of claustrophobia and snake/spider phobias: Fear of arousal and fear of context. *Behaviour Research and Therapy, 33,* 197–203.

Fredrikson, M., Annas, P., Fischer, H., & Wik, G. (1996). Gender and age differences in the prevalence of specific fears and phobias. *Behaviour Research and Therapy, 34*(1), 33–39.

Kessler, R. C., McGonagle, K. A., Zhao, S., Nelson, C. B., Hughes, M., Eshleman, S., Wittchen, H. U., & Kendler, K. S. (1994). Lifetime and 12-month prevalence of *DSM–III–R* psychiatric disorders in the United States. *Archives of General Psychiatry, 51,* 8–19.

McNally, R. J. (1995). Preparedness, phobias, and the Panglossian paradigm. *Behavioural and Brain Sciences, 18,* 303–304.

McNally, R., & Foa, E. B. (1986). Preparedness and resistance to extinction to fear-relevant stimuli: A failure to replicate. *Behaviour Research and Therapy, 24,* 529–535.

Merckelbach, H., de Jong, P. J., Muris, P., & van den Hout, M. A. (1996). The etiology of specific phobias: A review. *Clinical Psychology Review, 16,* 337–361.

Moore, R., Brodsgaard, I., & Birn, H. (1991). Manifestations, acquisition, and diagnostic categories of dental fear in a self-referred population. *Behaviour Research and Therapy, 29,* 51–60.

Öst, L. G. (1987). Age of onset in different phobias. *Journal of Abnormal Psychology, 96,* 223–229.

Öst, L. G. (1989). One-session treatment for specific phobias. *Behaviour Research and Therapy, 27,* 1–7.

Öst, L. G. (1996). Long-term effects of behavior therapy for specific phobias. In M. R. Mavissakalian & R. F. Prien (Eds.), *Long-term treatments of anxiety disorders* (pp. 121–170). Washington, DC: American Psychiatric Press.

Page, A. C. (1994). Blood-injury phobia. *Clinical Psychology Review, 14,* 443–461.

Rachman, S. (1990). The determinants and treatment of simple phobias. *Advances in Behaviour Research and Therapy, 12,* 1–30.

Seligman, M. E. P. (1971). Phobias and preparedness. *Behavior Therapy, 2,* 307–320.

Thorpe, S. J., & Salkovskis, P. M. (1995). Phobia beliefs: Do cognitive factors play a role in specific phobias? *Behaviour Research and Therapy, 33,* 805–816.

Janet Woodruff-Borden and Sarah E. Jeffery

SPEECH AND LANGUAGE DISORDERS. The study of the psychology of speech and language disorders is difficult because of definition variability, differing models of speech and language or development, and problems in separating acquired disorders from developmental disorders of communication. (Speech and language disorders associated with aphasia or hearing loss are not covered here, since these each comprise an extensive literature of their own.)

Language is defined as a conventional symbolic system used for communication purposes. It refers to the expression and reception (comprehension) of ideas and feelings. Separate parts of language include phonology (sound system), grammar (syntax, morphology), semantics (symbolic meaning), and pragmatics (functional use). Speech is the product of oral-motor movement resulting in articulation of language expression. A third component that must be included in order to understand speech and language disorders is verbal mediation, which is frequently referred to as central language function. Verbal mediation is the use of the symbolic language system in thinking. Pure speech disorders may include misarticulation, dysphonia, dysfluency (e.g., stuttering), dysarthria (a sensorimotor musculature control problem), and dyspraxia (deficit in programming verbal-motor output); these also may be accompanied by language deficits. Severe language problems are sometimes seen in the absence of speech problems; however, most language disorders are accompanied by speech disorders. (I use the terms *speech* and *language* together here since most diagnostic systems incorporate these together in their models.)

Historical Overview

The early history of the study of speech and language disorders (SLD) is tied to the adult aphasia literature. The early studies are observations and autopsy findings of individuals with SLD. Paul Broca initially identified individuals with lack of speech but with intact ideas and coined the term *aphemia* to distinguish this from aphasia, which referred to the lack of speech caused by the lack of ideas. Carl Wernicke later associated aphasia with left temporal lobe damage (Wernicke's aphasia), and the term *aphemia* was renamed Broca's aphasia, which was associated with damage to the left prefrontal areas. These differentiations were the early beginnings of the current emphasis on subtyping communication disorders. A continuing controversy is whether the aphasia model applies to developmental SLD and whether these disorders are also due to deficient left hemisphere functioning. [*See* Aphasia; *and the biography of Broca.*]

Another early development that associated language functions to left cerebral lateralization rather than damage also continues (Corballis, 1983). The emphasis in child developmental speech and language disorders shifted away from the adult brain damage model to a developmental model similar to developmental dyslexia. This shift resulted in the classification referred to as developmental language disorders. This was a classification not related to a specific etiology such as brain damage, psychiatric disorder, general intellectual impairment, or hearing loss, but to a typology of speech and language symptoms. The classification of developmental speech/language disorders (SLD) led to a renewed emphasis on studies of the development of normal language and how abnormal language acquisition occurred.

Language development studies showed that there are some innate infant auditory abilities across human languages, and toddlers gradually lose the ability to discriminate sounds irrelevant to the language to which they are exposed. This suggests that the spoken language may strengthen synapses in certain circuits and weaken others. According to Isabel Rapin (*Journal of Child Psychology and Psychiatry*, 1996, 37, 643–655), studies of pragmatics and semantic language show early association with environmental stimulation and specific brain regions. Thus, deviations of either environmental stimulation and/or neuromaturational development may lead to various types of speech and language disorders. It is not surprising that given the complexity of neuromaturation and environmental stimulation that there would be a variety of different developmental speech and language disorders and numerous explanations for their occurrence.

Etiology and Epidemiology

The etiology of SLD is usually unknown. Although there are many hypotheses regarding the causes of SLD, most neurological hypotheses related to possible brain damage or left hemisphere abnormalities remain largely unproven. One of the most recent etiological hypotheses relates to a perceptual deficit in auditory function. This hypothesis suggests that there may be deficits in auditory discrimination, auditory sequencing, short-term memory, or rate of auditory processing. However, it is likely that these hypotheses may only explain etiology for specific subgroups of children with SLD. There probably are multifactorial etiologies for SLD due to the heterogeneity across and within subtypes of SLD. Jeff Gilger (*Journal of Speech and Hearing Disorders*, 1997, 40, 1126–1142) has reviewed the evidence for genetic etiology of SLD.

Epidemiological studies of children with SLD show a wide variability in prevalence estimates; the variances are based on the type of SLD being considered and the severity of the speech and language problem considered. Developmental language disorders occur in approximately 5% of the childhood population. Dennis Cantwell and Lorian Baker (*Psychiatric and Developmental Disorders in Children with Communication Disorder*, Washington, D.C., 1991) report numerous prevalence estimates ranging from 1 to 33% for speech and language disorders, with approximately 17% for language disorders only. Speech and language disorders that are severe enough to warrant treatment during preschool years are approximately 5 to 10%, with 50 to 80% of the children continuing to show difficulties into adolescence and early adulthood. Prevalence estimates and prognosis vary according to type of SLD. Articulation disorder shows the highest prevalence (3–32%),

and pure receptive language disorder shows the lowest prevalence (1–13%). However, isolated articulation or phonological disorders have the most positive outcome, whereas more general language disorders (receptive–expressive) have the least favorable outcome. Despite the widely ranging prevalence estimates of SLD, it is second in prevalence only to learning disorders among handicapping conditions found in school children. Most research indicates that SLD occurs more often in males than females, although the estimated ratios vary widely.

Related Conditions

Speech and language disorders are often associated with learning disorders, behavior disorders, and emotional disorders. Many children with SLD, regardless of subtype, show deficits in short-term auditory memory, word retrieval, and rapid object naming, symptoms often described as dysnomia. This may occur as an isolated problem or may be accompanied by any of the more severe language symptoms. Children with even the isolated form may show only mild speech and language symptoms during preschool years, although they often show a reading disability later. Since early reading is tied to phonological memory and retrieval, as well as word recall and naming ability, it is not surprising that even mild forms of SLD are associated with reading and learning disabilities. (For an extensive review of the relationship of speech and language disorder subtypes to specific learning disorders and treatments, see L. C. Richman and K. Wood, S. Netherton, D. Holmes, and C. E. Walker, Eds., in *Child and Adolescent Psychological Disorders*, New York, 1999.)

Behavioral and emotional disorders are often associated with SLD. For example, Cantwell and Baker followed children with SLD from a community speech and language clinic and found that 5 years later, 60% showed some sign of a psychological disorder, with attention deficit/hyperactivity disorder (ADHD) most prevalent (37%) and anxiety disorders second (14%). Beitchman followed children with SLD from 5 to 12 ½ years of age and found different levels and types of psychiatric disorders associated with different types of SLD (*Journal of the American Academy of Child and Adolescent Psychiatry*, 1996, 35, 815–825). Children with more general language disorders were the most disturbed later, showing externalizing behavior disorders, and were likely to show some social competence problems according to their mothers' ratings.

Subtypes of SLD

There have been many recent attempts to develop empirically derived classification systems for subtyping SLD. There are generally overlapping subtypes, although some minor differences also occur across differing subtype systems, and different names are sometimes used for similar subtypes. For purposes of simplicity, this review will use the classification names of the *Diagnostic and Statistical Manual* of the American Psychiatric Association (Washington, D.C., 1994) to review SLD subtypes. One additional subtype not in *DSM–IV* (1994) is supported by the research literature: disnomia—auditory memory disorder.

Expressive Language Disorder. This disorder is characterized by verbal production difficulties. The typical symptoms include problems in naming and efficient use of words in sentences, along with decreased vocabulary. This disorder often includes symptoms of articulation and/or phonological errors, especially at younger ages. Problems with expressive language can be assessed on tests of fluency, naming, vocabulary, and rapid verbal memory. Clinical symptoms include hesitancies in responding, telegraphic speech, verbal omissions, and circumlocutions. Children with expressive disorder often have oral reading difficulties and may read at slow rates. Since they may struggle with the expressive component of reading, they may lose the meaning. They often perform better on silent reading exams. Due to their halting speech patterns and difficulty in communicating their ideas, these individuals are often teased or shunned by peers and are vulnerable to the development of low self-esteem and social withdrawal. Although research shows that this subgroup exhibits less severe psychological problems than other SLD subgroups, they do show mild degrees of social inhibition and frustration related to verbal interactions.

Phonological Disorder. The *DSM–IV* classification of this disorder includes both the phonological disorder and the earlier *DSM–III* (1980) articulation disorder. The characteristics of this disorder include sound substitutions, omissions, and articulation errors. This disorder also incorporates symptoms of verbal dyspraxia or speech-motor programming deficits in some classification systems. These children usually have intact comprehension skills. This disorder may interfere with the ability to blend phonemes into words and in its severe form produces a disability in phonetic processing or awareness. Children with milder forms of this disorder (e.g., articulation errors or mild phonetic errors) perform well on most cognitive and educational tests. However, those with more severe phonological processing deficits invariably show severe language deficits and a language-based dyslexia. Even mild forms may interfere with early learning of letter-sound associations and sound blending, which are integral parts of early reading. Tests of sound blending and auditory discrimination are important in assessing these symptoms. Those individuals with associated problems in vocal production (dyspraxia, dysarthria) often show other neuromotor deficits on neuropsychological testing. One group with both articulation and graphomotor problems usually shows later reading disorders and handwriting

problems. Recent therapeutic approaches that appear promising in treating children with fundamental phonemic processing deficits include direct teaching of phonemic awareness and synthesis.

Mixed Receptive-Expressive Language Disorder. This disorder combines the symptoms of expressive language disorder with the symptoms of semantic comprehension problems. This leads to difficulty with word associations, categorization, and verbal mediation in general. Often this condition is referred to as a global, general, or pervasive language disorder. It is the type of language disorder usually seen in children diagnosed as autistic (usually referred to as semantic-pragmatic disorder), although it often occurs unassociated with autistic features. Unique forms of this disorder occur when auditory memory is intact or even superior, including hyperlexia, when children learn to read words without meaning; or fluent dysphasia, when vocalizations occur fluently but without clear meaning. Individuals with receptive-expressive language disorders perform poorly on all language tests. Neuropsychological tests of receptive language, pictorial associations, and analogies are particularly important in identifying visual-spatial reasoning strengths. Due to the severe deficit in associative language, verbal mediation of behavior of self and others is impaired, creating significant externalizing behavior disorders, such as conduct disorders or ADHD. Severe educational problems are usually associated with this disorder, and self-contained educational settings are often necessary, along with extensive behavioral conditioning paradigms. Early and intensive language therapy using an aphasia model may be helpful.

Stuttering Disorders. Stuttering is a disorder in the timing and fluency of speech. Sounds may be elongated or repeated. Dysfluencies are normal in preschool children. This disorder has many controversial theories regarding etiology, with extreme positions ranging from total environmental to no environmental cause. Most recent research suggests a strong genetic component to stuttering, and it is rarely associated with other learning disorders or other neuropsychological deficits, as are most SLDs. Stuttering is usually treated by speech pathologists using operant speech programs, delayed auditory feedback, and other behavioral paradigms. Psychologists are infrequently involved with examination or treatment of stuttering, and when they are it is usually because of an unrelated learning disorder or a secondary emotional problem. Although stuttering has been associated with an increase in other speech and language problems, there are no specific psychological characteristics associated with stuttering, although many early theories suggest a quite extensive psychological interpretation. Two types of stuttering can be identified: idiopathic, with no known cause, and acquired, which may occur after brain injury. A review of research on stuttering by Gavin Andrews shows 84% of all children who stutter will recover by age 16, some with and some without therapy (*Journal of Speech and Hearing Disorders*, 1983, *48*, 226–245).

Dysnomia–Auditory Retrieval Disorder. One important SLD not classified in *DSM–IV* (1994) is a disorder associated with dysnomia, a problem of word retrieval, object naming, and auditory memory. This group of children may show only mild symptoms during preschool years, but they may then show unexplained dyslexia later. The symptoms of this disorder are relatively similar to those of expressive language disorder, and this disorder is often subsumed under that diagnostic category. However, it has been identified as a separate diagnostic entity by some researchers. An important distinction is that individuals with dysnomia or auditory retrieval disorder often do not show signs of reduced verbal output, as seen in the expressive language disorder. This disorder may be most evident in sequencing or serial order memory. The individual may have difficulty remembering meaningful information such as sentences or stories in a sequential fashion even though they may show good expressive language skills. Sequential memory tests may show a difference in auditory versus visual memory skills. School problems often include forgetting letters, numbers, words, math facts, and spelling. The memory deficit may mimic an attention deficit disorder. Behavior is rarely a problem for individuals with this disorder, although in childhood this may produce frustration secondary to associated learning disorders, especially if these are not identified.

Selective Mutism. Selective mutism is the persistent withholding of speech by a child in a selective situation despite reasonably adequate ability to communicate and comprehend language. Thus, this is not a primary SLD. This disorder usually begins during preschool years or at school entrance time and occurs in approximately 0.5% of psychiatric clinics. It has been associated with an increased frequency of articulation and expressive language problems (20–28%) but not with receptive language disorders or stuttering. Intellectual skills are reported to be generally average, at least for nonverbal IQ. Selective mutism is considered to be a symptom of shyness, social anxiety, or generalized anxiety, although some cases show oppositional characteristics. It is reported to occur equally or more often in females than males, unlike other SLDs. It has also been associated with preschool somatic symptoms of eating problems, sleeping difficulties, and elimination disorders. Although early theories suggest a deep-seated psychoanalytic problem, there is evidence to indicate that intensive behavior and emphathetic treatment is quite effective. Although there are suggestions in the literature that early speech problems and over-enmeshed maternal-child relations may contribute to this disorder, there appear to be no unique or universal conditions contributing to this disorder. It is likely that there are either anxiety or oppositional factors involved in most children with this disorder, with the primary behavioral features being internalizing problems. Educational problems in learning are reported in 25% of children with selective mutism.

Cleft Lip and Palate. Children with cleft lip and palate often experience speech and language impairment. Those with both cleft lip and palate often show expressive language disorders and sometimes phonological disorders, whereas speech and language problems associated with cleft palate only often include expressive-receptive language disorder. Cleft is a frequently occurring condition occurring in approximately 1 to 2% of births. Associated problems include behavioral inhibition, which has been associated with peer teasing; neuropsychological patterns, indicative of language-based learning disorders; and self-esteem problems secondary to social aspects of early feeding difficulties, speech problems, and facial disfigurement. Although most treatments include oral surgery, speech therapy, and dental restoration, the psychological aspects of this condition warrant frequent psychological assessment and treatment. Early development is often delayed due to speech and language delay, feeding difficulties, and social stigmatization that results in less interactive play with peers. Reading disability is the most frequent type of learning disability associated with cleft. Reading disability usually occurs due to early speech difficulties that limit early phonological development. It is important that children with cleft who experience expressive language disorder receive psychological assessment for reading problems and early remedial reading focusing on oral-phonics. Those with more expressive-receptive language disorders often require intensive language therapy and extensive special learning assistance. Research does show that adolescents who have cleft often show signs of low self-esteem and over-internalizing behaviors, which may warrant psychological intervention.

Bibliography

Bishop, D. V. M. (1992). The underlying nature of specific language impairment. *Journal of Child Psychology and Psychiatry, 33,* 3–66. An extensive review of numerous theories; evaluates research support of these.

Corballis, M. (1983). *Human laterality.* New York: Academic Press.

Felsenfeld, S., & Plomin, R. (1997). Epidemiological and offspring analysis of developmental speech disorders, using data from the Colorado adoption project. *Journal of Speech and Hearing Disorders, 40,* 778–791.

Korkman, M., & Hakkinen-Rihu, P. (1994). A new classification of developmental language disorders. *Brain & Language, 47,* 96–116.

Krohn, D. D., Weckstein, S. M., & Wright, H. A. (1992). A study of the effectiveness of a specific treatment of elective mutism. *Journal of American Academy of Child and Adolescent Psychiatry, 31,* 711–718.

Kuhl, P. K., William, L. F., Stevens, K. N., & Lindbloom, B. (1992). Linguistic experience alters phonetic perception in infants by 6 months of age. *Science, 255,* 606–608.

Richman, L., & Eliason, M. (1992). Psychological characteristics associated with cleft palate. In K. T. Koller & C. D. Starr (Eds.), *Cleft palate: Interdisciplinary issues and treatments.* Austin, TX: Pro-Ed. An extensive review of psychological aspects of this condition.

Lynn C. Richman

SPEECH PRODUCTION. The ability to produce speech is the most complex cognitive-motor skill of *homo sapiens.* Wilhelm Wundt was the first psychologist to give a systematic account of this ability and its evolution in *Die Sprache* (Leipzig, 1900). Rudolf Meringer and Karl Mayer, in their *Verlesen und Versprechen* (Stuttgart, 1895), pioneered a major research method, the analysis of speech errors. In 1861, Paul Broca discovered an area in the frontal left hemisphere specifically dedicated to speech production.

The core setting for speech production is conversation, in which participants take turns in contributing to some joint theme. The proximal aim for speakers is that their communicative intentions are recognized from the utterances produced. The construction of such utterances involves several steps, as follows.

Conceptual Preparation

The speaker must select and organize the relevant information to be expressed. If the goal is to give the interlocutor some route direction, the speaker will construct or retrieve a mental map of the appropriate area, decide on a shortest or easiest route, and chunk it in pieces from landmark to landmark, to be delivered in a particular order. The linearization of information to be expressed, to decide on what to say first, what next, and so on, is a core ingredient of conceptual preparation. The selection of information is further guided by the speaker's model of the listener's state of mind. What is the common ground? What information is given? What will be new to the listener? This model of mind is underdeveloped in autistic speech. In order to achieve their communicative goals, speakers have access to a range of rhetorical devices—ways of organizing information effectively—such as asserting, requesting, threatening, and apologizing. The ultimate message constructed by the speaker consists of lexical concepts, concepts for which there exist words in the target language. Languages differ in their repository of lexical concepts, and conceptual preparation differs accordingly.

Grammatical Encoding

To construct an utterance, the speaker will select words (or lemmas) and arrange them in the correct syntactic order. Lexical concepts are part of the mental lexicon, the mental repository of words. Lexical selection is theoretically modeled as activation spreading from a lexical concept node to the corresponding lemma node in a lexical network. In normal fluent speech, lemmas are selected at a rate of two to three per second. Still, selection errors, such as *don't burn your toes* (instead of *fingers*), are rare. They tend to be semantic (as in *toes* for *fingers*) because activation spreads among related concepts. Semantic selection errors are quite frequent in both Broca's and Wernicke's aphasia. The syntactic properties of lemmas drive their syntactic assemblage; they must behave as noun (count, mass, etc.), as verb (transitive, intransitive, etc.), as adverb, as preposition, or as other syntactic category. The utterance is incrementally built up within the constraints of syntactic feasibility. This construction process requires that the syntactic properties of lemmas remain available during some critical time span. Such availability is not guaranteed in Broca's aphasia, typically resulting in agrammatism.

Morpho-phonological Encoding

Each selected lemma spreads its activation to its morphemes in the network. Many words (such as *us, dog, blue,* and *select*) are monomorphemic; others (such as *bill-board, work-ing, eye-s* and *frank-ly*) are multimorphemic. Each morpheme contains a phonological code. It consists mainly of the morpheme's segments, for instance /s/, /i/, /l/, /ɛ/, /k/, and /t/ for the morpheme *select*. When a morpheme is successfully activated, the code becomes available. Still, accessing a morpheme can be problematic. In the tip-of-the-tongue (TOT) state, access is blocked, although the lemma can be available with all of its syntactic properties (such as a noun's gender in gender-marking languages). This is also the major problem in certain types of anomia. Generally, accessing a low-frequency morpheme (such as *marsh*) is slower than accessing a high-frequency one (such as *mouth*).

Phonological encoding involves the building up of a syllable structure for the word in its context. When producing the utterance *Peter will select us,* the phrase *select us* will be syllabified as a whole. This proceeds strictly from left to right, as it were, by concatenating the spelled-out segments of the phonological codes: /s/ and /i/ form the first syllable, then /l/, /ɛ/, and /k/ form the second syllable, and finally /t/, /ʌ/, and /s/ form the last syllable: si-lɛk-tʌs. Notice that the last syllable, tʌs, straddles a word boundary. This is often the case in syllabification.

Phonological encoding also involves the construction of larger units. Particularly important is the construction of intonational phrases, sense units with a characteristic pitch contour. When asserting *Peter will select us*, the speaker will provide the syllable lɛk with a (raised) pitch accent and then make a dropping boundary tone on the last syllable tʌs. But when questioning the state of affairs, the speaker will render a falling pitch accent on lɛk and provide tʌs with a high boundary tone. The assignment of pitch is strongly affected by the limbic system and hence expressive of emotion.

Phonetic Encoding

As soon as a syllable (such as lɛk or tʌs) is composed, the corresponding articulatory gesture is prepared. We do most of our speaking with no more than a few hundred different syllables. These overlearned articulatory routines are probably all stored in the premotor cortex and retrieved on the fly as syllables are composed. Still, speakers are also able to compose new syllabic gestures for the occasional new or low-frequency syllable. Syllabic routines have highly expressive free parameters for pitch, duration, and amplitude that are independently set during phonological and phonetic encoding.

Articulation

The articulatory gestures are executed by an intricate articulatory apparatus, consisting of the respiratory system, providing the acoustic energy; the laryngeal system, controlling voicing and loudness; and the vocal tract, whose resonance chambers control the timbre of vowels and whose articulators (tongue, velum, and lips) control the place and manner of sound formation. The control of articulation is a major topic in phonetics. [*See* Phonetics.]

Self-Monitoring

Speakers can attend to their own overt and internal speech. When they detect an error or other trouble that may jeopardize the intended communicative effect, they can self-interrupt and make a repair.

[*See also* Aphasia.]

Bibliography

Bock, J. K., & Levelt, W. J. M. (1994). Language production: Grammatical encoding. In M. A. Gernsbacher (Ed.), *Handbook of psycholinguistics* (pp. 945–984). New York: Academic Press.

Clark, H. H. (1996). *Using language*. Cambridge, UK: Cambridge University Press.

Fromkin, V. A. (Ed.). (1973). *Speech errors as linguistic evidence*. The Hague: Mouton.

Kent, R. D., Adams, S. G., & Turner, G. S. (1996). Models of speech production. In N. J. Las (Ed.), *Principles of experimental phonetics* (pp. 3–45). St. Louis: Mosby.

Levelt, W. J. M. (1989) *Speaking*. Cambridge, MA: MIT Press.

Levelt, W. J. M. (Ed.). (1993). *Lexical access in speech production*. Cambridge, UK: Blackwell.

Levelt, W. J. M., Roelofs, A., & Meyer, A. S. (1999). A theory of lexical access in speech production. *Behavioral and Brain Sciences, 22*, 1–38.

Liberman, A. (1996). *Speech: A special code*. Cambridge, MA: MIT Press.

Willem J. M. Levelt

SPENCE, KENNETH WARTINBEE (1907–1967), American psychologist. Spence was born in Chicago, Illinois, where his father was an electrical engineer. The family moved to Montreal, Canada, when he was a young child. In high school, he was active in sports and, later, at McGill University, injured his back in track competition. As part of his convalescence, he went to live with his grandmother in Wisconsin, where he attended LaCrosse Teachers College and majored in physical education. There he met and married Isabel Temte. He returned to McGill, switched his major to psychology, and took his bachelor's degree in 1929 and a master's degree in 1930.

From McGill, Spence went to Yale University, where he was a research assistant in the laboratory of Robert M. Yerkes, under whose direction he completed a dissertation on visual acuity in the chimpanzee and received a doctorate in 1933. While at Yale, Spence began an intellectual association with Clark L. Hull. With Walter Shipley, he performed an experimental test of one of Hull's deductions concerning the order of difficulty of blind alleys in maze learning, which Spence published "on the side" while doing his dissertation (Hilgard, 1967). This research revealed Spence's great promise at designing experiments relative to theory, a feature of his style that became the hallmark of his theoretical-experimental work.

After graduating, Spence spent four years at the Yale Laboratories of Primate Biology at Orange Park, Florida, where he did seminal work on discrimination learning in the chimpanzee. Following a year at the University of Virginia, he went to the University of Iowa, where he spent 26 years, 22 of which he served as head of the department of psychology, before moving to the University of Texas in 1964, where he died 2 years later.

Spence's name and Hull's appeared together on a paper just once, in 1938, in a methodological article on correction versus noncorrection procedures in maze learning. Their names, however, are linked to identify the most influential neobehavioristic theory of the 1940s and 1950s that encompassed conditioning, learning, and motivation. Spence's contribution to this theory was explicitly acknowledged in the preface to Hull's *Principles of Behavior* (New York, 1943), but it can also be inferred from the correspondence they maintained. The volume, the time span, and the theoretical content of this correspondence make it, from a historical standpoint, perhaps the most extensive and important in the history of the psychology of learning.

The 13 papers Spence published in the *Psychological Review* between 1936 and 1966 are independent testimony to his contributions, which fall into three categories: learning and motivation theory; the experimental psychology of learning and motivation; and methodology and philosophy of science. (In some of the latter writings, his collaborator was the philosopher Gustav Bergmann.)

Spence's contributions to learning theory, apart from his collaboration in the Hull-Spence system, were of two kinds. One was as a systematist, as a commentator on and interpreter of the theories and systems of others. His chapters in 1951 in the edited volumes of Stone and in Stevens's *Handbook of Experimental Psychology* are examples of this skill. Edward Tolman, whose theorizing in animal learning and motivation provided the major alternative to the Hull-Spence position, is reported to have said he never fully comprehended the structure of his theory until he saw Spence's analysis of it.

Spence's second, and arguably major, theoretical contribution began with his famous papers in the 1930s on discrimination learning, which included the derivation of transposition from stimulus-response gradients of excitation and inhibition, and of the seemingly sudden solutions to discrimination problems from stimulus-response contiguity rather than Gestalt principles. This early work, a product of Spence's time at the Orange Park laboratories, became the focus of much later research at Iowa and remains among his most influential contributions. His later, more formal, theoretical contributions to the study of learning and motivation are summarized in his Silliman Lectures at Yale University (Spence, 1956).

Spence's research career can be divided into two phases. The first phase, beginning in the 1930s and ending about 1950, is marked by work on discrimination learning in animals and some preoccupation with philosophical-methodological matters. From about 1950 on, while still supervising research at Iowa on instrumental learning and interactions between motivation and reinforcement, his own research papers began to focus on Pavlovian eyeblink conditioning in humans.

The eyeblink conditioning experiment represented for Spence a "psychological vacuum" for teasing out the fundamental principles of association and the relative roles of habit and drive in simple learning. Spence (1966) forcefully demonstrated that human conditioning data could be "contaminated" by cognitive factors (a little air creeping into the "vacuum") and that such factors accounted for the greater extinction rates in Pavlovian conditioning in humans than in animals. He and his students showed that if participants were told a "cover story" to mask the true purpose of the experiment, the transition to extinction was much slower than when the participant was aware of it. The "vacuum" under these masked conditions was restored, thus coming closer to revealing the fundamental form of the process.

Spence did not live to see the full flowering of the "cognitive revolution" in psychology, and his stance vis-à-vis the cognitivists is not well understood. Although influenced by Pavlov and the early Watsonian behaviorism, Spence was not a thoroughgoing behaviorist in the mold of Watson or the post–1950 B. F. Skinner. His position, like Hull's and Tolman's before him, is now characterized as a form of neobehaviorism (although he was a behaviorist in every methodological sense). Like other neobehaviorists he did not take the more extreme positivistic stance of the later Skinner—of avoiding the use of empirical constructs defined operationally. Indeed, much of his later work had as its major purpose the separation of habit and motivational factors in the eyeblink conditioning experiment. Some of his work also involved the concept of "level of anxiety," leading to the construction of the Taylor Manifest Anxiety Scale, in collaboration with I. E. Farber and Janet A. Taylor (later Janet Taylor Spence).

No account of Spence's intellectual history can overlook, or underestimate, another facet of his contribution—the many (about 75) doctoral students who came out of his Iowa laboratory, a large number of whom went on to make significant contributions of their own. The recipient of many honors, Spence was elected to the National Academy of Sciences and the Society of Experimental Psychologists, receiving the latter's Howard Crosby Warren Medal for outstanding research in psychology. He also received the Distinguished Scientific Contribution Award of the American Psychological Association in 1956, the first year it was offered.

[*Many of the people mentioned in this article are the subjects of independent biographical entries.*]

Bibliography

Works by Spence

Spence, K. W. (1951). Theoretical interpretations of learning. In S. S. Stevens (Ed.), *Handbook of experimental psychology* (pp. 690–729). New York: Wiley.
Spence, K. W. (1951). Theoretical interpretations of learn-

ing. In C. P. Stone (Ed.), *Comparative psychology* (pp. 239–291). Englewood Cliffs, NJ: Prentice Hall.

Spence, K. W. (1956). *Behavior theory and conditioning.* New Haven, CT: Yale University Press.

Spence, K. W. (1960). *Behavior theory and learning: Selected papers.* Englewood Cliffs, NJ: Prentice Hall.

Spence, K. W. (1966). Cognitive and drive factors in the extinction of the conditioned eye blink in human subjects. *Psychological Review, 73,* 445–458.

Works about Spence

Amsel, A. (1995). Kenneth Wartinbee Spence. In *Biographical memoirs* (Vol. 66, pp. 335–351). Washington, DC: National Academy of Sciences.

Hilgard, E. R. (1967). Kenneth Wartinbee Spence. *American Journal of Psychology, 80,* 314–318.

Kendler, H. H. (1967). Kenneth W. Spence. *Psychological Review, 74,* 335–341.

Abram Amsel

SPENCER, HERBERT (1820–1903), English philosopher. Born and raised in Derby, Spencer was the only surviving son of Nonconformist parents. Self-taught, he joined the staff of the railway as a civil engineer from 1837 to 1841, became an occasional journalist and inventor undertaking and abandoning the most varied projects, dallied with phrenology, joined the railroads again between 1844 and 1846, and finally, in December 1847, became subeditor of the *Economist.* The bequests of two uncles and his father subsequently allowed him to devote all his time to the development of his theories.

Spencer's *System of Synthetic Philosophy* was a serious attempt to generalize an important scientific idea, that of evolution, by applying it to the fields of psychology, sociology, and ethics. The *System* eventually grew to some 10 large volumes: *First Principles* (1862), *Principles of Psychology* (1855/1870), *Principles of Biology* (1863–1865), *Principles of Sociology* (1876–1896), and *Principles of Ethics* (1884–1893). Spencer's ultimate purpose, in his own words, was "finding for the principles of right and wrong in conduct at large, a scientific basis." The *Ethics* was the culmination of the whole system.

The original edition of *Principles of Psychology* preceded the *Synthetic Philosophy* but was later reworked by Spencer and incorporated into it. Here Spencer adopted associationist psychology and gave it a new basis in evolutionary biology. Théodule Ribot in his *English Psychology* (New York, 1874, p. 158) accurately summarized Spencer's two fundamental ideas: "That of the continuity of psychological phenomena; [and] that of the intimate relation between the being and its medium. These two points virtually contain his doctrine." The first idea significantly advanced the conception of psychology as a biological science and of mind as evolving from life. A strict adherence to the law of continuity meant that there was no precise line of demarcation between physiological and psychological facts, and that every absolute distinction between the two was illusory, thus undermining the special status of consciousness and faculty psychology.

Spencer arrived at the second idea by generalizing Karl Ernst von Baer's law that progress in individual organisms consisted in the passage from a homogeneous to a heterogeneous structure and applying that principle to all development. The development of the earth, of life on its surface, and of society all supposed the same evolution of the simple into the complex by successive dynamic adjustments of internal relations to external circumstances. Thus, the "complication of the mind" arose by "insensible steps": "it is certain that between the automatic actions of the lowest creatures, and the highest conscious actions of the human race, a series of actions displayed by the various tribes of the animal kingdom may be so placed as to render it impossible to say of any one step in the series—Here intelligence begins" (Spencer, 1855, p. 349).

The key doctrine of Spencer's *Principles of Psychology* was his solution to the "controversy between the disciples of Locke and those of Kant." With it, Spencer was able to rescue associationist psychology at its weakest point: its inability to explain species or individual differences. In Spencer's own words: "The familiar doctrine of association here undergoes a great extension; for it is held that not only in the individual do ideas become connected when in experience the things producing them have repeatedly occurred together, but that such results of repeated occurrences accumulate in successions of individuals: the effects of associations are supposed to be transmitted as modifications of the nervous system" (Spencer, 1904, Vol. 1, p. 470). What were, from the point of view of the individual, a priori axioms were now revealed as being the inherited experience of the species. Forms of thought might thus be likened to reflex actions and instincts, which are also the result of experiences far back in the development of the race. In this way, Spencer was able to maintain the basic position of sensationalism while avoiding having to explain such complex phenomena as instincts solely on the basis of individual experience. The mechanism of heredity at work in this process was the "Lamarckian" inheritance of acquired characteristics. This theory was current in Spencer's lifetime and was also present in Darwin's work (as was natural selection in Spencer's).

Spencer shared with Darwin the establishment of psychology on a biological, evolutionary basis, and with Alexander Bain the close alliance of associationist psychology with sensory-motor psychophysiology. His significance can be measured by the importance of those he influenced, such as William James and John Dewey in functional psychology, George J. Romanes in animal and comparative psychology, John Hughlings Jackson in sensory-motor psychophysiology, and Ivan P. Pavlov's classical conditioning experiments.

[*Many of the people mentioned in this article are the subjects of independent biographical entries.*]

Bibliography

Works by Spencer

Spencer, H. (1855) *Principles of psychology.* London: Longman, Brown, Green. (1872). (2nd ed., 2 vols). London: Williams and Norgate.
Spencer, H. (1862). *First principles* London: Williams & Norgate.
Spencer, H. (1904). *Autobiography.* (2 vols.). London: Williams and Norgate.

Works about Spencer

Duncan, D. (1909). *Life and letters of Herbert Spencer.* New York: D. Appleton.
Magoun, H. W. (1960). Evolutionary concepts of brain function following Darwin and Spencer. In S. Tax (Ed.), *Evolution after Darwin: Vol. 2. The evolution of man.* (pp. 187–209). Chicago, IL: University of Chicago Press.
Peel, J. D. Y. (1971). *Herbert Spencer: The evolution of a sociologist.* New York: Basic Books. This work places Spencer in the context of provincial dissent in England during the close of the heroic period of industrialization. Despite being centered on sociology, it discusses all the main works and is a handy one-volume treatment of Spencer.
Richards, R. J. (1987). *Darwin and the emergence of evolutionary theories of mind and behavior.* Chicago, IL: University of Chicago Press. The author focuses on Spencer's evolutionary theory of morality and shows how each of his works developed concepts that helped further Spencer's attempt to found morality on science.
Stocking, G. W. (1968). *Race, culture, and evolution.* New York: Free Press.
Young, R. M. (1971). *Mind, brain, and adaptation in the nineteenth century.* Oxford: Oxford University Press. The author shows how Spencer's education and especially his early attraction for phrenology influenced his mature psychological theories.

Daniela S. Barberis

SPERRY, ROGER WOLCOTT (1913–1994), American psychologist. A "research program" is broadly defined as a long-term, carefully crafted series of studies that attempt to answer important questions. Roger Sperry formulated the questions that fueled his 50-year program of research during the first day of R. H. Stetson's Introduction to Psychology class at Oberlin College. The questions, which were the themes for the American Psychological Association's centennial conference, were (1) In what proportion does behavior come from nature or nurture? and (2) What is the purpose of consciousness? These questions reflect the influence of Stetson's own mentor, William James. Interestingly, Sperry had actually read James's *Psychology* as an adolescent after his father had brought the book home from the public library.

To answer these questions, Sperry set out to obtain the necessary skills for research. After obtaining a bachelor's degree in English (1935) and essentially a minor in psychology, he stayed at Oberlin to obtain a master's degree (1937) in psychology with Stetson—the professor who exerted the greatest influence on his thinking. After developing strong ideas about the connections between movement, brain activity, and consciousness, based on the interactions with Stetson, Sperry proceeded to work with Paul Weiss, a prominent neuroembryologist at the University of Chicago. Weiss believed that peripheral nerve functions were malleable. After completing a series of carefully crafted and elegant studies with a variety of species and nerves, Sperry came to the conclusion that Weiss's belief was in need of revision.

After receiving his doctoral degree in zoology in 1941, Sperry went to the Yerkes Laboratories of Primate Biology in Orange Park, Florida, as a postdoctoral fellow to work with Karl Lashley. Lashley had developed critically acclaimed theories of brain functioning—primarily the theory of equipotentiality. This theory suggested that all portions of the cerebral cortex are equally responsible for the acquisition of information and the production of behavior. With similar tenacity, Sperry worked on a series of studies that addressed both equipotentiality and mass action. During these formative years at Yerkes, Sperry interacted with important figures including Frank Beach, Henry Nissen, Austin Riessen, and Donald Hebb.

In 1946, Sperry left the idyllic surroundings of Yerkes to return to the University of Chicago. There he expanded some of his peripheral nerve regeneration studies and began asking similar questions of the central nervous system. Despite his prodigious scholarly output and the beginnings of split-brain research, the department of anatomy failed to grant him tenure. He spent one more year, without tenure but with funding and an appointment from the National Institutes of Health, in the department of psychology before finally leaving Chicago. Thereafter, Sperry spent a year fighting tuberculosis in the Adirondack Mountains with his new bride, Norma Deupree. This difficult time allowed Sperry to further develop his thinking about the brain and consciousness, which received mention in his 1952 paper published in *Neurology.*

On the recommendation of the biologist Norman Horowitz, Sperry was invited to deliver the prestigious

Hixon Lecture in Psychobiology at the California Institute of Technology. The Division of Biology was so impressed with his nerve regeneration research that it offered him the newly created Hixon Chair of Psychobiology—a position he held until his retirement. During the next 4 decades at Caltech, Sperry worked closely with almost 100 graduate students, postdoctoral fellows, and visiting scientists representing every continent and a variety of disciplines ranging from molecular neurobiology to Jungian philosophy.

Throughout the 1950s, 1960s, and 1970s, Sperry added to his nerve regeneration studies and the burgeoning split-brain research. He initially worked with cats, then monkeys, and finally humans. Together with Joseph Bogen, probably his closest colleague, he embarked on what is now considered historic research. Cutting the largest nerve tract of the brain, the corpus callosum, resulted in two cognitively isolated halves of the cerebrum. Together with students and colleagues such as Giovanni Berlucchi, Alice Cronin-Golumb, Robert Doty, Michael Gazzaniga, Harold Gordon, Charles Hamilton, Brenda Milner, Ronald Meyer, Richard Nebes, Colwyn Trevarthen, Theodore Voneida, Eran and Dahlia Zaidel, and others, he performed a series of ingenious studies that revealed that commissurotomized patients appeared to have two independent minds. This work resulted in widespread recognition of hemisphericity and laterality.

Sperry had concluded that the two independent sides of the brain worked in unison, giving rise to one consciousness. In other words, consciousness emerged from the unified working brain. As early as 1964, Sperry had hypothesized (in a lecture to colleagues at Caltech) that this emergent consciousness, in turn, had a downward effect on specific brain function: specifically, downward causation affected neuronal function. Thus, consciousness was, in fact, an emergent quality and a causal force simultaneously. This bimodal model of consciousness was developed further by Sperry during the last two decades of his life. Acceptance of the subjective in brain research had two important outcomes. First, it helped to shift the focus from behaviorism to cognition. For Sperry this was indeed the beginning of the consciousness revolution. Second, acceptance of the subjective in psychology allowed the inclusion of values as the determining agent in the development of consciousness. These values, however, were biologically, not environmentally, based, having evolved for the survival of the organism. Appropriate values could, in turn, address overpopulation, pollution, and other modern crises. Thus, this value-laden consciousness revolution would represent a new *Zeitgeist*, originated by psychology and affecting other sciences as well as the world around us.

Half a century of research, 300 publications, and 100 students and colleagues resulted, not surprisingly, in many honors and awards for Sperry. He was particularly proud of his recognition by fellow psychologists (the American Psychological Association's Lifetime Achievement Award in 1993) and by scientists (the 1981 Nobel Prize in Physiology, which he shared with David Hubel and Torsten Weisel). Sperry, the only individual to have obtained a graduate degree in psychology who won a Nobel Prize, died of amyotrophic lateral sclerosis in Pasadena, California.

Bibliography

Puente, A. E. (1995). Roger Wolcott Sperry. *American Psychologist, 50,* 940–941.

Sperry, R. W. (1951). Mechanisms of neuronal maturation. In S. S. Stevens (Ed.), *Handbook of experimental psychology.* New York: Wiley.

Sperry, R. W. (1952). Neurology and the mind-brain problem. *American Scientist, 40,* 291–312.

Sperry, R. W. (1962). Problems in molecular coding. In E. O Schmitt (Ed.), *Macro-molecular specificity and biological memory.* Cambridge, MA: MIT Press.

Sperry, R. W. (1964). The great cerebral commissure. *Scientific American, 210,* 42–52.

Sperry, R. W. (1965). Brain bisection and mechanism of consciousness. Pontifical Academy Seminar on Study of Brain and Consciousness. In J. C. Eccles (Ed.), *Brain and conscious experience.* Heidelberg, Germany: Springer-Verlag.

Sperry, R. W. (1967). Mind, brain and humanist values. In J. R. Platt (Ed.), *New view of the nature of man.* Chicago: University of Chicago Press.

Sperry, R. W. (1968). Hemispheric disconnection and unity in conscious awareness. *American Psychologist, 23,* 723–733.

Sperry, R. W. (1969). A modified concept of consciousness. *Psychological Review, 76,* 532–536.

Sperry, R. W. (1974). Science and the problem of values. *Zygon, 9,* 7–21.

Sperry, R. W. (1983). *Science and moral priority.* New York: Columbia University Press.

Sperry, R. W. (1993). The impact and promise of the cognitive revolution. *American Psychologist, 48*(3), 878–885.

Antonio E. Puente

SPINAL CORD INJURY. *See* Rehabilitation Psychology.

SPINOZA, BARUCH (BENEDICTUS DE) (1632–1677), Dutch philosopher. Spinoza was born in Amsterdam on 24 November 1632 into a family of Jewish Marrano immigrants from Portugal. Although his given name was Baruch, he published his most important works in Latin under the name Benedictus de Spinoza. Those appearing during his lifetime included the *Philosophical Principles of René Descartes* (1663), and *Theological-Political Treatise* (1670). His two most important works for psychology were published shortly after his death in 1677: *On the Improvement of the Understanding* and his masterpiece, *Ethics Demonstrated with Geometrical Order*.

Although famously characterized as "God-intoxicated" by Novalis (Garrett, 1996, p. 1) and as "the noblest and most lovable of the great philosophers" by Bertrand Russell (1965, p. 569), Spinoza was widely shunned and excoriated as an atheist during his lifetime. A brilliant student, he encountered the writings of Descartes while still a teenager and adopted views in reaction that led to his excommunication from the synagogue. He subsequently earned his living as a lens-grinder while developing his philosophy in private. He had some contact with leading intellectual figures of the day including Christiaan Huygens, Gottfried Leibniz, and the British Royal Society's Henry Oldenburg but never formed a school. Leibniz, who unquestionably benefited from seeing a prepublication draft of the *Ethics*, timidly downplayed its influence because of Spinoza's notoriety.

Spinoza's disrepute derived from his formulation of what is now called the "double aspect" conception of the mind-body relationship. He rejected Descartes's postulation of two separate but interacting "substances" of mind and matter, both created by an independent God. Spinoza posited instead a single substance, which he equated with God, having separate "attributes" of thought and extension. These attributes do not interact, as in Cartesian dualism. Thoughts give rise only to other thoughts, and physical events only to other physical occurrences. But as separate aspects of the same underlying universal substance, minds and bodies are ultimately consistent with each other. Spinoza held all mental and physical phenomena to be strictly determined by the laws of nature. Individual free will is thus an illusion, although by appreciating the laws of nature one may come to experience a psychologically liberating sense of harmony with the universe and of oneness with God. Spinoza also wrote incisively about the emotions and the passions—which he differentiated on the grounds that the causes of the former are consciously understood while those of the latter are not—and about aspects of learning and memory.

Spinoza's denial of free will and of a personal God led to his being branded an atheist during his lifetime. Actually pantheistic rather than atheistic, his worldview became much more acceptable and even fashionable following its rediscovery and espousal by early-nineteenth-century German romantic philosophers, who in turn influenced American transcendentalism and aspects of Victorian agnosticism. Although Spinoza does not receive much space in many history of psychology textbooks, Walter Bernard has documented Spinoza's direct influence on the nineteenth-century psychological pioneers Johannes Müller and Gustav Fechner and argued that his actual importance to psychology surpasses that of Descartes. In a similar vein, Alexander and Selesnick (1966, p. 137) maintain that Spinoza's influence on the general German intellectual climate "was so pervasive that many of his basic concepts became part of the general ideological climate that influenced Freud without his knowing its origin."

[*Many of the people mentioned in this article are the subjects of independent biographical entries.*]

Bibliography

Alexander, F. G., & Selesnick, S. T. (1966). *The history of psychiatry*. New York: Mentor Books. See pp. 133–138 for an appreciative account of Spinoza's general influence on German thought.

Bernard, W. (1972). Spinoza's influence on the rise of scientific psychology: A neglected chapter in the history of psychology. *Journal of the History of the Behavioral Sciences, 8*, 208–215.

Garrett, D. (Ed.). (1966). *The Cambridge companion to Spinoza*. Cambridge: Cambridge University Press. Contains essays by ten contributors on various aspects of Spinoza's life and work.

Robinson, D. N. (1981). *An intellectual history of psychology* (Rev. ed.). New York: Macmillan. Pages 265–271 present a useful summary of Spinoza's psychological thought, while denying its major direct influence on the development of modern psychology.

Russell, B. (1965). *A history of western philosophy*. New York: Simon and Schuster. Book Three, Chapter X (pp. 569–581) of this classic text contains an appreciative account of Spinoza as an ethicist and "the noblest and most lovable of the great philosophers."

Spinoza, B. (1967). *Ethics, preceded by On the improvement of the understanding*. (Edited with an introduction by James Gutmann). New York: Hafner. These two most important of Spinoza's psychologically related works have been published in numerous English translations and editions.

Raymond E. Fancher

SPIRITUALISM. *See* Religious Experience, *article on* Belief and Faith.

SPORT PERFORMANCE INTERVENTIONS. Sport psychology started to grow and come into prominence in the 1960s and 1970s. The original research focused on the relationship between personality and performance, attempting to determine whether highly able athletes have different personality styles from less successful athletes or nonathletes. Investigating whether certain personality types are more likely to be successful in different sports or positions within sports was another area of interest. This was followed by a focus on testing mainstream psychology theories (e.g., attribution theory, achievement motivation theory, social facilitation theory) in laboratory settings using motor performance as the major outcome variable. These early studies yielded some interesting findings that helped lay the foundation for our body of knowledge in sport psychology. However, in the 1980s a number of sport psychologists felt that these highly controlled, mostly laboratory studies compromised the generalizability of these findings to the extent that applications to the real competitive sport environment were limited. At the same time, there was an increased interest from coaches and athletes regarding the mental side of sport performance, with many individuals feeling that this aspect was being neglected and needed to be developed.

As the field started to progress in the 1980s and 1990s the focus became more applied, investigating how various psychological techniques such as anxiety management, goal-setting, imagery, self-talk, and concentration training might enhance athletic performance. Many practitioners started to become interested in using some of these psychological skills (i.e., mental skills) to enhance their own performances or the performances of their athletes. However, a debate started to emerge among sport psychologists regarding the research basis for the effectiveness of these interventions. Specifically, although sport psychologists had become more interested in applied issues and the development of mental training programs to enhance performance, skepticism remained as to whether the accumulated scientific evidence warranted the use of psychological interventions with athletes. For example, Dishman said that "it is not clear to what extent contemporary sport psychology possesses a clearly defined and reliable technology for interventions in applied settings" (1983, p. 127). However, Gould (1988) argues that it is rare (if not impossible) for a profession to have a complete scientific database to guide application, so sport psychologists should be guided by a careful integration of existing empirical data and professional practice experience. In either case, it would be instructive to determine exactly what is the existing scientific knowledge concerning the effectiveness of psychological interventions in competitive sports.

Sport Psychology Intervention Research

The first comprehensive review of psychological interventions in competitive sport settings was conducted by Greenspan and Feltz (1989). A total of 23 interventions using psychological techniques to enhance performance in competitive sport settings (going as far back as Suinn's 1972 work with downhill skiers) were utilized for the analysis. Results revealed that educational relaxation-based interventions and remedial cognitive restructuring interventions were effective in improving competitive performance in 83% of the studies. As a follow-up to Greenspan and Feltz's work, Vealey (1994) and Weinberg and Comar (1994) more recently examined the effectiveness of sport psychology interventions. Their combined results also revealed that over 80% of the studies found positive performance improvements for cognitive, cognitive-behavioral, and behavioral interventions. In summary, 45 studies employing psychological interventions to enhance competitive sport performance were reviewed, and 38 (85%) found positive performance effects, although causality could only be inferred in 20 of these studies. It should be noted that most recent interventions have employed more multimodal approaches using a variety of psychological techniques within a package approach to help enhance performance. Thus, it is often difficult to determine which of the mental skills included in the intervention package was primarily responsible for any potential performance increments. However, a number of studies have also focused on the effectiveness of individual particular interventions; their findings are as follows. (It should be noted that a number of methodological issues still prevail regarding the psychological skills-intervention literature.)

Imagery

Imagery has been studied using various terms such as *mental rehearsal, mental practice,* and *visualization.* The early literature dating back to the early 1900s (and continuing until the early 1980s) used the term *mental practice,* and studies were virtually always conducted in the laboratory. These studies focused on the learning of motor skills, and a meta-analysis of 60 studies (Feltz & Landers, 1983) revealed that participants in the mental practice groups performed approximately one standard deviation higher than participants in the no-practice groups. In addition, these effects were greater for cognitive tasks than for motor or strength tasks. More recent reviews (Hall, Schmidt, Durand, & Buckolz, 1994; Murphy, 1994) also indicate the effectiveness of enhancing various types of performance through the use of imagery. Finally, an evaluation of U.S. and Canadian Olympic athletes reveals that over 90% of the athletes regularly use imagery as part of their training and preparation, thus attesting to their belief of the benefits of imagery in enhancing performance as well as increasing confidence and reducing anxiety.

A number of theories have been put forth over the years to explain the effectiveness of imagery, including psychoneuromuscular theory (Jacobson, 1934), symbolic rehearsal theory (Sackett, 1934), and bioinformational theory (Lang, 1979). Some empirical support has been found for each theory, although more research is necessary to draw more definitive conclusions regarding the underlying mechanisms contributing to the positive effects found for imaginal rehearsal.

Recently, imagery research has focused on precompetition interventions, with the emphasis on improving athletic performance. Although in general, research has indicated the potential beneficial effects of imaginal rehearsal on improving performance, several mediating variables seem to be critical for determining imagery effectiveness. Specifically, imagery effectiveness is enhanced when images are more controllable and vivid, individuals have good imagery ability, the images are positive (as opposed to negative), and the imagery uses multiple senses (e.g., visual, kinesthetic, auditory, olfactory). Research has also indicated that other variables such as imagery perspective (internal versus external) and relaxation prior to imagery are helpful, although not critical, for enhancing imagery effectiveness.

Arousal Regulation

Sport psychologists have long been interested in the relationship between arousal and performance. Although numerous recent theories and approaches such as the zone of optimal functioning hypothesis, multidimensional anxiety theory, catastrophe theory, and reversal theory provide different explanations for the relationship between arousal and performance, there is general agreement that performers must find the appropriate mixture of arousal-related states that lead to best performance. Moreover, if athletes are not in this ideal state, then strategies must be employed to regulate arousal (i.e., arousal needs to be either increased or decreased).

The focus of attention in the sport psychology literature has been on identifying techniques (e.g., biofeedback, mental/physical relaxation, cognitive-behavioral interventions, mental preparation routines) to reduce arousal with the goal of enhancing performance. Biofeedback, which involves the use of instrumentation that provides individuals with information regarding their physiological states, has been found to improve either arousal control or performance in 83% of the 42 studies reviewed by Zaichkowsky and Fuchs (1988). Relaxation-based interventions such as the relaxation response, progressive relaxation, and autogenic training have been the most commonly employed techniques to teach athletes how to relax when encountering a stressful situation. In a review of the effectiveness of these techniques, Gould and Udry (1994) state that although there appears to be some performance enhancement resulting from relaxation-based training, most of the positive performance results were correlational as opposed to causal in nature. More research is necessary to establish causal links between relaxation procedures and enhanced performance.

In contrast to relaxation-based interventions that focus primarily on lowering physiological arousal, cognitive-behavioral interventions emphasize cognitive restructuring techniques combined with physical relaxation and imagery in an effort to assist an athlete in lowering arousal and enhancing performance. Special attention is placed on replacing negative self-statements and images with positive affirmations and images of desirable performance. The three most popular programs used in the sport domain include stress inoculation training (SIT), stress management training (SMT), and visuomotor behavior rehearsal (VMBR). Comprehensive reviews and meta-analysis of the effectiveness of cognitive behavioral interventions have clearly shown that these interventions can be effective in helping athletes lower arousal-related states. Unfortunately, many studies have not examined performance as a dependent variable, so conclusions need to be viewed cautiously.

Mental Preparation Routines

Studies employing in-depth interviews with Olympic athletes (e.g., Gould, Eklund, & Jackson, 1992; Orlick & Partington, 1988) have identified the development and consistent adherence to preperformance mental preparation routines (systematic, routinized patterns of physical actions and preplanned sequences of thoughts and arousal-related cues) as being a critical factor discriminating between more versus less successful athletes. It has been suggested that these routines facilitate performance by helping athletes divert their attention from task-irrelevant to task-relevant thoughts and by assisting them in achieving optimal arousal levels. Although controlled empirical studies of the use of these techniques are limited, initial evidence is promising. For example, in a series of studies, Crews (1993) has demonstrated that individuals can be taught to develop routines and that these routines can help enhance their performance.

Arousal Energizing Strategies

Unfortunately, little original research has been conducted on the efficacy of arousal energizing strategies in sport. This probably results from the fact that athletes more often report difficulties from being overaroused prior to and during competition rather than being underaroused. However, there are certainly times when athletes must become more energized and aroused if they are to achieve their optimal level of arousal.

There has been some research that has focused on identifying and describing psyching-up (mental preparation) strategies used by athletes and then examining whether these techniques actually enhance performance. For example, Weinberg, Gould, and Jackson (Gould, Weinberg & Jackson, 1980; Weinberg, Gould, & Jackson, 1980) found that preparatory arousal techniques (e.g., getting mad, charged up, or pumped up) facilitated performance significantly more than other mental preparation strategies, although these effects were found only on strength tasks and not on tasks requiring balance, precision, and fine-motor coordination. This finding is consistent with the notion that optimal arousal levels are task specific and that high levels of arousal seem most appropriate for strength tasks. In addition, although there is not a great deal of empirical evidence regarding the use of specific techniques for increasing arousal and subsequent performance, a number of applied sport psychologists working with athletes have recommended the following arousal-inducing techniques: (a) increase breathing rate, (b) act energized, (c) use mood words/positive statements, (d) listen to upbeat music, and (e) use energizing imagery.

Goal Setting

Goal setting and its effects on productivity and performance has been one of the most studied areas within industrial/organizational psychology since the seminal work of Edwin Locke in the 1960s. In fact, a review of the goal setting literature in organizational settings produced over 400 studies and found overwhelming consistent support (90%) for the notion that specific, difficult goals produce significantly greater performance than do-your-best goals, easy goals, or no goals (Locke & Latham, 1990). The research focusing on goal setting and its effect on performance in sport and exercise settings started in earnest in the middle 1980s with the publication of Locke and Latham's article (1985) on the application of goal setting to sports. Locke and Latham suggested that goal setting could work even better in sports than in business because the measurement of an individual's performance is typically more objective in sport than in organizational settings.

Of approximately 40 studies investigating the effect of goal setting in sport and exercise settings, 70% showed significant positive effects on performance. Most of the studies conducted in sport and exercise settings have emphasized the areas of goal difficulty, goal specificity, and goal proximity, which is consistent with the industrial psychology focus. In addition, a meta-analysis (Kyllo & Landers, 1995) found that overall, setting goals improved performance by 0.34 of a standard deviation and that moderately difficult, absolute, and combined short- and long-term goals were associated with the greatest effects.

Although these results suggest a positive relationship between goal setting and performance, they are not as impressive as the organizational psychology findings. Researchers (Burton, 1993; Weinberg, 1994) have suggested the reason for this resides in the different methodologies employed in sport and exercise settings along with moderator variables that mediate the goal setting–performance relationship. Some of these methodological and design considerations include spontaneous goal setting in control groups, subject motivation and commitment, task characteristics, and competition among subjects. In addition, athletes and exercise participants simply differ in their motivations and perform under different task conditions than do subjects in the organizational psychology studies. Furthermore, Kyllo and Landers (1995) suggest that low statistical power might be another explanation for why the goal setting studies conducted in sport and exerciser settings have not been as overwhelmingly positive in enhancing performance as those conducted in organizational settings.

In an extension of previous goal setting research, some qualitative and quantitative research (Weinberg, Burton, Yukelson, & Weigand, 1993; Weinberg, Burke, & Jackson, 1997) has assessed coaches' and athletes' perceptions of the frequency, effectiveness, and importance of different goals to enhance performance. Descriptive results revealed that virtually all athletes practiced some type of goal setting to enhance performance, and they found their goals to be moderately to highly effective. Athletes also reported that improving overall performance, winning, and fun-affiliation were the three most important goals, but qualitative analysis revealed that athletes felt that these were interdependent, as opposed to independent (i.e., if we play well we are likely to win, and winning is fun). In addition, athletes preferred moderately difficult goals over difficult and moderate goals and felt that the main purpose of setting goals was to provide direction and to help keep focused. Few coach-athlete differences were found, although coaches tended to use a wide variety of goal setting strategies more often than athletes and found them more effective.

Based on the research conducted in sport and exercise settings, a number of guidelines have been suggested by researchers (Weinberg & Gould, 1999; Weinberg, 1996) to facilitate the effectiveness of goal setting. These included the following: (a) set specific, measurable goals, (b) set realistic but challenging goals, (c) set both short-term and long-term goals, (d) reevaluate goals periodically, (e) set goals for practice and competition, (f) write goals down and make them public, (g) develop goal-achievement strategies, (h) set performance (self-improvement) goals in addition to outcome (winning) goals, (i) set individual and team goals (but individual goals should not conflict with team goals), and (j) provide for goal evaluation.

Team/Group Cohesion

The interventions just discussed have focused on the use of various psychological skills to enhance individual performance. However, most sport performance involves groups of individuals working together as a cohesive unit. In essence, the individual ability of team members may not be as important as their ability to work together toward common goals while understanding their individual roles within the team concept. This point is highlighted by the following quote from Michael Jordan, the basketball player formerly of the Chicago Bulls:

> Naturally there are going to be some ups and downs, particularly if you have individuals trying to achieve at a high level. But when we stepped in between the lines, we knew what we were capable of doing. When a pressure situation presented itself, we were plugged into one another as a cohesive unit. That's why we were able to beat more talented teams. (1994, p. 23)

This same perception has been recognized for years by practitioners and researchers. In fact, Mullen and Cooper (1994) conducted a meta-analysis that showed that the effect of cohesion on performance is stronger among real groups than on artificial groups and is due primarily to commitment to the task rather than interpersonal attraction or group pride. In addition, in a review of 30 studies, Widmeyer, Carron, and Brawley (1993) found that 83% reported a positive relationship between cohesion and performance, with higher team cohesiveness associated with greater team success.

However, the relationship between cohesion and performance has been shown to be mediated by several variables, including the measurement of cohesion, task characteristics, and direction of causality (see Widmeyer, Carron, & Brawley, 1993, for a review). First, more positive results between cohesion and performance are typically found when assessing task cohesion (common goals) than when assessing social cohesion (friendship, interpersonal attraction). Second, positive cohesion-performance relationships are reported most often for team sports that require extensive interaction, coordination, and cooperation among team members such as basketball, hockey, soccer, and volleyball. Conversely, little or no relationships have been found for tasks that are predominantly coactive, requiring independent performance with little integration and interaction, such as riflery, archery, and bowling. Third, regarding the direction of causality, performance seems to have a stronger effect on cohesion than does cohesion on performance. In fact, the relationship appears to be circular, with performance apparently affecting later cohesion and then changes in cohesion affecting subsequent performance.

However, in most of these studies, no intervention attempting to manipulate cohesion was performed. Rather, cohesion was simply measured at different points in time along with performance. Team-building interventions have been studied in both the sport and exercise settings (see Carron, Spink, & Prapavessis, 1997, for a review). Strategies to build cohesion were somewhat different for sport versus exercise groups, but they included such areas as role clarity and acceptance, leadership, distinctiveness, group goals and objectives, cooperation, interactions and communication, group norms, and individual sacrifices for the group. Results for the exercise groups revealed that the classes undergoing the cohesion intervention showed higher levels of cohesion and significantly fewer dropouts and late arrivals than the classes not exposed to team building. In addition, the team building program offset the negative impact that increased class size had on the perceptions of cohesiveness, with large classes having the same level of cohesion as smaller classes. Since this is a relatively new area, more interventions that attempt to build group cohesion are needed in both sport and exercise settings before more definitive conclusions can be reached.

[*See also* Intervention.]

Bibliography

Burton, D. (1993). Goal setting in sport. In R. N. Singer, M. Murphey, & L. K. Tennant (Eds.), *Handbook of research in sport psychology* (pp. 467–491). New York: Macmillan.

Carron, A., Spink, K., & Prapavessis, H. (1997). Team building and cohesiveness in sport and exercise settings: Use of indirect interactions. *Journal of Applied Sport Psychology, 9*, 61–72.

Crews, D. (1993). Self-regulation strategies in sport and exercise. In R. N. Singer, M. Murphy, & L. K. Tennent (Eds.), *Handbook of research in sport psychology* (pp. 557–568). New York: Macmillan.

Dishman, R. (1983). Identity crisis in North American sport psychology: Academics in professional issues. *Journal of Sport Psychology, 5*, 123–134.

Feltz, D. L., & Landers, D. M. (1983). The effects of mental practice on motor skill learning and performance: A meta-analysis. *Journal of Sport Psychology, 5*, 25–57.

Gould, D. (1988). ABC Nightline news telecast focus on sport psychology (editorial). *Sport Psychologist, 2*, 95–96.

Gould, D., Eklund, R. C., & Jackson, S. A. (1992). U.S. Olympic wrestling excellence: I. Mental preparation, precompetitive cognition, and affect. *Sport Psychologist, 6*, 358–382.

Gould, D., & Udry, E. (1994). Psychological skills for enhancing performance: Arousal regulation strategies. *Medicine and Science in Sport and Exercise, 26*, 478–485.

Gould, D. R., Weinberg, R. S., & Jackson, A. (1980). Mental preparation strategies, cognitions and strength performance. *Journal of Sport Psychology, 2*, 329–339.

Greenspan, M. J., & Feltz, D. L. (1989). Psychological interventions with athletes in competitive situations: A review. *Sport Psychologist, 3*, 219–236.

Hall, C., Schmidt, D., Durand, M. C., & Buckolz, E. (1989). Imagery and motor skills requisition. In A. E. Sheskh and E. R. Korn (Eds.), *Imagery in sports and physical performance* (pp. 121–134). Amityville, NY: Baywood.

Jacobson, E. (1934). Electrophysiology of mental activities. *American Journal of Psychology, 11,* 677–694.

Jordan, M. (1994). *I can't accept not trying.* New York: HarperCollins.

Kyllo, L. B., & Landers, D. M. (1995). Goal setting in sport and exercise: A research synthesis to resolve the controversy. *Journal of Sport and Exercise Psychology, 17,* 117–137.

Lang, P. J. (1979). A bio-informational theory of emotional imagery. *Psychophysiology, 17,* 495–512.

Locke, E. A., & Latham, G. P. (1985). The application of goal setting to sports. *Journal of Sport Psychology, 7,* 205–222.

Locke, E. A., & Latham, G. P. (1990). *A theory of goal setting and task performance.* Englewood Cliffs, NJ: Prentice Hall.

Mullen, B., & Cooper, C. (1994). The relation between group cohesiveness and performance: An integration. *Psychological Bulletin, 115,* 210–227.

Murphy, S. N. (1994). Imagery intervention in sport. *Medicine and Science in Sport and Exercise, 26,* 486–494.

Orlick, T., & Partington, J. (1988). Mental links to excellence. *Sport Psychologist, 2,* 105–130.

Sackett, R. S. (1934). The influence of symbolic rehearsal upon the retention of a maze habit. *Journal of General Psychology, 10,* 375–395.

Suinn, R. M. (1972). Behavior rehearsal training for ski racers. *Behavior Therapy, 3,* 519–520.

Vealey, R. (1994). Current status and prominent issues in sport psyhchology intervention. *Medicine and Science in Sport Exercise, 26,* 495–502.

Weinberg, R., Burton, D., Yukelson, D., & Weigand, D. (1993). Goal setting in competitive sport: An exploratory investigation of practices of collegiate athletice. *Sport Psychologist, 7,* 275–289.

Weinberg, R. S. (1994). Goal setting in sport and exercise: A review and critique. *Medicine and Science in Sports and Exercise, 26,* 459–477.

Weinberg, R. S. (1995). Goal setting in sport and exercise: Research to practice. In J. Van Raalte & B. W. Brewer (Eds.), *Exploring sort and exercise psychology* (pp. 3–24). Washington DC: American Psychological Association.

Weinberg, R. S., Burke, K. L., & Jackson, A. (1997). Coaches' and players' perception of goal setting in junior tennis: An exploratory investigation. *Sport Psychologist, 11,* 426–439.

Weinberg, R. S., & Comar, W. (1994). The effectiveness of psychological interventions in competitive sport. *Sports Medicine, 18,* 406–418.

Weinberg, R. S., & Gould, D. (1999). *Foundation of sport and exercise psychology* (2nd ed.). Champaign, IL: Human Kinetics.

Weinberg, R. S., Gould, D., & Jackson, A. (1980). Cognition and motor performance: Effect of psyching-up strategies on three motor tasks. *Cognitive Therapy and Research, 4,* 239–245.

Widmeyer, W. N., Carron, A. V., & Brawley, L. R. (1993). Group cohesion in sport and exercise. In R. N. Singer, M. Murphy, & K. Tennant (Eds.), *Handbook of research on sport psychology* (pp. 672–692). New York: Macmillan.

Zaichkowsky, L., & Fuchs, C. (1988). Biofeedback applications in exercise and athletic performance. *Exercise and Sport Science Review, 16,* 381–421.

Robert S. Weinberg

SPORT PSYCHOLOGY. [*This entry comprises four articles:* History of the Field; Research; Assessment; *and* Social Psychology Perspectives. *The first article provides an overview of the broad history of the field from its inception to the present. The second article discusses the major research designs, methodologies, trends, and theories in the field. The third article examines the assessment methods used in the field. The fourth article surveys the social psychological factors in sport psychology influencing the athlete, athletic performance, and the audience. For independent entries related to sport psychology, see* Exercise and Physical Activity; Rehabilitation Psychology; *and* Stress, *article on* Impact on Health.]

History of the Field

Sport psychology is a field of study in which the principles of psychology are applied in a sports and/or exercise setting. These principles are often applied to enhance performance. The sport psychologist, however, is interested in more than performance enhancement and views sport and exercise as a vehicle for human enrichment.

Sport psychology as a distinct field of study is extremely young and evolving. Perhaps the first clear historical example of research being conducted in the area of sport psychology was reported by Norman Triplett in 1897. Drawing on field observations and secondary data, Triplett analyzed the performance of cyclists under conditions of social facilitation. He concluded from this milestone research that the presence of other competitors was capable of facilitating better cycling performance (Davis, Huss, & Becker, 1995).

While Triplett provided an example of one of the earliest recorded sport psychology research investigations, he was not the first person to systematically carry out sport psychology research over an extended period of time. This distinction is attributed to Coleman Roberts Griffith (1930), often referred to as the father of sport psychology in North America (Gould & Pick, 1995). Griffith is credited with establishing the first sport psychology laboratory at the University of Illinois in 1925. Over an extended period of time, Griffith studied the nature of psychomotor skills, motor learning, and the relationship between personality variables and physical performance. Griffith, a psychologist, was selected by George Huff, head of the department of physical education at the University of Illinois, to develop this new laboratory. From Huff's vision, Griffith developed a laboratory devoted to solving psychological and physiological problems associated with sport and athletic performance. Thus, the historical trend for the next 60 years was established in this early event. Physical education, a cross-disciplinary entity, would provide the academic home for the application of psychology to sport and athletics.

While Coleman Griffith was credited with the development of the first sport psychology research laboratory, others followed his lead. Following the Second World War, such notables as Franklin M. Henry at the University of California, John Lawther at Pennsylvania State University, and Arthur Slater-Hammel at Indiana University pioneered graduate level courses and developed research laboratories of their own.

Dan Landers (1995) refers to the period of time from 1950 to 1980 as the formative years for sport psychology. During this time, sport psychology began to emerge as a discipline somewhat distinct from exercise physiology and motor learning. This is especially true of applied sport psychology; prior to its emergence, most research related to sport psychology was conducted within a laboratory setting and was referred to as motor learning research. During the formative years, a number of important research initiatives and textbooks were published. These early sporadic initiatives paved the way for the emergence of sport psychology as an academic subdiscipline within physical education and psychology. Some of the early textbooks included *Psychology of Coaching* by John D. Lawther (1951), *Problem Athletes and How to Handle Them* by Bruce Ogilvie and Tom Tutko (1966), *Motor Learning and Human Performance* by Robert Singer (1968), *Psychology of Motor Learning* by Joseph B. Oxendine (1968), *Psychology and the Superior Athlete* by Miroslaw Vanek and Bryant Cratty (1970), *Social Psychology and Physical Activity* by Rainer Martens (1975), and *Social Psychology of Sport* by Albert Carron (1980).

Important sport psychology research initiatives emerged during the formative years. Some of these initiatives were Warren Johnson's work with hypnosis and athletic performance (1960s), the development and testing of anxiety inventories by Rainer Martens (1970s and 1980s), Dan Landers and Rainer Martens's research with Zajonc's model of social facilitation (1970s), Albert Carron and P. Chelladurai's work with sport leadership and team cohesion (1970s and 1980s), Ronald Smith and Frank Smoll's research with coaching behaviors of youth sport coaches (1970s and 1980s), and Bill Morgan's work with the "iceberg profile" of the mentally healthy athlete (1970s and 1980s).

Development of Professional Organizations

A number of professional sport psychology organizations have evolved since the 1960s. In 1965, the International Society of Sport Psychology (ISSP) was formed. Organized in Rome, the purpose of ISSP is to promote and disseminate information about the practice of sport psychology throughout the world. In North America, a small group of sport psychologists from Canada and the United States met in Dallas, Texas, to discuss the feasibility of forming a professional organization distinct from the American Association of Health, Physical Education, and Recreation (AAHPER). The efforts of this small group came to fruition in 1966 when it was recognized by ISSP. The new organization, called the North American Society for the Psychology of Sport and Physical Activity (NASPSPA), held its first annual meeting prior to the 1967 AAHPER National Convention in Las Vegas. Since that time, NASPSPA has evolved into an influential academic society focusing on sport psychology in the broadest sense. It provided a forum for researchers in the areas of sport psychology, sport sociology, motor learning, motor control, and motor development to meet and exchange ideas and research. Shortly after the emergence of NASPSPA in the United States, another significant professional organization came into existence in Canada in 1969, the Canadian Society for Psychomotor Learning and Sport Psychology (CSPLSP). Originally organized under the auspices of the Canadian Association for Health, Physical Education, and Recreation (CAHPER), CSPLSP became an independent society in 1977. Somewhat concurrent with the emergence of the Canadian association, the Sports Psychology Academy (SPA) emerged in the United States as one of six academies within the National Association for Sport and Physical Education (NASPE)—an association within AAHPERD. In order to better address the interests and needs of sport psychologists interested in applying the principles of psychology to sport and exercise, the Association for the Advancement of Applied Sport Psychology (AAASP) was formed in the fall of 1985 (Silva, 1989). The AAASP has emerged in the 1990s as the dominant association for the advancement of applied sport psychology, as well as for research in North America and perhaps in the world.

In addition to these specialized organizations, two significant North America–based associations created interest areas dedicated to sport psychology within their organizations. These are the American Psychological Association (APA), with its Division 47 (formed in 1968), and the American College of Sports Medicine (ACSM). Paralleling the emergence of professional sport

SPORT PSYCHOLOGY: History of the Field. Table 1. Journals completely or partially dedicated to sport and exercise psychology

Journal Name	Abbreviation	Affiliation
International Journal of Sport Psychology	IJSP	ISSP
Journal of Applied Sport Psychology	JASP	AAASP
Journal of Sport Behavior	JSB	None
Journal of Sport & Exercise Psychology	JS&EP	NASPSPA
Medicine and Science in Sports and Exercise	MSSE	ACSM
Research Quarterly for Exercise and Sport	RQES	AAHPERD
Sport Psychologist	TSP	ISSP*

*Not an official affiliation.

psychology organizations are journals that provide an outlet and forum for research generated by members of these organizations. Research journals that are completely or partially dedicated to the advancement and/or application of knowledge in sport and exercise psychology are listed in Table 1.

The Issue of Certification

Historically, sport psychology emerged as a discipline from the broad field of physical education. A significant interest in the discipline has developed, however, among individuals prepared in psychology and counseling. This has raised the issue among practicing sport psychologists as to who are qualified to call themselves sport psychologists and to provide services to athletes. Some have argued that only licensed psychologists should be allowed to call themselves sport psychologists and have suggested that the appropriate title for a non-licensed sport psychologist would be mental training consultant. Most agree, however, that even licensed psychologists should have significant academic training in the exercise and sport sciences before practicing applied sport psychology. A partial solution to the issue of professionalization of sport psychology was proposed by the United States Olympic Committee (USOC) in 1983 and 1986. The USOC developed the Sport Psychology Registry to identify three categories in which a person could demonstrate competence, corresponding to three types of sport psychologists: the clinical/counseling sport psychologist, the educational sport psychologist, and the research sport psychologist. The purpose of the Sport Psychology Registry was to identify individuals in the area of sport psychology who could work with specific national teams within the Olympic movement. The registry was not meant to be a licensing or authorizing committee.

As described by USOC, the clinical/counseling sport psychologist is a licensed psychologist who has experience and training in the exercise and sport sciences, with a deep interest and understanding of the athletic experience. Consistent with his or her academic training, the clinical/counseling psychologist is prepared to deal with emotional and personality disorder problems that may affect some athletes. The educational sport psychologist is not a licensed psychologist and is trained to use the medium of education to teach correct principles of sport psychology to athletes and coaches. In general, the mission of the educational sport psychologist is to help athletes develop psychological skills necessary for performance enhancement. Finally, the research sport psychologist provides the academic knowledge base that allows the applied sport psychologist to function. In order to enjoy professional credibility, the practices of the applied sport psychologist must be based on a credible scientific body of knowledge.

In addition to the USOC's clarifying statements, AAASP took the issue a step further and adopted a certification document outlining the requirements an individual must meet to be given the title of Certified Consultant, Association for the Advancement of Applied Sport Psychology. Included in these are requirements that the applicant hold an earned doctorate in an area related to sport psychology (e.g., counseling/clinical psychology, sport science, or physical education). In addition, numerous specific courses and experiences are identified. While the certification process adopted by AAASP may not be the final one, it is a good beginning, since it recognizes that an individual needs specialized training in psychology and physical education (sport and exercise science) to be certified as a practicing sport psychologist.

Ethics in Sport Psychology

The practice of sport psychology, whether by a coach or by a licensed psychologist, involves two diverse components. The first involves teaching; the second is clinical in nature. For example, the sport psychologist uses teaching principles to help an athlete learn how to use imagery and/or relaxation techniques effectively. A well-trained and informed coach or teacher should be able to provide such service. However, when the sport psychologist is called on to provide such services as crisis counseling, psychotherapy, or psychological testing, it is important that person be specifically trained and licensed.

To help the sport psychologist deal effectively with the issue of ethics in the delivery of sport psychology services, NASPSPA issued its Ethical Standards for Provision of Services by NASPSPA Members in 1982. These standards were summarized in a set of nine principles. While the ethical standards published by NASPSPA served a useful purpose, they have become woefully inadequate. In 1982, there were very few practicing sport psychologists; this situation changed dramatically in the 1990s. To address the obvious need for a detailed set of ethical principles and a code of conduct to govern the practices of sport psychology consultants, AAASP generally adopted the published guidelines of the American Psychological Association (APA) to govern the behavior of the AAASP certified consultant.

Bibliography

American Psychological Association. (1992). Ethical principles of psychologists and code of conduct. *American Psychologist, 47,* 1597–1611.

Carron, A. (1980). *Social psychology of sport.* Ithaca, NY: Mouvement Publications.

Davis, S. F., Huss, M. T., & Becker, A. H. (1995). Norman Triplett and the dawning of sport psychology. *Sport Psychologist, 9,* 366–375.

Gould, D., & Pick, S. (1995). Sport psychology: The Griffith era. *Sport Psychologist, 9,* 391–405.

Griffith, C. R. (1930). A laboratory for research in athletics. *Research Quarterly, 1,* 34–41.

Landers, D. M. (1995). Sport psychology: The formative years, 1950–1980. *Sport Psychologist, 9,* 406–417.

Lawther, J. D. (1951). *Psychology of coaching.* Englewood Cliffs, NJ: Prentice Hall.

Martens, R. (1975). *Social psychology and physical activity.* New York: Harper & Row.

Ogilvie, B. C., & Tutko, T. A. (1966). *Problem athletes and how to handle them.* London: Pelham Books.

Oxendine, J. B. (1968). *Psychology of motor learning.* New York: Appleton-Century-Crofts.

Silva, J. M., III (1989). The evolution of AAASP and JASP. *Journal of Applied Sport Psychology, 1,* 1–3.

Singer, R. N. (1989). Applied sport psychology in the United States. *Journal of Applied Sport Psychology, 1,* 61–80.

Singer, R. N. (1968). *Motor learning and human performance.* London: Macmillan.

Taylor, J. (1994). Examining the boundaries of sport science and psychology trained practitioners in applied sport psychology: Title usage and area of competence. *Sport Psychologist, 6,* 185–195. In this work, Taylor takes a position on who may call themselves sport psychologists and what he believes the boundaries should be.

Triplett, N. (1897). The dynamogenic factors in pacemaking and competition. *American Journal of Psychology, 9,* 507–533.

United States Olympic Committee. (1983). U.S. Olympic Committee establishes guidelines for sport psychology services. *Journal of Sport Psychology, 5,* 4–7. This is an important article in terms of differentiating among the different kinds of sport psychologists and what each may do.

Vanek, M., & Cratty, B. J. (1970). *Psychology and the superior athlete.* London: Macmillan.

Wiggins, D. K. (1984). The history of sport psychology in North America. In J. M. Silva & R. S. Weinberg (Eds.), *Psychological foundations of sport* (pp. 9–22). Champaign, IL: Human Kinetics. From the perspective of a sport historian, Wiggins provides one of the first renditions of the development of sport psychology in North America.

Richard H. Cox

Research

Describing and defining research and theory in sport and exercise psychology is a difficult task because there are so many different perspectives on the field. One view is that the field consists of sport, exercise, rehabilitation, and health psychology (Rejesky & Brawley, 1988). Another view (Smith, 1989) considers sport psychology a subdiscipline within the field of psychology and thus defined as an applied psychology. Simply stated, sport and exercise psychology is the scientific study of people and their behavior in sport and exercise contexts. Most researchers in sport and exercise psychology focus on the following objectives: (a) investigating how psychological factors affect an individual's physical performance and participation and (b) understanding how participation in sport and exercise environments affects a person's psychological development, health, and well-being. Typical questions studied under these two approaches might include the following: (a) Does self-confidence influence a child's ability to learn to swim? (b) Does running reduce anxiety and depression? (c) Does imagery training facilitate the recovery process in injured athletes and exercisers? Although the focus of early research in the field was on sport and athletic performance, interest has grown in psychological factors related to exercise and physical activity.

Approaches to Sport and Exercise Psychology

As with any discipline, researchers in sport and exercise psychology approach the study of different topics from somewhat different perspectives. In addition, different researchers adopt different orientations to similar areas of study. Some of the main orientations and approaches to the study of sport and exercise psychology are as follows.

Researchers taking a behavioral orientation view the primary determinants of an athlete's or exerciser's behavior as coming from the environment, with relatively little emphasis on thoughts, personality, and perceptions. Instead, the focus is on how environmental factors such as reinforcement and punishment influence behavior. In typical research studies using the behavioral approach, the environment is systematically manipulated to produce behavior change. For example, giving baseball players money for higher batting averages attempts to change performance through a behavioral manipulation.

Studies taking a psychophysiological approach to sport and exercise typically examine the physiological processes of the brain and their influences on physical activity and performance. Measures such as heart rate, brain wave activity, respiration rate, and muscle action potentials are taken, and relationships between these psychophysiological measures and sport and exercise behavior are drawn. For example, Landers (1985) used biofeedback to train elite marksmen to fire between heart beats to improve accuracy, since even minute movement shifts (such as a beating heart) can influence shooting accuracy.

In recent years, probably the most popular approach to examining behavior in sport and exercise contexts is an interactional one. This approach assumes that behavior is determined by an interaction between the environment and a person's cognitions (thoughts) in that environment. This interactional perspective between individuals and the environment in which they are placed appears to be the dominant one in sport and exercise psychology. In essence, how individuals appraise and interpret the environment is central in determining their behaviors. For example, studies (e.g., Gould, Eklund, & Jackson, 1992) have assessed the relationship between Olympic athletes' cognitions prior to performance and actual performance outcome (i.e., winning/ losing). Results indicated that before their best matches, athletes following specific mental preparation plans and routines were highly confident, totally focused, and optimally aroused. However, before their worst matches athletes experienced many negative and task-irrelevant thoughts, were not confident, had inappropriate arousal states, and deviated from mental plans. Thus, linkages between athletes' thoughts and behaviors were clearly evidenced.

Trends in Content

Sport and exercise psychology has evolved greatly in the past 30 years in terms of the different topics that are seen as central to the field. When the field started to grow in the 1960s, the study of personality dominated the literature. This is not surprising since the dominant paradigm at that time within psychology was the trait approach, and trends in sport and exercise

psychology have tended to parallel those in general psychology. The trait approach argues that an individual's behavior is consistent across situations due to personality traits that are relatively stable and enduring (this is opposed to the situational approach, which argues that behavior is determined predominantly by the situation in which people are functioning). For example, making comparisons and predicting behavior based on personality between team and individual sport athletes, elite and less elite performers, and male and female athletes was typical of the trait approach taken at that time.

The publication of Zajonc's classic article (1965) provided a reconceptualization of the social facilitation (effect of spectators on performance) literature using a drive theory approach. This provided an impetus to study the effect of spectators on sport performance as well as the arousal-performance relationship (since drive theory is an explanation for how arousal affects performance), which was a focus of research in the late 1960s and 1970s. For example, many studies using a social facilitation framework were conducted focusing on the perceived home court advantage. In essence social facilitation theory predicts that well-learned skills are facilitated by increases in arousal that occur when playing in front of a supportive crowd, and this in turn enhances performance. In addition, in the 1960s and 1970s, many studies investigated the arousal-performance relationship using the Yerkes-Dodson theory, which predicts an inverted-U relationship between arousal and performance, so that there is an optimal level of arousal where performance is maximized and performance deteriorates when arousal is too low or too high. Thus, research from 1965 to 1975 was characterized by a social analysis approach, selecting one theory at a time from mainstream psychology and testing the theory in the area of sport and motor performance. In addition to social facilitation and the arousal-performance relationship, such topics as social reinforcement, modeling, and achievement motivation were studied during this period. These theories and models had researchers asking questions such as "How do high and low achievers differ in their motivation in achievement situations?" "Is providing rewards more conducive to enhancing performance than using punishment?" and "What are the factors that maximize the effectiveness of modeling sport performance?"

In the 1980s and 1990s, researchers began to focus more on an interactional approach in trying to understand behavior in sport and exercise settings. Biddle (1997) conducted a review and content analysis (using major sport and exercise psychology journals—over 500 articles) detailing trends in sport and exercise psychology topics; the topics that received the most attention fall into these general categories: (a) motivation,

(b) anxiety, (c) self-efficacy/confidence, (d) exercise and mental health, and (e) group dynamics.

Motivational themes of theoretical significance included intrinsic motivation, motivational orientations (e.g., ego- versus task-orientation), motivational climate, attribution theory, and measurement of motivation (e.g., self-motivation, enjoyment), whereas more applied research on motivation focused on topics such as participation-dropout motives, motive for exercise participation-adherence, and coach-athlete relationships. In addition, motivation has been studied in the context of the anxiety-performance relationship. Specifically, research on competitive anxiety has made a great many theoretical advances from the early approaches of drive theory and the inverted-U hypothesis (which are no longer seen as viable explanations for the anxiety-performance relationship) to more recent approaches such as individual zones of optimal functioning, multidimensional anxiety theory, catastrophe theory, and reversal theory. Anxiety has also been studied in the exercise psychology literature, with several meta-analyses (e.g., Long & van Stavel, 1995) finding that aerobic exercise moderately reduces both state and trait anxiety. Further research began to focus on coping strategies as a means of effectively dealing with high levels of stress and anxiety.

The potential of imagery (also termed mental rehearsal and mental practice) to enhance performance, has been consistently investigated. A number of variables that affect imagery effectiveness have been studied, including skill level, type of task, cognitive style, imagery ability, and type of imagery (internal versus external). Different theories of imagery have been proposed in the past, such as psychoneuromuscular theory and symbolic learning theory, and newer approaches, including bioinformational theory (Lang, 1979) and triple code theory (Ahsen, 1984) have been advanced. Finally, research has focused on the potential positive effects of imagery on psychological states, for example, reducing anxiety, improving confidence, and redirecting anger, as well as on the use of imagery in rehabilitation from injury.

The interest in studying self-efficacy and self-confidence in sport and exercise stemmed from Bandura's seminal paper (1977), in which he developed his theory of self-efficacy. Specific topics addressed within the self-efficacy/confidence framework include gender differences, competitive orientation, sources of self-confidence, movement confidence, cognitive strategies, and high-risk sports. The role of expectations has also been studied in relation to coach-athlete and teacher-student relationships. Specifically, it has been demonstrated that the expectations teachers and coaches have of their athletes and students can have a profound effect on the coaches' behavior and subsequently on the

athletes' responses (sometimes called the Pygmalion effect). Finally, self-efficacy has been recently studied in the exercise psychology literature in relation to its impact on adherence to physical activity and understanding of exercise behavior (McAuley, 1992).

The relationships between physical activity and mental health gained increasing attention in the 1990s. This health orientation (as opposed to an earlier performance orientation) has potential application to a wide array of individuals across all ages. Along these lines, Biddle's content analysis (1997) revealed that exercise and mental health studies in the literature have addressed a wide range of topics. For example, meta-analyses have been reported on the effects of exercise on anxiety, depression, self-concept and self-esteem, cognitive functioning, stress reactivity, personality and adjustment, and mood. In general, despite some methodological problems, the literature is fairly clear in showing the potential for physical activity to make a positive impact on psychological health.

In the area of group dynamics, studies have focused on group motivation and group cohesion. Research on group motivation has included such topics as social loafing, collective efficacy, group size, and member characteristics; research on group cohesion has focused on the cohesion-performance relationship in sport and exercise, exercise adherence, group disruption, and measurement issues. Significant attention to and advances in the measurement of group cohesion have occurred with specific reference to task and social cohesion and the view of cohesion as a multidimensional construct. Using this multidimensional approach, research has found that group cohesion is related to lower state anxiety, higher adherence to exercise, and superior team performance.

Trends in Sport and Exercise Psychology Methodologies

As sport psychology started to expand in the 1960s and 1970s, the research efforts were dominated by empiricism with a focus on logical positivism. Specifically, most research studies were laboratory based, emphasizing strict controls of independent and dependent variables (high internal validity) and testing the dominant psychological theories noted earlier. However, Martens (1979), in his a critique of the reliance on laboratory studies, argued that in order to build sport-specific theories and generate data useful for practitioners, researchers also needed to study the behavior of athletes and coaches in authentic settings. This article helped provide a springboard for the move of research from the laboratory to the field in the 1980s, with researchers beginning to focus on conducting field studies and field experiments in actual competitive environments. Of course, no one method is best; laboratory and field-based studies offer different but equally valuable information to the field of sport and exercise psychology.

Biddle's review of research designs in the sport and exercise psychology literature (1997) found that the survey method was the most often used research design, followed by experimental and quasi-experimental methods, qualitative, and archival/historical approaches. However, the journals surveyed were mostly traditional in nature; other mainstream sport and exercise psychology outlets (e.g., *the Sport Psychologist* and the *Journal of Applied Sport Psychology*) show a trend toward more qualitative methodologies and case-study approaches. For example, a number of researchers have begun to use in-depth interviews to study such topics as peak performance (flow), sources of stress, imagery, mental preparation and coping strategies, and goal setting. An inductive content analysis approach is typically taken, with researchers attempting to use the content of the interviews to develop themes that represent consistent trends in the data. The richness of this type of approach, combined with traditional quantitative methodologies, appears to offer researchers a more comprehensive understanding of behavior in sport and exercise psychology settings. Another emergent methodology is the case-study approach, which has been typically employed in the investigation of the effectiveness of psychological skills training. Specifically, introduction of a psychological skills training program that might include components such as relaxation, self-talk, attentional control, goal-setting, or imagery is typically followed by a careful observation and documentation of behavioral changes of one person or a small group of individuals over time. This type of in-depth longitudinal analysis forms the cornerstone of the case-study approach.

Bibliography

Ahsen, A. (1984). ISM: The triple code model for imagery and psychophysiology. *Journal of Mental Imagery, 8,* 15–42.

Bandura, A. (1977). Self-efficacy: Toward a unifying theory of behavioral change. *Psychological Review, 84,* 191–215.

Biddle, S. (1997). Current trends in sport and exercise psychology research. *Psychologist, 10,* 63–69.

Gould, D., Eklund, R., & Jackson, S. (1992). U.S. Olympic wrestling excellence: I. Mental preparation, precompetitive cognition and affect. *Sport Psychologist, 6,* 358–382.

Landers, D. M. (1985). Psychophysiological assessment and biofeedback: Application for athletes in closed skill sport. In J. Sandweiss & S. Wolf (Eds.), *Biofeedback and sport science* (pp. 65–105). New York: Plenum.

Lang, P. J. (1979). A bio-informational theory of emotional imagery. *Psychophysiology, 17,* 495–512.

Long, B. C. & van Stavel, R. (1995). Effects of exercise training on anxiety: A meta-analysis. *Journal of Applied Sport Psychology, 7,* 167–189.

McAuley, E. (1992). Self-referent thought in sport and physical activity. In T. S. Horn (Ed.), *Advances in sport psychology* (pp. 101–118). Champaign, IL: Human Kinetics.

Martens, R. (1979). About smocks and jocks. *Journal of Sport Psychology, 1,* 94–99.

Rejeski, W. J., & Brawley, L. R. (1988). Defining the boundaries of sport psychology. *Sport Psychologist, 2,* 231–242.

Smith, R. (1989). Applied sport psychology in the age of accountability. *Journal of Applied Sport Psychology, 1,* 166–180.

Zajonc, R. (1965). Social facilitation. *Science, 149,* 269–274.

Robert Weinberg

Assessment

While there were pockets of research activity and scholarly inquiry evident during the first half of this century, not until the first International Congress of Sport Psychology was held in Rome, Italy, in 1965 was a concerted effort made by an international group of scholars to share and disseminate research on the psychological aspects of sport and related physical activity. Subsequently, numerous professional organizations, academic training programs, and textbooks and journals devoted to the professional and disciplinary advancement of sport psychology emerged. In fact, in the late 1990s there were over 100 graduate training programs in sport psychology located in the United States, Canada, Australia, Great Britain, and South Africa (Sachs, Burke, & Gomer, 1998).

Sport psychology as an academic discipline examines how personality traits and states, motives, cognitions, values, attitudes, interests, and behaviors effect and have been affected by participating in or observing sport. Sport psychology as a profession focuses on appropriate models of educational training, accreditation of training programs, credentialing issues (e.g., certification versus licensure), and ethical concerns. Success in advancing sport psychology as an academic discipline and profession is clearly dependent on the adequacy, richness, and diversity of the assessment approaches that have underscored the field.

Within sport and exercise psychology settings, psychological assessment has played an important role in at least four domains: health and exercise (e.g., mood changes as a function of exercise participation); clinical (e.g., evaluation of eating disorders); performance enhancement (e.g., evaluation of an imagery training program); and special purposes (e.g., talent identification) (Heil & Henschen, 1996). Goals of the sport psychology assessment program have included the generation of hypotheses for the purposes of description, explanation, prediction, and (perhaps) modification of behavior; the efficient and accurate description of psychological characteristics and concerns of the test taker; and a determination of the progress of behavioral change (Etzel, Yura, & Perna, 1998).

As a subdiscipline of psychology, assessment in sport psychology has paralleled (and sometimes lagged behind) advances that have occurred in the general field of psychological testing and assessment. For example, during the 1960s and early 1970s the dominant mode of psychological assessment in the sport sciences was the use of general personality trait measures, such as the Cattell Sixteen Personality Factor Questionnaire (Cattell 16 P-F), the Eysenck Personality Inventory, the Minnesota Multiphasic Personality Inventory, and the Edwards Personal Preference Schedule, to compare the personality traits of elite versus nonelite athletes, combative versus noncombative sport participants, male athletes versus female athletes, and so forth. Much of the impetus for this effort, albeit unsuccessful, was to identify any underlying personality structure predictive of athletic success. Widespread dissatisfaction emerged, both conceptually and methodologically, with this approach to sport psychology assessment (e.g., Singer, Harris, Kroll, & Sechrest, 1977).

For example, Rainer Martens (1973), a well-recognized sport psychology researcher, noted that, despite the publication of more than 200 studies on sport psychology at the time, there was little information on the accurate prediction of behavior in sport. Martens and others felt that this stemmed from a lack of understanding of the theoretical premises of the assessment approaches undertaken, a reliance on a shotgun approach to personality assessment in sport, a failure to adequately operationalize terms such as *elite athlete*, and the use of univariate statistical approaches to evaluating measurement data when, in fact, the accurate prediction of behavior in sport required multivariate solutions.

Perhaps more than any other issue, however, was the concern that general personality inventories such as the Cattell 16 P-F failed to account for the potential situational specificity and idiosyncratic organization of behavior in sport. The theoretical work of such distinguished psychologists as Walter Mischel (1968, 1973) and Norman Endler (1973) led sport psychology researchers in the late 1970s to abandon their strict reliance on the use of general personality trait inventories and to turn their attention toward developing sport-specific personality tests that were based on an interactionist perspective of human personality.

Perhaps the best example of this new orientation was the development of the Sport Competition Anxiety Test (SCAT) by Martens and his colleagues. A conceptual framework for the understanding of the sport competitive process was proposed. Within this framework, competitive trait anxiety was viewed as a characteristic of the individual that mediated perceptions of potentially stressful situations, such as negative social appraisal, within a competitive sport context. The SCAT was then developed to assess individual differences in the tendency to view competitive situations as threatening and respond to these situations with changes in state anxiety.

The SCAT has been employed in several thousand research investigations. For example, researchers have determined that participation by young children in sport is not necessarily stressful but there may be a propensity toward stress among children evaluated as high on competitive trait anxiety. The SCAT also gave rise to the Competitive State Anxiety Inventory-2 (CSAI-2), the most widely used instrument for assessing cognitive and somatic forms of state anxiety (as well as confidence) in sport (Martens, Vealey, & Burton, 1990). Since the early 1980s there has been a proliferation of self-report, situationally specific psychological tests used within sport settings. Almost all of these tests are used for research purposes rather than diagnosis. The vast majority of tests are not commercially published.

A review of published articles (1989–1992) in five prominent sport psychology journals revealed that tests have played a major role in the development of the field (Fogarty, 1995). What became readily apparent, however, was that there was a lack of a comprehensive list of sport-specific psychological tests that professionals could access. A list of this nature would not only facilitate the use of appropriate instruments within applied sport psychology settings but would also allow a determination of future needs in terms of psychological test development (Anshel, 1987).

Several hundred sport- and exercise-specific psychological scales, questionnaires, and inventories have since been summarized and catalogued in Ostrow (1996). This directory provides information on the purposes, foci, construction procedures, psychometric properties, normative data, and reference support for 314 sport- or exercise-specific psychological tests. Thus, the reader can readily find information on tests used in sport to measure confidence, motivation, attitudes, aggression, attention, anxiety, cohesion, psychological skills, and other important psychological constructs. Some of the more widely used and better validated sport-specific psychological tests reported in the directory include the Task and Ego Orientation in Sport Questionnaire, which assesses task versus ego achievement orientations within sport settings, the SCAT and CSAI-2 described earlier, the Sport Anxiety Scale, which provides a multidimensional assessment of competitive trait anxiety, the Group Environment Questionnaire, which examines team cohesiveness, the State and Trait

Sport-Confidence Inventories, the Leadership Scale for Sports, which assesses perceptions of coach leadership behaviors, and the Athletic Coping Skills Inventory, which evaluates an array of sport psychological skills such as coping with adversity, goal setting, mental preparation, confidence, and coachability.

Also noteworthy within the second edition of the directory is the marked increase in the number of exercise-specific psychological tests that have been developed to assess exercise motivation, attitudes toward exercise and physical activity, perceptions of physical competence, and adherence to exercise rehabilitation programs. Prominent instruments that have evolved include the Physical Self-Efficacy Scale, which is employed to assess individual differences in perceived physical ability and confidence in physical self-presentation in social situations, the Physical Self-Perception Profile, a multidimensional measure of physical self, the Personal Incentives for Exercise Questionnaire, which evaluates 10 categories of personal incentives for exercise participation (e.g., mastery, affiliation), and the Sport Injury Rehabilitation Adherence Scale.

While the directory was developed to provide comprehensive summaries of psychological tests employed in sport, it has several shortcomings. First, several popular psychological tests used within sport settings, while not sport specific, are not reported in the directory. These instruments include the Profile of Mood States (POMS), which has been widely used to evaluate mood manifestations such as depression, vigor, and fatigue in response to exercise interventions, and the Test of Attentional and Interpersonal Style (TAIS), which has been heavily employed to evaluate the width and direction of attentional focus as well as preferred attentional styles in sport.

Second, there is now general consensus (Duda, 1998) that a sport psychology assessment package should not be delimited to self-report paper and pencil measures. Qualitative self-report, behavioral observation scales, such as the Coaching Behavior Assessment System, and psychophysiological measures, such as the use of electromyography to measure muscle tension and the electroencephalogram or the magnetoencephalogram to measure the electrical activity of the brain, have added to our understanding of how constructs such as anxiety and attention impact sport performance. Futher, the addition of these measures may provide consensual validation for the use of self-report inventories.

Third, the directory does not provide critiques of these instruments. Toward this end, a reference work, *Advances in Sport and Exercise Psychology Measurement*, edited by Joan L. Duda, a prominent sport psychology researcher (1998), serves as a definitive review and critique of psychological assessment approaches in the sport and exercise sciences. Over 50 of the world's leading experts on sport psychology assessment contributed 29 chapters that overview the linkages of theory to sport psychology assessment, evaluate and critique sport psychology assessment approaches, and offer suggestions for future conceptual and methodological assessment directions.

This important work makes clear that a number of common issues transverse sport psychology assessment. These issues include the extent to which response sets (such as social desirability) contaminate self-report data; the need to distinguish between psychological traits versus states in the assessment design; the extent to which personal attributes versus situational characteristics impact sport participation and performance; the generality versus specificity of personality traits; the extent to which cognitions or psychological drives, personality traits, and/or motives mediate performance; and the interpretation of human personality as multidimensional rather than unidimensional in structure. Thus, the development and employment of a psychological assessment package is intricately related to the professional's underlying philosophy and theoretical orientation regarding the nature of human personality.

Of further concern are ethical issues surrounding the use of psychological tests in sport. For example, Vealey and Garner-Holman (1998) reported data on the ethical concerns of 68 certified consultants of the Association for the Advancement of Applied Sport Psychology and other well-known practicing sport psychology consultants. Their concerns (in order of identified importance) included: a lack of training or competence by persons administering psychological tests; issues of confidentiality; questionable psychometric properties of the instruments; a failure to give feedback to those tested; the inappropriate use of inventories; the misinterpretation of results; and excessive emphasis on psychological inventory results.

Sport psychology professionals come from diverse backgrounds. Approximately half of the members of the Association for the Advancement of Applied Sport Psychology have had formal training in physical education and sport science, while the remaining membership has professional roots in psychology. These professionals may view ethics differently. Nevertheless, several publications by the American Psychological Association (such as *Standards for Educational and Psychological Testing*, 19) provide guidance in terms of ethical principles and standards (Etzel, Yura, & Perna, 1998). Informed consent, confidentiality, test security, the provision for test feedback, and the use of tests that are valid and not obsolete are all important considerations when designing and delivering sport psychology assessment programs.

During the 1990s more rigor was evident in sport psychology test construction and validation; there was a better articulation of the links between theory and test design; more sophisticated statistical techniques were employed; and there was a concerted effort to disseminate test results. Inevitably, the foundation of knowledge and effectiveness of sport psychology interventions rely on in the validity and applicability of the assessment process.

Bibliography

Anshel, M. H. (1987). Psychological inventories used in sport psychology research. *Sport Psychologist, 1*, 331–349.

Duda, J. L. (Ed.). (1998). *Advances in sport and exercise psychology measurement.* Morgantown, WV: Fitness Information Technology.

Endler, N. S. (1973). The person versus the situation—A pseudo-issue? A reply to Alker. *Journal of Personality, 41*, 287–303.

Etzel, E., Yura, M., & Perna, F. (1998). Ethics in assessment and testing in sport and exercise psychology. In J. Duda (Ed.), *Advances in sport and exercise psychology measurement* (pp. 423–432). Morgantown, WV: Fitness Information Technology.

Fogarty, G. J. (1995). Some comments on the use of psychological tests in sport settings. *International Journal of Sport Psychology, 26*, 161–170.

Heil, J., & Henschen, K. (1996). Assessment in sport and exercise psychology. In J. L. Van Raalte & B. W. Brewer (Eds.), *Exploring sport and exercise psychology* (pp. 229–255). Washington, DC: American Psychological Association.

Martens, R. (1973, March). *Sport personologists have problems-other sport personologists.* Paper presented at the Midwest Convention of the American Alliance for Health, Physical Education, and Recreation, Columbus, OH.

Martens, R., Vealey, R. S., & Burton, D. (1990). *Competitive anxiety in sport.* Champaign, IL: Human Kinetics.

Mischel, W. (1968). *Personality and assessment.* New York: Wiley.

Mischel, W. (1973). Toward a cognitive social learning reconceptualization of personality. *Psychological Review, 80*, 252–283.

Ostrow, A. C. (Ed.). (1996). *The directory of psychological tests in the sport and exercise sciences* (2nd ed.). Morgantown, WV: Fitness Information Technology.

Sachs, M. L., Burke, K. L., & Gomer, S. (Eds.). (1998). *Directory of graduate programs in applied sport psychology* (5th ed.). Morgantown, WV: Fitness Information Technology.

Singer, R. N., Harris, D., Kroll, W., & Sechrest, L. J. (1977). Psychological testing of athletes. *Journal of Physical Education, 48*, 30–32.

Vealey, R. S., & Garner-Holman, M. (1998). Applied sport psychology: Measurement issues. In J. L. Duda (Ed.), *Advances in sport and exercise psychology measurement* (pp. 433–446). Morgantown, WV: Fitness Information Technology.

Andrew C. Ostrow

Social Psychology Perspectives

The social psychological aspects of sport psychology include motivation, leadership, group/team cohesion, socialization, aggression, audience, and exercise psychology.

Motivation

Motivation is generally defined as the study of goal directed behavior that involves examining personal and situational factors that influence the direction, intensity and duration of behavior. The study of sport-related motivation has taken different forms. An early emphasis on attempting to identify a personality profile that consistently discriminates athletes from nonathletes or successful athletes from unsuccessful athletes met with little success. More recent sport motivation research has emphasized the study of individual differences as one aspect of a dynamic system.

Interest in youth sport motivation has developed in response to the worldwide spread of organized youth sport programs and the posited physical, psychological, and social benefits of those programs. Descriptive research has identified a number of reasons for participating in and conversely for ceasing to participate in youth sport programs. Reasons for participating include: social (being with friends, making new friends), sensory (enjoying activity), health (developing fitness), status (recognition of peers and others), and achievement (improving skills, performing better than others). Reasons for dropping out include: time pressures, choosing to spend time on other activities, loss of interest in or enjoyment of the particular activity, lack of skill or personal success in the activity, dislike of the leadership, or some other aspects of the experience.

In attempting to extend understanding of sport motivation beyond a simple descriptive level, researchers have employed a number of different social–cognitive theoretical perspectives. Attribution theory has been applied in an attempt to understand athletes' thought processes, more specifically their causal attributions for sport outcomes as a means of understanding their feelings about sport (e.g., satisfaction) and their future behavior. Much of this research has been limited in scope, essentially applying American psychologist Bernard Weiner's dimensional analysis of achievement attributions to sport contexts. The sport research has generally replicated results from other achievement contexts. Self-serving biases are evident, in that although athletes tend to attribute both success and failure to internal factors, typically more internal, stable, and controllable attributions are given for success than for failure (e.g., "I won the game because of my athletic ability and effort," but "I lost because I wasn't feeling well or had bad luck."). Much of this research has been limited to an objective definition of success as winning a sport competition and failure as losing; however, evidence indicates that individuals define personal success and failure more subjectively, in terms of how satisfied they are with their performance rather than objectively, in terms of game outcome. In sport, as in other achievement contexts, the particular attributions made have important consequences for feelings and for expectations concerning future performance behavior. Athletes take greater pride in a successful performance if they attribute it to internal and controllable factors (e.g., effort, superior teamwork) than to external and uncontrollable factors (e.g., weak opposition, superior equipment). Stable and controllable attributions (e.g., ability, effort) are related to expectations for success in future situations.

Attributions of success to personal ability fosters perceptions of competency, mastery, or self-efficacy, which are central elements of a number of different motivational theories that are prominently represented in the sport psychology literature (e.g., Harter's competence motivation theory, Deci and Ryan's self-determination theory, Bandura's self-efficacy theory, and Csikszentmihalyi's flow theory). While each of these theoretical positions provides a different emphasis, they are similar in emphasizing the importance of thoughts concerning one's ability to meet the challenge of different tasks for motivation and performance (see, e.g., Roberts, 1992). The following discussion addresses the social-cognitive perspective of achievement goal theories.

Drawing upon the education-oriented child motivation research of such University of Illinois researchers as Carole Ames, Carol Dweck, and John Nicholls (later of Purdue University), sport psychology researchers Glyn Roberts, Joan Duda, and colleagues have emphasized the importance of personalized meanings and goals to understanding children's sport behaviors. Research has indicated that in youth sport contexts, as in school-based educational contexts, children adopt different types of achievement goals that have important implications for performance, satisfaction, and continued involvement. While different researchers use different labels and differ somewhat in the emphases within their theoretical orientations, there is general agreement that there are two types of achievement goals. One type of goal is more process oriented, emphasizing learning, developing one's skills, and mastering the task(s) at hand. The second goal type is more outcome oriented, emphasizing doing better than others. These two types of goals can be referred to as task-oriented and ego-oriented goals, respectively.

Research in educational and sport contexts has indicated that generally task-oriented goals are advantageous for learning, performance, satisfaction, and persistence. Task-oriented individuals tend to set moderately difficult or challenging goals, persist in the face

of difficulty or failure, and take considerable satisfaction from goal attainment, as they attribute it largely to their own effort and ability (internal attributions). Ego-oriented individuals, in contrast, often evidence maladaptive achievement behaviors characterized by setting either excessively easy or difficult goals and exhibit decreasing effort and performance over time, which subsequently leads to lack of persistence and leaving the activity.

Both ego- and task-oriented individuals may be attracted to competitive sport situations, and both are interested in winning, but they differ in how they perceive the situation and success in it. By emphasizing individual mastery and improvement regardless of game outcome, task-oriented individuals can experience subjective success regardless of the difficulty of the challenge and the particular game outcome. Ego-oriented individuals, on the other hand, have less opportunity for experiencing success. They exhibit adaptive achievement behavior patterns only when they have high perceived ability for the task. When they have low perceived ability, they exhibit poor motivation and are prone to leaving the competitive sport context.

While individual differences in goal predispositions have important implications for achievement behavior, so too does the environmental climate. A competitive, outcome-oriented environment predisposes the setting of ego-oriented task goals. To foster healthy task-oriented goals in youth sports, coaches, sport organizers and parents must work to counteract a dominant outcome-oriented sport philosophy. Research indicates that through rewarding appropriate process behaviors, rather than performance outcomes, teachers and coaches can foster the development of task-oriented goals. Stress associated with excessive pressure to win reduces enjoyment and contributes to dropping out of sport.

Leadership

While much of the motivation research has implications for leadership, research dealing directly with leadership in sport has been largely restricted to two areas. First, Ron Smith, Frank Smoll, and their associates at the University of Washington have made a distinctive contribution to youth sport leadership through their development of the Coaching Behavior Assessment Scale (CBAS). This rating scale for classifying reactive and spontaneous coaching behaviors evidenced in different sport contexts has proven useful in distinguishing between more effective and less effective coaches in terms of their effect upon players' self-esteem, attraction to teammates, and desire for continued sport involvement. Furthermore, youth sport coach training programs based on the research has been shown to result in more positive youth sport experiences for participants.

At a more theoretical level, Chelladurai and associates have attempted to synthesize and extend earlier leadership theories in developing a multidimensional model of leadership. This model takes situational, leader, and member characteristics into account in assessing how leadership behavior effects performance and satisfaction. The required behavior for a situation, what the situational demands and organizational requirements dictate, and the behavioral preferences of the members influence a given leader's actual leadership behavior. In addition, these required and preferred leadership behaviors interact with actual leadership behaviors in shaping performance and satisfaction outcomes.

A Leadership Scale for Sports (LSS) has been developed to measure five dimensions of leadership: training and instruction, democratic behavior, autocratic behavior, social support, and positive feedback. Considerable research using the LSS has been conducted to test predictions from the model. Evidence supports the predictions that situational characteristics (organizational goals, task type) and member characteristics (personality, age, sex, ability, level of sport involvement) effect preferred leadership behavior. Generally younger and less experienced athletes prefer more social support and more democratic and less autocratic coaching behavior then do older, more experienced athletes. Females tend to prefer more democratic behavior from coaches while males evidence stronger preference for autocratic behaviors. These differences tend to disappear at higher levels of competition. Highly task-motivated individuals indicate higher preferences for training and instruction while affiliation-motivated individuals express stronger preferences for social support. Research supports the importance of the congruence of actual and preferred leadership behavior to satisfaction. There is less support for the proposed effects of leadership behavior on performance. No systematic research, however, has been carried out to test the causal linkages of the overall model.

Group Cohesion

While leadership is important to sport performance and satisfaction, so too are group dynamics and the group behavior of participants. The most prominent small group research in sport has dealt with group cohesion. Bert Carron, together with colleagues at the universities of Waterloo and Western Ontario, has conducted a program of research over the past two decades that has contributed substantially to theory and instrumentation concerning group cohesion. Cohesion is viewed as the tendency for a group to stick together and remain united in pursuing its goals. Carron views overall cohesion, comprised of task and social cohesion components, as part of a dynamic process with a number of antecedents and two major sets of consequences: group

and individual outcomes. Antecedent factors include environmental, personal, team, and leadership factors. The two outcome components include both performance and satisfaction aspects.

The Group Environment Questionnaire, a psychometrically sound instrument, was developed to assess different components of cohesion. It produces four scores, task and social scores for both group integration (a member's perception of the group as a totality) and individual attraction to the group. Research using this instrument has shown task cohesion to be more closely related than social cohesion to performance and that it is more important for interacting sports (e.g., soccer, basketball) than coactive sports (e.g., track and field, swimming). The relation between performance and task cohesion appears to be circular. Although clear causal links have not been established, cohesion has been shown to be positively related to individual satisfaction with a group, conformity of group members to the normative attitudes and behaviors of the group, stability of membership in the group, and acceptance of group goals.

Socialization

Frequently espoused goals for youth sport programs are the development of the sense of fair play, positive attitudes, values, and good citizenship. Although much research has been conducted concerning these and other desired outcomes, few definitive conclusions can be drawn concerning the socialization effects of sport. Given the diverse sport opportunities available and the widely divergent leadership practices involved, it should not be surprising to find divergent results, with desirable character development outcomes reported from some programs and undesirable outcomes observed from others. Rather than a simplistic, "How does sport involvement affect 'x'?" perspective, it is preferable to ask, "What are the necessary organizational, leadership, and supporting social environment conditions for producing specified types of outcomes?" In this regard, the previously discussed leadership research of Smith, Smoll, and colleagues, as well as recent qualitative research into youth sport experiences, is particularly valuable. A number of youth sport coach development programs have been developed, which although not always substantiated by strong empirical research, do educate coaches in the use of practices thought conducive to desirable outcomes.

Aggression

One area pertaining to socialization that has been of particular interest is that of sport and aggression. Research on aggression in sport has been beset by definitional and measurement problems. Sport participants and spectators alike often refer to the need for athletes to be aggressive in order to be successful (i.e., perform at a high level and win important competitions). In this context the term *aggression* is used inappropriately as a synonym for assertiveness or working hard in pursuing one's athletic goals. To be appropriately considered aggressive or to indicate aggression, there must be the emission of a behavioral response with the intent to injure. While it might appear that the intent to injure would clearly differentiate aggressive behavior from highly motivated, but nonaggressive, goal-directed behavior, this is not the case. Aggression may be part of a goal-oriented strategy. American psychologist Arnold Buss (*The Psychology of Aggression*, New York, 1961) differentiated between hostile aggression (actions intended to harm another person who has angered or provoked an individual), and instrumental aggression (an impersonal attack designed to facilitate goal attainment). In sport, this takes the form of attempting to injure or otherwise impair an opponent's performance to facilitate winning a competition, accomplishing one's competitive goal. The distinction of hostile and instrumental aggression in sport is a murky area. The two terms lie on a continuum rather than constitute a dichotomy. Whereas a hard hit on a quarterback may lead to an incomplete pass, a harder hit may put the star player out of the game for a few plays, and a more severe act may put him out for the game or for the season. This ambiguity poses difficulties for those who argue that sport encourages good aggression but helps to control bad aggression. What does theory and research suggest about the effect of sport on the aggressive tendencies of athletes and spectators?

Various instinct theories posit that humans, like other animals, have basic survival instincts that result in aggressive acts in the struggle to survive. According to these perspectives, socially acceptable forms of aggression in sport can serve a cathartic function of releasing or draining off aggressive tendencies that, if not released, result in an increased build-up of pressure until the energy explodes in more violent, destructive forms of aggression. Although such a rationale is used by apologists for maintaining aggression in sport (e.g., the argument against banning fighting from the National Hockey League), there is little empirical support for this position.

Extensive evidence from sport, as well as from general aggression research, supports a social learning perspective that much aggressive behavior, like other forms of behavior, is learned through modeling and reinforcement processes. Seeing others rewarded for aggressive acts or being personally rewarded for them increases the prevalence of such behaviors. There is a potential to learn through sport to either control aggressive acts or to commit them more readily depending on which behaviors are modeled and reinforced. Unfortunately, evidence indicates that the generalized effect of organized sport on aggression is to increase aggressive tendencies. Researchers such as Michael Smith and Brenda Bredemeier have reported that the tolerance for aggression both within and outside sport increases in parallel with involvement in competitive sport. Athletes tend to view aggression in sport as a form of bracketed reality—they view many aggressive acts as acceptable in sporting environments that are unacceptable in nonsport settings. Similarly, the viewing of aggressive sport by spectators has not been shown to produce cathartic effects on aggression. Such viewing has been shown to have no effects or a tendency to elevate aggression levels.

Audience

Although spectators are a central element of many sport situations, this is a largely undeveloped research area. The research that has been done essentially focuses on two issues. First, in terms of understanding spectators themselves, what are the motives of spectators? Why do they chose to spend their time, and often considerable money, to watch sporting events? Second, how does the presence of spectators or an audience effect athletic performance?

Spectators may be attracted to sport for various reasons. One line of inquiry holds that sport spectatorship is based on affective dispositions to derive positive affect from the successes of allied teams. Fan alliance with a team might be based on affiliation related to such shared aspects as community, nation, institution, race, or gender. Fans have been shown to engage in aspects of ego enhancement or impression management through what has been termed *basking in the reflected glory (BIRGing)* of successful sport teams. There is a greater tendency to wear team colors and use more affiliative pronouns when speaking of a team (we/us versus they/them) after a successful performance than following an unsuccessful outcome. Although attendance is higher when a team is winning, most fans who attend games have allegiance to the chosen team and stick with it through good and bad. This emotional appeal can extend to dislike of competing teams or athletes who have a strong rivalry with one's favorite. Emotional reactions are triggered by team success (liking, positive reactions) or failure of disliked rivals.

The opportunity to observe outstanding athletic performance is undoubtedly another factor underlying the appeal of sport to spectators. Nevertheless, research on team sports by Dolf Zillmann and his colleagues at Indiana University indicates that fan enjoyment and disappointment is more dependent on team success and failure than an impartial appreciation of athletic excellence or innovative play. While it would appear that the appeal of such sports as figure skating, diving, and gymnastics is based largely on aspects of beauty and aesthetics, there is a lack of research to substantiate the importance of aesthetic appreciation to sport spectators. Even in these sports where grace and beauty of movement are emphasized, spectator interest is greatly enhanced when an element of rivalry between adversaries is added. This point is clearly evident in the use of national rivalries to promote interest in the Olympic Games and other major sport spectacles. The linking of aggressive acts to this rivalry by sports reporters has been shown to augment fan interest.

Although there has been extensive research on the effects of small numbers of spectators on task performance, there has been little systematic research on sport audience effects. Limited evidence suggests that generalizations from other areas also apply to sport. For example, whereas the presence of an audience or spectators may facilitate the performance of easy or well-learned skills, it may impede the learning of new skills or the performance of complex skills.

Sport audiences differ from many of the audiences of controlled research in that they are often passionate about the sporting event being watched and they become actively involved in responding to the observed events. Correlational research indicates that playing in front of a supportive audience in the form of a home crowd may have a performance advantage. As many factors may be involved in playing home and away games, however, it is not possible to determine how much of this is due to an audience effect. Research has not substantiated any clear effects of crowd size on athletic performance. It is a common occurrence, however, to hear athletes offer testimonials to the importance of a large, supportive home crowd for successful team performance. Apart from the motivational, inspirational effect of an encouraging crowd, a supportive audience may provide directional and cuing effects to influence performance and outcome. The cheering of aggressive behaviors by fans can reinforce aggressiveness. It is now routine behavior for fans to attempt to influence game events directly through distracting athletes (i.e., distracting movements during basketball free throws or place kicks in football) or through strategic crowd roar to drown out on-field communication of the opposing players. Fans may also indirectly influence game outcome through influencing officiating through differential cheering and booing of actions of home and away players.

Exercise Psychology

The exercise psychology aspect of sport psychology focuses on two aspects. First, what are the psychological consequences of sport and physical activity involvement? Second, given that there are positive outcomes (physiological, social, as well as psychological) to be gained from physical activity, how can psychology contribute to more effective promotion of the necessary physical activity to produce these benefits?

Although the most clearly documented health benefits of physical activity are of a physiological nature, there is also mounting evidence that appropriate physical activity can also produce a number of psychological benefits. At the most general level, people commonly report feeling better after engaging in physical activity. Survey research indicates a positive association between regular physical activity and mental health.

Positive self-concept, which is important to individual achievement, happiness, and social adjustment, is one of the more useful indicators of mental health. Correlational research has implicated physical activity in the development of a positive self-concept. In addition, there is increasing support for the view that physical activity affects self-concept through its effects on self-efficacy and physical self-worth. Self-efficacy beliefs concerning one's competency for performing physical skills are developed through experiences in physical activity and sport situations. Positive experiences, based on improving one's skills and experiencing success in meeting realistic challenges, foster the development of positive physical self-worth (evaluative reactions about one's body and its capabilities), which enhances overall self-concept. This process can be related to the earlier discussion of the importance of a task rather than an ego orientation in the development of young sport participants.

With adults, much of the attention concerning the psychological benefits of physical activity have focused on the use of exercise as a treatment modality for, or a preventive action to, anxiety and depression. Physicians increasingly prescribe regular physical activity as a treatment for mild forms of these two common maladies. Correlational as well as experimental research evidence supports the utility of exercise or physical activity for treating both state and trait anxiety. In addition, physical activity has been associated with decreased levels of depression. It has not been established, however, that physical activity causes these psychological outcomes, as no underlying mechanisms for the effects have been established. Little empirical evidence is available to substantiate the various physiological, biochemical, and psychological mechanisms that have been suggested to account for the effects.

Although the underlying mechanisms have not been specified, progress has been made in demonstrating a number of important considerations for enhancing positive psychological effects from physical activity. When considering immediate effects of a single bout of activity, both state anxiety and depressed mood state have been shown to benefit from activity. Activity type, intensity, and duration all seem important. Most evidence supports aerobic type activity of a regular rhythmic variety such as running, cycling, or swimming. There is less evidence to support the utility of such other activities as yoga, martial arts, and weight training. With such aerobic activities, a duration of at least 20 minutes has been shown to be effective. In terms of intensity, moderate activity (50 to 60% of maximum heart rate) appears to be most effective. Too high intensity can be counterproductive, resulting in increased chance of injury and increased stress. Beyond objective activity characteristics, personalized subjective reactions to the exercise context are important. Enjoyment of the activity, or at least of the larger activity experience, has been shown to be important to deriving psychological benefits. If the activity experience is not enjoyed, it has the potential to become just another stressor, with attendant negative psychological impacts. The physical environment and the social situation, as well as the activity itself, are important to the subjective experience and psychological outcome.

More enduring psychological effects in the form of reduced trait anxiety and lessened general or chronic levels of depression are susceptible to cumulative training effects. Those with nonpathological but chronically high levels of anxiety or depression have been shown to benefit from regular physical activity. In this area, the frequency, regularity, and duration of an activity program become important, in addition to the intensity, type, and duration considerations pertinent to single exercise bouts. Current evidence indicates that moderate aerobic activity bouts of at least 20 minutes at a frequency of at least twice a week for a program duration of 10 weeks or more are most effective. Further research into the mechanisms underlying physical activity effects and how different personal and environmental factors impact these mechanisms is required to develop more precise and effective treatment modalities.

Limited research attention has addressed the role of physical activity and sport in enhancing positive affect. Although sport has long been accepted as a major component of recreation programs offered by public, private, and commercial agencies provided for the enjoyment and well-being of clients, the value of such programs has largely been based on the personal testimonials of participants. Only recently have researchers attempted to systematically assess the nature of enjoyment and positive affect in physical activity settings. While much remains to be explored, the importance of enjoyment to psychological outcomes and alternately as a motivational factor underlying regular activity involvement has been recognized. Research has supported the perspective that enjoyment is a positive emotional state that is subjectively attached to a variety of different sources of enjoyment. These enjoyment sources might pertain to the activity itself, the social setting, or to the outcomes from the activity.

Recognition of the considerable physical and psychological health benefits of physical activity has spurred a major public health interest in encouraging people to be more active. Within academia, exercise adherence or physical activity motivation has emerged as a prominent research area within sport and exercise psychology. This research may be grouped into two categories: (1) research generally of a correlational, cross-sectional nature pertaining to the determinants of physical activity and (2) research, generally of an experimental or quasi-experimental nature, pertaining to interventions to enhance exercise involvement. The determinants research has been descriptive and atheoretical in nature. A number of environmental (climate, access to facilities), personal (health status, age, sex, skill level, socioeconomic level, education), psychological (beliefs, expectancies, attitudes, habits), social (social support, models), activity (intensity, perceived exertion), and situational (time, program availability) factors have been associated with activity involvement.

Interventions to enhance exercise adherence have been based upon a number of different theoretical orientations. Behaviorist orientations have emphasized the provision of appropriate cues to elicit desired behaviors (e.g., posters, written, or oral messages) and/or the implementation of appropriate reward programs to reinforce desired changes. Research across a range of subjects in both individual and group settings using a variety of specific reinforcers such as monetary, token, equipment, praise, and encouragement has indicated that behaviorist principles can be used to increase the intensity and regularity of activity involvement. As the studies have all been of short-term duration, a question remains as to the long-term effectiveness of these programs.

The bulk of the research has been based on some form of social-cognitive theoretical orientation, with Bandura's self-efficacy (SE) theory and Ajzen's theory of planned behavior (TPB) being particularly popular. General support has been provided for both approaches. Although some attempts have been made to test the relative utility of the two approaches, it seems that they are generally complementary. They rely on beliefs concerning one's ability to successfully engage in the targeted activity behavior (self-efficacy expectancies in the case of SE; perceived control beliefs in TPB) and beliefs pertaining to the probable outcomes resulting from engaging in those behaviors (outcome expectancies in SE theory, behavioral beliefs underlying attitudes, and normative beliefs underlying social norms concerning the behavior in TPB). While these theoretical models have been useful in organizing psychological factors influencing intentional physical activity behavior and have been demonstrated to have some utility for predicting and/or explaining physical activity involvement of different individuals and groups, they typically account for only a small proportion of the behavioral variance. This has resulted in a recognition that more complete models must also take other factors—not just psychological factors—into consideration. In addition, the inadequacy of such static models for explaining dynamic changing physical activity behavior has been recognized.

Jim Prochaska and his associates have developed a transtheoretical model of behavior change as one attempt to view behavior change in a more dynamic way. This model holds that in making a health-related behavior change, such as changing from a sedentary to an active lifestyle, change proceeds through a series of stages. In addition, individuals use a number of common behavioral and experiential (cognitive) processes in making these changes. Different processes are more useful at different stages. Initial research indicates that interventions to assist individuals to become regularly active will be more effective if they target the processes that are most pertinent to the stage of change of the target group. It appears that such stage-targeted interventions might be particularly useful in working with fairly large populations or institutional groups. At the individual level, a more clinical, in-depth approach is indicated.

Bibliography

Cox, R. H. (1998). *Sport psychology: Concepts and applications* (2nd ed.). Boston: WCB/McGraw-Hill. Very readable introduction to sport psychology. Intersperses sport examples with principles derived from theory and research. Offers concrete suggestions for sport practice.

Dishman, R. K. (Ed.). (1994). *Advances in exercise adherence.* Champaign, IL: Human Kinetics. Review articles by leading researchers provide an excellent source of information on psychological effects of physical activity and especially psychology of exercise adherence.

Horn, T. S. (Ed.). (1992). *Advances in sport psychology.* Champaign, IL: Human Kinetics. Good review of major areas of research within sport psychology excluding exercise psychology.

Kremer, J. M., & Scully, D. (1994). *Psychology in sport.* Bristol, PA: Taylor & Francis. Valuable source for a broader perspective of sport psychology research and how it relates to the main field of psychology.

LeUnes, A., & Nation, J. R. (1996). *Sport psychology: An introduction.* (2nd ed.). Chicago: Nelson-Hall. Good introductory text. Geared for a broader psychology audience than most sport psychology texts.

Roberts, G. C. (Ed.). (1992). *Motivation in sport and exercise.* Champaign, IL: Human Kinetics. Extensive coverage of motivation research pertaining to sport and exercise with an emphasis on social-cognitive approaches. Emphasis on research adopting a self-efficacy or achievement goal perspective.

Russell, G. W. (1993). *The social psychology of sport.* New York: Springer-Verlag. Provides more extensive coverage of sport spectatorship and aggression in sport than do most general sport psychology texts.

Singer, R. N., Murphey, M. & Tennant, K. (Eds.). (1992). *Handbook of research on sport psychology.* New York: Macmillan. Comprehensive reference on theory and research for major topics in sport and exercise psychology. Presents extensive literature reviews of most topics covered here.

Weinberg, R. S., & Gould, D. (1995). *Foundations of sport and exercise psychology.* Champaign, IL: Human Kinetics. Easy-to-read popular introductory textbook in the field. Synthesizes theoretical and practical information; provides case studies to illustrate applications.

Willis, J. D., & Campbell, L. F. (1992). *Exercise psychology.* Champaign, IL: Human Kinetics. Most comprehensive text available on the psychology of exercise and fitness. Extensive review of research and practical applications targeted to those beginning to specialize in exercise psychology.

Leonard M. Wankel

SPOUSE ABUSE. *See* Domestic Violence.

SPRANGER, EDUARD (1882–1963), German philosopher, pedagogue, and psychologist. During his professorship of philosophy in Leipzig (1911–1920), Spranger (1914/1928) published an influential monograph on personality psychology and its connection to ethics. As a professor of philosophy and pedagogy in Berlin (1920–1946), he published in 1924 a widely successful developmental treatise on the psychology of young people. Spranger was a prolific and respected writer, not only in psychology, philosophy, and education, but also in political and cultural studies (Spranger, 1969–1980).

Spranger was a student of Wilhelm Dilthey, the German philosopher who emphasized the autonomy of the *Geisteswissenschaften* ("cultural sciences") against the natural sciences. Spranger, incorporating German classical philosophy (particularly that of G. W. F. Hegel), drew on Dilthey for his elaboration of a *geisteswissenschaftliche* psychology. Spranger conceptualized a psychological performance as part of a meaningful life totality that requires knowledge and "understanding" of the psychological-mental whole. The term he used, *verstehen* ("to understand"), does not denote the act of sympathizing with another person, but refers to transcending the immediate consciousness of the individual's psyche and grasping mental structures as meaningful in cultural relations, while providing objectively valid knowledge.

Using a *verstehende* psychology, Spranger (1914/1928) proposed in his personality psychology six ideally basic types of individuality. *Each* type fulfills the quality of a Gestalt and corresponds to an ethical system. The theoretical type accords with the ethics of general legality and the value of objectivity; the economic type with utilitarian ethics and the value of utility; the aesthetic type with the ethics of inner form and the value of proper form and harmony; the social type with the ethics of helpful love and loyalty; the political type with the ethics of a will to power; and the religious type with the ethics of blessedness in God. Spranger argued that his system of types has implications for research and practical life, and that individuals may not belong exclusively to one type because mixed and historically determined types exist.

In his developmental psychology, Spranger (1924) offered a holistic characterization of adolescence (from age 13 to 19 for girls, and 14 to 22 for boys). Adolescence is characterized, in general, by the discovery of a self, the emergence of a life plan, and the growth of the adolescent into different domains of human life. Using material from history, literature, and the method of understanding, Spranger describes, in a detailed manner, the fantasy and creativity of adolescents, pubertal eroticism and sexuality, the ethical and social development of youth, and the legal, political, ideological, work-related, and religious consciousness of young people. As with his personality psychology, Spranger identifies several different types of adolescent emotions, in the domains of "life" and the "ego."

The Americanization of West German psychology after World War II led to a decline of the *geisteswissenschaftliche* psychology in Germany. From a contemporary psychological point of view, Spranger's approach would not be considered scientific because it is based mainly on philosophical-intellectual authority and the *verstehende* competence of the psychologist. Despite a gender-biased and elitist position, Spranger still offers insights into human psychological life and its complexity.

Bibliography

Spranger, E. (1924). *Psychologie des Jugendalters* [Psychology of youth]. Leipzig: Quelle & Meyer.

Spranger, E. (1928). *Types of men: The psychology and ethics of personality* (P. J. W. Pigors, Trans.). Halle: Max Niemeyer. (Original work published 1914 under the title *Lebensformen: Geisteswissenschaftliche Psychologie und Ethik der Persönlichkeit*)

Spranger, E. (1969–1980). *Gesammelte Schriften* [Collected writings] (Vols. 1–11) (H. W. Bähr et al., Eds.). Heidelberg: Quelle & Meyer.

Thomas Teo

SPURZHEIM, JOHANN G. *See* Phrenology.

STANDARDIZED TESTS. Psychological assessment is a procedure for evaluating an individual on certain psychological characteristics including (but not limited to) intellectual functioning, personality functioning, and emotional and social functioning. A variety of uses for psychological assessment exist: mental health screening, sanity determinations for court cases, placing children for adoption, school achievement or school problems, learning disabilities, special abilities, career selection, job advancement, hiring for special jobs, and classifying military personnel. The psychologist conducting the assessment uses information from past behavior, present behavior, and psychological tests to arrive at hypotheses. Past history, projective methods, objective methods, and interview material are integrated into the final assessment.

Historical Perspective

Psychological testing developed from early attempts to identify and classify the mentally deficient. As early as 1838, Jean Esquirol differentiated between various levels of intelligence among individuals by their relative abilities to use language. Francis Galton, using measurement of vision and hearing, muscular strength, and reaction time, was the first experimental psychologist to develop instruments, questionnaires, rating scales, and statistical methods to measure intelligence. The trend to restrict testing to relatively simple and specialized abilities changed when Alfred Binet developed the first scale individual test of intelligence in 1905 (Goldenson, 1970).

Interest in assessment expanded in the early twentieth century with evaluation of intellectual functions and personality traits and characteristics. During this time, Hermann Rorschach developed a method to study personality characteristics using inkblots. In 1920, Woodworth introduced the first formal self-report questionnaire for screening mental health problems. Development of assessment tools continued, between World War I and World War II, with an emphasis on diagnostic techniques and improved statistical methods. Due to the growing demands of mobilizing extensive military operations during World War II, the application of newly developed assessment technologies provided an early foundation for contemporary personality assessment. At this time, psychologists were responsible for the development and further refinement of assessment methods in the areas of pilot and officer candidate selections and potential in learning radio and navigation skills (Corsini, 1994). After World War II, the use of personality tests in personnel selection came to be widely recognized and accepted. Today, psychological assessment plays one of the most central roles in applied psychology.

Assessment Techniques

Several different techniques are used in psychological assessment.

Behavioral Observation. In behavioral observation, the individual's overt motor and verbal behavior are assessed. Direct observation may be done by a psychologist or a designated person such as a parent or a teacher. Then presence of a behavior, its frequency, antecedents and consequences of behavior are recorded for evaluation. A behavior checklist or rating scale might be used by the clinician to structure or standardize the assessment.

Interviews. Face-to-face interviews are the most common technique used for assessing psychological status. In a structured interview, specific questions are asked in order to gather specific information. Questions are presented in a preselected order, and responses are checked to ensure that the obtained data are clear and relevant. In an open-ended interview, the interviewee is asked to talk about a certain topic in general terms. If the interviewee has not covered specific areas, the interviewer will ask more direct questions.

Objective Techniques. Objective tests, referred to as paper-and-pencil methods, consist of the evaluation of an individual's responses to specific questions and the subsequent comparison of the answers with the known answers of groups of individuals. This approach is used in the assessment of intelligence and personality. Objective inventories are standardized and can be administered to a large number of people at the same time. This method is thought to be more amenable to scale validation.

Projective Techniques. Projective techniques rose out of the traditions of psychoanalysis and ego psychology to focus on the conscious demonstration of psychological wants and needs. It is believed that an individual's thoughts, conflicts, impulses, and feelings can be projected onto ambiguous stimuli, such as inkblots, which may be perceived in varying shapes or involved in varying movements. The personality of the person is thought to determine what shapes are seen, how they are seen, and what activities appear (Corsini, 1994).

Reliability and Validity

In order that a psychological test be considered to demonstrate scientific and practical value, it must have reliability and validity. A reliable test is one that is dependable, stable, and reproducible. The test items must be similarly interpreted by different participants, produce the same results when administered by different examiners, and consistently measure whatever is being assessed. A test is usually considered reliable if two independent scores for the same individual are approximately equal.

The validity of an assessment instrument is determined by whether the test measures what it is designed to measure. This quality is an important requirement for a psychological test. After an independent criterion or criterion score is set, validity is determined by whether the test score correlates highly with or predicts the criterion (Goldenson, 1970).

Personality Assessment

Personality tests are designed to assess motivational processes, attitudes, beliefs, values, temperament, self-concepts, interpersonal relations, emotional states, and trait characteristics. The most widely used objective personality test is the Minnesota Multiphasic Personality Inventory (MMPI-2). A fifth- or sixth-grade level of reading is sufficient for comprehension of the items (Butcher, 1987). In addition to paper-pencil forms, audiocassette or computer-automated administration is also available. The MMPI-2 provides information in several areas: attitudes toward assessment, cooperation, mood and affect, conflicts, coping styles, diagnostic considerations, and treatment recommendations. In addition, the MMPI-2 has the highest level of comprehensive validity to assess the subject's attitudes, cooperation, and honesty in responding to the test items of all personality assessments (Graham, 1993). The MMPI-2 is an example of objective personality assessment with documented national and international credibility. This test is currently available in 25 languages and is in use in 45 countries across the globe. This is evidence to the utility of personality assessment across the world. Other examples of objective tests include the Millon Clinical Multiaxial Inventory, the 16PF, and the Neuroticism Extroversion Openness Personality Inventory-Revised, Neo-PI-R (Cohen, Swerdlik, & Philipps, 1996).

The most commonly applied projective technique for assessing personality development and the presence of psychopathology is the Rorschach Inkblot Test, in which an individual is evaluated according to the characteristics and pattern of their responses to a series of ambiguous inkblots. The Thematic Apperception Test (TAT) is another projective technique, in which the individual is asked to develop a story in response to the presentation of pictures. The Children's Apperception Test (CAT) was developed for use with children. Other projective formats included word association, sentence completion, and drawing tests.

Neuropsychological assessment is a procedure used to assess brain-behavior functioning and to determine the impact of brain dysfunction on intelligence and/or personality. One example of such a technique is the Bender-Gestalt test, which measures the individual's ability to reproduce certain geometric designs by direct copying and from memory (Corsini, 1994). For a comprehensive discussion of neuropsychological tests, see Lezak (1995).

Utility of Personality Tests

Psychological tests are used in various fields, as follows.

Legal Systems. In determining responsibility in legal matters, the use of psychological tests to measure personality is considered fairly objective and more reliable than subjective means of appraisal. Courts rely on the use of these tools to determine whether a person charged with a criminal offense can understand reality the way an ordinary person does, if he or she can think logically and rationally, and whether he or she can plan and organize behavior in such a way as to be held responsible for a criminal offense. In determining the possibility of malingering, whereby an offender attempts to feign mental illness to escape punishment for a crime, the use of psychological tests enhances the ability of psychologists to make accurate decisions. An example of such a test is the MMPI-2, which has special scales that detect test-taking attitudes and indicate whether an individual is likely to exaggerate symptoms.

Personality assessment is also utilized in the determination of suitability for child custody. Through methodological appraisal, the psychologist may be able to assess whether a person has genuinely good parental characteristics or is just pretending. For example, information about parental style can be inferred from the Thematic Apperception Test. Furthermore, the content of Rorschach responses can be used as further evidence concerning the emotional depth of the person relative to warmth and nurturance (Corsini, 1987, 1994).

Vocational Counseling. Through personality assessment, it is possible to determine vocational choices for individuals seeking counseling. Whether an individual is better suited for work involving close contact with people, more structured and formal contact, or no contact at all is best assessed through instruments measuring personality. Stress tolerance and problem solving at a time of crisis are important factors in determining workers' and public safety for sensitive occupations. By using indirect psychological tests such as projective methods and empirically derived inventories, it is possible to obtain a more objective appraisal of an individual's fitness for a particular type of career.

Counseling and Clinical Settings. Furthermore, assessment of personality can be used to plan psychotherapeutic intervention. It can be predicted that some people will respond well to introspective techniques that lead to insight, others may benefit from social skills training in a group setting, and still others may benefit most from individual record-keeping and behavioral assignments. Through attempting to match the client to the method, the chance of success is increased (Corsini, 1987, 1994).

Computerized Personality Assessment

The surge of interest in computer technology has influenced the field of psychological and, specifically, personality assessment. While computers do not replace the clinical experience of psychologists, they have proven effective in assisting psychologists in the assessment process. Computers have been successfully used in one or more areas of assessment including administration, scoring, and interpretation. For example, MMPI-2 can be administered and scored by a computer. In addition, computers can generate automated reports. An extensive list of psychological assessment software since 1987 is available in Butcher (1987).

[*See also* Testing.]

Bibliography

Butcher, J. N. (1987). *Psychological assessment.* New York: Basic Books.

Butcher, J. N., & Williams, C. L. (1992). *Essentials of MMPI-2 and MMPI-A interpretation.* Minneapolis: University of Minnesota Press.

Cohen, R. J., Swerdlik, E. S., & Philipps, S. M. (1996). *Psychological testing and assessment. An introduction to tests and measurement.* (3rd ed.). Mountain View, CA: Mayfield.

Corsini, R. J. (1987). *Concise encyclopedia of psychology.* New York: Wiley.

Corsini, R. J. (1994). *Encyclopedia of psychology* (2nd ed.). New York: Wiley.

Gall, S. (1996). *The Gale encyclopedia of psychology.* Detroit, Michigan: Gale.

Goldenson, R. M. (1970). *The encyclopedia of human behavior: Psychology, psychiatry, and mental health.* Garden City, NY: Doubleday.

Graham, J. R. (1993). *MMPI-2: Assessing personality and psychopathology* (2nd ed.). New York: Oxford University Press.

Lezak, M. D. (1995). *Neuropsychological assessment.* New York: Oxford University Press.

Wolman, B. B. (1970). *Children without a childhood: A study of childhood schizophrenia.* New York: Grune & Stratton.

Wolman, B. B. (1977). *International encyclopedia of psychiatry, psychology, psychoanalysis and neurology.* New York: Aesculapius Publishers/Van Nostrand Reinhold.

Elahe Nezami

STANFORD–BINET INTELLIGENCE SCALE. Alfred Binet and Théodore Simon originally introduced an intelligence test in 1905 that consisted of a series of developmental screening tasks intended to differentiate varying abilities among school children. They revised the tasks in 1908 and 1911, adding items and clustering these by the age at which most children could pass them (i.e., introducing the concept of *mental age* to indicate an average mental level at which items should be successfully completed). Adult tasks were also added to give the test more range.

While the work of Binet and Simon was groundbreaking in its formulation of the intelligence test items and initial configuration, it was the Stanford–Binet Intelligence scale (the first to be called by that name) developed by Lewis Madison Terman in 1916 that became widely used. While Terman conceptually adhered to much of Binet and Simon's work, he revamped the test organization, changed scoring and administrative procedures, improved representative sampling, and introduced the world to the concept of the Intelligence Quotient (IQ) based on the formula:

$$(\text{Mental Age} / \text{Chronological Age}) \times 100$$

The second version of the Stanford–Binet, developed by Terman and Merrill in 1937, was recognized as a landmark achievement in the evolution of individualized testing of intelligence (Sattler, 1988). Two new forms of the test were designed (Forms L and M), featuring better standardization procedures and psychometric properties, and now covering ages ranging from two through adult. In 1960 Terman and Merrill produced the third revision of the Stanford–Binet, which was a merging of the best tests of the 1937 L and M forms, combined to produce just one form, the Stanford–Binet L-M. The traditional ratio IQ score was discarded in favor of the Deviation IQ, based upon a normalized standard score similar to the way in which Wechsler scores were calculated. In 1972 Thorndike restandardized the L-M, which had not been done in 1960, leaving the test items virtually intact.

In 1986 Thorndike, Hagen, and Sattler gave the Stanford–Binet's Fourth Edition (SB:FE) its most substantial revision. The SB:FE no longer employed groups of items appropriate for children of particular ages, opting instead for items of varying difficulty organized by type. Thus, the SB:FE used subtests in the same way as the Wechsler scales. These subtests were further organized into four different ability factors.

The SB:FE can be administered to individuals aged 2 years through adult in approximately 60 to 80 minutes. This is a practical advantage over other methods of assessing intelligence, which generally are designed for either children or adults. The range of ages is possible due to the developmental nature of the SB: FE subtests, many of which change task requirements within a subtest depending upon the age of the examinee (a carryover from the age-scale format philosophy). The SB:FE contains a total of 15 subtests; between 8 and 15 of them are administered to an individual, depending on chronological age. The subtests are grouped into four factor areas: Verbal Reasoning, Abstract/Visual Reasoning, Quantitative Reasoning, and Short-Term Memory. Verbal Reasoning is comprised of subtests that require knowledge, understanding, and application of verbal skills. This includes subtests like Vocabulary (oral definition of words) and Verbal Relations (finding common characteristic of a set of words). Abstract/Visual Reasoning measures abilities in organizing and interpreting visually perceived stimuli. For example, in the subtest matrices, a pattern of four figures contains one missing element, and the individual must select the best logical alternative to complete the matrix. Quantitative Reasoning involves basic arithmetic skills and the use of reasoning to solve problems. The subtest Equation Building contains items with a set of numbers followed by several arithmetic operation signs. The numbers and signs must be arranged to make a coherent number sentence. Short-Term Memory may involve sequencing, attention, and concentration skills, as well as memory. For example, in the Bead Memory subtest, subjects are shown a model of differentially shaped and colored beads arranged on a vertical post. After 5 seconds the model is removed and the subject must reproduce the beads in the same arrangement that was shown on the model.

Each individual subtest has a mean of 50 and a standard deviation of 8, a scale unlike those used in many other intelligence tests. The four factor areas described above yield a standardized score called a Standard Age Score (SAS), with a mean of 100 and a standard deviation of 16, as does the test composite, which is based upon the sum of the four area SASs.

Clearly, the Stanford–Binet scale established the historical parameters for the practice of intelligence testing. The subject of literally thousands of research papers and books since its inception, the current and previous versions of the scale continue to rank as one of the most widely used instruments in school, clinical, and hospital settings (Hutton, Dubes, & Muir, 1992). The Stanford–Binet, along with the work of Binet and Simon, established the standard for how general ability is measured. General ability was assessed using a series of tasks designed to evaluate a range of skills. These skills have been interpreted as strengths and weaknesses using this test and other general ability measures such as the Wechsler scales.

In summary, the contributions of the Stanford–Binet in its various revisions to the field of intelligence testing can only be described as profound. Binet and Simon laid the groundwork for tests that followed, especially the Wechsler scales. [See Wechsler Memory Scale.] Like the Wechsler scale, the Binet scale has been synonymous with intelligence testing because of its longevity and research base, and both have been valuable tools used by psychology since the early twentieth century. The field of intelligence testing is changing, however. The concepts underlying the Stanford–Binet have come under scrutiny due to recent developments in theories of intelligence. Whereas in the past the Stanford–Binet has been evaluated in comparison to tests built during the same period, now its value is being contrasted to newer measures based on more modern concepts. Ultimately, the ability of these approaches to meet the needs of users and withstand the critical examination of researchers will determine which instruments psychologists will use in the future.

[*See also the biography of Binet.*]

Bibliography

Hutton, J. B., Dubes, R., & Muir, S. (1992). Assessment practices of school psychologists: Ten years later. *School Psychology Review, 21,* 271–284.

Sattler, J. M. (1988). *Assessment of children* (3rd ed.). San Diego, CA: Author.

Anthony W. Paolitto and Jack A. Naglieri

STARTLE REFLEX. *See* Fear and Terror.

STATES OF CONSCIOUSNESS. *See* Consciousness and Unconsciousness.

STATISTICAL POWER. *See* Data Analysis.

STATISTICAL PROCEDURES. *See* Data Analysis.

STATISTICAL SIGNIFICANCE. The basic process of determining statistical significance is uncontroversial. Suppose a researcher wishes to make a claim, supported by an observed pattern in the data. For example, an experimenter might test the effect of two treatments, observe that the average for one treatment was higher than the average for the other, and wish to claim that the one treatment was more effective than the second. A null hypothesis is constructed, representing the hypothesis that the observed pattern occurred just by chance. For example, the null hypothesis would be that the two treatments were equally effective. Even if the null hypothesis was correct, there would be a discrepancy between what was observed and what would be expected given the null hypothesis. The probability of achieving the observed discrepancy or a larger discrepancy is calculated, assuming the null hypothesis is correct. When this value, p, is less than some criterion, α, the null hypothesis is rejected. The difference between the observed pattern and the expected observation given the null hypothesis is then deemed statistically significant, and the observed pattern is accepted as true. For example, with p less than 0.05 and a lack of confounds, the experimenter could conclude that one treatment was more effective than another.

Most textbooks allow researchers to set their own value of α. This would allow α to reflect the costs, benefits, and probabilities of the various outcomes of the statistical test. However, in practice α seems to be set by the field of psychology, at 0.05.

History

The precursor to the modern statistical test is the critical-ratio test, developed and used in the early 1900s. The leading developers of modern statistical testing are Karl Pearson, Ronald Fisher, Jerszy Neyman, and Egon Pearson. Fisher differed vehemently with the justifications proposed by Neyman and E. Pearson, even though current statistical textbooks present a combination of their ideas.

Justification

Justifying the procedure of statistical testing is not easy. It might seem as though the null hypothesis is being rejected because the observed outcome was very unlikely given the null hypothesis. However, all particular outcomes are unlikely given the null hypothesis. For example, it is unlikely that exactly 100 heads would occur in 200 tosses of an unbiased coin, but this low probability would not support the conclusion that the coin is biased.

Why then do some outcomes allow rejecting the null hypothesis while others do not? Neyman and Pearson suggested the following justification. Define the rejection region as those outcomes that will allow rejecting the null hypothesis. Next, fix the probability of rejecting a true null hypothesis at the predetermined value of α. Finally, select the rejection region that maximizes the probability of rejecting a false null hypothesis. This leads to rejecting the null hypothesis when an outcome is too discrepant from the expected outcome given the null hypothesis.

Another issue is the need for a criterion—there is something illogical about accepting a claim when $p = 0.049$ and not accepting it when $p = 0.051$, given that these two values are so close. However, scientists apparently need to classify the data of a study as either sufficient or insufficient to support the claim the researcher is making. Faced with a need for classification, there must be some criterion distinguishing suffcient from insufficient data.

A third issue is that most conventional statistical tests make assumptions that are difficult to justify, such as the data being normally distributed on an interval scale. In response to this problem, nonparametric statistical tests were developed that avoid these questionable assumptions in determining *p*. Nonparametric tests are not widely used, perhaps because they usually give approximately the same answer as conventional tests. However, when data are obviously not normally distributed, researchers will often transform their data so that it is approximately normally distributed.

Finally, it is mathematically convenient to assume that the data were produced by random sampling from a population, even though this rarely if ever occurs. This has led to a number of attempts to locate or define some population, real or hypothetical, to which the results of the statistical test apply. In practice, the notion of samples and populations is usually ignored. The concern is the plausibility of the observed pattern occurring just by chance. Statistical significance is then interpreted as implying that in the study, the observed pattern did not occur just by chance.

Limitations

There are also limits to what statistical significance accomplishes. The probability of achieving statistical significance is influenced by the size of the effect, with larger effect sizes making statistical significance more likely. But other factors are relevant, such as the number of subjects tested. Therefore, contrary to whatever might be implied by the term significant, statistical significance cannot be interpreted as necessarily meaning that the size of an effect was large or important. This has led psychologists to distinguish clinical or practical significance from mere statistical significance.

As Bayesians are fond to note, statistical significance also is not a reliable guide as to whether or not a claim should be believed. Instead, belief in a claim should be influenced by all knowledge regarding the claim. Statistical significance indicates only that the research study itself contains a criterion amount of evidence for a claim.

Thus, there are a number of reasons for not being fond of researchers' ubiquitous concern with achieving statistical significance. However, it continues to serve a necessary function in psychology, demonstrating that a criterion level of evidence has been provided against the possibility that an observed pattern occurred in the data just by chance.

[*See also* Data Analysis; *and* Hypothesis Testing.]

Bibliography

Berger, J. O. (1986). Bayesian salesmanship. In P. Goel and A. Zellner (Eds.), *Bayesian inference and decision techniques* (pp. 473–488). Amsterdam: Elsevier Science Publishers. Criticizes null hypothesis testing from a Bayesian perspective.

Cohen, J. (1994). The earth is round (*p* < .05). *American Psychologist, 49*, 997–1003. Criticizes the logic of null hypothesis testing.

Frick, R. W. (1996). The appropriate use of null hypothesis testing. *Psychological Methods, 1*, 379–390. Defends the use of statistical significance while pointing out its limitations.

Gigerenzer, G., Swijink, Z., Porter, T., Daston, L., Beatty, J., & Kruger, L. (1989). *The empire of chance*. Cambridge: Cambridge University Press. History and use of statistical testing in psychology.

Hagen, R. L. (1997). In praise of the null hypothesis statistical test. *American Psychologist, 52*, 15–24. Explains and defends the standard justifications for using statistical significance.

Loftus, G. R. (1996). Psychology will be a much better science when we change the way we analyze data. *Current Directions in Psychological Science, 5*, 161–171. Criticizes the need for statistical significance.

Robert W. Frick

STELLAR, ELIOT (1919–1993), American physiological psychologist. Stellar's academic career spanned more than 45 years. He was renowned for his research in the complex behavioral, physiological, and chemical interactions underlying human and animal ingestive behaviors, but also gained wide distinction for the development of behavioral neuroscience as an interdisciplinary subject, for his educational leadership, and for his work on the National Commission for the Protection of Human Subjects of Research, as well as for his manifold efforts for the rights of scientists through the National Academy of Sciences.

Stellar was born in Boston, attended the Boston Latin School and Harvard University and received a master's degree in 1942 and a doctorate in psychology in 1947 from Brown University. During World War II, he served in the military as a psychologist.

Stellar's first appointment was at the Johns Hopkins University, where he coauthored with Clifford Morgan the second edition of C. T. Morgan's pioneer textbook *Physiological Psychology* (Morgan & Stellar, 1950) and published a now classic paper, "The Physiology of Motivation" (Stellar, 1954), which clearly identified the hypothalamus as the center of motivated behavior. It was one of eight papers selected by the *Psychological Review* for its centennial edition as one of the most influential papers of the twentieth century.

With Nelson Krauss, Stellar developed a stereotaxic instrument to produce accurate lesions in the hypothalamus of the rat. The Stellar–Krauss instrument was a major step in the advancement of research in hunger and satiety but also in other areas of behavioral neuroscience. Not only did this instrument enhance the replication of behavioral experiments with animals and their scientific validity, but it also reduced the number of animals needed to demonstrate a statistically significant result.

In 1954, Stellar joined the anatomy department of the University of Pennsylvania Medical School. He worked with Louis Flexner, James Sprague, William Chambers, John Brobeck, and Per-Olar Therman to develop the then fledgling Institute of Neurological Sciences, which served as a paradigm for other neuroscience centers in the United States and abroad.

When Stellar began his career, physiological psychology was in its infancy. Largely due to his efforts, the 1950s became known as the age of the hypothalamus in physiological psychology. The problems he explored still remain central to the field. Stellar collaborated with Philip Teitelbaum and Alan Epstein on motivated behaviors involved in hunger and satiety and on oral and postingestive control of eating and drinking in rats. Later in his career, with Albert Stunkard, Henry Jordan, and Theresa Spiegel, he began the measurement of food intake in human participants.

Stellar made other pivotal contributions to psychology and other scientific disciplines. With Louis and Josepha Flexner and Gabriel de la Haba, he elaborated the chemical substrates of memory; with James Sprague, William Chambers, John Liu, and Melvin Levitt, he studied brainstem mechanisms of arousal, attention and affect; and he collaborated with Jeri Sechzer and Thomas Meikle on early studies of interhemispheric transfer of learning and memory in "split-brain" cats.

At the University of Pennsylvania, Stellar became professor of physiological psychology in the anatomy department and served as director of its Institute of Neurological Sciences from 1965 to 1973 and as provost from 1973 to 1978.

In 1968, Stellar was elected to the National Academy of Sciences and in 1972 to the American Academy of Arts and Sciences. From 1974 to 1978 he served on the National Commission for the Protection of Human Subjects of Biomedical and Behavioral Research. Stellar's work with the commission culminated in *The Belmont Report: Ethical Principles and Guidelines for the Protection of Human Subjects of Research* (1978), which established the first federal regulations for the use of human research participants in the United States.

In 1984 Stellar became chair of the National Academy of Sciences Committee on Human Rights, achieving remarkable success in intervening on behalf of political prisoners of totalitarian regimes (e.g., Andre Sakharov). In 1989 he received the medallion of the National Academy of Sciences for contributions to cooperation between the U.S. and U.S.S.R. academies of sciences. Stellar was a member of the Institute of Medicine. He was elected to the American Philosophical Society, serving as president from 1987 to 1993. Stellar was given the Warren Medal of the Society of Experimental Psychologists and in 1993 was awarded the American Psychological Foundation's Gold Medal for Life Achievement in Psychological Science. He was also the recipient of numerous honorary degrees and citations by many countries.

Regardless of these appointments and honors, Stellar always returned to his research on eating and satiety. Toward the end of his life his work extended to hedonic experiences in ingestive behavior. In another classic paper, "Brain Mechanisms in Hunger and Other Hedonic Experiences," Stellar (1974) hypothesized that the neural mechanisms of the hedonics of eating and drinking evolved from and overlapped with mechanisms that control ingestive behavior.

Stellar authored or coauthored many books. The one that provided the most special fulfillment and pleasure was *The Neurobiology of Motivation and Reward* (Stellar & Stellar, 1985), which he wrote with his son James.

Stellar's work continued to be recognized posthumously for many years. Shortly after his death, the Polish Academy of Science honored him with the Copernicus Medal, the highest Polish award for foreign scientists. This was in recognition of the 30 years he spent, initially with Jerzy Konorski and Jerzy Rose, in developing research projects at the Nencki Institute in Warsaw and of his work in organizing exchange programs with the University of Pennsylvania. Other recognition has come in conferences and symposia from his former students and colleagues honoring his research and its far-reaching influences on the variety of disciplines he engendered.

Bibliography

American Psychological Foundation. (1993). Eliot Stellar: Gold medal for life achievement in psychological science. *American Psychologist, 48,* 721–723.

Dethier, V. G., & Stellar, E. (1961). *Animal behavior.* Englewood Cliffs, NJ: Prentice Hall.

Meikle, T. H., Jr., Sechzer, J. A. & Stellar, E. (1962). Interhemispheric transfer of tactile conditioned responses in corpus-callosum conditioned cats. *Journal of Neurophysiology, 25,* 530–543.

Morgan, C. T., & Stellar, E. (1950). *Physiological psychology.* New York: McGraw-Hill.

National Commission for the Protection of Human Subjects of Biomedical and Behavioral Research. (1978). *The Belmont report. Ethical principles and guidelines for the protection of human subjects of research* (OS-78-0012). Washington, DC: United States Department of Health, Education, and Welfare. *Appendix:* Volumes 1–2 (DHEW OS-78-0013, DHEW OS-78-0014).

Sechzer, J. A. (1995). Eliot Stellar (1919–1993). *American Psychologist, 50,* 387–388.

Stellar, E. (1954). The physiology of motivation. *Psychological Review, 61,* 5–22.

Stellar, E. (1974). Brain mechanisms in hunger and other hedonic experiences. *Proceedings of the American Philosophical Society, 118,* 276–282.

Stellar, J. A., & Stellar, E. (1985). *The neurobiology of motivation and reward.* New York: Springer-Verlag.

Jeri Altneu Sechzer

STEREOTYPES. In this 1922 book *Public Opinion*, Walter Lippmann introduced the term *stereotype* to refer to beliefs about social groups. A journalist, Lippmann borrowed the term from printing terminology, where it denoted fixed casts of metal used to repeatedly produce the same sets of letters. He used it to refer to the way in which humans form "pictures in their heads" of other groups of people, repeatedly applying the same attributes to people belonging to the same group. Lippmann regarded the stereotyping process as arising from both cognitive-perceptual and motivational factors (though he did not use these specific terms), and thus laid the groundwork for future psychological research.

What Is a Stereotype?

The term *stereotype* may be defined as a perceiver's knowledge, beliefs, and expectancies about some social group. Although this definition seems straightforward, some important definitional issues arise upon further consideration. First, social scientists have debated whether or not stereotypes are consensually shared across society. Many regard a stereotype as any individual's beliefs about social groups, while others have used the term only to indicate those beliefs that are widely shared within a culture. In addition, controversy has surrounded the issue of whether or not stereotypes are faulty, invalid overgeneralizations, and therefore necessarily inaccurate. To argue that stereotypes are completely inaccurate is to assume that there are no actual differences among groups, which flies in the face of common experience. Many stereotypes, then, probably contain some "kernel of truth." On the other hand, as overgeneralizations applied to all members of a group, stereotypic characterizations immediately become inaccurate descriptions of at least some (and often many) group members, given the diversity within any large social group on virtually any psychological attribute. Furthermore, stereotype inaccuracy may arise from the individual or group-based motivations of at least some perceivers.

Social scientists have adopted three main conceptual approaches in their efforts to understand and to investigate stereotyping (Ashmore & Del Boca, 1981). The *psychodynamic* approach, with its roots in Freudian thought, regards stereotypes as manifestations of unacceptable human impulses. According to this view, beliefs about groups of people are used to cope with internal conflicts or satisfy the motivational needs of the perceiver; for example, by projecting negative views of the self onto members of the derogated group. This approach's greatest influence was in the work on the authoritarian personality (Adorno, Frenkel-Brunswik, Levinson, & Sanford, 1950), which viewed stereotypes and prejudice as manifestations of a personality syndrome that included adherence to conventional norms, submission to authority, and intolerance of those who violated these prescriptions. The *sociocultural* approach has viewed stereotypes as the product of broad sociological forces in conflict. Here, stereotypes are viewed predominantly as consensually shared beliefs that rationalize the existing order of intergroup relations. These beliefs are an inherent part of culture, transmitted and maintained through pervasive forces of socialization. The *cognitive* approach has concentrated on basic cognitive processes in human functioning that underlie stereotyping. It emphasizes the extent to which stereotypes result from human processes of categorization that arise from the individual perceiver's attempts to efficiently deal with large amounts of information. The cognitive approach generally analyzes stereotyping as it occurs at the individual level, with a focus on the human information-processing mechanisms that lead to stereotyping rather than on the content of particular stereotypes. While the psychodynamic and sociocultural approaches have had a large impact on the history of stereotyping research, the cognitive orientation has been extremely influential in recent years (cf., Hamilton & Sherman, 1994; Hamilton, Stroessner, & Driscoll, 1994).

How Are Stereotypes Measured?

In one of the first empirical studies of stereotypes, Katz and Braly (1933) presented people with a large list of traits and instructed them to check those that best described the people in a given social group. The traits checked most frequently were viewed as constituting the stereotype of that group. The Katz–Braly checklist method became the standard procedure for measuring the content of stereotypes for many years.

Studies of stereotype content have provided information about people's consensually shared beliefs about large social categories. Most research has focused on stereotypes of groups defined by gender, age, and race. Research on gender stereotypes has shown that women are typically regarded as kind and nurturing, but not very skillful, while men are regarded as skillful and domineering, but not very kind. Studies of age stereotypes have usually concerned views of the elderly rather than the young. The aged are viewed in paradoxical terms: stereotypes about them include negative traits such as senile, disabled, and grumpy, as well as positive traits such as wise and generous. Racial stereotype research has gathered generalizations about a variety of different racial groups, generally consisting of Anglo Whites' beliefs about minority group members.

Research involving stereotype content concerning gender, age, race, and other groups often reflects only the views of those in majority-advantaged groups toward those in minority-disadvantaged groups, and it is always restricted to a given culture within a particular historical period (cf., Fiske, 1998).

Because the content of a stereotype in the Katz–Braly method is defined by consensus among participants, the extensive use of this technique implicitly includes the assumption that stereotypes are widely shared cultural beliefs, a consequence of the methodology rather than a strong theoretical orientation. This constraining assumption, as well as a focus on linguistic stereotype content alone, imposed significant limitations on the breadth of questions and issues studied in stereotyping research. As the cognitive approach developed, the assumption of consensus was replaced by an emphasis on the individual's belief system, and the focus on measuring stereotype content was replaced by investigating the processes underlying the formation and maintenance of stereotypes, how and when stereotypic judgments are made, and mechanisms of stereotype change (Hamilton et al., 1994).

Why Stereotype?

Why do people form generalized beliefs about the members of other social groups? The answer to this question is more complex than it may seem at first glance.

The first step in stereotype formation is that of categorizing others into groups and thereby viewing all members of the group as interchangeable and functionally equivalent. Why do people categorize others into groups? Why don't they perceive each person as an individual? Categorization occurs as the result of both cognitive and motivational factors. One major cognitive factor underlying people's use of categorizations in their perceptions of others is that they simply do not have the processing resources to attend to and retain the vast amount of social information with which they are continually bombarded. By using generalized categories, they gain cognitive efficiency, for they can make broad differentiations between categories of people and assume similarity within categories without trying to preserve all the information they learn about each individual person. Moreover, category-based stereotypes provide perceivers with functional "knowledge" (beliefs, expectations) about the characteristics of category members. People can then use group stereotypes to make inferences about any given individual they might interact with, especially when other kinds of information are not available. Such inferences will be useful to the extent that the stereotype is relatively accurate or diagnostic, even though unique information about the individual will be lost.

Differentiation between groups can also result from a cognitive bias known as the distinctiveness-based illusory correlation. When processing information, perceivers are highly attentive and responsive to unusual or distinctive stimulus events, and when two such events co-occur, their infrequency can bias the observer to associate these distinctive events with each other. Thus, distinctive behaviors (e.g., negative behaviors) performed by a distinctive group (i.e., a minority) tend to be associated with one another and best remembered in the context of developing beliefs about groups. The consequence is that perceivers may differentially evaluate two groups even though they are described by evaluatively equivalent information (Hamilton & Gifford, 1976). [*See* Illusory Correlation.]

A second major factor underlying categorization lies in people's desire to enhance their own self-evaluation through their identification with groups to which they belong (in-groups). If people feel good about their in-groups, then they can feel good about themselves, with positive consequences for their self-esteem. It is, of course, a subjective judgment as to how "good" one's group is. However, evaluations of groups to which one does not belong (out-groups) are equally subjective. Therefore, comparisons of in-groups with out-groups can often enhance in-group evaluations and hence feelings of positive self-worth, especially if one chooses the comparison group carefully and selects the attributes on which they are compared in a biased but beneficial manner. These ideas are at the heart of social identity theory, developed by psychologist Henri Tajfel, which has had enormous impact on psychological thinking about and research on intergroup relations (Tajfel & Turner, 1986).

Thus, both cognitive and motivational factors lead people to classify others into categories. What bases do people use for forming such categorizations? With so much information in the social environment, which information do they choose to select as a means for dividing people into groups?

Race, gender, and age have often been considered the basic social categories as a result of their highly prevalent use by social perceivers. One reason these categorizations might be used so extensively is that they are easily identified through visual cues; it is difficult upon encountering a person not to recognize that person's gender, race, and age group. However, visual salience alone does not explain the dominance of these categorizations in the social-perceptual field; other potential categorizations, such as height and hair color, are equally visually accessible, but rarely used. It is likely that race, gender, and age are given special preference for categorization because people believe that these categorizations are diagnostic of behavior and they note their prevalent use by others throughout society.

Having formed social categories in which to place others, people gain knowledge and develop beliefs and expectancies about the people within them. Stereotyping does not consist of categorization alone, but rather the association of such knowledge, beliefs, and expectancies to the categories. Once these associations are made, people are quite willing to mentally imbue any individual included in a given categorization with the characteristics implied by it.

Categorizations are often made not only at broad, inclusive levels (such as gender and race) but also at more specific "subtype" levels. As perceivers interact with more members of a social group and gain more information about that category, they are increasingly likely to encounter group members that do not "fit" the general conception of the group. As this happens, perceivers recognize smaller segments within the overall group. Each subgroup is seen as possessing some attributes that define the overarching category but also sharing other characteristics that differentiate it both from the overall group conception and from other subgroups within the category. Perceivers may also develop generalized conceptions of these subtypes, and hence will not only have a stereotype about the total group (e.g., women) but also have and use stereotypes about the subtypes (e.g., housewives, feminists, etc.). When a person adequately fits within any particular subtype categorization, he or she will more likely be categorized in terms of that subtype than in terms of the larger categorization. As noted above, a large number of subtypes exist within the broad, well-known categorizations such as gender, age, and race, and these basic-level categorizations may be employed more frequently than the superordinate category classifications. Subtypes tend to contain richer information than do larger social categories, while retaining a sufficient amount of generality to still allow for relatively widespread application.

Categorization processes may be greatly affected by the situation and circumstances at hand. A given attribute is highly likely to be employed for categorization purposes under conditions when it is made salient to the perceiver, when it is relevant to immediate interaction goals, and when it represents a noticeable differentiation within the present social context. For example, a perceiver is likely to use weight as a basis for categorization when it has been quite recently discussed, when it is important to the goals of the situation (e.g., purchasing new clothes), or when there are obvious weight differences among the people present in a given situation.

While these cognitive factors lead to categorization because they provide a means to functionally simplify the social world for the perceiver, motivational factors lead social perceivers to categorize others as belonging to the same group or a different group than the self, that is, into ingroups and outgroups. This type of categorization seems to be one of the most predominant and natural in any social situation. In-group–out-group categorizations allow people to enhance their own positive self-evaluations by finding ways to view their groups in a favorable light.

What Are the Consequences of Stereotypes?

Once people form stereotypes of others, numerous consequences ensue. Just as they underlie the original formation of stereotypic categories, both cognitive and motivational factors also influence the use of those stereotypes.

Considerable research evidence shows that people's information processing is biased in several ways toward the confirmation of their own stereotypes (Hamilton, Sherman, & Ruvolo, 1990). People pay greater attention to information that is consistent with their beliefs, tending to ignore inconsistent information and interpreting ambiguous information in such a way as to support their own expectancies. Furthermore, they seek information that confirms their stereotypes through the (often unintentional) use of directional and misleading questions, and they uphold their information search until their own expectancies have been substantiated. Moreover, their attributions for group members' behaviors are biased in a stereotype-consistent manner. Finally, when they remember information about social groups, they do so in a biased manner. Stereotype-confirming information is often easiest to retrieve, and additional retrieval biases occur as people guide their information search toward stereotype-confirming information. In these ways the very use of the stereotype serves to perpetuate its apparent usefulness.

Similarly, the motivation to see ourselves, and our own groups, in a favorable light has important ramifications on interpersonal perception and behavior. In fact, the in-group–out-group categorization by itself has important consequences. As Tajfel et al. (1971) documented, even arbitrarily categorizing people into groups is sufficient to induce in-group bias (the tendency to evaluate one's own group more favorably than others) and discriminatory behavior (making resource allocations that benefit their own group). Another consequence lies in the tendency to perceive greater within-group similarity in out-groups than in-groups, a bias that has been termed the *out-group homogeneity effect* (cf., Linville, 1998).

The knowledge, beliefs, and expectancies contained within stereotypes may also have a large influence on behavior, through a process known as the self-fulfilling prophecy. When a stereotype is activated upon contact with a member of a stereotyped group, people often behave in ways guided by their stereotypic beliefs, which in turn can induce the stereotyped person to act in accordance with those expectancies. When perceivers observe such expectancy-confirming behavior, they view it as additional evidence confirming their beliefs. In this manner, stereotypes can lead to a circular pattern of behavioral confirmation that can result not only in the strengthening of stereotypes held by the social perceiver, but also in the long-term adoption of stereotype-consistent behaviors by the stereotyped (Olson, Roese, & Zanna, 1996).

Once people form beliefs about certain social groups, those stereotypes can be transmitted to others in a variety of ways. Stereotypes are learned through the comments and behaviors of family and friends, are conveyed through jokes about ethnic groups, and, on a wider scale, are promoted through portrayals of minority groups in television, movies, and the print media. Even the linguistic properties of descriptions of members of stereotyped groups are biased in a manner that perpetuates the preexisting belief system (Maass and Arcuri, 1996).

In addition, within society, members of certain groups are often disproportionately placed within particular roles, which leads social perceivers to form false beliefs that these people are naturally suited to such roles (Eagly & Steffen, 1984). Moreover, people gradually learn the social norms that govern their society, and their inherent tendency to conform to such norms leads them to accept certain behaviors as appropriate for interaction with members of a given social group. Thus, transmission processes can influence both the types of categorizations made and the content of stereotypes about people within such categorizations.

Can Stereotypes Be Changed?

Everyday experience suggests that stereotypes often do not change over time. In fact, a series of studies replicating Katz and Braly's (1933) research documents that white Americans' stereotype of Blacks has been quite consistent across several decades. Such findings indicate that stereotypes can be highly resistant to change. On the other hand, studies have also shown that the stereotype of the Japanese, highly favorable in the Katz and Braly study, became extremely negative during the World War II period, and then returned to a more favorable characterization in the decades that followed. Thus, stereotypes can change. Given these conflicting patterns, research has sought to identify the factors that determine which course any given stereotype will follow.

One line of research has investigated the effects of intergroup contact as a mechanism for alleviating inter-group hostilities and changing stereotypes. Although this research has specified a number of such conditions that facilitate positive change, those conditions also impose limits on expectations for such change following interaction with out-group members (Hewstone, 1996). [See Intergroup Relations.] A second line of research, studies of the subtyping process discussed earlier, has shown that experiences with members of stereotyped groups can result in the perceiver mentally grouping disconfirming cases into a separate subcategory. Such subtyping can have diverse effects. On the one hand, it can preserve the existing stereotype by isolating atypical group members from the prevailing conception of the out-group, thereby undermining the impact of stereotype-disconfirming evidence. On the other hand, mentally establishing several such subgroups can increase the perceived variability of the overall group. Increasing the perception of within-group diversity can in turn diminish the perceiver's ability to make sweeping generalizations about the group, thereby undermining one of the hallmarks of stereotyping.

[See also Discrimination.]

Bibliography

Adorno, T. W., Frenkel-Brunswik, E., Levinson, D. J., & Sanford, R. N. (1950). *The authoritarian personality*. New York: Harper.

Ashmore, R. D., & Del Boca, F. K. (1981). Conceptual approaches to stereotypes and stereotyping. In D. L. Hamilton (Ed.), *Cognitive processes in stereotyping and intergroup behavior* (pp. 1–35). Hillsdale, NJ: Erlbaum.

Eagly, A. H., & Steffen, V. J. (1984). Gender stereotypes stem from the distribution of men and women into social roles. *Journal of Personality and Social Psychology, 34*, 590–598.

Fiske, S. T. (1998). Stereotyping, prejudice, and discrimination. In D. T. Gilbert, S. T. Fiske, & G. Lindzey (Eds.), *Handbook of social psychology* (4th ed., Vol. 2, pp. 357–411). Boston: McGraw-Hill.

Hamilton, D. L., & Gifford, R. K. (1976). Illusory correlation in interpersonal perception: A cognitive basis of stereotypic judgments. *Journal of Experimental Social Psychology, 12*, 392–407.

Hamilton, D. L., & Sherman, J. W. (1994). Stereotypes. In R. S. Wyer, Jr., & T. K. Srull (Eds.), *Handbook of social cognition* (2nd ed., Vol. 2, pp. 1–68). Hillsdale, NJ: Erlbaum.

Hamilton, D. L., Sherman, S. J., & Ruvolo, C. M. (1990). Stereotype-based expectancies: Effects on information processing and social behavior. *Journal of Social Issues, 46*(2), 35–60.

Hamilton, D. L., Stroessner, S. J., & Driscoll, D. M. (1994). Social cognition and the study of stereotyping. In P. G. Devine, D. L. Hamilton, & T. M. Ostrom (Eds.), *Social cognition: Impact on social psychology* (pp. 291–321). San Diego, CA: Academic Press.

Hewstone, M. (1996). Contact and categorization: Social psychological interventions to changing intergroup relations. In C. N. Macrae, C. Stangor, & M. Hewstone

(Eds.), *Stereotypes and stereotyping* (pp. 323–368). New York: Guilford Press.

Katz, D., & Braly, K. W. (1933). Racial stereotypes of 100 college students. *Journal of Abnormal and Social Psychology, 28,* 280–290.

Lippmann, W. (1922). *Public opinion.* New York: Harcourt Brace.

Linville, P. W. (1998). The heterogeneity of homogeneity. In J. Darley & J. Cooper (Eds.), *Attribution and social interaction: The legacy of Edward E. Jones* (pp. 423–462). Washington, DC: American Psychological Association.

Maass, A., & Arcuri, L. (1996). Language and stereotyping. In C. N. Macrae, C. Stangor, & M. Hewstone (Eds.), *Stereotypes and stereotyping* (pp. 193–226). New York: Guilford Press.

Olson, J. M., Roese, N. J., & Zanna, M. P. (1996). Expectancies. In E. T. Higgins & A. W. Kruglanski (Eds.), *Social psychology: Handbook of basic principles* (pp. 211–238). New York: Guilford Press.

Tajfel, H., Flament, C., Billig, M. G., & Bundy, R. P. (1971). Social categorization and intergroup behavior. *European Journal of Social Psychology, 1,* 149–178.

Tajfel, H., & Turner, J. C. (1986). The social identity theory of intergroup behavior. In S. Worchel & W. G. Austin (Eds.), *Psychology of intergroup relations* (pp. 7–24). Chicago: Nelson-Hall.

David L. Hamilton and A. Neville Uhles

STERN, LOUIS WILLIAM (1871–1938), German psychologist and philosopher. An only child, Louis William Stern was born in Berlin to Jewish parents of modest means, Rosa and Sigismund Stern. William (as he would come to be known) was educated at the Friedrich-Wilhelms-University in Berlin, where his studies in philology, philosophy, and psychology were guided primarily by Friedrich Paulson, Moritz Lazarus, and Hermann Ebbinghaus. In 1897, Stern followed Ebbinghaus to the University of Breslau (now Wroclaw, Poland). Two years later, Stern married Clara Joseephy, and the couple would have three children: Hilde in 1900, Günther in 1902, and Eva in 1904.

Beginning with Hilde's birth and continuing for the next 18 years, Clara and William Stern kept diaries recording observations relevant to the psychological development of their three children. This material grounded two coauthored (German language) monographs dealing, respectively, with *Children's Speech* (1907) and *Recollection, Testimony and Lying in Early Childhood* (1909). William Stern would also consult the diary material for parts of what would prove to be his most popular book, *The Psychology of Early Childhood Up to the Sixth Year of Age* (1914). These three works would solidify Stern's status as one of the most important developmental psychologists of the first half of the twentieth century.

Stern contributed significantly to many areas of scientific psychology. His 1900 book *On the Psychology of Individual Differences* and its 1911 sequel, *Methodological Foundations of Differential Psychology*, are cornerstones of modern differential psychology. In 1906 he founded, with Otto Lipmann, the German-language *Journal of Applied Psychology*, which served as an outlet for many works dealing with intelligence testing, procedures for identifying gifted children, the effectiveness of various pedagogical practices, and forensic psychology—especially the psychology of legal testimony.

After moving to Hamburg in 1916, Stern was a major figure in the establishment of the university there 3 years later, and he served that institution for the next 14 years as professor of psychology and philosophy. He directed a research institute concerned primarily with the problem of identifying gifted and talented children by means of psychological tests, supplemented by extensive investigations of individual cases according to methods he termed psychographic. Concurrently, he continued with his *magnum opus*, a three-volume series entitled *Person and Thing: A Systematic Philosophical World View* (*Philosophical Foundations*, 1906; *The Human Personality*, 1918; *Philosophy of Values*, 1924). Setting forth a conceptual and theoretical framework Stern labeled critical personalism, these books give full expression to Stern's views on the problem that, by his own account, centered and guided his scholarly life: the problem of human individuality.

Taking as irreducible and inviolable the distinction between persons and things, Stern hoped to realize, through critical personalism, a system of thought "as far removed from a one-sided individualism recognizing only the rights and happiness of the single individual, as from a socialism in which individuality and personal freedom are choked by the pressures of supra-personal demands" (Stern, 1918, p. xi). Early on, he seems to have viewed intelligence testing in particular (it was he who first proposed the intelligence quotient in 1912), and the study of individual differences more generally, as possibly helpful means to this end. Increasingly, however, Stern would distance himself from the investigative methods he had once so ably promoted. He did so on the grounds that *psychotechnology*, a term he had invented to refer to the practical use of psychometric instruments in nonacademic settings, was effacing the person-thing distinction and, in the process, compromising the socioethical principles of critical personalism. Stern's thinking on these matters was, and has remained, outside of the mainstream. Consequently, although the correlational research methods he first espoused but later eschewed remain prominent in the landscape of late twentieth-century psychology, critical personalism has remained a system of thought known to very few.

Following Hitler's accession to power in 1933, Stern

was summarily dismissed from the faculty of the University of Hamburg, and in the fall of that same year, Stern's two closest colleagues, Martha Muchow and Otto Lipmann, committed suicide. Profoundly shaken, Stern fled Germany in 1934. He resided briefly in the Netherlands, where, despite the tragic developments, he still managed to complete his last major work, *General Psychology from a Personalistic Standpoint.*

Stern then accepted William McDougal's offer of a position in the department of psychology at Duke University. Because he was burdened by his limited familiarity with the English language, concerned for his children and grandchildren, and crestfallen by developments in his native country, the last years of this remarkable scholar's life were difficult ones. William Stern died in Durham, North Carolina.

Bibliography

Works by Stern

Stern, W. (1900). *Über Psychologie der individuellen Differenzen (Ideen zu einer differentiellen Psychologie)*. Leipzig: Barth. The first textbook in differential psychology; documents the birth of a field.

Stern, W. (1906). *Person und Sache: System der philosophischen Weltanschauung*. Vol. 1: *Ableitung und Grundlehre*. Leipzig: Barth. Volume 1 of Stern's major three-volume work, *Person and thing*, this work describes the philosophical foundations of critical personalism.

Stern, W. (1911). *Die Differentielle Psychologie in ihren methodischen Grundlagen*. Leipzig: Barth. Stern himself said he wrote this book instead of a revised edition of the 1900 book. As its title suggests, this work is essentially a methods handbook. It is much more systematic and comprehensive than the 1900 book. Because of the efforts of Kurt Pawlik of the University of Hamburg, this volume was reprinted by the German publishing house Hogrefe (Göttingen) in 1994, the seventy-fifth anniversary of the University of Hamburg, which Stern had helped to found.

Stern, W. (1912). *Die psychologischen Methoden der Intelligenzprüfung*. Leipzig: Barth. In this monograph Stern first proposes that a child's level of intelligence should be indexed not as the difference between mental age and chronological age but instead as the ratio of the former to the latter—hence the intelligence quotient.

Stern, W. (1917). *Die Psychologie und der Personalismus*. Leipzig: Barth. This short book offers a concise, densely packed introduction to critical personalism.

Stern, W. (1918). *Person und Sache: System der philosophischen Weltanschauung*. Zweiter Band: *Die menschliche Persönlichkeit*. Leipzig: Barth. Volume 2 of *Person and thing*, this discussion of the human personality is the most thoroughly psychological work in the series.

Stern, W. (1924). *Person und Sache: System der kritischen Personalismus*. Dritter Band: *Wertphilosophie*. Leipzig: Barth. The third and last of the *Person and thing* series, this work brings Stern's outlook to full expression. It is

centered on his treatment of the role of human values, and the human activity of valuation, in the psychological functioning of individuals and, by extension, in the realization of the human community.

Stern, W. (1930). Self-portrayal. In C. Murchison (Ed.), *A history of psychology in autobiography* (pp. 335–388). (S. Langer, Trans.). Worcester, MA: Clark University Press. As its title suggests, this article offers a retrospective view of Stern's intellectual life through his own eyes.

Stern, W. (1933). Der personale Faktor in Psychotechnik und praktischer Psychologie. *Zeitschrift für angewandte Psychologie, 44,* 52–63. In this article, the reader can experience firsthand Stern's mounting frustration with developments in mainstream differential psychology and see the basis for his rejection of that framework to achieve a proper understanding of human individuality.

Stern, W. (1938). *General psychology from a personalistic standpoint*. Trans. H. Spoerl. New York: Macmillan. (Original work published in 1935.) The last and most fully developed statement of Stern's personalistic perspective on psychology's specific domains of inquiry.

Stern, C., & Stern, W. (1907). *Die Kindersprache*. Leipzig: Barth. Drawing extensively on their diary material, the Sterns address themselves in this work to the development of children's speech.

Stern, C., & Stern, W. (1999). *Recollection, testimony, and lying in early childhood*. (J. T. Lamiell, Trans.). Washington, DC: APA Books. (Original work published in 1909.) The second of the two monographs published by the Sterns on the basis of their diaries. The work is remarkable in its anticipation of much current thinking regarding young children's ability to observe what is going on around them, to remember what they have experienced, and to report those experiences accurately later on. This is a landmark work offering, among other things, a vivid illustration of the use of diaries as a research tool.

Works about Stern

Bühring, G. (1996). *William Stern oder Streben nach Einheit*. Frankfurt am Main: Peter Lang Verlag. The only currently available biography of William Stern. It is limited as a critical treatment of Stern's substantive contributions to psychology, but nevertheless it offers an informative and sensitive glimpse into Stern's domestic and professional life.

Deutsch, W. (Hg.). (1990). *Die verborgene Aktualität von William Stern*. Frankfurt am Main: Verlag Peter Lang. Revised versions of contributions to a symposium held in Berlin in 1988 on the fiftieth anniversary of Stern's death. It offers relatively brief commentaries on Stern's contributions to many different areas of psychology, as well as a lengthy discussion of the Stern-Freud controversy concerning the practice of psychoanalytic psychotherapy with children and juveniles. Includes a reminiscence by Eva Stern, the youngest of the three Stern children.

Lück, H. E., & Löwisch, D.-J. (1994). *Der Briefwechsel zwischen William Stern und Jonas Cohn: Dokumente einer Freundschaft zwischen zwei Wissenschaftlern*. Frankfurt am Main: Verlag Peter Lang. Offers an interesting glimpse into Stern's professional life, as conveyed through letters Stern sent to his friend and colleague, the Freiburg philosopher Jonas Cohn. Unfortunately, the letters from Cohn to Stern have been lost.

Schmidt, W. (1994). William Stern (1871–1938) und Lewis Terman (1877–1956): Deutsche und amerikanische Intelligenz- und Begabungsforschung im Lichte ihrer andersartigen politischen und ideologischen Voraussetzungen. *Psychologie und Geschichte, 6,* 3–26. This article vividly contrasts Terman's and Stern's respective outlooks on psychological testing—particularly intelligence and ability testing—and helps to explain why Stern gradually distanced himself from this enterprise.

James T. Lamiell

STEVENS, STANLEY SMITH (1906–1973), American psychologist. Stevens was born in Ogden, Utah, and came to the discipline by way of religion. He worked as a Mormon missionary in Europe from 1924 to 1927 and remained a member of the church while an undergraduate at the University of Utah and later at Stanford University, where he received a bachelor's degree in 1931. After a brief period of occupational uncertainty, Stevens settled on experimental psychology. He enrolled at Harvard University and wrote his doctoral dissertation, "The Volume and Intensity of Tones" (1933) under the direction of Edward G. Boring.

Although trained in experimental psychology, Stevens first came to prominence for his work in the philosophy of science. Stevens was convinced that the divisiveness of psychology was due largely to the ambiguities of language. Searching for a way to "silence useless controversy" in psychology and guard against "hazy, ambiguous, and contradictory notions," he found a solution in the operationist philosophy of Rudolf Carnap and Percy Bridgman (Stevens, 1935a, p. 323). Both scholars proposed to define scientific concepts by the procedures or "concrete operations" used to measure them. Believing operationism to be a "revolution that would put an end to the possibility of revolutions," Stevens (1935a, p. 323) wrote a series of articles in the 1930s encouraging psychologists to adopt operational analysis (1935a, 1935b, 1936a, 1939). His work fuelled the spread of operationism within psychology, and by 1940 the "operational definition" had become a standard feature of American psychological research (Leahey, 1980; Rogers, 1989).

The philosophical investigations undertaken by Stevens were closely connected to problems he had encountered while conducting empirical research on the psychophysics of hearing. His primary concern involved a basic question that had been posed by a committee of the British Association for the Advancement of Science: Was it possible to measure human sensation? Stevens believed it was. He published a scale for the measurement of the psychological magnitude of loudness as a function of the acoustic amplitude of the stimulus (1936b) and a year later published a similar scale for the measurement of the psychological magnitude of pitch as a function of frequency of vibration (Stevens, Volkmann, and Newman, 1937). Nevertheless, his position encountered stiff opposition from scientists who argued that "there was no way of adding two sensations together in a way that was comparable to putting two lengths end to end or two weights on the same scale" (Miller, 1974, p. 283). To counter this argument, Stevens drew on operational philosophy. He suggested that measurement should be evaluated according to the operations that are used rather than the tangibility of the object or events to be measured. Reflecting on the issue further, he concluded that "measurement exists in a variety of forms and that scales of measurement fall into certain definite classes" (Stevens, 1946, p. 677), which he termed nominal, ordinal, interval, and ratio. This work helped clarify the nature of measurement in psychology, and his classification of scales of measurement remains a core concept in statistics.

Academic success propelled Stevens into positions of administrative leadership. In 1940, he was appointed director of the Harvard Psychoacoustic Laboratory, and from 1949 to 1962 he also took on additional responsibility as director of the Harvard Psychological Laboratories. Never completely satisfied in the role of administrator, Stevens maintained an active interest in empirical research and in the 1950s began publishing works on his most significant empirical finding: the "power law," or "Stevens law" (Stevens, 1957, 1961). The research was the culmination of Stevens's longstanding interest in the classic problems of psychophysics and in particular Fechner's law. Gustav Fechner had suggested that the subjective intensity of a stimulus equals the logarithm of its physical intensity times a constant. Drawing on extensive empirical studies, Stevens noticed anomalies in Fechner's law and proposed a new law that would explain both the incongruities and Fechner's original findings. The power law states that the subjective intensity of the stimulus is a function of its physical intensity raised to a particular power times a constant: $S = kP^n$. One of the most robust findings in psychology, the power law remains a central concept in modern psychophysics.

Stevens was awarded several professional honors throughout his career, including the Warren Medal of the Society of Experimental Psychologists in 1943, the Distinguished Scientific Contribution Award of the American Psychological Association in 1960, and the

Rayleigh Gold Medal Award of the British Acoustical Society in 1972. Despite his many successes, Stevens's sense of connection to psychology grew weaker over the course of his career. Committed to a vision of the field as laboratory-based objective science, he viewed the rise of clinical psychology and socially relevant "action research" with dismay. Never one to conceal his opinions, Stevens eventually abandoned the term psychologist altogether in favor of the title professor of psychophysics (Stevens, 1974, p. 418).

An accomplished and eclectic scientist, Stevens helped shape the language of American psychology and was one of the foremost American experimentalist psychologists of the twentieth century.

Bibliography

Works by Stevens

Stevens, S. (1935a). The operational basis of psychology. *American Journal of Psychology, 47,* 323–330.

Stevens, S. (1935b). The operational definition of psychological concepts. *Psychological Review, 42,* 517–527.

Stevens, S. (1936a). Psychology: The propaedeutic science. *Philosophy of Science, 3,* 90–103.

Stevens, S. (1936b). A scale for the measurement of a psychological magnitude: Loudness. *Psychological Review, 43,* 405–416.

Stevens, S., Volkmann, J., & Newman, E. B. (1937). A scale for the measurement of psychological magnitude: Pitch. *Journal of the Acoustical Society of America, 8,* 185–190.

Stevens, S. (1939). Psychology and the science of science. *Psychological Bulletin, 36,* 221–263.

Stevens, S., (1946). On the theory of scales of measurement. *Science, 103,* 677–680.

Stevens, S., & Boring, E. G. (1947). The new Harvard Psychological Laboratories. *American Psychologist 2,* 239–243.

Stevens, S. (1957). On the psychophysical law. *Psychological Review, 64,* 153–181.

Stevens, S. (1961). To honor Fechner and repeal his law. *Science, 133,* 80–86.

Stevens, (1974). S. S. Stevens. In G. Lindzey (Ed.), *A history of psychology in autobiography* (Vol. 6, pp. 395–420). Englewood Cliffs, NJ: Prentice Hall.

Works about Stevens

Leahey, T. (1980). The myth of operationism. *Journal of Mind and Behavior, 1,* 127–143.

Miller, G. (1974). Stanley Smith Stevens: 1906–1973. *American Journal of Psychology, 87,* 279–288.

Rogers, T. (1989). Operationism in psychology: A discussion of contextual antecedents and an historical interpretation of its longevity. *Journal of the History of the Behavioral Sciences, 25,* 139–153.

Ian A. M. Nicholson

STIGMA refers to an attribute of a person that is deeply discrediting, and reduces him or her "in our minds from a whole and usual person to a tainted, discounted one" (Goffman, 1963, p. 3). The stigmatized person is devalued, spoiled, or flawed in the eyes of others (Jones et al., 1984). Goffman (1963) described three types of stigmas: tribal stigmas, which are familial, or passed from generation to generation, and include membership in devalued racial, ethnic, or religious groups; "abominations of the body," which are uninherited physical characteristics that convey a devalued social identity, such as physical handicaps of various sorts, disfiguring conditions, and obesity; and blemishes of individual character, which are devalued social identities related to one's personality or behavior, such as being a substance abuser, juvenile delinquent, or homosexual.

Stigmatizing conditions differ along at least six dimensions (Jones et al., 1984): (1) concealability—whether a stigmatizing condition can be hidden from others; (2) course—the way the condition changes over time, and its ultimate outcome; (3) disruptiveness—how much the condition hampers social interactions; (4) aesthetic qualities—how much the attribute makes the individual ugly, repellent, or upsetting to others; (5) origin—how the stigmatizing condition was acquired, and who was responsible; and (6) peril—the kind and degree of danger that the stigmatizing condition poses to others. Each of these dimensions has implications for how the stigma affects social interactions (Jones et al., 1984).

Goffman's (1963) analysis of social stigma focused attention on the psychological experience of those who are stigmatized. Four aspects of this experience are particularly noteworthy. First, stigmatized individuals must deal with prejudice and discrimination. The nature of incidents involving prejudice and discrimination may range from blatant to subtle—from epithets or physical attacks to being passed by an empty taxicab or neglected by a salesperson. Second, stigmatized individuals are frequently aware that they are devalued or regarded as flawed in the eyes of others. Third, the stigmatized are likely to be aware of the specific stereotypes that others hold of their social groups. African Americans, for example, are often aware that stereotypes accuse them of being intellectually inferior and aggressive; women know that stereotypes accuse them of being emotional, bad at math, and lacking in leadership aptitude. Fourth, the stigmatized may feel uncertainty, or attributional ambiguity, about the causes of events in their lives (Snyder & Wicklund, 1981; Crocker & Major, 1989). Negative outcomes could be due to one's lack of merit, or they could be due to prejudice and discrimination based on one's devalued social identity. Positive outcomes could be due to one's merit, or they could be due to another's sympathy for one's stigmatized status, or the desire to avoid the appearance of being prejudiced.

Most classic discussions of stigmatization conceptualize the experience of being stigmatized as involving some internalization of the stigmatizing images and stereotypes of one's group. Thus, it is often assumed that the experiences of stigmatization lead to low self-regard among the stigmatized. Surprisingly, however, empirical research contradicts this widely held assumption. Crocker and Major (1989) reviewed studies comparing the self-esteem of a wide variety of stigmatized groups, and concluded: "In short, this research, conducted over a time span of more than 20 years, leads to the surprising conclusion that prejudice against members of stigmatized or oppressed groups generally does not result in lowered self-esteem for members of those groups" (p. 611). In general, research suggests that although some stigmatized individuals are vulnerable to low self-esteem, diminished life satisfaction, and particularly depression, the vast majority of individuals, even severely stigmatized individuals, are able to maintain positive views of themselves, of their groups, and of their lives. Although stigmatized individuals confront many threats to their self-concepts, they also actively cope with those threats. Of course, some individuals cope with the self-threats posed by stigma more effectively than others. Research has focused on comparisons of stigmatized with nonstigmatized individuals on measures of well-being, such as self-esteem, positive affect, and life satisfaction, and tends to find small or nonsignificant effects. The absence of significant between-group effects may mask important differences within stigmatized groups in terms of which individuals are vulnerable to distress, and why (Friedman & Brownell, 1995).

A more subtle consequence of social stigma is its effect on cognitive and intellectual performance. According to Steele (1998; Steele & Aronson, 1995), awareness of negative stereotypes about intellectual ability can undermine the academic achievement and performance of members of devalued or stigmatized groups. This effect of *stereotype threat* occurs in particular situations in which one's performance may be interpreted in light of those stereotypes. African American college students underperform relative to White students on a difficult English test when they are told that the test is diagnostic of intellectual ability; when told that the same test is not diagnostic of ability, African American students perform as well as White students (Steele & Aronson, 1995). Similarly, women underperform on very difficult math tests relative to men when they are told that the test shows gender differences but perform as well as men when told that the test does not produce gender differences.

Stigmatization is primarily a situational threat, the predicament of being in a situation where one's stigma could influence how one is treated and judged (Goffman, 1963; Katz, 1981). No internalization of devaluation or stigmatizing stereotypes is necessary for this predicament to influence the person's experience. Furthermore, stigmatized individuals actively cope with the predicaments that their stigma poses, using the same coping strategies that nonstigmatized individuals use when faced with self-threats: social comparisons with others in a similar predicament; devaluing of the domains in which one is disadvantaged by the stigma; and attributing negative outcomes to external factors, in particular, prejudice and discrimination (Crocker & Major, 1989). Although these coping responses have costs for the stigmatized, both psychological and otherwise, these costs are more context specific, less internalized and permanent, and less inevitable and universal than is often assumed (Crocker, Major, & Steele, 1998).

Bibliography

Crocker, J., & Major, B. (1989). Social stigma and self-esteem: The self-protective properties of stigma. *Psychological Review*, 96, 608–630.

Crocker, J., Major, B., & Steele, C. M. (1998). Social stigma. In Gilbert, D., Fiske, S. T., & Lindzey, G. (Eds.), *The handbook of social psychology* (4th ed., Vol. 2, pp. 504–553). New York: McGraw-Hill.

Friedman, M. A., & Brownell, K. D. (1995). Psychological correlates of obesity: Moving to the next research generation. *Psychological Bulletin*, 117, 3–20.

Goffman, E. (1963). *Stigma: Notes on the management of spoiled identity*. Englewood Cliffs, NJ: Prentice Hall.

Jones, E. E., Farina, A., Hastorf, A. H., Markus, H., Miller, D. T., & Scott, R. A. (1984). *Social stigma: The psychology of marked relationships*. New York: Freeman.

Katz, I. (1981). *Stigma: A social-psychological perspective*. Hillsdale, NJ: Erlbaum.

Synder, M. L., & Wicklund, R. A. (1981). Attribute ambiguity. In J. H. Harvey, W. J. Ickes, & R. F. Kidd (Eds.), *New directions in attribution research* (Vol. 3, pp. 197–221). Hillsdale, NJ: Erlbaum.

Steele, C. M. (1998). Suspected by reputation: The stereotype vulnerability, disidentification, and intellectual performance of women and African Americans. *American Psychologist*, 52, 613–629.

Steele, C. M., & Aronson, J. (1995). Stereotype vulnerability and the intellectual test performance of African-Americans. *Journal of Personality and Social Psychology*, 69, 797–811.

Jennifer Crocker

STIMULANTS. The primary therapeutic use of psychostimulants is for attention-deficit/hyperactivity disorder (ADHD). The vast majority of treated patients are children and, increasingly, adolescents and adults. Pharmacological intervention with one of the central nervous system (CNS) stimulant drugs is the most common mode of treatment for ADHD, and has been for 30 years.

Psychostimulants include methylphenidate (MPH; Ritalin), pemoline (Cylert), and amphetamine compounds (Dexedrine, Adderall), with the majority of children receiving MPH. Stimulants act by facilitating release and blocking reuptake of dopamine and norepinephrine. Psychostimulants produce effects quickly (in 20 to 60 minutes, depending on the preparation) and wear off quickly (in 4 to 6 hours for immediate release and 8 to 12 hours for pemoline and sustained-release preparations). MPH and amphetamine are typically given with breakfast and lunch (or slightly after), and sometimes in a late, third afternoon dose to extend into the evening, while the timed-release preparations and pemoline are usually given only with breakfast. Dosing should be done to cover the times of day and situations in which the child has impairment.

The dose ranges that are described in pharmacology texts and ADHD treatment articles are considerably higher than those typically used in actual practice. Doses at the lower end of the MPH range (0.25 to 0.4 mg/kg per dose, with amphetamine requiring half as much medication and pemoline six times as much) are more common in practice than doses in the higher range, particularly when medication is combined with behavioral intervention. Most of the gains from stimulant therapy derive from relatively low doses, with diminishing incremental gain from increased doses. Compared to average ADHD children, obese children, adolescents, and adults may require less stimulant per weight to obtain a maximally beneficial response.

Beneficial effects of stimulants in ADHD children are among the best documented short-term effects in the field of treatments for childhood mental-health disorders (Greenhill, 1995; Spencer et al., 1996; Swanson, McBarnett, Christian, & Wigal, 1995). Stimulants have positive acute effects on a variety of laboratory measures of cognition (e.g., attention, inhibition, and response execution), classroom measures of disruption and daily academic task completion, teacher and parent ratings of behavior and attention, parent-child interactions, aggression, and peer interactions. Acute stimulant effects are often dramatic.

Seventy to 80% of children with ADHD show beneficial responses to stimulant medication; the others show either no response or an adverse response. Among the children who show a positive response, however, there are large individual differences in magnitude of response, dose-response functions, and responses across situations, and individual responsiveness cannot be predicted (Pelham & Smith, in press). Children also do not respond similarly to all stimulants (Pelham, Hoza, Kipp, Gnagy, & Trane, 1990), suggesting that all three major stimulants (MPH, amphetamine compounds, and pemoline) should be tried before a child is switched to nonstimulant drugs. Although most studies have focused on children, recent research has shown that beneficial effects continue into adulthood as long as medication continues to be taken (Smith et al., 1998; Spencer et al., 1996).

Side effects or treatment emergent symptoms (TESS) are sometimes associated with stimulant treatment. Loss of appetite and insomnia are the most common adverse reactions. Other common TESS include stomachaches and headaches. Some symptoms dissipate with repeated administration (e.g., stomachaches), while others do not dissipate (e.g., appetite loss) but can be controlled by reducing the dose of medication. Stimulants can exacerbate or precipitate motor tics and motor movements, particularly of the mouth, jaw, and tongue. However, in most affected cases the drugs do not appear to precipitate or worsen Tourette's syndrome.

Long-term stimulant treatment (2 to 4 years) with high doses and daily dosing results in a reduction in the rate of weight gain and to a lesser extent height gain, perhaps due to the anorectic effect. This can be minimized or avoided by keeping the dose low, medicating during school hours and on school days only, and giving high-calorie nutrition to the child at meals and snack time when he or she is not medicated.

Stimulant medication can also cause cognitive overfocusing, social withdrawal, and dysphoria—a response that has been popularized as the "zombie effect" of medication. However, reports of such substantive adverse effects of low to moderate doses are rare. It has been argued that stimulants have "psychotoxic" effects through which they make children psychologically dependent on them. There is no evidence to support this belief and much evidence to the contrary (e.g., Pelham, Hoza, Kipp, Gnagy, & Trane, 1997).

Many of the most serious TESS are rare, and irreversible side effects (e.g., liver toxicity) are extremely rare. However, their potential impact means that medicated children should be carefully monitored, especially when medication is initially prescribed, to ensure that these adverse side effects are not caused or exacerbated by stimulant therapy.

Despite widely validated salutary effects, the stimulants have limitations in their clinical efficacy. First, as mentioned above, stimulants are not effective for all children, and even with drug responders there is still room for improvement for many stimulant-treated ADHD children.

Second, psychostimulant effects are limited to the time when the drugs are physiologically active. The brief half-life of the immediate-release medications means that they must be administered at least twice daily or in long-acting form to ensure adequate treatment throughout a child's school day, with a possible third dose after school to affect late afternoon behavior. The fact that the child must be given a pill at school is often problematic because some ADHD children and school personnel actively avoid or prohibit medication at school, resulting in poor compliance, which increasingly becomes a problem in early adolescence.

Finally, there is no evidence that stimulants have a long-term beneficial effect. ADHD children have a poor outcome in adolescence and adulthood, and pharmacotherapy alone does not alter that outcome.

Therefore, the current standard of care is that stimulants should be given only as one component of intensive, long-term treatment that includes behavioral parent training, classroom management strategies, and behavioral interventions with the child. The only way to know when stimulants are no longer needed for a child is to have annual trials off medication and to stop the medication when such probes reveal no worsening in functioning.

Bibliography

Greenhill, L. L. (1995). Attention-deficit hyperactivity disorder: The stimulants. *Child and Adolescent Psychiatric Clinics of North America, 4,* 123–168.

Greenhill, L., & Osman, B. (in press). *Ritalin: Theory and patient management* (2nd ed.). New York: Liebert.

Hinshaw, S. P. (1994). *Attention deficits and hyperactivity in children.* Thousand Oaks, CA: Sage.

Pelham, W. E., Greenslade, K. E., Vodde-Hamilton, M. A., Murphy, D. A., Greenstein J. J., Gnagy, E. M., Guthrie, K., Hoover, M., & Dahl R. E. (1990). Relative efficacy of long-acting CNS stimulants on children with attention-deficit/hyperactivity disorder: A comparison of standard methylphenidate, sustained-release methylphenidate, sustained-release dextroamphetamine, and pemoline. *Pediatrics, 86,* 226–237.

Pelham, W. E., Hoza, B., Kipp, H. L., Gnagy, E. M., & Trane, S. T. (1997). Effects of methylphenidate and expectancy on ADHD children's performance, self evaluations, persistence, and attributions on a cognitive task. *Experimental and Clinical Psychopharmacology, 5,* 3–13.

Pelham, W. E., & Smith, B. H. (in press). Prediction and measurement of individual responses to Ritalin by children and adolescents with ADHD. In L. Greenhill & B. Osman (Eds.), *Ritalin: Theory and patient management* (2nd ed.). New York: Leibert.

Smith, B. H., Pelham, W. E., Evans, S., Molina, B., Gnagy, E., Bukstein, O., Greiner, A., Myak, C., Presnell, M., & Willoughby, M. (1998). Dosage effects of methylphenidate on the social behavior of adolescents diagnosed with attention deficit hyperactivity disorder. *Journal of Experimental and Clinical Psychopharmacology, 6,* 187–204.

Spencer, T., Biederman, J., Wilens, T., Harding, M., O'Donnell, D., & Griffin, S. (1996). Pharmacotherapy of attention-deficit/hyperactivity disorder across the life cycle. *Journal of the American Academy of Child and Adolescent Psychiatry, 35,* 409–432.

Swanson, J. M., McBurnett, K., Christian, D. L., & Wigal, T. (1995). Stimulant medications and the treatment of children with ADHD. In T. H. Ollendick & R. J. Prinz (Eds.), *Advances in clinical child psychology* (Vol. 17, pp. 265–322). New York: Plenum Press.

William E. Pelham

STONE, CALVIN P. (1892–1954), American psychologist. Stone was born on a farm near the small town of Portland, Indiana, the seventh of eight children. At the age of five, he experienced two family tragedies: His father died, and on the day of the funeral the family home burned to the ground. His mother's persistence and determination to rebuild and remain on the farm perhaps influenced Stone, for these were two traits that he often displayed in his career. Stone completed as much education as was locally available and, at the age of 15, entered Valparaiso University, where he earned the equivalent of a high school diploma and a few college credits. For 3 years after completing the work at Valparaiso, Stone taught high school, eventually becoming superintendent. He then entered Indiana University, where he completed both his undergraduate (1914) and master's degrees (1916). The master's thesis was supervised by the comparative and educational psychologist M. E. Haggerty. Stone enrolled at the University of Minnesota in 1919, after spending a year as a research psychologist at a reformatory and 2 years in the military.

At Minnesota, Stone earned his doctorate in psychology under Karl Lashley (1921) and began a program of research into sexual behavior that continued for two decades and resulted in numerous publications. In 1922, Stone accepted a position at Stanford University, where he remained for the rest of his career.

Stone's research was always marked by its thoroughness and precision. His early work on sexual and maternal behavior in rats is considered today as classic. Stone's sex research program was generously supported by the Committee for Research in Problems of Sex and illustrates Stone's interdisciplinary interests and critical role in developing the new borderland of the scientific study of sex. After World War II, Stone began a research program on the effects of electroconvulsive shock that continued until his death in 1954. His hypophyseal research, begun just 2 years before his death, was his last.

Throughout his career, Stone involved his students in his research, as well as collaborating with them on their own projects. His collaborative work included topics both within and outside his principal interests. He was also intensely interested in abnormal behavior. His course in abnormal psychology was among the most popular of electives at Stanford. He also edited a volume of case studies in abnormal behavior. As a teacher, Stone was admired for his thoroughness and exactness. He was the first American psychologist to offer a course in Freudian psychology (1923). The ideas of Freud were important to Stone, though he often criticized Freud for inexactness. In a trip to Europe in 1932, Stone spent a morning with Freud's disciple, Ernest Jones, in discussion about the hypotheses of Freud. [*See the biography of Freud.*] During the last week of his life, Stone was reading the letters of Freud and writing comments on them to his friends.

Stone was an important contributor to the discipline and profession of psychology. He served on various national committees and was elected president of the American Psychological Association in 1941. He also was editor of the *Journal of Comparative and Physiological Psychology* (1947–1950) and the *Annual Review of Psychology* (1950–1955). Among his many honors, perhaps the most significant was his election to the National Academy of Sciences in 1943.

Bibliography

Dewsbury, D. A. (1984). *Comparative psychology in the twentieth century*. Stroudsburg, PA: Hutchinson Ross Publishing Company. Dewsbury provides an overview and assessment of Stone's work and importance in the history of comparative psychology.

Hilgard, E. R. (1994). Calvin Perry Stone, February 28, 1892–December 28, 1954. *Biographical memoirs of the National Academy of Sciences of the United States of America, 64*, 396–419. Washington, DC: National Academy Press. A fine brief biography of Stone by someone who knew him well.

Stone, C. P. (1922). The congenital sexual behavior of the young male albino rat. *Journal of Comparative Psychology, 2*, 95–103. This paper, Stone's first on sexual behavior, is considered a classic of comparative sex research.

Stone, C. P. (1932). Wildness and savageness in rats of different strains. In K. S. Lashley, C. P. Stone, C. W. Darrow, C. Landis, & L. L. Heath (Eds.), *Studies in the dynamics of behavior* (pp. 3–55). Chicago: University of Chicago Press.

Stone, C. P. (1943). Multiply, vary, let the strongest live and the weakest die. *Psychological Bulletin, 40*, 1–24.

Wade Pickren

STOUT, GEORGE FREDERICK (1860–1944), British philosopher. George F. Stout was a philosopher who wrote extensively about psychology. His education began at St. John's College, Cambridge, where he studied the classics and received distinction for his work in ancient philosophy and metaphysics. A fellowship at St. John's College came in 1884, followed in 1894 by an appointment as University Lecturer at Cambridge. Stout then held the Anderson Lectureship in comparative psychology at Aberdeen between 1896 and 1898, when he became the Wilde Reader in mental philosophy at Oxford. Stout completed the remainder of his career (1903–1936) as a chair of logic and metaphysics at St. Andrews.

Stout edited the prestigious journal *Mind* between 1891 and 1920. During that time he wrote several books that examined psychology using philosophical analysis. His first book was *Analytic Psychology*, published in 1896. This text was followed by the *Manual of Psychology*, first published in 1898. The *Manual* became a popular primer of introductory psychology at English universities and was released in five editions. *Studies in Philosophy and Psychology* contained a collection of Stout's previously published papers.

There are several reasons why Stout is not better recognized for his contributions to the early history of psychology. First, his style of writing was not easily accessible and lacked the compelling flare of his contemporaries in psychology. C. A. Mace (1945), who coauthored the last edition of the *Manual*, observed that Stout "rarely adapt[ed] his exposition to the tempo of an impatient reader."

Another contributor to obscurity is the fact that Stout was a philosopher who wrote about psychology during a time when psychologists were busy adopting the mantle of empiricism and distancing themselves from the speculative methods of philosophy. During the first quarter of the twentieth century, psychology experienced rapid growth within the walls of academe. The new generation of psychologists founded departments of psychology in America, England, and the European continent upon the foundation of empirical research not philosophical analysis. Characteristic of this prejudice was Edward B. Titchener, who accused Stout of ignoring the advances of empirical psychology to focus on what philosophers *thought* about psychology.

Stout should not, however, be discounted as a member of an obsolete order of philosopher-psychologists who was born and trained at the wrong time and incapable of assimilating the emergence of psychology as an independent and empirical discipline. Stout joined fellow English philosophers F. H. Bradley and James Ward in a substantive assault on the associationist psychology that evolved from the works of John Locke, James, and John Stuart Mill, and Alexander Bain. As Mace (1954) noted, Stout's critique of the laws of association produced many concepts readily accepted by a later generation of psychologists. For example, his principle of relative suggestion describes what psychologists now recognize as stimulus and response generalization. Similarly, his analysis of perception anticipated much of the work of the Gestalt movement. Thus, Stout's legacy is a reminder that careful analytic analysis is a component of a discipline's vitality.

[*Many of the people mentioned in this article are the subjects of independent biographical entries.*]

Bibliography

Hamlyn, D. W. (1968). Bradley, Ward, and Stout. In B. B. Wolman (Ed.), *Historical roots of contemporary psychology*. New York: Harper & Row.

Mace, C. A. (1945). George Fredrick Stout. *Proceeding of the British Academy*, 31, 307–316.

Mace, C. A. (1954). The permanent contributions to psychology of George Fredrick Stout. *The British Journal of Educational Psychology*, 24, 64–75.

David J. Pittenger

STRATTON, GEORGE M. (1865–1957), American psychologist. As an undergraduate at the University of California, Berkeley (A.B. 1888), Stratton first encountered the new scientific approach to philosophical questions through the philosopher George H. Howison. He then spent 2 years at Yale (A.M. 1890), where he grew "tired of the hair-splitting of philosophy," and returned to California to teach high school. In 1893, Stratton became instructor in philosophy at Berkeley, and the following summer began (with Howison's blessings) his graduate study in psychology with Hugo Münsterberg at Harvard. A University of California fellowship then allowed him to spend 2 years with Wilhelm Wundt at Leipzig. His dissertation was titled "The Perception of Changes of Pressure at Varying Rates." In 1896, he returned to Berkeley as an instructor. [*See the biographies of Münsterberg and Wundt.*]

At Berkeley he established a psychological laboratory, where he performed the experiments that made his reputation as an outstanding experimentalist. By wearing over a period of 8 days a set of lenses that reversed the retinal image, he investigated "vision without inversion of the retinal image." He readily adapted to an upside-down world and concluded that experience determines a person's sense of up and down. The 1897 publication of his report of these experiments in the *Psychological Review* attracted much attention, both because they confirmed long-held notions about the relativity of visual orientation and because they illustrated human functional adaptability.

Stratton continued to investigate other visual phenomena, and for many years he annually reviewed literature on the subject in the *Psychological Bulletin*. By 1899, however, he began to address the broader implications of experimental psychology with a popular article, "The Psychological Evidence for Theism." A 1903 book, *Experimental Psychology and Its Bearing upon Culture*, reviewed for lay readers conclusions that psychologists had drawn from their laboratory investigations. Some of his colleagues argued that the book made its points largely by attacking straw men, but most also admitted that it effectively illustrated much that their science had to say about everyday life.

In 1904, the offer of the professorship drew Stratton to Johns Hopkins University. In 1908, he was elected president of the American Psychological Association and returned to the University of California. There he continued to address social phenomena from a psychological perspective. In 1911, for example, his *Psychology of the Religious Life* focused on the role of human impulses, instincts, and other motives in religion. Unlike most contemporaneous studies in the psychology of religion, Stratton's book looked beyond Christianity and Judaism to examine the rites and practices of Islam, Buddhism, Taoism, Zoroastrianism, and other "oriental religions." As Europe mobilized for war, Stratton wrote pamphlets for the American Association for International Conciliation entitled "The Double Standard in Regard to Fighting" and "The Control of the Fighting Instinct." Once the United States entered World War I, Stratton joined the army as a captain in the aviation section of the Signal Corps, where he developed, with collaborators, heavily used psychological tests for the selection of aviators. This work led eventually to his appointment as head of the psychology section of the Air Service's Medical Research Laboratory. In the 1920s, Stratton served as chairman of the National Research Council's Division of Anthropology and Psychology, and he was elected to the National Academy of Sciences in 1928.

Stratton had meanwhile begun arguing that an understanding of emotion could help avert war. This belief led to such books as *Anger: Its Religious and Moral Significance* (1923) and *The Social Psychology of International Conduct* (1929), and popular articles such as "Human Nature and War" and "Reeducation for International Affairs." Through the 1930s, he and his students experimentally studied emotion and its relation to such factors as race, cephalic index, eye and hair color, and disease. As war seemed ever more likely, Stratton published pamphlets entitled "Is World Peace an Attainable Ideal?" and "Conflict Can Be Eliminated in the Community of Nations." In 1944, his last professional papers addressed the "deeper sources" of "Violence Between Nations" and the "treatment" of "Violence Within the Nation." His last book, *Man, Creator or Destroyer* (1952), argued that communal ties among nations would lead to lasting peace.

Bibliography

Bridgman, O. (1958). George Malcolm Stratton: 1865–1957. *American Journal of Psychology, 71,* 160–461.

Brown, C. W. (1958). George Malcolm Stratton, social psychologist. *Science, 127,* 1432–1433.

Peirce, C. S. (1904). Review of *Experimental psychology and its bearing upon culture. Nation, 79,* 402–403.

Sokal, M. M. (1980). Graduate study with Wundt: Two eyewitness accounts. In W. G. Bringmann & R. D. Tweney (Eds.), *Wundt studies: A centennial collection* (pp. 210–225). Toronto: Hogrcfc.

Tolman, E. C. (1961). George Malcolm Stratton, 1865–1957. *Biographical Memoirs of the National Academy of Sciences, 35,* 292–306. Includes a fairly complete bibliography of Stratton's writings.

Michael M. Sokal

STRESS. [*This entry comprises three articles. The lead article discusses various definitions of stress and the physiological components and manifestations of stress. The two companion articles provide overviews on the measurement of stress and on its effects on health.*]

Definition and Physiology

The challenge of stress physiology is to elucidate the mechanisms that underlie the relationship between the risk factor of stress and the outcome measure of health. How and under what conditions does stress promote disease?

For far too long stress physiologists have relied on the rather barren concept of homeostasis as the basis for understanding the concept of organisms fighting tenaciously to maintain physiological systems within the range of some ill-defined set point. Within this framework, a stressor is simply any event that threatens homeostasis. This was a useful starting point for the contributions of Canon and others in the 1930s, but the time has long passed since this idea was of value to health scientists (Sterling & Eyers, 1988). Such simplistic notions defy Darwinian biology (Weiner, 1992). Life is full of struggle against the obstacles, challenges, and threats in our environment. Success is most often measured not in the defense of set points, but in our ability to adapt to such conditions, and the ease with which such adaptations occur. Adaptation, not stability, is the essence of life, biological fitness, and health (Selye, 1978).

Adaptation may be considered a set of changes that occur in order to maintain a normal level of function. One of the most important innovations in stress research is the understanding that illness is best understood not in terms of the nature of the stressful events to which an individual is exposed, but in terms of the magnitude of the individual's physiological and psychological responses to the stressor that are necessary to maintain function. The magnitude of these responses determines the likelihood of disease. The same set of responses that are activated in order to survive a stressor and maintain function can produce vulnerability to disease. This idea was advanced by Selye, who referred to many forms of chronic illnesses as "diseases of adaptation."

The brilliance of Selye's science was to recognize the common set of reactions that occurred in response to a wide variety of conditions, including various disease states, and involved fatigue, loss of appetite, and muscle wasting. These reactions formed the general adaptation syndrome, which lay at the heart of the relationship between stress and disease.

Physiological Responses to Stress

For Selye, the first phase of the general adaptation syndrome was the alarm reaction, a set of responses designed to meet the immediate needs of the body and analogous to a fight/flight response (Canon, 1929). Two systems have always been considered primary here. The hypothalamic-pituitary-adrenal (HPA) axis, emphasized by Selye, produced adrenocorticosteroids, mainly cortisol, and mineralocorticoids, including deoxycortisol and aldosterone. Second, the sympathetic nervous system, emphasized by Canon, focused on adrenomeduallary catecholamines, including adrenaline and noradrenaline (or epinephrine and norepinephrine). Together, these hormones furnish the front line of defense for mammals in response to stressors.

As Selye pointed out, there are common pathways that mediate any attempt to adapt to environmental demands and sustain function. A primary concern here is the change in metabolism that occurs in response to a stressor. One reasonably simple way to see how stress can compromise health is to simply appreciate the demands placed on the body during a period of stress. During a stress reaction, many cells are working harder to meet the demands of the situation. If these cells are more active they require more fuel—a greater ability of energy substrates. In the absence of a sufficient level of energy substrates, cells begin to shut down and can even run the risk of ischemic death. A basic feature of the body's response to a stressor is designed to ensure the adequate availability and distribution of energy substrates to specific organs in the body, notably those involved in assuring survival (Sapolsky, 1992). The resultant increase in plasma glucose levels also assists cognitive performance levels during periods of distress.

First, high levels of stress hormones, including the catecholamines, adrenaline, and noradrenaline, as well as the glucocorticoids, principally cortisol in humans, are produced from the adrenal gland. These hormones orchestrate a move to catabolism, increasing lipolysis and mobilizing glucose reserves. Glucose, fatty acids, and amino acids are then liberated from their macromolecular storage forms of glycogen, fat, and protein. Glycogen is converted into glucose and released into the bloodstream. The increase in lipolysis serves to break down fats and thus elevate circulating levels of fatty acids and glycerol (Brindley & Rolland, 1989), both of which can be used effectively as energy substrates by cells. Certain protein stores are broken down into amino acids, which then serve to fuel the stress hormone–induced increase in hepatic gluconeogenesis. These actions serve to defend blood glucose levels during stress. In addition, both the catecholamines and the glucocorticoids serve to antagonize the effects of insulin, decreasing the tissue response to it. This is no time to be storing sugars away in the form of glycogen. Rather, glycogen stores are broken down into glucose and poured into the bloodstream. Collectively, these responses serve to increase the availability of energy substrates. This is essential for survival.

Second, not only does the production of energy substrates increase, but so does their distribution. During stress, sympathetic activity increases arterial blood pressure through vasoconstriction as well as through heart rate. These actions increase blood flow. Interestingly, these actions are highly selective. Blood flow to active muscles, the liver, and the brain are increased. In contrast, circulation to the skin and mesentery is decreased. Digestion is thus compromised—this is no time for an all-dressed pizza.

Third, we also respond to stress as if performing a small cost-benefit analysis of our investment of resources. During a period of serious threat, survival is at risk. Growth hormone production is shut off and anabolism is suppressed. The elevated levels of glucocorticoids also serve to dampen tissue sensitivity to growth hormone. These events ensure that during a crisis growth-related processes are not draining energy reserves from vital organs. This is no time to be investing precious energy substrates into bone density and muscle mass. These processes can wait until the threat has subsided. Likewise, since processes such as ovulation are not essential to survival at this time, we turn off our reproductive function. Leutinizing hormone production from the anterior pituitary is suppressed during periods of stress as part of a general suppression of anabolism.

Fourth, there are cognitive responses to stressors that include systems that mediate attentional processes as well as learning and memory. During a stress reaction, we become hypervigilant; the level of attention directed to the surrounding environment is increased at the expense of our ability to concentrate on a focused set of tasks that are not essential for survival. As a function of these changes in attentional processes, as

well as the effects of glucocorticoids on brain structures such as the hippocampus, episodic memory is less functional during periods of stress. At the same time, glucocorticoids act on areas of the brain such as the amygdala to enhance emotional learning and memory (Lupien & McEwen, 1997). These changes in psychological function obviously greatly depend on changes in central nervous system activity and are associated with altered emotional states (Davis, 1992; Le Doux, 1995). Feelings of apprehension and fear predominate during a stressful experience. Thus, stress has effects on cognition and emotions that are consistent with the demands of the situation.

Corticotropin-Releasing Hormone

Perhaps one of the most significant advances in stress research is the identification of a neural hormone, corticotropin-releasing hormone (CRH), which appears to initiate and coordinate behavioral, emotional, autotonic, and endocrine responses to stressors. The CRH is a 41-amino-acid peptide, and while it is widely distributed throughout the brain, two CRH pathways appear to be principally involved in the expression of autotonic, behavioral/emotional, and endocrine response to stress (Sawchenko & Swanson, 1981). The first is a CRH pathway from the paraventricular region of the hypothalamus (PVNh) to the hypophysial-portal system of the anterior pituitary, a system that serves as a principal network for the neural regulation of the HPA axis. In response to stressors, CRH, and often arginine vasopressin (AVP), are released from PVNh neurons into the portal blood supply of the anterior pituitary, where they provoke the synthesis and release of adrenocorticotropin hormone (ACTH; Plotsky, 1991). In turn, pituitary ACTH causes the release of glucocorticoids from the adrenal gland. This hypothalamic-releasing factor system thus serves as the means by which a neural signal associated with the stressor is transduced into an endocrine response.

Another subset of hypothalamic CRH neurons project to midbrain sites regulating autonomic activity, resulting in changes in sympathetic nervous system activity (Brown, 1989). The second CRH pathway arises from the central nucleus of the amygdala and projects to the noradrenergic cell body regions of the locus coeruleus, the n. tractus solitarius, and the parabrachial n. as well as the serotonergic cell bodies in the raphe nuclei. Activation of these CRH projections results in an increase in the firing of targets and an increased release of serotonin and noradrenaline (Dunn & Berridge, 1990). These monoaminergic responses mediate behavioral/emotional responses to stress (Koob et al., 1994). The CRH antagonists can attentuate or even block the behavioral/emotional responses to stressors (Le Doux, 1995; Davis, 1992; Koob et al., 1994). These CRH systems therefore play an essential role in mediating the effects of stressors on emotional and behavioral states, as well as regulating autonomic activity.

Chronic Stress

Chronic, intermittent, or chronic continuous stress generally has two important effects on stress hormone levels. First, it increases basal plasma levels of glucocorticoids and cathecholamines. In response to chronic stressors, there are increases in the resting levels of heart rate and blood pressure, as well as in the circulating levels of triglycerides, cholesterol, and fatty acids. The second effect is an increase in reactivity to new forms of stress. This effect is referred to as facilitation by neuroendocrinologists studying the HPA axis, and sensitization by neurochemists studying either peripheral or central catecholamine responses to novel forms of stress. In addition, chronic stress, at least in studies of rodents, can serve to prolong the stress hormone response, such that the hormonal response persists even following the termination of the stressor. Together, these effects increase the cumulative exposure to stress hormones.

While these changes have been seen as the hallmarks of chronic stress, it appears that the long-term effects of a serious form of acute stress may have been underestimated. Severe forms of acute stress produce enduring changes in both basal HPA activity (Tannenbaum et al., 1997) as well as hypothalamic-releasing factor systems.

Chronic stress increases CRH and/or AVP gene expression in both the PVNh and CRH expression in the central nerve of the amygdala (Schulkin, McEwen, & Gold, 1994). These effects form the basis for the chronic stress–induced increase in endocrine, autotonic, and emotional responses to acute stress. Increased CRH activity has been associated with depression and anxiety disorders (Stout & Nemeroff, 1994), and may provide a neural basis for stress-induced affective disorders. Interestingly, antidepressant drugs have been found to serve as useful prophylactic substances, dampening the effects of chronic stress. These compounds have been found to decrease CRH gene expression in both the PVNh and the central n. of the amygdala (Brady et al., 1991). These findings may underlie the anxiolytic effects of certain antidepressant medications.

Resistance, Adaptation, and Illness

Allostasis. Allostasis is the establishment of a new level of activity in the brain and the rest of the body in response to the demands imposed on an individual over an extended period of time (i.e., chronic stress). Stability of function is maintained through allostasis. This is the essence of adaptation. For example, under conditions of stress we experience an increase in blood pressure and higher levels of fat metabolites, triglycerides, and fatty acids in circulation. When the conditions become chronic, the body begins to establish a higher baseline level of blood pressure and fat metabolism, and seems to defend this new state with appropriate changes in the circulatory system and increased fat consumption. The net result of these changes is the allostatic load—the burden an individual carries around as a result of adapting to adversity. In this case the burden is represented by increased blood pressure and circulating fat levels, but the reader can certainly add to this list. Irritability (perhaps associated with higher vigilance), listlessness, fatigue, and changes in appetite and digestion come readily to mind (see Sapolsky, 1992; Weiner, 1992, for reviews).

The critical assumption here is that the greater the allostatic load, the greater the risk of illness (McEwen, 1998). Seeman, Singer, and Charpentier (1995) recently tested this hypothesis using a cumulative index of allostatic load based on a variety of measures, including systolic blood pressure, urinary cortisol and cathecholamine levels, hip-to-waist ratio, glycosylated hemoglobin, measures of serum-high density and lipoprotein, and cholesterol. Based on a 3-year follow-up, it was found that individuals with higher allostatic loads were more likely to have cardiovascular disease and declines in physical and cognitive functioning. In our longitudinal studies with an otherwise healthy population of elderly clients, we found that basal cortisol levels over several years were negatively correlated with hippocampal volume and cognitive performance (Lupien et al., 1998).

Chronic Stress and CHD. The concept of allostasis leads to an understanding of the relationship between stress and disease. Disease emerges not directly as a function of the stressor but rather as a function of responses to the stressor. The constant pressures of a hated job does not directly promote heart disease. What leads to illness is the increased blood pressure and heart rate along with the elevated levels of fat metabolites produced in response to stress. Likewise, the suppression of immune function, the antagonism of insulin action, and the inhibition of growth hormone release are all natural features of response to stress, and all are conditions in which stress can promote illness. The question then becomes one of whether stress will promote illness.

In attempting to address the complex question of individual differences I have always found it useful to return to basics. Lazarus defined stressful conditions as those in which the demands of a situation exceed the resources of an individual (Lazarus & Folkman, 1984). This effort follows in the tradition of Mason (1975), in emphasizing both the stressful stimulus and the individual. This is a simple yet important definition, for it recognizes not only the stimulus event and its impact on the individual, but also the fact that individuals differ in their resources. Moreover, and this is essential, the definition crosses disciplinary boundaries. The stimulus event can refer to verbal abuse, a horrible recurrent image, or the presence of an antigen. Likewise, the resources can refer to the ability of certain neurotransmitter systems to maintain normal function, the capacity of an individual to call upon a social network of friends and family, or the capacity of the immune system to attack and destroy the viral assailant.

There are features of a situation that can produce greater stress responses very reliably. Obviously, the intensity or severity of a stressor is a major factor, but so too are the features that determine the nature of cognitive responses or appraisals. When there is a high degree of uncertainty surrounding events, when outcomes are unpredictable—these are situations generally seen as being far more effective in producing physiological responses. Perhaps the critical feature is that of controllability: Conditions in which we feel we have no effective means of coping with events produce the greatest set of stress responses. This is, of course, entirely consistent with the definition of Lazarus, who suggested that a situation is seen as stressful when one appraises it as being beyond control.

There are at least two obvious sources of individual difference here. The first lies in the appraisal of the meaning of the stressor; the second lies in the resources available to the individual. The two are intimately related. A stressor is evaluated by an individual in terms of available resources. We respond not to events, per se, but rather to our perception of events. There is clearly room for tremendous individual variation in the appraisal of stressors; the same events can have very different meaning and significance to different people, and thus elicit very different reactions. Such variations are partly associated with stable individual differences in activity in the left and right prefrontal cortex (Davidson, 1992), which are, in turn, associated with individual difference in stress hormone release (Wittling, 1995). It is tempting to think that these findings might provide a neurobiological basis for the effect of optimism on responses to stress, and a relationship between optimism and allostatic load.

The research of Hellhammer and colleagues provides a wonderful insight into the basis for individual differences in hormonal responses to stress. Following years of study, Hellhammer found that the single most influential factor in determining individual differences in cortisol responses to acute stress was self-esteem (Seeman, Singer, & Charpentier, 1995). Individuals high in self-esteem showed far more modest hormonal responses to an acute social stressor than did persons low in self-esteem: The assessment of one's resources, reflected in the measure of self-esteem, determined the magnitude of the response to stress. This idea seems to parallel the older ideas of mastery (White, 1960) and would seem to be an essential feature in determining the psychological basis for individual differences in stress reactivity. The greater our estimation of our resources, the smaller the stress response. Interestingly, early developmental histories that undermine self-esteem also increase the sensitivity of neural CRH pathways to stress.

There is obviously a long path to travel before we can clearly understand these issues, but more recent studies provide the basis for some fascinating hypotheses concerning the mechanisms through which social support, self-esteem, and optimism might influence health (Taylor, Repetti, & Seeman, 1997). Do these factors produce good outcomes because, over the lifetime, they serve to dampen the impact of stressors and reduce allostatic load? In addition to self-esteem, it appears that a case could be made for the effect of social support on cardiovascular, endocrine, and immune responses to provocation (Uchino, Kiecolt-Glaser, & Cacioppo, 1996), allostatic load, and health outcomes (Cohen, 1988).

The same logic can potentially be applied to understanding why psychotherapy might serve to decrease the risk of illnesses such as heart disease or diabetes, or assist in the management of these disorders. Several forms of psychotherapy, such as cognitive-behavioral or interpersonal therapies, can be viewed as increasing the resources of the individual (or the perception of existing resources) in the face of existing demand. Therapies that focus on coping skills and decision-making as a means of enhancing controllability can decrease stress hormone response (e.g., Dienstbier, 1989). Increased resources and a greater sense of control should thus serve to dampen stress hormone responses, decrease allostatic load, and improve health outcomes.

We must accept that stress research involves a degree of ambiguity. We are not unique here. The concept of heart disease is equally vague and nonspecific. Heart disease takes many forms and frequently involves kidney dysfunction, metabolic disorders such as diabetes, as well as the myriad effects associated with circulatory failure. Yet we continue to pursue the study of heart disease despite the fact that we know its form will differ for each individual—so too is it with stress research. The advantage of the allostatic model is that it provides a clear set of hypotheses concerning the mechanisms through which stress can influence health, as well as a basis for collaboration between individuals whose focus is psychosocial or psychological mediators. Only through such multidisciplinary efforts will we fully understand how stress promotes illness.

Bibliography

Baxter, J. D., & Tyrrell, J. B. (1987). The adrenal cortex. In P. Felig, J. D. Broadus, & L. A. Frohman (Eds.), *Endocri-*

nology and metabolism (pp. 385–511). New York: McGraw-Hill.

Brady, L., Whitfield, H. W., Jr., Fox, R., Gold, P. W., & Herkenham, M. (1991). Antidepressant drugs regulate corticotropin-releasing factor and tyrosine hydroxylase messenger RNAs in rat brain. *Journal of Clinical Investigation, 87,* 831–837.

Brindley, D., & Rolland, Y. (1989). Possible connections between stress, diabetes, obesity, hypertension, and altered lipoprotein metabolism that may result in atherosclerosis. *Clinical Science, 77,* 453–461.

Brown, M. R. (1989). Neuropeptide regulation of the autonomic nervous system. In Y. Taché, J. E. Morley, & M. R. Brown (Eds.), *Neuropeptides and stress* (pp. 107–120). New York: Springer-Verlag.

Canon, W. (1929). The wisdom of the body. *Physiological Reviews, 9,* 399–431.

Cohen, S. (1988). Psychosocial models of the role of social support in the etiology of physical disease. *Health Psychology, 7,* 269–297.

Cohen, S., Doyle, W. J., Skoner, D. P., Rabin, B. S., & Gwaltney, Jr., J. M. (1997). Social ties and susceptibility to the common cold. *Journal of the American Medical Association, 277,* 1940–1944.

Darlington, D. N., Chew, G., Ha, T., & Dallman, M. F. (1990). Corticosterone, but not glucose, treatment enables fasted adrenalectomized rats to survive moderate hemorrhage. *Endocrinology, 127,* 766–772.

Davidson, R. J. (1992). Anterior cerebral asymmetry and the nature of emotion. *Brain and Cognition, 20,* 125–151.

Davis, M. (1992). The role of the amygdala in fear and anxiety. *Annual Review of Neuroscience, 15,* 353–375.

Dienstbar, R. A. (1989). Arousal and physiological toughness: implications for mental and physical health. *Psychological Review, 96,* 84–100.

Dunn, A. J., & Berridge, C. W. (1990). Physiological and behavioral responses to corticotropin-releasing factor administration: Is CRF a mediator of anxiety or stress responses? *Brain Research Reviews, 15,* 71–100.

House, J. S., Landis, K. R., & Umberson, D. (1988). Social relationships and health. *Science, 241,* 540–545.

Kirschbaum, C., Prussnes, J. C., Stone, A. A., et al. (1995). Persistent high cortisol responses to repeated psychological stress in a subpopulation of healthy men. *Psychosomatic Medicine, 57,* 468–474.

Koob, G. F., Heinrichs, S. C., Menzaghi, F., Pich, E. M., & Britton, K. T. (1994). Corticotropin releasing-factor, stress, and behavior. *Seminars in Neuroscience, 6,* 221–229.

Lazarus, R. S., & Folkman, S. (1984). *Stress, appraisal, and coping.* New York: Springer.

Le Doux, J. E. (1995). In search of an emotional system in the brain: Leaping from fear to emotion and consciousness. In M. Gazzaniga (Ed.), *The cognitive neurosciences* (pp. 1049–1061). Cambridge, MA: MIT Press.

Lupien, S. J., Lecours, A. R., Lussier, I., Schwartz, G., Nair, N. P. V., & Meany, M. J. (1994). Basal cortisol levels and cognitive deficits in human aging. *Journal of Neuroscience, 14,* 2893–2903.

Lupien, S. J., & McEwen, B. S. (1997). The acute effects of corticosteroids on cognition: Integration of animal and human model studies. *Brain Res. Review, 24,* 1–27.

Lupien, S. J., Sharma, S., Nair, N. P. V., Hauger, R., McEwen, B. S., de Leon, M., & Meany, M. J. (1998). Glucocorticoids and human brain aging. *Nature (Neuroscience), 1,* 69–73.

McEwen, B. S. (1998). Protective and damaging effects of stress mediators. *New England Journal of Medicine, 338,* 171–179.

McEwen, B. S., & Steller, E. (1993). Stress and the individual: Mechanisms leading to disease. *Archives of Internal Medicine, 153,* 2093–2101.

Meany, M. J. Aitken, D. H., van Berkel, C., Bhatnagar, S. & Sapolsky, R. M. (1988). Effects of neonatal handling of age-related impairments associated with the hippocampus. *Science, 239,* 766–768.

Pickering, T. G., Devereux, R. B., James, G. D. (1996). Environmental influences on blood pressure and the role of jab strain. *Journal of Hypertension, 14(Suppl.),* S179–S185.

Plotsky, P. M. (1991). Pathways to the secretion of adrenocorticotropin: A view from the portal. *Journal of Neuroendocrinology, 3,* 1–9.

Sapolsky, R. M. (1992). *Why zebras don't get ulcers.* New York: Freeman.

Sawchenko, P., & Swanson, L. (1981). Central noradrenergic pathways for the integration of hypothalamic neuroendocrine and autonomic responses. *Science, 214,* 683–687.

Schulkin, J., McEwen, B. S., & Gold, P. W. (1994). Allostasis, the amygdala, and anticipatory angst. *Neurosciences and Biobehavioral Review, 18,* 1–12.

Seeman, T. E., Singer, B. H., & Charpentier, P. (1995). Gender differences in patterns of HPA-axis response to challenge: MacArthur studies of successful aging. *Psychoneuroendocrinology, 20,* 711–725.

Seeman, T. E., Singer, B. H., Rowe, J. W., Horwitz, R. I., & McEwen, B. S. (1997). The price of adaptation—allostatic load and its health consequences. *Archives of Internal Medicine, 157,* 2259–2268.

Selye, H. (1978). *The stress of life.* New York: McGraw-Hill.

Sterling, P., & Eyers, J. (1998). Allostasis: A new paradigm to explain arousal pathology. In S. Fisher & J. Reason (Eds.), *Handbook of life stress: Cognition and health* (pp. 631–651). New York: Wiley.

Stout, S. C., & Nemeroff, C. B. (1994). Stress and psychiatric disorders. *Seminars in Neouroscience, 6,* 271–280.

Tannenbaum, B., Sharma, S., Diorio, J., Walker, M., Steverman, A., & Meany, M. J. (1997). Dynamic changes in plasma CBG and sustained elevations in basal corticosterone levels in the 24 hours following acute stress in the rat. *Journal of Neuroendocrinology, 9,* 163–168.

Taylor, S. E., Repetti, R. L., & Seeman, T. (1997). Health psychology: What is an unhealthy environment and how does it get under the skin? *Annual Review of Psychology, 48,* 411–447.

Uchino, B. N., Kiecolt-Glaser, J. K., & Caciopppo, J. T. (1996). The relationship between social support and physiological processes: A review with emphasis on underlying mechanisms and implications for health. *Psychological Bulletin, 119,* 488–531.

van Bockstaele, E. J., Colago, E. E. O., & Valentino, R. J. (1996). Corticotropin-releasing factor-containing axon terminals synapse onto catecholamine dendrites and may presynaptically modulate other afferents in the rostral pole of the nucleus locus coeruleus in the rat brain. *Journal of Comp. Neurology, 364,* 523–534.

van Dijken, H. H., de Goeij, D. C. E., Sutanto, W., Moss, J., de Kloet, E. R., & Tilders, F. J. H. (1993). Short inescapable stress produces long-lasting changes in the brain-pituitary-adrenal axis of adult male rats. *Neuroendocrinology, 58,* 57–64.

Weiner, H. (1992). *Perturbing the organism.* Chicago: University of Chicago Press.

White, R. (1960). *The psychology of mastery.* New York: McGraw-Hill.

Wittling, W. (1995). Brain asymmetry in the control of autonomic-physiologic activity. In R. Davidson & K. Hughdahl (Eds.), *Brain asymmetry* (pp. 305–357). Cambridge, MA: MIT Press.

Michael J. Meaney

Measurement

Stress is an individual's generalized, systemic mind-body response to demands and stressors. The environmental stress perspective focuses on external demands and stressors; the psychological stress perspective focuses on how the individual evaluates these demands; and the biological stress perspective focuses on physiological responses. Valid, reliable stress measurement requires multiple psychological, environmental, and biomedical measurements. Stress instruments and measures fall into four construct categories. They are:

1. Environmental demands and stressors
2. Healthy, normal stress response
3. Modifiers of the stress response
4. Psychological, behavioral, and biomedical distress and strain.

Environmental Demands and Stressors

There are few broadly applicable, standardized, generally accepted measures of environmental demands and stressors. Commonly used self-report measures include the Life Events Scale, the Life Experiences Scale, the Perceived Stress Scale, and the Hassles and Uplifts Scale. Work is a specific, important life domain where occupational and organizational demands are measured. More than a dozen measures of work and occupational demands are available. The two most established and used are the Michigan Stress Assessment and the Occupational Stress Indicator. Emerging work stress measures include the Job Stress Survey and the NIOSH General Job Stress Questionnaire. Environmental demands and stressors may also be measured using interviews, observational methods, and instruments for the physical environment (e.g., noise and temperature).

The Life Events Scale (LES)

The LES is a 43-item checklist for measuring stress and long-term health risks. Medical, especially psychiatric, professionals in the psychobiological tradition consider major life-change events as sources of stress with accompanying health risks. Measuring life-change events is an important component of health risk assessment because these events account for about 25% of the variance in symptoms. Life-change researchers consider events in five life arenas: personal, family, financial, social, and work. Measuring life change events separately from their presumed effects and having a normative group scale of their intensity has the advantage of separating the impact from an ill person's perceptions, defenses, and coping activities. Both positive and negative life-change events appear to cause stress and a health risk.

The Life Experiences Scale

This is a 57-item measure of recent life events, including 17 specific events and 10 specific items for students. Impact is rated on a 7-point Likert scale from negative (-3) to positive $(+3)$. Test-retest reliability was significant $(p < .001)$ in two tests for total change scores $(r = .63, .64)$, positive scores $(r = .19, .53)$, and negative scores $(r = .56, .88)$. Negative change scores have been significantly correlated with Beck Depression Inventory (BDI) scores $(r = .24, p < .05)$.

The Perceived Stress Scale (PSS)

The PSS measures the degree to which life situations are viewed as stressful due to their unpredictability, uncontrollableness, or overloading. The PSS is a 14-item, 5-point Likert scale measure with good internal reliability $(.84, .85)$ and correlates positively with LES scores in two studies $(r = .20, .35, p < .01)$. The PSS has test-retest correlations of .85 (2-day) and .55 (6-week), and was more highly correlated with depressive symptomatology $(r = .76, .65)$ and physical symptomatology $(.52, .65)$ than was the LES.

The Hassles and Uplifts Scale

The Hassles and Uplifts Scales focus on work and non-work demands of a more minor, short-term nature. The Hassles Scale contains 117 items identified as irritants (from minor annoyances to fairly major pressures, problems, or difficulties) and the Uplifts Scale contains 136 items identified as sources of good feelings, peace, satisfaction, or joy. The scales measure the frequency and intensity of events. In one study, the Hassles Scale predicted concurrent and subsequent psychological symptoms such as anxiety, depression, and psychoticism better than the LES. The Uplifts Scale was positively related to symptoms for women but not for men.

The test-retest reliability was 0.79 for frequency and 0.60 for intensity of the Uplifts Scale.

The Michigan Stress Assessment

This is a self-report stress measure originally developed to identify demands and stressors in the industrial environment implicated in coronary artery disease. The principal demands and stressors in the assessment are: role ambiguity, workload, role conflict, responsibility for persons, responsibility for things, participation, and relationship with a work group. The assessment used 5-point Likert scales for each item, and the constructs (item clusters) were factor analytically derived. In addition to the self-report scales, the Michigan Stress Assessment has a tally sheet for obtaining objective workload data (e.g., phone calls, office visits, meetings, and other daily activities) from a third party observer, such as an administrative assistant.

The Occupational Stress Indicator (OSI)

The OSI is a self-report measure of three domains of occupational adjustment: occupational stress, personal strain, and coping resources. The occupational stress section has 60 items measuring six demand or stressor categories: role overload, role insufficiency, role ambiguity, role boundary, responsibility, and physical environment. The personal strain section has 40 items measuring four strain, or distress, categories: vocational (problems in work quality or output); psychological and/or emotional problems; interpersonal problems; and physical illnesses. The coping section has 40 items measuring four stress management categories: recreational activities, self care, social support, and rational/cognitive coping. Responses to the instrument's 140 items are made on a 5-point scale that gauges the frequency with which an item applies. The various subscales have demonstrated good test-retest reliability, and occupational norms are available. Plotting standardized scores yields an individual stress profile.

Healthy, Normal Stress Response

The stress response is a healthy mind-body response to change, challenge, demand, and threat. The key physiological parameters (e.g., blood pressure) for the biomedical measurement of this normal stress response as a biological construct are discussed in detail in a separate article. While physiological parameters may be reliably measured, assessing their validity as stress measures is more difficult. The validity of a biomedical test must consider both the sensitivity and specificity of the test. Sensitivity is the ability of a test to identify people with a given condition, while specificity is the ability of a test to separate people with the condition from people without the condition.

Modifiers of the Stress Response

Individual differences play an important role in the modification of the normal mind-body stress response. These modifiers of the stress response may enhance vulnerability for various forms of individual distress or serve as protective, preventive agents. These modifiers include anger, cognitive style, sex, age, ethnicity, social support, and diet. The action of these modifiers rests on the Achilles heel, or organ inferiority, hypothesis, which is well established in psychosomatic medicine from the 1950s.

Anger and Hostility. The identification of anger and hostility as modifying risk factors emerged from the original research on the type A behavior pattern, which used a *structured interview* (SI) to measure the behavior. The State-Trait Anger Inventory (STAXI) was developed as a self-report measure of state and trait anger expression. The STAXI is a three-part, 44-item measure of anger using 4-point Likert responses. State-trait anger scores have been correlated with anxiety, neuroticism, psychoticism, and blood pressure, with no significant correlation with extroversion. Anger scores above the 75th percentile are related to anger expression that may interfere with optimal functioning; scores above the 90th percentile on the subscales of anger directed at self and others are associated with vulnerability for coronary artery disease and heart attacks.

Locus of Control. Locus of control is a personality characteristic that may modify an individual's perception of stressful events and one's response to them. This characteristic concerns the degree to which individuals perceive that they have control over events in their lives. An individual with an external locus of control perceives that circumstances, bad or good luck, other people, or events are responsible for what occurs in life. An individual with an internal locus of control perceives that individuals are the masters of their own destinies and responsible for what happens to them. The most established measure is a 29-item, forced-choice measure of the tendency toward an internal or external locus of control. This scale includes 6 filler items intended to disguise the aim of the test and 23 items used to determine an individual's locus of control. The measure has demonstrated internal consistency, test-retest reliability, and discriminant validity. A 16-item measure of generalized control beliefs in the work setting shows good reliability.

The Life Orientation Test (LOT)

Optimism and pessimism are two alternative explanatory styles people use to understand the good and bad events in life. These explanatory styles are habits of thinking learned over time. Pessimism is a major risk factor for depression and is implicated as a risk in physical health problems and low levels of achievement. The LOT is an 8-item scale, plus 4 filler items, designed to measure dispositional optimism. The items have 5-point Likert response choices from 0 to 4. The LOT demonstrates both good internal reliability (r = .76) and test-retest reliability (r = .79). Construct validity results showed factor loading >.50. Dispositional optimism has been studied in adult as well as adolescent populations.

Distress and Strain

Distress and strain may take one of three forms: psychological, behavioral, and medical. While many individuals of most human populations exhibit healthy responses to stressful events and circumstances, there are significant minorities who develop distress symptoms and strain, not all of which may be clearly traced to specific demands nor stressors.

Psychological Distress. The major forms of psychological distress implicated in the stress process are depression, burnout, anxiety disorders, and conversion reactions. Several self-report measures of psychological distress have demonstrated sufficiently good construct reliability and validity to use in diagnostic assessments. The Profile of Mood States (POMS) is a well-known, well-validated 65-item adjective checklist using 5-point Likert-type scales to measure five independent forms of psychological distress (tension-anxiety, depression-dejection, anger-hostility, fatigue-inertia, and confusion-bewilderment) and one form of psychological health (vigor-activity). The tension-anxiety subscale is highly correlated with the State-Trait Anxiety Inventory (r = .78, p <.002 for STAI-T; r = .69, p < .002 for STAI-S). Other components of the POMS are significantly correlated with several worry and anxiety measures (r > .40, p < .002). The Beck Depression Inventory (BDI) is a 21-item measure of the intensity of depression. Items are rated from 0 to 3 for intensity. The BDI has been tested in psychiatric and nonpsychiatric populations, demonstrated excellent internal consistency (alphas from .73 to .95), and very good test-retest reliability (r = .48 to .86). Thirty-five concurrent validity studies show significant correlations between the BDI and the MMPI-D (.41 to .86 in psychiatric populations; .56 to .80 in nonpsychiatric). The Maslach Burnout Inventory is a 22-item measure of three aspects of the experience: emotional exhaustion, depersonalization, and lack of personal accomplishment.

Behavioral Distress. The major forms of behavioral distress include alcohol and drug abuse (including tobacco) accidents, violence (verbal or physical), and eating disorders. Self-report measures of these behaviors tend to underestimate their occurrence, especially with regard to alcohol, drug, and tobacco consumption. Frequency counts using tally sheets or other behavioral observation recording methods lead to more accurate measures of these behaviors. However, the causal contributions of demands and stress to these behavioral consequences, especially accidents and violent events, is not well established in comparison to the contributions of other causal factors.

Biomedical Distress. Measuring the major forms of biomedical distress opens the whole domain of medical diagnosis, which is beyond the scope of the present survey. The Cornell Medical Index (CMI), one of the oldest and most widely used standard questionnaires for medical symptoms, and daily logs of stress-related symptoms are among the measures used to examine medical distress. The Sickness Impact Profile (SIP) is an interviewer-administered, behaviorally based 235-item/question measure of the impact of sickness. The SIP also includes two 7-point self-rated items, on dysfunction and one on sickness.

Bibliography

Beck, A. T., Steer, R. A., & Garbin, M. G. (1988). Psychometric properties of the Beck Depression Inventory: Twenty-five years of evaluation. *Clinical Psychology Review, 8*, 77–100.

Bergner, M., Bobbitt, R. A., Pollard, W. E., Martin, D. P., & Gilson, B. S. (1976). The Sickness Impact Profile: Validation of a health status measure. *Medical Care, 14*, 57–67.

Brodman, K., Erdmann, A. J., Jr., Lorge, I., & Wolff, H. G. (1949). The Cornell Medical Index. *Journal of the American Medical Association, 145*, 152–157.

Cohen, S., Kessler, R. C., & Gordon, L. U. (1995). *Measuring stress: A guide for health and social scientists.* New York: Oxford University Press.

Kanner, A. D., Coyne, J. C., Schaefer, C., & Lazarus, R. S. (1981). Comparison of two modes of stress measurement: Daily hassles and uplifts versus major life events. *Journal of Behavioral Medicine, 4*(1), 1–39.

Maslach, C., & Jackson, S. E. (1981). *Maslach burnout inventory: Research edition.* Palo Alto, CA: Consulting Psychologists Press.

Quick, J. C., Quick, J. D., Nelson, D. L., & Hurrell, J. J., Jr. (1997). *Preventive stress management in organizations.* Washington, DC: American Psychological Association.

Rahe, R. H. (1994). The more things change. *Psychosomatic Medicine, 56*, 307.

Rotter, J. B. (1966). Generalized expectancies for internal versus external control of reinforcement. *Psychological Monographs* (80, Whole No. 609).

Sarason, I. G., Johnson, J. H., & Siegel, J. M. (1978). Assessing the impact of life changes: Development of the Life Experiences Survey. *Journal of Consulting and Clinical Psychology, 46*, 932–946.

Scheier, M. F., & Carver, C. S. (1985). Optimism, coping, and health: Assessment and implication of generalized outcome expectancies. *Health Psychology, 4*, 219–247.

Spielberger, C. D. (1991). *State-Trait Anger Expression Inven-*

tory, Revised Research Edition. Odessa, FL: Psychological Assessment Resources.

*James Campbell Quick, Jonathan D. Quick,
and Joanne H. Gavin*

Impact on Health

Stress has broad effects on mood, behavior, and health. It involves changes in response of nearly every system in the body, affects how we feel, and influences our behavior. By causing these whole-body changes, stress contributes directly to disease processes and affects health by increasing high-risk behavior and reducing quality of life. Evidence for these broad effects is increasing despite the difficulty in doing research on stress and illness. Recent data suggest that stress can affect health in many different ways and that it can be managed so that its effects are reduced.

Stress has been hard to define, but most investigators agree that it is caused by events or thoughts that convey threat, harm, or loss. These stressors are appraised or interpreted, and to the extent that they are perceived as dangerous, stress is experienced. Stress is a general term referring to a state or response pattern characterized by changes in most bodily systems, mood, and behavior. Biological and psychological arousal alters mood and behavior and elicits coping responses directed at reducing or eliminating the source of stress or its effects. This arousal is characteristic of stress and heightens the motivation to cope with the stressor and increases attempts to eliminate or reduce its impact.

Stress responses appear to have been naturally selected. Walter Cannon, a noted American physiologist (writing in 1929) believed that stress evolved to serve as a general energizer and regulator of emergency reactions and response to life threat. Often referred to as the fight/flight response, stress has helped people survive by increasing their strength, alertness, and stamina. Stress increases the body's metabolism and blood flow to skeletal muscles and the brain, and enhances peoples' ability to react. Biological aspects of stress are initiated by the nervous and endocrine systems, principally by sympathetic nervous system (SNS) arousal. Release of epinephrine, norepinephrine, and cortisol (among other hormones and neurotransmitters) is characteristic, and these actions signal bodily systems to break down and release stored energy and to increase the speed and efficiency of its distribution, resulting in an alert, stronger, and more robust organism. Digestive processes are slowed, and the availability of glucose is increased in circulating blood to fuel the major muscle groups. Heart rate, blood pressure, and respiration increase to improve circulation and the delivery of nutrients to muscles and brain. These readying responses work well when stressors are acute and/or

amenable to coping characterized by physical responses. However, when stress is unusually intense or prolonged, or when activity is not appropriate, wear and tear on the organism results and health may be compromised.

This wear and tear was described by Hans Selye, an endocrinologist who is considered the most prolific stress researcher of this century. He observed three changes in the body that occurred as a consequence of any stressor. These changes included an increase in the size of the adrenal glands, shrinkage of the thymus gland and lymphoid (immune) tissue, and increased incidence of ulcers in the digestive tract. In his 1956 book *The Stress of Life*, Selye theorized that organisms are born with a fixed capacity to resist stressors, but that repeated exposure to danger and activation of stress responses can deplete these reserves and cause tissue and organ damage. Although this theory has been criticized and psychological components have been added, research suggests that repeated or prolonged exposure to stress can harm our health.

The nature of stress makes investigation of some of these relationships very difficult. For example, many clinicians and researchers suspect that stress has a role in the development of heart disease, cancer, AIDS, and other illnesses. However, these diseases often develop over decades of life. Correlating or even identifying stressors or critical disease points over such a long period is difficult. Animal models provide an important complement to decades-long naturalistic study of humans under stress. Evidence of stress as a factor in the etiology of chronic diseases has been reported, although it is considerably more controversial than findings suggesting that stress plays a role in progression, recurrence of, or recovery from disease.

There are three main pathways through which excessive stress affects health. First, it causes changes in biological systems in the body, including the endocrine, cardiovascular, and immune systems. These direct effects include tissue damage caused by the repeated release of stress hormones that irritate the lining of arteries and contribute to atherosclerosis. In vulnerable individuals, acute stress can cause platelets to aggregate and form clots that can induce heart attack or stroke. Prolonged stress responding may compromise the immune system, allowing infections and some forms of cancers to develop. For example, Sheldon Cohen, a noted health psychologist, has found that stress affects whether people catch colds or experience viral infections.

Stress also affects behaviors that in turn have effects on physiological systems. Stress can increase cigarette consumption, alcohol and/or drug abuse, and diet. These behaviors may help decrease the tension or discomfort associated with stress, but they have negative physiological consequences and may interact with the direct effects of stress and affect subsequent coping. Third, stress affects health behaviors; to the extent that it affects whether people follow medical advice or utilize screening, it can also affect the recovery and recurrence of disease. Complex interactions among these pathways appear to contribute to the development and/or progression of hypertension, cancer, depression, asthma, cardiovascular disease, diabetes, and AIDS.

Reducing the Effects of Stress

Given this impact of stress on the body, what aspects of the stress process can be modified to reduce its health consequences? Perhaps the most effective way to reduce stress is to eliminate its source, either by moving away from it, eliminating it, or reducing its effects on us. If people experience stress because of their commute to work, they can change their route, time of commute, or other aspects of the stressor to reduce stress. However, most stressors are not time-limited and are generally beyond our control to eliminate them. An important aspect of coping is accommodation or adapting to a stressful situation and "learning how to live with it." Most stress management interventions focus on modifying people's responses to stressors, innoculating them against stress, and/or learning new coping skills that help people accommodate. One such approach capitalizes on the importance of appraisal and coping in the stress process. In a very influential book (*Psychological Stress and the Coping Process*, 1966) Lazarus argued that psychological appraisal is critical in determining the extent to which stress is experienced. Consequently, stress may be reduced if the threatening event is appraised as less harmful or threatening. Many of the stress-reduction techniques that have been used are targeted at these appraisals. Other interventions are based on learning and conditioning principles, or on increasing people's self-efficacy and perceived control.

People are inclined to cope with stress because it is an unpleasant state. This coping can be detrimental to health if it involves increases in health-impairing behaviors such as smoking or if it reduces that likelihood of health-protective behaviors (such as exercise or safer sex). When coping increases harmful conditions, stress-related illnesses are more likely. Because this can cause absenteeism and lost productivity, organized stress management programs have become increasingly popular in workplace settings. By helping people cope more effectively and/or maintain the physical conditioning that reduces its affects on the body, these programs are intended to reduce stress and its health consequences.

Stress inoculation training involves three phases of treatment: education, rehearsal, and the application of coping skills. The education phase of stress involves identifying sources of distress that stem from negative self-talk. These cognitive distortions may include overgeneralization, personalization, magnifying failures, and minimizing successes. Therapeutic intervention involves showing people the problems with these thoughts and substituting positive statements. Once the stressor is identified and the particular problems accurately interpreted, individuals may prepare to cope with future stressful events by practicing coping skills in increasingly stressful situations.

Extreme stress or fears related to objects or situations associated with harm can be alleviated using a technique called systematic desensitization. This approach requires the client to substitute relaxation for anxiety in response to a particular object or situation. Deep-muscle relaxation is paired with anxiety-provoking images or statements. The therapist and client construct a hierarchy of items ranging from games evoking low levels of anxiety to those causing very uncomfortable levels of anxiety. The individual learns to relax while being led through increasingly difficult imagined situations. Eventually, the client can relax while imagining his or her most stressful situation and ultimately can learn to relax while confronting stressful situations in real life.

Systematic desensitization involves progressive muscle relaxation. This intervention is based on the observation that relaxation and stress responses are incompatible, that is, relaxation and stress cannot exist simultaneously, and deep relaxation can actually inhibit anxiety. This method is called progressive muscle relaxation because it proceeds through all of the major groups one at a time until a completely relaxed state is reached. Muscles in the feet are tensed for 6 to 8 seconds, then relaxed. Other muscle groups are tensed and then relaxed, working up to the face. The client learns to identify states of tension and relaxation, and with practice can benefit by unwinding after stressors and by being prepared for future stressful encounters. Progressive muscle relaxation is effective in lowering blood pressure, reducing the side effects of chemotherapy, and has been used to treat ulcers, insomnia, asthma, and headaches. Systematic desensitization is particularly useful for treating phobias, including anticipatory stress associated with medical procedures.

Biofeedback is also useful in reducing stress. Most biofeedback involves learning to control visceral responses such as heart rate or brain activity. It encourages a sense of efficacy and control as well as a direct means of stress reduction. For example, skin temperature, neuromuscular activity, blood pressure, heart rate, and brain-wave activity can be targeted and, with feedback, people learn to control or alter these bodily functions and learn to control physiological responses and reduce stress-related activity. Biofeedback is often combined with other stress reduction techniques for the treatment of stress-linked illnesses such as hypertension or headache.

A very different approach to stress management focuses on increasing physical fitness and overall well-being so that episodes of stress have shorter or less intense impact. Although data are not conclusive, they suggest that diet and exercise may reduce the impact of stress and its effects on health. The plasticity of bodily systems, their ability to refract and respond again, and the habituation of response are all important in this regard. General good health may increase coping ability by augmenting the ability to unwind after stressful encounters or by minimizing physiological reactivity. Vigorous exercise may lead to subsequent deep relaxation and better sleep, both of which are beneficial. Exercise appears to be related to well-being, reduction of anxiety, and depression, may help disperse the arousal associated with stress, and can substitute for negative coping behaviors such as overeating, smoking, and using alcohol to unwind.

The stress response is adaptive in that it motivates and enables an individual to either fight or flee a noxious agent. However, repeated or prolonged activation of the stress response can be detrimental to health. Stress can affect health through several pathways. These include the prolonged presence of stress hormones and the wear and tear of disruptions of homeostasis, the influence of stress on lifestyle variables such as smoking and alcohol consumption, and the influence of stress on seeking health care and adhering to medical advice. Stress, among other modifiable and non-modifiable factors, contributes to a wide variety of disorders and diseases. Stress reduction techniques enable people to reinterpret events, assert themselves, and relax in times of tension. Ultimately, stress reduction should contribute to better health and a better quality of life.

Bibliography

Baum, A., Herberman, H., & Cohen, L. (1995). Managing stress and managing illness: Survival and quality of life in chronic disease. *Journal of Clinical Psychology in Medical Settings, 2,* 309–333.

Brown, G. W., & Harris, T. O. (Eds). (1988). *Life events and illness.* New York: Guilford Press.

Cohen, S., & Williamson, G. (1991). Stress and infectious disease in humans. *Psychological Bulletin, 109,* 5–24.

Cohen, S., Tyrrell, D. A., & Smith, A. P. (1991). Psychological stress and susceptibility to the common cold. *New England Journal of Medicine, 325*(9), 606–612.

Krantz, D. S., & Raisen, S. E. (1988). Environmental stress, reactivity, and ischemic disease. *British Journal of Medical Psychology, 61,* 3–16.

Lazarus, R. S. (1966). *Psychological stress and the coping process.* New York: McGraw-Hill.

Lazarus, R. S., & Folkman, S. (1984). *Stress, appraisal, and coping.* New York: Springer.

Levy, S., Herberman, R., Whiteside, T., Sazo, K., et al. (1990). Perceived social support and tumor estrogen/progesterone receptor status as a predictor of natural killer cell activity in breast cancer patients. *Psychosomatic Medicine, 52*(1), 73–85.

Mason, J. (1975). A historical view of the stress field: Part 2. *Journal of Human Stress, 1*(2), 22–36.

Schneiderman, N. (1983). Animal behavior models of coronary heart disease. In D. S. Krantz, A. Baum, & J. E. Singer (Eds.), *Handbook of psychology and health* (Vol. 3). Hillsdale, NJ: Erlbaum.

Selye, H. (1976). *The stress of life.* New York: McGraw-Hill.

Zakowski, S., Hall, M. H., & Baum, A. (1992). Stress, stress management, and the immune system. *Applied and Preventive Psychology, 1,* 1–13.

Tonya Y. Schooler, Angela Dougall, and Andrew Baum

STROKE. *See* Alzheimer's Disease.

STRONG, EDWARD KELLOGG, JR. (1884–1963), American psychologist. Strong was born in Syracuse, New York, the son of Edward Kellogg Strong and Mary Elizabeth Graves. He entered the University of California at Berkeley, graduating with a bachelor's degree in biology in 1906 and a master's in psychology in 1909. In 1911, Strong received his doctoral degree in psychology at Columbia University where he worked as an assistant at Barnard College and as a fellow at Columbia University. His dissertation, "The Relative Merit of Advertisements: A Psychological and Statistical Study," was an early reflection of his interest in applied issues from an empirical perspective.

After graduation, Strong worked as a research fellow in advertising before accepting a position as professor of psychology and education at George Peabody College for Teachers in Nashville, Tennessee, in 1914. He enlisted in the armed forces in 1917 and was assigned to the Department of the Adjutant General of the United States Army. Strong was a member of the Committee on the Classification of Personnel where he became actively involved in issues of occupational and personnel classification. He aided in the development of a personnel selection system, played a central role in the preparation of the *Index of Occupations,* and was a leader in the education and training of personnel officers. After the war, Strong went to the Carnegie Institute of Technology as professor and head of the department of vocational education (1919) and then as head of the Bureau of Educational Research (1921).

At Carnegie, Strong was part of a pioneering group of psychologists that helped to lay the foundation of applied psychology in America, especially in the application of psychology to personnel work and business practice. Initially, Strong worked on issues of occupational analysis and was later assigned to the development and delivery of a three-month course of training for life insurance salesmen. Publication of the *Psychology of Selling Life Insurance* (1922) and *Job Analysis and the Curriculum* (1923) were outcomes of his work. In 1923, the graduate program in psychology and education was disbanded, and Strong accepted a position as professor of psychology in the Graduate School of Business at Stanford University, becoming director of Vocational Interest Research in 1927.

While Strong would continue to write books and publish articles on a variety of topics, his name became synonymous with the Strong Vocational Interest Blank (SVIB; now referred to as the Strong Interest Inventory, SII), an interest inventory that he developed and that remains one of the most widely used career assessment instruments in industry, education, and counseling. The idea for the interest inventory came from Strong's association with his colleagues at Carnegie Institute of Technology who published the *Carnegie Interest Inventory* in 1921. Karl M. Cowdery, a graduate student of Strong's at Stanford, had developed a modified version of the Carnegie Interest Inventory and worked with Strong to develop a means of scoring the blank so that patterns of interests could be used to differentiate occupational groups from one another. Revising and extending Cowdery's work, Strong introduced the *Vocational Interest Blank* in 1927. The original blank contained 420 items that could be scored to yield scores on 34 occupations. The items that made up the blank referred to various types of occupations, activities, and interests, and respondents were to indicate whether they liked, disliked, or were indifferent to the content of the items. Strong refined methods of contrasting the interests of an occupational criterion sample with that of a general reference sample. Item responses that showed distinct differences between members of a particular occupational group and people in general would be grouped together and weighted to form scales representing occupational groups, a practice still used today. He was a detailed methodologist, which is exemplified in his 1943 publication, *Vocational Interests of Men and Women*. Strong retired from Stanford in 1943 but continued working on the interest blank and produced another major work on the topic, *Vocational Interests 18 Years After College* in 1955.

Strong's research contributions were recognized by numerous awards including the Butler Silver Medal Award given by Columbia University in 1944 and the American Personnel and Guidance Association Research Award in 1953. In 1958, he was selected to give the Walter Van Dyke Bingham lecture at the University of Minnesota. Strong, who had worked closely with colleagues in the psychology department at the University of Minnesota, left all his materials on the SVIB to the newly established Center for Interest Measurement Research upon his death in 1963. The center has continued to develop the interest inventory, and a revision appeared in 1994.

Bibliography

Darley, J. G. (1964). Edward Kellogg Strong, Jr. *Journal of Applied Psychology, 48*, 72–74. Obituary written by a colleague at the University of Minnesota.

Harmon, L. W., Hansen, J. C., Borgen, F. H., & Hammer, A. L. (1994). *Strong Interest Inventory: Applications and Technical Guide.* Stanford, CA: Stanford University Press. The test manual for the most current revision of the Strong Interest Inventory.

Hansen, J. C. (1987). Edward Kellogg Strong, Jr.: First author of the Strong Interest Inventory. *Journal of Counseling and Development, 66*, 119–125. Provides biographical material on Strong as well as transcripts of interviews with his daughter and a colleague at the University of Minnesota.

Layton, W. L. (1960). *The Strong Vocational Interest Blank: Research and uses.* Minneapolis, MN: University of Minnesota Press. Papers from a conference held to honor Strong. Provides a historical perspective on the development of interests research and Strong's impact on the field.

David B. Baker

STRONG INTEREST INVENTORY. The current version of the Strong Interest Inventory (known as the Strong), revised by Lenore Harmon, Jo-Ida Hansen, Fred Borgen, and Al Hammer (1994) is used to assess interests of college-age and adult populations who are participating in vocational decision-making processes. The instrument also is used in basic research to operationalize vocational interests. Occasionally, the Strong is used in selection evaluations or to assist an employee in finding the right position within an organization.

The first version of the Strong, the Strong Vocational Interest Blank, was published in 1927 by E. K. Strong, Jr., making it one of the oldest psychological inventories. Its long life can be attributed to revisions throughout its history that updated the instrument to meet increasingly demanding psychometric and social standards. The most notable revisions include (a) the addition of Basic Interest Scales (BIS) to the profile by

Strong, David Campbell, Ralph Berdie, and Kenneth Clark (1964), (b) the addition of General Occupational Themes to the profile and the merger of the separate sex women's and men's forms by David Campbell (1974), and (c) the addition of Occupational Scales by Jo-Ida Hansen and David Campbell (1985) to provide sexual equity for career exploration.

The Strong test items are presented in a Like, Indifferent, Dislike response format. The profile includes the General Occupational Themes (GOT), the BIS, the Occupational Scales, and the Personal Style Scales. The GOT, constructed to measure John L. Holland's (1985) six vocational types (realistic, investigative, artistic, social, enterprising, and conventional), and the BIS are composed of items with substantial intercorrelations. These sets of scales are used to explore an individual's interest in various work and leisure activities, occupational and recreational environments, and types of people.

The Occupational Scales measure the interests of people in a wide variety of occupations and were constructed using the empirical method of contrast groups. This technique involves contrasting the item responses of women or men in general with those of women and men in specific occupations. Items that differentiate the in-general group from the occupational sample are selected to represent the interests of people in that occupation.

The Personal Style Scales are designed to measure how people prefer to learn or work. The Work Style Scale measures an interest in working with people versus working with ideas, data, and things. The Learning Environment Scale separates people who prefer applied learning from those who prefer academic learning. The Leadership Scale identifies individuals who prefer to direct others. The Risk Taking/Adventure Scale separates those who are cautious from those who are thrill seekers.

The psychometric properties of every revision of the Strong have been thoroughly studied. The conclusion generally is that the Strong is among the most technically sound of the available interest inventories. For example, 3-month test-retest reliabilities typically are in the 0.80 to 0.90 range. Alpha coefficients for the homogeneous BIS and GOT range from 0.87 to 0.90. Evidence of predictive validity for the Strong usually takes the form of examining the relationship between an individual's Occupational Scale scores at Time one and the occupation in which the person is engaged at Time two after an interval of several months or years. Results show that the percentage of people engaged in work that matches their earlier scores on the Strong exceeds chance. Evidence for the use of the Strong with diverse populations, though tentative, suggests that the instrument is robust across groups of varying ethnicities and countries of origin, sexual preferences, and disabilities.

Bibliography

Campbell, D. P. (1974a). An informal history of the Strong Interest Inventory. In D. P. Campbell (Ed.), *Handbook for the Strong Vocational Interest Blank* (pp. 341–365). Stanford, CA: Stanford University Press.

Campbell, D. P. (1974b). *Manual for the SVIB-SCII.* Stanford, CA: Stanford University Press.

Chernin, J., Holden, J., & Chandler, C. (1997). Bias in psychological assessment: Heterosexism. *Measurement and Evaluation in Counseling and Development, 2,* 68–76.

Dewitt, D. (1994). Using the Strong with people who have disabilities. In L. Harmon, J. C. Hansen, F. Borgen, & A. Hammer (Eds.), *Strong Interest Inventory applications and technical guide* (pp. 281–290). Palo Alto, CA: Consulting Psychologists Press.

Fouad, N., Harmon, L., & Hansen, J. C. (1994). Cross-cultural use of the Strong. In L. Harmon, J. C. Hansen, F. Borgen, & A. Hammer (Eds.). *Strong Interest Inventory applications and technical guide* (pp. 255–280). Palo Alto, CA: Consulting Psychologists Press.

Hansen, J. C. (1984). *User's guide for the Strong Interest Inventory* (2nd ed.). Stanford, CA: Stanford University Press.

Hansen, J. C. (1994). The measurement of vocational interests. In M. G. Rumsey & J. H. Harris (Eds.). *Personnel selection and classification* (pp. 293–316). Hillsdale, NJ: Erlbaum.

Hansen, J. C., & Campbell, D. P. (1985). *Manual for the SVIB-SCII* (4th ed.). Stanford, CA: Stanford University Press.

Harmon, L., Hansen, J. C., Borgen, F., & Hammer, A. (1994). *Strong Interest Inventory applications and technical guide.* Palo Alto, CA: Consulting Psychologists Press.

Holland, J. L. (1985). *Making vocational decisions* (2nd ed.). Englewood Cliffs, NJ: Prentice-Hall.

Strong, E. K., Jr., Campbell, D. P., Berdie, R. F., & Clark, K. E. (1964). Proposed scoring changes for the Strong Vocational Interest Blank. *Journal of Applied Psychology, 48,* 75–80.

Jo-Ida C. Hansen

STRUCTURALISM. *See* Psychology, *articles on* Early Twentieth Century *and* Post–World War II.

STUDENT CHARACTERISTICS. Students begin their schooling endowed with distinctive personal characteristics, such as age, intelligence, affect states, race, and gender, that will affect their subsequent academic success. Historically these characteristics have been conceptualized as singular unchanging traits, but researchers have discovered extensive individual differences within these categories as well as significant relations between these characteristics and sociocultural or instructional factors. Currently, students' academic achievement is interpreted widely to be an interaction of personal biological characteristics and environmental influences.

Types of Student Characteristics

Age or Readiness. One of the most widely discussed aspects of students is their age. Chronological age provides a rough estimate of a student's developmental level, the period when certain skills or abilities are typically observed. Although development is age-related, it is not age dependent because growth proceeds at different rates depending on the individual, task, and circumstances. Stage theorists such as Piaget and Kohlberg have recommended the use of qualitative stage notions to describe students' overall cognitive developmental level; however, educators have generally relied on quantitative tests of readiness to guide instructional decision-making in each academic content area. Readiness refers to certain minimum levels of cognitive, linguistic, and motor development that are necessary to learn specific skills. Readiness for instruction is defined in terms of normative developmental expectations, sequences of content knowledge, or hierarchies of motor skills. A wide variety of causes of readiness are recognized, including physical and mental maturation, motivational activation, prerequisite learning, or an enriching environment. Because of its flexibility and usefulness, the construct of readiness has been widely adopted in schools.

Intelligence. No student characteristic has garnered more attention by educators than intelligence. The classical view of intelligence as a general mental ability, or g factor, has been increasingly criticized. Although the predictiveness of classical intelligence tests are moderately high for success in school, these measures are not predictive of many other types of human performance, such as employment success or achievement in specialized areas such as art or drama. Some investigators have developed tests of social or practical intelligence to predict expertise on everyday tasks (Sternberg & Wagner, 1986). Other efforts to develop new intelligence tests have sought to expand beyond g factor measures of logical-mathematical and verbal reasoning to measure musical, spatial, bodily-kinesthetic, interpersonal, and intrapersonal abilities (Gardner, 1993). These intelligences are viewed as separate domains of performance, such that achievement in one area, such as music, art, or physical movement, is not necessarily related to the level achieved in other domains. This multiplicity conceptualization bridges the gap between single-factor definitions of intelligence and descriptions of giftedness that treat human talents as discrete domains.

Retardation and Learning Disabilities. From the time of Binet, intelligence tests have been used to assess retardation in students, and they continue to be used for this purpose in contemporary practice. Students with mental retardation not only record low scores on tests of intelligence, but also display diminished levels of personal independence and social responsibility for their age and background. However, many students of normal intelligence still fail to learn effectively in school. Only 13% of all students with learning disabilities are mentally retarded (U.S. Department of Education, 1991). Learning disabilities are a diverse group of disorders characterized by significant difficulties in the acquisition and use of listening, speaking, reading, writing, reasoning, or computing skills. The vast majority of students who are learning disabled receive the designation because of failures in learning to read; as a result, attention has focused on reading disabilities. On average, students with learning disabilities tend to have lower self-perceptions than nondisabled students and to resemble other low achievers.

Affect States. The emotional states of students can profoundly influence their learning and academic achievement. For example, many gifted writers, artists, scientists, and musicians have struggled throughout their lives to cope with manic depression, which dramatically altered their motivation and periods of productivity. In addition to these motivational effects, personal affect can affect the quality of one's thinking and memory. For example, recall can be mood dependent: students remember better if their emotional state during recall matches their mood during learning. In general, positive affect enhances learning and cognitive organization whereas negative affect depresses them. A negative relation exists between measures of anxiety and learning, but this relation is influenced by variation in task difficulty, effort, and instructional treatment (Helmke, 1989). Anxiety actually enhances performance on easy tasks and does not impair learning when efforts to relax are successful or when nonthreatening instruction is provided.

Causal attributions about why an event occurred can also influence students' emotional reactions. In general, attributing failures to effort sustains students' optimism better than attributions to fixed ability (Schunk, 1994). Attributing failures to deficient strategies provides even further benefits because it prompts learners to consider making changes in the direction of learning rather than merely increasing a failing effort. Students who are taught to attribute their failure to ineffective strategies demonstrate higher expectations for future success and have more positive self-judgments than those who are taught to attribute failure to a lack of ability or effort.

Gender. The role of gender differences in school performance, achievement, and intelligence has been debated for centuries. Historically, males have surpassed females in numerous areas of achievement, such as mathematics, art, and science, but research has, with few exceptions, discredited claims of biologically based differences in intelligence or academic achievement. Although there is evidence of some minor differences in brain structure and hormonal patterns that can affect emotions and reasoning of males and females, most evidence of gender differences in academic performance points to origins in distinctive socialization experiences, including differential reinforcement by one's family or teachers (Wigfield, Eccles, & Pintrich, 1996). Children enter school having been socialized into appropriate sex-role behaviors by parents who often hold widely different expectations for boys than for girls that can affect their attitudes, behaviors, and school readiness. Once in school, boys and girls are often treated differently by their teachers. Despite these treatment differences during socialization and instruction, male-female differences on any measure of intellectual ability have been very small and so variable that they have few if any practical consequences.

Race or Ethnicity. One of the most intense areas of current research on students' characteristics concerns the role of race or ethnicity in academic achievement. Initially these differences were attributed to the genetic variable of race; however, most American students have mixed racial backgrounds, which has prompted researchers to treat even self-designations of race as a cultural rather than a genetic variable. For this reason, the term *ethnicity* has been preferred. Reliable differences in achievement have emerged in both cross-ethnic studies as well as cross-national studies. In general, Asian American students display the highest achievement, European American students are intermediate, and African American and Hispanic American students fare most poorly. The underlying question for debate is the cause of these differences. Sociocultural influences play a greater role than purely economic factors. For example, educational attainment of the parents, especially the mother, is more predictive than the financial resources of the family, and this has prompted increased attention to the influence of the parenting processes on children's achievement in school. Parents serve as role models for their children. Parents' affective tone, academic involvement, and styles of supervision are highly correlated with their offsprings' attitudes toward schools and achievement outcomes. Regardless of their ethnic background, parents who fail to monitor their children's school performance or participate at school are less effective in mobilizing their children to achieve.

The ethnicity of a student is also an important determinant of the peer group with which he or she associates. The academic orientation of peer groups can have either a positive or negative effect on students' achievement, and Asian American students often benefit from having academically oriented peers (Steinberg,

1996). Although peers become increasingly influential during schooling, they are more effective in reinforcing existing dispositions than in changing a student's achievement orientation in a major way. This occurs because low achievers usually seek out other low achievers, leading them to do even worse in school, and high achievers associate with other high achievers, which helps them even further. Despite the increasing influence of peers, students generally agree with their parents on major issues, such as the importance of education, religion, politics, and morality, and thus parents who are deeply engaged in their children's schooling can play a major role in how peers are selected.

Academic Self-Beliefs. Students display increasing differentiation in their self-beliefs by task as they mature and progress through school. This process begins early, and by the time youngsters enter school, they base their self-concepts on broad classes of activities, such as academic, social, and physical ones, rather than on a general sense of worth (Harter, 1983). Even more focused measures of self-belief have been used with older students; distinctive self-concept measures for math and reading have proven successful in predicting students' achievement in those academic areas. The most task-specific measure of academic self-beliefs are self-efficacy judgments, which refer to one's capability to learn or perform designated skills, such as math division problems or reading comprehension tasks. Self-efficacy measures have been predictive of students' motivation and use of learning strategies as well as their academic achievement (Bandura, 1997).

Strategy Use. Investigators have begun to study a relatively new psychological characteristic of students—their strategies to learn. Learning strategies are cognitive procedures that students can use to help them understand tasks and perform actions to attain a goal, such as self-instruction, verbal elaboration, text comprehension monitoring, goal setting, and self-recording. Use of learning strategies is distinct from but correlated with measures of mental ability (Zimmerman & Martinez-Pons, 1988). Students who use a greater diversity and number of learning strategies display substantially higher levels of academic achievement. Students' use of learning strategies is related to their ages, giftedness, and sociocultural backgrounds, with young, normal ability, and minority youth displaying lower levels. However, strategy use remains highly predictive of academic success regardless of a student's age, talent, or sociocultural background.

Classroom Accommodations for Student Characteristics

Schools as an institution and teachers as instructional agents have historically coped with student differences by using a number of adaptive or compensatory techniques, such as grouping, individualized instruction, cooperative learning, reciprocal teaching, self-regulated learning, and mastery learning. There has been widespread use of ability grouping and tracking to adapt instruction to student differences. Ability grouping begins with separate reading ability groups in grade 1 and continues through the end of high school, with advanced placement courses for the most able students and vocational education classes for students of lesser ability. Forming homogeneous classes with regard to students' ability does not increase academic achievement overall (Slavin, 1990), but it does affect the quality of instruction. Students assigned to lower track classrooms receive less instructional time, more punishment, less homework, and less response to their questions than students assigned to upper track classrooms. Although students in the upper track typically learn more and those in the lower track learn less than their untracked counterparts, these differential effects of tracking cancel each other when considering the achievement of the entire student population. In contrast, the use of in-class instructional groups formed for limited purposes and durations, such as basic skills in mathematics or reading, typically has beneficial effects on the achievement of students of all abilities.

The literature on individualized instruction indicates that the needs of many students with special needs can be met in the regular classroom with little or no outside assistance if the teacher allocates personal time for working with individual students or uses teacher aides or peer tutors to provide such instruction. Many teachers accommodate foreign students with limited English-speaking skills by assigning them a peer interpreter who is fluent in their mother tongue. Students with learning disabilities can be given individualized instruction in their area of limitation by the classroom teacher, aides, or a special education instructor. United States Public Law 94-142 requires that special education students be placed in minimally restrictive environments; as a result, there has been widespread adoption of mainstreaming, in which the needs of mildly retarded or emotionally troubled youngsters are met through individualized instruction in regular classrooms. Mainstreaming is designed to facilitate these youths' adaptation to regular academic settings and their acceptance by typical classmates.

Cooperative learning is an instructional method in which students work together in small groups to help each other learn. Students in cooperative leaning groups display higher achievement, higher self-esteem, and more positive attitudes toward school than classmates given traditional forms of instruction. However, there is evidence that students should be individually accountable if optimal participation and achievement is desired (Slavin, 1990). When students in a cooperative group are required to turn in their own work or show their personal contribution to a group project, it discourages any seeking of a free ride and rewards constructive participation. Generally, research on cooperative learning shows that when it is used in classrooms, children are more accepting of one another, and fewer children are socially isolated (Johnson & Johnson, 1986).

Reciprocal teaching involves the teacher conducting an instructional dialogue with small groups of students in which all members of the group take turns in the role of teacher. This method of instruction grew out of Vygotsky's assumption that knowledge is gradually internalized from adult modeling to student self-verbalization and out of constructivists' assumption that learners must individually discover and transform information if they are to learn. Recent reviews indicate that reciprocal teaching significantly increases the achievement for all ability groups of students but that its effects were much greater when it was preceded by explicit strategy teaching (Rosenshine & Meister, 1994).

Self-regulated learning methods treat students' learning as personally directed activity involving self-generated thoughts, feelings, and actions intended to attain specific educational goals, such as analyzing a reading assignment. Students are given explicit training in goal setting, strategy use, self-monitoring, and systematic practice as they engage in self-directed study. Use of these processes is highly predictive not only of students' achievement in school, but also of their perceptions of self-efficacy, self-reactions, and goal setting (Zimmerman & Bandura, 1994). Efforts to teach component skills in self-regulation, such as goal setting and verbal self-instruction, have led to significant increases in skill, academic achievement, and perceptions of self-efficacy (Schunk, 1994).

Another way of adapting instruction to the needs of different students is *mastery learning*. Mastery learning assumes that human knowledge and skill is hierarchical in organization, and as a result, students must achieve subordinate instructional objectives before they move on to higher order objectives. It is also assumed that every student can learn the essential skills in the curriculum if given adequate time and practice. Slower students often fail to profit from conventional group instruction because the teacher moves to new objectives before they've mastered previous ones. Keller's model of mastery learning (1968) advocates self-directed study, whereas Bloom's model (1971) relies on group instruction. Mastery learning has proven more successful in bringing students to a preestablished level of mastery (usually 90% criterion of success on tests) than conventional forms of instruction, although the differences in time to mastery varies considerably among students. However, students prone to procrastination need to be carefully monitored when using Keller's self-directed method of mastery learning.

[*See also* Exceptional Students: *and* Teachers.]

Bibliography

Bandura, A. (1997). *Self-efficacy: The exercise of control.* New York: Freeman.

Bloom, B. J. (1971). Mastery learning and its implications for curriculum development. In E. W. Eisner (Ed.), *Confronting curriculum reform* (pp. 17–55). Boston: Little, Brown.

Gardner, H. (1993). *Multiple intelligences: The theory and practice.* New York: Basic Books.

Harter, S. (1983). Developmental perspectives on the self-system. In P. Mussen (Ed.), *Handbook of child psychology: Socialization, personality and social development* (Vol. 4, pp. 275–385). New York: Wiley.

Helmke, A. (1989). Affective student characteristics and cognitive development: Problems, pitfalls, perspectives. *International Journal of Educational Research, 13,* 915–932.

Johnson, D., & Johnson, R. (1986). *Learning together and alone* (2nd ed.). Englewood Cliffs, NJ: Prentice Hall.

Keller, F. (1968). Goodbye Teacher . . . *Journal of Applied Behavior Analysis, 1,* 79–89.

Rosenshine, B., & Meister, C. (1994). Reciprocal teaching: A review of the research. *Review of Educational Research, 64,* 479–530.

Schunk, D. (1994). Self-regulation of self-efficacy and attributions in academic settings. In D. H. Schunk & B. J. Zimmerman (Eds.), *Self-regulation of learning and performance: Issues and educational applications.* Hillsdale, NJ: Erlbaum.

Slavin, R. (1990). *Cooperative learning: Theory, research, and practice.* Englewood Cliffs, NJ: Prentice Hall.

Steinberg, L. (1996). *Beyond the classroom.* New York: Simon & Schuster.

Sternberg, R. J., & Wagner, R. K. (1986). *Practical intelligence: Nature and origins of competence in the everyday world.* New York: Cambridge University Press.

Wigfield, A., Eccles, J. S., & Pintrich, P. R. (1996). Development between the ages of 11 and 25. In D. C. Berliner & R. C. Calfee (Eds.), *Handbook of educational psychology.* New York: Simon & Schuster Macmillan.

Zimmerman, B. J., & Bandura, A. (1994). Impact of self-regulatory influences on attainment in a writing course. *American Educational Research Journal, 29,* 663–676.

Zimmerman, B. J., & Martinez-Pons, M. (1988). Construct validation of a strategy model of student self-regulated learning. *Journal of Educational Psychology, 80,* 284–290.

Barry J. Zimmerman and Anastasia Kitsantas

STUMPF, CARL (1848–1936), German psychologist. Although comparatively little known today, Carl Stumpf can be regarded as one of the foundational figures in the emergence of psychology as an independent scientific discipline. Stumpf was born on 21 April 1848, in a small village in Bavaria, Germany. He took up his academic studies in 1865 at the University of Würzburg, where he came into contact with the famous philosopher-psychologist Franz Brentano, who had a strong influence on his thinking. In 1867, on Brentano's recommendation, Stumpf moved to the University of Göttingen, where he completed his dissertation ("The Relation between Plato's God and His Idea of Goodness") under Rudolf Hermann Lotze in 1868, and his Habilitation (on the axioms of mathematics) in 1870. In 1873, he became Brentano's successor in Würzburg. Subsequently, Stumpf took up successive professorships at the universities of Prague (1879), Halle (1884), Munich (1889), and finally at the Friedrich-Wilhelms University in Berlin (1893), where he spent the rest of his academic career (until 1921) as professor of philosophy and director of the Institute of Psychology. Stumpf died in Berlin on 25 December 1936, at the age of 88.

Stumpf's scientific work covers a diversity of themes in philosophy as well as in theoretical and empirical psychology. His philosophical contributions include a theory of parts and wholes, articles on probability theory and the classification of sciences, and works on epistemology and research methodology. His contributions to theoretical psychology comprise, for example, studies on the nature and classification of mental phenomena and the mind-body problem. With respect to empirical psychology, Stumpf was best known in his time for his fundamental contributions to the psychology of auditory perception and music. He wrote an authoritative two-volume work, *Tone Psychology* (1883, 1890), and enriched musicology with a large number of empirical and theoretical studies. In 1888, he also founded a new journal in this area, *Contributions to Acoustics and Musicology.* Other important contributions of Stumpf were his works on emotion, reviewed later.

Stumpf's style of approach as a theoretician has been compared to the piecemeal conceptual clarification characteristic of later analytic philosophers, and his writings were often praised for their clarity of thought. At the same time, Stumpf was regarded as one of the foremost experimental psychologists of his time.

Of Stumpf's scientific works, his publications on emotion belong to those that still deserve to be read today. His main contributions to this area of psychology consist of a cognitive-evaluative theory of emotions that in many respects anticipates contemporary cognitive emotion theories; a complementary theory of sensory pleasures and displeasures; and a comprehensive and incisive critique of the main opposing (noncognitive) theories of emotion of his time, those of William James and Wilhelm Wundt. Stumpf's own theory of emotions may have been influenced by Lotze; it exemplifies the elaboration of an emotion theory within the school of psychology established by his teacher Brentano, usually known as act psychology or intentional psychology. These names tend to be misleading; what Brentano emphasized was the object-directedness, or the representational character, of mental states. If one, for example, perceives, believes, desires, loves, or hates, then one always perceives, believes, desires, or loves or hates something; this something—which may not actually exist—is the intentional object of the respective mental state.

Object-directed mental states can therefore be construed as special types of relations between the person and an intended object; different intentional states differ with regard either to their objects or to the kind of intentional relation, the mode of mental apperception that links person and object. Elaborating these ideas, Stumpf proposed that, in contrast to simple sensory pleasures and displeasures, emotions proper (e.g., anger, fear, hope, etc.) have states of affairs (or propositions) as objects. According to Stumpf, this indicates that proper emotions presuppose a judgment or belief directed at the same propositional object. For example, if one is happy that a friend has recovered from illness (= the propositional object of happiness, p), one must also believe that the friend has recovered from illness. Accordingly, Stumpf defined an emotion as an affective state that is directed at a judged state of affairs, and hence is based on a judgment. More precisely, an emotion is a positive or negative evaluation of a state of affairs that is (a) caused by beliefs and (b) semantically linked to the belief contents. For example, happiness about p can be defined as a positive evaluation of p, which is, in part, caused by the belief that p.

It is important to note that the evaluations that form the affective core of emotions were conceptualized by Stumpf as unique psychological modes of relating to objects that are fundamentally different from the believing-mode. In particular, taking a positive or negative evaluative stance toward p is fundamentally different from forming an evaluative belief about p, that is, thinking it good or bad that p. Stumpf furthermore emphasized that judgment must be understood broadly, and he proposed that differentiations among emotions that go beyond the pleasant-unpleasant distinction are due to their cognitive presuppositions, that is, to the judgments on which they are based.

In addition to his scientific contributions, Stumpf's achievements in the politics of science are noteworthy. The most important of these were, first, the establishment of the Berlin Institute of Psychology, which became one of the world's largest and most efficient experimental institutes of its time; second, the foundation of a center for research on anthropoids on Tenerife, where his student Wolfgang Köhler conducted his well-known studies on problem solving in apes; and third, the founding of an archive of phonograms for use as a collection of ethnomusicological data. Stumpf also succeeded in attracting a sizable number of gifted students and coworkers, most notably Wolfgang Köhler, Kurt Koffka, Kurt Lewin, and Max Wertheimer, the founders of the Berlin school of Gestalt psychology. Other students or coworkers included the psychologists Johannes von Allesch, Hans Rupp, and Erich Moritz von Hornbostel. Finally, Stumpf was in close contact with many leading psychologists of his time, including Gustav Theodor Fechner, Georg Elias Müller, Hermann Ebbinghaus, and Ewald Hering. Together with Edmund Husserl and Alexius Meinong, he belonged to the inner circle of Franz Brentano's students, and he was a friend of the famous American philosopher and psychologist William James, with whom he shared in many respects a common view of psychology. This included the belief that experimental psychology and its mother science philosophy needed one another, and that to sever their fundamental connection would be to the disadvantage of both disciplines.

Bibliography

Ash, M. G. (1995). *Gestalt psychology in German culture, 1890–1967. Holism and the quest for objectivity.* (Cambridge studies in the history of psychology). Cambridge: Cambridge University Press. Locates Stumpf within the broader context of German Gestalt psychology.

Lewin, K. (1937). Carl Stumpf. *Psychological Review, 44,* 189–194.

Reisenzein, R. (1992). Stumpfs kognitiv-evaluative Theorie der Emotionen. [Stumpf's cognitive-evaluative theory of emotion]. In L. Sprung & W. Schönpflug (Eds.), *Zur Geschichte der Psychologie in Berlin* (pp. 97–137). Frankfurt am Main: Lang. Presents a reconstruction of Stumpf's theory of emotion and places it into a wider theoretical context.

Reisenzein, R., & Schönpflug, W. (1992). Stumpf's cognitive-evaluative theory of emotion. *American Psychologist, 47,* 34–45. Contains a condensed reconstruction of Stumpf's theory of emotion and points out the relevance of Stumpf's contributions to today's emotion psychology.

Sprung, H. (1997). Carl Stumpf. In W. Bringmann, H. E. Lück, R. Miller, & Ch. E. Early (Eds.), *A pictorial history of psychology* (pp. 247–250). Chicago: Quintessence.

Sprung, H. (1997). (Ed.). *Carl Stumpf—Schriften zur Psychologie* [Carl Stumpf—psychological writings]. Frankfurt am Main: Lang. A newly edited selection from Stumpf's psychological writings, including articles on the nature and classification of mental states, the mind-body problem, methods of developmental psychology, and most of Stumpf's writings on emotion. The volume also contains a biographical introductory essay, an introduction to the reprinted articles, and a complete bibliography of Stumpf's writings and of publications on Stumpf.

Sprung, H., & Sprung, L. (1996). Carl Stumpf (1848–1936), a general psychologist and methodologist, and a case study of a cross-cultural scientific transition process. In W. Battmann & S. Dutke (Eds.), *Processes of the molar regulation of behavior* (pp. 327–342). Lengerich: Pabst Science Publishers. A study of Stumpf as a general psychologist and methodologist, and his relationship to William James.

Rainer Reisenzein and Helga Sprung

SUBLIMATION. *See* Defense Mechanisms; *and* Psychoanalysis, *article on* Theories.

SUBLIMINAL PERCEPTION. Whenever stimuli presented below the threshold or limen for awareness are found to influence thoughts, feelings, or actions, subliminal perception has occurred. The term *subliminal perception* was originally used to describe situations in which weak stimuli were perceived without awareness. In recent years, the term has been applied more generally to describe any situation in which unnoticed stimuli are perceived.

The concept of subliminal perception is of considerable interest because it suggests that people's thoughts, feelings, and actions are influenced by stimuli that are perceived without any awareness of perceiving. This interest was reflected in some of the earliest psychological studies conducted during the late 1800s and early 1900s. In these early studies, people were simply asked whether or not they were aware of perceiving. For example, visual stimuli such as letters, digits, or geometric figures were presented at such a distance from observers that they claimed either not to see anything at all or to see nothing more than blurred dots. Likewise, auditory stimuli such as the names of letters were whispered so faintly that observers claimed that they were unable to hear any sound whatsoever. To test whether these visual or auditory stimuli may have been perceived despite statements to the contrary, the observers were asked to make guesses regarding the stimuli. For example, if half the stimuli were letters and half the stimuli were digits, the observers may have been asked to guess whether a letter or a digit had been presented. The consistent result found in these early studies was that the observers' guesses regarding the stimuli were more correct than would be expected on the basis of chance guessing. In other words, despite the observers' statements indicating that they were unaware of perceiving the stimuli, their guesses indicated that they did in fact perceive sufficient information to make accurate guesses regarding the stimuli. Over the years, there have been literally hundreds of studies following a similar format. Taken together, these studies show that considerable information capable of informing decisions and guiding actions is perceived even when observers do not experience any awareness of perceiving.

Another way in which subliminal perception has been demonstrated in controlled laboratory studies is by showing that stimuli can be perceived even when they are presented under conditions that make it difficult if not impossible to distinguish one stimulus from another stimulus. The classic studies were conducted in the 1970s by the British psychologist Anthony Marcel. These experiments were based on previous findings indicating that a decision regarding a stimulus is facilitated or primed when the stimulus follows a related stimulus. For example, if an observer is asked to classify a letter string as either a word (e.g., doctor, bread) or a nonword (e.g., tocdor, dread), a letter string such as the word *doctor* will be classified as a word faster when it follows a semantically related word (e.g., nurse) than when it follows a semantically nonrelated word (e.g., butter). Marcel found that words facilitated or primed subsequent word-nonword decisions to letter strings even when the words were presented under conditions that made it difficult if not impossible for the observers to distinguish when the words were present from when the words were absent. Since the time of Marcel's original experiments, there have been many other studies that have used similar methods. Not only have these studies confirmed Marcel's original findings, but they have shown that other stimuli such as pictures, faces, and spoken words can also facilitate subsequent decisions when they are presented under conditions that make it difficult to discriminate one stimulus from another stimulus. Although questions have been raised regarding whether the observers in these studies were completely unable to discriminate one stimulus from another stimulus, the one firm conclusion that can be made on the basis of these studies is that considerable information is perceived even when observers experience little or no awareness of perceiving as indicated by their difficulty in discriminating one stimulus from another stimulus.

Examples of subliminal perception are found in studies of patients with neurological damage. A striking characteristic of a number of neurological syndromes is that patients claim not to see particular stimuli but nevertheless respond on the basis of information conveyed by these stimuli. One example is a syndrome called *blindsight*. Patients with blindsight have damage to the primary visual cortex. As a result of this damage, they are often unaware of perceiving stimuli within a restricted area of their visual field. For example, if the visual field is thought of as consisting of four quadrants, a blindsight patient may have normal vision for stimuli presented in three of the quadrants but be completely unaware of stimuli presented in the fourth quadrant. However, even though these patients may claim not to see stimuli located within the "blind" quadrant, they are still able to guess the size, shape, or orientation of the stimuli that they claim not to see. Another neurological syndrome in which subliminal perception occurs is prosopagnosia or face agnosia. Patients with prosopagnosia are unable to recognize familiar faces. Although they may be aware that they are looking at a person's face, they are unable to say who the person may be. Thus, prosapagnosics have no awareness of perceiving any information regarding whose face they may be viewing. However, despite this absence of awareness, some patients with prosapagnosia are able to choose which of two names goes with each familiar face that they claim not to be able to recognize.

Perception without an awareness of perceiving can also occur in surgical patients undergoing general anesthesia. One goal of general anesthesia is to ensure that surgical patients are completely unaware of all events that occur during anesthesia. This goal is satisfied in the vast majority of cases because when patients are asked following surgery to report anything they remember that happened during surgery, just about every patient claims not to remember anything. However, when memory is assessed by more indirect methods, there appears to be some memory for events during anesthesia. For example, during surgery, patients may wear earphones and a tape recording of a number of repetitions of a series of words may be played to the patients. If following surgery, these patients are presented word stems such as *gui__* or *pro__* and asked to complete these stems to produce a common English word, there are numerous possible completions (e.g., guilt, guild, guile; prove, prowl, probe). However, if the words *guide* and *proud* had been presented during anesthesia, then the patients may be more likely to complete the stems *gui__* and *pro__* with letters that reproduce *guide* and *proud* than with letters that produce other possible words. Given that patients undergoing general anesthesia are unaware of events in the external environment, memory for specific stimuli presented during anesthesia shows that information is at times perceived without any awareness of perceiving during general anesthesia.

Over the years, some extraordinary claims have been made concerning the power of subliminal perception. Perhaps the most widely known claim was made in 1957 by James Vicary, a market researcher. He claimed that over a 6-week period, 45,699 patrons at a movie theater in Fort Lee, New Jersey were shown two advertising messages, "Eat Popcorn" and "Drink Coca-Cola," while they watched the film *Picnic*. According to Vicary, a message was flashed for 3/1000 of a second once every 5 seconds. The duration of the messages was so short that they were never consciously perceived. Despite the fact that the customers were not aware of perceiving the messages, Vicary claimed that over the 6-week period the sales of popcorn rose 57.7% and the sales of Coca-Cola rose 18.1%. Vicary's claims are often accepted as established fact. However, Vicary never released a detailed description of his study, and there has never been any independent evidence to support his claims. Also, in an interview with *Advertising Age* in 1962, Vicary stated that the original study was a fabrication. The weight of the evidence suggests that it was indeed a fabrication.

Other claims regarding the extraordinary efficacy of subliminal perception also lack substance. In the 1970s, Wilson Bryan Key wrote such books as *Subliminal Seduction* and *Media Sexploitation* in which he claimed subliminal sexual symbols or objects are often used to entice consumers to buy and use various products and services. One of Key's most famous claims is that the word *sex* was often embedded in products and advertisements. For example, he claimed that the word *sex* was printed on Ritz crackers and was embedded in the ice cubes of the drink shown in a well-known ad for Gilbey's Gin. According to Key, despite the fact the embedded words are not consciously perceived, they are unconsciously perceived and can elicit sexual arousal which in turn makes the products more attractive to consumers. Although Key's claims are widely known, there is no independent evidence indicating that embedded subliminal words, symbols, or objects are used to sell products. Furthermore, even if such embedded subliminal stimuli were used, there is no evidence to suggest this would be an effective method for influencing the choices that consumers make.

Belief in the power of subliminal perception to induce changes in the way people feel and act is so widespread that a number of companies have been able to exploit this belief by marketing subliminal self-help audio- and videotapes. The companies that market these tapes claim that regular use of the tapes can cure a variety of problems and aid in the development of many skills. Each company markets a number of different tapes. Presumably, what distinguishes the different tapes marketed by each company are the embedded subliminal messages that can be neither consciously seen nor heard. Some of the more popular tapes are claimed to help individuals stop smoking, lose weight, or reduce stress; other tapes are claimed to help people increase their reading speed, improve their memory, or develop their skills at tennis (or golf or baseball, etc.). Given the extraordinary nature of these claims, there have been a number of controlled studies specifically designed to test of the efficacy of the tapes. All of these studies have failed to find any evidence consistent with the claims of the companies that market these tapes. There is simply no evidence that regular listening to subliminal self-help audiotapes or regular viewing of subliminal self-help videotapes is an effective method for overcoming problems or improving skills. In fact, there is even evidence to suggest that many subliminal self-help tapes do not even contain subliminal messages that could possibly be perceived under any circumstances by a human observer.

A common theme that links all extraordinary claims regarding subliminal perception is that perception in the absence of an awareness of perceiving is somehow more powerful or influential than perception that is accompanied by an awareness of perceiving. This idea is not supported by the results of controlled laboratory investigations of subliminal perception. Rather, the findings from controlled studies indicate that subliminal perception, when it occurs, reflects a person's usual interpretations of stimuli. Furthermore, there is no evidence to suggest that people initiate actions on the basis of subliminal perception. The weight of the evidence indicates that people must be aware of perceiving stimuli before they initiate actions or change their habitual reactions to these stimuli. Thus, although subliminal perception may allow us to make accurate guesses regarding the characteristics of stimuli, subliminal perception cannot lead a person to drink Coca-Cola or to eat Ritz Crackers, and it cannot be used effectively to improve a person's tennis skills or to cure a person's bad habits.

Bibliography

Dixon, N. F. (1971). *Subliminal perception: The nature of a controversy*. New York: McGraw-Hill. Comprehensive review of all research findings prior to 1970.

Greenwald, A. W. (1992). New look 3: Unconscious cognition reclaimed. *American Psychologist, 47,* 766–779. A review and discussion of recent research findings.

McConnell, J. V., Cutler, R. L., & McNeil, E. B. (1958). Subliminal stimulation: An overview. *American Psychologist, 13,* 229–242. This paper was published shortly after the original claims regarding the effectiveness of embedded messages such as "Eat Popcorn" and "Drink Coca-Cola" became widely known. It provides an in-depth evaluation of these claims.

Merikle, P. M., & Daneman, M. (1996). Memory for unconsciously perceived events: Evidence from anesthetized patients. *Consciousness and Cognition, 5,* 525–541. Presents and discusses the aggregate results of all studies investigating memory for events during general anesthesia.

Merikle, P. M., & Daneman, M. (1998). Psychological investigations of unconscious perception. *Journal of Consciousness Studies, 5,* 5–18. Overview of scientific approaches to the study of subliminal perception. Includes some speculations regarding the consequences of subliminal perception.

Pratkanis, A. R. (1992). The cargo-cult science of subliminal persuasion. *Skeptical Inquirer, 16,* 260–272. Evaluates many of the extraordinary claims regarding subliminal perception.

Vokey, J. R., & Read, J. D. (1985). Subliminal messages: Between the devil and the media. *American Psychologist, 40,* 1231–1239. A review and evaluation of the claim that some rock music contains subliminal backward messages.

Weiskrantz, L. (1986). *Blindsight: A case study and implications*. New York: Oxford University Press. This is the classic case study of a patient with blindsight.

Young, A. W. (1994). Covert recognition. In M. J. Farah & G. Ratcliff (Eds.), *The neuropsychology of high-level vision* (pp. 331–358). Hillsdale, NJ: Erlbaum. Detailed summary of many of the studies of prosapagnosic patients.

Philip Merikle

SUB-SAHARAN AFRICA. [*This entry discusses the history of the field of psychology in the English-speaking countries of the region including Botswana, Cameroon, Ethiopia, Gambia, Ghana, Kenya, Liberia, Malawi, Nigeria, Sierra Leone, Somalia, Sudan, Tanzania, Uganda, Zambia, and Zimbabwe.*]

Sub-Saharan Africa, as a major geographic area, was subject to colonization by Britain or domination by other European countries from the late 1800s to the latter half of the twentieth century. These contacts resulted in the introduction of the English language as the official language for education and business and in the introduction of Euro-American educational systems. By the mid-1900s the colonized countries of sub-Saharan Africa achieved independence from colonizers, and the governments of the newly independent countries created universities in order to educate their nationals for positions of leadership. With the advent of universities in the 1950s the field of psychology formally began in sub-Saharan Africa.

The very first departments of psychology in Anglophone Africa were opened in Nigeria (University of Nigeria, Nsukka) in 1964 and in Ghana (University of Ghana) in 1967. The first experimental psychology laboratory was opened at the University of Zambia in 1965, and a department of psychology was opened there in 1966. Following these early developments, departments of psychology were opened in Kenya in 1970, in Zimbabwe in 1974, in Uganda in 1975, and in Malawi in 1980. A School of Psychology and Kindergarten Education was opened in the Sudan in 1967 and a department of educational psychology was opened in Ethiopia in 1974. A department of educational psychology was also opened in Tanzania in 1990. The year in which psychology was established in Cameroon is not known.

Departments of psychology or educational psychology still do not exist in Botswana, Sierra Leone, or Somalia. There is to date no university in Gambia, and no information is available regarding Liberia.

In spite of the fact that there are so few departments of psychology in Anglophone Africa, it has been and continues to be common practice for most universities to employ at least one or two psychologists, whose main role is to teach a few psychology courses to students who are studying in other disciplines. The students most likely to study psychology courses are enrolled in social studies or social sciences (sociology, anthropology, economics, and political science), social work, education, health sciences, rehabilitation, nursing, medicine, and psychiatry. The courses the students usually enroll in are: Introduction to Psychology, Social Psychology, Developmental Psychology, Educational Psychology, Health Psychology, and Organizational Psychology.

Departments of psychology initially offered the B.Sc. (bachelor of science) or B.A. (bachelor of arts) degree; they began to add the postgraduate degrees of M.Sc. (master of science) and M.A. (master of arts) in the 1970s and 1980s. The highest level of postgraduate training in psychology is the Ph.D. degree, and the only country to offer this level of training has been Nigeria.

The standard throughout sub-Saharan Africa is that two degrees in psychology, a B.Sc. or B.A. and an M.Sc., are required in order to be a fully qualified professional psychologist. Professional psychologists are qualified to teach at universities, conduct psychological research, and practice in the applied fields of clinical, educational, and occupational psychology. Most professional psychologists in sub-Saharan Africa are employed as teaching faculty at universities, medical schools, and teacher-training colleges. Only in Zimbabwe and Nigeria are a large proportion of psychologists in independent practice in the applied fields of clinical, educational, and occupational psychology.

Early Contributions to the Development of Psychology

The development of the field of psychology in sub-Saharan Africa was assisted by several notable psychologists from developed countries who went to Africa for the specific purpose of conducting research on persons of African origin. Sir Frederick Bartlett, the leading British psychologist of the 1930s, conducted research in Nigeria in the 1930s on the impact of culture on memory processes. In the 1960s and 1970s, John W. Berry, from Canada, conducted research in Sierra Leone and the Central African Republic on visual perception and cognitive style. Marshall H. Segall, from the United States, conducted research on visual perception in 12 countries in Africa, and Michael Cole, Sylvia Scribner, and John Gay, from the United States, worked in Liberia on learning and thinking.

Several psychologists from the United Kingdom took up teaching and research positions at universities or related institutions in sub-Saharan Africa in the 1960s and 1970s. These included Jan Deregowski, Alistar Heron, and Robert Serpell, all of whom worked in Zambia; Gustav Jahoda, who worked in Ghana; and Mallory Wober, who worked in Nigeria and Uganda. Wober published an important book, *Psychology in Africa* (London, 1976), in which he describes 600 pieces of writing and research that are related to Africa. Of all of the psychologists who have worked in Africa, Alistair Mundy-Castle has the longest and most distinguished record of teaching and research, which began in 1948. He has worked in South Africa, Ghana, Nigeria, and Zimbabwe.

Fields of Psychology

Almost all universities that developed in sub-Saharan Africa after 1950 were national universities that received their funding from their national governments. The goal of these universities was to create graduates who could contribute to national development. National development meant changes in economic activity away from pastoral and agricultural subsistence economies to modern industrial economies that could compete in a global economy. To accomplish this transition, most governments were interested in providing Western-style primary school education to all citizens. Thus the field of educational psychology was universally accepted by the governments in sub-Saharan Africa. Educational psychology was seen as a welcome component in universities and teacher training colleges in order to ensure that teachers understood the learner, the learning process, and the learning situation.

The field of social psychology, which deals with the individual in relation to groups, was also viewed by national governments as useful in national development. Changes in the economy resulted in changes in human behavior as people moved from rural to urban areas and took up employment in modern factories and offices. This rapid socioeconomic change led to changes in attitudes, value systems, motivations, and life styles. Governments were concerned with creating attitudes that would modernize their citizens and make them more accepting of the need to compete in a global economy, which was dominated by western countries.

In the 1960s and 1970s, the applied fields of occupational, industrial, and organizational psychology were relevant to only certain countries. In the heavily industrialized countries of Ghana, Nigeria, Zambia, and

Zimbabwe, for example, industrial and organizational psychology were viewed as providing practical inputs into areas such as personnel selection and training, industrial relations, and human resource management. Organizational psychology became relevant in Malawi in the 1980s and has expanded in the 1990s in Uganda as the country has embarked on a new scheme of national development.

The field of psychometrics, that is, the assessment of mental abilities and skills, was imported from South Africa into Zimbabwe and Zambia in the 1960s. It was used mainly in personnel selection for the mining industry. It has recently become a focus of attention in Uganda, where the government is reforming the public service and utilizing psychometric tests. Psychometrics has been and continues to be a controversial area not only in Africa but worldwide, as many people question whether tests that are imported from one culture can accurately measure mental abilities and skills in people in a different culture (Greenfield, 1997). Over the years there has been more emphasis on developing tests within each country (the cultural approach), rather than importing tests from other countries (the cross-cultural approach).

The field of psychology toward which there has been a great deal of ambivalence is clinical psychology, which deals with the assessment and treatment of mental illness. In Africa, physical illness, mental illness, bad luck, and accidents are usually attributed to witchcraft, magic, or ancestral spirits, and people usually seek help from traditional healers who know the local cultural beliefs. However, in attempts to modernize the health care systems, most national governments have introduced Western-style medical, psychiatric, and psychological treatment, and people can choose from the two systems, traditional versus Western. (See Peltzer, 1995).

Conferences

Very few psychology conferences have been held in sub-Saharan Africa. The first and probably the key conference, "Social Psychology and National Development," was held at the University of Ibadan in Nigeria in 1966. Another important conference, "Human Behavior and the Challenges of National Development," was held at Ife, Nigeria, in 1985. In 1989, a conference entitled "The Current Status of Teaching of Psychology and Psychological Research in Eastern and Southern Africa" was held in Nairobi, Kenya. The International Association for Cross-Cultural Psychology, which has many members from African countries, has held regional conferences in Ibadan, Nigeria (in 1973) and Nairobi, Kenya (in 1975). In addition to the conferences just mentioned, which were attended by international delegates, conferences have been held in individual countries for the nationals of those countries.

Employment in Psychology

In sub-Saharan Africa, there are no specific jobs for a person who has only one degree in psychology; such graduates are usually employed in positions in which a university degree in any of the social sciences is acceptable, for example, teaching in schools, assisting in mental health centers or early childhood education programs, or positions in administration, personnel, and management.

The majority of professional psychologists (those with two or more degrees in psychology) are based at universities, teacher training colleges, and medical schools. Those who work outside academic settings are usually employed in government positions in mental health and educational psychology, in private counseling centers or early childhood education centers, or in administrative, personnel, or managerial positions.

Psychology in Individual Countries

The importance of psychology in each country can be partly determined by comparing the year in which a particular university opened and the number of years that elapsed before a department of psychology was established; the six countries that show the most development in psychology in sub-Saharan Africa are Ethiopia, Kenya, Nigeria, Sudan, Uganda, and Zimbabwe.

British Commonwealth Countries. The countries of the British Commonwealth share a common educational and political history because of their early contacts with Britain and Christian missionaries.

Botswana. Botswana, located in southern Africa, became a British protectorate in 1885 and gained its independence in 1966. There is only one university in Botswana, the University of Botswana, located in the capital city of Gaborone, and it was founded in 1976. There is currently no department of psychology, but three psychology courses are taught in the department of social work. Plans are currently under way to discuss the establishment of a department of psychology.

Cameroon. Cameroon, located in West Africa, was colonized by the Germans in 1884, but after World War I the French had a mandate over 80% of the area, and the British had a mandate over 20% of the area. French Cameroon became an independent state in 1960, and it was enlarged to include British Cameroon in 1961. Cameroon joined the British Commonwealth in 1995.

The first university was the University of Yaounde, which was established in the capital city of Yaounde in 1962. Both English and French were used as teaching languages. After 1991, the university expanded, and there is currently a University of Yaounde I and a University of Yaounde II. There are four additional universities in Cameroon; of these, classes are taught in French in three and in English in one.

Detailed information is not available about the field

of psychology in Cameroon. A. Bame Nsamenang, who is associated with the Institute of Human Sciences in Bemenda is well known for his recent book, *Human Development in Cultural Context: A Third World Perspective* (Newbury Park, Calif., 1992).

Gambia. Located in West Africa, Gambia has no university.

Ghana. Located in West Africa, Ghana became a British colony in 1874 and achieved independence in 1957. There are five universities in Ghana. Only the University of Ghana has a department of psychology; the university is located in Legon, near the capital city of Accra. The university was granted university status in 1961. The department of psychology was established in 1967. In the late 1990s the department offered bachelor's degrees as well as master's degrees in clinical, industrial, and organizational psychology and social and developmental psychology.

Most research in psychology in Ghana is conducted at the university, and focuses on issues that are relevant to national development, for example, gender issues, job stress, moral development, adjustment to college, drug use among Ghanaians, attitudes toward the use of condoms, and the mental health of refugees. Psychological research is published in the *Legon Bulletin of Psychology*.

Psychologists in Ghana who have made significant contributions to the field of psychology are S. Danquan, C. R. Fiscian, and G. Jahoda (from Scotland).

Kenya. Located in east Africa, Kenya became an official Crown Colony of the British Government in 1920; it gained independence in 1963. There are five universities in Kenya; only two have departments of psychology: the University of Nairobi and the United States International University Africa (USIU-Africa). The University of Nairobi was established in 1956; the department of psychology, established in the 1990s, offers degrees in educational psychology, not general psychology. USIU-Africa, a private university, is located in Nairobi, and is affiliated with the United States International University in San Diego, California. The university opened in 1970, and psychology degrees have been offered since that time. Bachelor's and master's degrees are offered as well as a certificate in chemical dependency.

The majority of professional psychologists in Kenya are employed in academic posts. The field of educational psychology has been and remains highly developed in Kenya. There are a few clinical and counseling psychologists who practice in the community; most research is conducted at the universities and colleges and is focused on educational problems as well as social problems such as drug abuse and teenage pregnancies.

The Kenya Psychological Association was established in 1997. There are no journals specifically devoted to the field of psychology in Kenya.

Psychologists who have made significant contributions to the development of psychology and educational psychology in Kenya are Patricia Kariuki, D. Kiminyo, S. Munywoki, F. Okatcha, E. Okech, and Sam Tumuti.

Malawi. Located in south-central Africa, Malawi became a British protectorate in 1889 and became independent in 1964. The one university in Malawi, the University of Malawi, founded in 1964, is located in Zomba. A department of human behavior, founded in 1964, consisted of philosophy, sociology, and psychology, and the full department of psychology was established in 1980. Degrees in psychology are not awarded, but psychology is studied as part of a social science degree.

The majority of professional psychologists in Malawi are employed in academic settings. Most research in psychology is done at the university and focuses on the problems facing national development in Malawi, for example, human immunodeficiency virus/acquired immunodeficiency syndrome (HIV/AIDS), orphan care, and marketing and personnel selection.

Psychological articles appear in the *Journal of Social Science*. The major contributors to the development of psychology in Malawi are Kathleen Myambo (from the United States), who was the first psychologist to teach at the university, Stephen Buggie (from the United States), who was appointed in 1980 to establish the Department of Psychology, and Howard Mzumara.

Nigeria. Located in west Africa, Nigeria became a protectorate of Britain in 1885 and became independent in 1963. The first department of psychology was established in 1964 at the University of Nigeria, Nsukka. There are 37 universities in Nigeria; 10 have psychology departments. Training is provided at the bachelor's, master's, and doctorate levels in most of these departments. The first doctorates were awarded in Nigeria in 1984.

Most professional psychologists are employed in academic settings, but Nigeria is one of the few countries in sub-Saharan Africa where a large percentage of psychologists are employed in the private sector or work as self-employed consultants in the applied areas of clinical, industrial, organizational, and occupational psychology.

Research is conducted mainly at the universities. Research topics include work productivity, motivation, job satisfaction, leadership, drug abuse, conflict, stress management, and developmental issues related to children and families.

There are three psychological associations in Nigeria: the Association of Nigerian Industrial/Organizational Psychologists (ANIOP), the Nigerian Association of Clinical Psychologists (NACP) and the Nigerian Psychological Association (NPA). The NPA is a member of the International Union of Psychological Science (IUPsyS).

Nigeria has more journals devoted to psychological research than any other country in sub-Saharan Africa: the *Nigerian Journal of Psychological Research* (founded in 1980), *Ife Psychologia: An International Journal* (founded in 1982), the *Nigerian Journal of Psychology* (founded in 1984), the *Nigerian Journal of Basic and Applied Psychology* (founded in 1987), and the *Journal of Psychology in Africa* (founded in 1988).

Ife Psychologia and the *Journal of Psychology in Africa* are the only two journals in sub-Saharan Africa that are Pan-African in scope and are included in *Psychological Abstracts*, published by the American Psychological Association.

Psychologists who have made a significant contribution in Nigeria are A. Babalola, E. U. Egwu, I. E. Eyo, B. A. Folarin, I. S. Obot, 'Sola Olowu, D. C. Uguro-Okorie, C. E. Ugwuegbu, A. F. Uzoka, A. Mundy-Castle (from England), and the late M. O. Okonji, who taught at the University of Zambia, the University of Lagos in Nigeria, and Makerere University in Uganda.

Sierra Leone. Located in west Africa, Sierra Leone became a British protectorate in 1896 and was granted independence in 1961. Its one university, the University of Sierra Leone, located in Freetown, has no department of psychology nor educational psychology. A few courses in educational psychology are taught to students in other degree programs.

Tanzania. Tanzania, in east Africa, became a British mandate in 1919 and achieved independence in 1961. None of the three universities in Tanzania have a department of psychology. The University of Dar Es Salaam, located in the port city of Dar Es Salaam, founded in 1961, has had a department of educational psychology since 1990. Most of the graduates from this department work in the field of education as teachers or administrators. The department offers a master's degree in social psychology and intends to offer a master's degree in applied social psychology that has an emphasis on community counseling and mental health.

The majority of research is conducted on effective counseling methods regarding human immunodeficiency virus/acquired immunodeficiency syndrome (HIV/AIDS). The names of journals that publish psychological articles are not available.

Significant contributers to the field of psychology are P. Biswalo, A. S. Mbise, I. M. Omari, and M. K. Possi.

Uganda. Located in east Africa, Uganda became a protectorate of Britain in 1896 and became independent in 1962. Of its three universities, only Makerere University (located in the capital city of Kampala), which was founded in 1949 and achieved university status in 1970, has a department of psychology. The department was established in 1975. B.Sc. and B.A. degrees in psychology are awarded. Master's degrees in organizational psychology, counseling psychology, and clinical psychology are offered.

Professional psychologists are based mainly in academic settings. Most research is conducted at the university and is in areas that are relevant to national development, that is, child development and the applied fields of industrial, organizational, health, and environmental psychology. There is a psychology testing department in the public service, and psychologists from Makerere University are involved in this development.

The Uganda National Psychological Association (UNPA) was established in 1992 and is a member of the International Union of Psychological Science. Psychological research is published in the following journals: the *East African Journal of Education*, the *Makerere Medical Journal*, and the *Journal of Psychology in Africa*.

Psychologists who have made significant contributions are P. Baguma, J. Iluko, John Munene, J. Opolot, V. Owens, O. Tom, and A. Okumu.

Zambia. Located in south central Africa, Zambia came under direct British government in 1924 and became an independent country in 1964. There are two universities in Zambia; there is a department of psychology at the University of Zambia in the capital city of Lusaka. The university was established in 1965, and developments in the field of psychology began immediately. The first laboratory of experimental psychology in independent Africa south of the Sahara was opened in 1965, and the department of psychology was established in 1966. This department of psychology had a strong orientation toward mental testing, and the early graduates from the department were recruited into the applied fields of educational psychology and industrial psychology.

Most professional psychologists are based at the university, but a small number work in government positions in educational psychology and in the mining industry. Most research is conducted at the university and is aimed toward community applications such as community health, the impact of social change on behavior, and social problems associated with alcohol consumption.

Articles with a psychological content are accepted by the *African Social Research Journal* and the *Journal of Adult Education*.

Psychologists who have made significant contributions are J. Deregoswki (from Scotland), A. Heron (from England), Peter Machungwa, Ravinder Kathuria (from India), Phil Kingsley (from the United States), M. Mwanalushi, and R. Serpell (from England).

Zimbabwe. Located in southern Africa, Zimbabwe, formerly known as Rhodesia, had associations with Britain dating back to 1889. Zimbabwe became a fully independent country in 1980. Of the three universities in Zimbabwe, only one has a department of psychology: the University of Zimbabwe, which opened in 1955 and achieved full university status in 1970.

The department of psychology began in 1974; the

university offers a B.Sc. degree in psychology and post-graduate degrees in clinical psychology and occupational psychology. Zimbabwe is probably the only country in sub-Saharan Africa where a larger number of psychologists work outside of academic settings than within academic settings. Many psychologists are employed as educational psychologists with the ministry of education, and a large number of professional psychologists are in independent practice and offer services in clinical, educational, and occupational psychology.

The majority of research is conducted at the university, although a small amount of research is carried out in government departments. The current research at the university focuses on problems that are relevant to national development, that is, HIV/AIDS, human sexuality, forensic psychology, unemployment, and organizational psychology.

The Zimbabwe Psychological Association (ZPA), formed in 1971, is a member of the International Union of Psychological Science. Formal legislation that governs the practice of psychology in Zimbabwe is incorporated in the Psychological Practices Act of 1971.

There is no specific publication that specializes in psychological research, but the following journals accept psychological articles: *Zambezia*, the *Zimbabwe Journal of Educational Research*, and the *Central African Journal of Medicine*.

Psychologists who have made significant contributions are K. Myambo (from the United States), who also taught in Malawi and Zambia, and A. Mundy-Castle (from England), who has worked in several countries in sub-Saharan Africa. Other well-known psychologists are Donald Munro (from Scotland), Sally Nyandiya-Bundy, and David Wilson.

Non-British Commonwealth Countries. These countries have unique histories with regard to their relationships to Western powers, and there are few historical and political similarities among them.

Ethiopia. Located in northeastern Africa, Ethiopia has never been colonized. There are two universities in Ethiopia, and psychology is taught at one of them, Addis Ababa University (AAU), which was founded in 1950 and gained full university status in 1961. The department of educational psychology was founded in 1974 and currently offers a B.A. degree in general psychology (with an emphasis on guidance and counseling), an M.A. degree in measurement and evaluation, and an M.A. degree in guidance and counseling.

Most research is conducted at the university. The topics of research are concerned with the applications of psychology to the field of education and social problems such as gender studies, ethnic stereotypes, and domestic violence.

The Ethiopian Psychologists Association (EPA) was formed in 1991. Psychological research is published in the *Ethiopian Journal of Education*.

The following people have made significant contributions to the development of psychology: Y. Abdi, H. Berhane, A. Eshete, A. Husain, A. Meshesha, H. Wondimu, D. Wole, and M. Yimer.

Liberia. Located in West Africa, Liberia was established in 1847 when 3,000 emancipated slaves from the United States arrived. It has never been colonized. The only university in Liberia, the University of Liberia, located in the capital city of Monrovia, was founded as Liberia College in 1862 and gained university status in 1951. No information is available as to whether or not there is a department of psychology at the university. However, it is noteworthy that a great deal of the early cross-cultural research in cognitive psychology was conducted in Liberia in the 1960s and 1970s by three Americans: M. Cole, S. Scribner, and J. Gay.

Somalia. Located in northeast Africa, Somalia has one university, the Somali National University in the capital city of Mogadishu; the university was founded in 1955 and achieved university status in 1969. There is no department of psychology; psychology courses are taught in the faculty of medicine.

Sudan. Located in northeast Africa, Sudan has eight universities. The major one, the University of Khartoum, was founded in 1956 and uses Arabic as the official language. No information is available from this university; information about the development of psychology in Sudan was provided by the Ahfad University for Women, which was established in 1966 and has a School of Psychology and Preschool Education, which was founded in 1967. Courses are taught in English and Arabic. The department awards B.Sc. degrees; there is an emphasis on counseling and health psychology.

The Sudanese Psychological Association was registered in 1987. Psychologists who have contributed to the development of psychology include G. Badri, M. E. Badri, T. Bashar, T. E. G. Doleeb, and E. B. Taha.

[*See also* North Africa; *and* South Africa.]

Bibliography

Cole, M., Gay, J., Glick, J., & Sharp, D. (1971). *The cultural context of learning and thinking.* New York: Basic Books.

Deregowski, J. B., & Bentley, A. M. (1986). Perception of pictorial space by Bushmen. *International Journal of Psychology, 21,* 743–752.

Gay, J., & Cole, M. (1967). *The new mathematics in an old culture.* New York: Holt, Rinehart and Winston.

Greenfield, P. M. (1997). You can't take it with you: Why ability assessments don't cross cultures. *American Psychologist, 52,* 1115–1124.

Ife Psychologia: An International Journal. Ife Centre for Psychological Studies, P. O. Box 1548, Ile-Ife, Nigeria. E-mail: solowu@oauife.edu.ng

Jahoda, G. & McGurk, H. (1974). Pictorial depth perception in Scottish and Ghanaian children: A critique of some findings with the Hudson Test. *International Journal of Psychology, 9,* 255–267.

Journal of Psychology in Africa. IKO Publisher, Postfach 900421, D-60444, Frankfurt/M. Germany. E-mail: ikoverlag@t-online.de

Kingsley, P. R. (1983). Technological development: Issues, roles and orientation for social psychology. In F. Blackler (Ed.), *Social psychology and developing countries* (pp. 131–153). New York: Wiley.

Montero, M., & Sloan, T. S. (1988). Understanding behavior in conditions of economic and cultural dependency. *International Journal of Psychology, 23,* 597–617.

Mundy-Castle, A. C. (1983). Are western concepts valid in Africa? A Nigerian review. In S. H. Irvine & J. W. Berry (Eds.), *Human assessment and cultural factors* (pp. 81–84). New York: Plenum Press.

Myambo, K. (1990). Social values and community development in rural Africa. *International Journal of Psychology, 25,* 767–777.

Nsamenang, A. B. (1992). *Human development in cultural context: A third world perspective.* Newbury Park, CA: Sage.

Okonji, O. M. (1971). The effects of familiarity on classification. *Journal of Cross-Cultural Psychology, 2,* 39–49.

Peltzer, K. (1995). *Psychology and health in African cultures: Examples of ethno-psychotherapeutic practice.* Frankfurt, Germany: IKO.

Segall, M. H., Campbell, D. T., & Herskovits, M. J. (1966). *The influence of culture on visual perception.* Indianapolis, IN: Bobbs-Merrill.

Serpell, R. (1993). *The significance of schooling: Life-journeys in an African society.* Cambridge, UK: Cambridge University Press.

Wober, M. (1975). *Psychology in Africa.* London: International African Institute.

Kathleen Myambo

SUBSTANCE ABUSE DISORDERS. *See* Alcoholism; Drug Abuse; *and* Smoking.

SUBURBAN COMMUNITIES. About 55% of Americans live in suburban communities, a percentage that demographers believe will increase. Many social scientists believe that living in the suburbs is likely to influence attitudes and social behaviors in particular ways. If so, we would like to know what those influences are, what effects result, and how both might be modified should we wish to do so.

An initial challenge facing students of suburban communities is to define them. This is not simple, because American suburbs vary considerably in population, income, ethnicity, employment base, economic outlook, and in self-perception. A metropolitan area of any size might contain dozens of suburbs, sometimes many dozens, that might range from older working-class or ethnic communities bordering the central city, to stereotypical middle-income suburbs attracting young families, to rapidly growing communities on the outer ring, with many gradations inbetween. But all these communities are conventionally called suburbs, and self-identify as suburbs, even though they may differ from each other at least as much as from the larger city at their hub.

To compound the definitional challenge, the traditional lines between suburb and city are blurring. This is because suburbs are increasing in population and in dominance relative to their central cities. They are sometimes evolving into satellite cities, or "edge cities" of their own, attracting offices, jobs, and commerce. They are touching the borders of other similarly growing metropolitan areas, forming contiguous urbanized expanses stretching for miles, where the urban-suburban distinction is harder to discern. And with their growth has come increased suburban economic and political power, not simply in purchasing or voting, but power in economic production—witness Silicon Valley—and the power over transportation, land use, and environmental quality that accompanies it.

These sociological, economic, and political changes, and their probable continuance, threaten the descriptive and explanatory value of the term "suburb" as a useful construct. But while recognizing these changes, the starting premise here is that there remain significant shared qualities among most suburbs, and that living in suburban communities as such can and does have identifiable and meaningful social and psychological consequences. What are these qualities, and what consequences follow?

Theoretical Perspectives

A suburb may be defined as an independently governed community, generally between 10,000 and 100,000 in size, located near a large city in a metropolitan area. Compared to city dwellers, suburban residents as a group are better educated and have higher household incomes. They are more likely to be employed, in better-paying jobs, and also to live in single-family housing, in their own homes, and in nuclear family structures. They are less likely to be foreign-born or non-White, and are less likely to experience crime.

Each of these demographics may influence behavior; but one additional quality of suburban communities is lower population density. Suburbs almost always contain fewer people per unit area than cities. This is of special interest to social scientists, because density has sometimes been considered a stronger predictor of behavior than size, and because it relates closely to earlier theories of urban life.

In his landmark analysis of cities, the sociologist Louis Wirth argued in 1938 (*American Journal of Sociology, 44*, 1–24) that density, size, and heterogeneity of population shape much of urban behavior. Given the city's size and density, the city-dweller would inevitably come into daily contact with more people than would be possible to know or even recognize. But given the city's diversity, one would also have more difficulty finding people of similar backgrounds, attitudes, and values for affirmation, friendship and support. For Wirth, as for sociologists such as Georg Simmel and Robert Park preceding him, and for psychologists such as Stanley Milgram a generation later, social relationships in the city would therefore tend to be anonymous, fragmentary, and fleeting. Their lack of richness and depth would foster loneliness, anxiety, and alienation. As by-products, community feeling would be eroded and social cohesion would be reduced.

The suburbs could offer an alternative—increased open space, decreased heterogeneity, less inevitability of contact, more freedom in contact choice, and therefore a healthier social and community climate. Though suburban communities in America were well-established even in the nineteenth century, the combination of population expansion and a strong domestic economy after World War II, coupled with high housing demand, low mortgage rates, increased automobile production, and postwar highway construction, brought the suburbs into prominence. Suburban lifestyle came to define mainstream culture. The social climate that resulted, however, has been criticized and debated.

The critique stems in part from the environmental characteristics and design of most suburbs themselves. One viewpoint, contrasting with Wirth's, draws different conclusions from the same density concept. Suburban density is lower; but when residents are more spread out, in single-family homes on private lots, they are less likely to come into everyday contact with each other. In addition, lower density means that shopping areas are more likely to be beyond easy walking distance, which in turn implies the use of a private automobile, reducing contact further. As a result, neighbors may visually encounter each other infrequently, though such physical seeing is usually a precondition for deeper and more meaningful social relationships to develop.

In community life that viewpoint continues; there is a natural progression from seeing, to knowing, to liking, to trusting, to acting. Each element depends upon the one preceding it. If neighbors do not see each other with sufficient frequency, then the other elements in the sequence cannot easily become activated, and the fabric of community life will tend to be weak. And in suburban communities, to which residents often move intentionally so as to lower the population density around them, and where they typically ensure additional privacy by fences, shrubbery, and other visual barriers, such physical encountering may be further minimized, with the hypothesized consequence of added social isolation, equaling or exceeding that found in the city.

The question of suburban versus urban differences is of more than theoretical concern. The qualities and output variables of interest—community feeling, satisfaction, social contacts, and participation among them—are highly valued by most community-oriented psychologists. And these same qualities have frequently been shown to be associated with other desirable social outcomes; for example, lower crime rates, more vigorous economic activity, greater social competence among children, better emotional and physical health, and longer life span. If proper community design could improve community social climate and confer such added benefits at the same time, that would be a major step forward for psychology and for social welfare.

Empirical Evidence

Precisely how suburban social behavior may in fact differ from urban behavior and from behavior in smaller community settings can best be answered by data. The data presently available, however, do not appear conclusive. Part of the reason is methodological: it is difficult to compare community types directly while holding other variables constant. In addition, psychological studies of American suburban communities are relatively rare: research has emphasized urban settings, where more obvious social problems exist. These limitations notwithstanding, a summary of the evidence is given below.

Qualitative Data. Many accounts of suburban behavior do emphasize separateness, psychological distance, and social remoteness. A reference point is M. P. Baumgartner's *The Moral Order of a Suburb* (New York, 1988), based upon participant observation and interviews in a predominantly upper-middle-income suburb in New Jersey, and which concludes: "People in the suburbs live in a world characterized by nonviolence and nonconfrontation, in which civility prevails and disturbances of the peace are uncommon." Along with conflict avoidance, though, goes diminishment of public life and withdrawal from personal engagement: "Weak social ties breed a general indifference and coldness, and a lack of conflict is accompanied by a lack of caring." The overall pattern is seen as "moral minimalism."

While Baumgartner's is one of the only in-depth behavioral field studies of suburbia, her conclusions are echoed by many other scholars and expert commentators, such as the suburban historian Kenneth Jackson ("Residential neighborhoods have become a mass of small, private islands"), environmental-design critics such as Philip Langdon and James Howard Kunstler, and architect and town planner Andres Duany ("The classic suburb is less a community than an agglomeration of houses, shops, and offices connected to one another by cars").

But it is not clear to what extent these conclusions apply across the board. There is also some research evidence that suburban-style communities can be particularly welcoming, participatory, and friendly. In their study of Seaside, in the Florida panhandle, Plas and Lewis (*American Journal of Community Psychology*, 1996, 24, 109–143) found that large majorities of residents interviewed reported that their community met their personal needs, made them feel at home, and allowed them to make friends easily. Because Seaside is a planned community, with housing and townscape features deliberately designed to encourage social contact, this study supports the position that prosocial community behaviors can be environmentally shaped. Yet precisely because Seaside is planned, and is also not a traditional metropolitan suburb, the question of generalization to other suburban communities again arises.

In sum, though, the sparse qualitative data, as distinct from the more subjective commentary, do not give firm support either to the argument that suburban social behavior is notably constricted, or that it is reliably distinct from urban or small-town settings.

Quantitative Data. Quantitative studies of suburban social behavior have most often focused on attitudinal measures of satisfaction and attachment, and behavioral measures of social contact and community participation. Among the most significant findings:

1. Compared to urban residents, suburban residents in most studies seem to express more self-rated satisfaction with their neighborhoods and communities, both overall and also with respect to specific community features, such as public schools or the performance of local government. The same holds true for summarized measures of community attachment.

2. Suburban residents tend to report a moderate to strong sense of community, as measured by several scales to assess that concept. One of the better validated scales is the Neighborhood Cohesion Index (NCI), developed by John Buckner (*American Journal of Community Psychology*, 1988, 16, 771–791). Buckner also found that NCI scores were significantly higher among suburban residents in a planned neighborhood with cooperative housing than among residents in a secluded housing complex. Comparative studies on this scale with urban residents, however, have not been reported.

3. With respect to reported social behaviors, as contrasted with attitudes, the most extensive research studies have been conducted by Claude Fischer in *To Dwell among Friends* (Chicago, 1982), using structured interviews with over 1,000 residents in 50 diversified northern California communities. He and others have found that suburban residents tend to know more neighbors,

have more neighborhood friends, and engage in more neighboring activities than urban residents. However, this does not mean that urbanites are more socially isolated, for Fischer notes that urban living makes available more options for social contact. The social network of the urban resident is less dense, and less interconnected, but also more diverse, and more extended in space; the urbanite has at least as many social ties, and also a larger combined number of friends.

4. The evidence on actual participation and involvement in one's community—going beyond friendship and neighboring—is mixed. While there is some evidence that suburbanites belong to more groups and organizations than urban residents, and volunteer more readily, other studies conclude that any social involvement differences appear to be small, and several studies report no differences at all.

5. The evidence reviewed so far has been based upon self-reports. However, a few studies have observed social behaviors in the field in communities of different sizes. Frequency of eye contact with strangers, and related measures of trust, appear to vary inversely with community size; but the general pattern for helpfulness may be more curvilinear, with somewhat greater helping behavior in mid-size communities of suburban population range. Moderate density may also predict helping behavior better than absolute size.

Three apparent general conclusions emerge from the empirical evidence on hand. First, suburban social behavior is highly variable across settings. Second, such behavior overall cannot be accurately described as either social or asocial, nor accurately categorized by other unidimensional scales. And third, while suburban residents as a group tend to report more community satisfaction and more community-oriented behaviors than urban residents, these differences seem to be relatively weak, and are not always demonstrable.

But the cautions in interpreting this evidence are worth restating: (a) studies directly comparing suburban and urban behaviors are infrequent; (b) direct comparisons with smaller towns and villages are less frequent still; (c) behavior may vary considerably even among different neighborhoods within the same suburb; (d) methodological problems of comparison are difficult to surmount; (e) other variables may explain observed differences; and (f) those variables sometimes interact, with each other and with output variables, in complex ways.

Regarding those other variables, research in primarily urban neighborhoods has shown with some consistency that numerous nonresidential factors influence neighboring and community involvement. Specifically, attitudes toward one's community are more positive, and community-related social behaviors more frequent, for people of higher income, for those with longer schooling, for women, for married residents, with young children, for residents of middle age, for residents in better health, for homeowners (particularly those who have lived in the community for a moderate length of time), and for those living in homogeneous community settings. These findings may tentatively be applied to suburban communities as well, and may explain suburban social behavior at least as much as community size or type.

However, the fact that environmental, residential, and setting-based variables have been shown to influence such behavior, on community-wide, neighborhood, as well as individual block levels, suggests that with proper environmental planning and design such influences could be both more pronounced and more socially beneficial. At least some of the knowledge to modify suburban social environments to achieve desired goals does exist; more is attainable. This point gives rise to an agenda for community research and practice.

A Research and Practice Agenda

Research. Although little psychological research has been done on suburban communities, although theories of suburban life are undeveloped, and although the behavioral effects of suburban living are not fully understood, the research questions themselves seem clear. A research program on suburban communities might include study of these central issues:

1. What are the observed variations in sociopsychological response measures across suburbs, or in neighborhoods within the same suburb? This will require the collection of presently nonexistent baseline data on reliable, meaningful, and agreed-upon variables, ideally measured over time, across a representative spectrum of suburban communities and neighborhoods.

2. To what extent are any of the measured differences attributable to place of residence—such as the city-suburb dimension—as contrasted with other environmental or individual sources of variation? Multivariate analyses will be helpful here, but the answer is most likely to emerge from the accumulation of studies using diverse methods, both quantitative and qualitative.

3. What cultural or racial differences might exist in these response measures? The percentages of African-, Hispanic-, and Asian-Americans living in the suburbs have each been increasing faster than their respective percentage increases in the population as a whole. Little is known about what behavioral differences may follow, either in culturally mixed or culturally homogeneous environments.

4. To what extent can planned interventions impact upon these behaviors? And what forms of interventions might those be? For example, what degree of privacy is most conducive to formation of a strong sense of community? Or, if we wished both to increase and measure neighborliness or any similar variable, what action steps will work, and how should they be carried out?

These questions should be resolvable. And if one accepts the premise that where one lives—city, suburb, town, or village—leaves its mark upon the dweller, then addressing these questions should be useful as well as feasible. Usefulness is essential: for despite the fundamental importance of research studies, community-minded psychologists should not be satisfied until their findings are applied to everyday community life. In other words, research should be accompanied by practice.

Practice. A practice agenda might emphasize participation in suburban town planning. This could range from involvement in the formation and study of entire planned communities, down to the analysis of existing small-scale public spaces, and to assistance in the creation, utilization, and evaluation of new ones. A specific practice issue, also researchable, might focus on the study and application of neotraditional or "new urbanist" environmental design principles, formed largely in response to suburban sprawl, and advocated by such architects and planners as Duany, Langdon, Kunstler, Elizabeth Plater-Zyberk, and Peter Calthorpe.

With such principles, the neighborhood is the basic planning unit, designed to attract a diverse population. Most residents live within walking distance of a neighborhood center. Buildings are mixed-use and relatively close together; local automobile use is discouraged; public spaces are plentiful; public squares are prominent; and, with optimum density and variety, casual social interaction is facilitated. While new urbanist principles have been increasingly discussed in the development of planned communities across the United States, and also in smaller neighborhood-level redesign, their actual behavioral effects are imperfectly known and provide fertile ground for investigation.

There are also multiple practice opportunities apart from environmental design. Practice could involve assistance to service providers regarding the best methods to reach and serve suburban target populations who, in their particular ways, are often isolated, poorly informed, and resistant to seeking agency-based help. Practice could also mean consultation to suburban governments and organizations to encourage citizen involvement in community life—or the direct education or training of citizens in community-building skills, on the grounds that setting-appropriate training and involvement could benefit both community and citizen. Through thoughtful communication and carefully chosen incentives, public institutions can stimulate contributions from everyone.

Future Prospects

The suburbs are a changing social phenomenon, whose rate of change shows no signs of slowing. Some additional trends already in evidence are the rapid growth of gated communities, the rise of home offices and tele-commuting, and the increasing multicultural immigration previously cited. A generation from now, the suburbs may be described and understood differently; the underlying nomenclature may itself change. Yet there will continue to be some community settings intermediate between large city and small town, with distinct structure and dynamics, with high psychological salience for their residents, and with both measurable and modifiable impacts upon the behavior of at least half the U.S. population. These settings will continue to be worthy of study.

Most suburbs are not likely to become places where everyone knows one another, where neighbors meet on a daily basis, and where the community is the primary focal point of life. Residents will have additional priorities, or different priorities altogether; even the best environmental and organizational interventions will have limited success in changing them. Still, suburban communities can be places of greater human warmth and connectedness, of broader neighborly awareness and support, and of deeper personal satisfaction for those who live there, with all the social benefits that follow. And they can be places that provide for the full expression of individual potential within a rich community context. Psychologists and other social scientists, who already know in part how to create those conditions, share responsibility for doing so.

Bibliography

Adams, R. E. (1992). Is happiness a home in the suburbs? The influence of urban versus suburban neighborhoods on psychological health. *Journal of Community Psychology 20*, 353–372.

Baldassare, M. (1992). Suburban communities. *Annual Review of Sociology, 18*, 475–494. A review chapter. Baldassare's definition of suburban communities has been followed for this Encyclopedia article.

Bell, P. A., Greene, T. C., Fisher, J. D., & Baum, A. (1996). *Environmental psychology* (4th ed.). Fort Worth: Harcourt Brace. A good example of a general text, summarizing current evidence relevant to suburban and other community design.

Blakely, E. J., & Snyder, M. G. (1997). *Fortress America: Gated communities in the United States.* Washington, DC: Brookings Institution Press.

Garreau, J. (1991). *Edge city: Life on the new frontier.* New York: Doubleday.

Guterbock, T. M., & Fries, J. C. (1997). *Maintaining America's social fabric: The AARP survey of civic involvement.* Washington, DC: American Association of Retired Persons. A national survey including discussions of social involvement by community type.

Jackson, K. T. (1985). *Crabgrass frontier: The suburbanization of the United States.* New York: Oxford University Press.

A definitive source on the history of suburban development.

Kunstler, J. H. (1996). *Home from nowhere: Remaking our everyday world for the twenty-first century.* New York: Simon & Schuster. A strong and often biting critique of prevalent suburban environmental design, written for a popular audience.

Langdon, P. (1994). *A better place to live: Reshaping the American suburb.* Amherst, MA: University of Massachusetts Press.

Langdon, P. (1996). Neo-traditionalist architect Andres Duany explains how to build better communities. *The American Enterprise, 7(6)*, 46–50. Contains a brief and excellent summary of new urbanist design principles. The journal issue in which this article appears also contains several other insightful essays on the suburbs, as well as comparative poll data.

Unger, D. G., & Wandersman, A. (1985). The importance of neighbors: The social, cognitive, and affective components of neighboring. *American Journal of Community Psychology, 13*, 139–169. A research review summarizing the determinants of neighboring.

Willis, A. (1993). *American suburbs rating guide and fact book.* Milpitas, CA: Toucan Valley Publications. Contains demographic data for individual U.S. suburban communities.

Wilson, G., & Baldassare, M. (1996). Overall "sense of community" in a suburban region: The effects of localism, privacy, and urbanization. *Environment and Behavior, 28*, 27–43.

Bill Berkowitz

SUICIDE. Over the centuries, there have been constantly shifting moral views about the social acceptability of suicidal behavior. This has varied from viewing suicide as an appropriate social response to disgrace. The Japanese code of Bushido in the seventeenth century held that the disgrace of failure to one's lord could be expiated by the ritual taking of one's own life. Litman (1980) noted that in traditional Western society it was necessary to assign blame for every death either to God or to man (i.e., homicide, suicide); that if God was responsible for the death, nothing more needed to be done, but if a human being was to blame, then there must be a punishment for the guilty.

In Western societies, although attitudes have become more tolerant toward suicide, there are still undercurrents of ambivalence and social condemnation (Litman, 1980). Judicial attitudes toward suicide have moved away from assessing "guilt and enforcing punishment toward protecting suicidal persons when possible, and toward efforts to care for or compensate the surviving victims of suicide deaths" (Litman, 1980, pp. 841–842). Litman also noted that because of this undercurrent of social condemnation, the friends and relatives of the person who committed suicide feel themselves to be not only bereaved but also stigmatized. These significant others often attempt to persuade, coerce, or otherwise influence the certifying authorities against a verdict of suicide, thus influencing the accuracy of suicide statistics.

The United States suicide rate of approximately 11.2 per 100,000, accounting for over 31,000 deaths per year (Hirschfeld & Russell, 1997), places it in the average category for industrialized countries. Higher rates have been reported in eastern Europe, German-speaking countries, Scandinavia, and Japan (rates often over 25 per 100,000). Lower rates, that is, rates below 6 per 100,000, are often seen in countries such as Greece, Ireland, and some Mediterranean countries (e.g., Italy).

Some authorities have pointed out that communities and social groups that are subject to conditions like economic instability or deprivation (e.g., unemployment) or to the breakdown of traditional family group structures, interpersonal violence, and so forth are at high risk for an increase in suicides (particularly among the young).

Throughout the twentieth century, the combined suicide rate in the United States during this century has remained at approximately 11 to 12 per 100,000. Suicide rates are the highest for men over 69 but are increasing alarmingly for youth (those aged 15–24). The rates for older persons have decreased during this same time period. Although in the United States, suicide accounts for roughly 2% of all deaths, it accounts for more than 15% of the deaths among adolescents Hirschfeld & Russell, 1997).

Hirschfeld and Russell (1997) noted that having thoughts about killing oneself is very common in the United States, and that up to one third of persons in the general population have suicidal ideation at some point in their lives. Maris (1981) found that nonfatal suicide attempts occur approximately six to eight times more often than completed suicide and that the risk of eventual completed suicide among attempters is roughly 15%; while Hirschfeld and Russell (1997) observed that there are approximately 18 suicide attempts for every completed suicide in the United States. Various other estimates of the ratio of attempters to completers have placed it at 1:8, or approximately 12.5%.

Although suicide in young children had been thought to be nonexistent, Murphy (1987) reported that a recent study of suicide in children ages 5 to 14 found that their attempts were very grave, with attempted hanging as the most common method, followed by running in front of vehicles and multiple methods. He concluded that the suicide attempt of a child is a very serious event and that researchers and medical examiners should vigilantly examine any cases of equivocal accidental deaths in this population.

Suicide statistics also differ by sex and ethnicity. For example, completed suicide is more than three times as likely in males as in females. (Hirscheld & Russell, 1997, place the ratio at closer to 4:1.) Hirschfeld and Russell (1997) pointed out that 73% of all suicides in the United States are committed by White males, and that firearms account for the largest proportion (nearly 60%) of deaths, followed by poisoning among women and hanging among men.

Suicide rates for Black men and women are roughly half as great as for Whites. However, one authority noted that suicide among Blacks is a youthful phenomenon. Suicide is the third leading cause of death in Black youths, after homicides and fatal accidents, and the suicide rate for Black youths age 15 to 24 has more than doubled in the past 25 years, with Black males accounting for most of the increase.

Suicide is currently the second leading cause of death, after accidents, for young Native Americans aged 20 to 24. Suicide rates vary considerably among the various tribes. The data on Hispanic suicides also show that the suicide rate is lower than for non-Hispanic Whites but higher than for Blacks in the same geographic locale. Again, the peak age for Hispanic suicide occurs between the ages of 20 and 24.

Few studies have examined the rates of suicide among Asian Americans. The current available data indicate that Chinese, Filipino, and Japanese male suicide rates are in general lower than those of other American males, except in the older age groups.

Understanding Suicide

Social-demographic theories of suicide have been historically prominent in effecting an empirical understanding of suicidal phenomena. The most cogent exponent of the sociological view was the French sociologist, Emile Durkheim (Maris, 1981). *Le Suicide*, first published in 1897, was Durkheim's comparative study of suicide in postindustrial society. This work continues to generate extensive research and discussion. Durkheim's general thesis is that the suicide rate varies inversely with external constraint and that external societal constraint has two dimensions, which Durkheim called integration and regulation (Maris, 1981). Roy (1988) spoke of three categories that Durkheim used to demonstrate this relationship: egoistic (lack of meaningful family ties or social integrations); anomic (the relationship between the person and society is broken by economic or social adversity); and altruistic (excessive integration, e.g., hara-kiri, suttee).

The more recent research on understanding suicide has focused on a number of different approaches (Shneidman, 1989) including:

1. psychological—identifying psychological states in suicide victims as well as the examination of cognitive, behavioral, and emotional components of suicidal acts;

2. psychodynamic—the turning against oneself of angry and destructive impulses, unconscious hostility, the splitting of ego states, self-destructive instincts, and so on (Maltsberger, 1986);
3. sociocultural—assessing the impact of social and cross-cultural factors, or the correlation of social change with suicide;
4. biological, biochemical, and constitutional—looking at the relationship of genetics, neurotransmitters, biochemistry, etc., to suicide;
5. psychiatric and mental illness;
6. epidemiological and demographic—population identifying;
7. prevention, intervention, and postvention.

Other approaches of note have included the dyadic/familial; interpersonal; literary and personal document; architectural; systems theory; empathic; philosophical and theological; legal and ethical; global, political, and supranational. Other authorities have added to the preceding approaches, including the public health, economic, and historical perspectives.

Shneidman (1989) stated that diagnosis of suicide depends on an unambiguous definition. At the same time, suicide is a word that, historically, has both a core and a periphery. The unambiguous core is the simple formula that *suicide is the act of taking one's own life.* Shneidman (1989) proposed that an operational definition of suicide must limit the term "suicide" to acts of committed suicide (or efforts or attempts to be dead by suicide). This definition would follow the British tradition of separating self-inflicted, sublethal acts from suicide. An individual who has made a nonlethal, self-inflicted, injurious suicidelike act is said to have committed parasuicide.

The boundaries between self-mutilation, sensation seeking, and suicidal behavior are murky (Bongar, 1991). Historically, there is a lack of clarity about whether consciously expressed suicidal desire accompanying the behavior should be requisite in order to classify the behavior as suicidal (Fawcett, Clark, & Busch, 1993; Maltsberger, 1986; Motto, 1979; Pokorny, 1964).

However, in the heat of the emergent clinical moment, psychologists who must evaluate and triage acts of suicidal or life-threatening behavior might do well to adopt a definition of attempted suicide such as Stengel's in 1986:

> A suicidal attempt is any act of self-damage inflicted with self-destructive intention, however vague and ambiguous. . . . For the clinician, it is safer still to regard all cases of potentially dangerous self-poisoning or self-inflicted injury as suicidal attempts, whatever the victim's explanation, unless there is clear evidence to the contrary. Potentially dangerous means in this context: believed by the attempter possibly to endanger life.

With regard to the actual danger of eventual completed suicide for the suicide attempter, Maris (1981) stated that there is a body of evidence to indicate that, in general, suicide completers are likely to make one lethal attempt, while most suicide attempters make multiple low-lethality attempts. This is in accord with Stengel's observation that those who attempt suicide and those who complete suicide may constitute two distinct, yet overlapping populations. An estimated 10 to 20% of attempters eventually go on to complete suicide; therefore, a history of suicide attempts significantly increases the likelihood of subsequent suicide (Hirschfeld & Russell, 1997).

Suicide is one of the few fatal consequences of psychiatric illness, and thus the subject is a source of endless disquiet to the practicing mental health professional (Motto, 1979; Pokorny, 1964). Adding to the problem is the fact that the relationship between psychopathology, suicide attempting, and completed suicide is complex, dynamic, and not yet well understood (Bongar, 1991; Fawcett, Clark, & Busch, 1993; Maltsberger, 1986; Maris, 1981; Motto, 1979; Pokorny, 1964; Shneidman, 1989). Recent studies show changes in the identity of high-risk groups, and follow-up studies demonstrate that risk factors among attempters may be significantly different from those for the general population (Fawcett, Clark, & Busch 1993). Also, studies suggest that rates of suicide among the mentally ill and physically ill far exceed that of the population as a whole (Motto, 1979; Murphy, 1987). Taken together, these findings suggest that the weighty task of determining who is most at risk for suicide is a difficult undertakng (Maltsberger, 1986; Motto, 1979; Pokorny, 1964).

Recent empirical findings have shown that the average professional psychologist who is involved in direct patient care has almost a one-in-three chance of losing a patient to suicide at some time during his or her professional career (Greaney, 1995). In addition, one study found that a psychologist in training has a one-in-seven chance of losing a patient to suicide. One telling national survey found that psychologists responded to the loss of a patient to suicide in a manner akin to the death of a family member.

Assessment and Management of the Suicidal Patient

The mental health professional's assessment and treatment efforts represent an opportunity to translate knowledge (albeit incomplete) of elevated risk factors into a plan of action (Bongar, 1991). The management plan for patients who are at an elevated risk for suicide should ameliorate those risk factors that are most foreseeably likely to result in suicide or self-harm (Brent, Kupfer, Bromet, & Dew, 1988; Motto, 1979). Here, there are several general principles that should guide the treatment of patients at elevated risk for suicide and that apply across broad diagnostic categories:

The most basic principle is that, because most suicide victims take their own lives or harm themselves in the midst of a psychiatric episode, it is critical to understand that a proper diagnosis and careful management/treatment plan of the acute psychiatric disorder could dramatically alter the risk for suicide (Brent, Kupfer, Bromet, & Dew, 1988). The data on adult suicides indicate that more than 90% of these suicide victims were mentally ill before their deaths.

For acute management, there are special precautions that clinicians must take when assessing and treating patients who present with chronic suicidal ideation and behavior (e.g., where the clinician takes repeated calculated risks in not hospitalizing). Gutheil (1992) noted that here the mental health clinician will feel the tension between short-term solutions (e.g., a protected environment) and long-term solutions (e.g., actual treatment of the chronicity).

Family involvement for support and improved compliance.

Diagnosis and treatment of any comorbid medical and psychiatric condition.

The provision of hope, particularly to new-onset patients.

The restriction of the availability of lethal agents, and indications for psychiatric hospitalization (Brent, Kupfer, Bromet, & Dew, 1988).

To this list, a risk management perspective would add the critical necessity of assessing personal and professional competencies in order to treat at-risk patients (Bongar, 1991).

Meticulous documentation and the routine involvement of "a second opinion," through consultation (Bongar, 1991).

All of our assessment and management activities also should include a specific evaluation of the patient's competency to participate in management and treatment decisions, especially the patient's ability to form a therapeutic alliance (Bongar, 1991; Maltsberger, 1986; Motto, 1979). Bongar (1991) noted that an essential element in strengthening this alliance is the use of informed consent; that is, patients have the right to participate actively in making decisions about their psychological/psychiatric care. Clinicians need to directly and continuously evaluate the quality of this special relationship—to understand that the quality of this collaborative alliance is inextricably part of any successful treatment/management plan.

Suicidal phenomena are enormously complex. In order to fully understand the event of suicide, one must attempt to understand the varieties of human behavior, thinking, and reasoning (Shneidman, 1989). Arguably, the central issue in suicide is not death or killing; rather, it is the stopping of the consciousness of unbearable pain that, unfortunately, by its very nature entails the stopping of life. Shneidman (1989) points out that one of suicide's chief shortcomings is that it unnecessarily answers a remediable challenge with a permanent negative solution. By contrast, living is a long-term set of resolutions with often only fleeting results (Shneidman, 1989).

Bibliography

Bongar, B. (1991). *The suicidal patient: Clinical and legal standards of care.* Washington, DC: American Psychological Association.

Brent, D. A., Kupfer, D. J., Bromet, E. J., & Dew, M. A. (1988). The assessment and treatment of patients at risk for suicide. In A. J. Frances, & R. E. Hales (Eds.), *American Psychiatric Press review of psychiatry: Vol. 7* (pp. 353–385). Washington, DC: American Psychiatric Press.

Fawcett, J., Clark, D. C., & Busch, K. A. (1993). Assessing and treating the patient at risk for suicide. *Psychiatric Annals, 23,* 244–255.

Greaney, S. (1995). *Psychologists' behavior and attitudes when working with the non-hospitalized suicidal patient.* Unpublished doctoral dissertation, Pacific Graduate School of Psychology,

Gutheil, T. G. (1992). Suicide and suit: Liability after self-destruction. In D. Jacobs (Ed.), *Suicide and clinical practice* (pp. 147–167). Washington, DC: American Psychiatric Press.

Hirschfeld, R. M. A., & Russell, J. M. (1997). Assessment and treatment of suicidal patients. *New England Journal of Medicine, 333*(13), 910–915.

Litman, R. E. (1980). Psycholegal aspects of suicide. In E. A. Curran (Ed.), *Modern legal medicine, psychiatry and forensic science* (pp. 841–853). Philadelphia: Davis.

Maltsberger, J. T. (1986). *Suicide risk: The formulation of clinical judgment.* New York: New York University Press.

Maris, R. W. (1981). *Pathways to suicide: A survey of self-destructive behaviors.* Baltimore: Johns Hopkins University Press.

Motto, J. A. (1979). Guidelines for the management of the suicidal patient. *Weekly Psychiatry Update Series Lesson, 20,* Volume 3, 3–7. (Available from Biomedia, Inc., Princeton, NJ.)

Murphy, G. E. (1987). Suicide and attempted suicide. In J. O. Cavenar (Ed.), *Psychiatry* (Vol. 1, pp. 1–18). Philadelphia: Lippincott.

Pokorny, A. D. (1964). A follow-up study of 618 suicidal patients. *American Journal of Psychiatry, 122,* 1109–1116.

Roy, A. (1988, May 7). Risk factors in suicide. In D. G. Jacobs, & J. Fawcett (Chairs), *Suicide and the psychiatrist: Clinical challenges.* Symposium presented by the Suicide Education Institute of Boston, in collaboration with the Center of Suicide Research and Prevention, at the American Psychiatric Association Annual Meeting, Montreal, Quebec, Canada.

Shneidman, E. S. (1989). Overview: A multidimensional approach to suicide. In D. G. Jacobs & H. N. Brown (Eds.), *Suicide: Understanding and responding: Harvard Medical School perspectives on suicide* (pp. 1–30). Madison, CT: International Universities Press.

Stengel, E. (1965). *Suicide and attempted suicide*. Bristol, UK: MacGibbon and Kee.

Bruce Bongar

SULLIVAN, HARRY STACK (1892–1949), American psychiatrist. Sullivan made major contributions to the history of personality theory. He outlined an interpersonal approach to personalitics: that an individual's concept of selfhood is a reflection of others' attitudes toward that person. Influenced by the social psychology of George Herbert Mead and Charles Cooley, Sullivan understood a person's ego-concept to be the result of what is mirrored back to that person by mother, father, and social surroundings.

Thus, Sullivan's theory of personality derived from his ideas regarding the evolution of the self-concept, a perception of the self that is gradually developed and elaborated from appraisals showered upon us by others. Although the personal self-concept develops slowly, the need for personal security is present from the very beginning of existence. Sullivan hypothesized that threats to an individual's self-respect are experienced as anxiety, which in turn produces defensive measures to relieve that anxiety and protect the self. These assaults on self-esteem emanate from sources outside the person, especially from the mother, who is a person's principal nurturing other. The origins of this way of thinking are probably found in Sullivan's life experience as the only surviving child of a demanding and rejecting mother. He recalled:

> I escaped most of the evils of being an only child by chief virtue of the fact that mother never troubled to notice the characteristics of the child she had brought forth. And her son was so different from me that I felt she had no use for me except as a clothes horse on which to hang an elaborate pattern of illusions. (Sullivan, 1974, p. 49)

In his 1931 article, "Environmental Factors in Biology and Course Under-Treatment of Schizophrenia," Sullivan states that the occurrence of this illness must be explained primarily on the basis of experimental rather than hereditary or organic factors. Because of personal experience, some people, caught up in the course of difficult events, undergo a change in total activity, behavior, and thought. This he identified as schizophrenic psychosis. Sullivan felt that, although heredity and genetic factors may contribute to a person's illness, once measured these factors will be found to be of little importance in the etiology of the disease.

The basis of schizophrenia's etiology, according to Sullivan, must be discovered within actual events involving the person and other significant individuals. The realization that dealings with other people are de-cidedly the most difficult actions for anyone to handle does not occur until a person's early teenage years. Although the individual may have learned to manage parents and other authority figures during childhood, it is only after a need for real, interpersonal intimacy appears that delicate adjustments of personality are developed, which foster relationships with others. Such a subtle level of personality growth is never achieved by the schizophrenic.

As a result, the schizophrenic male, who has suffered such a disastrous loss of self-esteem, retreats into a dreamlike state, building a barrier between himself and other people who threaten him. And since the development of such a barrier deprives the individual of consensual validation, the schizophrenic becomes interpersonally incompetent. As his behavior becomes increasingly inappropriate, he may begin to feel persecuted, and his behavior gradually deteriorates. Sullivan prescribed a sympathetic environment as the cure for such progression of the disease. Thus, he initiated his unique technique of therapy he labeled "Treatment Milieu" for the schizophrenic adolescent. For this kind of treatment he trained and coordinated a team of subprofessionals selected on the basis of personalities that were suited, in his mind, to dealing with schizophrenics.

Sullivan was one of the major American personality theorists of the twentieth century and contributed to the modification of Freudian psychoanalysis. Sullivan was a neo-Freudian (although he rejected the term as applied to himself), but it is important to stress the significant revision that he introduced into Freudian theory. Whereas Freud believed in an intrapsychic model of personality, Sullivan held to an interpersonal model of the self, the idea that personality is a product of the mutual interaction between the human organism and the familiar-social. Whereas Freud emphasized libidinal forces as determinates of personality, with particular focus on the Oedipal complex, Sullivan shifted attention to the area of self-esteem and adjustment. Both Freud and Sullivan understood the adult personality as an arena upon which the unresolved conflicts of earlier life were played out, and this idea of a past haunting a present was their common grounding in psychoanalysis. In a lasting reconstruction of psychoanalysis, Sullivan demonstrated how the self is not only the product of inner forces but a result of the image of ourselves that society reflects back to us.

[*Many of the people mentioned in this article are the subjects of independent biographical entries.*]

Bibliography

Works by Sullivan

Sullivan, H. S. (1931). Environmental factors in etiology and course under treatment of schizophrenia. *Medical Journal and Records*, *133*, 19–22.

Sullivan, H. S. (1953). *Concepts of modern psychiatry*. New York: Norton.

Sullivan, H. S. (1953). *The interpersonal theory of psychiatry*. New York: Norton.

Sullivan, H. S. (1974). *Schizophrenia as a human process*. New York: Norton.

Works about Sullivan

Chapman, A. H. (1976). *Harry Stack Sullivan: The man and his work*. New York: Putnam.

Chatelaine, K. L. (1981). *Harry Stack Sullivan: The formative years*. Washington, DC: University Press of America.

Mullahy, P. (1973). *The beginning of modern American psychiatry. The ideas of Harry Stack Sullivan*. Boston: Houghton Mifflin.

Kenneth L. Chatelaine

SULLY, JAMES (1843–1923), British psychologist and philosopher. Although Sully is invariably characterized in standard histories as one of the early leaders of British psychology, founder of the first British psychological laboratory in 1897 at University College, London, and a founder member in 1901 of the British Psychological Society, his charming and gossipy autobiography, published in 1918, completely belies this stern pioneering image. Instead, we find a man of independent means, educated at some length and expense both in Britain and in Germany, with interests much wider than the narrow specialties embraced by modern academic psychologists. Indeed, like many other influential figures in nineteenth-century psychology, Sully viewed the subject as a two-way exchange of ideas from many different areas, including theology, literature, philosophy (British and European), aesthetics, biology, and physiology. Thus his writings helped to determine the somewhat eclectic form assumed by contemporary British psychology until Charles Spearman (among others) gave the discipline its current professional and experimental cast at the start of the twentieth century.

After graduating with a bachelor of arts degree from the Regent's Park Baptist College in London, an event coinciding with his loss of any real commitment to Christianity, he and a college friend traveled in 1867 to Göttingen in Germany to study under the psychologist Rudolph Lotze and the Hebrew scholar Heinrich Ewald. Sully's second important visit to that country took him to Berlin during the winter of 1871–1872, where he attended Helmholtz's lectures on physiology. In between, Sully practiced the life of the self-employed, highbrow literary hack, writing articles for worthy publications such as the *Cornhill Magazine* and the *Pall Mall Gazette* on a variety of topics from Alpine journeys to more serious accounts of child rearing. This work was neatly complemented by an intellectually formidable range of airings for his favorite philosophical *bêtes noires* (particularly the more obscure Germanic ones) and articles for more weighty outlets such as *Mind, Encyclopedia Britannica* (on aesthetics, evolution, and dreams), and Ribot's *Revue Philosophique*. Sully's circle of friends was equally catholic, and included Alexander Bain, Herbert Spencer, Croom Robertson, and William James, as well as literati such as George Meredith, George Eliot, and G. H. Lewes.

Sully had lectured for many years in London and in Wales and had designed several textbooks for this teaching (particularly the *Outlines of Psychology*, first published in 1884). However, it was not until 1892, at the rather advanced age of 49 and after several unsuccessful attempts, that Sully finally attained a senior academic position. He succeeded Croom Robertson as Grote Professor of the Philosophy of Mind and Logic at London's University College, largely on the strength of his latest book, *The Human Mind* (1892). Although this tome was seen by some as an English rival to William James's equally monumental *Principles of Psychology*, it was in essence a greatly expanded version of the 1892 revised edition of *Outlines* with all its attitudes intact. In the end, *The Human Mind* proved to be less successful than Sully had hoped, being judged too old-fashioned and not really sympathetic to the power of the new experimentalism then raging through the discipline. Sully retired at the age of 60 in 1903 and never seriously concerned himself with psychology again.

Although he was generally pigeonholed as a conventional child of British analytical philosophy, Sully's fundamental attachment to associationism (though with an evolutionary slant) is almost matched by his creative use of synthesis. Furthermore, his strongly nativist view that production (thought, reasoning, perception, and so on) presupposes reproduction (memory) places him philosophically well outside British empiricism, as does his quasi-sociological approach to the nature and growth of the self and to the more general problems of epistemology. In the closing chapter of *Illusions* (1881), for instance, he muses on the nature of reality, with science resting on "a stable consensus, a body of commonly held belief" (p. 357). Moreover, in the 1892 edition of *Outlines*, we find him airing his notion of "knowledge as social product," for which the purpose of language is to achieve conceptual consensus. Unfortunately, these teasing glimpses of a more radical alternative to a conventionally individualistic psychology were never really expanded upon, unlike his extended and careful account of the personal determinants of the act of memory (or reproduction) and reasoning that mixes analytical and synthetic insights (e.g., *Outlines*, 1884, Chapter 10).

Sully became a neglected figure even in his own lifetime because psychology, which now looked only to the controlled experiment for certainty, had turned its back on other equally fruitful sources of ideas.

Bibliography

Sully, J. (1877). *Pessimism*. London: Kegan Paul, Trench, Trübner. Although strongly critical of the German pessimist movement, this work was said to have lost Sully the chair of philosophy at Liverpool; the appointing committee thought that someone interested in such a topic might have an equally gloomy outlook on life that would be inappropriate for the then fledgling institution.

Sully, J. (1881). *Illusions: A psychological study*. London: Kegan Paul, Trench, Trübner. This is an early psychological exploration of errors of perception, memory, and reasoning.

Sully, J. (1884). *Outlines of psychology*. London: Longmans Green. This book is the most successful and accessible summary of Sully's work and ideas on key psychological topics such as sensation, perception, memory, thinking, and development.

Sully, J. (1892). *The human mind: A text-book of psychology*. (Vols. 1–2). London: Longmans Green. This book provides the fullest account of Sully's approach to psychology.

Sully, J. (1895). *Studies of childhood*. London: Longmans Green. This work looks at child development from an evolutionary perpective; it also contains some original studies on children's drawings.

Sully, J. (1918). *My life and friends: A psychologist's memories*. London: Fisher Unwin. This autobiography contains reminiscences of the people and events that shaped Sully's intellectual and social life, though giving away little about his own thinking.

A. D. Lovie and P. Lovie

SUMNER, FRANCIS CECIL (1895–1954), first African American to receive a doctor of philosophy degree in psychology in the United States. Born in Pine Bluff, Arkansas, Sumner attended elementary schools in Norfolk, Virginia, and Plainfield, New Jersey. Secondary education for Blacks was rare in the early 1900s, and Sumner did not have a formal high school education. Admitted to Lincoln University in Pennsylvania in 1911 by examination, Sumner graduated in 1915 with a bachelor of arts magna cum laude and received a master of arts from Lincoln in 1917. Sumner entered Clark University that same year and was awarded a doctorate in 1920, during a period in which innumerable social and physical factors mitigated against such achievements for Black Americans. Under the tutelage of G. Stanley Hall, Sumner defended his dissertation on the psychoanalytic theories of Sigmund Freud and Alfred Adler—work that was hailed as an outstanding interpretation of their theories. Sumner was Hall's last doctoral advisee.

Following his graduation he became a professor of psychology and spent his entire professional career teaching in America's racially segregated Black colleges and universities. He was a professor of psychology at Wilberforce College (Ohio) and Southern University (Louisiana) before chairing the psychology departments at West Virginia Collegiate Institute (now West Virginia State University) and Howard University (Washington, D.C.). Sumner's greatest contributions were in the area of training and preparing future Black psychologists. When appointed head of the burgeoning psychology department at Howard in 1928, he recognized the opportunity to increase the numbers of Black psychologists and developed curricula to accomplish this goal. He established classrooms and laboratories to facilitate his plan. Sumner was a leader, innovator, teacher, and mentor for many students. During World War II the Howard program produced more Black psychologists than all other American colleges and universities combined. Sumner's model programs at Howard led the way for other Black psychologists in America's Black universities. For many years, Sumner maintained and distributed an annual newsletter, which reported the progress of Howard's psychology graduates and provided historical data that detailed the work of Howard's Black psychologists.

Sumner was a generalist, and his research efforts were limited. He had a long-term interest, however, in the relationships among psychology, religion, and the administration of justice. He was among the first academicians to contribute to the understanding of each of these areas of study. His contributions to psychology and religion can be seen in his massive unpublished manuscript titled "The Structure of Religion: A History of European Psychology of Religion" (Howard University, 1934). He was the first to establish courses in the psychology of religion in the Black colleges and universities. His research assessing the attitudes of more than 2,000 Black and white college students toward the administration of justice was regarded as seminal. Performed by Black researchers, this study called for legal procedures that would facilitate the administration of justice on a more democratic basis. Sumner continued as a professor until the last year of his life, 1954, the year in which the Supreme Court outlawed the "separate but equal" doctrine.

Bibliography

Works by Sumner

Sumner, F. C. (1922). Psychoanalysis of Freud and Adler on sex determination and character formation. *Peda-*

gogical Seminary, 24, 139–168. Dissertation submitted by Sumner for his doctorate at Clark University.

Sumner, F. C., & Shaed, D. L., (1945). Negro-white attitudes towards the administration of justice as affecting Negroes. *Journal of Applied Psychology, 29,* 368–377.

Works about Sumner

Guthrie, R. V. (1998). *Even the rat was white: A historical view of psychology* (2nd ed.). Boston: Allyn and Bacon. Includes a chapter outlining the life and accomplishments of Sumner and the complete listing of his publications.

Robert V. Guthrie

SUPER, DONALD EDWIN (1910–1994), vocational psychologist. In 1950, Super began a program of research that eventually expanded the domain of vocational psychology from a narrow focus on choosing occupations to a broad vista on developing careers. During the first half of the twentieth century, vocational psychologists concentrated on a "matching model" for vocational guidance that emphasized the use of interest inventories, ability tests, and occupational information to help adolescents and young adults make initial occupational choices. Super contributed significantly to this model for matching people to positions, and his first two books codified existing knowledge about vocational guidance (*Dynamics of Occupational Adjustment,* New York, 1942) and vocational assessment (*Appraising Vocational Fitness,* New York, 1949).

Following the publication of these books, Super initiated a program of research that would, in due course, extend vocational psychology's purview from matching adolescents with occupations to developing careers over the life span. Super's most cited journal article, "A Theory of Vocational Development" (*American Psychologist,* 1953), presented the initial statement of his career theory. His definitive book, *The Psychology of Careers* (New York, 1957), more fully expounded the theory and offered empirical support for its ten propositions. The theory was tested and revised in a myriad of manuscripts and measures resulting from the Career Pattern Study (CPS) in which Super and his colleagues investigated the natural history of careers as they unfolded in the lives of 100 men over a period of 40 years.

In all of this work, Super's singular insight involved using models and methods from developmental psychology to conceptualize and study empirically the life course of careers through stages of growth, exploration, establishment, maintenance, and disengagement. He linguistically explicated and operationally defined each career stage by its characteristic vocational devel-

opment tasks and coping behaviors. He coined the term "career maturity" to denote individuals' attitudinal and cognitive readiness to master the developmental tasks of their life stage. The CPS staff devised numerous measures of career maturity still used by researchers and counselors. Most notably, Super and his colleagues constructed the Career Development Inventory to measure adolescents' attitudes toward exploring occupations and making plans, as well as their competence in using occupational information to choose from among educational and vocational options.

After his retirement in 1975 from Teachers College, Columbia University, where he worked for 30 years, Super dedicated the next years to expanding once again the purview of vocational psychology, this time from careers to life roles. To address life roles across the life span, Super constructed a heuristic model that portrays work as a salient but single arc in a rainbow of roles in the community, at home, and with friends. In collaboration with colleagues from 12 countries, Super developed a life-span, life-space framework that is used to research and develop careers of diverse individuals in manifold settings (*Life Roles, Values, and Career,* San Francisco, 1995). For these accomplishments, and many more, the American Psychological Association presented Super with the 1983 Distinguished Scientific Award for Contributions to Applied Psychology.

Bibliography

Savickas, M. L. (Ed.). (1994). From vocational guidance to career counseling: Essays to honor Donald E. Super. *Career Development Quarterly, 43,* (1). Includes Super's biography, a complete list of his publications from 1932 to 1994, and eight articles about his contributions to psychology.

Super, D. E. (1983). Assessment in career guidance: Toward truly developmental counseling. *Personnel and Guidance Journal, 61,* 5–562. Outlines Super's career counseling model and methods.

Super, D. E. (1985). Coming of age in Middletown: Careers in the making. *American Psychologist, 40,* 405–414. Describes the Career Pattern Study.

Super, D. E., Savickas, M. L., & Super, C. M. (1996). The lifespan, life-space approach to careers. In D. Brown & L. Brooks (Eds.), *Career choice and development: Applying contemporary theories to practice* (3rd ed., pp. 121–178). San Francisco, CA: Jossey-Bass. Explains Super's lifespan, life-space theory.

Mark L. Savickas

SUPEREGO. According to psychoanalytic theory, the superego is the seat of conscience, ideals and values, and moral codes. This structure is largely, but not entirely, unconscious and is involved in the generation of affect states, principally shame and guilt. While these two affects are intimately connected, guilt is generally regarded as a concern that one's thoughts or actions may be harmful to others, while shame refers to the failure to live up to one's expectations of oneself.

A related term is ego ideal, which Freud initially used interchangeably with superego. With the passage of time, the notion of the ego ideal has become subsumed under the broader concept of superego. While the superego is primarily involved in passing judgments and proscribing certain thoughts, feelings, and behaviors, the ego ideal is generally regarded as prescribing ideal standards of conduct to which one should adhere.

The construct of the superego is generally linked to Freud's classic 1923 paper "The Ego and the Id." However, in earlier contributions Freud had laid the groundwork for this idea. In his 1914 paper "On Narcissism," he suggested that the ego ideal was linked to a state of infantile bliss, while a separate agency served the function of comparing and observing real behavior with internalized standards.

The superego achieved its penultimate status with the publication of "The Ego and the Id." Freud conceptualized it as one of the three major intrapsychic agencies collectively known as the tripartite structural model. As the name implies, the superego has something of a supervisory function over the ego. It limits the satisfactions of the ego and to a large extent directs the defensive operations of the ego. It reproaches the ego when it appears to get out of line. The superego also closely monitors the id to be certain that aggressive and sexual forces from the unconscious are contained and controlled.

In Freud's view the superego was the "heir of the Oedipus complex" (1923/1961, pp. 47–48). The boy child, for example, ultimately realizes that he cannot compete with his father for mother's favor, so he internalizes his father and strives to be like this internalized version of his same-sex parent. Yet Freud also emphasized that the superego was based on identifications with both parents and was not by any means an exact replica of the external parents. In the process of internalizing the parents, the child's own aggressiveness may enter into the equation. For example, an excessively harsh superego may not represent an excessively harsh parent. Rather, it may represent a projection of the child's own propensity to aggression. In other words, it may reflect an exaggerated perception of the dangers of retaliation based on the child's own hostility. Moreover, to some extent the child's superego reflects the nature of the parents' superego rather than the parents' professed moral code. The subtleties of the parents' behavior and their nonverbal communication,

then, may be key components of superego formation. Arlow (1982) stressed this complexity by pointing out that the superego is not a uniform and coherent entity; it is actually a jumble of contradictions. He suggested that the superego is unreliable in the same way as a policeman, who is rarely around when you need him most.

While the aggressive, critical, and censuring aspects of the superego are often emphasized, Schafer (1960) called attention to the loving and beloved aspects of the superego. He stressed that the child's views of his or her parents are represented in the superego, and these parental "introjects" (internal representations) provide comfort, protection, and love when the child embodies the parental ideals, moral codes, and values.

While Freud implied that the mature superego was not in place until after the resolution of the Oedipal conflict, around the age of 5, there is a growing consensus that internalized standards of moral behavior are in place much earlier. Empirical research on moral development has made it clear that children can express empathy and manifest internalized prohibitions and rules regarding expectations of family roles as early as the age of 3. Buchsbaum and Emde (1990) used systematic play and narrative research technique that encouraged children to finish standard stories by providing the opportunity for enactments that expressed a variety of representational themes. Some of the 3-year-olds showed the capacity to struggle with and even to resolve moral dilemmas. Just as superego development is not confined to the resolution of the Oedipus complex, neither is it limited to early childhood. The superego continues to grow and be modified in the post-Oedipal period.

Superego pathology may take a variety of forms. A highly critical superego may be involved in conditions associated with intense guilt, such as depression or obsessive-compulsive personality disorder. Insufficiently developed superegos have been linked with antisocial personality disorder. However, we should be wary of reifying the superego as a fixed structure in any one individual. It is a dynamic structure that grows or shrinks according to demands for moral guidance. Nevertheless, many forms of self-destructive behavior involve forms of unconscious attack by the superego.

Much of the therapeutic action of psychoanalytic treatment with neurotic patients involves superego modification. Initially, the patient perceives the analyst as harsh and punitive. Over time, however, the patient starts to recognize that he is attributing his own harshness to the analyst. In this manner, the analyst is taken in as a new internal representation who modifies the harshness of the patient's superego.

[See also Ego; Id; and Psychoanalysis, article on Theories.]

Bibliography

Arlow, J. (1982). Problems with the superego concept. *Psychoanalytic Study of the Child, 37*, 229–224.

Buchsbaum, H. K., & Emde, R. N. (1990). Play narratives in 36-month-old children: Early moral development and family relationship. *Psychoanalytic Study of the Child, 40*, 129–155.

Freud, S. (1961). The ego and the id. In J. Strachey (Ed. and Trans.) *The standard edition of the complete psychological works of Sigmund Freud* (Vol. 19, pp. 1–66). London: Hogarth Press. (Original work published 1923)

Freud, S. (1961/1953). Introductory lectures on psychoanalysis. In J. Strachey (Ed. and Trans.) *The standard edition of the complete psychological works of Sigmund Freud* (Vols. 15–16, pp. 1–482). London: Hogarth Press. (Original work published 1916–1917)

Freud, S. (1963). On narcissism: an introduction. In J. Strachey (Ed. and Trans.) *The standard edition of the complete psychological works of Sigmund Freud* (Vol. 14, pp. 67–102). London: Hogarth Press. (Original work published 1914)

Schafer, R. (1960). The loving and beloved superego in Freud's structural theory. *Psychoanalytic Study of the Child, 15*, 163–188.

Glen O. Gabbard

SUPPES, PATRICK (1922–), American philosopher of science and mathematical psychologist. Suppes's scientific work spans an exceptionally large range of topics. A short list would necessarily include the following: foundations of physics, foundations of probability, decision theory, concept formation, education (especially educational technology), measurement theory, mathematical learning theory, and psycholinguistics. The last three of these topics are the focus of this article (for more extensive coverage, see Bogdan, 1979).

Born in Tulsa, Oklahoma, Suppes pursued undergraduate studies in physics and mathematics, receiving a B.S. in physics from the University of Chicago in 1943. After 2 years of military duty in the South Pacific, he began graduate studies in philosophy at Columbia University and obtained his doctorate in 1950. While at Columbia, he was strongly influenced by the philosopher Ernest Nagel. In 1950, he joined the department of philosophy at Stanford, where he remained all his life. After moving to Stanford, he collaborated with the logicians Alfred Tarski (from Berkeley) and J. C. C. McKinsey (from Stanford), who introduced him to the axiomatic and set theoretical methods that remained his trademark for the rest of his career. Together with Duncan Luce, he can be credited with introducing these methods into theoretical psychology. This rigorous formalism contrasts with the predominant style of earlier theorists. It enables the precise statement of theories and the systematic derivation of their predictions—rendering empirical testing feasible and generally raising the standards of scientific discourse.

Measurement Theory

Suppes's first published paper was on measurement theory, a topic that he regards as central to the foundations of psychology. Indeed, many scholars believe that any scientific discipline necessarily relies on an intrinsic set of fundamental measurement scales, as exemplified by length, mass, and time in the physical sciences. The existence of such scales for measuring specific psychological quantities remains controversial, however. In a major paper on this topic, Scott and Suppes (1958) laid down some foundational principles for measurement theories in general, in a framework that is now commonly accepted. A comprehensive presentation of the subject is given in the three-volume *Foundations of Measurement* (New York, 1971–1990) written by Suppes in collaboration with David Krantz, Duncan Luce, and Amos Tversky. An elementary introduction is contained in Suppes and Zinnes (1963).

Mathematical Learning Theory

Between 1955 and 1970, Suppes collaborated with W. K. Estes, R. C. Atkinson, and others in formalizing mathematical learning theory, especially in the guise of stimulus sampling theory, in terms of a collection of stochastic processes of the Markovian type (Estes & Suppes, 1959, 1974; Suppes & Atkinson, 1960). In simple learning situations, these Markov models were successful in representing the data, and this approach was generally regarded as notable progress over the informal learning theories proposed by Clark Hull, Edward Tolman, and others, whose ambiguous predictions led to controversies.

Psycholinguistics

In a longstanding controversy, linguists have challenged psychologists to provide an adequate stimulus-response theory of natural language learning. Suppes's main contribution to this debate (Suppes, 1969) takes the form of a mathematical result proving that, for any connected finite automaton, there exists a stimulus-response model (formulated in the framework of stimulus theory) that is asymptotically isomorphic to that automaton. Because Suppes's result contains no information regarding the learning rate, the implications of this mathematical result for possible mechanisms of natural-language learning within a realistic time are unclear. An account of the controversy is given by Batchelder and Wexler (in Bogdan, 1979).

Suppes also authored classic textbooks in logic and axiomatic set theory, and a very large number of papers on various topics. Some of his recent work focuses on machine learning and brain-wave manifestations of word recognition. Suppes has received numerous honorific distinctions, including election as a fellow of the American Academy of Arts and Sciences and as a member of the National Academy of Sciences. In 1972, he received the Distinguished Scientific Contribution Award of the American Psychological Association, and in 1990 the National Medal of Science.

Bibliography

Bogdan, R. J. (Ed.). (1979). *Patrick Suppes*. Dordrecht, Netherlands: D. Reidel.

Estes, W. K., & Suppes, P. (1959). Foundations of linear models. In R. R. Bush & W. K. Estes (Eds.), *Studies in mathematical learning theory* (pp. 137–179). Stanford, CA: Stanford University Press.

Estes, W. K., & Suppes, P. (1974). Foundations of stimulus sampling theory. In D. H. Krantz, R. C. Atkinson, R. D. Luce, & P. Suppes (Eds.), *Contemporary developments in mathematical psychology: Vol. 1. Learning, memory and thinking* (pp. 163–183). San Francisco: Freeman.

Scott, D., & Suppes, P. (1958). Foundational aspects of theories of measurement. *Journal of Symbolic Logic, 23*, 113–128.

Suppes, P. (1969). Stimulus-response theory of finite automata. *Journal of Mathematical Psychology, 6*, 327–355.

Suppes, P., & Atkinson, R. C. (1960). *Markov learning models for multiperson interaction*. Stanford, CA: Stanford University Press.

Suppes, P., & Zinnes, J. (1963). Basic measurement theory. In R. D. Luce, R. R. Bush, & E. Galanter (Eds.), *Handbook of mathematical psychology* (Vol. 1, pp. 3–76). New York: Wiley.

Jean-Claude Falmagne

SUPRA-CONSCIOUSNESS. *See* Meditation; Religious Experience; *and* Transpersonal Psychology.

SURVEY METHODOLOGY. In the social sciences, a survey is a technique for collecting information about some population of people. Survey research requires a melding of three different methodologies: sampling, designing questions, and collecting data. Usually, information is collected by asking people questions; most often data are collected from only a sample of a population, rather than from every single member. [*See* Data Collection, *article on* Field Research.]

Sampling

If a sample is drawn properly, the people in the sample will be very likely to have the same distribution of characteristics—opinions, feelings, and experiences—as the whole population. By accurately describing such a sample, one can produce an accurate description of the entire population. To select a representative sample, all members of the population ideally should have a known chance to be included; a sample will not reflect the characteristics of those who had no chance to be selected. Also, the process of selection should be determined by chance. If people are included because they volunteer or are readily available, the sample will include a disproportionate number of people with the characteristics of those who volunteer or are available, and the sample is likely to differ from the population. [*See* Sampling.]

The other issue affecting the representativeness of sample survey data is the percentage of those selected who respond. This percentage is called the *response rate*. The higher the response rate, the more likely it is that the sample data will accurately describe the population.

Designing Questions to Be Good Measures

Surveys are conducted by asking people questions; if a good question is asked, the answers accurately describe what the research is trying to measure.

When asking about objective events, characteristics, and experiences, in theory one could check the accuracy of answers against some other source. Only a small percentage of questions actually can be checked against reliable records. Cannell, Marquis, and Laurent (1979) summarized results showing that when such evaluations are done major events are reported more accurately than minor events, recent events are reported more accurately than those that occurred further in the past, and events that significantly affect respondents' lives are reported more accurately than those that have little effect on their lives. In addition, when the answers to questions might reflect negatively on respondents, accurate answers are less likely to be given.

When measuring subjective states, it is not possible to check the accuracy of answers. Lee J. Cronbach and Paul E. Meehl (*Psychological Bulletin*, 1995, *52*, 281–302) outlined the basic approach to evaluating the validity of answers by examining the extent to which they have predictable or orderly associations with other answers. There is a long history of psychometric evaluation in psychology, and researchers draw on that tradition to evaluate the validity and reliability of answers. [*See* Reliability; *and* Validity.]

Other important standards for survey questions are that they can be understood consistently by everyone, that they are easily answerable by respondents, and that their answers mean what the researcher wants them to mean. To see if questions meet these standards, it is increasingly common to do cognitive evaluations of questions. Prior to conducting a survey, a small number of test respondents are asked to explain how they understood the questions and what their answers mean. In this way, researchers can identify in advance and correct questions that are confusing or ambiguous or that elicit answers that do not accurately describe what the researchers are trying to measure.

Methods of Data Collection

Respondents can be asked to answer questions by filling out a questionnaire or by answering questions administered by an interviewer. Interviewers conduct interviews over the telephone and in person. Increasingly, data collection is being assisted by computers, sometimes by having interviewers enter answers directly into computers, in other cases having respondents themselves give answers by entering them into computers.

Like all forms of measurement, it is important that survey data collection be standardized: To the extent possible, people should all be answering the same question in the same context so that differences in answers can be attributed to differences in respondents.

When surveys are self-administered, variation in the way questions are presented to respondents is minimal. In contrast, in interviews the potential exists that answers may be affected by interviewers. [See Artifacts, article on Assessment.] There are three keys steps to minimizing the effects of interviewers on answers. (1) Survey questions should be designed so that they can be read exactly as worded, without elaboration or editing; interviewers are trained to read questions exactly as worded. (2) Inevitably there are occasions in an interview when respondents do not fully answer a question. At that point, interviewers are required to ask follow-up questions; interviewers are taught to use nondirective probes that do not influence the content of answers. (3) Although interviewers inevitably differ in obvious ways with respect to gender, age, ethnic background, and personal styles, interviewers are trained to create a professional interaction in which response accuracy is primary. Good interviewers will not express personal opinions and will not give feedback that implies preferences among answers. Studies have shown that well-trained and supervised interviewers, given a well-designed survey instrument, generally are successful at not affecting the answers of respondents.

Sometimes, surveys ask people questions that may evoke sensitive or socially undesirable answers. For example, surveys are done about drug use, alcohol consumption, and sexual behavior. When surveys deal with such issues, the mode of data collection affects the answers that are given. It has been consistently found that respondents are more likely to give socially undesirable answers (such as reporting cocaine use in the past year) on a self-administered form than when reporting to an interviewer. Entering answers into a computer, rather than reporting them to an interviewer, seems to have the same advantage. [See Social Desirability.]

Conclusion

How well statistics based on a survey provide accurate information about a population depends on the sample selection, question design, and data collection protocols. It is only when all three aspects of survey methodology are appropriately carried out that one can have confidence in the accuracy of survey results.

Bibliography

Biemrer, P., Groves, R. M., Lyberg, L. E., Mathiowetz, N. A., & Sudman, S. (Eds.), (1991). *Measurement errors in surveys.* New York: Wiley. A compendium with chapters on the various sources of error in survey research, for more advanced readers.

Cannell, C. F., Marquis, K. H., & Laurent, A. (1977). *A summary of research studies of interviewing methodology, 1959–1970.* (Vital and health statistics: Series 2. Data evaluation and methods research, no. 69; DHEW Publication No. HRA 77–1343). Rockville, MD: U.S. Department of Health, Education, and Welfare, National Center for Health Statistics.

Fowler, F. J., Jr., (1993). *Survey research methods* (2nd ed.). Newbury Park, CA: Sage. An introductory book that presents the basic issues in collecting good survey data.

Fowler, F. J., Jr., (1995). *Improving survey questions: Design and evaluation.* Thousand Oaks, CA: Sage. An introduction to the design and evaluation of survey questions.

Groves, R. M. (1989). *Survey errors and survey costs.* New York: Wiley. A very comprehensive examination of known sources and magnitudes of errors in surveys, for those with some statistical background.

Kalton, G. (1983). *Introduction to survey sampling.* Beverly Hills, CA: Sage. A good introduction to sampling.

Sudman, S., & Bradburn, N. (1982). *Asking questions.* San Francisco: Jossey-Bass. Another excellent book about how to choose or design survey questions.

Floyd J. Fowler, Jr.

SWEDEN. Psychology is a young discipline in Sweden. It was not until 1948 that the first professor of psychology was appointed, at Uppsala University. Prior to this, psychology was part of pedagogy. The first chairs in this discipline came in 1910 at the universities in Lund and Uppsala. Between 1948 and 1956 psychology departments were established at all four universities in existence at the time, Uppsala, Lund, Göteborg, and Stockholm. A decade later a fifth department was founded at Umeå University. The sixth university in Sweden to give training in psychology was Linköping University, at which the department of pedagogy and psychology was established in 1984. All six universities now offer undergraduate training and graduate training in psychology. Undergraduate teaching in psychology is also given at a dozen university colleges in the country.

Research

Sidney Alrutz introduced experimental psychology in Sweden at the turn of the century after studying with Georg Elias Müller in Germany. His research on sense perception and pain at the Department of Physiology in Uppsala led to a Ph.D. in 1901. Alrutz founded the first psychological laboratory in Uppsala in 1902, the first scientific journal in psychology, *Psyke*, in 1906, and the Institute for Psychological Research in Uppsala in 1909. In addition to his research on the perception of cold, heat, and pain, which reached international recognition, Alrutz was interested in hypnosis and parapsychology.

Although Alrutz was successful in taking the first steps in introducing scientific studies in psychology in Sweden, many years passed before psychology became an independent discipline at the various universities. For about four decades after Alrutz, psychology was part of pedagogy and philosophy. To the extent that research in psychology was carried out in Sweden during this time, the main orientation was differential psychology. Gustaf Axel Jaederholm, who was a professor in philosophy and pedagogy at Göteborg, was a key figure in Sweden in this field. Jaederholm, like Alrutz, received his scientific training in experimental psychology in Germany. Differential psychology was the main focus of interest in Swedish psychology all the way up to the beginning of the 1950s. Since psychology was strongly related to educational practice at the time, the study of principles of learning was also a major focus of interest. Whereas German psychology had been the main source of influence for the early pioneers in Swedish psychology, American psychology became the main source of inspiration and ever since the Second World War has dominated the Swedish scene.

The only exception to the new American influence was David Katz, who came from Müller's lab in Göttingen in Germany to become the first holder of the endowed Olof Eneroth Professorship in Stockholm. This chair was in pedagogy, but Katz's research interest was truly psychological. Katz reached international recognition for his research on the phenomenology of color perception. The recognition of Katz's research and the growing fame of the psychology department in Stockholm contributed to the fact that Stockholm was selected to be the host for the Thirteenth International Congress of Psychology in 1951, for which Katz was the president.

In 1962, Gösta Ekman succeeded Katz as professor on the Eneroth chair, which by now was a professorship in psychology. Ekman was very successful in his research on perception and psychophysics; his orientation became known as the Stockholm School. This tradition has continued with work by Gunnar Borg, Hannes Eisler, and Birgitta Berglund, among others. Borg's scale for ratings of perceived exertion, which is used in many applied settings worldwide, is an example of the impact of this line of research. David Magnusson, who succeeded Ekman on the Eneroth chair in 1969, gained an international reputation for his longitudinal research on individual development. The largest psychology department in Sweden is now at Stockholm University; Magnusson played a major role in this development. The department consists of separate sections in biological psychology (with Ulf Lundberg as professor), clinical psychology (Lars-Göran Öst), cognitive psychology (Henry Montgomery), perception and psychophysics (Birgitta Berglund), personality-social-developmental psychology (Lars R. Bergman), risk analysis and decision research (Ola Svenson), and work and organizational psychology (Gunn Johansson). In 1994, Lars-Göran Nilsson, who came from Uppsala and Umeå, became the fourth holder of the Eneroth chair.

Research interests in perception moved from Katz in Stockholm to Gunnar Johansson in Uppsala. Johansson, who was originally trained in philosophy and received his training in experimental psychology from Katz, became professor of psychology at Uppsala University in the 1950s and built a famous research laboratory for studies in movement perception. This laboratory had worldwide influence in this field for many years. Sten Sture Bergström at Umeå and Sverker Runeson and Claes von Hofsten at Uppsala have continued this tradition.

Psychology in Lund was for many years dominated by a psychoanalytically oriented theory aimed at exploring unconscious psychic conflicts and defense mechanisms. Gudmund Smith and Ulf Kragh, professors of psychology and applied psychology, respectively, directed this research. The psychology department in Lund was intellectually more homogeneous during these years than any other psychology department in Sweden. The percept-genetic approach of Smith and Kragh still plays an important role in Lund, but other research traditions are growing stronger, for example, the neuropsychological research of Jarl Risberg.

In Göteborg there have been two main traditions for many years. One line of research is that of cognitive psychology with Lennart Sjöberg and later Tommy Gärling, Erland Hjelmqvist, and Lars Bäckman as the main players. The other tradition is in animal models of human behavior, with Knut Larsson and Trevor Archer as the key figures. It is noteworthy that the psychology department in Göteborg has the only existing animal lab in the country.

Mats Björkman came to the new university in Umeå

in the late 1960s to hold the first chair of psychology. Ever since then, cognitive psychology has been the dominant theme of research in Umeå, with Lars-Göran Nilsson and Claes von Hofsten, in turn, succeeding Björkman. Ingvar Lundberg also played a major role in developing the psychology department in Umeå into a first-class research institution. Current main researchers at Umeå are Peter Juslin, Bo Molander, Timo Mäntylä, and Lars Nyberg.

Jerker Rönnberg, in cognitive psychology, and Rolf Sandell were the first professors of psychology to be inaugurated in 1997 at the newest university, in Linköping. Although not at any of the six universities in Sweden, the psychobiological research of Arne Öhman at the Karolinska Institute and the research on risk perception by Lennart Sjöberg at the Stockholm School of Economics should be noted also as two major themes of research that have developed in Sweden. Marianne Frankenhaeuser directed her influential research on stress for many years from her chair at Karolinska.

Research Funding

It was not until the 1930s and 1940s that governmental funding for basic research was organized for the natural sciences and medicine and later for the social sciences. Most researchers in academic psychology receive their grants from the Swedish Council for Research in the Humanities and Social Sciences and from the Swedish Council for Social Research. Research funding can also be obtained from the Bank of Sweden Tercentenary Foundation, which is a research council covering all areas of research. Funds for research in psychology are also available from the Medical Research Council. Funding of research on applied problems from various other sources than these increased considerably during 1980s and 1990s.

Teaching of Psychology

Undergraduate courses in psychology are offered in two different ways. One is a 5-year program leading to a degree in psychology, which after one year of practical work under supervision qualifies a person to become a state licensed psychologist. This psychologist program is offered at the six universities only. Another line of undergraduate courses in psychology does not lead to a profession as a psychologist but is combined with other subjects, mainly in the social sciences, to comprise a basic university degree of B.A. The students who take this course typically constitute the basis for recruitment to graduate school.

To qualify for graduate studies in psychology a student must have at least three full semesters of courses in psychology and three full semesters of teaching in other areas leading up to a B.A. degree. The standard time period to pass the Ph.D. is 4 years. For various reasons very few students keep to this ideal; most take 6 to 8 years to earn the degree. The Ph.D. degree consists of two parts; one third of the work consists of courses in various areas of psychology, and two thirds of the time the work is devoted to the dissertation. In a typical dissertation, the student includes four to eight articles that he or she has published in international journals with or without the superviser and others as co-authors. The requirement is that the student should be a single author or the main author of more than half of the articles included in the thesis.

Organization

The departmental organization in Sweden was originally modeled after the German system, with one professor for each discipline and department. The professor was usually assisted only by a secretary, one research-trained person with a Ph.D. called a *docent*, and a student as assistant for all sorts of practical work. The rapidly expanding body of students during the 1960s, however, prompted changes in teaching routines and the structure of positions.

A new type of position, university lecturer, was created during the 1960s to handle the teaching of large masses of students entering university at that time. Many university lecturers were employed at each department, but few had completed their Ph.Ds. Most undergraduate teaching was, therefore done by a relatively large group of people with very little scientific experience. As time went by, more and more of these lecturers worked through their graduate programs while they fulfilled a very heavy teaching load. Eventually, the research-oriented lecturers during the 1960s and 1970s got their Ph.Ds and are now professors at psychology departments in Sweden.

A psychology department in Sweden now has several professors whose main focus is research, with minimal teaching obligations, and several university lecturers whose focus is teaching, with few opportunities for research. Professors and lecturers are now always tenured positions. In addition to professors and lecturers, there are now typically also several nontenured postdoctoral positions in a psychology department. Thus, the departmental organization in Sweden has changed from a German to a North American system, with more than one professor. However, there is still a long way to go before there is a system of high integration between research and teaching at all career levels.

Psychology departments at Swedish universities belong to the faculties of social sciences, except for the Karolinska Institute, where the psychology department belongs to the Faculty of Medical Science. As noted, the connection to social sciences is also important when it comes to research funding.

There are more than 7,000 psychologists organized in the Swedish Psychological Association, an association primarily for professional psychologists, which was founded under a different name in 1947. There is no similar organization for academic psychology. However, the National Committee for Psychology was established at the Royal Swedish Academy of Sciences in 1985. The Swedish Psychological Association and, indirectly, the National Committee for Psychology are connected to the International Union of Psychological Science (IUPsyS). IUPsyS was established 1951 at the Thirteenth International Congress of Psychology, which was organized in Stockholm.

Journals

Alrutz was the first editor of the first journal in psychology, *Psyke*. This journal was published during the first two decades of the twentieth century. At present there is no scientific journal in Sweden. The *Scandinavian Journal of Psychology*, which is a joint enterprise of the Nordic countries (Sweden, Denmark, Norway, Finland), was founded in 1960. The journal is an outlet for academic psychology in general, publishing articles in English in all fields of psychology. There is also a scientific journal, *Nordisk Psykologi*, which publishes papers in any of the Nordic languages.

Bibliography

Hugdahl, K., & Öhman, A. (1987). Sweden. In A. R. Gilgen & C. K. Gilgen (Eds.), *International handbook of psychology* (pp. 461–483). New York: Greenwood.

Künnapas, T. (1976). Sweden. In V. S. Sexton & H. Misiak (Eds.), *Psychology around the world* (pp. 405–417). Monterey, CA: Brooks/Cole.

Nilsson, L. -G. (1988). The Swedish national committee of psychology. *International Journal of Psychology, 23*, 649–652.

Rönnberg, J. (1986). Cognitive psychology in Scandinavia. Attention, memory, learning and memory dysfunctions. *Scandinavian Journal of Psychology, 27*, 95–149.

Lars-Göran Nilsson

SWITZERLAND. To understand the history of psychology in Switzerland it is useful to keep in mind that this country is a confederation with 26 ministers of education and four national languages (German, French, Italian, and Romansh). The country is surrounded by especially important neighbors when considering the history of psychology: Austria, France, Germany, and Italy. The influence of Wundt and Freud was immediate as some of their disciples were active in the country. For scientific activity, Switzerland can be considered a bilingual country; the universities have been established in the most important German- or French-speaking cities.

Precursors

There is a long tradition of interest in education in Switzerland. The ideas of Jean-Jacques Rousseau (1712–1778) played such an important role that the institute in Geneva where psychology was studied and taught was named after him. Heinrich Pestalozzi (1746–1827), influenced by Rousseau's ideas, played an important role; he was strongly engaged in the social support of children and spent all his life in education. His experiences led him to the conclusion that education should be based on understanding the natural development of children. He advocated group activities in education. Johan Caspar Lavater (1741–1801), a pastor in Zurich, was another precursor of psychology; interested in physiognomy, he wrote four volumes about the description of individual character differences. These precursors drew attention to psychological problems and prepared the field on which scientific psychology developed at the end of the nineteenth century.

Early Steps and Oppositions

For a long time, the University of Geneva was the only one to have appointed professors of psychology; they were members of the scientific departments (in science or medicine). Théodore Flournoy (1854–1920) had been a student of Wundt in Leipzig. He became the first professor of psychology and physiology in Geneva where he established, in 1892, the second laboratory of experimental psychology in Europe. Flournoy and his nephew, Edouard Claparède (1873–1940), founded in 1901 the *Archives de Psychologie*, the first journal of psychology in Switzerland. Claparède had studied medicine but was appointed professor of psychology. He made important contributions in different fields, including the psychology of intelligence, educational psychology, and a biological theory of sleep. He criticized associationism and adopted a functionalist approach, studying numerous psychological phenomena in terms of their usefulness, that all behavior is directed toward the achievement of a goal.

Claparède and Pierre Bovet (1878–1965) founded the Institut Jean-Jacques Rousseau in 1911, the ancestor of the current Faculté de Psychologie et des Sciences de l'Education. Bovet, the first director of the institute, was a professor of philosophy in Neuchâtel and of education in Geneva. Claparède also introduced intelligence tests. He demonstrated how to apply them to the educational context (Claparède, 1924) and to methods of measurement as well as to theoretical foundations. [*See* Measures of Intelligence, *article on* Intelligence Tests.]

In 1921, Claparède called Jean Piaget, who was working in Paris at this time, to join the institute, a decision that turned out to be a key factor in strengthening the position of psychology at the University of

Geneva. As in several other countries, many of the first psychologists in Switzerland received their initial academic training in medicine and were interested in psychopathology and psychotherapy. This was the case in Geneva (Claparède was a physician), but this tendency was even stronger in Zurich.

There have been some tentative steps to integrate the discipline into the German-speaking universities. Moritz Lazarus was appointed professor in the faculty of philosophy in Bern and served for six years starting in 1860; he was in charge of teaching "in particular psychology and folks' psychology" (Heller, 1986). In Zurich a chair for inductive philosophy was created in 1870; the first professor was Friedrich Albert Lange (1828–1875). When he left Zurich, Lange was replaced by Wilhelm Wundt, who stayed only one academic year (1874–1875) before he moved to Leipzig. Richard Avenarius (1843–1896) was appointed as his successor; his work about thinking processes can be considered a pioneering step for the development of the Würzburg school.

However, the resistance seems to have been stronger than the will to establish empirical and scientific psychology in academic institutions. The reason was probably not mainly scientific, but rather academic or political. Because of the extreme decentralization of the political institutions, the influence of the local government was important in deciding the priorities of each university. This phenomenon has been analyzed in detail by Heller and Perrez (1990) in the case of Fribourg.

It should be mentioned that in Zurich modern psychiatry and psychoanalysis played important roles. The hospital Burghölzli contributed highly to the development of the study of psychopathology. It was the most famous institution in Switzerland, comparable to other European hospitals like La Salpêtrière in Paris. It was led after 1879 by the French-speaking naturalist and physician Auguste Forel. The psychiatrist Eugen Bleuler (1857–1939), who introduced the term schizophrenia in 1911, was strongly influenced by the ideas of Freud and tried to apply them to the therapy of psychotic patients.

Carl Gustav Jung (1875–1961), probably the most famous of Freud's disciples, later became his dissenter. He agreed with Freud that the unconscious exerts a powerful influence, but he contended that the unconscious contains more than the person's repressed thoughts and feelings, that is, the "collective unconscious" heritage of our early ancestors. Jung also developed a theory of personality based on psychological types and his description of the orientations of the personality (extroversion versus introversion) eventually became very popular.

Because psychology could not find a sufficient development in the academic institutions, private schools were created outside the university. Since the beginning of the 1920s, the training of practical psychologists was assumed in Zurich by an institute of applied psychology, outside of the university. Similarly the Jung Institute was created and is still active near Zurich. The concurrence between these schools and the universities is partly responsible for the delay in establishing the legal base for the profession of psychologist and psychotherapist.

Piaget and Cognitive Development

Jean Piaget's (1896–1980) primary interest was in epistemological questions such as the origins of intelligence and scientific knowledge in the human species. After his studies in biology, he became interested in psychology as a way to answer these fundamental questions using an empirical methodology. His work on children's thinking began in 1920. Instead of adapting children's intelligence tests, Piaget was more interested in the wrong answers and interviewed the children more deeply about their conceptions. Claparède read his first articles on these experiments and invited him to join the Rousseau Institute. Later he succeeded Claparède as a professor of psychology, and Bovet as director of the institute.

Instead of 5 years, as he anticipated at this time (Piaget, 1976), this detour into psychology lasted more than 50 years and, with the help of many coworkers, he organized a large set of quantitative observations about the four main stages of cognitive development from birth to adulthood, each stage being characterized by an operational structure. These studies were guided by the idea that mental organization depends on the interaction of external factors with internal structures. Piaget paid close attention to processes common to the biological and intellectual development (adaptation, assimilation, accommodation). He argued that children themselves play a role as active constructors of their own development. Knowledge is not a copy of reality, but it comes from modifying and transforming the world. Development can be sped up or slowed down by variations in the environment, but the basic sequence of changes is universal.

Piaget published many books and articles and was honored by more than 30 universities around the world. Among the most important works are those about schemata (Piaget, 1936), tasks of conservation (Piaget & Inhelder, 1941), biology and knowledge (Piaget, 1967), and the process of equilibration (Piaget, 1975). Bärbel Inhelder (1913–1997) collaborated on most of Piaget's books; later she published three books with other coworkers about learning (Inhelder, Sinclair, & Bovet, 1974), cross-cultural psychology (Dasen, Inhelder, Lavallée, & Retschitzki, 1978), and strategies (Inhelder & Cellérier, 1992).

Diagnostic Contribution

The interest in applied psychology in Switzerland resulted in the creation of many tests. Hermann Rorschach developed his well-known projective Inkblot Test in 1921. Lipot Szondi elaborated a method of psychodiagnosis based upon the idea that hereditary factors determine personality. Richard Meili, who had studied with Wolfgang Köhler and became a collaborator of Claparède, published a book in 1936 about diagnostic psychology. André Rey (1906–1965) was an assistant of Claparède whose Ph.D. thesis is about the practical intelligence of the child (Rey, 1934). He became professor of applied psychology and was highly productive in creating many tests intended to measure specific abilities (memory, spatial abilities, use of instruments, and others).

German-language psychology continues to be highly assessment oriented. Each student has to take a course in psychological assessment, which typically includes one or more laboratory courses in test construction, practical assessment work, and report writing (Pawlik, 1994). The weight of assessment in the curricula of French-speaking departments is lighter.

The Expansion

During World War II, Swiss psychologists could not easily keep in touch with their foreign colleagues, therefore, allowing them time to organize themselves within the country. The first national bilingual journal (*Revue Suisse de Psychologie Pure et Appliquée / Schweizerische Zeitschrift für Psychologie und ihre Anwendungen*) was first published in 1942. Recently (in 1994) the title was changed to the *Swiss Journal of Psychology* and the articles are now mostly written in English.

The Swiss Society of Psychology, the national academic organization, was created in 1943; Piaget was its first president and he was president for 3 years. This institutional consolidation finally reached the academic world, with psychology now in all the universities. Institutes of psychology were created in Bern (1954), Zurich (1966), Lausanne (1967), Neuchâtel (1970), Fribourg (1973), and Basel (1981). There has been an Institute for Work and Organizational Psychology at the Federal Polytechnic Institute in Zurich since 1972.

Applied psychology experienced monumental growth after World War II. Psychologists have found work in schools, businesses, and industry; more people suffering from psychological disorders consult psychologists for help. Psychological language has become part of everyday life. Nevertheless some reluctance still exists; applied psychology has evolved much more slowly in the rural parts of the country.

At the end of the 1990s, there is still no federal regulation regarding training in psychology or in private practice. Some cantons have a regulation about the practice of psychology or psychotherapy, others do not. However, a project of law for psychology is being discussed; it plans to create a federal examination that would apply to all psychology students.

Domains

In research domains there is no longer a Swiss "particular case" as it was when the influence of Piaget was dominant. Swiss psychology has joined the mainstream of the discipline. The large number of contacts beyond the nation's limits contributed to the emergence of new paradigms and fields of research. The most dynamic research domains are clinical psychology, social psychology, and cognitive psychology.

Psychotherapy and Clinical Psychology

Psychotherapy has a long history in Switzerland. Meili (1984) noted that an international conference on psychotherapy had taken place in 1920, under the presidency of Claparède. It is interesting to observe that, paradoxically, although psychoanalysis developed in German language and culture, it never succeeded to establish itself within academic psychology in German-speaking institutions in Switzerland, nor in Austria or Germany (Pawlik, 1994).

Clinical psychology can be studied in most psychology departments (e.g., Basel, Bern, Fribourg, Geneva, Zurich), and it is the most popular domain for the majority of students. Very few clinical psychologists have received special psychoanalytic training. Training is offered mainly in cognitive and behavioral therapy and in client-oriented psychotherapy. However, in French-speaking universities, as in France, psychoanalysis is clearly the main frame of reference.

Social Psychology

Social psychology is represented in each university, and many groups work with emphasis on different aspects: social influence of minorities, social interactions in cognitive development, social representations, and so on. To illustrate the importance of social psychology in Switzerland, the first volume of the *Swiss Monographs in Psychology* is devoted to it (von Cranach, Doise, & Mugny, 1992). The growing influence of the Vygotskian perspective was perceptible during the conference held in Geneva in 1996 on the occasion of the centennial of Piaget and Vygotsky.

Current Situation, Problems, and Tendencies

At least one department of psychology exists in each of the nine universities in Switzerland. Because of their public status, they are under the control of cantonal political institutions, which provide a significant part of the budget. Recently the federal administration has tried to promote better coordination between universities. Most of these departments offer academic training up to and including a doctorate degree. Universities differ as to how psychology is institutionalized academically: psychology may be part of a faculty of philosophy, of social sciences, of economics and law, or a separate faculty on its own (Geneva). In addition, universities differ widely in the size of their psychology departments (in terms of faculty and students—ranging from fewer than 100 up to over 1,200 psychology majors). The standard of an eight-semester curriculum for the training in psychology is widely recognized. In most systems, the training is broad during at least 2 years, and specialization, if any, occurs only in the second half of the curriculum. Research support comes mainly from outside the university sector; the Swiss National Foundation for Scientific Research funds individual grants for young researchers as well as research projects and nationwide programs.

Although Switzerland is not a member of the European community, several Swiss departments take part in ERASMUS or SOCRATES programs (promoting cooperation in education and supporting exchanges of students and teachers among European countries) and many Swiss psychologists cooperate with foreign colleagues all around the world. The language was never the key factor in determining the development of the field; the influences crossed the language fence. Pestalozzi was active in Yverdon, a French-speaking city; Forel worked in Zurich; and even Piaget studied there one year (1918–1919). German-speaking psychologists (e.g., Inhelder, Meili, Aebli, and Fischer) were trained in Geneva. Nevertheless, the language plays a role in favoring some contacts with foreign colleagues; German-speaking professors of psychology tend to cooperate primarily with German universities and to be members of German scientific societies; French-speaking professors are more in touch with Latin colleagues. Sometimes through international events, Swiss psychologists have opportunities to meet and cooperate. Most of them have frequent activities in scientific societies, and with the growing trend to use English as the main scientific language in most journals and congresses, they are able to go beyond linguistic borders.

Societies

The Swiss Society of Psychology (SSP, Schweizerische Gesellschaft für Psychologie / Société Suisse de Psychologie) is the national academic organization and a member of the International Union of Psychological Science. It publishes its own journal (*Swiss Journal of Psychology*; Bern: Huber) and, since 1992, the English-language proceedings of its biennial congresses (*Swiss Monographs in Psychology*, Lewiston: Hogrefe & Huber). The Federation of Swiss Psychologists (FSP, founded in

1987) functions as the umbrella organization of all Swiss psychological associations (more than 30 societies, including the SSP) and has a membership of 4,000 academically trained psychologists. Its periodical publication is *Psychoscope*.

[*Many of the people mentioned in this entry are the subjects of biographies in this encyclopedia.*]

Bibliography

Claparède, E. (1924). *Comment diagnostiquer les aptitudes des écoliers.* Paris: Flammarion.

Dasen, P. R., Inhelder, B., Lavallée, M., & Retschitzki, J. (1978). *La naissance de l'intelligence chez l'enfant baoulé de Côte d'Ivoire.* Berne: Huber.

Heller, D. (1986). Zur Geschichte der Psychologie an den Schweizer Universitäten—Moritz Lazarus in Bern. *Schweizerische Zeitschrift für Psychologie, 45,* 1–16.

Heller, D., & Perrez, M. (1990). Die Anfänge der experimentellen Psychologie in der Schweiz unter besonderer Berücksichtigung ihrer Entwicklung an der Universität Freiburg. *Schweizerische Zeitschrift für Psychologie, 49,* 57–65.

Inhelder, B., & Cellérier, G. (1992). *Le cheminement des découvertes de l'enfant.* Neuchâtel-Paris: Delachaux & Niestlé.

Inhelder, B., Sinclair, H., & Bovet, M. (1974). *L'apprentissage des structures cognitives.* Paris: PUF.

Meili, R. (1984). Psychology in Switzerland. In R. J. Corsini (Ed.), *Encyclopedia of psychology* (pp. 157–158). New York: Wiley.

Pawlik, K. (1994). Psychology in Europe: Origins and development of psychology in German-speaking countries. *International Journal of Psychology, 29,* 677–694.

Piaget, J. (1936). *La naissance de l'intelligence chez l'enfant.* Neuchâtel: Delachaux & Niestlé.

Piaget, J. (1967). *Biologie et connaissance.* Paris: Gallimard.

Piaget, J. (1975). *L'équilibration des structures cognitives.* Paris: PUF.

Piaget, J. (1976). Autobiographie. *Revue Européenne des Sciences Sociales, 14,* 1–43.

Piaget, J., & Inhelder, B. (1941). *Le dévelopment des quantités physiques chez l'enfant.* Neuchâtel: Delachaux & Niestlé.

Rey, A. (1934). *L'intelligence pratique chez l'enfant.* Paris: Alcan.

Von Cranach, M., Doise, W., & Mugny, G. (1992). *Social representations and the social bases of knowledge.* Lewiston, NY: Hogrefe & Huber.

Jean Retschitzki

SYMBOLIC INTERACTION THEORY. While spawning specific theories—e.g., affect control theory (Heise, *Understanding Events,* New York, 1979); identity theory (Stryker, in E. F. Borgatta and M. L. Borgatta, [Eds.], *Encyclopedia of Sociology,* Vol. 2, New York, pp. 871–875, 1992)—symbolic interaction theory is best understood as a theoretical framework, an approach to social psychology reflecting a sociological starting point, and not a theory explaining relationships among social psychological variables. Various versions of the frame exist; these share a common intellectual heritage, certain assumptions and concepts, imagery, and a very general proposition.

The general proposition holds that self reflects society and organizes social behavior. The imagery includes viewing society as a web of communication or symbolic interaction, conducted through meanings developed in persons' interdependent activity. Effecting interaction is the environment as defined or interpreted, rather than raw. Society is created and recreated as persons interact. Both society and person derive from interaction; each presupposes the other. Humans are minded; mindedness can be reflexive. When humans take themselves as objects of their reflection, they construct selves, doing so from the standpoint of those with whom they interact; selves are thus inherently social. Mind develops in response to interrupted activities and involves selecting from symbolically available alternative actions. Thus, humans are active and creative, constructing their interaction. Although constructions are not necessarily novel, they can be. There is consequently some indeterminacy in social life; outcomes of interaction cannot in principle be completely predicted from preexisting conditions.

This imagery leads to three assumptions. First, adequate accounts of behavior must reflect the perspectives of the actors engaged in that behavior and cannot rest on the perspective of observers alone. A second assumption assigns priority to social interaction with respect to the emergence of both social organization and the individual: "In the beginning there is society" (Stryker, in C. McGarty and S. A. Haslma, [Eds.], *The Message of Social Psychology*, New York, pp. 315–327, 1996). This assumption differentiates symbolic interactionism from social psychological approaches used by psychologists giving priority to the individual. The third assumption asserts that the self, people's reflexive responses to themselves, links societal processes to social interactions and behaviors.

The foregoing incorporates concepts basic to the approach. Meaning is fundamental; it refers to anticipations of future behavior invoked when symbols are attached to things, ideas, and relationships among things and ideas entering the experience of human beings. Meanings common among actors, significant symbols, organize behavior with respect to what they symbolize. To act in an organized manner on entering situations, persons build definitions of the situation. Defining who others are in a situation, critical to coherent action, is typically accomplished by locating those others as members of socially recognized categories of actors. Locating persons in this way invokes expectations for behavior symbolized by the categorical labels; these expectations are termed roles. Also critical to coherent action is defining who one is in the situation; doing so involves locating oneself as a member of a social category, invoking expectations for one's own behavior. To reflexively respond to oneself is to have a self.

People learn what to expect from others through role-taking, putting oneself in others' place to see the world as they do, using knowledge of the social categories in which they locate others, prior experience with others, and symbolic cues available in their interaction. Often, in ambiguous situations, they role-make (Turner, in A. M. Rose, [Ed.], *Human Behavior and Social Processes*, Boston, pp. 20–40, 1962), creating performances on the basis of roles imputed to others.

Differentiating contemporary from earlier versions of the approach is an assumption that persons have multiple selves. That is, current versions accept Willam James's (*Principles of Psychology*, New York, 1890) view that persons have as many selves as there are groups of persons responding to them. This assumption follows from the idea that self reflects society and the recognition that contemporary societies are highly differentiated internally.

Central to symbolic interactionism's intellectual heritage is George Herbert Mead (1934); others of import include John Dewey, Charles Horton Cooley, and William Isaac Thomas. Herbert Blumer (*Symbolic Interactionism*, Englewood Cliffs, N.J., 1969) is the pivotal albeit controversial figure linking these progenitors to more contemporary proponents including Erving Goffman, Anselm Strauss, Ralph Turner, Sheldon Stryker, Norman Denzin, David Maines, Gary Fine, and John Hewitt.

This list hides important diversity. For some, the frame applies broadly to sociology; for others, it is limited to social psychology. Some hold the constructed nature of social behavior implies only *posthoc* understanding of past events is possible, others that testable predictive explanations of social behavior are achievable. Naturalistic, observational methods are the only legitimate research path to some, while others are open to any social science method or technique. Some argue that observers' perspectives only distort accounts of behavior, others that participants' perspectives need be considered in achieving explanations but cannot in themselves constitute explanations. For some, social life is fluid, with definitions and interpretations continuously reworked in interaction, so effectively denying the utility of social structural concepts in social psychological analysis and denying as well the applicability of concepts developed in prior analyses. Others accept the reality of social structure, continuity of definitions and interpretations, and the possibility that concepts developed in prior analyses are useful in later analyses. Self is for some a first cause of behavior, itself independent of external causation; others take self to be the result of prior social structure effecting self through interaction. Some see self as continuously constructed anew in every situation of interaction, with novelty and creativity as endemic in social life; others see self as transsituational, the reconstruction of social life in preexisting patterns a typical outcome of interaction, and novelty a possible but relatively improbable outcome of interaction. Some attend primarily to the phenomenological worlds of persons they study, others to how concerted lines of social action are developed (drawing on the behavioristic elements in Mead [1934]), and still others to how social structures constrain or facilitate the impact of self on subsequent social behavior.

Although the meaning of self as used by cognitive social psychologists and symbolic interactionists differs, their common use of the term encourages a dialogue between sociology and psychology that, at least potentially, is mutually beneficial. For symbolic interactionists, viewing self as a cognitive schema gives the concept more precision and a more adequate basis for measurement than has heretofore been available. Cognitive social psychologists, on the other hand, can only benefit from recognizing that self and all other social cognitions are rooted in social structures and processes.

Bibliography

Cooley, C. H. (1902). *Human nature and the social order.* New York: Scribner's. A more phenomenological rendering of the meta-theoretical underpinnings of symbolic interactionism than is provided by Mead; places greater emphasis on emotion relative to cognition than is found in Mead.

Dewey, J. (1930). *Human nature and conduct.* New York: Modern Library. Friend and sometime colleague of Mead; together the two worked out implications of philosophical pragmatism for a social psychology.

Fine, G. A. (1987). *With the boys: Little league baseball and preadolescent culture.* Chicago: University of Chicago Press. An illustration of the preference of some symbolic interactionists for ethnographic methods in researching issues of the emergence of social order through interaction.

Goffman, E. (1959). *The presentation of self in everyday life.* Garden City, NY: Doubleday. Perhaps the best known writings of a sociologist whose insights into how interactions work are nearly legendary.

Maines, D. (1977). Social organization and social structure in symbolic interactionist thought. *Annual Review of Sociology, 3,* 235–259. A defense of traditional symbolic interactionism against the charge that it demonstrates an astructural bias.

Mead, G. H. (1934). *Mind, self, and society.* Chicago: University of Chicago Press. The classic statement of the meta-theoretical underpinnings of symbolic interactionist theory, drawing strongly on a pragmatic philosophical base.

Strauss, A. L. (1978). *Negotiations.* San Francisco: Jossey-Bass. Uses the metaphor of negotiation to trace through the processes by which persons with conflicting interests arrive at an ordered set of norms and rules, enabling them to meet the goals of the organizations in which they interact.

Stryker, S. (1980). *Symbolic interactionism: A social structural version.* Menlo Park, CA: Benjamin/Cummings. An argument that to be properly understood, social psychological processes involving cognitions of self must be seen as embedded in and heavily impacted by social structural settings.

Thomas, W. I., & Thomas, D. S. (1928). *The child in America.* New York: Knopf. "If men define situations as real, they are real in their consequences." While Thomas gave symbolic interactionism this methodological premise, he recognized (as some do not) the power of situations *per se* to override definitions or cognitions.

Turner, R. H. (1978). The role and the person. *American Journal of Sociology, 84,* 1–23. An insightful treatment of how, and the conditions under which, persons merge their roles and their selves.

Sheldon Stryker

SYMBOLISM. *See* Religious Symbol, Myth, and Ritual.

SYMPATHY. Although definitions of sympathy vary, it is frequently defined as an emotional reaction based on the apprehension or comprehension of another's emotional state or condition, a reaction involving feelings of compassion, sorrow, or concern for another person. Sympathy frequently may stem from empathy (a vicariously induced emotional response to another's emotion or condition that involves experiencing the same emotion as the other person or a highly similar emotion). [*See* Empathy.] However, sympathy also may occur as a consequence of either cognitively taking the perspective of another person or accessing stored information from memory relevant to understanding the other person's emotional state or condition. Some investigators use the terms *empathy* and *sympathy* interchangeably; however, according to these definitions, the latter, and not the former, involves an orientation to another's needs rather than the mere reflection of the other person's real or inferred emotional state. It also is important to differentiate sympathy from personal distress. Personal distress is an aversive, self-focused emotional reaction to another's emotional state or condition, such as anxiety or discomfort, that frequently stems from empathy.

Personal distress occurs when an individual experiences empathic overarousal in reaction to another's emotion, whereas sympathy is associated with somewhat less physiological arousal. Thus, individuals prone to frequent and intense negative emotions would be expected to be prone to personal distress, as should people who are not skilled at regulating their emotions and emotion-related reactions. In contrast, individuals who are well regulated are expected to be prone to sympathy. Findings for children and adults generally support these hypotheses. Moreover, self-reported emotional reactivity to both positive and negative emotions has been linked to adults' sympathy, whereas adults' reports of children's intense and frequent negative emotionality have been correlated with low dispositional sympathy for boys. Adults' reports of boys' negative emotionality likely reflect children's displays of externalizing emotions, such as anger, rather than emotions such as concern, sadness, or worry. Thus, it appears that personality and temperamental differences in emotionality and emotion-related emotion are linked to sympathy and personal distress.

Developmental Theory and Trends

According to Martin Hoffman (1982), sympathy develops from the ability to empathize early in life. Infants in the second year of life sometimes react to the negative emotional states of others, although they often seem uncertain who is experiencing the pain or distress. Sometime around the second or third year of life, toddlers can clearly differentiate between their own and others' emotional states and therefore can respond with concern to other people's distress. As children's abilities to understand others' internal states develop, they increasingly are motivated to put themselves in the other's place and locate the source of another's distress. Thus, they become more sympathetic and capable of providing appropriate, sensitive assistance. Hoffman further hypothesized that during childhood and early adolescence, as children become aware of their own and others' continuing existence beyond the immediate context, they gradually begin reacting to others' general condition as well as to another's immediate distress. Consequently, adolescents often can comprehend and respond sympathetically to the plight of an entire group or class of people, such as the economically impoverished, politically oppressed, or developmentally disabled.

Empirical evidence provides some support for Hoffman's ideas. Prosocial behaviors based on infants' observations of others' negative emotion emerge between one and two years of age and increase in frequency and variety over this time span. Early prosocial behaviors often are linked to children's expressions of concern, as well as children's efforts to understand and experience the other person's plight. Although two-year-olds are especially responsive to their mothers' distress, they also show some sensitivity toward unfamiliar adults.

Children report more empathy with age in child-hood, but there are few data on changes in sympathy in the school years. It is likely that children can sympathize in more situations as their sociocognitive skills (e.g., perspective-taking) develop. In any case, sympathy is stable (i.e., is correlated across time) from early adolescence into early adulthood.

Gender Differences in Sympathy

Researchers have found fairly consistent gender differences favoring girls and women for questionnaire measures of sympathy, modest self-reported gender differences in sympathy in reaction to empathy-inducing stimuli, occasional differences in facial reactions and observed concern (generally favoring females), but no consistent gender differences in physiological markers of sympathy. Whether the self-reported difference in males' and females' sympathy reflects a real difference or the desire to perceive or present oneself in sex-stereotypic ways is unknown, although the overall findings suggest that females are actually at least slightly more sympathetic than are males.

The Relation of Sympathy to Prosocial Behavior

Psychologists frequently have hypothesized that sympathy is associated with prosocial behavior (voluntary behavior intended to benefit another regardless of motive) or altruism (i.e., nonegoistically motivated prosocial behavior). In contrast, people who experience personal distress are expected to try to alleviate their own distress and, thus, to assist others only if that is the easiest way to decrease their own distress.

The empirical data generally support these hypotheses. In studies of adults, C. Daniel Batson found that inducing adults to attend to the misfortune of others resulted in more reported sympathy as well as the increased helping of distressed or needy individuals (1991). Other manipulations have produced similar results, and sympathy appears to increase adults' valuing of another's welfare. Moreover, inducing adults to feel sympathy for a stigmatized group (e.g., AIDS victims) improves attitudes toward the group as a whole. In contrast, adults who experience personal distress tend not to help others if it is easy to avoid contact with them. Similarly, children's sympathy, as assessed through facial and physiological reactions to empathy-inducing films, has been positively associated with their helping and sharing. In contrast, children's personal distress reactions have been uncorrelated with prosocial behavior or correlated with low prosocial behavior. Thus, sympathy has been positively associated with other-oriented behavior, although sympathy for an individual may increase the helping of the individual at a cost to that of the larger group.

An ongoing debate in social psychological research is whether sympathy is associated with true altruism or if all prosocial behavior, including that motivated by sympathy, is egoistically motivated. C. Daniel Batson has argued that sympathy is associated with the selfless desire to benefit another and that sympathetically motivated altruistic behavior is not due to the desire for external rewards, the desire to avoid guilt, or the expectation of feeling good because of the vicarious sharing of a person's joy when his or her condition has improved. Although Batson and other researchers have gathered considerable data consistent with this argument, other findings suggest that people experiencing sympathy sometimes help to alleviate their own negative mood because of perceived oneness with the other person or to experience empathic joy. Thus, the debate regarding the motivational status of sympathy is not resolved.

The Socialization of Sympathy

Although there is evidence from studies of twins that there is a genetic basis to sympathetic concern, there also is an association between children's socialization experiences and their sympathy. Children's sympathetic helping has been associated with the quality of the mother-child attachment early in life and with supportive parenting. In addition, parents' self-reported sympathy and perspective-taking have been positively correlated with same-sex elementary school children's sympathy and negatively correlated with their personal distress reactions.

Parents may model or communicate acceptance of a variety of emotional responses, including sympathy, through their own expression of nonhostile emotions or their acceptance of others' emotions in everyday interactions. Women and girls (but not males) from homes high in expression of submissive (nonassertive) negative emotions are relatively likely to report responding emotionally (for women) or to react with sympathy (for girls) to empathy-inducing films. The expression of hostile negative emotions (e.g., anger) in the home has been unrelated to women's sympathy but associated with low levels of sympathy in children.

Parental verbalizations regarding the expression of emotion and others' emotions are also related to children's sympathy. For boys, parental emphasis on controlling emotion seems to be associated with high levels of personal distress and low levels of sympathy, whereas discussion of ways to deal instrumentally with stressful situations has been associated with sympathy in response to another's distress. Maternal verbalizations linking the child's own experience to that of a distressed person have been correlated with children's vicarious emotional responses (sadness, sympathy, and distress). In contrast, mothers' reports to their children of feeling sad or sympathetic in an empathy-inducing context have been associated with boys' self-reported

sympathy. Moreover, mothers who try to involve their children when telling empathy-inducing stories tend to have sympathetic offspring. Finally, maternal-reported reinforcement of children's sympathetic and prosocial reactions has been associated with girls' sympathy and the sensitivity of boys' attempts to comfort others.

In summary, a number of parental characteristics and behaviors have been linked to the development of empathy, sympathy, or personal distress in children. However, there are few studies on this issue, so findings must be viewed as preliminary.

Acknowledgments. Work on this entry was supported by a grant from the National Institutes of Mental Health (1 R01 HH55052) and Research Scientist Development and Research Scientist Awards from the National Institute of Mental Health (K05 M801321).

Bibliography

Batson, C. D. (1991). *The altruism question: Toward a social-psychological answer.* Hillsdale, NJ: Erlbaum.

Batson, C. D., Batson, J. G., Todd, R. M., Brummett, B. H., Shaw, L. L., & Aldeguer, C. M. R. (1995). Empathy and the collective good: Caring for one of the others in a social dilemma. *Journal of Personality and Social Psychology, 68,* 619–631.

Batson, C. D., Turk, C. L., Shaw, L. L., & Klein, T. R. (1995). Information function of empathic emotion: Learning that we value the other's welfare. *Journal of Personality and Social Psychology, 68,* 300–313.

Batson, C. D., Polycarpou, M. P., Harmon-Jones, E., Imhoff, H. J., Mitchener, E. C., Bednar, L. L., Klein, T. R., & Highberger, L. (1997). Empathy and attitudes: Can feelings for a member of a stigmatized group improve feelings toward the group? *Journal of Personality and Social Psychology, 72,* 105–118.

Cialdini, R. B., Brown, S. L., Lewis, B. P., Luce, C., & Neuberg, S. L. (1997). Reinterpreting the empathy-altruism relationship: When one into one equals oneness. *Personality and Social Psychology, 73,* 481–494.

Davis, M. H. (1994). *Empathy: A social psychological approach.* Madison, WI: Brown & Benchmark.

Eisenberg, N., & Fabes, R. A. (1998). Prosocial development. In W. Damon (Series Ed.) & N. Eisenberg (Vol. Ed.), *Handbook of child psychology: Vol. 3. Social, emotional, and personality development* (5th ed., pp. 701–778). New York: Wiley.

Eisenberg, N., Fabes, R. A., Murphy, B., Karbon, M., Maszk, P., Smith, M., O'Boyle, C., & Suh, K. (1994). The relations of emotionality and regulation to dispositional and situational empathy-related responding. *Journal of Personality and Social Psychology, 66,* 776–797.

Eisenberg, N., Fabes, R. A., Murphy, B., Karbon, M., Smith, M., & Maszk, P. (1996). The relations of children's dispositional empathy-related responding to their emotionality, regulation, and social functioning. *Developmental Psychology, 32,* 195–209.

Eisenberg, N., & Mussen, P. (1989). *The roots of prosocial behavior in children.* Cambridge, England: Cambridge University Press.

Eisenberg, N., & Strayer, J. (1987). *Empathy and its development.* Cambridge, England: Cambridge University Press.

Hoffman, M. L. (1982). Development of prosocial motivation: Empathy and guilt. In N. Eisenberg (Ed.), *The development of prosocial behavior* (pp. 281–313). New York: Academic Press.

Hunt, M. (1990). *The compassionate beast.* New York: William Morrow.

Zahn-Waxler, C., Radke-Yarrow, Wagner, E., & Chapman, M. (1992). Development of concern for others. *Developmental Psychology, 28,* 126–136.

Nancy Eisenberg

SYMPTOM CHECKLIST-90-R. *See* SCL-90-R.

SYNAPSE. The nervous system consists of neurons and the glial cells that support and protect them. Processing of information in the nervous system takes place in circuits of interconnected neurons. Most neurons consist of a cell body (soma) to which is attached several dendrites and a single axon, which may divide into many branches. Each branch ends in a terminal button. [*See* Neuron.]

Neurons communicate by means of synapses—junctions between the terminal button of one neuron (the presynaptic neuron) and a small portion of the membrane of the dendrite or soma of another neuron (the postsynaptic neuron). The presynaptic and postsynaptic membrane do not touch each other; they are separated by a 20-nanometer gap called the synaptic cleft, which is filled with the extracellular fluid that surrounds all the cells of the nervous system (Figure 1).

The membrane of a neuron contains an electrical charge called the membrane potential. Normally, the outside of the membrane is positively charged. When a synapse becomes active, it produces a postsynaptic potential—a brief change in the membrane potential of the postsynaptic membrane. Excitatory postsynaptic potentials (EPSPs) decrease the membrane potential; inhibitory postsynaptic potentials (IPSPs) reduce it.

Up to several tens of thousands of terminal buttons can form synapses with an individual neuron. Some of these terminal buttons produce EPSPs and some produce IPSPs. The EPSPs and IPSPs are transmitted across the membrane of the dendrites and soma and eventually reach the junction of the soma with the axon—the axon hillock. Whenever the membrane po-

tential of the axon hillock becomes sufficiently reduced, the threshold of excitation is reached and the axon fires. (Firing refers to the production of an action potential.) At any given moment, some of the terminal buttons that form synapses with a particular neuron are active. If most of the active terminal buttons are those that produce EPSPs, the axon of the postsynaptic neuron will fire at a high rate. If IPSPs predominate, the rate of firing will be low.

Action potentials are transmitted to the terminal buttons at the ends of all the branches of an axon. When an action potential reaches a terminal button, it triggers the secretion of a small amount of a chemical called a neurotransmitter. Different types of neurons release one of at least a dozen different neurotransmitters. Molecules of the neurotransmitter dissolve in the extracellular fluid that fills the synaptic cleft, diffuse across this space, and encounter postsynaptic receptors, specialized protein molecules embedded in the postsynaptic membrane in a region called the postsynaptic thickening. Postsynaptic receptors contain binding sites—regions of the protein molecule to which molecules of the appropriate neurotransmitter can attach. The match between a binding site and a molecule of the appropriate neurotransmitter is similar to that between a lock and the appropriate key. When a molecule of the neurotransmitter binds with its receptor, it opens

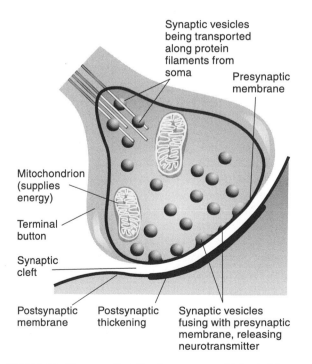

SYNAPSE. Figure 1. Details of a synapse. (Adapted from Carlson, 1998.)

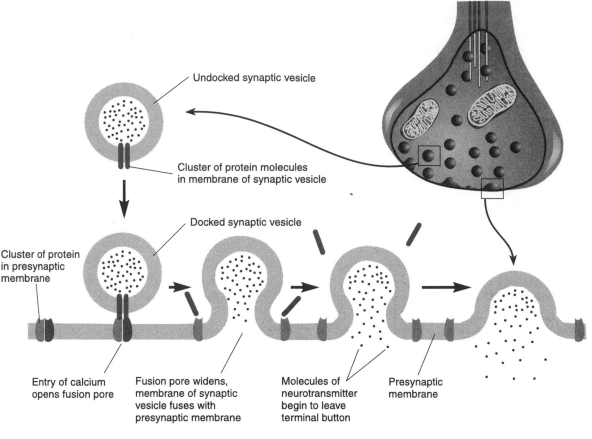

Undocked synaptic vesicle

Cluster of protein molecules
in membrane of synaptic vesicle

Docked synaptic vesicle

Cluster of protein
in presynaptic
membrane

Entry of calcium
opens fusion pore

Fusion pore widens,
membrane of synaptic
vesicle fuses with
presynaptic membrane

Molecules of
neurotransmitter
begin to leave
terminal button

Presynaptic
membrane

SYNAPSE. Figure 2. Release of a neurotransmitter. An action potential opens calcium channels. Calcium ions enter and bind with the protein embedded in the membrane of synaptic vesicles docked at the release zone. The fusion pores open and the transmitter substance is released into the synaptic cleft. The membrane of the vesicles fuses with that of the terminal button. (Adapted from Carlson, 1998.)

one or more ion channels, which permits a particular type of ion to flow in or out of the postsynaptic neuron. Some ion channels are part of the structure of the postsynaptic receptor, and open as soon as a molecule of the neurotransmitter attaches to the binding site. Other postsynaptic receptors trigger a chemical reaction that produces a second messenger—a chemical that opens ion channels located elsewhere in the postsynaptic membrane.

The opening of ion channels produces postsynaptic potentials. Ions are positively or negatively charged particles. The opening of sodium channels permits positively charged sodium ions to enter the neuron, which reduces the membrane potential and produces an EPSP. The opening of potassium channels or chloride channels permits positively charged potassium ions to leave the neuron or negatively charged chloride ions to enter the neuron, either of which increases the membrane potential and produces an IPSP.

Neurotransmitters are produced in the soma and stored in synaptic vesicles, small round sacs made of the same type of membrane that encases a neuron. The vesicles are delivered to the terminal buttons by axoplasmic transport, a process that involves long protein filaments that travel the length of the axon. Just across the synaptic cleft from the postsynaptic thickening is a region of the presynaptic membrane called the release zone. Synaptic vesicles eventually reach the release zone, where some of them become docked to the inside of the presynaptic membrane. When a synaptic vesicle is docked, a cluster of protein molecule embedded in the membrane of the vesicle attaches to another cluster embedded in the membrane of the release zone.

The arrival of an action potential causes some neurotransmitter to be released. The reversal of the membrane potential that accompanies an action potential opens voltage-dependent calcium channels, specialized protein molecules embedded in the membrane of the release zone. The opening of these ion channels permits calcium ions to enter the terminal button, where they attach to the clusters of protein molecules responsible for docking synaptic vesicles to the release zone. The protein molecules move in such a way that an opening appears in both the presynaptic membrane and the membrane of the synaptic vesicles at the point where they are attached. The membrane of the synaptic vesicles fuses with the presynaptic membrane, and the synaptic vesicles turn inside-out, releasing their contents into the synaptic cleft (Figure 2). A new batch of synaptic vesicles descends toward the release zone and becomes docked, taking the place of the vesicles whose membranes are now merged with that of the terminal button.

Normally, the synaptic activity triggered by an action potential lasts only a few tens of milliseconds. Docked synaptic vesicles release their contents, molecules of the neurotransmitter diffuse across the synaptic cleft and activate postsynaptic receptors, and then the neurotransmitter is deactivated or removed from the synaptic cleft. Embedded in the membrane of most terminal buttons are specialized protein molecules that transport molecules of the neurotransmitter from the synaptic cleft back into the terminal button, where they are stored into new synaptic vesicles and thus recycled. The removal of the neurotransmitter from the synaptic cleft is called reuptake. In a few cases, enzymes destroy the neurotransmitter soon after it is released. Drugs that block the process of reuptake of a particular neurotransmitter permit a higher than normal concentration of the neurotransmitter to accumulate in the synaptic cleft and thus prolong synaptic activity. For example, fluoxetine (Prozac) inhibits the reuptake of the neurotransmitter serotonin.

[See also Brain; and Neuron.]

Bibliography

Bear, M. F., Connors, B. W., & Paradiso, M. A. (1996). *Neuroscience: Exploring the brain.* Baltimore, MD: Williams & Wilkins.

Carlson, N. R. (1998). *Physiology of behavior* (6th ed). Boston: Allyn & Bacon.

Hall, A. (1992). *An Introduction to molecular neurobiology.* Sunderland, MA: Sinauer.

Kandel, E. R., Schwartz, J. H., & Jessell, T. M. (1992). *Principles of Neural Science* (3rd ed.). Norwalk, CT: Appleton & Lange.

Nicholls, J. G., Martin, A. R., Wallace, B. G., & Kuffler, S. W. (1992). *From neuron to brain* (3rd ed.). Sunderland, MA: Sinauer.

Rosenzweig, M. R., Leiman, A. L., & Breedlove, S. M. (1996). *Biological psychology.* Sunderland, MA: Sinauer.

Neil R. Carlson

SYNTAX. *See* Psycholinguistics, *article on* Syntax and Grammar.

SYSTEMATIC DESENSITIZATION has been one of the most widely used and well-known psychosocial treatments for fear and anxiety-related problems throughout the second half of the twentieth century. Broadly defined, systematic desensitization refers to strategies that decrease anxiety and fear by gradually exposing an individual to distressing stimuli and, at the same time, having the individual engaged in a state that is incompatible with such negative emotional responding.

Systematic desensitization dates to the 1950s, when Joseph Wolpe began exploring how competing responses could be used to reduce fear. Cats were repeatedly shocked while in cages, producing a conditioned fear response that interfered with feeding behavior in the "shock cages." In "shock-free" cages, however, cats showed little fear and were able to feed. The pairing of eating behavior, a response that competes with fear, with successive approximations of shock cages, alleviated fearful responding. Wolpe termed this process of gradual exposure with competing responses systematic desensitization and studied the effects of this procedure in humans with specific phobias. A relaxed state, produced by training, was the primary antagonistic activity used with people. It was found that individuals with specific fears who imagined distressing objects or situations in a relaxed state were able to confront such stimuli in the natural environment and thereby overcome their phobia.

Among the most popular theoretical explanations for the mechanisms of systematic desensitization are counterconditioning, extinction, habituation, cognitive restructuring, and nonspecific treatment factors (e.g., therapist-patient rapport). Given the scope of the present article, only the most fully accepted and widely known theory of counterconditioning is presented (Wolpe, 1958). In counterconditioning, a conditioned stimulus (CS) is presented with an unconditioned stimulus (US) that is different from the original US. Once learned, a conditioned response to the new US "competes" with the conditioned response produced by the original US, lessening the conditioned response to the original US. Wolpe (1990) termed the process of teaching a competing response reciprocal inhibition because the new response inhibits other problem states such as fear. One criticism of the theory of counterconditioning is that desensitization without a competing response can occur, a phenomenon termed "extinction" (Kazdin & Wilcoxon, 1976). Although studies that have directly examined theories of counterconditioning and extinction are inconclusive, competing responses and other nonspecific treatment factors (e.g., rapport) may serve to enhance a basic extinction process.

Systematic desensitization was the first major behavior therapy for anxiety disorders, but the procedure also has been used successfully with individuals who have a host of stress-related and other problems such as anger, asthma, chronic pain, motion sickness, nightmares, alcoholism, hypertension, stuttering, and headaches. Exposure conducted imaginally typically is referred to as systematic desensitization, but follow-up exposure *in vivo* (i.e., in the actual situation) is common. Also, fearful stimuli in desensitization can be presented through various sensory modalities (e.g., slides, videotapes, and virtual reality applications). Therapists have used various forms of relaxation training, anxiolytic drugs, hypnosis, and food consumption to evoke antagonistic responses; however, progressive muscle relaxation (Jacobson, 1938) is the most common and most extensively studied competing activity (McGlynn, Mealiea, & Landau, 1981). Therapists typically shorten Jacobson's original relaxation procedures in order to administer treatment in a timely manner. Although therapists differ in the details of application, the basic procedure remains generally the same, with the typical desensitization session lasting 15 to 30 minutes (Wolpe, 1990). Interestingly, automated desensitization procedures also have been used with success (Lang, Melamed, & Hart, 1970).

In one form of classic imaginal systematic desensitization, the client learns and practices progressive muscle relaxation (see Poppen, 1988, for a more detailed account of relaxation procedures) both in the office and through homework. Once the client is reliably able to produce a relaxation response, the client and therapist construct a hierarchy of approximately 10 to 15 fear items. Typically, a subjective units of distress scale (SUDs; Wolpe, 1958), in which 0 equals no anxiety and 100 equals extreme anxiety, is used to place items in their hierarchical order. The therapist verbally describes the scenes individually and asks the client to imagine each one as vividly as possible, but without any increase in anxiety. Pleasant, relaxing scenes are often used to prompt relaxation at the beginning and end of therapy sessions and between hierarchy items. Finger signals are used by the client to indicate image clarity and any significant increase in anxiety during scene presentations. Scenes are typically presented for 20 to 30 seconds, in order, with less distressing scenes first. Research has indicated, however, that the duration of exposure, rather than the order of the fear-relevant scenes, is particularly important for therapeutic efficacy (McGlynn et al., 1981). A SUDs ratings is taken, and the client is then instructed to stop imagining the fear-relevant scene

and relax for perhaps another 20 to 30 seconds. If the SUDs rating is below a specified criterion (e.g., 20), the next scene in the hierarchy is presented; if the SUDs rating is above the specified criterion, the original scene is repeated. This same procedure is followed in a stepwise fashion for all scenes. Systematic desensitization is usually conducted across several therapy sessions. Direct exposure to feared stimuli typically follows imaginal desensitization.

Paul (1969), in a classic review, observed that systematic desensitization greatly alleviates pathological anxiety across a broad range of disorders (see also Kazdin & Wilcoxon, 1976). Other researchers have drawn similar conclusions in more recent years (McGlynn et al., 1981); the procedure often results in long-term (i.e., years) positive behavior change (e.g., Liddell, Di Fazio, Blackwood, & Ackerman, 1994). Systematic desensitization is most effective for persons with a specific phobia (Evans & Kellam, 1973; Lang & Lasovik, 1963) who produce an elevated visceral response to specific fear-relevant stimuli (Lang et al., 1970) and do not have an underlying skill deficit (Wolpe, 1990). Overall, despite theoretical controversy regarding the mechanisms of systematic desensitization, the procedure is commonly used, and a great deal of empirical evidence supports its efficacy in the treatment of many fear- and anxiety-related problems.

Bibliography

Davison, G. C. (1968). Systematic desensitization as a counterconditioning process. *Journal of Abnormal Psychology, 73,* 91–99.

Evans, P. D., & Kellam, A. M. P. (1973). Semiautomated desensitization: A controlled clinical trial. *Behaviour Research and Therapy, 11,* 641–646.

Jacobson, E. (1938). *Progressive relaxation,* Chicago: University of Chicago Press. The original book on progressive muscle relaxation, which includes a detailed, unabbreviated description of the procedure.

Kazdin, A. E., & Wilcoxon, L. A. (1976). Systematic desensitization and nonspecific treatment effects: A methodological evaluation. *Psychological Bulletin, 83,* 729–758.

Lader, M. H., Gelder, M. G., & Marks, I. M. (1967). Palmar skin conductance measures of response to anxiety in phobic states. *Journal of Psychosomatic Research, 11,* 271–281.

Lang, P. J., & Lazovik, A. D. (1963). Experimental desensitization of a phobia. *Journal of Abnormal Psychology, 70,* 395–402.

Lang, P. J., Melamed, B. G., & Hart, J. (1970). A psychophysiological analysis of fear modification using an automated desensitization procedure. *Journal of Abnormal Psychology, 2,* 220–234.

Liddell, A., Di Fazio, L., Blackwood, J., & Ackerman, C. (1994). Long-term follow-up of treated dental phobics. *Behaviour Research and Therapy, 32,* 605–610.

McGlynn, F. D., Mealiea, W. L., & Landau, D. L. (1981). The current status of systematic desensitization. *Clinical Psychology Review, 1,* 149–179. A classic review article that provides a critical evaluation of the theoretical and empirical issues surrounding the use of systematic desensitization.

Paul, G. L. (1969). Outcome of systematic desensitization II. Controlled investigations of individual treatment, technique variations, and current status. In C. M. Franks (Ed.), *Behavior therapy: Appraisal and status.* New York: McGraw-Hill. Perhaps the most well-known and widely cited literature review of the systematic desensitization literature, focusing particularly on treatment efficacy and procedural modifications.

Poppen, R. (1988). *Behavioral relaxation training and assessment.* Elmsford, NY: Pergamon Press. Outlines the basic procedures for conducting progressive muscle relaxation training. The procedures are shorter and more contemporary than those of Jacobson (1938).

Wolpe, J. (1958). *Psychotherapy by reciprocal inhibition.* Stanford, CA: Stanford University Press. A classic text by the originator of systematic desensitization that outlines behavioral principles and their application in the treatment of anxiety-related problems.

Wolpe, J. (1990). *The practice of behavior therapy* (4th ed.). New York: Pergamon Press.

Daniel W. McNeil and Michael J. Zvolensky

SYSTEMATIC OBSERVATION. *See* Direct Observation.

SYSTEM ERROR ANALYSIS refers to the analysis, measurement, and prediction of the various potential and actual contributions to the output of criterion performance of a human–machine system operating in its intended environment. In industrial and military systems there normally is an agreed-on criterion of output or mission performance. In the case of industrial production systems, output may be in units produced per unit of time. In the case of military systems, it may be number of bombs on target, number of targets destroyed, and so on. Generally, these are subcriteria that contribute to overall system effectiveness. System reliability and availability are such subcriteria. At this level of description and potential measurement (e.g., mean time between failure), the interaction of the human performance with the machine (or information system), performance errors of operation may occur. The human operator's contribution to this error may be the result of inadequate training, aptitude, or skill. It also may be due to the error-prone design of the interface between the operator(s) and the system. For example, Grether (1947) investigated many accidents that occurred during the landing phases of military aircraft because of the altimeter scale design. Finally, systems effectiveness may also be affected by equipment or software failure.

The task of the human factors analyst or engineering psychologist is to identify the human–system interface error contribution to overall system error or, conversely, to system performance effectiveness. This process can occur at several stages in system development, from conceptual design through operational testing and implementation. Generally, the earlier the human factors analyst/psychologist can identify human–system interface error potentials, the more cost effective is the process. Frequently, early function analysis can identify potential error sources, which may stem from design engineers' misconceptions about humans' capabilities and limitations in performing certain functions and tasks. Later in systems development where tasks and jobs have been defined, the determination of the operator/maintainer's aptitudes, skill levels, and training requirements can be identified to minimize system error.

One way of characterizing the phases or elements of analyses is by a structural components of variance equation:

$$\sigma_H^2 + \sigma_M^2 + \sigma_H \sigma_M + \sigma_E^2 = \sigma_{SYS}^2$$

The first term (σ_H^2) refers to the systems variance contributed by the individual differences in human performance, differences in aptitude, skill, intelligence, attitudes, and so on. The second term (σ_M^2) refers to the variance contributed by the variable performance of the machine, within certain design constraints. In one sense this could be interpreted as the unreliable performance of the machine (i.e., machine error). The third term ($\partial_H \partial_M$) refers to the performance variance contributed by the human and machine interaction. This interaction can occur directly in the operation or maintenance of the system, or indirectly in its reliability. The last term (∂_E^2), on the prediction side of the equation, is the error that results from the inability to obtain precise measure of the prediction variables (i.e., error of measurement). Topmiller (1969) used this approach in an Air Force study designed to predict average maintenance times on three different weapon systems (The B-52, GAM-77, and KC-135). Using human engineering design criteria to represent the $\sigma_H \sigma_M$ term, a factor analytic–regression technique resulted in multiple coefficients from R = 0.513 to R = 0.812 explaining up to 46%, or nearly half, of the criterion variance of maintenance times.

Other approaches to system error analysis include real-time multioperator simulations by Howell (1967) and computer-generated Monte Carlo simulations by Siegel and Wolf (1969).

Major emphasis and further development of this quantitative methodology occurred as a result of the 1979 Three Mile Island nuclear power plant incident.

Congress and the Nuclear Regulatory Agency (NRC) mandated that the development of human system error analysis be included in the engineering risk analyses. performed on nuclear power plants. Alan Swain and L. Rigey (1971), who had developed human error probability prediction methods while at Sandia National Laboratories, expanded and refined the Sandia Human Error Data Bank (SHEDB) and published the mature version of this quantitative prediction methodology in NUREG/CR 1278. Topmiller, Eckel, and Kozinsky (1982) reviewed several other human reliability data banks. These data banks reflected the attempts, at that time, to quantify and predict human operator and maintainer performance reliability as a function of system design, training, procedural, and situational factors.

Since system error is a function of all of the components of variance elements and therefore involves more than just user error, these more complex simulation and modeling efforts are required to quantify and predict system error throughout system development and operation.

[*See also* Human Error Analysis.]

Bibliography

Grether, W. (1947). *The effect of variations in indicator design upon speed and accuracy of altitude readings.* (Rep. TSFAA-694-14) Wright-Patterson Air Force Base, OH: Aero Medical Lab, Wright Air Development Center.

Howell, W. C. (1967). Some principles for the design of decision systems. *A review of six years of research on a command-control system simulation.* TR-67-136, Wright-Patterson Air Force Base, OH: Wright Air Development Center.

Siegal, A., and Wolf, J. (1969). *Man-machine simulation models.* New York: Wiley-Interscience.

Swain, A. (1971). Development of a human error rate data bank. *Proceedings of U.S. Navy Reliability Workshop.*

Swain, A., and Guttman, H. (1980). *Handbook of human reliability analysis with emphasis on nuclear power plant application.* USNRC Report NUREG/CR-1278. Washington, DC: U.S. Nuclear Regulatory Commission.

Topmiller, D. (1969). Mathematical models of human performance in man-machine systems. In A. DeBrisson (Ed.), *La simulation du comportment humain.* Paris: Dunod.

Topmiller, D. (1981). Manned system design: Methods, equipment, and applications. In J. Moraal and K. Kraiss (Ed.), *Manned systems design* (pp. 3–30). Nato Conference. Series III: Human Factors, Vol. 17. New York: Plenum Press.

Topmiller, D., Eckel, T., and Kozinsky, E. (1982). *Human data bank for nuclear power plant operations.* A Review of Existing Human Reliability Data Banks. USNRC Report NUREG/CR 2744. Washington, DC: U.S. Nuclear Regulatory Commission.

Donald A. Topmiller

SYSTEMS THEORY views human behavior as a product of complex interactions between persons and their environments. Instead of focusing on either internal psychological processes or external forces, systems theory highlights the fluid process of mutual influence between individuals in relationships and between individuals and their environmental contexts. It challenges traditional notions of cause and effect based on single identifiable causes of human behavior. Developed originally within biological and information sciences in the 1940s, systems theory did not begin to influence psychology and related disciplines until the 1950s and 1960s, when it was first applied to the understanding of families.

Austrian biologist Ludwig von Bertalanffy, troubled by mechanistic models of biology in the 1930s and 1940s, sought to develop principles that would fit all living systems and explain their behavior in complex ways. In his pioneering book *General System Theory* (New York, 1968), von Bertalanffy defined a system as a "set of elements standing in interrelation" (p. 55). He maintained that every system is more than the sum of its parts, because the interactions among the parts are major constituents of the system itself.

The second historical source of systems theory was the development of cybernetics during and after World War II. Cybernetics is the science of informational feedback and control, in which the system has a goal, monitors information from the environment, and adjusts its internal state in order to stay on course towards the goal. For example, a thermostat maintains a steady temperature in a room (its goal) by reading the ambient temperature and accordingly turning the furnace on or off. These processes of self-monitoring and self-correction are essential to all living systems from cells to societies because every organism must maintain stability while adapting flexibly to environmental and internal changes.

Systems theory entered psychology and psychiatry first through the work of the anthropologist Gregory Bateson and his team in Palo Alto, California. Influenced by cybnerneticists and systems theorists, Bateson and his group first applied systems theory to families in the mid-1950s. In their studies of family communication, Bateson, along with Don Jackson, Jay Haley, John Weakland, and Virginia Satir, began to view the family as an interacting system that shares properties with all living systems, properties such as boundaries, subsystems, structures, and continuous inflow and outflow of energy and information. In the 1960s and 1970s, these ideas were expanded by family psychiatrists such as Murray Bowen, Lyman Wynne, and Salvador Minuchin, who pioneered the clinical application of family systems theory in the form of family therapy.

Psychologists were less prominent than psychiatrists

in the early development of family systems theory, but in the 1980s, the American Psychological Association formed the Division of Family Psychology in response to the growing number of psychologists interested in family systems theory and research. Contemporary family systems theory focuses on how the behavior of individual family members emerges from the interactional structures and processes of the family and its relations with other systems. An example is a child's oppositional behavior stemming from a negative interactional triangle consisting of the warring divorced parents and the child caught in a loyalty bind.

Prior to the 1980s there was relatively little empirical research to demonstrate the scientific validity of systems theory for understanding families. In that decade, however, researchers began to make important strides in empirically measuring aspects of family systems such as cohesion, adaptability, coalition dynamics, boundary disturbances, and other specific family patterns that relate to the adjustment of individuals. Although family systems theory is more an overarching conceptual framework than a specific, testable theory, its validity in psychological research and practice has been increasingly recognized.

During the 1980s and 1990s, developmental psychologists began to incorporate variations of systems thinking into their theories. For example, Donald H. Ford and Richard M. Lerner, in their book *Developmental Systems Theory* (Newbury Park, Calif., 1992), articulated a systems model for understanding human development as the outcome of dynamic interactional processes between persons and their contexts in which both the person and the context influence each other.

A recent variant of systems theory, sometimes termed chaos theory or dynamical systems theory, has become an important new venue for theory and research in a variety of subfields within psychology, in particular developmental psychology, cognitive neuroscience, social psychology, motor development, and language acquisition psychology. In addition to traditional systems notions of multiple interacting factors and emerging patterns, dynamical systems theorists stress nonlinear change and complex temporal patterning. That is, behavioral patterns do not always develop in a progressive, linear pattern following a fixed time sequence. Rather, discontinuous shifts sometimes occur that represent rapid qualitative changes that are not predictable in advance. For example, the psychologist Eugene Goldfield, in his *Emergent Forms* (New York, 1995) has successfully applied dynamical systems theory to extraordinarily complex domains of motor development such as infants learning to crawl.

Dynamical systems theories in developmental psychology and social psychology view persons and groups as complex systems akin to other kinds of complex, even turbulent systems in nature, such as weather patterns, whose precise configurations cannot be fully predicted in advance. The task of the psychologist is to track the evolution of systems of behavior and paths of change on a time scale long enough to identify the emerging patterns. For example, social relationships studied over long time periods can reveal patterns of small and large fluctuations in attitudes and commitment.

The major criticisms of systems theory are that (a) its concepts are so abstract and broad as to be not testable; (b) it tends to neglect the role of individual psychological factors because of its emphasis on interactional processes and contextual dynamics; and (c) it tends to neglect the contextual issues of gender, race, ethnicity, and social class in its pursuit of broad explanatory models. Family systems theorists have had more time than other systems theorists in psychology to absorb these critiques and adjust their theorizing and research.

Bibliography

Bateson, G. (1979). *Steps to an ecology of mind*. New York: Ballantine. A collection of papers by the originator of family systems theory and his colleagues.

Doherty, W. J., & Baptiste, D. A. (1993). Family theories emerging from family therapy. In P. G. Boss, W. J. Doherty, R. LaRossa, W. R. Schumm, & S. K. Steinmetz (Eds.), *Sourcebook of family theories and methods: A contextual approach*. New York: Plenum. A description of clinical theory derived from family systems theory, along with a discussion of critiques of family systems theory.

Montgomery, J., & Fewer, W. (1988). *Family systems and beyond*. New York: Human Sciences Press. A readable introduction to systems concepts and their application to families.

Vallacher, R. R., & Nowak, A. (Eds.) (1994). *Dynamical systems in social psychology*. New York: Academic Press. Sophisticated state-of-the-art chapters on the application of dynamical systems theory to various domains of social psychology.

van Geert, P. (1994). *Dynamic systems of development: Change between complexity and chaos*. New York: Harvester Wheatsheaf. A sophisticated introduction to dynamical systems theory for developmental psychology.

von Bertalanffy, L. (1968). *General system theory*. New York: Braziller. The classic work by the originator of systems theory in biology.

Whitchurch, G. C., & Constantine, L. L. (1993). Systems theory. In P. G. Boss, W. J. Doherty, R. LaRossa, W. R. Schumm, & S. K. Steinmetz (Eds.), *Sourcebook of family theories and methods: A contextual approach*. New York: Plenum Press. A good overview of systems theory, with applications to families.

William J. Doherty